A Review of the Events of 1971

The 1972 World Book Year Book

The Annual Supplement to The World Book Encyclopedia

Field Enterprises Educational Corporation

Chicago   London   Rome   Sydney   Tokyo   Toronto

Staff

Preface

Late in 1971, as in past years, THE YEAR BOOK Board of Editors and members of the staff met to discuss the events of the turbulent year. In the relaxed setting of a resort near Phoenix, Ariz., the board reviewed the happenings in their particular fields and presented proposals for their "Focus" articles for the 1972 edition.

As sometimes happens, one pervasive theme emerged from the three days of discussions. Alastair Buchan struck the note at the very outset: 1971 had been a year of startling change. The new relationship between the United States and the People's Republic of China, the United Nations membership for that Asian nation, the acceleration of West European integration, and the new U.S. economic policies marked the end of an era, he suggested. Jim Murray, attending his first meeting as a new board member, pointed out that the great change in U.S.-China relations was heralded, interestingly, by an athletic team —the U.S. Ping-Pong players who toured China in April.

James Reston, not long back from a lengthy visit to China, said he saw 1971 as a year of wide-ranging reappraisal by the United States—of moving away from old ideas about our economic system, from old assumptions about the Western Alliance, and from the old attitude that the United States can do anything. Enlarging on the idea of changes in attitude, Alistair Cooke cited a 1971 public-opinion poll that found that public respect for the leadership of many U.S. institutions—such as government, labor, and the military—had fallen drastically since 1966. Harrison Brown added that another significant shift in attitude was evidenced when Congress voted down funds for development of the supersonic transport, the first time any such project was scrapped primarily because of its potential danger to the environment.

Sylvia Porter assessed the "three towering events" that changed the world of economics in 1971, and Lawrence Cremin—relating the question of economics to education —noted that recent court rulings could lead to great changes in the way our financially troubled public schools are funded.

Change, of course, is inevitable. What made 1971 different was that the changes seemed more far-reaching than those of other years. What they will lead to is unknown, but it might be helpful to keep in mind some words of President Abraham Lincoln in his message to Congress on Dec. 1, 1862: "The dogmas of the quiet past, are inadequate to the stormy present . . . As our case is new, so we must think anew, and act anew." WAYNE WILLE

"Somehow, we've got to break that up."

Birdwatchers

Contents

15 Section One: The Year in Focus

The members of THE YEAR BOOK Board of Editors focus their
attention on the significant developments of 1971.

16 **Alastair Buchan: Focus on The World**

Professor of International Relations, Oxford University, England.

22 **James Reston: Focus on The Nation**

Vice-president of *The New York Times;* a Pulitzer Prize medalist
for national reporting.

28 **Sylvia Porter: Focus on The Economy**

Financial writer; columnist for the Publishers-Hall newspaper
syndicate; Editor, *Reporting on Governments.*

34 **Harrison Brown: Focus on Science**

Professor of Geochemistry and of Science and Government,
California Institute of Technology; Foreign Secretary,
National Academy of Sciences.

40 **Lawrence A. Cremin: Focus on Education**

Frederick Barnard Professor of Education, Teachers College,
Columbia University.

46 **Alistair Cooke: Focus on The Arts**

Journalist; broadcaster; Chief U.S. Correspondent for
The Guardian, Manchester, England.

52 **Jim Murray: Focus on Sports**

Sports columnist for *The Los Angeles Times.*

57 Section Two: Special Reports

Six special articles and THE YEAR BOOK Trans-Vision® give
special treatment to subjects of current importance.

58 **The Dark Side of the Green Revolution** by Mark Gayn

"Miracle" wheat and rice seeds are making the threat of world starvation
seem hollow, but there is another—and less happy—side of the picture.

76 **Caging the Inflation Monster** by Henry C. Wallich

President Richard M. Nixon's new economic policy of 1971 is but
one more weapon in the long and continuous war against rising prices.

92   **Crime in Paradise** by Jim Bishop
America's worldwide image as a relative utopia is being seriously
threatened by an unparalleled upsurge in crime throughout the nation.

118   **New Game Plan for Sports in the '70s** by William Barry Furlong
The new Golden Age of sports finds players showing a new awareness,
and owners seeking players, money, and places in which to play.

136   **A Freshman in the Senate** by Senator Adlai E. Stevenson III
After his first year in the U.S. Senate, a new member assesses
what has been called the "greatest deliberative body in the world."

160   **The American City: A special two-part feature**

161   **Making Our Cities Livable–THE YEAR BOOK Trans-Vision®**
Colorful, transparent overlays show some ways in which our
decaying cities can be modernized and, most of all, humanized.

179   **Taking a Closer Look at the City** by William H. Whyte
A long-time city-watcher suggests that our cities may have
more going for them than we realize—or care to admit.

197   Section Three: The Year on File
YEAR BOOK contributors report the developments of 1971
in alphabetically arranged articles, from "Advertising"
to "Zumwalt, Elmo Russell, Jr."

559   Section Four: World Book Supplement
Two important new articles—"Motion Picture" and "Environmental
Pollution"—are reprinted from the 1972 edition of THE WORLD
BOOK ENCYCLOPEDIA.

601   Section Five: Dictionary Supplement
Here is a listing of newly approved words and definitions that will be
included in the 1972 edition of THE WORLD BOOK DICTIONARY.

605   Section Six: Index
A 17-page cumulative index covering the contents of the 1970,
1971, and 1972 editions of THE YEAR BOOK.

A chronology of the most important events of 1971 appears on
pages 8 to 14. A preview of 1972 is given on pages 625 and 626.

Contributors

Alexiou, Arthur G., M.S., E.E.; Program Director, Office of Sea Grant Programs, National Science Foundation. [OCEAN]

Anderson, Joseph P., M.S., LL.D.; Consultant, National Association of Social Workers. [MEDICARE; Social Organizations]

Arnold, Rus, Photojournalism Editor, *Writer's Digest.* [PHOTOGRAPHY]

Banovetz, James M., Ph.D.; Professor of Political Science and Director, Center for Governmental Studies, Northern Illinois University. [CITY; City Articles; HOUSING]

Bautz, Laura P., Ph.D.; Assistant Professor of Astronomy, Northwestern University. [ASTRONOMY]

Bazell, Robert J., B.A., C. Phil.; News Writer, *Science* Magazine. [SCIENCE AND RESEARCH]

Beaumont, Lynn, Travel and Public Relations Consultant. [FAIRS AND EXPOSITIONS; TRAVEL]

Benson, Barbara N., A.B., M.S.; Graduate Assistant, Southern Illinois University. [BOTANY; ZOOLOGY]

Berkwitt, George J., B.S.J.; Senior Editor, *Dun's Review* Magazine. [MANUFACTURING]

Bishop, Jim, Editor; Columnist; Author; *The Day Lincoln Was Shot; The Day Christ Died.* [Special Report: CRIME IN PARADISE]

Bornstein, Leon, B.A., M.A.; Labor Economist, U.S. Dept. of Labor. [LABOR]

Bradley, Van Allen, B.J ; former Literary Editor, *Chicago Daily News.* [LITERATURE]

Brown, Kenneth, European Journalist. [Western Europe Articles]

Burnet, Alastair, M.A.; Editor, *The Economist.* [GREAT BRITAIN]

Cain, Charles C., III, B.A.; Automotive Writer, Associated Press. [AUTOMOBILE]

Carruth, Hayden, M.A.; Poet. [POETRY]

Collins, William G., B.S., M.A.; Research Meteorologist, National Meteorological Center. [WEATHER]

Conley, Clare, B.A.; Editor, *Field & Stream* Magazine. [HUNTING AND FISHING]

Cook, Robert C.; Population Consultant, National Parks Association. [POPULATION, WORLD]

Cromie, William J., B.S.; Vice-President and Editor, Universal Science News, Inc. [ASTRONAUTS]

Csida, June Bundy; Former Radio-TV Editor, *Billboard* Magazine. [RADIO; TELEVISION]

Cuscaden, Rob; Author; Architecture Critic, *Chicago Sun-Times* [ARCHITECTURE]

Cviic, Chris, B.A., B.Sc.; Editorial Staff, *The Economist.* [Eastern Europe Articles]

Dale, Edwin L., Jr., B.A.; Reporter, *The New York Times,* Washington Bureau. [INTERNATIONAL TRADE AND FINANCE]

Darby, Edwin W., B.S.J.; Financial Editor *Chicago Sun-Times.* [Business Articles]

Delaune, Lynn de Grummond, M.A.; Assistant Professor, College of William and Mary; Author. [LITERATURE FOR CHILDREN]

Dewald, William G., Ph.D.; Professor of Economics, Ohio State University. [Finance Articles]

Evans, Earl A., Jr., Ph.D.; Professor and Chairman, Department of Biochemistry, University of Chicago. [BIOCHEMISTRY; BIOLOGY]

Fantel, Hans, B.S.; Journalist; Science Writer; Historian. [ELECTRONICS]

Farr, David M. L., D.Phil.; Professor of History, Carleton University, Ottawa. [CANADA; MICHENER, ROLAND; TRUDEAU, PIERRE E.]

Fischer, Dean E., M.A.; Washington Correspondent, *Time* Magazine. [COURTS AND LAWS]

Flynn, Betty, B.A.; UN Correspondent, *Chicago Daily News.* [UNITED NATIONS]

French, Charles E., Ph.D.; Head, Agricultural Economics Department, Purdue University. [AGRICULTURE]

Furlong, William B., B.S.; Free-Lance Writer. [Special Report: NEW GAME PLAN FOR SPORTS IN THE '70s]

Gayn, Mark, B.S.; Asia Bureau Chief, *The Toronto Star;* Author. [CHINA; INDIA; PAKISTAN; Special Report: THE DARK SIDE OF THE GREEN REVOLUTION]

Goldner, Nancy, B.A.; Critic, *Dance News* and *Christian Science Monitor.* [DANCING]

Goldstein, Jane, B.A.; U.S. Representative, International Racing Bureau. [HORSE RACING]

Goy, Robert W., Ph.D.; Director, Wisconsin Regional Primate Research Center. [PSYCHOLOGY]

Grasso, Thomas X., B.A., M.A.; Associate Professor and Chairman, Department of Geosciences, Monroe Community College. [GEOLOGY]

Griffin, Alice, Ph.D.; Professor of English, Lehman College, City University of New York. [THEATER]

Havighurst, Robert J., Ph.D.; Professor of Education and Human Development, University of Chicago. [OLD AGE]

Hechinger, Fred M., B.A.; Education Editor, *The New York Times.* [EDUCATION]

Holmes, Jay E., B.A.; Policy Analyst, Field Center Development, National Aeronautics and Space Administration. [SPACE EXPLORATION]

Jessup, Mary E., B.A.; former News Editor, *Civil Engineering* Magazine. [Engineering Articles]

Joseph, Lou, B.A.; Assistant Director, Bureau of Public Information, American Dental Association. [DENTISTRY]

Kelly, John B., Jr., B.S.; President, Amateur Athletic Union. [SPORTS (Close-Up)]

Kind, Joshua B., Ph.D.; Associate Professor of Art History, Northern Illinois University; Author, *Rouault;* Midwest Correspondent, *Art News.* [VISUAL ARTS]

Knight, Arthur, B.A.; Professor, Cinema Department, University of Southern California; Author; Contributing Editor, *The Saturday Review;* Board of Trustees, American Film Institute. [MOTION PICTURES]

Koenig, Louis W., Ph.D., L.H.D.; Professor of Government, New York University; Author: *The Life and Times of William Jennings Bryan.* [CIVIL RIGHTS]

Lach, Alma, Diplome de Cordon Bleu; Author, *Cooking à la Cordon Bleu.* [FOOD]

Lewis, Ralph H., M.A.; Chief, Branch of Museum Operations, National Park Service. [MUSEUMS]

Litsky, Frank, B.S.; Assistant Sports Editor, *The New York Times.* [Sports Articles]

Livingston, Kathryn Zahony, B.A.; Feature Editor, *Town and Country.* [FASHION]

Luy, Mary Lynn M., B.A., M.S.J.; Chicago Correspondent, *Chemical Week* Magazine. [CHEMICAL INDUSTRY; DRUGS]

MacIntosh, Donalda A. ; Special Assistant to the Director, Census Division, Dominion Bureau of Statistics, Canada. [CANADA (Census Introduction)]

Maki, John M., Ph.D.; Vice-Dean, College of Arts and Sciences, University of Massachusetts. [JAPAN]

Malia, Thomas M., Ph.B.; Executive Editor, *Telecommunications Reports.* [COMMUNICATIONS]

Marsh, Robert C., Ed.D.; Music Critic, *Chicago Sun-Times.* [MUSIC, CLASSICAL]

Marty, Martin E., Ph.D.; Associate Editor, *The Christian Century.* [PROTESTANT; RELIGION]

McGaffin, William, B.A., B.Sc.; Washington Correspondent, *Chicago Daily News.* [Political and Government Articles]

Merritt, Malcolm, B.A.; Editor, *Research Institute Bulletin,* American Newspaper Publishers Association. [PUBLISHING]

Morton, Elizabeth H., LL.D.; Former Editor in Chief, Canadian Library Association. [CANADIAN LIBRARY ASSOCIATION; CANADIAN LITERATURE]

Mullen, Frances A., Ph.D.; Consultant on Education of the Handicapped. [CHILD WELFARE]

Nelson, Larry L., Ph.D.; Executive Vice-President, Snyder Associates, Inc. [AGRICULTURE]

Newman, Andrew L., M.A.; Deputy Director of Information, U.S. Department of the Interior. [Conservation Articles]

Norman, Lloyd H., B.S.; Military Affairs Correspondent, *Newsweek* Magazine. [ARMED FORCES OF THE WORLD; ESPIONAGE; NATIONAL DEFENSE]

O'Connor, James J., E. E.; Editor in Chief, *Power* Magazine. [ENERGY]

O'Leary, Theodore M., B.A.; Regional Correspondent, *Sports Illustrated* Magazine. [BRIDGE, CONTRACT; CHESS; GAMES, MODELS, AND TOYS; HOBBIES; PET]

Perloff, Harvey, Ph.D.; Dean, School of Architecture and Urban Planning, University of California, Los Angeles. [Consultant, Trans-Vision®]

Petacque, Art ; Investigative Reporter covering crime and government, *Chicago Sun-Times.* [CRIME]

Plog, Fred, Ph.D.; Assistant Professor, Department of Anthropology, University of California, Los Angeles. [ANTHROPOLOGY; ARCHAEOLOGY]

Pyle, Howard ; President, National Safety Council. [SAFETY]

Rabb, George B., Ph.D.; Associate Director, Research and Education, Chicago Zoological Park. [ZOOS AND AQUARIUMS]

Reed, Michael, B.S.; Associate Editor, WORLD BOOK SCIENCE YEAR. [Biographies; CELEBRATIONS]

Rogers, Morris E., B.S.; Chicago Area Editor, *Drovers Journal.* [INTERNATIONAL LIVE STOCK EXPOSITION]

Rowse, Arthur E., I.A., M.B.A.; President, Consumer News, Inc. [CONSUMER AFFAIRS]

Schaefle, Kenneth E., M.B.A.; President, The Communication Center, Inc. [AVIATION; TRANSPORTATION]

Schmemann, The Reverend Alexander, S.T.D., D.D., LL.D., Th.D.; Dean, St. Vladimir's Orthodox Theological Seminary, New York. [EASTERN ORTHODOX CHURCHES]

Schubert, Helen C., B.S.; Home Furnishing Writer. [INTERIOR DESIGN]

Shaw, Robert J., B.S.B.A.; Editor, *Library Technology Reports,* American Library Association. [LIBRARY]

Shearer, Warren W., Ph.D.; former Chairman, Department of Economics, Wabash College. [ECONOMY, THE]

Sheerin, John B., C.S.P., A.B., M.A., LL.D., J.D.; Editor, *Catholic World.* [ROMAN CATHOLIC CHURCH]

Shepherd, George W., Ph.D.; Professor, Graduate School of International Studies, University of Denver. [Africa Articles]

Spencer, William, Ph.D.; Professor of History, Florida State University; Author, *Land and People of Algeria.* [Middle East Articles; North Africa articles]

Stalker, John N., Ph.D.; Professor of History, University of Hawaii. [ASIA; Asia Articles]

Steffek, Edwin F., B.S.; Editor, *Horticulture* Magazine. [GARDENING]

Stevenson, Adlai E., III, LL.B; U.S. Senator. [Special Report: A FRESHMAN IN THE SENATE]

Swanson, Curtis E., B.A.; Manager, Public Relations, American Library Association. [AMERICAN LIBRARY ASSOCIATION]

Thompson, Carol L., M.A.; Editor, *Current History* Magazine. [U.S. Government Articles]

Tiegel, Eliot, B.A.; Special Issues Editor, *Billboard* Magazine. [MUSIC, POPULAR; RECORDINGS]

Treuting, Theodore F., M.D., F.A.C.P.; Professor of Medicine, Tulane University School of Medicine. [Health Articles]

von Smolinski, Alfred W., Ph.D.; Assistant Professor of Chemistry, University of Illinois at the Medical Center. [CHEMISTRY]

Vreeland, Diana ; Contributing Editor, *Vogue;* former Editor in Chief, *Vogue;* former Fashion Editor, *Harper's Bazaar.* [FASHION (Close-Up)]

Wallich, Henry C., Ph.D.; Professor of Economics, Yale University; former member President's Council of Economic Advisers. [Special Report: CAGING THE INFLATION MONSTER]

Weber, Robert H., B.A., M.A.; Director of Publications, Council of State Governments. [STATE GOVERNMENT]

Webster, Mary C., B.A.; Editor, *Noticias* Magazine. [LATIN AMERICA; Latin America Articles]

Weinstein, David, B.A.B.H.L., M.H.L., M.A., Ed.D.; President, Spertus College of Judaica. [JEWS]

White, Thomas O., Ph.D.; Physicist, National Accelerator Laboratory, Batavia Ill. [PHYSICS]

Whyte, William H., B.A.; Author: *The Organization Man; Open Space Action.* [Special Report: TAKING A CLOSER LOOK AT THE CITY]

Contributors not listed on these pages are members of the WORLD BOOK YEAR BOOK editorial staff.

Chronology 1971

January

Sun	Mon	Tue	Wed	Thu	Fri	Sat
					1	2
3	4	5	6	7	8	9
10	11	12	13	14	15	16
17	18	19	20	21	22	23
24 31	25	26	27	28	29	30

1   **Three-day New Year's cease-fire** in Vietnam ends amid reports that sporadic fighting continued throughout the period.

2   **The 91st Congress** adjourns, ending its second session—the longest held since 1950.

4   **Leon Howard Sullivan,** a Negro, is elected to the board of directors of General Motors Corporation, becoming the first black director in the world's largest industrial corporation.

6   **Two biochemists** at the University of California Medical Center in San Francisco succeed in synthesizing the hormone responsible for growth in the human body.

11   **Holy Cross College** of Worcester, Mass., founded by the Society of Jesus in 1843, announces it will admit women students in

September, 1972, thereby becoming the last of the 28 Jesuit colleges in the United States to go coeducational.

President Juan Jose Torres of Bolivia announces that a coup has been crushed.

Canadian diplomat John MacLeod Fraser arrives to set up Canada's embassy in China.

11-17   **New outbreaks of violence** sweep two Roman Catholic areas in Belfast, Northern Ireland.

12   **Philip F. Berrigan** and five others are indicted on charges they conspired to kidnap Henry A. Kissinger, assistant to the President for national security.

15   **The Republican National Committee** approves Senator Robert J. Dole of Kansas as the party's National Chairman.

20   **The first nationwide** postal strike in British history begins, idling 220,000 members of the Union of Post Office Workers.

21   **The 100th session** of the peace talks between representatives of the United States and North Vietnam is held in Paris.

The 92nd Congress convenes with Democratic majorities in both houses.

22   **President Richard M. Nixon** delivers annual State of the Union message before a joint session of Congress.

25   **President Apollo Milton Obote** of Uganda is ousted in a coup led by Major General Idi Amin Dada.

26   **The longest trial** in California's history ends in Los Angeles with the conviction of Charles M. Manson and three of his followers on charges of first-degree murder.

Russia announces that its interplanetary probe, *Venera 7,* landed on Venus on Dec. 15, 1970.

29   **Canadian Prime Minister** Pierre Elliott Trudeau returns to Canada after a 24-day tour of Asia, during which he took part in the Commonwealth conference of prime ministers in Singapore.

February

Sun	Mon	Tue	Wed	Thu	Fri	Sat
	1	2	3	4	5	6
7	8	9	10	11	12	13
14	15	16	17	18	19	20
21	22	23	24	25	26	27
28						

1   **Diplomat Hsu Chung-fu** and a 10-man Chinese delegation arrive in Ottawa to set up Peking's embassy in Canada.

4   **Rolls-Royce, Limited,** a world symbol of British engineering and craftsmanship, declares bankruptcy because of spiraling costs involved in developing the RB 211 engine for Lockheed Aircraft Corporation.

5   **Egypt and Israel agree** to extend a cease-fire in the Middle East for another 30 days, the third such cease-fire negotiated since June, 1970.

United States astronauts Alan B. Shepard, Jr., and Edgar D. Mitchell land their lunar module, Antares, on the moon while a third astronaut, Stuart A. Roosa, remains aboard the command-and-service module Kitty Hawk. The *Apollo 14* mission had lifted from Cape Kennedy Launch Pad 39A at 4:03 P.M. E.S.T. on January 31.

7   **A constitutional amendment** is approved by male voters in Switzerland giving Swiss women for the first time the right to vote in federal elections and to hold federal office.

8   **South Vietnamese troops,** backed by U.S. air, artillery, and logistical support, invade southern Laos, touching off considerable pro-and-con debate in international capitals.

9 The *Apollo 14* mission is successfully completed with a safe splashdown in the Pacific Ocean at 4:05 P.M. E.S.T.

11 A seabed treaty, barring the installation of nuclear weapons on the ocean floor, is signed by 63 nations in Washington, Moscow, and London.

15 A decimal currency system is adopted by Great Britain, ending the 1,000-year history of the pence-and-pound currency.

23 A nationwide dispute is touched off over the merits and accuracy of a CBS television documentary entitled "The Selling of the Pentagon."

March

Sun	Mon	Tue	Wed	Thu	Fri	Sat
	1	2	3	4	5	6
7	8	9	10	11	12	13
14	15	16	17	18	19	20
21	22	23	24	25	26	27
28	29	30	31			

1 A bomb allegedly planted by dissidents protesting the U.S.-supported invasion of Laos, explodes in the Senate wing of the Capitol at 1:32 A.M. Damages are estimated at $300,000.
Pakistan's President Agha Mohammad Yahya Khan postpones the opening of Pakistan's first popularly elected National Assembly because of disagreement over a proposed new Constitution.

1-10 The ruling New Congress Party of India's Prime Minister Indira Gandhi wins a landslide victory in nationwide elections held for the Lok Sabha, the lower house of Parliament.

8 Postal workers in Great Britain vote to end a 47-day wage strike that had cost the post office at least $64.8 million in revenue.

10 John G. Gorton is ousted as Australia's prime minister and leader of the Liberal Party; he is subsequently succeeded by former External Affairs Minister William McMahon.

12 South Korean troops replace U.S. troops along the 151-mile armistice border with North Korea for the first time since the end of the Korean War.
Lieutenant General Hafiz al-Asad is approved as president of Syria in a nationwide plebiscite.

15 United States discontinues requirement that all U.S. citizens obtain specially validated passports for travel to China.

16 A nationwide state of siege is declared by Ceylon's Prime Minister Sirimavo Bandaranaike following weeks of terrorist activity.

17 President Nixon signs bill providing for a 10 per cent increase in social security benefits.
A minority Labor government, headed by Trygve M. Bratteli, is sworn in, in Norway as successor to the government of Prime Minister Per Borten.

23 Brian Faulkner is elected the sixth prime minister of Northern Ireland, succeeding James D. Chichester-Clark, who resigned in a bitter dispute involving Roman Catholic terrorist activities in Northern Ireland.
A three-man military junta ousts Argentina's President Roberto Marcelo Levingston following a week of severe rioting in Cordoba.

24 The U. S. Senate votes to end government sponsorship of the supersonic transport.

25 Civil war erupts in East Pakistan;
East Pakistani leader Sheik Mujibur Rahman proclaims East Pakistan the independent nation of Bangla Desh.

26 Army commander Alejandro Agustín Lanusse, a member of the military junta that ousted Argentine President Roberto Marcelo Levingston, is sworn in as president.

28 In presidential elections in Honduras, Ramón Ernesto Cruz and his National Party win a decisive victory over Jorge Buesco Arias and his Liberal Party.

29 Yugoslav President Tito meets with Pope Paul VI during a formal state visit to Italy, thus becoming the first Communist leader ever to meet the Roman Catholic pontiff officially.
A U.S. Army court-martial jury finds Army First Lieutenant William L. Calley, Jr., guilty of the premeditated murder of South Vietnamese civilians at My Lai, and sentences him to life imprisonment at hard labor.

April

Sun	Mon	Tue	Wed	Thu	Fri	Sat
				1	2	3
4	5	6	7	8	9	10
11	12	13	14	15	16	17
18	19	20	21	22	23	24
25	26	27	28	29	30	

1 Argentina legalizes activities of political parties, ending a ban that had been in effect since 1964.

2 Rising violence in East Pakistan prompts the United States, Russia, and other nations to appeal to President Agha Mohammed Yahya Khan to halt the fighting and resolve the conflict peacefully.

4   **Chilean President** Salvador Allende passes the first popular test of his administration's policies by winning 49.73 per cent of the votes cast in 280 municipal elections.

5   **An armed rebellion erupts** in Ceylon; Prime Minister Sirimavo Bandaranaike orders a nationwide curfew and bans the militant Marxist People's Liberation Front.

6   **Richard J. Daley** wins his fifth term as mayor of Chicago. He had served 16 consecutive years, longer than any other man in the city's history.

7   **President Nixon** announces a plan to increase the rate of U.S. troop withdrawals from South Vietnam.

10   **The arrival** of a nine-member U.S. table tennis team in the People's Republic of China opens a new phase in U.S.-Chinese relations.

14   **President Nixon** orders a relaxation of the 20-year embargo on trade with China.

17   **Egypt, Syria, and Libya** sign an accord agreeing to form a federation subject to approval by plebiscites in the three countries.

18-24   **Earth Week,** an observance devoted to the environment, is held nationwide to direct attention to environmental problems in the United States.

20   **The U.S. Supreme Court** unanimously upholds busing of children as a means of achieving racially balanced schools.

21   **Prime Minister Siaka P. Stevens** is sworn in as president of the newly proclaimed republic of Sierra Leone.

22   **Jean-Claude Duvalier** is sworn in as president of Haiti, succeeding his father, François Duvalier, who had died the preceding day.

25   **Austria's President** Franz Jonas is re-elected to a new six-year term.

27   **South Korea's President** Chung Hee Park is re-elected to a third four-year term.

May

Sun	Mon	Tue	Wed	Thu	Fri	Sat
						1
2	3	4	5	6	7	8
9	10	11	12	13	14	15
16	17	18	19	20	21	22
23 / 30	24 / 31	25	26	27	28	29

1   **U.S. Secretary of State** William P. Rogers begins a five-nation tour of the Middle East to evaluate chances of settling the Arab-Israeli dispute.
Amtrak, a quasigovernmental corporation, inaugurates a new passenger rail service linking about 300 cities.

3   **Erich Honecker** is unanimously elected to succeed Walter Ulbricht as first secretary of East Germany's Socialist Unity Party.

3-5   **Thousands of antiwar protestors** are arrested in Washington, D.C., after they threaten to close down the capital by a massive civil-disobedience protest.

4   **A massive speculative** assault against the U.S. dollar sweeps the European money markets and threatens the value of the dollar.

12   **The Chilean government** passes a constitutional reform bill permitting the nationalization of the U.S.-owned copper industry in Chile.

16   **Albanian voters** approve a new Constitution that replaces the Presidium of the National Assembly with a State Council.

21   **U.S. Secretary of the Army** Stanley E. Resor resigns his post after six years in office, but agrees to remain until a successor is named.

22   **The $18.6-million** Lyndon Baines Johnson Library complex on the University of Texas campus in Austin is dedicated.

24-25   **Indian-Pakistani** troops clash along the East Pakistani frontier as millions of East Pakistani war refugees stream into India.

June

Sun	Mon	Tue	Wed	Thu	Fri	Sat
		1	2	3	4	5
6	7	8	9	10	11	12
13	14	15	16	17	18	19
20	21	22	23	24	25	26
27	28	29	30			

1   **Brazil announces** that its warships and planes will patrol the 200-mile territorial water limit that replaced the former 12-mile limit.

3   **A controversial bill** that could eliminate opposition to Vietnamese President Nguyen Van Thieu in the presidential elections scheduled for October 3 is approved by the lower chamber of the South Vietnamese National Assembly.

James R. Hoffa, president of the International Brotherhood of Teamsters, which he has headed since 1957, announces from prison that he is not a candidate for re-election.

5-6 **A series of bomb explosions** in Belfast, Northern Ireland, injure at least eight persons as Roman Catholics and Protestants alike are subjected to continuing terrorism.

7 **The World Health Organization** reports that an epidemic of cholera has broken out among the estimated 4.7 million East Pakistani war refugees who have sought asylum in India.
Massive traffic tie-ups occur in New York City as municipal employees strike over a proposed pension plan.

10 **Clashes between** Leftist students and armed groups of Right wing extremists in Mexico City result in 9 students dead and 160 wounded.

11 **U.S. marshals remove** 15 Indians from Alcatraz Island in San Francisco Bay, ending a 19-month occupation of the former federal prison by the Indians.

12 **Patricia Nixon,** President Nixon's daughter, and Edward Cox are married in the White House Rose Garden.

13 *The New York Times* begins publication of a series of articles and documents based on a secret Pentagon study ordered by U.S. Secretary of Defense Robert S. MacNamara during the Administration of President Lyndon B. Johnson.

17 **A U.S.-Japanese treaty** is signed under which the United States agrees to return to Japan in 1972 the Pacific island of Okinawa, the other islands in the Ryuku group, and the Daito Islands.

21 **The International** Court of Justice at The Hague

rules that South Africa's administrative control of South West Africa (Namibia) is illegal and should be relinquished.

23 **Great Britain** and the European Community reach final settlement of major obstacles that had obstructed British membership in the community.

30 **The U.S. Supreme Court** upholds by a 6 to 3 decision *The New York Times'* right to publish material from a classified Pentagon study of the Vietnamese war's origins.
Three Soviet cosmonauts, who set a 24-day endurance record for space flight in Russia's space laboratory *Salyut,* die as they re-enter earth's atmosphere.
The 26th Amendment to the U.S. Constitution, establishing 18 years as the minimum voting age for all federal, state, and local elections, is ratified when Ohio becomes the 38th state to approve it.

July

Sun	Mon	Tue	Wed	Thu	Fri	Sat
				1	2	3
4	5	6	7	8	9	10
11	12	13	14	15	16	17
18	19	20	21	22	23	24
25	26	27	28	29	30	31

1 **The 182-year-old** U.S. Post Office Department is officially replaced by the new semi-independent U.S. Postal Service.

3 **Indonesia's** ruling Sekber Golkar coalition government wins a sweeping victory in the nation's first parliamentary elections in 16 years.

5 **The 26th Amendment** to the U.S. Constitution is officially certified by President Nixon.

6 **Malawi's Hastings K. Banda** is sworn in as president for life in ceremonies also marking the fifth anniversary of the republic.

8 **U.S.-Russian delegates** open the fifth round of strategic arms limitation talks (SALT) in Helsinki, Finland.

10 **Moroccan King Hassan II** survives a coup launched at his summer palace at Skhirat, where he was celebrating his birthday.

13 **Relations between** Jordan, Egypt, Syria, and Iraq deteriorate after Jordanian armed forces launch an all-out attack against Palestinian commandos operating in northern Jordan.

14 **A Leftist coalition** government headed by Prime Minister Olafur Johannesson takes office in Iceland.

15 **President Nixon** discloses he will make an unprecedented visit to confer in Peking with leaders of the People's Republic of China in 1972; his action follows a secret visit made by his national security affairs adviser, Henry A. Kissinger, to Peking on July 9 to 11.

16 **The Belgian Chamber of Deputies** approves constitutional reforms designed to resolve long-standing discord between Belgium's French- and Flemish-speaking communities.

18 **Six Persian Gulf Emirates** announce they will merge into one single federation in 1971.

20 **The U.S. Selective Service** System, despite a congressional stalemate in extending the draft law, sets new draft lottery to determine which 19-year-olds will be called for induction in 1972.

22 **Sudan's Major General** Jafir Muhammad Nimeri, deposed in a Leftist-led coup three days earlier, is restored to power by military forces loyal to his regime.

26 **The moon-bound** *Apollo 15,* with three

astronauts aboard, is launched from Cape Kennedy, Fla., at 9:34 A.M. E.D.T. atop a 363-foot Saturn 5 rocket.

28 **The U.S. Army command** in South Vietnam announces that all U.S. servicemen returning to America from the area will be tested for heroin use.

August

Sun	Mon	Tue	Wed	Thu	Fri	Sat
1	2	3	4	5	6	7
8	9	10	11	12	13	14
15	16	17	18	19	20	21
22	23	24	25	26	27	28
29	30	31				

2 **The U.S. Department of State** announces it will support United Nations membership for the People's Republic of China, thus in effect ending 20 years of U.S. opposition to China's presence in the UN.

6 **U.S. Congress** begins a one-month recess. **Morocco's King** Hassan II appoints a new government headed by Prime Minister Mohamed Karim Lamrani.

7 **U.S. astronauts** splash down safely in the Pacific at 4:46 P.M. E.D.T. after successfully exploring moon's surface.

8 **Canadian Prime Minister** Pierre Trudeau ends a 10-day tour of the nation's Atlantic provinces, including Nova Scotia, Newfoundland, and Prince Edward Island.

9 **A 20-year friendship treaty** is signed by India and the Soviet Union in which both nations agree to avoid interfering in one another's internal affairs.
A new wave of Roman Catholic-Protestant rioting, reportedly the heaviest in 50 years, erupts in Northern Ireland.

12 **Syria breaks off** diplomatic relations with Jordan after military forces of both countries clash along the border.

13 **The North Atlantic** Treaty Organization, acting on a request made by the Malta government, announces it will close its naval headquarters on the Mediterranean island.

14 **Bahrain, a Persian Gulf** sheikdom, declares itself independent of Great Britain and renames itself the State of Bahrain.

15 **President Nixon,** in a surprise move designed to cope with the inflationary spiral in the United States, orders an immediate 90-day freeze on wages, rents, and prices. He also ends the traditional convertibility of the U.S. dollar to gold in order to defend it against international speculators, and orders a 10 per cent surcharge on imported goods.

20 **A new Constitution** for the proposed three-member Federation of Arab Republics is signed by representatives of Syria, Egypt, and Libya.
Malawi President Hastings K. Banda ends a state visit to the Republic of South Africa, the first black head of state to travel in that country.

20-23 **A major political crisis** develops in South Vietnam when General Duong Van Minh and Vice-President Nguyen Cao Ky withdraw from the presidential race, leaving incumbent President Nguyen Van Thieu as the sole candidate.

22 **A new Rightist** government headed by Colonel Hugo Banzer Suarez is installed in Brazil following the overthrow of the 10-month-old regime of Leftist President Juan Jose Torres.

23 **The United States,** France, Britain, and Russia reach agreement on a draft of principles for a Berlin settlement that includes "unimpeded access to the city."

September

Sun	Mon	Tue	Wed	Thu	Fri	Sat
			1	2	3	4
5	6	7	8	9	10	11
12	13	14	15	16	17	18
19	20	21	22	23	24	25
26	27	28	29	30		

1 **Voters in Egypt,** Libya, and Syria endorse a merger whereby the three nations become members of the Federation of Arab Republics.
Qatar, a Persian Gulf sheikdom, declares itself independent of Great Britain.

4 **Major General** Hassan al-Amri, forced to resign as prime minister of Yemen less than two weeks after forming a new Cabinet, takes up exile in Lebanon.

8 **U. S. Congress** reconvenes after its summer recess.

10 **The United States** completes removal of

poisonous gas stored at American bases in Okinawa.

11 **Egypt's President** Anwar al-Sadat announces that a new Constitution has been overwhelmingly approved in a national referendum.

13 **An uprising** by 1,200 inmates in the Attica Correctional Facility in Attica, N.Y., is quelled by nearly 1,500 state troopers, sheriff's deputies, and prison guards. The final death toll is 43.

17 **Associate Justice** Hugo L. Black resigns for health reasons after 34 years of service on the U. S. Supreme Court.

18 **Egyptian and Israeli** forces stationed along the Suez Canal exchange heavy fire for the first time since August, 1970, when a cease-fire went into effect.

21 **Congressional approval** is finally given to a draft bill extending military conscription through June, 1973. The draft had been suspended since June 30, when the old law expired.
The 26th session of the United Nations General Assembly convenes in New York City; Indonesia's foreign minister Adam Malik is elected as its president.

23 **Associate Justice** John M. Harlan resigns from the U.S. Supreme Court because of ill health.

25 **Associate Justice** Hugo L. Black dies a week after he resigned from the Supreme Court.

26 **President Nixon** meets with Japan's Emperor Hirohito in Anchorage, Alaska.
Representative Shirley A. Chisholm, the only black woman in Congress, announces she will enter the 1972 presidential primaries in Florida, Wisconsin, California, and North Carolina.

28 **The arrival** of Joseph Cardinal Mindszenty at the Vatican in Rome marks the end of a 15-year exile in the U.S. Embassy in Budapest, Hungary.

October

Sun	Mon	Tue	Wed	Thu	Fri	Sat
					1	2
3	4	5	6	7	8	9
10	11	12	13	14	15	16
17	18	19	20	21	22	23
24 / 31	25	26	27	28	29	30

1 **Ralph Bunche,** winner of the 1950 Nobel peace prize, and undersecretary-general for special political affairs for the United Nations, retires because of illness. He had helped negotiate the 1949 Middle East cease-fire.

3 **William Gopallawa,** the royal governor of Ceylon, signs a bill abolishing Ceylon's Senate. The House of Representatives becomes the nation's only legislative body.
South Vietnam's President Nguyen Van Thieu, in an uncontested election, is re-elected to a second four-year term.

4 **Egyptian President** Anwar al-Sadat is named president of the Federation of Arab Republics.

7 **President Nixon** announces Phase 2 of his plan to fight inflation in the United States. The wage-and-price restraint program is continued, and various boards and commissions are established to handle the administrative machinery.

8 **President Nixon** becomes the first U. S. President to visit all 50 states when he attends the 35th annual State Forest Festival in Elkins, W.Va.

11 **A minority government,** headed by Denmark's Social Democratic leader Jens Otto Krag, replaces the center-right coalition government of Hilmar Baunsgaard.

12 **Major General** Jafir Muhammad Nimeri, who had headed the government since October, 1969, is installed as the first elected president of Sudan; he received 98.6 per cent of the vote in a national referendum held over a two-week period.

14 **Iran holds** an elaborate celebration to mark the 2,500th anniversary of the founding of the Persian Empire by Cyrus the Great.

21 **President Nixon** nominates Lewis F. Powell, Jr., and William H. Rehnquist to the Supreme Court.

22 **Premier Lon Nol** imposes a state of emergency in Cambodia and abolishes constitutional rule as a measure to prevent a threatened outbreak of violence.

25 **The United Nations** General Assembly, by a 76 to 35 vote (with 17 abstentions), admits the People's Republic of China as a member and expels the Chinese Nationalist government of Formosa (Taiwan).

28 **A historic turning point** in Britain's 10-year effort to join the European Community is reached when the House of Commons approves the principle of British membership.

29 **The U.S. Senate,** by a vote of 41 to 27, refuses to authorize the continuation of U.S. foreign aid. It was the first Senate rejection of such aid in more than two decades.
Finnish Prime Minister Ahti Karjalainen and his center-left coalition government resign, and a caretaker government headed by Teuvo Auro is appointed by President Urho Kekkonen.

November

Sun	Mon	Tue	Wed	Thu	Fri	Sat
	1	2	3	4	5	6
7	8	9	10	11	12	13
14	15	16	17	18	19	20
21	22	23	24	25	26	27
28	29	30				

1   **A five-nation** Asian defense pact, signed by Malaysia, Singapore, Australia, New Zealand, and Great Britain, supersedes the British-Malaysian-Singapore defense treaty under which Britain had formerly assumed sole responsibility for security of the area.

4   **A new all-Socialist** Austrian government headed by Chancellor Bruno Kreisky is sworn in after winning a sweeping victory in national elections.

6   **Despite protests** by Canada and Japan, and by many scientists and ecologists, the United States explodes a five-megaton H-bomb on the Alaskan island of Amchitka in the Aleutian Islands.

10   **The U.S. Senate,** by an 84-6 vote, ratifies the treaty under which Okinawa and the other Ryukyu Islands will revert to Japan in 1972.

11   **Clifford M. Hardin** resigns as U.S. Secretary of Agriculture; President Nixon nominates Earl L. Butz, an agricultural official in the Eisenhower Administration, as his successor.

12   **The United States** enters Phase 2 of the economic stabilization program.

13   **The U.S. interplanetary** space probe, *Mariner 9,* goes into orbit around Mars after a 5½-month journey across 247 million miles. The $65-million spacecraft, which had been launched from Cape Kennedy, Fla., on May 30, is the first man-made craft to orbit another planet.

16   **The first working** session of the sixth round of U.S.-Russian strategic arms limitation talks (SALT) resumes in Vienna, Austria.

17   **In a bloodless** coup d'état, Premier Thanom Kittikachorn and a group of military and civilian leaders seize the government of Thailand, abolish the Constitution, and establish martial law.

30   **King Hussein of Jordan** appoints Ahmad al-Lawzi as premier, replacing Wasfi el-Tal, who was assassinated in Cairo while attending a meeting of the Arab League's Joint Defense Council.

December

Sun	Mon	Tue	Wed	Thu	Fri	Sat
			1	2	3	4
5	6	7	8	9	10	11
12	13	14	15	16	17	18
19	20	21	22	23	24	25
26	27	28	29	30	31	

1   **The U.S. government** suspends the licensing of all arms shipments to India, citing Indian incursions into Pakistani territory as its reason. The sending of U. S. arms to Pakistan had been stopped early in September.

2   **Britain's House of Commons** votes 297 to 269 to approve the government's proposals for a settlement of the long-standing dispute with the white-led government of Rhodesia.

2   **Earl L. Butz** is confirmed as U.S. Secretary of Agriculture in a 51 to 44 Senate vote.

3   **Six Persian Gulf** sheikdoms proclaim their independence as the Union of Arab Emirates at a meeting held in Dubayy. Sheik Zayd Ben, Sultan of Abdu Dhabi, is named the union's first president.
India launches a full-scale land, sea, and air attack against Pakistan without a declaration of war.

5   **General Motors,** in the largest recall in automotive history, announces it will correct at its own expense a defect involving the motor mounts in 6.7 million 1965–1969 Chevrolet cars and trucks.

8   **Russia announces** it has succeeded in landing a capsule on the surface of Mars and that it has transmitted television signals for a brief period.

15   **The United States,** in an effort to resolve the world monetary crisis, announces it is prepared to devalue the dollar as part of an international agreement to realign the rates of major currencies.

16   **India orders** a complete cease-fire on both fronts after Pakistan's surrender in the East.

17   **Steps are begun** to set up the government for the new nation of Bangla Desh, formerly East Pakistan.
The first session of the 92nd Congress adjourns after resolving the foreign aid controversy by temporarily extending the current program.
Col. Oran K. Henderson is acquitted of charges that he covered up the killing of about 100 civilians in the South Vietnamese hamlet of My Lai. The colonel was the last to be tried for having had a role in the affair.

18   **The International Monetary Fund** approves the new pattern of exchange rates among the world's leading currencies. The decision makes legal an agreement reached the day before by a group of 10 leading industrial countries, who had recommended that currencies be permitted to fluctuate 2.25 per cent above and below the new par values.

20   **President Nixon** announces that the 10 per cent surcharge on goods imported into the United States has been terminated.
Zulfikar Ali Bhutto, Pakistan's deputy premier and foreign minister, is sworn in as president and martial-law administrator of Pakistan, returning the nation to civilian rule for the first time since 1958. His predecessor, Agha Mohammed Yahya Khan, was forced to resign following Pakistan's defeat by India.

21   **Kurt Waldheim,** Austria's permanent representative to the United Nations is elected by the Security Council to succeed U Thant as secretary-general. Waldheim is the fourth man to head the secretariat in the organization's history.

23   **The ruling** Nationalist Chinese party, the Kuomintang, announces that the first national elections since 1947 will be held in Formosa in May, 1972. President Chiang Kai-shek had always refused to hold elections pending his government's return to mainland China, when all Chinese could participate.
President Nixon signs a bill to implement a much-expanded research attack on cancer. Some 137 guests are present at the White House for the occasion, including many research scientists.

24   **President Nixon commutes** the prison term of James R. Hoffa, former president of the International Brotherhood of Teamsters. Hoffa had served 4 years, 9 months, and 16 days of a 13-year term.

26-29   **U.S. Air Force** and Navy planes launch heavy bombing raids on military installations in North Vietnam. It was the first time since 1968 that a series of attacks against North Vietnam had lasted more than two days.

27   **Delegates representing** 18 Arab countries meet in Cairo, Egypt to discuss plans for coordinating military and economic strategy against Israel.

Section One

The Year In Focus

THE YEAR BOOK Board of Editors analyzes some significant developments of 1971 and considers their impact on contemporary affairs. The Related Articles list following each report directs the reader to THE YEAR BOOK's additional coverage of related subjects.

16   Alastair Buchan: Focus on The World

22   James Reston: Focus on The Nation

28   Sylvia Porter: Focus on The Economy

34   Harrison Brown: Focus on Science

40   Lawrence A. Cremin: Focus on Education

46   Alistair Cooke: Focus on The Arts

52   Jim Murray: Focus on Sports

Alastair Buchan

Focus on The World

In 1971, the international system underwent a radical transformation—primarily because of a redefinition of United States interests in the world, and the world's reaction to it

The network of interdependent relationships that bind together the 120 or so sovereign states of the world—relationships of friendship or hostility, cooperation or competition, trade or aid—is known by scholars as "the international system." It is never static. It is always in a process of continuous and gradual change, as if we were looking into a kaleidoscope whose eyepiece was being gently rotated. But from time to time, the forces of history impart a sudden jerk to the kaleidoscope so that the pattern changes swiftly. In 1971, the post-World War II international system underwent just such a change.

For 20 years or so, the system had possessed certain striking characteristics:

■ A basic hostility between the two postwar superpowers, the United States and Russia, which was muted and controlled by the possession of long-range nuclear weapons by both nations.

■ An equally hostile relationship between the two superpowers and China.

■ A close political and security relationship between the United States and most of the nations of Western Europe, plus many in the Far East, operating through military alliances and a network of economic arrangements, and based on U.S. economic and military power.

■ A high degree of Western influence in the developing nations, based on aid and trade and old affinities.

True, this system underwent minor modifications throughout the late 1960s. The Vietnam War had illustrated the limits of America's power to support a disorganized, small ally. The Nixon Doctrine of 1969 had put all the allies of the United States on notice that it could not indefinitely remain the master member of all the alliances of which it was a member, for a mixture of social and economic reasons. Arms-control negotiations with Russia had identified a certain degree of common interest between Moscow and Washington. The old emotional animosity toward "Red" China was clearly diminishing. Western Europe was beginning to acquire a political and economic coherence of its own.

Alastair Buchan

17

But until 1971, the postwar system remained basically unchanged. Then, in the second half of the year, the pace of change began to accelerate dramatically, primarily because of a redefinition of U.S. interests in the world, and the world's reaction to it.

The development that most caught the headlines was the change in Sino-American relations and in China's position in the world. It started in semicomic fashion with a Chinese invitation in April to an American and a British Ping-Pong team to visit Peking. Premier Chou Enlai used the visit as an opportunity to speak of "a new stage in the relations between the Chinese and American peoples." President Richard M. Nixon reciprocated in April and May by liberalizing U.S. restrictions on personal travel and trade with China, which had been in force for more than 20 years. In June, he lifted all embargoes, save those on strategic goods.

During 1970, more and more Western or Western-oriented countries—Austria, Canada, and Italy, to name only a few—had been entering into full diplomatic relations with China. And clearly a fundamental decision was made in Washington in the spring of 1971 that the United States would isolate itself, rather than China, by refusing to have any dealings with Peking. So it was not wholly surprising when Henry A. Kissinger, the President's adviser on national security affairs, appeared in Peking in July, and it was later announced that the President himself would go there early in 1972. On August 2, U.S. Secretary of State William P. Rogers expressed support for China's entry into the United Nations (UN), provided it did not prejudice the status of Formosa (Taiwan).

But in fact, the breaking of the Sino-American logjam precipitated a more rapid pace of events than Washington could control. On October 25, after two weeks of American rearguard action in the UN to protect Formosa, the General Assembly voted by a large majority—with only Australia, Japan, and a number of small Asian and Latin American nations supporting the United States—to give the Chinese seat in the UN to Peking. The delegation from Formosa withdrew, and, in November, the representatives from Peking took their seats in both the Security Council and the General Assembly. A chapter of history spanning nearly a generation had been closed.

The end of China's isolation set other processes in motion. Russia, which has long feared a Sino-American rapprochement, not only muttered its disapproval of the new trend in U.S. policy through its press, but also took positive steps to strengthen its position in Asia by concluding two long-term treaties of "Peace, Friendship, and Cooperation." The first of these was with Egypt, in May, and the second with India, in August. The treaties impose a direct obligation on the smaller power to consult with Moscow in a crisis, in return for arms and aid, and were the first such treaties Russia has signed with non-Communist countries since World War II. In December, Moscow and Peking backed India and Pakistan, respectively, in a brief war that saw a new nation, Bangla Desh, proclaimed after the collapse of East Pakistan.

When China took its UN seat, a long chapter of history closed

China in the UN

Russia's fear of any expansion of Chinese influence in the world did not snap the thread of Soviet-American communication. President Nixon wisely announced that he would visit Moscow after he had been to Peking, and the two superpowers' negotiations for a bilateral treaty on the limitation of strategic armaments (the SALT talks) moved toward fruition as the year closed. True, Russia continued to play its traditional game of trying to sow dissension in Western Europe and to divide the two halves of the Atlantic Alliance. It concentrated especially on France, to which Party Secretary Leonid I. Brezhnev, now the master of Russian foreign policy, paid a state visit in October.

There are limits to the diplomatic havoc Russia dare wreak in Europe

But there are other factors, which I will mention, making for greater unity in Western Europe. There also are limits to how much diplomatic havoc Moscow dare attempt to wreak there, since Russia needs Western technology, and wishes to capitalize on the readiness of West Germany to accept the status quo of a divided Germany. Thus, in September, after long negotiations, Russia signed a new agreement on access to Berlin, the first such agreement since 1947.

During the year, the prime concentration of Russian policy was on persuading the countries of Western Europe to agree to a grand European Conference on Security and Cooperation in 1972 at which all the 28 states of Europe, East and West, would be represented, as well as Canada and the United States. In Russian eyes, the main purpose of such a conference, even if it took several years to achieve agreement, would be to secure acknowledgment of the status quo in Europe—particularly recognition by the West of the sovereign status of East Germany. A second purpose would be to gain greater access to Western technology.

The smaller West European and neutral states, plus West Germany, are prepared to agree to such a conference. This is so not merely because they are ready to acknowledge the existence of different political systems in Eastern Europe (including East Germany), but also because they hope to negotiate in such a conference a mutual reduction of military-force levels in Europe, especially as the threat of unilateral American troop reductions looms larger and larger. The year's events showed that the countries dubious about accepting an invitation are Great Britain, France, and the United States. This is probably because each of them fears that a conference of this kind would provide a superb opportunity for Russian propaganda, and would encourage the tendency toward neutralism or isolationism in the public opinions of their own or allied countries without achieving greater security in Europe. This identity of interest was illustrated by President Nixon's decision to have private meetings with British Prime Minister Edward Heath and French President Georges Pompidou in December, as part of his consultation with allied leaders before he goes to Peking and Moscow.

War news in India

China has found its place once again in the councils of the world, thanks to years of patient and assiduous cultivation of the small developing countries. There is a new note of confidence in Russia's diplomacy in Europe, even if its diplomacy is motivated more by fear than by confidence in Asia. But nothing has occurred to alter the central balance of power in the world, even though Russia may have built a larger inventory of missiles than the United States has, as well as a modern navy. The United States still possesses an undisputed ability to destroy Russian civilization in a nuclear exchange, has 15 attack carriers at sea while Russia has none, and has an economy that is twice the size of Russia's. Nevertheless, there was an atmosphere of concern and pessimism in some Western capitals as the year ended. The reasons for it had more to do with the internal cohesion of the American alliance systems, and the influence they can exert elsewhere in the world, than with the actions or strength of the Communist powers.

The August 15 economic moves by the U.S. had great effects on world politics

In the first place, President Nixon's decision to seek rapprochement with China was made without any consultation with its Southeast Asia Treaty Organization allies and, above all, without consulting Japan, the second most economically powerful nation in the U.S. alliance systems. Consequently, it shook the confidence and the political credibility of Japanese Prime Minister Eisaku Sato's government, and undid most of the benefits of the new U.S.-Japanese agreement on the return of Okinawa to Japan.

But far more widespread were the political effects of the economic measures that President Nixon felt it necessary to announce on August 15, after the most serious downturn in the U.S. balance of payments since the 1930s. They included a 10 per cent surcharge on imports of manufactured goods, and a decoupling of the value of the U.S. dollar from the price of gold. The measures reinforced growing doubts in Japan and Western Europe as to whether the unified Western system of trade, payments, and political coordination that had existed for the quarter-century since World War II could be sustained into the last quarter of the 20th century—or whether the specter of economic and political nationalism might not be rising to haunt the world again. Mr. Nixon's December actions—suspending the surcharge and devaluing the dollar—restored stability to currency rates, although the final shape of a new Western monetary system was yet to be determined.

The effect of developments in U.S. policy upon Western Europe has been particularly complex. On the one hand, a fear that the United States may be becoming more nationalist in its attitudes—"American Gaullism" is a phrase one sometimes hears—has tended to draw Western Europe together. After nine years of French opposition to British entry into the European Community (Common Market), Prime Minister Heath and President Pompidou discovered by meeting in May that the differences in French and British outlooks on the future of Europe were now relatively trivial. In June, Britain secured terms of entry into the Common Market that met its principal requirements. And on October 28, the House of Commons voted by a large majority (including nearly half the opposition Labour Party) in favor of entry. There will be stormy debates as the legislation to bring British law into conformity with the market's rules winds its way through Parliament

Britain's Edward Heath

in 1972, but among other considerations affecting British attitudes to a more united Europe is Heath's view that the old "special relationship" between London and Washington is now virtually defunct. There is also a growing conviction in Britain, echoed in France and elsewhere, that Europe as a political entity will shortly have to assume a greater share of its own defense as well as adopt a more unified responsibility for the operation of the international monetary system.

On the other hand, the growth of unemployment in Europe has made for economic nationalism there, and has placed strains on the Franco-German relationship (the essential political basis of the Common Market) because of the differing strengths of the two economies and currencies. And this has made the community itself more difficult to operate. These difficulties will, I think, be overcome. But the fact remains that American eyes may see an enlarged European Community of 10 nations (the original 6 plus Denmark, Ireland, and Norway, as well as Britain), with preferential trade arrangements with some 40 other countries, as a threat to its economic interests instead of as that "equal and responsible partner" that has been the goal of the U.S. Department of State for many years.

Other bits of the kaleidoscope also began to shift in 1971, illustrating the diminishing influence of the great upon the small. They included the failure of patient American efforts to edge Israel toward a Middle Eastern settlement; the united stand of the oil-producing countries of the world, from Venezuela to Indonesia, under the leadership of the Shah of Iran, that forced a substantial raise in crude-oil prices on the great western oil companies; tiny Malta's successful blackmail of the North Atlantic Treaty Organization powers for an increase in payment for use of its naval facilities; and the U.S. Senate's growing disillusion with foreign aid.

The eyepiece of the kaleidoscope was still turning fast as 1971 ended, and the pattern of the new international system that will replace the postwar one is far from clear. But at its heart is one complex question. In an era when fear of Communism is no longer the driving force, can the developed nations of the Free World reconstitute a series of equitable monetary, trade, and defense relationships, based on an acknowledgment that the United States is still the only major strategic power among them, but no longer the dominant economic power? Or will all of them retire into forms of nationalism, of which Russia will be the diplomatic beneficiary in Europe, and of which China will reap the harvest in Asia and the developing world?

The pattern of the system that will replace the postwar one is far from clear

Related Articles

For further information on international relations in 1971, see the articles on the various nations in Section Three. In the same section, see also the following:

Africa	International Trade	Middle East
Asia	and Finance	Pacific Islands
Europe	Latin America	United Nations

James Reston

Focus on The Nation

The year 1971 in the United States was one of change and reappraisal in all fields—and it left hardly anyone feeling confident about where it was all going

For the United States, 1971 was a year of reappraisal, and in some cases even of retreat, from established positions and policies. Both at home and abroad, ideas that had long been accepted were directly challenged, political and economic theories once regarded as untouchable were torn up and reversed. Everywhere in America, leaders of the government, the political parties, business, and the universities seemed in 1971 to be adopting the pragmatic slogan: If it doesn't work, scrap it.

This, of course, is not a new idea in this country. Products that don't sell, coaches who don't win, and even marriages that don't hum have usually been abandoned in the United States quicker than elsewhere. But paradoxically, we have usually been slow to change political policies and ideologies, and even slower to admit we were changing them.

The year 1971 was an exception to this general rule. In the first years of his Administration, President Richard M. Nixon was defending the conservative economic doctrines of the Republican Party. He was arguing for balanced budgets and he was condemning those in the Democratic Party who insisted that the sluggish American economy, with its high rates of inflation and unemployment, needed more government spending, even at the risk of large federal deficits, and also wage and price controls.

Yet by the end of the year, Mr. Nixon had not only retreated from the conservative foundations of his economic policy, but he had also accepted the largest planned peacetime budget deficit in American history, had introduced wage and price controls, and was devaluing the American dollar.

Similarly, while President Nixon had been an outspoken critic of the welfare-state policies of the Roosevelt, Truman, and Kennedy administrations, he fought in 1971 for the principle of a guaranteed annual wage for all poor families. And while seeking basic reforms in the welfare system of the past, he emerged, not as an economic conservative, but as a self-proclaimed follower of the liberal economic theories of John Maynard Keynes.

James Reston

This did not mean that he had suddenly become a convert to liberal economic policies in all fields, or had adopted any new and rigid ideology. His new pragmatism took many different forms. For example, the liberal trading policies of the United States, which had been in operation since the days of Secretary of State Cordell Hull in the early 1930s, were suddenly changed in 1971 in favor of strict but temporary protectionist policies to defend the dollar and combat both inflation and unemployment.

Mr. Nixon moved in bold ways to prepare to run for re-election

If-you're-losing-change-the-game-plan became the national guideline in other fields. Part of the reason for this was obviously the approach of the 1972 presidential election. Every political party has its own particular nightmare, and the nightmare of the Republican Party is unemployment and economic depression. This has kept it out of the White House for most of the time since the so-called Hoover depression of the early 1930s. So Mr. Nixon moved in bold and even radical ways to put himself in a position to run for re-election on the popular and familiar platform of peace and prosperity.

He increased the pace of withdrawal of American troops from the Vietnam battlefields, and accepted the principle that U.S. ground troops would no longer be sent into Cambodia and Laos. At the beginning of 1971, there were 372,600 American fighting men in Indochina. At year-end, there were about 171,000, and on this schedule of withdrawal, it was planned to have no more than 50,000 men in that peninsula by mid-1972 providing air and logistic support for the South Vietnamese, but no ground troops. One result of this was that U.S. casualties in that war dropped from 9,414 in 1969, and 4,221 in 1970, to around 1,370 in 1971.

This did not stop the demands of many people in both parties for a policy of total withdrawal by a date certain, but it indicated the change in Mr. Nixon's tactics, strategy, and objectives. He was no longer talking of fighting on to "victory" against the menace of Russian and Chinese Communism. He was not only getting out of Vietnam, but he was also going to Peking and Moscow to negotiate what he called "a generation of peace."

Leaving Vietnam

President Nixon's approach to China was the most dramatic diplomatic initiative of the year. For a generation, China with its one-quarter of the human race had lived in isolation from the people of the United States. More than that, the foreign policies of the two countries were mutually hostile, and it was the assumption in Washington of a threatening and expanding China that contributed very largely to the policy of "containing Chinese Communism"—a policy that in turn helped involve the United States in the Korean and Indochina wars.

Mr. Nixon, though he had risen to prominence in American politics as a leader of the anti-Communist movement, set out early in his Administration to normalize diplomatic relations with China. And while he did not quite get that far in 1971, he did start the process.

His argument was that, while the United States did not like to see China under Communism, it had to deal with the world of reality.

Accordingly, he arranged to visit Peking in February of 1972, by which time the representatives of the Peking government were already representing China in the United Nations in New York City.

Thus, it was evident at the beginning of 1972 that the relations between the nations had entered a period of profound transformation, and America's new pragmatism was consciously designed to adapt to the changes. Not only was China taking a more active role in world politics, but the war in Indochina was winding down. There was a cease-fire between Israel and the Arab states in the Middle East. Russia, uneasy over its confrontation with China in Asia and with a million soldiers on the Chinese border, was negotiating a truce over Berlin, and was seeking new strategic arms agreements with the United States and new security arrangements in Europe, where Great Britain was moving toward membership in the European Community.

Instead of just two superpowers, there were five centers of power

With all this going on, there was a feeling in the world that the first postwar historical period—which had been marked by the domination of two nations, the United States and Russia—had come to an end, and that there were now actually five major centers of power: the United States, Russia, China, Japan, and a uniting Europe.

America's reappraisal of this changing political situation paralleled its reappraisal of the changing world monetary situation. The Bretton Woods system, created after World War II to maintain stability in the currencies of the major trading nations, was virtually scrapped in 1971. And by the beginning of 1972, the United States was negotiating a wholly new system in which it was obvious that the dollar was no longer going to be the dominant reserve currency in the world.

Even that least changeable of American institutions, the Supreme Court of the United States, was transformed in 1971. During President Franklin D. Roosevelt's long tenure in the White House, he appointed one chief justice of the United States and eight associate justices, and in the process tipped the balance of the court from a conservative to a liberal majority. But in 1969, President Nixon appointed a new chief justice; in 1970, an associate justice; and in 1971, two more associate justices—all of whom were widely regarded as being conservative in the field of criminal law—to turn the balance of the court back again toward a conservative majority.

This, then, seemed to be the pattern of the year in government policy: a pulling back from the war in Indochina; a reduction of American military and economic aid commitments elsewhere; a less ideological attitude toward the major Communist nations on the control of arms and the reduction of tensions; and, at home, stricter control over wages and prices and sterner punishment of criminal elements, particularly those connected with the traffic in drugs.

Moreover, this tendency toward less ambitious goals was fairly obvious in nongovernmental institutions as well. In the universities of America, for example, there was a noticeable decline in the use of violence in 1971 to achieve political or social ends. Even the radical campus leaders of the late 1960s and of 1970 seemed to have concluded that violent confrontations were not achieving their goals but were raising up opposition to their objectives. Accordingly, the student bodies all over the United States were quieter in 1971, more studious, and as a result of the unemployment and inflation, they were more concerned about the serious business of getting an education, and finding and keeping a job.

At least in part because of this return to more moderate or normal political action by the young people of the nation, the Congress took a much more sympathetic attitude toward the movement to lower the voting age from 21 to 18. The House of Representatives, on March 23, 1971, passed, by a 401 to 19 roll-call vote, a proposed constitutional amendment to this effect.

Giving the vote to 18-year-olds could prove to be one of 1971's most significant acts

The amendment stated: "The right of citizens of the United States, who are 18 years of age or older, to vote shall not be denied or abridged by the United States or by any state on account of age." Ohio ratified the amendment on June 30, thus assuring its adoption by two-thirds of the states, and enfranchising an estimated 11 million new voters in local and state as well as in federal elections. This could be one of the most significant events of the year, depending on how the 18- to 21-year-olds accept their new opportunities and responsibilities in the presidential election of 1972.

Here again was evidence of the capacity of the American people to change well-established attitudes, habits, and laws when confronted with a quickly changing world. Increasingly in recent years, young people have been getting more education and more responsibility than their parents had at the same age, and have been taking a more assertive position on the politics and policies of the nation. Accordingly, the Congress and the states have put them in a position, not only to vote, but also to hold the balance of power in presidential elections. In this sense, the 26th Amendment, adopted in 1971, could set new and historic patterns in the conduct of the nation's public affairs.

Signing new amendment

This gave to the 1972 presidential election, already well underway in 1971, an air of uncertainty, and there were other reasons for wondering how the struggle for executive power would come out. For the American people themselves were also reappraising their crises, their traditions and beliefs, and their political parties.

Seldom in this century had there been so much doubt among the people about giving their allegiance to one or the other of the two major political parties. There was still a *tendency* toward conservative policy in the Republican Party, and a *tendency* toward liberal, innovative, progressive, or even radical policies in the Democratic Party. But there was no clear ideology or set of principles that distinguished the Democrats from the Republicans.

Each party had its factions. President Nixon was too progressive, too Keynesian, and too unpredictable for the conservative or "regular" Republicans. The governor of Alabama, George C. Wallace, who regarded himself as a "regular" Democrat, was not only more conservative than most Democratic Party presidential hopefuls, but more conservative than President Nixon's brand of Republicanism as well.

The Democratic Party, therefore, could not count on the support of the urban industrial workers, who were the foundation of the Roosevelt New Deal, and the Republicans could not count on the support of the declining farm population, which traditionally had been loyal to the Republican banner.

Even the potential presidential candidates in 1971 were not quite sure of their allegiances. For example, the mayor of New York City, John V. Lindsay, a lifelong Republican, who was rejected by the Republicans in his successful race for city hall in the last New York mayoral election, switched to the Democratic Party. Eugene J. McCarthy, who ran for the presidency in 1968 as a Democrat, was thinking about trying for the White House again in 1972 as an independent. And Nelson A. Rockefeller, the governor of New York, who was rejected by the Republican Party for its presidential nomination in 1964 and 1968 as being too progressive, became increasingly conservative in 1971 and a confidant of President Nixon, whose conservative policies he had opposed in the previous three presidential elections.

So 1971 in America was not only a year of change and reappraisal in all fields, but also, not surprisingly, a year of confusion, shifting alliances, new loyalties, new young constituencies, new means of communication through cable television, new means of financing political campaigns, new techniques of international relations through communications satellites linking the continents, and new fears and hopes about human life and death through drugs and the other wonderful and terrible discoveries of science.

This convulsion of change affected not only the American government, but also the church, the university, the business enterprises, and the family. In short, all human relationships—husband and wife, parents and children, employers and employees, President, parties, voters, and all the rest—were caught up in this vast and exciting question about the meaning of life and the relationships of living human beings and institutions to one another.

There was much anxiety but also much hope in the reappraisal. But at the beginning of 1972 there was scarcely a man or woman who felt confident about where it was all going—and this was true not only of the President of the United States, with all his problems, but also of the other leaders of the republic as well.

The convulsion of change in the U.S. brought not only anxiety, but also some hope

Related Articles

For further information on national affairs in 1971, see also Section One, Focus on The Economy; and the following articles in Section Three:

American Party	Democratic Party	Nixon, Richard M.
Civil Rights	Economy, The	President of the U.S.
Congress of the United States	Elections	Republican Party
Courts and Laws	Labor	Taxation
	National Defense	U.S. Government

Sylvia Porter

Focus on The Economy

In the world of economics, time ran very fast in 1971, with three towering events that staggered the imagination and left the question of what they might lead to

Three economic events towered above all others during the economically tumultuous year of 1971. No one can yet foretell to what or to where each will lead. Nor can anyone yet be sure how each will ultimately affect the United States and the world:

■ On August 15, President Richard M. Nixon set the stage for a momentous revision of the basic U.S. economic system when he abruptly and spectacularly rejected his own do-nothing wage-price policies and announced an unprecedented wage-price freeze for 90 days. This was followed in mid-November by the first wage-price controls ever imposed in the United States while a war was winding *down*, not up; while there were *surpluses*, not shortages, of goods; while unemployment was *high*, not minimal. We entered a new economic era in the United States in 1971, and not in the foreseeable future will our economy be as free as it was in the weeks leading up to that fateful Sunday in summer.

■ Also on August 15, the U.S. President made it imperative for the world to create a new monetary system when he suddenly and unilaterally cut the U.S. dollar's link with gold, set the dollar "floating" in the world's money markets, and thereby tore apart the international monetary system created at the Bretton Woods Conference in 1944. Finding a lasting substitute for Bretton Woods will take skill. It will demand masterful give-and-take. And it will take lots of time. But on that Sunday in summer, a new phase in international money relationships opened, too.

■ Then, on October 28, Great Britain finally voted to become a member of the European Community and thereby telegraphed the emergence of a vastly enlarged, potentially far more powerful European Community of nations and the start of a new era of the stiffest competition in history between the United States and its world trading partners.

Sylvia Porter

So overwhelmingly significant can each of these events turn out to be that I would confuse rather than clarify their meaning by analyzing them together. Thus, let us first focus on the United States.

**On August 15,
Phase 2 ushered
in a new era of
economic controls**

The first economic era of this Nixon Administration spanned two years and seven months. It began in January, 1969, when President Nixon entered the White House, and ended in August, 1971, when he slapped on the 90-day wage-price freeze. In this short period, your cost of living soared a hair-raising 14.5 per cent and the purchasing power of the dollar you earn and spend in the U.S. market place shriveled another 8.5 cents to 59 cents*. During this time, unemployment climbed to close to 6 per cent, the United States slid into the first recession since the Eisenhower Administration, both consumers and businessmen sharply cut back their spending, and the stock market crashed. It was a near-disaster for tens of millions of Americans and an unmitigated disaster for all those who were living on fixed or small incomes, forced out of jobs, or pushed into bankruptcy.

The cumulative upsurge in the cost of living during this partial presidential term was greater than during any full term of any President going back to the global war years of the 1940s. But the Nixon Administration's failure—so cruel to so many millions, so wasteful, so threatening to the entire Free World—was hardly deliberate. Before this subject becomes utterly befuddled by 1972's election-year politics, let it be understood that most economists heartily approved of the traditional "indirect" anti-inflation policies in these months of Mr. Nixon's presidency: the credit squeeze, the federal budget restraints, the upsurge in interest rates. And indeed, the old-fashioned techniques cooled the economy to the point of recession.

But the policies did not touch the power of big unions to negotiate inflationary wage hikes and the power of big business to pass on the costs to us in the form of higher prices. The policies did not stop the leapfrogging of wages over prices, prices over wages, wages over prices. To be brutally objective about it, the danger in early August was that the United States was slipping from the recession of 1969-1970 into the recession of 1971—two economic downturns in less than four years. The record keepers were starting to argue that the weak recovery that began in late 1970 wasn't a recovery at all, but simply a hiccup in the downtrend. It was against that dreadful background that President Nixon initiated the most fundamental shift in economic policies in modern United States history.

The second economic era of this Nixon Administration began on Aug. 15, 1971; it will last until January, 1973, at least. Whatever the political events, this is a new era of economic controls: guidelines for wage increases, limits for profit hikes, curbs on dividends, restraints on profit margins, boards to dictate and arbitrate, and a network—a loose one, but still a network—for supervising and policing wages, prices, dividends, and profit margins.

In this new era, your cost of living will continue up, but at a slower pace. Your dollar will continue to lose buying power, but also at a slower pace. For even assuming the Phase 2 restraints that replaced

**Before the Freeze:
Cost of Living**

(1967=100)

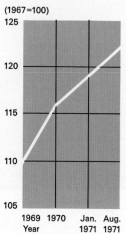

| | 1969 1970 | Jan. Aug. |
| Year | | 1971 1971 |

*Assumes 1948 as base year with price index in that year at 100 and dollar worth 100 cents.

the rigid freeze in mid-November turn out to be workable and successful over the long pull, our cost of living will rise an average of 2 to 3 per cent year after year into the distant future—with the pace at much higher percentages from time to time.

This 2 to 3 per cent degree of inflation we could live with. This would be almost "stability" in a dynamic, growing economy—which surely the United States will be—and anything under 2 per cent would be the equivalent of stability. This degree of inflation would affect our decisions on buying, building, investing, and saving, but it would not distort those decisions—a vital distinction.

Also, 1971's tax cuts, designed to stimulate spending both by consumers and by businessmen, are certain to spur the already strong underlying economic forces in the United States and quicken the upswing in 1972 and 1973. Thus, the odds as 1972 began were that the recession that started in 1969 did end in November, 1970, and that it was followed by a very sluggish pickup until November, 1971. And the odds were that the economic expansion would be broadening right into the presidential election in November, 1972.

Now, the world scene. Long before August 15, fundamental changes were obviously on the way in the Free World's international monetary system. For far too many years, the United States had continued to spend tens of billions of dollars more abroad than it had earned abroad—and had thereby permitted foreign governments and central banks to build up monstrous dollar claims against our dwindling gold reserves. For far too many years, the U.S. dollar had stood firm as the pivot around which all other paper currencies revolved—and had thereby taken on an awesome and increasingly intolerable burden. The U.S. dollar was not in danger as long as our foreign creditors had confidence in our economic stability, and as long, therefore, as they did not stage runs on our currency. The dollar also was protected throughout the 1960s by the fact that our exports of goods were much greater than our imports of goods—and by the widespread recognition that the tremendous annual deficits in our balance of payments were due primarily to U.S. military adventures and commitments abroad, huge spending by U.S. tourists, and other factors that had nothing to do with world trade itself.

But then, in 1971, the U.S. trade account also went into the red. Simultaneously, the continuation of steep inflation in the United States and President Nixon's hands-off wage-price policies led to a loss of faith in the U.S. dollar among our foreign creditors. In the spring and summer, there were increasingly serious attacks on the dollar, and the eerie feeling grew that the monetary system that had served the world so superbly for more than a quarter-century was cracking up before our eyes.

Then came August 15. The U.S. dollar's traditional link with gold was severed. The nations of the world were "invited" to let their currencies float up against the U.S. dollar in the world's money market. A heavy-handed 10 per cent surcharge was slapped on imports into

The feeling grew that the world monetary system was cracking up

Before the Freeze: Buying Power of the Dollar

(1967 = $1)

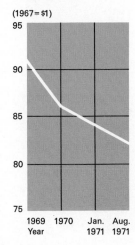

95

90

85

80

75

1969 1970   Jan.   Aug.
Year   1971   1971

the United States to give us some trade assistance and a bargaining lever in negotiations over future currency relationships.

Overnight, the great changes in the world's monetary system that were gradually on the way assumed deep urgency. The finance ministers of the wealthy "Group of Ten"–representing Belgium, Canada, France, Great Britain, Italy, Japan, the Netherlands, Sweden, the United States, and West Germany–immediately began a series of conferences that led to an interim settlement in mid-December, under which a new pattern of currency rates was established, resulting in what the United States sought: an effective devaluation of the U.S. dollar against other currencies of 12 per cent. As its contribution to the agreement, the United States itself devalued the dollar by raising the official price of gold 8.5 per cent, from $35 an ounce to $38 an ounce, and lifting the detested surcharge on imports.

Great Britain decided to join the European Common Market

With this restoration of the essential stability in world currency rates, the finance ministers, at year-end, turned to work on the shape and form of the new monetary system. A probable blueprint:

- Our proud but overburdened dollar will remain a key currency of the world–a first among equals–but it will no longer be the sole foundation for all other currencies.
- All currencies will be permitted to move up or down within fairly wide "bands" of as much as 2.5 per cent on either side of the new parities. This will give new, essential flexibility to the monetary system.
- "Paper Gold"–the Special Drawing Rights approved by the International Monetary Fund nations in 1969 as a new type of international money to supplement the U.S. dollar and gold in settlement of international debts–will help fill the gaps left by the dollar's changed role.
- And gold? Even though its official monetary price has been raised a bit by the United States to enhance the dollar value of all existing gold reserves, this yellow metal has now sunk to a lesser role in the world monetary system. The Special Drawing Rights are far more suitable as basic assets in the new monetary system.

Finally, in the third of 1971's towering economic events, Great Britain launched itself into one of the greatest European economic experiments since the empire of Charlemagne in the 800s when it voted to join the European Community. This will boost the Common Market's membership from the original Six to Ten, for following Britain will be Denmark, Ireland, and Norway.

This will create an economic bloc of 255 million people, perceptibly exceeding the population of our 50 states. The European Community is now the world's largest trading bloc, with total exports, including intracommunity trade, of $89 billion in 1970. With Britain added, the export total will jump to $108 billion, in contrast to the U.S. 1970 export total of $43 billion.

Of course, Britain's formal entry into the Common Market won't be until 1973. Of course, there will be differences that may not infrequently threaten to blow the nations apart. And of course, Europe's

London headline

fumbling toward political as well as real economic unity will be tortuous.

Even admitting all this, what might this event mean to the United States? It must lead to tougher competition for us as a trading nation. The impact on our exports to Britain—which totaled a huge $2.5-billion in 1970—may be especially adverse. At the same time, though, an enlarged Common Market could mean much brighter opportunities for U.S. corporations operating in the European Community. Our companies would benefit from faster economic growth in Britain, from more flexibility in locating their operations, and from more harmonized industrial standards, patents, and the like.

Britain in the Common Market almost surely will bring about some loosening of its special relationships with us. It must compel the United States to return to and pursue the goal of liberalization of trade barriers—if only to make sure there is an ever-larger total of world trade in which to maintain our share.

What I have written above will make the skeptics—of whom there are plenty—sneer that what Britain will be joining is merely a very loose tariff-free customs union. And who cares about that at a time when tariffs count less and less as trade walls?

But let us not forget that the heads of governments of the original Six reached a historic political decision back in December, 1969, to try to work toward full economic-monetary integration during the 1970s. Among their targets is a single European currency by 1980 and completion of the first steps toward monetary integration by early 1973. It could be, too, that "August 15" will harden Europe's determination to reach some sort of currency accord, if only to be in a better position to resist and bargain with the United States.

Let the skeptics sneer. But note how far Europe has progressed toward integration in less than 10 years and then reconsider the possibilities for the next 10 years. And, in perspective, how can you scoff at an event that, after a thousand years, symbolizes the reunification of the nations of Western Europe? How can you ignore the challenges to us that may be inherent in this event and not feel a bit queasy about how we will rise to meet them?

Any of the three towering economic events of 1971 would challenge the imagination—but the three together in a span of months? Time, in the sphere of economics, began to run very swiftly in 1971.

One must feel a bit queasy about the challenges ahead for the U.S.

Related Articles

For further information on economics in 1971, see also Section One, FOCUS ON THE WORLD; Section Two, CAGING THE INFLATION MONSTER; and the following articles in Section Three:

Agriculture	International Trade	Manufacturing
Banks and Banking	and Finance	Money
Economy, The	Labor	Stocks and Bonds

Harrison Brown

Focus on Science

It used to be confined to science fiction, but in 1971, the question of intelligent life on other planets was taken up by a conference of 50 scientists and scholars

A remarkable scientific conference was held in September, 1971, at the Byurakan Astrophysical Observatory of the Armenian Academy of Sciences. Some 50 scientists and other scholars gathered there to discuss the possibilities of our detecting and communicating with extraterrestrial intelligence. The conference had been jointly organized by the rather conservative academies of science of the United States and Russia, and most of the participants were from these two nations. They represented a variety of fields ranging from astronomy to chemistry and biology, from anthropology to history, and they engaged in imaginative, but nevertheless serious, discussion of the problems of establishing contact with civilizations associated with other planetary systems. Once again, a subject that had traditionally been confined to science fiction was transformed into a subject that was judged worthy of serious scholarly attention.

Many questions must be answered before we can assess in any truly meaningful way the chances that other intelligent creatures share the universe with us and have developed civilizations at technological levels equal to or superior to our own. Nevertheless, the conference concluded that, considering the insights we have gained in recent years into such questions as the origin of planetary systems, the origin and evolution of life, and the emergence of civilizations, "the promise of contact with such extraterrestrial civilizations is sufficiently high to justify initiating a variety of well-formulated research programs." The group added: "For the first time in human history it has become possible to make serious and detailed experimental investigations of this fundamental and important problem."

Harrison Brown

How many potential abodes of life might there be in the universe? As far as stars are concerned, which provide the flow of energy necessary for the support of life processes, the number is breathtakingly large. The galaxy to which our own sun belongs is fairly typical, and it is composed of about 200 billion stars. The Milky Way, though, is but one of some 10 billion galaxies of similar size within the range of our most powerful telescopes. There are probably many more billions of galaxies beyond that range. There are at least some 1,000 billion billion stars that would be candidates for the support of life.

But it is difficult to imagine life processes, at least as we now understand them, taking place on stars. Such processes involve complicated chemical reactions between very complex molecules. If the temperature is too high, such molecules cannot exist—they fall apart. As a result, the known life that is associated with our own star, the sun, exists on a small piece of relatively cold solid matter, the earth, which orbits the sun and is nourished by its radiation. Thus, one of the most fundamental questions concerns the abundance of planetary systems as distinct from stars.

It is difficult to imagine life processes taking place on stars

Studies of nearby stars indicate that a substantial proportion have cold, nonvisible companions. Such bodies must be very large (in planetary terms) to be detected, so it is tempting to conclude that planetary systems may well be the rule rather than the exception. Indeed, there is reason to believe that virtually all the visible stars have planets associated with them.

Given an abundance of planetary systems, then, what is the likelihood that life will come into existence on any particular planet? Thus far, we know of life only on earth. Did life appear here by accident—in other words, as the result of a miracle? Or did it appear as the result of a comprehensible sequence of physical and chemical processes? If we were repeatedly to make an earth exactly as it is with respect to size, chemical composition, and distance from the sun, would life repeatedly emerge? Or would it emerge perhaps only once in a million times—in other words, would it emerge miraculously?

We now know that the most fundamental element of life is the molecule that can *replicate* (reproduce) itself. We know that molecules that can accomplish this feat are enormously complicated aggregates of thousands of atoms of carbon, hydrogen, nitrogen, oxygen, and other elements. Such molecules cannot survive at very high temperatures. At very low temperatures, chemical reactions proceed but slowly, with the result that life processes cannot easily take place.

Thus, for replicating molecules to be born and to function, the temperature must be neither too hot nor too cold. Further, it is reasonable to suppose that some kind of a medium (such as water), in which chemical reactions can easily take place, can facilitate the evolution of such molecules. So, given a planet that is not too hot, not too cold, and with a medium in which reactions involving complex molecules can readily take place, life once begun can be supported. But what about the prelife stages?

During the past few years, a number of complex molecules have been detected in space. Among those clearly identified are carbon monoxide, formaldehyde, formic acid, water, methyl alcohol, hydrogen cyanide, and ammonia. Formamide, a compound of nitrogen, carbon, hydrogen, and oxygen, was discovered early in 1971. Later, Fred M.

Johnson, chairman of the physics department of California State College, announced the largest molecule yet to be detected in space. He appears to have identified a very complex, 57-atom porphyrin that is remarkably stable and is related in composition to both chlorophyll and cytochrome. On the basis of his observation, Johnson predicts the existence in space of other complex molecules essential to life on earth, including chlorophyll itself. The discovery of seven amino acids in a meteorite that fell in 1969 in Australia had already suggested that these basic building blocks of protein might also be synthesized in the primitive environments of outer space.

The evidence is rapidly accumulating that complex compounds of carbon, nitrogen, oxygen, and hydrogen may be abundant in space, providing the raw materials from which self-replicating molecules might eventually evolve, given suitable environmental conditions. On earth, which was formed neither too hot nor too cold and which was endowed with large quantities of water, such molecules clearly did evolve, and the process of chemical evolution was then transformed into the process of biological evolution. But the other bodies in our planetary system appear to have been less favored. We now know that the moon is lifeless. Venus appears to be too hot to support life processes, and the giant planets beyond the asteroid belt appear to be too cold. Mars appears to be marginal; conceivably life exists there now or perhaps it existed there in the remote past. It might well turn out, on the other hand, that life on earth is unique in the solar system, that earth alone among our sun's planets was favored.

If it is true that planetary systems are abundant and if it is also true that complex molecules from which self-replicating molecules can evolve are abundant, then it is plausible that life itself is also abundant in the universe. This is particularly true when we consider the great variation in the luminosities of stars, the probable diversity in the sizes and chemical compositions of the planets that are associated with them, and the likely variation of the distances of the planets from the central stars that warm them.

Even were we to concede that life of some sort might exist on perhaps 10 billion billion planetary bodies in the universe, however, we must admit that the road from a self-replicating molecule to an animal endowed with the power of conceptual thought and with the gift of language is a long one. We know, for example, that earth was formed 4,600 million years ago and that life has existed here for at least 3,000 million of those years. As eon followed eon, the primitive microscopic structures reproduced themselves. Equally important, they reproduced accidents that happened within their structures, so new structures were always being introduced into the environment. Most of the new structures perished, but those that survived did so because they had a special characteristic that gave them competitive advantage over their relatives. And thus began the tortuous path of biological evolution that led to the emergence of increasingly complicated life forms. Eventually, evolutionary processes led to the emergence some 2.5 million

It is plausible to assume that life is abundant in the universe

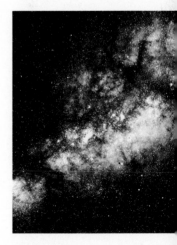

The Milky Way

years ago of *Australopithecus*, the first manlike creature, a toolmaker and apparent ancestor of modern man.

Viewed from a purely biological point of view, man is not unique—his biochemistry and physiology are virtually the same as those of other mammals. What is unique about man is his gift of language, which enables him to communicate with his fellow man in the past and future as well as in the present, and which made possible the development of agriculture, cities, and civilization. With the emergence of language, biological evolution was gradually replaced by cultural evolution as a dominant life force.

It is easy enough for us to perceive that language and the culture it makes possible has survival value in the biological world—by now it is amply clear that man is at present the dominant form of life on earth. Perhaps this means that at some point in time, cultural evolution is destined to become dominant over biological evolution on most planets that support life and have environments conducive to the evolution of animals that possess the necessary physiological complexity. We do not know, however, what the range of such environments might be. So we are in no position to assess the likelihood, given a planet with life, that a creature eventually will emerge endowed with the gift of language. And even were the probability high, the time scale might be such that the planets on which the breakthrough has actually taken place might be very few in number.

Yet another unknown is the rate of cultural evolution. For the greater part of the approximately 2.5 million years during which manlike creatures have inhabited the earth, they have lived, in spite of their tools, much like the other animals about them. Until agriculture was invented a few thousand years ago, culture—and with it, technology—changed very slowly. The development of agriculture triggered a sequence of events that eventually led to our learning how to concentrate enormous quantities of energy to accomplish specific tasks, and paved the way for the evolution of modern technology. Unfortunately, we do not yet understand why these rates of cultural change were what they were. Under different environmental conditions, they may have been faster or slower.

Thus, there are many imponderables. Planetary systems and planets that support life and biological evolution might well be very abundant. But planets that support language and cultural evolution might be extremely rare. And planets, other than earth, that support high levels of technology might be virtually nonexistent. In our ignorance, we simply cannot say.

Nevertheless, the participants in the Byurakan conference urged that we apply our technological genius to a systematic search for evidences of civilizations possessing advanced technologies. The group specifically recommended a search for signals and for evidence of astroengineering activities in the radiation of a few hundred nearby stars, and a search for signals from powerful sources within relatively nearby galaxies. The group also recommended the design of a number of

Radio telescope

The conference recommended a systematic search for signals from nearby galaxies powerful new astronomical instruments that would be particularly useful in such a search.

With respect to the detection of signals, it is important to realize that they can be of two types. First, and most likely, are those radiations generated by a civilization itself as by-products of its operations. For example, our civilization on earth is very close to being detectable by a distant observer because of the vast outpouring of radiation generated by television. A distant observer looking toward our sun and noting this radiation might well conclude that something very peculiar is going on. Were he smart, he might suspect the existence of a civilization with a high level of technology.

The second type of signal would be one sent on purpose in an attempt to establish communication with another civilization. It would be expensive to send such signals over long distances, but it would be feasible – and it is by no means impossible that it is being done. We also know that, thanks to the fact that mathematics is truly a universal language, it would be possible to send repetitive messages containing a wealth of easily decoded information. Communication between groups that really desire to communicate does not appear to be difficult.

All in all, a cosmic gambler, looking at the earth from afar, confronted by our array of knowledge and – even more important – by our array of ignorance, would probably give very high odds that no meaningful contact will be made with another civilization in the near future. The gambler would probably be right in giving such odds. But, nevertheless, he might well turn out to be a loser. In a very real sense, gambling is the lifeblood of science, for it makes possible the discovery of the unexpected and the unpredictable.

The Byurakan group concluded its deliberations on a philosophical note: "If extraterrestrial civilizations are ever discovered, the effect on human scientific and technological capabilities will be immense, and the discovery can positively influence the whole future of man. The practical and philosophical significance of a successful contact with an extraterrestrial civilization would be so enormous as to justify the expenditure of substantial efforts."

If contact is ever made, it will indeed make a quantum jump in human development. If contact is not made, the effort itself will probably endow us nevertheless with knowledge concerning our universe that was undreamed of by our ancestors.

Even if contact is not made with other worlds, we will have added to our knowledge

Related Articles

For further information on science and technology in 1971, see Section Two, THE DARK SIDE OF THE GREEN REVOLUTION; and the following articles in Section Three:

Anthropology	Chemistry	Nobel Prizes
Archaeology	Energy	Ocean
Astronomy	Environment	Physics
Biochemistry	Geology	Psychology
Biology	Health	Science and Research
Botany	Medicine	Zoology

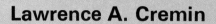

Focus on Education

The schools' financial problems of 1971 may lead to changes in the way America's commitment to education for all is carried out—and also in the way it is paid for

For the United States, 1971 was the year the schools and colleges ran out of money. Harvard, the nation's richest university with an endowment of a billion dollars, was reported in one study to be headed for serious financial difficulty. New York City, the nation's richest diocese, was struggling desperately to keep its parochial schools open. And California, one of the nation's richest states, saw several dozen of its local school districts literally go bankrupt.

The crisis was nationwide. It affected every manner of institution, large and small, public and private, old and new, famous and obscure. And it appeared destined to get worse before it got better. How had it come to pass in the wealthiest nation in the world?

With respect to public elementary and secondary education, the crisis seemed to reflect the final exhaustion of the local property tax as the historic mainstay of public school support. As is well known, the United States Constitution makes no mention of education, so that under the reserved powers provision of the 10th Amendment education is a function reserved to the states. The states, in turn, have delegated much of their authority in educational matters to local school districts, which are specifically empowered to build schools and operate them under guidelines set by the states. Some districts are very large—New York City is a single school district, as is the entire state of Hawaii. Other districts are so small that they maintain only a single one-room school or no school at all.

School districts tend to be independent of local government—political scientists refer to them as *coordinate* with villages, towns, and cities—but they are dependent on the state for the powers they exercise, including the power to tax. And generally state governments have given districts the power to tax real estate (land and buildings) but have kept for themselves the power to tax income and sales, in which so much of the wealth of a modern economy is reflected. The result has been to tie the schools

Lawrence A. Cremin

primarily to revenues that are local and static in character, with the states using their greater wealth to "equalize" differences that inevitably appear from district to district.

Now, of the $39.5 billion spent to operate public elementary and secondary schools in 1970-1971, roughly 52 per cent was raised by local taxes (mostly taxes on real estate), roughly 41 per cent was raised by state taxes (taxes on sales and income as well as on real estate), and roughly 7 per cent was contributed by the federal government under a variety of aid programs (authorized under the responsibility of Congress to "provide for the common defense and general welfare"). In one sense, the $39.5 billion was more than generous: During the 1960s, enrollment in the schools had risen around 30 per cent while expenditures had risen around 150 per cent. In another sense, however, the amount was grossly insufficient: Inflation had eaten up much of the gain; increases in teachers' salaries had accounted for a good deal of the remainder; and all too often little had been left for the smaller classes, the special remedial programs, and the individual attention to the needs of each child that the American people were demanding of their schools.

Americans wanted better schools, but didn't want to pay the bills

What is more, at the same time as Americans were demanding these improved educational services, they were increasingly refusing to vote the necessary funds at the local level. Thus, for example, the Investment Bankers Association reported that whereas voters in 1960 had rejected 19 per cent of the school bond issues put before them, voters in 1970 had rejected 52 per cent. Also, the percentage of school-budget defeats rose alarmingly, with many a local board having to return to its constituency two, three, and four times to gain approval of the most austere budget (in Ohio, the 1970 rejection rate was 71 per cent). To be sure, voters in 1970 seemed recalcitrant about expenditures in many realms, owing in part, no doubt, to the general sluggishness of the economy. But there is no denying the significance of the resistance in education, particularly in what it implied about public confidence in the schools.

At least one element in that resistance may well have been a widespread recognition that, despite a good deal of rhetoric about state equalization, there were vast inequalities in school expenditures from one district to another. Indeed, a high tax rate in district A often produced less money than a low tax rate in district B, because district B happened to have a valuable new factory (which it taxed most profitably) while district A housed the factory's employees (whose residences it was able to tax less profitably). One study, based on statistics for 1969-1970, revealed that the poorest district in Arizona spent $436 on each child during the year while the richest spent $2,223. The comparable figures for California were $569 and $2,414; for Kansas, $454 and $1,831; for Massachusetts, $515 and $1,281; and for Texas, $264 and $5,334. And these figures included state equalization payments. Clearly, not only were there glaring inequalities in the taxes raised by different districts, but those inequalities were not nearly compensated for by the allocation of state funds. In fact, other studies revealed that in many states the richer suburban districts were actually receiving more state aid per child than the poorer rural or central city districts, thus compounding inequality with more inequality.

The problem was as old as the public schools and the traditional ways in which Americans had supported them. But 1971 may have marked a turning point, for on August 30 the California Supreme Court in the case of *Serrano v. Priest* ruled that the state's system of financing its schools, based largely on local property taxes, violated the equal protection clause of the 14th Amendment to the U.S. Constitution. "We have determined," the court argued, "that this funding scheme invidiously discriminates against the poor because it makes the quality of a child's education a function of the wealth of his parents and neighbors." Six weeks later, in the case of *Dusartz v. Hatfield*, a U.S. District Court applied the Serrano doctrine to the state of Minnesota, thus making the issue a federal question.

The two decisions did not rule out the continuing use of school districts. Nor did they consider the question of inequalities from one state to another. Nor did they specify the ways in which California and Minnesota might remedy the situation. But they did insist on a prompt, reasonable, and honest attack on the problem. At the year's end, similar cases were projected or already on court dockets in a majority of the 50 states and there was little doubt that they portended fundamental changes in the nature and sources of public-school support.

With respect to the private elementary and secondary schools, the vast majority of which are affiliated with the Roman Catholic Church, the crisis of 1971 seemed to derive from a spiraling of costs coupled with a sudden constriction of public assistance. The rise in costs had been associated with many of the same factors as affected the public schools, especially inflation. But in the case of the Roman Catholic schools there was an additional problem. Historically, those schools had been conducted by priests, brothers, and nuns who contributed their services out of a sense of spiritual vocation and religious obligation and who required far less by way of financial compensation than lay teachers with families to support. With the marked decline in religious vocations during the 1960s, however, parish and diocesan authorities were forced to employ lay teachers in ever-greater numbers. And though many of those teachers worked with the same devotion as their religious colleagues, they insisted on salaries that would enable them to maintain their families at decent and dignified levels. The schools had no endowments, though, and drew their support almost wholly from tuition, contributions, and whatever funds could be raised from bingo games and bake sales. And to make matters even more difficult, church authorities felt obliged to care for many children whose parents could not afford to pay tuition at all.

The result was a growing gap between expenditures and income, with parishes and dioceses first going into debt and then reluctantly

Court decisions portended some great changes in school funding

Parochial school

beginning to close down schools. Not surprisingly, pressure for some form of public assistance mounted. Here, however, there were historic barriers to the support of religious institutions in both state and federal constitutional law, so that what legislatures tried to do was to pass laws that would assist the schools indirectly, by paying for curriculum materials or by subsidizing the teaching of "secular" subjects such as mathematics, foreign languages, or physical education. To some citizens, this seemed entirely reasonable: The parochial schools performed a useful public function, they argued, and at the same time relieved the public schools of a serious financial burden. To other citizens, however, it seemed equally unreasonable: Parochial schools were an arm of the church, they argued, and to aid the schools or any of their activities was no different from aiding the church.

Pressures mounted for some sort of public aid for parochial schools

A number of test cases were brought before the Supreme Court of the United States, and on June 28 the court struck down as unconstitutional two of the most ambitious state programs: Pennsylvania's, under which cigarette-tax revenues were used to reimburse nonpublic schools for the cost of textbooks and teachers' salaries in "secular" subjects, and Rhode Island's, under which the state paid up to 15 per cent of the salaries of teachers of "secular" subjects. The decisions represented a major setback for parochial schools across the country because they called into question similar arrangements in other states. And although a number of legislatures began to contemplate the possibility of direct payments to parochial-school parents (thus hoping to avoid the constitutional barrier to school support), the crisis of the parochial schools quickly deepened and the number of closings mounted.

With respect to higher education, the crisis of 1971 seemed in many ways a crisis of success. At the end of World War II, American colleges and universities had been asked to expand their facilities so that every young American who desired it and had the qualifications would have an opportunity to continue his studies after graduation from high school. And the colleges and universities had risen to the responsibility during a time of high birth rates and continuing inflation. By 1971, enrollments had passed 8 million and included as large a proportion of the young adult population (and as diverse a group of students) as had ever gone on to higher education anywhere. It was an unprecedented accomplishment, but the costs had been equally unprecedented.

Higher education has always been what economists call a "labor-intensive" operation. The "productivity" of a professor can be increased only so far by the use of machines (for example, closed-circuit television) before his "product" (the education his students receive) begins to be diluted or his "clients" (the students) begin to complain. Hence, expenditures for higher education have skyrocketed as colleges have reached out to the children of the poor, as the technical requirements of first-class teaching in fields such as medicine, physics, computer sciences, and agriculture have grown more complicated, and as the salary levels of faculties have increased to meet rising costs of living.

The Supreme Court

Part of the burden, of course, has been borne by the students and their families, who have paid more tuition almost every year for the past two decades. But tuition has never paid the entire cost of higher education, and what is more, tuition increases in general have not nearly matched cost increases. What made up the difference during the early 1960s was the vast upsurge of federal and state support and the continuing increase in philanthropic contributions. After 1967, however, the effects of the Vietnam War on federal spending, the effects of student unrest on state spending, and the effects of economic slowdown on private giving combined to create a widening gap between income and expenditures. By the time the colleges and universities had closed their books for 1970-1971, many found their reserve funds exhausted and debt staring them in the face.

The gap between income and costs has widened for higher education

During 1971, cutbacks in faculty, services, maintenance, and building programs were everywhere the rule, and hundreds of smaller private institutions literally teetered on the edge of bankruptcy. There was much talk about the uses of adversity, as politicians, trustees, and faculty members re-examined everything from the nature of tenure to the needs of libraries (one report in California went so far as to suggest that the state university at Berkeley sell its rare book collection and use the proceeds to meet current expenses). But there was no denying that if the crisis persisted it could lead to a serious erosion of academic quality and educational opportunity. Institutions facing bankruptcy are not likely to reach out for distinguished faculty members or impoverished students.

By the year's end, there was a flurry of activity aimed at resolving the financial crisis at all levels. Public and parochial school authorities were discussing possibilities for sharing staff and facilities. Legislatures were seeking new arrangements whereby they could support the public schools and assist the private schools without violating their own or the federal constitutions. Colleges and universities were developing new combinations of independent study and classroom instruction. And congressional committees were exploring new formulas for increasing the flow of federal funds. Ultimately, there seemed little chance that the American people would abandon their traditional commitment to widespread educational opportunity. But there was every indication that the way they would carry out that commitment, and in particular the way they would pay for it, would change dramatically during the decade immediately ahead.

Related Articles

For further information on education in 1971, see the following articles in Section Three:

Congress of the United States

Education
Handicapped

Parents and Teachers, National Congress of

Alistair Cooke

Focus on The Arts

The antihero has replaced the hero, and Hollywood–which is now a gigantic TV factory–is reflecting that fact in its abandonment of the old "star system"

One of the profound ideas of our time, only now coming into focus as a historical movement, is that of the "antihero." It can now be seen as a slowly gathering revolt against the Romantic Movement, which has had a fairly uninterrupted run of more than a century and a half. The effects of this shift on the Western world can only be guessed at. They are likely to be as considerable as the idea of chivalry, which dignified war, introduced the notion of the "gentleman," and led to the extraordinary practice of marrying for love.

Put very crudely, the Romantic Movement was one that believed in heroes. Although every civilization and every age has had its heroes, the conscious belief in heroes as the prime movers and shakers of the life around them began not much later than the American and French revolutions, and was solidly planted in Western literature at the beginning of the 1800s. Even the most elementary course in English literature notes the eclipse of the 18th-century ideas of order and reason by such heady romantics as Keats and Shelley, without ever hinting at the revolution this was to cause in the popular conceptions of government, war, art, and literature. Thomas Carlyle's *On Heroes and Hero-Worship* elevated into a philosophy of history the romantic idea of nations and empires created and invigorated by single powerful men.

I hope this rather forbidding preamble will serve as a student's springboard into the antihero doctrine as it has affected the arts, most of all the motion picture. Until television began to drain the box office, the motion picture was the most widespread popular art in history. It fattened on the hero, from the first filmed kiss (in, I believe, 1908) to James Bond's final defeat of Goldfinger. During all that time, the fadeout saw the leading man on top of the world. He was the hero, the star: William S. Hart, Clark Gable, Gary Cooper, Humphrey Bogart, Sean Connery, who trapped the rustlers, captured the daughter of old moneybags, asserted the dignity of the country boy against the city slickers, foiled

Alistair Cooke

47

the evil Nazis, out-smarted Smersh, and somehow always got the girl.

In the 1960s, the idea of the hero began to fade. It was, in fact, highly suspect. The term "antihero," coined by drama critics, described a general disillusion with the romantic formula. In the postwar devastation of Europe, and the crumbling of the values on which Europe had created the world's political establishment, there arose such playwrights as Bertolt Brecht, Samuel Beckett, and Harold Pinter. They saw Everyman neither as a hero nor as a being with any control of his destiny, but rather as a helpless cog in the machine of society, a cipher not much more effective than Shakespeare's "poor forked radish."

In the United States, the suspicion of heroes and hero worship has been powerfully reinforced by the experience of the war in Indochina. A generation has come to manhood and womanhood that has never known a "good" war, in the sense of a war in which an indisputably evil force (Hitler) was let loose on the world and would have to be destroyed. On the contrary, the origins and progress of the war in Indochina were so murky, so debatable, that it was possible for young people who would have jumped to arms in 1917, 1941, or even in 1950, to decide in good conscience to defect or desert—to do anything but enlist or be drafted into the armed service of their country.

Maybe young people need to be reminded that this is something quite new in the world. There were always conscientious objectors, in small numbers, and they were either derided as freaks or barely respected as admirable people suffering from a twisted moral impulse. In our day, however, they have appeared in such large numbers, and their sincerity is so palpable, that we have had to ask ourselves whether they aren't at least as thoughtful as the ones who leap to the colors.

However, no movement in the arts is as neat and pat as the professors find it convenient to pretend. The avant-garde has transformed playwriting and shocked the movies into a quite new direction. But the yearning for heroes can achieve the force of a dying kick when there appear to be so few of them around. And the dying hero is given new life in television, where he now takes such odd forms as the noble doctor (Marcus Welby, M.D., who is, at this writing, at the top of the ratings) and the incorruptible, and always successful, private detective (Mannix). But what television doggedly continues to exhibit as fiction is contradicted every evening by the news and documentary programs, which show hospitals run with nothing like Dr. Welby's dedicated humanity, and detectives living off bribes from narcotics pushers, not to mention nations fighting brutal wars out of naked self-interest and giant corporations fouling the rivers and the atmosphere. It seems to me that the television soap-opera and fiction series offer the hero his last stand.

Hollywood is now a gigantic television factory. As such, it is the last-ditch manufacturer of assembly-line heroes and heroines. But Hollywood as a motion picture metropolis is quite another story. Once the film capital of the world, it is now in a deeper depression than it was

Gary Cooper, hero

in the 1930s. The average actor earns about $2,500 a year, about half that of the average Negro family, and close to one-third of the annual income of the average Puerto Rican family.

Whatever the reason for this economic slump, Hollywood reflects the decline of the hero by its abandonment of the star system and the investment that protected it; namely, the long-term contract. The shrinking audience for the family film may simply believe that new stars have replaced the old. But the point is that the replacements now proceed at a furious rate. Under the influence of foreign films—from Sweden, Italy, England, and even Czechoslovakia—Hollywood has discovered that a famous face (what was once called a "reliable property") is no longer a guarantee of a thriving box office. No longer can the imprimatur of a famous studio automatically produce a hit. Only one studio manages to maintain itself in the manner in which a famous half dozen were accustomed to flourish.

Every movie is an experiment, a risk. And since labor and equipment costs have helped to price the old-time studio out of existence, the studio system has now been replaced by independent producers with bank loans gambling on a single hit. Paralleling this discovery—as a fact of life dictated by necessity—is the recognition that there need be nothing systematic about the creation of a new star. No long apprenticeship in minor roles, no studio publicity build-up, no incessant grooming of an image, is any longer necessary. (It may be a sign of how desperate is our hunger for heroes that the grooming treatment has now passed over to presidential candidates, who, sensing their mediocrity and their lack of heroic stature, are now dependent for their public image not only on speechwriters and public relations firms, but also on hair dye, hair stylists, and makeup men. Imagine Thomas Jefferson or Abraham Lincoln refusing to appear in public without the ministrations of a beautician and Max Factor No. 9.)

The motion picture audience has absorbed the antihero belief sufficiently to accept the notion that the extremely handsome male and the breathtakingly beautiful female are obsolete as fantasy gratifications. Thirty years ago, it would have been impossible to imagine Steve McQueen, Jack Nicholson, Elliot Gould, or Walter Matthau as leading men, not to mention a whole flock of leading ladies whose long, melancholy, poker faces, innocent of makeup, and seen through a Pre-Raphaelite mane of hair, make them indistinguishable from the type formerly cast as the dimwit maid or the village simpleton. To put it a little more objectively, one can say that there are thousands of agreeable young men and women who have little discoverable acting talent, but who can be depended on to do something far more acceptable to today's audiences: They can "behave" unself-consciously in front of a camera turned on them as mechanically as an electric fan. With clever coaching (this means that the *director* has now turned into the "reliable property"), any one of these can be made to emerge as something appealing and lifelike. They are people like ourselves to whom, in the current jargon, one can "relate." It was the special magic of

Elliot Gould, antihero

stars such as Rudolph Valentino, Greta Garbo, Fredric March, and Rita Hayworth that one would not have dared "relate" to them. The wicked pleasure of watching them was that of being privy, for an hour or two, to the intimate life of such unapproachable deities as Monsieur Beaucaire, Queen Christina, Christopher Columbus, and Salome.

It is a question whether the chicken came before the egg: whether, that is, the antihero cult made film personalities cheaper to buy, or whether the long economic recession of the movie industry made it essential to make films at one-fourth or one-tenth of the budgets that were once thought routine. There was a dizzy period a year or so ago, after the enormous success of *Easy Rider* (which was made for about $350,000), when legions of ambitious young men seized a camera and dashed out and shot reams of film from the shoulder. They concluded that two amateur actors, the American landscape, and a roving camera were much more essential than a plot, a script, and a star. This delusion produced a wave of defaulting backers. The system that evolved, however, when it was no longer possible to buy familiar faces at fancy prices, was to pick a couple of unknowns, make a hit, allow their new high salaries to last for one or two more pictures, and then go out and pick some more unknowns. The movie-going public, which is now mostly youthful as it was once mostly middle-aged, does not, of course, directly dictate the economics of the industry. But its preference for players who seem more like ourselves, and therefore less like actors and actresses, is strong enough to have anachronized the era of the long-term gods and goddesses.

The surest proof that the great age of Hollywood is over is the nightly lamentation over its passing that one hears on the television talk shows. Faded relics of the 1930s, wizened directors of famous westerns, and soured comics who made a killing as talented juveniles, regularly appear on the midnight confessionals of Johnny Carson, Dick Cavett, and Merv Griffin, expressing alarm at the disappearance of the "wholesome" (and profitable) family film, disgust at the rampant pornography, and nostalgic sighs for the days when men were knights and women were cream puffs. In truth, there is a steady taste of sour grapes about these litanies. The present feature film certainly no longer provides a chocolate-box escape from the realities of life outside. But there has never been a time when the realistic motion picture was so uncompromisingly true to life as most people honestly know and live it. Admittedly, there is a good deal of self-conscious "realism" by way of sex and violence, a gritty determination on the part of young directors to show that *their* integrity is finer than *your* integrity. But since realism is now the total fashion, these abuses are inevitable.

What is best about this trend is due, undoubtedly, to what is called the permissive era, to the failure or unwillingness of the courts of the Western world to find a workable definition of obscenity. What is worst about it is also a consequence of the general abolition of censorship: the opening up of thousands of old stores, lofts, failed little the-

Realism is the total fashion in our motion pictures now

Hollywood TV factory

aters, and city ratholes to exhibitions of the most stark and witless pornography. Badly lit films accompanied by muffled sound, in atrocious color, very often shot against a single background (a bedroom, usually): These X-rated "adult" films are the last word in the provision of clinical sex for cretins.

The only good news here is that such hard-core movies are doing pretty badly. The anticipated mobs of pathological voyeurs have not materialized. And in several of our big cities, the small porno theaters have switched to horror films or R-rated features at worst. The one great danger that I foresee is one that is all too typical of the American experience in politics as well as the arts: a period of blowzy liberty followed, in a rage of respectability, by a period of extreme repression. Arnold Toynbee's celebrated formula for historical action, *Challenge and Response*, may not be true of all civilizations. But too often in American history, too much liberty has provoked the fearful response of too little.

Too often, too much liberty results in our having too little

Related Articles

For further information on the arts in 1971, see the following articles in Section Three:

Architecture	Fashion	Nobel Prizes
Awards and Prizes	Interior Design	Personalities
(Arts Awards)	Library	Photography
Canadian Library	Literature	Pulitzer Prizes
Association	Literature for Children	Radio
Canadian Literature	Motion Pictures	Recordings
Dancing	Museums	Television
Deaths of Notable	Music, Classical	Theater
Persons	Music, Popular	Visual Arts

Jim Murray

Focus on Sports

There are teams that leave their mark on history, and—in 1971—a big mark was left by the United States table tennis players who gave the world "Ping-Pong diplomacy"

It was a year of high-level political intervention in the wonderful world of sports. Not since the Hitler Olympics of 1936 had the chancelleries displayed such a high interest in the goings-on on the playing fields as they did in 1971.

You could hardly win a football game, golf tournament, or World Series without the President of the United States coming on the hot line. He was such a fan of the Washington Redskins, a football team that lost more close ones than he did, that other teams were afraid he'd roll back and freeze scoring to mid-November levels to protect them from any late-season slump. He took to dropping in on their midweek practices for fight talks, which led some Cabinet members to speculate that, to get an audience with the President, they first had to get a tryout with the Redskins.

But nothing could prepare the world for the intervention of China in the American sports scene. When Chinese Premier Chou En-lai invited the U.S. table tennis team to Peking, the world couldn't have been more shocked if he had bid for the Republican National Convention.

The United States was startled at China's invitation to the table tennis squad because, up to then, Americans hadn't recognized either one of them. The rank-and-file sports fan was uneasy because he would rather the Chinese had invited the Kansas City Chiefs or the University of Southern California track team. Something he had *faith* in.

The United States had been determined that China could not shoot its way into the United Nations. But there was no objection at all to their *paddling* their way in. China had never invited the Seventh Fleet to give an exhibition; they pointedly ignored the Blue Angels flying team, the United States Marine Corps Band, the Central Intelligence Agency's dummy airlines, and other cultural exchanges. But the table tennis team looked harmless enough—and had the international record to prove it.

Every epoch has its teams that leave their marks on history. Usually, they are less than cosmic. The

Jim Murray

Babe Ruth-ian Yankees, the Notre Dame Four Horsemen, and the Bill Tilden Davis Cuppers, after all, stopped well short of brinkmanship. The 1971 U.S. table tennis team, though, put World War III temporarily on *hold*. They gave the world a new term—"Ping-Pong diplomacy." Talleyrand would have been flabbergasted. Metternich would have turned in his diplomatic pouch.

The team was perfect for the role. It had one of everything—like the old Warner Brothers war movies where the top sergeant assembled Able Company by singing out "Standish, Schultz, Shapiro, O'Brien, Swizowicz, Moretti, Wun Sing-ho, Fujihara, Swanson, MacGregor, and Uncle Tom." The table tennis team had (1) a hippie, (2) a college professor, (3) a housewife, (4) a black, (5) a chemist, (6) a Wall Streeter, (7) a computer programmer, (8) a collegian, and (9) a Detroit automobile executive.

As a team, their contribution to 1971—and maybe to the rest of the century—stands alone. By year's end, President Richard M. Nixon was preparing a trip to China, the Chinese were in the United Nations, Formosa was out, and 25 years of the United States saying "What elephant?" and pretending 772 million people didn't exist had come to an end.

The outstanding score of 1971 was 8-0, the margin by which the Supreme Court of the United States decided that Muhammad Ali could do his fighting in the ring and not in the rice paddies of Southeast Asia or the prison gym. The decision came too late to save his title. He rushed into a bout with Joe Frazier, who thrashed him narrowly in a prize fight that in part looked more like a bullfight. Later, some thought the Supreme Court should be impeached when Ali used his newly found freedom to beat up an ex-sparring partner and ersatz interim "champion," and "carry" an old, overweight, out-of-shape contender coming off a two-year "retirement" in a bout so Laurel-and-Hardy-ish that the American Broadcasting Company ran it on television as a silent and set it to a sound track of a waltz.

To give you an idea of the kind of year it was—the outstanding champion of 1971 was a gangling, cantankerous, asocial young (28) man from Brooklyn, a school drop-out who excels at the most cerebral game in the world: chess. Bobby Fischer never learned to field a punt, hit a curve, or sink a basket, but at age 14, he was champion in a sport historically restricted to old men, military geniuses, or European dictators. In the year 1971, Bobby Fischer finished a string of 20 consecutive chess games before he lost or tied one. Then he overpowered Russia's second-best player to win the right to play for the world championship against Russia's Boris Spassky in 1972. For most Americans, chess is a game played by two cobwebbed figures, presumably alive, and so boring that it can be played by mail—fourth class at that. But for those in the know, the 28-year-old Fischer is an American prodigy in the great tradition of Bobby Jones, Bill Tilden, or Billy Hitchcock—one who not only can beat the Europeans at their own game, but revolutionize it in the process.

Thanks to the
Ping-Pong team,
World War III
was on hold

Ping-Pong team in China

It was a year that saw the first on-field death in the history of professional football. The medics who attach themselves to pro football were quick to ascribe it to a sclerotic condition that had nothing to do with football—a finding that could not be successfully challenged by an Establishment that did not much want to anyway. Nonetheless, Chuck Hughes of the Detroit Lions had a fatal heart attack on the 15-yard line of the Chicago Bears. It seemed hard to explain what a man who should have been in an oxygen tent was doing there.

Some said the team physician should be Dr. Frankenstein

The incident remained isolated, but the football players themselves finally moved to question the high incidence of bone and joint injuries that plagued their sport. They were inclined to blame artificial grass, which coach Tommy Prothro of the Los Angeles Rams likened to "throwing a rug on a cement driveway and having a free-for-all on it." The chemical companies that make the fake turf sought to defend it, but had to do so against a backdrop of injuries that prompted one player to concede that "artificial turf is fine for crutches." The games continued to be exercises in sadomasochism, which led some to believe that artificial surfaces called for artificial players and that the team doctor should be Frankenstein.

It was a year in which the antihero dug in and consolidated himself. Even in the traditional sports, the word "champion" had to have an asterisk after it. Pro football, baseball, hockey, and basketball had fissioned into an expansion that diluted the word or churned it until it was pure cheddar. Pro football had tinkered with its selection system until it was perfectly possible for a team to become Super Bowl champion with 1 regular season win and 13 ties. Or, better yet, 1 win, 1 loss, 12 ties, and a coin flip.

Consider this: When the American Football League and the National Football League merged, they split each conference into divisions totaling three, which is neither company nor a crowd. To balance the play-offs, they decided to invite the team with the *second-best* record to the championship party. In the case of two teams with identical second-best records, they hit upon a coin flip. The survivor of this pie-throwing contest would be the world "champion."

The games became as farcical as the conditions. In an Oakland Raiders-Kansas City Chiefs game, 44-year-old George Blanda kicked a field goal from the *6-inch* line to ensure a 20-20 tie. "Ties don't count," sunnily observed Raider coach John Madden. As Grantland Rice said, "It's not whether you won or lost." It's how you tied the game.

Even the games that ended in a decision were, like as not, four 15-minute quarters of dock fights between sweating behemoths of 280 pounds and up—and then a jockey-size Cypriot or Norwegian or Hungarian who had never made a tackle or hit a line in his life would come off the bench to kick the clinching points. The league's leading scorer never touched a football with anything but his shoe.

Baseball served up a less fictional champion in 1971, although its system of split divisions was as susceptible to mediocrity as football's. As it was, the Pittsburgh Pirates' self-denigrated "no-name pitching

Football-field violence

staff" managed in the World Series to outpitch the Baltimore Orioles, who had so many 20-game winners that they used them in relief. Baltimore couldn't hold the younger, faster Pirates even though they used pitchers in some games whose combined wins for the year totaled 61. The critical game was won by a two-base hit by a banjo-hitting 36-year-old retread named Jose Pagan who was so little thought of that the Orioles waived his ineligibility for the series. He hit a double with none out, scoring Willie Stargell from first in the seventh game. Baseball's strict reconstructionists were not convinced. "He should have bunted," frowned the game's venerable Moe Berg, linguist and one-time catcher for Washington.

Kareem Jabbar stood out as the Himalaya of basketball

Golf got a reprieve from its galling anonymity in the person of a garrulous Mexican-American from El Paso, Tex., who showed up on the tour a few years ago with a little hooky swing and the guts of a train robber. Lee Trevino won the 1971 U.S. Open, Canadian Open, and British Open in the span of a month. That's a life's work for most golfers. He's still about 50 career tournament wins behind Arnold Palmer, however, and golf hopes his swing can hold together long enough to save the game from the 150 What's-His-Names? who win a tournament a week each.

Basketball continued to disappear into the maw of a 7-foot 5-inch center with the Milwaukee Bucks. Kareem Abdul Jabbar, a young man from the burning sands of Harlem, changed his name, his diet, and his wardrobe, but he still looked suspiciously like Lew Alcindor to the rest of the league when it came to dunking and rebounding—and winning. He doesn't play a game, he gives a recital. He is the Himalaya of the sport. Everything else is foothills.

Spectator tennis continued its self-immolation. Once called "the Balkans of sport" by a writer, it appeared to have errored itself to match point and was within one lob of extinction. Billie Jean King walked off the court in the Pacific Southwest finals because of a line call. Promoter Lamar Hunt withdrew his professionals from Forest Hills, where professionals have been trying to get in for 50 years, and the pros were reduced to playing in traffic on downtown streets to lure crowds. Presumably, without calliopes. A few more years of this and we'll be able to write, "What can you say of a 100-year-old sport that died?"

Related Articles

For further information on sports in 1971, see Section Two, NEW GAME PLAN FOR SPORTS IN THE '70s; and the articles on individual sports in Section Three.

Section Two

Special Reports

Six articles and the exclusive YEAR BOOK Trans-Vision® give special treatment to subjects of current importance and lasting interest.

58   **The Dark Side of the Green Revolution** by Mark Gayn

76   **Caging the Inflation Monster** by Henry C. Wallich

92   **Crime in Paradise** by Jim Bishop

118   **New Game Plan for Sports in the '70s** by William Barry Furlong

136   **A Freshman in the Senate** by Senator Adlai E. Stevenson III

160   **The American City:** A special two-part feature

    161   **Making Our Cities Livable**–THE YEAR BOOK Trans-Vision®

    179   **Taking a Closer Look at the City** by William H. Whyte

A Year Book Special Report

By Mark Gayn

The Dark Side of The Green Revolution

Planners, taking a look at the benefits of Asia's agricultural boom, are finding that it has also created unexpected social problems

In New Delhi, they still remember the dark days of 1965, when nature and man's folly joined in a terrifying alliance. Each year, the uncontrollable birth rate of India had been adding 10 or 12 million mouths to be fed. The grain yield, meanwhile, could not keep pace with the birth rate. A pattern for hunger was being formed. Then, the summer monsoon rains failed, and one of the century's worst droughts gripped much of India.

The government chartered foreign ships by the dozen to bring in grain—most of it a gift from the United States. Supplies were rushed to the hungry people. Rationing of cereals was ordered. But the ordeal was not yet ended. After the drought of 1965, the rainfall again was meager the next year.

I was in the northeastern Indian state of Bīhar on Christmas Day in 1966, and saw the thin-faced farmers who ate only one meal a day so that their children could have two. I saw the little girls who searched parched fields for a few blades of green grass to feed to the starving cattle, and the villagers who squatted on the ground of an evening, staring numbly at the drying community well.

But, even as much of the land lay cracked with thirst, something extraordinary was happening in some irrigated areas. India, in 1965, had imported a ton of special rice seed from the International Rice Research Institute (IRRI) in Los Baños, the Philippines, and 250 tons of "miracle" wheat seed from the International Maize and Wheat Improvement Center in Mexico. Both lived up to the most exuberant predictions. By 1970, some 12.5 million acres were planted with the new variety of wheat. This was only a fraction of the tilled land in India, but the yield was so bountiful that more than a third of the country's wheat harvest came from these fields. India, in one of its darkest hours, had stumbled upon the Green Revolution.

"This was a true miracle," an Indian planner said. "Not only did it end the threat of famine, it also gave us 20 years of breathing time. We now have enough to eat while we try to solve the problem of too many babies born each year."

India was not alone. The new seeds, as if by magic, totally changed the Asian food picture. Almost overnight, rice and wheat yields increased by 20, 50, and even 100 per cent. And with these increases, Asian ways of life and patterns of development also began to change. It was a massive revolution, though no blood was shed.

Today, the revolution continues. "Miracle" seeds are being replaced with still more miraculous ones. More and more acreage is being prepared for the high-yield plants, and modern farming techniques are now in use on selected farms from the Philippines all the way to Turkey.

Yet, as all this is taking place, uneasy voices are beginning to be heard. International conferences have been called to take a worried look at newly produced economic disruptions. Reformers, who have spent a lifetime struggling to change the barbaric age-old social structure in the Asian countryside, have discovered in dismay that the season of plenty has retarded much-needed reforms. Even plant geneticists—the first cousins of the miracle makers—have found reasons for anxiety. The miraculous Green Revolution has suddenly revealed a dark side. But this is running a bit ahead of the story.

In the IRRI files at Los Baños, there is a letter from William S. Gaud, executive vice-president of the International Finance Corporation in Washington, D.C., an affiliate of the World Bank, telling how he first thought of the term Green Revolution, and used it in a speech in March, 1968. The expression seized public imagination. What it described was the way in which scientists met the challenge of hunger— and, by and large, defeated it.

The author:
Mark Gayn was born in China and now lives in Hong Kong. He travels widely throughout the Far East as *The Toronto Star*'s Asia bureau chief.

The first victories were scored by the wheat specialists. Their search for types of seeds that would produce more wheat with an increased use of fertilizer had begun at least a century before. Japanese began experimentation in 1875 to produce one of these varieties, later calling it Norin. The variety's ancestry included two types of American wheat, Turkey Red and Fultz. To these, in 1917, they added a Japanese dwarf variety called Daruma. The famous Norin 10 was released in 1935, and Samuel C. Salmon, an agricultural adviser to the U.S. Army in Japan, saw these plants growing at the Morioka agricultural station on northern Honshu Island and brought them to the United States in 1947.

At about the same time, Mexico, its wheat production lagging, formed a plant research partnership with the Rockefeller Foundation, and a team of U.S. and Mexican scientists, headed by plant pathologist Norman E. Borlaug, began to work in Mexico. The team's first

Plants such as this high-yield variety of Mexican wheat are producing bountiful crops as part of the Green Revolution.

At the International Rice
Research Institute in
Los Baños, Philippines,
a farmer plows an
irrigated field to prepare
the ground for planting
new rice seeds.

hybrid plants were destroyed by plant rust, but in 1953 the scientists
began to transfer the genes of Norin 10 to a series of variants to produce dwarf wheats that were rust-resistant. In 1967 and 1968, the new
seeds yielded twice as much grain from each acre as Mexican farmers
had harvested seven years earlier.

The Mexican seeds found their way into laboratories in India and
Pakistan as early as 1963, but they attracted little attention until the
big drought. Then, India imported the newer seeds, and sent most of
the supply to the enterprising farmers of the Punjab region in northern
India. By 1970, more than 20 million acres in India and Pakistan were
planted in varieties of Mexican wheat. When I visited Pakistan's Punjab that year, the landlords, standing on the edges of their golden-
yellow fields, smiled happily when they spoke of the harvest, and the
economic planners in Islāmābād wondered where they might find
markets for their new wheat surplus.

The rice developers were somewhat tardier than the wheat specialists in Mexico, and a little less successful. It was not until 1959 that the
Ford and Rockefeller foundations agreed to invest in a rice-develop-
ment project in the Philippines, and appointed Robert F. Chandler, a
forest soil specialist and former president of the University of New
Hampshire, to direct it. The Los Baños research institute was set up in
1962 with some 30 scientists, including the remarkable trio of Peter
R. Jennings, Henry M. Beachell, and Te-Tzu Chang.

In their quest for a variety of "miracle" rice, Jennings, Beachell,
and Chang crossed three dwarf breeds that Chang had brought from
Formosa with a long-stem Peta rice from Indonesia. They made the
cross in 1962, and three years later they spotted what was to become
a renowned variety, IR-8. In November, 1966, the institute gave
about 60 tons of seed to farmers in the Philippines and some other
countries. The results were sensational. With proper amounts of ferti-

lizer and water, fields that once produced 1,500 pounds of rice an acre now produced six times as much.

Once the scientists had the IR-8, they began to add refinements to it—greater resistance to disease and cold, better taste, and (so demanding are the Asian rice eaters) better appearance. Late in 1967, they introduced IR-5, inferior to IR-8 in some respects but more resistant to blight. Then, late in 1969, came IR-20 and IR-22, which some regard as the present "queen" of the institute. In May, 1971, the scientists christened IR-24, a variety they promised would be particularly soft and moist when cooked.

Rice is a much more sensitive plant than wheat. A variety of rice that will flourish in one place may do badly 50 miles away. The farmers of East Pakistan prefer IR-20, perhaps because it is immune to some of the insects and diseases that trouble IR-8, which is widely used in India. "As yet," says Beachell, "we cannot quite explain why IR-20 has this immunity." Thus the IRRI rice requires experimentation and adaptation in each country where it is planted.

By and large, IR rice has done well wherever it is planted. About 10 per cent of India's paddy land is now under IR-8, and the rice crops in India and West Pakistan are millions of tons greater. Thanks to this rice, the Philippines is within sight of self-sufficiency.

IR-8 rice at the left is tall and straight. Older Philippine variety at right in this Los Baños field often bends to the ground, where the grain gets no sunlight and rots.

The problem with the high-yielding IR rice is that better seed alone is not enough. It is only one part of a trinity that includes ample and well-regulated supplies of water and great quantities of chemical fertilizer. And fertilizer and water may both cost more than a poor farmer can afford. In addition, the IR-8 grain, for all its virtues, is a rumpled country bumpkin compared to the long-cultivated aristocrat of Indian rices, Basmati. IR-8 looks untidy, it breaks during milling, and rice-eaters insist it does not taste good. In one field in Tamil Nadu, a state in southern India, a small landowner told me he was growing IR-8: "Its yield is so high that it brings me a good profit." But he will not eat it. "I think it tastes bad because of the pesticide we use on it." Experts at the Los Baños institute assured me that pesticide could not alter the taste of rice, but this farmer was beyond convincing: "For me and my family, I grow that rice over there–Basmati."

In the neighboring state of Kerala, a landlord stood in his field and watched 32 men, women, and children, all hired hands, work hard to gather in his harvest. He, too, did not like to eat IR-8, but he endorsed growing it. The yield was 50 per cent higher than his best previous crop, and it justified the investment in fertilizer and an electric pump for irrigation. Rice prices had dropped, but still he was doing handsomely. "All the farmers here think it is a wonderful rice," he said. "Some have even named their sons Ayar-Ate." It took me a moment to realize that this could also be spelled IR-8.

When I passed his field again six hours later, the crop had been harvested. Outlined against the red sky was a column of men, women, and children headed toward the village, carrying sheaves of rice on their heads. The landlord, a tall, middle-aged, bronzed man, was still in his field making sure no rice had been left behind. He had paid the 32 laborers 30 pounds of rice–nothing else–for six hours' work.

Adequate food is the moral right of all who are born into this world. Yet the United Nations Food and Agriculture Organization (FAO) says that 1.5 billion people will go to bed hungry on this day because of lack of food or an improper diet–and most of these will be Asians. It is also estimated that 10,000 persons will die of malnutrition on this day, again most of them in Asia. Only a decade ago, this human condition was thought unavoidable because too many infants were born and not enough food was grown. Because of the Green Revolution, however, hunger is no longer inevitable.

And yet, more and more specialists in Asia and in the West are beginning to cry alarm. They recognize the Green Revolution as the miracle and blessing it is, but they are also beginning to see it in the same light in which they once viewed DDT. It achieved its objective, but it did so by disturbing the delicate balance of life and nature. The "miracle" seeds make it possible to reduce the threat of hunger. Some of their unforeseen by-products, however, are proving to be disastrous.

To point this out is no bad reflection on the remarkable achievements of those involved in the Green Revolution. Borlaug won the

I Saw China Having Its Own Green Revolution

My visits to the "rice bowl" of South Asia were interspersed in 1971 with two tours of China, one in the spring and the other in the summer. In north China and south China, and in the Yangtze Valley in between, I went into the countryside to talk to commune officials and ordinary peasants. We sat under portraits of Chairman Mao Tse-tung and red banners denouncing "U.S. imperialism and its running dogs," drank endless cups of tea, and talked about grain and fertilizer. None of the men and women in blue denim had heard of the Green Revolution or of "miracle seeds." They were politely, but not excessively, interested. As I talked to them, however, it became apparent that, without the benefit of catchy names, China, too, was in the midst of a Green Revolution.

Typical were two huge communes, Hwa Tung (Yellow Flower) and Tom Tong (Tom Family Pond), in Kwangtung Province in the south. The rice seed they used came from the Kwangtung Agricultural Scientific Station, a sort of Red IRRI, in Canton. The station sent out a steady flow of seeds to be tested on the commune experimental plots. The Chinese counterpart of IR-8 is Pearl, a fistful of which was first tested a dozen years ago when the communes were still in their infancy. Although it is not as productive as the Los Baños varieties (an acre of Pearl will yield a maximum of 5,000 pounds as compared with 8,000 pounds for IR-8), it does not collapse with the weight of the grain, and it adapts well to various types of soil. Pearl is being used for the early crop, along with Southern Special and Iron Bone. For the late rice, the Chinese have been using Kwangtung No. 2, Bamboo, Well Stream, and Red Stream, the last one noted for its resistance to pests and typhoons. In one corner of the experimental plot at Hwa Tung, I saw a patch of tilled earth that was shielded from the burning sun. The commune had just planted a fistful of a new seed, Long Autumn, which they had received from the agricultural station in Canton. High-yielding, resistant to wind, and late-maturing, the new seed could be planted late in the year for what might be an unprecedented third crop.

At Tom Tong, in the mountains about 80 miles north of Canton, the commune had its own miracle man, Mo Chi-ming. He is an untutored, homebred genius in his late 30s. The commune had given him a team of helpers and a plot of land, and there he puttered about, crossing his own strains with those sent from Canton. At least four of the varieties he has developed are in use, and they have brought the commune yield to about 4,000 pounds per acre.

Impressive as all this is to anyone who remembers the meager yields and subsistence farming of old China, the most impressive thing is the physical change wrought in the terrain. From one of those eye-in-the-sky satellites hurtling over China, the land must look like an ant hill, with millions of people endlessly digging, moving, building, and altering the land. In the mid-1960s, in Shansi Province, I saw a vast fresh-water sea created in the mountains by 20,000 people, working in teams and brought in relays from the nearby villages. That project, however, was dwarfed by the elaborate irrigation system I found in the Hwa Tung commune. In the commune office, a contour map showed the farmland dotted with 26 large mountain reservoirs and veined with 15 miles of irrigation canals and 10 miles of dikes and dams. "We no longer fear drought," said the young and intense Communist Party boss, "because nearly all of our land is now irrigated. And our dikes protect us from floods." An incredible 1.2 million workdays had been put into the labor needed to create this irrigation system, over four arduous winters, with each adult doing roughly two months of work.

The Chinese, thus, have fair seed and good irrigation. What they lack is fertilizer, the third part of the essential trinity of the Green Revolution. Where a Japanese farmer might put 180 pounds of chemical fertilizer on an acre of land, workers at Hwa Tung will put only 10. The Chinese try to make up for this lack of chemical fertilizer with huge quantities of pig and green manure. (The latter is green leafy plants, such as clover or alfalfa, plowed under to enrich the soil.) The commune members wheedle chemical fertilizer from the government, and lucky is the commune that can get a little more than its neighbors. But it is only a fraction of what they need, and when a visitor comes, they try to rationalize. They say that one of the great crimes of the ousted chief of state, Liu Shao-chi, was that he urged the people to use more and more chemical fertilizer. "That scab, renegade, and traitor never told the people that too much chemical fertilizer is bad for the soil," I was told.

It is the lack of this essential ingredient, as much as anything, that has kept the rice and wheat yields of China far below those attained with Mexican and Los Baños "miracle" seeds. But such comparisons may be unfair. The fact is that the Hwa Tung commune has more than doubled its output of rice in a dozen years, and the yield is still going up. Throughout China, the irrigation network is being extended relentlessly. New chemical fertilizer plants are being built. Samples of IRRI rice have been obtained and are, at this moment, probably being crossed with Kwangtung No. 2, Pearl, and Red Stream.

There is an added element that India, Pakistan, and Indonesia do not have—a disciplined, politically motivated, rigidly organized, and ably led mass of peasants. When a Chinese commune needs a million workdays to dig a new irrigation canal, a million workdays are provided. The vast army of Chinese peasants, whether in units of 10 or a thousand persons, can be mobilized for almost any project in a remarkably short time, something that exists nowhere else in Asia. The result is that China's grain production is rapidly rising, and so are its exports of rice. This is beginning to provide competition for the traditional producers in Asia, a point to keep in mind in assessing the impact of the Green Revolution.

Despite crude methods, Chinese communes are raising more grain than ever before.

Nobel Peace Prize for 1970, and few scientists ever deserved it more. The two institutes that were the nurseries of the "miracle" plants have, deservedly, been given the United Nations Educational, Scientific, and Cultural Organization Science Prize. The scientists met their assignment with patience and imagination. They achieved fantastic results in a startlingly short time. But no agricultural revolution of this sort could have failed to have a deep—and often painful—social, economic, and even genetic impact. This fact needs to be closely watched, remedied, and counteracted, and, indeed, it needs to be widely publicized.

Until this age of miracles, the grain economy of Asia was reasonably stable. India, Pakistan, Indonesia, and the Philippines were the consumers shopping around for the best bargains. Thailand, Burma, and Cambodia were the providers of rice. Their sales were steady, and permitted their peasants to make a modest living. This, of course, is a greatly simplified picture. It ignores the princely gifts of wheat that the United States has been handing out for years to India, Pakistan, South Vietnam, and other Asian countries. It also ignores the wars, military coups, and political upheavals that cut down the rice production in Burma, Cambodia, and South Vietnam. But, providing for such exceptions, the pattern of Asian grain trade has been reasonably steady for generations.

Almost overnight, the Green Revolution upset this pattern. As countries grow more and more rice and wheat, they cease to be markets for the traditional suppliers. Worse, some of yesterday's buyers have now become selling competitors. The Philippines, for example, has always been a heavy buyer of rice. But in 1968, thanks to IR-8, it sold 50,000 tons of rice to Indonesia, which Thailand has always regarded as its own market. Japan, which only a few years ago imported great quantities of rice, now has a surplus of 8 million tons in its bulging elevators. Since 1969, Japan has been virtually giving rice away—to South Korea, the Philippines, and Indonesia. In the 1971-1972 growing season, Japan's fields will not only meet the entire domestic demand, but will add 2 million tons to its mountain of unsold rice. India, which expects to grow all the rice it needs in from two to four years, has already cut imports from 10 million tons in the grim year of 1966 to less than half that in 1971.

As the demand shrinks, anxiety among the traditional rice producers is growing. This has produced political pressure to do something about the glut. And, predictably, this has led to a series of conferences that so far have mainly been exercises in frustration.

At a meeting in late 1969, farm experts from Thailand, Burma, Cambodia, and the Philippines argued for international controls on rice acreage and prices. There was no agreement. In March, 1970, delegates from 15 countries met to look at what was delicately described as the "volatility of the rice situation." Once again the rice traders could not see eye to eye. India remained neutral, but Pakistan,

Storage bins in Thailand are filled to capacity, symbolizing changing
market patterns in Southeast Asia and the bounty of the Green Revolution.

Ceylon, and Indonesia wanted no controls. They were happy to be shopping in a buyers' market. More conferences were scheduled, and it is a safe wager that once they meet, Thailand will be demanding that the United States stop giving rice to the have-nots, while Indonesia and South Vietnam, both receivers of such gifts, will dissent.

Glut is easier to deal with than hunger, of course. One solution is to persuade farmers to turn from rice and wheat to other crops. Japan is already paying a fat bounty to any farmer who will do so. Thailand is also beginning the switch. And scientists at the "miracle" institutes in Mexico and the Philippines are working on high-yielding corn, sorghum, and other plants. But paddy land cannot always be used for other crops, and Asian farmers are bound to rice culture by powerful bonds of sentiment and tradition that are not easily broken. In addition, after many years of recurring famine, Asian governments are obsessed with the idea of self-sufficiency in rice and wheat—and they don't concern themselves with the market economy of the continent.

The market dislocations caused by the Green Revolution are harsh enough, but the miracles wrought in the fields have also served to deepen the already grave social injustice in the Asian countryside. This was underlined for me by what happened in a field in West Pakistan. I had gone into the countryside to talk to the sharecroppers about the "miracle" rice they were growing. The men, happy at this unscheduled break in the long day, were frank and talkative. But they turned silent when they saw a lean, dark, hard-looking man on horseback galloping toward us. He carried a rifle and a leather whip. The man brought his horse to an abrupt halt before us, and sat there silently. Finally, I asked him who he was. With obvious reluctance, he said he was a bodyguard for the landlord to whom much of this land belonged. The peasants, so informative only a few moments earlier, could now remember the answers to none of my questions—how much they paid to the landlord for the irrigation water; what part of the crops they had to give to the owner; or how much land the man owned in the village. Eventually, I gave up. When I returned to my car and looked back, I saw the horseman tapping the saddle with his whip for emphasis as he spoke to the peasants. In a few minutes, he was off, racing across the fields.

This is how it has always been in the countryside, and the Green Revolution has not changed the situation. Indeed, it has tended to solidify social injustice. The Green Revolution requires money—for irrigation, fertilizer, and pesticides. The landlords have money. Some of the small and independent farmers—those who own 5 or 10 acres—can also afford the new agriculture. In India's Punjab, for example, the small wheat farmer has been prospering. A farm implement dealer there told me this story:

"The other day, a group of peasants came to the yard. They were rather poor looking, and I was not paying much attention to them. They walked around the tractors, looked at the engines, tried the

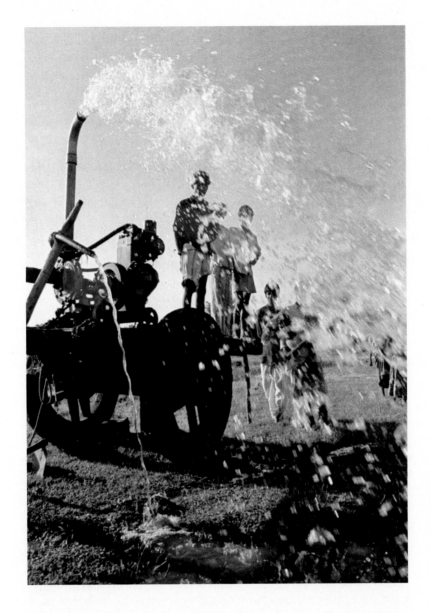

Only wealthy Indian farmers can afford the mechanical pumps needed to provide the water new rice seed requires. This pump can be wheeled easily from field to field.

seats. Then they asked me to put one of the tractors through its paces. One of them produced a thick wad of rupees and said, 'We'll take this one.' After he finished counting the money, he said, 'Now show us a combine.'"

But such farmers are in a minority. On a recent journey into Bihar, I found the land, which lay bare and brown in 1966, now lushly green. Not far from the roadside, I saw a young man near a pump that was driving a heavy stream of water into the irrigation ditch. Unlike the other farmers, who were bare to the waist and barefoot, this man was wearing a beige shirt and slacks and sharp-toed "city" shoes. He spoke fair English. Yes, he said, the pump belonged to his family, and so did the land with its rich harvest of IR-8 rice. The pump had cost the family a lot of money, some of which they borrowed from the state government. "It was well worth the money," he said. "You cannot raise IR-8 without all this water, and I now have enough water to sell some of it to the neighboring farmers." The fields, the water sparkling in the hot sun, the contented young man, were all proof that here the Green Revolution had succeeded.

I drove a few hundred yards down the road, and talked to other farmers, clad in loincloths. Some, in teams of two or three, were drawing water from old wells, using wooden levers with a water pail at one end and a heavy rock at the other. They emptied the water into irrigation ditches. It was slow, backbreaking, monotonous labor. Why weren't the men using a pump? They explained sullenly that they were sharecroppers and could not get a loan to buy a pump. Of course, there was the water that the young landlord was selling, but it was too expensive for them. They were not growing IR-8. "To grow it, you must have water and fertilizer. We know the yield is high, but we simply do not have the money for IR-8."

The sharecroppers, though, are well off compared to the seasonal workers, emaciated and ragged men and women whom I saw harvesting someone else's grain from Tamil Nadu in the south to Bīhar in the north. Lucky to have work 4 months in 12 and lucky to earn $40 a year, they are neglected and scorned, the true outcasts of the Indian and Pakistani countryside.

Some specialists believe the future will be worse for these forgotten people. (Early in 1971, a few months before his death, Dhananjay R. Gadgil, chairman of India's Planning Commission, told me that up to 40 per cent of the people in the countryside were landless peasants.) The new, rich yields have already boosted the price of irrigated land sky-high. In Kerala, a small farmer told me his 5 acres were now worth $20,000. A big landlord—and in Bīhar some manage to own as much as 5,000 acres—finds it makes no economic sense to rent out his land. Instead, he now uses every sly stratagem to force his tenants or sharecroppers off the land, and works it himself, using hired help. And many an owner has already realized that he can earn even higher profits if he uses tractors. As efficiency increases, the "miracle" seed produces ever-greater yields. The landlord becomes richer, and yesterday's sharecroppers, in ever-multiplying thousands, become today's seasonal workers, with an increasingly harsh life.

Credit at low cost could make things easier for Asia's small farmers, and it should be an essential part of the Green Revolution. But the old social structure in the countryside denies such credit to the half-acre farmer. Even when the government provides funds, these are allocated by local councils dominated by men of substance who are members of the "right" caste. One of Gadgil's senior assistants put it this way:

"The agencies meant to help the small farmer are so set up that they help the big owner and not the small one. If I am a big farmer

An important step in growing "miracle" IR-8 rice is spraying regularly with insecticides, as this man is doing in a field in Los Baños.

and I control the credit, you can be sure I'll give the small farmer only marginal help–only enough for me to obey the letter of the law. Take irrigation water. There are hundreds of ways I can deny it to the small owner, or charge him more for it. The pressures on the small farmer are much greater than you will ever see set down on paper. The chairman of one local council has been quoted as saying, 'It is public money, and I must have it repaid. If I lend it to my relatives, I know they will repay the loans.'"

The village councilman is wealth-, class-, and caste-conscious. The situation is worse in India's state assemblies, which are completely dominated by big landlords and their allies. A new kind of farmer is emerging, the enterprising, urban professional–doctors, lawyers, army officers, and businessmen–who, with the aid of an archaic tax system, now invests money in "gentleman farms." It is they who go into the modern, efficient farming that is, almost literally, the death of the landless peasant.

Some of the ardent champions of the Green Revolution argue that social reform is someone else's business. "It is a job for the politicians," they say, or "We saw a hungry Asia, and we made it possible to feed it," or "The Green Revolution was never meant to usher in rural revolution." All these arguments are beside the point if the Green Revolution results primarily in increasing the old injustices. As many Indian writers have already noted, the Green Revolution may turn Red, if the Communists can exploit the new tensions.

Landless peasants, no longer needed for the mechanized farming of the "miracle" seeds, now crowd into dilapidated shacks of India's slums.

Another worrisome problem produced by the Green Revolution has to do with genes, those minute biological substances through which heredity is transmitted. In selecting the best varieties of wheat and rice to cross, scientists have discarded inferior plants. The result has been the creation of a rather narrow group of high-yielding, virtually man-made plants. Mexi-Pak, the superior wheat developed in Mexico, now covers great parts of India and West Pakistan. This is all to the good, but it also means that if new types of rust disease outwit the defense mechanisms built into Mexi-Pak by the geneticists, all this wheat will be affected.

In the past, the yield was much lower, but then the farmers planted different varieties of rice, wheat, or corn. When disease struck one farmer's field, it did not necessarily affect his neighbor's crop. Tomorrow, thanks to the Green Revolution, everyone will be growing the same "miracle" rice or wheat. And if disaster comes, everyone will suffer together. In the United States, hybrid corn has recently suffered from just such a calamity.

At a recent international conference on plant genetics, one speaker after another deplored the disappearance of the primitive crops that may not have a high yield but that store an infinite range of genes. They pointed out that in Turkey, blessed by the Green Revolution, thousands of local varieties of wheat are no longer to be found. The same is true in Mexico, Ethiopia, and Afghanistan. The worried geneticists now urge the creation of vast banks of primitive wheats, rice, corn, and soybeans, to which they could turn for disease-immune genes in case a disaster wiped out the "miracle" plants.

Near the administration building in Los Baños, there is a cage in which brown plant hoppers, green leaf hoppers, and other pests are allowed to destroy rice. A green leaf hopper can kill a rice seedling in five days, and the pest is so tiny that its eggs can be spread by the wind. Outside the cage, rice is purposely infected with grassy stunt. The scientists at the Los Baños institute are thus seeking ways to build resistance to all these pests and diseases into successive generations of IRRI rice.

Some of the scientists now believe they can tailor rice to any demand. "If you want sticky, moist, or dry rice," says one, "we can produce it. We simply control the amount of amylose, a starch element, that we breed into the plant. We can also put aroma into it. Basmati has the aroma, and we have now dwarfed Basmati. Dwarfing prevents the rice from lodging—collapsing from top-heaviness. We can now get 9,000 pounds of rice from one acre. Five years ago, a Filipino farmer got only 1,500. We are now trying to reduce the time of maturing, so that in the future, the farmer can raise three crops a year instead of two."

Given time, science is bound to win all its battles. But the problem for Asia is to spread the scientific know-how so the Indians, the Pakistani, and the Vietnamese can deal with threats to their crops as they appear. By narrowing the genetic base of the "miracle" plants, the scientists have taken a bold gamble on their ability to find the antidote for all the wickedness that nature can provide—and find it quickly. Unfortunately, recent history is full of instances in which nature has outfoxed the scientist.

The Green Revolution has been one of the best gifts the have-not world has received in this century. It has brought food—and therefore hope—to hundreds of millions. It is changing the ways of living. But the last five or six years have also proven that the Green Revolution itself is not enough. Its benefits are limited if the old patterns of injustice remain. It does the poor farmer no good to be aware of the advantages of "miracle" seeds, if he cannot afford to use them. The scientist has done his bit, and now the political leader must do his share. The Green Revolution can fully serve mankind only if and when it is combined with social and political change. And, as important, Asia will have only gained breathing time—10 years, 20 at the most—if it fails to couple the Green Revolution with a vigorous campaign of birth control.

The Green Revolution, like all true revolutions, cannot be stopped. It will probably go faster as the vital protein content of the food grains is increased through plant breeding. Through this revolution, science has challenged nature, and such challenges, of course, ensure human progress. But nature is still full of secrets, and it has a way of rebuffing those who pry into them. One can only hope fervently that not too many such unpleasant surprises lie ahead for the Green Revolution.

By Henry C. Wallich

Caging the Inflation Monster

The first peacetime wage and price controls are a
new weapon in the old struggle against rising prices

Americans went about their Christmas shopping in 1971 with their fingers crossed. Was the new economic policy going to work? Would the Pay Board and Price Commission guidelines bring the long race of wages and prices to a halt?

Christmas shopping had been expensive—more than 3 per cent over 1970, according to the Consumer Price Index (CPI). Judging by the price tags, it often seemed worse than that. But here and there prices had stood still. The new policies seemed to be working, but would the line continue to hold?

For the people of the United States, trying to make ends meet, and for President Richard M. Nixon, trying to be re-elected, a great deal was riding on the answer. Six years of inflation had embittered con-

In a far less complicated era, the inflation monster is tightly
caged, lulled by the mandolin music of a golden troubadour.

sumers, who had watched their hard-earned income gains melt away. Inflation had bled savers, who lost something like $50 billion on roughly $1 trillion of deposits, bonds, insurance, and pension rights. Inflation had frustrated labor unions, and they responded with near-astronomical wage demands. Normally nonmilitant groups, such as firemen, policemen, and teachers, had become strikers. Home buyers had been priced out of the market by the highest interest rates in history and by skyrocketing construction costs. To top it off, the economic "game plan" to which the Nixon Administration had clung so resolutely until the 90-day wage-price freeze of August 15 had lifted the number of unemployed to about 6 per cent, while making only moderate progress toward stable prices.

The dollar, to be sure, had not suffered the galloping inflation of some European currencies that had gone up in smoke following wars and revolutions. There was no American counterpart of the extravagant heir who managed to salvage more of his inheritance after inflation by selling a collection of empty bottles than did his careful brother who had invested in government bonds. But it says something about the prevailing attitude toward the currency when a waiter, asked for change, returns a dollar bill, saying: "This *is* change."

From the spirit of bitterness and frustration into which inflation had helped plunge the American people, the new economic policy was born. Both the wage-price freeze, which ended on November 13, and the subsequent guidelines for wages and prices, also referred to as *incomes policy*, conflict sharply with the earlier philosophy of the Nixon Administration. The costs of the freeze were high in terms of lost wage increases, lost profits, and mounting imbalance in the economy. No country has yet pulled off either a successful freeze or a successful incomes policy. As of early 1972, therefore, the outlook could only be assessed as uncertain, although hopeful.

It is often argued, and not only by apologists of inflation, that price increases of from 1 to 2 per cent can, and should, be ignored. Small price increases of this sort may reflect improvements in products—more horsepower, finer tuning, greater durability—which are not fully allowed for in the various price indexes. In any event, economists believe these increases are too small to be observed by any but the most meticulous comparison shopper. They believe such rises are unlikely to cause businessmen or consumers to alter their buying habits.

This is a questionable proposition, however. Steady price increases of 2 per cent a year mean that anyone starting his first job will see the price level doubled—and the value of a life insurance policy taken out today cut in half—long before he or she retires. Faith in continuous upgrading of products is challenged, moreover, by the mounting evidence that "product improvement" often means deterioration of the environment—through greater air and water pollution, urban congestion, and solid-waste disposal problems.

In any event, history shows that prices need not always rise. There

The author:
Henry C. Wallich is professor of economics at Yale University and is also a columnist for *Newsweek* magazine. A former member of the President's Council of Economic Advisers, he is now a consultant to the Treasury Department.

Illustrations by George Roth

have been many periods when they were falling. A look at the historical record is revealing. The longest continuous record is the index of British prices, which began in 1264, during the reign of King Henry III. That index rose from 83 in 1264 to 3,825 in 1954, an increase of 4,508 per cent. This tremendous increase, however, was by no means continuous. For 344 of those 690 years, prices dropped or stood still from year to year. The long upward trend resulted because the increases, very often recorded in war years, were bigger than the declines, not because they were substantially more frequent. Yet, for many business and household decisions, it is the year-to-year movement that matters, rather than the long-term trend. Over the longer periods important to a person buying common stocks or life insurance, however, periods of price increase clearly predominated.

For the United States, the Bureau of Labor Statistics of the U.S. Department of Labor has compiled an index going back to 1720. Starting at 20, the index reached 113 in 1969, for an annual rise of 0.4 per cent. Nevertheless, our forefathers were kept guessing from year to year, because there were 130 annual increases as opposed to 119 years of decline or no change. On two occasions—after the peaks of the War of 1812 and the Civil War—the index moved steadily downward for about 30 years. These declines certainly lasted long enough to justify all kinds of plausible theories demonstrating that prices must always fall, just as today we "prove" to ourselves theoretically that they must always rise.

The second long decline, ending in 1896, gave rise to a strong inflationist movement in American politics—the campaigns of William Jennings Bryan, who favored free coinage of silver. The prolonged fall in prices particularly hurt farmers who had incurred heavy debts when prices were higher. The silverites blamed the price decline on the scarcity of gold, which was the basis of the nation's money. They argued that there would be more money and that prices would rise again if silver were included in that base.

Bryan was turned back in his three bids for the presidency, twice by William McKinley and then by William Howard Taft. In these elections, the supporters of stable prices defeated the inflationists. The issue vanished from American politics soon after, when huge gold discoveries in South Africa helped the money supply to expand without the aid of silver. After 1896, prices rose at a rate of about 3 per cent per year. Since people had not yet become index conscious, and in view of the long preceding decline, nobody seems to have been greatly troubled by that rise.

During World War I, prices took a big jump, followed by a small drop in 1920. During most of the 1920s, prices held stable or declined slightly in the face of almost continuous prosperity. This was the last time for a long period that the American economy enjoyed stable prices and full employment at the same time. Then the Great Depression of the 1930s brought a drastic price collapse. President Franklin

D. Roosevelt labored for years through his New Deal to *raise* prices in order to help distressed farmers and other producers.

World War II once more brought great inflationary pressures. They were kept under control, after a fashion, by wage and price ceilings imposed by the federal government. The exercise was only partly successful, and produced such unpleasant side effects as a shortage of merchandise and black markets. Those who worked for the Office of Price Administration (OPA) remember this period as an administrative nightmare. These recollections have acquired more than ordinary importance because they are shared by a former OPA official who, in 1969, became President of the United States. Mr. Nixon's long reluctance to impose wage and price controls can probably be traced back to what he witnessed while working in the OPA tire-rationing section in Washington, D.C., in 1942.

World War II gave a classic demonstration of *demand-pull inflation* (too much money chasing after too few goods). Much of the nation's output had to be set aside for the conduct of the war. The wages, salaries, and profits generated by war production converged on the restricted supply of civilian goods. Even very tight controls could not fully stem the pull of this excess demand.

The late 1950s brought what may have been our first clearly identifiable experience with *cost-push inflation* (wage increases in excess of productivity gains). After a brief period of stability from 1952 to 1955, the economy once more became overexpanded and prices began to rise in response to demand-pull. Excess demand was eliminated by creating tight money through the credit policies of the Federal Reserve System (Fed)—and by a strong effort at balancing the federal budget. But prices went right on rising under the pressure of cost-push. Wages had acquired a momentum of their own. Producers' profit margins were squeezed in the process and unemployment was high, but inflation did not end until wage increases slowed down to a reasonable level.

The early 1960s were our last period of substantial price stability, though, unfortunately, they were accompanied by high unemployment. Wage increases generally were limited to productivity gains— that is, to the percentage rate of increase of output per man-hour. This rate was computed at a little over 3 per cent per year for the early 1960s. Of course, productivity gains varied widely among industries. The high-technology industries, such as electronics, tended to have high increases, while stagnant industries (especially services) generally had low increases. Nevertheless, the nation's leaders correctly saw that productivity gains in each separate industry could not be the guideline for noninflationary wage increases. That would have led to intolerable interindustry wage differentials. Increasing wages by a more or less equal percentage for all industries would avoid such differentials. This would mean that prices would have to rise in industries with low productivity gains. But in high-gain industries, profit margins would tend to widen, so prices there could be cut. On the average, then, the price level would be stable.

Facing page:

The 1920s are a time of stability in the American economy. In a lush, green, overripe setting, the inflation monster is held in check by both stable prices and full employment.

81

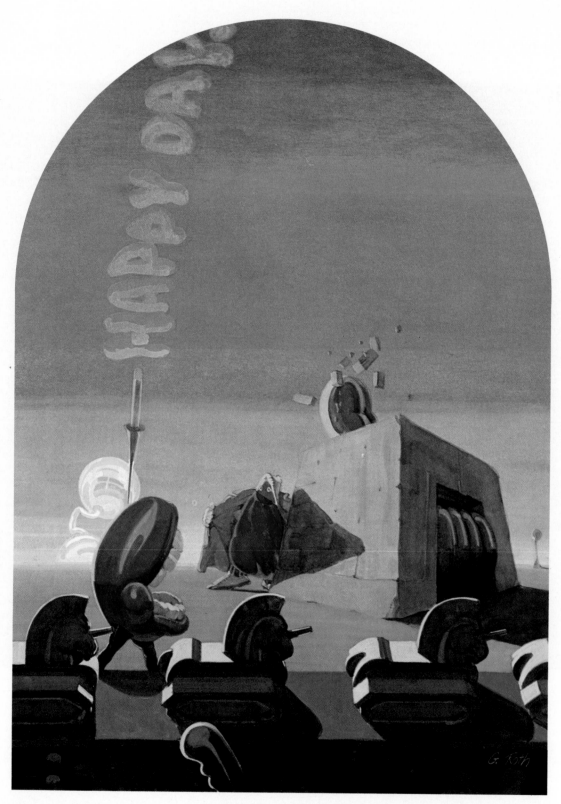

This was the "wage-price guidelines" theory underlying the efforts at keeping prices stable during the early and middle 1960s. It was reinforced by dramatic confrontations such as that of President John F. Kennedy and the steel industry in April, 1962, when Mr. Kennedy compelled U.S. Steel, the largest company in the industry, and others, to cancel an announced price increase. Many of the government's economists and advisers were not satisfied, however. They felt that the policy gave too much emphasis to price stability and too little to reducing unemployment. The ground was thus prepared for a more aggressive approach.

A theory had been developed based on the research of the British engineer-economist A. W. Phillips, which said that a country could have less unemployment if it were willing to tolerate more inflation. The theory held that, as the economy begins to boom and unemployment declines, labor demands higher wages and business is more willing to grant them. Prices then begin to rise, so that in *real terms* (dollars of constant purchasing power) labor's gains are no greater than before. But labor is not supposed to notice, or at least not to react to, this. It is assumed that labor will be satisfied with higher wages in *nominal terms* (more dollars but of diminishing purchasing power).

If this were so, much could be said for a policy of tolerating some inflation. A rise in prices hurts many people, but usually few of them are hurt severely. Unemployment, on the other hand, hurts only a small number, but it does real damage to these—unless it is very brief, or unless it affects only the second or third breadwinner in the family. It takes a great deal of faith in the stupidity of others, moreover, to believe that labor will never realize that it is being fooled by inflation. If labor wakes up to the facts, it will increase its demands in order to compensate for the loss of purchasing power. Then, inflation will accelerate, and the "Phillips Curve" game is over.

The economic advisers of Presidents Kennedy and Lyndon B. Johnson—Walter W. Heller, James Tobin, H. Gardner Ackley, Arthur M. Okun—and other top academic economists bought the Phillips analysis of the trade-off between inflation and unemployment. As a result, they were tempted to tolerate some inflation. This fitted in with the general orientation of the *New Economics*, which argued that the government should continuously press for maximum employment by means of easy credit and increased government spending. The earlier philosophy had been that these well-known instruments of policy should be used sparingly, mainly to cure recessions when they occurred.

Then, in 1965, President Johnson began to escalate the war in Vietnam. The economy, meanwhile, had reached full employment. Under the impact of added defense spending, it threatened to take off into inflation. But the President's economists were reluctant to urge restraint by means of tighter money and higher taxes. There is considerable debate now as to how and when proposals for a tax hike were finally put before Mr. Johnson. If the advisers said that higher taxes were needed, they did not say so very loudly. And, in any event,

Facing page:

After the Great Depression and the New Deal, come World War II and a sharp inflation. With industry turning out war material, fewer domestic goods are available, and hungry consumers turn to black markets. The inflation monster starts breaking loose.

the President did not listen. Instead, the American economy was asked to provide both guns and butter—military and domestic goods—at the same time, and inflation of the demand-pull variety resulted.

A 10 per cent surcharge on the income tax was put through in 1968, two and a half years after it had become necessary. Since Mr. Johnson had requested the surcharge in 1967, Congress bears the blame for much of the delay. The results, however, were disappointing. The Fed, fearing that a 10 per cent surcharge meant an "overkill" of the inflation that could trigger a recession, counteracted it by loosening credit restrictions to provide easy money. The result was a defeat for the New Economics with its faith in fiscal (budget) policy as a means of keeping the economy under control. It was a victory for the *monetarists*, who believed in controlling the money supply (volume of currency and demand deposits in banks). Inflation escalated further.

In November, 1968, the Republicans won the presidency. President Johnson bequeathed a booming economy to his successor with unemployment at the very low level of 3.3 per cent, with high wage increases and high profits, but also with mounting inflation. Most people enjoyed the boom, though many were dismayed by prices. In effect, the Democrats had thrown the party and the Republicans were left to clean up.

Public pressure to bring inflation to an end was becoming very strong. This had been one of the major Republican issues in the election campaign. The pressure came from the aged, who are the principal victims of inflation because they often live on fixed income from pensions and savings whose value is consumed by rising prices. It came from business, which was concerned about the increasing wage demands and future stability of the economy. It came from people, including many of the young, who questioned the merits of producing more and more goods instead of stressing the quality of life.

The big question was how to disinflate. One line of advice counseled President Nixon to step vigorously on the fiscal and monetary brakes—to raise taxes, cut spending, and tighten credit. This would knock inflation on its head, and the economy would then be on its way with stable prices and high employment a couple of years later. But this meant running the risk of a recession with high unemployment. Mr. Nixon, who had lost the presidential election in 1960 largely because of the high unemployment in the late 1950s when he was Vice-President under President Dwight D. Eisenhower, vetoed this line. Instead, he adopted a policy of *gradualism*. By putting on the brakes gently, inflation was to be brought down slowly without forcing unemployment up.

Gradualism proved no great success. To be sure, excess demand in the economy was gradually overcome by a moderately tight budget and tight money. But inflation actually accelerated during this long drawn-out exercise. In the process, it performed its familiar shift to a cost-push type of movement. Labor, seeing that small wage increases were not bringing workers more money, held out for previously unheard-of gains. Interest rates rose to the highest levels since

Facing page:

In the 1950s, the inflation monster, spurred on by high wage settlements and high prices, breaks out of its cage. But tight money and credit policies—the fiscal balancing act of the Fed—keep it in control. The delicately straddled guidelines of the early 1960s also help keep the monster in check. But the cost for both periods is a high rate of unemployment.

the Civil War as savers tried to prevent their assets from being eaten up. And unemployment rose to an inhumane and politically frightening 6 per cent before the rate of inflation had been brought down from 6.1 per cent in 1969 to a still excessive 5.7 in August, 1971.

What caused gradualism to fail? It had been supported by a great majority of both the New Economists and the monetarists. Both sides analyzed the problem according to their own techniques. The New Economists used large-scale mathematical models of the economy, running simulations of alternative policies through their computers. The principal defect of this procedure was that the models were derived from data compiled during periods with more stable prices, and probably with low expectations of price increases on the part of the public. Thus, the computer-simulated models could not cope with high inflation. In particular, they failed to distinguish between the *nominal* and the *real interest rate*. (The real interest rate equals the nominal rate minus the rate of inflation—that is, the rate that the saver gets after compensating for the inflation damage to his principal. Thus, a 7 per cent nominal interest rate, at 5 per cent inflation, represents a real rate of only 2 per cent.)

The monetarists, led by Professor Milton Friedman of the University of Chicago, were rapidly gaining in prominence during this period. They used much simpler methods, relying principally on the growth in the quantity of money. But their procedures, too, suffered from complications induced by inflation. A 7 per cent increase in the quantity of money means one thing when prices are stable, and another when prices grow at 5 per cent. In the latter case, 5 per cent is chewed up by the need to finance an unchanging volume of transactions at higher prices, and only 2 per cent is left to accommodate real growth in the economy. More importantly, perhaps, the economic theories underlying the monetarists' methods were less clearly worked out than those used by the New Economists. Nobody could deny the monetarists' thesis that changes in the volume of money and changes in the economy are closely related. But the suspicion always remained that it was the economy that influenced money, rather than money influencing the economy, as the monetarists claimed.

It seems that the main thing gradualism accomplished was gradually to disappoint both its New Economist and its monetarist sponsors. The defects in underlying economic analysis must be held principally accountable, but gradualism also suffered from a credibility gap. The failure of the gradualism-oriented Nixon Administration to initiate really drastic measures seems to have persuaded large numbers of corporate and labor leaders that the Administration did not mean business—that they would have to learn to live with inflation. Accordingly, exorbitant wage settlements, frequent price hikes, and abnormal interest rates became widely accepted. Inflationary *expectations* became harder to erase.

As inflation proceeded, it disrupted not only the domestic economy, but also our international economic relations. It undermined the international position of the dollar. Foreign goods flooded American

Facing page:

The most recent inflation begins with the escalation of the war in Vietnam in 1965. The U.S. economy cannot afford guns and butter at the same time, and war expenditures increase. "Gradualism" does not work, and the monster starts to go on a rampage.

markets. Prices of American goods rose in comparison to goods made abroad, causing our foreign sales to lag and our foreign purchases to boom. Demand rose for protection against import competition, protection that would benefit some industries but ultimately hurt the consumer by eliminating the remaining sources of cheap products. Foreign confidence in the dollar diminished. American gold stocks reached the lowest point since World War II, and the United States became a heavy short-term debtor to many other countries.

The international turmoil triggered by these developments came to a head in the summer of 1971, when the Administration was preparing to freeze prices and restimulate the economy. As part of his wage-price freeze, President Nixon decided to cut the dollar loose from gold and to impose a temporary surcharge of 10 per cent on most imports. Foreign countries were urged to *revalue* their currencies—that is, to raise their value relative to the dollar. The American inflation had broken apart the world monetary system that had rested firmly upon the dollar since World War II.

A large part of the public had believed all along that tight wage and price controls were the answer to inflation. Successive Gallup Polls made that clear. Most economists, however, aware of the hornet's nest of problems that controls would stir up, opposed them. But many were beginning to swing over to a method of dealing with wages and prices that fell short of full controls. This was usually referred to as incomes policy, an approach that rested essentially on the old wage-price guidelines of the Kennedy-Johnson Administrations.

Within the Nixon Administration, different groups had been arguing the pros and cons of an incomes policy. The President had sided with opponents of the policy. In the summer of 1971, however, he became convinced that the old game plan had been tried long enough, with unsatisfactory results. The time had come to switch policies.

In a dramatic reversal, he announced a 90-day wage-price freeze on August 15. This was followed by creation of a Pay Board and a Price Commission. The Pay Board, at labor's insistence, consisted of representatives of the interests involved—labor, business, and the public. The Price Commission had members of the public only. The two bodies began to issue guidelines and regulations, with some evidence appearing that the Pay Board was more generous. Both bodies, however, concentrated on the big wage and price decisions, leaving the majority of workers and businessmen subject largely to self-policing.

The incomes policy started off under auspicious conditions. The economy was free of demand-pull inflation. Halting the inflation simply required braking the forces of cost-push inflation. But the past history of similar efforts elsewhere offered little encouragement. Grumblings by organized labor were mounting. And pressure was mounting in Congress to take the lid off the budget, on the dubious grounds that it was now the job of the Pay Board and the Price Commission to worry about stability. The outcome remained in doubt.

Meanwhile, the recession brought on by the failure of gradualism was beginning to mend. The country was entering a new phase of

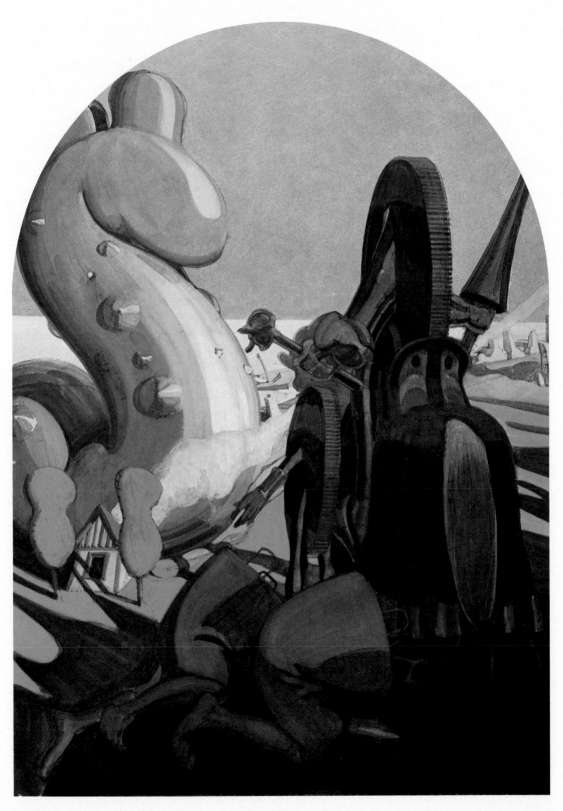

expansion. But, unlike 1961, the expansion did not start from a solid base of price stability. Inflation was still moving at a 3.3 per cent rate, with long-term interest rates at 7.5 per cent, and with first-year wage increases in major union contracts at 11.5 per cent. The incomes policy gave grounds for hope that inflation would be defeated. But the risk could not be ignored that a rapidly expanding economy would overrun these restraints and that a new round of inflation might start from a higher level.

What have we learned from our present bout with inflation that we did not know before? Some major lessons seem to stand out:

- The costs of inflation are higher than New Economics prophets have been willing to believe. For most people, the combined effects of wage increases and price hikes, or eroded savings and appreciated homes and common stocks does not balance out. There are gainers and losers, and the losers get angry. Social tensions mount at home, the world position of the dollar is undermined, protectionism makes headway, and financial security gives way to bankruptcy. Inflation damages the economic environment, much as pollution deteriorates the physical environment.
- The benefits of inflation have been overrated. Temporary gains in employment are important because they often benefit the poor and minority groups. But the long-run advantages are questionable. The benefits wear off as inflation increasingly comes to be expected, as wage demands and interest rates come to include a full insurance premium for future inflation. Unemployment then will be no lower than it would be with price stability. There are studies claiming that inflation never becomes fully discounted, and therefore always retains some beneficial effect. But these are studies based upon the data of the past, when the American public still had an illusion of price stability. Once this illusion is lost, so is the employment gain from inflation.
- The effort to push production to a maximum with the help of inflation has lost its appeal. The cult of unrestricted growth regardless of quality has lately been widely rejected. This might have occurred even without inflation, but the experience of inflation has helped to open our eyes.
- The costs of stopping inflation, once it has gained a foothold, have also been shown to be higher than expected. The history of gradualism demonstrates that. Inflation has been revealed as a form of addiction, requiring bigger doses to get the same kick as time goes on, and involving more agonizing withdrawal pains the longer the cure is postponed. If permanent wage-price controls—involving the distortions of a repressed inflation with their injustices and their black markets and disincentives—are the only way in which inflation can be brought to a halt, the cost of deflating would multiply.

What, then, is the outlook? The finding that inflation has diminishing returns and increasing costs over time suggests that we should end it, rather than try to live with it. But, recent experience of the high cost of unemployment, freezes, and guidelines raises doubt about our determination to stick it out to the end. Instead, we may find ourselves caught in a stop-go policy in which we never stop long enough to kill inflation, and always start going so fast again that we rekindle it. We would then be living with intermittent inflation. The economic spectrum of the past has ranged from full employment with moderately rising prices during booms to heavy unemployment with falling prices during recessions. The spectrum of the future may range from overfull employment with sharp price advances at the top to moderate unemployment with something less than price stability at the bottom.

A sequence of this kind would fit into the political pattern of the United States in the past 20 years. The Republicans won in 1952, at the end of a period of inflation that had contributed to the downfall of the Democrats. By 1960, the Republicans had defeated another bout of inflation, but at a cost in unemployment and slow growth that cost them the election. The Democrats took over an economy that had been thoroughly disinflated and was ready to go. They stepped on the gas and reaped the benefits of long expansion, but they overdid it and started a new inflationary spiral. That inflation, along with the Vietnam War issue, brought the Republicans back in 1968. Unless the tax cuts and other stimulation applied recently work remarkably well, unemployment is likely to loom as a major issue in the 1972 election. Should the Democrats win, history will have repeated itself: They would once more inherit a disinflated economy—one less disinflated than last time, but an economy ready to go.

The record suggests that the American people may be ready now to visit retribution upon the party they hold responsible for unemployment instead of upon the party responsible for inflation. There may be little logic in this attitude. While unemployment often is the consequence of a preceding inflation, inflation does not follow from earlier unemployment. But, if politicians conclude that such are the facts of political life, resistance to inflation will be further eroded and the spectrum of economic fluctuations will shift further toward the inflationary side.

This is not a happy prospect. The American people can do better than to inflict a painful cycle of alternating economic ills upon themselves. The key to progress lies in finding a way to ease the suffering of unemployment through better insurance, job training, job information, and labor mobility. We have already learned that attaining maximum output is not the end of all human endeavor. Stability also has value. But stability attained by inflicting a loss of income on those who can least afford it cannot be the permanent answer. It is barbaric to fight inflation with unemployment—just as it is barbaric to fight unemployment with inflation. To rid ourselves of this cycle, and of these alternatives, is one of the big jobs facing us in the 1970s.

See also Section One, FOCUS ON THE ECONOMY; Section Three, ECONOMY, THE; LABOR.

Crime in Paradise

The soaring crime rate confronts every state in the union,
including Hawaii, almost every American's dream of utopia

The green mountains stand like crumpled desk blotters and their
faces are deeply furrowed with lines of time and fretfulness; they dip
their edges into the cobalt blue of the sea, thinking they are absorbing
it, but it is the sea that is absorbing them. They have been lonely in
the Pacific Ocean for millions of years and they have stood witness to
the rise and fall of many cultures and many gods, but the day will
come when the final lip of lava will be laved by the first wave of the
sea, and Hawaii—all of it—will be gone.

The old volcanoes cool and billions of blades of grass climb the sides
bravely and spawn their young deep inside the craters where once
fountains of flame and flying rock ruddied the night sky. Great white
fleets of clouds sail from the north and northeast under full canvas

and spinnakers and they run hard aground on the peaks and are sheared into luminous bridal veils. Thin pencils of sweet water slip down the old furrows until they come to a precipitous cliff and they fall spangling in the warm sun into a ravine never seen.

This is Hawaii, a paradise unlike any other. Yet behind the façade of serene beauty there lurks a specter whose shadow similarly darkens every state in the Union. The name of the specter is crime.

In 1959, when Hawaii became the 50th state, there were 7,566 crimes reported by the police—less than 1 per 100,000 residents. In 1970, however, 26,148 crimes were reported—about 3 for every 100,000 people in the islands. Thus, in little more than a decade, crime had tripled. Since statehood, murders had risen from 2.7 to 3.6 per 100,000. Burglaries had almost tripled, as had car thefts. Robberies had quadrupled. Larceny had increased fivefold, as had aggravated assault. Other crimes ranging from gambling to vandalism had increased proportionately.

And as it was in Hawaii, so it was throughout the United States—which to much of the world is the same kind of "paradise" that Hawaii is to mainland Americans. Nationwide, according to the Federal Bureau of Investigation (FBI), 5,568,200 crimes were reported in the United States in 1970, nearly three times as many as the 2,014,600 in 1960. Over that 10-year period, crimes of violence, such as murder and assault, rose 156 per cent while crimes against property, such as burglary and larceny, increased 180 per cent. In terms of a 24-hour day, this meant that in 1970, a burglary was committed every 15 seconds; a larcenous act ($50 and over) was perpetrated every 18 seconds; a murder occurred every 33 seconds; an auto was stolen every 34 seconds; a robbery was committed every 91 seconds; an aggravated assault took place every 96 seconds; and a forcible rape happened every 14 minutes. This, in a nation that considers itself law-abiding.

Changing concepts of crime

Nationwide, there are a number of reasons for the increase. First, there is the ever-changing definition of crime itself and what constitutes a crime. A dictionary describes crime as "an action or an instance of negligence that is deemed injurious to the public welfare or morals." The dictionary is short of the truth. Crime is any act of commission or omission that the current culture decrees is an offense against persons or property. In Hawaii, it was once a crime to step on the shadow of the king, and the punishment was death. It was an act of friendship for a Hawaiian to share his wife with a few friends. Now the king and his shadow are gone but it is an adulterous crime to share a wife. Each year, too, state legislatures add new misdemeanors and new felonies to their books; this, of course, increases the ways in which to perpetrate a wrong. In New York it is a crime for a pedestrian to cross a street against a red light. In California a pedestrian has the right of way at all times and swift-moving traffic must

The author:
An internationally known columnist and author, Jim Bishop began his career as a reporter covering crime in New York City. His many books include *The Day Lincoln Was Shot; The Day Christ Died;* and, his newest, *The Days of Martin Luther King, Jr.*

come to a grinding, screeching halt when the pedestrian enters the lanes. Prostitution is illegal in 49 states but it is legal in Nevada. Rape, which may be punishable by death in some Southern states, may draw only a 2-to-5-year sentence elsewhere.

The so-called "youth explosion" plays an important role in the enormous upswing in crime. The median age in the United States today is 28, the lowest recorded in the nation's history, and the predominance of this age group in the population is reflected in the nation's crime statistics: Persons under 15 years of age made up 9 per cent of the total police arrests in 1970; those under 18 accounted for 25 per cent; under 21, 39 per cent; and under 25, 52 per cent. By and large, it was the under-25 age group that accounted for most of the misdemeanors reported in 1970.

Most of these youthful offenders come from middle- or upper-middle-class families. They are the children who required, according to some psychologists, an emotional corral beyond which they could not stray, but whose permissive parents allowed them to roam and mature unrestrained and unpunished.

Honolulu's "finest" line up for an inspection at police headquarters. The soaring crime rate has forced police officials on the islands to beef up their forces and open a school for new recruits.

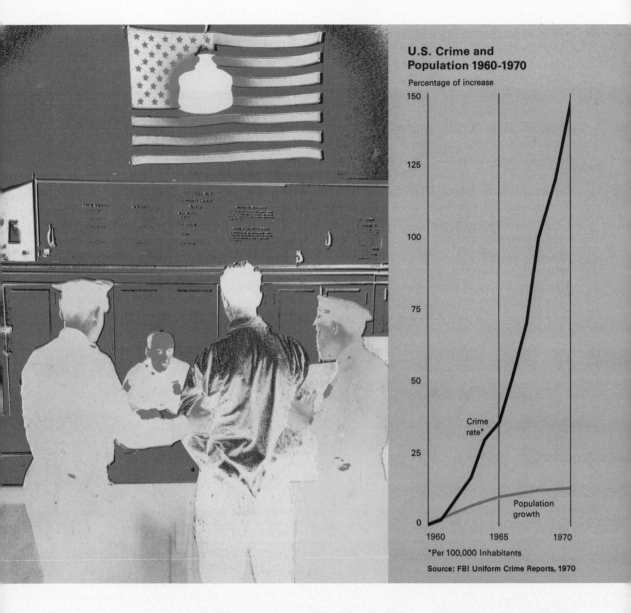

U.S. Crime and Population 1960-1970

Percentage of increase

Crime rate*

Population growth

*Per 100,000 Inhabitants

Source: FBI Uniform Crime Reports, 1970

Add to permissiveness another factor: The cement of American society—the old neighborhood in which generations had remained rooted, in which children shared infancy, adulthood, marriage, and even grandparenthood with other neighborhood children—has practically disappeared. America has become a fluid society. United States census figures show that between March, 1969, and March, 1970, alone some 36.5 million Americans—18.4 per cent of the population—packed their belongings and moved. A classic example of the disintegrating concept of neighborliness is expressed in the boast of the typical apartment dweller in any metropolis who says: "I don't even know who lives next door." It is best exemplified by an incident that occurred in New York City a few years ago, when 40 couples leaned on apartment window sills in the middle of the night, watching a girl across the street screaming for help as she was being stabbed to death. When she died, and her screams ceased, the apartment lights went out one by one and the "neighbors" returned to their beds.

There is what some psychologists and psychiatrists call "the basic human flaw—a predilection for violence." Until Nov. 22, 1963, the United States considered itself a peaceful and nonviolent nation. Although there was no basis for this aura of smugness, it permeated the population. Then came revelation: A shot fired from the window of a schoolbook depository building in Dallas on that day killed John F. Kennedy, the 35th President of the United States. The ensuing shock wave reverberated around the world.

The easy thing to say is that on that tragic day America lost its innocence. But it would not be accurate. The country was never innocent. Histories yellow with age show that the world's richest nation has always been afflicted with a frontier mentality. Robbery, rape, murder, and fraud were well known in the early days of the republic. Even the presidency has not always been held sacrosanct— Abraham Lincoln was murdered in 1865, James A. Garfield in 1881, William McKinley in 1901. On the day President Kennedy was killed, however, America for the first time faced itself in a mirror and saw the venom, the violence, and the vengeance in its eyes. Later, when Robert F. Kennedy and Martin Luther King, Jr., were assassinated, the republic's collective self-esteem dropped further.

Perhaps Dr. Lester Keiser, chief of the psychiatric division of the Hollywood Memorial Hospital in Hollywood, Fla., sums it up best: "Everybody has a criminal element within him. Animals are aggressive. They will kill to eat, and they will fight over a mate, or to protect their nests. But not to the death. Man is the only innately hostile animal."

Ethnic aspects of crime

All of these factors play a part in the rise in crime. The largest single factor in recent years, however, has been the increasing urbanization of American society and the emergence of the blacks as a major segment of that urbanity. The nation's larger cities account for the most crimes, and because blacks are concentrated more heavily there, they are at the statistical core of crime in the United States. Caged in environmental prisons, frustrated by inequalities in education, stymied by discriminatory practices, yearning for equality and determined to have it, blacks express their frustrations in assaults, robberies, and even murder. Blacks constitute only 11 per cent of the U.S. population, but they account for an overwhelming percentage of all the violent crime that is reported.

Most U.S. communities are so overweighted with ethnic-oriented crime that to present a sensible, undistorted report on crime in current U.S. society, it became necessary to find a state where race was not an important issue. Hawaii met the requirements. In Hawaii,

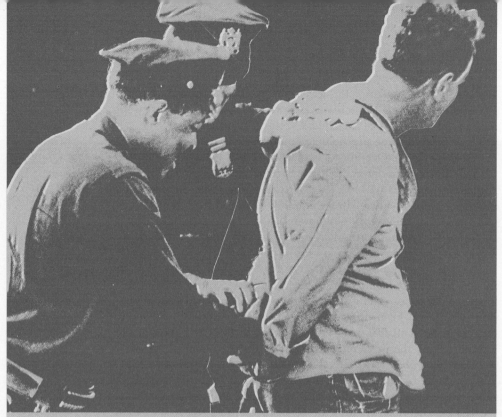

Increase in Crimes of Violence 1960-1970*

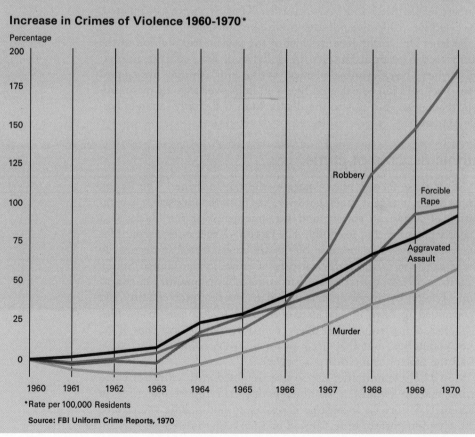

Percentage

Robbery

Forcible Rape

Aggravated Assault

Murder

1960 1961 1962 1963 1964 1965 1966 1967 1968 1969 1970

*Rate per 100,000 Residents

Source: FBI Uniform Crime Reports, 1970

blacks make up only a miniscule portion of the population; altogether, there are only 5,000 black "immigrants" on the islands. Hawaii was thus chosen as the focal point for this report because it offers a view of crime and crime prevention that is largely undistorted by ethnic considerations.

This does not mean, however, that racial animosities do not exist among the state's 770,000 people. Although it is nonviolent, a low-keyed feeling of prejudice exists among the Caucasians (whites), the Japanese, the Chinese, the Portuguese, and the native Hawaiians—the groups that, for the most part, make up the state's polyglot population. Some Japanese, for example, will not sell a house to a white, even though the state has an open-housing law, because they think that the white might run the neighborhood down. The white man in turn often looks down on the Hawaiian as indolent, and Hawaiians of all colors complain of discrimination. They complain, for example, that they are not permitted to surf on some beaches because they are privately owned—by the whites. There is even a civilian-versus-military prejudice in the islands: Hawaiians of all ethnic backgrounds resent the fact that Molokini Island had to be totally evacuated because the U.S. military establishment required it for bombing practice, and that a large part of Kahoolawe, an island southwest of Maui, is marked on all maps as a "Military Reserve," which to Hawaiians means "keep off." To repeat, racial prejudice in Hawaii does indeed exist but it is passive, a passivity that is reflected in a wry catch phrase coined by the islanders: "The Chinese run the economy; the Japanese run the politics; the Caucasians run the plantations; and the Hawaiians run for the hills."

Statehood's unwanted "dividends"

The crime rise in Hawaii is due, according to the local police authorities, primarily to an influx of residents, both transient and permanent, who have infected the paradise state with sophisticated crime brought in from the mainland. This is not to imply that crime was nonexistent before the huge aluminum jets moved the islands to within four and a half hours of California instead of the four and a half days it used to take by ship. Crime has soared because more and more native-born Hawaiians have been exposed to and are emulating their Caucasian teachers in the use of narcotics and in committing crimes ranging from embezzlement and burglary to such specialized criminal pursuits as counterfeiting. The vacationer is important to the islands and his wallet adds much to the local economy, but Hawaii is learning that its outstretched palm cannot accept affluence without accepting also the unconscionable elements within an affluent society. In 1970, more than a million tourists spent $460 million on vacations to Hawaii. During that same year, tourists committed about 15 per cent of all crimes reported on the islands.

It is useless to explain to Chief of Police Abraham Aiona that Hawaii is not alone in its predicament, that the U.S. crime rate too has

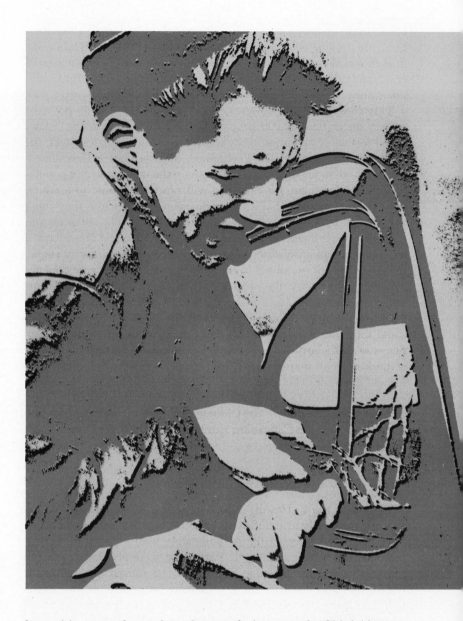

been rising even faster than the population growth. Chief Aiona—a big, beaming man with molasses-colored skin and a broad nose—refuses to take solace in the overall statistic that shows a 144 per cent crime rise in the United States versus only a 13 per cent population increase over the last decade. Maui is an example close to home. Between 1965 and 1970, he points out, the population actually dropped from 51,215 to 46,156—but major crimes increased 121 per cent. In 1970, property on the island valued at $131,905 was stolen, but only $16,189—about 12 per cent—was recovered. To add to Aiona's chagrin, this took place on an island from which a thief cannot escape except by plane or seaworthy boat. Furthermore, the police chief notes, it took place despite intense police surveillance; his

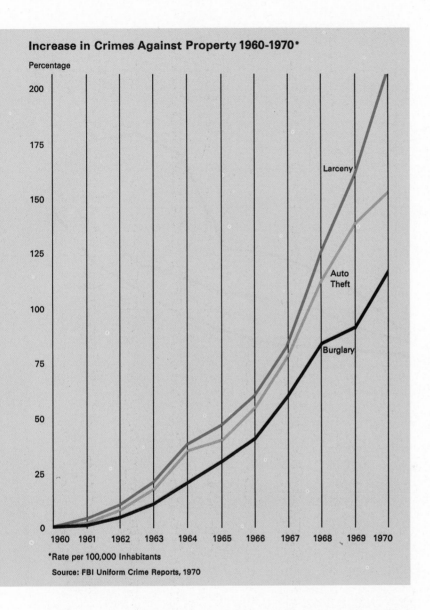

Increase in Crimes Against Property 1960-1970*

Percentage

Larceny

Auto
Theft

Burglary

1960 1961 1962 1963 1964 1965 1966 1967 1968 1969 1970

*Rate per 100,000 Inhabitants

Source: FBI Uniform Crime Reports, 1970

squad cars, which patrol Maui, Lanai, and Molokai–three of the state's six main islands–logged 1,606,257 miles of duty in 1970, although the six islands have only about 3,200 miles of surfaced highways among them.

Aiona is chronically unhappy that only 33.9 per cent of all crimes committed in 1970 on the three islands under his jurisdiction were "cleared"–that is, resolved by arrest and conviction. Again, working to better the record, he finds no comfort in the fact that his percentage of cleared crimes in 1970 was far above that of the United States as a whole, which scored only about 20.1 per cent. The chief worries, too, because the rise in crime has been accompanied by a parallel rise in expenses. The cost of protecting the three islands in 1967 was $1,361,-

Increases in Robbery and Theft 1960-1970

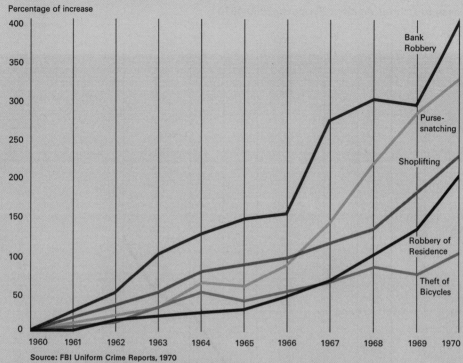

Percentage of increase

Bank Robbery

Purse-snatching

Shoplifting

Robbery of Residence

Theft of Bicycles

Source: FBI Uniform Crime Reports, 1970

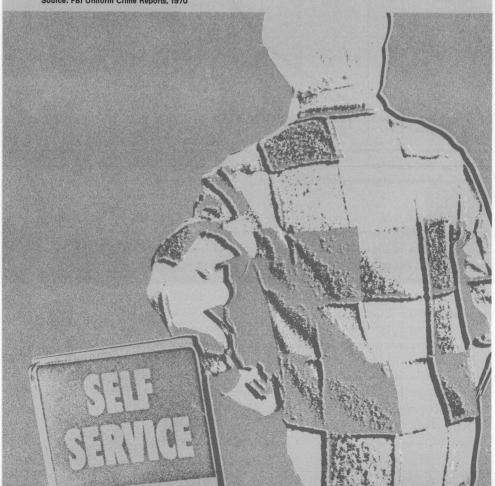

SELF SERVICE

000. By 1970, the cost had risen to $1,891,000, and Chief Aiona was forced to increase his expenses by opening a school for additional police recruits.

One particular crime statistic both mystifies and frustrates Aiona. He would like to know why some of the 36 cars stolen in his district in 1970 were never found. Joy-ride theft is to be expected now and then, and most of the automobiles so stolen are discovered abandoned the following morning. But what does a *true* car thief do with a stolen car on a small island in the middle of the Pacific Ocean? How does he disguise it? To whom does he sell it? Chief Aiona takes little comfort from the fact that he has administrative power over the one community on the islands where there is no crime. It is called Kalaupapa, a community whose 200 adults live on a lip of land located beneath the forbidding cliffs of Molokai. This tiny paradise is a leper colony.

Drugs a major problem

So with the incoming tide of humanity has come an upsurge in crime. The range is all-inclusive—from forgery and fraud to purse-snatching and pocket-picking, from vagrancy and vandalism to drunkenness and disorderly conduct. None of these were unknown to Hawaii in the past. It is the volume that has become alarming, and in no category is this more true than in drug law violations. The "drug scene" is large in the United States today and it is spreading. Nation-wide, arrests for narcotic drug law violations in 1970 were up 44 per cent over 1969. Even more frightening, arrests for drug violations increased 741 per cent between 1960 and 1970.

In Hawaii, drug abuse is a serious problem and just as difficult to combat as it is in the other 49 states. In the shadow of Oahu's Diamond Head crater, for example, lies Fort De Russy, a broad strand of lawn and palm trees on the edge of Waikiki Beach. About 600 U.S. veterans of the war in Vietnam sit on the grass with their backs to the late afternoon sun, their arms around wives or fiancées as they sway to the sweet sad strains of "Aloha Oe." They are here for a week of rest and recreation; their young faces register pure joy. One face on the edge of the crowd is grim, however. It belongs to Lieutenant John Borges, a tall Hawaiian with slick, jet-black hair, who works in the narcotics division of the Honolulu Police Department. As his eyes wander over the crowd, Borges wonders how many of these happy servicemen have small bags of heroin sewed into their collars. Those who have may use it, or they may sell it along Kalakaua Avenue, where almost anyone except a policeman can buy a "three cap" of heroin for $10. Borges' forehead wrinkles in a worried frown of frustration. He knows heroin is there somewhere, but he also knows he can't break up a musical luau to frisk hundreds of war heroes.

The narcotics-smuggling techniques are limited only by the ingenuity of the human mind. Nor are GI's from Vietnam the sole source. Drugs arrive in Honolulu, by plane and by ship, from California to the east and from Laos, Cambodia, Thailand, and Vietnam to the west. They enter via sailors, tourists, islanders, ships' crews, and airline employees.

To help stem the tide, the U.S. Treasury Department keeps John Maxcy as special agent in charge of customs in Honolulu. He is a young man with curly brown hair and with energy to burn. Honolulu, as Maxcy is well aware, is the fourth busiest port of entry of the United States. To cope with the ever-increasing traffic in illegal goods, Maxcy keeps 30 inspectors at the airport and 10 at the harbor docks. He is realistic enough to know, as most customs men do, that he cannot eradicate smuggling in general or the drug traffic in particular; at best he can only hope to control it at its lowest level. Sometimes, though, he feels that he is sweeping the incoming tide with a toothpick instead of with a fine-toothed comb.

Since 1970, according to Maxcy, something new has been added: Cocaine is now showing up in large quantities in Hawaii. The customs agents know where the cocaine is coming from. It starts its journey from several countries in South America and then moves northward into Mexico. From there it goes to San Diego or Los Angeles and—eventually—into Hawaii. But it is smuggled in under so many disguises by so many innocent-looking parties that it is virtually impossible to intercept all the shipments.

Addicts send crime zooming

The immediate effect of the drug influx has been twofold. It has forced the Hawaiian police department to increase the strength of its narcotics division—from 3 in 1965 to 19 today. A second effect has been a collateral increase in other crimes in the islands with the result that, overall, the roster of police department employees has risen from 1,118 (in 1960) to 1,730 (in 1970)—a phenomenal increase. The major responsibility for the increase in nonviolent crimes appears to lie with the addicts themselves. "Our burglary rate is zooming," explains one police officer, "because the drug user needs between $40 and $60 a day to support his habit. To raise that amount, a man who is hooked must steal at least $150 a day in goods in order to get $50 or $60 from a fence willing to handle it."

With a habit that costs $60 a day to support, the addict must produce $420 a week or $21,840 a year to satisfy it. The clever ones, long before they are overwhelmed by the economics of their plight, surrender to the police, or turn themselves in at a hospital emergency room. Some do so because they are desperately sincere in their desire to kick the habit. The devious ones, however, surrender solely to be detoxified and brought back to a point where the effects of one $10 fix will again last 24 hours.

There are the exceptions. As a general rule, the addict who is truly trapped will prefer to remain dependent on the fruits of crime to satisfy his cravings. It is this hard-core group of drug users, and the spiraling cost of their addiction, that is helping to send the crime statistics soaring.

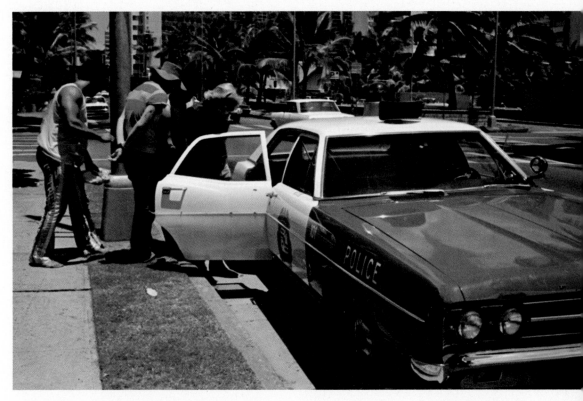

A colorfully disguised Hawaiian undercover agent, left, herds suspected narcotics users into a squad car. The increase in drug traffic has spurred a rise in such crimes as theft and burglary.

The cost of crime in Hawaii as measured by operating expenses is still no more than $2 million annually. And while this is steep enough, it is a mere drop in the bucket for the United States as a whole. In 1955, according to the FBI, the annual cost of law enforcement in the United States was $2.23 billion. By 1965, it had more than doubled— to $4.9 billion. By 1970, it stood at $6.3 billion. These statistics, however, do not reflect the true cost of crime.

According to some authoritative estimates, the job of protecting 205 million Americans in their homes and on the streets costs the U.S. government about $20 billion annually. The true figure is probably much higher; it may even be impossible to gauge. To reach an accurate figure, for example, it would be necessary to know not only the total number of prisoners incarcerated in all federal, state, county, and municipal jails, but also the cost to the taxpayers of their confinement: the value of the real estate on which the jails stand; the cost of erecting the prisons themselves; the sums involved in their maintenance; the salaries and civil service retirement pay of wardens, guards, and even kitchen help; the cost of equipping and stocking medical infirmaries; and the cost of supplying the food the prisoners eat and the clothing they wear.

Next to be included in the overall sum would be the cost of all police departments in the nation, not only in salaries but also in operating expenses. This latter ingredient would reflect an appalling finan-

Recidivism—The High Rate of "Repeaters"

Percentage of persons released in 1965 and rearrested within 4 years

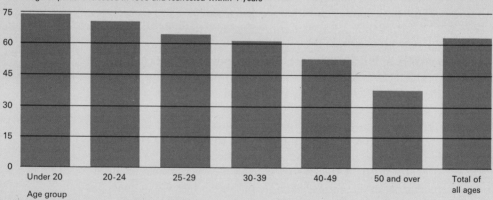

Source: FBI Uniform Crime Reports, 1970

cial overlap because of jurisdictional confusion, in which municipal police frequently find themselves at a crime scene fighting for authority with county or state police. Add, too, the operating budget of the FBI and the U.S. Secret Service, the value of their buildings, their real estate, and their crime-detection equipment; the cost of the U.S. Customs operation and its installations; the salaries of all county district attorneys and their staffs as well as those of their federal counterparts. Bolster these figures with the costs of local, state, and federal courts and their upkeep, the salaries of court employees, and the pensions of retired ones—and an even greater sum emerges.

Nor are these the only factors to be considered if one is to obtain a reasonably accurate figure of the cost of crime in America. To do so, it would be further necessary to add the cost of private detectives in department stores; security police in all the big hotels; and the night watchmen who patrol warehouses and industrial plants. Add to this the retail value of all stolen merchandise—estimated at $8 million a day, nearly $3 billion annually—and the economic cost of crime approaches the astronomical.

All of the cost, which is obviously much greater than the estimated $20 billion, is borne by the law-abiding citizens, whether it be in the form of direct taxation or the markup on the price of a dress or shirt. One could go on—and on: the cost in lost tax revenue from pilfered goods; even the precautionary locks on the doors and windows of the average American home help swell the total. Other elements of the crime scene contribute to the costs, too: Expenses connected with rehabilitation programs, for example, reach hundreds of millions of dollars—for probation officers, parole officers, their offices and their office help, salaries, even the cost of the typewriters on which they tap out their weekly or monthly reports.

A waste of money—and lives

All these and more contribute to the exorbitantly high cost of crime. No cost inquiry would be complete, however, without the inclusion of a factor that involves not only money but a waste of human lives as well. It is known as *recidivism*—a word meaning repeated relapses into crime. Contrary to the general belief, the crime rate is mushrooming because of crime-hardened recidivists, or repeaters, and not because of new "recruits." And while it is important that an all-out effort be made to eliminate the causes of crime and thereby reduce the number of first offenders, it is equally important that sustained efforts be made to prevent the one-time offender from becoming a repeater.

Recidivism runs appallingly high. In 1963, for example, a special follow-up study was inaugurated by the FBI covering 18,567 prisoners released during that year. Within six years, the records show, 65 per cent had been rearrested. A specific breakdown reveals that 57 per cent of those released on probation by court order were later rearrested on another charge. Those who were paroled returned at the rate of 76 per cent. In the category of court acquittals or dismissals of charges, 95 per cent were rearrested during that same six years.

In its report covering 1970, to cite a more recent example, the FBI reported that a study of 37,884 federal offenders arrested in 1969 showed that 68 per cent had been arrested previously. These 37,884 offenders had an average criminal career of five years and five months. During this time, too, they were arrested on criminal charges an average of four times each for a total of 158,000 charges. Altogether, the study group had chalked up a total of 52,936 convictions and 22,240 imprisonments of six months or more.

In general, criminologists tend to agree that the high rate of recidivism is directly linked to the nation's antiquated prison system, a system that dates back to the Pilgrims. Long prison sentences, they maintain, do not chasten convicts; reform schools neither reform nor rehabilitate; and probation and parole systems do not accomplish what they should. Capital punishment, they point out, is not a deterrent to homicide—nor is a life sentence. In support of their contention, they point out that despite 1,284 executions in the United States between 1940 and 1949, the murder rate increased. Since 1966, there have been but two executions—one in California and one in Colorado —and all scheduled executions for murder have since been suspended pending a ruling by the Supreme Court of the United States on several cases appealing the death sentence as unusual and inhumane punishment. Nevertheless, the life sentence still stands—and the number of murders committed in the United States continues to increase. In the first three months of 1971, the homicide rate in America rose 11 per cent, and *that* rate was computed from a 12 per cent increase in 1970 over 1969.

Experiments in prison reform

The hope that criminals can be reformed by merely confining them in cells for varying lengths of time is dashed by J. Edgar Hoover, director of the FBI, who has called prisons "a proving ground for the breeding of an unlimited supply of criminals." And, he might have added, all too often the hardened repeaters are more than willing to teach the tricks of their trade to the newcomers. "Anything can be bought [in prison]—with narcotics high on the list," he says. "These things cannot happen without prison personnel being involved; too much money is involved to stop it." Homosexuality, he continues, is the norm in prison; the rape of the young and weak by the strong and aggressive is a crime of shame that is rarely reported.

Penal systems, and this includes not only facilities but correctional and rehabilitation programs as well, vary widely throughout America. In some states, the prisons are Bastille-like fortresses; in other states, archaic road gangs are the norm. But a few have instituted new and forward-looking approaches to the problems of recidivism.

In Hawaii, a most progressive and relatively successful penal system is in operation. The techniques it has evolved in its criminal rehabilitation programs might well be emulated in the continental United States.

The key person who supervises Hawaii's entire system is a balding, middle-aged man who has the improbable title of Administrator, Corrections Division of the Department of Social Services and Housing. His name is Ray Belnap. Some 30 years ago, Belnap was a prison guard, or in prison slang, a "screw." Today, he sits in a big, sunny office listening to the tapping of a couple of typists on the other side of the wall. "At one time," says Ray Belnap, "Hawaii held all records for the longest terms of imprisonment." His own philosophy on penology has undergone a radical change, he says. In middle age, he now favors short prison terms, or probation, but he thinks that there is more to the incidence of crime than criminal minds. He finds a correlation, for example, between the rise in unemployment and the rise in the crime rate.

"When the economy sags," he asks, big hands outstretched, "who is laid off first? The unskilled worker. Where is he going to go for work? If times are bad, they are bad all over. The moment I notice my charts on house burglaries inching up, I know that within 30 to 60 days, I will read that business suffered a recession."

Not a game of cat-and-mouse

To ascertain how Hawaii's liberal penal system works, one turns to Russ Takaki. Takaki, who is 52 years old and part Japanese, has been working in the correctional field since 1943. He has a small desk in a small office in a downtown building in Honolulu. His job is chief executive to the Board of Paroles and Pardons, a unit that consists of five members, all unpaid, who are appointed by the governor of Hawaii and confirmed by the state Senate. The board, each of whose members serves four years, meets frequently in a second floor office at Oahu State Prison. These are the five men who have the power to chop a court sentence in Hawaii from 10 years to 18 months. The committing judge, of course, has the right to impose sentence and put on probation a person convicted of any crime except the following: murder first degree; murder second degree; rape; carnal abuse of any child under 12; incest; arson; kidnaping; armed robbery; burglary when armed with a deadly weapon; embezzlement of public money; or bribery of a public official.

In cases where a prisoner is convicted and is placed on probation, he remains under the jurisdiction of court-appointed probation officers. If he goes to prison, however, his future is determined by the Board of Paroles and Pardons. In 1970, 1,590 convicts were out on court probation; 112 were paroled. Those who must serve time are under Takaki's astute eye. Of all those paroled during 1969, only 6.7 per cent had their paroles revoked. In the late summer of 1971, the figure was 5.1 per cent. This is surprisingly low and supports Takaki's notion that a good parole system does not play cat-and-mouse with a convict; rather, it assists him with his daily problems at home and at work—not to "rehabilitate" him but, instead, to "reintegrate" him into society.

The cost is incredibly small. Takaki has but 19 parole officers for the entire state; his budget amounts to only $206,000 a year. "We think that the longer anyone remains in prison," he says, smiling from behind his desk, "the more likely he is to commit another crime. The shorter the time we keep him confined—well, look at the record."

Takaki talks about an Adult Furlough Center operated by the Corrections Division. Three months before release from prison, the convict is taken to a big Quonset hut located just off Oahu State Prison grounds. There he lives with others who are nervously waiting to make the perilous leap from prison to freedom.

"They live two to a room," Takaki says. "They have their own kitchens, a TV set, and table tennis. Most citizens think that it is easy to jump from a cell to city life. It isn't. The prisoner feels that everybody can see on his face that he has done time; he feels like a pariah. When he gets to the Adult Furlough Center, we begin to ease him back into the outer world, step by step. We help him to find work according to his skill and, if he gets a job at once, he is permitted to go to his place of business every day, even though he hasn't been paroled. Most of them like this because they don't want to be sprung out overnight, without job, money, friends, or security. As they work, we help them to save money and assist them to find proper housing, too. That 90-day period provides a most important cushion against the ex-convict's returning to criminal life."

A "prison" without bars

To visit another of Hawaii's innovative rehabilitation centers—known as Halfway House—one drives west on Kalakaua between Diamond Head and Pearl Harbor, the landscape flashing alternate glimpses of exotic tropical beauty and skyscrapers. The car continues west until it becomes a twig in the swift flow of traffic streaming along Nimitz Highway.

Soon, the car passes over the Kapalama Drainage Canal. Off to the left stands Honolulu Harbor, almost empty of World War II hulls, and beyond it, Sand Island. On three sides, Sand Island has military reservations. On the land side, there are stands of pines and tall green tropical shrubs. It is lonely and empty on the landward side, except for surfers teetering on boards between Mokauea Island and Sand. Swinging left on Puuhale, the car approaches Oahu State Prison—grayish, depressing stones with watchtowers like geranium pots at the corners and, deep inside, a huge capital X of cells and a prison yard. Jet planes climb out of Honolulu International Airport and clear the prison with their mighty thunder day and night. Here live Hawaii's hardened criminals, many of whom have been inside since the days when there were no jet planes. Here those who were once young and tough grow old behind bars; eventually they die in the tick-tack-toe of sunlight on cell floors.

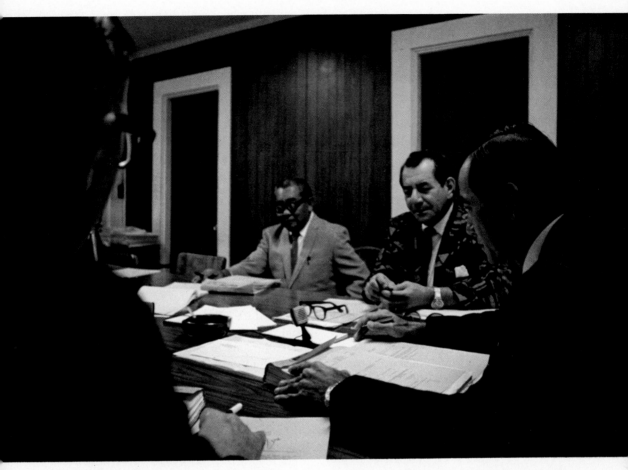

The car turns left in front of Oahu prison, then right on Laumaka Street and there it is—Halfway House. This is where Hawaii sends first offenders who are considered promising rehabilitation prospects. Halfway House consists of a group of long one-story bungalows. There are no prison gates, no bars, no keepers, no warden. In concept, Halfway House seeks to refute the old truism familiar to bird lovers who say that when a canary is put in a cage, it will try to peck its way to freedom. Leave it there long enough and it becomes "institutionalized"; it doesn't want to leave. At Halfway House, the young "canaries" have sofas, rugs, color television, screen doors, a kitchen with a big coffee urn, and a play yard. They are not trying to peck their way to freedom; they are in no danger of being institutionalized.

No prisoners play in the yard because they are too busy leaving for college or jobs in the mornings and, when they return, they're hungry to start a talk session and have dinner. There are 15 men in each building. Each pays $100 a month for room and board. They are self-governing. Between 5:30 P.M. and 6:30 P.M., each group must have a round-table discussion of mutual problems. There is no counselor present, just 15 men in trouble trying to get out of it. No action may be

Reintegrating convicted criminals into society is the special concern of Hawaii's Board of Paroles and Pardons. Its members meet regularly in a paneled office in the Oahu State Prison.

taken on getting a job, or going to school, unless the vote among the men is unanimous.

A young man with a low educational level and a speech impediment serves as a good example of how Halfway House works. An experienced truckdriver, he was anxious to take a job that would put that experience to use. His peers pondered, and voted permission. The young man, tawny-haired and timid, consulted the newspaper want ads and found a job. He felt good working at something productive. He also knew that, according to the rule, he must put some of his earnings in a thrift account against the day of freedom. Within a month, however, his stuttering became worse. At an evening session, one of the prisoners noted that the young man was not working steadily. His trucking boss used him 3 hours one day, none the next, and 12 on the third. The matter was put to a vote, and the decision was reached that the man quit the job at once.

The young man felt the tears coming. It was the first honest job he had had in a long time and they were taking it away from him. Under Hawaiian law, he must obey the unanimous vote of his fellows or return to Oahu State Prison. He had no option. He agreed to quit the job. At once, smiles spread around the table. One man spoke. "We've been discussing your job and we feel that it is making you nervous. We will now take a vote to ask the state to put you in speech school." It was unanimous. After 10 months in speech school and a crash study program, the young man became a white-collar worker with a promising future.

Screening the candidates

"The system," says another inmate of Halfway House, "is only five years old. Before that, the courts were harsh and practically everybody went to a county or state prison. Somewhere around 1966, the police, the courts, the probation system, the parole system, the prisons—everything was changed. It came about so quickly and naturally that I can't think of any one governor or legislature that inaugurated it.

"Under the new system, when the defendant is convicted—either by jury or judge—the court must impose the maximum sentence. If it is 10 years for grand theft or for embezzlement, as it was in my case, you go to prison—the real one—for a few months until the parole board gets individual reports on the prisoner. These reports are put together by parole board workers assigned to your case. They get depositions from your attorney, your church pastor, your parents, relatives, your former employers, neighbors, and—in addition—a psychiatric report from the prison. Even the keepers at the prison are permitted to write their observations of you.

"All of it is placed on a copying machine and the entire report is sent to the members of the parole board one week before they are scheduled to meet. This is done so that they do not have to meet and then riffle through the reports. They have time to read everything, pro and con, and assess the prisoner. Under the law, they can cut the

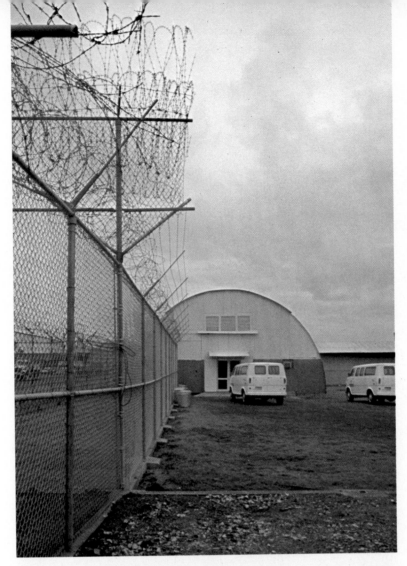

Three months before Hawaiian convicts are released from prison, they are transferred to quarters in a Quonset hut just outside Oahu State Prison, *left.* Their return to normal life is made easier by parole officers who help them find jobs and arrange family reunions, *below.*

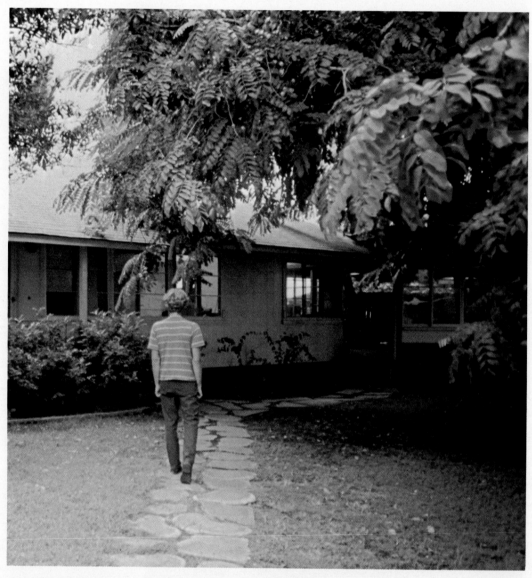

Hawaii's first offenders who are considered rehabilitation prospects are sent to a conditional release center known as Halfway House. To give inmates a psychological boost, there are no prison walls or barred windows at the center.

sentence of the court. In my case, because I showed up pretty good on the reports, my sentence was dropped at once from 10 years to 18 months. Then they decided what to do with me. Fortunately, I was transferred here."

Ultimately, because of Hawaii's system, the young man—and dozens like him—will return to society as useful citizens. It is this reassuring thought that the visitor to Halfway House carries with him as his car again takes him past Oahu State Prison, out along Nimitz Highway and, eventually, back into downtown Honolulu. There, seemingly far removed from the stark realities of crime, all is white sunlight and aloha sport shirts, shopping malls and taxicabs and bearded hippies and middle-aged tourists who tire easily and sit on bus benches consulting their watches. It is members of a religious sect —shaven-headed except for long narrow tufts of hair hanging down the backs of their orange-colored saris—beating drums as they prose-lytize along the sidewalks. Honolulu is yacht harbors, sunbathers, sailors in whites, glassy skyscrapers, the odors of burning sandalwood and jasmine, a picket fence of hotels screening the beach, ancient craters, and old unpainted gabled houses on side streets.

It is warehouses, Sony shops, and bespectacled schoolteachers in flowered muumuus. It is police cars drifting along curbs, stacks of surfboards on sand, coconut palm trees in attitudes of fatigue, stately royal palms reaching high for the sun, and torches blazing outside Polynesian restaurants. It is the bleak harmony of ukuleles, of poin-settias nodding in the breeze, of banyan trees lost in their own roots and, behind it all, the sharp-toothed volcanic peaks shearing the fabrics of the clouds.

This is Honolulu. But in a larger sense it might also be Miami, Las Vegas, San Francisco, New Orleans, or Detroit. It is an American city. It is America.

And America, as mirrored in its crime-ridden cities, has a problem. To solve it will not be an easy matter. Establishing a uniform code of crime will be but one step. Prison reform will be yet another. New approaches to correctional programs and new emphases on rehabilita-tional techniques will be a third step. But first and foremost, there

Each bungalow in Halfway House holds 15 men. All must be self-supporting if they want to remain there. Inmates meet nightly in the recreation room to discuss and resolve problems they encounter "on the outside" during the day.

must be an evaluation of precisely what role the individual citizen plays in the moral climate of the times. America must again reach for the mirror of truth as it did when John F. Kennedy was assassinated.

It is easy enough to say, smugly, that two-thirds of all crimes are perpetrated by slum dwellers. It is less easy to acknowledge the fact that the remaining one-third of all crimes reported are committed by the affluent—or that hundreds of crimes are being committed unwittingly or otherwise by people who would be the first to deny they are criminals. The automobile driver who keeps a $20 bill behind his driver's license in case he is stopped for a traffic infraction counts himself a law-abiding citizen. But he is not. The apartment-house owner who passes cash to a building inspector is not charged with a crime even though his building may burn to the ground because it lacked adequate fire protection. He is nevertheless morally guilty of criminal negligence. The housewife with a zero bank balance who deliberately writes a check at the supermarket a day before payday thinks nothing of it—although she is indulging in a deceptive practice, an illegal act. The millions of small wage earners who list church donations on their income tax returns far in excess of what they gave in any one year are

The hubbub of automobile and pedestrian traffic in Honolulu reflects life in other cities, but the exciting facade too often masks the grim face of urban crime.

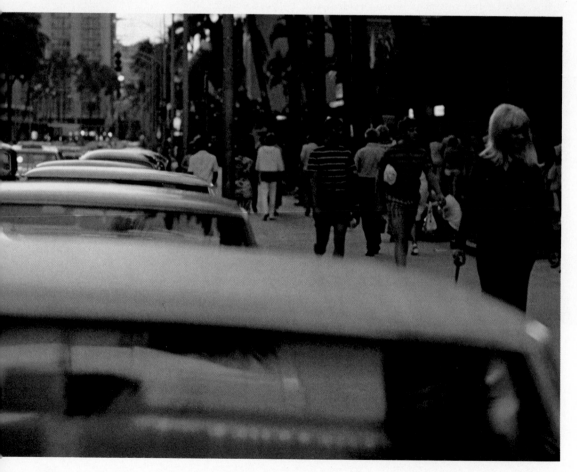

practicing their own personal form of larceny. The banker who charges 9 per cent for a mortgage on a $25,000 house and then demands two "points"—or $500 more—under the table for granting the mortgage is committing a crime. The traveler who files an inflated claim for lost luggage is playing a fraudulent game.

Even the forces of law and order are not above moral reproach. Lawyers have been known to bribe jurors; judges have been known to take bribes. Highly placed government officials, not only in city halls and statehouses but in the halls of Congress and on the White House staff itself, have been convicted of crimes. Policemen, sworn to uphold the law, have been known to subvert it. Most criminologists drop the subject at this point by conceding that crime, on any rate except small scale, is impossible without the connivance of law-enforcement officers and politicians. But, they say, a policeman who has never been tempted by a bribe is a policeman who has never left his precinct station. How many succumb is anybody's guess.

Thus, it seems fair to conclude that crime is not confined to just one class of citizen but seeps across the spectrum of the country. It includes not just known criminals, but also the average man in the street, the legal profession, the judiciary, high government officials, and the forces of law and order.

A call for positive action

The conscience of the country calls for more positive action than is currently being taken, a call that is clearly justified by the findings of such groups as the National Commission on Reform of Federal Criminal Laws and the National Commission on the Causes and Prevention of Violence. "To millions of Americans," says the latter's report, "few things are more pervasive, more frightening, more real today than violent crime and the fear of being assaulted, mugged, robbed, or raped." Warren E. Burger, chief justice of the United States has said, "Judicial processes for resolving cases and controversies have remained static for 200 years and must be updated before the system loses the people's faith." And it is perhaps with this overriding concern in mind that a number of citizens' groups are proposing the formation of a national committee consisting of supreme court justices from the 50 states, as well as representatives from the Supreme Court of the United States and the attorneys general of the states. In accordance with the proposal, they would meet, confer, and establish an equitable system of trial and punishment so that American society would be protected from its predators without sacrificing the freedom of those who may be saved.

For unless some such far-reaching step is taken soon, America may find itself not a utopia but a fool's paradise. Secure in the belief that crime is being vanquished, the nation may find itself living an illusion not unlike that affecting Hawaii's mountains, which dream they are absorbing the blue Pacific, whereas in reality it is the Pacific that is slowly absorbing them.

By William Barry Furlong

New Game Plan for Sports in the '70s

Players are showing a new awareness, while owners are
seeking new ways to find men, money, and places to play

Before the Super Bowl game in January, 1971, a reporter tried to
draw some expression of the "overwhelming" drama of that football
event from Duane Thomas, then the Rookie-of-the-Year halfback for
the Dallas Cowboys.

"After all," said the reporter, "this is the *ultimate* game."

Thomas calmly responded, "If this is the *ultimate* game, then how
come they're playing it again next year?"

The insight—and skepticism—of that remark reflects a new and
growing attitude in sports. To some people, it is only cynicism, but to
others, it is a new realism. To all, it is a change from an innocent
past—a new awareness that has profoundly affected the fundamental
aspects of professional sports: finding men, money, and a place to
play the game.

It was just over 10 years ago that sports entered a new Golden Age.
With the increase in leisure time, there was an explosive increase in
the nation's interest in sports. Baseball, football, basketball, and

There's more to the old ball game than just the ball—even such unlikely
sports equipment as computers, tax loopholes, and city governments.

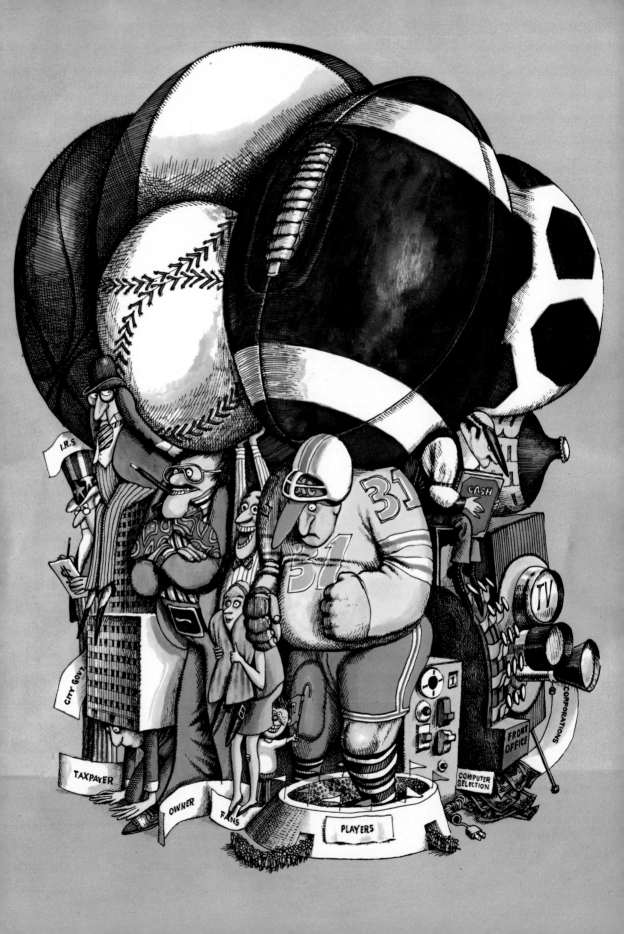

hockey expanded exponentially. Television was there to pave, and pay, the way. The professional sports franchises—long run as family enterprises—were taken over by anybody and everybody anxious to get into the big-money game, including insurance salesmen, singing cowboys, restaurant-chain operators, show-business agents, and even a butterfly collector.

They didn't even have to be playing the game or financing it to seek their fortune in sports. Dr. James Robert Cade of the University of Florida, a researcher in renal medicine, developed a liquid that seemingly refreshed sweating athletes faster than water. It was called Gatorade, and he managed to make a fortune from it. A retired garment maker, Ed Sabol, combined his home-movie hobby with his passion for professional football and won the rights to make movies of the pro football title game. He eventually turned the whole project into some of the finest and most prosperous sports programming on television. A 22-year-old fireman named Craig Breedlove bought a jet engine for $500, built a racing car around it, and set a land speed record on Utah's Bonneville Salt Flats. During the speed run, his brakes melted away, his safety chute ripped loose, and his car sheared off a telephone pole before hurtling into a canal some 18 feet deep. ("For my next act," said Breedlove, "I'm going to set myself on fire.") A 37-year-old advertising agency president, George Lois, who was an athlete in his spare time, paid quarterback Joe Namath of the New York Jets some $10,000 to shave off his Fu Manchu mustache for a razor-blade commercial. The executive then became so ecstatic with the "sell" of Namath's name that he started a series of employment agencies called Namath Girls, Inc.

Through it all, there was an exhilarating sense of opportunity, a feeling that the men and the money would always be there, and that massive profits would come to whoever took part in the action. Joe Namath got $400,000 on a four-year contract with the Jets, and quarterback John Brodie of the San Francisco 49ers got $921,000 on a five-year contract. But there was never a doubt that the cost of these players was worth it, for both payments made possible the merger of the two professional football leagues into one. The payment to Brodie avoided an antitrust suit that might have halted the merger. The payment to Namath was amply returned when he led the Jets to the first Super Bowl triumph ever recorded by the infant American Football League over the older National Football League (NFL), justifying, at least for fans, the merger of the two leagues. So, even though they complained bitterly over the demands of labor—as do many proprietors—the owners of professional sports knew they were getting their money's worth.

Today, much of this has changed. Craig Breedlove fell into financial problems. The doctor who developed Gatorade found his profits in litigation. The commissioner of baseball, faced with the second team bankruptcy in as many seasons, cast around anxiously for somebody

The author:
William Barry Furlong has long had his eye on the sports scene as a free-lance writer and a special correspondent for Sports Illustrated.

Illustrations by John Huehnergarth

The professional athlete is seen by the coach as an animal and by the owner as a money-making machine – but *he* knows he is a deep thinker.

to take over the tottering Washington Senators. Failing in this, the club was allowed to move to Arlington, Tex., when Texas sources provided a $7.5-million advance at low interest rates to the financially strapped owner, Robert E. Short. Also, 25 of the 28 teams in professional basketball lost money in 1971, and 400 of the schools in the National Collegiate Athletic Association reported their sports programs were in the red. And even the new enterprises that spring up around sports were in trouble: The new Off-Track Betting Corporation in New York City, for one, indicated that it would turn only $25 million over to the city – instead of the expected $50 million – after its first year of operation.

The players felt the change in egocentric as well as economic terms. Football player Alex Karras, a popular man on television and on the lecture circuit, was cut from the Detroit Lions squad in 1971 just as he was to appear in a nationwide advertising campaign. The advertisements were to feature Karras endorsing a new copying machine, and were to identify him as the "All-Pro Tackle of the Detroit Lions." The Lions action in removing him from the squad, however, made the advertisements instantly untrue. Karras felt it was less a reflection on his athletic than on his commercial and declamatory skills. "Perhaps there is no room in the world of sports these days for an athlete who has an opinion on anything except his own sport," said Karras. "I have opinions. I think I am entitled to the same consideration as other human beings. That includes having the right to express myself on something other than playing defensive tackle."

Candor has never been what sports owners sought in their hirelings. They have preferred players who were close-mouthed, close-minded, hard-working, and perhaps not too intelligent. The frustration of

Because of dwindling gate receipts, some teams move from city to city in a game of musical chairs, with owners calling the tune.

Karras reflected that of a rising number of players in the 1970s who suddenly demanded to be treated as human beings. Some of these players turned author, writing books that inferred that big-time sports was "dehumanizing." (And it was. The highest accolade a coach could deliver about a particular player in football or basketball was, "He's a real animal!")

The treatment of players was sometimes brutish. Certain front-office men did not care what they did to a player as long as the team's "image" was maintained. When Alex Johnson, the 1970 American League batting champion, was suspended by the California Angels for indifferent, even sulky, play in 1971, he claimed that he had been the target of hostility in the team's clubhouse and had once been attacked by a gun-wielding teammate. Dick Walsh, the executive vice-president and general manager of the Angels, said that Johnson lied, that no such attack had ever taken place. Walsh went so far as to tell Johnson's wife that her husband was having hallucinations. Later, in testimony taken under oath, Walsh admitted he was lying. The attack had taken place, and Walsh knew about it. He had ordered that the gun be hidden so the incident could be kept secret. Here, among the vast and highly touted ideals of baseball, there was apparently no room for simple concepts of justice and human dignity.

But sports executives were not so much concerned about flaws in themselves, in 1971, as about the baffling changes that were occurring in the players. In the hunt for men, the front office could no longer be altogether sure what they were getting. One top professional football player, Steve Thompson of the New York Jets, quit to turn to God; and a top professional baseball player, Ken Harrelson of Cleveland, suddenly quit to take up golf. To be sure, owners had encountered trouble with players in the past, but those were troubles that

the owners could understand. When Paul Hornung, a superb halfback for the Green Bay Packers, was suspended for a year during the 1960s for betting on football games, the old hands were not deeply distressed. They had once done a little "investing" themselves. In fact, two or three of the founding families of the game made their original fortunes through betting and bookmaking. They also knew there was nothing sinister about Paul Hornung. He was simply a fun-loving rover. Once he was thrown off an all-star team when he showed up 45 minutes late for practice and inquired casually of an assistant coach, "What's the record for breaking curfew?" He'd just set it—two days.

The problem that adventurous players such as Hornung created for the owners was that they spoiled the system—in particular, the man-hunting system. According to the system, Hornung—a Notre Dame man, a three-time all-American, and a Heisman Trophy winner—should have been the ideal player, one who accepts the game with monkish fervor. But the man-hunting system was then new and didn't take a player's temperament into account. "Ten years ago, you'd see guys walk into the pro football draft meeting with nothing more than a marked copy of the *Street & Smith Football Annual* under their arms," says Gil Brandt, director of personnel for the Dallas Cowboys of the National Football League. By 1970, though, at least 17 professional football teams were using computers to sift and rank the talent of some 3,000 college football prospects. The Cowboys had become so sophisticated in the use of a computer that their talent hunt turned up everything from a player's IQ ("Average IQ of 20 top cornerbacks in the NFL last year was 95.5.") to how much he favors turning right instead of turning left. Every bit of information is recorded objectively through a numbering system devised by the Cowboys so that it can be fed easily into a computer. The latter sifts, analyzes, and processes

the information, gives each player a score, and then ranks all the players by score from the best to the worst.

The computer can deliver any information that the Cowboys seek: "Name five best tight ends who are 6 feet 4 inches and over, 200 pounds and over, and can run 40 yards in 4.6 seconds or less." In a matter of milliseconds, the computer begins printing out the names on a teletypewriter next to Brandt's office. The most important command the computer obeys is to deliver the names and details on the 600 top college prospects in the country, from best to worst. Only 450 or so of these will be drafted—442 in 1971, to be exact. The Cowboys do not like to go into the draft with the 1,000 to 2,000 names that some other teams now use. Their system is designed to be different in a number of ways.

Dallas does not rate the players against each other. Instead, they use the computer to rate them against a highly intricate mathematical model of perfection at each position. Dallas considers the usual pro football best-to-worst list, which rates quarterbacks against linebackers against receivers against rushmen, similar to comparing apples, oranges, and pears. The Cowboys figure out a "perfect" score for each position and then measure players against that score. A score of 898 for a quarterback would mean that the quarterback prospect was 102 points below the "perfect" quarterback—for Dallas purposes. A score of 890 for a linebacker would mean that this prospect was 110 points below the "perfect" linebacker. A score of 885 for a receiver would mean that the prospect was 115 points below the "perfect" receiver. The numbers mean nothing in reference to each other (though the scores provide a handy way to list the prospects on a best-to-worst list). Thus, where other teams use a scoring system that compares prospects with a single nonexistent concept of the "perfect" football player, the Dallas system provides a comparison of every prospect with a "perfect" player at a specific position.

Dallas does not draft by position, however, as do other teams. Instead, the club drafts the best prospect available when its turn comes in the draft, no matter what position he plays. Every time a player is selected by another team in the NFL draft, Brandt crosses that player's name off the best-to-worst list compiled by Dallas. Then, when the Cowboys get their chance to pick a player, Brandt simply looks for the highest name that hasn't been crossed off. In 1969, for example, the Cowboys were the 24th team to get a draft pick. The fifth name on this list—Calvin Hill, a halfback from Yale—was still available. Dallas picked Hill, and he went on to become Rookie of the Year with the Cowboys in 1969. "Some teams in the league didn't even have Hill in the first 100 names on their lists," says Brandt. On the second round, when Dallas had the 49th pick from the start of the draft, they found the ninth man on their best-to-worst list still un-

Old 885 probably will make a good running back. But that's not his speed or his uniform number—it's his rating, churned out by a computer.

picked. He was Richmond Flowers of Tennessee, who became a regular member of the Dallas secondary. If Dallas had been drafting by position, they probably would have ignored these two players because the players didn't help fill a particular gap in the team's strength. The Cowboys believe that if they keep drafting the best prospect available, round after round, year after year, gaps will never develop–they'll simply have the best men available for every position. "Oh sure, if we've drafted six straight tight ends and, in the seventh round, find that the best player available is another tight end, we might drop down the list to the next-best player available," says Brandt. "But not if we have to go down a hundred names to find him."

Dallas was in next-to-last place in 1961, when it became the first NFL team to develop a computer system. It moved up steadily in the standings as it began to perfect the system. Then, with the system working smoothly, the Cowboys won five division titles and played three times in the league championship game, and once in the Super Bowl, all in the period from 1966 through 1970. More than that, the Dallas computer system was developing player quality to an incredible depth: 38 of the players that the team traded or let go wound up on other NFL teams in 1970. That means that the Dallas system picked two full teams capable of playing NFL football, one that works in Dallas as the Cowboys and the other scattered throughout the league as Cowboy opponents.

Nevertheless, the system has a flaw. It cannot predict the temperament that a player brings to the game. In most cases, particularly during the 1960s, this did not matter much. But with the development of a new attitude of skepticism among players in the 1970s, temperament has become more important. Duane Thomas, Dallas' first draft choice before the 1970 season, had been given a three-year contract that, with bonuses, raised an $18,000-a-year wage to $71,000 for the first year. In his second year, he wanted to rewrite the contract, reportedly to make the $71,000 his basic wage. He was apparently acting out a need for recognition as a human being, and when that need wasn't met in the way he hoped it would be, he began lashing out temperamentally at the team's management. Thomas called Dallas head coach Tom Landry "a plastic man"; general manager Tex Schramm "sick, demented, and dishonest"; and director of personnel Brandt "a liar." ("Not bad," commented Brandt drolly. "He got two out of three.")

To be sure, Dallas has a category called "character" in its computer analyses, but that refers to the earnestness with which a player views practice and discipline more than the way a player views himself or the world. It is based on an understanding of the player as he existed in the 1960s, a player motivated primarily, if not exclusively, by a lust for money.

Players were certainly getting their fair share of money in the 1970s, at least in professional football. Quarterbacks now draw an

average of $39,860 a year; receivers, an average of $26,000 a year; and ball carriers, $27,400 a year. At the same time, three of the four basic offensive positions were getting an average of $26,000 or more, and only the offensive linemen ($23,000) were below that figure. None of the defensive positions, however, were that well paid. Defensive linemen averaged $25,000, linebackers averaged $24,500, and defensive backs averaged $23,300. Perhaps it was a matter of the most money going to the players who put the points on the scoreboard. But, it was also a matter of the players at the "skill" positions—play calling, ball carrying, ball handling—getting more financial recognition than the players at the "brute" positions—blocking and tackling. The only high-skill, low-pay position was kicking. Punters and place-kickers averaged only $19,600 a year, even though they put more points on the scoreboard than anybody else. In fact, the three highest scorers in pro football history—George Blanda, most recently of Oakland, Lou Groza of Cleveland, and Gino Cappelletti of Boston—were all field-goal kickers, a position called on to perform for only a few seconds in any game. "You can't feel too sorry for them at their rate of pay," says a player on a defensive unit. "They get a lot more money per 'bump' than anybody else in the game."

In any case, the computer programmers have omitted a temperament category in the hunt for athletes in the 1970s, a category that is increasingly upsetting the sports scene. To add this would be to acknowledge the more complex dimensions of the modern athlete, who today is looking not only for money but also for self-fulfillment. The owners, apparently, don't fully understand this. They themselves are still looking primarily for money.

No longer is money so easy to find. To be sure, the gross income of professional sports is impressive—$360 million for professional football, baseball, basketball, and hockey combined in 1970. And there is still an urgent clamor for tickets to certain events. In Washington,

As the more learned insiders often view it, sports is the *arbor pecuniaria*—money tree.

D.C., for example, one woman walked into the office of the Washington Redskins to pick up a pair of highly coveted season tickets held for years by her husband. The ticket manager gave them to her, and a little later had to face her irate husband, who said that he and his wife had been separated for two years. Nevertheless, there are signs that all this does not reflect a high and universal prosperity. Half the teams in major league baseball lost money in 1970. Owner William Clay Ford of the Detroit Lions said that the financial situation in the NFL was so critical that some teams might go under—thus contracting, not expanding, pro football, the sport that was thought to be impervious to such troubles. And it is estimated that one-third of all the teams in professional basketball—perhaps nine franchises—will collapse and disappear once the two professional leagues are merged. ("Sure, some teams are losing money," said Leonard Fleisher, an attorney for a number of pro basketball players, "but what law says every business must be a success?")

Moreover, there were signs of a new resistance among fans to the ticket-sale practices of the professional leagues. In Buffalo, N.Y., Angelo Coniglio filed an antitrust suit against pro football for forcing fans to buy exhibition-game tickets in season-ticket packages. The fan claimed this was an effort by the owners to unload an inferior product (exhibition games) on the fans who wanted to buy only a superior product (regular-season games). In Washington, Senator William Proxmire (D., Wis.) criticized professional football for banning telecasts of home games from stadiums built with public money. "In most cities, the local stadium has been built with public funds or the public subsidized the stadium in other ways," he said. "Yet the local taxpayer can neither get a ticket to a home game nor see it on television." In Baltimore, the defending Super Bowl champion Colts, who had sold 50,246 season tickets every year for six years, drew only 16,200 fans to an exhibition game in 1971. Club president Steve Rosenbloom, skirting the allegation that the fans felt his team was exploiting their loyalty, snapped: "Baltimore's reputation as a great sports town may be a myth." The next week, the Colts drew only 13,000 for a game against the Chicago Bears.

Baseball also was feeling the pinch. It saw Seattle go bankrupt in 1970 and Washington in 1971. There might even have been more bankruptcies had television money not helped to offset losses at the gate. To be sure, there had been warnings in baseball for years. In the 1960s, major league baseball was playing more games and had more teams in more cities with greater population than ever before, yet attendance failed to rise rapidly until after 1968. In fact, it took 20 years for baseball to break conclusively the overall attendance record it had set, with fewer teams and fewer games, in 1948. Even then, the new record was set only because organized baseball adopted the dog-

The most valuable "player" on a team today may well be a good accountant with a highly sophisticated understanding of tax-depreciation matters.

Today's athlete may be looking for more self-fulfillment, but the owner is still looking for more money— and no longer is it so easy for him to find.

ma of a man most of the owners despised as a "clown." This was Bill Veeck, who introduced the midget batter, the exploding scoreboard, and many other gimmicks into baseball.

Veeck was out of baseball during most of the 1960s, but the owners adopted his methods to increase attendance. They ran Bat Days, Ball Days, Helmet Days, T-Shirt Days, even Hot Pants Days and Panty-hose Days. Oakland ran greased-pig races to promote its ball games, St. Louis ran country and western concerts, and Philadelphia built not one but two exploding scoreboards. Some of the promoters didn't seem to know where to stop. Charles O. Finley, owner of the Oakland Athletics, went to pitcher Vida Blue in the early days of the 1971 season with a "spectacular" idea. "I'll give you $2,000 if you'll go over to city hall and have your name changed legally to Vida True Blue." Finley envisioned headlines reading: "True Blue wins again. . . ." Vida turned him down. The name Vida was his late father's name, and the pitcher hoped his performance would bring honor to his father's memory. "Besides," said Vida to one of Finley's emissaries, "if Mr. Finley thinks it's such a great name, why doesn't he call himself True O. Finley?"

And all this time, there were also significant changes in the pattern of the game itself, changes that helped to alter the attendance out-look. From 1968 to 1970, the number of home runs increased about 75 per cent—from 1,995 to 3,429—and team batting averages rose from .237 to .253. As a result of all this clout and clowning, baseball attendance rose from 23.1 million in 1968 to 28.7 million in 1970.

The development of baseball as a corporate property was another change in the perennial money hunt. This mushroomed after Veeck discovered a way to handle tax matters within baseball that changed the game from a dowdy, floundering, family-owned enterprise to a glamorous, alluring, business-oriented venture. Veeck, who labored hard to keep his less spectacular dimensions a secret, had studied accounting in night school for seven years. But somehow he never let that fact get around in baseball circles. He wanted other owners to view him only as a clown, not as a shrewd, rather perceptive operator who understood every figure that went into their accounting ledgers. His discovery involved a highly sophisticated understanding of tax depreciation.

The process can be explained this way. Suppose an individual buys a ball club for $10.2 million. It is important that he buy almost all of the stock (80 per cent will do the trick in most locations). That means the former owners must give up complete control of the club. Once that is done—and under the tax laws it must be done within a year—the new owner can reorganize the club into a new corporation. He can then list all the club assets for which he just paid, and estimate how fast those assets will depreciate. It may take 10, 20, 30, or 40 years for some assets—the franchise, the ballpark, the lighting system for night games, the scoreboard, and the equipment used to mow the grass—to reach the end of their "useful" life. But other assets reach the end of their useful life in a short time. Ballplayers do, for example. Ask any manager. Their "value" can be written off, or depreciated, in from three to five years. The aim of the new owner is to get as high a depreciation in the first few years of ownership as possible, because the depreciation can be deducted from the profits that the ball club earns—and that radically reduces the taxes. Here's how the owner who has paid $10.2 million for a ball club could handle it:

■ He'll set the value on those assets that depreciate over a long period of time as low as possible, because he can then realize greater tax-depreciation allowances in the first few years of ownership. He may decide that all the long-term assets—the franchise, the ballpark, and so on—are worth only $200,000. If it takes 40 years for those assets to depreciate, he is able to deduct $5,000 a year from his profits on his tax reports, assuming the most common system of accounting for depreciation.

■ He'll set the value on those assets that depreciate in a short period of time as high as possible. He may say, for example, that his ballplayers are worth $10 million and that they'll have a useful life of only five years. In this way, he can deduct $2 million in depreciation from the profits the ball club earns every year for five years. Thus, if his ball club earns $2 million a year in profits, and he can deduct the $2 million in depreciation, he will pay no taxes at all on his profits. He would normally have to pay almost $1 million in taxes on that $2-million in profits. So the owner actually has his $2 million a year in profits in his pockets. The depreciation deduction—though it offsets profits on a tax report—is a bookkeeping entry; it doesn't actually take any money from the owner, as taxes would.

Over the first five years that he owns the club, the new owner can make $10 million in profits, knowing that with the fast write-off on

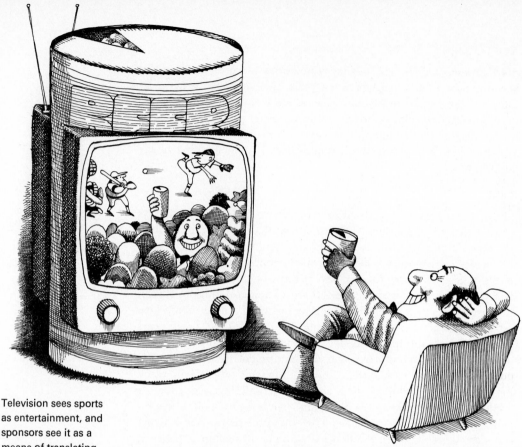

Television sees sports as entertainment, and sponsors see it as a means of translating fans' team loyalties into brand loyalty.

depreciation of certain assets he won't have to pay a penny of tax on that profit. There's one limitation, however: He *must* make a profit. None of the depreciation is of any use if his ball club is mired in losses year after year.

This financial razzle-dazzle doesn't benefit the old families whose ancestors started the various baseball franchises. They can't suddenly decide to turn their teams into new corporations just to get depreciation allowances. The only way the founding families can make money by this process is to sell their stock at a somewhat inflated price to somebody who *can* use the scheme. The result has been a trend within baseball to sell ball clubs from family ownership into more impersonal ownership. Only Calvin Griffith (of Minnesota *née* Washington) and Horace Stoneham (of San Francisco *née* New York) remain as representatives of the early families in baseball. At the same time, the new owners who have bought into the game have given it a great deal more color and vitality. They have had to make a profit in order to make the depreciation deduction work, and so they have jettisoned some of the old promotional methods and introduced new ones in the hope of attracting profits.

The tax-saving-through-depreciaton program may soon be less advantageous, though. For one thing, the federal government is tightening up on the process of scheduling depreciation in sports enterprises so that it doesn't lose so much in taxes. For another, some ball clubs simply have been unable to make a profit on their operations and therefore cannot take advantage of this kind of fast write-off on depreciation. The Washington Senators, in particular, faced constant losses. They had the highest ticket prices and the poorest constituency in baseball. As it sank toward bankruptcy, the owner of the ball club said he would sell it for about $13 million. Veeck, however, said that if it came up for auction under baseball rules, it would go for about $6-million. It was clear that the only thing that could save the club was a massive infusion of new capital, or new fans—and the new fans could come only by moving the club to a new city. Robert E. Short, the beleaguered Washington owner, favored moving the franchise and won out, although baseball commissioner Bowie Kuhn had sought new capital from one or another corporation that might rescue the Senators to be "near the seat of government."

The difficulty in courting corporations lies in the fact that the profits from depreciation on ballplayers are not much of a motive for a large corporate overlord. The biggest corporations in America are almost 4,000 times as large as the better baseball franchises, and the tax savings in baseball—though large for an individual owner—are small for a large corporation. Only two ball clubs have thus far been purchased by large corporations: The New York Yankees are owned by the Columbia Broadcasting System (CBS), and the St. Louis Cardinals are owned by the Anheuser-Busch brewery. Neither corporation went into baseball ownership as a bailout, or rescue, operation, but because the game had some relationship to its corporate interest. CBS saw baseball as entertainment, like TV, and the brewery hoped to establish a brand loyalty based on the fans' sports loyalty.

Another important factor in raising money is finding an adequate place to play. Almost any change gives an enormous, if brief, surge to

City fathers do not want to lose a team that brings them fame, so there is no limit to what they might promise a ball club to keep it in town.

profits. A new ballpark offers the chance to raise ticket prices and still play to a larger attendance. In baseball, the Philadelphia Phils more than doubled their attendance—with a last-place ball club—by moving to a new park in 1971. But the new dimension was provided by those professional football clubs that sought a new constituency by moving out of the city into the suburbs. The Boston Patriots built a new park in Foxboro, Mass., south of Boston, and changed their name to the New England Patriots. The Dallas Cowboys built their new stadium in suburban Irving, Tex. The Detroit Lions accepted an invitation to move their games to Pontiac, Mich., in the near future, and the New York Giants said they would move their games to suburban New Jersey by the mid-1970s. The Baltimore Colts planned to build a new stadium in suburban Columbia, Md., but paused in the face of an angry fan reaction. The Chicago Bears announced a move to suburban Evanston, Ill., but backed down in the face of resistance from local citizenry and a ban by the Big Ten Conference on their planned use of the Northwestern University stadium.

The Bears' case is significant because it shows that professional football teams are not seeking merely a suburban constituency but, if possible, a collegiate one. In 1971, the Detroit Lions played Baltimore in an exhibition game in the University of Michigan stadium at Ann Arbor and drew 91,745 fans. Los Angeles and Oakland played in the University of California stadium in Berkeley and drew 67,939 to an exhibiton game. The Chicago Bears and Cleveland Browns drew only 43,000 fans, however, to an exhibition game in the University of Notre Dame stadium in South Bend, Ind. It was the only time in nine years that Notre Dame stadium was not filled to capacity for a football game, but this was not a suburban location for either Chicago or Cleveland. Since it was an attempt to find a constituency among college fans through a mediocre game between two mediocre teams, it was not surprising that it did not draw a capacity crowd.

The change to a suburban locale was becoming infectious for several reasons. Toll roads and expressways often make it easier to reach a suburban ballpark than one surrounded by dense inner-city traffic problems, and the suburbs offer more parking space or room to build new parking lots. Too, the constituency in the suburbs has more money than the throngs in the inner city—and pro football's owners were hoping to attract more fans to more games at higher ticket prices than ever before.

The earliest returns were more than satisfactory to sports owners. The New England Patriots, who had difficulty filling Fenway Park (capacity 37,216) found that at Foxboro they drew 60,000 fans to their first home game. But few suburbs have the ability—or inclination—to finance the building of a huge new stadium and virtually give it away to a sports club, as do most big cities. Clubs that moved to the suburbs either had to find a stadium waiting for them—as the Chicago Bears hoped might occur in moving to Evanston—or finance the construction of their own new stadium. The Patriots built one at a cost of $6.1 million. The Cowboys tied the financing of the suburban stadium to the sale of season tickets. Every Dallas fan who bought a season ticket also had to buy up to $1,000 worth of low-yield bonds to help build the stadium. By the start of the 1971 season, the Cowboys had financed approximately half the cost of this $27-million project by means of such bond sales.

The leaders of the inner cities, however, didn't want to give up the teams that brought them fame. There was virtually no limit to what politicians might promise a ball club to stay in town. Chicago paid $770,000 to improve aging Soldier Field to assure the Bears a mid-town location, and then promised to build a new $55-million football stadium on the lakefront. The Wayne County Board of Commissioners of Detroit tried to lure the Lions back into town by announcing plans for a $126-million domed stadium in a downtown location. And the taxpayers of the entire state of Louisiana were asked to guarantee loans for the costliest stadium of all time—a $130-million domed structure in New Orleans that would accommodate baseball, football, and basketball. The proprietors of sports thus found that either they could move to the suburbs, or they could use the *threat* of moving to the suburbs to get inner-city politicians to build opulent new stadiums. By their very lavishness, these stadiums would attract large crowds, even to see poor teams (as the Astrodome in Houston did for several years). The next step was to seek the best of both possible worlds—to seek a suburban location, and to get the politicians of the entire state to use taxpayer financing to build an extravagant stadium at little or no cost to the sports proprietor.

Behind these changes in the hunt for men, money, and a place to play is a new lucidity about the nature of sports on the part of the sports fan. Until now, the dream of sports was what gripped the fan, the conviction that somehow athletes possess a purity, honor, and ethic all their own. Those who won did so because somehow they were more *deserving* in a vaguely spiritual as well as physical sense. As the athlete became a gladiator representing his community or school, those he won for also became more deserving. Thus sports became a shared ecstasy in which the fan wallowed in dreams of idealism, not only about sports but also about himself.

To be sure, the dreams of man have always been exploited in sports. Even in ancient Greece, the winners of the games on the plains of Olympia were likely corrupted. As soon as they got home, they were wined and dined lavishly at public expense, given many gifts, and exempted from taxes. But rarely in the past did athletes, or those who rewarded them, talk openly about this. The tradition has always been to conceal the corruption and profit from the dream. The test of sports in the 1970s will be whether the candor of the times, or the cynicism, will touch the dreams of man. For it is in those dreams that sports endure.

A Year Book Special Report

By Senator Adlai E. Stevenson III

A Freshman
In the Senate

One of its newest members provides an inside look
at "the greatest deliberative body in the world"

The hundreds of thousands of schoolchildren, tourists, and others who visit the nation's capital each year are often disappointed—perhaps even disillusioned—when they watch the United States Senate in session. From their seats in the galleries they look down into the historic chamber, with its 100 old-fashioned desks and armchairs in four semi-circular rows—only to realize that most of the senators' seats are empty.

The few senators present seem to pay scant attention to whoever is speaking. There is no Daniel Webster among today's debaters; the tone is generally conversational, with one senator drawing the response he wants from a like-minded colleague or trying to snare an opponent in an accidental admission or inconsistency. Whatever high tensions may exist are usually concealed by the relaxed manner of debate.

Occasionally, of course, spectators in the galleries will hear an impassioned speech (but no outbursts to match Webster's "Liberty and Union, now and forever, one and inseparable!"). Or they may witness a moment of high drama, such as a particularly close roll-call vote on an issue of national controversy.

For every such moment of drama in a senator's life, however, there are countless long hours devoted to committee meetings. Others are spent on the vast range of additional chores that demand every senator's time and attention.

Much of the work of the Senate is conducted by its 16 standing committees. The hundreds of bills and resolutions introduced each year are referred to the appropriate committees for consideration. On important legislation, a committee may spend many days listening to arguments pro and con. It hears Cabinet members and other public officials, professors and professionals whose expert opinions it seeks, and spokesmen for special interests and groups claiming to represent the public interest. The legislation may be amended or wholly rewritten by the committee in executive sessions. All this comes before the bill even reaches the Senate floor, where it may be amended even more before it is passed or voted down.

The magnitude and complexity of the problems facing our society and the volume of legislation that is proposed each year have required the standing committees of the Senate to create a maze of specialized subcommittees. Each senator serves on two major committees (mine are the committees on labor and public welfare and on banking, housing, and urban affairs) and several subcommittees (I am chairman of the one on migratory labor and serve on 11 others).

The tip of an iceberg

Vital as this activity is, however, the proceedings on the Senate floor and committee business represent only the tip of the iceberg. Every senator faces an endless variety of tasks at his office desk. For instance:

- My incoming mail—most of it from Illinois—averages about 10,000 letters a month. About two-thirds urge me to vote for or against legislation of interest to the writer. With the help of my staff, I try to respond to all of this mail. Handling the load is difficult, but the number of people who want their voice to be heard is heartening. And I consider it important that they know someone in Washington is listening.

- Many citizens with personal problems, frustrated in their efforts to deal with government agencies, appeal to their representative or senators for help. Members of my staff try to be helpful in such cases, and I often talk with individuals who have come to us for assistance. In a society such as ours, the individual citizen is too often known to his government only by his social security number. Too often he finds himself pleading with an indifferent or insensitive bureaucrat or corresponding with a computer. Hence, such personal contacts are important.

- Visitors from Illinois—my constituents—seem to stream endlessly into my office. A businessman from Decatur has come to Washington to dis-

The author:
A former Illinois legislator and state treasurer, Adlai E. Stevenson III was elected to the U.S. Senate in 1970.

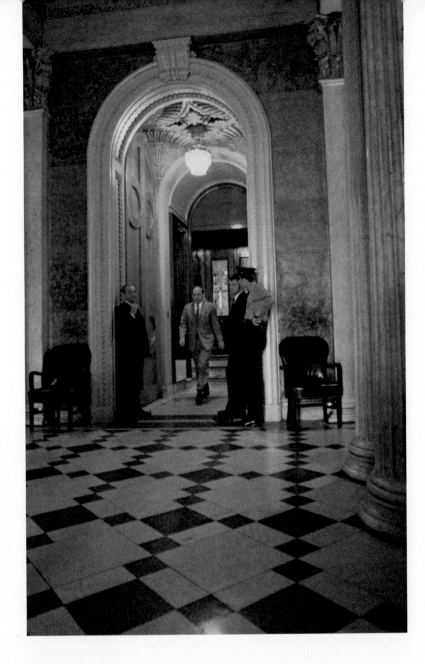

Leaving the Senate chamber, the author heads back to his office to continue the myriad tasks that fill the day of a U.S. senator.

cuss a ruling by one of the federal regulatory agencies. A delegation of 4-H members from downstate and a state official who is in town to discuss federal grant programs administered by the U.S. Office of Education may add to the flow. So do the president of a labor union lobbying for new trade legislation and a delegation of women's club members.

I see as many visitors as I can. But at the moment they reach my office I may be hurrying to the floor of the Senate for a vote on an amendment. By the time they get to the galleries and are admitted, the roll call may have been completed and I am hurrying to a subcommittee meeting. I suspect they sometimes go back to Illinois wondering what their senator does all day, having found me neither in my office nor in the Senate chamber.

I meet intermittently throughout the day with various members of my staff, often during lunch—a bowl of soup from a hot plate and a couple of crackers—at my desk. My legislative assistant comes in to summarize developments in a committee meeting that I was unable to attend because of a conflicting meeting. Another assistant comes in to report on his conversations with the Department of the Interior regarding a home-state project I am backing. Then we are interrupted by the buzzer in the big clock on my office wall, ringing insistently to signal the start of a roll-call vote.

As I leave for the Senate chamber, my secretary hands me a briefing memo that helps to prepare me for a midafternoon meeting, and a newspaper reporter who has been waiting comes along to ask my reaction to a noontime White House announcement. He tries to take notes while we half-run down the stairs to the basement of the Old Senate Office Building, climb aboard the subway that carries us to the Capitol, step onto an escalator up to the Senate wing, and crowd our way into an elevator that goes up to the corridor leading to the Senate chamber. The activity is often hurried, but many members of the Senate follow a similar schedule.

An allowance problem

This would, of course, be an impossible pace without the help of an overworked staff. Each senator receives an annual allowance for the payment of staff salaries and the purchase of typewriters and other office equipment. There are additional allowances for stationery and supplies, telephone and telegraph, postage, travel, and the maintenance of state offices. But there are also many expenses that are not covered by these allowances. To meet these extra costs, many senators —myself included—find it necessary to supplement their $42,500-a-year salary by accepting honorariums for occasional lectures and articles.

Because the workload is heaviest in the offices of senators representing the most populous states, the allowance for staff salaries and equipment for my office ($407,868 per year) is greater than the allowance for senators from smaller states. But the formula for the allocation of these funds is inequitable; on a per capita basis, the allowance for such sparsely populated states as Wyoming and Alaska ranges from 90 cents to $1, while the per capita allowance for Illinois works out to less than 4 cents.

This inadequate allowance does not provide the staff capacity that a senator from a heavily populated state needs. I have 24 people in my Washington office, 6 in my office in Chicago, and 2 in Springfield, the Illinois state capital. That sounds like a large staff, but three-fourths of this manpower, and womanpower, is devoted to the handling of mail, to casework and other services for constituents, and to working with local officials and federal agencies on matters of importance to communities in Illinois. All of these functions are important, but the time that my staff and I must devote to them makes it difficult, without

Part of the massive mail load gets a
dictated reply, *above left*. The flow
of visitors to a senator's office is
also heavy, *above right*. Meetings
with his Washington staff, *left*, and
conferences with individual advisers,
above, are essential, but make heavy
inroads into efforts to attend to
his main business—legislating.

A small subway takes Stevenson to the Capitol from the Old Senate Office Building, *left*. In the high-ceilinged committee rooms, much of the Senate's work is carried out.

additional staff, to give sufficient attention to the most important part of a senator's work—the legislative initiatives and judgments that a senator must exercise if he is to fulfill his responsibility to the people he represents.

My day generally begins at 8:30 A.M. when I ease my Ford out of our driveway in northwest Washington. Even in rush-hour traffic, home is only about 30 minutes from the Old Senate Office Building.

I seldom get home for dinner before 7:30. After the dinner hour with my family, it is time to retire upstairs to the study to concentrate on unfinished business—accumulated correspondence, unwritten speeches, and the like. I use a small recorder to dictate letters, speech drafts, and comments to my staff on memoranda they have prepared for my overnight reading. If I am to take part in the questioning of a witness at an important committee hearing the next day, I may review the transcript of previous testimony and other documents on the subject. If an important floor vote is coming up, I may make notes for a statement that I plan for the final hours of debate. Finally, late at night, I may take a magazine article that someone has urged me to read or, too rarely, a book to bed with me. All of this leaves little time for the "glamorous" embassy receptions and black-tie dinners that are supposed to be essential to Washington life.

It leaves precious little time, too, for a family tennis match or an evening of Monopoly. But my long workdays, my "homework," and my frequent trips away from home are nothing new to my wife Nancy and our children, Adlai IV, Lucy, Katie, and Warwick. We lived in Chicago during the two years I was a member of the Illinois legislature and the four years I served as state treasurer, and I spent much of my time during those years in Springfield.

At a luncheon meeting, the author discusses policy with Admiral Elmo R. Zumwalt, innovative chief of naval operations.

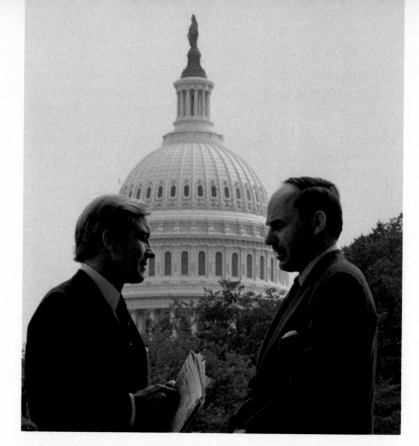

Senator Stevenson talks over legislative issues with Illinois's other U.S. senator, Republican Charles H. Percy, in front of the Capitol dome. His party's leader in the Senate, Mike J. Mansfield of Montana, chats with Senator Stevenson, *on facing page.*

When I first came to Washington following my election to the Senate in November, 1970, I lived out of a suitcase in the home of friends for six weeks. Nancy divided her time between housekeeping in Chicago and house-hunting in Washington. We rented a furnished house in Washington for three months, and during that time we bought and redecorated a 30-year-old red brick home in a hilly, wooded section of the city. We needed a house with space enough for not only our four children, but also for two college students who live with us. One of them works as an "intern" in my Senate office as part of her college program, and the other helps Nancy with the children. We needed a house big enough, as well, to accommodate Joe, our Belgian shepherd; Hamlet, our hamster; and two rabbits.

Our three younger children attend Sidwell Friends School, a co-educational Quaker day school not far from our home. Adlai IV is at the Middlesex School in Concord, Mass.

I try to spend as much time as I can on weekends with Nancy and our children, but many of my weekends must be spent in Illinois, speaking at a luncheon meeting of the United Nations Association in Chicago, perhaps, or addressing the Peoria Association of Commerce, meeting with staff members and constituents in my Chicago or Springfield offices, and making stops in three or four towns to maintain my political fences. This sort of scheduling problem must confront many senators, especially those from larger states with as many and varied needs as Illinois has.

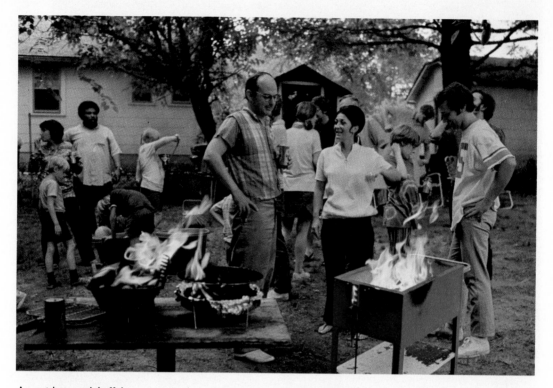

An outdoor social affair gives Stevenson, his family, and his staff an opportunity to relax together and exchange the small talk that keeps everyone up to date.

The demands of a senator's schedule do not leave much time for thinking, the kind of unhurried reflection that ought to be possible—indeed, mandatory—for all 100 members of the Senate.

From its earliest days, the Senate has been looked upon as a great deliberative body—"a temperate and respectable body of citizens" as envisioned in The Federalist papers. Its members were to ponder and debate the great issues of their time, ratify treaties with foreign powers, and consent to the President's appointments in the executive and judicial branches.

The Senate was created by a compromise—the "Great Compromise" negotiated by the framers of the Constitution in 1787. The size of each state's delegation in the House of Representatives is determined by population. The smaller states feared domination of the lawmaking process by the relative Goliaths, so the Constitutional Convention, after long and sometimes violent debate, agreed that each state should have equal representation in the Senate. Thus, New York today has 41 members in the House of Representatives to Wyoming's 1, while each state has 2 senators.

That spirit of accommodation continues today in the institution created by the Great Compromise. Because Senate rules governing debate and the amending process are less restrictive than those in the House, the Senate is better able to reconcile differences arising from the conflicting interests of a diverse people.

For many men in elective politics, the ultimate goal is to serve someday in the Senate. That was my ambition from the beginning of my political career, which started with my election to the Illinois legislature in 1964, when I was 34. I intend here to weigh that ambition and the Founding Fathers' expectations against the experience of my first year in the Senate. These observations will be colored by the awe of a freshman senator and by the reverence of a public servant for the Senate as an institution.

That reverence for the institution is reflected in the extraordinary deference that each member accords the next. Senate debate, even at its most contentious, goes on with great civility. However bitter their differences, a senator rarely refers to a colleague in other than terms of high esteem. I recall how one of my fellow freshmen took care to observe this custom during one lively exchange. He referred to his adversary, a very senior committee chairman, as "the distinguished chairman," but he then proceeded immediately to liken the distinguished chairman to a wily possum.

The courtesies so carefully observed on the floor of the Senate may strike visitors as vestiges of an archaic ritual. But they are more: They are, among the senators, an acknowledgment of a mutual respect that transcends ideological and sectional differences. Considering its diversity of philosophies, prejudices, and personalities, the Senate might be unable to endure, or at least unable to function, without the courtesies that have evolved over the years.

Much of the business on the Senate floor is conducted by *unanimous consent*. This is a device by which, for example, all senators agree to reduce delay by dispensing with a normally required procedure such as the reading aloud of a particular document. The record of a single, randomly selected day showed 71 separate actions that were made pos-

The dinner hour at home brings the Stevenson family and their guests together nearly every evening before the senator's homework session must begin.

To complete unfinished business, Senator Stevenson works in the upstairs study of his Washington home virtually every evening.

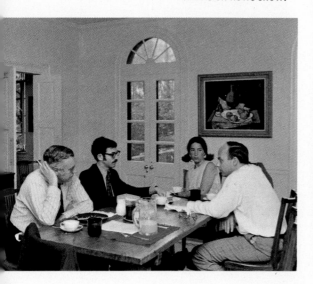

The author meets with staff members at home to prepare himself for an appearance on NBC's early-morning "Today" television news show.

sible by unanimous consent. A lone senator, by withholding his consent to such moves, can disrupt the legislative process.

Under the principle of unlimited debate, a minority of senators can use long, delaying speeches to block action on legislation they oppose. Such obstructive tactics have been resorted to often in recent years— notably (but by no means exclusively) by Southern senators opposing civil rights legislation. Hence, there has been recurring pressure to modify the Senate's much-debated Rule 22, which requires a two-thirds vote to invoke cloture and thus stop a *filibuster* (a purposeful delay that often depends on time-consuming speeches).

It is not easy to muster this two-thirds vote. In 58 roll calls on cloture motions since the adoption of Rule 22 in 1917, the Senate has voted only 9 times to limit debate.

Those who want to change the rule contend that it allows a willful minority to thwart the will of the majority. But those who support the two-thirds rule point out that the men who framed the Constitution did not intend all questions before the Congress to be resolved by a simple

Interviews and informal
chats with journalists
such as Edward P.
Morgan are a part of
Senator Stevenson's day.

majority. Thus, the Constitution requires a two-thirds vote on a number of questions—for example, to ratify treaties and to override presidential vetoes. The same men regard the filibuster as an essential safeguard against minority rights being trampled on by the rash action of a hasty majority. The right of unlimited debate can be used as a last line of defense by any kind of minority. It is most commonly associated in the public mind with efforts to obstruct civil rights legislation. But, in a society grown weary of dissent and disorder, this right of unlimited debate might well be utilized one day by the defenders of civil rights.

This controversy dates back many years. I was pointedly reminded of that fact during the first weeks of the 92nd Congress, when the Senate was again debating Rule 22. I was presiding—a chore that is rotated among junior senators in the Vice-President's absence—during a long speech by Senator Sam J. Ervin, Jr., of North Carolina, a vigorous defender (and practitioner) of prolonged debate. Turning toward me, Senator Ervin said he wanted the Senate "and particularly the present occupant of the chair" to hear a "very wise statement made by a

A flight to a Democratic function, the Jefferson-Jackson Day dinner in Charleston, W. Va., provides time for extra work, *above left*. Trips to Illinois include an appearance at a parade, *above;* the chance for a young citizen to get an autograph, *left;* and the opportunity for a strong-minded constituent to register her opinion with her senator, *below*.

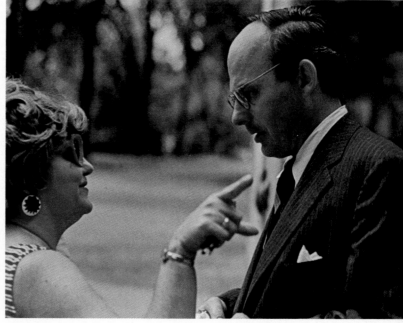

great American" many years ago. The statement was a rejoinder to "those who clamor against the Senate and its method of procedure." Senator Ervin was quoting from remarks made by my own great-grandfather, the first Adlai Stevenson, while presiding over the Senate as Vice-President during President Grover Cleveland's second Administration. Senator Ervin glanced at me as he continued to quote my great-grandfather: "Great evils often result from hasty legislation, rarely from the delay which follows full discussion and deliberation. . . ."

Even in the short time I have been in the Senate I have witnessed the impact of sudden public passion on members of the Congress. The conviction of Lieutenant William L. Calley on charges of murdering helpless women and children in a Vietnam village provoked outrage in many Americans who regarded the young Army officer as a scapegoat and a victim of gross injustice. Members of the Congress were besieged by angry telephone calls, telegrams, and letters demanding that Calley be set free. The public's indignation was echoed in oratory on the Senate floor. Very few stood to say that the nation must not make a hero of a convicted murderer. Very few stood to say that justice must be done and the orderly processes of the law upheld. In this instance, the public fury subsided quickly. But on another day those very few might find it necessary to stand on the floor of the Senate, there to hold the line with extended debate, until, once again, the nation regained its senses.

To make the majority prevail

The filibuster, as I have already noted, is known primarily as a tactic employed from time to time by a minority of senators to prevent the passage of legislation and thus thwart the will of the majority. But in my early months in the Senate, a filibuster was used to make the will of the majority prevail.

One of the most controversial issues before the 91st Congress was President Richard M. Nixon's request for an appropriation of $290-million in continued federal subsidies for the aviation industry's development of a supersonic transport (SST). Opposition to the SST was based on several factors, including public apprehension about noise levels and scientific concern about the effects of supersonic flights on the earth's upper atmosphere. Aside from these considerations, I opposed the SST because I felt there were better uses for the hundreds of millions of dollars that development of this aircraft would ultimately cost—money that could be used instead for schools, hospitals, mass transit, and other urgent national needs.

The House of Representatives had approved the President's request for continued federal subsidies for the SST. The Senate showdown came on an amendment to delete the $290 million from the Department of Transportation appropriations bill already passed by the House. On a 52-41 roll call on Dec. 3, 1970, the members of the Senate voted to "kill" the SST.

As is always necessary when there are differences in legislation

A Senator's Crowded Schedule

A senator's duties are diverse almost beyond measure. One of my busiest—and most interesting—periods of 1971 came during May when the Senate majority leader, Mike J. Mansfield of Montana, proposed cutting in half the number of U.S. troops stationed in Europe under the North Atlantic Treaty Organization (NATO). With two others, I co-sponsored a substitute amendment asking President Richard M. Nixon to negotiate with Russia for a mutual reduction of forces in Europe; to negotiate with our European allies for greater financial and manpower support from them for NATO; and to report to the Congress on progress. As a co-sponsor, I was to take part in Senate debate for the first time. But meanwhile, other senatorial duties also continued their demands. An abbreviated log of activity for part of the three days beginning Tuesday, May 18, illustrates what a senator's day includes.

Tuesday. Breakfast with Secretary of State William Rogers. Several senators were invited so Rogers could lobby against both Mansfield's move and the substitutes. Our proposal did not compel any Administration action, but it was opposed, nevertheless, on the grounds that it intruded on the President's authority.

After breakfast, rushed to an executive session of the Labor and Public Welfare Committee. It was called to work on legislation to postpone a threatened railroad strike.

Next, hurried to the Senate floor to deliver my speech in support of our substitute for the Mansfield proposal. Senator Birch Bayh of Indiana had offered a different substitute.

In the afternoon, taped a television show with Republican Charles H. Percy, Illinois's other senator, for showing in Illinois.

Wednesday. One of my longest days in the Senate. On the way to an 8:30 breakfast with a co-sponsor of our NATO troop proposal, stopped at my office long enough to empty my briefcase of work done at home, including the draft of a commencement speech I was to deliver at Illinois Wesleyan University. Breakfast conversation focused on strategy for our proposal, due for a Senate vote today. Said I wanted to speak during the debate.

After breakfast, went to a 10 A.M. meeting of the banking committee. Arthur F. Burns, chairman of the Federal Reserve Board, and Paul A.

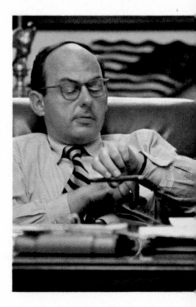

Volcker, an undersecretary of the treasury, testified on the state of the nation's economy.

At 11 A.M., conducted a hearing of the manpower and poverty subcommittee on an emergency food and medicine act—for which the Administration had virtually no funds. As a subcommittee member, I took over for the chairman, Senator Gaylord A. Nelson of Wisconsin, who had to be in the Senate chamber to support his proposal on NATO troop withdrawal. He would make it effective only in the absence of negotiations with Russia on mutual withdrawal, then spread it over three years.

Lunch at my office desk. Then took the subway to the Capitol, moved into my back-row seat in the Senate chamber, and waited to be called on. Debate was under an agreement on the time to vote, so speaking time available to each side was strictly limited. Was given two minutes to say why our amendment should be passed. At the vote, all reduction proposals lost.

During the afternoon and evening, shuttled between the floor and my office, trying to sandwich some desk work into time not spent at debate. Dinner at my desk. Finally left the Senate when it adjourned at 11:29 P.M. Besides disposing of all NATO troop proposals, it had stopped a House move to revive the government subsidy for the supersonic transport—a subsidy supposedly killed earlier.

Thursday. Had about 30 high school youngsters from Chicago in my office in the morning to talk to them.

Also held a news conference to discuss what should be done with Fort Sheridan, a half-empty Army base on the Lake Michigan shore just north of Chicago. We had counted 124 vacant buildings there. Seems a better use could be found for this resource.

Throughout the day, worked on a backlog of correspondence, dictated the first draft of a speech on national priorities, and met with various members of my staff on matters ranging from a flood control-water resource project in the Wabash Valley of Illinois to the war in Vietnam.

Service in the Senate can be frustrating at times. But it is always interesting, and it can be very satisfying. For me, each hectic day brings a measure of satisfaction if, at the end of the day, I know that in some way—however small—we have served the public interest.

passed by the House and Senate, the appropriations bill was referred to a conference committee. In their effort to resolve the dispute over the SST, the conferees—nine members of the House and seven senators —agreed on a compromise that would have continued its development, but at a reduced level of federal funding. When the conference report was taken up in the Senate, leaders of the opposition to the SST argued that a majority of senators had voted to stop work on the project, and that adoption of the compromise proposed by the conference committee would thus thwart the will of the Senate.

Because this controversy was the last remaining obstacle to adjournment of the 91st Congress, leaders of the fight against the SST feared that some senators who had voted to kill the project would accept the compromise if the conference report were brought to a quick vote. To prevent such a vote, the leaders of the anti-SST bloc resorted to a filibuster. Twice within a week, supporters of the SST moved to cut off the debate, but they could not muster the two-thirds vote necessary under Rule 22 to invoke cloture, and the filibuster continued. In the final days of the session, the issue was put aside with the understanding that it would be brought up again in the early months of the next Congress.

In addition to blocking the new appropriation for the SST, the long Senate debate served to focus public attention on the arguments against continued development of the plane. There was a marked increase in mail urging senators and representatives to abandon the project, and both the House and the Senate voted to do just that when the issue came up again three months later.

Some senators who in past years had advocated changing Rule 22 to make it easier to limit debate were among those who took part in the filibuster against the SST. In the 92nd Congress, some of the same senators supported two filibusters against extension of the military draft. On both of these occasions, cloture was invoked to shut off the debate on the floor of the Senate.

"I sometimes become impatient"

As a result of these experiences, several senators — myself included — have come to appreciate more fully the merits of extended debate. At the outset of the 92nd Congress in 1971, I supported a move to reduce the majority required for cloture from two-thirds to three-fifths. But I am no longer inclined to favor the termination of debate by a narrower majority.

In common with many younger members—and some not so young— I sometimes become impatient with the Senate's performance. That it works at all is a tribute to the durability of the procedures that have evolved over the years and to the patience and skill of the members.

That is not to say that the Senate's procedures cannot be improved and its work conducted far more efficiently and more responsively to that elusive quantity known as the public interest. But the Senate's rules and customs are cogs in a delicately balanced mechanism. If we are to tamper with them, we must be certain to do so with great care.

Nor do I agree that the Senate would somehow be transformed into a marvel of efficiency if only the seniority system were abolished. The system automatically selects as chairman the committee member from the majority party who has been on the committee for the longest time. It is true that senators from some of the less populous states—often Southerners—hold a disproportionate share of committee chairmanships solely because of their seniority. But I find that most committee chairmen act fairly and responsibly. Many people would like to abolish the seniority system. But few can suggest an alternative plan that would assure better performance.

The appointment of committee chairmen on the basis of seniority is a custom, not a rule, of the Senate. As a step toward reform, the Democratic membership agreed in 1971 that in the future the appointment of Democratic chairmen and members of committees will be subject to the approval of all the party members in the Senate. It is not hard to imagine the wheeling and dealing likely to result if the selection were thrown completely open. The new procedure is called a timid

Senator Stevenson is briefed by U.S. advisers to South Vietnam during a fact-finding trip to a settlement project called Ky Ngoc, near the city of Da Nang.

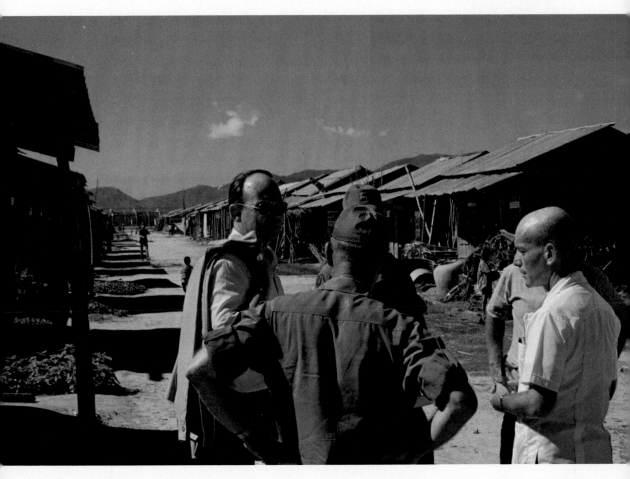

step, but it is at least a step in the right direction. And in the future, it may prove to have been a giant stride.

There are many things we can do to make the Senate a more efficient institution, more readily responsive to the needs of the nation and the will of its people. A computerized information-retrieval system, for example, would save senators and their staffs vast amounts of time. More adequate office space would surely increase the productivity and the creativity of senators' staffs—the 24 members of my Washington office staff are crammed into six noisy rooms where the constant ringing of telephones is muffled only by the ceaseless clacking of the typewriters.

We must recognize, however, that, in a democratic society, the legislative process will never be a model of efficiency—certainly not in so diverse a society as ours. Inefficiency is inherent, so cynicism comes easy. The work of the Senate is infinite in its possibilities, infinite in its array of concerns and in the magnitude of their importance. Inefficiencies can be minimized, but it is extremely doubtful that they will ever be eliminated.

Money a corrupting influence

We can tolerate procedural inefficiencies. But, if our political system is to endure, we can no longer tolerate practices that impair the impartiality of the legislative process. At every level of government—federal, state, and local—money is a corrupting influence in our politics. The costs of seeking public office have soared in recent years, mainly because of the extremely high costs of television time. It has become increasingly difficult for a man of moderate means, let alone a poor man, to seek elective office. To do so, many candidates are obliged to accept substantial campaign contributions from special interests, thereby impairing their ability to serve the public interest.

Existing state and federal laws on campaign financing are inadequate. We must have enforceable and stringent limits on campaign spending if government of, by, and for the people is to survive. And I believe that all campaign contributions should be made a matter of public record.

It is not satisfactory for a public official to say, as too many do, that his personal financial affairs are his own business and nobody else's. Quite the contrary: One who becomes a public servant should be prepared to make his private affairs the public's business. Legislation requiring public disclosure by the members of the Congress of their sources of outside income has been advocated for years by such scrupulous men as former Senator Paul H. Douglas of Illinois, but without avail. I began making personal financial reports at regular intervals following my election as state treasurer of Illinois in 1966, and I continue to do so. Several other members of the Congress make similar reports voluntarily.

The integrity of the legislative process is clouded by conflicts of interest, real and imagined. Some members of the Congress, for instance, own stock in businesses whose earnings may be significantly

With his son, Adlai IV, the author walks past a bust of the first Adlai E. Stevenson, who was U.S. Vice-President from 1893 to 1897. The bust is in the Senate wing of the Capitol.

affected by some of the legislation that the stockholder-legislator must vote on.

Until public disclosure of personal financial affairs is required of all officeholders, public confidence in the integrity of government will be shaken. All public officials will be suspect—however scrupulous their conduct—whenever it is discovered, as happened in Illinois not long ago, that a man had secretly amassed a fortune during his years in public service.

Any consideration of the deficiencies in our present system of self-government must lead to consideration of the ever-increasing power of the executive branch of the federal government. For years, the Congress has accepted this trend, and, on occasion, has abetted it. Yet this has been at the expense of its own right to participate in shaping national policy and in making the great decisions of war and peace.

Under our constitutional system of checks and balances, the Congress —and especially the Senate—is charged with restraining the exercise of excessive executive power. But recent years have witnessed an erosion of the Senate's role, particularly in regard to foreign affairs. As a result, we see a growing imbalance in the federal system.

Too late, the Congress learned how little it knew—and how little the people knew—about the depth of America's military commitments in Indochina. It is imperative that the Congress reclaim its constitutional prerogatives—most importantly, the warmaking power.

Without advice and consent

Through its committees, the Congress can interrogate the secretary of state, the secretary of defense, and other members of the President's Cabinet. But Presidents now surround themselves with a growing number of personal assistants, who are appointed without the Senate's advice and consent. Their influence in both foreign and domestic affairs often appears to exceed the Cabinet's. Shielded by claims of executive privilege, these assistants cannot be called before committees. They are accountable only to the President—not to the Congress and not to the people.

The legislative branch should reassert its power—limiting the warmaking authority of the executive branch, reordering national priorities by means of its power to appropriate money, playing its proper role in forming national policy. Whether it does so depends ultimately on the quality of the men and women who serve in the Congress. And that, in a self-governing society, depends on the good sense and judgment of an informed electorate.

I often recall a statement my father made in his great faith in the capacity and durability of our system of government: "Trust the people," he said. "Trust their good sense, their decency, their fortitude, their faith. Trust them with the facts. Trust them with the great decisions." I can think of no better mandate for the government of a free people.

See also Section Three, CONGRESS OF THE UNITED STATES (Close-Up).

The American City:
A *Year Book*
Trans-Vision® and
Special Report

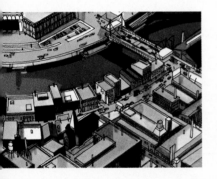

Making Our Cities Livable

Our major cities contain the greatest portion of our nation's wealth, industrial might, and brainpower. Yet we have allowed parts of them to decay. American cities need to be modernized and, most of all, humanized. This *Year Book* Trans-Vision®, prepared by the *Year Book* staff with the assistance of Professor Harvey S. Perloff of the University of California, Los Angeles, uses transparent overlays to show some relatively modest ways in which this could be done.

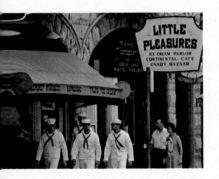

Taking a Closer Look at the City

We must have a realistic diagnosis of what ails our cities before we can prescribe remedies. When we look closely, we find that many "known" facts and "obvious" conclusions about cities are not supported by the evidence. In this *Year Book* Special Report, William H. Whyte takes us on a leisurely tour of the American city and points out that things are not always what they seem. In fact, our major cities may have quite a bit more going for them than we may realize or care to admit.

160

Making Our Cities Livable

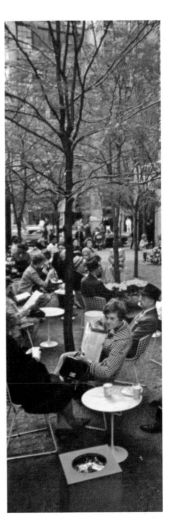

Introduction

American cities urgently need to be transformed. They must be modernized and humanized. To indicate how this might be done, this Trans-Vision® unit deals with a hypothetical American metropolis. It points out some of the serious problems of our cities and then examines some possibilities for making urban life more satisfying. It is not a blueprint for change, but an attempt to show some of the ways we can make cities happier, brighter places in which to live.

Cities in Trouble

Our major cities contain the greatest portion of our wealth, they are the cradle of the nation's industrial might, they house most of the nation's brainpower, and they represent our cultural aspirations. Yet, we have permitted parts of our cities to decay and become overcrowded, filthy, and dangerous.

During the past 100 years, city population in the United States has grown at a phenomenal rate (from 25 per cent of the total population in 1870 to 70 per cent today). This unprecedented growth resulted from both immigration from Europe and migration from rural areas. Urban problems have multiplied with growth, and the unplanned way in which cities have been allowed to develop has caught up with them.

Change and More Change. At the beginning of the 1900s, cities were dominated by factories and mills that processed farm and mine products. These plants were clustered in the central parts of cities along railroad lines, and workers tended to concentrate nearby. Immigrants streamed in from Europe and from rural areas to become the blue-collar workers of the central-city factories and mills.

Then, in the 1920s, plants manufacturing products for new industries—electronics, chemicals, and communications—came to the forefront. With the advent of automobiles, trucks, and airplanes, railroads became less important, and the new manufacturing plants were no longer restricted to the central part of the city. Larger plants were built on the less expensive land farther and farther from the crowded inner city. The whole urban structure began to spread out. More and more middle-class urbanites moved out to the suburbs. After World War II, the move to the suburbs became a veritable flood. As the middle-class city dwellers and industries fled the inner city, the city's tax base, and hence its services, declined. Almost all new growth took place in outlying areas.

Soon, manufacturing itself was pushed into the background. Trade and services—professional, business, educational, and governmental—began to dominate the economic life of the inner city. Demand for administrative, professional, and clerical

Our cities are overcrowded and hopelessly clogged with traffic.

A blanket of smog often covers many cities.

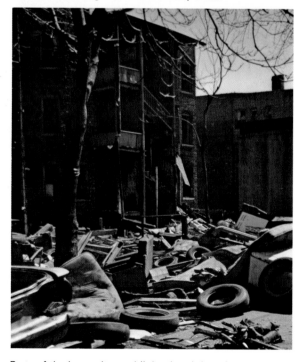

Parts of the inner city are blighted and decaying.

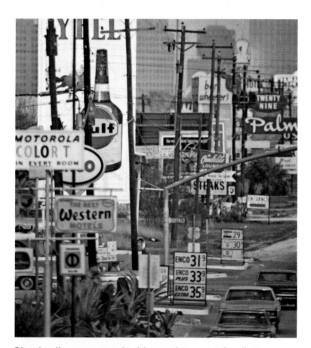

City dwellers are assaulted by environmental ugliness.

Children are the real victims of the inner city.

workers grew, and the need for factory workers declined. As immigration slowed down, however, the migration of black farmworkers, particularly from the South, greatly increased. With them came Mexican-Americans, Puerto Ricans, Asians, and American Indians. But these minority groups found few of the factory jobs they sought. Factories had moved out to the suburbs, far from the inner-city areas where these newcomers were forced to live. Untrained for more skilled jobs, many had to turn to welfare. The places where they lived soon showed signs of their poverty and disadvantage.

The creation of inner-city ghettos was only one of the multitude of problems created by the changing uses of the city and the way it grew. The whole physical plant of the city began to show signs of breakdown. Government machinery, including the tax structure, largely designed to cope with the problems of an earlier time, could not keep up with the new and complex problems of a more modern era. In the past few decades, urban problems have proliferated, turning our urban communities into the vast, violent, and dehumanizing cities that we struggle to live in today.

The City Today is a complex system, every part of which is intimately interlocked. The physical plant of the city has to provide facilities for industrial, commercial, governmental, residential, recreational, educational, and many other activities. It has to provide for transportation for both people and freight over short and great distances. It must provide for all forms of communication.

When major parts of this system are inadequate and obsolete, urban life tends to get bogged down and become unpleasant. That has been happening to American cities. They are choked with traffic, for example. Streets that were originally built for trolley cars and horses and buggies cannot accommodate today's flood of automobiles, buses, and trucks. The more superhighways and freeways that are built, the worse traffic becomes, since more vehicles are attracted to them. People, automobiles, buses, and trucks are all thrown together. Pedestrians risk their lives when they cross the street. There is not enough off-street parking, so streets tend to become vast parking lots. In some cities, as much as half of the downtown area is used for the movement and parking of vehicles. In addition, motor vehicles create much of the air pollution (60 per cent in New York City) that puts a dark pall over the cities and endangers the health of the people. The street noise is nerve-racking.

In the older parts of the city, houses and other structures are decaying. Many are as obsolete as the streets. Open spaces and structures often are jumbled together—junkyards and used-car lots and factories and homes and shops—adding up to an environment that is as ugly as it is inefficient. Not

only are many houses run-down, but so are public services and facilities. People in need of medical care wait in overcrowded hospitals and clinics for treatment. Many schools are dilapidated and poorly equipped. There are few recreation facilities; children have no place to play but the streets. The poor are forced to live in these decaying, forbidding parts of the inner city, which often turn into racial ghettos, and their anger, frustration, and alienation grows. The decay and the blight spread like a rapidly growing disease.

The physical and social problems of the city thus tend to aggravate each other. Racial tensions sometimes burst into violence. Crime becomes so rampant that people rarely dare to venture out after dark. The nighttime city is dark and forbidding. There are few brightly lit, pleasant areas—its great potential for play and fun is thus hardly utilized.

In many ways, the suburbs are better off than the central cities. They are newer and have more space and amenities. But most of their development (estimated at the rate of 500,000 acres annually in the United States) is speculative and unplanned. Often they are too spread out to provide adequate public services. Governments are fragmented—some 1,100 local governmental units surround Chicago, for example. This means that areawide services, such as sewage disposal, are inadequate. Schools and hospitals are poorly financed, and in some cases recreational facilities are almost non-existent. Because of the sprawl and the lack of public transportation, family members are dependent on the automobile. The mother becomes a chauffeur for the children. The father often has to travel great distances to and from work and has little time to spend with his family. Young people often find the suburban atmosphere stifling.

Some white city residents move to the suburbs to escape the inner-city problems and minority groups. They set up rigorous building, planning, and zoning regulations to keep out lower-income families. The result, as a presidential commission has pointed out, is a polarized society—of poor and middle class, of blacks and whites. The problems of cities and suburbs alike cannot be solved as long as this polarization exists.

What Can Be Done? The demand by city people for improvements has become more and more persistent. They want cities that are more livable and more human. The search for solutions has become more serious, and there are many exciting ideas to consider.

Can our cities be transformed and modernized—good places in which to live, work, learn, and play? The answer is yes. But it is a yes with a big *if* attached. *If* the nation puts city improvement high on its political agenda. *If* the nation really wants to build better cities.

The City as Part of a System

The stylized drawing below shows a typical metropolitan area. The city's central business district (CBD) is at the core, and is surrounded by the inner city. The lightest tone shows the suburban fringe. In reality, of course, most cities are oddly shaped—the suburban zone is anything but continuous—and suburbs are scattered more widely.

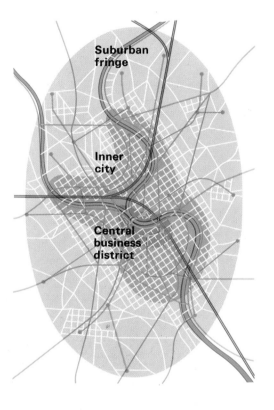

Our major cities today are the central parts of such complex systems, generally called metropolitan areas. All parts are closely intertwined; each part depends on every other part. Workers in plants and shops come from every part of the metropolitan area. Customers come from every corner of the region. Transportation, communications, water, sewerage, electric power, and other utilities are all parts of regional networks. Clearly, then, any attempt to improve and modernize the city must start with an understanding of this interdependence and must be done on a systemwide basis covering the entire metropolitan area. This will require a massive effort. Yet, there are some relatively simple things we can do—things that have, in fact, already been done in a few cities—to make our cities more livable and satisfying. The pages that follow will provide a look at some of them.

Turn the entire double page

Transformation of a City

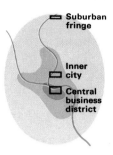

Suburban fringe
Inner city
Central business district

The rectangles on the following page represent the three areas in the drawing at the left. The bottom rectangle shows a part of the CBD; the middle, a part of the inner city; the top, the beginning of the suburban fringe.

The City Today: Paper-Page Drawings

Each section of the metropolis has its own functions, its own character—and its own problems. Some of the problems are shown on the paper-page base drawing. As you read this text, take the time to search a bit to try to identify these problems.

In the CBD, at the bottom of the page, the obsolete layout of buildings and streets can be seen. Pedestrians, trucks, buses, and automobiles are dangerously jammed together. Many of the buildings that house mills, power plants, and warehouses are old, decaying, and in the wrong place. They were needed there decades ago when workers were unable to travel far to work. Now, they clutter up the CBD and make it ugly as well as inefficient.

The inner city, in the middle rectangle, also shows the result of unplanned development. Much of the housing is run-down, unsanitary, or overcrowded. The streets cannot handle the increased traffic. At night, the inner city is bleak and forbidding, with no well-lit places for people to gather.

The newer suburban fringe, at the top of the page, also shows the results of inadequate planning. Houses, factories, and stores are scattered and mixed, almost at random. While there is open space in the suburbs, it is haphazardly distributed and provides little recreation or beauty. There is little or no public transportation.

Change Begins: First Overlay

Even limited changes, if continuous and carefully planned, can make a big improvement in a city in a decade or two. Some realistic possibilities can be seen by turning the first transparent page.

More modern concepts of urban transportation are now being applied throughout all sections of the metropolitan area. Highways and streets are built or relocated to avoid unnecessary crisscrossing of traffic, and in some areas some traffic is eliminated. New forms of mass transit, which take many of the cars off the street, reduce traffic congestion and make it easier for pedestrians to move about. The need for commuting is reduced by clustering homes and workplaces in high-density centers in the inner city and the suburban fringe.

Lift the folded page

Slum housing beyond repair is cleared, but most older homes and neighborhoods are rehabilitated. A program of building new, low-cost, subsidized housing to provide good in-town living is undertaken. Public services and facilities are improved in the poorer sections to fit the needs of residents. Older schools, hospitals, and recreation centers are remodeled and rebuilt to meet the new demands. Decentralized facilities and mobile library, health, education, and recreation units, bring public services close to the people.

A Modernized City: Second Overlay

A well-planned, soundly paced improvement program, as shown on the second transparent page, has now begun to produce a modern, more human city—a good place in which to live, work, and have fun. It has also provided institutions that can cope with inevitable continuing change.

Each section of the metropolitan area is carrying out those functions for which it is best suited. The CBD has caught up with the service age. Business services, education, cultural activities, professional services, and recreation are now dominant there; only a few smaller-scale manufacturing plants remain. Traffic has been disentangled so that mass transit, trucks, automobiles, and pedestrians move along on separate routes and surfaces.

The old, dull, dirty, inner city has been given new life and vitality through the creation of "new towns intown," with lighted centers. These new "intowns" are planned areas that bring together stores, public services, workplaces, and other activities in a uniquely urban setting. Businesses in new intowns are in specially designed industrial estates geared specifically to intown manufacturing, warehousing, and other economic activities. Housing has been rehabilitated. High-rise apartments and townhouses are clustered to provide a feeling of open space. A lighted center offers safe and pleasant nighttime recreation.

The scattered suburban fringe has been redeveloped into more clustered communities with some high-density centers. Governments have become more centralized to cope with areawide problems and services. Transportation facilities have been increased; people have more choice in travel modes. Low-cost housing has been provided. Man and nature have developed a friendlier partnership; waterways, forests, marshes, and other natural features are protected.

Some of the improvements can be accomplished quickly; others will take more time. Some are relatively simple; others require large-scale commitment and funds. Some of the more important of these new features—most of them in existence now—are highlighted on the third transparent page and on the double-page paper foldout following it.

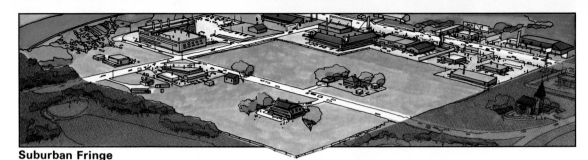

Suburban Fringe

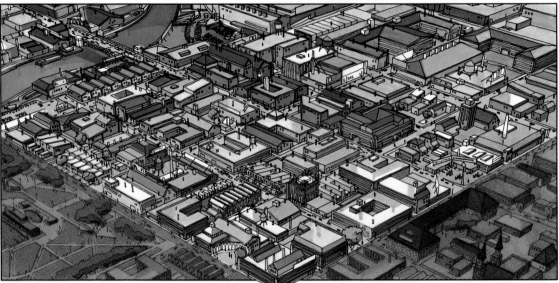

Inner City

Central Business District

A Modernized City: 10 Highlights

1 Recreational Green Belt Along River

A green belt along the banks of a river offers welcome open space, much of which is ideal for water-related and other recreational facilities. Trees and grass protect the river basin and help to prevent flooding. In addition, keeping the banks of the river free of both factories and homes helps to reduce water pollution.

2 Suburban Mobile-Home Park

Well-designed and fully serviced mobile-home parks expand the housing possibilities in the suburban fringe. Less expensive and easier to finance than houses, mobile homes make it possible for low-income families, including members of minority groups, to live closer to job opportunities that have opened up in suburban areas. The mobile-home park thus offers a relatively painless step in the process of breaking down the economic and racial barriers that now exist in many suburbs.

3 Multigrade Educational Campus

Modernizing public services is critical to the transformation of the inner city. And no service is more important to the inner city than education. A multigrade educational campus can provide community-oriented facilities not available through separate elementary, junior high, and high schools. Adult education facilities and multimedia facilities – film centers, experimental laboratories, computers, community newspaper plants, shops, and various services – would be run by students working closely, in many cases, with other interested people of the community, thus creating a new environment for learning and community service.

Lighted center

4 Large-Scale Rehabilitated Housing

The most difficult task in adjusting to rapid urban change comes in updating and improving housing that was built in an earlier era. Such improvement must be done on a large scale – involving many inner city homes – so that the impact is widely felt and economies can be achieved. Residents and owners have to be involved in the rehabilitation process from the beginning. This rehabilitated section of the inner city has once again been made a good place to live and rear a family.

Disentangling traffic

5 Lighted Center of New Town Intown

The construction of a new town intown with a lighted center can bring new life and vitality to the vast gray areas of the inner city. The new town intown incorporates many features associated with outlying new towns and cities, but does so in a uniquely urban manner. The lighted center shown above provides a safe shopping and recreation area where people of all ages can gather, and a variety of public services, such as educational, health, recreation, day-care, and teen centers.

6 City-Within-a-City

We are already building tall towers in our cities that provide many needed urban services and facilities as well as living space. Skyscrapers with apartments, offices, shops, restaurants, pedestrian plazas, recreation, and parking add a vertical dimension to urban space. The modernized city can take full advantage of our architectural and engineering capacities to open these towers to a wide range of features, such as rent-supported schools for children of residents.

7 Disentangling Traffic

Each mode of transportation, including walking, has its own uses and its own requirements. A disentangled, well-planned movement system can work for, instead of against, the people of the city. Shown at the left is a multilayer system that provides channels for trains, trucks, buses, and automobiles. Pedestrians have safe walkways. People movers – automated guideways, and personal rapid-transit vehicles – reduce the need for automobiles.

8 Rooftop Use

There are many ways to introduce beauty and a sense of space into the central city. Malls and plazas with fountains, benches, kiosks, charming outdoor furniture, sculpture, and a blending of natural and man-made features all help to make the crowded city more satisfying. They are new ways to add zest to city living. Among the least-used spaces in cities are rooftops. The potential of rooftops, especially in the CBD, for recreation, dining, or simply as a relaxing haven from hectic city life is limitless.

9 Subsurface Malls

Possibilities for opening up urban space exist below the city as well as above. Arcades below street level can provide theaters, shops, restaurants, gymnasiums, and many other desirable urban functions and services and, at the same time, pedestrian walkways and people movers can help to reduce the concentration at crowded street levels.

10 Vest-Pocket Parks

Many small spaces within the central city can be turned into delightful parks and resting areas. These vest-pocket parks, such as the one shown below, offer a place to escape – to stop and relax and to enjoy a feeling of space and beauty.

Vest-pocket park

Turn the entire double page

Beyond the Metropolis

Many of our present metropolises are already much too large and crowded to permit good living. And, by the year 2000, population will have increased by some 100 million persons. By 1980, it is estimated, 26 million new dwelling units will be needed. Clearly the cities and the suburban fringe, where the bulk of this growth is expected, cannot hope to accommodate a 50 per cent increase in population during this period of time without straining present facilities to the breaking point. Interest in new

For the Next 100 Million

Even with sound modernization programs, our cities will not be able to support the anticipated increase in population. The regional map below shows how new cities can supplement our existing hypothetical city.

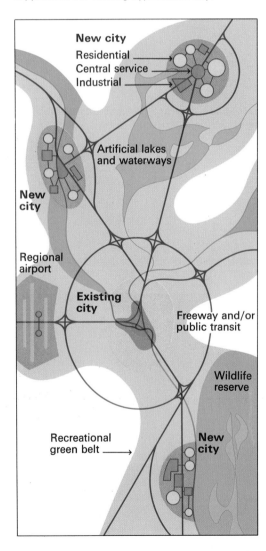

New city
Residential
Central service
Industrial

Artificial lakes
and waterways

New city

Regional airport

Existing city

Freeway and/or public transit

Wildlife reserve

Recreational green belt

New city

Lift the folded page

urban forms is thus growing, particularly in the creation of new towns and new cities.

A small number of such communities are already being built in the United States, following the lead of Great Britain and the Scandinavian countries. Many more could be built in the future. A report by the National Committee on Urban Growth Policy urged the creation, with federal assistance, of 100 new towns of 100,000 population and 10 with a population of 1 million by the year 2000. These would be entirely new communities developed by private companies in partnership with government or with government assistance. Most of these new communities would be fairly close to existing metropolitan centers, allowing them to take advantage of the city's unique services and business and entertainment facilities, but they would be fully or partly self-supported by their own business enterprises and other economic activities.

If well-planned, new towns and cities would share certain attractive features. First, they would be carefully developed to provide for growth and change. The plans would seek to bring homes and workplaces closer together, thus reducing the need for commuting. Traffic patterns would be designed to avoid congestion. There would be an effort to combine natural and man-made features into a harmonious whole. For example, residential areas could be built around lakes with areas provided for "nature walks."

Recreation could play a large role in this new kind of urban living. Artificial lakes and waterways would provide an attractive setting not only for daily living, but also for swimming, water skiing, and sailing. Imaginative indoor recreation facilities could be readily available.

Public and community services would be given new physical, social, and organizational forms to better fit them to human needs and aspirations. Comprehensive health services, with convenient and flexible facilities, would be furnished. A great variety of educational facilities and opportunities would be provided, taking advantage of multi-media facilities, so that young people and adults would find daily living a rich learning experience.

Future urban communities may provide at least some scope for commune living, to which many young persons are currently attracted. The future city, if it is to be a healthy setting for modern living, will have to provide for many different life styles and many different patterns of living. Whether such new towns and new cities can integrate racial and income groups more successfully than have existing urban centers remains an open question.

Once we permit ourselves to dream about the urban future, all sorts of possibilities can challenge us. Some of these ideas that are now actually in existence are shown here.

Clustered housing is built in natural settings.

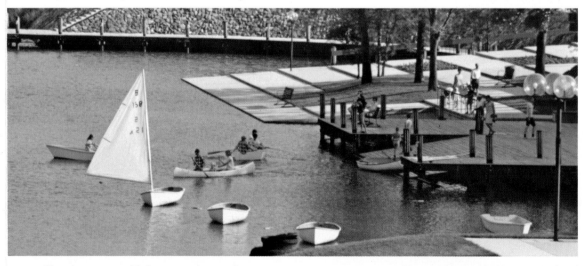

Abundant water adds beauty and recreation.

Many elements blend through planning.→

Recreational facilities are imaginative and fun.

Shopping centers can be attractive, too.

Decorative elements add variety and liveliness.

Suggestions for Further Reading:

This Trans-Vision® unit has presented a brief overview of the problems and prospects of the American city. The discussion of some highly complex issues was necessarily condensed. For a more complete view of the problems of cities and what the city has been, is, and can be, you might be interested in consulting some of the books and publications listed below. These books have been selected not only for their valuable information, but also for their liveliness and readability. Some of them are classics in the field.

Cities in Trouble:

Perhaps the best-known presentation of the crisis in our cities is Jane Jacobs' *The Death and Life of Great American Cities* (Random House, 1961). This is the book that jolted city planners and government officials into reconsidering the sterile high-rise projects and wholesale bulldozing techniques prevalent during the 1950s. A recent analysis of the social and economic problems that plague our cities today can be found in Anthony Downs's *Urban Problems and Prospects* (Markham, 1970). A classic work in tracing the emergence of cities to the present time is Lewis Mumford's *The City in History* (Harcourt, 1961).

What Can Be Done?

There are a number of important books on planning, designing, and modernizing American cities. One of the best known is Victor Gruen's *The Heart of Our Cities* (Simon & Schuster, 1964), the subtitle of which is "The Urban Crisis: Diagnosis and Cure." One of Gruen's major themes is that automobiles are choking our cities to death. His solution of separating pedestrians and automobiles led to his well-known Fort Worth plan, which created a square mile of pedestrian islands. Lawrence Halprin's *Cities* (Reinhold, 1963) is a well-illustrated and imaginative treatise on smaller-scale urban design: street furniture, fountains, malls, squares, plazas, and other public gathering places. A more recent work by Halprin on a similar theme is *New York New York: A Study of the Quality, Character, and Meaning of Open Space in Urban Design* (Chapman, 1968). The summary of existing urban problems and proposals for solutions in *The City Is the Frontier* (Harper, 1965) by Charles Abrams, one of the outstanding U.S. housing experts, deals mainly with older American cities. The Fall, 1968, issue of *Daedalus* is devoted to the "conscience of the city." Its various contributors offer suggestions as to how specific economic and political objectives can be obtained and why "an exhortation to change is not enough." Harvey Perloff's "New Towns Intown" (*Journal of the American Institute of Planners*, May, 1966) presents his proposal for a comprehensive approach to rebuilding older sections of cities and to bringing new life to the inner city. *Building the American City*, the report of the National Commission on Urban Problems (Government Printing Office, 1969), presents a thoughtful analysis of the nation's urban crisis and suggests national policies that might point the way to a better future.

Beyond the Metropolis:

The fountainhead of the new town movement in Great Britain and Continental Europe and, later, in the United States, was Ebenezer Howard's *Garden Cities of Tomorrow* (M.I.T. Press, 1965). For an analysis of new towns in the United States today, see *The New City*, Donald Canty, ed. (Praeger, 1969). This report, prepared for Urban America, Inc., by the National Committee on Urban Growth Policy, proposed the construction of 100 new towns to alleviate the problems of the older cities and to stimulate urban growth in the United States in a planned and orderly fashion. Ian McHarg's *Design with Nature* (Natural History Press, 1969) is an ecologically oriented study of urban civilization. McHarg, a landscape architect, stresses the idea that man must plan his urban development in harmony with nature.

Prepared by the staff of *The World Book Year Book*.

Text by Harvey S. Perloff, dean, School of Architecture and Urban Planning, University of California, Los Angeles.

Unit designed by Leon Bishop.

Printed in U.S.A. by the Trans-Vision® Division, Milprint Incorporated.

By William H. Whyte

Taking a Closer Look at the City

When it comes to examining the
life and problems of America's cities,
there may be more than meets the eye

Never has the city seemed in such bad shape. Its services are bad and getting worse. Its taxes are high and getting higher. City air is polluted, its waters fouled, its streets dirty and choked with cars. It is little wonder some observers have concluded that the central city is obsolete. Cities are beyond rescue, they argue, and the United States should channel its growing population into entirely new, moderately sized outlying communities.

This requiem may be premature, however. Our major cities, in fact, may well be on the verge of a resurgence. By being forced to shed those functions they do not perform well and to concentrate on those they do best, American cities are undergoing a process of change from which they may emerge, in the long run, better off.

This is not to herald utopia. Americans tend to alternate between extremes of pessimism or optimism about their cities. Not so many decades ago we conjured futuramic visions of dream cities as enthusiastically as we now condemn them. But utopias and anti-utopias tend to obscure the real alternatives. In sounding a moderate optimism, this tempering premise is useful: The city has always been something of a mess, and it probably always will be. If we recognize this, we may find practical ways of making it more livable.

We cannot, of course, discuss cities apart from their surrounding metropolitan areas. It is vital, however, to recognize the differences between cities and the areas surrounding them. Because of the stagger-

The author:
William H. Whyte wrote *The Last Landscape,* a book that examines urban sprawl in America. An authority on cities and city planning, he served as consultant on critical issues for the 1969 *Plan for New York City.*

ing population shift from rural to urban areas, many people – influential legislators among them – assume that cities have become hopelessly choked with people. They see its density as the cause of many other ills.

But they are looking through the wrong end of the telescope. Too many people is not the problem of the cities. Nearly all of the population growth in the United States over the past 20 years has taken place in the suburbs. Most central cities have hardly grown at all; in some, population has actually declined. Slums are still overcrowded, to be sure, but some surprising movements have occurred within them. New York City's Harlem, for example, has lost more than 25 per cent of its population in only 10 years. One consequence of such

People tend to see the inner city as gray and run-down, even bleak. But what else can we see when we look more closely?

movements is more crowding elsewhere; but many city neighborhoods do not work well because they have too *few* people.

The real problem is the shift in the population mix. Most of the people moving to outlying areas from our inner cities have been young, white, and middle class. Most of those moving into the inner city are black and Puerto Rican. The newcomers, it should be noted, are by no means the least able of the nation's migrants. The popular image of hordes of rural Southerners arriving in northern cities on buses and trains in order to get on the welfare roles is cruelly misleading. Most black migrants move from one city to another in hopes of finding work. Few move looking for welfare. The majority of welfare cases tend to be home-grown. Basically, the in-migration is only a variation of the kind of cycle that has operated in U.S. cities since their beginning. Throughout U.S. history, minority groups have come to the cities in hope, not despair.

But this time there is a key difference. Hobbled by their color, language, or lack of education, the blacks and Puerto Ricans are stuck at the bottom of the ladder in a way previous groups were not. The consequence for the city has been a crushing welfare load and isolation and bitterness that may deepen even more.

This despair has been magnified by changes in the cities' job opportunities. In many ways, the great economic boom since the end of World War II seems to have hurt cities more than it has helped them. The growing prosperity that accelerated the population move to a more affluent suburbia also impelled industry to begin looking outward. Cities began to lose industrial firms—not the marginal ones, but the prosperous ones that were expanding and needed space. They have been moving to outlying areas, taking the blue-collar jobs with them. The firms needed new plants and the trend was to single-story structures surrounded by acres of parking space for cars. The cities had few such sites left.

The city's blue-collar workers, however, among them the blacks and Puerto Ricans, have had a difficult time following industry to the suburbs. A few have been able to do so by reverse commuting. Paralleling the morning expressway traffic jam carrying suburbanites to office jobs downtown, one sees more and more cars headed the other way, filled with blacks who cannot afford to live in the suburbs where they work, or would not be allowed to if they could. For the great bulk of the city's blue-collar workers, however, suburbia's jobs are out of reach.

As blue-collar work has been declining in the city, white-collar office work has been expanding. The total number of jobs has not changed much, but the character of them has. There has been a marked expansion of office work in almost every major city. The shift in the cities' work force is international, and one that many official planning bodies—London's and Moscow's among them—have tried to curb. Office building has boomed, nonetheless. One result for U.S.

cities has been a sharp upgrading in the quality of the city's job mix – better jobs, better-paying jobs, and jobs that offer advancement.

But for whom? In most cases, for suburbanites. Relatively speaking, the low-income people who live in the city are worse off than before. For them, unemployment figures are sharply higher, and a great many of those who do work have part-time jobs that pay little and lead nowhere. Even worse, unemployment is concentrated among the younger, unskilled workers. A look at the help-wanted ads shows that many jobs are going begging – but they are for such white-collar skills as key punch operators and computer programmers. Most low-income people cannot qualify for these jobs; they lack the educational requirements. There are few jobs that do not require a high school education. And there are language and cultural barriers as well.

Assorted crash training programs have been set up to fill the gap in skills, and the coined words, or acronyms, for them – UP, CAREER – are charged with promise. So far, however, the results have not been very encouraging. The training too often has been set up by boards of education out of touch with the needs of business. Much of it has been for obsolete skills.

In time, schools may provide the answer. They are not up to it yet. In only one generation, city school systems that were geared to white and middle-class aspirations have had to take on a different clientele. Much of our education system, designed for another age, is breaking down. As in job training, there have been a succession of innovative crash programs – SEEK, PACE, CUE, STEP – but the harsh fact is that the hopes spelled out in these names have not been realized. If the cities ever do go to hell, the path will surely be paved with acronyms.

Shouldering the burden of these and other programs has sorely strained the city's depleting finances. A U.S. Bureau of the Census study shows that for the fiscal year 1970, cities spent $34.2 billion but took in $1.5 billion less than that. The gap between expenditures and income is steadily widening, and cities are finding it harder than ever to make up the difference. If they continue to raise their property taxes, they will risk speeding up the middle-class exodus from the city. Most cities have already raised the sales and various nuisance taxes to the breaking point. For salvation, the cities have

People are jammed together in the city. Congestion often is blamed for many of the cities' social and economic ills.

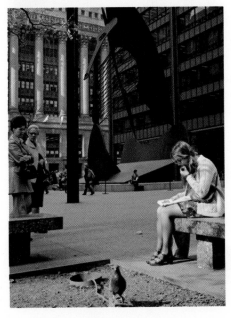

But some of the crowding is voluntary, and chance encounters on the street plus places to get away from the crowds contradict the image of hopeless congestion.

been asking for more state and federal aid. But for all their anguished cries, they have not been getting much of an increase, and they are not likely to in the near future.

On big-capital projects, such as transportation systems, cities are not too bad off. They can forestall payment by floating bond issues. Also, most federal aid funds tend to be earmarked for capital projects. The real pinch is in operating costs—the costs of day-to-day maintenance, paid out of city taxes. While the number of citizens to be serviced remains fairly constant, the number of people who do the servicing—the police, the firemen, the caseworkers—has grown greatly, and so has their pay. As one example, New York City 10 years ago had about 250,000 employees and an expense budget of $2.5 billion. Today there are more than 380,000 employees and the budget is $8.5 billion.

Taxpayers might find the cost tolerable if the services were better. But they have worsened. Despite more workers and new equipment, man-hour productivity in municipal departments has failed to improve. Other institutions—the telephone company, the electric power company, and the postal service, for example—are having the same trouble. Year after year, there seem to be more people providing less service at higher rates.

The general level of services is acknowledged to be acceptable in only one major city—Chicago—and this is an illuminating exception. Mayor Richard J. Daley is the master of an old-line political machine, and through a shrewd mixture of rewards and sanctions he has seen to it that the housekeeping machinery delivers a fair product. Eventually, however, the bill for such accommodations becomes very steep—in social problems unmet and problems deferred—and so it may prove to be for Chicago.

Elsewhere, the old political machines have disappeared, and the institutions that replaced them are in their own way growing obsolete. The civil service apparatus with its nearly 3 million federal employees has hardened into a mechanism that too often rewards mediocrity and smothers ability. The same is true of the civil service apparatus of most cities. Administrators who want to introduce new approaches and new people find it difficult to do so. In the critical task of setting and enforcing job standards, furthermore, the rise of the municipal unions has led to their seizing many of the functions

The vitality and diversity of a city can be seen in its architecture and its neighborhood shops, on its streets, in its parks, and in its little pleasures.

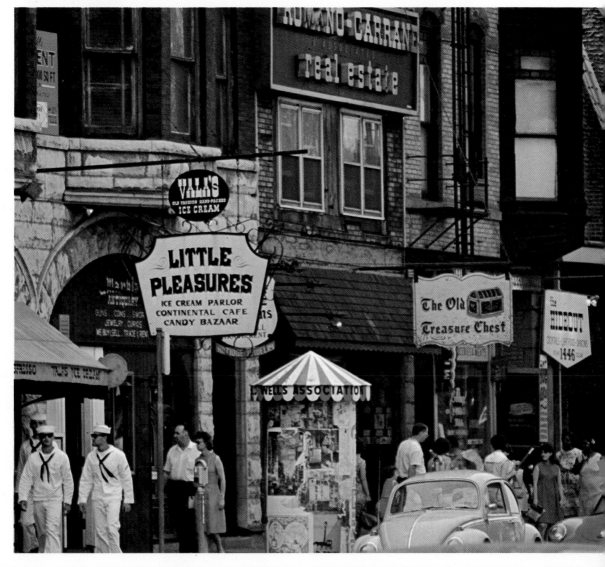

of the civil service. And, the unions, too, are growing old and ingrained.

Corruption remains a problem, but equally troublesome is the proliferation of machinery developed to prevent corruption. Over the years, city councils and state legislators have passed a host of laws and safeguards and, though these measures do not seem to stop ingenious sinners, they can make it unbelievably difficult for ordinary people to get things done. For example, so many reviews, certifications, and approvals are necessary in negotiating contracts that cities often pay more in extra personnel and time than if they were being cheated outright.

The undramatic, day-to-day job of running the city, then, is one of the biggest obstacles to an effective attack on the city's problems. Any comprehensive plan that does not take this into account is bound to fail. Mayors can come and mayors can go. Unless the machinery is overhauled, the city will be run—and not very well—by the tenured civil servants and other bureaucrats.

If the city is in such dismal shape, how can one be optimistic about its chances? History helps. Cities have always caught the brunt of social and economic change. But, while the initial shock effects were often adverse, there were long-term effects that were otherwise. So today. Many of the highly visible woes that have befallen the city are the result of trends that are not necessarily bad in themselves. The shift of factories to outlying areas, for example, has much common sense behind it. So has the outward migration of people to the suburbs; there they generally find better housing bargains for their money. So far, we have been examining the bad side of such changes for the city. There is a good side, too, and it is just as worthy of consideration.

The city, it is often said, is fast becoming a place only for the very rich and the very poor. Some observers believe that the routes to a better life are now so sealed off that the very poor may be congealing into a sort of permanent laboring class. The facts belie such gloom. The cities do have the extremes, to be sure. But even in what is supposed to be the most polarized city of all—New York—the middle class is clearly the largest. With a few exceptions, the same is true of most U.S. cities. They are still basically middle class and there are reasons for believing that they will continue to be.

The shift to office work provides one reason. Its most immediate effect has been a cruel mismatch of jobs and people, but in the long run, it can provide greater opportunity. For compelling economic reasons, employers are going to have to bring many more blacks and Puerto Ricans into the white-collar world. For compelling political reasons, city governments are already doing this. The city bureaucracies, often the biggest urban employers, have been hiring blacks and Puerto Ricans at an increasing rate. Some big corporations are hiring people they would not have even interviewed a decade ago. The transition has not been easy. But the fact is that it is being made, and it will be made by many more organizations in the future.

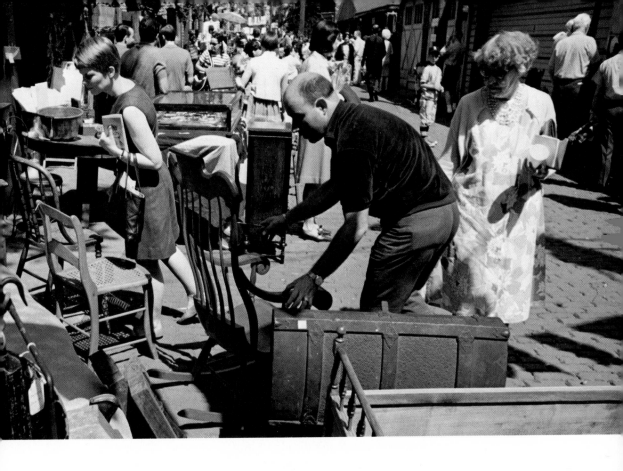

The city remains unique in the richness and variety of
its artistic and creative activities and happenings.

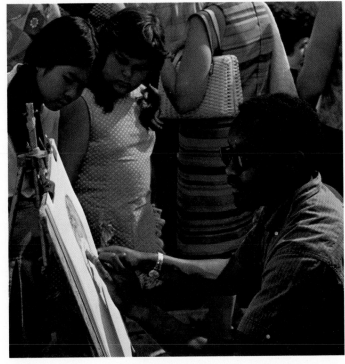

The routes outward will be opening up, too. For the time being, the exodus of industry has put blue-collar jobs farther out of reach of the city's poor—but it has also set counterforces in motion. Suburbia is being put on the rack. In exchange for the tax revenues that industry brings, the suburbs will have to give up restrictive zoning requirements that keep out minority groups. Many white-collar suburbanites still do not want blue-collar people around, but employers most emphatically do, and so do commercial and residential developers. Suburbanites cannot expect much more industrial growth unless there are more places nearby for workers to live—low-rent, higher-density developments. While such housing developments are still denounced by many local zoning boards, practical considerations, if not humanitarian ones, are forcing businesses to the more equalitarian view. In legal attacks on single-family residential zoning, corporations are well wishers, if not always *amici curiae* (friends of the court). And in one recent case, it was a corporation that launched the suit.

If the trend of recent court decisions is any indication, such suits will be increasingly successful, and the zoning bars to suburban housing for blue-collar blacks and other minorities, as well as whites, will be coming down. The result will not be any massive movement from slums to suburbia. As with so many migrations, there will be many intermediate steps on the way. But the breach is being made.

Suburbia is undergoing so many changes that it is tempting to speculate on a sizable middle-class return to the city. But this is unlikely. There have always been some families moving back from suburbia to the city, willing to give up their suburban lawns for downtown apartments closer to city activity. If the relative advantages of suburban living decline further, this flow could get larger. In sheer numbers, however, it will probably continue to be far outweighed by the outward migration of younger people, and by natural growth of the population already in suburbia.

But numbers alone are only part of the story. A small but significant fraction of younger people are electing to live in the city. They are difficult to pin down statistically; they cut across a number of occupational and professional lines. Some were born in the city, some elsewhere. They do seem to be bound together, however, by several common characteristics. They tend to be college educated and somewhat left of center politically. They take culture rather seriously. Above all, they *like* the city.

They like its diversity. They have been moving into mixed neighborhoods, rehabilitating run-down houses, and setting up block organizations. These are the people who have been responsible for the revival of brownstone neighborhoods in Brooklyn, for the transformation of the rows of boarding houses built on the "wrong side" of San Francisco's hills. They are only a small fraction of the population, but they may well be the critical fraction for the life and spirit of the city.

They like to say that they are at the center of things. But the great concentration of activities in the central city is precisely what many ecologists and planners condemn as what is most wrong with the city. Documentary films on the urban plight invariably fasten on the crowded downtown streets as a symbol of the city at its worst. It is a frightening scene: hordes of tense, harried people; sirens wailing; traffic lights flashing. Almost obligatory are somber references to recent experiments that show how rats get tense and harried and eventually suicidal when they are crowded together.

Images have a way of shaping our perceptions. City people themselves join in the condemnation. With downright gusto, they try to top each other's horror stories about the miseries of the workplace. They might be miserably homesick if they had to live out in one of the planners' often dull utopias, but they find the idea of decentralization attractive. The one element of the city-funded 1969 *Plan for New York City* most universally criticized by its citizens is the program for expanding the central business district. Younger people have been particularly critical.

But it is this very concentration that has made the city pre-eminent as a market place. The business centers of today are carrying out the most historic function of the city. They are not doing it as efficiently and comfortably as they might, but then cities never have. Imperial Rome at its height was reviled for its noise and bustle. Victorian London was an abomination.

But it does not follow that concentration means congestion – and that the two must go together. They all too often do, but this may be because of bad planning, or none at all. Sidewalks, for example, are crowded because their width has not been changed to match the increase in the size of the buildings, holding more people, that now line them. No research study or technological breakthrough is needed to resolve this problem. Wider sidewalks would do it.

Until recently, most cities left such matters up to individual builders. As a result, buildings went up without much relationship to one another, and the little touches that can mean so much were not provided, or were ineffective. A low wall to sit on, for example – if provided – was probably at the wrong height for sitting. Now cities are beginning to lay down some design standards and to see that they

Many a city dweller's individuality is expressed in the place where he lives.

The real enemy, uniformity, can be found in endless rows of identical houses in the suburbs or in the bleakness of housing projects in the inner city.

are followed. They are inducing private builders to provide more pleasing public amenities – the wider sidewalks, for example, and covered arcades and plazas, and vest-pocket parks. This kind of planning works. It harnesses the growth forces rather than denies them, and it can make the central city considerably more attractive than it is today and relieve much of the congestion.

But good design, fine as it may be, is not the central factor. What makes a city center is a coming together of people. Attractive architecture helps, but it is not the key. Some of the liveliest, most successful commercial streets are quite dreadful visually. Nor is machinery and advanced technology critical; in fact, the more complicated the machinery becomes, the more reason there may be to relocate it on the outskirts.

What the center does best is provide people with opportunities for face-to-face meetings with other people. In the late 1940s, it was widely expected that advances in communications and electronics would greatly reduce the need for such face-to-face relationships. One would be able to conduct business from anywhere, it was reasoned, and the best place would appear to be out in the pleasant countryside. It has not turned out that way. Some offices have moved out, but expansion within the center, particularly in service activities requiring high accessibility to people, has more than made up for this.

Since 1970, the writer has been making a study of the life of the streets, parks, and open spaces of the center city, using time-lapse photography to observe detailed changes in the city's activity. The findings so far indicate that in the supposedly impersonal city, the frequency of face-to-face contact is, if anything, rising. One phenomenon that can be charted is the surprising number of chance encounters and impromptu discussions that occur on the street. (For some reason difficult to fathom, the longer the talk, the more likely conferees are to stand in the center of the pedestrian traffic.) But the meetings are not really by chance. They are statistical probability. By concentrating so many people

in a relatively small network of paths, the city maximizes such contact—far more than the roomier suburban centers.

Is too much crowding the price? At times and in spots, yes. It is the choke points that cause the problem—a narrow entrance to a subway, for example—and even a few of them can color our perception of a whole area. But check the actual pedestrian flows and you will find that most of the time most of the pedestrian space is not crowded.

You will also find that the places people go to by chance are not the empty ones, but the busy ones. Various street "professionals," such as beggars and vendors, are keenly aware of this; watch their patterns and you have a guide to the action. People attract people—that splendid human activity of exchanging news and gossip called "schmoosing," girl watching, demonstrations—to watch the crowd go by you need a crowd, and complain as they may, people will cooperate. They are the amused spectators at each other's parades.

If the automobile falls from grace it will be a boon for the center. It is long overdue. The millions of automobiles and the great spread of highways has had a disintegrating impact on the city. It has promoted a diffuse pattern of urban sprawl, and it has fouled the center city with exhaust emissions. It also happens to be a very inefficient way of moving a few people. Private automobiles account for about 30 per cent of the vehicles on the street, but they carry less than 10 per cent of the people. Banning them from the center city would ease the traffic jam, and it would vastly improve the environment.

Until recently, agitation in U.S. cities to restrict traffic or close streets was shrugged off as impractical. But these projects—such as Nicollet Mall in Minneapolis and Maiden Lane in San Francisco—get more serious attention now. It seems clear that once people get a taste of life in the center without cars, they like it. The city's thralldom to the automobile is not over, but it appears to be waning.

On the other side of the coin, better mass transportation is badly needed. At the moment, highway construction still gets most of the available dollars, but the momentum for better mass transportation is building. With improved mass transportation, the city centers should be strengthened in contrast to the diffused sprawl we know now. As old rail systems are rejuvenated and new ones laid down, the

A city's future is a series of choices. It can turn its streets and open spaces over to the automobile, for example, or it can become more livable for people.

center city should become more accessible than ever to the rest of the metropolitan region. Other city centers will be growing, too, however. Mass transit needs concentrations to be profitable and it stimulates concentrations. San Francisco's $1-billion, 75-mile, Bay Area Rapid Transit (BART) system, the first new U.S. rapid transit system built since 1909, should lead to a strengthening of the existing centers in the region and the nurturing of some new ones.

There will be interruptions. Business goes in cycles and a downward trend may well be in store. Much new office-building construction started during a period of expansion several years ago is now available for use at a time when vacancy rates have been increasing. There will be quite a few empty offices in business centers for some time to come, and rents will come down. One possible by-product of this softening, however, may be that the city will regain some competitive economic advantage over suburbia.

Ecological problems will continue to be immense. It is important to remember, however, that they are metropolitan problems, not just city problems. A high concentration of people within cities accentuates waste and pollution problems; that same concentration, however, makes more practical new technological methods to handle them. High-efficiency installations such as disposal plants work best in areas where population is concentrated, rather than in areas where the population is scattered.

So far the cities have not been showing much imagination in this respect. For some reason, municipal engineers seem to be among the most tradition-bound technicians. They are beginning to agree, however, that simply expanding conventional systems will not do the job, and that the eventual goal must be a complete recycling system. What we do now is use and discard. We throw our solid wastes away – by dumping, land-fill, and other methods most cities use for disposing of their waste. It is a one-way process. By contrast, the idea of recycling is to regard all waste as raw material to be utilized – to be used over and over again – with the waste from one operation furnishing energy for another. Recycling is now technically feasible. Some rudimentary steps have already been taken – high-temperature incinerators, for example, which use the heat produced in burning a city's refuse to provide electric power.

Looking at the good side of the city's problems is not to slight the bad ones, nor is it a forecast that the city's future will be a rosy one. It probably will not be. It is important to remember that a dynamic is still at work in our cities, and as long as it is, the good and the bad will be inexorably bound together.

As soon as the city begins to master one problem, it will be bedeviled by another and still another. Every change that affects the country will be writ largest in our cities. Our cities will continue to be crowded, messy, exasperating. But they will also continue to be our major centers of vitality, diversity, activity, and – most of all – change.

The Year On File, 1971

Contributors to THE WORLD BOOK YEAR BOOK report on the major developments of 1971 in their respective fields. The names of these contributors appear at the end of the articles they have written. A complete roster of contributors, giving their professional affiliations and listing the articles they have prepared, appears on pages 6 and 7.

Articles in this section are alphabetically arranged by subject matter. In most cases, titles refer directly to articles in THE WORLD BOOK ENCYCLOPEDIA. Numerous cross references (in bold type) are a part of this alphabetical listing. Their function is to guide the reader to a subject or to information that may be a part of some other article, or that may appear under an alternative title. *See* and *See also* cross references appear within and at the end of articles and similarly direct the reader to related information contained elsewhere in THE YEAR BOOK.

ADEN. See SOUTHERN YEMEN, PEOPLE'S REP. OF.

ADVERTISING. It was a drab year at best for the advertising industry in 1971. Estimated total volume for national and local advertising in the major media increased by less than 4 per cent, and this gain was wiped out by inflation.

The modest gain in volume was even less impressive than it first appears. In 1970, the industry suffered because of a 57-day strike by the United Auto Workers against General Motors (GM). Because of the strike, the nation's second largest national advertiser canceled most of its automobile advertising for weeks during the big 1971-model introductory season.

In 1971, Procter & Gamble retained its title as the number-one national advertiser, leading GM by a large margin. The others in the top 10 were, in order: Bristol-Myers, General Foods, American Home Products, Colgate-Palmolive, Ford Motor, Sterling Drug, Lever Brothers, and Warner-Lambert.

Public Opinion. A Louis Harris opinion survey conducted for *Life* magazine indicated deep public concern with deceptive advertising. Most persons interviewed indicated they would overwhelmingly support drastic federal sanctions against an advertiser found guilty of making false or misleading statements. Fully 81 per cent of those surveyed approved the idea of prohibiting a guilty advertiser from advertising for a period of time.

Ten Facts
Parents Should Know About
Marijuana

Newsweek

Newsweek magazine's ad received the most votes as the year's best public-service advertisement in the *Saturday Review* annual Advertising Awards competition.

The Harris survey also looked at what the public likes and dislikes most about advertising. Top on the list of preferences was the disclosure of useful information about products. Misrepresentation and exaggeration were the most disliked.

The public's displeasure was reflected in the halls of Congress and in federal regulatory agencies. "Very soon, Congress and the federal agencies will take the field for the big game and they're going to use us as the ball," warned Dan Seymour, president of J. Walter Thompson Company, the world's largest advertising agency.

Seymour cast a skeptical eye at the lengthy hearings on modern advertising practices held by the Federal Trade Commission (FTC) in October and November. The agency held a series of 16 hearings on the impact of television advertising on the public, especially the impact of advertising on children. Although the hearings were billed as "for information only," admen suspected that they would be used as a platform to launch new restrictive legislation or FTC regulation.

FTC Action. In an unprecedented move, the FTC required advertisers to prove their claims publicly. The main thrust of the FTC in 1971 was in demanding that automobile manufacturers present proof to substantiate advertising claims of quality and superiority. The order required advertisers unable to do so to carry retractions in future ads for as long as a year. The FTC order, issued in July, resulted in 1,100 pages of sworn data from the four major U.S. automobile manufacturers and the three leading foreign importers. Later in the year, similar orders were issued to manufacturers of air conditioners and electric razors.

The first advertiser required to provide "corrective" information under the FTC's new stand was International Telephone and Telegraph's subsidiary, Continental Baking Company, for its Profile Bread. Under an order signed in July, 25 per cent of the product's advertising budget for one year had to be devoted to correcting previous claims that Profile Bread contained fewer calories than other breads and that it possessed dietary advantages over other breads. The corrective ads were required to explain that Profile Bread contained fewer calories only because it was sliced thinner than other brands.

The FTC campaign delayed action in Congress on a truth-in-advertising bill sponsored by Senators George S. McGovern (D., S. Dak.) and Frank E. Moss (D., Utah). One provision of the bill would force advertisers and agencies to turn over their files to any interested party.

Prior to the FTC hearings, advertising industry leaders, responsive to the growing public criticism, joined together to create a comprehensive system of self-regulation. Enforcement of advertising standards was to be maintained by a newly formed National Advertising Division of the Council of Better

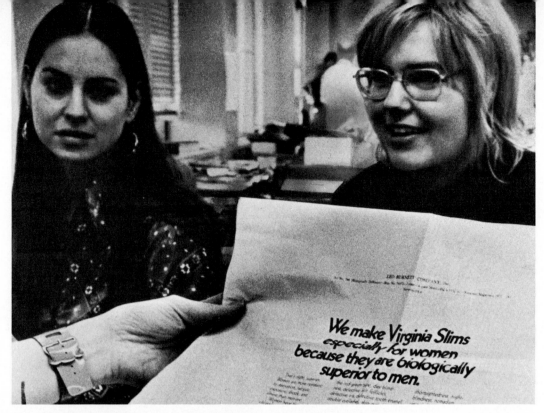

Members of the Media Action Committee of the National Organization for Women voiced their objection to the new "female stereotype" in a cigarette ad.

Business Bureaus and by an independent National Advertising Review Board. The review board, with Charles W. Yost, former ambassador to the United Nations, as chairman, consisted of 50 members – 30 representing advertisers, 10 representing advertising agencies, and 10 members of the general public. According to the new system, an appropriate government agency would be notified if any advertiser did not voluntarily change advertising that the board found objectionable.

Broadcasting Revenue Up. In a year that saw *Look* magazine fold for want of sufficient advertising revenue, the National Broadcasting Company claimed a record for commercial time charges – $86,000 per minute for spot advertising on the "Flip Wilson Show." Outdoor advertising, with revenue up 1,000 per cent, benefited the most from the Jan. 2, 1971, radio and television ban on cigarette advertising. A study of 14 magazines, reported by the University of Minnesota in May, indicated cigarette advertising in magazines had doubled during the first three months of the ban.

A study commissioned by Action for Children's Television, issued in September, found that 23 per cent of the viewing time on children's shows was devoted to commercials. The study also found that only 10 of 406 commercials during 1,125 minutes of total time studied gave any indication of product cost, and most lacked "essential data."   Edwin W. Darby

AFGHANISTAN. A political crisis brought on by economic difficulties in 1971 endangered efforts to introduce representative democracy to this remote mountain kingdom. Prime Minister Nur Ahmad Etemadi resigned in May after a series of student demonstrations and after Parliament threatened to censure the government for failure to improve the economy. King Mohammed Zahir Shah chose his personal physician, Abdul Zahir (no relation), as the new prime minister, and prudently closed schools a month early to avoid further demonstrations.

The major problem facing the new Cabinet was a two-year drought that had crippled agricultural production and threatened famine. Some Afghans were reported eating grass, and others began mass migrations in search of food. Emergency aid was provided by the United States and Russia. Japan sent a team of hydrology experts to Afghanistan to locate underground water supplies.

The economic crisis delayed action on the budget, on a law to permit political parties to operate openly, and on the new five-year development plan. Afghan schools and universities, however, opened on schedule for the 1971-1972 academic year.

Facts in Brief. Population: 17,579,000. Government: King Mohammed Zahir Shah; Prime Minister Abdul Zahir. Monetary Unit: afghani. Foreign Trade: exports, $81,000,000; imports, $134,000,000. Principal Exports: fruits and nuts.   William Spencer

AFRICA

The major issues for Africa increasingly took on a black-white racial character in 1971. During the year, the International Court of Justice handed down a major advisory opinion on the status of South West Africa, which is also known as Namibia. Controversy arose over Great Britain's planned restoration of arms sales to South Africa and the establishment of a black African dialogue with South Africa. Britain reached a controversial settlement with the white regime in Rhodesia in November.

There was also internal political turmoil in several African countries. In several nations, the military sought to end political failure as coup followed coup. Many African leaders went to jail, were executed, or barely escaped with their lives.

South West Africa has become a major point of struggle between the Republic of South Africa and the United Nations (UN). The issue has come to symbolize the opposition of the outside world to South African apartheid (complete separation of the races) and the extension of South Africa's influence beyond its traditional boundaries.

The UN-South African struggle for control of South West Africa dates back to 1966. Seeking to compel South Africa to withdraw its control over South West Africa, the UN in 1966 declared the old League of Nations mandate of South Africa terminated. South Africa refused to relinquish its control, so the UN sought an advisory opinion from the International Court of Justice in 1970 on whether South Africa has a continuing legal claim to jurisdiction over South West Africa.

On June 21, 1971, the court ruled, 13 to 2, that South Africa no longer has legal power there. It further ruled, 11 to 4, that UN member states should refrain from any actions that indicated support of South Africa's claim to jurisdiction.

As a result of the decision, the UN renewed its demands that administration of the area be handed over to the UN Council for Namibia. However, South Africa refused to consider the UN demands and angrily denounced all attempts to interfere with South African rule.

Dialogue with South Africa became a major point of controversy among black African states in 1971. President Felix Houphouet-Boigny of the Ivory Coast raised the possibility of initiating discussions between black African states and South Africa late in 1970. The increasing desire of some African states to open trade and economic relations with South Africa led Houphouet-Boigny to make this proposal.

During the 1960s, South Africa doubled its economic production and created the strongest military force on the African continent. A few black African

Thousands of South Africans greeted Malawi's President Banda in August. He was the first black African head of state to visit white-ruled South Africa.

states, such as the Ivory Coast and Malawi, want to establish ties for economic reasons, but the majority of African states oppose such a move.

African states that oppose South Africa's racial policies and fear its new power increased their protests in 1971. Among their most forceful spokesmen was President Kenneth David Kaunda of Zambia. English-speaking Africans, with the exception of a few, such as President Hastings Kamuzu Banda of Malawi and Prime Minister Kofi A. Busia of Ghana,

were greatly angered by the suggestion that they should end their boycott of South Africa.

More moderate African states indicated they would be willing to engage in talks, provided the South Africans were prepared to discuss apartheid and the self-determination of black Africans in South Africa, South West Africa, and Rhodesia. However, South African Prime Minister Johannes Vorster would not consider discussing these matters.

The question of dialogue became a major issue for the Organization of African Unity (OAU). It was first raised at the OAU Council of Ministers meeting in June, when Tanzania and Somalia introduced a resolution that specifically repudiated dialogue with South Africa.

The OAU summit meeting in July adopted a "no dialogue" resolution by a vote of 28 to 6. The Ivory Coast, Lesotho, Malawi, Mauritius, Madagascar, and Gabon favored opening the dialogue. There were five abstentions – Dahomey, Togo, Niger, Upper Volta, and Swaziland. Ghana shifted its earlier position and voted for the "no dialogue" resolution.

Banda was the leading advocate of establishing contacts with South Africa. In August, he became the first black African head of state to visit that country. See MALAWI.

Liberation Movements did not fare well in 1971, even though assistance from sympathetic African states, from the West, and from Communist nations continued to grow. The World Council of Churches, which caused a furor when it decided in September, 1970, to give funds to liberation groups, on September 9 again allocated $200,000, a major portion of its resources, to support the humanitarian aspects of groups "combating racism." The greatest share, $130,000, was granted to the African liberation movements for educational and medical programs.

Increasing support came from some official Western sources, such as the Swedish government, which promised $1.5 million for humanitarian aid. The Joseph Rowntree Charitable Trust in Britain allocated almost $70,000 to the Mozambique Institute.

There was competition for the increased aid between rival liberation groups. The OAU tried to distribute aid fairly and effectively, but had immense problems in dealing with the rival groups. Further complicating the situation was the competition for African influence between China and Russia and, to a lesser extent, between pro-Western and pro-Communist groups within the African nations.

The rebel struggle in the Portuguese territories was stalemated in 1971. However, sabotage and terrorism spread to Portugal. The Armed Revolutionary Action (ARA), a liberation group inside Portugal, claimed credit for two bombing incidents in and near Lisbon in 1971. The bombings were described as protests against Portugal's colonial policies in Angola, Mozambique, and Portuguese Guinea. The ARA was also blamed for an explosion aboard a Portuguese cargo ship off the coast of Mozambique that killed 23 crewmen in April.

During late August and early September, a delegation from the Mozambique Liberation Front (Frelimo) visited Peking. At about the same time, three journalists from the Central Committee of the Russian Communist Party visited Tete Province in Mozambique, which is under Frelimo control.

In South Africa, fighting broke out periodically between members of the South West African People's Organization and the security police in the Caprivi Strip, a narrow strip of land in South West Africa that borders on Zambia, Rhodesia, Botswana, and Angola. After one such strike, South Africa threatened to pursue the guerrillas across the border into Zambia.

The major military contingents of the Zimbabwe African National Union (ZANU) and the Zimbabwe African People's Union (ZAPU), operating against Rhodesia, were virtually paralyzed because of internal political differences. In October, a new liberation group, Front for the Liberation of Zimbabwe, was formed as an attempt to consolidate ZANU and ZAPU.

Rhodesian Settlement. The British-proposed settlement with Rhodesia in November was vigorously opposed by all liberation factions, as well as their supporting governments. In its attempt to reach a settlement with Rhodesia, Great Britain sharply modified its earlier stand of NIBMAR (no independence before

majority African rule). This threatened to heighten tensions between the Commonwealth African states and Great Britain. Relations were already strained. Britain's plan to supply arms to South Africa had been a major point of dissent at the Commonwealth of Nations conference in Singapore in January.

African leaders such as Kaunda and President Julius K. Nyerere of Tanzania declared that the independence issue was no longer a matter between Britain and Rhodesia, but was an international matter that should be settled by the UN Security Council.

African and Asian nations pressed vigorously for continuation of UN economic sanctions against Rhodesia and refused to accept Rhodesia as a sovereign state, even though Great Britain plans to grant independence soon. See RHODESIA.

Growing Chinese Influence. In 1970, the People's Republic of China regained a prominent position on the African continent. After its unsuccessful revolutionary attempts in Gabon, the Congo, and Kenya in 1964 and 1965, China reduced activities in Africa. In 1971, however, China was recognized by a majority of the African nations, including some of the more conservative ones. Emperor Haile Selassie I made a state visit to Peking and returned with a generous $80-million long-term, interest-free, development loan to be paid for with exports.

China surpassed Russia in the amount of economic assistance granted to African states. Its two largest commitments, $200 million each to Tanzania and Zambia, are helping to build the Tanzam Railroad. The terms of the loan are more liberal than any previous major loan, including the Russian loan to Egypt for the Aswan High Dam. Repayment does not begin for 5 years and there is no interest over the 30-year repayment period.

The vigorous efforts of Tanzania and the switch from an anti-Peking attitude in many French-speaking African states made the admission of China to the UN easier. Among the African-Malagasy-Mauritius Common Organization states, the trend toward recognizing Peking started with Cameroon in April. By mid-September, 23 African states had recognized Peking and 16 had made economic aid agreements.

Military Coups. Major General Idi Amin Dada's take-over in Uganda in January was an example of the fact that the military is a growing political force in Africa (see AMIN, IDI; UGANDA). Scarcely a major nation in Africa has been untouched by military intervention since it became independent. Several countries, such as Ghana, have returned successfully to civilian rule. Major General Yakubu Gowon has promised civilian rule in Nigeria by 1976, and Amin also promised to restore civilian rule in Uganda, but did not specify a date.

The coup that ousted Uganda's President Milton Obote on January 25 caused serious difficulties for the East African Community, composed of Kenya, Tanzania, and Uganda. Tanzania refused to recog-

Facts in Brief on the African Countries

Country	Population	Government	Monetary Unit*	Foreign Trade (million U.S. $1) Exports	Imports
Algeria	14,587,000	President Houari Boumediene	dinar (4.9 = $1)	934	1,009
Angola	5,645,000	Governor-General Camilo Augusto de Miranda Rebocho Vaz	escudo (28.65 = $1)	423	342
Botswana	687,000	President Seretse Khama	rand (1 = $1.40)	18	43
Burundi	3,688,000	President and Prime Minister Michel Micombero	franc (87.5 = $1)	24	22
Cameroon	6,045,000	President Ahmadou Ahidjo	CFA franc (277.71 = $1)	226	242
Central African Republic	1,635,000	President Jean Bedel Bokassa	CFA franc (277.71 = $1)	31	34
Chad	3,670,000	President François Tombalbaye	CFA franc (277.71 = $1)	28	52
Congo (Brazza.)	915,000	President Marien N'Gouabi	CFA franc (277.71 = $1)	31	57
Congo (Kinshasa)	18,254,000	President and Prime Minister Joseph Mobutu	zaire (1 = $2)	644	410
Dahomey	2,876,000	Presidential Council President Hubert Maga	CFA franc (277.71 = $1)	24	51
Egypt, Arab Republic of	35,000,000	President Anwar al-Sadat; Prime Minister Mahmoud Fawzi	pound (1 = $2.30)	762	773
Equatorial Guinea	301,000	President Francisco Macias Nguema	peseta (70 = $1)	23	18
Ethiopia	26,362,000	Emperor Haile Selassie I; Prime Minister T. T. Akilou Abte-Wold	dollar (2.5 = $1)	122	172
Gabon	500,000	President and Prime Minister Albert Bernard Bongo	CFA franc (277.71 = $1)	121	80
Gambia	380,000	President Dawda Kairaba Jawara	dalasi (2.08 = $1)	16	17
Ghana	9,316,000	President Edward Akufo-Addo; Prime Minister Kofi A. Busia	new cedi (1.02 = $1)	375	409
Guinea	4,189,000	President Sékou Touré	franc (277.71 = $1)	65	45
Ivory Coast	4,491,000	President Felix Houphouet-Boigny	CFA franc (277.71 = $1)	469	388
Kenya	11,447,000	President Jomo Kenyatta	shilling (7.14 = $1)	217	397
Lesotho	1,010,000	King Motlotlehi Moshoeshoe II; Prime Minister Leabua Jonathan	rand (1 = $1.40)	5	33
Liberia	1,217,000	President William R. Tolbert	dollar (1 = $1)	214	114
Libya	2,084,000	Revolutionary Command Council President and Prime Minister Muammar Muhammad al-Qadhaafi	dinar (1 = $2.80)	2,366	554
Malagasy	7,112,000	President Philibert Tsiranana	franc (277.71 = $1)	145	170
Malawi	4,764,000	President Hastings Kamuzu Banda	kwacha (1 = $1.20)	59	99
Mali	5,165,000	President and Prime Minister Moussa Traoré	franc (555.4 = $1)	24	39
Mauritania	1,210,000	President Moktar Ould Daddah	CFA franc (277.71 = $1)	71	39
Morocco	16,454,000	King Hassan II; Prime Minister Mohamed Karim Lamrani	dirham (5.04 = $1)	488	686
Mozambique	7,690,000	Governor-General Eduardo de Arantes e Oliveira	escudo (28.65 = $1)	156	326
Niger	4,234,000	President Hamani Diori	CFA franc (277.71 = $1)	23	45
Nigeria	68,580,000	Federal Military Government Head Yakubu Gowon	pound (1 = $2.80)	1,242	1,053
Rhodesia	5,594,000	President Clifford Dupont; Prime Minister Ian D. Smith	dollar (1 = $1.40)	318	279
Rwanda	3,827,000	President Grégoire Kayibanda	franc (100 = $1)	25	29
Senegal	4,035,000	President Leopold Sedar Senghor; Prime Minister Abdou Diouf	CFA franc (277.71 = $1)	152	193
Sierra Leone	2,625,000	President Siaka P. Stevens	leone (1 = $1.20)	103	116
Somalia	2,957,000	Supreme Revolutionary Council Chairman Mohamed Siad Barre	shilling (7.14 = $1)	31	45
South Africa	21,065,000	President Jacobus Johannes Fouche; Prime Minister Balthazar Johannes Vorster	rand (1 = $1.40)	2,175	3,922
Sudan	16,498,000	President Jafir Muhammad Nimeri	pound (1 = $2.87)	298	288
Swaziland	448,000	King Sobhuza II; Prime Minister Makhosini Dlamini	rand (1 = $1.40)	67	53
Tanzania	13,952,000	President Julius K. Nyerere	shilling (7.14 = $1)	239	271
Togo	1,955,000	President Etienne Eyadema	CFA franc (277.71 = $1)	52	66
Tunisia	5,154,000	President Habib Bourguiba; Prime Minister Hedi Nouira	dinar (1 = $1.90)	181	305
Uganda	8,981,000	President Idi Amin Dada	shiiling (7.14 = $1)	249	121
Upper Volta	5,618,000	President Sangoulé Lamizana; Prime Minister Gerard Kango Ouedraogo	CFA franc (277.71 = $1)	18	46
Zambia	4,612,000	President Kenneth David Kaunda; Vice-President Mainza Chona	kwacha (1 = $1.40)	1,073	437

*Exchange rates as of Sept. 30, 1971

nize Amin's military regime as the legal government of Uganda. At the East African Legislative Assembly in April, Tanzania challenged the credentials of the Ugandan delegation, but was overruled. President Nyerere refused to meet with General Amin to discuss community matters. Finally, in October, the two nations agreed to settle some of their differences so that the community could continue functioning.

A similar situation developed within the OAU. Tanzania urged the organization not to recognize Amin's government. However, on June 11, the OAU voted to seat Uganda's representatives.

On March 23, the commander of Sierra Leone's armed forces, Brigadier General John Bangurah, tried to overthrow the government of Prime Minister Siaka P. Stevens. The rebel troops attacked Stevens' residence and his office, but loyalist troops put down the insurrection and arrested Bangurah. Under the terms of a mutual defense pact, soldiers from Guinea were brought in to protect Stevens. Bangurah and three other officers were executed on June 29. Meanwhile, in April, Sierra Leone declared itself a republic. Stevens became its first president on April 21.

Two other unsuccessful coups were attempted in 1971. A group of leftist army officers briefly seized power on July 19 in Sudan, but within 72 hours Major General Jafir Muhammad Nimeri regained control of the government. Nimeri then executed those accused of involvement in the plot, including the leader of the Sudanese Communist Party (see NIMERI, JAFIR MUHAMMAD; SUDAN). On August 27, a former deputy of Chad's National Assembly led an unsuccessful attempt to overthrow the government. Chad accused Libya of being involved in the plot and broke off diplomatic relations. See CHAD.

Unemployment Problems in Africa worsened in 1971. At the root of the problem are millions of young black Africans, most of them elementary-school drop-outs, who leave rural areas to seek work in the cities. They are educated just enough to be dissatisfied with village life, but they have no job skills. The economies of the developing African nations cannot provide enough jobs to employ them.

Even though several countries have programs designed to keep youths in rural areas, the situation threatens to grow worse. An estimated 68 per cent of all African youths do not continue their education beyond the elementary school level. In Zambia, there are only about 350,000 jobs, but every year 50,000 youths drop out of the seventh grade, presumably to find work. In 1971, it was estimated that one-third of the work force was unemployed in Kinshasa, Zaïre; one-half, in Lagos, Nigeria.

Increasing unemployment has created fear of a rising crime rate throughout Africa's major cities. In Uganda and Nigeria, the crime rate has already begun to grow. As a deterrent, Nigeria instituted the death penalty for armed robbery.   George Shepherd

See also articles on various African nations.

AGNEW, SPIRO T., spent a great part of 1971 traveling, and again stirred controversy with hard-hitting speeches. The Vice-President visited 13 state legislatures to promote President Richard M. Nixon's revenue-sharing plan. In July, he made a good-will tour of Asia, Africa, the Middle East, and Europe. In October, he visited Turkey and his father's homeland, Greece. He was a guest in Persepolis at the Shah of Iran's celebration of the 2,500th anniversary of the founding of the Persian Empire.

The Good-Will Trip began when Agnew flew to South Korea for the July 1 inauguration of President Chung Hee Park. After a stop in Singapore, he went to Kuwait and Saudi Arabia for talks on the Middle East situation.

In Africa, Agnew met with Ethiopian Emperor Haile Selassie I, Kenya's President Jomo Kenyatta, and President Joseph Mobutu of Zaïre, formerly Congo (Kinshasa). He concluded his tour with visits to Spain, Morocco, and Portugal. During his October trip to Greece, Agnew visited his father's hometown of Gargalianoi and met with Greek Prime Minister George Papadopoulos.

His Controversial Comments were directed at the news media and at politicians who criticized Administration policies. Agnew charged that a Columbia Broadcasting System television documentary, *The Selling of the Pentagon*, was a "vicious broadside against the nation's defense establishment." He also charged that some U.S. news coverage of the Indochina war unintentionally assists North Vietnam.

He irritated many of America's black leaders when he said that most of them "could learn much" from the African leaders he saw in Ethiopia, Kenya, and Zaïre. He said that the African leaders "impressed me with their understanding of the internal problems and their moderateness" in contrast to "the querulous complaints and constant recriminations" of most black American leaders.

Agnew defended himself against charges that he was dividing the American people. "I not only plead guilty to this charge," Agnew said, "but am somewhat flattered by it." The Vice-President explained that he practiced a "politics of positive division" while "radical liberals" practice a "politics of negative division," seeking to split the nation "along lines of racial, generational, economic, and cultural difference."

In October, he declared political war on the "radical liberals" in Congress. "Be assured," he said, "we intend to strengthen the hand of the President during the second Nixon Administration by removing most, if not all, of these afflicted souls."

He infuriated Democrats when he attempted to link the views of four Democratic presidential hopefuls, who had called for cuts in military spending, with the views of Gus Hall, secretary of the U.S. Communist Party.   William McGaffin

See also REPUBLICAN PARTY.

AGRICULTURE struggled again in 1971 with the problem of inadequate income. It also developed a potential political issue when President Richard M. Nixon nominated Earl L. Butz to succeed the resigning Clifford M. Hardin as secretary of agriculture. Many Congressmen and farmers opposed Butz on the grounds that he favored large-scale, or corporate, farming. But after several days of bitter debate the U.S. Senate confirmed Butz on December 2 by a close vote, 51 to 44.

The basic issues revolved around who will control agriculture and what type of farm-income programs will be maintained. Agriculture can be divided into four segments according to the degree of commercialization. First are the large commercial enterprises with farm sales in excess of $100,000. Many of them are parts of large industrial conglomerates. That segment of agriculture once again enjoyed substantial growth during the year. Second are the modern, commercial, family farms. Although still in a minority, they produce most of the nation's food and fiber. Their sales range between $40,000 and $100,000 per farm per year. Third are the many marginal farmers, who are making a poor living in commercial agriculture and are being squeezed out. They comprise the largest agricultural group, yet they account for only a small percentage of farm sales. Marginal farmers generally have annual sales

of less than $10,000. Fourth are part-time farmers. Many in this group are successful business executives and professionals using agriculture either as a hobby or as a means of converting ordinary income into capital gains.

The Farm Price Picture was somewhat mixed in 1971. The index of all prices received by farmers stood at 114 (1967=100) in November, 1971, compared with 106 a year earlier. The wage-price freeze of 1971 did not apply to raw farm products.

Livestock prices improved greatly by year-end over late 1970 and early 1971 levels. Hog prices averaged $18.90 per hundredweight (cwt) and beef cattle averaged $29.50 per cwt during November, 1971, compared with $15.40 for hogs and $25.10 for cattle a year earlier. Even though hog prices were improving, they were still far below the $28 per cwt level reached in early 1970. The index of all livestock and products prices stood at 119 (1967=100) in November, 1971, compared with 109 in November, 1970.

Milk prices and broiler prices were near 1970 levels. November egg prices, at 29.7 cents per dozen, were 6 cents below November, 1970.

Overall crop prices were up. The November, 1971, index was 108 (1967=100) compared with 102 a year earlier. Most of the increase was in cotton, tobacco, fruits, and vegetables. Food-grain and feed-grain prices were depressed from the high 1970

Corpses of horses killed in an outbreak of Venezuelan equine encephalomyelitis in the United States in 1971 are bulldozed into a city dump in Port Isabel, Tex.

levels. The reduction was caused by a combination of sharply expanded production and curtailed export sales due to longshoremen strikes. Corn prices fell below $1 per bushel in late 1971. The 1970 price was more than 30 per cent higher.

Prices paid by farmers for supplies and services continued to rise. The index of prices paid in November, 1971, was 121 (1967=100), up over 5 per cent from 1970.

Retail food prices were estimated at an average of 3 per cent above 1970, and per capita food consumption was up 1 per cent. But the proportion of income American consumers spend for food, already the lowest of any country in the world, continued to decline. In 1960, U.S. consumers spent 20 per cent of their income for food. By 1970, this had fallen to only 16.6 per cent, and in 1971 dropped still further to approximately 16.2 per cent.

Crop Production. United States farmers produced a bumper harvest of crops in 1971. Many new records for production and yield were established. The index for "all-crops" production and yield both achieved record levels in 1971. The all-crops production index was at 113 (1967=100), 13 per cent over 1970. The all-crops yield index was 110 (1967=100), up 8 per cent from 1970. Production of the feed grains (corn, oats, barley, and sorghum) led the increase, up by 29 per cent over 1970. Of the feed grains, only oats showed a decline in production.

Corn production, rebounding from the Southern Corn leaf blight infestation of 1970, was expected to be over 5.5 billion bushels, up 35 per cent from 1970. The yield was the highest ever–86.6 bushels per acre compared with 71.7 bushels per acre in 1970 and 83.9 in 1969. Sorghum and barley production also increased dramatically over 1970, with sorghum up 28 per cent and barley up 14 per cent.

Soybean Production pushed to a record 1.2 billion bushels. A record yield of 28 bushels per acre helped achieve the increased production. Rice production was up almost 2 per cent over 1970 but 7 per cent below 1969, although a record-high yield of 4,641 pounds per acre was achieved. Cotton production was up 5 per cent and tobacco production down 5 per cent over 1970.

Livestock Production. Very high corn prices and low hog prices in late 1970 and early 1971 resulted in declining hog production as 1971 progressed. Hog slaughter during early 1971 was as much as 20 per cent above the previous year's levels. By late 1971, however, slaughter was below the unusually high levels of late 1970. An estimated 10 per cent reduction in Corn Belt farrowings was expected to result in reduced hog slaughter in early 1972.

Beef production in the first half of 1971 was 1 per cent above a year earlier. During the last half of the year, beef production was approximately the same as in 1970.

Consumption of meat (beef, veal, lamb, mutton,

and pork) was more than 192 pounds per person in 1971, up 3 per cent from 1970. All the increase was in pork consumption with beef unchanged and small decreases in veal, lamb, and mutton.

Farm Income Figures for 1971 were estimated to be somewhat lower than the $15.7 billion net income of 1970. Declining numbers of farms, however, kept net income per farm near the $5,374 level of 1970. The record high net income per farm was $5,654 in 1969.

A late-year study by the United States Department of Agriculture (USDA) shows that off-the-farm income of farmers now exceeds net income from farming. Based on 1970 data, the study reports that the average farm family realized $5,374 net income from farming and $5,833 income from nonfarm sources. This same study also reported that farms with over $40,000 in gross sales made up 8 per cent of all farms in 1970, yet accounted for over 52 per cent of cash receipts and over 36 per cent of net farm income. In 1960, by contrast, this same group of farms made up only 3 per cent of all farms, and had 33 per cent of cash receipts and 18 per cent of net income.

Farm Exports and Imports increased during the fiscal year ended June 30, 1971. The dollar value of farm exports hit a record high of $7.8 billion, 15 per cent over the previous year and 14 per cent above the previous record of $6.8 billion set in the 1966-1967 fiscal year. An estimated two-thirds of the increase in export value was due to increased volume, while one-third was attributed to higher prices. Record sales of $1.77 billion to the European Community (Common Market), 25 per cent above last year, plus increased sales to Japan and Canada, accounted for nearly 75 per cent of the increase in farm exports.

Agricultural exports take the output of 1 out of every 4 harvested acres of U.S. cropland. In 1971, export markets accounted for 80 per cent of the production of dried peas, nearly 60 per cent of the rice, more than 50 per cent of the wheat and soybeans, about 40 per cent of the cattle hides, tallow, and raisins, and more than 30 per cent of the cotton and tobacco. Feed grain exports represented about 20 per cent of sales by U.S. farmers. A longshoremen's strike that began on July 1, 1971, in West Coast ports and on October 1 in Gulf and East Coast ports sharply curtailed exports during the latter half of the year.

Imports of farm products were also up in the year ended June 30, 1971. The dollar value of imports was $5.8 billion, up 4 per cent from the previous year. All of the increase in dollar value was due to price increases, however, as the quantity of goods remained essentially unchanged from the 1969-1970 fiscal year.

The announcement of sales of grain to Russia in November was hailed by Agriculture Secretary Hardin as a "historic arrangement leading to sale of approximately 3 million tons of corn and other grains

Agricultural Statistics, 1971

U.S. Production of Animal Products
(millions of pounds)

	1957-59†	1970	1971*
Beef	13,704	21,800	22,100
Veal	1,240	600	550
Lamb and Mutton	711	540	550
Pork	10,957	13,160	14,700
Eggs (a)	5,475	5,860	5,975
Chicken	5,292	10,950	10,717
Turkey	1,382	2,157	2,250
Total Milk (b)	123.2	116.8	118.7
Cheese	1,396	2,182	2,360
Butter	1,477	1,122	1,121

†Average; *Preliminary.
(a) 1,000,000 dozens; (b) 100,000,000 lbs.

Output of Major U.S. Crops
(millions of bushels)

Crop	1962-66†	1970	1971*
Corn	3,862	4,104	5,552
Sorghums	595	708	890
Oats	912	891	885
Wheat	1,230	1,360	1,628
Soybeans	769	1,134	1,200
Rice (a)	742	844	840
Potatoes (b)	275	323	318
Cotton (c)	125	104	107
Tobacco (d)	2,126	1,874	1,804

†Average; *Preliminary.
(a) 100,000 cwt.; (b) 1,000,000 cwt.;
(c) 100,000 bales; (d) 1,000,000 lbs.

World Crop Production
(million units)

Crop	Units	1964-68†	1970	1971*	%U.S.
Barley	Metric Tons	101.0	114.3	127.4	8
Corn	Metric Tons	(NA)	(NA)	293.5	48
Oats	Metric Tons	45.9	49.0	52.3	24
Wheat	Metric Tons	276.3	279.8	304.2	15
Rice[1]	Metric Tons	261.0	(NA)	294.0	1
Coffee	Bags[2]	68.5	57.0	58.0	.06
Cotton	Bales	51.2	52.0	53.9	19
Soybeans	Bushels	1,113[3]	1,527	44.3	74

†Average; *Preliminary; (NA) not available.
[1]Excluding Communist Asia; [2]132.276 lbs.

[3]1962-66 average

Food's Share of Total Expenditures In Selected Countries

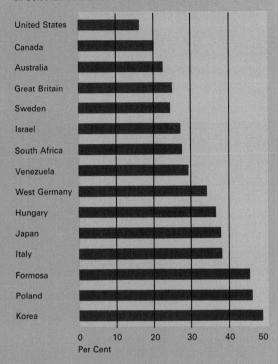

Food Expenditures and Income in U.S.
Billions of dollars

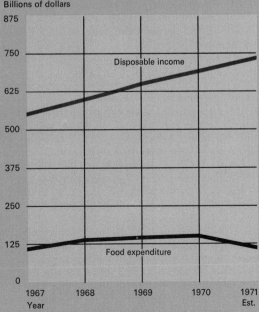

Visitors strolling on the White House lawn view an exhibition organized by the U.S. Department of Agriculture as a tribute to modern agricultural methods.

to Russia [that] holds great promise for American farmers." Agricultural spokesmen repeatedly pointed out that agricultural trade was one of the key positive factors in the U.S. trade balance deficit.

New Feed-Grain Programs for 1972 began in 1971. Aimed at lowering crop production and raising prices and incomes, the new programs were designed to idle 38 million acres, more than double 1971's 18 million.

The Freeze. Agriculture was pleased to have only nominal controls placed on it by President Nixon's 90-day wage-price freeze, which was announced on August 15. However, it was somewhat chagrined that it had essentially no partisan representation on the high levels of the new administrative boards. Undersecretary of Agriculture J. Phil Campbell explained that "by exempting raw farm products from the freeze, the President recognized that farmers aren't the cause of inflation but the victims of it. . . ."

Total Farm Debt at the beginning of 1971 stood at $61.2 billion–up from $58.1 billion the previous year. Investment in agriculture totaled $318.9 billion, of which 19 per cent was borrowed capital. Commercial banks, the largest of all institutional lenders, supplied slightly more than 25 per cent of all farm loans. A recent study by the Farm Credit Administration showed that the credit needs of agriculture will continue to rise during the 1970s. Credit was affected by the same factors that caused rapid

credit expansion during the 1960s–substitution of capital for labor and other inputs, rising input prices, the changing financial structure of farming, and changing attitudes of borrowers. By 1980, capital needs are expected to rise to between $91 billion and $140 billion, and yearly capital flow is projected to reach about $19 billion from 1975 to 1979.

Bargaining Power was a major issue with farmers in 1971. Congressional hearings on several bargaining bills were sustained and serious, and bargaining legislation of some type is expected to result in 1972. Such legislation would probably put emphasis on agricultural cooperatives. Undersecretary Campbell said in October, "It is more important than ever before that cooperatives be market pacesetters." Substantial cooperative power blocs were evident in 1971. For example, four milk cooperatives marketed over 70 per cent of the milk in the Midwest and South. President Nixon addressed the annual meeting of one of these groups, comprising more than 40,000 farmers, in Chicago in September. Setting government price supports for milk was a national issue with broad news coverage dealing with the political power of these groups.

Environmental Issues were of increasing concern, and agricultural consultation was an important part of Environmental Protection Agency decisions in 1971. USDA officials recognized the responsible action demanded of agriculture but decried the "super-emotionalism which has attached itself to environmental issues."

The environmental program of the USDA had five chief elements: (1) identification, retention, and protection of land for agricultural production; (2) design of new approaches in using land released from agriculture for esthetic and recreational purposes; (3) stimulation of selected small and medium-sized growth centers around the nation; (4) increasing efforts to determine the capacity of land to absorb waste and to find ways to use wastes; and (5) modification in use of agricultural chemicals.

Agricultural Poverty loomed big in 1971. Congressional concern was voiced in many bills. For example, Senator Herman E. Talmadge (D., Ga.) cited the following in support of new legislation: "The percentage of people living in poverty in non-metropolitan areas was nearly twice as high in 1969 as those living in urban areas. Rural areas compare poorly with urban areas with respect to health and education."

Deadly Horse Virus. Venezuelan equine encephalomyelitis, a sleeping sickness virus spread by marsh mosquitoes, swept into Texas from Mexico in July, and quickly spread to several other states. The disease killed more than 1,000 horses in Texas in July and struck about 1,500 horses in other parts of the Southwest. Secretary Hardin called the spread of the disease a "national emergency," and channeled federal funds from other programs for massive inoculation and spraying programs.

World Agricultural Production was generally up in 1971. Soybean production, due largely to the large U.S. crop, set a new record for the seventh consecutive year, up 4 per cent from 1970. Production of wheat and rye also was up. The 304-million-ton wheat harvest was up almost 6 per cent from 1970.

World livestock production continued to increase. As of Jan. 1, 1971, cattle numbered 1.211 billion head, a new record. Hog and sheep numbers also established record high levels with hogs numbering 615 million head, up 8 per cent over 1970, and sheep up 1 per cent to 1.037 billion head.

Data released during 1971 show that world red-meat production in 1970 went up 3 billion pounds to 136 billion, exceeding the record set in 1969. Most of the increase came from increased pork production. Argentina was the leading per capita consumer of beef and veal, with an average of 176 pounds consumed per person. Pork consumption was highest in Denmark at 88 pounds per capita. New Zealand had the highest red-meat consumption in the world, averaging 230 pounds per person per year. The United States ranked fifth in total red-meat consumption at 186 pounds.   Charles E. French and Larry L. Nelson

AIR FORCE, U.S. See NATIONAL DEFENSE.
AIR POLLUTION. See ENVIRONMENT.
ALABAMA. See STATE GOVERNMENT.
ALASKA. See STATE GOVERNMENT.

ALBANIA continued to open itself up to the outside world in 1971 but maintained its strong ties with China. The reconciliation was most marked with Albania's Balkan neighbors, Yugoslavia and Greece. Albania established full diplomatic relations with Yugoslavia in February and with Greece and Norway in May. More Western tourists and a few Western journalists were allowed into the country.

But Albania did not better its relations with Russia. The press and radio continued their bitter attacks on the so-called Brezhnev Doctrine of limited sovereignty for Socialist countries. Several high-ranking Chinese delegations visited Albania during the year.

National plans call for large increases in the output of gasoline, raw materials, and electric energy (some of which will be exported to Yugoslavia). But the main priority goes to modernizing agriculture. In August, collective farms were converted into state farms to "narrow the gap between urban and rural areas." The size of private plots was reduced from almost 1,200 square yards to less than 360.

Facts in Brief. Population: 2,254,000. Government: Communist Party First Secretary Enver Hoxha; Premier Mehmet Shehu; People's Assembly Presidium Chairman Haxhi Lleshi. Monetary Unit: lek. Foreign Trade: exports, $80,000,000; imports, $143,000,000. Principal Exports: metal ores, crude petroleum, bitumen, tobacco.   Chris Cviic

ALBERT, CARL BERT (1908-), was elected the 46th speaker of the U.S. House of Representatives, the third highest office in the land, on Jan. 21, 1971. A Democrat from Oklahoma, Albert maintained a middle-of-the-road position throughout his 25 years in the House. He represents a 22-county rural district in southeastern Oklahoma called "Little Dixie." Nearly two-thirds of its residents have incomes below the poverty level.

Albert, who stands only 5 feet 4 inches tall, was mistaken for a page by another congressman when he started his first term in 1947. But he quickly rose to a position of leadership. A protégé of the late Speaker Sam Rayburn of Texas, he became Democratic whip in 1955 and majority leader in 1962. He served as the permanent chairman of the Democratic National Convention in August, 1968.

Albert was born on a farm near McAlester, Okla., the oldest of five children of a coal miner. The family moved to Bug Tussle in 1911, where Albert attended a two-room school. In 1923, they returned to McAlester. Albert graduated from high school there, winning national honors and touring the United States as a debater. He graduated from the University of Oklahoma in 1931 with a B.A. degree in political science, a Phi Beta Kappa key, and a Rhodes scholarship. In 1942 he married Mary Harmon. They have two children.   Allan Davidson

ALBERTA. See CANADA.

ALGERIA elected People's Communal Assemblies for the country's 691 communes in February, 1971, as the government of President Houari Boumediene continued the gradual re-establishment of parliamentary government. About 77 per cent of the electorate voted, compared to 71 per cent in the 1967 municipal elections. Of the 21,000 candidates, two-thirds were members of Algeria's only political party, the National Liberation Front. Nine women were elected to the assembly for Algiers. With the regional assemblies already formed, the way was open for the election of a new National Assembly as the next step.

Release of the nephew of former President Ahmed Ben Bella from prison was another indication of Algeria's move toward more normal times. Ben Bella, under house arrest since 1965, was married during the year.

The government banned the National Students Union in January after six of its members were arrested for alleged links with the outlawed Avant-Garde Socialist Party. Students in the nation's three universities struck in protest. Student unrest was actually relatively limited. Major causes of dissatisfaction were the shortage of teachers and dependence on foreign, especially French, teachers. In April, President Boumediene opened a teacher-training institute at Ben Aknoun. It is to train 640 primary teachers annually to help meet the shortage.

A long-term dispute with France over preferential economic and trade arrangements for French companies developed into a serious crisis during the year. Algeria was determined to control its national resources and receive its full share from them. Its negotiators were equally motivated by agreements that had given other oil-producing countries a greater share in profits. In February, Algeria nationalized French-owned companies, and adopted a new Algerian Oil Code that would require ownership of 51 per cent by Sonatrach, Algeria's national oil trust. France retaliated by reducing production by two-thirds, a blow to Algeria since 70 per cent of its oil is exported to French markets. In June, the French agreed to the 51 per cent rule.

Algeria continued to diversify its industry and agriculture in order to reduce dependence on France. Trade agreements were signed with Belgium, Italy, Poland, and Romania. West Germany agreed to build a dry-battery plant at Sétif. About 55,000 acres of vineyards were to be converted to other crops, but Boumediene reversed his field, promising to help winegrowers improve the quantity and quality of their production. France had virtually embargoed Algerian wine.

Facts in Brief. Population: 14,587,000. Government: President Houari Boumediene. Monetary Unit: dinar. Foreign Trade: exports, $934,000,000; imports, $1,009,000,000. Principal Exports: crude petroleum, wine, natural gas.   William Spencer

AMERICAN LEGION. See VETERANS.

AMERICAN LIBRARY ASSOCIATION (ALA). President Richard M. Nixon named a 14-member National Commission on Libraries and Information Science on May 19, 1971. The ALA's Washington, D.C., office was instrumental in the establishment of the commission, which will recommend plans for use of the nation's educational resources.

Keith Doms, director of the Free Library of Philadelphia, was inaugurated as president of ALA at the 90th annual ALA conference, held in Dallas from June 20 to 26. Katherine Laich, lecturer and coordinator of programs at the School of Library Science, University of Southern California, took office as vice-president and president-elect.

The principal winner of the $25,000 J. Morris Jones-World Book Encyclopedia-ALA Goals Award for 1971 was a project, "Total Community Library Service: A Conference and Follow-Up Activities," a project of the ALA and the Joint Committee of the National Education Association. The remainder of the year's award went to the Freedom to Read Foundation of the Intellectual Freedom Committee to support its program. The principal award will be used to set up a conference in May, 1972, in the Washington, D.C., area to discuss the need to coordinate school, college, and public library service.

Two-year grant awards from the School Library Manpower Project, funded by the Knapp Foundation, Incorporated, of North Carolina and administered by the American Association of School Librarians, were given to Arizona State University, Tempe; Auburn (Ala.) University; Mankato (Minn.) State College; Millersville (Pa.) State College; University of Denver, Colorado; and the University of Michigan, Ann Arbor.

ALA members, polled by mail, voted 6,917 to 981 to ratify amendments to ALA bylaws calling for re-organization of the ALA Council. Another mail vote brought approval of the merger of ALA's Adult Services Division (ASD) and Reference Services Division (RSD). Members of ASD voted 674 to 43 and RSD members voted 1,434 to 366 in favor.

ALA publications in 1971 included: *Future of General Adult Books, Reading in America, Acronyms in Education and the Behavioral Sciences, Educational Media Selection Centers, Books for Children 1969-70, American Library Laws, Guides to Educational Media, Science Fiction Story Index, Melcher on Acquisition, Fundamental Sources,* and *Non Book Materials.*

The ALA Council approved a Program of Action for Mediation, Arbitration, and Inquiry, with responsibilities related to tenure, status, fair employment, due process, ethics, and intellectual freedom as set forth in ALA council policies. The council also approved a statement of responsibility for ALA's American Association of State Libraries and gave approval for it to change its name to Association of State Library Agencies.   Curtis Swanson

See also AWARDS AND PRIZES.

AMERICAN PARTY. George C. Wallace, the Democratic governor of Alabama, delayed a formal announcement in 1971 of his plans to seek the presidency as the 1972 American Party candidate. But Wallace has never really stopped running since his last presidential attempt in 1968. His campaign headquarters in Montgomery, Ala., never closed. Money for the campaign fund came from contributions sent to P.O. Box 1972, from the sale of $15.95 George Wallace wrist watches, and from Wallace newsletter subscriptions at $12 a year. Additional funds were raised in 1971 at $25-a-plate "appreciation dinners," at which Wallace spoke.

Wallace appeared undeterred by the fact that his strength in the South as the third-party champion of states' rights and segregation may have weakened. He freely discussed his 1972 campaign plans with reporters, including his interest in entering a few Democratic primaries. Opinion polls showed that Wallace held about the same percentage of the vote as in 1968, when he captured almost 10 million votes. The American Party machinery was ready to put Wallace's name on the ballot in all 50 states.

An American Party candidate, William E. Smith, came in a poor fourth in the Kentucky governorship race on November 2. Smith received only 7,509 votes. William McGaffin

See also DEMOCRATIC PARTY; ELECTIONS; REPUBLICAN PARTY; WALLACE, GEORGE CORLEY.

AMIN, IDI (1925?-   ), led a military coup that deposed President Apollo Milton Obote of Uganda on Jan. 26, 1971. Obote was in Singapore at the time. On Feb. 20, the government announced Major General Amin had been named president and promoted to full general by "the soldiers and officers of the Ugandan Army."

Amin was born in Koboko, a northern Uganda village, and helped to tend his family's goats as a boy. He attended primary school there when his father could pay the costs. He joined the British Army in 1944 and served against Mau Mau terrorists in Kenya in 1953. Amin was an enthusiastic rugby player, and praised military life as "the finest physical training a footballer could have." For nearly 10 years, he was his country's heavyweight boxing champion.

After Uganda achieved independence on Oct. 8, 1962, Amin became an officer in the new nation's army. He rose to command Uganda's armed forces.

Amin and Obote were close friends, but Amin became increasingly dissatisfied with Obote's "move to the left" and his plans to nationalize many businesses. On May 1, Amin announced he would limit the number of businesses in Uganda that would be nationalized. Ed Nelson

ANGOLA. See AFRICA.

ANIMAL. See AGRICULTURE; CONSERVATION; INTERNATIONAL LIVE STOCK EXPOSITION; ZOOLOGY.

ANTHROPOLOGY. Raoul Naroll of the State University of New York, Buffalo, in 1971 summarized the most important conclusions about social evolution that anthropologists have reached by using cross-cultural comparisons. Not surprisingly, observations showed that men have increased their control over the natural environment, and their societies have become more complex and urbanized.

Other trends, however, are surprising. Naroll says that economic relationships that once spread wealth evenly through a society have been replaced by those that concentrate it in a few hands. Leadership has tended to become formal and authoritative. Originally, it was informal and by mutual consent. The élite, or privileged few, of societies have begun to act for their own benefit rather than for the good of all. And, warlike societies have spread.

In a specific application of cross-cultural methods, Melvin and Carol Ember of Hunter College in New York City investigated changes in the housing patterns of married couples. They found that where newlyweds in our society live after marriage varies considerably. In tribal societies, it is common for the couple to live with either the wife's or the husband's family. Some anthropologists have argued that where the females provide the food, the couple will live with the wife's family (matrilocal). Where the husband is the major provider, the couple will live

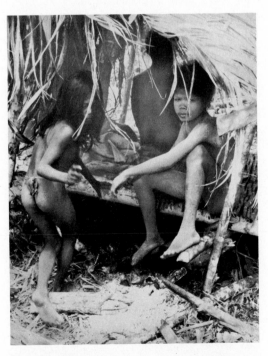

A group of Stone Age tribesmen were found in the Tasaday rain forest of the Philippines in June. They thought they were the only human beings in the world.

with his family (patrilocal). But after examining a sample of the world's societies, the Embers found that this hypothesis could not be supported. Instead, they concluded, patrilocal residence tends to occur in societies where neighboring communities fight. According to the Embers, if residence were not patrilocal, fathers, sons, and brothers would be forced to fight each other. In societies where warfare usually occurs only between distant communities and where it interferes with some critical subsistence activities, matrilocal residence predominates.

American Indians Today. Anthropologists' studies usually are focused on American Indian cultures at the time of first white contact or on the more traditional aspects of their current cultures. Jack O. Waddell and Michael O. Watson of Purdue University have published *The American Indian in Urban Society*, a collection of articles on Indian conditions today, particularly those of the Indians that live in cities. The authors demonstrate that the extreme poverty in which most Indians live cannot be traced to the Indians' traditional culture or incomplete acculturation. It results from specific problems that the Indians encounter in new social situations and because of governmental policies.

One chapter, written by Joseph Jorgensen of the University of Michigan, considers the plight of the Northern Ute Indians, whose reservations are in Utah. Jorgensen shows that government policy has consistently been to purchase resources on the Ute reservation for exploitation by white outsiders, rather than to help the Indians develop the resources for their own use.

Effects of Apartheid. Mary Lystad of the National Institute of Mental Health analyzed the themes of stories written and told by black adolescents in Swaziland and South Africa in an effort to determine the effects of apartheid on the children. She found that the South Africans, who live under this policy of racial separation, showed an irrational approach to social situations and viewed the world as threatening to their well-being.

Australopithecines. Kelton R. McKinley of Michigan State University compared a large number of fossil remains of the prehistoric apelike men, *Australopithecus robustus* and *Australopithecus africanus*. Using differential wear patterns on teeth as a measure of age, McKinley determined that the average age at death was 22.9 years for *A. africanus* and 18.0 years for *A. robustus*. Most anthropologists believe that *A. africanus* was a direct ancestor of man, but that *A. robustus* was not. McKinley's finding suggests that *A. africanus* enjoyed at least one selective advantage over *A. robustus*—longer life.   Fred Plog

ANTI-POVERTY PROGRAM. See POVERTY; SOCIAL SECURITY; SOCIAL WELFARE.

ARAB EMIRATES, UNION OF. See PERSIAN GULF EMIRATES.

ARABIA. See SAUDI ARABIA.

ARCHAEOLOGY. For several decades, archaeologists have debated the probable date of man's arrival in the New World. Richard S. MacNeish of the Peabody Foundation, Phillips Academy, Andover, Mass., said in 1971 that there is evidence that man was present in South America between 14,000 and 19,000 years ago. While such early dates had previously been suggested for the arrival of man in South America, there was never sufficient evidence to convince most archaeologists of their validity.

MacNeish found man-made tools and datable animal bones in the Pepper and Flea caves near Ayacucho, some 200 miles southeast of Lima, Peru. Considering the amount of time that it might have taken for early men to travel from the Bering Strait through Alaska and North America to Peru, and the age of Asian tools similar to those MacNeish found, he believes that man may have crossed the strait 40,000 to 100,000 years ago.

Domestication of Animals. Investigations of the early domestication of animals have been handicapped by the inability to determine whether fossil bones belonged to domesticated animals or to their wild ancestors. Some investigators have assumed that domesticated animals would not be slaughtered until they reached a specific age, while the bones of wild beasts might be those of either young or old animals. The archaeologists have thus sought to establish the presence of domestication by studying the age structure of collections of bones. This assumption, however, is difficult to demonstrate.

Isabella M. Drew, Dexter Perkins, and Patricia Daly of Columbia University used a different method to study the bones of these two types of animals. They noted that the bones of domesticated animals always feel greasy, and reasoned that this should be reflected in the internal composition of the bones. The team cut thin sections from bones of domesticated and wild sheep, goats, and cows. When they examined the sections under a microscope with polarized light and a gypsum filter, they found that the crystalline microstructure in bones of the domesticated group differed from that in bones of the wild group. If further research validates this finding, archaeologists will be able to trace the history of domestication far more precisely.

Tools or Arithmetic? Alexander Marshack of the Peabody Museum, Harvard University, published in 1971 the results of seven years of research on the markings on bone tools that were made in Europe from 10,000 to 32,000 years ago. Archaeologists have long believed that the grooves and other markings on these bones were made either as decorations or to create a firmer grip. Marshack reasoned that if this were so, the grooves on any one tool should all have been cut at the same time with the same tool. Using a microscope to examine each groove, he found that they were made with different tools and, presumably, at different times. Moreover, Marshack showed

Vanessa Knight, an archaeological assistant, studies the grave of an Iron Age chieftain, discovered at Driffield, England, that dates back to 200 B.C.

that the marks occur in definable sets, subsets, and sums. He argued that the bones may have been used as calendars, with the marks indicating cycles of the moon. While much work is still needed to demonstrate this thesis, it is likely that the marks do represent some early system of counting.

Illegal Archaeology. Three men in England—Martin Aitken of Oxford University, Peter Ucko of London University, and Roger Moorey of the Ashmolean Museum—used a technique called thermoluminescence to demonstrate that some of the pottery in a number of museums in Europe and the United States was fake. The pottery was supposed to have come from an Anatolian neolithic site, Hacilar, but they found it was of recent manufacture. Thermoluminescent dating is based on a measure of the electrons trapped in the clay when it was fired.

The sale of fake artifacts is but one indication of an increasingly grave problem facing archaeologists—illegal activities on the part of untrained persons. In most countries, it is illegal for anyone who does not have a degree in archaeology to remove artifacts or otherwise disturb a site. But some individuals and teams are looting sites, sometimes using power equipment, to obtain artifacts for their own use or for sale. This phenomenon poses a grave threat to the continued practice of archaeology. The problem has become the focus of discussion at meetings and in archaeological journals. Fred Plog

ARCHITECTURE. Louis Kahn, an almost legendary figure with a great international reputation, received his share of more general recognition in the United States in 1971. The 70-year-old Kahn, architect and teacher, was the subject of several newspaper and magazine articles during the year. These accolades culminated in Detroit at the annual convention of the American Institute of Architects (AIA) in June, when he received the AIA's highest honor, its Gold Medal.

A slight figure with a thatch of unruly white hair, Kahn outlined his almost mystical approach to architecture in his acceptance speech: "When it is in service and finished, a building wants to say, 'Look, I want to tell you about the way I was made.'"

Preservation Problems. Across the land, professional preservationists and concerned citizens fought a losing battle to save historic works of architecture. Economic pressures, especially in the larger cities, resulted in one building after another being torn down and replaced by much larger, more profitable structures.

This was true even of buildings universally recognized as major works of art, such as architect Louis H. Sullivan's Chicago Stock Exchange Building of 1894, probably the finest example of this master's work in the commercial high-rise field. In November, a wrecking company's scaffolding was up around the building, and one more piece of the country's cultural heritage was now being destroyed.

Preservationists sometimes went to bizarre lengths to try to save historic buildings. Typical was the latest in a long series of plans to save the Old Post Office in St. Louis. The scheme involved converting the 89-year-old landmark into a luxury hotel, some of whose guest rooms would have 16-foot ceilings.

New Towns is a concept that has proven very successful in Europe, but has yet to work well in America. The few communities that have been built, such as Columbia, Md., and Reston, Va., have turned out to be not so much "new towns" as just very large subdivisions. There was housing, but practically none of the recreational and cultural amenities that make up a genuine, livable new community.

In 1971, enthusiasm was growing, instead, for new towns within the old towns. Why, architects and planners asked, attempt to create wholly new cultural entities when these already exist in the large urban centers?

Thus, a $400-million new community was announced for a site in downtown Philadelphia that was occupied mainly by parking lots and obsolete factories. The 50-acre development, called Franklin Town, will be financed by five leading Philadelphia corporations and one of its major banks.

Famed architect Philip Johnson created Franklin Town's master plan, which consists of a new in-town residential neighborhood built around a 2-acre "town square," to have offices, hotels, and shopping facilities.

A similarly innovative plan for Chicago was devised by the architectural firm of Holabird & Root. The architects envision several new communities located on relatively undeveloped tracts of land along the Chicago River. They planned communities complete with medium- and high-density housing, schools, health-care facilities, municipal and commercial space, and recreational and cultural facilities. By their plan, the river would become a basic transportation artery for residents going downtown, much as is done in Amsterdam, Netherlands, and Venice, Italy. Much of the land is currently being used only for coal storage, truck parking, and other service installations.

Convention Centers were very much in the news during 1971. Architect Charles Luckman's Los Angeles Convention and Exhibition Center opened for business in July and claimed the largest column-free space in the United States. But its 458,000 square feet was no record. C. F. Murphy & Associates' new McCormick Place in Chicago, a huge, exposed steel and glass facility, contains 600,000 square feet of exhibition space on two levels.

Ground was broken for two other centers. Welton Beckett & Associates designed one for Milwaukee

Christensen Hall, a dormitory on the University of New Hampshire campus at Durham, won a 1971 Honor Award of the American Institute of Architects.

Westbeth Artists Housing in New York City won an American Institute of Architects Honor Award as an example of the rehabilitation of an obsolete structure.

containing 365,000 square feet, and which may have second-floor, enclosed "sky bridges" linking it to other buildings in the immediate area. A very striking plan for the Niagara Falls, N.Y., International Convention Center, which will be located a scant 1,800 feet from the American falls, was created by architects Philip Johnson and John Burgee.

Notable New Buildings. Two of the largest and most expensive structures of the year also generated the most controversy. The John F. Kennedy Center for the Performing Arts opened with suitable pomp and ceremony on September 9 in Washington, D.C. But critics dubbed it "an inflated Greek Temple" and "a national tragedy." The $76-million, marble-clad, three-theater building was designed by Edward Durell Stone.

Skidmore, Owings and Merrill's Lyndon Baines Johnson Library, on the University of Texas Austin campus, fared little better. It may contain 31 million documents, but to most architects it just looked like an outsized concrete mausoleum.

Sibyl Moholy-Nagy, professor of architectural history at Pratt Institute, and author of a number of important books, died on Jan. 8, 1971. In her last book, *Matrix of Man*, published in 1968, she wrote, in her characteristically humane fashion, "The computer cannot be taught the meaning of urban environments."   Rob Cuscaden

See also Awards and Prizes.

ARGENTINA. A three-man junta, the commanding officers of the army, navy, and air force, assumed power on March 23, 1971, after deposing President Roberto Marcelo Levingston. On March 26, Lieutenant General Alejandro Augustín Lanusse, commander in chief of the armed forces, was sworn in as president. The take-over marked the ninth change of government since September, 1955, when the military ousted the flamboyant strongman Juan D. Perón.

Levingston was ousted because of his inability to cope with the severe sociopolitical-economic crisis confronting the nation. The new regime, in a move to attract the support of labor and business, abolished the ceiling on wage increases and promised to "readjust" price controls to reflect the wage settlements. It also reportedly approved a 19 per cent pay hike for all employees, although in March, when more than 600 wage contracts were due to expire, labor leaders had talked in terms of 40 to 50 per cent increases. During the spring, wage increases ranging from 12 to 50 per cent were granted. Due to soaring living costs, however – up nearly 10 per cent in the first two months of 1971 and from 45 to 50 per cent by the end of the year – the pay increases were soon absorbed. As a result, labor unrest grew as business and construction activities slowed down. Early in September, the government froze prices and raised all wages about $10 a month.

On April 1, the new government announced that all political parties except the Perónist party would be legalized. They had been banned since a military take-over in 1966. It was also announced that the republic would return to a civilian, constitutional government on May 25, 1973, following elections scheduled for March 25 of that year. President Lanusse, meanwhile, began a complex political maneuver to draw the Perónist movement into a plan for "national pacification." Without the cooperation of the Peronistas, who control Argentina's powerful labor movement and probably one-third of the electorate, there was little chance of an early return to the promised constitutional government.

Economic Downtrend. The business and financial sectors were so shaken by economic uncertainties that investment funds grew scarce, thus contributing to a high level of unemployment. A maze of cumbersome government regulations and interference paralyzed business to an increasing degree. Agriculture also was depressed, and the regime had to ban domestic sales of beef on alternate weeks to rescue the beef export trade. It also ordered special credits to meat-packing firms specializing in exports so they could reopen. As a result, the nation's exports could not pay for the high level of imports, and exchange reserves fell to critically low levels.

Trade Imbalance. In an apparent move to avert a balance-of-payments crisis, the regime in September ordered an almost complete halt in new imports.

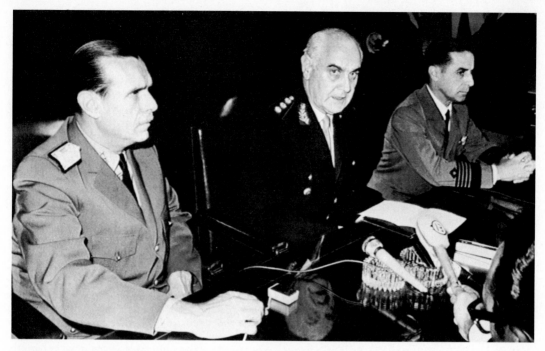

A three-man junta headed by Lieutenant General Alejandro Lanusse, center, assumed power in Argentina in March, 1971. Lanusse was later named president.

But within two weeks of its announcement, it was compelled to issue a long list of exemptions in order to keep the economy moving. During the year, the peso was devalued frequently. The currency shrank some 4 per cent every month, about the same as the rate at which living costs were rising. Argentina introduced a "two-tier" exchange rate for the peso on September 20 in a move to save scarce foreign exchange and help the critical balance of payments problem. One rate resulted in devaluation of the peso over 40 per cent.

During the year, the government approved various projects to stimulate the economy, including the construction of a $300-million Puerto Madryn aluminum plant. The plant will produce up to 165,000 tons per year when completed. It would be the world's ninth largest and South America's biggest. Celulosa Argentina started an $87-million pulp and paper plant expansion. The state-owned Fabricaciones Militares contracted for large-scale copper exploration and mining in the Andean foothills in Neuquén province.

Facts in Brief. Population: 25,079,000. Government: President Alejandro Augustín Lanusse. Monetary Unit: peso. Foreign Trade: exports, $1,775,000,000; imports; $1,710,000,000. Principal Exports: meat, corn, wheat.   Mary C. Webster

ARIZONA. See STATE GOVERNMENT.

ARKANSAS. See STATE GOVERNMENT.

ARMED FORCES OF THE WORLD. Russia challenged the United States ranking as the number-one superpower in 1971. In intercontinental ballistic missiles (ICBM's), the Russians took about a 60 per cent lead over the United States, and they were building Polaris-type missile submarines at the rate of about eight a year. If this rate continues, they were expected to overtake the United States by 1974. Russia was also building about 80 new missile silos. Apparently, these new silos were to be used for advanced ICBM's.

The pace of the Russian build-up puzzled and disturbed U.S. military planners, especially in view of the Strategic Arms Limitation Talks (SALT) that have been going on for more than two years between the United States and Russia. Since a rough level of strategic parity had been reached, U.S. officials had expected the Russians to slow their missile-site construction. But they could not fathom Russian intentions when space satellite photos showed some 20 new ICBM silos larger than the SS-9 and 60 others larger than the SS-11, on ICBM similar to the U.S. Minuteman in size.

The expansion of Russian military power is interpreted by some U.S. military analysts as a bid for supremacy that would enable Russia to exert its influence throughout the world without resorting to warfare. Other analysts believe Russia is trying to establish itself as an equal superpower, but more importantly, as the clearly defined leader of the Communist world.

In spite of the Russian build-up, the first concrete results were produced by the SALT negotiations in 1971. On September 30, Russia and the United States signed agreements aimed at strengthening the Moscow-Washington, D.C., "hot line" and limiting the possibility of an accidental nuclear war.

Russia, U.S. Defenses. Russian strategic forces were still behind those of the United States in deliverable warheads (see table). This was largely because of the U.S. lead in long-range bombers and multiple-warhead missiles.

The Russians, however, had a heavy air defense system with massive radars, more than 3,000 jet in-

The Strategic Balance in 1971

	United States	Russia
ICBM's	1,054	1,600
Polaris-type missile submarines	41	25*
Submarine missiles	656	420
Long-range bombers	550	200
Deliverable nuclear weapons	7,500†	2,500

*With 15 more under construction.
†Includes triple warheads on about 120 Minuteman III ICBM's and 64 missiles with 10 warheads each on Poseidon submarines.

terceptor planes, and 10,000 surface-to-air (SAM) missiles. By comparison, the U.S. force was small, with about 500 interceptors and 900 SAM missiles. The Russian Galosh antiballistic missile (ABM) system, with four complexes totaling 64 missiles, had no counterpart in the United States. The U.S. was still building its Safeguard ABM system.

Russian nuclear forces included 700 medium-range bombers, 400 land-based naval bombers, 5,000 light bombers and fighter bombers, and about 600 medium-range missiles.

Russian Army conventional forces increased during the year to more than 160 divisions, including the reinforced 40 divisions along the Chinese border. The total of 2.2 million Russian troops was about double the size of the U.S. force. The Russian Navy had 220 major warships, 90 nuclear-powered submarines, 265 diesel submarines, and 675 other ships. The U.S. fleet was still credited with superior overall striking power, however, largely because of its 16 aircraft carriers.

Warsaw Pact Nations and NATO. Bulgaria, East Germany, Czechoslovakia, Hungary, Poland, and Romania augmented the 31 Russian divisions in Eastern Europe with 60 divisions and overall ground forces of 800,000 troops. The East European navies had 8 major warships, 470 other ships, 8 diesel submarines, and about 3,000 tactical planes.

The North Atlantic Treaty Organization (NATO) forces were considerably weaker than those of the Warsaw Pact. In central Europe, NATO could muster only about 20 divisions, including 4⅓ U.S. divisions. The Institute for Strategic Studies (ISS) in London estimated that NATO had 7,750 tanks and

2,850 planes against the Warsaw Pact's 21,700 tanks and 5,360 planes. The United States backed NATO with 7,200 tactical nuclear weapons, compared with 3,500 for the Communist bloc.

China's Capability. China may have enough nuclear material for 120 bombs and missiles, and may have at least 30 TU-16 Soviet-type bombers, according to the ISS. American military analysts suspect that China conducted a reduced-range ICBM test late in 1970 and would be able to deploy such missiles as early as 1973. By the end of 1971, the Chinese already had a small number of medium-range nuclear weapons. They were producing the TU-16 jet bombers and reportedly were building a nuclear submarine.

China had the largest army in the world—more than 140 divisions with 2.6 million ground troops.

Comparative Military Manpower

	United States	Russia	Communist China
Army	1,050,423	2,200,000	2,600,000
Navy	826,952*	450,000	150,000
Air Force	755,855	800,000†	180,000
Total	2,627,230	3,450,000	2,930,000

*Includes 204,045 Marines as of Sept. 30, 1971
†Includes strategic rocket force of 350,000.

The Chinese also had more than 4,000 planes (mostly jet fighters) and 870 warships. Most of the ships were small. They included about 40 attack submarines and several dozen missile patrol boats.

According to U.S. military analysts, China could mount major offensives against Russia, South Korea, India, and countries in Southeast Asia. However, the Chinese Army would be handicapped by supply and transportation problems if it tried to fight on more than one front.

Other Asian Countries. North Korea had the equivalent of 25 divisions with 360,000 troops. There were 600 tactical fighter planes in the North Korean Air Force, plus some light bombers, transports, and helicopters. The navy had 150 ships, most of them motor torpedo boats and missile patrol boats. It had four small submarines.

North Vietnam had about 13 divisions with some 315,000 troops within its borders. There were also 100,000 North Vietnamese and Viet Cong in South Vietnam, 125,000 in Laos, and 60,000 in Cambodia. The navy had about 40 gun and torpedo boats; the air force, about 200 jet fighters.

South Korea had 20 divisions, with 600,000 troops, and more than 200 planes. Formosa (Taiwan) had 16 divisions, with a potential of 600,000 troops, and 400 planes. There were 480,000 troops in South Vietnam's regular armed forces, plus 700,000 in paramilitary forces. Cambodia had 200,000 troops, but not all were armed or trained.   Lloyd Norman

ARMY, U.S. See NATIONAL DEFENSE.

ART. See ARCHITECTURE; DANCING; LITERATURE; MUSIC, CLASSICAL; POETRY; VISUAL ARTS.

ASIA

The outbreak of a new war – and the new direction taken by an old one – made Asia the focus of world attention in 1971. The new war erupted between India and Pakistan early in December. It was not just political in its ramifications; it had religious and ethnic overtones as well (see Close-Up). The fact that it lasted only two weeks belied the ferocity with which it was fought. See INDIA; PAKISTAN; UNITED NATIONS (UN).

The old war, which found North and South Vietnam still locked in combat after two decades, nevertheless moved in a new direction as the South Vietnamese Army assumed greater responsibility and more autonomy in its pursuit of the enemy. It was in this latter context that 1971 would also be recorded as the year in which the West began a major withdrawal from direct military involvement in Asian problems. Throughout the year, the United States and Great Britain, joined by Australia and New Zealand, coordinated their actions in reducing their commitments to a number of Asian nations. Conversely, the year also marked the emergence of the People's Republic of China as a major power on the international scene. The reduction of the Western presence in Asia paired with the emergence of China had tremendous repercussions throughout Asia and the world.

Western Withdrawal, which was led by the United States, took several forms. The most obvious one was the military withdrawal from the mainland of Asia. Vietnam, where the largest component of Western forces were concentrated, witnessed a continuing pullout of Western troops. The cutback in the number of U.S. military personnel stationed there reduced U.S. strength to 157,000 troops as of December 31. Similarly, Australian and New Zealand units – except for small wind-up forces – had been removed from South Vietnam by the end of the year.

But the withdrawals were not limited to Vietnam. American military personnel stationed at bases in Thailand were sharply reduced. American forces operating unofficially in Laos were also pulled out. Nor was the withdrawal limited to the Indochinese peninsula. Huge American bases in the Philippines had their manpower reduced, and in some cases the bases themselves were turned over to the Philippines. Most U.S. bases on Formosa (Taiwan) reverted to the Chinese Nationalists in 1971, and only a skeletal U.S. Air Force unit remained.

The United States had assured South Korea that there would be no reduction in American forces there until the republic was ready to shoulder the increasing burden of defense. Because this requirement was evidently being met, however, some American units were pulled out during the year, leaving about 40,000 U.S. troops. While a contingent of American troops would remain on Okinawa, the island was to revert to Japan in July, 1972, and American forces would be reduced. Similarly, Britain, once responsible for the huge naval base at Singapore, made its final exit, though it maintained certain defense commitments in the area with Australia and New Zealand.

Economic Actions. Even as the Western powers were pulling their military forces back to various

Indian troops, obeying a cease-fire order in the India-Pakistan war, pass one of their own tanks destroyed during a major battle in East Pakistan.

Pacific island strongholds, reductions were also being effected in the economic sphere. Ever since 1945, the United States and other Western powers had poured an immense amount of capital into Asia in an effort to promote economic development and stability. But America's own economic position and its increasingly serious balance-of-payments deficit forced a change in 1971. In September, a restive U.S. Congress defeated the Administration-proposed foreign-aid legislation that contained approximately $1 billion in aid for the Asian countries. Although the foreign aid program was later extended until February, 1972, it appeared that the end result would be a marked decrease in the amounts available for Asia.

The United States faced up to the growing problem of Japan in the economic sphere. In August, after years of trying to persuade Japan to exercise some restraints on its U.S.-bound exports, to ease restrictions on the import of U.S. goods, and to revalue the yen, the United States took a drastic step. It placed a 10 per cent surcharge on all imports and demanded that the Japanese allow the yen to float freely in relation to other world currencies. The Japanese protested sharply that this would mean an upward valuation of the yen.

After the December dollar devaluation, however, the Japanese yen was revalued upward by 8 per cent and both the Japanese and European trading partners of the United States agreed to trading concessions in exchange for dropping of the import sur-

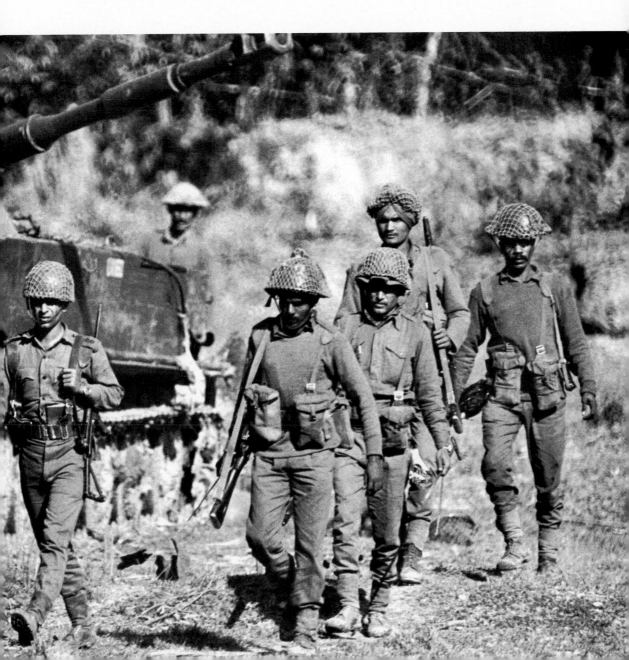

The Seeds
Of Prejudice

A brief but brutal war erupted between India and Pakistan on Dec. 3, 1971, and out of the carnage rose a new country – Bangla Desh. Power politics were undoubtedly part of the cause, but there were two basic issues that have bedeviled the Asian subcontinent for centuries: religious hatred and ethnic rivalry.

The issue of religion arose as far back as A.D. 700, when the Moslems who invaded India sought to suppress the Hinduism already entrenched there. The ethnic question has existed since about 1500 B.C., when light-skinned Aryans who migrated to India set up social barriers between themselves and the darker-skinned Dravidians who already occupied the land. Both issues have repeatedly thwarted all efforts by subsequent rulers to weld the nation's people into one unified nation, beginning with Alexander the Great in 326 B.C. and extending through Great Britain, which took over rule in India in 1858. The reli-

Divided Pakistan

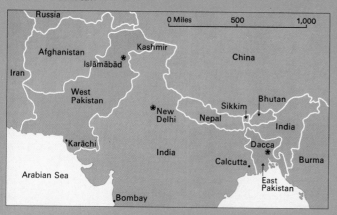

gious and race issues also played a major role in Britain's decision to grant India its independence in 1947.

The Indians began clamoring for independence during World War II, and Britain agreed to grant it. The only question was when and in what form. Here the trouble began. The British wanted to free a unified India. So did the all-powerful Congress Party of India, which was predominantly Hindu. The second major party, the

Moslem League, also wanted freedom. But it made no bones about representing, exclusively, the interests of the Moslems. It maintained that the Congress Party – because of its Hindu orientation – would continue to dominate and exploit the Moslems. To end this dominance, the Moslem League demanded that a separate Moslem state be created. It insisted that the new state – to be called Pakistan – be carved from those parts of India where Moslems were in the majority.

The British, in the face of mounting tensions and the threat of a civil war, abruptly accepted the league's demands and created a separate state in 1947. Half of Punjab province was set aside for the western portion of Pakistan; half of Bengal became the eastern portion. Unfortunately, this "partition" solved nothing. In the first nine months of independence, about 6 million Hindus and Sikhs fled from Pakistan to India, and about 7 million Moslems fled from India to Pakistan, as unbridled religious persecution broke out. Within months, too, India and Pakistan were at war over Kashmir, a territory whose population was 80 per cent Moslem but whose ruler was a Hindu.

Nor did the uneasy peace that followed end the explosive problem. The new nation of Pakistan itself was riddled with bigotry. West Pakistan included among its people such ethnic groups as the Punjabis and Pathans. Tall, erect, light-skinned, and martial in outlook, they speak Urdu, prefer wheat to rice, and feel an affinity for the Moslems of nearby Arab countries. By contrast, the Bengalis of East Pakistan (now the newly proclaimed state of Bangla Desh) are dark-skinned and shorter in stature. They speak Sanskritized Bengali and feel closer to the Hindu Bengalese in neighboring India, a feeling that is reciprocated in India.

Thus, East Pakistan's pursuit of autonomy in 1971, and India's support of it, were only manifestations of the same religious and ethnic divisions that have set Indian against Indian throughout history. The seeds planted in 1500 B.C. and A.D. 700 continued to blossom and bear fruit in India – and Pakistan – in 1971.   Paul C. Tullier

East Pakistani refugees, fleeing from the civil war between West Pakistan and Bengalis early in 1971, head for India with their few, paltry belongings.

charge and the 7 per cent "buy American" investment tax credit. See INTERNATIONAL TRADE AND FINANCE.

Diplomatic Maneuvers. United States moves in the military and economic fields were more than matched by a major change in American foreign policy in Asia. It began on April 10, with a weeklong visit to China by an American Ping-Pong team, and continued with a secret visit to Peking, July 9 to 11, by the President's assistant on national security, Henry A. Kissinger. Talks between Kissinger and Chinese Premier Chou En-lai, the second-most-powerful leader in China, led to a startling announcement by President Richard M. Nixon. On July 15, the President announced to an international television audience that the talks had taken place and that, because of the frank and cordial exchange, he would make an unprecedented visit to Peking before May, 1972, to continue such exchanges. The major thrust of the talks would be an effort by both sides to establish more normal relations between China and the United States (see PRESIDENT OF THE UNITED STATES). The United States, as part of that effort, announced later in the year that it would no longer oppose China's admission to the United Nations (UN).

The "China question" was quickly put on the agenda of the UN when it convened in September. The United States had favored and tried to win sup-

port for a policy under which the Peking government would occupy a seat in the Security Council and the Nationalist Chinese would be represented by a seat in the General Assembly. The Communist Chinese, however, had made it clear that they would not accept membership in the UN on such a basis and in the final vote the Peking regime was seated. The Chinese Nationalists were expelled. See FORMOSA (TAIWAN); UNITED NATIONS (UN).

China's emergence as a member of the UN – and the American withdrawals and accommodations – stimulated large-scale diplomatic shuffling among the Asian nations. Thailand, the Asian hub of the South East Asia Treaty Organization and a nation long considered a bastion of anti-Communism, began making overtures to Peking. Both Nepal and Malaysia sent special trade missions to the Chinese capital. Japan, although caught off guard by the Nixon announcement, quickly readied a number of trade missions to China; Japanese Prime Minister Eisaku Sato began to face up to the importance of a peace treaty with China. Among the Western nations, Canada not only continued to expand its own trade with China, but also on occasion helped stimulate China's contacts with the rest of the West.

The Indochina Fighting. China's new role, however, did not mean that peace had arrived in Asia. Fighting not only continued on the continent in 1971, but it also expanded.

221

ASIA

The most enduring of the conflicts remained in Vietnam and the countries contiguous to it. Throughout the year, the Army of the Republic of (South) Vietnam (ARVN) demonstrated new-found military muscle in a variety of ways. To bolster the Cambodians, the ARVN made several incursions to protect the Cambodian capital of Phnom Penh from Viet Cong attacks and safeguard the all-important Route 1 connecting Phnom Penh with Saigon, South Vietnam's capital.

Early in 1971, the South Vietnamese launched a major drive into southeastern Laos, in an effort to cut the complex Ho Chih Minh trail, a Communist supply route leading into the south. The intensity of the Communist response to this move indicated the importance they placed on defeating the strategy. Although the South Vietnamese were forced to withdraw a few weeks ahead of the timetable they had originally set, they inflicted such extensive damage to this basic Communist supply artery that it effectively stalled the possibility of a major Communist offensive for the rest of the year.

Although the move into Laos provoked an adverse reaction among many nations, the move was in effect merely an acknowledgment that the war in Vietnam had always involved both Laos and Cambodia. The South Vietnamese, by their action, also made it clear that neither Cambodia nor Laos would be permitted to serve as privileged Communist sanctuaries in the future. American air power continued to support such efforts and made occasional strikes at selected targets in North Vietnam. The air attacks were stepped up for four days late in December. The Paris peace talks ground on in 1971 without any breakthroughs on such all-important questions as the release of U.S. prisoners of war or a definite date for total U.S. withdrawal.

Elsewhere in Asia, civil conflicts were much in evidence during the year. Sporadic Communist guerrilla activities cropped up in Malaysia, Thailand, and Burma. More serious fighting erupted in April in Ceylon, where a rebel group aligning itself with the Maoist movement and North Korea attacked the government of Prime Minister Sirimavo Bandaranaike. The government forces suppressed the rebels, but only after bitter fighting and widespread terrorist activities.

The most bitter civil conflict, which finally broadened into an international war, was one involving, first, East and West Pakistan, and eventually India.

The crisis was rooted in separatist sentiment prevalent in East Pakistan, where the Bengalis sought greater autonomy from West Pakistan, which firmly opposed it. On March 25, Sheik Mujibur Rahman, head of East Pakistan's Awami League, called for separation from West Pakistan and the creation of a new nation to be known as Bangla Desh. Within 24 hours, West Pakistani troops had moved into East Pakistan, arrested Mujibur Rahman, and launched

Thousands of sympathizers give their ardent support to a demonstration organized in Washington, D.C., in April, 1971, by the Vietnam Veterans Against the War.

fierce attacks on such major cities as Dacca, Jessore, and Chittagong. The violence was such that a flood of between 6 and 8 million East Pakistani refugees poured into neighboring India.

International relief supplies forwarded to India for refugee aid proved hopelessly inadequate, and in June, India again called for international intervention to help stop the anti-Bengali pillage in East Pakistan. India, meanwhile, was secretly aiding the guerrilla forces of Bangla Desh, whose independence it favored. Its troops, too, clashed more and more frequently with the West Pakistani forces along the border. On December 3, all restraint ended; six Indian divisions crossed East Pakistan's borders and began a drive to dislodge the Pakistani troops from their strongholds. Pakistan struck back in the west, driving hard into Kashmir, long an area of contention between India and Pakistan. In the war in Kashmir, Pakistan heavily damaged Indian positions. On December 16, Pakistani troops in East Pakistan – badly outnumbered and cut off from West Pakistan – were forced to surrender. Indian troops had taken Dacca, the capital, as well as most of the major cities.

Largely because of Pakistan's defeat by India, President Agha Mohammed Yahya Khan was forced to resign. On December 20, Zulfikar Ali Bhutto was sworn in as president and martial-law administrator of Pakistan, returning the nation to civilian rule for the first time since 1958. One of his first acts was to order the retirement of General YahyaKhan. In East Pakistan, India announced that the area, which it referred to as Bangla Desh, was free and independent of West Pakistan. East Pakistani leader Mujibur Rahman was named head of the new nation.

Although the Indian-Pakistani war dominated the headlines in the latter part of 1971, other major events were happening far from the fighting. In the capitals of the major powers – the United States, Russia, China, and Japan – diplomatic maneuvers were taking place that might determine the fate of Asia. While Japan had military power to compare with that of the other three powers, its undisputed economic capacity was indeed a major force to be considered in Asia. Japan continued to depend on the United States as its defensive shield, but there were signs among the Big Three of an increasing willingness to accept a larger build-up of Japan's armed forces as well as greater Japanese responsibility for its defense. A rearmed Japan with its great industrial capacity would introduce a new component in Asia that might counterbalance the dominance of Russia and China.

The cordial reception given by the Chinese to the U.S. gestures in 1971 may have been prompted by continuing Chinese concern over its border problems with Russia. As the Chinese and Americans gingerly moved toward one another, Russia and Japan began more serious talks, and the Sato government sought increased understanding from both China and America. While China and Japan jockeyed for positions, the two superpowers, Russia and the United States, began what could be termed both advances and withdrawals. United States troop withdrawals from Asia were being balanced by a quiet but steady build-up in Pacific bases. While some troop withdrawals were projected for the North Atlantic Treaty Organization forces in Europe, it was hoped these would be balanced by a reduction in Russian force levels in the Warsaw Pact nations. Considerable hope was seen, too, in the steady progress being made in the Strategic Arms Limitation Talks between Russia and the United States to limit the missile race. See ARMED FORCES OF THE WORLD.

The major obstacle to a possible agreement between Russia and the United States was the enormous build-up taking place in the Russian Navy. For the first time in history, Russian naval units regularly cruised the Indian Ocean. In the Pacific, considered an American lake since 1945, Russian naval units held maneuvers regularly, even venturing within eyesight of Hawaii, the U.S. defensive bastion. Submarine activity on both sides quickened as hunt-and-seek missions became commonplace. There was an ominous quality in the placid waters of the Pacific, and it reflected the tensions and agonies of the world's most populous region – Asia.   John N. Stalker

See also the various Asian country articles.

ASTRONAUTS made two successful moon landings in 1971. *Apollo 14* astronauts Alan B. Shepard, Jr., and Edgar D. Mitchell spent 33½ hours on the lunar surface in February, while Stuart A. Roosa orbited overhead. The 12-day *Apollo 15* mission in July and August was an outstanding success. Astronauts David R. Scott and James B. Irwin conducted scientific experiments on the moon, and Alfred M. Worden took photographs and measurements from lunar orbit. See SPACE EXPLORATION.

Scientist Named. Thirteen of the 45 astronauts on flight status with the National Aeronautics and Space Administration (NASA) in 1971 were scientist-astronauts. Following the significant scientific achievements of *Apollo 15*, NASA responded to demands from the scientific community by assigning the first scientist-astronaut to the prime crew of a manned space flight. Harrison H. (Jack) Schmitt, a 36-year-old geologist from Santa Rita, N. Mex., was named lunar module pilot for *Apollo 17*, the last flight of the Apollo series, scheduled for the summer of 1972. Schmitt replaced pilot-astronaut Joe H. Engle, famed test pilot of the X-15 rocket plane, on a crew that had trained together for two years.

Selection of the last Apollo crew left 26 astronauts without space experience or a flight assignment. These men must compete for nine additional assignments on three earth-orbital missions to be flown on

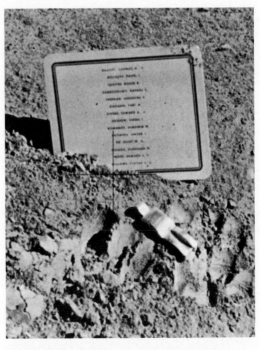

Apollo 15 astronauts David R. Scott and James B. Irwin left this plaque on the moon in memory of the 14 astronauts and cosmonauts who have lost their lives.

the Skylab program in 1972 and 1973. No other manned space missions are presently planned.

Tragedy Struck the Russian space program on June 30, when three astronauts were killed in *Soyuz 11*, a space ferry that carried them to a *Salyut* space station. Georgi T. Dobrovolsky, Vladislav N. Volkov, and Viktor I. Patsayev died when their craft re-entered the earth's atmosphere after setting a 24-day endurance record for space flight. The deaths were apparently caused by improper sealing of the spacecraft hatch after leaving the space station.

Personnel Changes. Edwin E. (Buzz) Aldrin, Jr., who walked on the moon during the *Apollo 11* mission, left the astronaut corps in July to take command of the Air Force's Aerospace Research Pilot School at Edwards Air Force Base in California. He was the last of the three-man crew of the historic *Apollo 11* mission to leave the astronaut corps. Neil A. Armstrong, who quit in 1970, became a University of Cincinnati engineering professor in August.

James A. Lovell, Jr., left active flight status in May to become Deputy Director of Science and Applications at the Manned Spacecraft Center in Houston. Walter Cunningham, who spent 11 days in earth orbit on the first manned Apollo flight (*Apollo 7*), resigned in June to go into private business. Thomas P. Stafford was named Deputy Director of Flight Crew Operations at the Manned Spacecraft Center in June. William J. Cromie

ASTRONOMY. Three California research institutions gathered new data in 1971 on a hidden galaxy. Scientists from the University of California at Berkeley, the Hale Observatories, and the California Institute of Technology reported that interstellar dust has long obscured one of the brightest of the nearby galaxies. It is 1 of about 17, called the Local Group, that appear to be bound together by gravity. Until this year, only two of them, the Milky Way and the spiral nebula in Andromeda, were known to be large, bright, massive stellar systems. The rest are fainter collections of stars that act as satellites to the two dominant members.

The newly discovered galaxy, which is called Maffei 1 because it is the first entry in a catalog compiled by Italian astrophysicist Paolo Maffei, is a slightly flattened elliptical system of perhaps 100 billion stars. It is about 3 million light-years away, which places it at the edge of the Local Group. The galaxy is moving away from us with such speed that it is probably only a temporary neighbor, not a permanent member, of the Local Group.

View from *Uhuru*. Throughout 1971, new data on X-ray stars were gathered by a 300-pound satellite observatory put into orbit around the earth on Dec. 12, 1970. The observatory was launched from a platform in the Indian Ocean off the coast of Kenya on the seventh anniversary of Kenya's independence, so it was named *Uhuru*, the Swahili word for freedom.

This was the first satellite devoted exclusively to observing cosmic X-ray sources. The earth's atmosphere blocks out X rays, so astronomers can observe them only through rockets and satellites that are orbited above the atmosphere. Previous observations from sounding rockets had shown that there are many X-ray sources in our galaxy, but each rocket provided only a few minutes of observing time before it re-entered the atmosphere. *Uhuru* provides longer and repeated observations of known sources and enables scientists to look for new sources.

Many new X-ray sources have now been discovered within the Milky Way and in other galaxies. A nearby object in the constellation Cygnus fluctuates in intensity and may be emitting X-ray flashes once each 73 thousandths of a second. An exploding galaxy far beyond the Perseus constellation is radiating as much energy in the hitherto unobservable X-ray form as it does in visible light that can be observed from earth.

Organic Molecules. In past years, there have been several reports of organic molecules found in meteorites. Most such reports were dismissed or attributed to contamination of the meteorite after it landed on the ground. But a new investigation by Cyril Ponnamperuma of the Ames Research Center of the National Aeronautics and Space Administration at Moffett Field, California, has revealed the first case where the organic material almost certainly was present in the meteor before it entered the earth's atmosphere.

The Murchison meteorite was recovered shortly after it fell near Victoria, Australia, on Sept. 28, 1969. Chemical analysis of its interior indicated 18 different amino acids, 6 of which are found in living cells. Contamination is ruled out because of the unusual mixture of molecular structures. Subsequent work on a meteorite that fell near Murray, Ky., in September, 1950, revealed the same amino acids.

Radio astronomers continued to expand the list of chemical molecules found by observing energy waves from interstellar clouds. They have revealed the presence of 21 molecules so far. Various combinations of hydrogen, carbon, nitrogen, oxygen, and sulfur have been detected. To date, the most complex molecule found has been methylacetylene, CH_3C_2H.

Promethium. Some peculiar stars with surface temperatures of about 18,000°F. have unusually large amounts of rare elements. They are especially rich in heavy elements such as silicon, chromium, europium, manganese, and platinum. Little is known about the source of these elements or the reason for their being in these stars. Now, astronomers at the University of Michigan have heightened the mystery with their discovery of promethium in a bright star, HR 465.

Promethium is an unstable element that quickly decays by emitting a beta particle from its nucleus. The average lifetime for the longest-lived form of

The world's largest movable radio telescope, which stands on the Eifel Plateau near Bonn, West Germany, began operating in May. It weighs about 3,200 tons.

promethium is less than 18 years. Such an element could not have survived since the star was formed millions or billions of years ago, so the star must have manufactured the element recently.

Normally, a star fuses light nuclei into heavier ones in its extremely hot interior. Scientists do not believe, however, that these elements are mixed and brought to the surface layers. The discovery of such a highly unstable element as promethium suggests that stars are capable of forming elements in their surface layers as well as in their interiors by some process that is not yet understood.

Pluto. Estimates of the mass of the small, distant planet Pluto have been steadily decreasing. The latest estimate, made in 1971 by the U.S. Naval Observatory in Washington, D.C., indicates that Pluto has a mass about one-tenth that of the earth. This would make the planet similar in mass and density to Mars. It is quite unlike the other outer planets, Jupiter, Saturn, Uranus, and Neptune, which are much larger and more massive. The new data tend to strengthen the belief that Pluto is an escaped satellite of Neptune.

Clouds of Venus. The clouds around Venus were measured in 1971 by a new technique developed by astronomers at Harvard University and the Smithsonian Astrophysical Observatory. Nathaniel Carleton, Wesley Traub, and Richard Wattson were attempting to determine the structure and compo-

sition of these clouds. With their specially designed spectrometer, they were able to measure the exact shapes of the spectral lines formed in the atmosphere of Venus. Their results indicated the existence of layering in the clouds.

In other studies of the planet, James E. Hansen and Albert Arking of the Institute for Space Studies in New York City found that the planet's cloud particles must be spherical, probably liquid, and have a refractive index of between 1.43 and 1.47. No known material fits these specifications, according to Hansen and Arking, so they could not determine the nature of the matter that forms the clouds of Venus. Their study included a detailed mathematical analysis of a large amount of data on the polarization of light from Venus collected in recent years.

Project Astra. One of the prime concerns of astronomers is the accurate measurement of light from stars. Starlight is absorbed and scattered by its passage through the earth's atmosphere. Because smog and dust decrease the transparency of the sky, making the stars appear fainter from the ground, astronomers have had to develop techniques to provide an index of the level of air pollution near observatory sites.

Paul W. Hodge of the University of Washington has now applied this astronomical know-how to air pollution studies. He heads Project Astra, designed to investigate the long-range changes in atmospheric transmission over the Mount Wilson Observatory near Pasadena, Calif. Hodge found that the sky had become measurably more opaque during the 50 years between 1911 and 1961. A vertical column of air over the observatory now transmits approximately 10 per cent less light in the yellow and blue range of the spectrum and 20 per cent less light in the ultraviolet range than it did in 1911. This comparison is all the more striking because the 1961 data were taken on nights that were chosen because they were smog-free.

Gum Nebula. In 1955, astronomer Colin S. Gum of Australia discovered a nearby complex of interstellar gas on photographs of the Southern Hemisphere constellations Vela and Pupis. At the time, this was considered just another example of gas glowing from the radiation of hot stars. The discovery of a pulsar, a rapidly flashing radio star, in the same general direction renewed interest in the Gum Nebula. Pulsars are currently regarded as rotating, extremely dense neutron stars that result from gigantic stellar explosions. In February, 1971, a group from the Goddard Space Flight Center and the Kitt Peak National Observatory proposed that the Gum Nebula was formed from a supernova explosion that generated the Vela pulsar. They theorized that the explosion occurred about 10,000 years ago, and that the light we now see is "fossil" radiation from that outburst. Laura P. Bautz

ATOMIC ENERGY. See ENERGY.

Former Australian Prime Minister John Gorton, left, ousted in a no-confidence vote, stands with his successor William McMahon, right, outside Parliament House.

AUSTRALIA. A crisis brought on by the resignation of a cabinet minister cost Prime Minister John G. Gorton his post in 1971. Gorton was ousted by his own Liberal Party, and William McMahon was sworn in as prime minister on March 10.

Gorton's government had survived a no-confidence motion in Parliament on its handling of the economy by a 57 to 52 vote on February 18. However, another no-confidence motion on March 10 resulted in Gorton's deposition both as prime minister and as leader of the Liberal Party. The motion was triggered by the resignation of Defense Minister Malcolm Fraser on March 8. Fraser had accused Gorton of failing to uphold him in a dispute involving a high-ranking army official who, in a newspaper article, had accused Fraser of "disloyalty" to the army. Fraser, who knew that Gorton had seen the letter before publication, concluded that Gorton supported the army. By its no-confidence vote, the Parliament agreed with Fraser.

On May 27, Prime Minister McMahon announced the creation of a new ministry for environment, aborigines, and the arts – thus increasing the government ministry to 27 departments. Peter Howson was named to the newly created post.

Fighting Inflation. As prime minister, Gorton had tried to control the cost of living, which had increased by 5 per cent over a 12-month period ending on March 1, 1971. Although Gorton resisted pressures to introduce new or higher taxes, or impose price controls, he did issue orders designed to curb both federal and state-level government spending. Restrictions were also placed on private investment projects, especially those involving the construction of large building complexes. The government cut its own expenditures by $85 million during the year, with the biggest cut involving a $23.3-million allocation originally scheduled for defense spending. Funds allocated for Australia's immigration program were cut back in May. By cutting its immigration target for fiscal 1972 from 180,000 to 140,000, the government expected to save about $7.3 million in passage money it provides to assist immigrants.

National Defense. Early in 1971, the government announced that Australian, British, and New Zealand military forces to be stationed in the Malaysia-Singapore region would be organized as a combined force under an Australian commander. It was also announced that the Australian and British navies would share submarine patrol duty in the Malaysia-Singapore region following a scheduled pullout of British land forces in 1972.

Between March 30 and June 30, 1,000 Australian service personnel were withdrawn from South Vietnam. The withdrawals left about 6,000 Australian forces in South Vietnam. Australian air force jet bombers ended four years of service in South Vietnam on May 31.

Labor Problems. A three-week strike by 2,000 Qantas Airways ground crewmen at Sydney Airport ended on January 29 when the 14 unions involved agreed to return to work pending final settlement by an arbitration board. The strike started on January 7 with the dismissal of a shop steward who had allegedly threatened apprentices with expulsion from the Amalgamated Engineering Union if they did not observe a union overtime ban.

The Australian Council of Trade Unions continued to press for a 35-hour, four-day workweek in some industries. In July, coal mine workers in New South Wales, Queensland, and Tasmania changed over to the 35-hour week. About 14,000 miners at 80 collieries as well as 4,000 clerical and administrative employees were affected by the changeover.

On April 18, the world's first laser beam lighthouse was officially opened at Point Danger, Southport, Queensland. The new facility offers ships at sea better visibility during inclement weather and it also costs less to maintain and operate than the conventional lighthouse.

Australia's first direct air link with Russia was inaugurated on April 1 through a new service offered by Thai International Airlines. Initially, flights would be made once a week from Sydney to Moscow via Bangkok. Meanwhile, French engineers were studying the feasibility of installing aerotrain systems that would link the centers of Australia's major cities with their airports. The trains would operate on elevated steel or concrete beams at speeds of about 100 miles an hour. A pilot project was planned to link downtown Melbourne with its new international jetport, Tullamarine, located north of the city.

Mineral Production. In midyear, plans were announced for the development of one of eastern Australia's biggest copper lodes, a 7-million-ton deposit at Tarago, near Lake George. Two U.S.-owned companies were to carry out the mining operations.

A large deposit of a rare mineral, tantalite, was discovered in northeastern Victoria. The metal extract, tantalum, is exceptionally resistant to heat, having a melting point of 2996° C. Some 39 tons of the extracted metal were exported to the United States in 1971.

The ministry of mines and mining announced in October that over a 10-year period, mining companies had spent $471.6 million on new rail and road work, as well as town and community facilities associated with mining ventures. An additional $316.3 million was spent for mine development and ore handling. Export income from minerals reached about $1.1 billion in 1970-1971.

Facts in Brief. Population: 13,049,000. Government: Governor General Sir Paul M. C. Hasluck; Prime Minister William McMahon. Monetary Unit: Australian dollar. Foreign Trade: exports, $4,766,-000,000; imports, $5,096,000,000. Principal Exports: wool, wheat, meat.   Paul C. Tullier

AUSTRIA. Chancellor Bruno Kreisky and his Socialist Party won an absolute majority in parliament in elections held on Oct. 10, 1971. The Socialists won 93 seats in the National Assembly, a majority of 1 over the total for the conservative People's Party and Freedom Party. The election was the first in Austria's democratic history to give one party an absolute majority in the Assembly. Kreisky quickly announced he would not seek a coalition with the Freedom Party. Socialist President Franz Jonas had won re-election April 25 in what was regarded as a political good omen for Kreisky. In July, the Socialists cut the period of compulsory military service from nine months to six, abolished the privileged status of police and uniformed municipal employees, raised family allowances, and reduced some taxes.

Revaluation. On May 9, the government raised the value of the schilling 5.05 per cent. Industrial leaders had wanted a 3 per cent rise. The change hurt trade with Yugoslavia and countries of the Council for Mutual Economic Assistance, the East European trade group. Minister of Finance Hannes Androsch drafted measures, accepted by the Assembly, to help exporters. They included rebates to promote exports.

South Tyrol Accord. A 50-year-old dispute between Austria and Italy, born of the World War I peace terms and the breakup of Austria-Hungary, ended on July 18. The foreign ministers of the two countries signed a document concerning the Trentino-Alto Adige, a German-speaking region of South Tyrol in northern Italy. The settlement gives the region considerable legislative and administrative autonomy and provides for maintenance of its mainly German culture. Any disputes are to go before the International Court at The Hague. In 1969, Italy had promised autonomy for the area by 1974. The pact ended almost 10 years of terrorist activity by German-speaking separatists in which 37 lives were lost.

Boom Slackens. The intense business activity of the preceding two years slowed in 1971, but with no threat of a serious recession. Austria's gross national product, which increased by 7 per cent in 1970, grew about half that amount in the first half of 1971. Major problems were a growing trade deficit and inflationary pressures. On July 22, Austria told the European Community (Common Market) that it accepted the Common Market proposal for free trade in industrial goods in a widened market, but asked for a special arrangement for agricultural trade. Austria is one of the six members of the European Free Trade Association that have not applied for Common Market membership.

Facts in Brief. Population: 7,482,000. Government: President Franz Jonas; Chancellor Bruno Kreisky. Monetary Unit: schilling. Foreign Trade: exports, $2,857,000,000; imports, $3,549,000,000. Principal Exports: iron and steel.   Kenneth Brown

AUTOMOBILE. New-car sales in the United States in 1971 topped the 10-million mark for the first time in history. Automakers set the new high despite a host of problems, including safety and ecology issues and high taxes.

Final sales totals reached 10,155,411 cars. This included 1.5 million imports, the most foreign cars ever sold in the United States. The previous record was 9.8 million sold in 1968.

The big three U.S. manufacturers – Ford Motor Company, Chrysler Corporation, and General Motors Corporation (GM) – predicted another record in 1972. They estimated sales would total between 10.5 and 11 million vehicles.

Production in U.S. auto plants for 1971 totaled 8,580,311 cars, the most since 1968's 8,848,000. Free World car and truck sales set a record at 29.5 million in 1971. The strength of the overseas auto market was shown not only in sales in those countries, but also in the sales of foreign products in the United States. The U.S. battle to slow down the imports had some success as foreign makers got a smaller percentage of the market.

American carmakers faced up to the challenge of the imports in 1971. GM touted its Vega, Ford its Pinto, and American Motors Corporation (AMC) its Gremlin, all subcompacts. Chrysler brought in two subcompacts manufactured overseas, the Cricket and the Colt. More customers bought Volkswagens, however, than any of the domestic manufacturers' subcompacts.

Toyota Motor Sales Company said it reached agreement with a U.S. manufacturer to begin in late 1971 to build some parts for small Toyota trucks and to complete their assembly. Nissan Motor Company, another Japanese manufacturer, said in November it was seeking to conclude a similar arrangement. Import duties were much lower on trucks valued under $1,000, so foreign makers sought ways to import them while their value was below the limit.

The 1972 Models. Virtually all the 1972 cars looked like the 1971 models. With large industry allocations to the auto safety field, the reduction of air pollution, and the testing of equipment for future cars, styling changes were held to a minimum.

The decline in the use of convertibles continued. Neither Chrysler nor American Motors offered any in their 1972 models. GM offered 13, compared with 16 for 1971, and Ford had 4, compared with 5 for 1971. The new emphasis was on sliding sun roofs.

The effectiveness of bumpers got major attention in the 1972 models, and will get even more in 1973, when a new and tough federal safety standard takes effect. Beginning with the 1973s, the front bumper must withstand a 5-mile-per-hour (mph) impact against a barrier, and rear bumpers a 2½-mph impact, without damage to safety components, such as lights and door latches. The standard will be even tougher for 1974. Test crashes against barriers are considered especially severe since barriers are virtually unyielding while another car in a highway crash would yield somewhat as it is crushed.

Another problem confronting auto manufacturers is the issue of exhaust pollution. The 1972s claim an 80 per cent reduction in unburned hydrocarbons and 65 to 70 per cent less carbon monoxide than from the 1960 models.

As a result, U.S. automakers talked less in 1971 about "hot" engines and powerful "muscle" cars. Instead, they discussed their gains in emission control. They also stressed the fact that virtually all 1972 engines run well on low-lead or nonlead gasoline instead of on premium fuels. They conceded, for the most part, that there was a slight sacrifice of fuel economy and overall power.

Warranties came in for some attention in the 1972s. American Motors gave buyers an unprecedented unconditional guarantee for 12 months or 12,000 miles on all parts of the car. Only tires, which are covered by a separate warranty, were excepted. Other firms kept their 12-month-or-12,000-mile policy in effect. It covered the power train and many parts of the car, but was not as broad as AMC's coverage.

In March, the Federal Trade Commission (FTC) joined in support of a proposed Senate bill that would improve warranties for automobiles and other products. A key section specified that warranties

Imported v. Domestic Car Sales

Millions of dollars

*1971 figures are for 10 months.
Source: U.S. Department of Commerce

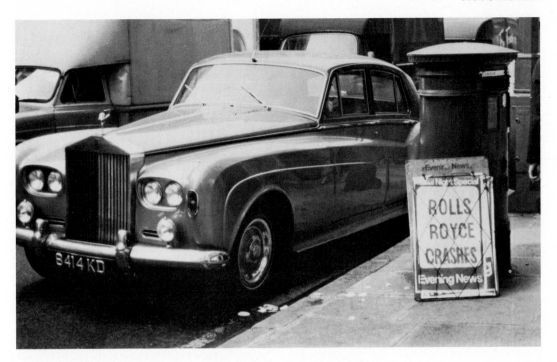

An international symbol of luxury – a Rolls-Royce – is parked at the curb behind
a London newspaper bulletin board headlining the collapse of the automobile firm.

would be labeled "Full Warranty" only if they provided for free repair or replacement of products or parts that had failed. Any that provided lesser or more restricted protection would be labeled merely "Partial Warranty," giving buyers an opportunity to distinguish them easily. The Nixon Administration, instead, proposed a version that would label all such agreements simply "Warranty."

The Senate passed the stricter version on November 9 with some amendments that broadened its coverage. The FTC said passage in 1972 in the House of Representatives seemed likely.

Experimental Engines. After more than 10 years of talk, large numbers of cars driven by rotary-piston engines reached the United States. Mazda Motors of America, a subsidiary of Toyo Kogyo of Japan, estimated U.S. customers bought 13,000 Japanese-built rotary-piston cars in 1971. The engine is based on a system devised by German inventor Felix Wankel, and avoids the power losses inherent in familiar reciprocating pistons. Ford and GM have indicated interest in using such an engine.

United States manufacturers continued their experiments with the gas turbine, the electric-powered engine, the steam engine, and other power plants. But 1971 passed with no major breakthrough.

Two steps by President Richard M. Nixon helped auto industry economics. They were the elimination of the 7 per cent federal excise tax on new cars and the imposition of a 10 per cent surtax on foreign goods – including automobiles.

The surtax, however, was in effect for only four months until President Nixon announced its discontinuance in December. The charge to foreign carmakers thus put the prices of U.S.-built cars in a much better competitive position only temporarily.

The Price Picture for U.S. cars was confused because the Nixon freeze on wages and prices came just as American-made 1972 cars were to be introduced. Carmakers rolled back price increases they had announced and waited for official clarification on the changes they could make.

Ultimately, most prices were raised from 2 to 3 per cent. An average 1972 GM model with average added equipment, for example, went up $118, or 2.6 per cent, from freeze levels. Other companies posted similar increases.

With the repeal of the federal tax going into effect in early December, auto companies refigured their prices. They announced the tax reduction meant price cuts ranging from $113 to $424.

The major personnel change of the year came at GM. Chairman of the board of directors James M. Roche reached the retirement age of 65 and was replaced on December 31 by Richard C. Gerstenberg, 62, who had been vice-chairman of the board. Thomas A. Murphy, 56, replaced Gerstenberg as vice-chairman.   Charles C. Cain III

AUTOMOBILE RACING. Their cars are tiny and fragile, their purse money often insignificant, and they race in such far-off sites as Zandvoort, Le Camp du Castellet, Silverstone, Adenau, and Zeltweg. But the drivers who race Formula One cars in 11 Grand Prix races in 11 nations for the world drivers' championship are the élite of their sport.

They consider Jackie Stewart, a 31-year-old Scotsman with shoulder-length hair, as the most talented of their group. In 1971, Stewart proved them correct. With 6 victories in the 11 races, he won the championship, as he did in 1969, and earned so much money outside racing that he moved to Switzerland to escape high British taxes.

Stewart's Grand Prix car had a Tyrrell chassis with a British Cosworth-Ford 3-liter engine. For the third straight year, Porsche won the world manufacturers' championship in another international series for sports cars and prototypes, taking 8 of the 11 races. These cars had larger engines, with displacement of 5 liters generating 600 horsepower.

But barring a last-minute reprieve, these magnificent sports cars – Porsche 917K, Ferrari 512M, and others, about 50 in all – were doomed to antiquity in 1972, outlawed by the Commission Sportive Internationale, auto racing's world governing body. For 1972, engines for the world manufacturers' championship series are limited to 3 liters. The commission cited the high cost ($30,000) of the 5-liter engines. Porsche said it would not build smaller engines, and Ferrari and Alfa Romeo said they would build them for factory teams only.

American Racing. Few Americans raced in the two world championship series. Most American interest centered on the United States Auto Club (USAC) Championship Trail for Indianapolis-type cars, the National Association for Stock Car Auto Racing (NASCAR) Grand National series for late-model sedans, and the Canadian-American Challenge Cup series (the Can-Am) for sports cars.

For the second consecutive year, Al Unser of Albuquerque, N. Mex., won the $1,001,604 Indianapolis 500, feature of the 12-race USAC series, in May. Unser won in a P. J. Colt-Ford, and split a record $238,454 purse with the car's owners. Mark Donohue of Media, Pa., won USAC's Pocono, Pa., 500-mile race in July. Joe Leonard of San Jose, Calif., won the Ontario, Calif., 500-mile race in September and the USAC driving championship.

Richard Petty of Randleman, N.C., became NASCAR's overall champion and the third driver in history to reach career earnings of $1 million.

Peter Revson of New York and Denis Hulme of New Zealand drove factory McLaren M8F's with Chevrolet V-8 engines to the Can-Am series title. It was McLaren's fifth straight.   Frank Litsky

World champion driver Jackie Stewart heads his car toward victory in the Formula One Grand Prix race in Monaco. The 1971 world title was his second.

AVIATION. The U.S. aviation industry continued to struggle through one of the most difficult periods in its history in 1971. Widespread cost-control programs and fare increases helped the airlines in their battle against rising costs, but traffic growth was disappointing because of the sluggish economy. Air carriers also continued to receive pressure from the public to increase service to small communities and to reduce aircraft noise and air pollution. Aircraft manufacturers suffered a bleak year as a result of a continuing decline in the demand for both military and commercial planes.

Airline Profits. Deficits for domestic scheduled airlines deepened in the first half of 1971. First-half losses for the 12 major and 9 regional airlines were more than double those for the same period in 1970 – $132.4 million compared with $58.1 million. However, industry earnings began to improve in the second half, even though anticipated traffic gains failed to materialize during the summer.

The upturn in earnings after four consecutive years of decline was due primarily to the establishment of massive cost-control programs by the carriers and to approval by the Civil Aeronautics Board (CAB) of a 6 per cent fare increase, which became effective on May 7. As a result of these two factors, pretax 1971 earnings of the 11 trunk carriers were estimated at $25 million compared with losses of $87-million in 1970. An additional factor in the difference between 1970 and 1971 was repayment during the year of previously posted delivery positions on the canceled supersonic transport.

The 11 trunk carriers estimated that cost control had reduced expenses by more than $250 million in 1971. These cost-control programs included trimming flight schedules to cut excess capacity, canceling or lengthening orders for new aircraft, and reducing the work force.

Air Cargo posted a particularly gloomy year from a financial viewpoint. During the first half of the year, domestic and international air cargo tonnages declined 7.8 and 2.1 per cent, respectively. These declines were in direct contrast to massive increases in freight capacity produced by the additions of new and larger aircraft to airline fleets.

The leveling off in the volume of air tonnage in 1971 was particularly disappointing. As recently as 1969, industry and government experts had projected an annual growth rate of 11 to 19 per cent for the 1969-1973 period.

Regulation. The CAB found itself being criticized by the government. The Administration wanted the CAB to reduce its role in regulating routes, schedules, and fares. The 1971 Economic Report of the President charged that regulation of air transportation "has probably resulted in rates that in many cases are higher than they would otherwise be." The report added that the airlines' "problems will be recurrent if prices are held substantially

above what they would be in a more openly competitive market." Airlines pointed out, however, that fares in 1971 were at the same average level that they were 10 years ago.

Airline Mergers have become an important force that could significantly influence the future structure of the industry. The American Airlines-Trans Caribbean Airways merger was completed in March, and consolidations involving 10 other carriers were in process during the year.

Industry experts believed that the proposed mergers, if approved without major modifications, would make changes by other carriers inevitable. Such moves could significantly reduce the number of airlines and restructure the industry as carriers seek more balanced route structures.

Airways-Airports Legislation. Aviation and other interests complained that the Department of Transportation (DOT) was attempting to divert funds from the Airways-Airport Trust Fund to pay Federal Aviation Agency (FAA) expenses instead of using them for needed airport development and planning grants. Consequently, Congress passed, and the President signed, legislation that established priorities for use of revenues from the fund. The fund was created by the Airways-Airport Development Act of 1970. In June, the FAA proposed its first set of rules for safety requirements for airports. They range from rules for adequate fire-fighting equipment to bird discouragement.

In August, the DOT reported that the government-industry program to fit airline engines with smoke-reduction devices was nearly half finished. All engines were expected to be equipped by the end of 1972.

Airplane skyjackings tapered off significantly during 1971. According to the DOT, there were 35 hijackings throughout the world in 1968, 87 in 1969, and more than 90 in 1970. However, the number dropped to 67 as of Dec. 1, 1971. Thirty-one of these involved U.S. aircraft. The decline in the number of skyjackings reflected increased security measures taken by the United States and other governments.

Nevertheless, some of the year's incidents provided dramatic moments. On November 24, a hijacker parachuted from a Northwest Airlines 727 with $200,000 of ransom in one of the most bizarre crimes in history. It was the first time a hijacker parachuted from an airliner, and the ransom was the highest ever paid in U.S. hijacking.

The Aircraft Manufacturers' financial situation continued to worsen in 1971 as demand for both military and commercial aircraft deteriorated. Industry sales dropped to $12.7 billion in 1971 from $13.6 billion in 1970 and the 1968 peak of $17.4-billion.

Of particular concern was the possibility of Lockheed Aircraft's financial collapse. Lockheed averted bankruptcy in September when the U.S. govern-

Unhappy Boeing employees listen from the cockpit of a supersonic transport mock-up as a company spokesman announces the layoff of 7,000 employees in May.

ment and a 24-bank consortium signed a $750-million financing program with the company, including a $250-million federal government loan guarantee, to support the L-1011 400-passenger jet-building program and, hopefully, permit delivery of planes starting in April, 1972.

At the same time that Lockheed's L-1011 program was in a critical stage, its C-5A all-cargo jet program continued to have technical problems with another budget overrun of $300 million. The unit cost for each of the 81 planes on order was approximately $60 million.

New Aircraft. The first full year of operating experience with the Boeing 747 was favorable. It showed average daily flight time of each 747 exceeding eight hours. The average load was about 50 per cent, and the number of passengers averaged 180 per flight. Mechanical reliability was nearly 90 per cent. Operating seat-mile costs for the 747 were 32 per cent lower than those of the 707.

Late in the year Boeing announced it was considering cutting 747 production from 2.5 to 1 per month. Of the 207 aircraft on order, 150 had been delivered with no new orders in sight.

The wide-bodied tri-jet era began in August when the McDonnell Douglas DC-10 was introduced into service by both American Airlines and United Air Lines. As of December 31, five U.S. airlines had introduced a total of 13 DC-10s into service.

The DC-10 performed well in terms of low noise levels and low emissions from jet engines. The 230- to 345-passenger capacity of the wide-bodied jet was a major step forward in efficiently transporting large numbers of people in fewer aircraft.

International Air Fares. On November 18, 24 transatlantic airlines tentatively agreed to a compromise that will reduce many air fares between North America and Europe in 1972.

The table below shows round-trip fares from New York City to three different cities in three different trip categories that will be in effect in 1972. Peak fares run from June 1 through August 31 on eastbound flights and from July 1 through September 30 on westbound flights. Basic or middle fares cover the rest of the year. Winter off-season fares are for the period from November 1 through March 31:

Normal Economy Class (No limit on duration)	London	Paris	Frankfurt
Winter	$400	$420	$460
Basic	450	470	500
Peak	552	596	636
Excursion (22 to 45 days)			
Winter	200	210	220
Basic	220	235	240
Peak	290	300	310
Group Travel (40 or more originating eastbound; 30 or more originating westbound)			
Winter	180	185	190
Basic	200	210	220
Peak	270	280	290

Supersonic Transport (SST). On two separate occasions—March 18 and May 19—Congress voted against supplying additional federal funds for the SST program. More than $1 billion had been spent on the project since the aircraft was first proposed in 1963.

The termination of the U.S. program to develop the 280-passenger, 1,800-mph plane apparently left the non-Communist SST market open primarily to the smaller British-French *Concorde*. The *Concorde* was expected to enter commercial air service late in October, 1974.

Russia's TU-144 SST was scheduled to be put into commercial service on a domestic route sometime in 1972. Previously, such service had been scheduled to start in 1974 with a 150-passenger version of the prototype airplane.

The tabulation below shows how the *Concorde* and TU-144 compare in major features:

	Concorde	TU-144
Cost ($ in millions)	31	20
Length (feet)	193	188½
Wingspan (feet)	84	72
Passenger capacity	112	120
Cruising speed (mph)	1,450	1,560
Ceiling (feet)	55,000	60,000

French and Russian spokesmen, reacting to arguments in the United States against the SST, said that they had not encountered any unsolvable noise or pollution problems with their planes. Kenneth E. Schaefle

AWARDS AND PRIZES presented in 1971 included the following:

Arts Awards

American Institute of Architects. *Gold Medal*, Louis I. Kahn, Philadelphia architect. *Architecture Critics' Medal*, Sibyl Moholy-Nagy (posthumously). *Fine Arts Medal*, Anthony Smith, sculptor.

Brandeis University. *Creative Arts Medal Awards*, Richard P. Wilbur and James Wright for poetry, Earl Kim and John Harbison for music, Louise Nevelson and Claes Oldenburg for sculpture, Charles Chaplin and Bruce Baillie for film, and George Balanchine for dance.

Capezio Dance Award. Arthur Mitchell, principal dancer with the New York City Ballet and founder-director of the Harlem Dance Theater.

National Academy of Design. *Benjamin Altman Prize for Figure Painting*, Alice Neel ($2,500) and Sidney Laufman ($1,250). *Benjamin Altman Prize for Landscape Painting*, Anne Poor ($2,500) and Philip Evergood ($1,250).

National Academy of Recording Arts and Sciences. *Grammy Awards: Best Album*, "Bridge over Troubled Waters" by Simon and Garfunkel. *Best New Artists*, The Carpenters. *Best Song*, "Bridge over Troubled Waters" by Simon and Garfunkel. *Best Classical Album*, "Les Troyens," with Colin Davis conducting the Royal Opera House Orchestra and Chorus. *Best Contemporary Vocal Performance, Female*, Dionne Warwick for "I'll Never Fall in Love Again." *Best Contemporary Vocal Performance, Male*, Ray Stevens for "Everything Is Beautiful." *Best Contemporary Vocal Performance, Group*, The Carpenters for "Close to You." *Record of the Year* and *Album of the Year*, "Bridge over Troubled Waters" by Simon and Garfunkel.

National Academy of Television Arts and Sciences. *Emmy Awards: Best Actor and Actress in a Single Dramatic Performance*, George C. Scott in "The Price" and Lee Grant in "The Neon Ceiling." *Best Supporting Actor and Actress*, the late David Burns in "The Price" and Margaret Leighton in "Hamlet." *Best Actor and Actress in a Dramatic Series*, Hal Holbrook in The Senator segment of "The Bold Ones" and Susan Hampshire in "The First Churchills." *Best Actor and Actress in a Comedy Series*, Jack Klugman in "The Odd Couple" and Jean Stapleton in "All in the Family." *Best Supporting Actor and Actress in a Comedy Series*, Edward Asner and Valerie Harper, both in "The Mary Tyler Moore Show." *Best Director of a Single Dramatic Program*, Fielder Cook for "The Price." *Outstanding Single Program*, "The Burt Bacharach Special." *Best Comedy Series*, "All in the Family." *Best Variety Show – Music*, "The Flip Wilson Show." *Outstanding Variety Series – Talk*, "The David Frost Show."

National Institute of Arts and Letters. *Awards in Painting and Sculpture*, painters Ilya Bolotowsky, Robert Goodnough, Alfred Leslie, Norman Lewis, Ludwig Sander, and Hedda Sterne, and sculptor Harold Tovish. *Richard and Hinda Rosenthal Foundation Award for Painting*, Donald Perlis. *Rosenthal Foundation Award for the Novel*, Christopher Brookhouse. *Marjorie Peabody Waite Award*, Ben Benn, painter. *Arnold W. Brunner Award*, John Andrews, Canadian architect. *Awards for Creative Work in Musical Composition*, Sydney Hodkinson, Fred Lerdahl, Roger Reynolds, and Loren Rush. *Gold Medal for Sculpture*, Alexander Calder. *Gold Medal for Music*, Elliot C. Carter. *Brunner Memorial Prize in Architecture*, John Andrews.

Journalism Awards

American Newspaper Guild. *Heywood Broun Award*, Donald Singleton, *The New York News*, for a 20-part series on crime in New York City.

Long Island University. *George Polk Memorial Awards: Foreign Reporting*, Gloria Emerson, *The New York Times*. *National Reporting*, The Knight newspapers. *Metropolitan Reporting*, Richard Oliver, *The New York Daily News*. *Television Reporting*, Alan Levin, producer of "Who Invited Us?" *Magazine Reporting*, *The Washington Monthly*. *News Photography*, John Darnell, John Filo, and Howard Ruffner, Kent State University students. *Criticism*, Pauline Kael, *The New Yorker*.

National Cartoonists Society. *Reuben*, Alfred Andriola for "Kerry Drake."

George Foster Peabody Awards. *Radio: News*, Douglas Kiker, NBC news correspondent, for "Jordan Reports." *Education*, NBC, for "The Danger Within: A Study of Disunity in America." *Public Service*, WAHT (AM) Lebanon, Pa., for "Medical Viewpoint" and "Pearl Harbor, Lest We Forget." *Television: News*, CBS, for "60 Minutes," and WPBT, Miami, for "Politithon '70." *Education*, ABC, for "The Eye of the Storm." *Children's Programs*, NBC, for "Hot Dog," and CBS, for Dr. Seuss programs. *Special Award*, CBS, for "The Selling of the Pentagon."

Sigma Delta Chi, Professional Journalistic Society. *Newspaper Awards: General Reporting*. Staff writers of *The Washington Post* for their 1970 election coverage. *Editorial Writing*, John R. Harrison, *The Ledger*, Lakeland, Fla., for editorials urging federal funds for health care and family-planning centers. *Washington Correspondence*, Jared D. Stout, Newhouse News Service, for a study of military surveillance of civilians. *Foreign Correspondence*, Hugh Mulligan, Associated Press, for stories on Biafra and on the war in Cambodia. *News Photography*, John P. Filo, Kent State University, for photograph of Kent State violence. *Editorial Cartooning*, Paul Conrad, *Los Angeles Times*, for his 1970 cartoon, "There's a Bomb Set to Go Off." *Public Service*, *Newsday*, Garden City, N.Y., for stories on the questionable ethics of Long Island public officials. *Magazine Awards: Reporting*, David L. Chandler, *Life*, for a report on criminal activity and corruption in Louisiana government. *Public Service*, *The Washingtonian Magazine*, Washington, D.C., for article on judges in the Washington area. *Radio Awards: Reporting*, Robert White, KRLD, Dallas, for coverage of Hurricane Celia. *Public Service*, WWDC, Washington, D.C., for 28-part series on drug hazards. *Editorializing*, WLPR Radio, Mobile, Ala., for editorial criticizing lieutenant governor-elect of Alabama for addressing secret Ku Klux Klan meeting. *Television Awards: Reporting*, KBTV, Denver, Colo., for coverage of fatal crash of plane carrying Wichita State University football team. *Public Service*, KING-TV, Seattle, for programs examining Puget Sound region environmental and social questions. *Editorializing*, WCCO-TV, Minneapolis, Minn., for editorial on abortion. *Research About Journalism*, William Small, CBS News, Washington, D.C., for his book *To Kill a Messenger*, which examines the impact of television news on American culture. *Distinguished Teaching in Journalism*, Ralph O. Nafziger, former director, school of journalism, University of Wisconsin, "for his outstanding achievement in the field of journalism education and for his contributions toward maintaining the highest standards of the profession."

Literature Awards

Academy of American Poets. *1971 Fellowship*, Howard Nemerov, professor of English, Washington University, St. Louis, for "distinguished poetic achievement." *Lamont Poetry Selection Award*, Stephen Dobyns for *Concurring Beasts*.

Columbia University. *Bancroft Prizes*, Erik Barnouw, for *The Image Empire*; David M. Kennedy, for *Birth Control in America: The Career of Margaret Sanger*; and Joseph Frazier Wall, for *Andrew Carnegie*.

AWARDS AND PRIZES

National Book Committee. *National Book Awards: Arts and Letters*, Francis Steegmuller, for *Cocteau*. *Children's Literature*, Lloyd Alexander, for *The Marvelous Misadventures of Sebastian*. *Fiction*, Saul Bellow, for *Mr. Sammler's Planet*. *History and Biography*, James MacGregor Burns, for *Roosevelt: The Soldier of Freedom*. *Poetry*, Mona Van Duyn, for *To See, To Take*. *Science*, the late Raymond Phineas Stearns, for *Science in the British Colonies of America*. *Translation*, Frank Jones, for *Saint Joan of the Stockyards*, and Edward G. Seidensticker, for *The Sound of the Mountain*. *National Medal for Literature*, E. B. White, author and an essayist for *The New Yorker* since 1925, "for the excellence of his total contribution to the world of letters."

Poetry Society of America. *Alice Fay di Castagnola Award*, Marsha Lee Masters, Chicago; and Cornel Lengyel, Georgetown, Calif. *John Masefield Award*, Sallie Nixon, Nebraska, for "This Is the Year." *Shelley Memorial Award*, Louise Townsend and Adrienne Rich, New York City.

Prix Goncourt of France, Jacques Laurent, for *Les Betises*, a novel.

Yale University. *Bollingen Prize in Poetry*, Richard P. Wilbur, for *Walking to Sleep* and Mona Van Duyn, for *To See, To Take*.

Nobel Prizes. See NOBEL PRIZES.

Public Service Awards

Albert Einstein Commemorative Awards, presented by the Albert Einstein College of Medicine, Yeshiva University, New York City, for outstanding contributions in various fields of human endeavor. *Communication Arts*, David Frost, television host. *Human Rights*, Governor Luis A. Ferré of Puerto Rico. *Medical Science*, Dr. Julius Axelrod, who shared the 1970 Nobel Prize in physiology and medicine. *Performing Arts*, actor-comedian Danny Kaye. *Public Affairs*, Paul A. Samuelson, winner of the 1970 Nobel Prize for economic science.

American Library Association. *Beta Phi Mu Award*, Leon Carnovsky, University of Chicago Graduate Library School, for distinguished service to education for librarianship. *Caldecott Medal*, Gail E. Haley, author and illustrator of *A Story, A Story*. *Francis Joseph Campbell Citation*, Mrs. Ranald H. Macdonald, New York City, in recognition of her outstanding contribution to the advancement of library service to the blind. *Melvil Dewey Medal*, William Joseph Welsh, Library of Congress, Washington, D.C., for distinguished contributions to the profession of librarianship. *Joseph W. Lippincott Award*, William S. Dix, librarian, Princeton University Library, Princeton, N.J., for his distinguished service in the profession of librarianship. *Newbery Medal*, Betsy Byers, author of *Summer of the Swans*.

Freedoms Foundation. *George Washington Award*, Bill Pearson, San Diego State College, for "loyal patriotism so dramatically demonstrated when, for 3½ hours, he stood alone and defenseless defying a screaming, heckling, menacing group of dissident students bent on tearing down and destroying an American flag."

National Association for the Advancement of Colored People. *Spingarn Medal*, Leon H. Sullivan, clergyman, activist, and prophet, "in admiration of the singular steadfastness with which he has melded religious leadership and social vision for the advancement of black folk."

Planned Parenthood—World Population Center. *Margaret Sanger Award*, Louis M. Hellman, M.D., obstetrician-gynecologist, and deputy assistant secretary for population affairs, Department of Health, Education, and Welfare, for long service to the birth control movement with great distinction.

Rockefeller Public Service Awards for "distinguished service to the government of the United States and the American people." *Administration*, Samuel M. Cohn, assistant director for budget review, Office of Management and Budget; and Robert C. Moot, assistant secretary, Department of Defense. *Human Resource Development and Protection*, Mary Lee Mills, nurse-consultant, community health service, Department of Health, Education, and Welfare. *Intergovernmental Operations*, Joseph J. Sisco, assistant secretary for Near Eastern and South Asian Affairs, Department of State. *Physical Source Development and Protection*, Luna B. Leopold, senior research hydrologist, U.S. Geological Survey, Department of the Interior. *Professional Accomplishment and Leadership*, Robert Solomon, adviser to the board of governors and director, division of international finance, Federal Reserve System.

United Nations Educational, Scientific, and Cultural Organization. *Kalinga Prize*, Margaret Mead, anthropologist, for the popularization of science.

Pulitzer Prizes. See PULITZER PRIZES.

Science and Technology Awards

American Chemical Society. *Priestley Medal*, Frederick D. Rossini, vice-president for research and professor of chemistry, University of Notre Dame, for "distinguished services to chemistry."

American Institute of Physics. *Dannie Heineman Prize for Mathematical Physics*, Roger Penrose, department of mathematics, Birksbeck College, London, "for his contribution to general relativity including new mathematical techniques, new conservation laws and his theorem on singularities in space-time."

American Physical Society. *Bonner Prize in Nuclear Physics*, Maurice Goldhaber, Brookhaven National Laboratory, "for his many ideas and discoveries, spanning the field of nuclear physics that have played vital roles in establishing the nature of nuclei, the electromagnetic interactions, and the validity of conservation laws central to all physics." *Buckley Solid State Physics Prize*, Erwin Hahn, University of California, Berkeley, "for his study of the transient response of solids under the action of electromagnetic pulses." *Compton Gold Medal*, Ralph A. Sawyer, formerly vice-president for research and dean of the Horace H. Rackham School of Graduate Studies, University of Michigan, Ann Arbor, for "outstanding statesmanship in science."

Atomic Energy Commission. *Ernest O. Lawrence Memorial Awards*, Robert L. Fleischer, physicist, General Electric Research Laboratory, Schenectady, N.Y.; P. Buford Price, professor of physics, University of California, Berkeley; and Robert M. Walker, McDonnell Professor of Physics, Washington University, St. Louis, for their fundamental contributions, in collaboration, to "the discovery and understanding of the phenomenon of etching charged particle tracks in solids . . . and for the application of the technique in a broad spectrum of scientific fields. . . ."; Thomas B. Cook, Jr., vice-president, Sandia Laboratories, Albuquerque, N. Mex., "for his significant contributions to the study of nuclear weapons effects;" and Robert L. Hellens, chief physicist, Combustion Engineering Inc., Windsor, Conn., for numerous pioneering contributions to the field of light-water reactor physics.

Robert J. Collier Trophy, William M. Allen, chairman of The Boeing Company, in recognition of Boeing as leader of the industry-airline-government team that successfully introduced the 747 into commercial service.

Columbia University. *Louisa Gross Horwitz Prize*, Hugh E. Huxley, a fellow of Churchill College, Cambridge University, England, for his "sliding filament hypothesis," which explains the chemical mechanism of muscle contraction.

Franklin Institute. *Franklin Medal*, Hannes Alfven, University of California, San Diego, for "his outstanding pioneer work in establishing the field of magnetohydrodynamics, and for his many revolutionary contributions in that field to plasma physics, space physics, and astrophysics."

Geological Society of America. *Penrose Medal*, Marshall Kay, professor of geology, Columbia University, for his contributions to geology in the field of stratigraphy and its relation to tectonics. *Arthur L. Day Medal*, Hans P. Eugster, professor of geology, Johns Hopkins University, in recognition of his technique for the control of oxygen content in laboratory experiments to influence the chemical reaction of iron-bearing solutions in forming igneous and metamorphic rocks.

Albert and Mary Lasker Foundation Awards. *Albert Lasker Award for Basic Medical Research*, Seymour Benzer, professor of biology, California Institute of Technology; Sydney Brenner, Medical Research Council Unit of Molecular Biology, Cambridge University, England; and Charles Yanofsky, professor of biology, Stanford University, for showing that the gene is the blueprint for making the body's protein. *Albert Lasker Award for Clinical Medical Research*, Edward D. Freis, senior medical investigator, Veterans Administration Hospital, Washington, D.C., for demonstrating the effectiveness of drugs in treating hypertension.

National Academy of Engineering. *Founders Medal*, Clarence L. Johnson, senior vice-president of Lockheed Aircraft Corporation, Burbank, Calif., for his experimental and theoretical investigations in aerospace sciences.

National Academy of Sciences. *Daniel Giraud Elliot Medal*, Richard D. Alexander, professor of zoology and curator of insects, University of Michigan, for his outstanding work on the classification, evolution, and behavior of crickets and other insects. *J. Lawrence Smith Medal*, Edward Anders, Enrico Fermi Institute, University of Chicago, for his basic studies on the origin and history of meteorites. *Henry Draper Medal*, Subrahmanyan Chandrasekhar, Laboratory for Astrophysics and Space Research, University of Chicago, for his contributions to theoretical astrophysics, particularly for his studies of the structure, evolution, and dynamics of stars. *U.S. Steel Foundation Award in Molecular Biology*, Masayasu Nomura, co-director of the Institute for Enzyme Research, University of Wisconsin, for "studies on the structure and function of ribosomes and their molecular components." *Benjamin Apthorp Gould Prize*, Elizabeth Roemer, professor of astronomy, University of Arizona, in recognition of her distinguished contributions in the field of cometary astronomy. *Gibbs Brothers Medal*, Henry A. Schade, researcher in ship architecture and professor emeritus, University of California, Berkeley, for outstanding contributions in the design, construction, and performance of ships. *John H. Carty Medal*, James D. Watson, Nobel laureate biochemist, Harvard University, for his accomplishments in molecular biology.

National Medal of Science, the U.S. government's highest award for distinguished achievement in science, mathematics, and engineering, to Richard D. Brauer, professor of mathematics, Harvard University, "for his work on conjectures of Dickson, Cartan, Maschke, and Artin, his introduction of the Brauer group, and his development of the theory of modular representations"; Robert H. Dicke, professor of physics, Princeton University, "for fashioning radio and light waves into tools of extraordinary accuracy"; Barbara McClintock, distinguished service member, Carnegie Institution of Washington, Cold Spring Harbor, N.Y., "for establishing the relationship between inherited characters in plants and the detailed shapes of their chromosomes, and for showing that some genes are controlled by other genes within chromosomes"; George E. Mueller, senior vice-president, General Dynamics Corporation,

"for his many individual contributions to the design of the Apollo system"; Albert B. Sabin, president of the Weizmann Institute of Science, Rehovot, Israel, "for numerous fundamental contributions to the understanding of viruses and viral diseases"; Allan R. Sandage, staff member, Hale Observatories, Carnegie Institution of Washington, California Institute of Technology, "for bringing the very limits of the universe within the reach of man's awareness and unraveling the evolution of stars and galaxies. . . ."; John C. Slater, professor of physics and chemistry, University of Florida, "for wide-ranging contributions to the basic theory of atoms, molecules, and matter in the solid form"; John A. Wheeler, professor of physics, Princeton University, "for his basic contributions to our understanding of the nuclei of atoms, exemplified by his theory of nuclear fission"; and Saul Winstein (posthumously), former professor of chemistry, University of California, Los Angeles, "in recognition of his many innovative and perceptive contributions to the study of mechanism in organic chemical reactions."

Vetlesen Prize. S. Keith Runcorn, director of the school of physics, University of Newcastle-upon-Tyne, England; and to Allan V. Cox, professor of geophysics, Stanford University; and Richard R. Doell, U.S. Geological Survey, "geophysicists whose studies in paleomagnetism have increased man's knowledge of the history of the earth."

Theater and Motion Picture Awards

Academy of Motion Picture Arts and Sciences. *"Oscar" Awards: Best Picture*, Patton, 20th Century-Fox. *Best Actor*, George C. Scott in *Patton*. *Best Supporting Actor*, John Mills in *Ryan's Daughter*. *Best Actress*, Glenda Jackson in *Women in Love*. *Best Supporting Actress*, Helen Hayes in *Airport*. *Best Director*, Franklin J. Schaffner for *Patton*. *Best Foreign Language Film*, *Investigation of a Citizen Above Suspicion*, directed by Elio Petri.

Antoinette Perry (Tony) Awards: *Best Dramatic Play*, *Sleuth*, by Anthony Shaffer. *Best Dramatic Actor*, Brian Bedford in *The School for Wives*. *Best Dramatic Actress*, Maureen Stapleton in *The Gingerbread Lady*. *Best Director of a Dramatic Play*, Peter Brook, for *A Midsummer Night's Dream*. *Best Musical*, *Company*. *Best Actor in a Musical*, Hal Linden in *The Rothschilds*. *Best Actress in a Musical*, Helen Gallagher in *No, No, Nanette*. *Best Director of a Musical*, Harold Prince, for *Company*. *Composer of the Best Music*, and *Writer of the Best Lyrics*, both to Stephen Sondheim for *Company*.

Cannes International Film Festival. *Golden Palm*, *The Go-Between*, directed by Joseph Losey. *Special Jury Prize*, *Taking Off*, directed by Milos Forman; and *Johnny Got His Gun*, directed by Dalton Trumbo. *Best Actor*, Ricardo Cucciolla of Italy in *Sacco and Vanzetti*. *Best Actress*, Kitty Winn of the United States in *Panic in Needle Park*. *Special Super Festival Prize*, director Luchino Visconti of Italy, for *Death in Venice*.

New York Drama Critics' Circle Awards. *Best Play of 1970-1971*, *Home*, a British play written by David Storey. *Best American Play*, *The House of Blue Leaves* by John Guare. *Best Musical*, *Follies*, with music and lyrics by Stephen Sondheim.

New York Film Critics Awards: *Best Starring Performances*, George C. Scott in *Patton* and Glenda Jackson in *Women in Love*. *Best Supporting Performances*, Karen Black in *Five Easy Pieces*, and Chief Dan George in *Little Big Man*. *Best Film*, *Five Easy Pieces*, presented by Columbia Pictures. *Best Director*, Bob Rafelson for his *Five Easy Pieces*. *Best Screenwriting*, Eric Rohmer for his *My Night at Maud's*. Lillian Zahrt

See also CANADIAN LITERATURE; CHEMISTRY; LITERATURE FOR CHILDREN.

BAHAMAS. See WEST INDIES.

BALLET. See DANCING.

BALTIMORE. City Council President William D. Schaefer was elected mayor of Baltimore on Nov. 2, 1971. Schaefer, a Democrat, defeated his Republican opponent, Ross Z. Pierpont, by building a black-white coalition. Schaefer had won the Democratic nomination for the office by defeating City Solicitor George L. Russell, Jr., and four other candidates in the September 14 primary election. Three of Schaefer's opponents in the primary, including Russell, were blacks.

Although black candidates failed to muster even a majority of the votes in the Democratic primary, the time seems not far off when black voters will control city elections in Baltimore. According to the 1970 census, 46.4 per cent of Baltimore's 905,759 residents are black, and the percentage of black residents in the city continues to rise. The city's total population fell by 3.5 per cent during the 1960s, but its black population rose by 29.1 per cent.

Suburban Growth. While the central city's population declined, the Baltimore metropolitan area had the second most rapid rate of growth among major metropolitan areas in the northeastern United States. Thanks to rapid suburban growth, the Baltimore area population increased 14.8 per cent during the 1960s, reaching 2,070,670 in 1970 and making Baltimore the 11th largest U. S. metropolitan area.

Problems and Progress. Like other major eastern cities, Baltimore has been experiencing severe problems. Its budget for public education more than tripled in the last 10 years, rising from $57 million in 1961 to $184 million in 1971. Baltimore also had a 15.2 per cent relief dependency rate, the highest of any major U.S. city.

Despite its financial problems, the city was launching new public-service programs. In cooperation with private agencies, it plans to develop a new approach to the problem of training unskilled and semiskilled workers from impoverished neighborhoods. Construction also began on 1,500 public housing units, and ground was broken for 387 units of moderate-income housing on urban-renewal land. This included the first neighborhood-owned, nonprofit housing development.

In January, the Maryland State Public Service Commission granted a construction permit to the Baltimore Gas and Electric Company for a nuclear power plant on the western shore of Chesapeake Bay. However, a July 23 court ruling halted construction on the $387-million Calvert Cliffs plant until its effect on the environment could be established.

To give students of Baltimore greater understanding of various cultures and ethnic groups, qualified teachers throughout the world have been recruited to teach for a limited time in the city's public schools. "Teacher ambassadors" have come from Ghana, Latin America, Japan, the Philippines, Scandinavian countries, and the Middle East. J. M. Banovetz

BANGLA DESH. See Asia; Pakistan.

BANKS AND BANKING. The Federal Reserve System (Fed) aimed at an annual rate of growth in the money supply in excess of 5 per cent for the first quarter of 1971. Money actually increased at 9.3 per cent, about what some Administration leaders had been hoping for. The increase was well above the levels that Fed chairman Arthur Burns had labeled as inflationary. The money supply was increasing at an 11 per cent annual rate by midyear, far above the 3 to 4 per cent rate that historically has been associated with noninflationary economic growth. Burns told the Joint Economic Committee in late June that the Fed had fully done its job in providing money for expansion and that monetary growth would probably slow down. The increase did halt during the third quarter, dropping to a snaillike 1.5 per cent annual growth rate—about 6 per cent for the year.

The increase in the money supply brought relief to thousands of businesses that were short of ready cash. Corporate cash rose to $68.9 billion by midyear, up from only $63 billion a year earlier. The surge of depreciation funds under the Department of the Treasury's new rulings on accelerated depreciation was an important factor, although the Fed's stimulation of rapid monetary growth was the major underlying stimulant. Interest rates remained somewhat lower than in 1969 and 1970, but well above earlier levels.

First Security Bank employees in Boise, Ida., piece together slivers of checks worth an estimated $843,000 that were accidentally shredded as trash.

Burns rejected suggestions from abroad that the United States raise its interest rates to slow the persistent outflow of dollars. Instead, he proposed an incomes policy to damp inflation, a policy that had been rejected by the Administration. In February, however, Burns gained an important ally in John B. Connally, who replaced David M. Kennedy as secretary of the treasury.

The Dollar Threatened. Capital outflow and an unprecedented trade deficit – the highest in U.S. history – made the December devaluation of the dollar seem inevitable. It was precipitated by a congressional committee report concluding that the United States had no choice but to devalue or let the dollar float. The multibillion-dollar international rush to sell dollars finally helped trigger an incomes policy – President Richard M. Nixon's new economic policy announced on August 15. Gold sales were halted, allowing the foreign currency value of the dollar to float. Import prices were raised by imposing a 10 per cent import surcharge until mid-December. Prices, wages, and rents were frozen for 90 days. Proposed tax cuts were enacted in December.

Trade and financial interests of Canada and Japan were severely affected by the import surcharge that was part of the new Nixon program. Major issues about reforming world trade and payments were being resolved at year's-end.

International Monetary Fund (IMF) managing director Pierre-Paul Schweitzer, had cautioned the United States earlier to rely more on expansionary fiscal policies that would tend to increase interest rates and induce capital inflows. Schweitzer said it was imperative that the $10-billion U.S. deficit in international payments in 1970 be improved. Instead, the actual balance of payments deficit on official settlements had doubled by the first half of 1971.

In May, the West German, Swiss, Dutch, Austrian, and Belgian central banks withdrew support of the old dollar parities. The German Deutsche mark and the Dutch guilder were permitted to float. Higher parities were set for the Swiss franc and the Austrian schilling. The Belgian franc was restored to its old parity to keep it in line with the French franc.

The dollar crisis sent shock waves through the countries of the European Community (Common Market), which are seeking to establish a common currency. Germany and the Netherlands favored floating the common currency against the dollar. France, Belgium, and Luxembourg, however, wanted a two-tier system, with one currency value for commercial transactions and another for capital transfers.

The British Scene. The changeover to the decimal system in Great Britain in February closed 14,000 bank offices over a four-day weekend to convert 25-million accounts to new pence, each worth one-hundredth of a pound. In its bid for Common Market membership, Britain agreed to phase out the use of its currency as an international reserve currency. Recession and the dollar crisis in Great Britain made the pound a relatively safer haven for foreign capital than it generally had been during the 1960s. British foreign exchange reserves rose to the highest levels in history.

Despite near-record domestic inflation, Prime Minister Edward Heath, unlike President Nixon, avoided the price and wage controls that existed in Britain under the previous government. Instead, he announced tax cuts to stimulate consumption.

Home Building in the United States, partly financed by record federal aid, rose to a record 2.2-million units in August, although it dropped somewhat thereafter. Under the 1970 Emergency Home Finance Act, home financing agencies started buying "conventional" mortgages. Only federally insured mortgages had been purchased previously. More than 50 per cent of new home mortgages were being financed indirectly by the federal government.

Commercial Banks. The Federal Deposit Insurance Corporation (FDIC) put up a record $100 million in temporary loans to establish a successor to a defunct Michigan bank. The FDIC hoped to recover about 90 per cent of the loan by selling the bank's assets. The bank had been one of several worth about $3 billion controlled by an investor's group headed by Donald H. Parsons. Excessive investment in long-term municipal securities that depreciated during 1969 and 1970 brought the bank to insolvency. Parson's group was also forced to give up control of the giant Bank of the Commonwealth in Detroit, the Union Commerce Bank in Cleveland, and several other banks through sale or foreclosure.

A Texas-sized stock scandal forced the collapse of Houston's Sharpstown State Bank. Losses of up to $16 million by depositors with more than the $20,000 in FDIC insurance coverage were estimated. Ironically, the scandal involved politicians speculating in bank stock at the same time they were trying to pass a state bank insurance law.

First National City Bank of New York City agreed to sell to Canadians its 75 per cent interest in the Mercantile Bank of Canada. The agreement ended a three-year dispute over Canadianization of Canadian banks.

Many of the largest banks adopted a floating prime rate on loans to their best customers, abandoning the conventional method of making periodic prime rate changes. The floating prime rate was to be set one-half percentage point above the 90-day commercial paper rate, and reviewed weekly.

Amendments to the Bank Holding Company Act of 1956 brought one-bank holding companies under the same regulations as multibank groups. One-bank holding companies were required to register by June 29. About 1,100 bank-holding companies are now prohibited from any new nonbanking activities. The Fed can force the 70 groups with significant non-bank activities that were formed before June 30, 1968, to get rid of such holdings if their association reduces competition unduly.

The Fed took several steps to modernize the payments system. It widened the zones of same-day settlement on check collections, and made it easier for banks to transmit money electronically. It was spending more than $135 million to collect checks, though it handled only one-third of the more than 20 billion checks that are written each year.

A partial removal of the 4.5 per cent interest ceiling on government bonds with maturities of five years or more was passed in July, 1971. The law allows sales of up to $10 billion in long-term government bonds outside the ceiling. A new 7 per cent, 10-year bond was sold—the first bond issue since 1965.

The Fed amended its margin requirements on stock purchases—that part of the total purchase price of securities that must be put up in cash—to apply to borrowers as well as to lenders. In the past, borrowers had circumvented the requirements by borrowing abroad.

In a precedent-shattering move, the federal government moved in August to guarantee up to $250-million in bank loans to the Lockheed Aircraft Corporation. Lockheed was facing bankruptcy because of the impending collapse of Great Britain's Rolls-Royce, a major subcontractor. William G. Dewald

BANZER SUAREZ, HUGO (1926-   ), became president of Bolivia on Aug. 22, 1971. He was named to the post by the armed forces, which had deposed General Juan Jose Torres. See BOLIVIA.

Banzer was born on July 10, 1926, in Santa Cruz, the capital of Bolivia's eastern department. An army man all his life, Banzer began his career after graduating from military college as a lieutenant in the cavalry. He served in various posts, including that of commanding officer of the Fourth Cavalry Regiment. In 1955, he attended a United States Army school in Panama. In 1960, he attended the Armored Cavalry School at Fort Hood, Tex. In the mid-1960s, he served as Bolivia's military attaché in Washington, D.C., and Argentina.

In 1969, he was named director of Bolivia's Military College, a prestigious position that carried considerable influence in the nation's top military and political circles. In October, 1970, however, shortly after a military coup in which he supported the losing side, Banzer was exiled to Argentina. His arrest in October, 1971, while on a secret visit to Santa Cruz, helped touch off the coup that brought him to power.

President Banzer and his wife, the former Yolanda Parra, have four children. He is a prolific reader whose taste ranges from James Bond to books on Latin American history.   Paul C. Tullier

BARBADOS. See WEST INDIES.

BASEBALL. The Pittsburgh Pirates and the Baltimore Orioles won major league baseball's pennant races in 1971. This fact was not surprising, but the Pirates' seven-game victory over the Orioles in the World Series was. It was also a memorable season for such players as Vida Blue, Ferguson Jenkins, Tom Seaver, Joe Torre, and Henry Aaron, and a nightmarish year for the Washington Senators. Near the season's end, the Senators received American League approval to move to Arlington, Tex., in 1972, where they became the Texas Rangers.

The Pirates won the National League's Eastern Division by 7 games, the Orioles the American League East by 12 games, and the Oakland Athletics the American League West by 16 games. The only close race was in the National League's Western Division, where the San Francisco Giants, who once led by 10½ games, entered the final night of the season leading the Los Angeles Dodgers by only 1 game. The Giants won that game and finished first.

The Giants, managed by Charlie Fox, were a hard-hitting team with aches and pains. Willie McCovey, their most feared slugger, played despite a torn cartilage in his left knee and arthritis in his right knee. Their one-time boy wonder Willie Mays, now 40 and showing his age, had bursitis in his shoulder.

The Pirates were managed by Danny Murtaugh, who always kept calm because he had a heart condi-

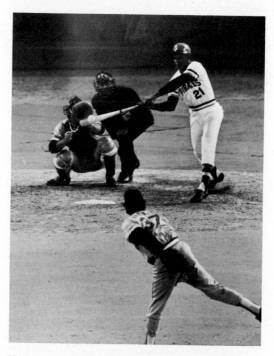

Pittsburgh's Roberto Clemente was the leading hitter in the World Series. He had ended the regular season needing just 118 hits for a lifetime total of 3,000.

Final Standings in Major League Baseball

American League	W.	L.	Pct.	GB.
Eastern Division				
Baltimore	101	57	.639	—
Detroit	91	71	.562	12
Boston	85	77	.525	18
New York	82	80	.506	21
Washington	63	96	.396	38½
Cleveland	60	102	.370	43
Western Division				
Oakland	101	60	.627	—
Kansas City	85	76	.528	16
Chicago	79	83	.488	22½
California	76	86	.469	25½
Minnesota	74	86	.463	26½
Milwaukee	69	92	.429	32

Leading Batters
Batting Average—Tony Oliva, Minnesota .337
Home Runs—Bill Melton, Chicago 33
Runs Batted In—Harmon Killebrew, Minnesota 119
Hits—Cesar Tovar, Minnesota 204

Leading Pitchers
Games Won—Mickey Lolich, Detroit 25
Win Average—Dave McNally, Baltimore (21-5) .808
Earned-Run Average—Vida Blue, Oakland 1.82
Strikeouts—Mickey Lolich, Detroit 308

Awards
Most Valuable Player—Vida Blue, Oakland
Cy Young—Vida Blue, Oakland
Rookie of the Year—Chris Chambliss, Cleveland
Manager of the Year—Dick Williams, Oakland

National League	W.	L.	Pct.	GB.
Eastern Division				
Pittsburgh	97	65	.599	—
St. Louis	90	72	.556	7
Chicago	83	79	.512	14
New York	83	79	.512	14
Montreal	71	90	.441	25½
Philadelphia	67	95	.414	30
Western Division				
San Francisco	90	72	.556	—
Los Angeles	89	73	.549	1
Atlanta	82	80	.506	8
Houston	79	83	.488	11
Cincinnati	79	83	.488	11
San Diego	61	100	.379	28½

Leading Batters
Batting Average—Joe Torre, St. Louis .363
Home Runs—Willie Stargell, Pittsburgh 48
Runs Batted In—Joe Torre, St. Louis 137
Hits—Joe Torre, St. Louis 230

Leading Pitchers
Games Won—Ferguson Jenkins, Chicago 24
Win Average—Don Gullett, Cincinnati (16-6) .727
Earned-Run Average—Tom Seaver, New York 1.76
Strikeouts—Tom Seaver, New York 289

Awards
Most Valuable Player—Joe Torre, St. Louis
Cy Young—Ferguson Jenkins, Chicago
Rookie of the Year—Earl Williams, Atlanta
Manager of the Year—Walter Alston, Los Angeles

tion. He also had heavy-hitting Willie Stargell, whose 48 home runs led the majors; Roberto Clemente, one of the game's greatest all-round stars; and Manny Sanguillen, who became baseball's best catcher. The Pirates' pitching, except for starter Dock Ellis and reliever Dave Giusti, was undistinguished.

The Play-Offs. In 1970, the Pirates won the National League East but lost the pennant play-offs to the Cincinnati Reds. This time, the Giants beat the Pirates, 5-4, in the first game of the three-of-five-game play-offs. Then the Pirates swept the next three games, 9-4, 2-1, and 9-5, as Bob Robertson hit three home runs in one game and one in the next.

The American League play-offs followed a familiar pattern. The Orioles beat the Athletics in three straight games, 5-3, 5-1, and 5-3, behind the pitching of Dave McNally, Mike Cuellar, and Jim Palmer. This was the Orioles' third consecutive sweep of the Western Division winners since 1969.

The pennant was the Orioles' fourth in six years. They won the World Series in 1966 and 1970. They became the second team in history (the first was the 1920 Chicago White Sox) to have four 20-game winners—McNally, Cuellar, Palmer, and Pat Dobson. They also had good hitting and fielding, and they had an astute, verbose manager, Earl Weaver. "In baseball knowledge," said Frank Robinson, the Oriole outfielder, "Weaver is second to no one."

The Athletics were strong everywhere except in catching. They had baseball's prime box-office attraction in Blue, a 22-year-old left-handed fireball pitcher. They also had a new manager, Dick Williams, who brought discipline to a team that needed it. But the Athletics took a beating from the Orioles, and the betting was 2 to 1 that the Pirates would, too.

World Series. The Orioles, playing at home, started the Series as a favorite should. They won the opener, 5-3, as McNally pitched a three-hitter and retired 21 of the last 22 batters. They won the second game, 11-3, behind Palmer, mustering 14 singles and 7 walks.

Then the Series moved to Pittsburgh. The Pirates won the third game, 5-1, as Steve Blass pitched a three-hitter. They won the fourth game (the first night game in Series history), 4-3, as rookie Bruce Kison pitched 6⅓ innings of one-hit relief. They took the fifth game, 4-0, on Nelson Briles's two-hitter.

Suddenly, the Pirates had a 3-2 lead in games, and Weaver wondered aloud, "I can't tell if it's their pitching or our hitting." But when the competition returned to Baltimore, the Orioles won the sixth game, 3-2, on Brooks Robinson's 10th-inning sacrifice fly.

Before the seventh and deciding game, Blass was so nervous that he could not finish breakfast that morning, but he pitched a four-hitter as the Pirates won, 2-1, to become world champions. After the Series, Murtaugh retired because of his health. Coach Bill

Virdon was named to succeed him as manager of the Pirates.

The outstanding player of the Series was the 37-year-old Clemente, who made 12 hits (1 short of the record) in 29 times at bat. In 17 seasons with the Pirates, Clemente had a lifetime batting average of .318. He had won four National League batting titles, but none in the last three years when he hit .345, .352, and .341. At season's end, he needed only 118 hits to reach 3,000, a plateau achieved by only 10 men in baseball history. "This guy," said Weaver, "plays like he's 16 years old."

The Season's Stars. Earlier in the year, the big star was Vida Blue of the Oakland A's. After losing the season opener, he won 10 straight games—a two-hitter, two three-hitters, three four-hitters, two five-hitters, and two six-hitters. By midseason, his won-lost record was 17-3, and 30 victories seemed assured.

They never came. Blue became increasingly uncomfortable with the public interest that surrounded him, and the fact that he got only three days of rest between pitching assignments seemed to take a toll on his arm. His record for the rest of the season was only 7-5. The final figures, however, were glowing—a 24-8 record, a 1.82 earned-run average (best in the American League), 24 complete games, 8 shut-outs, and 301 strikeouts in 312 innings. On October 26, Blue was named the winner of the Cy Young Award as the best pitcher in the American League. He is the youngest player to win this honor. In November, he was named the league's Most Valuable Player. See BLUE, VIDA.

The lowest earned-run average in the major leagues, 1.76, belonged to Seaver of the New York Mets. His record became 20-10 when he won the last game of the season. Torre of the St. Louis Cardinals led the major leagues in batting (.363), hits (230), and runs batted in (137). Tony Oliva of Minnesota (.337) won his third American League batting title.

Aaron, like Clemente a young 37, hit 47 home runs, second only to Stargell in the majors. Aaron finished the year with 639 career home runs, which gave him a good chance to break baseball's most revered record, Babe Ruth's lifetime total of 714 homers. Mays, with 646 home runs, was ahead of the Atlanta outfielder, but Mays's major league career seemed almost over.

Baseball's Problems. The Senators had many difficulties. Owner Bob Short, desperately trying to attract fans, had acquired two controversial players in Denny McLain and Curt Flood. McLain was suspended much of the 1970 season for his involvement with a bet-taking operation. Flood sat out the 1970 season while suing professional baseball, contending that its reserve clause was illegal.

Both had disastrous 1971 seasons. McLain, drawing a salary of $100,000, lost 22 games, the most in the majors. Flood, whose salary was $110,000, quit the team after three weeks and hibernated in Europe, a victim of financial problems.

On October 19, the Supreme Court of the United States announced that it would hear Flood's challenge to the reserve clause, which binds a player to the team that first signs him, unless he is sold or traded. Flood charged this was a form of involuntary servitude, and that by forbidding players to bargain freely with club owners, professional baseball violates federal and state antitrust laws.

Controversy surrounded Alex Johnson of the California Angels. The 28-year-old outfielder was fined 29 times during the season and often suspended for not doing his best. "I'm not mentally ready," Johnson said. An arbitrator ruled that Johnson needed psychiatric help and thus could not be suspended without pay. After the season, Johnson was traded to Cleveland, his fifth team in eight years. During the major-league meetings in November and December in Phoenix, Ariz., 18 of the 24 clubs traded a total of 54 players.

Major league attendance set an all-time record of more than 29,100,000 (17,300,000 for the National League, 11,800,000 for the American). Thirteen of the 24 teams drew fewer spectators, but the Philadelphia Phillies, playing in a new stadium, attracted 1.5 million, almost double their 1970 figure.   Frank Litsky

See SECTION TWO, NEW GAME PLAN FOR SPORTS IN THE '70s.

BASKETBALL. The Milwaukee Bucks and the Utah Stars, two teams that had never come close before, won professional basketball championships in the 1970-1971 season. The University of California, Los Angeles (UCLA), which knew all about winning, captured the National Collegiate Athletic Association (NCAA) championship for the fifth straight year and for the seventh time in eight years, all under coach John Wooden.

More significant, however, was the continuing love-hate relationship between the two professional leagues—the 25-year-old National Basketball Association (NBA) and the 4-year-old American Basketball Association (ABA). While battling each other for veteran players and outstanding collegians, they agreed to merge and asked the Congress of the United States for approval.

A focal point of their battle was Spencer Haywood, the hero of the United States basketball team's 1968 Olympic triumph. Haywood, then a University of Detroit sophomore, was signed in 1969 by Denver of the ABA as a "hardship case." NBA rules barred the drafting or signing of any player before his college class had graduated. But the ABA allowed its teams to sign players who still had college eligibility if the players showed that the system used by the NBA worked a financial hardship. Haywood became an immediate professional star. In 1970, contending that Denver had breached his contract, he quit the

Superstars Oscar Robertson (with the ball) and Lew Alcindor (33), now Kareem Abdul-Jabbar, led the Milwaukee Bucks to the NBA championship.

team, and Seattle of the NBA signed him to a six-year contract.

Denver then sued to get Haywood back. The NBA also called the Seattle club's action illegal, citing the NBA rule on signing of college players. A U.S. District Court ruled, however, that Seattle's signing was legal and the NBA rule illegal.

By that time, ABA teams had signed three of the best college undergraduates. Johnny Neumann of Mississippi, a sophomore who led the nation in scoring with 40.1 points per game, signed with the Memphis Pros. Julius Erving of Massachusetts, joined the Virginia Squires, and George McGinnis left Indiana University to join the Indiana Pacers. NBA club owners, furious at Seattle, reluctantly changed their rule and like the ABA, staged a hardship draft.

Merger Talks. In 1970, the NBA Players Association had obtained a federal court order barring an NBA-ABA merger without congressional approval, citing possible antitrust violations. The two leagues took their merger request to Congress in 1971 saying that only a merger could save them from financial suicide. Meanwhile, the costly bidding war between the two leagues continued.

The NBA added three teams (Buffalo, Cleveland, and Portland) and reorganized into four divisions. Milwaukee, which already had the NBA's finest young player in 7-foot 2-inch Lew Alcindor, ob-tained Oscar Robertson, one of the greatest guards in basketball history, from Cincinnati, and signed him to a three-year, $700,000 contract. "Oscar is a leader," said Milwaukee coach Larry Costello. "He will make Lew a better player."

The Champion Bucks. The 32-year-old Robertson did just that. The Bucks won 34 of their 36 home games, a record. They also won 28 games on the road, another record, and during the season they won 20 games in a row, still another record. They won their division title by 15 games and swept through the play-offs, winning 12 of 14 games. They crushed the Baltimore Bullets in four consecutive games in the play-off finals to become champions in their third year of existence.

Alcindor, only 24, swept every available honor. He was voted the outstanding player of the regular season and the play-offs. He won the scoring title, averaging 31.7 points per game. He led the voting for the All-Star team (the other All-Stars were John Havlicek of Boston, Billy Cunningham of Philadelphia, Jerry West of Los Angeles, and Dave Bing of Detroit). After the season, Alcindor changed his name to Kareem Abdul-Jabbar.

In the ABA, there were three franchise shifts – New Orleans to Memphis, Los Angeles to Utah, and Washington to Virginia. Virginia and Indiana won the division titles, but Utah captured the play-offs, beating Kentucky in seven games.

Final Standings in Major League Basketball

National Basketball Association

Eastern Conference

Atlantic Division	W.	L.	Pct.
New York	52	30	.634
Philadelphia	47	35	.573
Boston	44	38	.537
Buffalo	22	60	.268
Central Division			
Baltimore	42	40	.512
Atlanta	36	46	.439
Cincinnati	33	49	.402
Cleveland	15	67	.183

Western Conference

Midwest Division	W.	L.	Pct.
Milwaukee	66	16	.805
Chicago	51	31	.622
Phoenix	48	34	.585
Detroit	45	37	.549
Pacific Division			
Los Angeles	48	34	.585
San Francisco	41	41	.500
San Diego	40	42	.488
Seattle	38	44	.463
Portland	29	53	.354

Leading Scorers	G.	FG.	FT.	Pts.	Avg.
Lew Alcindor, Milwaukee	82	1,063	470	2,596	31.7
John Havlicek, Boston	81	892	554	2,338	28.9
Elvin Hayes, San Diego	82	948	454	2,350	28.7
Dave Bing, Detroit	82	799	615	2,213	27.0
Lou Hudson, Atlanta	76	829	381	2,039	26.8
Bob Love, Chicago	81	765	513	2,043	25.2
Geoff Petrie, Portland	82	784	463	2,031	24.8
Pete Maravich, Atlanta	81	738	404	1,880	23.2
Bill Cunningham, Philadelphia	81	702	455	1,859	23.0
Tom Van Arsdale, Cincinnati	82	749	377	1,875	22.9
Chet Walker, Chicago	81	650	480	1,780	22.0

American Basketball Association

Eastern Division	W.	L.	Pct.
Virginia	55	29	.655
Kentucky	44	40	.524
New York	40	44	.476
Floridians	37	47	.440
Pittsburgh	36	48	.429
Carolina	34	50	.405

Western Division	W.	L.	Pct.
Indiana	58	26	.690
Utah	57	27	.679
Memphis	41	43	.488
Texas	30	54	.357
Denver	30	54	.357

Leading Scorers	G.	FG.	FT.	Pts.	Avg.
Dan Issel, Kentucky	83	938	604	2,480	29.8
Rick Barry, New York	59	613	451	1,734	29.3
John Brisker, Pittsburgh	79	809	430	2,315	29.3
Mack Calvin, Floridians	81	727	696	2,201	27.1
Charlie Scott, Virginia	84	886	456	2,276	27.1
Larry Cannon, Denver	80	733	606	2,126	26.5
Larry Jones, Floridians	84	719	471	2,044	24.3
Don Freeman, Texas	66	596	367	1,559	23.6
Joe Caldwell, Carolina	72	679	302	1,678	23.3
Zelmo Beaty, Utah	76	659	420	1,744	22.9
Steve Jones, Memphis	83	692	332	1,836	22.1

In College Basketball, UCLA was ranked first after the regular season by both the Associated Press and United Press International. The only major undefeated teams during the regular season were Marquette and Pennsylvania. Marquette had won 39 consecutive games over two seasons until losing to Ohio State in the NCAA regional competition. Pennsylvania had won 28 in a row until an astonishing 43-point loss to Villanova in an NCAA regional final. In the national final on March 27 in the Houston Astrodome, UCLA defeated Villanova, 68-62.

Villanova's elation at reaching the NCAA final was short-lived. Howard Porter, its 6-foot 7-inch star, had become the object of a tug-of-war between the NBA and ABA, and he signed with the Chicago Bulls of the NBA after the NCAA championships. The Pittsburgh Condors of the ABA, claiming prior ownership, revealed in court that Porter had signed an ABA contract in midseason and had accepted a down payment of $15,000, violating NCAA rules. Villanova forfeited its second-place tournament finish. Porter stayed with the Bulls.

Austin Carr of Notre Dame was chosen Player of the Year, and he was a popular all-America choice along with Sidney Wicks of UCLA, Jim McDaniels of Western Kentucky, Artis Gilmore of Jacksonville, Dean Meminger of Marquette, and John Roche of South Carolina.

Frank Litsky

BELGIUM. After a yearlong struggle, the government in 1971 settled the long-standing language dispute between French-speaking Walloons and Dutch-speaking Flemings, who constitute about 60 per cent of the population. The last two bills in a complex deal were approved by the Senate on July 19. The legislation reduces tensions between the two groups by decentralizing decision-making processes. The Flemings live in the north and the Walloons live south of Brussels. The regions were given special powers for economic and cultural planning, and the French-speaking minority received guarantees that it will not be outvoted in parliament on crucial issues. A compromise on Brussels, largely French-speaking, confirmed the present city limits, but let parents there pick their children's schools.

The Socialist Party decided in January to pick two presidents, one to represent the Flemish community and one the Walloon. The step was seen as a sign of Belgium's move toward becoming a federal state, a goal that extremists from both communities seek.

General Election. Prime Minister Gaston Eyskens moved a general election set for spring, 1972, up to Nov. 7, 1971. Eyskens' coalition, the Roman Catholic Christian Social Party and the Socialists, held its majority. The new membership of the Chamber of Representatives, however, seemed to have a more regionalist outlook, suggesting more rapid moves toward federalism for Belgium.

Shops, cafes, gasoline stations, and movies were closed for 24 hours on February 18 by a "strike without a cause." The Confederation of Independent Workers called the strike to protest against a demand for two months' advance payment on Value-Added Tax collected. The government yielded, but about 800,000 small traders – a fifth of the working population – struck anyway to show the strength of the official middle classes, who have their own government minister.

When West Germany and the Netherlands revalued their currencies in May, Belgium angered its neighbors by refusing to float the franc against an incoming flow of speculative dollars. Belgium decided that its two-tier exchange system, with both an uncontrolled and an official market, was enough protection.

Lower Production. Full utilization of industrial capacity and a tight labor market slowed production growth to about 5 per cent. In 1969, it had been 11 per cent and in 1970, 7½ per cent. Introduction of the Value-Added Tax in January raised the cost of living by 2.5 per cent and increased inflation dangers.

Facts in Brief. Population: 9,821,000. Government: King Baudouin I; Prime Minister Gaston Eyskens. Monetary Unit: Belgian franc. Foreign Trade: exports, $11,610,000,000; imports, $11,363,000,000 (including Luxembourg). Principal Exports: iron and steel, machinery. Kenneth Brown

BELLOW, SAUL (1915-   ), became the first author to receive three National Book Awards when he was honored in March, 1971, for his novel *Mr. Sammler's Planet*. The hero of the book, septuagenarian Artur Sammler, lives on New York City's West Side with his niece and daughter. There, he scrutinizes history, the city, and friends and relatives. Bellow also won National Book Awards for *The Adventures of Augie March* in 1954, and for *Herzog* in 1965. He also received the $10,000 Prix International de Littérature for *Herzog*.

Bellow was born in Lachine, Canada, on July 10, 1915. His parents had moved to Canada from St. Petersburg (now called Leningrad), Russia. When he was 9 years old, the family moved to Chicago. He entered the University of Chicago in 1933 and Northwestern University in 1935, and graduated with honors in anthropology and sociology from Northwestern in 1937. Briefly, he taught at a Chicago teachers college and worked for the *Encyclopaedia Britannica*. Bellow then taught writing and literature at the University of Minnesota, Princeton University, and Bard College in New York state before joining the faculty at the University of Chicago. His first published novel, *Dangling Man* (1944), won high critical acclaim. Bellow, who has been married three times, has three sons. He teaches literature and chairs the Committee on Social Thought at the University of Chicago. Lillian Zahrt

BIOCHEMISTRY. The primary structure of the human growth hormone (HGH) was apparently definitely established in 1971. HGH, first isolated and purified in 1956 by biochemist Choh Hao Li of the University of California Medical Center, San Francisco, is composed of a sequence of 188 amino acids. In 1970, Li and Donald Yamashiro, also of the University of California Medical Center, reported that they had synthesized the amino acid chain for the structure in accordance with the sequence previously thought to be correct. However, the synthetic product proved to have only 5 to 10 per cent of the physiological activity of the naturally occurring material.

In March, 1971, biochemist Hugh D. Niall and his colleagues at the Massachusetts General Hospital in Boston suggested that the synthetic growth hormone was inactive because Li's sequence of the 188 amino acids was incorrect.

By transposing a sequence of 15 amino acids occupying positions 17 to 31 in Li's model to positions 77 to 91, and by adding two additional amino acids that had not been included in Li's original analysis, Niall said, the hormones would more closely resemble the naturally occurring material. When this new structure is used, Niall reported, approximately 80 per cent of the amino acid residues are identical in sequence to those of human growth hormone.

Li announced a revision of his structure for HGH at the International Symposium on Growth Hormone in Milan, Italy, on May 5. It was essentially identical with that proposed by Niall. Researchers will get final proof when a structure corresponding to the new formula is synthesized and tested for physiological activity.

Parathyroid Hormone. Calcium metabolism is controlled by two hormones, parathyroid hormone and calcitonin. The first increases the amount of calcium in the bloodstream, and the second decreases the amount. In December, 1970, Bryan Brewer and Rosemary Ronan, biochemists at the National Institutes of Health (NIH) in Bethesda, Md., isolated cattle parathyroid hormone and determined its structure. The hormone consists of a single chain of 84 amino acids.

In January, 1971, investigators from NIH and from the Massachusetts General Hospital reported that they had synthesized the cattle parathyroid hormone. Tests of their synthetic material showed the surprising fact that a segment of only 34 amino acids corresponding to the terminal sequence of the whole hormone – something less than half of the structure of the whole hormone – exhibited the complete physiological activity of the whole hormone. The synthetic segment was also found to be more potent in test-tube experiments than in test animals. This may mean that the portion of the hormone that was missing in the synthetic segment may protect

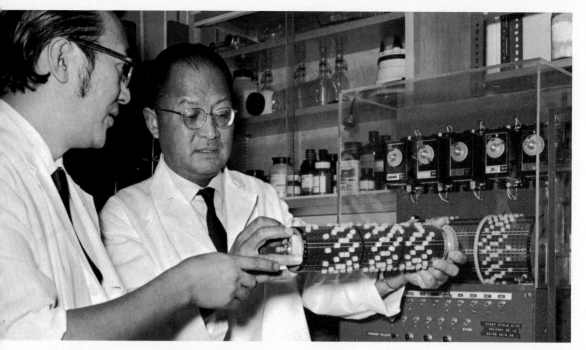

Donald Yamashiro, left, and Choh Hao Li of the University of California
announced a revised structure for synthetic human growth hormone in 1971.

the whole hormone from any type of rapid metabolic breakdown.

Since this development, the structure of the opposite hormone, calcitonin, has also been determined. This turns out to be only one-third the size of the parathyroid hormone and has no apparent similarities in structure.

Multiple Sclerosis victims suffer from a variety of symptoms attributed to degeneration of the central nervous system. The precise cause is unknown, but some biochemists have suggested that the patient has, in some fashion, become sensitized to the tissue of his own central nervous system. Although exact analogies do not exist in the animal world, there has been great interest in a condition known as experimental allergic encephalomyelitis (EAE), a paralytic disease that can be induced in monkeys, rabbits, guinea pigs, and rats. The disease is caused by injecting a protein into the animals' blood stream.

The protein A1 is one of two proteins that form the myelin membrane surrounding the central section of nerve cells in any animal or human body. One of these is a complex protein associated with a variety of lipid materials and the other, present in somewhat smaller amounts, is the A1 protein. When the A1 protein is injected in small amounts into experimental animals, it causes EAE.

The complete amino acid sequence for the A1 protein from humans and from cattle was determined in 1970 by Edwin H. Eylar at the Salk Institute, San Diego, Calif. Eylar showed that human A1 protein has 172 amino acids and cattle A1 protein has 170. The Salk Institute investigators also found that they could split the A1 protein with enzymes, and that relatively small fragments of the whole protein can induce EAE. By chemical analysis of the smaller fragments, they were able to demonstrate that the sequence had to contain the amino acid tryptophan followed by any four amino acids, and then glutamine and lysine or arginine, in order to cause EAE. However, it appears that the tryptophan-containing sequence may not be essential to induce the disease in every species. In rabbits, for example, a segment containing 49 amino acids of the original A1 protein, but not containing the tryptophan sequences can also cause EAE. This has been confirmed by workers at the University of California Medical Center in San Francisco. They found that any chemical modification of the tryptophan residue makes the A1 injection ineffective for guinea pigs, whereas it continues to cause EAE in rabbits. Scientists note with great interest that guinea pigs that have been given the inactivated tryptophan material become resistant to the effects of the original A1 protein.

Definite proof that A1 protein causes multiple sclerosis is still missing. However, these experimental results on animals are promising and of great medical interest.

Earl A. Evans

BIOLOGY. Scientists learned more about satellite DNA in 1971. In most cells, DNA is present primarily in the nucleus, where it constitutes genetic material. However, DNA also is found elsewhere in many plant and animal cells and is different from the nuclear material. This DNA is known as satellite DNA. In a recent survey of mammals, satellite DNA was discovered in the cells of 48 of the 90 species that were examined. At least two satellite DNA fractions are known to exist in human beings.

In 1971, Edwin M. Southern of the University of Edinburgh analyzed the sequence of nucleotides present in one specimen of satellite DNA, the alpha-satellite DNA from a guinea pig. Two other types of satellite DNA are also found in guinea pigs, and the alpha satellite that Southern studied accounts for only about 5 per cent of the total DNA. He found that the sequence of nucleotide bases in the alpha-satellite DNA had a structure of six nucleotides repeated over and over in each of its two strands. One strand sequence is cytosine, cytosine, cytosine, thymine, adenine, and adenine; the complementary strand contains guanine, guanine, guanine, adenine, thymine, and thymine.

Despite its widespread presence, however, satellite DNA has resisted all the efforts of scientists to determine its function. It is unlikely that satellite DNA produces protein, as does other DNA. If it did, the protein would consist simply of a series of repeating amino acid sequences, a series that the cell apparently could not use. On the other hand, satellite DNA may play some unforeseen role in the development of the cell's structure.

A group at Yale University, under the direction of Joseph G. Gall, found that satellite DNA appears to be localized in the cell nucleus at certain times during cell division. The researchers are not yet certain that this is true for every type of cell. But if this is the case, it may explain both the function and the reason for the unique structure of satellite DNA. Repetitive sequences of nucleotide bases are particularly effective in holding DNA strands together as a cell nucleus divides, and this may be what the nucleotide bases of satellite DNA do.

There are, however, unanswered questions. For example, why do some species have much more satellite DNA than other species, and what has been the evolutionary history of the appearance of DNA in the cell? One suggestion is that the satellite DNA may arise by duplication of a short sequence of nucleotide pairs followed by the transfer of some of these pairs to every chromosome in the cell. Perhaps the selection of a particular sequence for duplication confers some as yet unknown advantage to the cell in which it resides.

Nerve Impulses. In many nerves, the nerve impulse, on reaching the synapse, releases a chemical substance called acetylcholine. This substance then travels to a receptor cell in which the nerve impulse is converted into some physiological activity, such as muscle contraction. An enzyme known as choline esterase is present in or near the receptor cell. It breaks down the used acetylcholine to acetic acid and choline, so that more acetylcholine must be released to continue the nerve-impulse action. The process of neural transmission thus assumes a pulse-like character.

New information about some aspects of this process was obtained, in 1963, by using the venom of a Formosan snake. Researchers found that the snake venom blocked the effect of acetylcholine at neuro-muscular junctions. In 1971, investigators in London demonstrated that the same snake venom also blocks the transmission of nerve impulses in the electric tissue of the Torpedo eel. The London group added radioactive material to the purified snake venom so that they could follow its actions in the electric tissue of the eel.

The researchers found that the venom reacted with a membrane protein in the eel's tissues. Each protein unit appeared to have only a single binding site for one molecule of the snake venom. In other words, the number of molecules in the protein and in the hydrolyzing enzyme is the same, although they can be physically separated and do not have a common subunit.   Earl A. Evans, Jr.

BLINDNESS. See HANDICAPPED.

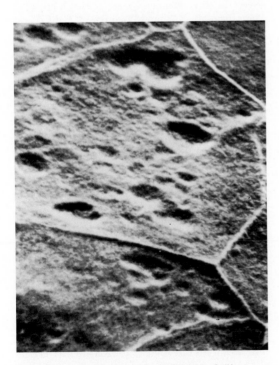

A scanning electron microscope in Berkeley, Calif., revealed amazing structural details of the nerves on the outermost surface of the cornea of a human eye.

BLUE, VIDA (1949-   ), became a pitching sensation with the Oakland Athletics in 1971, his first full season of major league baseball. The tall, slender left-hander lost the opening game of the season, then won 10 games in a row. He won a total of 24 games and lost only 8, and led the American League in complete games pitched (24) and shut-outs (8), and had the lowest earned-run average (1.82) among starting pitchers. In addition, Blue was the starting and winning pitcher in the annual major league All-Star game, won the Cy Young Award as the league's best pitcher, and was named the American League's Most Valuable Player.

Blue's sensational pitching made him the American League's biggest drawing card. When the New York Yankees held a special "Blue Tuesday" on June 1, a crowd of 30,052, the largest to see a night game in Yankee Stadium in three years, came to see him pitch. Five days later, 40,246 watched him pitch against the Washington Senators, the largest Sunday crowd in seven years there.

Blue was born in Mansfield, La., the oldest of six children. He began pitching while in high school. An outstanding high school quarterback, Blue received several offers to play college football. But his father, a laborer in an iron foundry, died suddenly, leaving the family with no means of support. Soon after, Blue signed a bonus contract with the Oakland club.

Joseph P. Spohn

BOATS AND BOATING. The boating industry made strides in 1971, despite a general consumer fall-off in major purchases during the year. A statistical report, issued jointly in September by the two major trade organizations, cited an 11.8 per cent increase over the previous model year in the combined factory value of boat, motor, and trailer shipments.

The report, covering the model year ended Aug. 31, 1971, was issued by the National Association of Engine and Boat Manufacturers and the Boating Industry Association. A sampling of manufacturers showed dollar increases in outboard motor sales (up 21.4 per cent), sailboats (14.4), canoes (9.5), houseboats without cabins (7.4), boat trailers (5.9), and inboard-outdrive boats (1.4). Dollar volume dropped in inboard boats (down 21.3 per cent), houseboats with cabins (15.6), and outboard boats (0.3).

In summary, it was a bad year for the more expensive boats. Overall figures, however, showed a 29 per cent increase in August over August, 1970, and the industry was optimistic about the future. Builders of fiber glass boats predicted a 10 to 12 per cent increase in sales in 1972.

The industry estimated that 45 million persons participated in recreational boating in 1971. There were 539,000 boats of all types sold in 1970, and 550,000 in 1971. Retail expenditures on boating increased from $680 million in 1950 to $3.4 billion in 1970. The number of recreational boats in use rose from 3.5 million in 1950 to 8.8 million in 1970.

On August 11, President Richard M. Nixon signed the Federal Boat and Safety Act, giving the Coast Guard power to set up stricter controls over boating and establish construction standards.

Turbine Engines. Turbine power plants, which offered more horsepower per pound, less vibration, less noise, and a cooler exhaust, were introduced to pleasure craft in 1971. Chris-Craft adapted a new Ford turbine for larger boats, starting with its 55-foot Commander fiber glass yachts. Pacemaker installed Ford turbines on its 48-foot Sportfisherman fiber glass boats. The turbine engines are cleaner than the diesel engines they replace and they require less maintenance.

Powerboat Races. Bill Wishnick, a New York City chemical company executive, and Bob Magoon, an eye surgeon from Miami Beach, Fla., were the leading drivers in offshore powerboat racing in 1971. Wishnick won the world championship, and Magoon succeeded him as American Power Boat Association inboard champion, each in a Cigarette hull.

The world title was decided in a series of 17 races, and Wishnick used two boats so he could compete easily on both sides of the Atlantic Ocean. His closest rival was Vincenzo Balistrieri of Italy.

The 37-year-old Magoon entered six American title races and won them all. He became the first to sweep the three Hennessy races at Key West, Fla.; Point Pleasant, N.J.; and Long Beach, Calif. Those three races and the Sam Griffith Memorial in Fort Lauderdale, Fla., also won by Wishnick, counted toward the world and American titles.

Hydroplanes. Unlimited hydroplanes–30-foot, 3-ton monsters with airplane engines that can deliver nearly 4,000 horsepower–staged nine races to crown a national champion. *Miss Budweiser*, driven by Dean Chenoweth of Xenia, Ohio, and powered by a Rolls-Royce engine, won for the third consecutive year. Maintenance cost the boat's beer sponsor $150,000 a year. The major race, the Gold Cup, was held at Madison, Ind., an Ohio River city of about 13,000. The crowd of 110,000 was delighted when a hometown boat, community-owned *Miss Madison*, won.

Sailing. In yachting, the North American champions included John Kolius of Houston among the men, Mrs. Romeyn Shethar Everdell of Duxbury, Mass., among the women, and Charlie Scott of Annapolis, Md., among juniors. Kolius was the junior champion in 1968. Mrs. Everdell won three previous women's titles, the first in 1939.

In ocean racing, the 73-foot sloop *Windward Passage*, owned by Mark Johnson of Maui, Hawaii, was the first finisher and handicap winner of the 2,225-mile race from Los Angeles to Honolulu. *Windward Passage* also was first to finish in the 811-mile race from Miami to Montego Bay and the 403-mile race from St. Petersburg to Fort Lauderdale.

Frank Litsky

BOLIVIA. The 10-month-old left-wing regime of President Juan Jose Torres was overthrown on Aug. 22, 1971. Hugo Banzer Suarez, a former education minister and military college director, was proclaimed president by the heads of the armed forces (see BANZER SUAREZ, HUGO). During four days of fighting that preceded Torres' ouster, an estimated 120 Bolivians were killed. Only quick action by the military prevented full-scale civil war.

Banzer sought to consolidate his support by declaring that the new government was "nationalistic, revolutionary, and loyal to the fatherland." Elections for a constitutional government, he indicated, would be postponed indefinitely. He also called for unity between the military forces and political parties—outlawed under the previous regime–in order to strengthen the economy.

The new regime began to revise investment laws to revive the inflow of foreign capital into such important areas as oil and mining. The nation's first tin refinery had begun operating at Vinto on January 9.

Facts in Brief. Population: 5,189,000. Government: President Hugo Banzer Suarez. Monetary Unit: peso. Foreign Trade: exports, $182,000,000; imports, $165,000,000. Principal Exports: tin, antimony, tungsten.   Mary C. Webster

BOOKS. See CANADIAN LITERATURE; LITERATURE; LITERATURE FOR CHILDREN; POETRY.

BORDABERRY, JUAN MARIA (1928-   ), apparently won a very close presidential election held in Uruguay on Nov. 28, 1971. Final results were not expected until early in 1972. One of 11 candidates, Bordaberry was hand-picked by outgoing President Jorge Pacheco Areco as his successor. Pacheco was prevented by the Constitution from succeeding himself. See URUGUAY.

Bordaberry was born on June 17, 1928, in Montevideo. He attended law school at the University of the Republic in Montevideo but did not graduate. For a number of years, he operated a large cattle ranch in Durazno Department. From 1959 to 1962, he was president of the National Meat Board. In March, 1964, he was named president of the Federal League for Rural Action (FLRA), a landowners group somewhat similar to the U.S. Chamber of Commerce.

Bordaberry was elected to the Senate as a member of the Blanco Party in November, 1962. He resigned in 1968, however, because of differences with the Blanco-dominated government over agricultural policies. From 1966 to 1969, he resumed the presidency of the FLRA, then he returned to government as minister of livestock and agriculture under Pacheco.

Bordaberry is married and the father of eight children. He is an expert horseman and an avid reader of Latin American history.   Paul C. Tullier

Members of the Revolutionary Nationalist Movement, which ousted Bolivia's left-wing regime in August, demonstrate in La Paz for the new government.

BOSTON. Kevin H. White won a second term as mayor of Boston in November, 1971, when he defeated Congresswoman Louise Day Hicks, an outspoken opponent of school busing. White won 62 per cent of the vote. See ELECTIONS.

On June 23, the Massachusetts Commission Against Discrimination ordered Boston to complete a sweeping integration of the city's public schools. In September, the Boston School Committee tried to integrate a new $8-million elementary school located in a black neighborhood. However, parents of about 300 children, both black and white, refused to enroll their children there. As a result, the committee abandoned its effort, leaving the school with a ratio of four black students to each white student. On December 1, the federal government charged Boston with operating a dual school system and threatened to cut off federal funds.

A federal report released in July showed that 16.6 per cent of Suffolk County's residents were receiving welfare. This was the highest percentage of welfare recipients among the nation's largest urban areas. In August, the Department of Labor added Boston to its list of metropolitan areas with an unemployment rate of at least 6 per cent.

The 1970 census showed that Boston's population had dropped 8.1 per cent since 1960 to 641,071. But the metropolitan area increased 6.1 per cent to 2,753,700.　　　　　　　　　　　　J. M. Banovetz

BOTANY. P. L. Neel and Richard W. Harris of the University of California, Davis, found in 1971 that trees that are shaken periodically will not grow as tall as trees that are undisturbed. They performed their experiment on sweet gum (*Liquidambar*) trees growing in a greenhouse. Researchers shook one tree from each of eight pairs for 30 seconds once a day over a period of 27 days to simulate the action of wind on trees growing in the open. The other tree of each pair was not touched. The shaken trees were found to grow an average of 20 per cent less than the unshaken trees, and six of the eight shaken trees formed terminal buds. These are the growths that appear at the end of a branch when it stops growing and begins to produce side branches. None of the unshaken trees formed terminal buds.

Microscopic examination of fibers in each tree showed that the shaken trees had shorter fibers, but the diameter of the fibers was the same as in the unshaken trees. The scientists concluded that any study of the inhibiting effects of wind on plant growth should include movement as well as the commonly considered effects of wind on transpiration, intake of carbon dioxide, and injury to leaves and branches.

Florigens. Evidence for the probable existence of flower-promoting substances called florigens has accumulated, but so far, none has been identified. David D. Gibby and Frank B. Salisbury of Utah State University conducted a series of experiments on the cocklebur (*Xanthium*) in an attempt to discover these elusive substances, and found reasons for the lack of success. The cocklebur flowers in response to short days of light. After exposing individual cocklebur leaves to selected amounts of light, the scientists found that the bottom half of a leaf on a long-day exposure inhibits the top half response to a short day. They also found that a leaf exposed for a long day of light inhibits the response of a leaf exposed to a short day if it is on the stem between the bud and the leaf exposed for the short day.

After conducting many other tests, the scientists hypothesized that although flower production may involve florigens, the limitation of florigen production does not inhibit flowering. The flowering mechanism seems to result from a push-pull mechanism, in which a leaf not actively producing florigens is actively inhibiting leaf growth. Any attempt to isolate florigens by applying substances thought to be florigens to plants exposed to long days of light will not show a flower-promoting response because the amount of light apparently destroys florigen.

Disease-free Tree. U.S. Department of Agriculture botanists believe they are close to stopping Dutch Elm disease in trees. They are developing a tree resistant to the disease. "Next year we hope to have the first resistant tree to release to the public," a spokesman said in June.　　　　Barbara N. Benson

BOTSWANA. See AFRICA.

BOWLING. Johnny Petraglia of Brooklyn, N.Y., won five bowling tournaments and the most money in 1971. Mike Limongello of North Babylon, N.Y., however, won the two most important tournaments – the Professional Bowlers Association (PBA) championship and the U.S. Open.

The PBA staged 35 tournaments, and the 24-year-old Petraglia won in Washington, D.C.; New Orleans; Houston; Akron, Ohio; and Winston-Salem, N.C. He captured three successive tournaments, finishing with the $100,000 Tournament of Champions, held from March 30 to April 3 in Akron. The $25,000 first prize was the richest in bowling history. During the 1971 tour, he earned $85,065 – a record for one-year earnings.

Limongello's Victories. In the $75,000 U.S. Open (formerly known as the All-Star Tournament), held in January in Akron, Limongello beat Teata Semiz of River Edge, N.J., 194-186, in the title game. In the final game of the PBA championship in Paramus, N.J., on October 16, Limongello defeated Dave Davis of St. Louis, 207-202. It was the 10th time in two years that Davis had finished second, and, as he did six of those times, he lost in the last frame.

Don Johnson of Akron, with $81,349, also broke the old one-year earnings record while winning six tournaments. Johnson was runner-up in the American Bowling Congress Masters Tournament in May in Detroit as Jim Godman of Lorain, Ohio, beat him in two four-game sets, 992-864 and 922-880. Godman averaged a record 229.8 for the 40 games.

Scoring Records. The South Bend (Ind.) Open, held from August 27 to 30, was the highest scoring tournament in history. Barry Asher of Costa Mesa, Calif., won and set PBA records of 1,585 for six games (an average of 264) and 10,380 for the tournament's 42 games (an average of 247). Johnson's 247 average for the 18 qualifying games broke still another record.

The *National Bowlers Journal* All-America team consisted of Petraglia; Johnson; Dave Soutar of Gilroy, Calif.; Nelson Burton, Jr., of St. Louis; Mike McGrath of El Cerrito, Calif.; and Dick Weber of St. Louis.

Mrs. Mildred Martorella of Rochester, N.Y., won the Woman's International Bowling Congress Queens tournament for the third time in five years, and Paula Sperber, a 20-year-old from Miami, won the Women's All-Star title.

Four of the six Women's All-Americans, including Mrs. Martorella and Miss Sperber, were left-handers. So were Petraglia, Davis, McGrath, and many other leading men. The left-handers had their finest hour when they produced all 16 finalists in the San Jose (Calif.) Open. A month later, in the Buckeye Open in Toledo, Ohio, the highest left-hander (Petraglia) finished 34th.   Frank Litsky

BOXING. The most talked-about sports event of 1971, and the richest single sports event in history, was the world heavyweight title fight between Joe Frazier and Muhammad Ali. Frazier won it on a 15-round decision on March 8 in New York's Madison Square Garden. But the fight itself, as stirring and bizarre as it was, was all but overshadowed by the excitement it created.

Each man was undefeated as a professional. Each claimed the title and had supporters who vociferously agreed. Most important, Ali, as always, was a master showman, a hero to many fellow blacks and some whites because he stood up to the Establishment. To many other whites and some blacks, he was a villain because he refused to live and play according to Establishment rules.

Ali's Conviction. In 1964, when Ali was known as Cassius Clay, he became heavyweight champion. At that time, he announced that he had also become a member of the Nation of Islam, better known as the Black Muslims, and that he wanted to be known by his Black Muslim name, Muhammad Ali. Further, he refused to be inducted into the U.S. Army, claiming exemption as a Black Muslim minister. Eventually, the courts found him guilty of draft evasion and sentenced him to five years in prison. He remained free while appealing, however, and on June 28, 1971, the Supreme Court of the United States unanimously reversed the conviction, saying he had

been drafted improperly. Meanwhile, most organizations that governed boxing vacated his title, and for 3½ years Ali could not get a fight. The governing bodies awarded the title to Frazier, who won a series of title bouts after Ali was dropped from contention. Ali returned to the ring in 1970, his public appeal as wide as ever. That fact was recognized by Jerry Perenchio, the theatrical agent who put together the unprecedented Frazier-Ali fight package.

The fight attracted a sellout crowd of 20,455, with tickets selling for up to $150. Of course, scalpers got much more. Satellites and cables carried the bout on television to 300 million people in 46 nations. There were 369 closed-circuit theater and club showings in the United States and Canada. The fight grossed about $20 million.

The Fight. Most people agreed that they probably got their money's worth. They had expected a classic confrontation between the 27-year-old Frazier, a Philadelphia brawler in the mold of the late Rocky Marciano, and the 29-year-old Ali, a Louisville puncher with probably the fastest hands in heavyweight history. They got the brawling of Frazier, but not the speed or finesse of the old Ali.

Ali spent much of the fight resting on the ropes, allowing Frazier to swing away at him. Ali made no effort to stop Frazier, partly because he was showing off, partly because he was tired. Ali was knocked

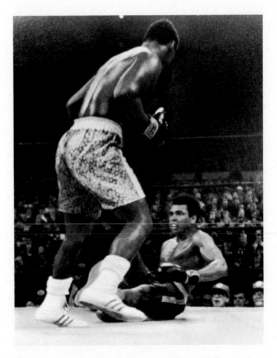

Muhammad Ali lands on the canvas after a 15th-round punch from Joe Frazier in their heavyweight title bout in New York City, March 8. Frazier won it.

World Champion Boxers

Division	Champion	Country	Year Won
Heavyweight	Joe Frazier	U.S.A.	1968
Light-heavyweight	Bob Foster	U.S.A.	1968
(disputed)	Vicente Rondon	Venezuela	1971
Middleweight	Carlos Monzon	Argentina	1970
Junior-middleweight	Koichi Wajima	Japan	1971
Welterweight	Jose Napoles	Mexico	1971
Junior-welterweight	Nicoline Loche	Argentina	1968
(disputed)	Bruno Arcari	Italy	1970
Lightweight	Ken Buchanan	Scotland	1970
(disputed)	Pedro Carrasco	Spain	1971
Junior-lightweight	Ricardo Arrendondo	Mexico	1971
(disputed)	Alfredo Marcano	Venezuela	1971
Featherweight	Kuniaki Shibata	Japan	1970
(disputed)	Antonio Gomez	Venezuela	1971
Bantamweight	Ruben Olivares	Mexico	1971
Flyweight	Masao Oba	Japan	1970
(disputed)	Betulio Gonzalez	Venezuela	1971

down in the last round and ended the night in a hospital for treatment of a swollen jaw. Frazier was hospitalized a few days later with headaches.

A month after the fight, Frazier became the first black man since Reconstruction days to speak before the legislature of his native South Carolina. At a state luncheon in his honor, Frazier's 10-year-old daughter, Jacquelyn, was introduced. In true Ali tradition, she read an original poem: "Fly like a butterfly, sting like a bee, Joe Frazier is the only one who can beat Muhammad Ali."

Frazier also spent much of his time touring with his rock music group, the Knockouts, and for a while was undecided whether to fight again. Ali made an extensive speaking tour of college campuses. Between speaking engagements, he kept fighting, hoping for a return bout with Frazier. Despite the defeat, Ali was as fast-talking as ever.

"Unlike a lot of young people," said Ferdie Pacheco, Ali's physician, "Ali has never fooled around with drugs. He doesn't have to. He can always get high on himself."

Other Winners. In other weight divisions, the most impressive fighters included bantamweight Ruben Olivares of Mexico, lightweight Ken Buchanan of Scotland, and middleweight Carlos Monzon of Argentina.   Frank Litsky

BOY SCOUTS. See YOUTH ORGANIZATIONS.

BOYS' CLUBS. See YOUTH ORGANIZATIONS.

BRATTELI, TRYGVE M. (1910-   ), became Norway's prime minister on March 17, 1971. His Labor Party assumed power when the coalition government of Prime Minister Per Borten collapsed. Borten resigned after he denied, then admitted, divulging the contents of a confidential document on negotiations for Norwegian membership in the European Community (Common Market) to opponents of the move.

Bratteli was born in the hamlet of Nøtterøy, about 50 miles south of Oslo, on Jan. 11, 1910. He began working as a messenger boy at the age of 14. From 1929 to 1933, he worked in the building trades and was active in Labor Party youth groups. During World War II, he worked as a logger until he was imprisoned by the Nazi occupation forces in 1942. In 1945, he was found near death in a prison camp in Germany.

Since returning to Norway, he has held a series of party and government positions. He had been chairman of the Labor Party since 1965.

Reserving a dry wit and moments of gaiety for an inner circle of friends, Bratteli is not an exciting public personality. He is described by those who know him as unassuming and introverted.

Bratteli married the former Randi Larssen in 1946. They live only a few blocks from the *Storting* (parliament) and Bratteli customarily walks to work. The couple have one son and two daughters.   Ed Nelson

BRAZIL. The military government of President Emílio Garrastazú Médici entered its eighth year of power in 1971. Under it, Brazil had made sizable gains toward social, political, and economic stability, despite charges of repression and censorship by the only official opposition party, the Brazilian Democratic Movement (MDB).

Economic Progress. For the fourth consecutive year, the economic boom continued, and it was predicted that the 1971 gross national product would reach $44 billion. Exports were expected to total $3-billion for the first time, with manufactured goods contributing $600 million, or 20 per cent of the total. Gross monetary reserves at the end of September totaled a record $1.6 billion, up from $1.1 billion the year before and from $505 million in the third quarter of 1969. They were the highest in South America, and sufficient for Brazil to cover almost seven months of imports. The annual inflow of foreign capital was near the $1.5-billion mark but, in September, foreign indebtedness had risen by $2.8 billion over a 30-month period to a total of $5.5 billion.

Statistics for the first six months of 1971 showed automotive production up 23 per cent over the same period in 1970; rubber consumption up 16 per cent; tractor output, 43 per cent; Portland cement, 22 per cent; and electrical output, 12 per cent. It was predicted that installed power capacity would climb from some 11.4 million kilowatts in 1971 to 17 mil-

A disastrous flash flood that followed a heavy downpour inundated a downtown section of Rio de Janeiro in February, 1971. Thousands were left homeless.

lion by 1974 and 30 million by 1980. The January-May total value of industrial production was 16 per cent higher than in the first five months of 1970.

Minimum wage hikes of from 20.5 to 26 per cent went into effect in May to compensate for an estimated 21 per cent increase in the cost of living during 1970. In the first nine months, living costs in Guanabara state alone climbed by 14.4 per cent. This was an improvement, nevertheless, over the 16.7 per cent hike registered in 1970. Observers believed that the country, for the first time in over 25 years, might close the year with an inflation rate of less than 20 per cent.

New Goals Set. Despite the economic boom in the overall statistics, only the southern region prospered. Elsewhere, the economy of much of the country stagnated and one-fourth of the population of 99.26 million persons still subsisted on incomes of only $100 annually. In the industrialized south, however, 25 million people had a per capita income of $800.

On September 15, President Médici moved to eliminate the imbalance. He presented to Congress a three-year development program designed to continue the growth rate, raise per capita income to $500 a year, and convert Brazil into a fully developed industrial nation within a generation. The program continued the Médici Government's attack on three of Brazil's major problems: illiteracy, backward agri-culture, and the uneven distribution of income. Among various priority investment targets listed were steel, petrochemicals, shipbuilding, highway construction, and electric power.

Expansion Programs Started. Brazil scheduled an $800-million expansion program to raise steel output from the 5 million tons produced in 1970 to 10 million by 1975 and 20 million by 1980. The World Bank loaned $96 million to develop the 375-million-ton Aguas Claras iron ore deposit; part of the funds would also provide for the transportation of the ore by rail some 400 miles to the Sepetiba Bay marine terminal south of Rio de Janeiro. The government-owned oil agency, Petrobras, planned to invest some $2 billion over a three-year period in domestic and foreign exploration and to expand production, distribution, refining, and transportation.

On March 29, Brazil extended its sovereignty over sea waters to 200 miles from its coast. Later, its patrols harassed United States shrimp boats operating within the strip, which most nations regarded as international waters. On June 30, in retaliation, the United States Congress allowed the International Coffee Agreement to lapse.

Facts in Brief. Population: 99,263,000. Government: President Emílio Garrastazú Médici. Monetary Unit: new cruzeiro. Foreign Trade: exports, $2,739,000,000; imports, $2,406,000,000. Principal Exports: coffee, cotton, iron ore.   Mary C. Webster

BRIDGE, CONTRACT. The Aces, originally known as the Dallas Aces, retained their World Bridge Team Championship in May, 1971, in Taipei, Formosa. The American team defeated France in the finals. The Aces started the final session with a lead of 45 international match points. The French whittled the lead to 29 points, but the Aces put on a final surge to win, 243 to 181. The foursome of Jim Jacoby, Bob Wolff, Mike Lawrence, and Bob Goldman did the bulk of the playing, with Bill Eisenberg and Bob Hamman playing only 16 of the 128 deals.

The Aces also won the Harold A. Vanderbilt Trophy at the spring national tournament of the American Contract Bridge League (A.C.B.L.) in Atlanta, Ga., in March. Their margin of 156 international match points was the largest ever achieved in a national final.

For the fourth time in the 37-year history of the event, a team successfully defended its Spingold Cup title, at the summer national tournament of the A.C.B.L. in Chicago in July. Members of the winning team were Joel Stuart, Gene Neiger, Peter Weichsel, and Steve Altman, all of New York City, and Tom Smith of Greenwich, Conn. Theodore M. O'Leary

BRIDGE. See BUILDING AND CONSTRUCTION.

BRITISH COLUMBIA. See CANADA.

BRITISH COMMONWEALTH OF NATIONS. See GREAT BRITAIN and articles on various countries of the Commonwealth.

BUILDING AND CONSTRUCTION expenditures rose 18 per cent in 1971 to an estimated $107 billion. This was a new high and represented an 18 per cent increase over the 1970 figure of $91.5 billion, according to the U.S. Bureau of the Census. The bureau attributed the rise to inflation and to a 50 per cent increase in residential building.

Contractors, struggling with a staggering rise in construction costs, were relieved by the 90-day wage-price freeze announced by President Richard M. Nixon in August, and by the continuation of the controls during the post-freeze period.

Engineering News-Record magazine, assuming that controls will continue through 1972, forecasts a sharp decline during this period in the rate of construction-cost inflation. Despite this optimistic outlook, the magazine's Building Cost Index, which measures changes in the prices of basic materials and the wages of skilled workers, reported that construction costs in 20 major cities were nearly 16 per cent higher at the end of the third quarter of 1971 than they were during the same period in 1970.

In several large cities, bricklayers, ironworkers, and carpenters received more than $10 an hour. New York City workers in these skilled trades were earning from $11 to $12.25 per hour. A sharp easing in the manpower shortage, however, especially in the South, was expected to help contractors in their contract bargaining with the construction unions.

Prior to the wage-price freeze, contractors were facing the worst materials-cost inflation since the end of World War II. Prefreeze price hikes of from 7 to 10 per cent on most construction steel products contributed heavily. Prior increases in the cost of cement, asphalt, and lumber also hiked prices.

An abrupt drop in interest rates, however, accompanied the announcement of the wage-price freeze and helped to ease financing costs during the latter part of the year.

New Building Techniques. A seven-story, 123-apartment complex for the elderly, completed near Washington, D.C., in 1971, features the first use in the United States of precast-concrete panels that incorporate doors, windows, and utilities. Workers erected the individual apartments with room-sized floor slabs and wall panels that had been precast at an on-site factory. The procedure cut costs in half.

In July, the Department of Housing and Urban Development (HUD) signed its last contract under its Operation Breakthrough program. The $125-million, 21-city project is designed to develop innovative, low-cost methods of building housing.

Building Codes and Specifications. The four model-code-writing organizations in the United States jointly published two specialized model national codes in 1971, for one- and two-family housing and for rehabilitation of old buildings. The new codes are part of HUD's drive to achieve uniformity of building codes. Currently, there are some 5,000 separate U.S. building codes. A similar experimental program was initiated in Japan in July with private industry footing the bill.

As a result of several fatal skyscraper fires, the General Services Administration ruled in October that all new high-rise federal buildings must have fire-safety systems. The Sears Tower (109 stories and 1,450 feet high) under construction in Chicago will be fully equipped with sprinklers, even though the city code requires sprinklers only below ground level in office buildings.

Outstanding Buildings. Canada's tallest building, Commerce Court, a 784-foot-high, 57-story office tower, was nearing completion in Toronto. Part of a $105-million, four-building project owned by the Canadian Imperial Bank of Commerce, the tower also ranks as the world's tallest stainless steel-clad building.

The Kennedy Center for the Performing Arts, under construction for eight years, opened in Washington, D.C., in September. The $70-million, marble-faced structure, housing a 2,500-seat opera house, a concert hall, and a theater under one roof, posed a major problem in soundproofing. Also notable are the fine acoustics achieved in the various halls.

The World Trade Center, nearing completion in New York City, was named the Outstanding Civil Engineering Achievement for 1971 by the American Society of Civil Engineers. As of 1971, the twin tow-

Freely suspended cables supported by massive corner piers hold the new, 12-story Federal Reserve Bank of Minneapolis 40 feet above street level.

ers, each 110 stories and 1,353 feet tall, were the tallest buildings in the world.

Bridges. In September, construction crews closed the final gap on one of the widest bridges in the U.S. interstate highway system. The $21-million span, 108 feet wide, will carry six lanes of Interstate 95 over the Piscataqua River between Portsmouth, N.H., and Kittery, Me. Designed as a three-span, continuous tied-arch truss, it consists of a 756-foot center span flanked by 294-foot anchor spans. The structure's bracing members are sealed boxes filled with nitrogen to prevent corrosion on the inside surfaces.

Detailed designs were underway for a $68-million post-tensioned concrete-box girder bridge over the Columbia River at Portland, Ore. The 7,700-foot crossing, a link in Interstate 205, by-passes Portland and Vancouver, Wash., and will have a 620-foot main span, longer than any bridge of its type in North America. It was anticipated that work on a similar crossing – the Three Sisters Bridge over the Potomac River between Virginia and the District of Columbia – will be resumed following completion of extensive tests on a $500,000 model of the bridge. The safety of the structure, which has a main span 750 feet long, had been questioned by the Federal Highway Administration.

In July, Italian bridgebuilders completed the world's longest concrete cable-stayed bridge in northern Libya. It is part of a new highway linking Tunisia and Egypt. The unique, three-span structure, which crosses a valley, has a center span 940 feet long and 313-foot side spans. Although most of the cable-stayed bridges in the world are made of steel, the Libyan bridge was made of concrete because of concrete's tolerance to the area's extreme variations in day and night temperatures.

Dams. In Formosa, work went ahead on the $150-million Tsengwen Dam project. The dam is the key structure in the multipurpose Tsengwen Reservoir system. Located in the deep tropics of southern Formosa, the dam will be a 427-foot-high rolled earth-fill structure, 1,312 feet long at the crest. It will hold up to 574,000 acre-feet of water.

Construction was well along on two record-breaking hydroelectric dams in Russia. Inguri Dam, near the Black Sea, will be the world's highest concrete arch at 886 feet. Nurek Dam, on the Vaksh River near the Afghanistan border, will be a 1,017-foot-high earth- and rock-fill structure – the highest of its type in the world.

In the United States, construction was postponed on three major hydroelectric dams in the Pacific Northwest when the governors of Oregon, Washington, and Idaho joined ecology groups in protesting their construction. Despite the critical power shortage in their states, the governors claimed that the destruction of areas supporting a great variety of wildlife could outweigh the benefits of the dams. The projects involved are the Mountain Sheep and Pleasant Valley dams in the last undeveloped stretch of the Snake River and the Lower Teton Project on a tributary of the Snake.

Tunnels. Swiss contractors began enlarging twin highway tunnels in Lucerne from pilot bore to full size, 34.5 feet in diameter. The expanded tunnels will run 5,100 feet south from the city, passing under two hills 300 feet high. They are a key link in National Highway 2, which will traverse the country, running south from Basel to Chiasso on the Italian border. Below Lucerne, the highway will go through a 10-mile tunnel being built under Saint Gotthard Pass.

Japan completed plans for driving a 14-mile-long railroad tunnel through the mountains of central Japan. The project will be a key structure in a new $1.6-billion express rail line, which will run 180 miles between Tokyo and Niigata on the Sea of Japan. Construction of the line, which will carry 150-mph express trains, started in October.

In the United States, work resumed on the Straight Creek Tunnel high in the Rocky Mountains after a year's delay caused by rock shifts and disputes between Colorado and the contractor over financial responsibility for a $16-million cost overrun on the project. The 8,148-foot, two-lane tunnel, now about half-finished, will carry Interstate 70 through the Continental Divide west of Denver.   Mary E. Jessup

Gondolas, riding cables that span the 2,952-foot-wide Dutch Delta, drop two of the 200,000 25-ton concrete blocks to form base for new Netherlands dam.

BULGARIA reorganized its government and continued on its pro-Russian path in 1971. A new Constitution was adopted by a national referendum on May 16, and the government was reorganized. Todor Zhivkov resigned as premier, and Stanko Todorov succeeded him on July 7. But Zhivkov retained his position as Communist Party first secretary and also became chairman of the newly formed state council, which will direct foreign and domestic policy. A well-known Stalinist, Angel Solakov, was replaced as minister of the interior and later was expelled from the party. But promises of more democracy and representative rule did not end government pressure on the intellectuals to conform.

Leonid I. Brezhnev, general secretary of Russia's Communist Party, addressed the Communist Party Congress on April 21. The congress formally adopted plans stressing a more centralized economy and closer integration with Russia. The government combined 120 industrial trusts into 64 and tightened control over individual firms.

Lŭchezar Avramov, deputy premier and minister of foreign trade, was dropped from the Politburo at the party congress and then was relieved of his government posts. He had signed a five-year trade agreement with Czechoslovakia on January 10, and was considered a potential rival of Zhivkov.

Foreign Relations. Bulgaria proposed an eight-point plan for improved economic relations with Greece on February 13. On July 2, Greece and Bulgaria announced the formation of a joint commission to study economic, technological, industrial, and scientific cooperation between the two countries. The two share a 300-mile border and have long been antagonists.

Bulgaria's ambassador, Stoyan Zaimov, was expelled from the Sudan on August 2. The African nation charged that Zaimov had taken part in an attempted coup against the Sudanese government on July 19.

After visiting Yugoslavia and other East European countries, Brezhnev returned briefly to Bulgaria on September 26. He decorated Zhivkov with the Order of Lenin.

Bulgaria announced in September that it was extending $10 million in credit to Peru for the purchase of fish-processing machinery. The loan is to be repaid to Bulgaria over 12 years at an interest rate of 2.5 per cent.

A Russian-built Bulgarian airliner crashed January 18 while attempting to land at the airport near Zurich, Switzerland, on a flight from France. Of the 35 aboard, only a child and the pilot survived.

Facts in Brief. Population: 8,614,000. Government: Communist Party First Secretary and State Council Chairman Todor Zhivkov; Premier Stanko Todorov. Monetary Unit: lev. Foreign Trade: exports, $2,009,000,000; imports, $1,815,000,000. Principal Exports: clothing, tobacco, fruit. Chris Cviic

BURMA. General Ne Win and his 200,000-man army maintained rigid control over the country in 1971. Although there was continuing opposition to the Ne Win regime among the Karens and the Kachins and in Shan State, it was mostly limited to occasional acts of terrorism or sabotage.

During the year, former Prime Minister U Nu, in exile, tried to solidify opposition to Ne Win. In January, he reportedly established headquarters just across the border in Thailand.

The major problem facing Burma in 1971 was economic stagnation. Ne Win's brand of military Socialism, with state control of all industry and commerce, produced very little production. Rice, once a major export, continued to decline as a money earner as demand dwindled among Burma's traditional Asian markets. Teak, another big export commodity in past years, suffered a general decline, and the volume of shipping was half what it had been in 1940. Increased smuggling was also responsible in part for the economic slump. Inflation was rampant despite government efforts to control commodity prices.

Facts in Brief. Population: 28,800,000. Government: Union Revolutionary Council Chairman and Prime Minister Ne Win. Monetary Unit: kyat. Foreign Trade: exports, $105,000,000; imports, $144,-000,000. Principal Exports: rice, teak. John N. Stalker

BURUNDI. See AFRICA.

BUS. See TRANSPORTATION.

BUSH, GEORGE H. W. (1924-), former Republican congressman from Texas, became United States representative to the United Nations on March 2, 1971. He replaced Charles W. Yost.

Bush was born in Milton, Mass., the son of former Republican Senator Prescott Bush. He attended Phillips Academy in Andover, Mass., served as a Navy pilot in World War II, for which he received several decorations, and graduated from Yale University in 1948 with a B.A. degree in economics. Bush then moved to Houston, where he helped to organize the Zapata Petroleum Corporation in 1953. He was named president of the Zapata Off Shore Company of Houston in 1956 and became chairman of its board of directors in 1964. That same year, he campaigned for U.S. senator, but lost to Democrat Ralph W. Yarborough.

In 1967, he was elected to Congress, and he held that post for two terms. In November, 1970, he lost his second bid for the Senate to Democrat Lloyd M. Bentsen, Jr.

Bush is considered an expert in international oil operations, and is also an energetic and compassionate worker in the areas of unemployment, education, urban affairs, population, and earth sciences.

Bush married the former Barbara Pierce in 1945. They have four sons—George, John, Neil, and Marvin—and a daughter, Dorothy. Foster Stockwell

BUSINESS. See ECONOMY, THE.

BUTZ, EARL L. (1909-), became secretary of agriculture on Dec. 2, 1971. The Senate confirmed his nomination by a narrow margin of 51 to 44, and President Richard M. Nixon gave him the oath of office a few hours later. Butz replaced Clifford M. Hardin, who resigned to accept a position with the Ralston Purina Company.

Opposition to his appointment developed especially among Midwestern senators, who felt that Butz favored the large farm operators over small farmers. Butz denied this, and promised to support the family-farm system.

President Nixon nominated Butz at a time when grain prices were low and Midwest farmers were disenchanted with the Administration. Political observers felt that Butz would be a more vigorous spokesman for farmers than his predecessor.

Butz was born in Albion, Ind., on July 3, 1909, and grew up on a farm. He studied agriculture at Purdue University, earning his Ph.D. in 1937. Butz then began teaching at Purdue and became head of the agricultural economics department in 1946. From 1954 to 1957, he served as an assistant secretary of agriculture under President Dwight D. Eisenhower. Butz returned to Purdue in 1957 as dean of agriculture, and became dean of continuing education in 1968.

Butz married Mary Emma Powell in 1937. They have two sons. Darlene R. Stille

CABINET, U.S. The number of Cabinet posts was reduced from 12 to 11 when the new U.S. Postal Service went into operation on July 1, 1971. The position of postmaster general, which had been a Cabinet post since 1829, was transferred from the Cabinet when the new corporate-style postal agency officially came into being. Winton M. Blount continued as head of the nation's mail service under the new system until October, when he resigned to run for the U.S. Senate in Alabama. See POSTAL SERVICE.

President Richard M. Nixon proposed an elaborate plan for reorganizing the Cabinet in January. He suggested reducing the number of Cabinet posts to eight. The President would retain the Departments of State, Defense, Justice, and the Treasury. The other seven would be incorporated into four new departments—Natural Resources, Human Resources, Economic Affairs, and Community Development.

The plan was criticized by congressmen, farmers, businessmen, and government officials. Particularly strong opposition was directed at the idea of dismantling the Department of Agriculture and parceling out its functions to four separate departments.

On November 11, Secretary of Agriculture Clifford M. Hardin resigned to become vice-chairman of the Ralston Purina Company in St. Louis. The President named Earl L. Butz, dean of continuing education at Purdue University, to replace Hardin (see BUTZ, EARL L.). At the same time, Mr. Nixon announced that the Department of Agriculture would not be included in the reorganization plan,

U.S. Cabinet as of Dec. 31, 1971

(In order of succession to the presidency)

Secretary of State	William P. Rogers
Secretary of the Treasury	John B. Connally
Secretary of Defense	Melvin R. Laird
Attorney General	John N. Mitchell
Secretary of the Interior	Rogers C. B. Morton
Secretary of Agriculture	Earl L. Butz
Secretary of Commerce	Maurice H. Stans
Secretary of Labor	James D. Hodgson
Secretary of Health, Education and Welfare	Elliot L. Richardson
Secretary of Housing and Urban Development	George W. Romney
Secretary of Transportation	John A. Volpe

but would continue as a separate department. This was seen as a move to placate farmers becoming disenchanted with the Nixon Administration.

John B. Connally, who was sworn in as secretary of the treasury on February 11, appeared to be second only to Attorney General John N. Mitchell in power and influence. Connally was in charge of President Nixon's wage and price freeze and the Phase 2 economic program.   Darlene R. Stille

CALIFORNIA. See LOS ANGELES; SAN FRANCISCO; STATE GOVERNMENT.

Postmaster General Winton M. Blount announces birth of the new U.S. Postal Service on July 1, and the elimination of postmaster general from the Cabinet.

CALLEY, WILLIAM LAWS, JR. (1943-   ), a first lieutenant in the U.S. Army, was sentenced to life imprisonment on March 29, 1971, for the premeditated murder of at least 22 Vietnamese civilians in 1968 at My Lai, South Vietnam. The court-martial verdict prompted such great public protest that President Richard M. Nixon ordered Calley released from the stockade at Fort Benning, Ga., and, instead, confined to his quarters until legal appeals were completed. Calley's sentence was subsequently reduced to 20 years. See NATIONAL DEFENSE (Close-Up).

Calley was a platoon leader in an operation against the hamlet of My Lai on March 16, 1968, in which the Army reported that 128 of the enemy were killed. More than a year later, the public learned what really happened at My Lai. The soldiers had not killed enemy guerrillas, but had massacred defenseless men, women, and children. Calley was accused by the Army of murdering 102 of these civilians. Calley testified that he was only obeying orders, and many critics of the court-martial believed he was being made a scapegoat for higher-ranking officers.

Calley was born in Miami, Fla., and grew up there. He attended Palm Beach (Fla.) Junior College for a year. After a succession of jobs, he tried to join the Army, but was rejected. In 1966, however, he was allowed to enlist. He was commissioned a second lieutenant on Sept. 7, 1967.   Foster Stockwell

CAMBODIA. The republic managed not only to survive in 1971, but even displayed a toughness and resiliency that few observers would have thought possible when the year began. The twin problems posed by the need to create an army and fight a war while simultaneously establishing some stability in government were huge obstacles, further complicated by the ill health of the head of the government, General Lon Nol. Lon Nol, after suffering a stroke in February, received medical treatment in Hawaii, and although he returned to Cambodia in March, he was unable to resume a full work schedule until late in the fall. Although he offered his resignation, it was not accepted, and while he retained the title of prime minister, it was General Sirik Matak – an able, if aristocratic administrator – who actually handled the daily affairs of government during Lon Nol's recuperation.

The most pressing problem facing Lon Nol, and later Sirik Matak, was the disruptive presence of Viet Cong and North Vietnamese guerrillas within Cambodia. To expel them and clear the major supply routes to Phnom Penh, the capital, became the over-riding concern of the Cambodian government. Starting the year with fewer than 50,000 badly equipped and ill-trained troops, the government turned for help to the United States. The U.S. Congress agreed to extend aid totaling some $225 million, of which most would be allocated for military

Cambodia's Premier Lon Nol, right, was temporarily relieved of his duties by a deputy, Sirik Matak, after suffering a serious illness in February, 1971.

spending. By the end of the year, the Cambodian forces totaled over 200,000 men, and more than half had received special training. These forces began to show their capacity as they cleared various routes to Phnom Penh that had been controlled by the North Vietnamese. With the help of South Vietnamese troops operating along the eastern sector, Route 4 was generally cleared and usable. The Cambodians themselves cleared Route 3 to the south. The Mekong River was also cleared for traffic between Phnom Penh and the sea. More important, the Cambodian pacification program seemed to be gaining popular support for the government. The Lon Nol government also had firm backing from the Buddhist monks, as the Communists made a major blunder in executing some of their religious leaders. On October 22, Lon Nol abolished constitutional rule. He said he would govern by "ordinance" to prevent anarchy by a "fifth column."

Economically, the fledgling government was hard pressed. Phnom Penh suffered from fuel and food shortages. American and international aid, however, enabled the government to weather its economic difficulties.

Facts in Brief. Population: 7,153,000. Government: Chief of State Cheng Heng; Prime Minister Lon Nol. Monetary Unit: riel. Foreign Trade: exports, $63,000,000; imports, $77,000,000. Principal Exports: rice, rubber.   John N. Stalker

CAMEROON. Old difficulties with the militant opposition group, Union of Cameroon Peoples (UPC), flared again in 1971. In several instances, UPC guerrilla leaders were given death sentences or prison terms for kidnaping, arson, and rebellion.

Trials and Executions. Ernest Ouandie, leader of the violent wing of the UPC, and two other guerrillas were publicly shot on January 15. Three others, including the Roman Catholic bishop of Nkongsamba, were also sentenced to death for planning to assassinate President Ahmadou Ahidjo. Later, their sentences were commuted to life imprisonment. Appeals from the International Federation of Jurists and the Vatican may have helped save their lives.

Ouandie refused to defend himself, but the bishop admitted his "mistakes." The executions of Ouandie and the other two guerrillas were carried out in the Bamileke region in the south, where the UPC was founded in 1955.

Support for the leftist rebels has dwindled, due largely to Ahidjo's efforts to bring members of the Bamileke tribe into his government. Reportedly, government troops have almost completely stamped out the rebellion in the central highlands.

Foreign Affairs. Cameroon became the first of the states belonging to the African-Malagasy-Mauritius Common Organization to recognize the People's Republic of China. This represented an important shift of diplomatic position for these nations.

President Ahidjo opposed the Ivory Coast's new policy of dialogue with South Africa. This was a major point of dispute at the Organization of African Unity (OAU) summit meeting in July (see AFRICA). Ahidjo did not attend the OAU meeting because he wanted to avoid a confrontation with President Felix Houphouet-Boigny of the Ivory Coast.

Relations with the Ivory Coast had been embittered by Cameroon's decision to withdraw from the joint airlines agreement of Air Afrique. Cameroon claimed that the arrangement was dominated by the Ivory Coast, to the exclusion of trade for other members, and decided to establish its own airline.

Major General Yakubu Gowon of Nigeria visited Cameroon in April, and the two countries agreed on a maritime border settlement.

Economy. The budget of the federal government was up by 17.5 per cent in 1971. A substantial portion of the increase was slated for reducing the national debt. The economy suffered from price fluctuations for exports and inflation from increasingly costly imports. The 1970 droughts in the north and heavy rains in the south also had adverse effects on the economy in 1971.

Facts in Brief. Population: 6,045,000. Government: President Ahmadou Ahidjo. Monetary Unit: CFA franc. Foreign Trade: exports, $226,000,000; imports, $242,000,000. Principal Exports: coffee, cocoa, aluminum.   George Shepherd

CAMP FIRE GIRLS. See YOUTH ORGANIZATIONS.

CANADA

Prime Minister Pierre Elliott Trudeau's government in 1971 erased the political violence that had threatened Canada's internal stability, and it introduced new fluidity in Canada's international relations. But its management of the economy was less successful.

There was no further political violence attributed to the Front de Libération du Québec (FLQ), and the revolutionary movement seemed to lose its appeal as an outlet for French-Canadian resentments. Paul Rose, 27, and Francis Simard, 23, were sentenced to life imprisonment for the 1970 kidnap and murder of Quebec Minister of Labor Pierre Laporte. Trudeau's firm handling of the crisis suited the mood of the country.

Canada activated diplomatic relations with China and improved its ties with Russia. But economic problems mounted.

During the year, federal policymakers shifted their attack from inflation to unemployment, recognizing a problem more serious than in any year in the past decade. President Richard M. Nixon's import surcharge, announced on August 15, dealt a heavy blow to the Canadian economy. This action threatened to undermine the intimate economic relationship that had grown between the two countries since World War II.

The 10 Per Cent Surcharge was a severe shock to Canada, which does 70 per cent of its export trade with the United States ($11 to $13 billion annually). Finance Minister Edgar J. Benson led a delegation to Washington, D.C., on August 19 to protest the surcharge. The Canadian delegation asked for exemption, saying that Canada was not guilty on either of the two grounds that U.S. Secretary of the Treasury John B. Connally cited for the surcharge. The Canadian dollar was not artificially undervalued against the U.S. dollar. On the contrary, it had been allowed to "float" beginning in May, 1970. Since then, it had gained about 6 per cent in value, closely approaching parity with the U.S. dollar. To Connally's other complaint–that countries had imposed discriminatory barriers against U.S. exports–Canada replied that its tariff structure had no such obstacles. In fact, 1970 was the first year since 1950 that Canada exported more to the United States than it imported. From 1950 to 1969, Canada's trade deficit in relation to the U.S. totaled almost $14 billion. Thus, until recently, Canada had helped to reduce the U.S. balance of payments deficit.

Surcharge Effects on Canada. While the U.S. government promised to consider Canada's objections, Canada measured the results of the new duties on its trade with the United States. It appeared that one-fourth of Canada's exports to the United States would be affected; the balance would not be subject to the surcharge. Trade under the Automotive Pact of 1965 and the Defense Production Sharing Agreement of 1959, for example, would be exempt. Such important Canadian exports as crude oil, natural gas, industrial raw materials, newsprint, wood pulp, and fertilizers would continue to flow unhindered to the U.S. market. But another group of exports–aluminum, electrical apparatus, machinery, paper, plywood, and whiskey–would be subject to the duty.

The United States quickly showed that it was unwilling to abandon its protectionist policies until it saw that other nations were willing to buy more from the United States and sell less to it. Treasury Secretary Connally said the United States would draw up "lists of particulars" describing barriers that other nations had erected to U.S. trade.

An outline of such a list applying to Canada appeared in a Chicago newspaper on October 11. It listed 17 grievances in trade matters that it said the United States would like to take up with Canada. The most important was one that Secretary Connally had mentioned earlier: the U.S. conviction that Canada was gaining the major benefits from the trade in vehicles and component parts under the 1965 auto agreement. Before the pact was signed, the United States had a $400-million surplus in car and truck exports to Canada; it now had a $400-million deficit. This turnaround was thought to result from the transitional safeguards Canada had insisted on writing into the pact in order to protect its industry in the North American market for automotive products. These guarantees included the preservation of a ratio between production and sales in Canada, and specified a minimum "Canadian content" in each vehicle made in Canada. With the increased popularity of the "compact car," many of which were Canadian-made, Canada had greatly increased its automobile sales in the United States.

The Defense Production Sharing Agreement was another item on the U.S. list. Allowing Canadian firms to compete on equal terms for U.S. defense contracts, it had provided Canada with a favorable balance of trade of $505 million over 11 years. Other complaints on the unofficial U.S. list included the point that Canadian tourist allowances in the United States were lower than those for Americans visiting Canada. Canadian industrial tariffs were considered too high. And such foreign industries as the Michelin tire company of France were induced to locate North American plants in Canada even though they sold most of their production to the United States.

Prime Minister Pierre Elliott Trudeau and his bride, the 22-year-old former Margaret Sinclair, leave their wedding reception, smiling through a confetti shower.

The Ministry of Canada
In order of precedence

Pierre Elliott Trudeau, prime minister

Paul Joseph James Martin, leader of the government in the senate

Mitchell Sharp, secretary of state for external affairs

Arthur Laing, minister of public works

Allan Joseph MacEachen, president of the queen's privy council

Charles Mills Drury, president of the treasury board

Edgar John Benson, minister of finance

Jean-Luc Pepin, minister of industry, trade, and commerce

Jean Marchand, minister of regional economic expansion

John James Greene, minister of energy, mines, and resources

Joseph Julien Jean-Pierre Côté, post-master general

John Napier Turner, minister of justice and attorney general of Canada

Jean Chrétien, minister of Indian affairs and northern development

Bryce Stuart Mackasey, minister of labor

Donald Stovel Macdonald, minister of national defense

John Carr Munro, minister of national health and welfare

Gérard Pelletier, secretary of state of Canada

Jack Davis, minister of the environment

Horace Andrew Olson, minister of agriculture

Jean-Eudes Dubé, minister of veterans affairs

Stanley Ronald Basford, minister of consumer and corporate affairs

Donald Campbell Jamieson, minister of transport

Robert Knight Andras, minister of state for urban affairs

James Armstrong Richardson, minister of supply and services

Otto Emil Lang, minister of manpower and immigration

Herb Gray, minister of national revenue

Robert Stanbury, minister of communications

Jean-Pierre Goyer, solicitor general of Canada

Alastair William Gillespie, minister of state for science and technology

Martin Patrick O'Connell, minister of state

Premiers of Canadian Provinces

Province	Premier
Alberta	Peter Lougheed
British Columbia	William A. C. Bennett
Manitoba	Edward R. Schreyer
New Brunswick	Richard B. Hatfield
Newfoundland	Joseph R. Smallwood
Nova Scotia	Gerald A. Regan
Ontario	William G. Davis
Prince Edward Island	Alexander B. Campbell
Quebec	J. Robert Bourassa
Saskatchewan	Allan Blakeney

Commissioners of Territories

Northwest Territories	Stuart M. Hodgson
Yukon Territory	James Smith

The Canadian Responses. The first move in the Trudeau government's contingency plan was an Employment Support Act, passed in Parliament by the end of September. It provided $80 million in grants over the next seven months for companies that exported at least 20 per cent of their 1970 production to the United States. The grants would pay up to two-thirds of the surcharge. If the surcharge lasted three months, the government estimated a loss of $400 million in export sales and 40,000 jobs. If it lasted a year, the loss would be $900 million and 90,000 jobs. This was bad news for a country where unemployment was already high. More serious still were other U.S. economic policies on the horizon. One was the planned Domestic International Sales Corporation. It might hurt U.S. subsidiaries in Canada and, as a further result, add difficulty to efforts to control the rate of unemployment in Canadian manufacturing.

While Canadians were stunned by the cruel consequences of the Nixon measures, they realized that the United States was not deliberately trying to create permanent restrictions on Canada's trade. "They don't seem to realize what they're doing to Canadians," complained Prime Minister Trudeau. If the United States continued to refuse to take Canadian manufactured goods, if it insisted that Canada become simply a supplier of raw materials and natural resources, he said, "We will have to reassess fundamentally our relations with them, trading, political, and otherwise." Clearly, as 1971 ended, the "special relationship" between the United States and Canada was entering a difficult phase, although Canadian pleasure greeted the December 20 dropping of the surcharge by President Nixon.

Domestic Politics. The Trudeau government lost a tempestuous member on April 29 when Eric W. Kierans, the minister of communications, resigned from the Cabinet because he disagreed with the government's policies favoring industries that export natural resources. Kierans held that these resources should be converted into manufactured goods while in Canada – by Canadian labor.

A Government Reorganization Act led to the creation of a Department of Environment, grouping a wide range of services from other departments. The government began the appointment of ministers of state, junior ministers assigned to carry out specific policy functions rather than departmental responsibilities.

The standing of parties in the House of Commons changed little in 1971. Six by-elections resulted in a Liberal loss of two seats. Party standings late in the year were: Liberals 150; Progressive Conservatives 71; New Democratic Party 25; Social Credit (Ralliement Créditiste) 13; Independents 2; Independent Liberal 1 in a 264-seat House. Two seats were vacant.

©Toronto Star Syndicate

Russian Premier Aleksei N. Kosygin was uninjured by an attack from a Hungarian refugee in Ottawa during his visit to Canada in October.

Legislation. The third session of Canada's 28th Parliament opened on Oct. 8, 1970, and ran until its summer adjournment on June 30. It resumed again on September 7 to complete its legislative program. The Trudeau government listed 68 bills at the October opening of the session. But the kidnaping of British trade commissioner James Cross diverted attention to legislation needed to deal with civil disturbances. The government replaced the War Measures Act, its original weapon against FLQ terrorists, with the Public Order (Temporary Measures) Act of 1970, which outlawed the FLQ Party. It was allowed to lapse on April 30, 1971.

By the June adjournment, 48 of the government's 68 bills had been approved. An important measure designed to give the government a more active role in developing Canadian businesses and resources was approved by the House of Commons and Senate. It created the Canada Development Corporation, a $2-billion venture capital fund that would combine private savings and public funds to start large-scale, Canadian-controlled enterprises.

Pollution Measures were passed in 1971. One provides standards to define air contamination and prescribes penalties for offenders. Another regulates pollution in navigable waters and assigns liability for spill damages. A packaging and labeling bill was approved for consumer protection. Unemployment insurance benefits were extended to cover virtually all working people except the self-employed. Old-age pensions were shifted from a universal basis to a more selective approach using guaranteed income supplements for those with lower incomes.

Constitutional Reform. The objections of Quebec stalled efforts at constitutional reform. Prime Minister J. Robert Bourassa made it clear at a preliminary conference in February that Quebec would insist on full jurisdiction over all social programs before agreeing to a formula for amending the constitution. Definitive proposals were offered at a crucial conference in Victoria, B.C., in June. The provinces were given until June 28 to accept or reject them. But, after discussions with his government, Bourassa announced on June 23 that Quebec could not accept them because some points were "unclear." The decision was a setback to Prime Minister Trudeau, who had emphasized plans to reform the Canadian constitution.

Foreign Affairs. Canada, which extended diplomatic recognition to China in 1970, maintained its initiative in 1971 by moving toward friendlier relations with Russia. In May, Prime Minister and Mrs. Trudeau made an 11-day visit to Russia. The party visited ancient Tashkent and Samarkand, the new Arctic industrial center of Noril'sk, and the bustling port of Murmansk, as well as Leningrad and Moscow. Trudeau repeatedly emphasized that Canada had a great deal to learn from the Soviet

Union in terms of trade, science, and technology, because the northern location of the two countries meant that they faced many of the same problems. During his visit, he signed an agreement in which the two countries agreed to hold high-level talks at least once a year on subjects of mutual interest. The possibilities for increasing trade between Canada and Russia were also discussed.

Soviet Premier Aleksei N. Kosygin returned Trudeau's visit in October. Kosygin arrived in Ottawa on October 17 for an eight-day tour that was marked by both applause and protests. On October 18, a Hungarian refugee broke past guards and jumped on Kosygin while he was walking with Trudeau. Guards quickly subdued the man before he could injure Kosygin.

After three days of talks in the capital, Kosygin moved on to Montreal and then to British Columbia, where he toured Vancouver harbor. He signed a four-year renewable Canadian-Russian agreement to expand relations in many fields during his visit.

In November, President Josip Broz Tito of Yugoslavia spent six days in eastern Canada and signed a scientific and technical agreement with Canada. Canada's ambassador to China, Ralph E. Collins, took up his new post in June. His counterpart in Ottawa was Huang Hua, an experienced diplomat who was later asked to represent China in the United Nations. In July, Jean-Luc Pepin, minister of industry, trade, and commerce, led a strong trade mission to Peking, thus initiating a series of visits by commercial groups.

Trudeau attended the Commonwealth Prime Ministers Conference in Singapore in January. It was the first regular meeting to be held outside London. At the conference, he helped Britain and African member states reach an accommodation over the proposed British sale of arms to South Africa. An agreement worked out in private discussions prevented the withdrawal of African members from the conference.

Defense Policy Changes. Late in August, the government issued a 48-page statement of policy on national defense. The document amplified guidelines Trudeau laid down for Canada's defense forces in 1969. It said Canada would continue to cooperate with the United States in North American defense and with its allies in the North Atlantic Treaty Organization. But Canadian forces would increasingly be used for obtaining information "on what is happening on Canada's land mass, in her airspace, and on and under her coastal waters." The report also foresaw a larger role for the defense forces in supporting the civil power, a need that was vividly demonstrated during the FLQ crisis in 1970. The government announced it would scrap its two squadrons of Bomarc nuclear-tipped missiles after 10 years of service in North American defense. As a bomber defense, the missiles could do little to protect the

U.S. strategic retaliatory forces in contemporary conditions. Canada will keep 48 CF 101-Voodoo interceptor aircraft that carry nuclear missiles at three bases across Canada. Armed forces strength for 1973 was set at 83,000. The military spending freeze imposed in 1969 was to be lifted gradually.

Financial Messages. A worsening economic situation brought three budget messages from Finance Minister Edgar John Benson in 10 months. As 1970 ended, he rejected the notion of tax cuts as a way to stimulate the Canadian economy. Instead, he proposed to spend additional funds in the winter to assist provincial public works projects. This strategy was based on a jobless rate averaging a little less than 6 per cent of the labor force.

On June 18, however, Benson introduced more dramatic measures to restore business confidence and accelerate consumer spending. He proposed moderate tax relief for middle-income taxpayers and exempted about 1 million low-income and elderly taxpayers. He warned higher-income individuals that taxes would be increased through a capital gains tax after Jan. 1, 1972. Revenue for fiscal 1971-1972 was estimated at $13.7 billion; spending was to be increased to $14 billion.

But the expectations behind the June budget were not realized; in September, the unemployment rate had climbed to 7.1 per cent, the highest level in a decade. As a result, Benson made his third budget adjustment on October 14. This time he cut personal income taxes by 3 per cent retroactive to July 1 and corporate income taxes by 7 per cent. He also announced measures to expand federal spending in vocational training, job-creating capital projects, and new loans for housing. They were to cost nearly $1.1 billion.

The Domestic Outlook. Canada's domestic economy seemed on a long-term growth path although the nation still faced problems in generating enough activity to provide full employment. The gross national product was expected to pass $91 billion, an increase of 8 to 9 per cent. In real output, growth was estimated at 5.5 per cent, an improvement over the showing in recent years.

Exports and imports continued to grow in 1971, although imports grew faster. Total exports reached $13 billion in the first nine months, 4.6 per cent above 1970 figures. This growth was achieved despite the Canadian dollar's increase of 6 to 7 per cent in value since May, 1970. Total imports for the first nine months of 1971 reached nearly $11.3 billion, an increase of 6.8 per cent over 1970. Imports were higher from most of Canada's principal suppliers – the United States, Japan, and the six-nation European Community (Common Market). The faster growth of imports reduced the trade surplus by 8 per cent for the first nine months.

The most worrisome feature of the economy was the persistent growth in unemployment. The labor force increased to 8,622,000–more than had been expected. While inflation was not overcome, it was held at a slower rate than in the United States and in most of Western Europe. The consumer price index was expected to rise about 3.5 per cent in the year.

Canada gained its first winner of the Nobel Prize in the natural sciences. Gerhard Herzberg of the National Research Council received the prize in chemistry for his work in molecular spectroscopy.

The Provinces

Alberta. After 36 years in power, the conservative Social Credit Party was swept out of office on August 30. It had held power longer than any other government in Canadian history. A rejuvenated Conservative organization led by a vigorous 43-year-old Calgary lawyer, Peter Lougheed, won the election. Charging age and lack of imagination in the province's government, the Conservatives won 49 of the 75 seats in the legislature, jumping from 6 at the last election. The Social Credit Party strength dropped from 55 to 25. One New Democratic Party member was elected.

British Columbia. Premier William A. C. Bennett, who is also minister of finance, presented a record $1.3-billion budget on February 5, claiming it would generate 25,000 new jobs to ease the province's high unemployment rate. In September, British Columbia became the first Canadian province to ban liquor and tobacco advertising.

Queen Elizabeth II, Prince Philip, and Princess Anne spent 10 days in British Columbia in May during celebrations commemorating the 100th anniversary of the province's entrance into the Confederation.

Manitoba. The New Democratic Party government of Premier Edward R. Schreyer completed a busy legislative session on July 27, 1971. After 75 days of debate, the legislature approved 113 bills. The most controversial abolished Greater Winnipeg's 12 municipalities and a metropolitan council in favor of an amalgamated city council of 50 aldermen. A compulsory, government, no-fault automobile insurance plan, Autopac, took effect on November 1.

New Brunswick. Premier Richard B. Hatfield's new conservative administration presented its first budget to the legislature on March 16, 1971. Finance Minister Jean-Maurice Simard forecast revenues of $481 million and record spending of $512 million. He criticized the previous Liberal Party government, saying it had saddled New Brunswick with "costly programs" that required thorough investigation.

Newfoundland saw another long-standing provincial government appear to fall. As the year drew to a close, however, results of the provincial elections were unclear. Premier Joseph R. Smallwood's Liberal Party, in power since the island province entered the Confederation in 1949, appeared to win 20 seats. The Progressive Conservatives, under Frank Moores, won 21. A Labrador independent agreed to support the Liberals. Several cases required recounting, however, and in one instance, some of the ballots had inadvertently been burned. The issue was in the courts at the end of 1971. Smallwood continued to hang grimly onto his office, although Newfoundland could be on the edge of a new political era. One possible result was a court order that a new election be held for the disputed seat. The issue was further complicated by the fact that the majority party appoints a member as nonvoting speaker.

A serious economic blow was postponed in October when the Smallwood government announced that it had secured an option until next June 30 to purchase the vast paper mill of Bowaters Newfoundland, Limited, at Corner Brook. The company had previously decided it would have to shut down part of the mill because of declining markets for paper products.

Nova Scotia. Oil was discovered on October 4 on Sable Island, a 20-mile bar of shifting sand dunes about 100 miles off Nova Scotia's east coast. The discovery was made by Mobil Oil Canada, Limited, at a depth of nearly 12,000 feet. It remained to be determined whether the flow of oil would be sufficient to justify drilling and marketing costs.

The new Liberal Party government of Gerald A. Regan presented its first budget on March 22. It estimated ordinary expenditures of $472 million, re-

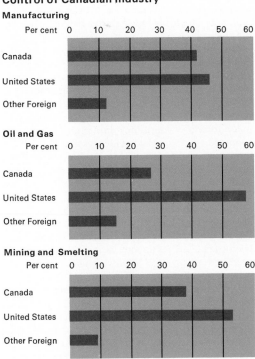

Control of Canadian Industry

Manufacturing

Per cent 0 10 20 30 40 50 60

Canada

United States

Other Foreign

Oil and Gas

Per cent 0 10 20 30 40 50 60

Canada

United States

Other Foreign

Mining and Smelting

Per cent 0 10 20 30 40 50 60

Canada

United States

Other Foreign

Source: Dominion Bureau of Statistics

Thousands of imported cars jammed port facilities at Vancouver, B.C., in a shipping boom generated when longshoremen struck at ports on the U.S. West Coast.

quiring a deficit of about $12 million to meet sinking fund payments. This made it the first Nova Scotia budget in 13 years not to attempt a balance of expenditures and revenues.

Ontario. Canada's largest province welcomed a new leader and gave him a solid vote of confidence in 1971. On February 13, William G. Davis, 41, minister of education and a member of the ruling Progressive Conservative Party, became the fourth leader of the party in its 27-year rule in Ontario. Davis was sworn in as Ontario's 18th prime minister on March 1. He proposed a large package of legislation to the legislature, which opened on March 30. The budget, presented by new Provincial Treasurer Darcy McKeough on April 26, totaled $4.26 billion and included a deficit of $415 million.

The most startling event of the session was Davis' announcement halting the controversial Spadina Expressway in Toronto after part of the route had been completed. As an alternative, the government promised to provide improved public transit in urban areas. See DAVIS, WILLIAM G.

Davis won a massive vote of confidence at a provincial election on October 21. Holding 68 seats when the legislature was dissolved, the Conservatives increased their strength to 78 in the 117-seat House. The Liberals dropped from 27 to 20 seats, while the New Democratic Party lost 2 seats to hold 19 in the new legislature.

Prince Edward Island faced pressing financial problems in 1971. To counter an increase of 45 per cent in government operating costs over the past two years, the Liberal government of Premier Alexander B. Campbell increased the sales tax from 7 to 8 per cent and the provincial portion of federal income tax 5 per cent. Ordinary expenditures in 1971 and 1972 were expected to reach a record $84,169,925, with capital expenditures adding an additional $13 million to the province's obligations. An overall deficit of $2.9 million was forecast.

Quebec. Prime Minister J. Robert Bourassa's plans for economic growth met frustration in 1971 in a sluggish Quebec economy marked by high unemployment. Plans for social reform were upset by the FLQ crisis in late 1970 and by a series of confrontations between the government and organized labor, physicians, teachers, and the police.

The province announced plans for the James Bay project, an immense water power, mining, and forestry development in northern Quebec. To cost $6 billion over 10 years, the project involves the harnessing of five large rivers flowing into James Bay to provide a hydroelectric power output 2½ times as large as that of the huge Churchill Falls project in Labrador. Bourassa hopes to sell the bulk of the power produced in the United States. In April, provincial officials held talks with Consolidated Edison Company, New York City. The first budget presented by Quebec's new Finance Minister Raymond Garneau, on March 25, estimated spending at $4.15-billion leaving a deficit of $271 million.

One of the worst natural disasters in Canadian history struck Quebec on May 4 when a giant landslide destroyed the little settlement of St. Jean Vianney on the Saguenay River, 115 miles north of Quebec City. Thirty-one persons died in the disaster.

Saskatchewan voters elected the New Democratic Party, headed by 45-year-old labor lawyer Allan Blakeney, on June 23. The New Democrats won 45 of the 60 seats in the legislature, leaving the ousted Liberals with 15. Six former Cabinet ministers and the speaker of the house were defeated.

The retiring premier, W. Ross Thatcher, died of a heart attack on July 23 after relinquishing the office to Blakeney. He had been premier of Saskatchewan for seven years.

The new socialist government announced that it would not back a major pulp mill planned for northern Saskatchewan. It cited as its reason uncertainties regarding the financial health and management of the project.

Facts in Brief. Population: 22,248,000. Government: Governor General Roland Michener; Prime Minister Pierre Elliott Trudeau. Monetary Unit: Canadian dollar. Foreign Trade: exports $16,861,-000,000; imports, $14,526,000,000. Principal Exports: motor vehicles, paper and pulp, nonferrous metals, wheat.   David M. L. Farr

Canadian Census Report

With tables of the preliminary population count

By Donalda A. MacIntosh, Special Assistant to the Director, Census Division, Statistics Canada

All of Canada's 10 largest census metropolitan areas showed significant population growth over their 1966 figures, according to the census conducted on June 1. The increases ranged from just over 5 per cent in the Winnipeg area to 21 per cent for Calgary. The Census Metropolitan Areas (CMA's) are roughly similar to the Standard Metropolitan Statistical Areas established by the U.S. Bureau of the Budget to help the study of metropolitan areas.

Not all the growth in CMA's took place in the central cities for which the areas are named, however. The population within the city limits of Montreal and Winnipeg actually declined. And, had it not been for changes in the boundaries, the same would have been true for Halifax, N.S.; Saint John, N.B.; and Quebec City. In fact, about three-fourths of the population increase in Canada's metropolitan areas took place in the fringe municipalities that ring the central cities.

Montreal, with a population close to 1.2 million, is still Canada's largest city, although it has lost about 2 per cent of its population since the 1966 count. Toronto, the second-largest city, is far behind.

Edmonton, Alta., based on central-city population alone, moved ahead of Vancouver, B.C., to become the third-largest city. In the Vancouver metropolitan area, as in most others, the increase – of 14.9 per cent – was concentrated in municipalities outside the city itself. Edmonton's city limits were newly enlarged, however, and included the area in which most of the metropolitan area's gain of 16.1 per cent took place.

Overall, early calculations indicated the CMA's held more than 54 per cent of the Canadian population. In 1966, they held just over 53 per cent.

The 1971 census was Canada's 11th decennial count since they began in 1871, four years after the nation's confederation. Five-year censuses in 1956 and 1966 supplemented the decennial count to keep closer track of trends in the population's changing social and economic characteristics.

Such major trends as the shift to the suburbs are clearly apparent, even in the preliminary population counts such as those used in this report. Preliminary totals do not include those people away from home during the count – at school, for example, or in hotels or general hospitals.

The 1971 count for Canada's total population was to become available when the bureau gets the first results from its computer, probably in March, 1972. Based on the 1966 count, and a record of changes since then, however, census workers estimated Canada's total population on June 1 was 21,681,000. The 1966 count was 20,014,880.

For the first time in the history of Canada's censuses, householders were asked to complete their own questionnaires. One-third of the households received a special long form with extra, "sample" questions. Careful sampling gave statisticians information about general changes in the population without covering every individual household. Officials expected that this and the high householder participation would improve the quality of information they received, help to make it more timely, and reduce the cost of the census.

Census records were microfilmed by automatic, high-speed cameras and transferred directly to computer tape with a special optical device. The only information that could not be fed into the computer, and therefore could never come out of it, was names or other information that could identify individual respondents to the census.

Largest Census Metropolitan Areas

1971 Rank		1971 Metropolitan Area	Central City	1966 Metropolitan Area*	Central City	Per Cent Change Metropolitan Area	Central City
1	Montreal	2,720,413	1,197,753	2,570,960	1,222,255	+ 5.8	− 2.0
2	Toronto	2,609,638	698,634	2,244,833	664,584	+16.3	+ 5.1
3	Vancouver	1,071,081	422,278	932,272	410,375	+14.9	+ 2.9
4	Ottawa	596,176	298,087	529,105	290,741	+12.7	+ 2.5
5	Winnipeg	534,685	243,208	508,759	257,005	+ 5.1	− 5.4
6	Hamilton	495,864	307,473	450,167	298,121	+10.2	+ 3.2
7	Edmonton	490,811	434,116	422,918	376,925	+16.1	+15.2
8	Quebec	476,232	182,418	435,787	166,984	+ 9.3	+ 9.1
9	Calgary	400,154	400,154	330,575	330,575	+21.0	+21.0
10	Niagara-St. Catharines	301,108	109,636	285,453	97,101	+ 5.5	+12.9

*Because most metropolitan-area boundaries were enlarged for 1971 census purposes, the figures in this column do not correspond, in most cases, to those published in 1966 census reports.

CANADIAN CENSUS (Preliminary)

ALBERTA

Population 1,634,000

Place	Pop.	Place	Pop.	Place	Pop.	Place	Pop.	Place	Pop.	Place	Pop.
Acme	300	Castor	1,157	Falher	900	Irma	412	New Norway	200	Spirit River	1,072
Airdrie	1,086	Cayley	122	Ferintosh	127	Irricana	139	New Sarepta	198	Spruce Grove	3,012
Alberta Beach	319	Cereal	220	Foremost	572	Irvine	193	Nobleford	401	Standard	264
Alix	563	Champion	323	Forest Lawn	12,211	Island Lake	20	Norglenwold	41	Stavely	351
Alliance	225	Chauvin	345	Forestburg	654	Itaska		Okotoks	1,239	Stettler	4,106
Amisk	124	Chinook	59	Fort		Beach (S.V.)	*	Olds	3,378	Stirling	434
Andrew	468	Chipman	181	Assiniboine	174	Jasper Place	30,417	Onoway	496	Stony Plain	1,772
Argentia Beach	2	Claresholm	2,957	Fort MacLeod	2,725	Kapasiwin	*	Oyen	930	Strathmore	1,161
Arrowwood	165	Clive	247	Fort McMurray	6,749	Killam	841	Paradise Valley	144	Strome	216
Athabasca	1,763	Cluny	87	Fort Saskat-		Kinuso	253	Peace River	4,951	Sundance Beach	
Barons	232	Clyde	236	chewan	5,743	Kitscoty	321	Penhold	450	(S.V.)	5
Barrhead	2,786	Coaldale	2,795	Fox Creek	1,282	Lac la Biche	1,783	Picture Butte	1,007	Sundre	937
Bashaw	753	Cochrane	1,053	Frank	221	Lacombe	3,407	Pincher Creek	3,231	Sunset Point	26
Bassano	858	Cold Lake	1,279	Gadsby	47	Lakeview	8	Plamondon	184	Swan Hills	1,380
Bawlf	182	Coleman	1,526	Galahad	164	Lamont	900	Point Alison	10	Sylvan Lake	1,601
Beaverlodge	1,128	Consort	659	Ghost Lake	11	Lavoy	115	Ponoka	4,422	Taber	4,790
Beiseker	414	Coronation	874	Gibbons	562	Leduc	3,994	Poplar Bay	*	Thorhild	502
Bellevue	1,244	Coutts	406	Girouxville	327	Legal	569	Provost	1,482	Thorsby	596
Bentley	621	Cowley	200	Gleichen	359	Lethbridge	40,706	Radisson	513	Three Hills	1,352
Berwyn	464	Craigmyle	72	Glendon	345	Linden	229	Radway	170	Tilley	254
Betula Beach	*	Cremona	187	Glenwood	200	Lloydminster (Alta.		Rainbow Lake	355	Tofield	920
Beverly	8,994	Crossfield	638	Golden Days	19	and Sask.)	4,653	Raymond	2,168	Torrington	121
Big Valley	301	Crystal Springs	8	Grand Cache	2,605	Lodgepole	501	Red Deer	27,428	Trochu	743
Bittern Lake	100	Czar	199	Grand Centre	2,068	Lomond	165	Redcliff	2,266	Turner Valley	756
Black Diamond	945	Daysland	584	Grande		Longview	190	Redwater	1,290	Two Hills	973
Blackfalds	910	Delburne	382	Prairie	12,797	Lougheed	202	Rimbey	1,453	Val Quentin	41
Blackie	168	Delia	243	Grandview (S.V.)	16	Magrath	1,208	Rochon Sands	20	Valleyview	1,678
Blairmore	2,041	Derwent	203	Granum	324	Ma-Me-O Beach	84	Rocky Mountain		Vauxhall	1,005
Bon Accord	331	Devon	1,465	Grassy Lake	196	Manning	1,048	House	2,975	Vegreville	3,696
Bonnyville	2,536	Dewberry	161	Grimshaw	1,681	Mannville	639	Rockyford	288	Vermilion	2,900
Bonnyville Beach	*	Didsbury	1,829	Gull Lake	57	Marwayne	351	Rosalind	203	Veteran	267
Botha	98	Donalda	221	Hairy Hill	99	Mayerthorpe	1,038	Rosemary	208	Viking	1,170
Bow Island	1,159	Donnelly	262	Halkirk	126	McLennan	1,088	Ross Haven	20	Vilna	305
Bowden	568	Drayton Valley	3,916	Hanna	2,561	McMurray	1,181	Rumsey	95	Vulcan	1,374
Bowness	9,082	Drumheller	5,428	Hardisty	580	Medicine Hat	26,058	Rycroft	452	Wainwright	3,791
Boyle	462	Duchess	228	Hay Lakes	211	Milk River	778	Ryley	426	Wanham	250
Breton	355	Eaglesham	198	Heisler	189	Millet	462	St. Albert	11,800	Warburg	460
Brooks	3,999	Eckville	657	High Level	1,606	Milo	117	St. Paul	4,171	Warner	410
Bruderheim	349	Edberg	145	High Prairie	2,329	Minburn	106	Sandy Beach	22	Warspite	110
Burdett	206	Edgerton	293	High River	2,663	Mirror	365	Sangudo	358	Waskatenau	231
Calgary	400,154	Edmonton	434,116	Hill Spring	213	Montgomery	5,020	Seba Beach		Wembley	338
Calmar	803	Edmonton		Hines Creek	418	Morinville	1,483	(S.V.)	165	West Cove	9
Camrose	8,648	Beach	148	Hinton	4,916	Morrin	198	Sedgewick	724	Westlock	3,265
Canmore	1,542	Edson	3,817	Holden	444	Mundare	508	Sexsmith	532	Wetaskiwin	6,266
Carbon	342	Elk Point	723	Hughenden	257	Munson	54	Silver Beach	27	Whitecourt	3,200
Cardston	2,744	Elnora	213	Hussar	171	Myrnam	403	Silver Sands (S.V.)	2	Wildwood	382
Carmangay	230	Empress	266	Hythe	467	Nakamun Park	3	Slave Lake	2,029	Willingdon	315
Caroline	338	Entwistle	352	Innisfail	2,468	Nampa	272	Smoky Lake	881	Yellowstone	14
Carstairs	881	Evansburg	527	Innisfree	252	Nanton	990	South View	19	Youngstown	305
Castle Island	*	Fairview	2,051								

BRITISH COLUMBIA

Population 2,196,000

Place	Pop.	Place	Pop.	Place	Pop.	Place	Pop.	Place	Pop.	Place	Pop.
Abbotsford	695	Enderby	1,159	Keremeos	584	Natal	818	Port Edward	1,017	South Fort	
Alberni	4,544	Fernie	4,170	Kimberley	7,441	Nelson	9,168	Port McNeill	939	George	1,279
Alert Bay	743	Fort Nelson	2,281	Kinnaird	2,838	New Denver	645	Port Moody	10,780	Squamish	1,536
Armstrong	1,631	Fort St. James	1,479	Ladysmith	3,656	New West-		Pouce Coupe	595	Tahsis	1,344
Ashcroft	1,867	Fort St. John	8,243	Lake Cowichan	2,368	minster	42,083	Prince George	32,755	Taylor	605
Burns Lake	1,227	Fraser Lake	1,296	Langley	4,634	North		Prince Rupert	15,355	Telkwa	741
Cache Creek	984	Fruitvale	1,371	Lillooet	1,520	Kamloops	6,406	Princeton	2,487	Tofino	445
Campbell River	3,547	Gibsons	1,936	Lion's Bay	396	North		Qualicum		Trail	10,843
Castlegar	3,068	Golden	2,929	Logan Lake	3	Vancouver	31,863	Beach	1,237	Ucluelet	977
Chase	1,213	Grand Forks	3,169	Lumby	935	Oliver	1,598	Quesnel	6,224	Valemount	690
Chetwynd	1,253	Greenwood	863	Lytton	486	100-Mile		Revelstoke	4,717	Valleyview	3,700
Chilliwack	8,848	Harrison Hot		Marysville	1,044	House	1,103	Rossland	3,911	Vancouver	422,278
Clinton	888	Springs	587	Massett	706	Osoyoos	1,279	Salmo	870	Vanderhoof	1,647
Comox	3,884	Hazelton	347	McBride	647	Parksville	2,137	Salmon Arm	1,228	Vernon	12,921
Courtenay	6,968	Hope	3,067	Merritt	5,161	Pemberton	159	Sayward	464	Victoria	60,897
Cranbrook	11,710	Houston	687	Midway	502	Penticton	17,702	Sechelt	590	Warfield	2,137
Creston	3,175	Invermere	1,066	Mission City	3,193	Port Alberni	19,749	Sidney	4,859	White Rock	10,244
Cumberland	1,720	Kamloops	25,599	Montrose	1,141	Port Alice	1,508	Silverton	246	Williams Lake	4,071
Dawson Creek	11,488	Kaslo	747	Nakusp	1,159	Port		Slocan	341	Zeballos	186
Duncan	4,391	Kelowna	19,089	Nanaimo	14,762	Coquitlam	19,570	Smithers	3,772		

MANITOBA

Population 988,000

Place	Pop.	Place	Pop.	Place	Pop.	Place	Pop.	Place	Pop.	Place	Pop.
Altona	2,123	Carman	2,010	Ethelbert	526	Hamiota	822	Morris	1,409	Powerview	666
Arborg	865	Cartwright	338	Flin Flon	8,839	Hartney	577	Napinka	135	Rapid City	371
Beauséjour	2,225	Crystal City	560	Foxwarren	257	Killarney	2,056	Neepawa	3,216	Rivers	1,164
Benito	478	Dauphin	8,860	Garson	301	Lac-du-Bonnet	957	Niverville	930	Riverton	795
Binscarth	468	Deloraine	957	Gilbert Plains	850	MacGregor	753	Notre Dame de		Roblin	1,742
Birtle	877	Dunnottar	202	Gimli	1,986	Manitou	881	Lourdes	606	Rossburn	638
Boissevain	1,511	East		Gladstone	935	McCreary	541	Oak Lake	332	Russell	1,515
Bowsman	440	Kildonan	29,722	Glenboro	699	Melita	1,131	Pilot Mound	765	St. Boniface	46,661
Brandon	30,832	Elkhorn	558	Grandview	965	Minitonas	610	Plum Coulee	479	St. Claude	675
Brooklands	4,302	Emerson	826	Great Falls	199	Minnedosa	2,629	Portage la		St. James	70,768
Carberry	1,308	Erickson	528	Gretna	521	Morden	3,276	Prairie	12,722	St. Lazare	429

*No figure in preliminary report.

St. Pierre......844	Selkirk......9,158	Stonewall.....1,570	Transcona....22,085	Wawanesa......485	Winnipeg...243,208
St. Vital....32,613	Shoal Lake.....835	Swan River....3,487	Treherne......636	West	Winnipeg
Ste. Anne.....1,048	Somerset......643	Teulon........830	Tuxedo......3,245	Kildonan...23,728	Beach.......661
Ste. Rose-du-	Souris......1,673	The Pas......6,072	Virden......2,778	Winkler.......2,942	Winnipegosis....891
Lac........819	Steinbach.....5,161	Thompson...16,219	Waskada.......246		

NEW BRUNSWICK

Population 632,000

Alma........408	Chatham.....7,812	Gonningsville..1,679	Moncton.....47,781	Rexton.......748	Saint John...87,910
Aroostook.....530	Chipman....1,965	Grand Anse.....539	Nackawic....1,324	Richibucto...1,829	St. Joseph......682
Atholville.....2,112	Clair..........701	Grand Falls....4,364	Nashwaaksis...7,197	Riverside-Albert..489	St. Leonard....1,469
Baker Brook....562	Dalhousie....6,247	Grand Harbour....565	Neguac.....1,488	Riverview	St. Louis De Kent.993
Barker's Point..1,875	Dieppe......4,261	Hampton.....1,703	Nelson	Heights......6,411	St. Martins......486
Bath........898	Doaktown......935	Hartland......998	Miramichi...1,536	Rivière Verte...1,655	St. Quentin....2,078
Bathurst....16,404	Dorchester....1,183	Harvey......383	Newcastle.....6,347	Rogersville....1,061	St. Stephen....3,300
Belledone......789	Douglastown.....631	Hillsborough....766	Nigadoo......599	Rothesay.....1,011	Salisbury......1,077
Beresford.....2,307	Drummond......637	Jacquet River....854	North Head....649	Sackville......3,176	Seal Cove......615
Bertrand.....1,099	East Riverside-	Kedgwick.....1,065	Norton.....1,097	St. André......320	Shediac......2,201
Blackville......917	Kingshurst....832	Lac Baker......360	Oromocto....11,518	St. Andrews...1,743	Shippegan....2,029
Bridgedale......421	East Shediac....591	Laméque......851	Pamdenec......417	Ste. Anne De	Silverwood......919
Buctouche....1,978	Edmundston..12,089	Lancaster....13,693	Paquetville......461	Madawaska...1,242	Stanley......388
Cambridge-	Eel River	Lewisville.....3,710	Perth Andover..2,049	Saint-Antoine...756	Surrey......268
Narrows......416	Crossing...1,066	Loggieville......878	Petitcodiac...1,570	St. Anselme...1,142	Sussex.....3,840
Campbellton..10,232	Fairvale.....2,015	Lower Caraquet.1,667	Petit Rocher...1,618	St. Basile....3,085	Sussex Corner....679
Canterbury.....523	Florenceville....577	Marysville.....3,802	Plaster Rock...1,317	St. François De	Tide Head......797
Caraquet.....3,411	Fredericton..23,612	McAdam.....2,204	Pointe Verte......522	Madawaska....511	Tracadie......2,188
Cap-Pelé......2,074	Fredericton	Meductic......172	Port Elgin......534	St. George......963	Tracy......609
Centreville......550	Junction......596	Milltown.....1,814	Quispamsis...2,179	St. Hilaire......199	Westfield......452
Charlo......1,617	Gagetown......613	Millville......352	Renforth.....1,567	St. Jacques....1,060	Woodstock....4,775
Chartersville.....320	Gondola Point...829	Minto........3,841			

NEWFOUNDLAND

Population 524,000

Badger......1,190	Channel-Port	Gaultois........508	Lawn..........981	Port Union.....572	Springdale....3,221
Baie Verte....2,406	aux Basques.5,870	Glenwood......980	Lewisporte....3,166	Pouch Cove...1,451	Stephenville...7,723
Bay de Verde....810	Clarenville.....2,207	Glovertown....1,921	Little Catalina....717	Ramea.......1,199	Stephenville
Bay Roberts....3,629	Glarke's Beach...869	Grand Bank...3,465	Lumsden......629	Robert's Arm...1,040	Crossing....2,110
Belleoram......530	Corner Brook.25,929	Grand Falls....7,659	Main Brook......587	Roddickton...1,232	Trepassey......1,027
Bishop's Falls..4,108	Cupids.......692	Greenspond......441	Marystown....4,982	St. Alban's...1,962	Twillingate.....1,438
Bonavista.....4,217	Deer Lake....4,403	Happy Valley..4,954	Mount Pearl...7,110	St. Anthony...2,586	Upper Island
Botwood.....4,109	Dunville.....1,736	Harbour	Newtown......513	St. George's...2,085	Cove......1,797
Brigus........737	Elliston......551	Breton......2,188	Norris Arm....1,188	St. John's...86,290	Wabana......5,256
Burgeo.....2,225	Englee......1,045	Harbour Grace.2,726	Old Perlican....591	St. Lawrence...2,147	Wesleyville....1,148
Burin......2,580	Fogo......1,155	Hare Bay....1,484	Pasadena......964	South Brook....801	Whitbourne....1,184
Carbonear.....4,673	Fortune......2,138	Holyrood.....1,269	Placentia.....2,174	South River....548	Windsor......6,651
Catalina......1,126	Freshwater....1,527	Jerseyside....1,050	Point	Spaniard's Bay.1,735	Winterton......780
Change Islands..592	Gander......7,720	Lamaline......545	Leamington...940		

NOVA SCOTIA

Population 770,000

Amherst......9,898	Dartmouth...64,002	Kentville......5,129	Mulgrave.....1,200	Port	Sydney Mines..8,957
Annapolis Royal.723	Digby.......2,324	Liverpool.....3,610	New Glasgow.10,792	Hawkesbury.3,427	Trenton......3,319
Antigonish....5,403	Dominion......2,860	Lockeport.....1,202	New Waterford.9,549	Shelburne.....2,699	Truro......12,968
Berwick......1,402	Glace Bay....22,276	Louisbourg.....1,578	North Sydney..8,498	Springhill.....5,195	Westville......3,844
Bridgetown.....1,012	Halifax....121,086	Lunenburg.....3,201	Oxford......1,409	Stellarton.....5,334	Windsor......3,626
Bridgewater....5,197	Hantsport......1,444	Mahone Bay...1,280	Parrsboro.....1,751	Stewiacke....1,003	Wolfville......2,831
Canso......1,202	Inverness.....2,066	Middleton....1,813	Pictou.......4,247	Sydney......32,459	Yarmouth.....8,291
Clark's Harbour, 1,079					

ONTARIO

Population 7,815,000

Acton........5,033	Bayfield......493	Brampton....41,238	Chatham....34,601	Crystal Beach..1,881	Erie Beach......221
Ailsa Craig.....608	Beachburg.....549	Brantford....62,853	Chatsworth.....395	Deep River....5,661	Erin.........1,455
Ajax.......12,509	Beachville......999	Bridgeport....2,374	Chelmsford....2,551	Delhi........3,837	Espanola......6,059
Alexandria....3,230	Beamsville....2,501	Brighton......2,953	Chesley......1,700	Deloro......253	Essex......4,034
Alfred.......1,228	Beaverton....1,462	Brockville...19,707	Chesterville...1,250	Deseronto....1,864	Exeter......3,379
Alliston......3,174	Beeton......1,053	Bruce Mines....509	Chippawa.....3,238	Drayton......751	Fenelon Falls..1,606
Almonte.....3,708	Belle River....2,879	Brussels......866	Clifford......554	Dresden......2,364	Fergus......5,415
Alvinston......698	Belleville...34,498	Burk's Falls....891	Clinton......3,113	Dryden......6,935	Finch........397
Amherstburg...5,115	Belmont......796	Burlington...86,125	Cobalt......2,191	Dundalk......1,022	Flesherton......525
Arkona......466	Blenheim....3,483	Cache Bay.....725	Cobden......937	Dundas......17,211	Fonthill......2,319
Arnprior......6,017	Blind River....3,393	Caledon East....905	Cobourg....11,214	Dunnville.....5,509	Forest......2,351
Arthur......1,421	Bloomfield.....724	Caledonia....3,184	Cochrane.....4,296	Durham......2,439	Forest Hill...19,998
Athens......1,071	Blyth.......818	Campbellford...3,470	Colborne.....1,578	Dutton......876	Fort Erie....23,099
Aurora......13,534	Bobcaygeon...1,517	Cannington....1,092	Coldwater......760	Eastview....23,764	Fort Frances...9,698
Aylmer.....4,697	Bolton......2,977	Capreol......3,471	Collingwood...9,719	Eganville......1,404	Fort William..44,563
Ayr.........1,272	Bonfield......698	Cardinal......1,867	Coniston.....2,917	Elmira......4,722	Frankford......1,851
Bala........469	Bothwell......812	Carleton Place..5,044	Cookstown......846	Elmvale......1,110	Galt.......38,134
Bancroft.....2,267	Bowmanville...8,894	Casselman....1,342	Copper Cliff...3,344	Elora......1,894	Gananoque....5,072
Barrie......26,985	Bracebridge...6,936	Cayuga......1,083	Cornwall....46,429	Embro......677	Georgetown...15,793
Barry's Bay...1,422	Bradford.....3,390	Chalk River....1,095	Courtright......592	Englehart....1,721	Geraldton.....3,145
Bath........812	Braeside......521	Charlton......131	Creemore......976	Erieau......511	Glencoe......1,385

*No figure in preliminary report.

CANADIAN CENSUS (Preliminary)

ONTARIO (Continued)

Goderich......6,804
Gore Bay......770
Grand Bend......702
Grand Valley....880
Gravenhurst...7,101
Grimsby.....15,742
Guelph.....58,364
Hagersville......2,281
Haileybury.....5,257
Hamilton....307,473
Hanover.....5,034
Harriston.....1,792
Harrow.....1,981
Hastings.......938
Havelock.....1,223
Hawkesbury...9,256
Hearst......3,484
Hensall......980
Hepworth......374
Hespeler......6,252
Highgate......424
Hilton Beach....165
Huntsville....9,577
Ingersoll....7,780
Iron Bridge......837
Iroquois......1,225
Iroquois Falls..7,248
Jarvis........965
Kapuskasing..12,789
Kearney......306
Keewatin....2,099
Kemptville...2,383
Kenora.....10,889
Killaloe Station..813
Kincardine....3,200
Kingston.....61,870
Kingsville....4,078
Kitchener...109,954

Lakefield......2,248
Lanark........858
Lancaster......590
Latchford......530
Leamington...10,589
Leaside.....18,356
Levack......2,943
Lincoln.....14,262
Lindsay....12,705
Lion's Head......464
Listowel......4,677
Little Current...1,559
Lively......2,988
London.....221,430
Long Branch..10,801
L'Orignal.....1,297
Lucan......1,179
Lucknow.....1,046
Madoc......1,361
Magnetawan.....201
Markdale......1,239
Markham....36,636
Marmora.....1,342
Massey.......1,288
Matheson......826
Mattawa.....2,878
Maxville......842
Meaford.....4,055
Merrickville......932
Midland....10,995
Mildmay......965
Millbrook......913
Milton.....7,023
Milverton.....1,165
Mimico....17,878
Mississauga .155,667
Mitchell.....2,549
Morrisburg....2,069

Mount Forest..3,031
Napanee......4,600
Nesterville......80
Neustadt......585
New Hamburg .2,998
New Liskeard..5,487
New Toronto .13,282
Newboro.......305
Newburgh......618
Newbury.......338
Newcastle....1,918
Newmarket...18,974
Niagara Falls .65,271
Niagara-on-the-
Lake......12,501
North Bay....49,063
Norwich.....1,796
Norwood.....1,187
Oakville.....61,365
Oil Springs.....570
Ojibway.........6
Omemee.......779
Orangeville....8,030
Orillia.....24,016
Oshawa.....91,113
Ottawa.....298,087
Owen Sound .18,281
Paisley.......794
Palmerston....1,849
Paris.......6,474
Parkhill.....1,177
Parry Sound....5,840
Pelham......9,949
Pembroke....16,130
Penetan-
guishene....5,491
Perth......5,539
Petawawa....5,657
Peterborough .57,498
Petrolia.....4,030
Pickering.....2,548

Picton......4,860
Plantagenet....909
Point Edward..2,780
Port Arthur...44,404
Port Burwell.....694
Port Carling.....518
Port Colborne .21,388
Port Credit....9,443
Port Dover....3,403
Port Elgin.....2,853
Port Hope.....8,747
Port McNicoll..1,457
Port Perry.....2,977
Port Rowan......862
Port Stanley...1,724
Port Sydney....193
Powassan.....1,148
Prescott.....5,178
Preston.....16,530
Rainy River....1,151
Renfrew......9,048
Richmond....2,133
Richmond Hill .32,399
Ridgetown.....2,836
Ripley.......447
Riverside....18,000
Rockcliffe Park .2,045
Rockland......3,654
Rodney.....1,017
Rosseau.......263
St. Catharines 109,636
St. Clair Beach .1,974
St. Isidore de
Prescott......613
St. Mary's....4,569
St. Thomas...25,062
Sarnia.....56,727
Sault Ste.
Marie.....78,175
Seaforth......2,138

Shallow Lake....384
Shelburne.....1,803
Simcoe......10,800
Sioux Lookout .2,495
Smiths Falls....9,598
Smooth Rock
Falls......1,216
South River...1,052
Southampton..2,038
Springfield......523
Stayner......1,940
Stirling......1,500
Stittsville.....1,991
Stoney Creek..8,364
Stratford.....23,863
Strathroy.....6,594
Streetsville....6,833
Sturgeon Falls .6,661
Sturgeon Point...34
Sudbury....89,898
Sundridge......721
Sutton West...1,456
Swansea.....9,544
Tara.........654
Tavistock.....1,502
Tecumseh.....5,157
Teeswater......982
Thamesville....1,018
Thedford......719
Thessalon.....1,858
Thornbury.....1,196
Thornloe.......138
Thorold.....15,042
Thunder
Bay......107,805
Tilbury.....3,626
Tillsonburg....6,611
Timmins....28,252
Tiverton......566
Toronto....698,634

Tottenham....1,615
Trenton......14,405
Trout Creek......587
Tweed......1,738
Uxbridge.....3,068
Vanier......21,859
Vankleek Hill..1,693
Vaughan.....15,839
Victoria
Harbour......1,233
Vienna........387
Walkerton....4,364
Wallaceburg..10,553
Wardsville......388
Wasaga Beach .1,921
Waterdown...2,142
Waterford.....2,418
Waterloo....37,245
Watford......1,390
Webbwood......586
Welland.....44,222
Wellesley......815
Wellington......989
West Lorne....1,090
Weston......9,557
Westport......599
Wheatley.....1,652
Whitby.....25,291
Whitchurch-
Stouffville..11,277
Wiarton.....2,173
Winchester...1,578
Windermere......137
Windsor....199,784
Wingham.....2,910
Woodbridge...2,299
Woodstock..25,559
Woodville......474
Wyoming.....1,274
Zurich........771

PRINCE EDWARD ISLAND

Population 111,000

Alberton......972
Borden.......630
Bunbury......522
Cardigan......268
Central Bedeque .213
Charlottetown 18,631

Cornwall......633
Crapaud......244
Georgetown....765
Kensington....1,079
Kinkora.......272
Miminigash.....417

Miscouche.....744
Montague....1,594
Morell........368
Mount Stewart..413
Murray Harbour..366
Murray River....471

North Rustico...746
O'Leary.......763
Parkdale.....2,321
Port Borden....677
St. Eleanors...1,611

St. Louis......151
St. Peters......360
Sherwood.....3,792
Souris......1,365
Summerside...9,315

Tignish.....1,045
Tyne Valley.....151
Victoria......148
Wellington......347
Wilmot.......736

QUEBEC

Population 6,030,000

Abercorn......365
Acton Vale....4,572
Adamsville.....495
Albanel......781
Alma......22,353
Amos......6,845
Amqui........3,777
Ancienne
Lorette.....8,282
Andréville......446
Ange-Gardien...521
Angers........887
Angliers......403
Anjou......33,842
Annaville......463
Armagh......982
Arthabaska....4,483
Arvida
(Ville de)...18,433
Asbestos.....9,760
Aston-Jonction..348
Auteuil......2,592
Ayer's Cliff......874
Ayersville.....2,938
Aylmer......7,160
Bagotville.....6,019
Baie-Comeau .12,108
Baie-Trinité......731
Baie-de-
Shawinigan...848
Baie-d'Urfé....3,886
Baie-St.-Paul...4,156
Baieville......507
Barkmere.......52
Barraute.....1,291
Barville........107

Beaconsfield..19,328
Beauceville....2,084
Beauceville-Est 2,186
Beauceville-
Ouest.....1,611
Beauharnois...8,141
Beaulac......514
Beaulieu......651
Beauport
(Ville de)...14,739
Beaupré.....2,853
Beaurepaire..2,400
Beaurivage.....518
Bécancour....8,163
Bedford......2,789
Beebe Plain..1,236
Bélair......4,485
Belleterre......614
Beloeil.....12,248
Bernierville...2,405
Berthierville...4,076
Bic.....1,154
Bishopton......331
Black Lake....4,140
Blainville.....9,641
Bois-des-
Filion......4,060
Boischatel....1,579
Boucherville .20,000
Boulanger......513
Bourlamaque...3,233
Brome........273
Bromont.....1,088
Bromptonville..2,766
Brossard....23,421
Brownsburg...3,387

Bryson.......815
Buckingham..7,267
Cabano......3,055
Cacouna......832
Cadillac.....1,105
Calumet......743
Campbell's
Bay.......1,192
Candiac.....5,189
Cap-à-l'Aigle...684
Cap-aux-Meules.836
Cap Chat....3,855
Cap-de-la-
Madeleine..31,120
Carignan......3,333
Carillon.......402
Causapscal...2,974
Chambly....11,466
Chambord....1,103
Champlain......633
Chandler....3,842
Chapais......2,906
Chapeau.......516
Charlemagne..4,174
Charlesbourg .33,484
Charny......5,192
Chateau d'Eau .1,039
Châteauguay .15,759
Châteauguay
Centre....17,897
Châteauguay
Heights....1,233
Château-
Richer.....3,099
Chénéville.....725
Chesterville.....323

Chibougamau..9,741
Chicoutimi....32,990
Chicoutimi-
Nord......14,058
Chomedey (Abord-à-
Plouffe)....29,930
Chute-aux-
Outardes....1,934
Clarenceville....332
Clermont.....3,386
Coaticook....6,566
Como.......806
Compton......498
Contrecoeur...2,688
Cookshire......1,490
Cote-St.-Luc .24,358
Cote St.
Michel.....52,719
Coteau-du-Lac..838
Coteau Landing..850
Coteau-Station.1,031
Courville......6,217
Cowansville..11,906
Crabtree......1,683
Danville......2,589
Daveluyville...1,002
Deauville.....1,490
Dégelis......3,049
De Grasse......102
De Léry......1,929
Delisle......1,287
Delson.....2,930
Desbiens.....1,831
Deschaillons.....290
Deschaillons-sur-
St.-Laurent .1,174

Deschambault...994
Deschênes....1,802
Deux-
Montagnes...8,598
Disraeli......3,394
Dixville.......545
Dolbeau......7,656
Dollard-des-
Ormeaux ...25,284
Donnacona...5,846
Dorion......6,195
Dorval.....20,471
Dorval Island......2
Douville.......3,288
Drummond-
ville.......39,438
Drummondville
Ouest......2,046
Drummondville-
Sud.........9,003
Dunham.......488
Duparquet......771
Durham-Sud.....464
Duvernay....10,473
East Angus....4,747
East Broughton .1,089
East Broughton
Station......1,118
East Farnham....341
Eastman.......527
Estérel........95
Évain........609
Fabreville.....5,181
Farnham......6,462
Ferme-Neuve..2,003
Forestville....1,617

Fort-Chambly..1,983
Fort-Coulonge .1,785
Fortierville......521
Fossambault-
Sur-Le-Lac....135
Foster.......451
Francoeur.....1,193
Frelighsburg....349
Gagnon......3,773
Garthby Station..507
Gaspé
(Ville De)...16,842
Gatineau.....22,356
Gentilly.......657
Giffard......13,087
Godbout......671
Gracefield....1,049
Granby
(Ville De)...33,958
Grand' Mère
(Ville De)...17,144
Grande Riviere .1,141
Grandes-
Bergeronnes...804
Greenfield
Park......15,277
Greenlay.....1,010
Grenville.....1,464
Grindstone
Island.......751
Grondines......492
Hampstead....7,035
Hatley.......215
Hauterive....13,204
Hébertville....1,587

*No figure in preliminary report.

Hébertville
Station.....1,162
Hemmingford...802
Henryville.....665
Howick.......575
Hudson......4,321
Hudson
Heights.....1,519
Hull.......62,842
Huntingdon...3,069
Iberville.....9,300
Île-Cadieux....45
Île-D'Entrée. ...247
Île-Dorval.......7
Ile Perrot....4,043
Iles-Laval.....789
Inverness.....359
Isle Cadieux.....18
Isle-Maligne...2,070
Isle-Verte....1,485
Jacques
Cartier.....40,157
Joliette.....19,497
Jonquière...28,080
Kamouraska....505
Kénogami....10,955
Kingsbury.....225
Kingsey Falls...562
Kirkland.....2,920
Knowlton.....1,352
La Baie.....562
La Baie
Shawinigan..1,076
Labelle.....1,492
Lac-À-La-
Croix.....586
Lac au Saumon.1,307
Lac-Bouchette...944
Lac-Brome....4,071
Lac Carré.....660
Lac-Delage....59
Lac-des-Ecorces.595
Lac-Etchemin..2,789
Lac-Mégantic..6,756
Lac-Poulin.......2
Lac-St.-Joseph....7
Lac-Ste.-Croix...521
Lac-Sergent.....150
Lachine....44,345
Lachute....11,789
Lacolle.....1,226
Laflèche....15,036
Lafontaine....2,976
La Guadeloupe.1,923
La Malbaie....4,032
Lambton.......766
L'Annonciation.2,148
La Patrie.....446
La Pérade.....1,125
La Petite-Rivière-
St.-Francois.4,704
La Pocatière...4,246
La Prairie.....8,310
La Providence..4,671
La Reine.......430
La Salle....72,916
La Sarre.....5,095
L'Assomption..4,885
La Station-du-
Coteau.......883
Laterrière.....581
La Tuque....13,071
Laurentides....1,745
Laurier Station...945
Laurierville.....922
Lauzon......12,801
Laval
(Ville De). 228,101
Laval des
Rapides....19,025
Laval Ouest...5,395
Laval-sur-le-Lac. 619
Lavaltrie....1,265
L'Avenir.......366
Lawrenceville....549
Lebel-sur-
Quevillon...2,935
Leclercville.....417
Le Moyne.....8,162
Lennoxville...3,867
L'Épiphanie...2,757
Léry......2,238
Les Becquets....493
Les Cedres.....434
Les Saules....4,066
Lévis......16,566
Linière.....1,231

L'Islet.......1,187
L'Isle-Verte....1,356
L'Islet-sur-Mer...883
L'Isletville....1,135
Longueuil
(Ville De)..97,483
Lorraine.....3,134
Lorrainville.....906
Lorretteville..11,646
Lotbinière.....543
Louiseville....4,015
Luceville.....1,410
Lyster.........871
Macamic.....1,675
Magog.....13,280
Malartic.....5,357
Maniwaki.....6,457
Manseau.......742
Maple Grove...1,705
Marbleton.....869
Marieville....4,521
Marsoui.......601
Martel.........970
Mascouche...8,783
Maskinongé.....995
Masson.....2,348
Massueville.....631
Matagami.....2,350
Matane.....11,826
McMasterville..2,502
Melbourne.....457
Melocheville..1,592
Mercier.....4,007
Métabetchouan 1,238
Metis Beach....211
Métis-sur-Mer...173
Mistassini.....3,607
Mont-Gabriel....36
Mont-Joli....6,707
Mont-Laurier...8,196
Mont Royal..21,470
Mont St. Hilaire 5,966
Mont-St.-Pierre...364
Montarville....6,643
Montauban.....246
Montauban-les-
Mines........321
Montebello...1,289
Montmagny...12,378
Montmorency..4,947
Montréal (Ville
De)....1,197,753
Montreal East..5,793
Montréal-Est...5,048
Montréal-
Nord......88,038
Montréal-
Ouest.....6,364
Montreal West.6,266
Mount
Royal......22,521
Murdochville...2,858
Napierville...1,993
Naudville....4,467
Neuville.......797
New Glasgow...127
New Richmond 3,942
Nicolet.....4,716
Nominingue.....702
Noranda....10,670
Norbertville.....283
Normandin....1,794
North Hatley....726
N.D.-
D'Hebertville.1,516
N.D.-Des-
Anges.......800
N.D.-Des-
Laurentides..5,087
Notre-Dame-du-
Bon-Conseil.1,057
Notre-Dame-du-
Lac.......2,116
Oka-sur-le-Lac
Omerville....1,109
Ormstown....1,517
Otterburn Park.3,506
Outremont
(Ville De)..28,402
Papineauville..1,407
Parent........452
Pascalis.......39
Percé......5,598
Phillipsburg.....388
Pierrefonds
(Ville De)..33,046

Pierreville.....1,456
Pincourt.....5,903
Plessisville....7,224
Pointe-au-Pic..1,228
Pointe-aux-
Dutardes.....836
Pointe-aux-
Trembles..35,521
Pointe-Calumet 2,226
Pointe-Claire. 27,310
Pointe-des-
Cascades.....683
Pointe-du-
Moulin.......185
Pointe Fortune...336
Pointe-
Gatineau...15,607
Pointe-Lebel....751
Pont Rouge...3,226
Pont Viau...19,174
Port-Alfred....9,191
Port-Cartier...3,738
Portage-du-
Fort.........431
Portneuf.....1,300
Preville.....1,003
Prévost.......298
Price.......2,752
Princeville....3,827
Quebec
(Ville de)..182,418
Quebec Ouest..8,681
Quyon.......874
Rawdon.....2,752
Repentigny...19,441
Richelieu.....1,762
Richmond....4,275
Rigaud.....2,145
Rimouski....26,546
Rimouski-Est..2,069
Ripon.......588
Riverbend.....266
Rivière-
Beaudette....226
Rivière-Bleue..1,501
Riviere des
Prairies.....8,548
Rivière-du-
Loup......12,423
Rivière-du-
Moulin.....4,391
Robertsonville.1,293
Roberval.....8,286
Rock Island...1,346
Rosemere....6,727
Rougemont.....866
Rouyn.....17,804
Roxboro.....7,654
Roxton Falls...1,139
Roxton Pond....770
Sacré-Coeur-de-
Jésus.....1,258
Saguenay.......39
St. Agapitville..1,493
St. Aime.......574
St. Alban.......765
St. Alexandre...408
St. Alexis.......455
St. Ambroise..1,627
St. Andre-
Avellin.....1,090
St. Andre de
Kamouraska...550
St. Andre-du-Lac-
St. Jean......602
St. André-Est..1,160
St. Andrews
East.......1,181
St. Anselme..1,412
St. Antoine...5,828
St. Antoine des
Laurentides..2,975
St. Apollinaire...966
St. Augustin....434
St. Basile de
Portneuf...1,729
St. Basile-le-
Grand.....4,383
St. Basile-Sud..1,692
St. Benoit......556
St. Bernard.....577
St. Boniface-de-
Shawinigan..2,586
St. Bruno....1,282
St. Bruno-de-
Montarville.15,822
St. Casimir....1,227

St. Casimir-Est...466
St. Celestin.....368
St. Césaire...2,273
St. Charles.....968
St. Charles-des-
Grondines.....420
St. Charles-sur-
Richelieu.....341
St.
Chrysostome.1,073
St. Clet.......249
St. Couer-de-
Marie.....1,225
St. Cyrille....1,129
St. Damase....1,119
St. David-de-
L'Auberivière. 3,808
St. Denis.......898
St. Denis-Riviere-
Richelieu....1,042
St. Dominique..1,732
St. Elzear-de-
Laval......4,101
St. Elzear......519
St. Emile.....2,636
St. Ephrem-de-
Beauce......988
St. Ephrem-de-
Tring.......954
St. Eustache..9,464
St. Eustache-sur-
le-Lac.....7,236
St. Félicien...4,955
St. Félix-de-
Valois.....1,455
St. Ferdinand..2,706
St. Flavien.....653
St. Francois...5,058
St. Francois-du-
Lac.........987
St. Fulgence....954
St. Gabriel...3,362
St. Gedeon.....884
St. Gédéon...1,180
St. Gedeon-de-
Beauce......905
St. Georges...7,570
St. Georges...2,036
St. Georges-de-
Cacouna.....991
St. Georges-de-
Windsor.....317
St. Georges-
Ouest.....6,002
St. Gérard.....629
St. Germain-de-
Grantham...1,109
St. Grégoire....666
St. Grégoire-de-
Greenlay.....694
St. Guillaume...803
St. Henri.....1,161
St. Herméné-
gilde........172
St. Hilaire-Est..2,867
St. Honoré....1,053
St. Hubert...21,753
St. Hugues.....463
St. Hyacinthe.24,192
St. Isidore.....738
St. Jacques...1,973
St. Jean
(Ville de)..32,484
St. Jean-
Chrysostome.1,911
St. Jean-de-
Boischatel...1,678
St. Jean Eudes.2,846
St. Jean-Vianney.177
St. Jérôme...1,931
St. Jérôme..26,131
St. Joseph...4,944
St. Joseph-de-
Beauce.....2,886
St. Joseph-de-la
Rive.........333
St. Joseph-de-la-
Riviere-Bleue 1,411
St. Joseph de St.
Hyacinthe..3,772
St. Joseph de
Sorel......3,279
St. Jovite....2,844
St. Lambert
(Ville de)..18,590
St. Laurent...63,067
St. Léonard..52,013

St. Léonard-
d'Aston.....995
St. Leonard-de-Port-
Maurice.....4,752
St. Liboire......667
St. Luc......4,852
St. Ludger.....268
St. Marc des
Carriéres...2,664
St. Nicolas...1,969
St. Noël......904
St. Norbert
d'Arthabaska..292
St. Ours......843
St. Pacôme...1,171
St. Pamphile..3,553
St. Pascal...2,491
St. Patrice-de-
Beau Rivage..466
St. Paul-de-
Chester.....318
St. Paulin.....808
St. Pie......1,695
St. Pierre.....356
St. Pierre....6,762
St. Pierre les
Becquets.....451
St. Placide.....259
St. Polycarpe....528
St. Prime....2,327
St. Prudentienne .799
St. Raphaël...1,220
St. Raymond..4,000
St. Redempteur 1,655
St. Rémi....2,297
St. Romuald-
d'Etchemin..8,439
St.-Sauveur-des-
Monts.....1,827
St. Sebastien....419
St.-Siméon...1,184
St. Stanislas....562
St. Sylvere.....214
St. Sylvestre....465
St. Theophile....469
St. Timothée..1,572
St. Tite.....3,136
St. Ubald.......811
St. Ulric......920
St. Vallier......571
St. Victor....1,014
St. Vincent-de-
Paul......11,028
St. Wenceslas...410
St. Zacharie...1,394
St. Zotique...1,230
Ste. Agathe..1,285
Ste. Agathe....644
Ste. Agathe-des-
Monts.....5,525
Ste. Agathe-
Sud.........963
Ste. Angele-de-
Laval.......484
Ste. Angèle-de-
Merici.......693
Ste.-Anne-de-
Beaupré...1,778
Ste. Anne-de-
Bellevue...4,932
Ste. Anne-de-la-
Perade.....1,179
Ste. Anne-de-la-
Pocatière..4,253
Ste. Anne-des-
Monts.....5,577
Ste. Anne-du-
Lac.........382
Ste. Anne-du-
Lac...........2
Ste. Clothilde-
de-Horton....393
Ste. Croix....1,559
Ste. Dorothée.5,231
Ste. Félicité....814
Ste. Foy
(Ville de)..67,834
Ste. Geneviève.2,847
Ste. Gertrude...361
Ste. Helene-de-
Bagot.......342
Ste. Jeanne-
D'Arc......926
Ste. Madeleine.1,106
Ste. Marie......184
Ste. Marie...4,308
Ste. Marthe.....198

Ste. Monique....227
Ste. Petronille..510
Ste. Rosalie...2,202
Ste. Rose.....7,434
Ste. Rose de-
Lima......2,950
Ste. Scholastique
(Ville de)..14,778
Ste. Thècle...1,723
Ste. Thérèse..17,161
Ste. Thérèse-
Ouest.....7,282
Saraguay.......438
Sault-au-
Mouton.....954
Sawyerville.....851
Sayabec.....1,799
Schefferville...3,277
Scotstown.....918
Senneterre...4,305
Senneville....1,418
Sept Iles....24,289
Shawbridge.....963
Shawinigan..27,502
Shawinigan-
Sud......11,452
Shawville....1,746
Sherbrooke..80,457
Sillery.....13,950
Sorel......19,317
Soulanges.....426
South Durham...427
South Stukely...393
Stanstead.....1,120
Stanstead Plain.1,195
Stukely-Sud.....388
Sutton.....1,694
Sweetsburg.....937
Tadoussac....1,004
Temiscaming..2,430
Templeton...3,696
Terrebonne...9,208
Thetford
Mines.....21,662
Thurso.....3,243
Tracy......11,845
Tring-Jonction.1,286
Trois Pistoles..4,654
Trois-Rivières.52,240
Trois-Rivières-
Ouest.....8,071
Upton.......814
Val Barrette....527
Val-Brillant.....698
Valcourt.....2,505
Val David....1,625
Val-d'Or....17,419
Val-Jalbert......39
Val-St.-Michel.2,063
Vallée-Jonction 1,276
Valleyfield
(Salaberry-
De)......29,776
Vanier......9,716
Varennes....2,368
Vaudreuil....3,831
Vaudreuil-Sur-
Le-Lac......288
Verchères....1,843
Verdun.....74,520
Victoriaville..22,088
Village de
Lafontaine...1,547
Village
Richelieu....1,563
Ville-de-
Tracy......8,106
Ville Marie...1,995
Ville
St. Georges..4,006
Ville St. Pierre..6,667
Villeneuve....4,044
Wakefield.....325
Warden.......385
Warwick.....2,841
Waterloo.....4,949
Waterville....1,435
Weedon-Centre 1,429
West Shefford...400
Westmount...23,570
Wickham......520
Windsor.....6,047
Wotton.......716
Wottonville.....682
Yamachiche...1,135
Yamaska......478
Yamaska-Est...323

SASKATCHEWAN

Population 928,000

Abbey.........246
Aberdeen......291
Abernethy......252
Adanac..........20
Admiral..........79
Alameda........470
Alida..........210
Allan..........704
Alsask.........849
Alvena.........147
Amulet..........48
Aneroid........164
Antler.........115
Arborfield......419
Archerwill......300
Arcola.........520
Ardath..........24
Ardill...........26
Arelee..........52
Arran.........123
Asquith........354
Assiniboia.....2,609
Atwater..........60
Avonlea........388
Aylesbury........88
Aylsham........171
Balcarres.......676
Balgonie........518
Bangor..........68
Bateman........106
Battleford.....1,792
Beatty..........97
Beechy.........339
Belle Plaine......62
Bengough.......615
Benson..........82
Bethune........292
Bienfait........803
Big River.......824
Biggar........2,598
Birch Hills......694
Birsay.........123
Bjorkdale.......223
Bladworth.......125
Blaine Lake.....672
Borden.........187
Bounty..........49
Bracken.........65
Bradwell........100
Bredenbury.....446
Briercrest.......129
Broadview......953
Brock..........195
Broderick.......115
Bromhead........97
Brownlee.......117
Bruno..........731
B-Say-Tah (S.V.) .37
Buchanan.......439
Buena Vista......28
Bulyea.........109
Burstall.........507
Cabri..........739
Cadillac........221
Calder.........186
Cando..........183
Canora........2,612
Canwood.......325
Carievale.......224
Carlyle.......1,076
Carlyle Lake
Resort (S.V.)...11
Carmichael.......21
Carnduff......1,035
Carragana.......137
Carrot River.....942
Central Butte....522
Ceylon.........259
Chamberlain....161
Chaplin........368
Choiceland.....454
Churchbridge....969
Climax........341
Coderre........163
Codette........169
Coleville.......462
Colgate..........62
Colonsay.......525
Conquest.......261
Consul.........203
Coronach.......363
Craik..........502
Craven.........126
Creelman.......178
Creighton.....1,857
Cudworth.......800
Cupar.........580
Cut Knife.......560
Dafoe...........46
Dalmeny........418
Darmody.........48
Davidson.....1,035
Debden.........344
Delisle.........659
Denholm.........71
Denzil.........289
Dilke..........129
Dinsmore.......422
Disley..........54
Dodsland.......384
Dollard..........92
Domremy.......209
Drake..........238
Drinkwater......117
Dubuc.........152
Duck Lake......584
Duff............91
Dunblane........57
Dundurn........354
Duval..........133
Dysart.........246
Earl Grey.......241
Eastend........794
Eatonia........615
Ebenezer.......143
Edam..........333
Edenwold.......131
Elbow.........356
Elfros.........253
Elrose.........567
Elstow.........150
Endeavour......195
Englefeld.......218
Ernfold........100
Esterhazy.....2,886
Estevan......8,930
Eston........1,428
Etters Beach......2
Evesham.........63
Eyebrow........184
Fairlight........107
Fenwood........111
Ferland........105
Fielding.........38
Fife Lake........84
Fillmore........383
Findlater.........94
Flaxcombe.......99
Fleming.........173
Flin Flon, Sask.
pt. (4).......468
Foam Lake....1,332
Forget.........113
Fort Qu'Appelle 1,592
Fosston........120
Fox Valley......494
Francis.........158
Frobisher.......220
Frontier........247
Gainsborough...352
Gerald.........175
Girvin..........86
Gladmar........111
Glaslyn........355
Glenavon.......326
Glen Ewen.....216
Glenside........94
Glentworth.....106
Glidden.........70
Golden Prairie...144
Goodeve........169
Goodsoil.......219
Goodwater.......71
Govan.........356
Grandview Beach..2
Gravelbourg...1,375
Grayson........262
Grenfell.......1,302
Guernsey.......142
Gull Lake.....1,156
Hafford........585
Hague.........423
Halbrite........146
Handel..........73
Hanley.........391
Hardy..........37
Harris.........249
Hawarden.......190
Hazenmore.....107
Hazlet.........198
Hepburn........305
Herbert.......1,010
Herschel.........89
Heward.........79
Hodgeville......399
Holdfast.......393
Horizon..........23
Hubbard.......117
Hudson Bay...1,955
Hughton.........84
Humboldt.....3,889
Hyas..........217
Imperial........491
Indian Head...1,789
Insinger.........72
Invermay.......410
Ituna..........955
Jansen.........240
Jasmin..........30
Jedburgh.........61
Kamsack......2,779
Kandahar.......111
Kannata Valley.....7
Katepwa Beach
(S.V.).........46
Keeler..........58
Kelfield..........27
Kelliher........459
Kelvington....1,057
Kenaston.......401
Kendal..........90
Kennedy........244
Kerrobert.....1,192
Khedive..........91
Killaly.........138
Kincaid.........295
Kindersley.....3,402
Kinistino.......747
Kinley..........74
Kipabiskau........*
Kipling.........888
Kisbey.........265
Krydor.........136
Kyle...........507
Lafleche........689
Laird..........218
Lake Alma......150
Lake Lenore.....391
Lampman.......792
Lancer.........198
Landis.........278
Lang..........183
Langenburg...1,233
Langham.......536
Lanigan......1,438
La Ronge.......898
Lashburn.......491
Lawson..........60
Leader.......1,108
Leask..........437
Lebret.........279
Leipzig.........87
Lemberg.......410
Leney..........26
Leoville........391
Leross..........91
Leroy..........436
Leslie...........87
Lestock........450
Liberty.........142
Limerick.......158
Lintlaw........213
Lipton.........400
Lloydminster (Sask.
and Alta.)...3,889
Lockwood.......61
Loon Lake......351
Loreburn.......252
Love..........133
Loverna..........55
Lucky Lake.....371
Lumsden.......904
Lumsden Beach
(S.V.)..........*
Luseland.......725
Macklin........832
MacNutt.......186
Macoun.........170
Macrorie.......120
Madison..........58
Maidstone......686
Major.........165
Makwa.........126
Manitou Beach
(S.V.)........118
Mankota.......399
Manor.........385
Mantario.........48
Maple Creek...2,268
Marcelin.......307
Marengo.......133
Margo.........218
Markinch.........80
Marquis........126
Marsden.......241
Marshall.......197
Martensville.....870
Maryfield.......403
Mawer..........72
Maymont.......168
Mazenod.........72
McLean........172
McTaggart.......56
Meacham......184
Meadow Lake..3,426
Meath Park.....254
Medstead.......179
Melfort.......4,740
Melville.......5,243
Mendham......163
Meota.........231
Mervin.........198
Metinota........11
Meyronne.......122
Midale.........644
Middle Lake....288
Milden.........239
Milestone......466
Minton........195
Mistatim.......165
Montmartre.....509
Moose Jaw ..31,284
Moosomin....2,359
Morse.........453
Mortlach.......309
Mossbank......440
Muenster.......280
Naicam.........720
Neilburg.......298
Netherhill.......68
Neudorf.......471
Neville.........151
Nipawin......4,060
Nokomis.......530
Norquay.......511
North
Battleford..12,453
North Portal.....179
Odessa........224
Ogema........434
Orkney..........90
Osage..........55
Osler..........182
Outlook......1,790
Oxbow.......1,330
Paddockwood...230
Palmer..........58
Pangman.......222
Paradise Hill....346
Parkside........112
Paynton........205
Pelly..........400
Pennant........215
Pense.........273
Penzance.........81
Perdue.........412
Piapot.........160
Pilger..........110
Pilot Butte......399
Plato...........66
Plenty.........208
Plunkett........152
Ponteix........791
Porcupine Plain..828
Portreeve........58
Preeceville....1,117
Prelate........407
Primate..........82
Prince Albert..27,613
Prud'homme....262
Punnichy.......441
Qu'Appelle.....454
Quill Lake......568
Quinton........197
Rabbit Lake.....206
Radisson.......414
Radville........988
Rama..........186
Raymore.......525
Redvers........824
Regina.....137,759
Regina Beach...333
Revenue.........96
Rhein..........295
Richard..........39
Richmound.....205
Ridgedale......166
Riverhurst......263
Robsart..........53
Rocanville......848
Roche Percée...147
Rockglen.......555
Rockhaven......53
Rose Valley.....589
Rosetown.....2,543
Rosthern......1,436
Rouleau........397
Ruddell..........25
Rush Lake......163
Ruthilda..........50
St. Benedict.....195
St. Brieux......361
St. Gregor......126
St. Louis.......380
St. Victor.......85
St. Walburg.....655
Saltcoats.......511
Salvador.........78
Sandy Beach......*
Saskatchewan
Beach..........9
Saskatoon..125,079
Sceptre........233
Scott..........236
Sedley.........268
Semans........329
Senlac..........96
Shackleton......56
Shamrock......105
Shaunavon....2,253
Sheho.........317
Shell Lake......254
Shellbrook....1,034
Silton..........59
Simpson.......239
Sintaluta.......271
Smeaton.......308
Smiley.........124
Southey........547
Sovereign.......91
Spalding.......329
Speers.........117
Spiritwood......719
Springside......349
Spring Valley.....71
Springwater.....103
Spruce Lake....103
Spy Hill........384
Star City.......540
Stenen.........232
Stewart Valley...138
Stockholm......354
Stornoway.......40
Storthoaks......167
Stoughton......711
Stranraer.........66
Strasbourg......756
Strongfield......110
Sturgis.........617
Success........101
Summerberry.....39
Swift Current .15,048
Tantallon.......174
Tessier..........40
Theodore.......426
Tisdale.......2,789
Togo..........219
Tompkins.......351
Torquay........361
Tramping Lake...241
Tribune........126
Truax...........76
Tugaske........196
Turtleford.......419
Tuxford........153
Unity........2,295
Val Marie......307
Valparaiso.......50
Vanguard.......317
Vanscoy........245
Vawn..........116
Veregin........196
Vibank.........277
Viceroy........130
Viscount.......398
Vonda.........257
Wadena......1,376
Wakaw.......1,008
Wakaw Lake
(S.V.)..........3
Waldeck.......241
Waldheim......609
Waldron.........80
Wapella........509
Warman........798
Waseca........115
Watrous......1,549
Watson........845
Wauchope.......72
Wawota........515
Webb..........105
Weekes........183
Weirdale.......107
Weldon........254
Welwyn........211
West Bend.......41
Weyburn......8,576
White City......130
White Fox......355
Whitewood....1,055
Wilcox.........191
Wilkie........1,648
Willow Bunch...461
Willowbrook.....70
Windthorst......179
Wiseton........181
Wishart........268
Wolseley........936
Wood Mountain..85
Woodrow........73
Wroxton.........91
Wynyard.......1,922
Yarbo..........160
Yellow Creek....164
Yellow Grass....484
Yorkton.....13,149
Young.........496
Zealandia.......144
Zelma...........51
Zenon Park.....350

YUKON

Population 17,000

Dawson.......745
Faro..........850
Mayo..........332
Whitehorse...11,084

*No figure in preliminary report.

CANADIAN LIBRARY ASSOCIATION (CLA)

held its 26th annual conference in Vancouver, B.C., from June 19 to 25, 1971. More than 1,100 persons attended. A goal of the conference was to encourage individual participation in small workshops discussing vital professional problems. Seated at tables in groups of from six to eight, participants discussed such topics as modern management techniques applied to libraries, training of library technicians, shared cataloging, book collections development, new techniques in technical services, new methods in planning and budgeting, and automation.

For several years, Canadian book publishers have faced financial difficulties that culminated in 1971 in the sale of one company to foreign interests and the possible sale of a second. CLA joined with other concerned groups in protesting such sales.

Medals and Awards. The Book of the Year for Children Medal was awarded to William Toye for *Cartier Discovers the St. Lawrence* and to Henriette Major for *La Surprise de Dame Chenille.* The Amelia Frances Howard-Gibbon Medal for illustrators, awarded for the first time by the Canadian Association of Children's Librarians, was won by Elizabeth Cleaver for *The Wind Has Wings.* The Canadian Library Trustees' Association Award of Merit went to Alex Smith of the Vancouver Island Regional Library. The third Howard V. Phalin-World Book Graduate Scholarship in Library Science was awarded by a CLA standing committee to Beryl Lapham Anderson, associate professor at the McGill University Graduate School of Library Science in Montreal. The scholarship was sponsored by World Book-Childcraft of Canada, Limited.

National Library. Two task groups were established to work toward the development of a national information network and central data bank. CLA members are included in both groups.

Future National Library plans were announced by National Librarian Guy Sylvestre at the American Library Association Conference in Dallas and by Associate National Librarian Lachlan F. MacRae at the CLA conference.

University Libraries. The Killam Library of Dalhousie University in Halifax, N.S., was opened in March. It houses collections formerly scattered throughout the university. The University of Toronto's humanities and social sciences research library, a three-building complex, was named the John P. Robarts Library in recognition of Premier Robarts' great contribution to education.

Library Education. The University of Toronto School of Library Science began a graduate program leading to a doctoral degree in library science. The University of Western Ontario School of Documentation and Library Science inaugurated a doctoral program in historical bibliography. Both programs indicate recognition of the need for advances in library education. Elizabeth Homer Morton

CANADIAN LITERATURE

in 1971 reflected the nation's wide range of concerns. The year's works discussed the Indian and the Eskimo, the French and the English, Quebec, the creative arts, and political problems.

Fiction. *St. Urbain's Horseman* by Mordecai Richler looks into the meaning of being a human being today. *Whir of Gold* by Sinclair Ross describes the experiences of a talented prairie lad trying to break into the pop-music world in Montreal. First novels of promise are *The Weekend Man* by Richard Wright, *Ceremony of Innocence* by Ruth Nichol, and *The Edible Woman* by Margaret Atwood.

Poetry. Three interesting anthologies appeared. *How Do I Love Thee: Sixty Poets of Canada (and Quebec) Select and Introduce Their Favourite Poems from Their Own Work,* edited by John Robert Colombo, a collection of 60 poems with brief comments by the editor, is bilingual and truly representative of Canada's best poetry. *Made in Canada: New Poems of the Seventies,* edited by Douglas Lochhead and Raymond Souster, is a collection of 150 recent poems by 64 poets, some of whom are little known. *Soundings,* edited by Jack Ludwig and Andy Wainwright, presents works from 14 of Canada's newer poets.

Rag and Bone Shop by Earle Birney; *Power of Politics* and *Procedures for Underground,* both by Margaret Atwood; *The Cave* by John Newlove; *The Mysterious Naked Man* by Alden Nowlan; *Acknowledgement to Life: The Collected Poems of Bertram Warr,* edited by Len Gasparini; and *Nail Polish* by Irving Layton are some of the better efforts of individual poets.

Biography. *James Douglas: Father of British Columbia* by Dorothy B. Smith and *John Sandfield Macdonald* by Bruce E. Hodgins are about fascinating personalities in an important time in history. *General Mud: Memories of Two World Wars* by E. L. M. Burns and *Not a One-Way Street* by James S. Duncan are autobiographies of a general and an industrialist. *The Man from Margaree: Writings and Speeches of M. M. Coady,* edited with commentary by Alexander F. Laidlaw, reveals the ideas of this internationally influential priest, educator, and reformer. *The Mackenzie King Record,* volumes 3 and 4, edited by J. W. Pickersgill and D. E. Forster, cover the years 1945 to 1948 in the life of Canada's "most successful prime minister and wiliest politician" and complete this biography. *Words and Occasions* by Lester B. Pearson collect many of the speeches and letters of this national and international statesman.

Canada. *Wilderness Canada,* edited by Borden Spears, aims "to capture the feelings of Canadians for the forests and rivers of this vast land." *Forts of Canada* by Leslie F. Hannon tells Canada's history through that of some 100 of its 600 forts. *Canada and the Canadians* by George Woodcock is a very personal travel book. *Portrait of Canada* by Jay and Audrey Walz explains "something of Canada to Americans, much of Canada to Canadians."

CANADIAN LITERATURE

Indians. In *There Is My People Sleeping: Ethnic Poem – Drawings*, Sarain Stump, a Shoshone Indian who works as an Alberta ranch foreman, describes Indian culture with the aid of his superb drawings. *Great Lakes Indians*, written and illustrated by William J. Kubiak, is a mostly accurate, encyclopedic account of Indian history in the Great Lakes vicinity. *The Ecstasy of Rita Joe and Other Plays* by George Ryga deals in the title play with an Indian girl's unhappy experiences on coming to the city. *Hunters of the Arctic* by Roger Frison-Roche, with photos by Pierre Tairraz, describes a two-week hunting trip with a Chipewyan band and an expedition with Eskimos. *Harpoon of the Hunter* by Markoosie, an Eskimo pilot, is a welcome forerunner of a written Eskimo literature evolving from traditional Eskimo storytelling.

Language and Art. *Speaking Canadian English* by Mark M. Orkin is a readable treatment of a lively topic. *The French Language and Culture in Canada* by René de Chantal and others, includes four essays, of which De Chantal's "The Middle Way" is valuable for its assessment of recent and future progress of the French language. *Robert Harris 1849-1919: An Unconventional Biography* by Moncrieff Williamson revives interest in this 19th-century portraitist who painted *Fathers of Confederation. Canadian Art: Vital Decades* by Paul Duval introduces Canadian paintings from the important McMichael collection.

Politics. *Gentlemen, Players & Politicians* by Dalton Camp and *The Party's Over* by James Johnston portray recent developments in the Progressive-Conservative Party. *Living in the Seventies*, edited by Allen M. Linden, contains the study papers of the Liberal Party's Conference at Harrison Hot Springs and deals with the liberation of the individual. *The Liberal Rip-Off: Trudeauism vs the Politics of Equality* by Ed Broadbent deals with numerous Canadian problems. *White Niggers of America* by Pierre Vallières is the confession of a revolutionary who grew up and was confined by poverty and deprivation in Montreal. It is one of an avalanche of books – including such titles as *Terror in Quebec: Case Studies in the FLQ* by Gustave Marf and *The Second Conquest: Reflections II* by Solange Chaput-Rolland – on the political situation in Quebec.

Governor-General's Literary Awards for books published in 1970 went to Monique Bosco for *La Femme de Loth* (French fiction); Jacques Brault for *Quand Nous Serons Heureux* (French play); Fernand Ouellette for *Les Actes Retrouvés* (French essays); David Godfrey for *The New Ancestors* (English fiction); B. P. Nichol for *Beachhead, Still Water, The True Eventual Story of Billy the Kid* (English poetry); Michael Ondaatje for *The Collected Works of Billy the Kid* (English prose and poetry). Fernand Ouellette refused his award for political reasons.

Stephen Leacock Memorial Award for humor went to Robert Thomas Allen for *Children, Wives and Other Wildlife.*

Elizabeth Homer Morton

CELEBRATIONS and anniversaries observed in 1971 included the following:

Chicago Fire Centennial. On Oct. 8, 1871, a raging fire swept through Chicago, driving its panicked residents into the streets. The old city was almost totally destroyed. Now the largest city in the Midwest, Chicago celebrated the centennial of its famous fire in 1971 with a number of activities, including: an exhibit called "Great Chicago Fire" at the Chicago Historical Society; a centennial exposition at Navy Pier from October 7 through 10; and a fire department parade on State Street on October 9. The Chicago Historical Society issued bronze and silver medallions commemorating the fire and the rebuilding of the city. The front of the medallion depicts Chicago's famed Water Tower, which survived the fire, and the old Chicago Historical Society building and the Second Presbyterian Church, both destroyed. Also shown are four skyscrapers from today's skyline. The second side of the medallion bears the seal of the city.

Emily Dickinson Commemorative Stamp. Amherst, Mass., held a three-day celebration from August 26 through 28, in honor of poet Emily Dickinson, who was born and lived there from 1830 to 1886. The celebration ended on August 28 with the first-day-of-issue ceremonies for the Emily Dickinson commemorative stamp, held at Amherst College's Johnson Chapel. The 8-cent stamp was the second issued in the American Poetry series.

Albrecht Dürer Quincentennial. Albrecht Dürer, the German artist who was born on May 21, 1471, in Nuremberg, was honored in 1971 in a yearlong celebration. Highlight of the event was an exhibition of more than 500 of Dürer's works–drawings, paintings, and original prints–in the Germanic National Museum in Nuremberg. Among the paintings were all three of Dürer's self-portraits, one on loan from the Bavarian State Collection of Paintings in Munich, another from the Louvre in Paris, and the last from the Prado in Madrid. It was the first time the three portraits were ever exhibited together.

Göteborg's 350th Anniversary. Göteborg, Sweden, was founded in 1621 by King Gustavus Adolphus (Gustav II). The city celebrated in 1971 with a program of cultural, sports, and other events. Included were the world ice skating championships, held on February 13 and 14; an international folk-dance festival, held August 11 to 16; and many fairs and congresses.

Iran's 2,500th Anniversary. On Oct. 14, 1971, the shah of Iran presided over an opulent anniversary party that took place in huge, richly appointed silk tents, amid the ruins of the ancient city of Persepolis. The 500 guests included royalty and political leaders from 70 nations. The elegant party, celebrating the 2,500th anniversary of the founding of the Persian Empire, lasted about 4½ hours and included cocktails, a dinner prepared by world-famous Maxim's of Paris, and a finale of blazing French fireworks.

Missouri Statehood Sesquicentennial. Missouri became a state on Aug. 10, 1821, and celebrated its 150th anniversary in 1971. A Missouri commemorative postage stamp was issued on May 8, during ceremonies at the Harry S. Truman Library in Independence. It features a part of a picture painted by Missouri artist Thomas Hart Benton. Commemorative bronze and silver medallions were struck. One side depicts the restored old state capitol in Jefferson City. Between the two buildings is the inscription "150 Years of Statehood." On the reverse side of the medallion, modes of transportation through the years surround a map of the state. There is a Mississippi paddlewheel boat, a covered wagon, the *Spirit of St. Louis* airplane, and a space capsule. Among the many festivities was a

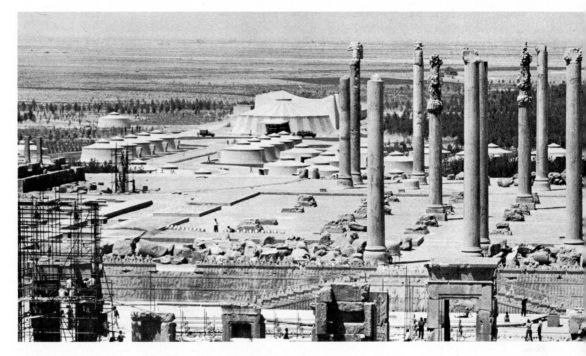

Iran built lavish tent villas and gardens amid the ruins of Persepolis for a celebration marking the 2,500th anniversary of the Persian Empire.

Missouri Folklife Festival from June 24 to 26 in St. Louis; an 1821 carnival on July 3 in Molden; and a celebration in St. Charles from August 10 to 15 that featured many events, including a coronation ball, fashion contest, beard-judging contest, and antique automobile show.

Proust Centennial. French novelist Marcel Proust's childhood home, the hamlet of Illiers, was renamed Illiers-Combray in 1971 to honor him on the centennial of his birth on July 10, 1871. Proust wrote about Illiers, using the fictional name Combray in his greatest work, *Remembrance of Things Past.* Mayor René Compére took many of the visitors on tours around the town. Many of those who know of Proust's work began their visit with a stop at a *pâtisserie* (pastry shop) on the *Place du Marché* where they sampled a shell-shaped confection called a madeleine. In his *Swann's Way,* Proust began his remembrance by recalling himself dunking a madeleine in tea: "No sooner had the warm liquid, and the crumbs with it, touched my palate, than a shudder ran through my whole body, and I stopped, intent upon the extraordinary changes that were taking place."

Sir Walter Scott Bicentennial. In 1971, Scotland celebrated the anniversary of Sir Walter Scott, who was born in Edinburgh in 1771. Scott's romantic historical novels made him a national hero. They reminded his countrymen of their proud heritage and introduced many in the outside world to Scotland and its people. The anniversary was celebrated throughout the country, and thousands visited the huge Scott Memorial on Princes Street in Edinburgh. But most impressive and popular was the tour of Abbotsford, Scott's mansion near Melrose, a town southeast of Edinburgh. Scott's great-great-great-granddaughter, Patricia Maxwell-Scott and her sister, Jean Maxwell-Scott, guided the visitors through the rooms, which still look as they did when Sir Walter worked, ate, and slept in them.

Stanley and Livingstone Centennial. In 1871, foreign correspondent Henry Morton Stanley of *The New York Herald* tracked down missing Scottish missionary David Livingstone. He found him in the African village of Ujiji on Lake Tanganyika. Upon confronting Livingstone, Stanley reportedly said, "Dr. Livingstone, I presume?"–now one of the most famous quotes in American folklore. In 1971, a commemorative postage stamp was issued in Tanzania, the country in which Ujiji is located. Otherwise, the anniversary was ignored by a populace anxious to forget their colonial past. An emphatic example of this attitude was a letter from the town clerk of Ujiji to the Royal Geographic Society in London. In the letter, he asked that the Stanley-Livingstone plaque in his town be replaced with a new one with the legend in Swahili rather than English.

Tønsberg's 1,100th Anniversary. Tønsberg, Norway, the oldest town in Scandinavia, was founded in 871. It celebrated its 1,100th year in 1971 with festivities in May, June, and July that included historical plays, a fair, an anniversary pageant, sailing regattas, and a brass-band contest.

1,900th Birthday of York. Founded in the year 71 by the Roman governor of Britain, Quintus Petillius Cerealis, the English city of York has withstood an explosive history of intrigue, plunder, and violence. Thousands of visitors flocked to the quaint cobblestoned city for the lavish 1971 celebration. Most impressive was the re-enactment of an English Civil War battle in which York fell to Oliver Cromwell's troops in 1644. Another highlight was a re-creation of the funeral of Roman Emperor Lucius Septimius Severus, whose death put an end to his despotic rule of York in 211.   Michael Reed

CENSUS, U.S. Reports released by the U.S. Bureau of the Census in 1971 showed definite racial migration patterns in the United States. Based on data from the 1970 census, they showed that whites continued to flee from the central cities to the suburbs, and blacks continued to move from the South to cities in the North. At the same time, whites were migrating to the South in record numbers.

During the 1960s, 1.8 million whites moved into southern states, while 1.4 million blacks moved out. This gave the South a net gain of more than 400,000 persons and reversed the South's recent trend toward population losses. Southern states with the greatest population gains through migration were Florida, Maryland, Texas, and Virginia.

In 1970, 53 per cent of all Negroes in the United States lived in the South, as compared with 77 per cent in 1940. Blacks accounted for 24 per cent of the South's total population in 1940, but only 19 per cent in 1970.

Urban Blacks. Of the 203 million persons in the United States in 1970, 22.7 million, or about 11 per cent, were black. Almost half the U.S. Negro population lived in 50 of the nation's largest cities. New York City had the largest Negro population, almost 1.7 million. Chicago ranked second with 1.1 million blacks; and Detroit was third, with more than 660,000.

A census report released in February showed that four major U.S. cities had a majority of black residents: Washington, D.C. (71.1 per cent); Atlanta, Ga. (51.3); Newark, N.J. (54.2); and Gary, Ind. (52.8). More than 40 per cent of the population was black in Baltimore; Birmingham, Ala.; Detroit; New Orleans; Richmond, Va.; St. Louis; and Wilmington, Del.

As the central-city black populations increased, the white populations decreased. Washington, D.C., lost 39.4 per cent of its white residents; Newark, 36.7 per cent; St. Louis, 31.6; Detroit, 29.2; Baltimore, 21.4; Atlanta, 20.0; Chicago, 18.6; and New York City, 9.3.

United States suburban areas, as a whole, were overwhelmingly white. But there were substantial increases in the number of blacks moving to the suburbs in scattered places. In the Cleveland area, Negro suburban residents increased by 452.8 per cent during the 1960s. Blacks increased by 106 per cent in the Los Angeles suburbs, and by 102 per cent in suburbs surrounding Washington, D.C.

Other Minorities. The nation's second largest minority is made up of persons of Spanish-speaking descent, according to an April report by the Bureau of the Census. Based on figures collected in November, 1969, the census bureau set the Spanish-American population at about 9.2 million persons, or 5 per cent of the U.S. total. Mexican Americans form the largest group (4.3 million) in this minority. Most persons of Mexican origin live in the Southwest. The second largest group (1.45 million) comes from Puerto Rico; the third largest (565,000), from Cuba. Most other Spanish Americans come from Central and South America.

The report also showed that 80 per cent of the Spanish-American population was born in the United States or its territories. The remaining 20 per cent comprised the largest group of foreign-born persons living in the United States. However, some Spanish-American leaders disputed these figures, claiming that there could be as many as 12 million persons of Spanish origin in the United States.

Another census study showed that families of Spanish origin earn more income than black families. In 1970, the median income was $7,330 for Spanish families, but only $6,280 for black families. That is, half the group earns more than that figure and half earns less. The median income for whites was $10,240. The median income for all races was $9,870.

American Indians, long considered a vanishing race, experienced a marked population increase during the 1960s. There were 792,730 Indians in 1970 as compared with 523,591 in 1960, and the 1970 count was more than double that of 1950. The Indian population grew at a rate of more than 5 per cent, about four times as fast as the total U.S. population. Improvements in public health service, resulting in a longer life expectancy and a lower infant mortality rate, were credited with the population gain.

Orientals made up about 1 per cent of the 1970 U.S. population. Filipinos were the fastest-growing ethnic group. They showed a 95 per cent population increase during the 1960s to a total of 343,060. The 435,062 persons of Chinese origin represented an 83.3 per cent increase over 1960. There were 591,290 Japanese, a gain of 27.4 per cent.

The Average U.S. Family in 1970 was smaller, older, and wealthier than in 1950. The typical 1970 family consisted of a 45-year-old father, a 42-year-old mother, and two children, ages 17 and 19. In the average family of 1950, the parents were about two years younger and had three children. The 1970 median family income of $9,870 had about twice the purchasing power of 1950's $3,330 income. The typical 1970 family owned a home in the suburbs. It was equipped with plumbing, heating, a washing machine, at least one television set, radios, and a telephone. See HOUSING.

The number of single-person households increased 57 per cent during the 1960s to a total of 11.1 million. Nearly 7.8 million of these were females. These figures reflect an increasing number of single (19.4 per cent) and divorced (3.7) women 14 years of age and older. The 104.3 million women make up 51 per cent of the population. The median age for both sexes in 1970 was 27.8. This meant that half the population was under 28 years of age.   Darlene R. Stille

CENTRAL AFRICAN REPUBLIC. See AFRICA.

CENTRAL AMERICA. See LATIN AMERICA.

Selected Census Statistics

Population Distribution by Sex, 1910 to 1970

	1910*	1920*	1930*	1940*	1950	1960	1970
Male	47,332,000	53,900,000	62,137,000	66,062,000	75,187,000	88,331,000	98,882,000
Female	44,640,000	51,810,000	60,638,000	65,608,000	76,139,000	90,992,000	104,284,000

*Does not include Alaska or Hawaii

Population Distribution by Race and Ethnic Group

	1960	1970	Per Cent of Total 1970 Population
White	158,831,732	177,748,975	87.5
Negro	18,871,831	22,580,289	11.1
American Indian	523,591	792,730	0.4
Japanese	464,332	591,290	0.3
Chinese	237,292	435,062	0.2
Filipino	176,310	343,060	0.2
Other*	218,087	720,520	0.3

*Mainly Aleuts, Hawaiians, Koreans, Malayans, and Polynesians

Population Distribution by Age, 1970*

Age	Number	Per Cent of Total Population
13 and under	53,813,865	26.4
14 to 19	23,165,338	11.4
20 to 24	16,371,650	8.1
25 to 34	24,908,490	12.3
35 to 44	23,071,631	11.4
45 to 54	23,202,735	11.4
55 to 64	18,582,398	9.1
65 and over	20,049,592	9.9
Total	203,165,699	100.0

*Based on 1970 census Advance Report, General Population Characteristics, February, 1971

Urban and Rural Population, 1940 to 1970

	1940*	1950*	1960	1970
Rural	43.5%	36.0%	30.1%	26.5%
Urban	56.5†	64.0	69.9	73.5

*Does not include Alaska or Hawaii

†Does not include unincorporated parts of urbanized areas

Urban and Suburban Population, 1950 to 1970

	1950	1960	1970
Standard metropolitan statistical areas	94,579,000	119,595,000	139,387,000
In central cities	53,817,000	59,964,000	63,816,000
Outside central cities	40,762,000	59,631,000	75,570,000

Population Distribution by Region, 1940 to 1970

	1940	1950	1960	1970
Northeast	35,977,000	39,478,000	44,678,000	49,041,000
Midwest	40,143,000	44,461,000	51,619,000	56,572,000
South	41,666,000	47,197,000	54,973,000	62,795,000
West	14,379,000	20,190,000	28,053,000	34,804,000

Urban Negro Population, 1950 to 1970

	1950	1960	1970
Standard metropolitan statistical areas	8,850,000	12,710,000	16,786,000
In central cities	6,608,000	9,950,000	13,097,000
Outside central cities	2,242,000	2,760,000	3,689,000

Source: U.S. Dept. of Commerce, Bureau of the Census

CEYLON. The Socialist Government of Prime Minister Sirimavo Bandaranaike began 1971 confidently pushing its nationalization program. On the surface, there was little cause for alarm. To combat a rise in world shipping rates, the government began expanding its merchant marine and harbor facilities. Government controls were further extended over most aspects of the economy, in a range that included rice marketing, film imports, and the exportation of precious gems.

Suddenly, and almost without warning, the Bandaranaike government was confronted early in April by a violently disruptive movement from the far left. The leftists, spearheaded by students and supported by a large number of the unemployed, styling themselves as either Maoists or Che Guevarists, centered their activities in the Kegalle district and eight southern and central provinces. The rebels seized roads and bridges and attacked government installations in 25 separate incidents. They called for the overthrow of the government.

Outside Aid Needed. The army was given full authority to stamp out the rebellion. It was authorized to use search and seizure techniques, 24-hour curfews were set, and martial law was imposed. The rebel forces, however, proved formidable. Ceylon, which had always prided itself on keeping its defense budgets small, suddenly found itself incapable of containing the rebellion with the limited military equipment on hand.

Prime Minister Bandaranaike called for outside military assistance, and Russia, Egypt, India, Yugoslavia, Pakistan, Great Britain, and the United States sent arms and equipment. The rebels, making full use of jungle cover, proved difficult to combat. Sporadic fighting continued into the summer, with the government issuing amnesty calls for those who would surrender. By September, about 9,000 insurgents had turned in their arms, while another 5,000 had been captured. Over 3,000 were killed, many of them summarily executed by army firing squads. An estimated 15,000 insurgents were put in special detention camps, and though thousands were later released, about 10,000 were still there at the end of the year.

The disruption proved costly, forcing the government to double its defense budget. It was forced, too, to spend more than $16 million to repair roads and other installations destroyed by the rebels. It was ironic that the rebels, who aligned themselves ideologically with the Maoists, should find the Chinese government giving Ceylon some $32 million to ease its precarious fiscal position.

Facts in Brief. Population: 13,143,000. Government: Governor-General William Gopallawa; Prime Minister Sirimavo Bandaranaike. Monetary Unit: rupee. Foreign Trade: exports, $340,000,000; imports, $389,000,000. Principal Exports: tea, rubber, coconut products.   John N. Stalker

CHAD moved toward a settlement of the long-standing civil war between the Africans in the south and the Arabs in the north in 1971. Until they were withdrawn in June, French troops assisted the government of President François Tombalbaye against the rebelling Arab tribes in the north.

Agreement with Rebels. After four months of negotiation, agreements were signed on January 6 and January 18 between President Tombalbaye and rebel leaders of the Chadian National Liberation Front (Frolinat). However, Frolinat headquarters in Algiers, Algeria, denounced the agreements and vowed to continue fighting the government of Chad.

In keeping with the agreements, the reconciled rebels gave up their arms and appointed representatives to the political bureau of the ruling Chad Progressive Party. In May, political prisoners were released, and representatives of the rebels were appointed to government ministries. Djibrine Kerallah, a rebel leader who had been imprisoned from 1965 to 1969, was named minister of finance. Two other former political prisoners were brought into the government, Baba Hassane, in charge of foreign affairs, and Mohamed Abdel Kerim, in charge of stock breeding.

Agreements were drawn up regarding the development of the north, and Moslem Arabs were appointed to civil service posts. However, the unofficial cease-fire did not bring peace to the north. Fairly heavy fighting continued during the first half of the year, and most observers agreed that President Tombalbaye could not have survived without French military support.

The Progressive Party Congress in May asked the government to take all possible measures to integrate the Moslem dissidents. It called upon all the people of Chad to fight tribalism, nepotism, and political corruption. But the Frolinat office in Algiers again denounced the attempts at reconciliation.

Attempted Coup. An unsuccessful attempt to overthrow the government occurred on August 27. The accused leader of the attempt, a former deputy in the National Assembly, reportedly committed suicide after his capture. Tombalbaye imposed a news blackout on the events surrounding the coup.

Chad charged Libya and a "major imperialist power" with involvement in the August incident. Chad immediately broke off diplomatic relations with Libya. Libya had repeatedly been accused by the Chad government of aiding the Arab rebels.

In early June, a cholera epidemic broke out in Chad that took over 2,300 lives. With the help of the World Health Organization, the disease was brought under control by late July.

Facts in Brief. Population: 3,670,000. Government: President François Tombalbaye. Monetary Unit: CFA franc. Foreign Trade: exports, $28,000,-000; imports, $52,000,000. Principal Exports: cotton, meat.   George Shepherd

CHEMICAL INDUSTRY. Business was off slightly in early 1971, but it began improving during the third quarter. National recovery from the recession was slow and the industry's gains failed to match those of the mid-1960s. Nevertheless, shipments of chemicals and allied products totaled $53.5 billion, almost 7 per cent over those in 1970. In general, the industry moved cautiously on purchases and kept inventories at low levels.

Most segments of the industry contributed to the overall growth. Shipments of plastics and resins reached an estimated $5 billion, up 11 per cent over 1970, but still below the 14 per cent annual average growth during the 1960s. The fertilizer market accelerated 1970's upturn; prices generally were higher and shipments were up 5 per cent to $1.9-billion. Profits for fertilizer producers were relatively modest, mainly because of higher costs, although they were better than any year since 1967.

Foreign trade in all chemicals failed to grow as rapidly as in 1970, but exports were up nearly 7 per cent, and imports went up about 10 per cent. The four-month 10 per cent surcharge on imports briefly improved the competitive position of many U.S. processed products, and the December devaluation of the dollar was expected to aid U.S. exports.

Environmental Issues stirred up considerable legislative and regulatory activity that affected the chemical industry. Early in the year, the Environmental Protection Agency (EPA) announced a pollution-control permit program, based on the 1899 Refuse Act. But bureaucratic red tape and the sheer immensity of the project, which required processing permits for every effluent pipe in the country, tied up the program. Even though the July 1 deadline was not met, the program exemplified the tough stand the EPA was beginning to take against industrial pollution. A number of companies were cited and prosecuted in 1971 by the Department of Justice on charges of violating this 1899 act.

Vermont attempted to become the first state to require polluters to pay for untreated wastes. Delaware passed a law banning new heavy industry from state coastal areas. A petrochemical complex and oil refinery planned by the Shell Oil Company was the first complex affected. Other states raised environmental quality standards and stiffened penalties.

On the whole, the chemical industry increased its own efforts for pollution control, spending more than $260 million on control measures in 1971.

Pesticide producers continued researching nonpersistent (not permanent), selective pesticides. Dow Chemical's new Zectran, a carbamate insecticide, received federal approval for certain uses at midyear. Meanwhile, the EPA banned DDT and dieldrin and aldrin, both chlorinated hydrocarbon insecticides, for all except a few uses. Public hearings were held on several other pesticides to determine what usage limitations, if any, should be imposed.

Polychlorinated biphenyls (PCB) came under Food and Drug Administration scrutiny as a toxic pollutant, following reports that animals and foods had been contaminated by the persistent chemical. Monsanto, the only U.S. producer of PCB, immediately eliminated its use in paints, flame retardants, or plasticizers from which potential food contamination could occur.

Phosphate Detergents. In September, the Public Health Service (PHS) and the EPA urged states and localities to reconsider their bans on phosphate detergents. At the same time, the PHS and the EPA continued the ban on nitrotriacetic acid in detergents, and warned nonphosphate detergent producers to reduce product alkalinity to lower levels. National opinion was divided. Earlier in the year, several cities, including Akron, Ohio; Chicago; and Detroit passed ordinances banning phosphates in detergents. In turn, the Soap and Detergent Association filed suits seeking injunctions to prevent enforcement of the bans. Nonphosphate detergents captured nearly 15 per cent of the $2.8-billion detergent market in 1971.

Foreign Companies continued purchasing U.S. firms or divisions to further market development in this country. The most notable example was the acquisition of Atlas Chemicals by Imperial Chemical Industries of Great Britain.   Mary Lynn M. Luy

Production of Leading Chemicals:

Inorganics (1,000 tons)	1969	1970	1971*
Ammonia	12,918	13,098	6,848
Chlorine	9,414	9,755	4,538
Hydrochloric acid	1,911	1,918	1,017
Nitric acid	6,443	6,460	3,417
Phosphoric acid	5,373	5,686	3,084
Sodium carbonate	4,540	4,414	2,103
Sodium hydroxide	9,917	10,074	4,713
Sulfuric acid	29,537	29,576	14,874
Organics (million pounds)			
Acetic anhydride	1,748	1,615	784
Acetone	1,518	1,598	775
Acrylonitrile	1,157	1,037	497
Butadiene	3,123	3,054	1,474
Cyclohexane	2,232	1,817	821
Ethylene oxide	3,408	3,671	1,703
Formaldehyde	4,398	4,312	2,119
Methanol	4,206	4,945	2,419
Phenol	1,691	1,710	820
Phthalic anhydride	760	714	368
Propylene oxide	1,177	1,121	530
Styrene	4,648	4,353	2,008
Urea	5,944	6,430	3,091
Vinyl chloride	729	799	407
Plastics (million pounds)	**1969**	**1970**	**1971***
Phenolics	1,181	1,042	539
Polyethylene	5,490	5,872	3,051
Polypropylene	1,090	1,038	578
Polystyrene	2,789	2,837	1,511
Polyvinyl chloride	3,032	3,134	1,613

*First six months. Other years, latest revised figures
Sources: U.S. Department of Commerce (inorganics); U.S. Tariff Commission (organics and plastics)

CHEMISTRY. The introduction of new light-scattering photometers in 1971 greatly improved the study of particles that are too small to be seen through most microscopes. These instruments use lasers as light sources and automatically feed the output data into a computer.

Andrew M. Wims and Mark E. Myers of General Motors Research Laboratories in Warren, Mich., developed one type of light-scattering photometer to study particles in the 0.1-to-50-millimicron range. They claim that the new photometer has many advantages over the most commonly used technique of optical or electron microscopy. With light-scattering, a large number of particles can be examined simultaneously, and there is no need for secondary standards to calibrate the instrument.

Philip J. Wyatt, president of Science Spectrum, Incorporated, of Santa Barbara, Calif., announced that engineers of his company had developed an automatic differential light-scattering photometer that was particularly useful in testing microbes, spores, and antibiotics. Wyatt treated a suspension of *Pseudomonas aeruginosa* bacteria with 100 micrograms of neomycin, and then viewed them with the light-scattering photometer. This showed that the bacteria were dead within 10 minutes.

Cyanocarbon Synthesis. A group of chemists at Du Pont's central research department in Wilmington, Del., led by Owen W. Webster, have prepared diimino-succinonitrile (DISN) in high yields by adding two relatively inexpensive compounds, hydrogen cyanide and cyanogen, to the catalyzed triethylamine base. DISN can be used in manufacturing a wide variety of drugs and agricultural chemicals. The other members of the research team were Robert W. Begland, Allan Cairncross, Denis S. Donald, Donald R. Hartter and William A. Sheppard.

DISN condenses with low-molecular-weight ketones, yielding a new family of chemicals called dicyanoisoimidazoles. DISN can also be easily reduced to diaminomaleonitrile (DAMN). Condensation of DISN and DAMN leads to a vast array of heterocyclic products. Among these are thiadiazoles, isomidazoles, diazocyclopentadienone derivatives, tetrahydropyrazines, pyrazines, triazoles, imidazoles, and imidazolones. DISN and DAMN are also starting materials for the synthesis of commercially useful polymers.

New Isotopes. A team of scientists headed by Albert Ghiorso produced two new isotopes of hahnium (tentative name for element 105) in the heavy ion linear accelerator at the University of California Lawrence Radiation Laboratory in Berkeley. The two isotopes were hahnium-261 and hahnium-262. In 1970, Ghiorso's team synthesized hahnium-260.

Hahnium-261 resulted from bombarding californium-250 with nitrogen-15 and by bombarding berkelium-249 with oxygen-16. Hahnium-262 was produced by bombarding berkelium-249 with oxygen-18. Both isotopes were found to have a surprisingly high stability for such heavy isotopes. Hahnium-261 decays to lawrencium-257 in a half-life of about 1.8 seconds. Hahnium-262 decays to lawrencium-258 in a half-life of about 50 seconds, which is quite long for such a heavy element.

Wins Award. The 1972 American Chemical Society Award in Pure Chemistry was given to Roy G. Gordon, professor of chemistry at Harvard University. His research has revealed much new information about the shapes and strengths of forces between molecules. In his work, Gordon has developed new approaches in quantum mechanics, statistical mechanics, scattering theory, and spectroscopy.

Since he does not perform laboratory experiments himself, Gordon developed new methods for estimating theoretical errors in calculated quantities and applied them to evaluate the accuracy of stated intermolecular forces, spectral line shapes, vibrational energies, and electronic energies.

Although highly theoretical, Gordon's work has practical application in determining the temperature distribution in the earth's atmosphere from spectral line shapes. His research is also applicable to the study of conformations in many types of organic molecules.   Alfred von Smolinski

See also AWARDS AND PRIZES; BIOCHEMISTRY; NOBEL PRIZES.

CHESS. Bobby Fischer of the United States capped a spectacular year in 1971, advancing to a world title match and seriously threatening Russian chess supremacy. Fischer defeated Tigran Petrosian of Russia 6½ points to 2½, in a series played in Buenos Aires, Argentina, in October. The series determined who would challenge world champion Boris Spassky, also of Russia, in April, 1972. See FISCHER, BOBBY.

After winning his last seven games in a tournament in Palma, Majorca, in December, 1970, Fischer won consecutive 6-to-0 decisions over grandmasters Mark Taimanov of Russia in Vancouver in May and Bent Larsen of Denmark in Denver in July. This feat is unprecedented.

Fischer defeated Petrosian in the first game of their series in Buenos Aires, then lost (resigned) the second game. The next three were draws, and Fischer won games 6, 7, 8, and 9.

Besides Fischer, Larsen, Taimanov, and Petrosian, others who qualified to play for the right to challenge Spassky were Victor Korchnoi and Yefim Geller of Russia, Wolfgang Uhlmann of East Germany, and Robert Huebner of West Germany.

Walter Browne of Sydney, Australia, and Larry Evans of Reno, Nev., tied for first place in the U.S. Open Championship in Ventura, Calif., in July. Kenneth Rogoff of Rochester, N.Y., and Greg DeFotis of Chicago tied for first in the Junior Championship in Newburgh, N.Y.   Theodore M. O'Leary

CHICAGO. Mayor Richard J. Daley was re-elected to an unprecedented fifth term on April 6, 1971. Daley received 70 per cent of the vote in beating Richard E. Friedman, an independent Democrat running on the Republican ticket. Friedman had the support of black leader Jesse Jackson, who had failed to gain a place on the ballot as an independent.

Joseph Bertrand, a banker, was elected city treasurer. Bertrand became the first black politician ever elected to citywide office in Chicago.

Cook County State's Attorney Edward V. Hanrahan and 13 other law officials were indicted in August on charges of conspiring to obstruct justice. The indictment stemmed from a 1969 raid by police assigned to the state's attorney's office in which two Black Panther Party members were killed.

Food and Housing. Chicago antipoverty agencies continued to deliver free, hot food to 14 inner city locations for distribution to needy residents. At its peak in the summer of 1970, the Family Food Program fed 9,061 persons daily. By September, 1971, the number of persons seeking food on an emergency basis had dropped to between 350 and 400 a day. The drop was largely because of the success of the Department of Human Resources and other agencies in finding jobs or other forms of permanent assistance for the hungry. In July, the Office of Economic Opportunity gave the city a $473,000 grant to establish a follow-up program, which included a referral system for locating and aiding other hungry people.

Mayor Daley denounced a federal court order directing the Chicago Housing Authority to file a plan for building public housing in the city's white neighborhoods. Daley insisted that public housing units would be built only where the people wanted them.

Chicago's public-school teachers went on strike in January, and eventually won a contract that provided for an 8 per cent wage boost in 1971 and another 8 per cent in 1972.

Home Rule arrived for Chicago on July 1, when Illinois's new Constitution took effect. Although Chicago's new legal status brought no immediate changes, the Home Rule Commission was reactivated to study ways of improving the city's government.

Chicago lost population during the 1960s. According to the 1970 census, the city's population fell 5.2 per cent to 3,366,957 between 1960 and 1970. The city's black population rose by 35.7 per cent during the same period. Blacks accounted for 32.7 per cent of the city's 1970 population.

In 1971, Chicago became the first major U.S. city capable of incinerating all of its solid wastes. The city's new $23-million incinerator is the largest of its type in the Western Hemisphere.

Mayor Daley proposed building a major new sports stadium on Chicago's lakefront. The idea was shelved, however, after it met with strong public opposition. Instead, the city decided to renovate its present stadium, Soldier Field.   J. M. Banovetz

CHILD WELFARE. The year 1971 was one of discussion, alarm, and commendable proposals, but little action. The White House Conference on Children and Youth, held every 10 years, met in two sessions. The first, held in Washington, D.C., in December, 1970, considered children under 14 years of age. There were also five regional follow-up meetings held early in 1971. The second session, devoted to youth from 14 to 24, was held in April, 1971, in Estes Park, Colo.

The conference on children recommended a program in which community ombudsmen would represent the rights and interests of children before government and private social and educational organizations. Personnel in the Department of Health, Education, and Welfare were assigned to the program, and Senator Abraham A. Ribicoff (D., Conn.) introduced legislation to finance experimental local programs. Economic, military, and space programs, however, left little in federal funds for welfare proposals.

The conference on youth was criticized because of apparent efforts to discourage press coverage, and because many believed its delegates were hand-picked nonmilitants. It made many strong recommendations, however. It urged an immediate end to the war in Indochina, citizen participation in a national effort to improve the environment, lowering

A mother drops her child off at a day-care center on her way to work. Many new centers have been opened because of the growing number of working mothers.

to 18 the legal age to make contracts and marry without parental consent, allocation of 25 per cent of the federal budget to education (now 3.6 per cent), and legalization of marijuana with government control of its sale and purity.

Day-Care Centers for children of working mothers have, in the past, been of concern chiefly to desperate mothers and a few social workers and agencies. In 1971, however, the nation began to give the problem more attention. There are more than 5 million children under 6 years old in the United States whose mothers work, but licensed day-care facilities are available for only 600,000. A Department of Labor study showed that 2 out of every 5 women who wanted to work gave lack of adequate day-care facilities as the main reason they could not.

A federal bill for comprehensive day care, with $2.1 billion for two years, passed both houses of Congress. The bill was vetoed, however, by President Richard M. Nixon on December 9. He claimed that although he approved of child care for welfare families, he objected to provisions in the bill allowing families not on welfare to use the facilities. Previous efforts, most of which have been supported by industry or unions, have proved inadequate for a large-scale, community solution.

Child Therapy and Guidance. There was increased research in, and public attention to, the use of drugs and a variety of psychological therapies for behavior and learning problems. Sedatives have been used to control hyperactivity and other child-behavior problems. More recently, however, Ritalin and related amphetamines have been widely used for hyperactive children. Stimulants, not depressants, these drugs reduce hyperactivity by increasing the child's attention span.

In 1971, a panel of experts found strong evidence that such medication, properly used, improves the hyperkinetic child's attention, learning, and social abilities. It reported no evidence that proper use leads to subsequent addiction. The panel also issued guidelines for amphetamine medication of such hyperkinetic children.

The National Institute of Mental Health gave the University of Illinois a $140,000 grant for a three-year study of how stimulants and tranquilizers affect a child's learning ability and intellectual and emotional development.

On the psychological side, two disparate trends continued to attract followers. One is to use behavior-modification techniques with immediate reinforcement, with rewards for correct behavior and punishment for undesirable behavior. The other approach uses humanistic psychology, with its emphasis on the whole person, on freeing the individual to be himself, and using encounter groups to release an individual's potentials.   Frances A. Mullen

CHILDREN'S BOOKS. See LITERATURE FOR CHILDREN.

CHILE. President Salvador Allende Gossens, an avowed Marxist, continued his efforts to transform Chile into a Socialist state in 1971. Through such measures as price freezes, wage increases of up to 50 per cent, and the use of foreign exchange reserves to maintain a heavy flow of imports, Allende's Popular Unity coalition government gained considerable popularity early in the year. In proof of this, its candidates won about 49 per cent of the votes cast in the April 4 municipal elections. But the price, in economic terms, was high: Shortages developed in such categories as consumer goods, food, and spare parts.

Copper production fell to around 580,000 metric tons in 1971, far below the 990,000 expected. Private foreign investments were virtually at a standstill, foreign credit shrank, and monetary reserves fell by about $250 million. The country was forced to ask its foreign creditors to renegotiate payments due on its debts totaling between $2.2 and $3 billion. There was serious doubt whether the United States would agree to renegotiate until Chile agreed to compensate American copper firms whose properties it had nationalized on July 15.

Facts in Brief. Population: 10,271,000. Government: President Salvador Allende Gossens. Monetary Unit: escudo. Foreign Trade: exports, $1,068,000,000; imports, $907,000,000. Principal Exports: copper, iron ore, nitrates.   Mary C. Webster

CHINA, NATIONALIST. See FORMOSA (TAIWAN).

CHINA, PEOPLE'S REPUBLIC OF. By any yardstick, 1971 turned out to be a memorable year for China and the rest of the world. It included the extraordinary April visit of the United States table tennis team, when Chinese audiences cheered young American players. China's gates were opened for the first time in two decades to U.S. newsmen, who were allowed to travel widely and report. Then, on July 9, in one of the best-kept postwar secrets, Henry A. Kissinger, President Richard M. Nixon's assistant on national security affairs, slipped into Peking for two days of talks with Premier Chou En-lai. And on July 15, the President told the world that he himself would be going to China. Kissinger was back in China in late October to make arrangements for the President's visit in February, 1972. Then, on October 25, Peking at last won membership in the United Nations—and Formosa was voted out (see UNITED NATIONS).

Retreat from Isolation. All of these events reflected China's return from the isolation into which the nation plunged during the Cultural Revolution from 1966 to 1969. At that time, all but one of the Chinese ambassadors abroad were recalled and, one after another, the foreign missions in Peking were closed. But in late 1969, with the Cultural Revolution at an end, China's leaders decided isolation was unrewarding. Also, the United States appeared to be slowly withdrawing from its Asian outposts, and the continent seemed to be entering a new phase in which a flexible foreign policy was needed. Thus began the subtle process of change, which led Chairman Mao Tse-tung, in 1971, to invite President Nixon to visit Peking.

Hanoi Objects. The switch was not painless. It disturbed China's own revolutionaries, who had been taught that "U.S. imperialism" was the ultimate villain. Even more important, the policy change alarmed China's allies, and none more than North Vietnam. In midsummer, Hanoi sharply warned the Chinese that the fate of Vietnam would be decided not across a negotiating table in Peking but on a battlefield. To reassure the uneasy spirits, the Chinese theoretical journal, *Red Flag*, said on September 1 that "moods cannot make policy," and that China remained an implacable foe of U.S. imperialism. A few weeks later, with Hanoi still unhappy, Peking sweetened the argument with a gift of weapons and machinery.

Once embarked on the new course, Peking did not deviate from it. And the Americans were not the only ones to be wooed. Much to Russia's dismay, delegations from Romania and Yugoslavia were given a warm welcome. While Peking continually denounced the Japanese government, it encouraged a massive pilgrimage to China by Japanese politicians and businessmen. Canada opened an embassy in Peking early in 1971, and a host of other countries recognized the People's Republic. The visitors to Peking ranged from Romania's President Nicolae Ceausescu and Ethiopia's Emperor Haile Selassie I to the Black Panther leader, Huey Newton. While the United States remained a target of abuse, the heavy fire was now focused on "militarist" Japan and "social-imperialist" Russia.

Changes at Home. Peking's vigorous and imaginative foreign policy was coupled with changes at home. The huge bureaucracy had been trimmed down after the Cultural Revolution, with one-fourth to one-third of it sent into the countryside to do manual labor for "re-education." Also shipped out to the country were millions of high school students, for whom industry could not provide enough jobs and whom Mao wanted politically "reborn" through work in rural China.

The machinery of governing had been radically changed. Every province, city, commune, school, and store now acquired its own Revolutionary Committee, which embodied Mao's idea of "three-in-one." This meant that each committee included representatives from the army, the party cadres, and the young "revolutionary masses," as well as the old, the middle-aged, and the young. As important was the revival of the Communist Party, which had been disrupted by the Cultural Revolution. The rebuilding process began in December, 1970, with the creation of a party committee in Mao's native Hunan province. It ended in August, 1971, with the emer-

In April, members of the U.S. table tennis team, including George Braithwaite (white sweater) and Errol Reseck, were welcomed by large gatherings in China.

gence of committees in such border regions as Tibet and Heilungkiang.

Army to the Fore. Significantly, most of the Revolutionary Committees as well as the party organs were headed by army men. In 22 of the 28 provincial and special-area party committees, the first secretaries wore military uniforms, and roughly half the members of the Politburo, ruling body of the Communist Party, were army men. In August, *The People's Daily* still argued that the party controlled the gun, and not the other way around. But the year's events confirmed the army's role as the dominant and stabilizing force in the nation.

The year also saw the continued attrition of the small group of men at the top. Mao remained the undoubted political master, with 63-year-old Lin Piao as his seldom-seen deputy. Chou En-lai, at 73, was still the indispensable man who saw to it that grain was purchased from the peasants, that the economic priorities were honored, and that the new foreign policy, which he had fashioned, was pursued without detours.

Purges Continued. There was a concerted attack on political extremists of the Cultural Revolution period. One of the Leftist "ultras," Yao Teng-shan, an obscure diplomat who for a few summer weeks in 1967 ran the foreign ministry, was exhibited in handcuffs at a mass "rally of denunciation" at a Peking stadium on June 11. Chen Po-ta, Mao's field general

Henry A. Kissinger, presidential adviser on national security affairs, met with Chinese Premier Chou En-lai during his surprise Peking visit in July.

during the Cultural Revolution, also was removed from his exalted fourth place in the hierarchy of power.

In September and October, the capital was filled with rumors of a secret four-day debate at the very top. Key army men vanished from sight, and most military and civil aircraft were grounded. These happenings were variously linked with the purge of the Left, with a debate on China's U.S. policy, and with the long-delayed National People's Congress that was to ratify the drastic changes of the preceding six years.

The adulation of Mao, which reached awesome proportions during the Cultural Revolution, was muted, reportedly on his own orders. For the first time since the Communists came to power, the annual National Day parade on October 1 was canceled, to be replaced by far more modest song-and-dance performances in the parks. Less stress was being put on politics, and more on production. Law and order, enforced by the military, returned to the land. And most of the managers and party secretaries, humbled and maltreated in the harsh days of 1966 to 1968, regained their old posts.

Bumper Crop. Generally, life in China seemed to have returned to its balmier pre-1966 days. Nowhere was the return to normality clearer than in the economy. In October, Peking claimed that the nation was harvesting its 10th successive bumper crop.

Premier Chou reported a record 1970 grain yield of 240 million tons. In 1971, it may have been as high. In March, 1971, 40 million tons of grain were being kept in storage as a national reserve.

Premier Chou also put China's 1971 steel production at a record 18 million tons, and its gross national product (GNP) at $120 billion. The GNP figure was not comparable to those in the West, because China does not include services in computing its GNP. But Chou estimated that China's GNP was roughly double that of Canada, if services were subtracted from the latter. All this denoted unspectacular, but steady, progress.

China's fourth five-year-plan began on Jan. 1, 1971. Its details were kept secret, and some experts thought the third five-year-plan may not have been completed. According to a Chinese source, the new plan gave top priority to defense, including the space-nuclear program. Next came transport, which has long been a bottleneck, and then basic industry, with emphasis on coal, iron ore mining, and steel. After these came agriculture, especially the production of chemical fertilizer. Premier Chou estimated fertilizer output in 1971 at 14 million tons, to be brought up to 35 million tons annually in five years. Even that would leave China far behind Japan, but it would ensure a large boost in the grain yield.

China's Population continued to grow, to the obvious dismay of its leaders. Chou complained to foreign visitors that the birth control program, while reasonably successful in the great east coast cities, was lagging in rural areas. In July, he told visitors that the goal for the 1970s was to bring the population growth down to 1 per cent a year, and for the 1980s to lower this rate. Foreign specialists estimated the present birth rate at 2.2 per cent, with the population more than 800 million. Birth control pills were provided free of charge in 1970, and distributed through village and factory clinics. Inquiries in the countryside indicated meager acceptance of the pill, though it was widely used in the cities.

Childbirth was not the only reason for the steady increase in China's population. The greatly expanded and improved public health network, which made for prolonged life expectancy, was also an important factor.

Changes in Education. After a four-year lapse, universities reopened late in 1970. The 1971 students were workers, peasants, and soldiers who had done at least three years of manual work or military service, and who were recommended for their political zeal. The education system had also been radically changed. The university term was reduced from five and six years to two or three, with emphasis on science and technical skills. Both primary and secondary school students were required to do a specified amount of manual work. Factory schools were also created for workers chosen on the basis of their intelligence and political activity.

Cultural life in 1971 remained largely confined to what had become known as "Chiang Ching's 10" – the 10 stage and musical works created or revised during the Cultural Revolution under the guidance of Mao's wife, Chiang Ching. But the year also saw such new "revolutionary" works as *Fighting on the Plains*, *The Tuchuan Mountain*, and *Ode to the Dragon River* added to the familiar *Red Lantern*, *Red Detachment of Women*, and *The White-Haired Girl*.

There was still virtually no new fiction in the bookstores, but *The People's Daily* had already set down the guidelines for China's budding novelists. Their works were to be revolutionary, optimistic, and permeated with the thoughts of Mao Tse-tung.

The extraordinary year ended well for China. The grain bins were overflowing, industry was expanding, and major successes were scored abroad. If there were any question marks, they involved the age and growing frailty of the leaders of this great revolution. If a young leadership was emerging, it remained invisible either to the man in the street in China or to a foreign onlooker.

Facts in Brief. Population: 772,000,000. Government: Communist Party Chairman Mao Tse-tung; Premier Chou En-lai. Monetary Unit: yuan. Foreign Trade: exports, $2,200,000,000; imports, $1,800,-000,000. Principal Export: rice.   Mark Gayn

CHISHOLM, SHIRLEY ANITA (1924-   ), Democratic representative from New York, announced in August, 1971, that she would seek the Democratic presidential nomination. The nation's first black woman representative told a black women's caucus in Chicago in October that she would make the race "without seeking anybody's endorsement." She explained that she was seeking a coalition of poor whites, Spanish-speaking Americans, blacks, and other minority groups. Representative Chisholm, whose 12th Congressional District encompasses the impoverished Bedford-Stuyvesant ghetto of Brooklyn, said that she sees her candidacy as "expendable" while she alerts the nation to the problems these groups face.

Representative Chisholm was born in Brooklyn and spent her childhood on a farm in Barbados, West Indies, returning to Brooklyn when she was 11 years old. She received an A.B. degree from Brooklyn College *cum laude* and an M.A. in elementary education from Columbia University. Prior to election to the U.S. House of Representatives in November, 1968, she was a state assemblywoman for four years. A straight-talking defender of minority rights, she once said, "My greatest political asset – which professional politicians fear – is my mouth."   Allan Davidson

CHRONOLOGY. See Pages 8 through 14.

CHURCHES. See EASTERN ORTHODOX CHURCHES; JEWS; PROTESTANT; RELIGION; ROMAN CATHOLIC.

Chicago Sun-Times

CHINA THAW

"It *is* better to light a candle than to curse the darkness."

CITY. The plight of the cities showed no signs of improvement in 1971. The rising costs of municipal services caused serious financial problems for many of the nation's major cities. According to the U.S. Bureau of the Census, urban expenses are rising faster than revenue. The massive migration of both businesses and white residents to the suburbs threatened to turn large cities into black ghettos. Detroit was particularly troubled by the loss of business firms, and this problem also threatened New York City (see DETROIT; NEW YORK CITY). A new civil rights issue developed over the question of building low-income, multiracial housing in the suburbs.

The financial crisis of American cities caused the U.S. Conference of Mayors to organize a legislative action committee to get financial relief for the cities, promote revenue-sharing measures in Congress, and encourage the federal government to pay local welfare expenses. The committee lobbied in Washington, D.C., and dramatized its case by visiting Baltimore, New York, and San Francisco in a self-proclaimed "road show." Its efforts were credited with having some influence in getting the Nixon Administration to release almost $800 million more in Model Cities funds. The mayors underscored the seriousness of the urban problem by predicting that "some American cities will soon go bankrupt" if they do not get financial help.

City Spending Up. The census report issued in September showed that in fiscal 1970 the cities spent $34.2 billion – $1.5 billion more than they received in revenue. Total 1970 city expenditures were 12 per cent higher than in 1969. The census bureau also reported that city employment rose 17 per cent and municipal payrolls increased 66 per cent during the period from 1965 to 1970. There were 1,563,000 full-time municipal employees in October, 1970, an average of 118.4 city employees for each 10,000 urban inhabitants. These figures seemed to support the dire predictions of the big-city mayors.

The National League of Cities, meeting in Honolulu in November, took a more moderate stand than the mayors. Instead of asking for more federal help for the cities, the league called for urban soul-searching, self-help programs, and local reform. It refused to endorse the child-care bill that was passed by Congress in December, but vetoed by President Richard M. Nixon (see CONGRESS). Unlike the mayors' conference, most of the league's members are small-city and suburban officials.

Urban Crime continued to be a major problem in the cities and a growing threat to the tranquillity of suburbia as well. Figures released by the Federal Bureau of Investigation in 1971 showed that although the 1970 rate of increase in crime had slowed in such major cities as Chicago, Cleveland, Pittsburgh, St. Louis, Seattle, and Washington, D.C., crime in the large cities rose at the overall rate of 6 per cent during that year. This was over-

shadowed, however, by a 15 per cent increase in crime in the suburbs and a 14 per cent increase in rural areas.

Scattered outbreaks of urban violence, bombings, and isolated terrorist acts continued in 1971. The U.S. Department of Justice reported that there were 11 major civil disturbances in the first eight months of 1971. (Major disturbances include bombing, arson, looting, sniping, and disturbances that involve at least 300 participants and last more than 12 hours. They require outside law-enforcement aid and a curfew.) During the same period, there were 49 serious and 133 minor disorders that occurred in small towns as well as large cities. Rioting broke out in such places as Albuquerque, N. Mex.; Jacksonville, Fla.; and Newburgh, N.Y.

According to the International Association of Chiefs of Police, there were 1,425 bombing incidents in which 15 persons died between July, 1970, and June, 1971. A total of 87 policemen were killed in the line of duty during the first nine months of 1971. President Nixon moved to give financial aid to the families of slain police officers. See CRIME.

Effects of Migration. The 1970 census showed that the nation is rapidly becoming a suburban society. More than 15 million persons moved into suburbia during the 1960s. The number of suburbanites now exceeds both rural and big-city dwellers. Migration to the suburbs has caused many of the cities' present difficulties and promises to add further troubles.

The new population distribution had an impact on the reapportionment of seats in the U.S. House of Representatives. Because of the 1970 census, congressional seats apportioned to the nation's central cities dropped by 10, to a total of 100. This represents less than one-fourth of the total number of congressional seats. Suburban area representation, however, increased by 32 seats in the House, to a total of 130. Sixty-three other seats were divided between central-city and suburban constituencies. The nation's rural areas lost 29 seats, to a total of 142. See CENSUS.

Suburbia is where the voters and an increasing percentage of congressional representation are found. This demographic-political fact will have an impact on the funding of federal programs to solve the problems of the cities. It appears certain that no solution for city problems will come at the expense of suburban areas.

Census figures also indicate that whites are leaving big cities at an alarming rate. The flight of the whites, accompanied by rapid increases in the black population in the cities, has also stimulated the movement of middle-class blacks from the cities to accommodating suburban areas. Washington, D.C., and Newark, N.J., have been particularly affected by the exodus of middle-class blacks.

However, many white suburban areas do not wel-

These bridges — connecting Manhattan with the Bronx — and more than 20 others were left jammed open by striking New York City municipal workers in June.

come black residents. There were allegations during the year that some suburban communities have used zoning restictions to keep out low-income and inter-racial housing projects. President Nixon responded to this charge in July by promising federal prosecution in individual cases of blatant racial discrimination in zoning. However, he also said that the federal government would not try to force integrated, low-income housing on any community.

Blackjack, Mo., a suburb of St. Louis, posed an immediate test of the Nixon Administration's intentions. Blackjack incorporated and quickly rezoned 25 acres of land after plans for a federally supported, low-income, interracial housing project were announced. The federal government sued Blackjack on June 4, charging the rezoning action was a deliberate attempt to block construction of the project. The final decision in the Blackjack case could have a major effect on residential patterns in suburban areas. See ST. LOUIS.

Mayoral Elections highlighted 1971 in several cities. The Democratic Party retained control of the mayor's office in Chicago; Baltimore; Boston; Gary, Ind.; Philadelphia; and San Francisco. The Republican Party retained the office in Indianapolis and won an upset victory in Cleveland.

Black candidates won election as mayor in Kalamazoo, Mich., and Englewood, N.J. Gary's black Mayor Richard G. Hatcher easily won re-election.

But Carl E. Stokes, who declined to run for re-election in Cleveland, failed in his effort to transfer his mayoral seat to Arnold R. Pinkney, another black.

The youth vote, cast for the first time in November, seemed to have little effect on major mayoral contests. However, mayoral elections in the village of Ayrshire, Iowa, and the town of Newcomerstown, Ohio, were both won by 19-year-olds. A 24-year-old was elected mayor of Cedar Falls, Iowa, and a 22-year-old was elected to Boston's City Council. See DEMOCRATIC PARTY; ELECTIONS; REPUBLICAN PARTY.

Environmental Concerns were a major topic of debate in many cities. Pollution from automobile exhausts was a prime issue. Several cities experimented with banning or reducing vehicular traffic in certain areas. Plans prohibiting on-street parking or creating pedestrian malls were tested in Boston, Philadelphia, and San Francisco.

A population limit of 1.5 million persons was proposed for the Denver metropolitan area by the Colorado Environmental Commission in January. The commission wanted to set up a system of green-belt parks and agricultural projects in the present urban area. It also recommended limiting the number of construction permits issued as a means of reducing suburban growth.   J. M. Banovetz

See also EDUCATION; Section One, FOCUS ON EDUCATION; Section Two, THE AMERICAN CITY: A YEAR BOOK TRANS-VISION® AND SPECIAL REPORT.

CIVIL RIGHTS. The new executive director of the National Urban League, Vernon E. Jordan, Jr., called upon President Richard M. Nixon in 1971 to make a "spiritual pilgrimage to black America." Like many other black spokesmen, Jordan was troubled by what he termed the Nixon Administration's "ambiguity" toward black people. " 'What the right hand giveth,' " he said, " 'the left hand taketh away.' " He commended the Administration's welfare reform proposals, but pointed out that basic payment levels under the proposed federal plan would be lower than those now provided by 45 states and the District of Columbia. Jordan charged that while the Administration proclaimed disapproval of overt racial discrimination, it failed to act against implicit discrimination in the form of economic and zoning barriers that prevent decent housing for blacks.

Jordan was named in June to succeed Whitney M. Young, Jr., as the executive director of the Urban League. Young, 49, died on March 11 in Nigeria, where he was attending a conference. He apparently drowned while swimming at a beach in Lagos. See JORDAN, VERNON E., JR.

School Busing was the most emotional civil rights issue of 1971. In a unanimous opinion written by Chief Justice Warren E. Burger, the Supreme Court of the United States ruled that busing could be ordered to end "all vestiges of state-imposed segregation." President Nixon, however, declared himself opposed to busing and ordered Administration officials to restrict its use "to the minimum required by law."

Busing and school integration proceeded in most Southern communities with hardly a disruptive incident, however. Figures released in June by the Department of Health, Education, and Welfare showed that only 14.1 per cent of Southern black students had attended segregated schools during the 1970-1971 school year.

More unsettling were the responses to forced busing in cities outside the South. In Pontiac, Mich., 10 school buses were blown up. Protesters blocked the school bus depot, and nine youths were injured during demonstrations. San Francisco suffered a massive, citywide student boycott over the busing issue. Thousands of children were kept home on the schools' opening day. Many parents sent their children to privately operated "freedom schools" rather than have them bused.

The Black Political World in 1971 was a place of ferment and hope, even of optimism. The elections of black mayors, the increasing populations of Northern ghettos, and the growing number of Southern black voters made the political mainstream increasingly attractive to many black leaders. "If blacks use their votes intelligently," said Washington, D.C., Congressman Walter E. Fauntroy, "they can affect the outcome of every election from city council to the presidency."

Black politicians mapped strategies for the 1972 elections. Their plans ranged from bargaining within the two major parties and exercising a veto over the Democratic national ticket to backing a "third force" black candidate for President.

Change touched the most militant ghetto organization, the Black Panther Party. After attaining peak impact in 1970, the party appeared to be disintegrating in 1971. Its ranks were decimated by warfare with the police, party purges, and desertions. Its best-known leaders, Eldridge Cleaver and Huey P. Newton, were openly at odds.

The Panthers fared better in the courts. In New York City, 13 Black Panthers accused of bombing and conspiracy were acquitted. In New Haven, Conn., a jury was unable to reach a verdict in the murder conspiracy trial of national chairman Bobby G. Seale. The judge dismissed the charges and barred a retrial. The Illinois Supreme Court ordered a judge in Chicago to release a grand jury indictment charging 14 law-enforcement officials with conspiring to obstruct justice in the 1969 killings of two Black Panthers. The men were killed during a predawn police raid on an apartment.

Black Capitalism. The chief preoccupation of black leaders in 1971 was neither politics nor revolution, but economics. "The black liberation movement is moving into its final phase and that's eco-

Burial Squad

The congressional Black Caucus, composed of 13 Negro members of Congress, met with President Richard M. Nixon twice in 1971 but were disappointed with the results.

nomic," said Jesse Jackson, director of the Southern Christian Leadership Conference's Operation Breadbasket. Eager to get black people off the welfare rolls, black leaders looked to government and business for help in promoting black economic independence. The manipulation of black buying power, they believe, can be a powerful force. According to Jackson, "Black Americans now possess enough buying power to make the margin of profit in a lot of the country's businesses."

The year's economic downturn, however, dealt harsh blows to black capitalism. Soaring unemployment rates among blacks and reduced welfare checks crippled black buying power. Tight money conditions cut off investment capital for black enterprises.

Women's Rights. At the forefront of movements struggling to strengthen human rights was women's liberation. In Washington, D.C., women from various organizations gathered to form the National Women's Political Caucus. Among those attending were Congresswomen Bella S. Abzug (D., N.Y.) and Shirley Chisholm (D., N.Y.); Betty Friedan, founder of the National Organization of Women; and journalist Gloria Steinem. The caucus set as its goal increased representation of women in government and at the national political conventions in 1972. The caucus declared it would support any candidate pledged to fight "sexism, racism, violence, and poverty." The women adopted a strategy that in-

cluded women voter registration drives and the infiltration of women into decision-making roles in existing political organizations. See CHISHOLM, SHIRLEY ANITA.

The annual General Assembly of the United Presbyterian Church in the U.S.A. elected its first woman moderator, Lois H. Stair, a ruling elder from Waukesha, Wis. She declared that male dominance in the church was disappearing. A week earlier, Ruth Rohlfs of Seattle was elected president of the American Baptist Convention.

Prison Revolts. The spotlight of civil rights and liberties fell on the nation's prisons. The event that focused attention on the question of prisoners' rights was the September revolt at New York state's Attica Correctional Facility. There, prisoners negotiated for a series of rights, including religious freedom, a healthy diet, adequate medical care, and noncensorship of outside publications, except where prison security was endangered. The revolt ended when about 1,500 law-enforcement officers stormed the prison. Thirty-two prisoners and 11 hostages were killed as a result of the action.

Attica and other prison uprisings seemed to mirror the trouble and racial discord existing in the outside world. Militant inmates influence other prisoners with their rhetoric. Adding to the friction is the stark racial division between prisoners and guards. When the uprising occurred at Attica, 85 per cent of the inmates were black and Puerto Rican, while virtually all of the guards were white. See CRIME.

Wiretapping and other forms of government surveillance of individuals became increasingly controversial in 1971. Legislators, educators, lawyers, and others warned that indiscriminate information gathering endangers civil liberties.

Senator Edmund S. Muskie (D., Me.) charged that the Federal Bureau of Investigation had kept a record of his activities during an Earth Day rally in April, 1970. Other congressmen said they suspected their telephones were tapped. It was also revealed that the House Internal Security Committee had once kept files on certain congressmen.

The Nixon Administration claimed the legal right to use wiretapping, without a prior court order, to watch suspected subversives. This, the Administration said, was necessary for national security. However, White House press secretary Ronald L. Ziegler said that surveillance of private citizens was "repugnant" to the President.

The Supreme Court blocked the government's attempt to suppress publication of a secret Pentagon history of the Vietnam War. The so-called Pentagon Papers first appeared in *The New York Times* and, later, the *Washington Post*. The court decision was widely regarded as a powerful demonstration of the openness of U.S. society. See PUBLISHING (Close-Up).

Two Roman Catholic priests, Philip and Daniel Berrigan, were among several persons charged with plotting to kidnap Mr. Nixon's national security adviser, Henry A. Kissinger, and blow up heating tunnels in Washington, D.C. The priests, antiwar activists in prison for destroying draft records, denied the charges. They claimed the indictments were an attempt by the government to discredit the peace movement. See ROMAN CATHOLIC CHURCH.

Civil Rights Abroad. Russia reduced to a trickle the number of Jewish families allowed to emigrate. This stirred protests in many countries, particularly among Jews in the United States. See RUSSIA.

A Greek military court sentenced to prison Lady Amalia Fleming, Greek-born widow of the discoverer of penicillin. She was convicted of plotting the escape of a man imprisoned for trying to murder Prime Minister George Papadopoulos. Later, she was released because of poor health and deported. Reportedly, about 600 persons were being held as political prisoners in Greece in mid-1971. Charges of prisoner torture continued to be made.

In February, women in Switzerland were granted the right to vote in federal elections. The women's suffrage issue was voted down in neighboring Liechtenstein, however. Liechtenstein is the only Western country in which women are not allowed to vote.

The Women's Liberation Movement gained momentum in Great Britain. In March, 4,000 women staged a march in London, demanding equal pay and equal job opportunities.   Louis W. Koenig

CLEVELAND voters elected a new mayor, Republican Ralph J. Perk, on Nov. 2, 1971. Former Mayor Carl B. Stokes, one of the first black mayors of a major U.S. city, had announced in April that he would not be a candidate for re-election. Noting that he had served 14 years in local government, Stokes indicated that his service had been restricted to "a relatively small constituency" and that he now wanted to "expand [his] efforts." Perk, Cleveland's first Republican mayor in 30 years, defeated a Democrat and a Stokes-backed independent in the November election.

A Severe Financial Crisis forced the city to lay off 1,000 employees on January 1 and later dismiss another 700. Recreation and health programs were hit particularly hard by budget reductions. The recreation department's budget was cut by 80 per cent, all city recreation halls were closed, and 423 of the department's 500 employees were dismissed.

Although no manpower reductions were scheduled for the police and fire departments, plans to add more men were shelved and the police academy was closed. An era came to an end when the city's last 44 mounted policemen were forced to trade their horses for squad cars.

Voters had twice rejected proposals to increase the city's income tax rates. They voted down a proposed increase from 1 per cent to 1.8 per cent in November, 1970, and then vetoed a proposed increase to 1.6 per cent in February, 1971. The second rejection cost Cleveland $20 million in revenue. It also ruled out a proposed increase of more than 20 per cent in the city's budget.

The City Council failed to support Mayor Stokes's proposals for low-income housing. To express his disapproval, Stokes and his staff began boycotting the City Council's weekly meetings.

Census Results. Cleveland experienced the second largest population decline of any major U.S. city during the 1960s. Population fell 14.3 per cent, from 876,050 in 1960 to 750,903 in 1970. In 1970, the city's nonwhite population reached 38.3 per cent, lending support to speculation that Cleveland would have a nonwhite majority before 1985. While the city proper retained its rank as the nation's 10th largest, the Cleveland metropolitan area fell from 11th to 12th place. Its population increased by only 154,711 persons to 2,064,194.

When the new National Railroad Passenger Corporation (Amtrak) routes were announced in March, Cleveland was excluded from passenger rail service. It was later added, however, as a stop on the route between Chicago and New York City.

Cleveland and the federal Environmental Protection Agency agreed on efforts to curb water pollution. The proposed $500-million program included $270 million in federal funds.   J. M. Banovetz

CLOTHING. See FASHION.

COAL. See MINES AND MINING.

COIN COLLECTING. The United States mint began taking orders for the new Eisenhower silver dollar on July 1, 1971. This was the first U.S. silver coin of that denomination to be minted since 1935. The demand was so great that no more orders could be accepted after October 8.

The obverse (front) side of the dollar shows President Dwight D. Eisenhower in profile, while the reverse side shows an eagle bearing an olive branch landing on the moon. This commemorates the Apollo 11 space mission.

Two different versions of the coin, which contains 40 per cent silver, were offered. Proof coins, priced at $10 each, were made in high relief and struck twice by special polished dies. Uncirculated coins, priced at $3 each, were also of high quality but lacked the mirrorlike finish of the proof coins and may have had minor flaws. Each customer was allowed to order five coins, and by late September, about 6 million requests had been received for the uncirculated coins and 4 million for the proof coins. The mint was to begin accepting orders for uncirculated 1972 Eisenhower coins on Feb. 1, 1972, and for the proof dollars on May 1. They projected a sale of 130 million uncirculated dollars over a two-year period and 20 million proof coins over four years. An undetermined number of cupronickel Eisenhower dollars will be minted for general circulation.

In February, the Denver mint began producing cupronickel Kennedy half dollars to supplant the 40 per cent silver coins that thousands of collectors had hoarded. The advent of the new coins was expected to put half dollars in general circulation again.

Canadian Coins. Canada also began producing silver dollars, its first since 1967. Priced at $3 and commemorating the 100th anniversary of British Columbia joining the Canadian Federation, the coins could be obtained only from the numismatic section of the Royal Canadian mint.

Excitement ran high among collectors when some 9,000 coins, part of a trove of 17th century Spanish coins and precious metals from a sunken ship, were offered for sale in London and New York City. Salvaged by divers off Grand Bahama Island in 1964, the items were valued at about $500,000 and included coins of 8, 4, and 2 reals. Most were priced at from $25 to $200, with some rarities going for more.

The annual Congress of the International Association of Professional Numismatists, meeting in June in Estoril, Portugal, formulated plans to publish a pamphlet in English, German, and French on counterfeit coins. It will define the problems of counterfeit coinage and list all known issues of questionable numismatic value from all parts of the world. A book by Burton Hobson, *Historic Coins of the World*, published in August, is the first on coinage to carry all its illustrations in full color.   Theodore M. O'Leary

COLOMBIA. Violence erupted repeatedly in 1971, even as President Misael Pastrana Borrero pursued his policy of "social justice." A wave of civil unrest hit various cities in February. In mid-April, the government had to close five universities to put down a series of student uprisings.

President Pastrana Borrero declared on October 8 that "the entire society" was at stake. Colombian politics were in confusion. Both the Conservative and the Liberal parties were torn by internal struggles. Capitalizing in part on this, the National Popular Alliance of Gustavo Rojas Pinilla, who seized power in 1953 and ruled until 1957, was gaining strength.

In the background were rising living costs, higher wage demands from labor, listless business activity, sluggish industrial output, increasing unemployment, and unrest over the ineffectiveness of the agricultural reform program. The latter program became so chaotic it was suspended in September. Between January and August, gross monetary holdings fell by $44.6 million.

Facts in Brief. Population: 22,491,000. Government: President Misael Pastrana Borrero. Monetary Unit: peso. Foreign Trade: exports, $608,000,000; imports, $686,000,000. Principal Exports: coffee, petroleum.   Mary C. Webster

COLORADO. See STATE GOVERNMENT.

COMMON MARKET. See EUROPE.

There was a great demand among collectors for the new Eisenhower silver dollar, both sides of which were designed by Frank Gasparro, chief mint engraver.

COMMUNICATIONS

COMMUNICATIONS. The 81-member International Telecommunications Satellite Consortium (Intelsat) agreed in August, 1971, on new regulations to govern the development of a global satellite system. Since its inception in 1964, Intelsat has grown to a system that now has four satellites operating in synchronous orbit, with a total capacity of 8,600 two-way voice circuits, linked to 63 ground station antennas in 38 countries.

Three major developments contributed to the 1971 increase in international telecommunications facilities. The first of seven *Intelsat 4* satellites, which will serve transatlantic routes, was launched on January 25, and a second went up on December 19. A new major cable link between Great Britain and Spain was opened, and a cable link began providing service between Canada and Bermuda.

Direct telephone and telegraph service between mainland China and the rest of the world was restored late in the year. Earlier, plans were also laid for a satellite communications system "hot line" between the United States and Russia.

Phone Service Expanding. With international telephone facilities growing rapidly, the nations of the world were keeping pace with their own internal expansion programs. At the end of 1971, an estimated 288 million telephones were in service throughout the world. Of this total, about 122 million were in the United States, with the total passing the 100-million mark late in the year for Bell System companies. Another 21.9 million were served by approximately 1,800 independent telephone companies.

To meet the heavy demands for service, the Bell System spent $7.5 billion on construction, compared with $7.2 billion in 1970, and announced that up to $8.5 billion will be spent in 1972. The independents, who spent $1.7 billion in 1970, increased that amount to $2 billion in 1971.

The American Telephone & Telegraph Company (A.T.&T.) requested a long-distance telephone rate increase for $385 million to produce a 9.5 per cent rate of return. It accepted a Federal Communications Commission (FCC) ruling on Jan. 13, 1971, that gave A.T.&T. interim increases amounting to $250 million, or a 6 per cent return. The company reserved the right to file for higher rates after full hearings were conducted by the commission.

Labor Unrest marked the year. In Great Britain, telecommunications workers were among post office employees who struck for seven weeks starting on January 20. In the United States, a work stoppage of Bell System employees across the country lasted from July 14 to July 20, and the Western Union Telegraph Company was also hit by the first nationwide strike in its history. It lasted from June 1 to July 23. In New York City, however, beset for several years by communications service problems, local members of the Communication Workers of America continued their strike against Western Union until September 13, a total of 104 days. Telephone plant workers, spurning the nationwide agreement, remained off the job to add to the mounting difficulties encountered in trying to catch up with the staggering increase in demand for service.

FCC Rulings. The complexion of the industry continued to change in 1971. The FCC had under consideration 11 different proposals for providing domestic satellite communications service in the United States, indicating that this mode of service may be added to the nation's vast terrestrial network.

In a landmark "specialized common carrier" decision, the FCC, in June, announced what amounted to an open-entry policy for interstate specialized business communications data companies, and other private line services. The FCC ruled that price determination would be allowed to come largely from the forces of competition, rather than from the constraints of a regulatory agency. The decision, in effect, granted approval to the numerous applications for new interstate microwave stations.

The entry of the specialized common carriers, the advent of interconnection of customer-furnished terminal equipment and systems, and a final decision by the FCC in how computer services are to be provided, all contributed to a changing face in the domestic telecommunications industry that might be almost unrecognizable in a few years.   Thomas M. Malia

CONGO (BRAZZAVILLE). See AFRICA.

CONGO (KINSHASA) was renamed the Republic of Zaïre on Oct. 27, 1971. The government also changed the name of the Congo River to the Zaïre.

The country was troubled by student unrest during the year. In June, the government closed Lovanium University and forced the students to enlist in the army for two years. Those students who refused to enlist were sentenced to 10 years in prison.

President Joseph Mobutu claimed that foreign students had plotted his assassination. On July 27, 1971, Eastern European diplomats were expelled for their alleged involvement in the student disorders. On August 26, 10 students were sentenced to life in prison for plotting to overthrow the government.

President Mobutu paid a weeklong official visit to France, beginning March 29, to discuss increased foreign aid. He also visited Kenya, Liberia, Senegal, the Sudan, and Togo during 1971. In July, U.S. Vice-President Spiro T. Agnew visited the Congo.

In January, Christophe Gbenye, leader of the rebellion in 1964 and 1965, returned to Kinshasa under an amnesty declared by Mobutu in December, 1970. During 1971, more than 9,000 former rebels accepted the amnesty.

Facts in Brief. Population: 18,254,000. Government: President and Prime Minister Joseph Mobutu. Monetary Unit: zaïre. Foreign Trade: exports, $644,000,000; imports, $410,000,000. Principal Exports: copper, coffee, diamonds.   George Shepherd

CONGRESS OF THE UNITED STATES. The first session of the 92nd Congress moved sluggishly for much of 1971, resisting both the liberal Democrats' attempts at reform and the efforts of President Richard M. Nixon's Administration to prod it to legislative action. By year-end, however, Congress had given the President much of what he had requested.

When President Nixon sent Congress his first special message on January 26, he asked for action on 40 items of legislation not passed by the 91st Congress. But, in its first session, the Democrat-controlled 92nd Congress also failed to act on key Administration requests, such as revenue sharing and administrative reorganization. It did, however, extend the draft, enlarge social security benefits, approve the President's two nominees to the Supreme Court of the United States, and reduce income taxes.

A continuing recession marked by rising unemployment in an inflated economy was the number-one issue for Congress in 1971. The nightmare of unemployment and runaway inflation worried Congress more than the war in Indochina. As a result, several measures to aid the economy were passed, including giving the President authority to freeze wages and prices.

Democratic Majority. When the first session of the 92nd Congress convened on January 21, the

Workmen clean up debris in the Capitol after a bomb planted in a washroom exploded on March 1, causing more than $300,000 damage to the building.

Democrats controlled both houses. In the Senate, there were 54 Democrats and 45 Republicans, with 1 vacancy. In the House of Representatives, there were 254 Democrats and 180 Republicans, with 1 vacancy.

Mike J. Mansfield (D., Mont.) was again chosen majority leader in the Senate, but Robert C. Byrd (D., W. Va.) replaced Edward M. Kennedy (D., Mass.) as the Democratic whip. The Senate minority leader was Hugh D. Scott, Jr. (R., Pa.); minority whip was Robert P. Griffin (R., Mich.).

The new speaker of the House was Carl B. Albert (D., Okla.). He replaced John W. McCormack (D., Mass.), who retired. Majority leader was Hale Boggs (D., La.). Minority leader of the House was Gerald R. Ford (R., Mich.); minority whip was Leslie C. Arends (R., Ill.). A nonvoting representative from the District of Columbia was elected to the House in March, black Congressman Walter E. Fauntroy. See FAUNTROY, WALTER E.

Before the session convened, members of the House agreed to modify the seniority system. The selection of committee chairmen, they agreed, would in the future be approved by party caucus instead of by strict order of seniority. But the seniority system was slow to die and continued strong throughout the first session. In May, the Senate voted unanimously in favor of allowing girl pages. See Close-Up.

The Budget. On January 29, President Nixon sent Congress the Administration's budget for fiscal 1972. He told Congress that the new budget was "expansionary but not inflationary." The budget estimated spending at $229.2 billion and revenue at $217.6 billion. At that time, the estimated deficit for fiscal 1972 was $11.6 billion. In September, however, Secretary of the Treasury John B. Connally revealed that the 1972 budget deficit would be in the $28-billion range.

The Economy. In May, Congress gave the President the authority to establish wage and price controls through April 30, 1972. The President did not ask for this authority and was, in fact, opposed to the measure. Nevertheless, he used this congressional authorization on August 15 to set a 90-day wage-price freeze and establish the Phase 2 economic controls that followed. In December, Congress extended this authority to April, 1973. See ECONOMY, THE; PRESIDENT OF THE UNITED STATES.

Congress also passed a measure to combat high unemployment, and, on July 12, the President signed the Emergency Employment Act of 1971. The act will provide about 173,000 public service jobs in the next two years at an estimated cost of $2.25 billion. Under its provisions, state and local governments may apply for federal funds for public-works jobs.

On August 5, the President signed a public-works and economic-development bill authorizing the expenditure of $2.5 billion for various regions and another $1.5 billion specifically for Appalachia.

Members of the United States House

The House of Representatives of the 92nd Congress consists of 254 Democrats and 178 Republicans, with 3 seats vacant (not including representatives from the District of Columbia and Puerto Rico), compared with 245 Democrats and 189 Republicans, with 1 seat vacant, for the 91st Congress. This table shows congressional districts, legislator, and party affiliation. Asterisk (*) denotes those who served in 91st Congress; dagger (†) denotes "at large."

Alabama

1. Jack Edwards, R.*
2. William L. Dickinson, R.*
3. Vacant
4. William Nichols, D.*
5. W. W. Flowers, D.*
6. John H. Buchanan, Jr., R *
7. Tom Bevill, D.*
8. Robert E. Jones, D.*

Alaska

† Nick Begich, D.

Arizona

1. John J. Rhodes, R.*
2. Morris K. Udall, D.*
3. Sam Steiger, R.*

Arkansas

1. Bill Alexander, D.*
2. Wilbur D. Mills, D.*
3. J. P. Hammerschmidt, R.*
4. David Pryor, D.*

California

1. Don H. Clausen, R.*
2. Harold T. Johnson, D.*
3. John E. Moss, D.*
4. Robert L. Leggett, D.*
5. Phillip Burton, D.*
6. William S. Mailliard, R.*
7. Ronald V. Dellums, D.
8. George P. Miller, D.*
9. Don Edwards, D.*
10. Charles S. Gubser, R.*
11. Paul N. McCloskey, Jr., R.*
12. Burt L. Talcott, R.*
13. Charles M. Teague, R.*
14. Jerome R. Waldie, D.*
15. John J. McFall, D.*
16. B. F. Sisk, D.*
17. Glenn M. Anderson, D.*
18. Robert B. Mathias, R.*
19. Chet Holifield, D.*
20. H. Allen Smith, R.*
21. Augustus F. Hawkins, D.*
22. James C. Corman, D.*
23. Del M. Clawson, R.*
24. John H. Rousselot, R.*
25. Charles E. Wiggins, R.*
26. Thomas M. Rees, D.*
27. Barry M. Goldwater, Jr., R.*
28. Alphonzo Bell, R.*
29. George E. Danielson, D.
30. Edward R. Roybal, D.*
31. Charles H. Wilson, D.*
32. Craig Hosmer, R.*
33. Jerry L. Pettis, R.*
34. Richard T. Hanna, D.*
35. John G. Schmitz, R.
36. Bob Wilson, R.*
37. Lionel Van Deerlin, D.*
38. Victor V. Veysey, R.

Colorado

1. James D. McKevitt, R.
2. Donald G. Brotzman, R.*
3. Frank E. Evans, D.*
4. Wayne N. Aspinall, D.*

Connecticut

1. William R. Cotter, D.
2. Robert H. Steele, R.
3. Robert N. Giaimo, D.*
4. Stewart B. McKinney, R.
5. John S. Monagan, D.*
6. Ella T. Grasso, D.

Delaware

† Pierre S. du Pont IV, R.

Florida

1. Robert L. F. Sikes, D.*
2. Don Fuqua, D.*
3. Charles E. Bennett, D.*
4. William V. Chappell, Jr., D.*
5. Louis Frey, Jr., R.*
6. Sam M. Gibbons, D.*
7. James A. Haley, D.*
8. C. W. Young, R.
9. Paul G. Rogers, D.*
10. J. Herbert Burke, R.*
11. Claude D. Pepper, D.*
12. Dante B. Fascell, D.*

Georgia

1. G. Elliott Hagan, D.*
2. Dawson Mathis, D.
3. Jack T. Brinkley, D.*
4. Ben B. Blackburn, R.*
5. Fletcher Thompson, R.*
6. John J. Flynt, Jr., D.*
7. John W. Davis, D.*
8. Williamson S. Stuckey, Jr., D.*
9. Phillip M. Landrum, D.*
10. Robert G. Stephens, Jr., D.*

Hawaii

1. Spark M. Matsunaga, D.*
2. Patsy T. Mink, D.*

Idaho

1. James A. McClure, R.*
2. Orval Hansen, R.*

Illinois

1. Ralph Metcalfe, D.
2. Abner J. Mikva, D.*
3. Morgan F. Murphy, D.
4. Edward J. Derwinski, R.*
5. John C. Kluczynski, D.*
6. George W. Collins, D.
7. Frank Annunzio, D.*
8. Daniel D. Rostenkowski, D.*
9. Sidney R. Yates, D.*
10. Harold R. Collier, R.*
11. Roman C. Pucinski, D.*
12. Robert McClory, R.*
13. Philip M. Crane, R.*
14. John N. Erlenborn, R.*
15. Vacant
16. John B. Anderson, R.*
17. Leslie C. Arends, R.*
18. Robert H. Michel, R.*
19. Thomas F. Railsback, R.*
20. Paul Findley, R.*
21. Kenneth J. Gray, D.*
22. William L. Springer, R.*
23. George E. Shipley, D.*
24. Charles Melvin Price, D.*

Indiana

1. Ray J. Madden, D.*
2. Earl F. Landgrebe, R.*
3. John Brademas, D.*
4. J. Edward Roush, D.
5. Elwood H. Hillis, R.
6. William G. Bray, R.*
7. John T. Myers, R.*
8. Roger H. Zion, R.*
9. Lee H. Hamilton, D.*
10. David W. Dennis, R.*
11. Andrew Jacobs, Jr., D.*

Iowa

1. Fred Schwengel, R.*
2. John C. Culver, D.*
3. H. R. Gross, R.*
4. John H. Kyl, R.*
5. Neal Smith, D.*
6. Wiley Mayne, R.*
7. William J. Scherle, R.*

Kansas

1. Keith G. Sebelius, R.*
2. William R. Roy, D.
3. Larry Winn, Jr., R.*
4. Garner E. Shriver, R.*
5. Joe Skubitz, R.*

Kentucky

1. Frank A. Stubblefield, D.*
2. William H. Natcher, D.*
3. Romano L. Mazzoli, D.
4. Marion Gene Snyder, R.*
5. Tim Lee Carter, R.*
6. William P. Curlin, Jr., D.
7. Carl D. Perkins, D.*

Louisiana

1. F. Edward Hébert, D.*
2. Hale Boggs, D.*
3. Patrick T. Caffery, D.*
4. Joe D. Waggonner, Jr., D.*
5. Otto E. Passman, D.*
6. John R. Rarick, D.*
7. Edwin W. Edwards, D.*
8. Speedy O. Long, D.*

Maine

1. Peter N. Kyros, D.*
2. William D. Hathaway, D.*

Maryland

1. William O. Mills, R.
2. Clarence D. Long, D.*
3. Edward A. Garmatz, D.*
4. Paul S. Sarbanes, D.
5. Lawrence J. Hogan, R.*
6. Goodloe E. Byron, D.
7. Parren J. Mitchell, D.
8. Gilbert Gude, R.*

Massachusetts

1. Silvio O. Conte, R.*
2. Edward P. Boland, D.*
3. Robert F. Drinan, D.
4. Harold D. Donohue, D.*
5. F. Bradford Morse, R.*
6. Michael Harrington, D.
7. Torbert H. Macdonald, D.*
8. Thomas P. O'Neill, Jr., D.*
9. Louise Day Hicks, D.
10. Margaret M. Heckler, R.*
11. James A. Burke, D.*
12. Hastings Keith, R.*

Michigan

1. John Conyers, Jr., D.*
2. Marvin L. Esch, R.*
3. Garry Brown, R.*
4. Edward Hutchinson, R.*
5. Gerald R. Ford, R.*
6. Charles E. Chamberlain, R.*
7. Donald W. Riegle, Jr., R.*
8. James Harvey, R.*
9. Guy A. Vander Jagt, R.*
10. Elford A. Cederberg, R.*
11. Philip E. Ruppe, R.*
12. James G. O'Hara, D.*
13. Charles C. Diggs, Jr., D.*
14. Lucien N. Nedzi, D.*
15. William D. Ford, D.*
16. John D. Dingell, D.*
17. Martha W. Griffiths, D.*
18. William S. Broomfield, R.*
19. Jack H. McDonald, R.*

Minnesota

1. Albert H. Quie, R.*
2. Ancher Nelsen, R.*
3. William Frenzel, R.
4. Joseph E. Karth, D.*
5. Donald M. Fraser, D.*
6. John M. Zwach, R.*
7. Bob Bergland, D.
8. John A. Blatnik, D.*

Mississippi

1. Thomas G. Abernethy, D.*
2. Jamie L. Whitten, D.*
3. Charles H. Griffin, D.*
4. G. V. Montgomery, D.*
5. William M. Colmer, D.*

Missouri

1. William Clay, D.*
2. James W. Symington, D.*
3. Leonor K. (Mrs. John B.) Sullivan, D.*
4. Wm. J. Randall, D.*
5. Richard Bolling, D.*
6. W. R. Hull, Jr., D.*
7. Durward G. Hall, R.*
8. Richard H. Ichord, D.*
9. William L. Hungate, D.*
10. Bill D. Burlison, D.*

Montana

1. Richard G. Shoup, R.
2. John Melcher, D.*

Nebraska

1. Charles Thone, R.
2. John Y. McCollister, R.
3. David T. Martin, R.*

Nevada

† Walter S. Baring, D.*

New Hampshire

1. Louis C. Wyman, R.*
2. James C. Cleveland, R.*

New Jersey

1. John E. Hunt, R.*
2. Charles W. Sandman, Jr., R.*
3. James J. Howard, D.*
4. Frank Thompson, Jr., D.*
5. Peter H. B. Frelinghuysen, R.*
6. Edwin B. Forsythe, R.
7. William B. Widnall, R.*
8. Robert A. Roe, D.*
9. Henry Helstoski, D.*
10. Peter W. Rodino, Jr., D.*
11. Joseph G. Minish, D.*
12. Florence P. Dwyer, R.*
13. Cornelius E. Gallagher, D.*
14. Dominick V. Daniels, D.*
15. Edward J. Patten, D.*

New Mexico

1. Manuel Lujan, Jr., R.*
2. Harold L. Runnels, D.

New York

1. Otis G. Pike, D.*
2. James R. Grover, Jr., R.*
3. Lester L. Wolff, D.*
4. John W. Wydler, R.*
5. Norman F. Lent, R.
6. Seymour Halpern, R.*
7. Joseph P. Addabbo, D.*
8. Benjamin S. Rosenthal, D.*
9. James J. Delaney, D.*
10. Emanuel Celler, D.*
11. Frank J. Brasco, D.*
12. Shirley Chisholm, D.*
13. Bertram L. Podell, D.*
14. John J. Rooney, D.*
15. Hugh L. Carey, D.*
16. John M. Murphy, D.*
17. Edward I. Koch, D.*
18. Charles B. Rangel, D.*
19. Bella S. Abzug, D.
20. William F. Ryan, D.*

21. Herman Badillo, D.
22. James H. Scheuer, D.
23. Jonathan B. Bingham, D.*
24. Mario Biaggi, D.*
25. Peter A. Peyser, R.
26. Ogden R. Reid, R.*
27. John G. Dow, D.
28. Hamilton Fish, Jr., R.*
29. Samuel S. Stratton, D.
30. Carleton J. King, R.*
31. Robert C. McEwen, R.*
32. Alexander Pirnie, R.*
33. Howard W. Robison, R.*
34. John H. Terry, R.
35. James M. Hanley, D.
36. Frank Horton, R.*
37. Barber B. Conable, Jr., R.*
38. James F. Hastings, R.*
39. Jack Kemp, R.
40. Henry P. Smith III, R.*
41. Thaddeus J. Dulski, D.*

North Carolina

1. Walter B. Jones, D.*
2. L. H. Fountain, D.*
3. David N. Henderson, D.*
4. Nick Galifianakis, D.*
5. Wilmer Mizell, R.*
6. Richardson Preyer, D.
7. Alton Asa Lennon, D.*
8. Earl B. Ruth, R.*
9. Charles Raper Jonas, R.*
10. James T. Broyhill, R.*
11. Roy A. Taylor, D.*

North Dakota

1. Mark Andrews, R.*
2. Arthur A. Link, D.

Ohio

1. William J. Keating, R.
2. Donald D. Clancy, R.*
3. Charles W. Whalen, Jr., R.*
4. William M. McCulloch, R.*
5. Delbert L. Latta, R.*
6. William H. Harsha, R.*
7. Clarence J. Brown, Jr., R.*
8. Jackson E. Betts, R.*
9. Thomas L. Ashley, D.*
10. Clarence E. Miller, R.*
11. J. William Stanton, R.*
12. Samuel L. Devine, R.*
13. Charles A. Mosher, R.*
14. John F. Seiberling, Jr., D.
15. Chalmers P. Wylie, R.*
16. Frank T. Bow, R.*
17. John M. Ashbrook, R.*
18. Wayne L. Hays, D.*
19. Charles J. Carney, D.
20. James Stanton, D.
21. Louis Stokes, D.*
22. Charles A. Vanik, D.*
23. William E. Minshall, R.*
24. Walter E. Powell, R.

Oklahoma

1. Page Belcher, R.*
2. Ed Edmondson, D.*
3. Carl B. Albert, D.*
4. Tom Steed, D.*
5. John Jarman, D.*
6. John N. Happy Camp, R.*

Oregon

1. Wendell Wyatt, R.*
2. Al Ullman, D.*
3. Edith Green, D.*
4. John R. Dellenback, R.*

Pennsylvania

1. William A. Barrett, D.*
2. Robert N. C. Nix, D.*
3. James A. Byrne, D.*
4. Joshua Eilberg, D.*
5. William J. Green III, D.*
6. Gus Yatron, D.*
7. Lawrence G. Williams, R.*
8. Edward G. Biester, Jr., R.*
9. John H. Ware III, R.
10. Joseph M. McDade, R.*
11. Daniel J. Flood, D.*
12. J. Irving Whalley, R.*
13. R. Lawrence Coughlin, R.*
14. William S. Moorhead, D.*
15. Fred B. Rooney, D.*
16. Edwin D. Eshleman, R.*
17. Herman T. Schneebeli, R.*
18. H. John Heinz III, R.
19. George A. Goodling, R.*
20. Joseph M. Gaydos, D.*
21. John H. Dent, D.*
22. John P. Saylor, R.*
23. Albert W. Johnson, R.*
24. Joseph P. Vigorito, D.*
25. Frank M. Clark, D.*
26. Thomas E. Morgan, D.*
27. Vacant

Rhode Island

1. Fernand J. St. Germain, D.*
2. Robert O. Tiernan, D.*

South Carolina

1. Mendel J. Davis, D.
2. Floyd D. Spence, R.
3. W. J. Bryan Dorn, D.*
4. James R. Mann, D.
5. Thomas S. Gettys, D.*
6. John L. McMillan, D.*

South Dakota

1. Frank E. Denholm, D.
2. James Abourezk, D.

Tennessee

1. James H. Quillen, R.*
2. John J. Duncan, R.*
3. LaMar Baker, R.
4. Joe L. Evins, D.*
5. Richard H. Fulton, D.*
6. William R. Anderson, D.*
7. Leonard Ray Blanton, D.*
8. Ed Jones, D.*
9. Dan W. Kuykendall, R.*

Texas

1. Wright Patman, D.*
2. John Dowdy, D.*
3. James M. Collins, R.*
4. Ray Roberts, D.*
5. Earle Cabell, D.*
6. Olin E. Teague, D.*
7. W. R. Archer, R.
8. Robert C. Eckhardt, D.*

9. Jack Brooks, D.*
10. J. J. Pickle, D.*
11. W. R. Poage, D.*
12. James C. Wright, Jr., D.*
13. Graham Purcell, D.*
14. John Young, D.*
15. Eligio de la Garza, D.*
16. Richard C. White, D.*
17. Omar Burleson, D.*
18. Robert D. Price, R.*
19. George H. Mahon, D.*
20. Henry B. Gonzalez, D.*
21. O. C. Fisher, D.*
22. Robert R Casey, D.*
23. Abraham Kazen, Jr., D.*

Utah

1. K. Gunn McKay, D.
2. Sherman P. Lloyd, R.*

Vermont

Richard W. Mallary, R.

Virginia

1. Thomas N. Downing, D.*
2. G. William Whitehurst, R.*
3. David E. Satterfield III, D.*
4. Watkins M. Abbitt, D.*
5. W. C. Daniel, D.*
6. Richard H. Poff, R.*
7. J. Kenneth Robinson, R.
8. William Lloyd Scott, R.*
9. William C. Wampler, R.*
10. Joel T. Broyhill, R.*

Washington

1. Thomas M. Pelly, R.*
2. Lloyd Meeds, D.*
3. Julia Butler Hansen, D.*
4. Mike McCormack, D.
5. Thomas S. Foley, D.*
6. Floyd V. Hicks, D.*
7. Brock Adams, D.*

West Virginia

1. Robert H. Mollohan, D.*
2. Harley O. Staggers, D.*
3. John M. Slack, Jr., D.*
4. Ken Hechler, D.*
5. James Kee, D.*

Wisconsin

1. Leslie Aspin, D.
2. Robert W. Kastenmeier, D.*
3. Vernon W. Thomson, R.*
4. Clement J. Zablocki, D.*
5. Henry S. Reuss, D.*
6. William A. Steiger, R.*
7. David R. Obey, D.
8. John W. Byrnes, R.*
9. Glenn R. Davis, R.*
10. Alvin E. O'Konski, R.*

Wyoming

† Teno Roncalio, D.

Puerto Rico

Resident Commissioner
Jorge L. Córdova

District of Columbia

Nonvoting Representative
Walter E. Fauntroy, D.

Members of the United States Senate

The Senate of the 92nd Congress consists of 54 Democrats, 44 Republicans,
1 Independent, and 1 Conservative, compared with 57 Democrats and 43 Republicans
for the 91st Congress. Senators shown starting their term in 1971 were elected for
the first time in the Nov. 3, 1970, elections. Those shown ending their current terms
in 1977 were re-elected to the Senate in the same balloting. The second date
in each listing shows when the term of a previously elected senator expires.
For organization purposes, the one Independent will line up with Democrats,
the one Conservative with Republicans.

State	Term	State	Term	State	Term
Alabama		**Louisiana**		**Ohio**	
John J. Sparkman, D.	1946–1973	Allen J. Ellender, D.	1937–1973	William B. Saxbe, R.	1969–1975
James B. Allen, D.	1969–1975	Russell B. Long, D.	1948–1975	Robert Taft, Jr., R.	1971–1977
Alaska		**Maine**		**Oklahoma**	
Theodore F. Stevens, R.	1968–1977	Margaret Chase Smith, R.	1949–1973	Fred R. Harris, D.	1965–1973
Mike Gravel, D.	1969–1975	Edmund S. Muskie, D.	1959–1977	Henry L. Bellmon, R.	1969–1975
Arizona		**Maryland**		**Oregon**	
Paul J. Fannin, R.	1965–1977	Charles McC. Mathias, Jr., R.	1969–1975	Mark O. Hatfield, R.	1967–1973
Barry Goldwater, R.	1969–1975	J. Glenn Beall, Jr., R.	1971–1977	Robert W. Packwood, R.	1969–1975
Arkansas		**Massachusetts**		**Pennsylvania**	
John L. McClellan, D.	1943–1973	Edward M. Kennedy, D.	1962–1977	Hugh D. Scott, Jr., R.	1959–1977
J. William Fulbright, D.	1945–1975	Edward W. Brooke, R.	1967–1973	Richard S. Schweicker, R.	1969–1975
California		**Michigan**		**Rhode Island**	
Alan Cranston, D.	1969–1975	Philip A. Hart, D.	1959–1977	John O. Pastore, D.	1950–1977
John V. Tunney, D.	1971–1977	Robert P. Griffin, R.	1966–1973	Claiborne Pell, D.	1961–1973
Colorado		**Minnesota**		**South Carolina**	
Gordon L. Allott, R.	1955–1973	Walter F. Mondale, D.	1964–1973	Strom Thurmond, R.	1956–1973
Peter H. Dominick, R.	1963–1975	Hubert H. Humphrey, D.	1971–1977	Ernest F. Hollings, D.	1966–1975
Connecticut		**Mississippi**		**South Dakota**	
Abraham A. Ribicoff, D.	1963–1975	James O. Eastland, D.	1943–1973	Karl E. Mundt, R.	1948–1973
Lowell P. Weicker, Jr., R.	1971–1977	John Cornelius Stennis, D.	1947–1977	George S. McGovern, D.	1963–1975
Delaware		**Missouri**		**Tennessee**	
J. Caleb Boggs, R.	1961–1973	Stuart Symington, D.	1953–1977	Howard H. Baker, Jr., R.	1967–1973
William V. Roth, Jr., R.	1971–1977	Thomas Francis Eagleton, D.	1968–1975	William E. Brock III, R.	1971–1977
Florida		**Montana**		**Texas**	
Edward J. Gurney, R.	1969–1975	Mike J. Mansfield, D.	1953–1977	John G. Tower, R.	1961–1973
Lawton Chiles, D.	1971–1977	Lee Metcalf, D.	1961–1973	Lloyd M. Bentsen, Jr., D.	1971–1977
Georgia		**Nebraska**		**Utah**	
Herman E. Talmadge, D.	1957–1975	Roman Lee Hruska, R.	1954–1977	Wallace F. Bennett, R.	1951–1975
David H. Gambrell, D.*	1971–1973	Carl T. Curtis, R.	1955–1973	Frank E. Moss, D.	1959–1977
Hawaii		**Nevada**		**Vermont**	
Hiram L. Fong, R.	1959–1977	Alan Bible, D.	1954–1975	George D. Aiken, R.	1941–1975
Daniel Ken Inouye, D.	1963–1975	Howard W. Cannon, D.	1959–1977	Robert T. Stafford, R.†	1971–1977
Idaho		**New Hampshire**		**Virginia**	
Frank Church, D.	1957–1975	Norris Cotton, R.	1954–1975	Harry F. Byrd, Jr., Ind.	1965–1977
Leo B. Jordan, R.	1962–1973	Thomas J. McIntyre, D.	1962–1973	William B. Spong, Jr., D.	1967–1973
Illinois		**New Jersey**		**Washington**	
Charles H. Percy, R.	1967–1973	Clifford P. Case, R.	1955–1973	Warren G. Magnuson, D.	1944–1975
Adlai E. Stevenson III, D.	1970–1975	Harrison A. Williams, Jr., D.	1959–1977	Henry M. Jackson, D.	1953–1977
Indiana		**New Mexico**		**West Virginia**	
Vance Hartke, D.	1959–1977	Clinton P. Anderson, D.	1949–1973	Jennings Randolph, D.	1958–1973
Birch Bayh, D.	1963–1975	Joseph M. Montoya, D.	1964–1977	Robert C. Byrd, D.	1959–1977
Iowa		**New York**		**Wisconsin**	
Jack R. Miller, R.	1961–1973	Jacob K. Javits, R.	1957–1975	William Proxmire, D.	1957–1977
Harold E. Hughes, D.	1969–1975	James L. Buckley, Cons.	1971–1977	Gaylord A. Nelson, D.	1963–1975
Kansas		**North Carolina**		**Wyoming**	
James B. Pearson, R.	1962–1973	Sam J. Ervin, Jr., D.	1954–1975	Gale W. McGee, D.	1959–1977
Robert J. Dole, R.	1969–1975	B. Everett Jordan, D.	1958–1973	Clifford P. Hansen, R.	1967–1973
Kentucky		**North Dakota**			
John Sherman Cooper, R.	1956–1973	Milton R. Young, R.	1945–1975		
Marlow W. Cook, R.	1969–1975	Quentin N. Burdick, D.	1960–1977		

*Replaced the late Richard B. Russell
in February, 1971.

†Replaced the late Winston L. Prouty
in September, 1971.

Congressmen applaud Carl B. Albert (D., Okla.) after he was elected the new speaker of the House when the 92nd Congress convened on January 21.

In August, Congress passed a bill allowing the government to guarantee $250 million in bank loans to corporations whose failure would seriously damage the economy. The entire amount, it was expected, would go to the Lockheed Aircraft Corporation to prevent its bankruptcy. See AVIATION.

Foreign Aid. Congress shocked the world in October by voting to end the foreign-aid program. On October 28, Administration forces had succeeded in defeating the Cooper-Church amendment proposed by Senator John Sherman Cooper (R., Ky.) and Senator Frank Church (D., Ida.) attached to the foreign-aid authorization bill. The amendment forbade the President to use any funds in Indochina, except for the withdrawal of U.S. military forces. But, the following day, the Senate unexpectedly defeated the entire $3.2-billion foreign-aid bill by a vote of 41 to 27. Political observers gave many possible reasons for the Senate's action, including a reaction to the United Nation's vote admitting mainland China to membership and congressional anger at the Administration. See UNITED NATIONS.

Failing to complete action on a new foreign-aid bill during its first session, the 92nd Congress extended the expiring program until February, 1972.

Even though the Nixon Administration was clearly winding down the war in Indochina, Senate doves still pressed for a more rapid withdrawal of U.S. troops from Vietnam. In November, Congress passed a $21.4-billion military procurement authorization bill with an amendment calling for the withdrawal of all U.S. troops from Indochina by a "date certain," following the release of all U.S. prisoners of war. The original version, passed earlier by the Senate, called for total withdrawal within six months after all prisoners had been released. The amendment was sponsored by Senator Mansfield. President Nixon signed the bill on November 17, but he said he would ignore the Mansfield amendment.

Education. On July 11, the President signed the largest appropriation bill in the history of the Office of Education, $5.15 billion. The bill reflected popular dissatisfaction with student rioting. It banned granting funds to any person at an institution of higher learning who had been involved in force or the threat of force, aimed at interfering with its functioning, since Aug. 1, 1969. It also barred the use of funds to force further desegregation.

School-lunch funds were the subject of controversy throughout the session. On June 28, Congress completed action on a bill that authorized an additional $135 million for free or reduced-price lunches for needy children. The Department of Agriculture in August announced cutbacks in subsidies for the school-lunch program. But, on October 1, Congress ordered the Administration to increase spending. The Department of Agriculture then cut the program again by reducing the number of children to

A First For the Senate

Five high-school girls broke the United States Senate's 182-year tradition of all male pages in 1971. They were employed in the Senate as pages after it adopted a resolution on May 13 to authorize the appointment of female pages.

The five were Paulette Desell, 17, of Schenectady, N.Y.; Ellen McConnell, 17, of Dundee, Ill.; Barbara Wheeler, 16, of Lawton, Okla.; Mari Iwashita, 15, of Honolulu, Hawaii; and Melissa Hayes, 15, of Little Rock, Ark. The girls were sponsored, respectively, by Senators Jacob K. Javits (R., N.Y.), Charles H. Percy (R., Ill.), Fred R. Harris (D., Okla.), Daniel K. Inouye (D., Hawaii), and J. William Fulbright (D., Ark.).

The three senators who led the successful fight for passage of the authorizing resolution—Percy, Javits, and Harris—said girls were being barred by discrimination against their sex.

"Long hours, strenuous tasks, housing, crime, and the inability of female pages to enter the men's washrooms —all these factors have been invoked

The first four girls to serve as U.S. Senate pages are, from left: Mari Iwashita, Barbara Wheeler, Ellen McConnell, and Paulette Desell.

as arguments against girl pages," Percy observed. "What is really at issue, in my opinion, is a reluctance to break with tradition." The "practical considerations" were only excuses, he said.

Paulette Desell, the Senate's first girl page, said, "There was definitely an antigirl feeling when I first arrived. The boy pages were jealous because of the publicity I had re-

ceived and the attention paid me by the senators. But the resentment went away when the boys found out that I was doing my share of work."

The 5 girls were part of a force of 30 Senate pages, 50 House of Representative pages, and 4 Supreme Court pages. They were paid a little more than $600 a month, and were dressed in navy blue pants suits, white blouses, and black shoes.

To offset two problems—the considerable crime around the Capitol and the fact that no dormitory facilities are provided for pages—the senators appointing the girls assumed responsibility for them.

There were sometimes big bundles of papers, the records of hearings, that had to be delivered to the Senate floor. But this presented no problem. The girls did the same as the boys and got carts to carry them. Nor was there a problem over rest rooms; a number of public rest rooms for women are available.

About the only problem that seemed to bother the girls—and they learned to cope with it—was the fatigue of the long hours. "You go until you think you cannot go a minute longer, then you go some more," Paulette said. Some, like Barbara Wheeler, got blisters on their feet.

Their day began at 6:15 A.M., when classes commenced in the Capitol Page School in the Library of Congress. School let out at 9:45 A.M., and the pages spent the rest of the day in the Senate—filing material on the senators' desks, running errands for them, and carrying reading matter between the Senate chamber and the senators' offices.

When they got home at night they did their school homework, washed their hair, and turned in as early as possible to be ready for another day.

On the social side, the girls found that their jobs offered new dating opportunities. There was time for dating their new friends among the boy pages on weekends. All of them agreed that the job is well worth the hard work because of the unusual opportunity it provides for listening to interesting debates and learning something about how the government operates.　William McGaffin

whom it would offer the lunches. On October 20, Congress acted to order the free-lunch program restored to full operation.

The Supreme Court. On October 21, the President named Lewis F. Powell, Jr., and William H. Rehnquist to fill Supreme Court vacancies left by the retirement and death of Hugo L. Black and the retirement of John M. Harlan. Powell, a Virginia lawyer, was a former president of the American Bar Association. Rehnquist was an assistant U.S. attorney general.

The Senate confirmed the nomination of Powell on December 6 by a vote of 89 to 1. There was stronger Senate opposition to Rehnquist, mainly because some senators suspected he was not sympathetic to the rights of minorities. Nevertheless, Rehnquist was confirmed, 68 to 26, on December 10. See COURTS AND LAWS; POWELL, LEWIS F., JR.; REHNQUIST, WILLIAM H.

Social Security. In March, Congress passed and the President signed legislation providing for a 10 per cent increase in social security benefits. The new law raised the minimum monthly payment for a single retired person to $70.40; for a couple, to $105.60. The maximum monthly payments under the new law would be $213.10 for a single person and $413.71 for a couple.

The cost of the increase was estimated at $3.6-billion a year. To pay the cost, the payroll tax would rise to 5.85 per cent in 1979 and to 6.05 per cent by 1987. (The payroll tax in 1971 was 5.2 per cent.) The amount of individual income subject to taxation would rise from the first $7,800 of earnings to the first $9,000 in 1972. See SOCIAL SECURITY.

Selective Service. The law that authorized the nation's draft calls expired on June 30. On June 22, the Senate voted 57 to 42 to adopt an amendment to the Selective Service Act calling for the withdrawal of all U.S. forces from Indochina within nine months if all American prisoners of war were released. But, on June 28, the House rejected the amendment, and for three months there was no draft law.

As the Selective Service Act of 1971 was finally passed, it included a "sense of Congress" resolution asking the President to withdraw all U.S. troops from Indochina by a "date certain," subject to the release of all American prisoners of war.

The act, signed by Mr. Nixon on September 28, authorized the President to draft men on a national rather than a community basis and to abolish student deferments. It prohibited the drafting of more than 130,000 men in fiscal 1972 and 140,000 men in fiscal 1973 without congressional authorization.

Supersonic Transport. Public controversy over the supersonic transport plane (SST) intensified in 1971. Many Americans were afraid that the SST would seriously pollute the atmosphere and that the noise of its sonic boom would be intolerable. There was also some doubt about whether the giant plane

would be a profitable undertaking. After much debate, the House and the Senate voted in March to cut off funds for the development of the plane. On May 25, the President signed a bill appropriating $97.3 million to phase out the project. In an appropriation bill passed by the House on July 29 and by the Senate on August 2, Congress allotted $58.5-million for refunds to domestic airlines for phasing out the SST.

Constitutional Amendments. On March 23, the House completed congressional action on a constitutional amendment, lowering the voting age in all elections to 18, by voting 400 to 19 in favor of the proposal. The amendment was ratified by the necessary 38 states by June, and, with the President's signature, it went into effect on July 5.

A proposed amendment to permit voluntary prayers in public schools was defeated in the House on November 8. See U.S. CONSTITUTION.

An amendment to grant equal rights to women was passed by the House on October 12 and sent to the Senate.

Vetoes. There were two major presidential vetoes in 1971. In June, the President vetoed a $5.6-billion public-works bill, designed to alleviate unemployment by creating federal jobs. Mr. Nixon termed the measure inflationary.

On December 9, he vetoed a bill to create a national system of child-development and day-care centers. President Nixon said he feared such federally created institutions would weaken the family.

Other Congressional Actions. In May, Congress ordered railroad signalmen to return to work, placing a moratorium on signalmen's strikes until October 1, and providing an interim wage increase of 13.5 per cent. See LABOR.

On July 1, the President signed a one-year extension of the 1968 Juvenile Delinquency Prevention and Control Act. The bill authorized $75 million for the program.

On July 2, the President signed a bill increasing retirement benefits for railroad employees by 10 per cent, to bring these benefits into line with social security increases.

On August 5, the House completed congressional action on a law allowing the President to use his discretion in approving trade with specific Communist countries through the Export-Import Bank. The Export Expansion Finance Act of 1971, signed by the President on August 17, extended the life of the Export-Import Bank to June 30, 1974.

On December 9, Congress completed action on a bill cutting taxes by $15.8 billion, and the President signed it on December 11. The measure increased the standard income tax deduction for individuals.

On December 14, Congress passed a measure requiring able-bodied relief recipients to apply for jobs or enroll in job-training programs. Carol L. Thompson

CONNECTICUT. See STATE GOVERNMENT.

CONSERVATION. A backlash started in 1971, off-setting the intensified public concern about conservation and environmental problems. Some conservationists complained that government conservation efforts were being weakened by pressures from business leaders who feared the huge costs of environmental cleanup. In an address to the National Petroleum Council on July 15, Secretary of Commerce Maurice H. Stans reflected the misgivings of many businessmen when he declared it was time "somebody said 'wait a minute'" before undertaking quick solutions to complex environmental problems.

Testifying before the House Fisheries and Wildlife Conservation Subcommittee on August 8, conservationists charged that pressure from the Department of Commerce and the Office of Management and Budget had led to weakening of plans to implement the Clean Air Act of 1970, and an "unhappy surrender" to the Florida Power and Light Company over reducing the discharge of polluted water into Biscayne Bay, south of Miami.

Reorganization Plan. On March 25, President Richard M. Nixon sent legislation to Congress to create a Department of Natural Resources. The new agency would centralize the now-scattered administration of such activities as land and recreation; water resources; energy and mineral resources; oceanic, atmospheric, and earth sciences; and Indian and territorial affairs. It would embrace most of the agencies now in the Department of the Interior; the Forest Service and the Soil Conservation Service of the Department of Agriculture; the civil works planning functions of the Army Corps of Engineers; the power functions of the Atomic Energy Commission; and the National Oceanic and Atmospheric Administration of the Department of Commerce. The proposal received broad support because it would bring together often overlapping and conflicting responsibilities in the natural resource area. However, congressional approval appeared unlikely until after the 1972 presidential election.

Amchitka A-Test. On November 6, a 5-megaton nuclear explosion was set off by the United States beneath Alaska's Amchitka Island, at the far end of the Aleutian Islands chain. The test, code-named Cannikin, caused the largest earth tremor ever produced by man, but it did not create either the earthquakes or the tidal waves predicted by some environmental groups. Eight organizations, including conservation groups, had protested in court that the Atomic Energy Commission had not made full disclosures of the potential dangers in the environmental impact statement on the test that is required by the National Environmental Policy Act. Just hours before the blast, the Supreme Court of the United States voted 4-3 not to stop the test.

Ecotage, or sabotage for ecological reasons, was used increasingly by some conservation activists in 1971. Ecotage activities ranged from dumping dye into sewage-treatment tanks to show how pollution travels down waterways, to sawing down roadside billboards.

The Nixon Administration, which did not endorse 1970 Earth Day, officially supported 1971 Earth Week, which was observed from April 18 to 24. Earth Week activities included litter pickups and other quiet endeavors that contrasted with the dramatic 1970 observance.

Parks and Outdoor Recreation. On January 8, President Nixon approved legislation creating the Voyageurs National Park on 139,000 acres of Minnesota lake country near the Canadian border; the Gulf Islands National Seashore, embracing a series of offshore islands and keys stretching 150 miles from Gulfport, Miss., to Destin, Fla.; and the Chesapeake and Ohio National Historical Park, winding 184 miles along the Potomac River in Maryland.

The Ice Age National Scientific Reserve, composed of nine areas of glacial features in Wisconsin, was established May 29 by Secretary of the Interior Rogers C. B. Morton.

Legislation proposing a Gateway National Recreation Area, as an integral part of the President's "Parks for People" program, was considered by Congress. The legislation would authorize a park embracing 23,000 acres in the densely populated area near the entrance to the New York harbor.

"Name your poison."

An "animal graveyard" was featured during Earth Week at the Bronx Zoo. Each of the tombstones represents an animal that has become extinct since the 1600s.

On April 28, President Nixon urged Congress to add 1.8 million acres to the 10-million acre system of wilderness areas to be kept in their natural state. The National Park System recorded a record total of 199-million visits in 1971. This represented an increase of 15 per cent.

Wildlife. The remains of 48 illegally poisoned bald and golden eagles were found in Wyoming in May. This was followed, in August, by a report that 500 more eagles were shot from a helicopter over Wyoming. Despite considerable evidence to the contrary, some ranchers consider eagles to be major predators on lambs. Legislation to stiffen penalties for such eagle killings was endorsed by the U.S. Department of the Interior in September and approved by Congress on November 5. At the urging of the National Audubon Society, the Council on Environmental Quality launched the first comprehensive review of public and private predator-control programs.

A suit filed by Friends of Animals, Inc., on June 1 charged that Secretary of the Interior Morton had been negligent in failing to place polar bears on the endangered-species list. Secretary of Commerce Stans reported on July 15 that charges that seals were being slaughtered inhumanely on the Pribilof Islands off Alaska were unfounded. The world's population of wild whooping cranes increased to a record 59. Legislation to protect the wild horses

roaming public lands in the West was enacted by Congress in December.

Water Resources. President Nixon, on January 19, ordered a halt in the 107-mile Cross-Florida Barge Canal that would have provided a short cut between the Atlantic Ocean and the Gulf of Mexico. The action followed issuance of an injunction enjoining key construction on the canal under a suit by the Environmental Defense Fund. The suit charged that the canal's construction was in violation of the National Environmental Policy Act. In congressional testimony on June 3, Assistant Secretary of the Interior Nathaniel P. Reed said the U.S. Army Corps of Engineers and the Agriculture Department "pay nothing more than lip service to earnest environmental protection" in their stream channelization programs.

In Other Countries, the realization grew that conservation is an international concern. Preparations accelerated for the major United Nations Conference on the Human Environment, which will be held in Stockholm, Sweden, in June, 1972. The conference will be faced with the task of reconciling the desire of some undeveloped nations to speed up the development of resources with that of more developed countries to conserve environmental quality. *Andrew L. Newman*

See also ENVIRONMENT.

CONSTITUTION, U.S. See U.S. CONSTITUTION.

CONSUMER AFFAIRS. "Consumerism" appeared to be still on the ascendancy in 1971. Consumer interests and needs continued to command increasing attention from government, business, the news media, and the consumers themselves. The level of complaints and inquiries rose steadily despite all that was being done in response to them. Especially noticeable was a new citizen awareness of consumer problems in a society traditionally oriented toward production. Long-established assumptions that "progress" required constantly rising production were being questioned more than ever. A growing number of people thought that the costs of progress were beginning to exceed the benefits.

The rising concern for consumers was dramatically illustrated in two major ways during the 90-day wage-price-rent freeze imposed by President Richard M. Nixon on August 15. The unexpected move was an attempt to slow down, if not stop, the steady increase in the Consumer Price Index, which had been rising at a rate of about 6 per cent a year. Initial results of the freeze showed a leveling off of retail prices. As Phase 2 began on November 14, the government issued general guidelines that sought to limit wage increases to 5.5 per cent and price increases to 2.5 per cent. Consumer leaders were generally pleased with the idea of freezing prices, but they became increasingly critical of the numerous exceptions to the freeze and its dependence on voluntary compliance. Among items exempted from controls were raw food products and interest rates. The list of exceptions grew during Phase 2.

Consumer Leaders enjoyed sudden new stature as participants in White House discussions about Phase 2 controls. For the first time in many years, representatives of consumer groups found themselves apparently on a par with business and labor spokesmen in discussions with the President on the economy. Ironically, the Administration's decision not to include consumer advocate Ralph Nader in the consumer delegation drew further attention to the consumer point of view when Nader held a press conference to criticize Administration efforts to control prices as Phase 2 began. Although there were no recognized consumer representatives among the public members of the major boards and commissions, Mrs. Virginia Knauer, President Nixon's special assistant for consumer affairs, served on the Cost of Living Council, the overall planning unit.

On February 24, President Nixon issued his second consumer message. He re-emphasized "A Buyer's Bill of Rights," called for "a national attack on consumer fraud," and recommended strengthening the Federal Trade Commission (FTC). He also urged expansion of Mrs. Knauer's office and a change in its name to the Office of Consumer Affairs. Her budget rose to almost $1 million (from less than $250,000 when the office was set up in 1964).

On August 5, President Nixon announced estab-lishment of a second advisory unit within Mrs. Knauer's office, the National Business Council for Consumer Affairs. It included 108 business executives divided into seven subcouncils. The move was apparently designed to offset frequent complaints from businessmen about the lack of any business representatives on the 12-member Consumer Advisory Council, which continued in effect. Critics of the new council accused the Administration of playing politics, pointing to several dozen firms represented on the council that had government actions pending.

In Congress, the pace of legislation in behalf of consumers slowed noticeably. No major bills were enacted, but several were prepared for final action in 1972, an election year. Drawing the most attention was a bill introduced in the House of Representatives to establish an independent consumer agency with the power to intervene in matters before federal agencies. The measure received an unexpected boost when the Administration, which had opposed a separate consumer agency, switched to mild support of it. Battle lines soon formed around a proposal of consumer advocates, introduced as an amendment to the bill to give the agency power to intervene in informal hearings as well as formal agency actions. Amendment supporters, led by Nader, said most agency actions were of the informal type. Despite extensive lobbying by consumer activists, the amendment was defeated in committee and lost on the floor, 218 to 160, with Republicans and Southern Democrats leading the opposition. The bill, however, was passed 344 to 44, and sent to the Senate on October 14.

On November 8, the Senate displayed strong pro-consumer sentiments by passing a bill designed to clarify product warranties and strengthen FTC powers to deal with advertising claims. The key vote came on an amendment offered by Senator Roman L. Hruska (R., Nebr.) to strike out the section applying to the FTC. The amendment was defeated, 57 to 24, with most Republicans and Southern Democrats again lining up against the consumer position. The bill was passed, 76 to 2.

Laws that became effective in 1971 included one giving individuals the right to see their records at credit bureaus and to have false information removed. In some cases, individuals would be able to sue for damages. Another 1971 law bans unsolicited credit cards and limits cardholder liability to $50.

Regulatory Agencies. The FTC was the most active agency in the consumer's behalf during 1971. On June 9, it launched a campaign to tone down advertising claims. The agency later ordered makers of automobiles, television sets, electric razors, and air conditioners to submit documentation of claims within 60 days. See ADVERTISING.

Corporate Action. In an effort to stay abreast of the rising concern for consumers' welfare, private firms added consumer consultants, simplified warranties, and made toll-free telephone lines available to customers with complaints or inquiries. Changes were particularly noticeable in the food industry. Large chains set the pace in providing more information about nutritional values, comparative unit costs, and how long perishable products have been on the shelf.

The Consumer Federation of America reported it had 196 member organizations. New public-interest law centers included the Georgetown University Institute for Public Interest Representation and Public Advocates Inc., a San Francisco law firm. Both were funded by the Ford Foundation.

State Legislation slowed down somewhat, but there were considerable advances in consumer protection. Most popular were measures to provide comprehensive consumer protection against fraud and deception, and bills to require "cooling-off" periods for door-to-door sales. Efforts to establish "no-fault" automobile insurance plans faltered in many states despite endorsement of the idea by some insurance firms and by the Nixon Administration. Meanwhile, after six months of a limited no-fault plan, Massachusetts reported that the cost and number of claims were down more than 50 per cent. The state ordered premiums reduced. In 1971, six more states established consumer affairs offices, bringing the total to 45.   Arthur E. Rowse

COSTA RICA. See LATIN AMERICA.

COURTS AND LAWS. School desegregation was given major impetus by the Supreme Court of the United States in 1971. On April 20, the court ruled that busing, pairing, and zoning are constitutionally valid means of eliminating racial discrimination in the dual school systems of the South.

The ruling was intended to eliminate any further challenges to the doctrine of desegregation established in *Brown v. Board of Education of Topeka* in 1954. The court did not apply the concept of racial balance north of Mason and Dixon's line. It continued to distinguish between *de jure* (by law) segregation, created by state legislation, and *de facto* (in fact) segregation, the result of racial housing patterns. Because of this distinction, the court refused to hear arguments on the busing of pupils to achieve racial balance in Pontiac, Mich. See CIVIL RIGHTS.

Employment Discrimination. On March 8, in *Griggs v. Duke Power Co.*, the court ruled that the Civil Rights Act of 1964 barred employment requirements, such as a high school diploma and/or the successful completion of intelligence tests, unless an employer could demonstrate that the requirement was necessary for the satisfactory performance of a job. The court found that these requirements were used to discriminate against Negroes.

Criminal Law. In *Harris v. New York*, decided on February 24, the high court ruled, 5 to 4, that state-

A crowd lines up outside the Supreme Court Building in Washington, D.C., on June 26, waiting for the special hearing on the "Pentagon Papers" to begin.

ments made by a criminal suspect may be used to impeach his testimony at trial, even though he had not been warned of his right to silence and to counsel. The decision is not a rejection of the landmark *Miranda v. Arizona* ruling of 1966 (it does not apply if there is evidence of police coercion), but it does establish limitations on suspects' rights that did not exist before.

Electronic Surveillance. On April 5, the Supreme Court decided, 6 to 3, in *United States v. White* that the Fourth Amendment does not prohibit federal agents from using a microphone concealed on a voluntary informer to record his conversations with a suspect. Also, the court ruled that agents may testify about the monitored conversations, even though the government is not required to produce the actual informer at the trial.

United States v. White left constitutional questions about the proper use of electronic surveillance unresolved. A major case was whether the U.S. attorney general has the authority to tap the telephones of citizens suspected of subversion without first obtaining a court order. On January 25, a federal court in Michigan ruled that "such power held by one individual was never contemplated by the framers of our Constitution, and cannot be tolerated today." On April 8, a panel of appeals court judges upheld the ruling. The Supreme Court then agreed to hear arguments on the issue.

Pentagon Papers. The most publicized case decided by the Supreme Court in 1971 was *The New York Times v. United States*, the "Pentagon Papers" case. The case arose after publication by *The New York Times* of excerpts from government documents on the Vietnam War that had been classified "secret" or "top secret." After three installments appeared, the Department of Justice obtained a federal injunction against further publication.

The New York Times case, and a companion case against *The Washington Post*, which also published articles based on the classified documents, raced through the federal courts. On June 26, just 13 days after the first installment was published, the Supreme Court met in a special Saturday session to hear arguments on the cases. On June 30, the court ruled, 6 to 3, that the government had failed to meet the heavy burden of justifying prior restraint, and had therefore infringed on the First Amendment's guarantee of freedom of the press. See PUBLISHING (Close-Up).

In Other Important Cases, the Supreme Court held:

• On March 8, 8 to 1, that the First Amendment's freedom of religion clause does not allow conferment of conscientious objector status on a draftee who opposes only a particular war.

• On April 26, 5 to 3, that, because of the state's tradition of democratic referenda, California residents are entitled to vote on public housing proposals before such housing can be built. Although voters might exercise a veto that would adversely affect blacks and poor people, the court concluded that the California law was not intended to be discriminatory.

• On May 3, 6 to 3, that the procedures followed by juries in imposing the death penalty are not unconstitutional. The court also agreed to hear arguments on the ultimate capital punishment question— whether the death penalty violates the "cruel and unusual" punishment provision of the Eighth Amendment.

• On June 28, 8 to 1, that state financial aid to parochial schools is unconstitutional. The high court ruled that state aid represents "excessive entanglement between government and religion."

• On November 22, unanimously, that state laws giving preference to men over women violate the 14th Amendment's equal-protection clause. In its landmark ruling, the court extended the equal-protection clause to discrimination on the basis of sex.

Two Court Vacancies. On September 17, Senior Associate Justice Hugo L. Black, 85, retired from the Supreme Court. Eight days later, he died of a stroke. On September 23, Justice John M. Harlan, 72, afflicted with spinal cancer, also retired.

President Richard M. Nixon moved swiftly to fill the vacancies. His first choice to succeed Black reportedly was Representative Richard H. Poff (R., Va.), but Poff withdrew from consideration. The President was determined to name a Southerner to replace Black, so he considered Herschel H. Friday, a bond lawyer from Little Rock, Ark. To succeed Harlan, Nixon contemplated appointing the first female justice to the high court. His aides suggested Mildred L. Lillie, a judge of the California state appeals court.

The names of Friday and Judge Lillie, together with four other names, were submitted to the American Bar Association's (ABA) committee on judicial fitness. The committee reported that none was qualified.

On October 21, the President dramatically announced to a nationwide television audience his two surprise selections for the court: Lewis F. Powell, Jr., 64, an attorney from Richmond, Va., and a former ABA president, and William H. Rehnquist, 47, an assistant U.S. attorney general. Powell was confirmed by the Senate, 89 to 1, on December 6; Rehnquist was confirmed, 68 to 26, on December 10. See POWELL, LEWIS F., JR.; REHNQUIST, WILLIAM H.

Grand Jury Indictment. An unprecedented attempt to investigate the secret proceedings of a grand jury occurred in Chicago. In April, the jury voted an indictment against Cook County State's Attorney Edward V. Hanrahan and 13 other law-enforcement officers. They were accused of conspiring to obstruct justice in the killing of two Black Panthers during a police raid in December, 1969.

Chief Criminal Court Judge Joseph A. Power refused to accept the indictment, claiming that all pertinent witnesses had not been heard and that the jury had been pressured by Barnabas F. Sears, the special prosecutor. Sears charged that the judge was illegally interfering with the grand jury. Judge Power appointed a special investigator to probe the grand jury's proceedings. Finally, the Illinois Supreme Court ordered the indictment opened and the special investigation stopped. The indictments were made public on August 24. Hanrahan later moved to have them quashed.

Property-Tax Issues. On August 30, the California Supreme Court ruled, 6 to 1, that the state's system of financing public schools with property taxes was discriminatory. The court held that the system favored children from wealthy areas over those from poor neighborhoods. The lower courts were asked to work out a more equitable system for school financing.

In October, a federal court ruled that the property-tax system of financing Minnesota's schools is unconstitutional. At the same time, the U.S. Office of Education released a four-year study showing that about 52 per cent of school costs are paid through local property taxes. The report called this unfair and recommended increased federal aid for schools. See Section One, FOCUS ON EDUCATION. Dean E. Fischer

CRIME continued its upward spiral in the United States in 1971, but the rate of increase slowed. The Federal Bureau of Investigation (FBI) said that total reported offenses during 1970 increased by 11 per cent over 1969. In the first six months of 1971, however, the crime rate was up 7 per cent over the same period in 1970. In 1970, the crime rate rose less rapidly in cities than it did in the nation's suburbs and rural areas.

The value of securities stolen in the first six months of 1971 exceeded losses for all of 1969 and 1970. The FBI reported that stolen and missing securities totaled $175.8 million in 1969, $227 million in 1970, and $494 million in the first half of 1971.

To help cities and states fight crime, President Richard M. Nixon signed into law on January 2 a three-year program calling for federal expenditures of $3.55 billion. The new law, unlike previous legislation in this area, emphasized help for urban high-crime areas. Congress had earlier heard testimony that a disproportionate amount of funds under a previous program had gone to small towns rather than big cities.

Prompted by the rising number of police deaths, President Nixon in June sent Congress a bill proposing a payment of $50,000 to the family survivors of policemen killed in the line of duty. The FBI reported that in the first 9 months of 1971, 87 police-

New York State Correction Commissioner Russell C. Oswald surveys the aftermath of the Attica prisoner uprising, which ended in death for 43 persons.

men died violently, as compared with 76 during the same period in 1970.

Federal Crime Insurance became available in August, 1971. The program is administered by the Department of Housing and Urban Development. It grew out of the 1968 city riots that caused private insurance companies to cancel policies because of the high risk involved. As a result, it had become virtually impossible for some inner-city residents and businessmen to obtain insurance.

The new federal program sets uniform insurance rates throughout a central city and its suburbs. Coverage costs the same in high-crime areas as in the suburbs. The federal insurance provides maximum coverage of $15,000 for commercial property and $5,000 for residential property. It covers burglary, robbery, vandalism, and other crime-related losses.

Law Reform. Drastic changes in federal criminal laws were recommended in January by the Commission on Reform of Federal Criminal Laws after four years of study. The commission's report urged that possession of marijuana be made an infraction punishable only by a fine and never by a jail sentence. Under existing federal statutes, mere possession of marijuana without intent to sell is a misdemeanor that can bring up to one year in jail. The commission would make a distinction between "hard," or dangerous, drugs, such as heroin and potent hallucinogens, and marijuana and other "abusable," or nonaddictive, drugs.

The panel, headed by former California Governor Edmund G. (Pat) Brown, also proposed abolishing the death penalty for federal crimes and outlawing the manufacture, sale, and possession of handguns for other than law-enforcement purposes.

Prison Conditions led to outbreaks of violence at several institutions, but the worst occurred at the Attica (N.Y.) Correctional Facility. More than 1,000 convicts took over a cell block on September 9 and held 32 prison employees hostage. They presented a list of demands ranging from greater religious freedom to less pork in the prison diet, and called for an end to "brutal, dehumanized" conditions. State Correction Commissioner Russell C. Oswald agreed to 28 of the demands, but the negotiations deadlocked over demands for complete amnesty and the firing of the prison superintendent.

On September 13, about 1,500 state troopers, sheriff's deputies, and prison guards stormed the prison. Thirty-two inmates and 11 hostages were killed in the action or died later of wounds. First reports said inmates slashed the throats of the hostages, but autopsies showed the hostages died of gunshot wounds, which they probably received in the police cross fire. The tragic loss of life prompted wide criticism of the way the revolt was put down. Major prison uprisings also occurred in New Orleans, New York City, and in several New Jersey prisons.

Three inmates and three guards were killed during an escape attempt on August 21 at the San Quentin (Calif.) State Prison. One of the inmates was black writer George Jackson, accused of killing a guard at Soledad State Prison in 1970.

Widely Publicized Happenings in 1971 included the following:

- Philip Berrigan, a priest, and five others were indicted in January for plotting to kidnap presidential adviser Henry A. Kissinger. See CIVIL RIGHTS; ROMAN CATHOLIC CHURCH.
- Charles M. Manson and three women members of his "family" were sentenced to death in March in Los Angeles for the 1969 murders of actress Sharon Tate and six others. In October, Charles Watson was also convicted of the murders in a separate trial.
- The mutilated bodies of 25 migrant farmworkers were uncovered in an orchard near Yuba City, Calif., in May and June. Juan V. Corona, a farm-labor contractor, was indicted for the murders.
- Eight persons were shot to death in June in Detroit. Police attributed the gangland-style massacre to a continuing war for the control of Detroit's drug traffic.
- Joseph A. Colombo, Sr., a reputed leader of the New York City underworld, was shot and severely wounded on June 28. The man suspected of the attack, Jerome A. Johnson, was shot dead at the scene by an unknown gunman.   Art Petacque

See also Section Two, CRIME IN PARADISE.

CRUZ, RAMÓN ERNESTO (1903-   ), was elected president of Honduras on March 28, 1971. He took office on June 6 for a six-year term. Cruz, representing the Nationalist Party, narrowly defeated Jorge Bueso Arias, the Liberal Party candidate. He became the first freely elected president of Honduras since 1932. Cruz said he would try to develop the Honduran economy and solve the nation's border dispute with El Salvador.

The presidency was the only high office filled in the general election, held under a new national unity plan that sought a stable democratic government. The two traditional parties, the Liberals and the Nationalists, had agreed to divide the 64 seats in the legislature evenly. Cruz won about 51.5 per cent of the 1971 vote. Slightly more than 500,000 votes were cast, although about 900,000 voters were eligible. Cruz was the Nationalist Party's candidate in the 1963 campaign, cut short by a military coup.

Cruz had headed the National University of Honduras twice and has been a faculty or administration member there almost continuously since 1929. However, he is best known to Hondurans as a lawyer and diplomat. He has represented Honduras in its long-standing border dispute with El Salvador, and he also represented his country at The Hague while a disagreement with Nicaragua was being considered there. Cruz and his wife, a former stenographer who worked for him, have four children.   Ed Nelson

CUBA. Premier Fidel Castro made one of his rare trips outside Cuba in 1971. On November 9, he arrived in Chile for a 25-day state visit, his first to a Latin American country in nearly 12 years. His visit was part of an effort to end the diplomatic and economic isolation imposed on Cuba by the Organization of American States in 1964.

Earlier in the year, Castro had labeled 1971 "the year of productivity." Top priority was to be given to raising the abysmally low productivity of most workers, who, with little or no incentive, were generally apathetic. A new law was passed attacking labor absenteeism, but the economy was still being disrupted by the mobilization of thousands of persons from factories, schools, and offices as "volunteer" sugar cane cutters. There were serious housing, oil, and power shortages, and a serious outbreak of swine fever threatened the pork supply.

The tobacco harvest was in trouble, and the important sugar crop, which had as its target 6.65 million tons, yielded only 5.9 million, thus failing to meet its goal for the sixth year in a row. The short yield was attributed to a prolonged drought plus a lack of power, manpower, and transportation equipment.

Facts in Brief. Population: 8,807,000. Government: President Osvaldo Dorticos Torrado; Premier Fidel Castro. Monetary Unit: peso. Foreign Trade: exports, $650,000,000; imports, $1,095,000,000. Principal Exports: sugar, chemicals.   Mary C. Webster

Gustav Husak, Czechoslovakia's Communist Party leader, greeted Russian party leader Leonid I. Brezhnev, at left, warmly when Brezhnev visited Prague in May.

CZECHOSLOVAKIA continued its march back to full acceptance in the Russian orbit under Gustav Husak, who was re-elected Communist Party General Secretary at the party congress on May 29, 1971. The congress also unanimously approved Russia's 1968 invasion of Czechoslovakia as an act of "international aid." Former President Antonín Novotný and other Stalinists were restored to party membership. But Husak continued to resist holding mass trials of liberals.

Czechoslovakia's economic picture improved. Increased family allowances and pensions, following a May 3 price cut for consumer goods, increased the regime's popularity. The cereal grains harvest was the best in years. Industrial production for the first half of the year increased significantly. But poor labor discipline, a high absenteeism rate, and costly construction delays remained serious. They threatened scheduling of such key projects as the natural gas pipeline linking Russia with East Germany and the rest of Europe. Such difficulties cast a cloud over plans approved at the May congress to increase national income by 28 per cent by 1975. Alexander Dubček, Czechoslovakia's deposed first secretary, was reported by a West German publication to be managing a parks department garage in his hometown of Bratislava. Husak denied the story. Dubček's efforts to liberalize the Czechoslovak government led to the 1968 invasion by Russia.

Czechoslovakia signed a trade agreement with West Germany on May 19. But talks in March, May, and September failed to "normalize" relations between the two states. The Czechoslovaks insisted that West Germany declare that the 1938 Munich agreement, by which Adolf Hitler took over much of Czechoslovakia, was reached under duress and had never been valid. West Germany held such a declaration would create legal problems for many Germans who had lived in Czechoslovakia throughout World War II.

In June, the government broke off talks with Austria over compensation for Austrian property confiscated since the war. The Czechoslovak press had charged that Austria broke its pledge of neutrality, supporting pro-Dubček elements in Austria. The Austrians rejected the charges.

General elections were held November 26 and 27, and 98.8 per cent of the voters approved the candidates. Procedure set by the Federal Assembly called for elections every five years instead of four, to correspond to a new schedule set for party congresses.

Facts in Brief. Population: 14,635,000. Government: Communist Party General Secretary Gustav Husak; President Ludvik Svoboda; Premier Lubomir Strougal. Monetary Unit: koruna. Foreign Trade: exports, $3,958,000,000; imports, $3,698,-000,000. Principal Exports: machinery, fuels, consumer goods.   Chris Cviic

305

DAHOMEY. The troika-style government of Hubert Maga, Sourou-Migan Apithy, and Justin Ahomadegbe brought some measure of political stability to Dahomey in 1971. Maga continued to serve as head of the three-man Presidential Council that was formed in 1970. The three leaders will take turns heading the council for two-year terms.

The government took advantage of the calm political situation to try to solve Dahomey's economic difficulties. Dahomey's 1971 budget was a record $35 million. With French aid, construction work went ahead on the new national university, which was started in November, 1970. More primary and secondary schools and a new nursing school were planned. The 1971 budget also included funds for a 50-kilowatt national radio transmitter.

Dahomey took a step toward economic sufficiency with the completion of a cement factory in 1971. The factory was expected to supply all of the country's cement needs. Agricultural exports reportedly increased. Dahomey also considered plans for a refinery to process oil from newly discovered offshore deposits.

Facts in Brief. Population: 2,876,000. Government: Presidential Council President Hubert Maga. Monetary Unit: CFA franc. Foreign Trade: exports, $24,000,000; imports, $51,000,000. Principal Exports: palm nuts and oil, cotton.   Darlene R. Stille

DAIRYING. See AGRICULTURE.

DALLAS became an All-American City in 1971. The city won the coveted designation in the annual awards sponsored by *Look* magazine and the National Municipal League. Playing a significant role in its victory was the "Goals for Dallas" program, launched in 1965. The program provided a set of long-range objectives for the city's growth and development.

Mayoral Election. For the first time in four decades, Dallas voters elected a mayor in 1971 who was not backed by the Citizens Charter Association (CCA), an organization of Dallas businessmen. In a run-off election, television sportscaster Wes Wise defeated Avery Mays, the owner of a Dallas construction company. The run-off election brought a record 97,000 voters to the polls.

In the run-off campaign, Mays enjoyed the support of the CCA, the City Council, the firemen's and policemen's associations, and two daily newspapers. He reportedly had a campaign fund of $250,000. Against this array, Wise pitted a budget of about $15,000 and a promise to return government to the "little people."

Elections also played an important part in Dallas school affairs in 1971. One issue was the school board's policy of permitting principals – and, unofficially, teachers – to administer corporal punishment to pupils. Four incumbent board members who supported the policy were defeated in the election. The

four candidates who won favored even tougher school discipline policies.

Financial Problems plagued Dallas throughout the year, and plans for a new city hall had to be shelved. The City Council rejected the most recent bid on the project because it exceeded the $38 million that was approved by referendum in 1968 by approximately $12 million.

Despite the city hall postponement, plans were announced for a 10-acre office-building complex on Main Place. Planning also continued for an underground city garage approximately one mile long and one-half mile wide, for completion by 1985.

Federal funds were obtained for an experimental pollution-free bus. Fueled by a specially refined oil called toluene, the new bus replaced an earlier, unsuccessful model that used a steam engine.

Dallas was one of only three of the nation's largest cities to show a significant population increase during the 1960s. The 1970 census counted 844,401 persons in the city, an increase of 24.2 per cent since 1960. Dallas suburbs grew 61.8 per cent during the same period. The city's black population increased by 62.7 per cent during the decade, raising the percentage of black residents from 19.0 in 1960 to 24.9 in 1970. The Dallas urban area had one of the lowest relief-dependency rates in the nation in 1971, with 5 per cent of the population on welfare.   J. M. Banovetz

DAM. See BUILDING AND CONSTRUCTION.

DANCING, statistically, reached an all-time high in 1971 in the number of companies, performances given, and spectators. The heightened activity was due in large part to the increasing patronage of the National Endowment for the Arts and many state art councils, which gave outright or matching grants to dance companies for tours, residencies at universities, new productions, and educational programs within their home communities.

A New Company, The Dance Theater of Harlem, was born in 1971. This all-black classical ballet company, the first in the United States, was founded by Arthur Mitchell, a soloist with the New York City Ballet. With grants from private and public institutions and with the prestigious backing of the City Ballet, the troupe had a successful first year.

Mitchell's troupe debuted on January 8 at the Guggenheim Museum of Art in New York City. Other engagements quickly followed: a week in New York as part of the modern dance festival staged by the New York City Center and the American National Theater and Academy (ANTA), a brief appearance in the spring in Chicago, and a summer tour of Europe. In May, the young dancers shared the stage with the New York City Ballet at Lincoln Center in *Concerto for Jazz Band and Orchestra*, a work choreographed jointly by Mitchell and George Balanchine. The company's future is bright, both artistically and financially.

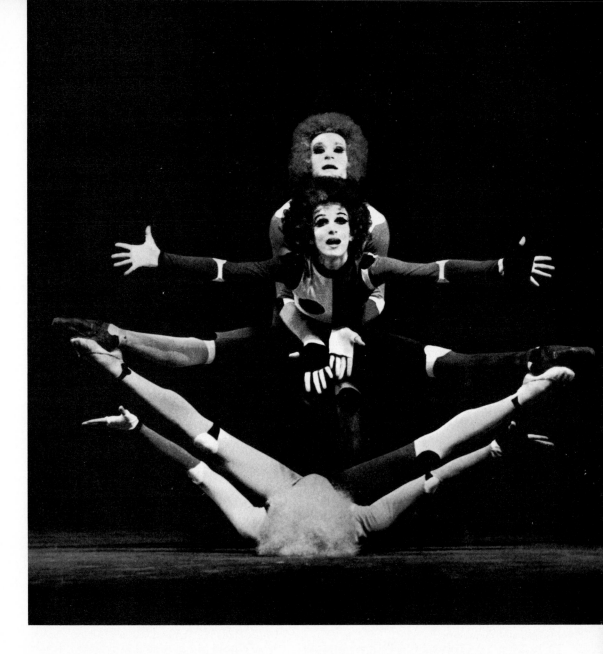

Virtuoso performances by the Stuttgart Ballet Company in 1971 included the U.S. première of John Cranko's *Ebony Concerto,* with music by Igor Stravinsky.

A Heralded New Ballet, Jerome Robbins' *The Goldberg Variations,* was premièred by the New York City Ballet in May, during its two-month spring season. Set to the famous variations of Bach, the ballet is as monumental as the music. Although the ballet is long and tells no story, it is fascinating for its varied exposition of the classical ballet vocabulary.

The American Ballet Theater's future stabilized when it became the official dance company of the John F. Kennedy Center for the Performing Arts in Washington, D.C. The company participated in the center's opening-week festivities in September, and followed with a two-week season.

With the Russian ballerina Natalia Makarova (who defected to the West in 1970) and such other luminaries as Erik Bruhn, Carla Fracci, and Lupe Serrano on its roster, American Ballet Theater drew large audiences on its spring transcontinental tour and during its six-week summer season at New York City's Lincoln Center in July and August. There were many outstanding performances in *Giselle* and *Swan Lake,* and in Bruhn's new staging of August Bournonville's *La Sylphide.*

Money Woes. Dancer and choreographer Eliot Feld announced in July that his American Ballet

Company was disbanding because of insufficient bookings and a lack of money. Feld founded the company in 1969, and it always received favorable reviews. Many observers rank Feld as a great choreographer, certainly the most talented young American to appear since Jerome Robbins came on the scene in the early 1940s. Yet audiences remained small. The troupe's final season at the Brooklyn Academy of Music, from April 20 to May 9, continued the paradox of an artistically acclaimed troupe playing to a half-filled house.

New ballets by Feld were *Romance, Theatre*, and *The Gods Amused*, each different in style and emotion but each a work of dramatic power and great imagination. Taking into account the quality as well as the quantity of Feld's work raises the alarming thought that the demise of the American Ballet Company might indicate that the dance picture in the United States is really not as rosy as statistics indicate.

The City Center Joffrey Ballet made its spring and fall seasons in New York, and appeared in Chicago and Washington, D.C., and on the West Coast. In May, the group made its first appearance in London. Critics there were impressed by the dancers' vitality, but faulted the choreography of Gerald Arpino, the group's resident choreographer. The company mounted eight new productions in 1971, including three by Arpino.

Dancers from Abroad. When the Bolshoi Ballet canceled its tour of the United States, the Stuttgart Ballet's visit was extended into a 10-week nationwide tour, preceded by a 6-week season beginning in April at the Metropolitan Opera House and followed by a 2-week season in July, with Dame Margot Fonteyn as guest artist. Once again, John Cranko's full-length narrative ballets were most popular.

Other visiting companies included the Australian Ballet, with Rudolf Nureyev as guest artist; Les Grands Ballets Canadiens, which toured with a dance production of *Tommy*, the rock opera; and ethnic groups from Cambodia, Iran, Korea, Mexico, Morocco, Poland, Senegal, Siberia, Sierra Leone, and Yugoslavia.

In Russia, the Leningrad Ballet premièred an elaborate, three-act version of *Hamlet*. It was choreographed by Konstantin Sergeyev and starred Mikhail Bayshnikov, 22, hailed as one of the world's great dancers. With the resignation of John Field, Great Britain's Royal Ballet fell under the sole directorship of Kenneth MacMillan. MacMillan's *Anastasia* was premièred in London on July 22. The first two acts, to Tchaikovsky, take place at the Russian court, but the third act, to electronic music and Martinu, centers around Anna Anderson, who claimed to be Anastasia, and her remembrances of childhood. Partly because of this unorthodox structure, the work provoked much controversy.

Modern Dance Groups. The Alvin Ailey American Dance Theater opened the ANTA dance season in January and scored a great success with Ailey's new *Flowers*. Based on the life and death of rock singer Janis Joplin, this production starred Lynn Seymour of Britain's Royal Ballet. Because this engagement was sold out, the troupe was invited for an "encore" season in May at the City Center. It performed there again in December after an American tour. On September 8, it became the first dance company to perform at the Kennedy Center, appearing in Leonard Bernstein's *Mass*. In addition to creating new works for his own group, Ailey mounted the new *Mingus Dances* and a revival of *Feast of Ashes* for the Joffrey Ballet and completed *The River* for the American Ballet Theater.

Modern dance's most comprehensive festival was that sponsored by ANTA and the City Center in a Broadway theater, for eight weeks beginning in January. The companies of Louis Falco, Eleo Pomare, Paul Taylor, Alwin Nikolais, Erick Hawkins and Don Redlich, as well as The Dance Theater of Harlem and the Ailey group, were presented.

The most controversial visitor from overseas was Maurice Béjart's Ballet of the 20th Century, which made its American debut at the Brooklyn Academy of Music in January. Many critics called Béjart's choreography vulgar and dated, with slick political messages covering up essentially dull choreography. Nevertheless, the group drew great crowds, primarily young people. Nancy Goldner

DAVIS, WILLIAM GRENVILLE (1929-), was sworn in as prime minister of Ontario, Canada's most populous and industralized province, on March 1, 1971. Davis hopes to persuade U.S. businesses to allow their Canadian branches to do more research and development work in Canada so that more technically skilled Canadians will remain in Ontario.

Davis was born in Brampton, Ont., near Toronto, the son of a prosperous attorney. He graduated from the University of Toronto in 1951 and studied law at Osgoode Hall, operated by the Law Society of Upper Canada. He practiced law briefly, and was first elected to the provincial Legislative Assembly in 1959. In 1962, when he was only 33, he was appointed minister of education by Prime Minister John P. Robarts. When Robarts retired, Davis was elected on Feb. 12, 1971, to succeed him as Progressive Conservative Party leader and Ontario's new prime minister.

On June 3, Davis' government halted work on Toronto's controversial Spadina expressway, which was to bring commuter traffic downtown. "The city does not belong to the automobile," he said, adding that the experience of other North American cities "demonstrates the ultimate futility of giving priority to the passenger car as a means of transportation into and out of cities." He plans to stress rapid transit instead. Ed Nelson

DEATHS OF NOTABLE PERSONS in 1971 included those listed below. An asterisk (*) indicates the person is the subject of a biography in The World Book Encyclopedia. Those listed were Americans unless otherwise indicated.

*Acheson, Dean G. (1893-Oct. 12), U.S. secretary of state from 1949 to 1953. He had been undersecretary to three secretaries of state and was closely associated with the development of President Harry S. Truman's foreign policy, including the Marshall Plan and the North Atlantic Treaty Organization.

*Adams, Roger (1889-July 6), organic chemist and winner in 1965 of the National Medal of Science. He joined the University of Illinois Chemistry Department in 1916 and served there as professor and head of the department until he became research professor emeritus in 1957.

Agagianian, Gregory Cardinal (1895-May 16), former chief of Roman Catholic worldwide missions and a member of the Sacred College of Cardinals.

Allen, James E., Jr. (1911-Oct. 16), educational administrator. After 14 years at the head of the New York state education system, he was appointed U.S. education commissioner in 1969. After little more than a year in office, he left because of policy differences with the Nixon Administration.

Anderson, Gilbert M. (Broncho Billy) (1881?-Jan. 20), pioneer motion-picture actor who appeared in *The Great Train Robbery*. Made in 1903 and running for 13 minutes, it was considered the first movie with a plot.

Andrews, George W. (1906-Dec. 25), Democratic congressman and senior member of the Alabama delegation. He was first elected to the House of Representatives in 1944.

*Armstrong, Louis (1900-July 6), celebrated jazz trumpeter and singer. He was called the first jazz soloist to attain worldwide influence. He began making recordings in 1923. See Music, Popular (Close-Up).

Bacci, Antonio Cardinal (1885-Jan. 20), highest ranking Latin scholar in the Roman Catholic Church and a conservative member of the College of Cardinals.

Balaban, Barney (1887-March 7), leading figure in the motion-picture industry. He was president of Paramount Pictures Corporation for nearly 20 years.

Ballard, Edna (1886-Feb. 10), leader of the "I Am" religious movement and widow of its founder. The movement does not believe in death.

Beall, J. Glenn (1895-Jan. 14), Republican congressman from Maryland from 1943 to 1953, and senator from 1953 until 1964.

Beberman, Max (1925-Jan. 24), professor of education at the University of Illinois and developer of "new math," a means of stimulating students to the discovery of mathematical principles.

*Black, Hugo L. (1886-Sept. 25), justice of the Supreme Court of the United States since 1937. Called a militant humanist, he often referred to himself as a "Clay County hillbilly."

Blanchfield, Florence A. (1884-May 12), the first woman to receive a commission in the Regular Army and superintendent of the U.S. Army Nurse Corps during World War II.

Bourke-White, Margaret (1906-Aug. 27), a photographer and writer, the first woman news correspondent accredited to go overseas during World War II.

*Boyd Orr, Lord (1880-June 25), British nutritionist and agricultural scientist who won the 1949 Nobel Peace Prize. He was the first director of the United Nations Food and Agriculture Organization.

Bragg, Sir William Lawrence (1890-July 1), British physicist who, with his father, found a way to use X rays to determine the structure of crystals. He shared the 1915 Nobel Prize in physics with his father, becoming the youngest person ever to receive it.

*Bunche, Ralph J. (1904-Dec. 9), winner in 1950 of the Nobel Peace Prize, the first awarded to a Negro. He had been an undersecretary of the United Nations since 1955, retiring from it in October because of ill health. Bunche, the grandson of an American slave, reached world prominence when he worked out an armistice agreement between Arab nations and Israel in 1949. The agreement ended a war in Palestine. His UN position was the highest ever held by a citizen of the United States.

Burnett, Leo (1891-June 7), founder of one of the world's largest advertising agencies, Leo Burnett Company, Incorporated.

Burns, David (1902-March 12), actor in dramatic and musical comedy productions. He made his Broadway debut in 1923, and starred in *Hello, Dolly*.

Byington, Spring (1893-Sept. 7), stage, screen, and television actress, was best known for her role as the mother-in-law in the TV series, "December Bride."

Cerf, Bennett (1898-Aug. 27), president of Random House, a book-publishing firm, and long-time panelist on the television quiz show, "What's My Line?" His overcoming government censorship in 1938 in court provided for publication of James Joyce's *Ulysses* and was a victory for publishing.

Chanel, Coco (Gabrielle B.) (1883-Jan. 10), queen of French high fashion. Timelessness was the trademark of her fashions and she enjoyed being copied. See Fashion (Close-Up).

Clark, Joseph James (1893-July 13), commander of the U.S. Navy Seventh Fleet in operations against North Korea. Clark retired from the Navy as a full admiral in 1953.

The widow of Nikita S. Khrushchev, right, and other family members stand at the open coffin during services for the former Russian premier.

A Music Master With Flair

He was wiry, strong, and incredibly energetic. He was urbane and witty, fiery-tempered and sharp-tongued. He could be glacially cold in his contempt for mediocrity but enchantingly warm in his kindness toward the struggling beginner. He was debonair, a man with a flair for fur-collared greatcoats, boutonnieres, walking canes, and, on occasion, beautifully tailored suede gloves and spats. He was a gourmet of exquisitely refined tastes—and a voracious reader of everything from Heraclitus and Suetonius to Agatha Christie and Ian Fleming. A connoisseur of fine jewels, he was also an enthusiastic hypochondriac who appreciated the finer points of an apothecary's wares.

He was Igor Stravinsky—an original in mind as well as in spirit—and his death in New York City on April 6, 1971, stilled a voice that through words and music had been addressing the world with eloquence and authority for more than 60 years.

Stravinsky, who was born in 1882, was never a true melodist in the sense that Peter Ilich Tchaikovsky was, nor was he a romantic in the Wagnerian tradition. But he was probably one of the greatest rhythmic innovators in the history of music. His scores, whether they were for a ballet, an opera, a symphony, a cantata, or a chamber group, were filled with rhythms that ranged from the undulant to the primitive to the bizarre. And the canopy of sound he erected over each—whether written in the traditions of "Russian" music, neoclassicism, or the 12-tone style he adopted in later years—never ceased to beguile the listener.

His scores breathed with rhythm: *Fireworks* (1908), which first brought him to the attention of Sergei Diaghilev, the great Russian impresario of the Ballets Russe; *Petrouchka* (1911); *The Rite of Spring* (1913); *The Soldier's Tale* (1918); *Symphony of Psalms* (1930); *Danses Concertantes* (1941-1942); *The Rake's Progress* (1951); *Agon* (1957); and *Requiem Canticles* (1966). And at the same time that one heard the music's pulsations, one also was aware that the score had been fashioned by a master craftsman who was in total intellectual control of the medium.

Igor Stravinsky

A tiny man in stature, Stravinsky was a giant in his musical crotchets and feuds, most of which were known throughout the musical world. A series of books he turned out in collaboration with Robert Craft over the years are unique in musical annals. His ongoing feuds with Paul Henry Lang of the now-defunct *New York Herald Tribune* and with Winthrop Sargeant of *The New Yorker* magazine are the stuff of which legends are—and have been—made.

His fondness for money was legendary, and it was one of his constant complaints that never in his lifetime would he receive adequate dollar compensation for his work. But he was forever trying. Once offered the gold medal of the Royal Philharmonic Society—a prestigious and highly coveted honor—he startled everyone by asking, "How many carats?" On another occasion, he was told he should have a monogram designed for his use. He promptly took a note pad and drew a dollar sign. Many of his works received their premières in Venice—but only after he had received, on demand, payment in advance. Consequently, among those musicians and critics who were unsympathetic or highly critical of his creative works, he was sneeringly known as "The Merchant of Venice." And Stravinsky did have his detractors who were as uncompromising in their disparagement of his musicianship as his admirers were unstinting in their praise of it. "For the past 25 years," said one critic, "he has been nothing but a sham." To which another added, "The sad and squalid panorama of his inexcusable decadence as documented in works composed in recent years is most displeasing to witness . . . they are bitter evidence of the aridity and dry senility of Igor Stravinsky." The master bridled over the comment—but continued in his own original way.

Once, just before leaving on a conducting tour of Africa, he joked with a friend: "If a lion eats me you'll hear the news from him. He'll say, 'The old man was tough—but he was a tasty meal.'" It might well serve as an epitaph on his tomb in San Michele, in Venice.   Paul C. Tullier

Clark, Walter Van Tilburg (1909-Nov. 11), author of *The Ox-Bow Incident* (1940).

Cleva, Fausto (1902-Aug. 6), a conductor at the New York Metropolitan Opera for more than 50 years.

Conniff, Frank (1914-May 25), former editor of the *New York World Journal Tribune*. He shared a 1955 Pulitzer Prize in international reporting for an interview with Russian Premier Nikita S. Khrushchev.

Constantine, Lord Learie N. (1901-July 1), Great Britain's first black peer and a former Trinidad and Tobago high commissioner (ambassador) to London.

Corbett, Robert J. (1905-April 25), Republican congressman from Pennsylvania.

Daniels, Bebe (1901-March 16), a motion-picture star in the 1920s and 1930s. She had been the leading lady with Harold Lloyd in the "Lonesome Luke" comedy series. She died in London.

Day, Helen H. (1890-Jan. 10), blind and editor of *The Searchlight*, a Braille magazine for blind children, from its founding in 1911 until she retired in the 1940s.

De Kruif, Paul (1890-March 7), author of *Microbe Hunters* (1926) and other popular books on science and medicine.

Derleth, August (1909-July 4), poet and novelist. His nearly 100 books included a fictional series about "Sac Prairie," presumably his hometown of Sauk City, Wis.

De Vaux, Roland (1903-Sept. 12), leader of a team that edited the Dead Sea Scrolls. A Dominican priest, he was head of the French École Biblique, a Biblical and archaeological school in Jerusalem.

Dewey, Thomas E. (1902-March 16), twice unsuccessful Republican candidate for President and governor of New York from 1943 to 1954.

Dobrovolsky, Georgi T. (1928-June 30), one of three Russian cosmonauts found dead in the *Soyuz 11* space capsule after an apparently successful landing June 30. Dobrovolsky was the flight commander.

Dodd, Thomas J. (1907-May 24), U.S. senator from Connecticut. He was censured by the Senate in 1967 for using funds contributed toward his political expenses to pay personal bills.

Duncan, Donald F. (1899-Jan. 15), founder of the Duncan Yo-Yo Company and initiator of a fad based on the whirling toy beginning in the late 1920s. Duncan also developed parking meters.

Dupré, Marcel (1886-May 31), internationally known as the grand master of French organists. He was performing in public at the age of 10 and, in 1920, presented a series of 10 recitals at which he played all of the more than 200 organ compositions of Johann Sebastian Bach from memory.

Duvalier, François (1907-April 21), dictator of Haiti since 1957. A country doctor and authority on voodoo before taking over the country, Duvalier had had himself proclaimed president for life in 1964.

Dyer, Rolla E. (1886-June 2), director of the National Institutes of Health from 1942 to 1950.

Eckert, William D. (1908-April 16), a former lieutenant general of the U.S. Air Force and commissioner of baseball from 1965 to 1969.

Edwards, Cliff (1895?-July 17), singer and motion-picture and stage performer known as "Ukulele Ike." He provided the voice for the character "Jiminy Cricket" in the movie *Pinocchio*.

Edwards, Philip A. (1907-Sept. 6), a Canadian physician and authority on tropical and chest diseases. He was a track star for Canada in the 1928, 1932, and 1936 Olympic Games.

Eisenhower, Edgar N. (1889-July 12), an attorney and older brother of the late President Dwight D. Eisenhower.

Eliot, George Fielding (1894-April 21), former military correspondent, analyst, and author. He was born in Brooklyn and grew up in Australia, but returned to the United States after World War I.

Evans, Herbert M. (1882-March 6), a researcher in factors of growth and reproduction, and the discoverer of vitamin E.

Fairchild, Sherman M. (1896-March 28), inventor of several cameras, including the Fairchild Flight Analyzer Camera, and an automatic photoengraving machine. He also developed new airplanes and aviation equipment.

Fanning, Lawrence S. (1914-Feb. 3), publisher of the *Anchorage* (Alaska) *Daily News*. He had been executive editor of the *Chicago Sun-Times* and later the *Chicago Daily News*.

Farnsworth, Philo T. (1906-March 11), who conceived the basic features of the electronic television system of today while he was a high school student in 1921. He became a pioneer in television engineering.

Fernandel (Fernand Contandin) (1903-Feb. 27), among the most popular and enduring comedy stars of French motion pictures. He had starred in nearly 150 films.

Fio Rito, Ted (1900-July 22), bandleader and composer during the "big band" era of the 1930s. Among songs he wrote are "Charlie My Boy," "Laugh, Clown, Laugh," and "Toot Toot Tootsie."

Fleming, Peter (1907-Aug. 19), British author and journalist. He became an established writer before his brother, Ian, won fame as author of the "James Bond" adventure series.

Fulton, James G. (1903-Oct. 6), Republican congressman serving his 13th term from a predominantly Democratic district in Pennsylvania.

Gallop, Sam (1915-Feb. 24), lyricist who wrote the words for such songs as "There Must Be a Way" and "Wake the Town and Tell the People."

Gilbert, Billy (1894-Sept. 13), long-time motion-picture comedy actor. He was known for his suspense-filled movie sneeze, and furnished the voice for "Sneezy" in *Snow White and the Seven Dwarfs*.

Glueck, Nelson (1900-Feb. 12), archaeologist, author, and president of Hebrew Union College-Jewish Institute of Religion. He used the Bible as a guide to find Middle Eastern artifacts.

Goetze, Albrecht E. R. (1897-Aug. 15), a leading scholar of Babylonian history and literature. He was widely honored for his translation in 1948 of clay tablets discovered near Baghdad. They illuminated a code of laws from the 20th and 19th centuries B.C.

Gomez, Thomas (1905-June 18), motion-picture character actor who specialized in villainous roles. He played "Big Daddy" in *Cat on a Hot Tin Roof*.

Goslin, Leon A. (Goose) (1900-May 15), one of the greatest hitters in major league baseball history. He won the American League batting championship in 1928 with an average of .379.

Guthrie, Sir Tyrone (1900-May 15), theater director, playwright, and producer. He had launched the Shakespeare Festival in Stratford, Canada, and regional repertory theater at the Tyrone Guthrie Theatre in Minneapolis, Minn. Guthrie was born in England but lived in Ireland.

Harlan, John Marshall (1899-Dec. 29), justice of the Supreme Court of the United States since 1955. He had retired on September 23.

Harridge, Will (1886-April 9), president of baseball's American League from 1931 until he retired in 1958.

Hart, Thomas C. (1887-July 4), commander of the U.S. Navy's Asiatic Fleet at the time of Pearl Harbor, and later a Republican U.S. senator from Connecticut.

Hayward, Leland (1902-March 18), producer of such hit Broadway shows as *South Pacific* and *Mister Roberts*, and co-producer of *The Sound of Music*.

Alfred Eisenstaedt, Life Magazine ©Time Inc.

Dean Acheson, secretary of state from 1949 to 1953, was architect of the U.S. Cold War strategy.

Hugo L. Black, a Supreme Court justice since 1937, called himself a "Clay County hillbilly."

Margaret Bourke-White recorded the world's joys and woes as its pre-eminent woman photojournalist.

Heflin, Van (Emmet Evan Heflin) (1910-July 22), versatile character actor in motion pictures and on the stage. He won an Academy Award for his role as a drunken scholar gone to seed in *Johnny Eager* in 1942.

Herbert, Sir Alan P. (1890-Nov. 11), British author, satirist, and social reformer. He began writing for the humor magazine *Punch* in 1918.

Hickenlooper, Bourke B. (1896-Sept. 4), former Republican U.S. senator from Iowa. He was the Senate sponsor of the Atomic Energy Act of 1954, which initiated the private development of atomic energy for nonmilitary uses.

Hodgins, Eric (1899-Jan. 7), journalist and publisher of *Fortune* magazine from 1937 to 1941. His first novel, *Mr. Blandings Builds His Dream House* (1946), was made into a motion picture in 1948.

Holland, Spessard L. (1892-Nov. 6), for 24 years a Democratic U.S. senator from Florida. The 24th Amendment to the U.S. Constitution, barring a poll tax as a qualification for voting, was considered one of his major legislative accomplishments.

Holman, Libby (1906-June 18), a Broadway blues singer of the 1920s and 1930s.

*Houssay, Bernardo Alberto (1887-Sept. 21), Argentine physiologist whose discovery of the role of pituitary hormones won him the Nobel Prize in physiology and medicine in 1947.

Johnson, Alvin (1874-June 7), a founder of the New School for Social Research in New York City and its president emeritus since 1945. Beginning in 1933, Johnson initiated a fund for non-Nazi intellectuals fleeing from Germany. They were the nucleus of the New School's Graduate Faculty of Political and Social Science.

*Jones, Bobby (Robert Tyre Jones, Jr.) (1902-Dec. 18), often called the greatest golfer of all time. He was the only man ever to win the U.S. and British opens and the U.S. and British amateur tournaments—the grand slam—all in one year, 1930. He then retired from the game.

Kaplan, Morris (1911-Sept. 15), pioneer consumer advocate and, for 25 years, technical director of Consumers Union, the publisher of *Consumer Reports*.

*Karrer, Paul (1889-June 18), a Swiss chemist and educator. He shared the Nobel Prize in Chemistry in 1937. From 1919 to 1959, Karrer was professor of chemistry at the University of Zurich, Switzerland.

*Kent, Rockwell (1882-March 14), artist, illustrator, author, and a stormy champion of liberal causes. He

commented, "The real art of living consists in keeping alive the conscience and sense of values we had when we were young."

*Khrushchev, Nikita S. (1894-Sept. 11), Russian premier from 1958 to 1964. He tried to raise the Soviet standard of living and started Russia's destalinization policy.

King, Dennis (1897-May 21), musical theater star best known for his role in the 1925 production of *The Vagabond King*. He also mastered the works of such playwrights as Shakespeare, Shaw, and Ibsen.

*Lawless, Theodore K. (1892-May 1), dermatologist who won the 1954 Spingarn Medal for "distinguished merit and achievement among American Negroes." As a boy, he had worked for $1 per day in New Orleans markets.

Lee, Manfred B. (1905-April 3), coauthor of the "Ellery Queen" mystery series that began in 1929. He and a first cousin, Frederic Dannay, also wrote under the name "Barnaby Ross." Publishers estimated their books had sold about 100 million copies.

Lemass, Sean F. (1899-May 11), former prime minister of the Republic of Ireland.

Leopold, Nathan F. (1904-Aug. 29), paroled in 1958 after conviction in 1924 for his part in the kidnaping and murder of 14-year-old Bobby Franks in Chicago. Since his parole, Leopold had worked in a church mission in Puerto Rico.

Lewis, Joe E. (1902-June 4), night club comedian with a gravelly voice.

Liston, Charles (Sonny) (1932-Jan. 5?), heavyweight boxing champion from Sept. 25, 1962, to Feb. 25, 1964.

*Lloyd, Harold (1894-March 8), one of the great motion-picture comedians. He made nearly 500 movies. Lensless horn-rimmed glasses were his trademark.

Lombardo, Carmen (1903-April 17), musician, songwriter, and singer. He was the music director and headed the saxophone section of his brother's band, known as Guy Lombardo and His Royal Canadians.

Lowe, Edmund (1892-April 21), pioneer motion-picture actor whose debut was in *The Silent Command* in 1923. He became famous as Sergeant Quirt in *What Price Glory*, made in 1926.

Mackey, Guy J. (Red) (1905-Feb. 21), athletic director at Purdue University from 1942 until his death.

Manry, Robert N. (1918-Feb. 21), former copy editor for the *Cleveland Plain Dealer* until the summer of 1965, when he crossed the Atlantic Ocean in *Tinkerbelle*, a 13½-foot sailboat.

Ralph J. Bunche, grandson of a slave, won a Nobel Peace Prize and was the top American at the UN.

Thomas E. Dewey served three terms as Republican governor of New York and twice ran for the presidency.

Outspoken artist Rockwell Kent was especially noted for his illustrations for classical books.

Manush, Henry A. (Heinie) (1901-May 12), one of the most aggressive and durable major league baseball players. He compiled a .330 batting average in 17 seasons in the big leagues.

McMahon, Horace (1907-Aug. 17), character actor who specialized in tough-guy and detective roles in motion pictures and on the stage and television.

Moholy-Nagy, Sibyl (1905-Jan. 8), professor of architectural history at Pratt Institute, Brooklyn, N.Y. Her last book was *Matrix of Man* (1968).

Mondadori, Arnoldo (1889-June 8), founder of one of Italy's largest publishing empires, Arnoldo Mondadori Editore. It includes the news magazine *Epoca*.

Morrison, James D. (Jim) (1943-July 3), lead singer of The Doors rock-music group. He was found dead in his Paris apartment.

Morse, Arthur D. (1902-June 1), executive director of the International Broadcast Institute, founded to help developing countries take part inexpensively in communications. He was reporter-director of the "See It Now" program of Edward R. Murrow.

Mulzac, Hugh N. (1886-Jan. 30), who became the first black captain of an American merchant ship in 1942. He was born on Union, a small island in the Caribbean Sea.

Murphy, Audie (1924-May 31), most decorated American hero of World War II. He became a motion-picture actor, beginning with a film based on his autobiography, but later went bankrupt. He was found dead in the wreckage of a private plane.

Murphy, Robert (1902-July 13), conservation authority and nature writer. His book, *The Pond*, won the Dutton Animal Book Award in 1964.

Nash, Ogden (1902-May 19), writer of more than 20 volumes of verse, almost all droll and witty. See POETRY (Close-Up).

Nevins, Allan (1890-March 5), an American historian, author, and educator who won Pulitzer prizes in 1933 for a biography of President Grover Cleveland and 1937 for a biography of Hamilton Fish, secretary of the state under President Ulysses S. Grant.

Niebuhr, Reinhold (1892-June 1), Protestant theologian of worldwide influence in both religion and politics. He was a leader in the liberal "social gospel" of Christianity. See RELIGION (Close-Up).

Nye, Gerald P. (1892-July 17), Republican senator from North Dakota from 1925 to 1945, and a foremost isolationist who opposed the United State's entry into World War II.

Palmer, Dewey H. (1898-May 14), physicist and founder of Consumers Union. When the staff of Consumers Research struck in 1935, Palmer joined them. In 1936, the strikers formed Consumers Union, publisher of *Consumer Reports*.

Patsayev, Viktor I. (1933-June 30), test engineer on the Russian space capsule *Soyuz 11*. He and two other crew members were found dead in the space capsule after an apparently successful landing.

Paumgartner, Bernhard (1887-July 26), Austrian conductor and composer, and president of Austria's annual Salzburg Festival.

Penney, James Cash (1875-Feb. 12), founder of the J. C. Penney department store chain.

Prouty, Winston L. (1906-Sept. 10), Republican senator from Vermont since 1959. He had been a congressman from 1951 until 1959.

Puller, Lewis B. (Chesty) (1898-Oct. 11), a lieutenant general and most-decorated member of the U.S. Marine Corps.

Reading, Lady Stella (Baroness Swanborough) (1894-May 23), first woman member of Great Britain's House of Lords. As the widow of a special ambassador to the United States, she toured America incognito, washing dishes and staying in cheap rooms, in order to get to know the people better.

Reed, William R. (1915-May 20), commissioner of the Big Ten athletic conference since 1961. He devised the grant-in-aid regulations that govern member universities' recruiting of athletes.

Reith, Lord John C. W. (1889-June 16), austere Scot who built the British Broadcasting Corporation into a great radio institution.

Rice, Charles D. (1910-Jan. 30), author, editor, and for 10 years writer of the column "Charlie Rice's Punchbowl" in *This Week*, a newspaper supplement that ended publication in 1969.

Robertson, A. Willis (1887-Nov. 1), Democratic U.S. Senator from Virginia for 20 years, and chairman of the Senate Banking and Currency Committee.

Rodale, J. I. (Jerome) (1898-June 7), a leading exponent of organic foods, and publisher of several magazines, including *Organic Farming and Gardening*.

Rojankovsky, Feodor (1891-Oct. 12), a Russian-American artist and illustrator of children's books. He won the Caldecott Medal in 1956 for illustrating *Frog Went A-Courtin'*.

Romanoff, Dmitri Michael (Mike) (1890?-Sept. 1), self-styled heir of White Russian nobility, but consid-

A Texas farm boy, Audie Murphy won 24 medals to become the most-decorated World War II hero.

Georgia Democrat Richard Russell was one of the most influential men in the United States Senate.

Whitney M. Young, Jr., fought for black progress as director of the National Urban League.

ered by immigration authorities to be Harry Gerguson. He maintained he was a Russian prince, although a Russian authority said the real prince had been killed.

Russell, Richard B. (1897-Jan. 21), one of the most influential members of the U.S. Senate. He was first elected to the Senate from Georgia in 1933.

Ryan, William M. (1893-June 3), special agent number one of the American Society for the Prevention of Cruelty to Animals and a member of its staff since 1921.

Ryerson, Edward L. (1886-Aug. 2), chairman of Inland Steel Company.

Sarnoff, David (1891-Dec. 12), often called the "father of American television," and the retired chairman of the board of the Radio Corporation of America, later renamed the RCA Corporation. He said he had hitched his wagon to the electron.

Seferis, George (1900-Sept. 20), Greek poet who won the Nobel Prize for literature in 1963. As George Seferiadhis, he was a veteran diplomat from a family of strong democratic tradition.

Siffert, Jo (1936-Oct. 24), Swiss race driver who won his first Grand Prix victory at Brands Hatch, England, in 1968. He died in a crash there.

Skouras, Spyros P. (1893-Aug. 16), former head of 20th Century-Fox motion-picture productions. He was president and operating head of the studio from 1942 to 1962, when he retired.

Sobolev, Leonid S. (1898-Feb. 17), Russian writer who publicly attacked Russian poet and novelist Boris Pasternak when Pasternak won the 1958 Nobel Prize in literature. Sobolev had headed the Russian Republic Writers Union since its founding in 1959.

Stanley, Wendell M. (1904-June 16), biochemist and specialist in virology. In 1946, he shared the Nobel Prize in chemistry.

Steiner, Max R. (1888-Dec. 28), Vienna-born composer who won Academy Awards for his scores for the movies *The Informer* (in 1935), *Now, Voyager* (1942), and *Since You Went Away* (1944).

Stravinsky, Igor (1882-April 6), Russian-born composer, widely considered one of the most important of the 1900s. He moved to Paris in 1920 and became a U.S. citizen in 1945. See Close-Up.

Svedberg, Theodore (1884-Feb. 26), Swedish nuclear scientist who won the Nobel Prize in chemistry in 1926. He developed the ultracentrifuge, which is used to measure very large molecules.

Tamm, Igor Y. (1895-April 12), Russian nuclear scientist whose research paved the way for the Russian

hydrogen bomb. He protested sharply against repressive Stalinist methods in the Soviet government. Tamm shared the Nobel Prize in physics in 1958.

Thatcher, W. Ross (1917-July 23), had been premier of Saskatchewan, Canada, for seven years. Although a member of the Liberal Party, he supported free enterprise strongly.

Thompson, William (1913-July 15), radio actor who played many parts on the "Fibber McGee and Molly Show."

Tiger, Dick (Richard Iheto) (1929-Dec. 13), Nigerian boxer, was world middleweight champion in 1962-1963 and 1965-1966 and light heavyweight champion from 1966 to 1968.

Tiselius, Arne (1902-Oct. 29), a Swedish physical chemist who worked out methods of protein analysis. He won the Nobel Prize in chemistry in 1948.

Tubman, William V. S. (1895-July 23), president of Liberia since 1944.

Ullman, James Ramsey (1907-June 20), author and mountain climber. His books included *None but Ourselves* (1970).

Volkov, Vladimir N. (1935-June 30), flight engineer on the Russian space capsule *Soyuz 11*. After an apparently successful landing, he and two other crew members were found dead in the capsule.

Warren, Constance (1880-June 15), president of Sarah Lawrence College, Bronxville, N.Y., from 1929 to 1945. She instituted highly individualized education that has influenced many other institutions.

Webster, Sir David (1903-May 11), adviser and retired administrator of the Royal Opera House in Covent Garden, London. In 25 years, he built it into what is recognized as one of the world's great opera and ballet houses.

Weigel, Helene (1900-May 6), East German actress and widow of dramatist Bertolt Brecht. Despite her staunch Communist views, she was also admired in West Germany and elsewhere for her interpretation of Brecht's work.

Wylie, Philip G. (1902-Oct. 25), novelist and critic of modern life. In *Generation of Vipers* (1942), he coined the term *momism* for mothers' excessive emotional domination of males, delaying their growing up.

Young, Whitney M., Jr. (1921-March 11), leader of the black struggle for civil rights and executive director of the National Urban League since 1961. He wrote several books, including *To Be Equal*. Ed Nelson

DELAWARE. See State Government.

DEMOCRATIC PARTY. In the 1971 off-year elections, the Democrats won back the Kentucky governorship that they had lost in 1967 to Louis B. Nunn. Democrat Wendell Ford won by a margin of 60,000 votes over Republican Thomas D. Emberton.

The Kentucky victory on November 2 made a total of 30 governorships under Democratic control to 20 under the Republicans. This gave the Democrats a strong political base for the 1972 presidential battle.

Other Elections. The Democrats' traditional control of most major cities continued with few exceptions. In mayoral elections, Democrats running on either partisan or nonpartisan tickets won in Boston; Chicago; Gary, Ind.; Philadelphia; and San Francisco. New York City also came into the Democratic ranks when Mayor John V. Lindsay, a former Republican, switched parties. The only major defeats suffered were in Cleveland and Indianapolis.

In Boston, Mayor Kevin H. White won a second term in a nonpartisan contest with another Democrat, Representative Louise Day Hicks. Most of Boston's blacks backed the liberal White against Representative Hicks, a vigorous foe of school busing. Chicago's Mayor Richard J. Daley won a landslide victory over Richard E. Friedman, an independent running with Republican support. Daley's victory assured him a major role in selecting the 1972 Democratic presidential candidate.

Former police commissioner Frank L. Rizzo was elected mayor of Philadelphia. In San Francisco, Mayor Joseph L. Alioto scored an easy re-election victory over 10 opponents.

In Gary, Ind., Mayor Richard G. Hatcher, a black Democrat, won re-election, defeating Republican Theodore Nering. Mayor Charles Evers of Fayette, Miss., a black Democrat running as an independent, lost the Mississippi governorship race to a moderate white Democrat, William Waller.

Mendel J. Davis (D.,S.C.) was elected to the House of Representatives in April to replace the late L. Mendel Rivers (D.,S.C.). Another Democrat, William P. Curlin, Jr., won a special Congressional election in Kentucky on December 4. He replaced the late John C. Watts (D.,Ky.).

The Democratic House leaders chosen in January were Carl B. Albert of Oklahoma, who replaced retiring John W. McCormack as speaker of the House, and Majority Leader Hale Boggs of Louisiana. Senate Democrats re-elected Mike J. Mansfield of Montana as their majority leader, but Robert C. Byrd of West Virginia replaced Edward M. Kennedy of Massachusetts as assistant leader, or whip.

Convention Plans. The Democratic National Committee in July picked Miami Beach, Fla., as the site for the 1972 Democratic National Convention. The Democrats had several prominent contenders

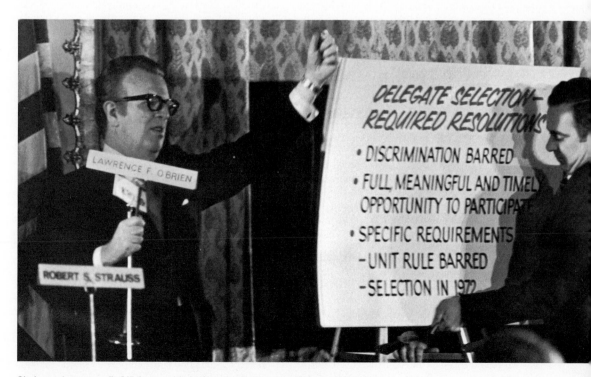

Chairman Lawrence F. O'Brien presided when the Democratic National Committee met in Washington, D.C., in February to map its 1972 convention procedures.

in the presidential sweepstakes. In January, Senator George S. McGovern of South Dakota became the first to announce his candidacy. Senator Fred R. Harris of Oklahoma declared his candidacy on September 24 but withdrew on November 10 because of lack of funds. Both Los Angeles Mayor Samuel W. Yorty and Senator Henry M. Jackson of Washington officially entered the race in November. The front runner, Senator Edmund S. Muskie of Maine, did not declare his candidacy until early 1972, however.

Other Democratic hopefuls included Mayor Lindsay, Senator Hubert H. Humphrey of Minnesota, Senator Kennedy, and Eugene J. McCarthy.

All the Democratic contenders trailed President Richard M. Nixon in most of the public opinion polls taken during the year. Also, the Democrats were hampered by a $9-million debt left over from the 1968 campaign. But, the Democrats held one political advantage over the Republicans—in addition to Democratic strength in state capitols and city halls, they controlled Congress.

Credentials Fight. A fierce struggle for the temporary chairmanship of the important credentials committee for the 1972 Democratic National Convention developed in October at a meeting of the Democratic National Committee. The chairman has the power to enforce or ignore new reform-oriented guidelines for selecting 1972 convention delegates. The guidelines had been drawn up to ensure fair representation in state delegations and to prevent the type of in-fighting that occurred at the 1968 convention.

Patricia Roberts Harris, a black lawyer backed by party regulars, won the post handily over reform-minded Senator Harold E. Hughes of Iowa. The bitterness of the contest seemed to reveal flaws in the façade of party unity so carefully constructed by Democratic national chairman Lawrence O'Brien.

Black Politicians banded together to try to influence the choice of the Democratic presidential nominee. Civil rights leaders, meeting in Mobile, Ala., in July and in Chicago in September, considered entering local black candidates in Democratic presidential primaries as a means of solidifying the black vote. See CIVIL RIGHTS.

Black Congresswoman Shirley A. Chisholm (D., N.Y.) announced in November that she would be a candidate in the North Carolina and Florida Democratic presidential primaries. Her appeal was aimed at youths, blacks and other minority groups, and women. *William McGaffin*

See also ALBERT, CARL B.; AMERICAN PARTY; CHISHOLM, SHIRLEY A.; ELECTIONS; FAUNTROY, WALTER E.; HUMPHREY, HUBERT H.; JACKSON, HENRY M.; KENNEDY, EDWARD M.; LINDSAY, JOHN V.; McGOVERN, GEORGE S.; MILLS, WILBUR D.; MUSKIE, EDMUND S.; PROXMIRE, WILLIAM; REPUBLICAN PARTY; WALLACE, GEORGE C.

DENMARK. An inconclusive general election on Sept. 21, 1971, toppled Denmark's center-right coalition government. Only 6,200 votes, or 0.3 per cent of about 3 million votes cast, separated government and opposition parties. Prime Minister Hilmar Baunsgaard's coalition was left with 88 seats in the Folketing, Denmark's legislature, 1 more than the opposition headed by the Social Democratic Party. After attempts to revive the coalition failed, Baunsgaard's government resigned on September 27. Jens Otto Krag of the Social Democratic Party formed a minority government on October 10.

An unofficial U.S. delegation of the Committee on the Atlantic Salmon Emergency visited Denmark to claim Danish fishing off Greenland deprived North American rivers of salmon. It reported it could not persuade Denmark to ban the fishing.

Common Market Entry. As Denmark's entry into the European Community (Common Market) neared, the divisions between its Scandinavian neighbors and the rest of Europe widened. As a concession to anti-Common Market pressure, the government accepted a demand for a 1972 national referendum on the issue. Many regarded Common Market entry as the best chance of solving Denmark's annual balance of payments deficit, which was running at $539 million, or 3.6 per cent of the gross national product. Higher export prices were needed for agricultural products—particularly beef, pigs, and cheese—sold to Germany. And higher Common Market prices in Great Britain and on the domestic market would stimulate an agricultural industry that, between 1950 and 1970, had dropped from employing 21 per cent of the country's workers to only 10 per cent. Agriculture employed 173,000 workers in 1971, or 8 per cent of the working population. An average of six farms a day have been closed over the last three years.

Higher Incomes. While incomes rose about 15 per cent, total direct taxes, such as social security contributions, went up 35 per cent. But higher taxes and a switch to a "pay-as-you-go" taxation system helped to dampen domestic demand.

The term of service for those drafted into the Danish Army was reduced from 12 to 9 months for a trial period starting in February. This was done despite opposition from the Social Democrats, who had proposed a new defense strategy that would have made it difficult for Denmark to fulfill its military role in the North Atlantic Treaty Organization.

Mrs. Inger Pederson, a judge of the Danish High Court, became the first woman judge of the European Court of Human Rights in Strasbourg, France.

Facts in Brief. Population: 5,029,000. Government: King Frederik IX; Prime Minister Jens Otto Krag. Monetary Unit: krone. Foreign Trade: exports, $3,355,000,000; imports, $4,403,000,000. Principal Exports: machinery, bacon and ham, butter. *Kenneth Brown*

DENTISTRY. Including dentistry in a national health program became the most crucial challenge facing the dental profession in the United States in 1971. Some of the proposed major health plans drew sharp criticism from the American Dental Association (ADA) because they "completely ignore dental care." The ADA House of Delegates, meeting in Atlantic City, N.J., in October, designed a blueprint that the dental profession can follow "in the consideration of a national health program." It was based on the report of a special Task Force on National Health Programs.

The new guidelines called for all dentists to "take an active position in the design and support of a program that includes a dental program that serves the needs of all people of this nation." The guidelines point out, however, that the dental profession "continues to be in opposition to any national health program that uses public funds to provide health care for persons who are financially able to pay for health services themselves."

Dental Research. An Eastman Dental Center scientist found that painting a plastic sealant on children's teeth has greatly reduced decay on the biting surfaces. Michael Buonocore of Rochester, N.Y., achieved a "99 per cent decay reduction . . . following a single application of an adhesive resin to seal the vulnerable areas." The reduction of decay lasted more than two years. The sealants do not cover the sides of the teeth, though. Therefore, they would not protect against smooth-surface or gumline cavities.

A University of California dental scientist predicted that laser treatment of teeth in the future may prevent cavities. Ralph Stern of Los Angeles told the International Association for Dental Research, meeting in Chicago in March, about a unique experiment in which a "mini-lab" was installed inside a gold bridge in the mouth of a fellow researcher. Pieces of laser-treated and untreated enamel from freshly extracted teeth were placed inside tiny openings in the bridge. The bits of enamel were shielded from tooth brushing by a thin gold plate. After four weeks, the samples that were not laser treated showed the typical chalkiness of beginning decay, while the teeth treated with laser beams showed no signs of decay.

Mistaken Toothache. Pain that dental patients often mistake for a toothache may actually be caused by far more serious maladies, including heart attacks, according to John I. Ingle, dean of the University of Southern California School of Dentistry. "Severe pain in the oral cavity may be referred there during a heart attack," Ingle said. "About 18 per cent of heart-attack cases have no symptoms in the chest, but rather have pain referred to the jaws and teeth." In such cases, the patient frequently goes to his dentist rather than calling a physician or going to a hospital.   Lou Joseph

DETROIT. The battle to resolve urban problems became especially urgent in Detroit in 1971. City officials fought to head off impending financial disaster and stem the exodus of business from the city.

Money was the immediate problem as Mayor Roman S. Gribbs drew up a "disaster plan" budget and faced the prospect of laying off 3,600 city employees. Detroit schools felt the financial pinch of an $11-million budget cutback. Two hundred substitute teachers were dismissed and class sizes were increased to as many as 40 pupils. New sources of revenue were difficult to find, because city taxes were being levied at their maximum legal limits. In 1970, the Michigan legislature had doubled the city's income tax rate on residents from 1 per cent to 2 per cent and had permitted the city to levy a 5 per cent tax on utility bills. It had also provided a $5-million grant.

The Business Migration. A steady migration of business from the city to suburban areas has in part both caused the financial crisis and resulted from it. Recent migrants have included such firms as Pan American World Airways, Delta Air Lines, and the S. S. Kresge Company. The Advanced Mortgage Corporation and the Michigan Automobile Club also moved out of Detroit. The J. L. Hudson Company reportedly lost $9 million in thefts from its downtown department store, but it stayed in the city. Estimates of the jobs lost by the moving of automobile companies in the last 12 years run as high as 100,000. To make matters worse, the owners of the Detroit Lions professional football team announced plans to move their future games to a new stadium in suburban Pontiac.

The migration was reflected in the final 1970 census figures. They showed a 9.5 per cent drop in population in the city between 1960 and 1970, while the suburbs enjoyed a 28.5 per cent gain. Detroit's total population of 1,511,482 ranked it fifth among the nation's cities. It ranked fourth in percentage (about 45) of nonwhite residents.

Two Major Blueprints for Detroit's future were unveiled in the fall of 1970 and spring of 1971. One was a five-year, $3-million study that called for reconstruction of the downtown area, construction of a new "twin" city 50 miles northeast, and development of 10 smaller satellite cities. The study proposed a new transit system and green belts and recreational areas. The other plan, produced by the Metropolitan Fund of Detroit, suggested pairing nine redeveloped inner-city areas with 10 newly developed suburban locations. This would provide closer ties between the city and its suburbs.

The Detroit Charter Study Commission worked on a proposed city charter, expecting to submit it to a referendum in 1972.   J. M. Banovetz

DICTIONARY. See Section Five. DICTIONARY SUPPLEMENT.

DIPLOMATIC CORPS. See U.S. GOVERNMENT.

DISASTERS. Natural disasters—earthquakes, floods, and tornadoes—took the lives of thousands of persons in 1971. A major earthquake in February killed 62 persons and caused extensive property damage in southern California. A huge section of earth caved in under a Quebec village in May, killing 31. The worst air disaster in history killed 162 in July in Japan, and a fire aboard a Greek ferryboat in August left about 100 persons dead or missing. Major disasters in 1971 included the following:

Aircraft Crashes

Jan. 1—Off Algerian Coast. A Nord 262 airliner on a chartered flight from Algiers to the island of Minorca crashed in the Mediterranean Sea. Of the 31 persons killed, 19 were members of the Algerian soccer club.

Jan. 2—Tripoli, Libya. A United Arab Airlines jet crashed while attempting to land during a sandstorm. All 17 persons aboard were killed.

Jan. 18—Zurich, Switzerland. A Bulgarian Ilyushin-18 turboprop crashed while attempting to land in heavy fog, killing 35 of the 37 persons aboard. The pilot and a 2-year-old boy survived.

Jan. 21—Near Privas, France. Twenty-one persons, including seven officers of the French Atomic Energy Commission and six high-ranking French military officers, died in the crash of a Nord 202.

April 15—Near Manila, Philippines. Thirty-nine persons were killed when a Philippine military plane crashed shortly after take-off. The only survivor was a 3-year-old child.

April 28—Near Manaus, Brazil. A Brazilian Air Force DC-6 crashed, killing 16 persons.

Rescue workers search for bodies in the wreckage of an express train that derailed near Rheinweiler, West Germany on July 21, killing 23 persons and injuring 120.

May 6—Near Coolidge, Ariz. An Apache Airlines plane crashed, killing all 12 persons aboard. It was the first U.S. air disaster involving a scheduled flight since November, 1969.

May 23—Rijeka, Yugoslavia. A Russian-built TU-134 jet crashed at Rijeka's airport, killing 76 persons.

May 26—Near Cape Town, South Africa. Several high-ranking South African air force officers were among the 11 persons killed when three planes crashed while practicing maneuvers for an air show scheduled to celebrate the 10th anniversary of the Republic of South Africa.

June 6—Near Duarte, Calif. A DC-9 Air West airliner en route from Los Angeles to Salt Lake City, Utah, collided with an F-4 Phantom jet above the San Gabriel Mountains. The 49 persons on the airliner and the pilot of the Phantom jet were killed. A radarman who was on the military craft managed to parachute to safety.

June 7—East Haven, Conn. An Allegheny Airlines Convair 580 prop jet crashed into three vacant cottages and burned while attempting to land at Tweed New Haven Airport. Twenty-eight of the 31 persons aboard were killed.

June 13—South Pacific. A U.S. Air Force C-135 transport disappeared while flying from Pago Pago in American Samoa to Hickam Air Force Base in Hawaii. The plane, which belonged to the research and development branch of the Air Force, carried 24 persons and was apparently on a secret mission.

July 3—Japan. A Japanese TOA Airlines plane crashed into a mountain in northern Japan, killing 68 persons.

July 30—Honshu Island, Japan. An All Nippon Airways Boeing 727 collided with a Japanese jet fighter plane about 200 miles north of Tokyo. All 162 persons aboard the commercial liner were killed, making it the worst disaster in aviation history. The pilot of the military plane, who was on a training mission, parachuted from his plane and survived the crash.

Aug. 11—Irkutsk, Russia. Travel officials reported that an Aeroflot jet crashed during take-off in late July, killing 97 persons.

Aug. 18—Near Pegnitz, West Germany. A CH-47 Chinook helicopter carrying U.S. soldiers to a field exercise crashed and burned, killing 37.

Aug. 28—Copenhagen, Denmark. A Hungarian Ilyushin-18 turboprop crashed while attempting to land at Kastrup International Airport. Thirty-one of the 34 persons aboard were killed.

Sept. 4—Near Juneau, Alaska. In the worst air disaster in U.S. history, an Alaska Airlines Boeing 727 jet crashed into a mountain 17 miles northwest of Juneau, killing all 111 persons aboard.

Sept. 28—Eastern Brazil. Thirty-two persons were killed when a Brazilian airliner crashed in the Amazon jungle while it was on a flight from Cruzeiro do Sul to Rio Branco.

Oct. 2—Near Ghent, Belgium. A British European Airways propjet crashed after an engine exploded. All 63 persons aboard were killed.

Oct. 16—Near Peach Springs, Ariz. The crash of a sightseeing plane killed 10 persons.

Oct. 21—Peoria, Ill. A Chicago and Southern Airlines plane struck a power line and crashed while attempting to land, killing 16 persons.

Dec. 21—Sofia, Bulgaria. A Bulgarian airliner crashed on take-off, killing 28 persons.

Dec. 24—Peru. A Peruvian airliner crashed in a dense jungle area, and 91 of the 92 persons aboard were killed.

Bus and Truck Crashes

Feb. 5—Western Iran. A bus plunged into a deep gorge near Ibjar, killing 30 persons and injuring 24 others.

Buckled pavement and a collapsed overpass on this
Los Angeles freeway reflect the damage caused by
the earthquake that hit southern California in February.

May 10—Near Kapyong, South Korea. An overloaded
bus ran off the road and plunged into a reservoir,
killing 77 persons.

May 24—Panama Canal Zone. A bus crashed through
the guard-rail on a bridge and fell 150 feet into the
Panama Canal, killing 38 passengers.

Aug. 18—Near Casablanca, Morocco. A bus left a
country road about 65 miles southwest of Casablanca
and plunged into a gorge, killing 45 and injuring 30.

Earthquakes

Feb. 6—Tuscania, Italy. Two earthquakes devastated
the historic town of Tuscania in central Italy. Many
art treasures, particularly Etruscan art, were severely
damaged or destroyed. At least 22 persons were killed
and 4,000 left homeless.

Feb. 9—Southern California. An earthquake jarred
the Los Angeles area, killing 62 persons, damaging
buildings, and buckling pavement. The quake weakened the Van Norman Reservoir Dam in the San
Fernando Valley, and some 120,000 persons were
evacuated from homes in the area. Among the dead
were 46 persons killed when walls collapsed at the
Veterans Hospital in Sylmar. Overall damage from
the quake was estimated by authorities at more than
$1 billion.

May 12—Burdur, Turkey. At least 54 persons were
killed when an earthquake struck in southwestern
Turkey.

July 8—Chile. At least 90 persons were killed when
an earthquake struck the provinces of Santiago, Val-

paraiso, and Aconcagua. Landslides and rain delayed relief efforts in the area.

Oct. 15—Aimaraes Province, Peru. At least 40 persons were killed by an earthquake in southeastern Peru.

Explosions and Fires

Jan. 4—Auch, France. An explosion ripped a six-story building and killed 16 persons. The explosion apparently was caused by gas that had accumulated beneath an underground garage.

Jan. 21—Off Sardinian Coast. Sixteen crew members were lost when the U.S. oil tanker *Universe Patriot* caught fire and exploded.

Feb. 23—Near Brunswick, Ga. An explosion and fire in a munitions plant killed at least 25 persons and injured 100.

Feb. 14—Near Zenica, Yugoslavia. Fire that ignited a train's diesel-fuel supply killed at least 34 passengers and injured 113 others. Most of the victims died of gas poisoning. The train stopped inside a tunnel after the fire broke out, and deadly gas was trapped inside the enclosure.

March 6—Burgholzli, Switzerland. Twenty-eight patients suffocated when they were trapped by a fire in the Zurich University psychiatric clinic.

April 20—Bangkok, Thailand. Fire in a hotel killed at least 24 persons. Nine of the victims were Americans.

April 25—Seattle. A fire in an apartment building killed 14 residents and seriously injured 9 others.

May 22—Off Vancouver, B.C. An explosion and fire in the crew's quarters of the Norwegian ocean liner *Meteor* killed 32 crew members.

July 24—New Orleans. Fire on the 12th floor of a downtown motel killed six persons and seriously injured six others.

Aug. 28—Adriatic Sea. A fire aboard a large Greek ferryboat, the *Heleanna*, killed more than 30 persons. About 70 were reported missing. The ferry, carrying several hundred passengers and about 200 automobiles, was sailing from Pátrai, Greece, to Ancona, Italy.

Oct. 19—Honesdale, Pa. Fire in a nursing home caused the deaths of 15 elderly patients. Most of the victims died of smoke inhalation.

Oct. 21—Glasgow, Scotland. The explosion of a gas main destroyed 15 stores in a shopping center and killed 13 persons. Some 100 others were injured.

Dec. 1—Frattaminore, Italy. Explosions caused an apartment building in a suburb of Naples to collapse, killing nine persons and injuring nine others.

Dec. 11—Port Huron, Mich. Twenty-one workers were killed when methane gas exploded inside a water tunnel being built under Lake Huron.

Dec. 25—Seoul, South Korea. Fire in a hotel, caused by an exploding propane gas tank, killed 159 persons. It was the worst hotel fire in history.

Floods

Jan. 5—Malaysia. Flooding, brought on by heavy rains, caused 114,000 persons to be evacuated from affected areas in 8 of West Malaysia's 11 states. Flood-related deaths were estimated at between 33 and 60.

Feb. 26—Rio de Janeiro, Brazil. A flash flood killed at least 130 persons, disrupted transportation, and left thousands of persons homeless.

April 26-28—Salvador, Brazil. Heavy rains caused floods that killed more than 140 persons, left 10,000 homeless, and caused property damage estimated at $6 million.

July 29—Afghanistan. Floodwaters pushed from a natural reservoir in the Hindu Kush mountain range by a landslide killed at least 1,000 persons.

Sept. 9—Northern India. The worst floods in Uttar Pradesh state and other northern points in more than a decade caused at least 300 deaths and forced 35,000 persons to leave their homes.

Sept. 14—Chester, Pa. Flooding caused by four days of torrential rain killed 10 persons.

Mine Disasters

March 23—Near Katowice, Poland. At least eight men died when a mine wall collapsed, trapping 11 miners 2,265 feet below the surface.

April 12—Near Golconda, Ill. Six miners were killed by hydrogen sulfide gas while working.

May 16—Sinjabi, West Pakistan. An explosion in a coal mine killed 32 miners.

Oct. 30—Humedoara, Romania. A landslide at a mining site killed 51 workers and injured 88.

Dec. 2—Near Keelung, Formosa. An explosion ripped through a coal mine, killing 41 persons and injuring 7. Seven others were sealed in the 7,260-foot-deep pit.

Shipwrecks

Jan. 11-12—English Channel. A Panamanian gas tanker exploded, broke in two, and sank after colliding with a Peruvian ship. Eight of the tanker's crew members were killed. The following day, a German freighter, the *Brandenburg*, crashed into the tanker wreckage and also sank. At least 7 members of the freighter's crew were killed and 14 others were missing.

March 29—Gulf of Tonkin. A Russian freighter smashed into a Chinese fishing boat. According to Chinese authorities, 11 fishermen were lost.

Nov. 21—The Philippines. An overloaded interisland cargo boat carrying about 200 passengers sank, killing at least 66 persons. The boat had a capacity of 11 passengers.

Tornadoes, Typhoons, and Storms

Jan. 13—Near Salisbury, Rhodesia. Eleven persons were killed by lightning during a severe storm.

Feb. 21—Louisiana, Mississippi, and Tennessee. Between 40 and 50 tornadoes ripped through the southern United States, killing more than 100 persons and leaving thousands of others homeless. A large part of Inverness, Miss., a town of about 1,600, was destroyed.

April 26—Central Philippines. At least 25 persons were killed by tropical storm Wanda, and more than 100 others were missing.

April 27-28—Kentucky. Ten persons were killed when a series of tornadoes struck the south and central parts of the state.

July 17—South Korea. A severe thunderstorm that brought 7 inches of rain to the central part of the country caused at least 35 deaths.

Aug. 5—Japan and South Korea. Typhoon Olive, with winds up to 73 miles per hour, killed at least 78 persons. The typhoon damaged or destroyed more than 1,500 buildings and sank 27 ships in Japan. The typhoon also forced 23,000 persons to evacuate the site of the 13th World Boy Scouts Jamboree at the foot of Mount Fuji.

Aug. 17—Hong Kong. Typhoon Rose, the worst typhoon to hit Hong Kong in almost 10 years, killed at least 25 persons and injured about 300 others. With violent winds up to 115 miles per hour, it tore 37 ships from their moorings and drove them ashore. Floods and landslides caused serious damage.

Oct. 13—The Philippines. Tropical storm Dadang killed at least 15 persons and left more than 70,000 homeless.

Oct. 23-24—South Vietnam. Typhoon Hester, with winds of up to 138 mph, ripped through the northern provinces. More than 100 persons were killed or missing, and hundreds were left homeless. The town of Namhoa was destroyed, and several U.S. combat bases were severely damaged.

Train Wrecks

Jan. 1—Near Atakpamé, Togo. Two trains collided in central Togo, killing 13 persons and seriously injuring 25 others.

Children wade through floodwaters at Bhadrakh in India's Orissa state, where a cyclone and tidal wave from the Bay of Bengal killed 10,000 in October.

Feb. 9—Near Aitrang, West Germany. The Trans-Europe Bavarian Express derailed about 50 miles southwest of Munich, and a local train ran into the wreckage. Twenty-eight persons were killed and 35 were seriously injured.

May 27—Near Wuppertal, West Germany. A passenger train carrying about 100 schoolchildren home from an outing collided head-on with a freight train. Forty-six persons (41 of them students) were killed.

June 10—Tonti, Ill. The *City of New Orleans*, a Chicago-to-New Orleans passenger train, derailed in southern Illinois. Ten persons were killed in the crash and fire that followed, and 94 were injured.

July 17—Near Sarajevo, Yugoslavia. A special holiday train carrying schoolchildren crashed into a freight train that was stopped at a station, killing 15 persons.

July 21—Near Rheinweiler, West Germany. Twenty-three persons were killed and more than 100 injured when an express train en route from Basel, Switzerland, to Copenhagen, Denmark, jumped the tracks on a curve, fell down a 15-foot embankment, and crashed into a house.

July 22—Italian-Swiss Border. A commuter train derailed in the Simplon Tunnel, killing 5 Italians.

Aug. 4—Near Belgrade, Yugoslavia. A six-car passenger train collided head-on with a freight train, killing 40 and injuring about 100.

Oct. 12—Seoul, Korea. After losing power, a train carrying schoolchildren rolled back down a hill and crashed into tank cars at a railroad station. At least 16 children were killed.

Oct. 25—Tsu, Japan. Thirteen persons were killed and 188 injured when two trains collided in a tunnel.

Other Disasters

Jan. 2—Glasgow, Scotland. A surging crowd, rushing to leave Ibrox Stadium after a soccer match, broke through a steel barricade at the head of a stairway, and 66 persons were killed.

Feb. 4—Belo Horizonte, Brazil. At least 63 construction workers were killed when a government exhibit hall on which they were working collapsed.

May 4—St. Jean de Vianney, Quebec. The earth under this small village caved in during heavy rains, killing 31 persons and engulfing 35 homes, several cars, and a bus. The cave-in left a sheer-walled pit about 1,000 feet long, 70 feet wide, and at least 100 feet deep.

May 15—Sallen, France. The floor of the village hall gave way during a wedding celebration, and guests fell into an old well 22 feet deep. Thirteen persons drowned in the well. Later, the mayor of the village committed suicide.

June 24—Sylmar, Calif. Seventeen workmen were killed by an explosion and fire in a tunnel that was under construction. Natural methane gas apparently caused the explosion.

Sept. 13—Near Liverpool, England. A chain-reaction collision of 200 automobiles and trucks in a patch of fog outside Thelwall killed 10 persons and seriously injured about 60 others.

Oct. 29—Orissa State, India. More than 10,000 persons were killed by a cyclone and tidal wave that swept in from the Bay of Bengal.

Nov. 10—Coblenz, West Germany. A bridge under construction collapsed, killing 20 workers.

Nov. 20—Rio de Janeiro. At least 21 persons were killed when a viaduct collapsed onto a busy street.

Nov. 29—Liston, England. About 100 cars and trucks collided on a superhighway 30 miles north of London, killing 8 persons and injuring 50 others.

Dec. 12—Alexandria, Egypt. Two apartment buildings collapsed, killing 34 persons. Darlene R. Stille

DOLE, ROBERT J. (1923-   ), U.S. senator from Kansas, was named national chairman of the Republican Party on Jan. 15, 1971. He replaced Representative Rogers C. B. Morton (R., Md.), who became secretary of the interior. A conservative with a reputation as a tough political and legislative infighter, Dole had actively sought the post.

Dole was born in Russell, Kans., and attended public schools there. He served in the Army during World War II, advancing from private to captain. He was decorated with a Purple Heart and the Bronze Star with cluster. Dole attended the universities of Arizona and Kansas, and received his law degree from Washburn Municipal University in Topeka, Kans., in 1952. He was serving in the Kansas House of Representatives at the time, having been elected to the legislature in 1951.

In 1953, he was elected to Congress, and served in the House of Representatives until 1969, when he won his Senate seat. Dole has vigorously assailed critics of President Richard M. Nixon's Vietnam policies, and defended the antiballistic missile project. He also supported the President's nominations of judges Clement F. Haynsworth, Jr., and G. Harrold Carswell to the Supreme Court.

Dole married the former Phyllis Eloise Holden in 1948, and they have one daughter, Robin. They were divorced in January, 1972.   Foster Stockwell

DOMINICAN REPUBLIC. See LATIN AMERICA.

DRUGS. President Richard M. Nixon took new steps to prevent drug abuse in 1971. On June 17, he set up a White House office to coordinate activities of the nine federal agencies involved in treating or preventing narcotics addiction. Mr. Nixon said that drug abuse had "assumed the dimensions of a national emergency," and he asked Congress for $155 million more for a campaign of rehabilitation, research, education, enforcement, and international control of drug traffic. He named Jerome H. Jaffe, former chief of the Illinois drug abuse program, to head the new Office of Drug Abuse Prevention.

The Department of Justice, following a recommendation from the U.S. Department of Health, Education, and Welfare, ordered the reclassification, in May, of most amphetamines and methamphetamines under Schedule II of the drug control law. Schedule II includes opiates and other potential abuse drugs. The shift puts the drugs under stricter regulation and prevents the automatic refill of old prescriptions.

Over-the-Counter Drugs also received closer federal scrutiny. A Senate committee investigating the drug industry, under the chairmanship of Senator Gaylord A. Nelson (D., Wis.), looked into the truth of claims made for drugs, as well as into the effectiveness and safety of drugs. Later, the Food and Drug Administration (FDA) moved to curtail excessive claims for sleep-inducing drugs by requiring manufacturers to present scientific data to support their claims.

In June, the FDA issued labeling regulations for certain prescription drugs. The order resulted from studies of nearly 3,000 prescription drugs made by joint panels of the National Academy of Sciences and the National Research Council. They rated each drug and placed it in one of five categories according to the effectiveness (or ineffectiveness) of each. The FDA order requires the category labeling on any prescription drug evaluated as other than "effective" by the National Academy of Sciences.

Throughout the year, the FDA asked the drug industry to voluntarily supply information needed for an exhaustive inventory of all drugs being marketed for human use. Firms were asked to supply names, dosage, ingredients, and production information on all drugs. Bills were introduced in Congress to make this cooperation mandatory.

Court Activity. In New York, a federal district court approved a settlement between five producers of the broad-spectrum antibiotic tetracycline, and numerous hospitals and Blue Cross agencies. The companies were Chas. Pfizer & Co., Inc; Bristol-Myers; American Cyanamid Company; Upjohn; and Squibb Beech-Nut, Incorporated. Pfizer, American Cyanamid, and Bristol-Myers had set aside $82.5 million to pay settlements. In 1961, the Department of Justice had charged the three with price-fixing and monopoly, and charged Upjohn and Squibb as co-conspirators. They were convicted in 1967, and the decision was reversed by a higher court in 1970. Midyear, the attorney general of California announced that the state planned to bring a class action suit against the five to reclaim partial refunds for purchases of the antibiotic during the years from 1954 to 1966.

Several drug companies merged with cosmetic firms. In January, Eli Lilly and Company announced the acquisition of Elizabeth Arden Sales Corporation. Then American Cyanamid filed a $120-million breach-of-contract suit, claiming it had had a prior agreement to purchase Elizabeth Arden. Also, American Cyanamid merged with Shulton, Inc. Revlon, Inc., agreed to buy Britain's BCA Pharmaceutical Ltd. And, after a two-year controversy, a Federal Trade Commission examiner recommended that antitrust charges be dismissed against Sterling Drug, Inc., for their acquisition of Lehn & Fink Products.

Drug Shipments totaled nearly $7.7 billion, up 10 per cent over 1970, and 22 per cent over the $6.3-billion shipped in 1969. Exports reached $515 million, a 20 per cent gain over 1970, while imports were up only 8 per cent to $95 million. After-tax profits were estimated at $1.3 billion. This represented a 9 per cent growth over 1970 profits, but was well below the 11 per cent annual profit increase enjoyed during the 1960s.   Mary Lynn M. Luy

DUVALIER, JEAN-CLAUDE (1951-   ), became Haiti's president for life on April 22, 1971, at the age of 19. He was sworn in on the night his father died. The elder Duvalier had declared himself president for life in 1964. Jean-Claude was designated his successor in a January, 1971, referendum in which no dissenting vote was announced.

Little is known about the new president. He had a sheltered childhood, rarely leaving the presidential palace without bodyguards. He attended elementary school in Port-au-Prince until foes of his dictator father tried to kidnap him. His high school diploma is from a Port-au-Prince school. In 1970, he began to study government at the University of Haiti.

Jean-Claude is a big man, about 6 feet tall and weighing perhaps 250 pounds. Friends describe him as introverted, and suggest that his reputation as a playboy is exaggerated. There is some confusion over his exact age because his father gave conflicting information while having the Haitian Constitution amended so Jean-Claude could meet presidential age requirements.

Observers speculated Jean-Claude might not last long in office, but in August he appeared to survive his first crisis. He apparently sided with a cabinet minister and against his sister, Marie-Denise Dominique, wife of Haiti's ambassador to France. Mrs. Dominique left Haiti for France.   Ed Nelson

EARTHQUAKES. See DISASTERS, GEOLOGY.

Newly elected Patriarch of the Russian Orthodox Church, 60-year-old Metropolitan Pimen of Kroutitzy, conducts services at the Holy Synod that chose him.

EASTERN ORTHODOX CHURCHES. The storm provoked in many countries of the world by the *autocephaly* (independence) of the former Russian Orthodox Church of America continued throughout 1971. The primate of the Church of Greece, Archbishop Ieronymos of Athens, in a letter to the Patriarch of Moscow, endorsed the protest made earlier by Patriarch Athenagoras I of Constantinople. At the same time, however, all churches involved in this controversy kept stressing the need for a common solution to the problem of the Eastern Orthodox *diaspora* (scattering) in the world.

In the United States, two Greek parishes joined the independent Orthodox Church in America (OCA) in 1971. The Greek archdiocese promptly instructed its priests to suspend sacramental communion with the new body. However, both clergy and laity disapproved of this measure. Relations were restored between the new group and the archdiocese at an October meeting between Metropolitan Ireney, head of the OCA, and Archbishop Iakovos, head of the Greek Archdiocese.

During the year, official representatives of the OCA visited the Eastern Orthodox Churches in Antioch, Turkey; Serbia; Bulgaria; and Romania. They discussed ecclesiastical problems arising from the establishment of the new independent church.

Meetings in the United States. The eighth Assembly of the International Association of Orthodox Youth Movements was held in Brookline, Mass., in July. This was its first meeting in the United States. The delegates adopted resolutions calling for greater Orthodox unity and a greater involvement in world problems. In August, the convention of The Antiochian Orthodox Christian Archdiocese of New York and All North America adopted a resolution asking Archbishop Philip to seek church unification.

In October, the Second All-American Council of the Orthodox Churches in America was held in South Canaan, Pa. The council defeated a motion to permit women to be elected as delegates from parishes. The council also protested the persecution of religion behind the Iron Curtain, and the closing by the Turkish government of the Patriarchal Theological School in Halki, Turkey.

Outside the United States. In June, a general council of the Russian Orthodox Church unanimously elected Metropolitan Pimen of Kroutitzy as Patriarch of Moscow and All Russia. He replaces the Patriarch Alexis, who died in April, 1970. In September, the Synod of Bishops of the "Russian Church in Exile," a body violently opposed to the official Moscow Patriarchate, said the election was invalid because it took place under pressure from the atheistic government of Russia. In July, the Orthodox Church in Bulgaria also elected a new patriarch—Maxim, the former Metropolitan of Lovets.   Alexander Schmemann

ECONOMY, THE. Americans will long remember 1971 as the year in which–for the first time during peace–the United States moved to price and wage controls. And 1972 will be the year that tests the success of that move. A careful examination of the U.S. economy's performance, both before and after the wage-price-rent freeze, announced with dramatic suddenness by President Richard M. Nixon on August 15, shows that the United States was slowly recovering from the recession of 1969 and 1970. Despite lingering unemployment and inflation, most citizens were at least as well off as ever.

What caused the President to impose the controls that only three weeks earlier he had denied were the solution to the economy's problems? His move was due primarily to a drastic outpouring of dollars that caused a negative U.S. balance of payments that reached an annual rate of $23 billion during the second quarter of 1971.

More significant than the domestic controls were the President's imposition of a 10 per cent surcharge on most imports, and his severing of the historical connection of the dollar to its gold base. No longer would the United States swap its dwindling supply of gold for dollars held by foreigners, and no longer would it strive to maintain the value of the dollar in terms of foreign currencies.

The immediate effect of the 10 per cent import tax was an international storm of protest. Many countries claimed, quite correctly, that the tax violated the General Agreement on Tariffs and Trade and canceled the effects of the latest round of reciprocal tariff reductions. Soon after the August pronouncement, the values of foreign currencies rose relative to the dollar. In what amounted to a partly free market, the Japanese yen and the West German Deutsche mark both rose about 8 per cent.

On December 1, the United States surprised members of the Group of Ten (the leading industrial nations of the Free World) at a meeting in Rome, Italy, by offering as much as a 10 per cent increase in the price of gold, which would effectively devalue the dollar. On December 18, President Nixon announced an agreement on a realignment of currency exchange rates among the 10 nations. It included dropping the import surcharge and devaluing the dollar by 8.57 per cent.

Foreign Import Barriers. United States officials have been particularly disturbed by the tendency of some foreign countries, notably Japan and France, to impose nontariff barriers on goods imported to their countries. These barriers, in effect, nullified the tariff reductions that had been negotiated, making it difficult for foreign goods to enter those countries. The eventual removal of nontariff barriers is a prime objective of the Nixon Administration, and lifting the 10 per cent surcharge on imports was initially conditioned upon progress being made in this direction.

For the first time in the 1900s, U.S. imports exceeded exports for a full calendar year. At year-end, the estimated balance-of-trade deficit was more than $1 billion. In past years, exports exceeded imports by more than $1 billion, but capital outflow created a negative balance of payments.

Inflationary pressure has been the most common reason cited for the rapid decrease in our balance of trade. Inflation is a contributing factor. The record indicates, however, that the major causes are the rapid growth of productivity abroad and the significantly lower wage rates that prevail there. The East, Gulf, and West Coast dock strikes in the United States during 1971 also contributed.

During the past year, U.S. productivity growth was lower than that of any other industrialized country, with the exception of Great Britain. On the other hand, prices abroad rose more rapidly than those in the United States. Among industrialized countries, only Canada had a lower rate of inflation than 1971's less than 4 per cent rise in the U.S. price index. Great Britain had the dubious distinction of being at the top of the list, with nearly a 10 per cent increase. Japan experienced a 7.4 per cent rise, and West Germany and France were about even at 5.6 per cent. These rates, of course, were well below the more than 15 per cent that is common to the developing countries of the world.

Some Hopeful Signs. The wage-price freeze and the international monetary turmoil that accompanied it almost overshadowed the more hopeful signs on the international economic front. Foreign trade continued to expand at an annual rate of nearly 10 per cent. As usual, however, the more industrialized countries appeared to be the chief beneficiaries of the increase. Canada, ranking sixth among the industrialized nations with $19 billion in exports, exported more than all of Latin America combined. The United States, still the leader with a total of more than $46 billion, sold more than Africa and Asia combined. Following the United States were West Germany, Japan, Great Britain, and France, in that order. Russian exports were well below those of Canada at $13 billion.

In late October, the British Parliament voted to join the European Community (Common Market), effective in 1973. The necessary legislation to accomplish the move was to be passed in 1972. This will unite Western Europe in an economic grouping that embraces all of the major powers with half a dozen other associate members. Ultimately, this is expected to lead to greater stability in the trading relationships within the Free World, although it will also unquestionably create an economic community that can speak as an equal to the United States on trade and financial matters. See EUROPE.

On the Domestic Scene, the United States made slow and, to some, inadequate progress toward a

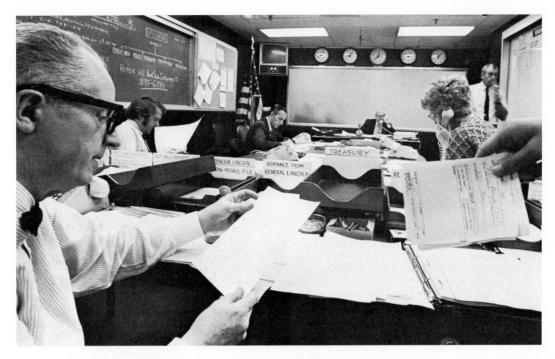

Staff members of the Office of Emergency Preparedness were given the thorny task of trying to interpret and answer questions about the wage-price freeze.

full recovery from the 1969-1970 downturn in the economy. The gross national product (GNP) for the year was slightly over $1 trillion, more than 7 per cent over the $974 billion registered in 1970. Of this gain, nearly 4.6 per cent was attributable to rising prices, which made real growth much less impressive than the raw statistics indicate. Nevertheless, achieving a trillion-dollar economy represented a record that indicates the economy's high productivity.

The rate of increase was disappointing, however, when compared with previous recoveries. The National Bureau of Economic Research, the authoritative arbiter in the measurement of business cycles, dates the recovery period as beginning in November, 1970. Real growth from this point to a date a year later was 4.1 per cent. In 1962, at a comparable point of recovery from the 1961 recession, the real rate was 6 per cent. These two figures represented the lowest rate of upswing of the four recessions that have occurred since World War II.

Other indicators also reflected this relative sluggishness. Industrial production rose by only 3.6 per cent, whereas recoveries from previous recessions showed gains ranging from 11.6 per cent to 26.9 per cent. Unemployment dropped only slightly, from 6 per cent to 5.9 per cent at year-end. It should be noted, however, that when the recession ended in 1970, unemployment was at a lower level

than it had been in previous postwar recessions.

Failure of industrial production to expand rapidly explains the relatively slight decline in unemployment. Union officials maintained that increased imports have also seriously reduced the number of jobs available in the United States.

On the brighter side, the unemployment rate among married males was running at only 3 per cent at year-end. This indicated that these most stable and generally higher-skilled members of the working force were able to find jobs. The percentage of unemployed blacks and teen-agers was much higher than for any other group. However, there was a tendency to overlook the fact that the total number of civilian jobs pushed close to the 80-million mark by the end of the year.

Levels of living, as measured by per capita income, also improved in 1971. The average rose from $2,595 in 1970 to $2,670 in 1971, both years being measured in terms of 1958 prices. Average weekly earnings in manufacturing also rose to nearly $130, up $6 during the year. Despite continuing inflation, the purchasing power of these wages regained most of the loss suffered in 1970. At year-end, it was only a few cents below the record level of 1969.

Farm Profits. Farmers did not fare so well. Net income per farm, measured in 1967 prices, fell for the second successive year, from $4,782 in 1970 to

$4,600 in 1971. Both years were well below the 1969 record level of $5,216. The principal cause of the decline was a drop in the parity ratio (what farmers receive for their crops relative to what they buy) from 77 to 74 (1914=100). A decline in export sales also contributed to the problem. Part of this decline was caused by a 57-day dock strike at East and Gulf coast ports. The strikes shut off normal grain shipments overseas. Harvested grain overflowed all storage facilities, and it piled up on farms and in Midwest grain elevators. As a result, American farmers lost an estimated $1 billion in foreign sales.

Corporate Profits, after taxes, recovered slightly from their 1970 lows, reaching $44.9 billion. This was well below the record level of nearly $50 billion set in 1965, however. Still, businessmen invested a record $81.5 billion in new plants and equipment, slightly above the previous high set in 1970. Continuing plant and equipment investment in the face of sluggish sales and profits would appear to indicate a continuing substitution of relatively low-priced capital for relatively high-priced labor. The inference is strengthened by the fact that most industries ran well below their rated capacity.

In past years, investment has generally tended to move with levels of capacity utilization, and the reversal of this tendency in 1970 and 1971 may indicate more about what businessmen expect about future wage costs and inflation than about their immediate prospects for profit. They are clearly more concerned about the former. This heavy investment was also encouraged by a general decline in interest rates from their high levels of 1970 as the Federal Reserve System (Fed) permitted the money supply to increase nearly 12 per cent during the first seven months of the year. This was far above 1970 levels, when the Fed's primary emphasis was to choke off inflationary pressures. This rate of increase in the money supply slackened substantially late in the year, and the total increase dropped to about 6 per cent. Some economists wondered if the rapid growth in the money supply during the first half of the year helped to increase inflationary expectations, especially abroad, thus contributing to the drastic midyear shift away from the dollar.

The Federal Budget, with a deficit of $22.3 billion in fiscal 1971 and an estimated deficit of more than $35 billion for fiscal 1972, also contributed to inflationary pressures. With the year-end tax cuts for 1972 and 1973, signed by President Nixon on December 10, this estimate could soar to over $45-billion unless a sharp increase in the economy were to result in unusually high tax collections.

Inflation Slows. The economy in 1971 certainly lacked luster, but it was by no means dismally unsuccessful. Even before the August wage-price freeze, the rate of inflation had begun to slow and unemployment was dropping. That neither movement was as vigorous as everyone would have liked

may serve to illustrate the difficulties of attempting to curb a past inflationary pressure while maintaining a relatively low level of unemployment.

The current inflation began in 1965 when the United States plunged into full-scale fighting in Vietnam. When the costs of that conflict began to soar, President Lyndon B. Johnson was warned by his economic advisers that higher taxes were desirable to curb an overheating economy. The advice was not taken, inflationary pressures started, and the federal budget has not been balanced since then.

Inflation did not really begin to pick up steam, however, until 1967. Employment levels remained high, with a resulting upward pressure on wage rates. In addition, people began to count on mild inflation, and adjusted prices and wage demands correspondingly. But when price increases began to exceed 2 or 3 per cent a year, and the U.S. balance of payments position became increasingly precarious, the traditional remedy was applied—tight money and higher interest rates. Although this policy succeeded in slowing investment and putting the brakes on the economy, it failed to halt inflation. Instead, a recession began in late 1969 and continued into the third quarter of 1970. Unemployment rose and prices continued to increase at approximately 5 per cent a year. To end this unsatisfactory state of affairs, the Fed began to expand the money supply early in 1971 at a 10-to-12 per cent annual rate. This was the situation that prompted foreign fears about the stability of the dollar.

The Wage-Price Freeze. It was in this setting that President Nixon made his historic announcement to the nation in August. Acting under powers granted him by Congress, he declared a 90-day freeze on all prices, wages, and rents, including those that had been previously negotiated and were scheduled to go into effect during the 90-day period. He also indicated that he would propose to Congress a 10 per cent one-year investment tax credit to industry for investment in new equipment; elimination of the 7 per cent automobile excise tax; and a reduction in individual income taxes in 1972, previously scheduled to go into effect in 1973. As a by-product of the President's December devaluation announcement, the United States agreed to cancel the short-lived investment credit program. See TAXATION.

After the initial surprise at this drastic reversal of policy, the public greeted the move with enthusiasm—with the single exception of labor leaders. Labor objected to President Nixon's failure to include interest rates in the freeze (although not even during World War II had this been attempted) and to barring previously negotiated wage increases.

Stock prices shot up. The Dow Jones average of 30 industrial stocks rose more than 30 points to 888 on the day following the announcement, and another 30 points were added in the ensuing two

Selected Key Economic Indicators

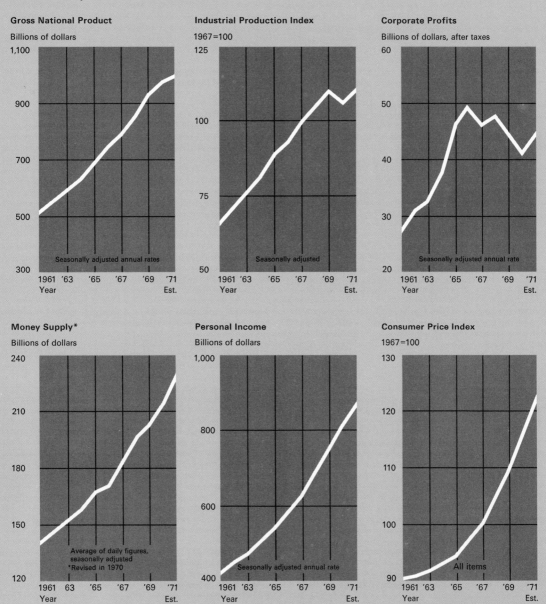

Gross National Product
Billions of dollars

1,100
900
700
500
300

Seasonally adjusted annual rates

1961 '63 '65 '67 '69 '71
Year   Est.

Industrial Production Index
1967=100

125
100
75
50

Seasonally adjusted

1961 '63 '65 '67 '69 '71
Year   Est.

Corporate Profits
Billions of dollars, after taxes

60
50
40
30
20

Seasonally adjusted annual rate

1961 '63 '65 '67 '69 '71
Year   Est.

Money Supply*
Billions of dollars

240
210
180
150
120

Average of daily figures,
seasonally adjusted
*Revised in 1970

1961 63 '65 '67 '69 '71
Year   Est.

Personal Income
Billions of dollars

1,000
800
600
400

Seasonally adjusted annual rate

1961 '63 '65 '67 '69 '71
Year   Est.

Consumer Price Index
1967=100

130
120
110
100
90

All items

1961 '63 '65 '67 '69 '71
Year   Est.

The most comprehensive measure of the nation's total output of goods and services is the *Gross National Product* (GNP). The GNP represents the dollar value in current prices of all goods and services plus the estimated value of certain imputed outputs, such as the rental value of owner-occupied dwellings. *Industrial Production Index* is a monthly measure of the physical output of manufacturing, mining, and utility industries. *Corporate Profits* are quarterly profit samplings from major industries. *Money Supply* measures the total amount of money in the economy in coin, currency, and demand deposits. *Personal Income* is current income received by persons (including nonprofit institutions and private trust funds) before personal taxes. *Consumer Price Index* (CPI) is a monthly measure of changes in the prices of goods and services consumed by urban families and individuals. CPI includes about 300 goods and services. All 1971 figures are *Year Book* estimates.

weeks. New-automobile sales began to boom as the new models were frozen at 1971 prices and, for the first October in history, U.S. manufacturers sold more than 1 million units. But uncertainties about what was to follow the end of the 90-day freeze period soon came to the front. Manufacturers of other durable consumer goods experienced little increased demand as consumers continued to save at the unprecedented rate of nearly 8 per cent. Americans apparently still had doubts about the ultimate course of incomes and prices. Investors, too, began to have second thoughts about what controls might be imposed after the freeze was over. In early September, the market began a steady decline that carried it below 800, its low point of the year, in late November, although it surged back after the year-end currency alignment.

Implementing the Controls. The President had promised that no massive government bureaucracy such as had administered the price controls during World War II would be established. It was thus a foregone conclusion that enforcement of whatever controls were adopted would fall most heavily on the largest corporations and on key labor contracts, and this proved to be the case. Voluntary compliance for the great bulk of business was the rule to be followed, with the threat of heavy fines for violations. Major companies were required to secure advance approval of price increases. Guidelines were established, permitting wage increases of 5.5 per cent, monitored by a Pay Board for contracts negotiated after the freeze was lifted and 2.5 per cent limits on prices, monitored by a Price Commission.

Wage increases negotiated prior to the freeze were permitted if they were "reasonable" (although not necessarily within the 5.5 per cent limitation), but no retroactive payment of wages that had been lost as a result of the freeze was permitted. Predictably, this latter decision touched off a wave of labor resentment. Labor claimed that the restriction represented a violation of contracts voluntarily entered into and that it was unconstitutional. Labor representatives served on the Pay Board, but labor continued to claim that the failure to place ceilings on profits represented a major inequity.

Controls on profits were not entirely lacking, however. Although total profits were expected to increase under the Phase 2 operations following the original 90-day period, profit margins (cents of profit per dollar of sales) were not permitted to rise above the average of the best two of the three immediately preceding years. In effect, this meant that the margins for most companies could not exceed the average they had attained in 1968 and 1969. Hopefully, increased volume of sales would permit

The President met with his key economic advisers—from left, Arthur F. Burns, John B. Connally, George P. Shultz, and Paul W. McCracken—before the freeze.

income, they will pour more than $15 billion into the economy by purchases of goods and services. In addition, if consumers were to spend from their past savings, accumulated in 1969 and 1970, the total could swell to more than $30 billion. While these sums in themselves would add pressure to the economy and normally result in more inflation, the increased output that such demand might generate would also serve to decrease unemployment, and profits might rise even if controls limited the increase in prices to 2.5 to 3 per cent.

Other targets for 1972 called for a drop in unemployment to about 4 per cent of the working force, and holding inflation to a 3 per cent pace. If these goals can be achieved, the great experiment will have succeeded, and the likelihood of removing controls from the economy by mid-1973 would appear good. If the nation does not reach these objectives, it may be a long time before the American economy returns to its free-market state. Most analysts predicted a better 1972 in terms of GNP, profits, and levels of employment. They were, however, far from certain that the present wage-price program would work effectively. The big news of 1972 will be how the American economy performs and how rapidly normal international monetary and trade relations can be restored. Warren W. Shearer

See also Section One, Focus on The Economy; Section Two, Caging the Inflation Monster.

profits to rise, thus providing funds for continuing investment in new plant and facilities and restoring profits to a level closer to their historical level—9 or 10 per cent of the GNP before taxes.

One of the first cases to come before the Pay Board was that of the soft-coal miners. On strike during most of October and early November, the miners had settled their dispute with an agreement that called for a 15.5 per cent first-year increase, nearly three times the limit set in the guidelines. The Pay Board promptly granted the increase with the explanation that it was not "seriously" out of line with reality, and that the miners had not shared fully in the general pay increases of the last two years. This illustrated the difficulties that attend attempts to control wages. Each bargain can, in one way or another, be argued as a special case, justifying the sought-for increase on the grounds of equity. This was a common occurrence during World War II. Granting such increases enormously complicates the administration of controls, however justified they may be. Each increase becomes, in turn, a precedent for similar increases. It can produce the familiar wage-price spiral that plagued the American economy for the past few years.

The key to the success of the effort to stimulate the economy and at the same time cool off the inflation probably rests with consumers. If they reduce their rate of savings to about 6 per cent of disposable

ECUADOR. A revolt against the regime of President José María Velasco Ibarra began and ended on April 1, 1971, without a shot being fired. The revolt was not aimed at the president, however, but at his nephew, Defense Minister Jorge Acosta Velasco, who had been instrumental in having General Luis Jácome Chavez dismissed as head of the war academy. Jácome Chavez retaliated by organizing the coup. To carry it out, he recruited 50 other officers from the academy. All surrendered to government forces at the end of the day. Late in the month, the president announced that constitutional amendments being prepared would be submitted to the voters and that elections would be held in June, 1972. On April 6, the president bowed to further army demands and dismissed his nephew.

In October, Ecuador pushed negotiations for arrangements for a $56-million loan from eight United States commercial banks. It hoped that the financial arrangement would relieve some of Ecuador's fiscal difficulties. The republic's monetary holdings, which totaled $55.1 million at the end of 1970, had fallen to $39.4 million by mid-1971, and to $37.56 million by September 3.

Facts in Brief. Population: 6,511,000. Government: President José María Velasco Ibarra. Monetary Unit: sucre. Foreign Trade: exports, $218,-000,000; imports, $247,000,000. Principal Exports: bananas, coffee, cacao. Mary C. Webster

EDUCATION. Peace returned to the American campus in 1971, but there was little peace of mind for educational administrators anywhere. Both the schools and the colleges were caught in the squeeze between inflation and recession. School districts across the country had to operate on austerity budgets, and many systems had to cut several weeks off the school year to save on maintenance and fuel.

Virtually all colleges registered deficits, many in the millions of dollars, as research funds were cut back and the costs of educating students continued to rise. For the first time in over a decade, gifts from private individuals and foundations declined. They totaled $1.78 billion, $20 million below 1970.

The Fiscal Crisis. The Carnegie Commission on Higher Education, headed by Clark Kerr, issued an extensive report on the fiscal crisis, entitled "The New Depression of Higher Education." Earl F. Cheit, director of the study, disclosed that 540 of the 2,300 institutions of higher learning in the United States were already in financial difficulty and another 1,000 were "rapidly headed for trouble." Even Harvard University, with its endowment of more than $1 billion, was just barely in the black. Columbia University had announced a deficit of $15 million. Stanford University mapped out a six-year plan with a $6-million spending cut spread over that period. Many colleges left vacant faculty positions unfilled; others asked all departments to reduce their budgets. The entire University of California system stopped faculty pay increases beyond cost-of-living raises and banned out-of-state travel at public expense for all its personnel.

The crisis came after years of expansion and relative affluence. In fact, Cheit's report said that "many institutions were undercapitalized, overextended, and moving into increased areas of responsibility . . . without permanent financing."

The Negro colleges were even more severely affected by the fiscal crisis. These approximately 110 institutions, about half of them privately financed and the rest state colleges, had already been hard-hit by the brain drain. Many of their best prospective students and increasing numbers of their faculty members had been attracted to predominantly white colleges. Now, the fiscal crisis left the Negro colleges without endowments and with few wealthy alumni, while the majority of their 160,000 students came from poor families and needed scholarship aid. Responding to the crisis, the Ford Foundation announced that it would spend $100 million over a six-year period to help about 10 of these colleges improve their academic and fiscal condition.

The California Supreme Court brought the school financing issue into focus on August 30 when it held that relying exclusively on real estate taxes was creating intolerable inequities in the amount of money spent by different districts to educate a child. In a case that involved the wealthy district of Beverly Hills and the less affluent Baldwin Park, the court found that the children's rights to "equal protection under the law" were violated in the poorer system. It ordered lower courts to seek more equitable methods of school financing. Similar suits have been filed in several other states.

In Chicago, the prospect of lopping 12 days off the public school schedule during 1971 was avoided only hours before the plan was to take effect. The means was to borrow $20 million from the 1972 portion of the budget. Even before that move was decided on, a 1972 deficit of $64 million was expected. And $40 million in contractually obligated raises for teachers was due Jan. 1, 1972. The superintendent of the Chicago system, the nation's third largest, commented: "With all these problems, we have not been improving our educational programs as we have to. We have been paring them down to save money."

The majority opinion in a New York state commission report called for state financing of all public schools. Indications were that the traditional system of school support will be subject to extensive reappraisal. See Section One, FOCUS ON EDUCATION.

Teachers and Enrollments. The total number of teachers at all levels was reported at 2.98 million in 1971, including 617,000 college faculty members. The national ratio of pupils per teacher (including auxiliary instructional personnel) stood at 22.3, the lowest in history. The National Education Association reported a surplus of more than 40,000 teachers. Teachers' salaries reached a national average of $9,200, while those of college and university faculty members averaged just below $13,000.

The total enrollment in both public and private institutions went up for the 27th consecutive year to 60.2 million. This was about 1 per cent above the 1970 total.

There were 36.7 million enrolled in the elementary grades, from kindergarten through grade 8, a decline of about 300,000. It followed a decline of 100,000 in 1970, the first year to break the steady growth on any level. About 32.5 million were in public schools, and the remaining 4.2 million attended private and parochial schools. Enrollment in public high schools, grades 9 through 12, was 13.6 million. Another 1.4 million were enrolled in nonpublic high schools. College and university estimates placed the total enrollment at 8.4 million, with 2.1 million in privately financed institutions.

The 1971 high school graduating class totaled 3.1 million students. The number of earned degrees for the 1971-1972 academic year was projected as follows: bachelor's and first-professional, 903,000; master's, 238,000; and doctorates, 34,600. Each level set a record.

School Expenditures. Public and private elementary and secondary schools spent an estimated

Charred school buses offer mute testimony to the violence of the
protest against school busing that broke out in August in Pontiac, Mich.

$54.1 billion in 1971-1972, compared with $49.6-billion in the previous fiscal year. Colleges and universities spent about $31 billion, an increase of $3-billion. Total education expenditures amounted to about 8 per cent of the gross national product of the United States, compared with 7.5 per cent the year before.

The federal government's subsidy for education was still growing. It rose from $8.6 billion in 1970 to $10.1 billion in 1971, and was expected to reach $11.4 billion in the fiscal year ending June 30, 1972. The average per-pupil expenditure in the nation's public schools had doubled during the past 10 years, reaching $858.

Parochial schools suffered setbacks. The Supreme Court of the United States, in cases from Rhode Island and Pennsylvania, held that public support of religious schools is unconstitutional. A national survey showed that Roman Catholic parochial schools continued to decline in number. It predicted that about 1,800 of the present 11,351 would be closed by 1975. More than 400 were reported to have closed during the past year, some to consolidate, but others because of lack of funds.

School Desegregation remained an issue of national debate. The Supreme Court, in a case from North Carolina, ruled that the use of school buses is a proper means of desegregation, provided the time children spend on buses is not excessive. President

Richard M. Nixon, however, ordered the Department of Health, Education, and Welfare, which administers and supervises the desegregation rules, to hold busing to "the minimum required by law." Harsh resistance to busing followed in several northern cities.

Open Admission. The City University of New York completed the first year of its new "open admissions" program. Under it, graduates of the city's high schools, regardless of their grades, are admitted to one of the institution's 20 campuses—some of them four-year schools and others two-year community colleges. The 1971 freshman class consisted of 40,000 students.

In the program's first year, 12 per cent of the freshman class of the senior colleges dropped out, compared with 7.7 per cent during the last year under the old requirements. But, except for severe space pressures, the institution, which enrolled almost 200,000 full- and part-time students, considered the initial results encouraging.

Remote Teaching. Under the auspices of the State University, New York opened its first "open university." It teaches its students largely by remote control—mailed assignments, television, tape recordings, and independent study. These are augmented by periodic guidance, discussion, and testing sessions with faculty members at specially designated learning centers.

EDUCATION

In another experiment, subsidized with federal funds, 20 colleges have joined in a program called University Without Walls, coordinated by Antioch College, in Ohio. Students may move from one participating campus to another, but they may also complete part of their credits in the field.

Public school reform movements focused on the British pattern called "open schools." Under that plan, pupils are encouraged to explore individually or in groups, with the teacher acting as a subtle guide rather than the presiding adult.

Women's Liberation began to have its impact on the campuses. Sex discrimination had been charged by many academic observers. The federal government reported that at least 250 specific complaints of discrimination—in employment, faculty promotions, and admission of students—had been filed and 40 investigations initiated. They were at such leading universities as Harvard, Brown, Michigan, and Wisconsin.

Too Many Doctorates. An oversupply of those with the Ph.D. degree resulted from cutbacks in research grants and a slowdown in hiring by universities, government, and industry. In reaction to the changed job market, applications to graduate schools, especially in physics and chemistry, fell off during 1971.

Unprecedented pressure for admission developed,

How Schooling Compares in 27 Areas

Metropolitan area	High School graduates per cent	College graduates per cent	Median Years in School
Atlanta	58.0	14.9	12.3
Baltimore	44.5	8.8	11.3
Boston	67.7	15.5	12.4
Buffalo	55.3	11.6	12.2
Chicago	58.4	12.6	12.3
Cincinnati	53.5	13.5	12.1
Cleveland	57.8	12.4	12.2
Columbus	65.9	14.7	12.4
Dallas	66.1	15.4	12.5
Denver	71.0	16.5	12.6
Detroit	53.2	9.3	12.1
Houston	55.6	11.9	12.2
Kansas City	61.5	12.3	12.3
Los Angeles-Long Beach	67.9	14.6	12.5
Memphis	54.6	8.5	12.1
Milwaukee	61.5	11.1	12.3
Minneapolis-St. Paul	70.6	15.3	12.5
New Orleans	48.7	10.2	11.8
New York	56.2	12.6	12.2
Newark	54.8	10.9	12.1
Philadelphia	53.8	11.9	12.1
Pittsburgh	53.8	8.7	12.1
St. Louis	48.6	9.5	11.8
San Diego	64.3	13.2	12.4
San Francisco-Oakland	71.4	18.0	12.6
Seattle	69.7	14.9	12.5
Washington, D.C.	72.9	25.4	12.7

Source: U.S. Bureau of the Census

Parochial school closings sparked protests such as this one in Colorado. Many urged financial aid for parochial schools as an economic necessity.

however, in schools of law and medicine. About 100,000 applicants took law school entrance tests in 1971, compared with 74,000 a year earlier. They competed for 35,000 places. An estimated 26,000 students applied to medical schools, compared with 24,000 in 1970, for just under 12,000 openings.

Educational Television. "Sesame Street," the program produced by the Children's Television Workshop for preschool children, concluded its second year of operations. It was widely hailed as a breakthrough in educational technology. Some authorities, though, including the British Broadcasting Corporation, found its use of repetition as a teaching method to be authoritarian.

Based on the success of the national experiment, its creators inaugurated a new program aimed at teaching youngsters between the ages of 5 and 11 how to read, as a supplement to classroom instruction. Called "The Electric Company," the five-day-a-week show had its première in October, 1971.

Student Unrest virtually dropped from the news in 1971. Some college observers reported a new mood ranging from apathy to serious but non-violent concern about national issues, possibly the result, in part, of the extension of the vote to 18-year-olds. But other observers thought that the economic pressures and concern over jobs and careers may also have turned students away from confrontation politics.

Fred M. Hechinger

EGYPT. President Anwar al-Sadat withstood a political challenge in May, 1971, that left him Egypt's undisputed leader and heir to the late President Gamal Abdel Nasser. Vice-President Aly Sabri and Interior Minister Sharawy Gomma led the challenge. Like Sadat, they were Nasser's long-time associates. They capitalized on fears that federating loosely with Libya and Syria in the Federation of Arab Republics would weaken Egypt's leadership in the Arab world. Plans for the federation had been announced on April 17.

Sabri and Gomma planned a coup to replace Sadat with a coalition, but Sadat was forewarned. On May 2, he dismissed Sabri by decree. The May 13 resignations of Gomma and other ministers failed to shake army and popular support for Sadat and his policies. A sweeping purge of government officials followed. A treason trial for 90 persons including Sabri and Gomma ended in October, with death sentences for eight. Sadat commuted the death sentences of Sabri and Gomma to life imprisonment. Sadat's new Cabinet retained Mahmoud Fawzi as prime minister and Mahmoud Riad as foreign minister, both considered moderates favoring peace with Israel.

New elections for the Arab Socialist Union (ASU), the nation's only political organization, began in July. Sadat had denounced the 1968 election as rigged. On July 23, the ASU congress elected a People's Assembly as Egypt's supreme legislature. Its prime job was to draft a new constitution.

In September, 99.98 per cent of the voters approved federation with Libya and Syria. Sadat became federation president on October 4. The new Constitution was also approved by a similar majority in September. It created a "super Cabinet" responsible directly to Sadat. The Constitution also changed Egypt's name from United Arab Republic to the Arab Republic of Egypt.

Problems Unsolved. Whether such changes could solve Egypt's long-term problems was another matter. Sadat's diplomacy produced little progress toward settling the Arab-Israeli conflict. Rising living costs and economic inequities, underlined by a steelworkers' strike, fed domestic discontent. Experts described the school system as "beyond repair."

Bright spots included two major oil discoveries in the western desert and the beginning of work on developing huge phosphate deposits. A West European consortium agreed to build a 206-mile pipeline from Port Suez to Alexandria.

Facts in Brief. Population: 35,000,000. Government: President Anwar al-Sadat; Prime Minister Mahmoud Fawzi. Monetary Unit: Egyptian pound. Foreign Trade: exports, $762,000,000; imports, $773,000,000. Principal Exports: cotton, textiles, rice. William Spencer

ELECTIONS. The scattered 1971 off-year elections produced contradictory results, and political analysts agreed that there were no clear-cut trends for either major party. In mayoral elections, the Democrats continued to hold most major cities. Black candidates did poorly, and the youth vote, cast for the first time on November 2, seemed to have no impact on most major contests.

The youth vote, with the voting age now lowered to 18, had its greatest effect in smaller cities and towns with large universities. Student-supported candidates were elected to the City Councils of Boulder, Colo., and East Lansing, Mich. Jon Crews, a 24-year-old graduate student at the University of Northern Iowa was elected mayor of Cedar Falls, Iowa, and 22-year-old Lawrence S. Dicara won a seat on Boston's City Council. Two 21-year-olds won City Council seats in Bassett, Iowa (population 152), and Marshall, Minn. (population 9,886).

Teen-agers won elective office in several small towns and villages. The incumbent mayor of Ayrshire, Iowa (population 248), was defeated by 19-year-old Jody Smith. Ron Hooker, also 19 and a student at Ashland College, won the mayoral race as a write-in candidate in Newcomerstown, Ohio. Teen-agers were elected to school boards in Pawtucket, R.I., and Bremerton, Wash.

Ohio State University students were credited with helping to unseat Maynard E. Sensenbrenner, Dem-

Egyptians gathered to hear President Anwar al-Sadat announce the resignations of nine top officials. All were arrested for their part in an attempted coup.

Patience Latting takes the oath of office on April 13, to become the mayor of Oklahoma City, Okla., and the only woman mayor of a major city in the United States.

ocratic mayor of Columbus, Ohio. Sensenbrenner, 69, had been mayor for 14 years, until his November defeat by Republican Tom Moody. The youth vote also was important in Democrat Francis X. Mc-Closkey's defeat of Republican Mayor John H. Hooker, Jr., in Bloomington, Ind. Because young people did not vote as a bloc along party lines, no one could predict how the youth vote would affect the 1972 presidential election.

The Economic Issue was a major factor in several elections. In a special Pennsylvania congressional election, Republican H. John Heinz III won by supporting President Richard M. Nixon's economic policies. However, Democrat Wendell Ford won election as Kentucky governor by criticizing the Nixon program. The special congressional election was held on November 2 to fill the seat left vacant by the death of Representative Robert J. Corbett (R., Pa.). Heinz, 33, a liberal Republican and an executive in the Heinz food-canning company, won by a 2-to-1 margin over his Democratic opponent, John E. Connelly.

Ford's victory over Republican Thomas D. Emberton returned the Kentucky governor's office to the Democrats. They had held it for 20 years prior to 1967, when Republican Louis B. Nunn was elected. Ford's election boosted to 30 the governorships under Democratic control.

The economy was also an issue in the Indianapolis

mayoral election. Republican Mayor Richard G. Lugar, a supporter of the Nixon economic program, easily defeated his Democratic challenger, John Neff.

Black Candidates were defeated in two major contests. In Mississippi, Fayette Mayor Charles Evers, a Democrat running as an independent, was badly beaten in the race for governor by William Waller, a moderate white Democrat. Arnold R. Pinkney, another black Democrat competing as an independent, lost a three-man race for mayor of Cleveland to Republican Ralph J. Perk. Perk appealed to the white ethnic vote. This was a setback for retiring Mayor Carl B. Stokes, who picked Pinkney and tried to elect him as a demonstration of black power politics. He had hoped a black victory would register on the 1972 Democratic convention. However, in Gary, Ind., black Democrat Richard G. Hatcher was re-elected mayor. He won an easy victory over Republican Theodore Nering. Black mayoral candidates also won in Englewood, N.J.; Benton Harbor, Mich.; and Kalamazoo, Mich.

The Law-and-Order Issue was tested in two mayoral contests. In Philadelphia, it enabled police commissioner Frank L. Rizzo, a Democrat, to defeat Thatcher Longstreth, a liberal Republican. Rizzo's victory was helped by his Italian ancestry, his reputation as a "tough cop," and a heavy Democratic registration.

In Boston, however, the law-and-order issue failed Representative Louise Day Hicks (D., Mass.) in her bid for mayor. Incumbent Mayor Kevin H. White coasted to a second term with a bigger margin than he won the first time they competed for the office, in 1967. Mrs. Hicks gained national prominence that year with her support of the law-and-order issue and her opposition to school busing. Her defeat in 1971 was not regarded by political observers as a weakening of these issues. Instead, it was attributed to the feebleness of her campaign in contrast to White's effective cultivation of ethnic groups.

Other Contests. In San Francisco, Joseph L. Alioto was re-elected mayor. Neither of his two principal opponents tried to exploit the fact that he had been indicted for allegedly bribing the former attorney general of Washington. Conservative Republican Harold S. Dobbs charged that Alioto had forgotten the middle-income voters. Dianne Feinstein, a left-of-center Democrat and president of the Board of Supervisors, contended that the city was no longer a safe place to live. School busing was opposed by Dobbs and backed by Mrs. Feinstein. Alioto urged the public to support busing until the courts settled the issue.

In Jersey City, N.J., Paul Jordan, a 30-year-old reform candidate, was elected mayor in November. This ended nearly half a century of political domination by the scandal-ridden Hudson County Democratic organization. Jordan defeated Morris T.. Longo, the organization-backed candidate; Thomas

Gangemi, Jr., son of a former mayor; and 14 other candidates. Jordan will complete the 18 months remaining in the term of former Mayor Thomas J. Whelan, who was sentenced in July to 15 years in prison on federal extortion conspiracy charges.

Henry E. Howell, a Democrat running as an independent was elected lieutenant governor of Virginia. He defeated Democrat George J. Kostel and Republican George P. Shafran.

Richard J. Daley won an unprecedented fifth four-year term as mayor of Chicago on April 6. The Democratic organization, fueled by jobs and money, was credited with Daley's landslide victory of 417,728 votes over Richard E. Friedman, an independent who ran with Republican support.

In other 1971 mayoral contests, Democrat William. D. Shaefer defeated Republican Ross Z. Pierpont in Baltimore. In San Diego, Republican Pete Wilson won a nonpartisan contest for mayor. Richard Marriott was re-elected mayor of Sacramento, Calif., and television sportscaster Wes Wise, an independent, was elected mayor of Dallas. The first Japanese-American mayor of a major U.S. city, Norman Y. Mineta, was elected in San Jose, Calif. Patience Latting, a 53-year-old housewife, was elected mayor of Oklahoma City.   William McGaffin

See also AMERICAN PARTY; DEMOCRATIC PARTY; REPUBLICAN PARTY; STATE GOVERNMENT.

ELECTRIC POWER. See ENERGY.

ELECTRONICS. Continuing refinements of existing methods highlighted developments in 1971. Some of these represented dramatic increases in technical sophistication. Among the most notable are a new electron microscope—the world's most powerful—and, at the opposite end of the scale of magnitudes, the world's largest radio telescope.

The giant new radio telescope is located at Westerbork, in the Netherlands, and, in the first year of its operation, it proved that radio waves emitted from distant galaxies can "picture" the heavens almost as accurately as the light waves seen through ordinary optical telescopes. Because radio waves from outer space reveal quite different data from those obtainable by visible light, however, scientists expect that this great electronic instrument will reveal heretofore unobtainable information about the nature of the universe. The giant radio telescope is now exploring galaxies so distant that the radio waves have been traveling for 12 million years before reaching the earth.

Exploring the microcosm will be greatly facilitated by the powerful new electron microscope at the University of Osaka in Japan. It can magnify up to 100,000 times. Built by Hitachi Company, the microscope uses extremely high voltages, permitting the image-forming electron beams to penetrate far thicker specimens of living tissue than any previous microscope of this kind, which is an important advantage in biological and medical research.

Space Exploration also stands to benefit from new electronic advances. Honeywell has developed a superior navigation device that consists of ring lasers embedded in a glass sphere. The ring-shaped lasers take the place of mechanical gyroscopes for sensing motion. The laser gyroscope is virtually immune to disturbance by shock or vibration, unlike the mechanical gyroscopes previously used for the inertial guidance of spacecraft and airplanes. The mechanical sensing devices often were sources of navigation errors.

Air Pollution. Electronics is also playing a growing role in efforts to combat air pollution. The Dutch Philips Corporation introduced an electronic air-pollution detector in the Netherlands that "sniffs" air samples, analyzes them for sulfur dioxide content, and automatically reports the result to a central computer. The computer then issues a special warning when the situation threatens to become critical. The device operates by electrochemical reactions set off by the pollutant, which generate an electric current proportional to the amount of pollution.

Production Technology. Electronics played an increasing part in 1971 in automated manufacturing methods. Chevrolet's Vega assembly plant in Lordstown, Ohio, introduced "Unimate" machines with electronic memories capable of "learning" from a skilled welder. The human welder guides the torch the first time it welds car bodies. The machine then automatically repeats the operation on subsequent jobs, assembling the entire Vega body with an accuracy of 1/16th of an inch.

A new device developed by Radio Corporation of America (RCA) has increased the efficiency of computers, telephone exchanges, and radar systems. It depends largely on speeding up switching operations. The fastest switch ever designed, the device can open or close a circuit in less than a billionth of a second. The switching action is accomplished without moving parts by using a solid state device.

A New Sound. Four-channel or "quadrasonic" records, which present music in an all-around perspective with separate stereo sound channels behind, as well as in front of, the listener, became a reality in 1971. A variety of four-channel sound equipment became available in retail shops. Four sound channels are compressed into a single record groove on these disks by an electronic method called matrixing. In effect, this method mixes the signals together for recording and then "unscrambles" them in playback so that they emerge separately—to be fed into four amplifiers and speakers. Unfortunately, the rival systems introduced by different companies are not entirely compatible.   Hans Fantel

EL SALVADOR. See LATIN AMERICA.

EMPLOYMENT. See ECONOMY, THE; EDUCATION; LABOR; SOCIAL SECURITY; SOCIAL WELFARE.

ENERGY. The electric utility industry added another 32 gigawatts (gw) to net generating capability in 1971, raising the U.S. total to 380 gw at year's end. Even after spending $15 billion for expansion, the industry's kilowatt-hour (kwh) sales were 3 per cent less than the average of 8 per cent for the previous five years. The drop in sales reflected the year's industrial slowdown; about 45 per cent of all utility sales are for industrial uses.

The U.S. Fuel Crisis. The availability for use of key fuels, rather than an overall world shortage, was the major problem during the year. Particularly crucial was the shortage of gas. New customers had to be turned down, and many old customers were rationed during the year. President Richard M. Nixon took an encouraging step in June when he announced a $20-million federal allocation, to be tacked onto an industry commitment of $10 million for augmenting the program to extract natural gas from coal.

The world fuel crisis was marked by an energy imbalance. The rich, readily usable fuels are abundant in those parts of the globe remote from industrial and population centers. A 1971 study reported a huge potential of 25 gw of hydroelectric potential power untapped in the Congo.

Russia was building two 48-inch gas lines from its north Siberian wells that eventually will alleviate some of the imbalance in Asia and Europe. One line will carry gas to the Ural Mountains to supply the growing industrial complex in that part of Siberia. The second line will supply Europe. The lines were being pushed hard above, on, and under the tundra, using European-supplied pipe to be paid for at a future date in gas.

Oil Industry Problems. With legislators pushing for wide use of less-polluting, low-sulfur fuels, the oil industry continued to build refineries that can remove the sulfur from the fuel. But progress is slow. More than two years are needed to design and build even a modest-sized refinery.

Crude oil entered the energy picture in 1971 when some utilities and users began to burn it as a substitute for low-sulfur fuel. Low-sulfur crude oil is cheaper and more plentiful although it presents some hazards because of its high volatility. About 85 per cent of all crude low-sulfur fuel oil is consumed on the East Coast where sulfur limits are appreciably tighter. A 1971 nationwide survey by the Environmental Protection Agency showed that New York City, Philadelphia, and the state of New Jersey, allowed only 0.3 per cent sulfur as the upper limit for residual fuel. Some other states and cities permit the burning of fuel oils exceeding 2 per cent sulfur.

The Electric Utility Industry had a modest year measured in terms of revenue, profit, and kilowatt hours (kwh) output. Industry figures for the year ending Dec. 31, 1971, were:

	1970	1971	% gain
	(in millions)		
Total capacity (kw)	367	389	9.1
Total production (kwh)	1,633,000	1,721,000	5.4
Utilities' output (kwh)	1,530,000	1,618,000	5.8
Utilities' revenue*	$18,610	$21,000	11.5

*For investor-owned companies

Electric utilities were expected to continue to expand during the 1970s. The industry spent an estimated $15 billion in 1971, and was expected to spend $23.1 billion by 1980 and $37.2 billion by 1990. The total for these two decades was expected to reach $490.6 billion, measured in 1971 dollars, or nearly $700 billion at the anticipated rate of inflation.

Underground Transmission showed a modest gain of 79 miles of new installation in 1971. A sharp increase was scheduled for 1972, however, as the utility industry tried to extend its system in this way. A total of 1,436 miles are planned by 1977. Although it is costly, underground transmission was a high-priority item in utility plans.

Gas Turbines continued to make an important contribution. The turbines were rushed into service when conventional generating capacity was expected to fall short of meeting summer peak-load requirements. More than 20 per cent of new generating capacity, some 6,500 megawatts (mw), were gas-turbine driven. One problem with gas-turbine exhausts is nitrogen oxide air pollution. However, a promising method of cutting emissions by nearly

Charles F. Luce of Consolidated Edison stands beside "Big Allis," million-kw generator in New York. It returned to service in June, 1971, after 10 months of repairs.

75 per cent was announced by General Electric (GE) in October. The GE plan calls for injecting steam into the combustion zone of a standard 60-mw power plant. The steam, totaling about 15 per cent of the fuel input, reduces temperature at the flame tip. GE claimed a reduction in harmful emissions, and an increase in the mass-flow of gas, thus increasing turbine output some 30 per cent.

Nuclear Power made little contribution in 1971. In fact, a drop in nuclear power plant construction activity forced the crash installation of many new gas turbines during the year. Delays that have become a part of nuclear plant construction—equipment availability, Atomic Energy Commission (AEC) licensing, objections by environmental groups—were expected to hold in the near future. There were 22 nuclear power plants in full operation in the United States in 1971.

Fossil-Fueled Plants, expected to carry most of the electrical load in the foreseeable future, grew in number in 1971. These plants generally take less time to build and do not have the obstacles that slow up nuclear-plant construction.

"Big Allis," the giant turbine generator in Queens, New York, out of service since July, 1970, had its second failure in January, less than three hours after its start-up. The huge, trouble-plagued Consolidated Edison (Con Ed) unit was started on January 24 and carried a modest load until electrical relays tripped the unit off line. Examination disclosed a breakdown in the stator-winding insulation, a different problem from the problem that caused the first breakdown. With a new stator rewinding, Big Allis did not get back into operation until early June. During the summer, a bearing failure took the trouble-prone unit off the line once again.

Environmental Concerns affected all electric utilities in 1971. Although attempts were made to reduce pollution during the year, industry spokesmen objected to what they believed were extreme proposals. Among these were proposals to abolish piston engines within five years, and develop a near-pure stack gas. The industry maintained that such goals must be tempered with the cold logic of engineering feasibility. Also, they questioned the public's willingness to pay the cost required to design, develop, and construct the necessary engineering alternatives.

Environmentalists countered that improved design was only a part of the problem. They rated checking unbridled growth as equally important. The view was perhaps expressed best by Professor Barry Commoner of Washington University in St. Louis, a leading environmentalist. "The environment got there first," he asserted, "and it's up to the economic system to adjust to the environment. Any economic system must be compatible with the environment, or it will not survive."

At year-end, however, there was little real sign

U.S. Power-Generating Capacity

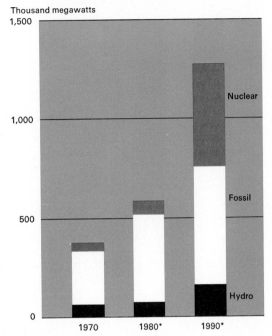

Thousand megawatts

*Projected
Source: Federal Power Commission

of any reduction in demand for goods and services.

Consumption of all energy sources was rising at an estimated 3 to 4 per cent a year, a rate that outstrips population growth. According to some projections, by the year 2000, some 320 million Americans (compared to 203 million in 1971) will be using from three to four times the present energy output. Both industry leaders and environmentalists agreed that this was the real issue.

Natural Power Sources. Early in the year, a United Nations report suggested using harnessed tides, dammed-up rivers, and underground heat to give the world pollution-free power. The report also speculated that "usable world resources of *geothermal energy* (the earth's internal heat) may have been considerably underestimated." The geothermal resources of California's Imperial Valley alone, the report said, could produce 20,000 mw of electricity, and Russian geothermal resources exceed its combined coal, peat, oil, and gas resources.

Energy Conferences. Some 1,900 energy specialists from throughout the world, met in July in Bucharest, Romania, for the World Energy Conference. They agreed that "for the next three decades, we will be in a race for our lives to meet our energy demands." But they held that recent oil and natural gas discoveries in the Arctic and the continental shelves of the world could fill the expected increase in demand by the year 2000. It was

U.S. Atomic Energy Plants

- Operable (22)
  (Kilowatt capacity 9,131,800)
- Being built (55)
  (Kilowatt capacity 46,605,000)
- Planned (49)
  (Kilowatt capacity 48,524,000)

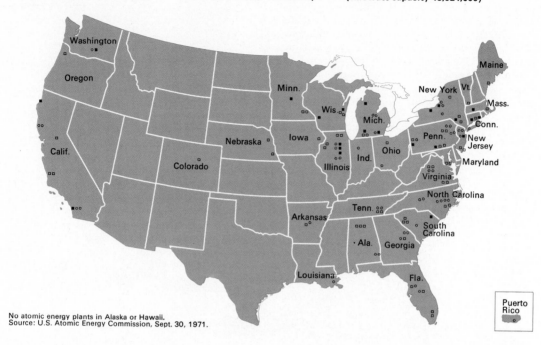

No atomic energy plants in Alaska or Hawaii.
Source: U.S. Atomic Energy Commission, Sept. 30, 1971.

generally agreed that nuclear power was still too expensive. Soviet delegate Pyotr S. Neporozhny, the outgoing president of the World Energy Conference, estimated "that by the end of the century, nuclear fuel will constitute [only] about 20 per cent of all energy fuels used." Neoporozhny claimed in an interview after the conference that he remained an optimist. "After a party when you have drunk all the bottles," he said, "there's always another half bottle of vodka to be found somewhere."

At the International Conference on the Peaceful Uses of Atomic Energy held in Geneva, Switzerland, in September, the future use of nuclear energy was vigorously discussed. Questions from the floor often brought tart replies from engineers representing the nuclear industry. The general conclusion reached was that nuclear energy for electric-power production should receive high priority in the coming years. A Russian spokesman warned of possible contamination of the world's oceans from nuclear power plants and called for effective measures to prevent it. He said the main danger was from radioactive zones in international waters and claimed there was a marked tendency toward an increase in their numbers, intensity, and dimensions. Other speakers tended to take a more defensive stance. The AEC's delegate dismissed the environmentalists, saying they were motivated by fear, misinformation, and misconceptions." He later praised

what he called "constructive criticism" from "responsible" groups.

Costs of new pollution-reduction equipment forced electric utility managers to take a fresh approach in pricing their product in 1971. They abandoned the old goal of producing a kwh at the lowest cost, reflected in low rates for customers. It was being replaced by midyear by escalating rates determined partly by the costs of operating pollutant-reduction equipment.

A typical boiler produces 50,000 tons a day of flue gas containing 0.25 per cent of sulfur dioxide (SO_2). Recent advances in electrostatic-precipitator designs allow the removal of more than 99 per cent of the particulates from stack gas. A number of schemes have been advanced for decreasing SO_2 emission, but only a few showed promise. In general, utilities were seeking new sources of low-sulfur fuels rather than attempting to remove sulfur from stack gas.

Power Costs, based on a 1971 survey of 24 modern steam stations, came to about 20 per cent above the 6.04 mills-per-kwh reported in an earlier survey. The largest single contributor to the 1.16-mill hike in total energy costs was from taxes and a hike in interest rates for new securities. Another substantial contribution was a 0.43-mill rise in the cost of fuel, attributed to the scramble for more expensive cleaner-burning coal.

James J. O'Connor

ENGINEERING. Unemployment was the major concern of the engineering profession in 1971. Unionization—long a subject for purely academic discussion at professional meetings—was being seriously considered in some design and engineering offices. Government cutbacks in defense and space-related industries laid off some 100,000 highly skilled engineers and technicians in 1970 and 1971. The Labor and Housing and Urban Development departments financed an experimental program aimed at retraining several hundred unemployed engineers for public-service jobs. Unemployment also was high among electrical and mechanical engineers. Civil engineers fared best with only 4.4 per cent unemployed, according to the National Registry of Engineers. Despite action taken by the Department of Labor in February to stem the flow of foreign engineers to the United States, about 9,300 engineers—mostly in civil, mechanical, and electrical engineering—entered the country in 1971.

Engineering Enrollments. Enrollments in the nation's engineering schools declined about 2 per cent from the 240,000 undergraduates enrolled in 1970, according to the Engineering Manpower Commission (EMC) of the Engineers Joint Council. Master's-degree enrollments were the only category showing an increase. They were up 14 per cent over 1970, but were still well below 1968 levels. In spite of a growing demand for more black engineers, only 2 per cent of all U.S. engineering students were black, according to a study by Robert Kiehl, of the Newark (N.J.) College of Engineering. Women constituted only 1 per cent of the total.

Despite the gloomy employment picture among the nation's engineers, EMC figures show that their salary level over the past two years continued its annual climb of 5 per cent. The median annual income for the 230,000 engineers surveyed was $15,500 in 1971.

The salary situation for graduating engineers, however, was less bright. The College Placement Council reported that starting salaries for 1971 engineering graduates were only slightly above those of the previous year's class. For Ph.D.-level engineers just starting out, the picture was even gloomier. Employers were offering them less money than their counterparts received a year ago.

Engineer Demand. Placement officers at colleges and universities across the nation reported that companies cut their recruiting visits by from 10 to 50 per cent from last year. In addition, companies that interviewed students had fewer jobs to offer than in 1970. Some went merely to maintain campus contacts in anticipation of future manpower needs. Typically, a June report from the University of Illinois placement office showed that 22 per cent of the 286 February, 1971, engineering graduates were still unemployed, compared to 3 per cent of the 1970 graduating class. Mary E. Jessup

ENVIRONMENT. The battle for a better environment intensified in 1971 with both the extent of the effort and the scope of the problems growing. In a message to Congress on February 8, President Richard M. Nixon called for a far-reaching "program to save and enhance the environment." He urged a stringent air- and water-pollution-control program and a national land-use policy to "end the plunder of America's heritage." Most of the proposed new initiatives to regulate noise, surface and underground mining, ocean dumping, and pesticides were still under congressional consideration at year's end.

In the second annual report of the Council on Environmental Quality (CEQ) on August 6, the President said, "I am pleased we have made considerable progress toward achieving our environmental objectives in the past 12 months." The President cited a decline in total emissions from automobiles and the use of persistent pesticides, but he conceded that the level of total pollutants is still rising.

Reflecting the concern about the costs of pollution control, the President warned, "It is simplistic to seek ecological perfection at the cost of bankrupting the very tax-paying enterprises which must pay for the social advances the nation seeks." The CEQ estimated that achieving federal antipollution standards by 1975 will cost the public and private sectors $105.2 billion. *Fortune* magazine estimated in July that American industry would spend $20 billion for direct pollution control in the next five years.

Air Pollution. The Environmental Protection Agency (EPA) published guidelines on August 14 to be followed by the states in developing plans to help clean the nation's air by mid-1975. National air quality standards for six of the most widespread air pollutants were published on April 7 under the 1970 amendments to the Clean Air Act. The states have until the end of January, 1972, to submit satisfactory plans to meet these standards.

The National Resources Defense Council, Inc., said the EPA guidelines were not as strict as originally proposed and that the EPA merely gave a "rubber stamp" to revisions imposed on it by the White House Office of Management and Budget (OMB). Consumer advocate Ralph Nader wrote to the governors of all 50 states on August 27, urging them to seek adoption of clean-air programs that would be more stringent than those required by the EPA guidelines.

Stagnated pockets of air caused an air-pollution crisis in Birmingham, Ala., on November 18, and threatened areas in the Northeast. Birmingham's count of dirty matter in the air reached 771 micrograms. The national urban average is 97. The EPA used its emergency powers under the Clean Air Act for the first time to obtain a federal court order that shut down 23 industrial plants in Birmingham. The order was lifted on November 19.

Henry Groskinsky, Life © Time Inc.

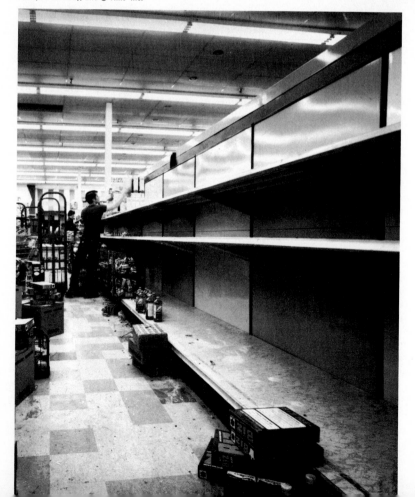

Local laws banning the use of phosphate detergents forced many stores to strip their detergent shelves almost bare. Later, federal officials said phosphates were safer than the substitutes.

The November inversion caused Pittsburgh to issue an air-pollution alert and order 29 industries to cut back on smoke emissions. In New York City, officials urged residents to limit the use of their cars.

Water Pollution. Key legislation making sweeping changes in the Federal Water Pollution Control Act of 1956 was approved 86-0 by the Senate on November 2. The legislation established a national policy barring the discharge of wastes into navigable waters by 1985, and it strengthened the use of federal permits to regulate such discharge. The bill also authorized spending $14 billion over four years to build municipal waste-treatment plants.

The Nixon Administration opposed the bill. On November 8, White House press secretary Ronald L. Ziegler said the Administration was not satisfied with much of the stringent legislation.

On April 12, a task force led by Nader charged that the federal government had failed to "reduce the level of pollution in any major body of water," despite spending $3 billion. The Senate Public Works Committee concluded in November that the national effort to reduce and control water pollution has been inadequate in every vital aspect.

Federal health and environmental officials on September 15 urged consumers to go back to using detergents containing phosphates. Phosphates have been linked to pollution that damages lakes and streams, and several states and major cities banned the use of phosphate detergents.

Surgeon General Jesse L. Stainfeld, however, said that the health dangers involved in swallowing or inhaling the substitutes were far greater than the environmental dangers posed by phosphates. Government officials expressed concern over the health hazards connected with such substitutes as NTA (nitrilotriacetic acid) and caustic substances, such as carbonates and silicates. The government's reversal created confusion. Many state and local officials differed sharply with the new federal approach and said they would continue to enforce antiphosphate curbs.

On September 24, the EPA asked the Department of Justice to prosecute 30 alleged industrial polluters. The action was taken against firms that had failed to apply for permits to discharge wastes in navigable waters.

Three members of Congress said on November 5 that the Armco Steel Company's contact with the White House over a court order that it stop dumping wastes into the Houston ship channel amounted to a "fix." Officials of EPA, which had obtained the court order, denied any improper influence. The original order of September 17 was amended on November 4 to permit the discharge to continue until the summer of 1972 while the company developed a system to control the discharge.

Solid Wastes. Under the Resource Recovery Act of 1970, which puts new emphasis on recycling solid wastes, the federal government changes its procurement specifications to require that paper purchased by federal agencies contain a specified amount of recycled material. More than 1,000 open dumps were closed under EPA's "Mission 5,000" drive to replace them with better methods of disposal, such as sanitary landfills.

Pesticide Control. Comprehensive legislation to replace the Federal Environmental Pesticide Control Act was proposed by President Nixon on February 8. On November 9, the House of Representatives approved a bill that environmental groups claimed was a retreat from effective pesticide regulation. The environmentalists said they would work in the Senate to toughen the bill.

In January, environmental groups won a federal court decision that pesticide cancellation notices should be issued for any substantial question of safety. Under this directive, EPA issued notices of cancellation for DDT, aldrin, dieldrin, and Mirex. Because of the complex appeals process, a final decision on banning these pesticides was not expected until sometime in 1972.

Energy. The conflicting demands for development of more energy resources on the one hand, and for the preservation of ecological balance on the other, led to a number of sharp clashes between environmentalists and the power industry. Environmental groups contended that smog from power plants in the Four Corners area of Colorado, Utah, New Mexico, and Arizona threatens Indian reservations and the Grand Canyon and other national park areas. On June 2, they asked the courts to delay power development in the area until a detailed environmental impact statement is filed.

In a landmark decision, a U.S. Appeals Court ruled on July 23 that the Atomic Energy Commission must investigate the environmental impact of nuclear plants before they are licensed. Action on the Administration's proposed Power Plant Siting Act, which would call for a long-range environmental review of power plant locations, was delayed in Congress when conservationists and industry spokesmen clashed.

Alaskan Pipeline. On January 13, the Department of the Interior issued an environmental statement on the 789-mile, $2-billion pipeline proposed to move oil across Alaska from the 10-billion-barrel oil field on the state's North Slope. The report said the pipeline should be constructed because it is "essential" to United States security.

In hearings in Washington, D.C., and Anchorage, Alaska, in February, conservation groups challenged the pipeline proposal. A final impact statement by the Interior Department was expected to recommend construction, but the pipeline still faced court challenges from conservation organizations.   Andrew L. Newman

EQUATORIAL GUINEA. See AFRICA.

ERIM, NIHAT (1912-   ), a former law professor, became Turkey's prime minister on March 19, 1971. Military leaders had complained to President Cevdet Sunay of "anarchy, fratricide, and social unrest" and called for a government "above party politics." They threatened to "seize power directly." Erim, a political moderate, was asked to form a new government when Suleyman Demirel resigned.

At Sunay's request, Erim resigned from the Republican People's Party when he formed the new government, saying, "Under the present conditions, I think I would be more productive as an independent." He gave first priority to restoring law and order, ending unrest in the armed forces, and adopting election reforms. Erim also said he would seek "a better way to make a living" for "our producers of opium." On March 26, he announced a new, relatively young cabinet with most of its 25 members from outside parliament. Many were technical experts with little political experience. One, Mrs. Turkan Akyol, was the nation's first woman cabinet member. The National Assembly approved the cabinet on April 7.

Born near Istanbul, Erim was educated at the University of Istanbul Law School and the Sorbonne in Paris. He was a member of parliament in the late 1940s. After his defeat in the 1950 election, he became a law professor at Ankara University. In 1961 he was returned to parliament.   Ed Nelson

"The Great Spy Scandal," a British television program, claimed that this film showed a Russian diplomat picking up material left for him by a British scientist.

ESPIONAGE. Great Britain ordered the largest expulsion of diplomats in history on Sept. 24, 1971, expelling 105 Russian officials. Oleg Lyalin, 34, described as a trade delegate and agent of the Russian secret service, reportedly defected after being arrested for a traffic offense, and turned over a list of Russians who were spying in Great Britain.

In Poland, Jean-Gabriel Auvray, 45, a code clerk in the French secret service, reinforced the conclusion of intelligence officers that electronics have not entirely displaced old-fashioned spy methods. Unhappy with the salary that scarcely provided for his seven children, Auvray fell under the spell of buxom Kristina Symanska, the attractive Polish maid who cleaned his office in Warsaw.

Auvray handled coding and the diplomatic pouch. But he hated Warsaw, and his superior, who was also having an affair with Kristina, constantly hounded him. He began to drink too much. In anger, Auvray told Kristina that he was disgusted with the French, and he offered to help Polish intelligence. She introduced him to a Polish colonel who paid him about $400 and promised $100 a month for his code books and other information. Auvray was tried in Paris and sentenced on January 20 to 13 years in jail.

In Lausanne, Switzerland, an engineer, Alfred Frauenknecht, 44, was sentenced to 4½ years in jail April 23 for selling secret blueprints of the Mirage jet engine to Israel. He admitted receiving about $200,000 for about two tons of documents.

A Russian Scientist Defected at the Paris air show May 27. Anatoly Fedoseyev slipped away to London, and reportedly took important technical intelligence on Russian missiles and space developments with him. Some reports later said his real name is Ignatily Alexandrovitch Nikitrine.

News stories described an elaborate scheme designed by British intelligence to spirit him out of France. British and U.S. intelligence services, however, played down Fedoseyev's importance.

U.S. Air Force Master Sergeant Raymond C. DeChamplain, 39, was found guilty on November 12 of security violations and sentenced to 15 years in prison by a military court on Guam. He had served at the big B-52 base at Utapao, Thailand, and at Don Muang air base near Bangkok. The inquiry was announced July 25, 1971, but few details were released. United States officials said he was suspected of trying to give secrets to two Russian Embassy employees in Bangkok. They left Thailand July 20, the day before DeChamplain's arrest.

Spy Flights Halted. The United States announced on July 29 that it was halting intelligence-gathering flights over China. The move was apparently in preparation for the planned visit to China by President Richard M. Nixon. The action recalled a summit meeting planned between President

Dwight D. Eisenhower and Russian Premier Nikita S. Khrushchev in May, 1960, which was canceled after Francis Gary Powers' U-2 spy plane was shot down over Russia. The flights over China used unmanned drones and twin-jet SR-71 planes, replacements for the U-2. They are capable of flying at 2,000 mph and an altitude of more than 80,000 feet.

Japanese police announced on August 4 that they had seized a Japanese electronics salesman accused of trying to buy secrets from a U.S. Air Force enlisted man for the Russian Embassy. Kazuo Kobayashi, 40, allegedly was hired by Lieutenant Colonel Lev D. Kononow, assistant military and air attaché at the Russian Embassy in Tokyo. Kononow left August 3 for Moscow.

Pierre Golendorf, a French photographer and journalist who had lived in Cuba for three years, was sentenced to 10 years' imprisonment for espionage in Cuba for the U.S. Central Intelligence Agency, the French newspaper *Le Monde* reported on September 3. Golendorf was arrested early in 1971 as he was preparing to leave Cuba.

The U.S. Department of State said on October 18 that it had granted political asylum to Anatoly Tchebotarev, a member of a Russian trade mission to Belgium who had exposed the Soviet Union's spy apparatus there, then defected. U.S. officials refused to answer questions about any connection between Tchebotarev and Lyalin. Lloyd H. Norman

ESPOSITO, PHIL ANTHONY (1942-   ), star center of the Boston Bruins, set a new scoring record for the National Hockey League (NHL) during the 1970-1971 season. A smooth skater and passer, the husky (6 feet 1 inch, 195 pounds) Boston center scored a record 76 goals and 76 assists for a record-breaking total of 152 points. In addition, Esposito and his linemates, wings Ken Hodge and Wayne Cashman, scored a total of 336 points, the most ever amassed by one line in a NHL season. In September, 1971, Esposito signed a four-year contract paying an estimated $400,000.

Esposito was born in Sault Sainte Marie, Canada, and began playing hockey as a small boy. With his brother, Tony, now the Chicago Black Hawks' goalie, he often played in the basement of their home with their mother serving as goalie.

The Black Hawks signed Esposito when he was 14, and he entered the NHL with Chicago in 1963. He had only ordinary success until he was traded to Boston in 1967. Then he became a star.

During the 1968-1969 season, Esposito scored 49 goals, then a record for a center, and 77 assists, also a record. With defenseman Bobby Orr, he has led the Boston team from last place to the top of the NHL's East Division. Esposito won the Ross Trophy, which is awarded to the league's leading scorer, in 1969 and 1971. He also won the Hart Trophy as most valuable player in 1969. Joseph P. Spohn

ETHIOPIA. The government declared a state of emergency in January, 1971, in an effort to put down the rebel Eritrean Liberation Front (ELF), and Emperor Haile Selassi I offered amnesty to the rebels. The ELF, reportedly financed by Syria, Iraq, and Algeria, wants to establish a separate state in the predominantly Moslem province of Eritrea. The emergency restrictions applied only to Eritrea and its border with the Sudan. Ethiopia and Sudan agreed on joint border controls to deny sanctuary to ELF members fleeing into Sudan.

Renewed Student Unrest. University students went on strike in May, protesting government restrictions on the newly formed National Student Union. They were joined by secondary and vocational school students in Addis Ababa. The government then closed the university and all other schools before the end of the academic year. Public buses, which had been the main target of the student rioting, were withdrawn from service, leaving the capital without public transportation.

The student unrest underscored growing discontent in Haile Selassie's feudal kingdom. The emperor, however, remained as vigorous as ever, taking an active role in African and world affairs. In March, he opened a French-built technical college that will offer training in urban planning, hydraulic engineering, and related fields.

Ethiopia received $10 million from the International Development Association for vocational training, and $2.4 million from the World Bank for teacher training institutes. The expanded educational facilities are needed to meet a projected increase of more than 3.3 million skilled jobs under the five-year development plan that begins in 1973.

The Economy was hard hit by a drop in world coffee prices. The foreign trade deficit reached $48-million, 10 times the previous year's deficit. Nevertheless, Ethiopia's relative internal stability continued to attract aid to the country.

The United States loaned Ethiopia $3 million for agricultural development. The largest project covered 116,000 acres and affected 80,000 farmers in Ada district near Addis Ababa. The World Bank granted $11 million for dairy cooperatives, and the United Nations Development Program provided $300,000 for phase two of the Awāsh Valley water power and land resettlement scheme. A new metal-working plant and a steel pipe factory opened in Akaki. It can produce up to 18,000 tons of steel pipe a year, four times Ethiopia's present needs. The two factories will employ 340 persons. Production also began at the East Africa Aluminum Company.

Facts in Brief. Population: 26,362,000. Government: Emperor Haile Selassie I; Prime Minister T. T. Aklilou Abte-Wold. Monetary Unit: Ethiopian dollar. Foreign Trade: exports, $122,000,000; imports, $172,000,000. Principal Exports: coffee, oil-seeds, hides and skins. William Spencer

EUROPE

The European Community (Common Market) during 1971 moved sharply toward a membership of 10 nations from its charter membership of 6. Such a community could serve 250 million people in 1973 and be second only to the United States in economic power. But European countries were unable to agree on a concerted monetary policy in the face of continuing currency crises. Four-power agreement on Berlin eased tensions on the continent and advanced the prospect of an East-West security conference in 1972.

Common Market Talks. The British membership in the community seemed imminent after October 28, when Parliament voted its approval of the terms in principle (see GREAT BRITAIN). But the actual breakthrough came with a dawn champagne toast in Luxembourg on June 23 after long talks in which the terms were negotiated. Almost 10 years after its first application to join the Common Market, Great Britain's negotiations were completed at 4:30 A.M. in the 23-story Kirchberg European Center. Weary negotiators ended a 48-hour meeting with a toast to "The Ten." Technical details were left on the table and negotiations for Denmark, Ireland, and Norway–the last 3 of the 10 nations–had not then begun. Nevertheless, enlargement of the original six on Jan. 1, 1973, was taken as a foregone conclusion.

As the early morning sun streamed down on the weary officials, Belgian Foreign Minister Pierre Harmel declared, "The dawn that is breaking is the most important for Europe for many years." Britain's chief negotiator, Geoffrey Rippon, said, "This is an historic day for Europe which opens the way for great achievements."

British Negotiations had faltered earlier on such key issues as New Zealand's dairy products, British Commonwealth sugar, and the future of the pound sterling. Britain sought provisions for food imports from other Commonwealth countries, but the community's protectionist agricultural tariffs were meant to guard the market for Europe's own food producers. The breakthrough came on May 20 and 21 when British Prime Minister Edward Heath met with French President Georges Pompidou in Paris. First signs of the "new understanding" between the two countries were seen when the negotiators met on June 7 and 8. Sterling balances, the pounds held in monetary reserves in such places as Hong Kong

British Prime Minister Edward Heath, left, and French President Georges Pompidou paved the way for British entry into the Common Market at a Paris meeting in May.

and Kuwait, in effect represent unpaid debts owed by Britain. They are an advantage to Britain since there normally is little pressure for immediate settlement and the practice enhances London's position as a world financial center. But if faith in the pound weakens, such debts could be cashed in. France, particularly, feared that Common Market countries might be called on for undue financial assistance. The pound sterling problem had seemed insuperable. All proposed solutions were scotched by the French representatives. After the Heath-Pompidou meeting, however, France made a complete about-face and accepted Britain's proposals to discuss ways to reduce the pound sterling reserve role after Britain's entry. The doubts of other delegations were cut short by French Finance Minister Valery Giscard d'Estaing's acceptance of the British commitment.

France also gave way on New Zealand, enabling the Common Market to raise its offer of a guaranteed market for New Zealand from 66 per cent to 71 per cent of current levels exported to Great Britain for five years after Britain joins. Britain originally had sought 100 per cent, with France asking for a gradual reduction to zero. The way was now clear for Britain to raise its initial offer—to contribute 3 per cent of the annual Common Market budget—to meet the community request of 8.64 per cent in the first year of British membership. This will cost $300 million in 1973 and will rise eventually to $850 million in 1977. On sugar, the Common Market decided to protect the interests of developing Commonwealth sugar-producing countries after the Commonwealth Sugar Agreement expires in 1974.

Other Decisions reached over the negotiating table: British agricultural tariffs have a six-stage transitional period over five years to come into line with community tariffs. British industrial tariffs are to be phased out in $4\frac{1}{2}$ years. Free movement of labor and capital is agreed on in principle. The rules of the European Coal and Steel Community and the European Atomic Energy Community will be applied in Britain with no transitional period. Voting rights for Britain are to be the same as those for West Germany, France, and Italy. And Britain will achieve an orderly and gradual reduction of sterling balances after joining the community.

The only big issue left unsettled after June 23 was the community's fishing policy. The Six recognized the objections of Britain, Denmark, Ireland, and Norway to the provision that fishermen from each member country have access to the territorial waters of the whole community. "Safeguarding" the new members' inshore fishermen will be discussed later.

Officials said that membership negotiations with the other three applicants—Denmark, Ireland, and Norway—"are bound to enjoy the same success" as those with Britain. Work of drafting the new Treaty of Accession in five languages began as the British Parliament prepared its vote. The treaty was to be signed by the year's end and ratified by Britain and the six present members—Belgium, France, Italy, Luxembourg, the Netherlands, and West Germany. Detailed legislation would then be needed to bring British law into conformity with the market's rules.

On July 14, Benelux, an economic union linking Belgium, the Netherlands, and Luxembourg, signed a trade agreement with Russia. The first between a Western European group and Russia, it was considered a possible blow to the barriers between the Common Market and the Soviet Union.

Financial Crises. Europe failed to solve its monetary problems in financial crises in May and August. The first was caused when an estimated $1 billion in foreign money flowed into West Germany. Germany wanted all Common Market currencies to float in unison against the U.S. dollar, but France rejected this plan, and the individual countries then made their own arrangements. Germany and the Netherlands decided to float their currencies for an indefinite period. The Swiss franc was revalued upwards by 7 per cent and the Austrian schilling by 5.05 per cent. Belgium pegged its franc to the dollar at its previous parity.

Efforts to adopt a common monetary policy failed again on August 15 when President Richard M. Nixon suspended convertibility of the dollar into gold, imposed a 10 per cent temporary surcharge on imported goods, and announced tax measures to encourage U.S. exports. Emergency meetings of the European Community's Council of Ministers and Commission could not agree on concerted action to avert serious damage to trade in Europe.

At a 16-Hour Meeting in Brussels on August 19 and 20, the Council of Ministers agreed to let member states choose between fixed and free rates of exchange in relation to the dollar. Germany continued to let the Deutsche mark float; the Italian lira fluctuated within wider margins; the Netherlands, Belgium, and Luxembourg operated a joint "float" for capital transactions while imposing a fixed rate for trade transactions. This two-tier system was also adopted by France. Britain supported Germany in opposing the two-tier method, while allowing the pound to float against the dollar. This approach created chaos in foreign exchanges.

Common Market Commission President Franco Maria Malfatti warned that common decisions must be taken to create an economic and monetary union. "Our defense of our interests as Europeans and the contribution we can make will be proportionate to our solidarity and the unity with which we act," he said. Vice-President Raymond Barre said the meetings had failed. He added, "Hope cannot altogether be lost that in the coming months the

community countries may reconcile their views and agree on action which will preserve the operation of the Common Market and contribute to the establishment of a new monetary system."

The first steps in an international trade and monetary settlement came on December 14 in a meeting between presidents Nixon and Georges Pompidou of France that led three days later to a broad realignment of currencies. The dollar was devalued by 8.6 per cent in terms of gold, the German mark revalued upward by 4.6 per cent, and the Japanese yen by 8 per cent. The net effect was a dollar devaluation of 12 per cent. See INTERNATIONAL TRADE AND FINANCE.

Toward *Détente*. A four-power settlement on Berlin, signed on September 3, eased tensions in Europe. Ambassadors from Britain, France, Russia, and the United States agreed that Berlin should become a four-power responsibility, with greater access from west to east. This cleared the way for detailed negotiations between the two Germanys and for West German ratification of the 1970 treaties with Russia and Poland.

More important, it led to hopes of an early East-West security conference. Calls for these talks go back to 1964 when Foreign Secretary Adam Rapacki of Poland suggested a European security conference. The Warsaw Pact countries supported the suggestion, and it has remained a constant theme of Russian and East European policy statements. But the North Atlantic Treaty Organization (NATO), while interested in easing tensions and reducing forces, has been cautious. In June, the NATO Council of Ministers said that such a meeting could only follow a Berlin settlement. See GERMANY, FEDERAL REPUBLIC OF (WEST).

In September, West German Chancellor Willy Brandt went to Yalta for talks with Russia's Communist Party Secretary Leonid I. Brezhnev. On October 5, NATO asked Manlio Brosio, its former secretary-general, to "explore" chances for talks on East-West troop reductions in Europe.

SALT Talks. The fifth round of the Strategic Arms Limitation Talks (SALT) ended in Helsinki, Finland, on September 24 with a communiqué declaring that "certain areas of common ground" had been achieved. Discussions included limitations on antiballistic missile systems and strategic offensive arms. "A clearer understanding has been achieved," the communiqué added.

In Geneva, Switzerland, a revised draft treaty on the prohibition of biological weapons was tabled on September 28 in disarmament talks by the NATO and Warsaw Pact nations. The revision banned the use of biological weapons under any circumstances. A final draft was sent to the United Nations General Assembly.

Malta-NATO Crisis. NATO withdrew its Mediterranean naval headquarters from Malta to Naples,

Italy, in August, at the request of the newly elected Maltese prime minister, Dom Mintoff. Negotiations continued on terms for continued NATO use of Maltese military installations.

An issue in the Maltese general election on June 13 had been its continued association with the Western Alliance, strengthened under G. Borg Olivier's Nationalist government and threatened by the known wish of Mintoff, Malta's Labour Party leader, for closer ties with Libya. Maltese voters elected, by a single seat, the island's first Labour government since its independence in 1964.

Ten days after the election, Admiral Gino Birindelli left his NATO command in Malta. He was said to be "unacceptable" to the new government. At the end of June, Malta nullified a 1964 defense agreement under which Great Britain paid $12.5-million for island facilities, including those for NATO naval, air, and land forces. In negotiations with the British, Mintoff sought to separate Britain's needs in Malta from NATO's.

Britain and its NATO allies offered to increase the rent for the island bases to $23 million. Mintoff, pressing for a better offer, withheld duty-free gasoline from British forces. The NATO nations debated how far they could help Britain in negotiating a new agreement when Mintoff demanded $72 million for continued use of military facilities. Britain

offered $22 million and Libya threatened to outbid Britain. Agreement was reached on September 23, when Britain agreed to pay $23.5 million, with a similar sum to come from other NATO countries.

Fighting Power. Imbalance of fighting power was highlighted by a report of the International Institute of Strategic Studies showing that the Warsaw Pact countries have three times as many tanks in Europe and 2,500 more tactical aircraft than NATO. General Andrew Goodpaster, supreme allied commander in Europe, described the Russian force on September 24 as "far exceeding defensive needs" and "in marked contrast to a policy of *deténte*."

In October, former Netherlands Foreign Minister Joseph Luns succeeded Manlio Brosio as NATO secretary-general. Brosio was appointed to explore possibilities of force reductions.

The Economy. Inflationary tendencies in most countries hurt European economic prospects. Twice during the year, the Organization for Economic Cooperation and Development warned that unless price increases were held within the rate experienced in the early 1960s, countries would find it hard to meet growth targets. The International Monetary Fund listed 14 countries with high inflation. Britain had the worst record with an 8.8 per cent rise on the basis of consumer price indexes.

The Changing European Community (EC)

■ EC members

▨ Candidates for admission to EC

▨ EFTA members

Miles
0   250   500   750

The ambassadors of France, Great Britain, Russia, and the United States signed
an agreement in Berlin on September 3 easing tensions in the divided city.

Sweden followed with 8 per cent. The UN Economic Commission for Europe forecast that economic growth rates in Western Europe would decline for the second successive year, with private consumption carrying most of the "rather modest expansion."

Fishing Limits. Iceland, where a new coalition government replaced the 12-year-old governing coalition in July, announced extension of its fishing limit to cover the continental shelf. The shelf extends 50 to 70 miles from Iceland's coast. Britain's delegate, John Simpson, told the UN Committee on the Peaceful Uses of the Seabed meeting in Geneva that this unilateral action was of grave concern for all who hoped for a success at the Law of the Sea Conference in 1973.

Tourist expenditures in Europe increased rapidly during the year, contributing 6 per cent to the total exports of goods and services. Tourism earned $10.4 billion. Eased restrictions on travel allowances in France helped the expansion, although strikes in both France and Italy discouraged expenditures in those countries and slowed tourism's growth.

No Vote for Women. In March, the all-male electorate of Liechtenstein decided by only 80 votes, 1,897 to 1,817, not to allow women to vote. The decision left the tiny principality the only country in Europe where women cannot vote.   Kenneth Brown

EXPLOSION. See DISASTERS.

FAIRS AND EXPOSITIONS. A thousand trade fairs and specialized exhibitions in more than 60 countries were included in more than 10,000 local, regional, national, and international fairs held throughout the world in 1971. Through the Department of Commerce, the United States exhibited at 19 international trade fairs and organized 58 exhibits of U.S. products in U.S. trade centers abroad.

Focusing attention on markets in developing countries, the Department of Commerce also began building a network of regional trade development centers in key developing countries, each of which serves several markets. The first unit in the network, the Southeast Asian Trade Development Center, opened in February in Bangkok, Thailand. It serves Formosa, Hong Kong, Indonesia, Malaysia, the Philippines, and Thailand.

Another U.S. program brought American suppliers and foreign buyers together in New York City at industry-sponsored "Visit, Investigate, Purchase" expositions. Two were held in 1971, a Design Engineering Show in April and a Chemical Industries Exposition in December. The U.S. Travel Service, an agency of the Commerce Department, sponsored travel trade marts in Chicago and Miami. About 100 foreign and 100 U.S. firms had representatives at the Miami meeting. Nearly $500,000 in travel services were sold there by the U.S. firms and more than $8 million in sales were expected from future commitments. The Chicago meeting, held in July, attracted 110 American and 175 foreign firms, and resulted in $1.1 million in on-the-spot sales and $4.2 million committed for the future.

The Paris Air Show in May was the largest aeronautical and space exposition in history. A million visitors viewed the 583 exhibits from 17 countries. Highlights of the show were the Russian supersonic airliner TU-144; the Soviet V-12, world's largest helicopter; and the Lockheed C-5A Galaxy cargo plane, the largest aircraft in the world and never before seen in France.

The Paris Automobile Show, held from October 7 to 17, drew 700,000 persons to view 1,000 exhibits from 22 countries. A million visitors had been expected, but a Paris subway strike held down attendance at the show.

The Frankfurt (West Germany) Book Fair, which opened its doors for the 23rd time in the postwar era, drew a collection of 270,000 books, including 78,000 new titles. The fair was staggering in its variety, with 3,522 exhibits from 58 countries. A council was created in 1970 (with the consent of the organizers of the fair, the German Publishers Association), to avert the violence that had marked the fair during the preceding three years. This council closed an exhibit of pro-Nazi books, but voted against purging the exhibition of works defending the governments of Greece, Spain, and Portugal.

More than 7 million people visited "Man and His World" during its three-month summer run in Montreal, and for the first time there was no admission charge. Half of the visitors came from the United States. More than 330,000 saw the American folk-art show, whose major sponsor was the Smithsonian Institution of Washington, D.C. The exhibit was coordinated by Disneyland Productions. In June, for example, there were performances by an Arizona cowboy singer, an Arkansas blues shouter, a blues pianist from Chicago, a Cajun band from Louisiana, and a Virginia string band.

The first U.S. travel exhibit in Russia opened in October at Leningrad's Systemotechnika '71. It featured Walt Disney's *America the Beautiful* in an air-supported theater that used a sophisticated nine-screen, nine-projector, nine-speaker audio-visual technique.

200th Birthday Party. Under the aegis of the U.S. Bicentennial Commission, cities and states across the United States are planning special events and programs for the bicentennial period that continues through 1983. Instead of one Expo 76, many will be held throughout the United States in a truly national celebration. Spokane, Wash., will hold the "World's Greatest Ecological Exposition" in 1974, which will also celebrate the cleaning-up of the Spokane River. An Air Expo is planned for the Washington, D.C., Dulles International Airport.

Boston will commemorate the event with Prologue '75 in 1975, and San Francisco will celebrate with a Mini-Culture Expo. An International Food Fair is planned for 1976 in Des Moines, Iowa, and a Marine Expo will be held in Hawaii. Though each state and some cities have already set up their own bicentennial planning groups, the U.S. commission in Washington, D.C., is the clearing house and ultimate judge in determining official events.

Disney World. For sheer size, excitement, and diversity, the year's major exhibition was Disney World. "Magic Kingdom," a huge, $400-million hotel-resort-amusement park-exhibit complex in Orlando, Fla., opened on October 1, and is expected to draw 10 million visitors and $100 million during its first year of operation. The $80-million hotel has 1,500 rooms and a monorail train that runs through its lobby. Disney World is more than 170 times as large as Disneyland in Anaheim, Calif., which took in $84 million during 1970. Disney World represents the largest recreation enterprise ever undertaken by a single company. Other phases of the total five-year Disney World development plan include a leisure-oriented residential community, an industrial park, an executive airport, and the Experimental Prototype Community of Tomorrow, the late Walt Disney's vision of a future community. See TRAVEL.   Lynn Beaumont

FARM MACHINERY. See MANUFACTURING.

FASHION. Irresolution, compromise, a swing to extremes, and excursions into the past characterized clothing styles in 1971 as fickle fashion and capricious consumer tried to reach accord. Zealously responding to outcries against the midi, designers in Paris, New York City, and just about every other major fashion center in the world shortened 1970's long hemlines to the knees. They decreed that peasants, cossacks, gypsies, and all ethnic-flavored clothes were out of fashion.

The "costume party" was to be replaced by "civilized classics"—clean-cut, ladylike silhouettes in traditional fabrics. Again, the fashion establishment was surprised by resistance. Sweeping city streets at high noon were skirts that grazed the anklebone—skirts that designers had intended for wear in the evening, for entertaining at home. The year's most extreme and curious fashion flash, hot pants, also "came up from the streets," which in trade terminology means they originated outside the design rooms of couturiers.

The overall mood of the Western world was reflected in two fashion trends. The nostalgia wave brought back a taste for nautical insignia and the movie-star glamour of the 1940s. The anticipation of culture contact with China prompted American designers to include several Chinese-inspired evening gowns in their collections. They became immediate sellers with socialites.

La Grande Demoiselle

CHANEL, Gabrielle Bonheur, better known as "Coco"; born, Auvergne province, France, Aug. 19, 1883; died, Paris, Jan. 10, 1971; inspiration for Broadway musical Coco, *which opened Dec. 18, 1969. Produced by Frederick Brisson. Lyrics by Allan Jay Lerner. Music by André Previn. Starring Katharine Hepburn.*

Coco Chanel, a French dressmaker, swung women from the bustles and the hobbles, the trussing and fussing of 19th century fashion, straight into the 20th century. Chanel saw the need for total simplification. Corsets, high heels, skirts dragging in the dust had to go. She anticipated the women of the 20th century.

By 1917, Maison Chanel, her shop at 31 rue Cambon in Paris, was established, and it still flourishes there. She became the Pied Piper of fashion, and smart women went to her shop for short, wool-jersey dresses, tailored suits, slacks, simple black evening dresses short to the knee, and pullovers much like those worn by English schoolboys.

By 1926, she employed more than 3,500 persons and owned perfume laboratories, textile mills, a fashion house, and a costume jewelry workshop. Chanel collections were the quintessence of modern luxury. Her instinct for what was necessary to dress women with dash and simple elegance came from a flair for combining many things—ropes of fake jewels, pearls strung on chains interspersed with cabochon emeralds and rubies, worn with a plain black sweater over white duck pants. She designed beige jersey tailored suits with knee-length skirts.

Before World War I, women felt they should wear an air of sorrow and experience. But with their new-found freedom of the late 1920s, they wanted to look forever young, forever gay. And Chanel was their leader. Even duchesses dressed like working girls.

In the 1930s, Chanel fashioned luxurious gypsy skirts of quilted, rhinestone-studded lamé and small boleros or spangled pajamas for evening wear. She also created the strapless dress. Chanel believed a strong,

Coco

well-proportioned body was more important than a pretty face—and more important than the clothes was how you looked in them.

The art of living was to Chanel as natural as her immaculate white shirts and neat little suits. Her beautiful house on the Faubourg St. Honoré was an exciting place, and she was an extraordinary hostess, filling her house with carefully selected guests. As a personality, Chanel was the wonder of Paris. Her personal charm was very great. She drew wit and intelligence around her. Her beautiful rooms above the shop were furnished with a herd of Chinese bronze deer, walls of great bindings on great books, masses of fresh white flowers, gleaming crystals, and Coromandel screens.

During the 1920s, she came to the rescue of Sergei Diaghilev when he needed money for his Ballets Russes. Composer Igor Stravinsky, surrealist painter Salvador Dali, and writer Jean Cocteau became her great friends. Pablo Picasso said of her, "She is the most sensible woman in France." Her great romances were with dashing, rich Englishmen—and the most handsome man in Europe, Grand Duke Dimitri.

Then came World War II, and Chanel went to live at the Ritz Hotel. She closed the Maison Chanel, and nothing was sold there except perfumes until February, 1954. Her Chanel No. 5, which she created in 1922, was her most famous product.

The Maison Chanel reopened in 1954. Soon her soft tweed suits with cardigan jackets and easy skirts, and quilted-cloth bags on gold chains became the most copied fashion creations in history.

By 1964, the now-famous Chanel suit was available to every woman at every price. It was copied all over the world. Chanel loved being copied and heartily encouraged it. She laughed with joy to see shopgirls, actresses, manicurists, and princesses all "dressed by Chanel."

The average dressmaker is important from 7 to 20 years. Chanel, exerting her rigorous discipline to the very end, maintained her position for more than 50 years. Diana Vreeland

Sporting the tailored look in casual clothes, young couples loved to dress alike, *left*, and to set the paces in the pants suit or hot pants, *above*.

Restudied Classics epitomized the compromise fashions. They took the shape of wrapped polo coats, blazers, Chanel-type suits, shirtwaist dresses, cloche hats, turtlenecks, shirts, vests, pants, and skirts with stitched-down pleats or gored seams. Executed in fine sportive fabrics—blanket plaids, camel hair, cashmere, deluxe country tweeds, tartans, argyle patterns, jacquard weaves, hide-side-out-fur-side-in leathers, subtle paisleys, and darkly floral challis prints—they were mixed or matched, to make up "The Layered Look."

American designer Bill Blass and Sonia Rykiel in France gave their layered looks a schoolgirl aura with collars and cuffs pulled under slim sweaters. Eye-riveting layered looks, such as those plotted out by Oscar de La Renta and Missoni of Italy, pitched striped or boldly patterned tank tops over shirts and skirts printed with floral or geometric motifs. The breath of fresh air in the revival of classics came from a spate of bright and amusing sweaters. Soft and snug, rather than bulky, they were knitted in bold, figurative motifs such as a single apple, an airplane, an elephant, a string of stars, bulls, numbers, or letters of the alphabet in crayon colors against a solid background—smack in the center of the chest, or arranged in a line across the bust.

Nostalgia for the 1940s showed clearly in Carmen Miranda necklaces hung with bananas and cherries. There were also turbans, silver fox chub-bies, glittery rhinestone stars worn as earrings or in triads on blazer lapels, square-shoulder toppers, bare-midriff halters, slinky and sophisticated black movie-star dresses that often sported rhinestone shoulder straps; and a revival of ruffled and rustling taffetas for bare-shoulder evening dresses. There was also the cascading hairdo once popularized by Rita Hayworth, and darker red lipstick. And in shoes—ankle-strap platform and wedge-heel sandals in black or navy suedes, or shiny leather combinations of red, wine, orange, and other cartoon colors. Yves Saint Laurent instigated the 1940s revival in his spring Paris collection that was panned by the fashion press but embraced by young trendsetters.

Nautical Themes were another echo of bygone times. Fashion's fleet came in on sailor suits, middy shirts, pea jackets, and wide-legged pants. They used trims of anchors, sailboats, sailors, and stars and stripes, and they were made in naval fabrics such as canvas, chino, cotton twill, and wool flannel. China incited the imagination of designers such as Giorgio di Sant'Angelo and Donald Brooks who adapted dolman and butterfly sleeves, chung-pow robes, quilting that simulated the Chinese fondness for padding, Mandarin collars, and long, flowing gowns. There also was a flowering of Chinese decorative motifs for American evenings.

Men's Fashions shed the aggressive styling and flamboyant "peacock" touches of recent years, but they managed to retain the sense of freewheeling and fun won during the so-called fashion revolution. The biggest news of the year were double knits used in tailored clothing. To their advantage was body-conformity and comfort. Their disadvantage: snagging, and alteration difficulties. Whalebone patterns, and waffle and jacquard weaves, freshened summer suits. Plaid that was subtly gentlemanly in city and brazen in the country, patchwork shirts, and velvets for day and evening wear livened the fall scene. The dominant shape for both knitted and woven suits was the two-button, single-breasted model with wide lapels, suppressed waist, accentuated shoulders, and deep back vents. Trousers remained slightly flared.

Awards. A national vote of more than 400 fashion editors elected Anne Klein to the Coty Hall of Fame for her high-fashion sportswear. "Winnies" went to Betsy Johnson and Halston for their individualistic young clothes. The 1971 Coty Men's Award went to Larry Kane of Raffles Wear for innovative separates. Special award winners were John Kloss of Cira for creative loungewear, Nancy Knox of Renegades for bringing excitement to men's shoes, and Walter A. Haas, chairman of the Board of Levi Strauss, for making the fundamental 120-year-old American fashion that now influences the world. Bill Blass was awarded a citation for his versatility. Kathryn Zahony Livingston

FAULKNER, ARTHUR BRIAN DEANE (1921-
), became prime minister of crisis-torn Northern Ireland on March 23, 1971, following the resignation of James D. Chichester-Clark (see GREAT BRITAIN). The hard-working Faulkner is considered by many observers to be the most able politician in the country. His main task is to bring stability and peace to a country split by virtual civil war between the Roman Catholic minority and the Protestant majority. Some observers believe his election represented the emergence of Ulster's industrious commercial class over the landed gentry that had long held power in Northern Ireland.

Faulkner was born in Belfast, the son of a wealthy shirt manufacturer. He attended boarding school at the College of St. Columbia near Dublin, and was planning to attend Yale University as an exchange student when World War II intervened. Then, at 20, he became manager of his family's shirt factory. He enlisted in the British Army at the end of the war.

At 28, Faulkner joined the Unionist Party and was elected as the youngest member of Parliament. When he was 35, he became the youngest chief whip of that body. He also served as home affairs minister from 1959 to 1963, commerce minister from 1963 to 1969, and minister of development from 1969 to 1971. He lost to Chichester-Clark by only one vote in the party election for prime minister in April, 1969. Foster Stockwell

FAUNTROY, WALTER EDWARD (1933-), a
Democrat, was elected the District of Columbia's nonvoting congressional delegate on March 23, 1971. A black Baptist minister, Fauntroy is the district's first member of the U.S. House of Representatives in a century.

Fauntroy was born on Feb. 6, 1933, in Washington, D.C., and grew up there. He graduated *cum laude* from Virginia Union University in Richmond, Va., in 1955, and from the Yale University School of Divinity in 1958. The following year he became pastor of the New Bethel Baptist Church in Washington, which he still heads.

During the 1960s, Fauntroy was active in the civil rights movement, and was Washington director of the Southern Christian Leadership Conference. He was a close friend of the late Martin Luther King, Jr. Fauntroy led many demonstrations and committees working to end segregation and discrimination. In 1963, he was a coordinator of the march on Washington. He also took part in the first James Meredith march in Mississippi in 1965 and in the march from Selma to Montgomery, Ala., in 1966.

He was named vice-chairman of the Washington City Council in 1967 by President Lyndon B. Johnson, but he resigned the next year to work for renewal of the Shaw section slum area where he was born. Fauntroy is married to the former Dorothy Sims, and they have a son, Marvin. Foster Stockwell

FINLAND.
Prime Minister Ahti Karjalainen and his coalition government resigned on Oct. 29, 1971, because the government's two main parties—the Social Democrats and the Center (Agrarian) Party—disagreed over a $4.5-million increase in farm subsidies. A caretaker government was established to rule the country until a general election could be held in January, 1972.

The October crisis was the second during the year. Communists voted themselves out of the coalition on March 17 and the government resigned. Nine days later, however, the coalition was reorganized without the Communists. Three ministerial posts that had been held by Communists were filled with Social Democrats. The four parties then remaining held 108 of the 200 parliamentary seats. The old coalition had held a more solid majority, with a total of 144 seats.

Russian Trade. Karjalainen went to Moscow on April 19 to seek new agreements that would increase Finland's trade with Russia. After five days, Karjalainen and Premier Aleksei N. Kosygin agreed on a formula of economic, technical, and industrial cooperation. Russia also agreed to deliver natural gas and a second 440,000-kilowatt nuclear power plant to Finland. Kosygin, praising the "high level of cooperation" between the two countries, pointed out that bilateral trade in the past five years was 26 per cent higher than their long-term trade agreement had provided for. Finnish internal political woes seemed to leave foreign relations unhurt.

Relations with Russia were further aided on July 28 when Finland said it would consider associating with the East European trade bloc. It would be the first non-Communist country to do so.

In September, the Finns asked East and West Germany for talks on diplomatic recognition of both countries. They also asked to discuss recognition of Finland's neutrality and a pact forbidding the use of force or threats of force.

Higher Taxes. In an attempt to bring the balance of payments under tighter control, the government increased the sales tax on durable consumer goods by 15 per cent in June. Imported goods, such as automobiles and refrigerators, were subject to an 18 per cent increase. The increases were to remain in effect only until the end of 1971.

The balance of payments showed a deficit of $330-million. Greater demand for imported goods and a high rate of inventory-building were blamed. The figures represented increases of 16 per cent in exports and 30 per cent in imports.

Facts in Brief. Population: 4,788,000. Government: President Urho Kekkonen. Monetary Unit: markka. Foreign Trade: exports, $2,307,000,000; imports, $2,637,000,000. Principal Exports: paper and pulp, lumber, ships and boats.   Kenneth Brown

FIRE. See DISASTERS.

FISCHER, BOBBY (1943-   ), scored 12 consecutive victories in world championship chess matches in 1971, a feat never before accomplished. Fischer shut out Mark Taimanov of Russia and Bent Larsen of Denmark by 6 to 0 scores. He followed this sensational performance by beating Tigran Petrosian of Russia in October, and will play world champion Boris Spassky of Russia for the world title in 1972.

Fischer has long been ranked as the strongest chess player in the United States. He began playing chess at the age of 6, and won his first U.S. title at 14. At 15, he became the youngest international grand master in the history of chess. He is noted for his aggressive, attacking style of play. He also writes articles on chess, and wrote a book, *Games of Chess.*

Robert James Fischer was born in Chicago. He dropped out of school at 14 because he was interested only in chess. He has been called the "Bad Boy of Chess" because he has often complained about playing conditions or dropped out of tournaments when he was dissatisfied. In 1961, he refused to compete for the U.S. title because he thought the $1,000 prize was not big enough. In 1962, he charged that Russian players used collusive tactics in world tournaments, and said he would never again play in tournaments sponsored by the International Chess Federation. The federation later adopted new rules to make collusion difficult.   Joseph P. Spohn

FISHING. See HUNTING AND FISHING.

FISHING INDUSTRY. Landings of fish and other marine products by the U.S. fishing industry in 1971 totaled about 4.94 billion pounds, an increase of about 60 million pounds over 1970. Its value, $584 million, represented a drop of $18 million from 1970, but it was still the second highest on record. The increase in the catch resulted primarily from heavier landings of menhaden, a fish used principally for processing into fish meal and oil. United States per capita fish consumption, however, was only two tenths of a pound less than the 1970 level of 11.4 pounds.

Fish consumption held despite the mercury scare in 1970 when some food fish were found to be contaminated. After a nationwide testing program conducted jointly by the industry and by the Food and Drug Administration (FDA), the FDA reported on September 21 that they found a hazard from mercury contamination of fish only in swordfish.

The Fishing War. The U.S. fishing industry was upset by competition from foreign fishing fleets off both the Atlantic and Pacific coasts and in the Gulf of Mexico. Russian trawlers damaged deepwater lobster gear off New England on May 19, and fishermen demanded that the U.S. territorial limit be extended to 200 miles. United States fishermen continued to ignore the claims of Ecuador and six other Latin American countries barring fishing with-

A delegation of U.S. fishing officials approaches the mother ship of Russia's Atlantic fishing fleet to resolve dispute over fishing off the New England Coast.

in 200 miles of their coasts. The United States claimed the Ecuadorians' control of the ocean extended only 12 miles from shore. Ecuador had seized about two dozen U.S. tuna boats for fishing within that limit by April, 1971, and fined the owners nearly $1 million. All of the boats were released after the fines were paid. The Ecuadorian seizures represented a new escalation of a long-smoldering dispute. Since 1951, more than 100 U.S. tuna boats have been seized off the coast of Ecuador. Heightened international tensions over fishing rights were also reflected in a "shrimp war" between Cuban and U.S. fishermen off the Florida coast.

Conservation Measures. Congress considered legislation to close the U.S. fish market to nations refusing to cooperate in international fishery conservation programs. The action was aimed principally at Denmark, which reportedly was still making large high-seas catches of Atlantic salmon despite fears the salmon stock was being depleted.

On April 19, Secretary of Commerce Maurice H. Stans ordered a halt, effective Dec. 31, 1971, to all whaling from the United States. The Department of the Interior had previously terminated all imports of whale products on that date. Legislation was introduced in Congress to give the secretary of the interior authority to ban the taking of all seals, sea otters, whales, polar bears, and other sea mammals without a permit.　　　　Andrew L. Newman

FITZSIMMONS, FRANK EDWARD (1908-　　), was chosen head of the 2-million-member Teamsters Union on June 21, 1971. He succeeded James R. Hoffa, who resigned the day before. As general vice-president of the union, Fitzsimmons had held the reins of power since 1967, when Hoffa began serving a federal prison sentence.

Fitzsimmons was born in Jeanette, Pa., where his father worked for the Pittsburgh Brewing Company. When he was 13 years of age, the family moved to Detroit. He had to drop out of school at 15 to support the family when his father became ill. Fitzsimmons became a bus driver for the Detroit Motor Company when he was 18, and later he was a truckdriver for the National Transit Corporation.

In 1934, Fitzsimmons joined Teamsters Local 299 in Detroit, the local that Hoffa served as president. Fitzsimmons became the local's business agent in 1937 and its vice-president in 1940. In 1943, he became the secretary-treasurer for the union's Michigan Conference. Hoffa, who had become international president of the union in 1958, selected him for the executive board as international vice-president in 1961.

Fitzsimmons married Mary Patricia O'Sullivan in 1952, after his first wife died. They have two children, Carol and Gary.　　　　Foster Stockwell

FLOOD. See DISASTERS.

FLORIDA. See STATE GOVERNMENT.

FOOD. The Food and Agriculture Organization (FAO) of the United Nations declared in 1971 that the Green Revolution was far from being complete. Nonetheless, world food production kept pace with population growth, and the search for new sources of foods high in protein was broadened. In developing countries, food supplies remained adequate, while in advanced countries, controversy raged over how to alleviate the seemingly permanent hunger of the poor.

In the United States, the day of the consumer dawned. Both the federal government and the food industry were forced by public pressure to tighten food inspection procedures and to enforce more truthful labeling and advertising practices. However, consumer groups held that there was still additional work to be done.

Food Production. In a report on a survey of food-deficit areas in eastern Asia, the FAO estimated that China's grain production reached a record 240 million tons in 1970. Rice yields also increased in Cambodia and South Vietnam, because conditions were somewhat more settled in the war zones. Food production remained unchanged in the developing countries of Africa, the Middle East, and Latin America.

In all of Eastern Europe, total food production declined 1 per cent, but it increased by 9 per cent in

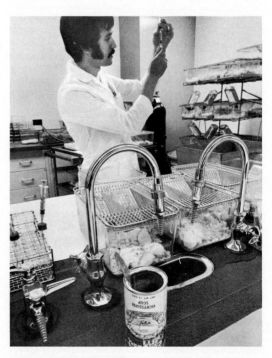

An FDA biologist tests soup for deadly botulism toxin. Discovery of the toxin led to the recall of millions of cans of soup and the financial collapse of one company.

Russia. Farm output in the United States and Canada remained unchanged, primarily because of government efforts to restrict production.

The Protein Search led the FAO to employ 100 vessels to fish throughout the world. The ships are equipped to study fish movements, locate new fishing grounds, and help train local fishermen in techniques that bring in larger catches.

American scientists successfully transplanted oysters and clams from Long Island Sound to the deep, cold waters surrounding the subtropical Virgin Islands. Experiments also were conducted with a new process for recovering high-grade protein from the cheese whey that is generally wasted. In addition, scientists at the University of Virginia worked on methods for extracting cellulose from solid wastes that could be converted into protein and added to human and animal foods.

The Food Stamp Program in the United States was modified. The new system enables poor families to buy stamps and to purchase food with them that is worth more than the stamps cost. The program is restricted to families whose able-bodied adults under 65, excepting mothers and students, are willing to accept work paying at least $1.30 per hour.

Contaminated Foods. Vichyssoise canned soup produced by Bon Vivant Soups Incorporated of Newark, N.J., was found to contain botulism toxins in July. A man died on June 30 in New York City after eating some of the soup. On July 7, the Food and Drug Administration (FDA) ordered the recall of all Bon Vivant soups, sauces, and other canned products. On August 22, the Campbell Soup Company announced the recall of its chicken vegetable soup from 16 southern and western states after discovering botulism contamination. This brought increased criticism from consumer groups already dissatisfied with the FDA's enforcement of federal standards.

Under public pressure, the FDA initiated criminal prosecution against farmers who ship livestock to market that contain illegal amounts of drug and hormone residues. It also warned the public on May 6 not to eat swordfish because 90 per cent of samples tested were found to contain excessive amounts of mercury. The Department of Agriculture also tightened its inspection procedures in meat-processing plants. The FDA set down preliminary guidelines for establishing the percentage of chemical residues "generally recognized as safe" in foods. Studies were also undertaken to determine the amounts of meat tenderizers and saccharin that may safely be added to foods.

The FDA dropped its prohibition against listing the fat content on labels, and some food chains began to include the amount, source, and type of fat on package labels. See CONSUMER AFFAIRS.

Food Trends. Sales in the United States rose more than 8 per cent. Frozen foods—especially

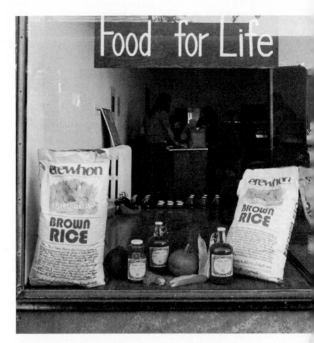

A health food store in Chicago promotes "natural" foods. Such stores sprang up as many Americans tried to improve their health through better diet.

snacks and toppings, ethnic foods, vegetables, and prepared meals—accounted for a large part of the increase. Beef, pork, chicken, and fish consumption increased, but less veal, lamb, and turkey was served. The average American ate 113.8 pounds of beef (110.5 in 1970), 66.2 pounds of pork (64.8), 42.3 pounds of chicken (39), and 11.4 pounds of fish and seafoods (11.1). Veal, lamb, and turkey consumption dropped just small fractions of pounds. Butter consumption, which was 8.2 pounds per person per year from 1957 to 1959, was only 5.3 pounds per person in 1970. Margarine consumption, which was 8.9 pounds per person per year from 1957 to 1959, was 11 pounds per person in 1970. Annual consumption of fresh fruits and vegetables has declined since 1957 by about 5 pounds per person. Potatoes and sweet potatoes, however, have become more popular—up by 12 and 2.5 pounds per person per year, respectively, since 1957. Yearly egg consumption has dropped since 1957 by about 37 eggs per person, but sugar has increased by 6 pounds. Cheese sales in 1971 reached a record high of about 11.5 pounds per person per year.

Drinks. In value of all food sales, beer moved into fourth place behind beef, provisions, and fresh vegetables, and ahead of fruits, milk, and bread. Coffee consumption declined by about a half-pound per person, and tea consumption rose by about one-fourth of a pound per person.   Alma Lach

FOOTBALL. The Dallas Cowboys, who were old hands at winning titles, and the Miami Dolphins, who never used to be winners, were professional football's most successful teams in 1971. The University of Nebraska dominated college football for the second straight year and defeated Oklahoma and Alabama in the season's two most heralded games.

Dallas won the National Football Conference (NFC) play-offs in the National Football League (NFL) and Miami won the American Football Conference (AFC) title. When they met in the Super Bowl in New Orleans on Jan. 16, 1972, Dallas smothered Miami, 24 to 3. Dallas back Duane Thomas gained 95 yards in 19 carries, and Roger Staubach passed for two touchdowns.

The NFL again played with two 13-team conferences, each conference consisting of three divisions. The six division champions qualified for the play-offs, along with the two second-place teams with the best records.

In the NFC play-off semifinals, the San Francisco 49ers beat the surprising Washington Redskins, 24 to 20, scoring the winning touchdown by recovering an errant Redskin's snapback for a punt in the Washington end zone. Dallas defeated the Minnesota Vikings, 20 to 12, as Minnesota lost the ball five times on interceptions and fumbles. In the NFC final, Dallas won from San Francisco, 14 to 3.

The AFC play-offs started with Miami's 27 to 24 victory over the Kansas City Chiefs on Garo Yepremian's 37-yard field goal. It came after 22 minutes 40 seconds of a sudden-death play-off, making the game the longest in professional history. Baltimore's defense led it to a 20 to 3 triumph over the Cleveland Browns, setting up a Miami-Baltimore battle for the AFC title. Miami won it, 21 to 0, capitalizing on two long passes from quarterback Bob Griese to wide receiver Paul Warfield.

The Division Races. In 1970, when the play-offs were first held, 14 of the 26 teams entered the final weekend with play-off aspirations. In 1971, only one play-off berth and two division titles were unsettled by closing day. San Francisco won its finale and beat out Los Angeles for the NFC Western title and a spot in the play-offs. Miami won while Baltimore was being upset by New England, thus giving Miami the AFC Eastern title (both teams had clinched play-off berths).

Don Shula became Miami coach in 1970 and led the Dolphins to their first winning season and first play-off berth. His 1971 team was even better. Griese was the AFC's leading passer, Warfield an exciting pass receiver, Larry Csonka and Jim Kiick the best running combination in the league, and Larry Little an exceptional guard. The team was young, well knit, and well coached.

Don McCafferty, who succeeded Shula as the Baltimore coach, fielded a defensive team in the Colts' tradition. It led the AFC in total defense,

pass defense, and fewest average points allowed per game (10). Johnny Unitas, the 38-year-old quarterback, suffered a ruptured Achilles tendon while playing paddle tennis during the off-season, so 37-year-old Earl Morrall filled in until Unitas was healthy again late in the season.

Dallas, despite obstacles, won its sixth consecutive division title. Its first problem came when Duane Thomas, its outstanding rookie runner of 1970, demanded a new contract. When the Cowboys refused, he boycotted training camp and assailed coach Tom Landry as "a plastic man . . . actually no man at all." The Cowboys then traded Thomas to the New England Patriots (formerly the Boston Patriots), but he walked out of their training camp and the deal was negated. Thomas rejoined the Cowboys after the season had started and eventually starred again.

The Cowboys got off to a sluggish start. Landry couldn't decide whether his best quarterback was Craig Morton, a classic dropback passer, or Roger Staubach, who tended to scramble. He used one, then the other. Against the Chicago Bears on October 31, he alternated them on every play. ("The dumbest thing I ever heard of," said Unitas.) The Cowboys lost that game, 23 to 19, making their midseason won-lost record 4-3. Then Staubach got the job and the Cowboys won their last seven regular-season games.

Staubach stayed in the pocket most of the time and became the NFC's leading passer. He had fine receivers in Bob Hayes and newly acquired Lance Alworth and excellent runners in Calvin Hill and Thomas. The Dallas defense was even better.

San Francisco came of age in 1970 and improved in 1971 by adding Vic Washington, for three years a dangerous running back in the Canadian Football League. Quarterback John Brodie triggered the offense, and the defense was aggressive.

Redskins' Resurgence. Perhaps the NFL's most exciting team was the Washington Redskins, who gained the play-offs for the first time since 1945. Their turnabout came with the hiring of coach George Allen, who had been dropped by the Los Angeles Rams.

Allen believed in winning now rather than building for the future. He preferred a veteran of 30 or older to a rookie, no matter how promising the rookie. Just before the draft of college players in January, he and the Rams swung a 15-man trade (7 players and 8 draft choices), the largest trade in NFL history. The Redskins acquired six Rams, including the three starting linebackers (all over 30). Allen also gave future draft choices for defensive linemen Verlon Biggs and Ron McDole, and for receiver Roy Jefferson—all-pro players who had become disenchanted elsewhere. In all, there was more than 50 per cent turnover of Redskin players. Despite a broken shoulder that sidelined first-string

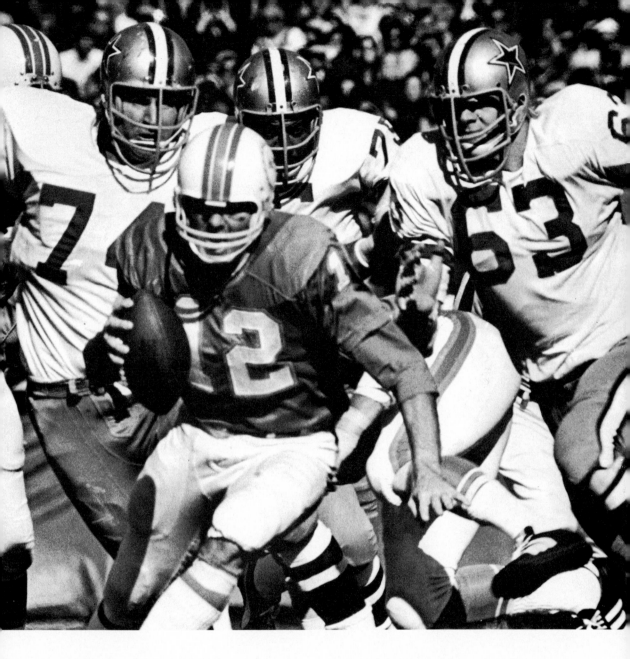

A stout Dallas defense completely throttled Miami in the Super Bowl. On this play, Dallas defenders dumped Dolphin quarterback Bob Griese for a 29-yard loss.

quarterback Sonny Jurgensen, the Redskins won their first five games, and they were tough all season. Allen was voted coach of the year.

The Disappointments. There were many disappointing teams. The Vikings, despite an 11-3 record and a division title, had almost no offense. They finished the season with third-stringer Bob Lee as their quarterback. The Detroit Lions broke down when their defense failed. The Oakland Raiders no longer were menacing, and quarterback Daryle

Lamonica was inconsistent. The New York Jets struggled after their best offensive player (quarterback Joe Namath) and their best defensive player (tackle John Elliott) underwent knee surgery, and George Sauer, all-pro wide receiver, quit football.

Chuck Hughes, a substitute wide receiver for the Lions, died of a heart attack during a game against the Bears in October. The great Gale Sayers of the Bears, still not fully recovered from 1970 knee surgery, appeared in just two games and carried the ball only 13 times all season. Joe Kapp, the colorful New England quarterback, sat out the season because of a contract dispute.

Coaching Changes. There were eight new coaches at the start of the season. Among them were Tom-

FOOTBALL

Standings in National Football Conference

Eastern Division	W.	L.	T.	Pc.
Dallas	11	3	0	.786
Washington	9	4	1	.692
Philadelphia	6	7	1	.462
St. Louis	4	9	1	.308
N.Y. Giants	4	10	0	.286
Central Division	**W.**	**L.**	**T.**	**Pc.**
Minnesota	11	3	0	.786
Detroit	7	6	1	.538
Chicago	6	8	0	.429
Green Bay	4	8	2	.333
Western Division	**W.**	**L.**	**T.**	**Pc.**
San Francisco	9	5	0	.643
Los Angeles	8	5	1	.615
Atlanta	7	6	1	.538
New Orleans	4	8	2	.333

Standings in American Football Conference

Eastern Division	W.	L.	T.	Pc.
Miami	10	3	1	.769
Baltimore	10	4	0	.714
N.Y. Jets	6	8	0	.429
New England	6	8	0	.429
Buffalo	1	13	0	.071
Central Division	**W.**	**L.**	**T.**	**Pc.**
Cleveland	9	5	0	.643
Pittsburgh	6	8	0	.429
Houston	4	9	1	.308
Cincinnati	4	10	0	.286
Western Division	**W.**	**L.**	**T.**	**Pc.**
Kansas City	10	3	1	.769
Oakland	8	4	2	.667
San Diego	6	8	0	.429
Denver	4	9	1	.308

National Conference Individual Statistics

Scoring	TDs.	E.P.	F.G.	Pts.
Knight, Wash.	0	27	29	114
Mann, Det.	0	37	22	103
Gossett, S.F.	0	32	23	101
Cox, Minn.	0	25	22	91
Ray, L.A.	0	37	18	91

Passing	Att.	Comp.	Pct.	Yds.	TDs.
Staubach, Dall.	211	126	59.7	1,882	15
Landry, Det.	261	136	52.1	2,237	16
Kilmer, Wash.	306	166	54.2	2,221	13
Berry, Atl.	226	136	60.2	2,005	11

Receiving	No. Caught	Total Yds.	Avg. Gain	Long Gain	TDs.
Tucker, N.Y.	59	791	13.4	63	4
Kwalick, S.F.	52	664	12.8	42	5
Jackson, Phila.	47	716	15.2	69	3
Jefferson, Wash.	47	701	14.9	70	4
G.Washington, S.F.	46	884	19.2	71	4

Rushing	Atts.	Yds.	Avg. Gain	Long Gain	TDs.
Brockington, G.B.	216	1,105	5.1	52	4
Owens, Det.	246	1,035	4.2	23	8
Ellison, L.A.	211	1,000	4.7	80	4
Brown, Wash.	253	948	3.7	34	4

Punting	No.	Avg. Yardage	Longest
McNeill, Phil.	73	42.0	64
H. Weaver, Det.	42	41.7	63
Widby, Dall.	56	41.6	59

Punt Returns	No.	Yds.	Avg.	Longest	TDs.
Duncan, Wash.	22	233	10.6	33	0
Barney, Det.	14	122	8.7	38	0
Vactor, Wash.	23	194	8.4	30	0

American Conference Individual Statistics

Scoring	TDs.	E.P.	F.G.	Pts.
Yepremian, Mia.	0	33	28	117
Stenerud, K.C.	0	32	26	110
O'Brien, Balt.	0	35	20	95
J. Turner, Den.	0	18	25	93
Muhlmann, Cin.	0	31	20	91

Passing	Att.	Comp.	Pct.	Yds.	TDs.
Griese, Mia.	263	145	55.1	2,089	19
Dawson, K.C.	301	167	55.5	2,504	15
Carter, Cin.	222	138	62.2	1,624	10
Hadl, S.D.	431	233	54.1	3,075	21

Receiving	No. Caught	Total Yds.	Avg. Gain	Long Gain	TDs.
Biletnikoff, Oak.	61	929	15.2	49	9
Taylor, K.C.	57	1,110	19.5	82	7
Vataha, N.E.	51	872	17.1	88	9
Shanklin, Pitt.	49	652	13.3	42	6
Fuqua, Pitt.	49	427	8.7	40	1

Rushing	Atts.	Yds.	Avg. Gain	Long Gain	TDs.
Little, Den.	283	1,133	4.0	40	6
Csonka, Mia.	195	1,051	5.4	28	7
Hubbard, Oak.	182	872	4.8	20	5
Kelly, Clev.	234	865	3.7	35	10

Punting	No.	Avg. Yardage	Longest
Lewis, Cin.	72	44.84	56
Wilson, K.C.	64	44.75	68
Walden, Pitt.	79	43.7	57

Punt Returns	No.	Yds.	Avg.	Longest	TDs.
Kelly, Clev.	30	292	9.7	74	0
Scott, Mia.	33	318	9.6	31	0
I. Hill, Buff.	14	133	9.5	68	1

1971 College Conference Champions

Conference	School	Conference	School
Atlantic Coast	North Carolina	Missouri Valley	Memphis
Big Eight	Nebraska	Pacific Eight	Stanford
Big Sky	Idaho	Southeastern	Alabama
Big Ten	Michigan	Southern	Richmond
Ivy League	Cornell-Dartmouth (tie)	Southwest	Texas
Ohio Valley	Western Kentucky	Western Athletic	Arizona State
Mid-America	Toledo	Yankee	Connecticut-Massachusetts (tie)

The Bowl Games

Bowl	Winner	Loser	Bowl	Winner	Loser
Bluebonnet	Colorado, 29	Houston, 17	Orange	Nebraska, 38	Alabama, 6
Cotton	Penn State, 30	Texas, 6	Rose	Stanford, 13	Michigan, 12
Gator	Georgia, 7	North Carolina, 3	Sugar	Oklahoma, 40	Auburn, 22
Liberty	Tennessee, 14	Arkansas, 13	Sun	Louisiana State, 33	Iowa State, 15

my Prothro of the Rams and Dan Devine of the Packers, the first college coaches to move into NFL head coaching jobs in 14 years. Prothro came from the University of California, Los Angeles, and Devine from Missouri.

The other new coaches were Nick Skorich at Cleveland, Harvey Johnson at Buffalo, Ed Hughes at Houston, Sid Gillman (returning to the job) at San Diego, Allen at Washington, and Bob Hollway at St. Louis. During the season, Harland Svare replaced Gillman at San Diego, Jerry Smith succeeded Lou Saban at Denver, and Ed Khayat took over for the ousted Jerry Williams at Philadelphia. After the season, Jim Dooley was fired by the Bears and Saban became coach at Buffalo. Pro football continued to dip into the college coaching ranks as Bill Peterson of Rice University replaced Hughes at Houston, and John Ralston, who coached Stanford to two straight Rose Bowl victories, replaced Saban at Denver.

Attendance for the NFL's 182 regular-season games totaled 10,362,448, the first time over 10-million. The average attendance was 56,937, or 95 per cent of seating capacity. College attendance (30,455,442) passed 30 million for the first time, helped by longer schedules.

Nebraska's Triumphs. The path to college football's top rung was not easy for Nebraska. The Cornhuskers, coached by Bob Devaney, won two key games before national television audiences, each against a previously undefeated and untied team ranked second nationally (Nebraska was ranked first all year).

On Thanksgiving Day, Nebraska scored a touchdown with 98 seconds left to play to beat Oklahoma, 35 to 31, at Norman, Okla. On New Year's Day, 1972, Nebraska routed Alabama, 38 to 6, in the Orange Bowl at Miami. The victory was Nebraska's 23rd in a row and its 32nd consecutive game without defeat.

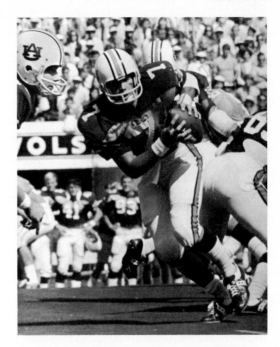

Quarterback Pat Sullivan of Auburn, Southeastern Conference passing leader, beat out Cornell's running back Ed Marinaro to win the Heisman Trophy.

All-America Team
(as picked by United Press International)
Offense
Ends—Terry Beasley, Auburn; Johnny Rodgers, Nebraska.
Tackles—Jerry Sisemore, Texas; Dave Joyner, Penn State.
Guards—Royce Smith, Georgia; Reggie McKenzie, Michigan.
Center—Tom DeLeone, Ohio State.
Quarterback—Pat Sullivan, Auburn.
Running Backs—Greg Pruitt, Oklahoma; Ed Marinaro, Cornell; Johnny Musso, Alabama.
Defense
Ends—Walt Patulski, Notre Dame; Willie Harper, Nebraska.
Tackles—Larry Jacobson, Nebraska; Mel Long, Toledo.
Linebackers—Jackie Walker, Tennessee; Mike Taylor, Michigan; Jeff Siemon, Stanford.
Defensive Backs—Tommy Casanova, Louisiana State; Bobby Majors, Tennessee; Clarence Ellis, Notre Dame; Brad Van Pelt, Michigan State.

In other New Year's Day games, Stanford upset Michigan, 13 to 12, in the Rose Bowl at Pasadena, Calif.; Oklahoma trounced Auburn, 40 to 22, in the Sugar Bowl at New Orleans; and Penn State surprised Texas, 30 to 6, in the Cotton Bowl at Dallas.

Alabama, Oklahoma, Texas, and Notre Dame were among the teams using the wishbone offense, a relatively new formation in which the quarterback has three options on every running play. The wishbone got its name because the three running backs line up in the shape of a wishbone.

In general, runners supplanted passers as the backfield stars. Ed Marinaro of Cornell broke 10 National Collegiate Athletic Association career and one-season records for major-college runners. His rushing yardage of 1,881 yards in one year and 4,715 in three years were the best ever. Eric Allen of Michigan State ran for a record 350 yards in one game (against Purdue). Quarterback John Reaves of Florida set a career passing record of 7,549 yards. The achievement was tainted, however, because the Florida defense allowed the opposition to score late in its final game so Reaves could get a chance to break the record. Quarterback Pat Sullivan of Auburn, also an outstanding passer, won the Heisman Trophy. The best runners included Marinaro, Greg Pruitt of Oklahoma, Johnny Musso of Alabama, and Lydell Mitchell of Penn State. Among the leading defensive players were Walt Patulski, a Notre Dame end, and Bobby Majors, a defensive back from Tennessee.   Frank Litsky

359

FOREST AND FOREST PRODUCTS. The long and heated controversy between the lumber industry, conservation groups, and members of Congress over logging in the national forests and other federal forestlands sharpened in 1971. Conservationists charged that the practice of "clear-cutting"—cutting down all trees in a given area—was threatening to destroy the forests. Industry spokesmen responded that clear-cutting was the most efficient way to harvest mature, overage, and diseased trees and to allow maximum sunlight and moisture to younger, healthy trees. They also claimed that the practice was necessary to meet the government goal of 2.6 million new and rebuilt houses annually. The 97 million acres of commercial timber in national forests provide 40 per cent of U.S. timber.

In his February 1 economic report, President Richard M. Nixon stated that "an increase in the timber harvest through intensified management" promised broad public benefits. On September 2, he appointed a new Presidential Advisory Panel on Timber and the Environment, naming Frederick A. Seaton, of Hastings, Nebr., a former secretary of the interior, as chairman of the panel. The panel, which will advise the President on "increasing the nation's supply of timber to meet growing housing needs while protecting and enhancing the quality of our environment" was to present its first report in 1972.

Congress considered several bills related to the controversy over clear-cutting. They ranged from the National Timber Supply Act of 1971, a compromise bill similar to the industry-supported legislation that was defeated in 1970, to the Forest Restoration and Protection Act of 1971, which requires federally approved state standards for all commercial forestlands. Debate over the legislation was expected to continue well into 1972.

Timber Sale Offerings for western Oregon forestlands managed by the Department of the Interior's Bureau of Land Management were reduced 48 million board feet for the fiscal year beginning on July 1. Secretary of the Interior Rogers C. B. Morton said the reduction was necessary to maintain sustained yields.

The demand for softwood construction lumber and plywood increased heavily over 1970, spurred by a record rate of new housing starts. Lumber and plywood prices rose about 30 per cent during the first quarter of 1971. When the President's 90-day wage-price freeze took effect on August 15, softwood lumber prices were about 33 per cent over 1970 levels.

Fires Devastate. The loss of national forest acreage to fires in 1971 was the greatest since 1934. Burned acreage totaled 556,000, including 276,800 acres in southern California and 152,599 acres in Washington.   Andrew L. Newman

FORMOSA, or TAIWAN. The world status of Nationalist China changed dramatically in 1971. On October 25, the United Nations General Assembly voted overwhelmingly to seat the People's Republic of China and expel the Nationalist Chinese government from the organization. Despite its ouster, which came after intense diplomatic efforts on the part of the United States to prevent it, the Nationalists insisted they were the true representatives of the more than 700 million Chinese on the mainland. "This government," said Nationalist President Chiang Kai-shek, "will continue its unalterable national purpose and holy task of restoring human rights and freedom" to mainland China. See UNITED NATIONS (UN).

Internal Unrest. A number of incidents involving an underground Formosan independence movement added to the tensions there in 1971. Members of the movement favored independence from any Chinese government, either Communist or Nationalist. They insisted that the 12 million native Formosans had their own interests and historical identity. On March 2, the government ordered the ouster of a U.S. missionary, M. L. Thornberry, and his wife. The Thornberrys were known to have been friendly with a number of Formosans opposed to the government. In May, five Americans assigned to duty with the U.S. Army Technical Group were withdrawn from Taipei, the capital, after the gov-

Truckers will be replacing these lumberjacks as soon as the new Dworshak Dam is completed on Idaho's Clearwater River. This last log run was on May 12.

ernment charged that they had assisted the outlawed independence movement. The Americans were accused of showing the Formosan dissidents how to use explosives and of helping them to contact countrymen living abroad through the clandestine use of U.S. military postal privileges. Several Japanese tourists were also arrested in April and May and charged with aiding the dissidents.

Speculation was rife during the year that President Chiang Kai-shek, who celebrated his 84th birthday in October, would not be a candidate for a fifth six-year term when the National Assembly convened in March, 1972, to elect a president and a vice-president. It was generally agreed, however, that if Chiang stepped down, he might well be succeeded by his son, Vice-Premier Chiang Ching-kuo, who was considered the second most powerful man in the government.

Despite its loss of international status, and domestic unrest, the Formosan economy—with a gross national product of $6 billion in 1971—remained one of the most stable in Asia.

Facts in Brief. Population: 14,992,000. Government: President Chiang Kai-shek; Vice-President and Prime Minister C. K. Yen. Monetary Unit: new Taiwan dollar. Foreign Trade: exports, $1,428,000,-000; imports, $1,524,000,000. Principal Exports: textiles, plywood.   John N. Stalker

FOUR-H CLUBS. See YOUTH ORGANIZATIONS.

FRANCE. With a half-million persons unemployed, labor unrest and prolonged strikes shook the economy and hit France's lucrative tourist industry in 1971. Industrial productivity increased 5.7 per cent, but inflation continued to cause concern.

Labor Troubles. The national minimum wage was raised by 3.7 per cent on January 6, and a rail strike was averted later in the month only by raising railroad workers' pay by 7.15 per cent. A wave of strikes followed in February that continued through most of the summer. Postal workers, miners, television and radio workers, and metalworkers all stopped work. The decision to close a mine in the Lorraine coal fields brought 26,000 men out for eight days and almost precipitated a nationwide pit stoppage. Airline pilots and navigators struck for more pay on February 18, resulting in a lockout by the airlines four days later. All flights by the country's leading airlines were suspended. One of France's longest strikes, by 1,700 metalworkers in the Loire district, ended after 45 days on March 2.

Police complained that they were misunderstood, and they staged a demonstration on March 4, handing out leaflets and giving street-corner talks. As the airline lockout entered its fourth week, dockworkers held a 24-hour work stoppage, their 11th in six months. Minor riots in Paris stirred fears of a return to the civil disturbances of 1968. Successive strikes were held in May and June by automobile workers, railroad workers, and air crews. A 10-day strike by 2,300 subway workers paralyzed Paris in October.

Five-Year Plan. The sixth economic five-year plan, for the period from 1971 to 1975, was approved by the Council of Ministers on April 28 and by the National Assembly on June 18. It emphasizes stepping up industrialization, with an annual growth rate of 5.4 per cent. Spending on roads (800 more miles of highways by 1975), housing, telephones, health, education, and technical training will increase by 9 per cent a year.

Financial Crisis. Floating of the (West) German Deutsche mark and Dutch guilder on May 10 provoked France to refuse to discuss European economic and monetary union as long as the currencies of some European Community (Common Market) countries were not stable. On May 26, President Georges Pompidou called for discussions with the United States on "the problem of the dollar."

Following U.S. moves to protect the dollar on August 15, France adopted a two-tier system—a financial, or special, franc for official transactions, and a standard franc for normal trading. On September 23, Pompidou reaffirmed France's aim of reforming the international monetary system, beginning with a return to fixed exchange rates and an end to the dollar's reserve role. On December 14, presidents Pompidou and Richard M. Nixon met in the Azores and worked out an international monetary agreement, starting with a formal devaluation of the dollar.

France's reaction to the U.S. surcharge on imports, imposed in August, was seen as one of the first signs of a feared shift toward protectionism in European trade. Henri Ziegler, a French aerospace industry leader, said in October that France had suggested that Common Market countries impose a customs barrier against U.S. imports to Europe in retaliation. The U.S. surcharge, however, was dropped on December 20.

European Negotiations. France played a leading role in negotiations to enlarge the Common Market. A critical point in talks with Great Britain was the role of the pound sterling as a reserve currency. After two days of talks in May with British Prime Minister Edward Heath, Pompidou declared, "On our general conception of Europe, its organization and its objectives, our views are close enough to allow us to go forward without pessimism" (see EUROPE). Diplomatic observers saw this summit meeting as laying the foundations of a new Anglo-French understanding. On June 24, President Pompidou called on an enlarged Common Market to cooperate with Eastern Europe and "give back to Europe her place in the world." Otherwise, he said, there was a risk of being "crushed" between the Communist bloc and the United States, which, although "our friend and ally, is not European."

Parading workers in Paris mark the 100th anniversary of the founding of the
Paris Commune with a huge portrait of Marianne, the symbol of French liberty.

In Local Elections in March, the government
(Gaullist) parties won about 50 per cent of the vote,
scoring gains in the traditionally left wing south and
winning a bare majority in the Paris City Council.
Hopes of the non-Communist left, extinguished in
1968 when the Federation of the Left ceased to exist,
were revived by a congress at Épinay, near Paris,
on June 13. A variety of Socialist splinter groups
merged to form a new Socialist Party with François
M. Mitterrand as first secretary.

On July 16, for the first time, steps by the Gaullist
government were held unconstitutional. France's
Constitutional Council invalidated governmental
restrictions on the right of free association.

Nuclear Tests. Nine nuclear strategic missiles
with 150 kiloton warheads and a range of 2,000
miles became operational at Albion Plateau near
Toulon on August 4. The third and fourth thermo-
nuclear devices to be set off since tests started in
1968 were exploded at the Murora atoll in the Pacific Ocean in August. Following protests from South
American countries, the tests were suspended.

Facts in Brief. Population: 51,701,000. Government: President Georges Pompidou; Prime Minister
Jacques Chaban-Delmas. Monetary Unit: franc.
Foreign Trade: exports, $17,935,000,000; imports,
$19,114,000,000. Principal Exports: machinery,
chemicals, motor vehicles.   Kenneth Brown

GABON. See AFRICA.

GAMBIA. In its first full year as a republic, Gambia was calm and stable in 1971. In conjunction
with the International Monetary Fund, Gambia
issued a new monetary unit, the dalasi, on July 1.
The new unit is equal to four shillings of the Gam-
bian pound. The introduction of the dalasi had no
relation to the fluctuating world money market and
represented no change, either upward or downward,
in the basic value of Gambia's currency.

In foreign relations, Gambia firmly opposed any
move by black African nations to open a dialogue
with the white-minority regime of South Africa.
Strong support for such a dialogue had been voiced
by Ghana, the Ivory Coast, and Uganda. On August 8, Senegal called for the admittance of Gambia
to the Senegal River States Organization and asked
that Guinea be expelled from that group.

During the debate on the entry of mainland China
to the United Nations, Gambia supported the United
States position that Nationalist China should retain
its seat. Gambia was also among the 35 nations that
voted against the resolution to expel the Formosa
government and seat the Peking regime. See UNITED
NATIONS (UN).

Facts in Brief. Population: 380,000. Government: President Dawda Kairaba Jawara. Monetary
Unit: dalasi. Foreign Trade: exports, $16,000,000;
imports, $17,000,000. Principal Exports: peanuts
and peanut oil.   Darlene R. Stille

GAMES, MODELS, AND TOYS. Controversy about the safety of toys increased in 1971. Legislators and consumer groups charged that thousands of children were being hurt by unsafe playthings, and some complained that the federal toy safety law, which went into effect in January, 1970, was not being enforced.

The Food and Drug Administration contended that it was doing the best it could to administer the law with limited funds and manpower. Meanwhile, the Department of Health, Education, and Welfare estimated that 700,000 children are injured annually in the United States by toys, not including bicycles, swings, or slides.

In a book titled *Toys That Don't Care*, Edward M. Swartz, a Boston lawyer, documented many charges relating to unsafe toys. He pointed out that common toys—such as electric irons, dolls, and cap pistols—can be dangerous, yet they carry no warning to children or parents. He also noted an increase in the marketing of "sadistic" toys and games, including toy hypodermic needles and plastic guillotine kits. Toy industry spokesmen defended their products as generally harmless. "No system would be quite good enough to prevent all accidents," said Fred Ertl, Jr., president of Toy Manufacturers of America, Inc.

A company that manufactures model rockets coordinated its model promotion program with the *Apollo 14* space flight. The company mailed out countdown information and instruction sheets for simulated launchings to the moon.

The trend toward games for adults reflecting social issues continued. One company brought out Couples, a game for male-female couples, and another produced a game called The Battle of the Sexes, with women's lib connotations.

Toy motorcycles that climb plastic mountains were big sellers, as were pieces of outdoor construction equipment called earth shakers. They were powered by tiny electric cells that could be readily recharged by "juice machines," sold with the toys. The growing popularity of snowmobiling was reflected in the appearance of scale models of snowmobiles, a snowmobile game, and a snowmobile bobsled that can carry four children. Popular dolls ranged from Raggedy Ann and Andy to a French doll that gives birth to a baby.

Model Making. Bucky Servaites of Kettering, Ohio, retained both his grand national and open national championships at the 40th National Model Airplane Championships at the Glenview (Ill.) Naval Air Station in July and August. The senior national championship went to Brian Webster of Manchester, Tenn., and Brian Pardue of Greensboro, N.C., took the junior national championship. The Dixie Whiz Kids took the team championship, and the club team championship went to the Greensboro Prop Twisters.   Theodore M. O'Leary

GARDENING. Ecology commanded considerable attention among gardeners in 1971. Polychlorinated biphenyls (PCB's), a DDT-like material, was discovered to be widespread in the environment. Indeed, tests for DDT had also been measuring PCB's, thereby giving false high DDT readings.

In a related incident, University of Wisconsin researchers opened jars of soil sealed for more than 60 years and tested the contents. They found residues of the recently banned insecticides aldrin and heptachlor. Neither of these pesticides were manufactured so long ago. This led to speculation that they may be produced in nature.

Undue alarm was generated in some areas by newspaper stories about purported dangers to children from poisonous plants. In recent years, no deaths have resulted in the United States from accidental plant poisoning, according to the National Clearing House for Poison Control Centers.

All-America Plants included "Peter Pan Plum" and "Peter Pan Pink" zinnias, "Queen of Hearts" dianthus, "Little Darling" snapdragon, and "Silver Puffs" dwarf hollyhock. Vegetable winners were "Extra Early Sweet" corn and "Red Head" cabbage.

"Southern Belle" perennial hibiscus won a Silver Medal, and the following gladioli received awards: "Anniversary" (lavender), "Cascade" (white), "Little Tiger," and "Orange Cascade." All-America roses were "Aquarius" (pink and white grandiflora), H. T. "Command Performance" (orange-red), and "Red-gold" floribunda.

Organizations and Awards. Donald Wyman, horticulturist emeritus of Harvard University's Arnold Arboretum won two top awards in 1971—the celebrated Scott Medal of the Arthur Hoyt Scott Horticultural Foundation, Swarthmore, Pa.; and the American Horticultural Society's highest award, the Liberty Hyde Bailey Medal.

The Massachusetts Horticultural Society presented the following awards: the George Robert White Medal to George S. Avery, director of the Brooklyn Botanic Garden; the Thomas Roland Medal to Edwin Menninger of Stuart, Fla., for work with tropical trees; the Jackson Dawson Medal to Charles E. Hess of Rutgers University, Brunswick, N.J., for work in propagation.

In Research. Scientists at Pennsylvania State University discovered that the number of grapes set by a vine correlates directly with day temperatures at flower-blooming time. Both high (90 to 95°F.) and low (60 to 65°F.) temperatures produced significantly smaller sets.

United States Department of Agriculture scientists found that bitter narigin from grapefruit and neohesperidin from bitter oranges can be converted into sweeteners, the first one-third as sweet as saccharin, and the second 100 times sweeter than table sugar.   Edwin F. Steffek

GEOLOGY. Scientists in April, 1971, found fossil spores of terrestrial plants that grew 30 million years earlier than any that had previously been found. The spores were discovered in rocks near Niagara Falls, N.Y., by Jane Gray of the Museum of Natural History at the University of Oregon, and Arthur J. Boucot of the department of geology at Oregon State University. The fossil spores were in sedimentary rocks nearly 425 million years old.

Previously, the earliest known forest in North America, one that contained abundant plants, was of the Middle Devonian Period, nearly 350 million years ago. Many fossil stumps of these primitive trees have been found in rock outcroppings near Gilboa, N.Y., about 40 miles southwest of Albany.

This Devonian flora, called the Gilboa Forest, covered nearly the entire state by the end of the Devonian Period.

The fossil record of terrestrial plants in rocks older than Middle Devonian is fragmentary, and until the discovery of fossil spores, it went back only as far as the late Silurian Period, about 410 million years ago.

The new discovery was unearthed in rocks of the early Silurian age, which began about 435 million

364

years ago, in the gorge of the Niagara River about 7 miles north of Niagara Falls. The spores were found near the base of the gorge in three layers of sandstone, known as the Whirlpool Sandstone (white), the Power Glen Formation (gray), and the Grimsby Sandstone (red). The Whirlpool Sandstone rests on top of the red shales of the late Ordovician age, thought to be nearly 465 million years old. Although these shales are totally barren of fossils, the sandstone yields spores and a few other fossils, such as worm tracks, small shelled invertebrates, and marine microfossils.

The shale and sandstone sequence represents part of a large delta that once spread across New York state from east to west. Whether this delta had lush vegetation is unknown because no definitive plant remains, such as stumps, stems, or bark, have been found with the spores.

Evidence of similar plants outside North America has been reported from sandstones in the Bohemia region of Czechoslovakia. The fossilized remains consist of a few rare spores that have yet to be authenticated but, if proven to be correct, will add another 25 million years to the geologic history of higher plants.

Plate Tectonics, the concept that sections of the earth's surface move laterally to produce continental drift, was studied further in 1971. An important contribution was a geodetic survey of the rift zone of Iceland, where plate-splitting presumably has occurred. It was conducted by Robert Decker of Dartmouth College, who surveyed the area in 1967 and again in 1970. A comparison of the results of the two surveys indicated a net movement at right angles to the axis of the rift zone of 6 to 7 centimeters (2.4 to 2.8 inches). The results of this survey lend substantial support to the plate tectonics theory. The National Ocean Survey also published information in 1971 on a seismic study that tends to confirm the plate tectonics theory.

New Father of Geology? William Maclure (1763-1840), a wealthy Scot shipping magnate who immigrated to America in the early 1800s, has long been considered the pioneer of American geology. In 1971, however, Edmund Speiker of Ohio State University published material showing that a German geologist, Johann David Schopf, preceded Maclure. Maclure became interested in natural history through his association with members of the Academy of Sciences in Philadelphia, an organization founded by Benjamin Franklin. This curiosity led him to make several studies of the Appalachian Mountains. He carefully recorded his observations, and in 1809 published *Observations on the Geology of the United States*, complete with a geologic map of the area east of the Mississippi River.

According to Speiker, Maclure was some 22 years behind Schopf, a German army surgeon who remained in America after the American Revolution

and published his observations in 1787. His work went unnoticed for more than a century and is still virtually unknown. Speiker cites it for historical exactness and for Schopf's attempts to interpret and explain the origin of the features he observed, something Maclure failed to do. Maclure's geologic map, the first of its kind in North America, is probably the reason Schopf's initial investigations have been overshadowed by Maclure's.

Los Angeles Earthquake. On the morning of Feb. 9, 1971, the densely populated Los Angeles area was shaken by an earthquake that measured 6.6 on the Richter scale of 10. Regarded as moderate in severity, this San Fernando earthquake caused an estimated $1 billion in property damage and killed 62 persons. Thousands of others were endangered by a fracture in an earth-fill dam.

Instruments indicated that ground motions during this earthquake were more severe than might have been suspected. The quake was centered in the Santa Susana-Sierra Madre fault zone along the base of the San Gabriel Mountains.

Meanwhile, research on earthquake prediction was given high priority by geophysicists. Although experts cannot yet predict when an earthquake will strike a given region, they have developed sensitive instruments that can measure stress and strain within the earth's crust.   Thomas X. Grasso

GEORGIA. See STATE GOVERNMENT.

GERMANY, DEMOCRATIC REPUBLIC OF (EAST). Walter Ulbricht, strong man of the republic since the postwar division of Germany, retired on May 3, 1971. Erich Honecker, 58, succeeded him as first secretary of the Central Committee of the German Socialist Unity Party (SED). Ulbricht, 78, retired from the post he had held since 1953 because of old age. He was reported ill and confined to bed when the SED party conference opened on June 15. Ulbricht remained as chairman of the State Council, or the head of state. The new party chief appeared ready to abandon Ulbricht's policy that saw the two Germanys as a natural whole. The words to the national anthem, with a reference to "Germany, united, fatherland. . . .," were de-emphasized. An East-West workers' conference and East Germany's state secretariat for West German affairs were dissolved. Honecker, who had long been groomed for succession, has close ties to Moscow military leaders. (See HONECKER, ERICH.)

Berlin Agreement. A chink in the wall that Ulbricht built 10 years earlier to divide Berlin appeared on September 3 when the ambassadors of Great Britain, France, Russia, and the United States signed the first part of a four-power agreement on the city. The signing, after 17 months of talks, had both East and West German approval. The agreement lays down four-power responsibility for the city, and confirms the ties between West

An era ended in East Germany when Chairman Walter Ulbricht, standing, resigned. Erich Honecker, seated at Ulbricht's left, succeeded him in May.

Berlin and West Germany. The 100-mile "ring round West Berlin," of which the wall is a part, still stands, but the agreement will ease movement between West and East and allow "facilitated and unimpeded" traffic from the West. There had been long delays earlier in the year. West Germany agreed not to hold federal assemblies and parliamentary meetings in Berlin. East Germany immediately began negotiating with Bonn representatives to settle outstanding issues. The East German government emphasized the significance of the agreement in easing tensions in central Europe. After the four-power agreement, West German Foreign Minister Walter Scheel raised the question of the two German states joining the United Nations (UN) in talks with UN Secretary-General U Thant and General Assembly members.

Prices Lowered. Rising production enabled East Germany to make extensive price reductions in February for textiles and consumer goods ranging from 9 to 34 per cent. Social services were improved.

Facts in Brief. Population: 17,157,000. Government: Communist Party First Secretary Erich Honecker; State Council Chairman Walter Ulbricht; Prime Minister Willi Stoph. Monetary Unit: mark. Foreign Trade: exports, $4,581,000,000; imports, $4,847,000,000. Principal Exports: machinery, fuels, clothing.   Kenneth Brown

366

GERMANY, FEDERAL REPUBLIC OF (WEST).
A four-power agreement on Berlin was signed on Sept. 3, 1971. The action came just over a year after West Germany and Russia agreed to renounce the use of force.

This new step toward easing central European tension was signed by the ambassadors of Great Britain, France, Russia, and the United States, subject to negotiations between the two German states on technical details. It opened the way for the long-awaited European security conference. The North Atlantic Treaty Organization (NATO) had made it clear in Lisbon in June that East-West talks, requested by Russia, were possible only after a Berlin settlement. And earlier, on January 30, Willy Brandt, West German chancellor, repeated his determination not to press for ratification of 1970 treaties with Poland and Russia until a Berlin settlement was reached.

Telephone service between Eastern and Western sectors of the city, interrupted when the Communists cut the circuits in 1952, resumed at 6 A.M. on January 31. Calls were limited to 750 per day from each side. Facilities were swamped and, by 8:30 A.M., West Berlin callers heard a recording: "Unfortunately, we can no longer accept bookings for the day."

Berlin became a four-power responsibility under the September 3 agreement, giving West Berliners access to the East. The wall that has divided Berlin for a decade still stands, but the harassment by East Germany of traffic on the way to Berlin was to end when the two Germanys ratified the agreement. Their talks on a way to implement it continued in December. On December 18, they agreed to allow civilian traffic between West Germany and West Berlin.

Visit to Russia. On September 16, Brandt went to Yalta for talks with Russia's Communist Party General Secretary Leonid I. Brezhnev. Main topics were East-West security and economic, technological, and cultural cooperation. The visit was seen in Europe as a political "coming of age" for West Germany.

Monetary Crisis. Demand for revaluation, or floating the Deutsche mark, without official restrictions on the rate of exchange, began in May when it was in danger of developing into a reserve currency. Efforts were made to keep the mark below its ceiling of 3.63 per U.S. dollar. On May 10, the government decided to float the mark. Brandt said the move would promote European stability. On June 14, Germany was under strong pressure from its five European Community (Common Market) partners to return to a fixed parity, but Finance Minister Karl Schiller refused to set a date. By year-end, after the December dollar devaluation, its official value dropped to a new low of 3.22 marks.

Inflation Dangers. With the worst inflation in 20 years and the cost-of-living index up 5.4 per cent for the year, the government cut public spending by 1 per cent. Increased taxes on gasoline, alcoholic beverages, and tobacco were announced on September 10 to take effect on Jan. 1, 1972. The budget anticipated an economic growth rate of 8 per cent. Slower growth, limited production gains, and new labor union militancy contributed to inflation.

Troop Cuts. In April, British Prime Minister Edward Heath assured West Germany in Bonn that British troops will remain "as long as there is a task for them to do and as long as you want them here to do it." Talks opened in June between the United States and West Germany on the cost of maintaining 210,000 U.S. troops on Federal Republic soil. The chancellor warned that unilateral reduction of U.S. forces in Europe would make efforts to achieve a balanced mutual reduction of both Eastern and Western troops and arms more difficult.

Germany's first jet airliner, the VFW 614, was completed in April, with deliveries scheduled for 1972. The 44-seat plane is designed for short take-off and landing, even from grass strips.

Facts in Brief. Population: 62,602,000. Government: President Gustav Heinemann; Chancellor Willy Brandt. Monetary Unit: Deutsche mark. Foreign Trade: exports, $34,188,000,000; imports, $29,-814,000,000. Principal Exports: machinery, motor vehicles, chemicals. Kenneth Brown

GHANA. The new civilian government which had come to power in 1970, replacing the National Liberation Council's military regime, consolidated its rule in 1971. In April, a student organization asked the government to grant amnesty to former President Kwame Nkrumah, who was ousted in 1966, and all other political exiles. The government denied the request.

In August, the National Assembly barred the return of Nkrumah's old Convention People's Party. However, a socialist opposition, the Ghanaian Popular Party, reportedly was formed in September.

Efforts were made during the year to reform local government. Local, district, and regional councils were set up. Local councils elect their own chairmen, but the prime minister appoints the chairmen of the district and regional councils.

Ghana was one of the first countries to recognize the new military regime in Uganda. Ghana's Prime Minister Kofi A. Busia favored establishing a dialogue with the white-minority government of South Africa.

Facts in Brief. Population: 9,316,000. Government: President Edward Akufo-Addo; Prime Minister Kofi A. Busia. Monetary Unit: new cedi. Foreign Trade: exports, $375,000,000; imports, $409,-000,000. Principal Export: cacao. George Shepherd

GIRL SCOUTS. See YOUTH ORGANIZATIONS.
GIRLS' CLUBS. See YOUTH ORGANIZATIONS.

GOLF. Lee Trevino and Jack Nicklaus, two of the most successful golf professionals in recent years, added to their laurels—and to their bankrolls—in 1971. In a four-week span, Trevino won the U.S., Canadian, and British Open championships. Nicklaus' major victory came in the Professional Golfers' Association (PGA) championship. During the year, Nicklaus ($244,490) and Trevino ($231,202) broke Nicklaus' 1967 all-time earnings record of $211,566. In November, Trevino was named PGA Golfer of the Year.

Trevino's success story resembles a Horatio Alger classic. He is the son of a Mexican immigrant grave-digger, and first worked as a caddie on public courses in Texas. By the age of 31, he had reached the top of the sport. A swarthy, colorful man who calls himself Super Mex, Trevino is quick with the quip and quick with the laugh. See TREVINO, LEE.

His year started well with victories in the $60,000 Tallahassee (Fla.) Open in April and the $175,000 Danny Thomas Memphis Classic in May. Then he won the $200,000 U.S. Open at Ardmore, Pa.; tied for 33rd place in the Cleveland Open; won the $150,000 Canadian Open at Montreal; and won the prestigious $108,000 British Open at Southport, England. In October, he captured the $135,000 Sahara Open in Las Vegas, Nev.

U.S. Open. In the U.S. Open, held June 17 to 21, Jim Simons, a 21-year-old amateur from Butler, Pa.,

Lee Trevino, winner of the U.S. Open at Ardmore, Pa., entertained the gallery during and after the contest with antics such as his dance of victory, *above*, and a ball-in-the-mouth gag after birdying on the 14th.

led after three rounds, but faltered. "Four days of heavy competition like this tends to weary the mind," said Simons. Trevino and Nicklaus took advantage of Simons' collapse to tie for first place at 280 for 72 holes. The next day, in an 18-hole play-off, the jaunty Trevino calmly shot a 68 and beat Nicklaus by three strokes.

In the British Open, from July 7 to 10, Trevino almost let victory slip away with a 7 on the next-to-last hole. But he birdied the final hole, and his 278 won by a stroke from Lu Liang Huan of Formosa. After accepting the winner's check of $13,200, Trevino sat down and wrote a $4,800 check for a British orphanage.

When Trevino returned to his home in El Paso, Tex., he was honored with a parade. In August, he underwent an emergency appendectomy in Truth or Consequences, N. Mex., and 24 days later he was back on the tour, playing tournament golf again. "But my golf clubs," he said, "don't know where they're playing."

The 31-year-old Nicklaus, from Columbus, Ohio, won five tournaments—the $200,000 PGA championship; the $165,000 Tournament of Champions at Rancho La Costa, Calif.; the $125,000 Byron Nelson Classic in Dallas; (with Arnold Palmer as his teammate) the $200,000 PGA team championship over Palmer's home course in Ligonier, Pa., and (with Trevino as his teammate) the World Cup at

Palm Beach, Fla. Nicklaus was second in the U.S. Open, Masters, World Series of Golf, and Piccadilly world match-play tournament.

The PGA Tournament was played from February 25 to 28 at North Palm Beach, Fla. Nicklaus shot 281 and beat Billy Casper by two strokes. The victory made Nicklaus the first golfer to win the world's four major titles—the U.S. Open, the British Open, the Masters, and the PGA—twice.

In the $198,000 Masters, held April 8 to 11 at Augusta, Ga., Charles Coody of Abilene, Tex., with a 279, beat Nicklaus and John Miller by two strokes. The 23-year-old Miller ruined his chances with bogeys on two of the last three holes. Ironically, Coody had led in the 1969 Masters until he bogeyed the last three holes.

The PGA circuit consisted of more than 60 tournaments. The richest was the $250,000 Westchester Classic in Harrison, N. Y., held in July, won by Palmer. After a few erratic years, Palmer had regained the form that previously made him the darling of the crowds. He also won the $140,000 Bob Hope Desert Classic at Palm Springs, Calif., in February, and the $150,000 Florida Citrus Open at Orlando in March. Two-time winners were Gary Player of South Africa, Coody, Tom Shaw, George Archer, Gene Littler, Tom Weiskopf, and J. C. Snead, the nephew of Sam Snead.

Trevino, Nicklaus, and Palmer helped the American professional team defeat the British, 18½ to 13½ in the biennial Ryder Cup matches, September 16 to 18, in St. Louis. The British did better in the Walker Cup matches, May 26 and 27, at St. Andrews, Scotland. Their amateurs upset the Americans, 13 to 11, for the first time since 1938 and for the second time in the history of the matches.

A week after the Walker Cup defeat, Steve Melnyk of Jacksonville, Fla., and Simons made partial amends by reaching the British amateur final. Melnyk won, 3 and 2. Canadian Gary Cowan of Kitchener, Canada, won his second U.S. amateur title.

Women Pros. The Ladies Professional Golf Association (LPGA) conducted 21 tournaments worth more than $600,000. Kathy Whitworth of Richardson, Tex., won five tournaments; Sandra Haynie of Fort Worth, Tex., four; Sandra Palmer two; JoAnne Gunderson Carner two; Jane Blalock two; and Judy Kimball two. Miss Whitworth, with $41,-192, was the leading money winner for the sixth time in seven years. She won the LPGA championship, and Mrs. Carner took the U.S. Open.

There were two memorable moments on the tour. One came in the richest women's tournament ever, the $60,000 Sears Classic at Port St. Lucie, Fla., when Ruth Jessen won a personal triumph over her five operations and cancer. The other came in the Lady Carling Open at Baltimore when Marilynn Smith carded a double-eagle 2 on a par-5 hole, the first in LPGA history.   Frank Litsky

GOOLAGONG, EVONNE (1951-   ), gained recognition as one of the world's best tennis players when she won the Wimbledon singles title in England in July, 1971. The attractive Australian aborigine decisively defeated her fellow Australian, Margaret Smith Court, a three-time Wimbledon champion and one of the world's best players, in the finals. She became the first teen-ager to win the Wimbledon crown since Maria Bueno of Brazil did it in 1959. Miss Goolagong also won the French Open singles title in June.

Miss Goolagong was born in a rural area of New South Wales, the daughter of a sheepshearer. The family moved to the village of Barellan, about 400 miles southwest of Sydney, when Evonne was 2 years old. Miss Goolagong started playing tennis when she was 6, and she won her first tournament at 10.

Soon after she began competing, she came to the attention of Vic Edwards, who has coached such Australian tennis stars as Fred Stolle. Edwards has coached Miss Goolagong ever since. At first, she went to Sydney for brief periods of special coaching, with Barellan townspeople raising funds to pay her expenses. She has lived with the Edwards family in a Sydney suburb since she was 14, however, and attended school there. Her parents and her brothers and sisters live in Barellan.   Joseph P. Spohn

GOVERNORS, U.S. See STATE GOVERNMENT.

GRAVELY, SAMUEL LEE, JR. (1922-   ), became the first black admiral in the history of the U.S. Navy on April 28, 1971. He was commander of the guided-missile frigate U.S.S. *Jouett* at the time of his promotion.

Gravely was born on June 4, 1922, in Richmond, Va. He attended the University of Virginia for three years before he entered the Navy. He concluded his studies later, and received a B.A. degree in history from the university in 1948.

When Gravely was 20, he entered the Naval Reserve. After officer training with a naval unit attached to the University of California, Los Angeles, he graduated from the midshipman's school of Columbia University in December, 1944, as an ensign in the Naval Reserve. In 1965, he transferred to the regular Navy. During World War II, he served aboard the submarine chaser U.S.S. *PC 1264*. During the Korean War, he was a communications officer aboard the battleship *Iowa*.

Gravely became the first black officer to command a U.S. warship when he was named skipper of the U.S.S. *Falgout* in January, 1962. In 1966, he became commanding officer of the destroyer *Taussig*. He was promoted to captain on Nov. 1, 1967.

Gravely likes to play tennis and handball, and his hobby is raising pigeons. He married the former Alma Clark in 1946, and they have two sons and a daughter. The family lives in San Diego. Lillian Zahrt

369

GREAT BRITAIN

For Prime Minister Edward Heath and his Cabinet, the crowning glory of 1971 was Britain's decisive march toward full membership in the European Community (Common Market). This grew out of the personal and political understanding achieved by Heath and French President Georges Pompidou when they met in Paris on May 20 and 21, and out of the patient diplomacy of Britain's negotiator at Brussels and Luxembourg, Geoffrey Rippon. It was climaxed by a remarkable 112-vote majority in the House of Commons on October 28, approving British membership as of Jan. 1, 1973.

For Heath, personally, it was the realization of a long-standing ambition. He had been the British negotiator when French President Charles de Gaulle cast his first veto against Britain's entry in 1963. His agreement with Pompidou was based on a mutual belief that signs of decline in U.S. military and economic power made a strong Western Europe essential. But they sought a Europe of nations, not one run by a supranational commission in Brussels. Where Heath had fears of American withdrawal, Pompidou was perturbed at growing West German strength.

France, however, put up a tough fight in the detailed talks the six Common Market nations held with Rippon. It took months to get special arrangements for New Zealand's butter exports to Britain and for the sugar trade on which several small and poor Commonwealth countries depended. Britain agreed to raise its food prices to the Common Market's levels over six years, to pay 20 per cent of its budget by 1977, and to take the risk of an adverse balance of payments immediately after joining. But the government and much of British industry were confident of economic success in an enlarged market of 250 million persons.

Reluctant Islanders. The British people, according to the opinion polls, were unenthusiastic about becoming Europeans. A majority steadfastly opposed entry, although it was prepared to let the House of Commons make the decision. Labour Party leader Harold Wilson, who had tried and failed to get British entry into the Common Market when he was prime minister, sided with public opinion. He attacked Heath's terms as a sell-out to France's farmers. He feared that capital would desert Britain for Europe and that New Zealand's farmers and the Commonwealth sugar growers

would suffer. A majority of the Labour Party, urged on by the big left-wing transport and engineering unions, backed Wilson.

But in the crucial Commons vote on October 28, 69 Labour members, led by former Chancellor of the Exchequer Roy Jenkins, voted with the government. Instead of taking the party line against Common Market entry, 20 more abstained. On the Conservative Party side, 39 rebels opposed entry into the community, led by the idol of the right wing, Enoch Powell. Only two abstained. Heath had allowed a free vote among Conservatives; Wilson had tried to whip Labour into the anticommunity camp. Although the anticommunity Labour left called for reprisals against Jenkins and

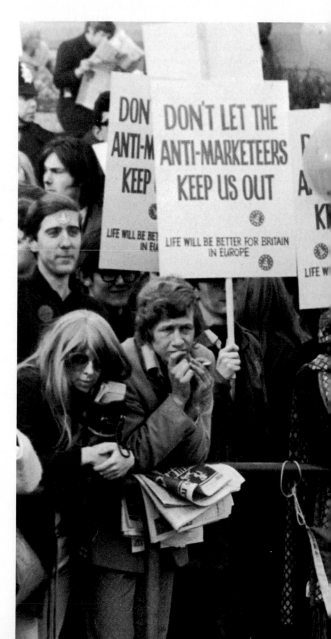

London backers of Great Britain's membership in the European Community confronted and heckled anti-market housewives holding a rally in Trafalgar Square.

other senior marketeers, including the entire treasury and foreign office teams from Wilson's tenure, Jenkins was re-elected the party's deputy leader on November 17. But Heath could no longer rely on Jenkins' support to pass further detailed legislation necessary to bring Britain into line with the community. Henceforward, he had to rely on Conservative and Liberal votes alone.

Sluggish Economy. The government's failure to persuade the public of the virtues of joining the Common Market came partly from the unpopularity it earned in failing to cope with price inflation (10 per cent during the year) and the highest unemployment since 1940. In a parliamentary by-election on May 27, the Conservatives lost the

"safe" seat of Bromsgrove, near Birmingham, and on September 30 hung onto another stronghold at Macclesfield only by the skin of their teeth. Cabinet ministers blamed excessive wage increases. Average earnings rose by 15 per cent during the year, with the automotive industry leading the way to even higher levels, while production rose very little and capital investment slumped. Government and employers seemed powerless to resist militant unions until a seven-week strike by the post office workers was beaten, and a wage rise of only 9 per cent granted in May. The workers had demanded a 13 per cent increase.

Barber's Tax Cuts. In two tax-cutting budgets, March 31 and July 19, Chancellor of the Exchequer

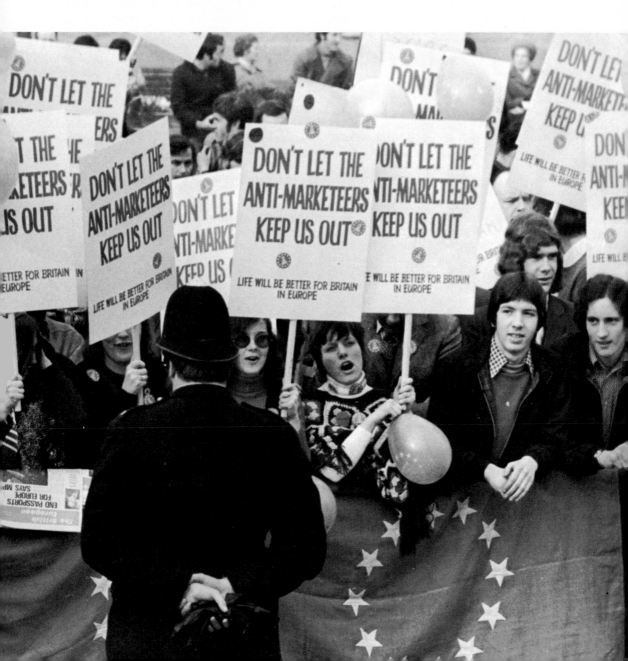

Anthony Barber tried to stimulate growth and investment through a consumer-led boom. He slashed the selective employment tax, purchase tax, corporation tax, and personal income taxes a total of 1.5-billion pounds sterling (about $3.7 billion) in the first 13 months of Conservative rule. To encourage acceptance of Barber's July measures, the employers in the Confederation of British Industry pledged themselves to keep price inflation down to 5 per cent for the next year. There were no promises from the unions. Consumption rose in the second half of the year but fitfully.

The Ulster Problem. Throughout the summer, the illegal Irish Republican Army (IRA) set off bombs in public buildings, factories, shops, and pubs in Northern Ireland, especially in central Belfast and Londonderry. The Roman Catholic minority rioted and demonstrated against 12,000 British troops who were attempting to keep militant Protestants and Catholics apart. The troops replied with tear gas and rubber bullets. Military searches for arms in Catholic strongholds sparked gunfire. After two civilians were killed in Londonderry, the Social Democratic and Labour Party, the Catholic community's chief political representatives, walked out of Stormont, the province's Parliament building in Belfast, on July 15. Tough, able Brian Faulkner, the Unionist prime minister who succeeded James Chichester-Clark in March, was under increasing Protestant pressure to crack down on the IRA (see FAULKNER, ARTHUR). Chichester-Clark had resigned on March 20 in the face of growing Protestant demands for firmer action against IRA terrorism.

The strife, which had taken almost 200 lives in 28 months, had grown from old religious animosities. The Protestant majority in the north demanded separation from the Republic of Ireland in 1921 because they feared domination by the Roman Catholic majority in the south. But Northern Ireland's Catholic minority has charged discrimination. Pressures for social and political reforms have met firm resistance from large elements of the Unionist Party, which has ruled the country since 1921.

Internment Without Trial. Faulkner paid a lightning visit to Heath and Home Secretary Reginald Maudling in London in August to secure their agreement to imprison suspected IRA activists without trial. Over 300 Catholics were picked up by troops in the first sweep on August 9, but IRA leaders, including Belfast commander Joe Cahill, escaped. Troops and the IRA shot it out. Bombings, riots, and arrests went on. By November, more than 800 suspects were in internment camps and some of them claimed they were brutally treated. The British Army had lost more than 40 men to terrorist action in Northern Ireland. Catholic girls who went out with British soldiers had their hair cut off and were tarred by Catholic women.

Faulkner offered the Catholics greater hope of representation at Stormont, but most of Ulster's Catholic politicians and Irish Prime Minister John Lynch in Dublin insisted on Stormont's abolition as a symbol of British rule in Northern Ireland. Protestant militants, under Ian Paisley, a Protestant minister, threatened outright civil war rather than give way. Heath, with dwindling support from Wilson, insisted that Britain would see the crisis through. Opinion polls showed, however, that 39 per cent of the British people wanted the troops brought home.

Talks in Rhodesia. Foreign Secretary Sir Alec Douglas-Home flew to Salisbury, Rhodesia, in November to see rebel Prime Minister Ian D. Smith in a final effort to settle the six-year quarrel. Conservative right-wingers sought to end Britain's trade blockade against its breakaway colony as ineffectual and costly. Liberal opinion hotly opposed such moves as a sell-out of Rhodesia's Africans. Britain had refused to agree to Rhodesian independence until whites there conceded eventual black majority rule—but that might not come in the next 100 years. On December 1, the House of Commons voted to accept the agreement reached by Douglas-Home and Smith, but the approval of the Rhodesian people was yet to come. See RHODESIA.

The Rolls Row. Rolls-Royce, the firm whose name was a worldwide symbol of British craftsmanship, went bankrupt on February 4. The company had contracted to develop and supply RB-211 engines for America's Lockheed Aircraft Corporation's Tri-Star airbus at too low a price. Heath commented, "For too long, much of our apparent prosperity has been based on illusions." With 30,000 jobs at stake at Rolls (and more at Lockheed) the affair even became an issue between Heath and U.S. President Richard M. Nixon. Britain kept Rolls in business until a U.S. Senate vote of $250-million for Lockheed in August gave the Tri-Star the go-ahead.

Upper Clyde Shipbuilders, Limited, whose John Brown yard had built the *Queen Mary*, *Queen Elizabeth*, and *Queen Elizabeth II*, also called in the receiver when a further government subsidy was refused on June 14. Angry unions talked of workers' control and began a work-in during August, supported by funds from friendly unions elsewhere, to protest unemployment.

In late September, the government established a company that would hopefully provide the nucleus for the remains of the bankrupt firm. John Davies, minister for trade and industry, said in Glasgow that the new organization would be called Govan Shipbuilders, Limited. The British government had owned 49 per cent of Upper Clyde.

Angry Brigade. A bomb attack was made on the home of Employment Minister Robert Carr on January 12, when his controversial bill to reform

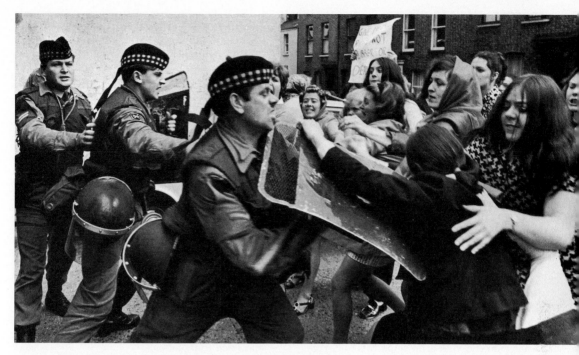

Goaded beyond self-control, British soldiers strike back at jeering Belfast women. Britain originally sent the troops to keep religious militants apart.

the trade unions was passing through the Commons. The attack seemed to threaten a return to political assassination in a country that had not known it for generations. The so-called Angry Brigade, a group purporting to side with such causes as workers' control and a united Ireland, claimed it was responsible for the attack. A bomb exploded on the 31st floor of the Post Office Tower in London on October 31, causing minor damage. Both the Angry Brigade and the IRA said they had planted it. Nearly 6,000 police guarded Queen Elizabeth II at the state opening of Parliament two days later.

Trials of Oz. Many who oppose firm controls over young people were outraged when three editors of the underground paper *Oz* were found guilty under the Obscene Publications Acts and sentenced on August 5 to prison terms of from 9 to 15 months for material published in their "Schoolkids' Issue." One of them, Richard Neville, was recommended for deportation to his native Australia. All three had their long hair shorn while in jail awaiting sentence. Amid wide controversy, the verdicts were set aside on a technicality by an appeals court.

Commercial Radio. The government pushed ahead with plans for a commercial radio system, based on advertising revenue, thus breaking the 50-year monopoly of the state-licensed British Broadcasting Corporation. In legislation proposed in November, posts and telecommunications minister

Chris Chataway envisaged 20 commercial stations operating in two years' time. One of the first two London stations would concentrate on an all-news output. The government expected up to 60 stations would be able to operate commercially. Labour spokesmen doubted the demand for any.

Sporting Princess. Despite more than one public spill, 21-year-old Princess Anne determinedly rode her way into the top flight of British equestrianism. She won the European Three-Day Event Championship at Burghley in September. A horse-loving nation loyally voted her Sportswoman of the Year. Her father, Prince Philip, reluctantly decided at 50 that old age disqualified him from his favorite sport, polo.

A House of Commons committee split along party lines on December 2 and voted, 8 to 7, to recommend an increase of 106 per cent in the salary of Queen Elizabeth II. It was meant to meet inflation's pressure on the royalty's public functions. Other members of the royal family also were to get raises. Members of Parliament were less divided over proposals to raise their own pay.

Facts in Brief. Population: 56,540,000. Government: Queen Elizabeth II; Prime Minister Edward Heath. Monetary Unit: pound. Foreign Trade: exports, $19,351,000,000; imports, $21,725,000,000. Principal Exports: machinery, motor vehicles, chemicals.   Alastair Burnet

GREECE. Prime Minister George Papadopoulos increased his powers on Aug. 24, 1971, by reshuffling the Cabinet. The change cut the number of ministries from 18 to 13. Three new committees, all headed by Papadopoulos, control national policy, defense, and economic affairs. He also presides over the Government Political Council, which develops economic, social, and national policy. Fifteen secretaries-general of existing ministries, all former military men, were called on to resign. Nikolaos Makareos and Stylianos Pattakos, Papadopoulos' closest colleagues in the 1967 military coup, became deputy prime ministers.

Regime Criticized. The 17-nation Council of Europe said on January 21 in Strasbourg, France, that repressive policies had cut the government off from the Greek people. Also in January, the government cut off visits to political prisoners by the International Red Cross. After investigators from the United States Senate Foreign Relations Committee visited Greece, U.S. Secretary of State William P. Rogers declared: "We have been disappointed that more has not been done to move towards the restoration of representative democracy." But the U.S. House Foreign Affairs Committee narrowly rejected a move to end U.S. arms shipments to Greece.

A law restricting the activities of journalists was published on August 4, but it was drastically revised 14 days later after protests. The second draft dropped all mention of obedience to Hellenic Christian traditions, or to "councils of honor."

Lady Fleming Jailed. In September, Lady Amalia Fleming, widow of the discoverer of penicillin, and a diabetic, was sentenced to prison by a Greek military court for her part in an effort to free Alexandros Panaghoulis from jail. He was convicted in 1968 of trying to kill Papadopoulos. Lady Fleming, 62, who had dual Greek and British citizenship, was later stripped of her Greek citizenship and exiled to Great Britain. She said she would continue to oppose the regime.

Expanding Economy. Inflation worsened, but the economy continued to expand. Much of the trade deficit was offset by foreign investments. A target was set of an average economic growth rate of 7.6 per cent over the next 10 years. After 31 years, Greece and Albania resumed diplomatic relations on May 6.

Facts in Brief. Population: 9,022,000. Government: Regent George Zoitakis; Prime Minister George Papadopoulos. Monetary Unit: drachma. Foreign Trade: exports, $642,000,000; imports, $1,956,000,000. Principal Exports: tobacco, fresh and dried fruit, cotton.   Kenneth Brown

GUATEMALA. See LATIN AMERICA.

GUINEA. See AFRICA.

Regent George Zoitakis, right, reviewed the parade held in Athens in March, when Greece observed its 150th anniversary of independence from Turkey.

GUYANA. Three major governmental changes took place in 1971. On January 1, two new ministries created by Prime Minister L. F. S. Burnham began operating. One, public corporations, was headed by Burnham; the other, mines and forests, was placed under the administration of Hubert O. Jack. On January 4, Sase Narain of the ruling National Congress Party was elected speaker of the Assembly.

Late in February, the government announced plans to nationalize the Canadian-owned Demerara Bauxite Company. It also indicated it would pay the owners, Canadian-based Alcan Aluminium, Limited, "reasonable compensation." Subsequently, Prime Minister Burnham signed into law a bill approving payment to Alcan Aluminium, Limited, of $53.5 million over a period of no more than 20 years.

On January 4, the joint Surinam-Guyana border commission held its first meeting in Georgetown. In an effort to establish closer relations between the two countries, delegates voted to establish a telecommunications link between Georgetown and Paramaribo, the capital of Surinam.

Facts in Brief. Population: 813,000. Government: President Arthur Robert Chung; Prime Minister L. F. S. Burnham. Monetary Unit: Guyana dollar. Foreign Trade: exports, $134,000,000; imports, $134,000,000. Principal Exports: sugar, bauxite, alumina.   Paul C. Tullier

Jean-Claude Duvalier, seated, was hand-picked to succeed his father François, standing, as president shortly before the latter's death in April, 1971.

HAITI. Jean-Claude Duvalier was sworn in as president for life on April 22, 1971. He succeeded his father, François Duvalier, who had died the day before of natural causes. The succession had been made possible in January when the Chamber of Deputies approved 13 constitutional amendments sponsored by the elder Duvalier, including one that lowered the age requirement for the presidency from 40 to 20.

The new head of state immediately named a Cabinet of 12 members, including four ministers who had served in his father's government. In his first policy statement after taking office, Duvalier indicated a desire to renew Haiti's ties with the United States. Because of the elder Duvalier's repressive regime, these ties had deteriorated badly. The United States, he said, "will always find Haiti on its side against Communism, especially in combating atheistic Marxism in Cuba and Chile." He promised to reorganize the nation's economy, as well as feed the hungry and "raise the national standard of living to one compatible with human dignity." He also declared an amnesty that would affect about 400,000 exiles who had fled Haiti because of disaffection with the elder Duvalier's regime. Under its terms, the exiles would be permitted to return and form opposition parties, but the Communist Party and revolutionary parties remained expressly forbidden. Later, the amnesty was modi-

fied to exclude about 1,000 persons imprisoned in Haitian jails for political crimes. In July, in a move to reduce the power and autonomy of the Ton Ton Macoute, an armed unit created by his father, President Duvalier dismissed the unit's leader.

A behind-the-scenes power struggle between two factions threatened the stability of the new Duvalier government. One faction, led by the young president's sister, Denise Dominique, and her husband, Colonel Max Dominique, Haiti's ambassador to France, apparently advocated a rapid liberalization of the Haitian regime. In direct opposition was a clique headed by Interior and Defense Minister Lieutenant Colonel Luckner Cambronne and Simone Duvalier, the president's mother. The young Duvalier sided with Cambronne, and Mrs. Dominique and her husband returned to Paris.

In August, acting on a request by the new government, the U.S. Department of State indicated it would arrange for U.S. technical advisers to help organize the Haitian customs and postal services. There were also indications that the U.S. government would permit Haiti to buy small arms and matériel to equip an antiguerrilla unit.

Facts in Brief. Population: 5,060,000. Government: President Jean-Claude Duvalier. Monetary Unit: gourde. Foreign Trade: exports, $40,000,000; imports, $42,000,000. Principal Exports: coffee, bauxite, sisal.   Paul C. Tullier

HANDICAPPED. A total of 291,272 disabled Americans were rehabilitated to productive activities in the United States during the fiscal year that ended on June 30, 1971. This was 9 per cent higher than the previous year's total, and represented the highest annual total ever reached, according to the Social Rehabilitation Service of the Department of Health, Education, and Welfare (HEW).

For the 10th consecutive year, Pennsylvania led all states with 20,064 individuals rehabilitated. Texas ranked second with 17,905, followed by California (14,430), Illinois (14,001), North Carolina (13,144), Florida (12,277), Georgia (11,512), New York (11,405), Virginia (11,042), and Kentucky (9,832).

Sidney P. Marland, Jr., U.S. commissioner of education, urged the adoption of a national goal to provide full educational opportunity for every handicapped child in the United States by 1980. Terrel H. Bell, deputy commissioner for school systems, and Edwin W. Martin, associate commissioner of education for the handicapped, were assigned to plan toward the 1980 goal.

Objectives for expanding education of the handicapped in 1972 included:

■ Extension of special-education programs to an additional 250,000 school-age children, raising the total to nearly 3 million.

■ Providing of appropriate career-education programs, including placement and employment services, for 250,000 teen-age handicapped students already receiving special education.

■ Qualifying, in 1972, of 17,000 trained teachers, teacher trainers, and other specialized personnel needed to conduct the additional special-education programs.

■ Training of 12,000 existing teachers to work with handicapped children in regular classrooms.

Deaf and Blind Center. Construction of a new national center for deaf-blind youths and adults started in 1971. The center will be operated by the Industrial Home for the Blind in New York City. The first training and research center of its kind in the nation, it was made possible through a grant of $2.5 million and an award of 25 acres of surplus government property from HEW.

From four to six satellite offices for the deaf and blind are also planned for other cities. They would identify and refer handicapped persons to the national center for training and services. Two of the offices, in Glendale, Calif., and Atlanta, Ga., began operating late in 1971.

Organizations. The 6th World Congress on the Deaf was held Aug. 2 to 7, 1971, in the United Nations Educational, Scientific, and Cultural Organization headquarters in Paris. Deaf persons and experts specializing in their problems attended.

A blind child tries to remember what items are behind doors covered with various textured materials. The learning device is called a tactile board.

The American Foundation for the Blind observed its 50th anniversary by sponsoring a series of events from October 25 to 29. The foundation also joined five other major organizations for the blind in the first semiannual meeting to discuss the needs of blind persons and nationwide trends and legislation that affect them. The five other participants: American Association of Workers for the Blind, American Council for the Blind, Association for the Education of the Visually Handicapped, National Council of State Agencies for the Blind, and National Federation of the Blind.

New Devices. The Bell System developed a new toy that enables blind children to enjoy sports. Called the "Audio Ball," it emits a constant beeping sound so that its movement can be tracked by sound, not sight. Teachers using the ball with blind youngsters find that students show better coordination and more confidence in moving around.

A new wheel chair may soon enable an estimated half-million handicapped persons to successfully cope with the stand-up world of water fountains, mailboxes, and pay telephones. Peter Bressler, a 25-year-old designer from Pittsburgh, has developed a "stand-up wheel chair." The seat tilts upward, raising the occupant while supporting him below the knees with a padded brace. Joseph P. Anderson

HARNESS RACING. See HORSE RACING.

HAWAII. See STATE GOVERNMENT.

HEALTH AND DISEASE. The World Health Organization announced in June that cholera had spread along the entire 1,350-mile West Bengal-East Pakistan boundary. Thousands of East Pakistan refugees died from the disease. The British foreign secretary, Sir Alec Douglas-Home, said that the size of the problem required coordination and direction by a central body. He called on the United Nations to assume that role.

In July, the Spanish government confirmed that there was also an outbreak of cholera in the northeast, centered on Saragossa. It said, however, that the situation was under control. A total of 7 persons were stricken in the province, whose more than 650,000 people were vaccinated against the disease. By August, a total of 2,011 persons had died in a cholera epidemic that started in May and swept through Chad in central Africa. Cholera was also reported spreading in 17 other African countries.

Measles Cases. The incidence of rubeola (red measles) reached a five-year high, despite the general availability of an effective vaccine. Cutbacks in federal funding of immunization programs were at least partly to blame, according to government sources. Figures for the rubeola "epidemiologic year"—an accounting period beginning in mid-October—indicated almost twice as many cases in the 1970-1971 period as were reported in 1969-1970. Rubeola is a major childhood disease that can cause inflamma-

tion of the brain, mental retardation, deafness, pneumonia, inflammation of the middle ear, and even death.

About 23 million children were vaccinated against rubella (German measles) during the 18 months prior to February, 1971, according to the U.S. Department of Health, Education, and Welfare. This was the largest number of children ever immunized in such a short time after licensing a new vaccine, according to Dr. David J. Sencer, director of the Center for Disease Control in Atlanta, Ga. The disease is mild when it occurs in children and most adults, but it can cause birth defects in an unborn child if it strikes a woman during pregnancy.

Venereal Disease. A new type of gonorrhea that stubbornly resists the usual treatment has aggravated an already "rampant epidemic" of venereal disease in California, according to public health officials. Dr. Warren Keterer, chief of venereal disease control for the California Public Health Department, said in April that the gonorrhea caseload was running 54 per cent ahead of the previous year and was substantially above the national level. The virulent new strain, called Asian or Vietnamese gonorrhea, is believed by some medical men to have been introduced into the United States by military personnel returning from Southeast Asia. Other authorities, including military doctors, say that the new strain may be the result of natural mutations that have made the gonorrhea organism more resistant to penicillin.

Abortions. Gordon Chase, New York City's health services administrator, reported in February that an estimated 69,000 abortions were performed during the first six months of legalized abortion in the state. Half of the abortions were performed on women from other states. The estimate did not include abortions performed in doctors' offices. The state law, which took effect July 1, 1970, permits abortions anywhere, but the city's health code was amended on Oct. 19, 1970, to require that the operation be performed only in hospitals or approved clinics. New York City residents accounted for 44.9 per cent of the total.

Health Insurance. In February, 1971, President Richard M. Nixon sent a national health insurance plan to Congress. Shortly thereafter, the American Medical Association presented its own health care plan, and other plans were introduced by various senators and congressmen. However, Dr. Harry Backer, a specialist in medical economics and professor of community health at Yeshiva University's Albert Einstein College of Medicine, said in August that none of the 45 bills before Congress was adequate. It is generally believed, however, that some form of national health insurance will be enacted within the next three years. Theodore F. Treuting

HIGHWAY. See BUILDING AND CONSTRUCTION; TRANSPORTATION.

HOBBIES

HOBBIES. A letter believed to be the first signed by President Richard M. Nixon after he took office brought $300 at an auction held in July, 1971, at the Charles Hamilton Galleries in New York City.

A few days earlier, the Hamilton Galleries had sold a Senate resolution expressing sympathy on the death of Senator Robert Taft for $775. The document bore the signature of the late President John F. Kennedy. A signed photograph of the late Senator Robert F. Kennedy sold for $65, and an 11-cent airmail sheet bearing the signatures of both Robert and Senator Edward M. Kennedy went for $75. Hamilton said the prices indicate that Kennedy autographs are increasing in value. Jacqueline Kennedy Onassis autographs are even more valuable than those of her late husband. Mrs. Onassis, however, has strongly protested the sale of any of her letters and documents.

A record price was paid for an antique Louis XVI writing table. It was auctioned for $415,800 in London in July, more than twice the previous record price for a piece of furniture. The table was part of the collection of 18th century French furniture of Mrs. Anna Thompson Dodge, widow of Horace Dodge, Detroit auto manufacturer. The collection went for $1,685,047.20, a record for a one-day auction of furniture.   *Theodore M. O'Leary*

See also COIN COLLECTING; GAMES, MODELS, AND TOYS; STAMP COLLECTING.

HOCKEY. The Boston Bruins went on a record scoring binge during the National Hockey League's (NHL) 1970-1971 season. But the Montreal Canadiens, despite dissension that cost their coach his job, rallied to win the Stanley Cup.

The NHL, for the first time, played with 14 teams. The two newcomers, Buffalo and Vancouver, finished fifth and sixth in the seven-team East Division. The Chicago Black Hawks, moved from the East Division to the West, easily won regular-season honors there.

The high-scoring Bruins finished first in the East Division and set 35 of the 47 new scoring records. Their leaders were Phil Esposito, who set all-time records with 76 goals and 152 points, and Bobby Orr, who made a record 102 assists (see ESPOSITO, PHIL). For the first time, one team produced the four top scorers—Esposito, Orr with 139 points, Johnny Bucyk with 116, and Ken Hodge with 105. The Bruins did not last long in the play-offs, however. In the first round, the Canadiens eliminated them in seven games. The Canadiens eventually advanced to the final round against Chicago.

The Canadiens coach was Al MacNeil, Claude Ruel had started the season as coach, with MacNeil as his assistant. But Ruel, unhappy with coaching, quit after two months and MacNeil replaced him.

Play-Off Finals. After the Canadiens and Black Hawks had split the first four games of the play-off

Standings in National Hockey League

East Division	W.	L.	T.	Pts.
Boston	57	14	7	121
New York	49	18	11	109
Montreal	42	23	13	97
Toronto	37	33	8	82
Buffalo	24	39	15	63
Vancouver	24	46	8	56
Detroit	22	45	11	55

West Division	W.	L.	T.	Pts.
Chicago	49	20	9	107
St. Louis	34	25	19	87
Philadelphia	28	33	17	73
Minnesota	28	34	16	72
Los Angeles	25	40	13	63
Pittsburgh	21	37	20	62
California	20	53	5	45

Scoring Leaders	Games	Goals	Assists	Points
Phil Esposito, Boston	78	76	76	152
Bobby Orr, Boston	78	37	102	139
John Bucyk, Boston	78	51	65	116
Ken Hodge, Boston	78	43	62	105
Bobby Hull, Chicago	78	44	52	96
Norm Ullman, Toronto	73	34	51	85
Wayne Cashman, Boston	77	21	58	79
John McKenzie, Boston	65	31	46	77
Dave Keon, Toronto	76	38	38	76
Jean Beliveau, Montreal	70	25	51	76
Fred Stanfield, Boston	75	24	52	76
Walt Tkaczuk, New York	77	26	49	75
Yvan Cournoyer, Montreal	65	37	36	73
Frank Mahovlich, Detroit-Montreal	73	31	42	73
Gilles Perreault, Buffalo	78	38	34	72

Leading Goalies	Games	Minutes	Goals against	Avg.
Ed Giacomin, New York	45	2,641	95	2.15
Gilles Villemure, New York	34	2,039	78	2.29
New York Totals	78	4,680	177	2.26
Tony Esposito, Chicago	57	3,325	126	2.27
Gerry Desjardins, Chicago	22	1,217	49	2.41
Chicago Totals	78	4,680	184	2.35
Ed Johnston, Boston	38	2,280	96	2.52
Gerry Cheevers, Boston	40	2,400	109	2.72
Boston Totals	78	4,680	207	2.65

Awards

Calder Trophy (best rookie of the year)
  Gil Perreault, Buffalo.
Hart Trophy (most valuable player)
  Bobby Orr, Boston.
Lady Byng Trophy (sportsmanship)
  John Bucyk, Boston.
Norris Trophy (best defenseman)
  Bobby Orr, Boston.
Ross Trophy (leading scorer)
  Phil Esposito, Boston.
Smythe Trophy (most valuable in Stanley Cup play)
  Ken Dryden, Montreal.
Vezina Trophy (leading goalie)
  Ed Giacomin and Gilles Villemure, New York.

Black Hawks' Dennis Hull (10) follows puck into net past Montreal's startled goalie Ken Dryden in Stanley Cup play-offs. The goal counted.

finals, MacNeil shuffled his forward lines. He used 22 line combinations in the fifth game, but the Canadiens still lost, 2-0. Henri Richard, who had been benched in the shuffle, was furious. The 35-year-old Richard, who had played on nine Montreal Stanley Cup championship teams, said of MacNeil, "This is the worst coach I ever played for. He is an incompetent coach." MacNeil took the criticism calmly, however, saying, "I've heard all that before."

Richard was back on the ice for the sixth game, which the Canadiens won, 4-3, to send the series into a seventh and deciding game, May 18, in Chicago. The Canadiens won that one, 3-2, as the graying Richard scored both the tying and winning goals.

Another Canadien hero was Ken Dryden, a 6-foot 4-inch graduate of Cornell University, who had played his first NHL game only two months before. Dryden became the Canadiens' regular goalie, and his play was decisive against the Bruins and Black Hawks. He won the Smythe Trophy as the Most Valuable Player in the play-offs.

The Stanley Cup was the 16th for the Canadiens and their appearance in the final round was their 21st, both records. It was also the beginning and the end for MacNeil. A month after the play-offs, he resigned under pressure and returned to a minor league coaching job. His replacement was Bill

(Scotty) Bowman, who had been general manager and coach of the St. Louis Blues.

Howe and Beliveau. It was the last season for Gordie Howe and Jean Beliveau, the league's two leading all-time scorers. Howe retired after a record 25 years, all with Detroit—not because of his age, 43, but because of an arthritic left wrist. Beliveau, 39, had completed 18 years with the Canadiens. Howe's career totals of 786 goals, 1,023 assists, 1,809 points, and 1,687 games were all records. Both became vice-presidents of their clubs.

Howe was one of the game's few $100,000-a-year players, and Beliveau earned almost as much. After the season, Orr and Esposito signed long-term contracts that made them the highest paid players in hockey history. Orr signed for $200,000 a year for five years, Esposito for $150,000 a year for four years. The All-Star Team consisted of Esposito at center, Bucyk and Hodge at wing, Orr and J. C. Tremblay of Montreal on defense, and Ed Giacomin of New York in goal.

Expansion Plans. The NHL announced in November that it would add new teams in Atlanta and Long Island, New York, for the 1972-1973 season. The action came after the new, 10-team World Hockey Association (WHA) announced it would start play in 1972. The WHA immediately filed a $33-million antitrust suit, contending the NHL action was taken to kill the WHA.   Frank Litsky

HOGNESS, JOHN RUSTEN (1922-   ), a physician known for his interest in all aspects of American health care, became president of the National Academy of Science's newly created Institute of Medicine on Aug. 1, 1971. The institute was created to identify and study the broadest, most difficult medical problems. Among its first activities are programs investigating whether physicians should allow incurable patients to die rather than prolong their suffering, and the desirability of a national health insurance plan.

Hogness was born in Oakland, Calif. He studied at Haverford College from 1939 to 1942. He received a bachelor's degree in chemistry in 1943 from the University of Chicago and his M.D. in 1946 from the University of Chicago School of Medicine.

After serving as a medical officer in the U.S. Army from 1947 to 1949, Hogness was assistant resident in medicine at the Columbia-Presbyterian Medical Center in New York City for a year, and then became chief resident in medicine at the University of Washington's King County Hospital in Seattle. He remained there until 1971, becoming director of the university's Health Service Center and chairman of its Board of Health Sciences.

Hogness married Katharine Ruenauver in 1944. They have 3 sons and 2 daughters.   Michael Reed

HOME FURNISHINGS. See INTERIOR DESIGN.

HONDURAS. See LATIN AMERICA.

HONECKER, ERICH (1912-   ), was elected first secretary of East Germany's Socialist Unity (Communist) Party on May 3, 1971. He succeeded Walter Ulbricht, who resigned. Honecker, a hard-line Communist leader and an Ulbricht disciple since 1945, had been in charge of East German security since 1958.

Honecker was born in Neunkirchen, a small Saar industrial town, the son of a miner. He became a member of the Young Pioneers, a Communist youth group, at the age of 10. At 14, he joined the Communist youth association, and, at 17, the German Communist Party. In 1935, he was sentenced to prison for illegal political activity. After 10 years in a Nazi prison, most of them in solitary confinement, Russian troops freed him in 1945. He promptly joined a small "Ulbricht group," which was flown to East Berlin to set up a government. From 1946 to 1955, he was chairman of the Free German Youth, the group that provided the force to drive democrats from the joint Berlin administration in 1948. It also helped to crush the workers' uprising of 1953 and provided the manpower to man the barricades that became part of the Berlin Wall in 1961.

Honecker married Edith Baumann, a minor party official, but divorced her in 1953. He then married Margot Feist, who was later appointed East Germany's minister of education.   Ed Nelson

HORSE RACING. Canonero II, a 3-year-old from Venezuela, surprised racing enthusiasts in 1971 by winning two of the Triple Crown events. Bred in the United States but previously raced only in Venezuela, the lightly regarded colt upset many of the best 3-year-olds with a stunning stretch run in the Kentucky Derby, the first Triple Crown event, on May 1.

Canonero II then won the Preakness on May 15, but physical problems proved his undoing in the final Triple Crown race, the Belmont Stakes on June 5. A long shot, Pass Catcher, won, with Canonero II coming in fourth. Canonero II did not race again in 1971, and was sold to U.S. interests.

Bold Reason and Run the Gantlet dominated the 3-year-old division later in the year. Bold Reason's victories included the American Derby, Hollywood Derby, and Travers. Run the Gantlet beat older horses in the Washington, D.C., International, the Man o' War, the United Nations Handicap, and other stakes races.

Among the better older horses were Ack Ack and Cougar II, consistent winners of California's major stakes races. In the East, Cougar II, a Chilean-bred horse, won the Woodward easily but was disqualified for cutting off another horse in the stretch.

Shuvee, a 5-year-old mare, was queen of the turf. She won the 2-mile Jockey Club Gold Cup against males for the second year in a row, and retired with career earnings of $890,445, a world's record for her sex. Other outstanding mares were Drumtop, Princess Pout, and 3-year-old Turkish Trousers, who compiled a record string of eight stakes victories in California.

Legal Off-Track Betting started in New York City on April 7. The Off-Track Betting Corporation accepted bets on all regular and harness-track racing in the state, as well as on some races elsewhere.

Investigation of the ownership of Santa Anita Derby winner Jim French led to suspensions of a prominent owner, Ralph C. Wilson, and two trainers, John P. Campo and George T. Poole. They allegedly had dealings with a man, barred from racing, who hid his ownership interest in Jim French.

Laffit Pincay, Jr., established a one-year earnings record as a jockey when his mounts' income exceeded the $3,088,888 mark set in 1967.

In Europe, 3-year-old Mill Reef was the champion of England and France, and Pistol Packer was the best 3-year-old filly in France. Both horses were bred in the United States.

Harness Racing. World time records highlighted the harness season. Steady Star paced a 1-minute 52-second mile in a time trial, and the 3-year-old pacer Albatross registered the fastest harness racing mile ever—1 minute 54 4/5 seconds. Both records were set in Lexington, Ky.   Jane Goldstein

HOSPITAL. See HEALTH AND DISEASE.

HOTEL. See TRAVEL.

Major U.S. Horse Races of 1971

Race	Winner	Value to Winner
American Derby Handicap	Bold Reason	$ 81,950
Belmont Stakes	Pass Catcher	97,710
Brooklyn Handicap	Never Bow	115,100
California Derby	Unconscious	72,900
Champagne Stakes	Riva Ridge	117,090
Charles H. Strub	War Heim	87,100
Coaching Club American Oaks	Our Cheri Amour	78,975
Colonial Cup Steeplechase	Inkslinger	63,000
Delaware Handicap	Blessing Angelica	80,860
Flamingo Stakes	Executioner	100,750
Florida Derby	Eastern Fleet	82,680
Futurity	Riva Ridge	87,636
Garden State Stakes	Riva Ridge	176,334
Gardenia Stakes	Numbered Account	110,625
Gulfstream Park Handicap	Fast Hilarious	77,040
Hawthorne Gold Cup	Twice Worthy	73,880
Hialeah Turf Cup	Drumtop	93,340
Hollywood Gold Cup	Ack Ack	100,000
Jersey Derby	Bold Reason	87,360
Jockey Club Gold Cup	Shuvee	66,900
Kentucky Derby	Canonero II	145,500
Man o' War Stakes	Run the Gantlet	67,200
Metropolitan Handicap	Tunex	72,960
Monmouth Handicap	West Coast Scout	65,000
Preakness	Canonero II	137,400
San Juan Capistrano	Cougar II	75,000
Santa Anita Derby	Jim French	88,400
Santa Anita Handicap	Ack Ack	100,000
Suburban Handicap	Twice Worthy	69,240
Sunset Handicap	Over the Counter	80,650
Travers	Bold Reason	$ 66,420
United Nations Handicap	Run the Gantlet	65,000
Washington, D.C., International	Run the Gantlet	100,000
Widener Handicap	True North	96,850
Woodward Stakes	West Coast Scout	67,860

Major Foreign Horse Races of 1971

Race	Winner	Value to Winner
Epsom Derby	Mill Reef	$154,062
French Derby	Rheffic	249,905
Grand National Steeplechase	Specify	38,750
Grand Prix de Paris	Rheffic	220,977
Irish Derby	Irish Ball	155,250
King George VI and Queen Elizabeth Stakes	Mill Reef	78,895
Prix de l'Arc de Triomphe	Mill Reef	262,997
Queen's Plate	Kennedy Road	54,389
St. Leger	Athens Wood	89,355

Major U.S. Harness Races of 1971

Race	Winner	Value to Winner
Cane Futurity Pace	Albatross	$ 53,397
Hambletonian	Speedy Crown	64,885
Kentucky Futurity	Savoir	31,707
Little Brown Jug	Nansemond	31,919
Messenger Pace	Albatross	57,488
Roosevelt International	Une de Mai	62,500
Yonkers Futurity	Quick Pride	55,397

HOUSING. The U.S. housing industry set a record with the number of new housing units started in 1971. The industry reached a record peak in July, when the adjusted rate of annual housing starts reached 2.215 million units. This broke a record that had stood since August, 1950. The industry went on to set a still higher record in August, when it hit an adjusted annual rate of 2.228 million units.

There were several reasons behind the spectacular increase in the volume of new housing units under construction. One was the upsurge in the number of apartment buildings under construction. New records were set in this category, too, as approximately 750,000 new apartment-house units were started in 1971. The previous high mark of 571,000 units started was set in 1969.

Declining Interest Rates on home mortgages helped spur the building boom. Mortgage interest rates, which had reached a high of 8.5 to 9 per cent in mid-1970, rapidly declined to 7 per cent or less by 1971. Tight money pressures in the mortgage market were eased considerably by the effects of the nation's wage-price freeze. The announcement of the freeze in August brought a sharp decline in long-term bond interest rates, which, in turn, diverted more funds into the residential-mortgage market.

The Federal Housing Administration's program to subsidize home ownership for low- and moderate-income families has been stimulating the construction of moderately priced dwellings. Authorized under the Housing Act of 1968, government subsidies can pay all but 1 per cent of the interest on 30-year mortgage loans of up to $24,000 for families earning between $5,000 and $10,000 a year.

Lower Cost Units. The 1971 housing boom was also stimulated by the industry's own shift in emphasis to the construction of less-expensive housing. Builders have been returning to the construction of small homes made of cheaper materials on smaller lots. Also, the increasing construction of townhouses and apartments reduced the per-unit cost of new housing.

Mobile homes, meanwhile, continue to be the nation's most popular form of inexpensive housing. Although mobile-home output was down to 414,000 units in 1970, it recovered in 1971. An estimated 450,000 mobile homes were produced during the year. Statistics released by the Mobile Home Manufacturers Association pointed out that nearly 6 million people now live in mobile homes and 85 per cent of all mobile-home residents are married couples. Nearly 50 per cent of all mobile homes are occupied by persons under 35 years of age.

Operation Breakthrough, in May, unveiled its first housing units. The prefab modules were placed on sites in Kalamazoo, Mich. Operation Breakthrough was begun by the U.S. Department of

This "high-rise" trailer project near Minneapolis, Minn., solves a space problem for parking mobile homes, a popular type of low-cost housing.

Housing and Urban Development in 1969 to foster large-volume, factory-built housing production. Breakthrough has housing sites under development in Indianapolis, Ind.; Jersey City, N.J.; Macon, Ga.; Memphis, Tenn.; St. Louis; Sacramento, Calif.; and Seattle.

The 1970 Housing Census revealed that the number of housing units in the United States increased by 18 per cent between 1960 and 1970, to a total of 68.6 million units. This compared unfavorably with the 26 per cent increase in the number of units built during the 1950s. In 1970, 63 per cent of the nation's families owned their homes, compared with 61.9 per cent in 1960 and 55 per cent in 1950.

The average number of persons per housing unit decreased during the 1960s. There were 3.3 persons per unit in 1960, but only 3.1 persons in 1970. The number of housing units with more than 1 person per room dropped from 6.1 million in 1960 to 5.2-million in 1970.

The average 1970 family home was much better than the average family home of a decade ago, according to the housing census. The typical family-owned home in 1970 had five rooms, was located in a metropolitan area, had complete kitchen and bathroom facilities, and contained piped hot water and central heating. It was worth approximately $17,000, representing a 43 per cent increase over the 1960 value of an average home.　　J. M. Banovetz

382

HOUSTON was rated in 1971 as the nation's fastest-growing major city. The 1970 census showed that the city's population rose 31.4 per cent during the 1960s to a 1970 count of 1,232,802. This was in striking contrast to many other large cities, which suffered population declines.

Houston also had one of the fastest rates of increase in black population, which rose by 47.2 per cent during the 1960s. Blacks made up 25.7 per cent of the total population in 1970. The relief-dependency rate of 4.2 per cent in Harris and Montgomery counties, where Houston is located, ranked as one of the lowest among major urban areas.

Integration Problems. A Houston desegregation plan pairing 22 elementary schools was ruled unacceptable by a U.S. district court on May 25. Pairing programs aim at attaining racial balance by exchanging selected students between two or more racially unbalanced schools. The court also ruled that Mexican-Americans were not entitled to relief under a court order issued in August, 1970, pairing 25 other elementary schools. Mexican-Americans charged that most of these pairings linked schools with predominantly Negro student bodies with schools with a high percentage of Mexican-Americans. Blacks account for little more than 8 per cent of the pupils in predominantly white schools.

In August, the Mexican-American Education Council called for a boycott of public schools. However, school officials reported that most of the city's 35,000 Mexican-American pupils attended public schools on opening day.

Minority Gains. Minorities and liberal whites made substantial gains in Houston's November elections. A black and a Mexican-American won seats on the school board, and, for the first time, a black was elected to the City Council.

Mayor Louie Welch, however, won a run-off election on December 7, defeating Fred Hofheinz, a 33-year-old lawyer. The running of the police department, repeatedly charged with brutality against minorities, had been a major campaign issue.

Environmental Issues. Between May and July, the federal government filed five criminal charges and one civil charge against six private firms in the Houston area. The firms were accused of discharging wastes into the Houston Ship Channel. Because of the extent of oil pollution, the channel is regarded as a fire hazard. In July, the city and the Texas Air Control Board filed charges against a chemical company for discharging poisonous gas.

City and county governments in the Houston area have launched the first phase of a three-stage program aimed at clearing up future drainage and flood-control problems. The first phase, costing $122.3 million, will be completed by 1974. The second and third phases, scheduled for completion before 1978, will cost $80 million.   J. M. Banovetz

HUMPHREY, HUBERT HORATIO (1911-   ), former Vice-President and an unsuccessful candidate for the presidency in 1968, told reporters on the occasion of his 60th birthday in May, "I've got my sails up. I'm testing the waters." Although he did not officially declare his intention to seek the Democratic nomination until January, 1972, Humphrey was a low-key candidate throughout 1971. In July, he informed the Wisconsin Democratic National Committee that he did not intend to enter that state's 1972 presidential primary, although, he said, he reserved the right to change his mind.

In November, 1970, Humphrey won the Minnesota Senate seat vacated by Eugene McCarthy. After his defeat in the 1968 election by Richard M. Nixon (Humphrey received 43.009 per cent of the popular vote to Mr. Nixon's 43.464 per cent), he returned to Minnesota, where he taught political science at Macalester College in St. Paul and the University of Minnesota in Minneapolis.

Humphrey was born in Wallace, S. Dak. He received a B.A. degree from the University of Minnesota in 1939 and an M.A. from Louisiana State University in 1940.

Prior to his serving as Vice-President under Lyndon B. Johnson, Humphrey was mayor of Minneapolis, from 1945 to 1948, and U.S. senator from Minnesota, from 1949 to 1964. In 1936, Humphrey married Muriel Buck.   Allan Davidson

HUNGARY continued to implement its consumer-oriented economic reform program in 1971. Its close adherence to the Russian foreign policy line, however, led to a temporary chill in relations with Romania and Yugoslavia. Hungary's relatively liberal foreign-trade policy continued despite dramatic growth in the balance of payments deficit, particularly with Western countries. Exports to the West grew slower than imports from the West, but the formation of several joint British-Hungarian firms for trade with third countries promised significant progress. In May, Hungary became the first Communist country since World War II to float a $25-million bond issue in the West.

To ease continuing tension in the investment field, the government made managers directly accountable for delays and failures in capital investment projects. To ease the financial burden of the housing program, rents were increased on July 1 to cover maintenance and repair costs. One of the government's major successes was relative price stability and continued improvement in the supply of consumer goods, a rising proportion of them imported from the West.

The Trade Unions' growing role in national policy as well as on the shop floor was highlighted when strong pleas were made at the May trade union congress to safeguard the position of lower-paid workers under the economic reform. Politics saw little actual change, although many seats were contested for the first time by several candidates at the much-publicized parliamentary and municipal elections on April 25. All campaigned as members of the Patriotic People's Front, the Communist Party organization. Only minor government changes followed. The most important was the promotion of Finance Minister Peter Valyi to deputy prime minister and chief delegate to the Council for Mutual Economic Assistance, the Russian-led East European trade bloc. Lajos Faluvegi replaced him as finance minister.

As Russia's close ally, Hungary played a prominent role in Moscow's summer war of nerves against Yugoslavia and Romania. Hungary's main target was the Romanian and Yugoslavian reconciliation with China. A leading member of the Hungarian Politburo criticized Romania in a June 24 speech. On August 13, a Budapest newspaper, *Magyar Hirlap*, spoke of an Albanian-Romanian-Yugoslav "axis" supported by China. But after Russian party leader Leonid I. Brezhnev's visit to Budapest in September, the whole campaign halted abruptly.

Facts in Brief. Population: 10,388,000. Government: Communist Party First Secretary Janos Kadar; President Pal Losonczi; Premier Jenö Fock. Monetary Unit: forint. Foreign Trade: exports, $2,317,000,000; imports, $2,506,000,000. Principal Exports: machinery, transportation equipment, chemicals.   Chris Cviic

HUNTING AND FISHING. Ten new world records in fresh- and salt-water categories were recognized during 1971. They spanned a range from 1 pound 3 ounces to 1,065 pounds. The official fresh-water world record list, kept by *Field & Stream*, added these five new records: a 16-pound 12-ounce bowfin caught by Joe Woods, Jr., at Lake Murvaul, Tex.; a 26-pound drum, caught by Larry L. Roberts at Jordan Lake, Ala.; a 4-pound 8-ounce red-ear sunfish, caught by Maurice E. Ball at Chase City, Va.; a 1-pound 3-ounce warmouth, caught by James W. Lorio at Atchafalaya Basin, La.; and a 42-pound 2-ounce rainbow trout (a steelhead), caught by David Robert White at Bell Island, Alaska. The trout record was set by an 8-year-old angler.

Five new records were accepted by the International Gamefish Association, official records keepers for salt-water records, during 1971. These were a 110-pound 5-ounce cobia, caught by Eric Tinworth at Mombasa, Kenya; a 50-pound 8-ounce permit, caught by Marshall E. Earnest at Key West, Fla.; a 296-pound yellowfin tuna, caught by Edward C. Malnar at San Benedicto Island, Mexico; a 38-pound blackfin tuna, caught by Archie L. Dickens in Bermuda; and a 1,065-pound bluefin tuna, caught by Robert Glen Gibson at Cape Breton, Canada.

Hunting. Although the hunting picture was generally bright in the United States in the fall of 1971, with good populations of most game birds and game animals reported by the states, one newsworthy change did take place. For the first time in many years, Minnesota did not have a firearms season on white-tailed deer. Bow hunting was allowed, however, because of its negligible deer harvest. This turn of events in Minnesota was the culmination of several years of trouble for the deer herds in the Gopher State and also in Michigan and Wisconsin. The winter range of deer in these states has been progressively reduced by allowing the forests to become increasingly made up of mature trees with few shrubs and small trees. Several hard winters and poor range conditions depleted the number of deer. According to the latest (1970) Federal Fish and Wildlife Service Big Game Inventory. Minnesota's deer harvest dropped from a high in 1965 of 128,000, to a 1968 total of 103,000, and a low in 1970 of 50,000. Michigan had a 1964 high of 143,000, a 1968 total of 99,000; and a 1970 low of 68,000 animals taken. Wisconsin had a 1967 high of 136,000; a 1968 total of 126,000; and a 1970 low of 72,000. Greater restrictions on deer hunting were also in effect in Michigan and Wisconsin in 1971.

By contrast, Texas, the biggest deer-hunting state since the elimination of a devastating parasitic fly, had a whitetail harvest of 279,000 in 1970 from its total herd population of 3.12 million animals. The Texas deer herd is nearly a million animals larger now than it was in 1964. Clare Conley

ICE SKATING. In recent years, the United States has always won at least one world figure skating championship, but has never come close to a speed skating title. The tables were turned in 1971. For the first time in six years, U.S. figure skaters failed to capture a title. But Anne Henning and Dianne Holum, two teen-agers from Northbrook, Ill., won two of the five world speed skating titles for women.

In the women's world championships on February 6 and 7 in Helsinki, Finland, 15-year-old Anne won the 500-meter title and 19-year-old Dianne became the 1,000-meter champion. In the overall standing, based on four races, Nina Statkevich of Russia, the European champion, finished 1st, Miss Holum 4th, and Miss Henning 15th.

Two weeks later, in the international sprint championships in Inzell, West Germany, Miss Henning finished second and Miss Holum third, behind Ruth Schleiermacher of East Germany. On successive days in that meet, Miss Henning became the first woman to better 43 seconds for 500 meters, setting world records of 42.91 seconds and then 42.75.

Ard Schenk of the Netherlands and Jack Walters of Brighton, Mass., were outstanding among the men. The 26-year-old Schenk won the men's world speed skating championship in Göteborg, Sweden, in February, winning 3 of the meet's 4 races. He lost his European title, however, to Dag Fornaess

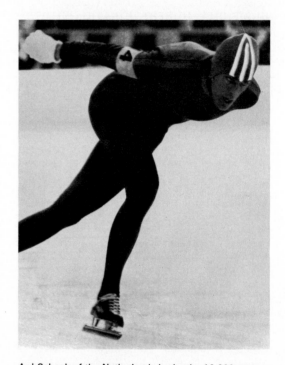

Ard Schenk of the Netherlands broke the 10,000-meter speed skating record in Göteborg, Sweden, in February and then beat his own record in Inzell, West Germany.

of Norway. The 25-year-old Walters ended Pete Cefalu's three-year reign as U.S. outdoor champion and tied Cefalu for the U.S. indoor title.

Figure Skating. European champions swept the four world titles in February in Lyons, France. Ondrej Nepela, 20, of Czechoslovakia, the European champion for three years, took the men's title and 19-year-old Beatrix Schuba of Austria became women's champion. Aleksei Ulanov and Irina Rodina of Russia won their third straight pairs championship.

In the U.S. figure skating championships in Buffalo, N.Y., in January, John Misha Petkevich of Great Falls, Mont., won the men's championship. Janet Lynn, 18, of Rockford, Ill., captured her third consecutive women's title. Jo Jo Starbuck and Kenneth Shelley of Downey, Calif., won their second straight pairs championship.

Petkevich also won the North American championship in February in Peterborough, Canada. Petkevich took the men's title, and Karen Magnussen of Vancouver, Canada, took the women's title. In the world championships in Lyons, the best American finishes were fifth by Petkevich among the men, and second by Julie Lynn Holmes of Littleton, Colo., and fourth by Miss Lynn among the women. Frank Litsky

IDAHO. See STATE GOVERNMENT.

ILLINOIS. See CHICAGO; STATE GOVERNMENT.

IMMIGRATION AND EMIGRATION. The problem of thousands of illegal aliens, working at a time of high unemployment in the United States, was investigated in 1971 by the House Judiciary Subcommittee on Immigration and Nationality. Representative Peter W. Rodino, Jr. (D., N.J.), subcommittee chairman, said that "unscrupulous persons" arrange for aliens to enter illegally or smuggle them in and then give them jobs at substandard wages.

Reportedly, 65 per cent of the illegal aliens come from Mexico, crossing the border secretly. Others from the Dominican Republic and Haiti enter with forged papers identifying them as U.S. citizens or permanent resident aliens.

Federal agents found illegal aliens from Mexico working in the food-processing plant of Romana A. Banuelos, President Richard M. Nixon's nominee for treasurer of the United States. Mrs. Banuelos said she was not aware that her company employed illegal aliens. Mrs. Banuelos' nomination was confirmed by the Senate in December.

The Administration sought to limit the types of jobs that could qualify aliens for visas to the medical, paramedical, and religious professions.

In fiscal 1971, 370,478 immigrants were admitted to the United States, compared with 373,326 in 1970. During the same period, 108,407 aliens became citizens. William McGaffin

INCOME TAX. See TAXATION.

Changing Sources of U.S. Immigrants

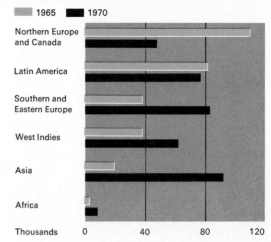

Increase in Immigration to the U.S.

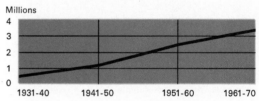

INDIA. An all-out, although undeclared, war broke out between India and Pakistan on Dec. 3, 1971. Each country maintained that the other had triggered the conflict. Although their claims and counterclaims were confusing, there was no doubt that the main cause of the conflict was East Pakistan's determination to set itself up as an independent nation. See ASIA; PAKISTAN.

Earlier in the year, Prime Minister Indira Gandhi won absolute control of the Lok Sabha, India's lower house of Parliament in elections held from March 1 to 10. As the results kept adding to Mrs. Gandhi's majority, the press took to calling it "a typhoon named Indira." In the 515-seat house, her New Congress Party captured 350 seats. No longer dependent on fickle allies, the 54-year-old prime minister could now go ahead with seeking answers to India's problems through a program of moderate socialism.

Even as Mrs. Gandhi was winning a mandate to lead her people to a better life, however, events were taking place only a few hundred miles away that would make this impossible. Within days of the Indian election, the Pakistani Army stationed in East Pakistan struck fiercely at Sheik Mujibur Rahman's Awami (People's) League, which was demanding independence for the eastern region. Within a week, frightened refugees were fleeing to India. By June, the number of refugees was put at 5-

Indian villagers, on their way to the polls, were among hundreds of thousands who gave Prime Minister Indira Gandhi a sweeping victory in the 1971 elections.

million; by late August, it was nearly twice that.

In May, cholera broke out among the refugees, and they fled south in terror, clogging the roads to Calcutta. By October, 5,869 had died from cholera and gastroenteritis. Doctors also estimated that some 150,000 children would die for lack of proper diet.

The Hawks. Mrs. Gandhi had argued all along that President Agha Mohammed Yahya Khan of Pakistan should settle his differences with Mujibur Rahman so the refugees could return home. But because this would involve prolonged negotiations, Mrs. Gandhi took other steps. A haven was offered to the self-proclaimed Bangla Desh (Bengal Nation) government in exile. Some arms and training were also provided to its force of guerrillas.

As the crisis deepened, Mrs. Gandhi increasingly found herself under pressure from the "hawks." All she had to do, they insisted, was to send Indian troops into East Pakistan, install the Bangla Desh government in Dacca, and send the refugees home. Mrs. Gandhi, however, felt war was a simple-minded solution. Instead, at the cost of a traditional policy of nonalignment, India on August 9 signed a 20-year treaty of peace, friendship, and cooperation with Russia. Although the pact was not quite as binding on the Russians as Mrs. Gandhi might have wished, India now had a strong friend for any emergency that might arise over the civil war in Pakistan. The decision to sign the compact was hastened by continued U.S. arms shipments to Pakistan, and by President Richard M. Nixon's efforts to ease strained relations with India's other rival, China.

Tensions Kept Mounting, however, and in late October India called up some 600,000 reservists to join its 825,000 army regulars. In October and November, Mrs. Gandhi toured the United States and other Western nations, pleading with them to exert pressure on President Khan. Then, in December, the two-week war broke out.

This drama was being enacted against the backdrop of "normal" problems. The rate of economic growth, which dropped to 4 per cent in 1970, dipped still lower in 1971. The 1971 census showed an increase of nearly 25 per cent in 10 years, thus giving India 15 per cent of the world population.

The Green Revolution presented the only bright spot. In 1970 and 1971, the yield of food grains reached nearly 108 million tons, against 94 million needed to feed the nation. With the storage sheds overflowing, the government announced that in June, 1972, it would end the agreement under which the United States supplied millions of tons of grain.

Facts in Brief. Population: 578,272,000. Government: President V. V. Giri; Prime Minister Indira Gandhi. Monetary Unit: rupee. Foreign Trade: exports, $1,957,000,000; imports, $2,130,000,000. Principal Exports: jute, tea, iron ore.   Mark Gayn

INDIAN, AMERICAN. Indian activists charged in 1971 that the Bureau of Indian Affairs (BIA) was thwarting efforts to give Indians more self-government. In August, the National Congress of American Indians and several other Indian groups sent President Richard M. Nixon a letter protesting BIA appointments made by Secretary of the Interior Rogers C. B. Morton. They particularly objected to the appointment of John O. Crow as deputy commissioner of Indian affairs.

The Indians charged that the appointments constituted a denial of the policy of Indian self-determination announced by President Nixon in July, 1970. On September 22, a group of Indians tried to make a citizen's arrest of Crow at BIA headquarters. They accused Crow of "criminal injustice" for allegedly blocking proposals aimed at giving Indians a greater voice in their own affairs.

Young Indians working in the bureau were angered by the threatened transfer of William H. Veeder from Washington, D.C., to Phoenix, Ariz. Veeder, an expert on Indian water rights, had criticized the way the rights were handled by the Department of the Interior.

Peter MacDonald, tribal chairman of the Navahos, charged that Indians were living under "a department that is hostile to our interests." On September 21, a group of Indian chiefs asked that the BIA be placed under direct White House control.

Bureau Shakeup. President Nixon, dissatisfied with the operation of the bureau, ordered Morton to "shake it up, and shake it up good." Morton announced that there would be greater emphasis on the advancement of Indian rights and economic progress through service contracts for Indians, road-building on reservations, and more self-government.

Morton's announcement received guarded approval from William Youpee, president of the National Tribal Chairmen's Association. "These are only beginnings," he said.

Indian Demonstrations dramatized their dissatisfaction. A group of Indians set up camp atop Mount Rushmore National Memorial in South Dakota. They were arrested on June 6. A force of U.S. marshals drove a band of Indians from Alcatraz Island on June 11. They had held the island since Nov. 20, 1969.

Militant Indians took over abandoned Army missile bases near Richmond, Calif.; in Chicago; and in Hinsdale, Ill., a Chicago suburb. They declared that old treaties gave them the right to claim unused federal property. Police evicted the Indians.

On December 14, Congress passed a bill granting Alaska's natives $926.5 million and 40 million acres of land in settlement of land claims.   A. L. Newman

INDIANA. See STATE GOVERNMENT.

INDONESIA. The military government of General Suharto made significant political and social gains in 1971. For the first time in 16 years, national elections were held on July 3 for 360 seats in the 460-member parliament. The government had reserved 100 of the seats for presidential appointments. About 85 per cent of the 57 million Indonesians eligible to vote turned out and endorsed the government-backed Sekber Golkar Party, giving it about 60 per cent of the total vote and thereby ensuring it of a 300-man majority in parliament.

Some restrictions were placed on traditional parties. The Indonesian Communist Party (PKI) was outlawed, giving rise to charges that the government had taken unfair advantage of its position during the election. There was little doubt, however, that Suharto had broadened his political base in the country.

By maintaining a hard-money policy and strict control over inflationary elements in the economy, the government was able to hold inflation below 9 per cent, as well as being assured of some $640 million in economic aid programs from international sources. Both the army and the civil service were given substantial pay increases, coupled with a tough anticorruption law. Some 50,000 soldiers were discharged in an effort to trim the defense budget.

Indonesia received special aid from the United States. Some $18 million went for roadbuilding

"Amazing what you can still buy with a handful of glass beads."

A paratrooper salutes Queen Juliana of the Netherlands and Indonesia's
President Suharto, right, during the queen's visit to the former Dutch colony.

projects, and another $5 million for light weapons. The United States also led the way in rescheduling Indonesia's $182-million debt by agreeing to repayment over a 30-year period, with interest on the debt repayable over 15 years beginning in 1985.

Communist activities were sharply curtailed, with some 42,000 political rebels in prison, and the Communists were largely disenfranchised. While unemployment and a high balance-of-payments deficit posed real problems, there were significant economic breakthroughs. The level of private foreign investments remained high, the United States contributing about $100 million for industrial development during the year. The Netherlands, Germany, and Great Britain made additional investments. Suharto was scheduled to step down in 1973, and, given the current momentum of the government, there was a good chance that he would do so, while backstopping a civil government with the army.

Late in August, Queen Juliana of the Netherlands paid an official 10-day state visit. She was the first reigning member of the House of Orange ever to visit the archipelago, which had been a Dutch possession until 1949.

Facts in Brief. Population: 125,908,000. Government: President Suharto. Monetary Unit: rupiah. Foreign Trade: exports, $811,000,000; imports, $679,000,000. Principal Exports: petroleum, rubber, coffee.   John N. Stalker

INSURANCE. For most people, the biggest insurance news of 1971 was the quickening trend toward lower costs for property insurance. Throughout the 1960s, homeowners, automobile owners, and other property owners were paying increasingly higher premiums as repair and replacement costs and jury awards in accident cases soared. In 1971, however, after years of huge losses, fire and casualty companies finally eased back into the profit column and were holding or reducing premium rates. Mutual companies were also increasing their dividends.

There were a number of reasons for the sudden new health of the insurance companies. For one, the rate increases of the past finally caught up with payouts. Ironically, the slower pace of the economy during the 1969-1970 recession meant fewer drivers and thus fewer accidents. Safety equipment built into cars in the past two years also resulted in fewer accidents and in less severe injuries.

No-Fault Insurance. For the long term, a more significant trend gathered momentum in 1971. After studying the massive $2-million report on auto insurance released by the Department of Transportation in March, the Nixon Administration recommended that the states enact no-fault insurance legislation. In essence, the no-fault plan eliminates the need to prove who caused an accident. If a policyholder is injured or his car is damaged, he collects immediately from his own insur-

INTERIOR DESIGN

ance company. There are a variety of no-fault plans now in existence or under study.

Features of the Administration program included full coverage of all medical benefits with small deductibles, income-loss benefits of up to $1,000 for up to three years, and a curtailment of the rights of the holder to sue for damages resulting from negligence. Richard J. Barber, former deputy assistant secretary of transportation, and head of the transportation department study, called the Administration plan "pale, anemic, and lacking in substance." Senators Philip A. Hart (D., Mich.) and Warren G. Magnuson (D., Wash.), co-sponsors of federal no-fault legislation, complained that leaving enactment up to the states could delay an overall program by five years. The transportation department study findings were highly critical of insurance companies. Among their conclusions were that auto insurance companies spent as much on lawsuits and sales promotion as on claims payments, and that the present liability system had "the highly dubious distinction of having probably the highest cost-benefit ratio of any [U.S.] major compensation system currently in operation."

No-fault advocates argue that the concept provides economic help quickly, that it lowers insurance costs by reducing the need for investigations and lawyer fees, and that it will eliminate many of the cases that now clog the courts.   Edwin W. Darby

INTERIOR DESIGN. New products presented in 1971 included modular furniture that is flexible, versatile, and adaptable in styling and design. It has simple lines, can be assembled to fit any need and can be moved easily to another home and reassembled. Manufactured of man-made materials, modular furnishings are durable and result from technological advances.

The use of bright new plastics and man-made fibers was widespread. Molded plastic furniture was popular, and automated manufacturing processes made it available at budget prices. As evidence of the importance of plastic furniture, the Society of Plastics Industry Furniture Council presented its Poly Award to Kenneth Booth of Ward Furniture of Fort Smith, Ark., for his pioneering use of plastic components in manufacturing. The presentation was made in January at a manufacturers meeting at the American Furniture Mart in Chicago.

More dual and multipurpose furnishings were shown and purchased during the year. Designers scaled furnishings to meet the requirements of smaller rooms and lower ceilings of today's housing.

Most Popular Design. A nationwide industry survey by the trade paper *Home Furnishings Daily*, published September 17, showed that the Mediterranean design was most popular in wood furniture selections. The favorite styling of upholstered furniture was traditional. Early American was the second choice in both categories. The survey also revealed that modern designs in chrome, steel, glass, and plastic had the greatest future.

Upholstered offerings by Italian designers at the September Milan showings included a look that was soft, smooth, deeply proportioned, and completely upholstered, with no exposed metal or wood frames. The Italians also presented a system of polyurethane foam blocks that could be assembled into divans and chairs. Totally flexible, the series of blocks could make a daybed, or be arranged around a table to form what designer Mario Bellini called a floating living center.

The High Point (N.C.) Furniture Market, held from October 22 to 29, featured modern cane furnishings. A cane-backed and steel étagère–a stand with open shelves for small ornaments–was shown, along with a rattan cane sling chair and a bamboo and cane bedroom grouping.

Unusual design concepts were offered at the Winter International Home Furnishings Market, held from January 3 to 9 in Chicago. They included a chromed-steel and hardwood chair in the shape of a tractor seat, a swivel-base lounge chair shaped like an airplane seat, and a bed frame called "sandbox." The box-shaped frame was laminated, with all four sides providing storage. It could house either a queen or a long, twin-size mattress.

Patterns, Prints, and Motifs on decorative accessories, drapery fabrics, clocks, wall plaques, china, glass, and porcelain were influenced by the ecology movement. Butterflies, birds, flowers, and nature scenes were presented realistically and romantically. These selections were seen in Chicago at the Winter Home Furnishings Market and the Gift and Accessories Market, held from January 25 to 30, and at the National Housewares Manufacturers' Association exhibitions.

Lighting and lamp selections placed an emphasis on function. New offerings were designed to provide simple, direct lighting and were made of metal, glass, and plastics.

Soft and hard surface floor coverings were offered in a wide range of colors, color combinations, and patterns. Shag carpeting was extremely popular and was offered in wide price ranges and in the man-made fibers as well as wool and cotton. Many carpeting pattern designs were inspired by South American and Eastern cultures, while others were sophisticated adaptations of colonial American motifs or geometric patterns.

The National Association of Furniture Manufacturers predicted sales of $8.2 billion by year's end for the entire home furnishings industry. The prediction was based on the fact that money was available because interest rates were lower. In addition, the all-industry promotion "Debut '72" was expected to stimulate interest in the home and in the purchase of furnishings.   Helen C. Schubert

389

INTERNATIONAL LIVE STOCK EXPOSITION.

The 215-pound international grand champion barrow (hog) stole the 1971 show, held in Chicago in November, when it sold for a world record price of $41 a pound. The final bid was by Bob Evans Farms of Rio Grande, Ohio. The hog was a crossbred Hampshire-Chester White from Jack Rodibaugh & Sons of Rensselaer, Ind. The Rodibaughs also had the champion trucklot of hogs, and daughter Betsy, 15, exhibited the champion barrow in the junior show. Her barrow brought $2 a pound.

The grand champion steer was an Angus that weighed 1,135 pounds. It was entered by Donald Overpeck & Sons of Clinton, Ind. It was sold for $7.75 a pound.

Grand champion steer in the junior show was also reserve grand champion in the open competition. It was a crossbred Charolais-Angus belonging to 16-year-old Debbie Haws of Chrisman, Ill. The steer sold for $1.45 a pound.

The grand champion wether lamb was a 115-pound Hampshire belonging to the Roger Snyder family of Aledo, Ill. The lamb sold to Mike Chiappetti of the Chiappetti Packing Company for $6 a pound and was donated to St. Michael School in Orland Park, Ill. Reserve grand champion was of the same breed and was entered by the University of Illinois. The lamb weighed 105 pounds and sold for $1.50 a pound.

Morris E. Rogers

INTERNATIONAL TRADE AND FINANCE

will never be quite the same again after 1971. It was a year of dramatic events, affecting international political relationships as well as the flow of goods and money among nations. In a year of turmoil, two events stood out.

First, and almost certainly the most important, was the devaluation of the dollar, announced by President Richard M. Nixon in December. It began on August 15, when President Nixon announced his wage-price freeze package and a set of decisions that, in practice, ended the post-World War II international monetary system established at the Bretton Woods, N.H., conference in 1944. The system, with its agreed rules, had been successful. It had played a major part in the vast increase in world trade and other transactions among nations.

The Old System. The essence of the system was a pattern of fixed, known, exchange rates among the leading currencies. But, as many economists had long warned, such a system could not work forever. Exchange rates among currencies gradually drifted out of line with one another. A host of factors were responsible for this, including different rates of inflation and different rates of technological progress. The problem showed up in a number of currency "crises" during the last decade, in which vast sums of money were moved from one country to another in anticipation of changes of exchange rates.

At the center of this system was the dollar. Only the United States offered to "cash" dollars held by foreign countries for gold—a major reason for the dollar's central role. But the dollar's exchange rate gradually became "overvalued" as many U.S. products became less competitive in price in the world market. Total U.S. transactions with the rest of the world, known as the balance of payments, swung into deficit, slowly at first and then with a great rush in 1970 and 1971. The balance of trade (included in the balance of payments) showed more imports than exports in 1971 for the first time in more than 75 years.

To remedy the situation, the President at first chose to suspend the convertibility of the dollar into gold. The clear aim was to devalue the dollar against the other leading currencies. And, without fixed exchange rates, the effect upon most other industrial nations was to force their currencies to "float" upward in daily trading in banks and exchange markets, from London to Tokyo.

The Official Devaluation of the dollar—ending the old monetary system of fixed, known, exchange rates—was announced on December 14 at a joint conference in the Azores between President Nixon and President Georges Pompidou of France. Mr. Nixon agreed to devalue the dollar in return for lower European trade barriers on U.S. goods, espe-

1971 Devaluation Chronology

Late March	Dollars flood into West Germany.
Early May	Wave of speculation against the dollar sweeps Europe; several countries refuse to accept dollars; West Germany floats its currency.
July	U.S. gold stock drops below $10-billion for first time since 1940s.
August 15	Dollar floated; U.S. 10 per cent import surcharge imposed; dollar no longer convertible for gold. Foreign exchange markets close.
August 23	All European currencies except French franc are allowed to float.
October	United States offers first hint it might consider devaluation.
December 1	Treasury Secretary John B. Connally surprises Group of 10 meeting in Rome with offer of 10 per cent devaluation.
December 14	President Richard M. Nixon meets with French President Georges Pompidou and agrees on need for dollar devaluation as part of overall currency realignment.
December 17-18	Group of 10 meets in Washington, D.C. United States agrees to 8.57 per cent dollar devaluation and end to 10 per cent import surcharge. Net effect is 12 per cent devaluation of dollar against other currencies.

cially farm products, and for upward changes in the relative values of currencies of some major U. S. trading partners.

On December 19, the President announced a major international monetary agreement that was "the most significant . . . in the history of the world." The agreement involved a realignment of currency exchange rates among the 10 leading industrial nations. The dollar devaluation became official with the United States agreeing to raise the price of gold from $35 to $38 an ounce. The effect was a dollar devaluation of 8.57 per cent on the old price of gold and 7.89 per cent on the new price. Other currencies were revalued in relation to the dollar. The net effect was an approximate dollar devaluation of 12 per cent. On December 21, the U.S. dollar successfully passed its first test in relatively quiet trading on the European exchanges.

The Import Surcharge, the other element in the President's August bombshell, placed a 10 per cent surcharge on many U.S. imports that pay duty. This immediately raised worldwide fears that the United States was, at bottom, trying to protect itself against import competition from abroad, and thus was threatening the long and painfully won progress of the world toward free trade. Mr. Nixon's position from the outset was that the new import tax was temporary, and that it would be removed once a more "realistic" pattern of exchange rates among currencies was established. And, in fact, this was precisely what happened. As part of the December devaluation agreement, the United States agreed to drop the import surcharge. For a while, though, there had been fears, both at home and abroad, that the new surcharge would be permanent— backed by the still-strong forces in the United States that are fearful of foreign competition. Many feared that it might lead to retaliation from America's trading partners.

The Common Market. The other great event of 1971 had much less immediate effect, but could be of vast importance in the future. This was the successful conclusion of negotiations, started 10 years earlier and interrupted by several failures, for British membership in the European Community (Common Market). The market is still primarily a free-trading customs union, but it has such high ambitions as establishing a common money and a unified foreign policy. It could not really represent "Europe" without Great Britain, but, at the same time, opinion polls demonstrated that an overwhelming portion of the British people still did not regard themselves as really "European." After sustained debate and a split in both major British political parties, the British House of Commons voted on October 28 to join the Common Market. But there remained some important legal steps before actual entry, scheduled for January, 1973. Along with Great Britain's entry, three smaller countries—

The U.S. Balance of Trade Tips

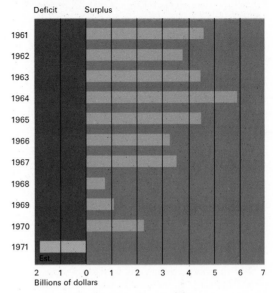

Source: U.S. Department of Commerce

The U.S. balance of trade, the difference between the value of its exports and its imports, suffered the first deficit over a full year since 1892.

Denmark, Ireland, and Norway—would be added, making 10 in all and an economic and political "bloc" of potentially major importance.

Trouble for Japan. The dramatic economic events of 1971, combined with President Nixon's new effort to resume relations with China, created a sense of shock in Japan. It was widely agreed throughout the world, if not always in Japan itself, that the exchange rate of the yen was the most "out of line" of all currencies and should be raised sharply. Apart from Canada, Japan's dependence on the United States as a market was greater than that of any other industrial country. As a result, the U.S. measures—the import surcharge, the yen's forced upward "float," and the formal upward revaluation of 16.9 per cent—caused major difficulties.

As 1971 ended, it was clear that the economic relations among nations had assumed a major, if not dominant, place in world politics. In the view of some, world prosperity was at stake, though world trade was still going on without major catastrophes. What loomed immediately ahead was an intricate set of negotiations on trade and money that would deeply test the will of the leading nations to cooperate and make sacrifices, rather than to try only to get the best of each other.   Edwin L. Dale, Jr.

See also ECONOMY, THE; Section One, FOCUS ON THE ECONOMY.

IOWA. See STATE GOVERNMENT.

IRAN celebrated the 2,500th anniversary of the founding of the Persian Empire with glittering ceremonies in October, 1971. Shah Mohammed Reza Pahlavi presided over festivities held in a specially built tent city at Persepolis, the ancient capital of Cyrus the Great. Some 50 crowned and uncrowned heads of state attended the celebrations. The cost of the affair, officially announced by the royal court as $16.6 million, aroused considerable criticism. But the shah was determined to emphasize Iran's place in the world and its unbroken tradition of sovereignty combined with a modern outlook. Several model projects, including hospitals and primary schools, were opened on the eve of the celebrations.

Another disturbing aspect of the event was the tight security measures, as the shah took no chances with potential opposition. Schools and universities were closed; several hundred persons were placed under house arrest; and soldiers ringed the tent city. Anti-shah elements bombed the Iranian consulate in San Francisco to protest his absolute rule.

Elections for Parliament in July assured the shah's Iran Novin Party, founded in 1963, of control. The shah's party won 230 seats to 15 for the opposition Mardom Party. A second opposition party, Pan-Iran, boycotted the elections.

Iran recognized mainland China on August 17. The nation also signed a trade agreement with Romania. Japan loaned $80 million for oil exploration in Iran's impoverished Luristan Province.

On February 16, Iran claimed that three small but strategically located islands at the mouth of the Persian Gulf were historically Iranian. Great Britain had ruled Greater Tunb, Lesser Tunb, and Abu Musa for more than a century, but British forces were being withdrawn before the end of the year. Shah Pahlavi said Iran would use force if necessary to regain control of the islands.

The British apparently proposed to the rulers of two small Gulf Emirates, Sharja and Ras al Khaymah, that they share sovereignty over the islands with the shah. Sheik Khalid al-Qasimi, who heads Sharja, and his cousin, Sheik Saqr al-Qasimi, the ruler of Ras al Khaymah, were reported to have rejected the British proposal.

On November 30, although British forces had not yet withdrawn, Iranian troops landed on the three islands. Prime Minister Amir Abbas Hoveyda told the Iranian Parliament, "The presence of some foreign elements in no way indicates that these islands are not now fully in Iranian control." Abu Musa had been administered by Sharja, and the Tunb islands by Ras al Khaymah.

Facts in Brief. Population: 30,478,000. Government: Shah Mohammed Reza Pahlavi; Prime Minister Amir Abbas Hoveyda. Monetary Unit: rial. Foreign Trade: exports, $2,355,000,000; imports, $1,658,000,000. Principal Exports: petroleum, carpets, cotton.   William Spencer

IRAQ. Friction within the ruling Ba'ath Party and the disenchantment of the Kurds undermined Iraq's stability in 1971, despite continued economic progress. The Kurds were unhappy with government failure to implement terms of the 1970 agreement ending the civil war, but they settled differences among themselves. The Kurdish Revolutionary Party merged with Mustafa Barzani's rival Kurdish Democratic Party and accepted his leadership. The government pledged $12 million for development of Kurdish regions, but it took few specific steps beyond opening a carpet factory in Irbīl. The Kurds' suspicions increased in September when assassins tried to kill Barzani at his mountain headquarters.

With President Ahmad Hasan al-Bakr reported seriously ill, a power struggle broke out within the Ba'ath Party. The foreign minister and vice-president were both dismissed, and party secretary-general Saadoun Takriti assumed both posts. In October, al-Bakr announced a new national charter.

Agreement with the Iraq Petroleum Company on June 7 for a higher oil export price was expected to nearly double Iraq's oil revenue for 1971.

Facts in Brief. Population: 9,492,000. Government: President and Prime Minister Ahmad Hasan al-Bakr. Monetary Unit: dinar. Foreign Trade: exports, $1,099,000,000; imports, $509,000,000. Principal Exports: petroleum, dates, cement, hides and skins, wool.   William Spencer

IRELAND. The bitter confrontation between the Roman Catholics and the Protestants of Northern Ireland raised a number of subsidiary issues in the Republic of Ireland in 1971. One of the most immediate involved the eventual reunification of Northern Ireland and the republic as the ultimate solution to Northern Ireland's domestic problems. Prime Minister John Lynch and most of the ruling Fianna Fáil Party favored such an eventuality but advocated a moderate approach. Other government leaders, however, favored direct action, including support of the militant Irish Republican Army (IRA). See GREAT BRITAIN.

The Fianna Fáil Party held its annual convention on February 20 and 21, in Dublin. Prime Minister Lynch was reaffirmed as party leader at the meeting, and all of the other principal party posts were won by supporters of his policies. In May, however, Kevin Boland, former minister for local government and social welfare, resigned from the party because of its moderate policies, particularly toward the IRA. His resignation was followed on August 18 by those of seven more high-ranking members of Fianna Fáil.

Birth-Control advocates continued to agitate for an end to a 1935 ban on the importation, sale, and advertising of contraceptive devices in Ireland. On March 31, the Senate refused to give a first hearing to a bill sponsored by Senator Mary Bourke Robinson to end the ban. It was generally believed, however, that the government favored the measure despite strong opposition from leaders of the Roman Catholic Church in Ireland.

On May 22, about 40 militant members of the Women's Liberation movement defied the ban by attempting to bring enormous stocks of birth-control devices into Dublin. When customs inspectors at the railroad station, where they had disembarked, attempted to confiscate the devices, a fight broke out during which the militants began hurling their supplies to a huge crowd of women sympathizers standing nearby. Calm was restored only when the militants were permitted to pass customs with the remainder of their supplies intact.

The Economic Growth of Ireland in 1971 was impeded by inflation, unemployment, and a severe balance of payments problem, according to a report published on April 14 by the Organization for Economic Cooperation and Development (OECD). To remedy the situation, the OECD recommended that the government adopt stricter price controls.

Facts in Brief. Population: 2,956,000. Government: President Eamon de Valera; Prime Minister John Lynch. Monetary Unit: pound. Foreign Trade: exports, $1,120,000,000; imports, $1,622,-000,000. Principal Exports: meat, cattle, dairy products.   Paul C. Tullier

ISRAEL held firmly throughout 1971 to its demand for a formal peace treaty recognizing its territorial integrity behind secure frontiers before it would withdraw from occupied Arab territory. The government accepted a February proposal by Egypt for a one-month extension of the cease-fire along the Suez Canal. The truce continued by mutual consent. There were no serious clashes.

Prime Minister Golda Meir received a vote of confidence in the Knesset (legislature) after the right-wing Gahal Party introduced a no-confidence resolution on the ground that her willingness to negotiate would endanger Israel's security. Aside from recognition and secure borders, Israel continued to insist on control of the Golan Heights in Syria, Sharm el-Sheikh at the tip of the Sinai Peninsula, and a demilitarized Sinai Peninsula as the price for a peace settlement.

UN Rebuffed. Israel's unyielding attitude, particularly on the difficult question of Jerusalem, aroused criticism even among some of its friends. It declared the city was its historic, irrevocable capital. In September, Jordan complained to the United Nations (UN) Security Council of Israeli measures to alter the character of occupied east Jerusalem. Jordan had claimed Israel planned to resettle Jews in part of the city that had been in Jordan. The United States complained of large new apartment

On her way to Israel's 23rd independence ceremony, Prime Minister Golda Meir reviews the honor guard at the presidential residence in Jerusalem.

ITALY

projects on similar grounds. In a 14 to 0 vote, the council called on Israel to rescind the changes. Israel said it would "continue the development of the city for the benefit of all its inhabitants" and bar proposed UN observers.

The high cost of military preparedness was reflected in the Israeli budget. Expenditures included $850 million for arms purchases out of total imports of $1.5 billion. Nevertheless, the economy continued to boom; the gross national product grew 6.9 per cent. The credit stability of previous years, however, gave way under inflationary pressures. Taxes as high as 50 per cent of income and rising prices more than offset wage increases. In August, the Israeli pound was devalued 20 per cent.

Large-Scale Immigration of Russian Jews to Israel took place as the U.S.S.R. relaxed its restrictions. An estimated 9,000 Soviet Jews arrived in their new homeland, most of them highly skilled workmen, teachers, artists, and engineers.

The occupied territories were relatively quiet. Arab workers benefited from the Israeli boom, some 30,000 holding regular jobs.

Facts in Brief. Population: 3,075,000. Government: President Zalman Shazar; Prime Minister Golda Meir. Monetary Unit: pound. Foreign Trade: exports, $781,000,000; imports, $1,438,-000,000. Principal Exports: diamonds, fruits, textiles. William Spencer

ITALY. Industrial unrest and political instability continued in 1971. Slowed production threatened the biggest recession since World War II and menaced the coalition government of Prime Minister Emilio Colombo. In January, a 24-hour work stoppage by seamen set the scene for a strike by 1.5 million building workers. This was followed by strikes by police, highway tollgate attendants, movie theater staffs, museum custodians, railroad workers, hotel workers, and soccer players. The climax was a one-day national strike on April 7.

President's Warning. On April 14, President Giuseppe Saragat warned that an economic slowdown could end workers' hopes for social reform. But further strikes against airlines, ports, and hotels, threatened tourism. Production was down and the cost of living up.

As President Saragat neared the end of his seven-year term on December 28, the electoral college took 23 ballots in 16 days before settling on a successor—Giovanni Leone, a Christian Democratic senator—on December 24.

Rioting in Reggio di Calabria against the choice of smaller Catanzaro as the seat of the regional government continued into February. Neo-Fascists were blamed for starting riots and strikes. They gained in local elections on June 14, getting 13.9 per cent of the vote as compared to 5.2 per cent in 1970 voting. Colombo reminded his countrymen

they had once lost their freedom under Fascism. On August 7, the Senate approved two important reforms. One streamlined the inefficient tax system; the other was to stimulate the construction of low-cost housing. Price controls were imposed on September 22.

Church and State. Demand for a referendum on the 1970 law legalizing divorce reopened conflict between civil and Roman Catholic Church forces. The Christian Democratic Party said in January that it would no longer oppose the law. On July 8, courts held the law constitutional. The Communist Party sought revision of the 1929 concordat between Pope Pius XI and Benito Mussolini regulating church-state relations.

Tuscania, an ancient Etruscan hill town 50 miles north of Rome, was virtually destroyed by an earthquake on February 6. The quake destroyed 100 buildings and killed 22 people. In Sicily, lava oozed down Mount Etna's slopes on April 3, cutting roads and terrifying the population. The lava flow subsided on June 8.

Facts in Brief. Population: 54,456,000. Government: President Giovanni Leone; Prime Minister Emilio Colombo. Monetary Unit: lira. Foreign Trade: exports, $13,186,000,000; imports, $14,944,-000,000. Principal Exports: machinery, transportation equipment, textiles. Kenneth Brown

IVORY COAST. See AFRICA.

JACKSON, GLENDA (1937-), won an Oscar in 1971 as the best actress for her 1970 performance as Gudrun in the motion picture version of D. H. Lawrence's book *Women in Love*. For this characterization, she was also voted best actress of 1970 by the New York Film Critics and the National Society of Film Critics.

Glenda Jackson was born in a small town near Liverpool, England. She was the oldest of four daughters of a bricklayer. At 16, she left school to join an amateur theatrical group. She won a two-year scholarship to the Royal Academy of Dramatic Art, and then performed in repertory theater for several years. In 1964, British director Peter Brook asked her to join the Royal Shakespeare Company and play in a Theater of Cruelty revue. Her performance was considered a highlight of the play.

In 1966, Miss Jackson won acclaim in London and New York City in Brooks's *Marat/Sade* as the mad Charlotte Corday. Since then, she has appeared as Ophelia in the Royal Shakespeare production of *Hamlet*, and in such motion pictures as *The Music Lovers, Negatives,* and *Sunday, Bloody Sunday*. She also appeared in a British television series in which she played Queen Elizabeth I from the age of 18 to 69.

Miss Jackson is married to former British actor Roy Hodges, who has an art gallery in Greenwich. They have a son, Daniel. Lillian Zahrt

JACKSON, HENRY MARTIN (1912-),United States senator from Washington, who throughout the first half of 1971 was an "official noncandidate," became the third declared candidate for the 1972 Democratic presidential nomination on November 19. One of the most powerful members of the Senate, he chairs the Interior and Insular Committee.

Jackson is seen by some observers as a perplexing study in political paradox. Long considered a "hawk" on military preparedness and a tenacious anti-Communist, he was President Richard M. Nixon's first choice for secretary of defense, a position he declined. On domestic issues, however, he is considered one of the leading liberals in the Senate. He has been a leading exponent of civil rights, school aid, environmental controls, and electoral reform. He opposed Nixon Administration policies on revenue sharing, calling them "misleading."

Jackson was born in Everett, Wash. He received a law degree from the University of Washington in 1935, and practiced law until he entered politics in 1938. One of the most remarkable vote-getters in American politics, Jackson received nearly 84 per cent of the vote in his 1968 election. He has not lost an election since he was elected prosecutor of Snohomish County in 1938. He served in the U.S. House of Representatives from 1940 to 1952. He has served in the Senate since then.   Allan Davidson

JAMAICA. See WEST INDIES.

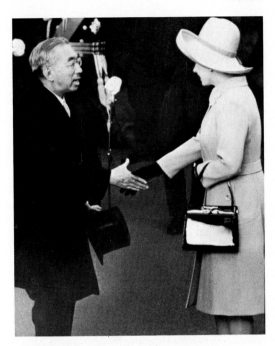

Emperor Hirohito of Japan is welcomed to Great Britain by Queen Elizabeth II during his unprecedented trip around the world in October.

JAPAN. Relations with the United States in 1971 entered their most difficult period since the end of World War II. The immediate causes were President Richard M. Nixon's dramatic decision to visit China and his new economic policy, particularly the brief 10 per cent surcharge on imports and the ending of the dollar's ties to gold. Both the economic and the diplomatic moves had great impact on Japan, particularly because they were made without prior consultation. See ECONOMY, THE; PRESIDENT OF THE UNITED STATES.

For several years, the U.S. government had been concerned about an increasingly adverse balance of trade with Japan, which was about $1.4 billion in 1970 and was running at a rate more than double that in 1971. The Japanese government's slowness in reducing barriers against imports from the United States and in liberalizing its regulations controlling foreign investments in Japan was a closely related problem.

On October 15, the two governments finally agreed on controls over Japanese textile exports to the United States, thus eliminating a difficult trade problem for the three-year period covered by the agreement. See INTERNATIONAL TRADE AND FINANCE.

The worsening U.S.-Japanese relations weakened the position of Prime Minister Eisaku Sato, who consistently followed a policy of close cooperation with the United States. In spite of his success in concluding an agreement on June 17, returning Okinawa to Japanese control in 1972, he was subjected to increasing attacks from inside and outside his Liberal Democratic Party. Sato also aligned himself with the United States by agreeing to cosponsor the American "Two Chinas" resolution in the United Nations debate over the China seat. See UNITED NATIONS (UN).

Sato's Liberal Democratic Party lost a little ground in the House of Councillors election June 26. It won 63 seats of the 126 involved, giving it a total of 137 (a loss of 1) of all 252 seats. The Japanese Socialist Party won 39 seats, an increase of 5 and the largest gain of any party. Okinawa elected 2 members to the House of Councillors and 5 to the House of Representatives, raising the membership in the latter to 491.

The Economy. In the fiscal year that ended March 31, Japan's gross national product (GNP) totaled $202 billion, exceeding the $200-billion mark for the first time. The nominal increase in the GNP was 16.5 per cent, the real increase – discounting for inflation – was 9.7 per cent. It was the first time since 1965 that the increase had fallen under 10 per cent. During calendar 1970, per capita income rose to $1,518, an increase of nearly $200, placing Japan about 15th in the world. About 0.76 per cent of the GNP went for foreign aid.

External monetary reserves were $13.4 billion as of October 1, making Japan second only to West Germany as a foreign currency holder. Although the government vigorously resisted revaluation of the yen, it allowed the yen to "float" on August 28.

Other Developments. In December, 1970, the National Diet passed 14 laws covering almost all aspects of Japan's serious pollution problem. A special law provided for criminal punishment of both individuals and corporations found guilty of environmental pollution. See ENVIRONMENT.

Emperor Hirohito and Empress Nagako made an unprecedented overseas journey in 1971. After a brief stopoff in Anchorage, Alaska, on September 26, for a visit with President Nixon, they visited Great Britain, West Germany, Belgium, France, Switzerland, Denmark, and the Netherlands. They returned to Japan on October 14, after a cool reception in Europe.

In preparation for the 1972 Winter Olympics scheduled to be held in Japan, a pre-Olympic winter sports competition was held in Sapporo in February.

Facts in Brief. Population: 105,735,000. Government: Emperor Hirohito; Prime Minister Eisaku Sato. Monetary Unit: yen. Foreign Trade: exports, $19,333,000,000; imports, $18,896,000,000. Principal Exports: machinery, transportation equipment, iron and steel.   John M. Maki

JEWS throughout the world protested the treatment of Jews in Russia in 1971. They circulated petitions and staged meetings, marches, and sit-ins, and some violence resulted.

Meanwhile, Russian Jews used similar tactics to fight for the right to be Jews and to live Jewish lives. Though considered unrealistic by many observers, mass emigration, assuredly selective emigration, remains the single hope for Russian Jews resisting spiritual and cultural extinction.

Under the impact of the Polish government's anti-Semitic campaign and the emigration of Jews that followed, Jewish life in Poland has virtually disappeared. Only 9,000 Jews remained in a country shorn of Jewish congregations and rabbis or other qualified religious personnel. Neighboring Czechoslovakia also continued its anti-Semitic policies. There was no open anti-Semitism in Hungary.

In Western Europe. British sympathy for Israel reached its lowest level during 1971. The Conservative Party election victory in 1970 accelerated the deterioration in British-Israeli relations. There was no significant change in the total number of Jews (425,000) in England, but there was concern about a slowly diminishing Jewish population.

France, with a Jewish population of 550,000, had the largest Jewish community in Western Europe. The influx of North African Jews thoroughly transformed French Jewry from a traditionally *Ashke-nazic* (European) community to one with a large *Sephardic* (Oriental) majority.

The small (35,000) Italian Jewish community was threatened both by a rising leftist anti-Semitism and by creeping assimilation. Italian Jews displayed strong ties to Israel, which has become the focal point of their religious pride. Relations between the Roman Catholic Church and the Jews, however, improved in 1971. This was because the Vatican displayed impartiality toward the Middle East conflict, reproaching both Israel and the Arabs in a more even-handed manner than in the past.

In the United States, public opinion remained heavily pro-Israel, though it had declined somewhat since the six-day war of 1967. The issue of using public funds for parochial schools in the United States created tensions among Jewish groups. The National Jewish Community Relations Advisory Council reaffirmed complete separation of church and state, and opposed the use of public funds to support religiously controlled schools. The Union of Orthodox Jewish Congregations in America, however, sided publicly with Roman Catholic exponents of federal aid to parochial schools.

The American Jewish community continued its concern over left-wing extremist groups that were strongly anti-Jewish and anti-Israel. Problems continued to arise in black-Jewish relations over the militancy and anti-Zionism of the Black Panthers and over crime and disorder involving Jewish victims in the black ghettos of the inner city.

Rabbi Meir Kahane, chairman of the militant Jewish Defense League (JDL), pleaded guilty in July to conspiracy charges involving the manufacture of explosives. The plea was part of an agreement between defense and government lawyers. The agreement cleared Kahane and 12 others of other charges involving firearms, provided all illegal firearms and explosives of the league were turned over to the government. The league also had to submit to a search of its camp in Woodburn, N.Y.

Few Jews remain neutral on the JDL. Many feel that the JDL has sparked a sense of urgency to answer threats to Jews here and abroad. Others feel that the real foe of the Jewish future is assimilation, promoted by the government in Russia, and by Jewish indifference in America.

World Population. The estimated world Jewish population at the end of 1970 was about 13,951,000, with about half, 6,963,000, being in North, Central, and South America. Over 4,000,000 were in Europe, some 2,668,000 in Asia, and the remainder were in Africa (196,000) and Australia and New Zealand (77,000).

Of the nearly 7,000,000 Jews in the Americas, 5,870,000 were in the United States, 280,000 in Canada, and 778,000 in Central and South America. Of the 2,668,000 Jews in Asia, 2,560,000 lived in Israel.   David Weinstein

JOHNSON, LYNDON BAINES (1908-   ), lived quietly at the LBJ Ranch in Texas in 1971, his third year of retirement from the presidency. Overseeing his land, golfing, watching football games, and collecting the paintings of Western artists, he stayed out of the limelight. The former President kept in close touch with the news, however, reading seven daily newspapers and keeping three television sets in his bedroom.

Mr. Johnson also received weekly briefings by federal government officials. On May 15, he declared that he was "totally in accord" with President Richard M. Nixon's opposition to a proposal that U.S. forces in Europe be reduced by half in 1971.

The Lyndon Baines Johnson Library in Austin, Tex., was dedicated on May 22. The library, built on the University of Texas campus, reportedly cost $18.6 million. The ceremony, which was attended by 3,000 guests and officials of both the Johnson and Nixon administrations, was slightly marred by about 2,000 antiwar demonstrators.

In June and July, *The New York Times* and other newspapers published the Pentagon Papers, classified documents dealing with Mr. Johnson's conduct of the Vietnam War, (see PUBLISHING). In October, Mr. Johnson's own account of his years in the presidency, *The Vantage Point: Perspectives of the Presidency 1963-1969*, was published.   Carol L. Thompson

JORDAN. King Hussein I won the long struggle in 1971 with Palestinian guerrillas who wanted to make Jordan a base for attacks against Israel. Government forces drove the two remaining organized brigades of the Palestine Liberation Army into Iraq and Egypt to be interned. The main guerrilla base at Irbid was almost abandoned. In July, Hussein said barely 200 guerrillas were still at large.

Arab criticism of Hussein's campaign against the guerrillas was muted although the Tunisian head of the truce supervision committee resigned, charging that Hussein never intended to make peace with the Palestinians. On July 14, Egypt canceled a visit that Hussein planned to make to Cairo, and on July 19, Iraq closed its border with Jordan. On August 12, Syria broke relations with Jordan.

The king proceeded with plans to reunite Jordan. He formed a Tribal Council headed by Prince Muhammad to supervise Jordan's 60,000 Bedouin tribesmen. On September 7, he proposed a National Charter. Prime Minister Wasfi al-Tal was assassinated November 28 in Cairo. Ahmed al-Lawzi replaced him.

Facts in Brief. Population: 2,374,000. Government: King Hussein I; Prime Minister Ahmed al-Lawzi. Monetary Unit: dinar. Foreign Trade: exports, $34,000,000; imports, $178,000,000. Principal Exports: phosphates, tomatoes.   William Spencer

Prime Minister Wasfi al-Tal, left, Prince Hassan, King Hussein, and the chief of staff celebrate Jordan's 50th anniversary. Tal was assassinated November 28.

JORDAN, VERNON EULION, JR. (1935-   ), was appointed executive director of the National Urban League on June 15, 1971. He succeeded Whitney M. Young, Jr., who drowned in Lagos, Nigeria, on March 11, 1971. Jordan said he would try to maintain "consistent dialogue" between black and white people.

Jordan was born on Aug. 15, 1935, in Atlanta, Ga., where his mother operated a food-catering business. Jordan graduated from DePauw University in 1957. He received a law degree from Howard University in 1960. He then became a law clerk in the office of civil rights lawyer Donald Hollowell.

From 1961 to 1963, Jordan was state director of the National Association for the Advancement of Colored People in Georgia. During this time, he led a boycott of Augusta stores that reportedly refused to hire Negroes. In 1961, he led student Charlayne Hunter into the University of Georgia, a landmark in Southern school integration.

While he was director of the Voter Education Project of the Southern Regional Council in Atlanta, he headed a campaign that registered 2 million black voters. On March 1, 1970, Jordan became the executive director of the United Negro College Fund, which supports 36 predominantly Negro colleges and universities. In June, 1971, he became a trustee of the Rockefeller Foundation.   Lillian Zahrt

KANSAS. See STATE GOVERNMENT.

KENNEDY, EDWARD MOORE (TED) (1932-   ), was a leading, though inactive, candidate for the Democratic presidential nomination in 1971. The Massachusetts senator stated repeatedly that he was not a candidate and would not compete in any primaries. Nevertheless, many opinion polls showed that he was the leading choice of Democratic voters.

Kennedy was an odds-on favorite for the 1972 nomination prior to an accident in 1969. A car he was driving plunged from a bridge on Chappaquiddick Island in Massachusetts and a girl passenger was drowned. Kennedy pleaded guilty to a charge of leaving the scene of an accident and received a suspended sentence of two months. In August, 1971, he said he would be content to play an "active role" in party affairs in 1972.

Kennedy was Democratic *whip* (assistant leader) of the Senate from 1969 to 1971. On Jan. 23, 1971, he was appointed to the Democratic Steering Committee by Senate Majority Leader Mike Mansfield.

Ted Kennedy was born in Boston, Mass. He graduated from Harvard University in 1956 and the University of Virginia Law School in 1959. Prior to being elected senator in 1962, he was an assistant district attorney for Suffolk County, Massachusetts. He married the former Virginia Joan Bennett in 1958. They have three children.   Allan Davidson

KENTUCKY. See STATE GOVERNMENT.

KENYA. President Jomo Kenyatta survived an attempted coup by army officers and high-level members of the government early in 1971. On June 8, 12 men were found guilty of conspiring to overthrow Kenyatta. Most of the plotters reportedly belonged to the Kenya People's Union (KPU), the outlawed opposition party. Among those implicated was Major General J. L. N. Ndolo, chief of staff of the armed forces. He resigned on July 1.

The accused leader of the plot was Joseph Daniel Owino, a former army officer. He had requested help from Tanzania's President Julius K. Nyerere, who reported the plot to Kenyan authorities.

Political Tensions eased somewhat after Oginga Odinga was released from prison in March. Odinga, leader of the KPU and a member of the Luo tribe, had been held as a political prisoner since 1969, when tribal rioting broke out between the Luo and the Kikuyu. Increasing public pressure forced the government to release him. In September, he rejoined the ruling Kenya African National Union (KANU), which he had left in 1966 to form the KPU.

John Washika, executive officer of the KANU, said that the party had fallen into a chaotic condition. He called for reorganization of KANU branches and suggested that annual delegates conferences be held. A conference had not been held since 1966. President Kenyatta postponed the local elections scheduled for 1972 until 1974.

Relations with White Africa. Kenya announced firm opposition to Great Britain's resumption of arms shipments to white-ruled South Africa. The government also declared that Kenya had never been in favor of establishing a dialogue with South Africa. Kenya called for the use of force against Rhodesia, because economic sanctions had failed to sway the white regime there. See RHODESIA; SOUTH AFRICA.

A detailed foreign policy statement was issued on April 1. It called for support of a nonalignment policy, African unity, liberation movements, and the East African Community. Kenya's relations with Uganda became strained following the January coup that overthrew Ugandan President Apollo Milton Obote. See UGANDA.

Famine and Plague swept Kenya early in 1971. A severe food shortage developed in February because of a severe drought that began in November, 1970. Malnutrition and dehydration killed and sickened animals, and 75 per cent of Kenya's cattle regions were quarantined. By late March, 140,000 persons were on famine relief. Then cholera broke out among the starving people in rural eastern and northeastern Kenya.

Facts in Brief. Population: 11,447,000. Government: President Jomo Kenyatta. Monetary Unit: shilling. Foreign Trade: exports, $217,000,000; imports, $397,000,000. Principal Exports: coffee, tea, petroleum products.   George Shepherd

KINSELLA, JOHN (1952-   ), a record-breaking Indiana University swimmer, was named the 41st winner of the Sullivan Trophy in January, 1971. The trophy is awarded annually to the outstanding amateur athlete in the United States. Only one other male swimmer—Don Schollander—has won it.

Kinsella set two world records in 1970. He won the greatest race of 1970 when he beat Olympic champion Mike Burton of Carmichael, Calif., by a foot in the 1,500-meter free style event in the national Amateur Athletic Union (A.A.U.) outdoor championships. Kinsella, then 17, swam the 1,500 meters in a record 15:57.1. It was the first time a swimmer had completed the event in less than 16 minutes. He also set a new world mark of 4:02.8 in the A.A.U. 400-meter free style. In addition, he swam on the U.S. 800-meter free style relay team that set a world record (7:48.0) in Tokyo in August, 1970.

Kinsella was born in Oak Park, Ill., and became an outstanding swimmer at Central High School in Hinsdale, Ill. At 16, he was the youngest male member of the U.S. team in the 1968 Olympic Games. He won a silver medal at the games in Mexico City when he finished second to Burton in the 1,500-meter free style with a time of 16:57.3. Kinsella hopes to compete in the 1972 Olympics in Munich, West Germany.   Joseph P. Spohn

KIWANIS INTERNATIONAL. See SERVICE CLUBS.

KOREA, NORTH. Relations with South Korea improved slightly in 1971. Red Cross officials representing North and South Korea met in Panmunjom on August 20. It marked the first bilateral meeting between representatives of the divided country since the Korean War.

The conferees met only briefly to discuss possible reunions of families divided since the Korean War but they agreed to resume further talks later. During August and September, both sides met several times in Panmunjom to try to establish a permanent liaison office at the armistice conference site. On September 16, however, they adjourned without setting a date for the next session.

Representatives of the Japanese and North Korean Red Cross organizations reached agreement in Moscow on February 5 on the repatriation of 15,000 North Koreans from Japan, and the emigration was completed in November. North Korean ties with China were strengthened on September 6 when an agreement was approved in Peking under which China agreed to provide military assistance.

Facts in Brief. Population: 14,323,000. Government: Chairman of the Presidium Choe Yong-kon; Prime Minister Kim Il-song. Monetary Unit: won. Foreign Trade: exports, $173,000,000; imports, $146,000,000. Principal Exports: metals, minerals, agricultural products.   Paul C. Tullier

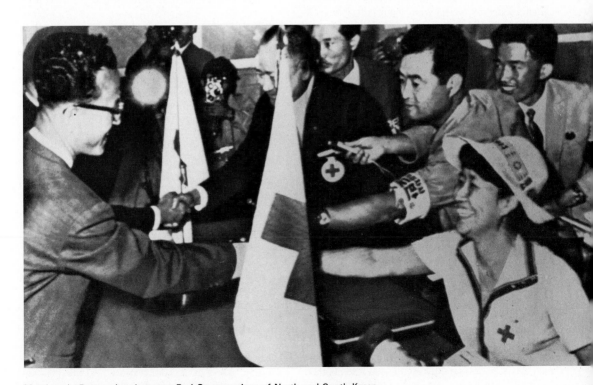

Meetings in Panmunjom between Red Cross workers of North and South Korea marked the first bilateral talks held between members of the divided nation since 1950.

KOREA, SOUTH. Chung Hee Park was re-elected to his third term as president of the Republic of (South) Korea on April 27, 1971, and was sworn in on July 1. President Park won a plurality of 946,928 votes over his principal opponent, Kim Dae Jung, in the April balloting. His ruling Democratic Republican Party, however, lost 56 seats in the National Assembly elections held on May 25. But it captured 113 of the 204 seats at stake.

Tentative moves toward reunification of the divided country occurred during the year. On August 15, President Park indicated in a speech that South Korea would be willing to join talks concerning reunification with North Korea if the talks were based on the premise that reunification would come only through "peaceful moves." Six days later, the North Korean Communist Party newspaper, *Worker's Daily*, quoted Park's proposal and suggested that reunification might be achieved through a referendum held in both segments of the country. If such a referendum were temporarily impractical, the article said, then a transitional confederation could be set up, leaving both political systems intact while reunification discussions were held.

Armistice Violations continued to create ill will between the North and the South, however. On May 14, a North Korean ship was sunk by South Korean naval and air force units in the Yellow Sea about 100 miles northeast of Seoul. All of the 15 men aboard the vessel were reportedly lost.

On June 18, a three-man North Korean team was thwarted in an attempt to infiltrate the demilitarized zone (DMZ) northwest of Seoul. Two men were killed and the third captured. Earlier, on June 16, another infiltrator was killed in a clash with South Korean patrols operating in the DMZ. In other clashes in August and September, 10 North Koreans and 6 South Koreans were slain.

U.S. Troop Withdrawals continued in 1971. On January 26, Defense Minister Jung Nai Hiuk announced that a joint U.S.-South Korea agreement had been signed under which United States military forces in South Korea would be reduced from 64,000 to about 43,000 by June 30. Under the terms of the agreement, South Korea would receive about $100 million in surplus military supplies left by the departing U.S. troops. On March 12, South Korean forces replaced U.S. troops guarding an 18-mile stretch along the armistice border with North Korea. The South Koreans thus became wholly responsible for guarding the 151-mile border. However, U.S. troops continued to stand guard at Panmunjom, the armistice conference site.

Facts in Brief. Population: 33,524,000. Government: President Chung Hee Park; Prime Minister Kim Jong Pil. Monetary Unit: won. Foreign Trade: exports, $835,000,000; imports, $1,984,000,000. Principal Exports: plywood, clothing, electronic products. Paul C. Tullier

KUBELIK, RAFAEL (1914-), chief conductor of the Bavarian Radio Symphony Orchestra in Munich, West Germany, was named music director of the Metropolitan Opera of New York on June 9, 1971. His three-year contract begins with the 1973-1974 season. The Czechoslovak conductor and composer is the first music director in the Met's 88-year history.

Kubelik was born June 29, 1914, in Býchory, near Prague, the son of Jan and Marianna (Szeel) Kubelik. Kubelik studied composition, conducting, piano, and violin at the Conservatory of Music in Prague. He came to the United States in 1935 as a piano accompanist for his father, one of the world's greatest violinists. From 1936 to 1939, he was conductor of the Czech Philharmonic Society in Prague. He was music director of Brno's opera house from 1939 to 1941, when he became chief conductor of the Czech Philharmonic Orchestra. He was music director of the Chicago Symphony Orchestra from 1950 to 1953, and later served as music director at Covent Garden Opera in London. He has been a guest conductor with various European orchestras and every major U.S. orchestra. He has also composed four operas and symphony and violin concertos.

Because of anti-Communist activity, Kubelik was deprived of his Czech citizenship in 1948. In 1967, he became a citizen of Switzerland. Lillian Zahrt

KUWAIT elected a new National Assembly on Jan. 23, 1971, and the Nationalist Party won seats for the first time. Nationalists won 10 of the 50 seats. The Assembly enacts laws and advises Emir Sabah al-Salim al-Sabah and his Cabinet. For the first time, the new seven-member Cabinet that took office had no members of the royal family.

Demonstrating its nonaligned foreign policy, Kuwait recognized China on March 22 and broke relations with Formosa (Taiwan). Relations with Iraq improved despite the March 30 murder in Kuwait of the exiled former Iraqi Air Marshal Hardan Takriti. A customs agreement exempted Iraqi dates from Kuwait customs duties. Kuwait and Saudi Arabia signed a similar agreement abolishing border traffic restrictions. An agreement with Afghanistan provided for the sale of 15,000 tons of fertilizers to that drought-stricken country.

Oil-rich Kuwait's per capita income in 1970 was reported at $4,859. The Kuwait Fund for Arab Economic Development (KFAED) reported a $7.6-million profit on its loans. New loans were made to Bahrain, Southern Yemen, Syria, and Iraq.

Facts in Brief. Population: 690,000. Government: Emir Sabah al-Salim al-Sabah; Prime Minister Jabir al-Ahmad al-Sabah. Monetary Unit: dinar. Foreign Trade: exports, $1,581,000,000; imports, $625,000,000. Principal Exports: crude petroleum and petroleum products. William Spencer

LABOR

"Stagflation" continued to bedevil American labor in 1971. The high rate of inflation began to moderate, but the Consumer Price Index (CPI) still stood at 4.0 per cent above the September, 1970, CPI. Gains for the Administration's anti-inflation policies seemed evident, however, because prices had risen an average of 5.9 per cent in 1970, and 5.4 per cent in 1969. Meanwhile, the unemployment rate remained high, partly as a result of past efforts to reduce inflation. It hovered around the 6 per cent mark most of the year, compared to an annual average of 4.9 per cent in 1970 and 3.5 per cent in 1969. Productivity began to rise, but was still considerably below the rise in compensation per man-hour, adding more fuel to the inflationary fires.

These indexes, combined with continuing substantial negotiated wage increases, were among the factors inducing President Richard M. Nixon to announce a 90-day wage-price-rent freeze on August 15, as part of his new economic policy.

George Meany scathingly denounced President Nixon's new economic policy at the AFL-CIO convention. He offered 20-to-1 odds that the program would fail.

Frank Fitzsimmons was elected Teamsters president at the union's July convention after imprisoned James R. Hoffa had declined to run.

The U.S. Bureau of Labor Statistics (BLS) figures for the first nine months of 1971 showed a slight decrease in the wage spiral that began in the mid-1960s. Settlement for 2.8 million workers in major collective bargaining agreements (1,000 or more workers) provided an average (mean) wage increase of 8 per cent a year over the life of the contracts. This represented a decrease from the 8.9 per cent for the full year of 1970.

First-year wage-rate adjustments averaged 11.8 per cent compared to 11.9 per cent in 1970. When combined with supplementary benefits, first-year wage changes in agreements covering 5,000 or more workers averaged 12.8 per cent, as opposed to 13.1 per cent in 1970.

Settlements affecting significantly fewer construction workers influenced the 1971 drop in wage gains. Substantial wage hikes for more than 700,000 construction workers had boosted the 1970 averages. The third quarter data showed 54 agreements for 186,000 construction workers, who received an average wage increase of 11.7 per cent over the contract life, compared to 14.9 per cent in 1970. The Construction Industry Stabilization Committee, established on March 29, approved 48 agreements averaging 11.3 per cent over the life of the contract. There were also six settlements averaging 16.9 per cent that were reached before the committee was created.

BLS preliminary estimates shown in the table below summarize major employment changes in 1971:

	1970	1971*
	(in thousands)	
Total Labor Force	**85,903**	**86,701**
Armed forces	3,188	2,859
Civilian employment	78,627	78,849
Unemployment	4,088	4,994
Unemployment rate	4.9%	5.9%
Change in real average weekly earnings		
(Private nonfarm sector)	−1.6%	1.3%
Increase in output per man-hour		
(Private nonfarm sector)	0.7%	2.8%†

*January-September average, seasonally adjusted, except for armed forces and weekly earnings data.
†Compared to the third quarter of 1970.

The 90-Day Freeze. President Nixon abandoned a "hands off" policy in his effort to slow inflation and reduce unemployment with dramatic suddenness on August 15. He announced a 90-day wage-price-rent freeze as part of "the most comprehensive new economic policy to be undertaken in this nation in four decades." The President signed an executive order authorizing the freeze under the Economic Stabilization Act of 1970. It applied to all forms of wage and salary compensation. A Cost of Living Council headed by Secretary of the Treasury John B. Connally was created to administer the freeze and to set up the mechanism for the post-freeze period (Phase 2). The Office of Emergency Preparedness was assigned the task of monitoring the freeze. Mr. Nixon also announced a 5 per cent reduction in federal employment and a $4.7 billion fiscal-year cut in federal spending.

Organized labor's initial response was generally unfavorable. AFL-CIO President George Meany led the condemnations, charging that the freeze was "patently discriminatory" against workers. He repeated labor's support of "even-handed" restraints if profits, dividends, and executive compensation were covered, along with wages and salaries.

Phase 2 began on November 14. President Nixon outlined his post-freeze plans on October 7. He announced the creation of a Pay Board to stop "inflationary wage and salary increases," and a Price Commission to "restrain prices and rent increases" and prevent "windfall profits." He said that both bodies would seek voluntary cooperation from labor and business, but that their decisions would be "backed by the authority of the law." The Cost of Living Council was assigned the task of supervising Phase 2, with the power to invoke government sanctions to back the Pay Board and Price Commission. The President emphasized the temporary nature of the controls.

The White House described the Pay Board's function as developing standards for permissible wage and benefit changes. It was to consist of 15 members, 5 each from labor, business, and the public, and was to be chaired by one of the public members. Although the board was to give "maximum latitude" to "free collective bargaining," it would review major settlements to see that they are "consistent" with its guidelines. If the guidelines are exceeded, the board can recommend sanctions. Top labor leaders agreed to serve on the board after receiving President Nixon's assurance that the Cost of Living Council "will not approve, revise, veto, or revoke specific standards or criteria developed by the Pay Board and Price Commission." An interim goal of an annual inflation rate of 2 to 3 per cent by the end of 1972 was set.

The Pay Board voted on November 8 to set an "aggregate" pay standard of 5.5 per cent in permissible annual wage and benefit increases after November 13. The vote was 10 to 5, with labor members voting against the limit. The board announced that it would review the "appropriateness" of this figure periodically, taking into account such factors as "the long-term productivity trend of 3 per cent," cost of living trends, and the aim of reducing inflation. Previously negotiated (deferred) wage increases would be allowed unless challenged by a "party of interest" or by five board members. The board would then review the deferred increase to determine whether it is "unreasonably inconsistent with the criteria established by the board." It also ruled against retroactive increases denied during the freeze, allowing exceptions in "specific

cases" approved by the board. A retroactive increase would be allowed if prices were raised in anticipation of wage increase; if a contract was negotiated after the freeze began to replace one that expired before August 26 where "retroactivity was established or had been agreed to by the parties"; and under any subsequent criteria set by the board to correct "severe inequities."

Among its later decisions, the Pay Board set a 1.5 per cent limit on exceptions to its 5.5 per cent guideline, for a maximum ceiling of 7 per cent. Allowable exceptions included tandem or "me-too" relationships in which settlements are historically based on prior contracts. The relationship had to be in existence for at least five years or two bargaining sessions.

Construction Stabilization. Prior to the freeze, the President had moved to curb wage and price increases in the construction industry. In February, he suspended provisions of the Davis-Bacon Act, which requires that contractors on federally assisted projects pay "prevailing" wage rates. He acted after asking union and management leaders in the industry to devise their own plan to curb the wage-price spiral. With no voluntary plan forthcoming, the President revoked his suspension of the Davis-Bacon Act in late March, and issued an executive order to moderate wage and price increases in the industry. Under the order's "cooperative" system

Selected Labor Indicators

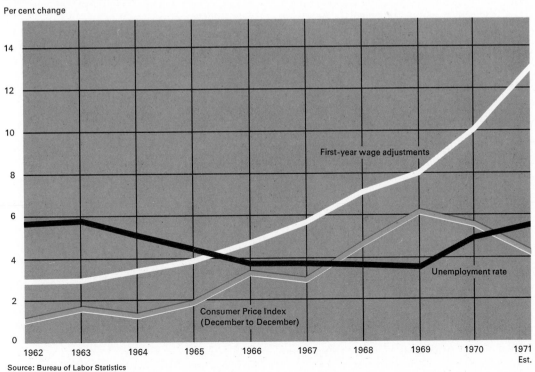

Source: Bureau of Labor Statistics

LABOR

of "constraints," 16 to 18 "craft-dispute boards" were to review settlements and determine whether they were acceptable. If a craft board found a settlement unacceptable, it would notify the Construction Industry Stabilization Committee. The committee would then have 15 days to determine whether the wage agreements violate the criteria set by the order.

The Unemployment Problems. The Administration announced programs to help specific groups of unemployed in addition to trying to reduce overall unemployment. In April, the Department of Labor set aside $42 million to help unemployed engineers and scientists find jobs in 14 areas hardhit by aerospace and defense cutbacks. In June, Secretary of Labor James D. Hodgson was named to head an intensive effort to find jobs and provide training for returning veterans. President Nixon signed the Emergency Employment Act of 1971 in July authorizing $1.15 billion over two years to finance some 150,000 new "public service" jobs.

Collective Bargaining in 1971 reflected the inflationary spiral that necessitated the wage-price freeze. Unions won sizable wage gains in their attempts to "catch up" with the sharp rise in the cost of living. They also sought to protect themselves against future price rises by either negotiating new cost-of-living escalator clauses or modifying existing clauses. Thus, three-year settlements in the steel, can, and aluminum industries provided wage and benefit packages of about 30 per cent over three years, and re-established escalator clauses that had been dropped in earlier settlements. The clauses provided for unlimited quarterly cost-of-living adjustments, beginning the second year, with 25 cents an hour guaranteed over the final two years. Copper industry agreements also established escalator clauses with unlimited adjustments.

A settlement on July 20 between the Communications Workers and the Bell System after a six-day strike by 500,000 workers provided a reported 31 per cent increase in wages and fringes over three years, and featured the adoption of a cost of living escalator clause. (The pact was rejected by locals in New York state, where the strike continued.) Other major settlements occurred in the apparel, West Coast paper, and petroleum industries. An agreement between the new United States Postal Service and seven unions came in July.

The first-year provisions of a November 13 agreement between the United Mine Workers and the Bituminous Coal Operators Association were approved by the Pay Board. The three-year settlement was valued at 39 per cent by management and 30 per cent by the union. Reached after a six-week strike and just prior to the start of Phase 2, the contract was subject to the board's review only if challenged by a "party of interest" or five or more of the board's members.

Meanwhile, the board delayed ruling on December settlements for over 100,000 aerospace workers until early 1972, amid indications that it might pare first-year wage increases. The pattern-setting agreement was reached on December 1 with the North American Rockwell Corporation for 11,000 Auto Workers. The three-year contract was reportedly similar to the industry pattern reached in late 1970 and early 1971, prompting Auto Workers' president Leonard Woodcock to say that he expected the board to approve the pact because of the aerospace industry's "tandem relationship" with the automobile industry. First-year wage increases averaged 51 cents an hour.

Railroad Bargaining turmoil continued in 1971. Rail unions were barred from striking until March 1, as a result of legislation passed by Congress that ended a one-day nationwide strike on Dec. 10, 1970, and provided for 13.5 per cent in retroactive wage increases. That increase represented the first two steps of a 37 per cent wage increase over three years recommended by a Presidential Emergency Board. The board also recommended that the unions modify some of their restrictive work rules. Three nonoperating unions settled with the nation's railroads in February on a package similar to the one suggested by the emergency board. However, it provided an additional 25 cents over an additional six months, for a total wage package of about 42 per cent over 42 months. The contracts, for 220,000 workers, included the recommended work rules changes, as well as improved holiday and vacation provisions.

The United Transportation Union (UTU), the largest of the operating unions, rejected the work rules changes and began a series of "selective" strikes on July 16 after the Supreme Court of the United States, in effect, upheld the legality of selective rail strikes. Most of the railroads then instituted work rules changes that resulted in layoffs and pay cuts for thousands of union workers. The selective strikes ended following an August 2 settlement with the nation's railroads that provided the 42 per cent wage pattern over 42 months and incorporated substantial work rules changes. The eventual outcome of the settlement for 150,000 workers remained in doubt because it was not ratified by UTU members before the freeze.

Union Affairs. Former Teamster president James R. Hoffa, imprisoned in 1967 for jury tampering and mail fraud, was released in December after serving 4 years and 9 months of a 13-year sentence. The sentence was commuted by order of President Nixon on the condition that Hoffa "not engage in the direct or indirect management of any labor organization prior to March, 1980."   Leon Bornstein

See also Section One, FOCUS ON THE ECONOMY; Section Two, CAGING THE INFLATION MONSTER; Section Three, ECONOMY, THE; FITZSIMMONS, FRANK.

LAOS. The tiny landlocked kingdom found itself unexpectedly thrust into the forefront of the Vietnamese conflict in 1971. In previous years, the Communist-backed Pathet Lao and the Royal Laotian forces had pursued their struggle in what had all the rhythm of a seasonal conflict. The Communist offensives usually took place in the dry season; the Royalist forces usually counterattacked in the monsoon season. But the rhythm was shattered on February 8. See ASIA.

On February 8, 14,000 crack airborne troops of South Vietnam moved into Laos. Backed by 800 American helicopters and an undisclosed number of U.S. B-52 heavy bombers, the South Vietnam troops had as their main objective the destruction of the Communist's supply artery through Laos. The Communists, in turn, moved between four and five divisions of regular North Vietnamese troops into Laos to stop the drive.

Although the South Vietnamese were outnumbered and outgunned, their greater mobility paid off. Using helicopters, they hopped from base to base, bombing Communist ammunition dumps and cutting fuel lines. Subsequently, as the extent of the Communists' troop and matériel commitment became apparent, another 10,000 South Vietnamese troops went into action in Laos. Losses on both sides were extremely heavy; entire battalions were destroyed in the fierce fighting that took place at Landing Zone Ranger and Hill 31. The South Vietnamese ground troops, however, did manage to reach the hub of the Communist trail at Tchepone, and, by destroying the supply network around it, effectively cut Route 9. On March 18, the South Vietnamese forces began a withdrawal.

On May 12, the Pathet Lao announced that the "unsuccessful conclusion" of the South Vietnamese incursion had tipped the balance of power in Laos in its favor. It offered to renew talks with the Royal Laotian government to end the fighting. One condition called for the United States to end its intervention and aggression in Laos. The second condition, predicated on acceptance of the first, called for an immediate cease-fire between its forces and the Royal Laotians. This, in turn, would lead to discussions on a provisional coalition government.

Premier Souvanna Phouma's response on June 30 in effect rejected the terms. He called for the holding of peace talks in Vientiane but without preconditions. The Pathet Lao, in turn, rejected the counterproposal.

Facts in Brief. Population: 3,106,000. Government: King Savang Vatthana; Prime Minister Souvanna Phouma. Monetary Unit: kip. Foreign Trade: exports, $4,000,000; imports, $83,000,000. Principal Exports: tin, timber, coffee. John N. Stalker

Loyal Meo tribesmen in northern Laos surround their tiny village with deep trenches to protect themselves from marauding antigovernment Pathet Lao forces.

LATIN
AMERICA

The disruptive internal events that disturbed most Latin American countries in 1971 delayed the continent from achieving the regional solidarity it had set as its goal for the 1970s. Military take-overs, guerrilla activities, and terrorism abounded—to the detriment of efforts to increase agricultural production and industrial development, combat illiteracy, expand communications, and improve roads.

International relations at times also contributed to the continent's frustrations, both internally as well as regionally. United States-Latin American relations in particular appeared to be fraying in a seemingly unprecedented variety of ways—over coffee and sugar trade, investments and foreign aid, nationalization without fair compensation, tariffs, and fishing rights. These issues mirrored to a great extent a new surge in Latin American nationalism and a mood in Washington, D.C., especially in Congress, that the United States had to stand up for its own rights. The Latins bitterly resented what they considered a lack of progress in the United States on various trade and aid measures, as well as the imposition by the United States of a 10 per cent import surcharge (see ECONOMY, THE).

Among themselves, the Latin Americans protested the way the U.S. Congress parceled out sugar import allocations as well as its refusal to act on enabling regulations covering the International Coffee Agreement. They were also unhappy that the United States stalled on granting tariff preferences on imports from the developing nations, whereas the European Community (Common Market) removed its duties for such countries, effective on July 1, up to a given ceiling for manufactured and semimanufactured products as well as 150 processed foodstuffs.

Economic Nationalism ran high in Latin America in 1971, as the republics tried to fulfill their aspirations. All seemed determined to make their own decisions and to play the central role in their own economies. Most of them were acutely aware that their people were not sharing in the "good life" as portrayed by television, motion pictures, and magazines. They felt exploited by the industrialized countries. Thus, several governments speeded up their take-overs of natural resources and such basic

Sign-carrying Chileans mark the nationalization of their copper industry in July. Many foreign-owned industries were taken over in Latin America in 1971.

industries as steel, communications, and banking. The result was an expected drying-up of foreign investments and loans for some of the republics.

All this occurred in a region with 265 million people, whose numbers were increasing at the rate of 2.9 per cent a year. The population growth rate, in turn, compounded and aggravated every economic and social problem in the region—from food supplies and clothing to housing, education, and employment. With slightly more than half of the population living in cities, the slum problem was growing from bad to worse.

The Alliance for Progress program marked its 10th anniversary on August 17. While there was much disenchantment with its accomplishments, if its results were measured against the short time it had been working, the alliance's achievements did stand out—particularly in view of such unanticipated obstacles as rapid population growth and the worsening of world trade conditions. In the decade of the alliance's existence, Latin America had invested $120 billion in its own development as compared to $10 billion from external sources. Furthermore, improvised policies were replaced with development-oriented planning. As a result, most republics had increased their gross national product (GNP) growth rate, and advanced their tax-reform programs. Agrarian reform was firmly established. New mineral-rich resources were located and developed, and had begun to pay dividends. Unfortunately, the program's impact on major problems such as unemployment, urban crowding, and bad distribution of income and land was mostly negligible.

U.S. Motives Questioned. The twelfth annual governor's meeting of the Inter-American Development Bank (IDB) was held in Lima from May 10 to May 14. It got off to a sensational start with an inaugural address by Peru's president Juan Velasco Alvarado. In it, he suggested that member nations might have to consider whether "in any significant sense it was worth their while" to continue their membership in the IDB, which "showed signs that it was being used as an instrument of political pressure against countries, such as Peru, which had decided to break with the past and initiate a policy of national liberation."

President Velasco's remarks implied that the United States did not like real reformist or revolutionary policies and was using its leverage as the IDB's richest member to reduce aid to those nations that did not follow the U.S. political line. Later, World Bank president Robert S. McNamara warned the developing nations that a "disquieting" trend of annulling agreements with foreign investors could "seriously imperil" their credit standing and inhibit investments in the region.

Secretary-General Galo Plaza Lasso of the Organization of American States (OAS), conversely, asserted: "Unless private investment is properly channeled into priority sectors and on terms compatible with national development objectives, its future is uncertain in Latin America; if foreign investment results in a mounting external-debt burden, environmental pollution, exhaustion of natural resources, or unemployment brought about by the introduction of capital-investive technology, it can foster a social and political strife."

The U.S. import surcharge spurred Latin America's efforts to expand its trade with other countries. During the year, trade accords were either signed or discussed with various Far East countries, including North Vietnam and China. Costa Rica concluded a trade agreement with Russia, and Guatemala sent a commercial delegation to Eastern Europe. Argentina signed a three-year nonpreferential trade agreement with the Common Market, which, in turn, sent one of its high-ranking officials to various other Latin American republics to discuss the market's overall trade relations with the region. In December, the U.S. surcharge was dropped.

Regional Trade Programs. The Latin American Free Trade Association (LAFTA) and the Central American Common Market (CACM) were at a virtual standstill. Scant results were expected from the 11th ordinary session of LAFTA, a 40-day series of meetings inaugurated on October 25 in Montevideo and attended by delegates from 11 republics. One problem was Argentina's growing trade deficit with Brazil. Another was the inability of the conferees to agree to a substantial number of tariff cuts on significant products. Still another was the failure of all the participating countries to comply fully with their liberalization commitments to LAFTA. The difficulties in LAFTA were caused by differences in the individual countries' approaches to economic and political questions, and such complicated issues as different stages of development, balance of payments problems, and a general lack of competitive spirit. The effectiveness of the CACM may have been permanently impaired by the new economic patterns that emerged following the so-called Soccer War between El Salvador and Honduras in 1969. As examples of the unbalanced regional arrangement that followed the altercation, Costa Rica and Honduras imposed import duties to protect themselves. In retaliation, El Salvador, Guatemala, and Nicaragua—the other CACM nations—sealed their frontiers to Costa Rican goods. In part, trade had resumed, but Honduras seemed determined to remain out of the market.

Despite the disappointing LAFTA and CACM situations, the impetus toward economic integration in Latin America remained alive. The Andean Group, which consists of Bolivia, Chile, Colombia, Ecuador, and Peru, worked out a common policy to deal with foreign investment involving minimum state participation in mixed companies. Although it was not universally popular, the policy had the advantage of laying down the ground rules formally and unequivocally.

Other Activities. Colombian and Venezuelan relations were strained in 1971 over conflicting claims to important petroleum deposits in the Gulf of Venezuela. Ill will was also created by a Venezuelan drive to eject Colombian migrant laborers without residence papers, and by a Colombian campaign to end the flow of contraband cattle into Venezuela. Brazil was beset by the continuing spread of coffee rust, which, it was feared, would eventually appear in Colombia. Mexico, meanwhile, carried out a massive campaign to vaccinate as many of its horses, mules, and burros as possible against equine encephalomyelitis, a serious disease affecting cattle that also appeared in the United States in 1971. See AGRICULTURE.

On March 6, the United States, Colombia, and Panama signed agreements calling for the construction of the final link of the 14,000-mile Pan American Highway, which extends from Alaska into Chile and Argentina. Involved in the last part of the project was the 250-mile Darien Gap, an area of swamps and rain forests, the crossing of which would cost an estimated $150 million and take five years.

Central America

Costa Rica. A return to a dual exchange-rate system was announced by the government on June 19.

Apparently this was an attempt to reduce the rising balance of payments deficit, but the colon–the nation's monetary unit–continued to slip. At the end of June, gross monetary reserves stood at a mere $8.49 million, down from $33.39 million in mid-1970. To help control inflation, the government fixed the wholesale and retail prices of some 40 essential goods, including foods, soaps, and gasoline.

El Salvador. Economic recovery made good headway during the year, and government officials were confident that the GNP would expand by some 6 per cent in real terms, up from 4.3 per cent in 1970. Official gross monetary reserves climbed from $62.8-million in January to $77.2 million by the end of July. To spur exports of nontraditional products, a new law granted various import duty and internal tax exemptions to industry.

Guatemala. For the first eight months of 1971, the GNP rose an estimated 6 per cent in real terms, while gross monetary holdings hit a record $98.4-million, up $20.2 million since January. Unemployment was widespread, but an agreement signed in February promised some relief. After 10 years of bargaining, the government and International Nickel of Canada reached agreement involving a $250-million venture that would bring Guatemala one of the largest mining projects in Central America and provide work for hundreds. Meanwhile, antigovern-

Facts in Brief on the Latin American Countries

Country	Population	Government	Monetary Unit*	Foreign Trade (million U.S. $) Exports	Imports
Argentina	25,079,000	President Alejandro Agustín Lanusse	peso (5 = $1)	1,775	1,710
Bahamas	162,000	Governor Sir Francis Cumming-Bruce; Prime Minister Lynden O. Pindling	dollar (1 = $1)	54	202
Barbados	263,000	Governor General Sir Arleigh Winston-Scott; Prime Minister Errol W. Barrow	East Caribbean dollar (2 = $1)	43	114
Bolivia	5,189,000	President Hugo Banzer Suarez	peso (11.88 = $1)	182	165
Brazil	99,263,000	President Emílio Garrastazú Médici	new cruzeiro (5.5 = $1)	2,739	2,406
British Honduras	132,000	Governor Sir John Paul; Premier George Price	dollar (1.66 = $1)	15	27
Chile	10,271,000	President Salvador Allende Gossens	escudo (12.23 = $1)	1,068	907
Colombia	22,491,000	President Misael Pastrana Borrero	peso (20.1 = $1)	608	686
Costa Rica	1,868,000	President José Figueres Ferrer	colón (6.65 = $1)	229	317
Cuba	8,807,000	President Osvaldo Dorticos Torrado; Premier Fidel Castro	peso (1 = $1)	650	1,095
Dominican Rep.	4,461,000	President Joaquín Balaguer	peso (1 = $1)	214	307
Ecuador	6,511,000	President José María Velasco Ibarra	sucre (25.25 = $1)	218	247
El Salvador	3,780,000	President Fidel Sánchez Hernández	colón (2.5 = $1)	229	214
Guatemala	5,495,000	President Carlos Arana Osorio	quetzal (1 = $1)	262	250
Guyana	813,000	President Arthur Robert Chung; Prime Minister L. F. S. Burnham	dollar (2 = $1)	134	134
Haiti	5,060,000	President Jean-Claude Duvalier	gourde (5 = $1)	40	42
Honduras	2,758,000	President Ramón Ernesto Cruz	lempira (2 = $1)	169	184
Jamaica	2,103,000	Governor-General Sir Clifford C. Campbell; Prime Minister Hugh Lawson Shearer	dollar (1 = $1.20)	299	522
Mexico	54,253,000	President Luis Echeverría Alvárez	peso (12.49 = $1)	1,398	2,461
Nicaragua	2,136,000	President Anastasio Somoza Debayle	córdoba (7 = $1)	155	170
Panama	1,562,000	Provisional Government President Demetrio B. Lakas	balboa (1 = $1)	114	353
Paraguay	2,531,000	President Alfredo Stroessner	guaraní (126 = $1)	64	76
Peru	14,536,000	President Juan Velasco Alvarado; Prime Minister Ernesto Montagne Sanchez	sol (38.7 = $1)	1,044	603
Puerto Rico	2,733,000	Governor Luis A. Ferré	dollar (U.S.)	1,606	2,262
Trinidad and Tobago	1,104,000	Governor-General Sir Solomon Hochoy; Prime Minister Eric Eustace Williams	dollar (2 = $1)	482	541
Uruguay	2,956,000	President Jorge Pacheco Areco	peso (250 = $1)	233	233
Venezuela	11,158,000	President Rafael Caldera	bolívar (4.5 = $1)	2,638	1,869

*As of Sept. 30, 1971

"Now, amigo, we'll go back to doing it my way."

LATTING, PATIENCE SEWELL (1918-   ), became mayor of Oklahoma City on April 13, 1971. Mrs. Latting is the first woman to head the government of a U.S. city of more than 200,000 population. Oklahoma City has more than 366,000 residents. She won the election easily, defeating businessman Bill Bishop, 32,000 votes to 22,000. Her first act as mayor was to appoint a committee to help revitalize the city's downtown area.

Mrs. Latting was born in Oklahoma City on Aug. 27, 1918, the daughter of Frank Sewell (now dead), the president of an Oklahoma City bank. When she was 19, she graduated from the University of Oklahoma with a degree in mathematics. When she was a junior, she was elected to Phi Beta Kappa. She earned a master's degree in economics and statistics from Columbia University, and then worked as a researcher for a short time for the Chase Manhattan National Bank in New York City.

She returned to Oklahoma and married Trimble B. Latting, an Oklahoma City lawyer and oil man. They have a son and three daughters.

Mrs. Latting is not a newcomer to politics, and is considered an astute politician. Before becoming Oklahoma City's $2,000-a-year mayor, she served four years on the eight-member City Council. She got into politics through her work with the League of Women Voters.   Lillian Zahrt

LAW. See CIVIL RIGHTS; COURTS AND LAWS; CRIME.

ment terrorists remained active, and in July, the International Commission of Jurists denounced what it called "a reign of terror" under which about 8,000 persons were assassinated in five years.

Honduras. National Party candidate Ramón Ernesto Cruz was inaugurated president on June 6. He succeeded President Oswaldo López Arellano, who remained as chief of the armed forces.

On November 22, the United States agreed to cede to Honduras the two Swann islets in the Caribbean. Located about 97 miles off the coast of Honduras, the islets have an area of about 3 square miles.

Nicaragua. On August 31, the Congress voted its own dissolution, thereby assuring that President Anastasio Somoza Debayle would remain in power until April, 1972. At that time, a new constitutional convention was scheduled to meet and alter the nation's Constitution.

Caribbean Islands.

Dominican Republic. The economy continued to expand, but the principal beneficiaries were the upper and middle classes. About 68 per cent of the people still lived in conditions of considerable hardship. Malnutrition was widespread and the nation became increasingly unable to feed itself. Some 33 per cent of a work force estimated at 1.2 million persons was unemployed.   Mary C. Webster

See also the various Latin American country articles.

LEBANON experienced unrest in 1971 despite the recovery of its economy from the dislocations of the Arab-Israeli war of 1967. Students protested the weaknesses of the educational system and their inability to get jobs after graduation. Dissatisfaction also reached groups hurt by inflation and shortages of consumer goods. Employees struck periodically in the electrical, telephone, and other service industries. A June decree raising duties on imported goods brought a nationwide strike by merchants until it was rescinded. The government announced a belated 5 per cent wage increase for public servants and a higher minimum monthly wage for trade union members to stimulate buying.

Lebanon's economy improved in 1971. Tourism, a major source of income, increased by 38 per cent over 1970, to $160 million.

The Israeli border remained relatively quiet as Palestinian guerrillas moved their bases back into Jordan or Syria. Their departure angered Lebanese students, many of them Palestinians. Another source of student unrest was an increase in fees at the American University of Beirut.

Facts in Brief. Population: 2,848,000. Government: President Suleiman Franjieh; Prime Minister Saeb Salaam. Monetary Unit: Lebanese pound. Foreign Trade: exports, $172,000,000; imports, $577,000,000. Principal Exports: fruits and vegetables, machinery, textiles.   William Spencer

LESOTHO. Prime Minister Leabua Jonathan and King Motlotlehi Moshoeshoe II were reconciled in February, 1971. The breach between the prime minister and the king had occurred in January, 1970, when Jonathan suspended the Constitution and declared a state of emergency. He claimed that the king had "technically abdicated" because of his involvement in plots against Jonathan's government. Jonathan then placed the monarchy under the regency of the queen. The king made his first official appearance in Lesotho since the January, 1970, incidents at a cocktail party in February, 1971.

Ntsu Mokhehle, the leader of the opposition Congress Party, who had been arrested during the 1970 political turmoil, was released from prison on June 8. Mokhehle reportedly was released and placed under house arrest after agreeing not to become involved in politics.

The United States appointed its first ambassador to Lesotho in June. Lesotho supported the U.S. position on China's entry into the United Nations (UN). On October 25, Lesotho voted against the resolution to seat mainland China in the UN.

Facts in Brief. Population: 1,010,000. Government: King Motlotlehi Moshoeshoe II; Prime Minister Leabua Jonathan. Monetary Unit: rand. Foreign Trade: exports, $5,000,000; imports, $33,-000,000. Principal Export: cattle.   Darlene R. Stille

LIBERIA. See AFRICA.

LIBRARY. Continued austerity in federal funding of library programs affected libraries of all types across the nation in 1971. Most notable were cuts in programs for public library construction, college library assistance, and training and research in librarianship.

As a result of local budget cuts or tax rate limitations, many libraries were faced with the prospect of reducing operations or closing. Among the libraries affected were the public libraries in Syracuse and Utica, N.Y., the Philadelphia Free Library, and the New York City Municipal Reference and Research Center. Public libraries in Hartford, Conn., and Akron, Ohio, faced similar difficulties. Programs funded under the Elementary and Secondary Education Act and the Medical Library Assistance Act, however, received about as much support as they had in 1970.

New Libraries. On the brighter side, plans were announced for the construction of several major libraries, and the newest presidential library, the Lyndon Baines Johnson Library, was dedicated.

Construction started on a $7.5-million "learning center" at Oberlin College in Ohio. The building will house 800,000 volumes, audio-visual facilities, and a computer center. The Meriden, Conn., court of common council approved a bond issue of more than $2.5 million for a new city library. The Houston Public Library announced plans for a new

$9.5-million library building. It was scheduled to open in 1975.

The Lyndon Baines Johnson Library, on the Austin campus of the University of Texas, was dedicated on May 22. President Richard M. Nixon and former President Johnson were among the 3,000 who attended the dedication. The University of Iowa received a grant of almost $2.5 million from the National Institutes of Health. The money will help finance the construction of a new health science library.

The Library of Congress received a $400,000 grant from the National Endowment for the Humanities and the Council on Library Resources, Inc. The grant will finance the library's cataloging in publication program. This program, which began in July, 1971, enables the Library of Congress to provide cataloging information for individual libraries at a fast rate. Thus, the individual libraries can circulate new books much sooner than they previously could. The experimental phase of the program will continue until June 30, 1973.

The 37th annual meeting of the International Federation of Library Associations was held in Liverpool, England. It featured exhibits of library equipment and supplies from several countries and the latest advances in information retrieval systems and in microfiche technology.   Robert J. Shaw

The massive, marble Lyndon Baines Johnson Library, on the campus of the University of Texas in Austin, is the largest presidential memorial library.

LIBYA. President Muammar Muhammad al-Qadhaafi climaxed his rapid rise to leadership among Arab statesmen on Aug. 20, 1971, when he and the leaders of Egypt and Syria signed a constitution for a proposed Federation of Arab Republics. Although Egypt's President Anwar Sadat was voted head of the federation's executive council by his two colleagues, the unity agreement was due largely to Qadhaafi's efforts to achieve Arab unity.

President Qadhaafi's tendency to make rash statements and publicly criticize "reactionary" Arab regimes created problems for him both abroad and at home. His announced support of an attempted military coup in Morocco in July strained relations between the two countries and caused the expulsion of the Libyan Embassy staff from Rabat, Morocco's capital. Later in that same month, Libyan authorities roiled pan-Arab relations when they forced a British airliner carrying Sudanese coup leaders to London to land at Benghazi. The two leaders were returned to Sudan and executed. In August, Chad accused Libya of backing a coup attempt against its government and of recognizing the Chadian Liberation Front based in Tripoli. Chad promptly broke off diplomatic relations. Later in the year, Qadhaafi accused the Philippine government of practicing genocide against the islands' 4 million Moslems.

Qadhaafi Resigns. Disagreements within the ruling Revolutionary Command Council (RCC) prompted Qadhaafi to resign as prime minister, president of the RCC, and chief of staff in September. He was particularly critical of the RCC for its failure to speed the pace of social and economic reform. Earlier, the Cabinet was reshuffled and five ministers, most of them military officers, were dismissed in an effort to bring competent civilians into the government. After Qadhaafi's resignation, he disappeared for two weeks, prompting speculation of an assassination attempt or mental depression. He later withdrew his resignation, but Libya's own future plans for the federation remained far from clear under its mercurial leader.

In October, a Peoples' Court sentenced 64 persons, including four former prime ministers, to prison terms of up to 15 years for political corruption and election rigging during the regime of deposed King Idris I.

A five-year agreement signed in April with the major oil companies raised the price for Libyan oil to $3.45 per barrel. The companies also agreed to pay Libyan income taxes of 55 per cent. The agreement would bring Libya $2 billion annually in oil revenue.

Facts in Brief. Population: 2,084,000. Government: Revolutionary Command Council President and Prime Minister Muammar Muhammad al-Qadhaafi. Monetary Unit: dinar. Foreign Trade: exports, $2,366,000,000; imports, $554,000,000. Principal Export: crude petroleum. William Spencer

LINDSAY, JOHN VLIET (1921-   ), Republican mayor of New York City since Jan. 1, 1966, officially switched his political allegiance to the Democratic Party on Aug. 11, 1971, and began building a power base of liberal Republicans, independents, and Democrats. In December, he announced plans to enter Democratic presidential primaries in seven states. He formally announced his candidacy on December 28.

Lindsay's switch surprised few political insiders. He had long been disenchanted with the Republican power structure—at odds with New York Governor Nelson A. Rockefeller, and increasingly critical of the Republican Administration in Washington. He claimed he left the Republican Party "because it has abandoned the fight for a government that will respond to the real need of most of our people." He particularly stressed what he claimed to be "the government's retreat from the Bill of Rights."

Energetic, handsome, and articulate, John Lindsay has been a prominent factor in American politics since his days as a progressive New York congressman from Manhattan's East Side from 1959 to 1965. When he became mayor of New York City in 1966, he took on what many consider to be the most monumental and thankless job in government. Allan Davidson

LIONS CLUBS. See SERVICE CLUBS.

LITERATURE. If the economic recession was making inroads on the book-publishing business, there was little surface evidence of it in 1971. Traditionally popular types of reading fare were abundant in all fields, but the key element of the literary year appeared to be diversity. In fiction, the range was from promising first novels by such writers as Sandra Hochman and George Cain to new offerings by the well-established storytellers Bernard Malamud, Joyce Carol Oates, John Updike, Herman Wouk, Walker Percy, and Wright Morris, to name only a few.

Nonfiction offerings were equally wide ranging—from autobiographical episodes by Edmund Wilson and Graham Greene to two books by, as well as two *about*, the good-bad boy of contemporary American letters, Norman Mailer. And there were a variety of books on the current and important topics of ecology and the preservation of our environment, the relationships between blacks and whites, and the war in Vietnam.

Fiction. Most of the year's fiction, especially from the established writers, was of a fairly predictable nature. Perhaps the surprise of the year was George Garrett's *Death of the Fox*, a marvelous re-creation of the life and times of Sir Walter Raleigh. The novel was a superb achievement by a young Southerner who had been building a firm literary reputation for two decades with poetry, fiction, and distinguished essays. It was a clear demonstration that the historical novel as an art form had not lost out entirely in an age when the richest rewards seemed too often to be reserved for sensationalism. The veteran novelist Herman Wouk also turned to history for a theme, coming to grips with the American experience in World War II in *The Winds of War*, a long and powerful narrative that was seven years in the writing. The first segment of a projected two-novel sequence, it was by far Wouk's best work since *The Caine Mutiny*.

Contemporary life and morals, complete with the drug scene, hippies, and racial conflict, were among the major preoccupations of other novelists. Joyce Carol Oates, a National Book Award winner for *them* in 1969, continued to explore the mysteries of human personality with intensity and compassion in her chilling and compelling novel *Wonderland*. John Updike created a sort of montage of the experience of the 1960s as he returned in *Rabbit Redux* to the tale of Harry (Rabbit) Angstrom begun in his second novel, *Rabbit, Run*, in 1960.

In Bernard Malamud's *The Tenants*, a black writer and a Jewish novelist share the same woman and the same problems as they face life's brutal truths in an abandoned New York tenement building. Philip Roth turned his fiercely comic imagination to literary satire to produce a well-honed attack on President Richard M. Nixon's political language in *Our Gang (Starring Tricky and His Friends)*. Wright Morris' *Fire Sermon* was a typically quiet and beautifully fashioned tale in which a hippie couple managed to take an 11-year-old orphan away from his 82-year-old uncle. Madison Jones, in *A Cry of Absence*, dealt with racial matters in a small Tennessee town following the Supreme Court's 1954 desegregation decision. In his ironic novel *Love in the Ruins*, Southern writer Walker Percy took a look at a future America in "a time near the end of the world," and found it strangely reminiscent of some of our present moral and environmental disasters.

A. B. Guthrie and Wallace Stegner, two veteran novelists who had previously written with fine craftsmanship about the pioneer West, came through again with first-rate performances–Guthrie with *Arfive*, a tale of the taming of a Montana frontier town, and Stegner with *Angle of Repose*, a quiet and distinguished novel of pioneering adventure.

Charles Newman and Jonathan Strong, two young novelists who had previously won critical acclaim, brought out creditable new work during the year. Newman produced a comic novel, *The Promisekeeper*, about a Chicago bachelor's troubles with people who are after his money. Strong's *Ourselves*, like his earlier success, *Tike*, dealt with the problems of a young man growing up.

Among the authors of first novels to attract attention were Sandra Hochman, whose *Walking Papers* concerned the affairs of a much-sought-after young woman; Earl Thompson, whose *A Garden of Sand* dealt with a lusty young man's growing up in Depression-era Kansas; and black novelist George Cain, whose *Blueschild Baby* was a polemical appeal for black unity.

Two other black novelists who brought out new work of more than ordinary interest were Ernest J. Gaines, whose *The Autobiography of Miss Jane Pittman* was the life story of a slave who was freed during the Civil War and lived until the 1960s, and John Oliver Killens, whose *The Cotillion* was a comic tale of a grand ball held at the Waldorf-Astoria Hotel by a Brooklyn black women's club.

Another black writer, Ed Bullins, who is better known as a playwright, produced a notable volume of short stories in *The Hungered One*. Other short-story collections of the year included Herbert Gold's *The Magic Will* (which also contained some lively essays); a 30-year gathering of work of the Irish writer Mary Lavin in *Collected Stories*; *Flannery O'Connor: The Complete Stories*, including 12 never published before by this Georgia writer, who died in 1964; *The Mortgaged Heart*, a collection of stories, essays, and poems by another Southern writer, the late Carson McCullers; Jorge Luis Borges' *The Aleph and Other Stories, 1933-1969*; *Franz Kafka: The Complete Stories*; and a collection of short stories, *Livingstone's Companions*, by the distinguished South African fiction writer Nadine Gordimer.

Three posthumously published novels from England attracted special interest. One was *The Bell Jar*, a story of a young woman's mental breakdown, by poet Sylvia Plath, who committed suicide in 1963. Another was E. M. Forster's novel of homosexuality, *Maurice*, which he wrote in 1913 and 1914 but himself suppressed. A third was Ivy Compton-Burnett's *The Last and the First*, another of her acid-tinged portrayals of English family life. Doris Lessing, one of England's finest novelists, produced a compelling story in *Briefing for a Descent into Hell*, about a professor who acquires sanity by going insane.

Biography and Autobiography. One of the year's most widely read and warmly reviewed works of biography was Joseph P. Lash's *Eleanor and Franklin*, a sympathetic portrait, by one of her closest friends, of Eleanor Roosevelt's relationship with Franklin D. Roosevelt from their marriage until his death in 1945. Former President Lyndon B. Johnson told his own story of his presidency in *The Vantage Point*, which contained few, if any, surprises. The life stories of two other presidents were ably documented in two solid biographies, Ralph Ketcham's *James Madison* and Harry Amman's *James Monroe*. Another political biography, long needed and exceptionally well written, was Gerald T. Dunne's *Justice Joseph Story*, the first full-scale work on this noted Supreme Court figure, who was a colleague of John Marshall.

In the literary field, there was the usual spate of intriguing books by and about notable figures, past and present. Two autobiographical segments that drew special interest were Graham Greene's *A Sort of Life*, in which the English novelist reviewed his first 27 years, and Edmund Wilson's *Upstate*, a moving personal record of the aging critic's latter-day years in the little New York state town where he grew up. In a somewhat similar vein, a less celebrated author, the Illinois-born novelist William Maxwell, published *Ancestors*, an absorbing study of his own family ties.

Perhaps the best of the year's literary biographies came from the F. Scott Fitzgerald specialist Arthur Mizener, who found a perfect subject for his talents in *The Saddest Story: A Biography of Ford Madox Ford*. It was by far the best and the most extensive portrait to date of that neglected Englishman. Enid Starkie completed her two-volume biography of Gustave Flaubert with the publication of *Flaubert the Master*, which covered the French novelist's active literary life from 1856 until his death in 1880.

Other books of the year offered peripheral or fragmentary biographical material of interest in the study of several modern writers. The private life of Ezra Pound, the poet who had so much influence on his contemporaries, was illuminated in two absorbing new books. The first was *Discretions*, by Mary de Rachewiltz, Pound's daughter. A memoir of her European childhood, it was filled with affectionate regard for Pound as father and poetic genius, as well as, ultimately, a foolish man beguiled by Mussolini. Direct evidence of Pound's shaping influence on T. S. Eliot and the latter's most famous work was offered with the publication of a facsimile and original drafts of *The Waste Land*, including the annotations in Pound's own handwriting. The book was edited by Valerie Eliot, the poet's widow.

Stanley Weintraub continued his studies of George Bernard Shaw with the publication of *Journey to Heartbreak*, a record of the Irish playwright's antiwar activities during the period from 1914 to 1918. Emily Dickinson continued to fascinate the psychobiographers. The latest, John Cody, published *After Great Pain*, a psychiatrist's fascinating inquiry into the tangled relationships of the poet's family.

Among the year's best in the field of popular biography was Turner Catledge's *My Life and Times*, in which that one-time Mississippi newspaperman reviewed his rise from a Southern newspaper to executive editorship of *The New York Times*. One of the more controversial books of the year was Mike Royko's *Boss*, a slashingly critical biography of Mayor Richard J. Daley of Chicago by the popular *Chicago Daily News* columnist.

History. One of the year's finest books of popular historical interest was Dee Brown's *Bury My Heart at Wounded Knee*, an account of how the Indians lost the American West to the white man. Its pro-Indian bias stirred controversy, but it was a telling indictment of the white man's bloody conquests, largely drawn from treaty-council records and the sorry facts of history. How the white man got to America in the first place was the broad subject explored in Admiral Samuel Eliot Morison's *The European Discovery of America*, a scholarly, but witty and highly readable, account of the early northern voyages of exploration that were carried out along the Atlantic seaboard.

The entry of China into the United Nations late in the year lent special interest to Barbara Tuchman's illuminating study of Joseph W. "Vinegar Joe" Stilwell and his relations with Chiang Kai-shek in *Stilwell and the American Experience in China, 1911-45.*

The Vietnam War books continued to roll from the presses. Among the more important ones were *The Roots of Involvement*, a compact history by Marvin Kalb and Elie Abel of the United States position in Asia from 1784 to today; Anthony Austin's *The President's War*, an account of the Bay of Tonkin incident of August, 1964, and how we got into the conflict; Dr. Ronald J. Glasser's *365 Days*, a physician's harrowing report of his encounters with Vietnam casualties; Don Oberdorfer's *Tet!*, a reporter's vivid account of the savage but largely ineffective Viet Cong offensive of 1968 that caused a complete turnabout in American public opinion; and Telford Taylor's *Nuremberg and Vietnam: An American Tragedy*, which discussed the war crimes issue in relation to our Vietnam involvement.

Social Criticism. Man's relationship to his environment was a continuing concern, and the most lucid commentary on the ecological problem came from scientist Barry Commoner in his sober, if sometimes frightening, book *The Closing Circle*. The concerns of young Americans in various areas of our national life were brilliantly reported by J. Anthony Lukas in *Don't Shoot—We Are Your Children!*, which consisted of interviews with 10 subjects. *Kent State*, by the well-known novelist James A. Michener, was a sober and exhaustive inquiry, involving interviews by Michener and a research team with scores of persons, into the shooting of four Kent State University students in May, 1970. In another troubled area of American life, Gilbert Moore, a black reporter for a national magazine, published *A Special Rage*, a sober and balanced account of his investigation of the Black Panther movement. Norman Mailer, who has turned from novels to nonfiction, produced two new books during the year—one of them *The Prisoner of Sex*, a free-swinging joust with the Women's Liberation movement, and the other, *Of a Fire on the Moon*, a diffuse and rambling report on the flight of *Apollo 11*. Late in the year, Mailer was the subject of a first major critical study in two volumes edited by the critic Robert F.

Chicago author Saul Bellow, left, who won his third National Book Award, chats
with Erich Segal, whose nominated book *Love Story* was rejected by the jury.

Lucid. One of the volumes was a selection by Lucid from Mailer's work over the last 25 years, issued under the title *The Long Patrol*. The other was a critical study, *Norman Mailer: The Man and His Work*.

Criticism. Of the handful of new books for the critical shelf, perhaps the most useful one published in 1971 was Robert Penn Warren's *Homage to Theodore Dreiser: August 27, 1871-December 28, 1945*, a much-needed revaluation of the Indiana novelist's work published on the anniversary of his birth. Among the others of more than passing interest were the two volumes of Leslie Fiedler's *Collected Essays*, thoughts and second thoughts of a controversial and sometimes abrasive critic; George Steiner's *In Bluebeard's Castle*, the British critic's lament for the "gardens of liberal culture" that were destroyed in Western Europe with the rise of Naziism; William H. Gass's scholarly discussions in *Fiction and the Figures of Life*; and *Selected Essays of Delmore Schwartz*, from the pen of the brilliant poet-critic who died in 1966.

Science. In the field of popular science, there were several books of special interest to the layman who wants to keep up with the world. Among the most interesting was Evgeny Riabchikov's *Russians in Space*, translated from the Russian by Guy Daniels. The book contains much hitherto-unavailable information on the Russian space exploration program. C. W. Ceram, author of *Gods, Graves and*

Scholars, a long-time favorite of armchair archaeologists, assembled in a new book, *The First American: A Story of North American Archaeology*, an enormous assortment of facts, some of them little known, about the first men in America. In *Microbes and Morals*, Theodor Rosebury argued for more knowledge and less moralizing in the continuing effort to end the scourge of venereal disease. Thor Heyerdahl, the author of *Kon-Tiki* and other scientific adventures, was back in print again, this time with *The Ra Expedition*, the story of the voyages he made in a balsa raft from Africa to South America in an effort to prove that culture could have come West in that manner. For the advanced science reader, there was Werner Heisenberg's *Physics and Beyond*, a profound account of his activities in atomic physics over half a century.

Art. Three of the year-end gift-season art books that appeared to have more than passing worth were Lloyd Goodrich's *Edward Hopper*, a well-illustrated survey of the work of an outstanding modern American realist; John Hayes's *The Drawings of Thomas Gainsborough*, two volumes; and Frederick George Marcham's *Louis Agassiz Fuertes & The Singular Beauty of Birds*, a collection of the painter's water-color work, together with a text drawn largely from his letters.   Van Allen Bradley

LITERATURE, CANADIAN. See CANADIAN LIBRARY ASSOCIATION; CANADIAN LITERATURE.

LITERATURE FOR CHILDREN. The year 1971 seems to have been the year when ecology really became a topic of major interest in children's books. This was evident in picture books, in older books with a story line, and also in science books, where the subject was dealt with in a straightforward manner without a story line. An interest in vanishing animal species and vanishing ways of life among various cultures on the periphery of civilization was also noticeable. Books showing minority ethnic groups continued to appear in large numbers, with quality varying widely.

Here are some of the outstanding books of 1971:

Picture Books

Gobble Growl Grunt, by Peter Spier (Doubleday). A wonderful picture book filled with page after page of beautifully drawn—and very much alive—animals and birds making their own sorts of noises and doing all manner of interesting things. This should hold the fascinated attention of a preschooler for many an hour. Up to age 6.

A Woggle of Witches, by Adrienne Adams (Scribners). Lively and imaginative full-color pictures, each covering two pages, show "a woggle of witches" doing all sorts of wonderful and ridiculous things as they fly through the air on their big night. Even a quite small trick-or-treater will enjoy this. Up to age 6.

Look What I Can Do, by José Aruego (Scribners). The title line—repeated at the beginning and the end—comprises the only text in the book, but what remarkable and amusing stunts take place in-between as the two carabaos in the pictures perform. The young child will enjoy their antics very much as he "reads" this one for himself. Up to age 6.

My Hopping Bunny, by Robert Bright (Doubleday). The fast-moving verse and simple illustrations add up to a very appealing little story of a frisky bunny whose little-boy owner understands his athletic feats. Delightfully childlike. Up to age 6.

Changes, Changes, by Pat Hutchins (Macmillan). Illustrations only—no words—show two wooden figures using a set of blocks to make a house. It catches on fire, so they use the blocks to make a fire engine. It pours out too much water, so they use the blocks to make a boat, and so on. These full-color pictures should be fun for the building-block set. Up to age 6.

Bear Circus, by William Pène DuBois (Viking). Rescued by the kangaroos, the koala bears show their gratitude by putting on a circus. Wonderfully illustrated by DuBois' beautiful—and large—full-color pictures. Up to age 6.

Impossible, Possum, by Ellen Conford, illustrated by Rosemary Wells (Little, Brown). A humorous story of a young possum who can't learn to hang upside down by his tail. After the use of an ingenious interim method, the little boy possum, with little sister's interference proving helpful, finally learns to sleep in proper possum fashion. Ages 6 to 8.

Sir Addlepate and the Unicorn, by Dahlov Ipcar (Doubleday). A delightful story of a knight's hunt for a unicorn and how he finds what he thinks is one and takes it home. Everything in the story could really have happened, which is one thing that makes the book—on such a subject—so appealing. Ages 6 to 8.

Mr. Biddle and the Birds, by Lonzo Anderson, illustrated by Adrienne Adams (Scribners). Mr. Biddle had always wanted to fly, and he finally figured out a way for his bird friends to help him do so. Things didn't work out at all as he had intended, but when the birds saw his disappointment, they helped. Up to age 8.

How Droofus the Dragon Lost His Head, by Bill Peet (Houghton Mifflin). Bright full-color pictures show the homely but appealing dragon—the king has offered a price for his head—as he makes friends with a little boy and performs various helpful tasks around the farm, until his whereabouts are reported to the king. The ingenious solution to the king's desire to have the dragon's head will amuse a reader of any age. Ages 5 to 8.

Me Day, by Joan M. Lexau, pictures by Robert Weaver (Dial). Rafer, a little black boy, wakes especially happy on his birthday but is disappointed when he doesn't hear from his father, who no longer lives with the family. The day becomes all he'd hoped for, however, when he finds his father has made arrangements to meet him so they can spend the day together. The fine black-and-white illustrations add much to the book. Ages 5 to 8.

Sixes and Sevens, by John Yeoman, pictures by Quentin Black (Macmillan). This tale of Barnaby's trip on a raft to Limber Lea and all the unexpected passengers he acquired, and the ingenious provisions he made to keep them busy, can be a delightful way to practice counting—or a just-for-fun picture book. Up to age 9.

Charles, by Liesel Moak Skorpen, pictures by Martha Alexander (Harper & Row). This is the story of a teddy bear first owned by a little girl who doesn't understand him and then by a little boy who does. The illustrations show a very lovable teddy bear and his boy owner having many good times together, bound by their close friendship and the little boy's complete understanding of how his teddy bear feels. Ages 4 to 8.

From Tomi Ungerer's *The Beast of Monsieur Racine*. A full-color picture book filled with comedy and pictorial splendor. Publisher: Farrar, Straus & Giroux.

Hermes, Lord of Robbers, translated by Penelope Proddow, illustrated by Barbara Cooney (Doubleday). An adaptation of Homeric Hymn Number Four, the text of this picture book tells the famous story of the first day in the life of Hermes. The beautiful paintings of the well-known illustrator are the charm of the book, with their careful attention to color and composition and their feeling of a classical Greek atmosphere.

Benjy and the Barking Bird, by Margaret Bloy Graham (Harper & Row). The dog Benjy is very jealous of all the attention Aunt Sarah's parrot Tilly gets and decides to get rid of her. Just as he is lifting her cage into the trash barrel, it opens and Tilly flies out. Later, it is Benjy who finds her and arranges her future satisfactorily for everyone. Up to age 8.

Dorrie and the Birthday Eggs, by Patrician Coombs (Lothrop, Lee, and Shepard). If anyone had listened to the little witch Dorrie's explanation instead of shushing her, as grown-ups will, Dorrie could have solved the mystery of the hen with mysterious powers right away. She does get a chance to help out eventually, however. The delightful illustrations add much to the story. Ages 6 to 10.

The Silver Whistle, by Jay Williams, illustrated by Friso Henstra (Parents Magazine Press). An amusing fairy tale—told with a difference that adds much to its charm (the heroine, for instance, has "a snub nose, a wide mouth . . . and so many freckles that it looked as if someone had sprinkled her with cinnamon" and later turns down a chance to become beautiful). The illustrations in color have an individuality and originality of their own while yet reminding one somewhat of Tenniel. Ages 4 to 10.

Art, Music, and Poetry

Haiku: The Mood of Earth, by Ann Atwood, with photographs in full color by the author (Scribners). The author says she hopes the words illustrate the photographs, and that is perhaps the best description for this book. The *haiku* poems show one the sudden wonder of beauty caught in these truly remarkable photographs. Anyone who has a feeling for and understanding of *haiku* at any age should find this book a memorable one.

A Visit from St. Nicholas, by Clement C. Moore; a facsimile of the original 1848 book (Simon and Schuster). Reproduced from one of the only two copies known to exist, this tiny volume has the original black-and-white engravings by 19th-century American artist T. C. Boyd, and includes a picture of Moore and a note about him by Kenneth A. Lohf of the Columbia University Libraries.

El Toro Pinto and Other Songs in Spanish, selected and illustrated by Anne Rockwell (Macmillan). Delightful full-color illustrations on every page—occasionally a picture for each verse, if it tells a story—give this book a very festive and attractive appearance. There is a treble piano notation of the melody with guitar chords indicated.

The Art of the Southwest Indians, by Shirley Glubok, photographs by Alfred Tamarin (Macmillan). Very good black-and-white photographs show the rock pictures, carvings, sand paintings, and sacred masks of the Indian tribes from the Southwestern United States, as well as their better-known pottery, rugs, and jewelry. Pictures and text together contribute a good bit to one's knowledge of the Indians' life and thought.

People, Places, and Things

The Mountain, written and illustrated by Peter Parnall (Doubleday). Starting in brilliant full color, this story of a mountain—people decided to make it a national park to protect its beauty—fades to black and white as its human visitors themselves destroy the beauty they had intended to preserve. Told with almost no text, this picture book makes its ecological point so tellingly

From John Burningham's *Mr. Gumpy's Outing.*
Mr. Gumpy collects a risky punt load of energetic passengers. Publisher: Holt, Rinehart & Winston.

that people of all ages might profit from looking at its pages—and perhaps the country would, too.

Julie Harris Talks to Young Actors, by Julie Harris with Barry Tarshis, illustrated with photographs (Lothrop, Lee, and Shepard). A must for anyone interested in acting as a career, this book gives what seems very sensible and considered advice on how to go about learning the art and craft of acting, how to increase one's chances to practice it professionally, and what many of the things one might expect to encounter are. This is not only fascinating reading, but strikes one as highly practical as well. Ages 12 and up.

I Am from Puerto Rico, by Peter Buckley (Simon and Schuster). This story of Federico Ramirez starts in New York City and follows the young teen-ager when he goes to live in Puerto Rico, to which the rest of his family has already returned. There, the reader learns, as Federico learns, about various ways of life on the island and watches the boy come to enjoy his new home. Ages 8 to 12.

Fourteen Hundred Cowries, and Other African Tales, by Abayomi Fuja, illustrated by Ademola Olugebefola (Lothrop, Lee, and Shepard). A collection of 31 Yoruba folk tales filled with stories of magic enchantments, helpful or deceitful jungle animals, butterflies that become beautiful maidens, and strong men performing brave deeds. Black-and-white primitive illustrations. Up to age 12.

Baron Munchausen and Other Comic Tales from Germany, by R. E. Raspe and others; edited by Stella Humphries and illustrated by Ulrik Schramm (Dutton). A collection of the ridiculous exaggerations that have delighted people for many years, this contains not only Munchausen's adventures, but also those of "The Men of Schilda." Ages 9 to 14.

This Is Australia, by M. Sasek (Macmillan). In his usual inimitable fashion, M. Sasek gives us another travel book filled with full-color paintings of all the famous and characteristic sights of "Down Under" and tells about them in his own distinctive fashion. Ages 8 to 12.

LITERATURE FOR CHILDREN

The Bread Book: All About Bread and How to Make It, by Carolyn Meyer, illustrated by Trina Schart Hyman (Harcourt Brace Jovanovich). A fascinating account of the history of bread from the accidental discovery of yeast by the ancient Egyptians on down to the workings of a large modern bakery. One of the delights of the book is the illustrations, accurate but full of humor and interest, which, coupled with the text, make this a book anyone could enjoy. Recipes are included. Ages 8 to 12.

Science, Animals, and Skills

Hot as an Ice Cube, a Let's-Read-and-Find-Out Science Book, by Philip Balestrino, illustrated by Tomie de Paola (Crowell). In simple, easy language and interesting drawings, this book explains something about the properties of heat and how it affects various substances. Some very simple experiments are given.

The Air We Breathe and *The Water We Drink*, by Enid Bloome (Doubleday). In these two books, very good photographs and simple text present the problems of pollution to the kindergarten-age child. The books grew out of the experiences of the author, a kindergarten teacher, in introducing her students to current ecological problems.

What Makes the Sun Shine? by Isaac Asimov, illustrated by Marc Brown (Atlantic-Little, Brown). This well-known science author has written an excellent and very understandable explanation of the changes taking place in hydrogen and helium atoms in the sun and how these changes result in the shining of the sun. Ages 8 to 12.

The Praying Mantis, Insect Cannibal, story and photographs by Lilo Hess (Scribners). An interesting text and remarkable photographs make this a fascinating and very informative book for anyone interested in these unusual insects. Excellent pictures are included of the mantis hatching, catching its prey, shedding its skin, and so on, and there is even information on the needs of a mantis as a pet. Ages 7 to 11.

Shelf Pets, by Edward R. Ricciuti, photographs by Arline Strong (Harper & Row). Subtitled "How to Take Care of Small Wild Animals," this book gives information on the habits and needs of toads, frogs, turtles, snakes, salamanders, lizards, snails, a variety of insects, and other living things that can be kept as shelf pets, as well as including information on hamsters and guinea pigs. The close-up photographs are excellent. Ages 10 and up.

Birds in the Street, The City Pigeon Book, by Winifred and Cecil Lubell (Parents Magazine Press). An interesting look at the bird most city dwellers know best, this book tells about the anatomy, life cycle, habits, and varieties of pigeons, and discusses some of the problems pigeons cause and some possible solutions. It is told in a brisk, informal style, and illustrated with many drawings. Ages 6 to 10.

Life on a Lost Continent: A Natural History of New Zealand, by Beth Day (Doubleday). A fascinating account of individual birds and beasts of New Zealand, including information on such famous oddities as the kiwi and the quatara, as well as many other, less-known ones. Photographs and an interestingly written text make this an information book adults will enjoy, too. Ages 8 to 12.

Mysteries from the Past, edited by Thomas G. Aylesworth (Natural History Press). Subtitled "Stories of Scientific Detection," this book interestingly tells about nine scientific mysteries (Stonehenge, Atlantis, Mayas, and so on), giving the reader some insight into archaeological methods and rousing his curiosity about fascinating questions still unanswered.

How to Play Hockey: A Guide for Players and Their Coaches, by Tom Watt, illustrated by Bob Berger (Doubleday). Starting with individual fundamentals and then giving information on team play, this book includes concrete, easily understood suggestions on many aspects of playing hockey and should be of value to anyone interested in taking part in the game. Black-and-white illustrations demonstrate the various maneuvers. Ages 11 and up.

Snowmobiling: The Guide, by John W. Malo (Macmillan). Concerned with what the author calls "our fastest-growing new sport," this book gives information on snowmobile manufacturers and models, maintenance of the vehicle, proper clothing, safe driving, games and competitions for snowmobiles, and a brief history of the machine. Illustrated by photographs. For adults as well as age 12 and up.

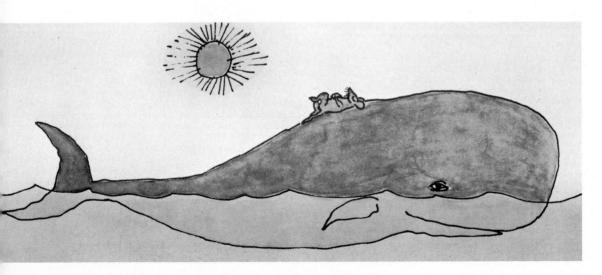

From William Steig's *Amos and Boris*. The story of a friendship between Amos the mouse and Boris the whale. Publisher: Farrar, Straus & Giroux.

Skiing for Beginners, by Bruce Gavett and Conrad Brown, photographs by Kim Massie (Scribners). This book shows the basic ski maneuvers in step-by-step photographs captioned by a description of what is being done, given by the youngster in the picture. A very understandable approach that should be the next-best thing to having an instructor present.

Auto Racing, by Charles Coombs (Morrow). Illustrated with 55 photographs, this book presents information on various types of racers, road courses and ovals, drivers, and mechanics, and finally takes the reader through an actual race showing driving strategy, what goes on during a pit stop, and so on. It contains a glossary of racing terms. Ages 10 to 14.

Fiction for the Middle Grades

Jingo Django, by Sid Fleischmann, illustrated by Eric von Schmidt (Atlantic-Little, Brown). A rousing adventure story enlivened by gypsies, a treasure map, and an unpredictable adventurer who lives by his wits. The air of mystery, and the ingenuity with which the predicaments are solved, make this a fascinating book.

The Finches' Fabulous Furnace, by Roger W. Drury, illustrated by Erik Blegvad (Little, Brown). A delightful tale about a family that moves into a house that mysteriously stays wonderfully warm with no heating bills; the real estate agent assures them there's really nothing unusual about it—except that it *does* have a small volcano in its cellar. There's lots of fun as the Finches try to keep the secret while the volcano grows.

The First Four Years, by Laura Ingalls Wilder, pictures by Garth Williams (Harper & Row). This first draft was found among Mrs. Wilder's papers after her death and though not revised, the book is still a vivid account of the difficult life on a homestead in South Dakota during the 1880s. Devotees of the series will be happy to have one more book about Laura.

The Case of the Ticklish Tooth, by Scott Corbett, illustrated by Paul Frame (Atlantic-Little, Brown). Another delightful mystery featuring Roger Tearle (nicknamed "Inspector") who gets involved in a small mystery when he finds his dentist bound and gagged in the dentist chair, and discovers his own bike has been stolen by the culprit as his getaway vehicle. Twin sister Shirley and his friend "Thumbs" Thorndyke add to the fun.

Teen-Age Fiction

Pennington's LAST TERM, by K. M. Peyton (Crowell). Pennington, 16, long-haired, lazy, indifferent to school, looked on by all as a confirmed troublemaker, is in his last term at school, a fact his teachers rejoice over. An outstanding book with the title character so real you feel you know him agonizingly well, this should hit home with many teen-agers.

Pulga, by S. R. Van Iterson, translated from the Dutch by Alexander and Alison Gode (Morrow Junior Books). Designated the best children's book of 1967 in the Netherlands, this realistic account of a 15-year-old boy from the slums of Bogotá, Colombia, not only captures the physical misery and helplessness of such an existence, but manages to do so without being a depressing book. The reader watches Pulga as, given a chance to become a truckdriver's helper, he begins to sense the possibility of another kind of life from the one he has known. One never doubts the feeling of truth that the book conveys.

A Room Made of Windows, by Eleanor Cameron, illustrated by Trina Schart Hyman (Atlantic-Little, Brown). A very good picture of 12-year-old Julia caught in the throes of growing up enough to accept —reluctantly—the fact that her widowed mother is going to remarry. The numerous characters are very real people whom the reader gets to know and care about. The book conveys well the sensitivity to words, to music, and to beauty in many forms that are char-

acteristic of Julia, as well as the more ordinary traits she shares with many 12-year-olds.

The Sorcerer, by Anne Eliot Crompton, illustrated by Leslie Morrill (Atlantic-Little, Brown). A book that captures the feel of the primitive life of the precave man when man's existence seemed only a little removed from that of the animals upon which his life depended. Told by Lefthand, whose sensitivity and ability to draw, as well as his lack of ability as a hunter, set him apart from the rest until the Sorcerer shows him that there is a place for one with his abilities.

Emma Tupper's Diary, by Peter Dickinson, illustrated by David Omar White (Atlantic-Little, Brown). Emma goes to spend the summer with her wealthy, eccentric, and fascinating McAndrews cousins and becomes involved in an exciting adventure when the McAndrews decide to put their grandfather's experimental two-man submarine back into operation, and stumble onto an exciting secret in their private lake in Scotland.

The Prisoners of Gridling Gap, by E. W. Hildick, illustrated by Paul Sagsoorian (Doubleday). A fast-moving suspense tale that has a murder and a disappearing corpse (later discovered alive) to get things off to a quick start, this mystery finds an 18-year-old brother and 14-year-old sister stumbling onto a menacing organization in what appears to be a quiet resort town.

Thin Ice, by Reginald Maddock (Little, Brown). A book that clearly conveys a boy's growing-up struggles as he gets involved with the wrong bunch of guys when he moves into a new school. Gradually, he begins to find the courage to stand up against the gang leader and starts to be able to see the members of his family, including his dictatorial father, as individuals apart from himself—a fast-moving and well-written book.

Awards in 1971 included:

American Library Association Children's Services Division Awards: The *John Newbery Award* for "the most distinguished contribution to American literature for children" was given to Betsy Byars for *The Summer of the Swans* (Viking). The *Randolph Caldecott Award* for "the most distinguished American picture book for children" was presented to Gail E. Haley for *A Story: An African Tale* (Atheneum); she was both reteller and illustrator of the book. The 1971 *Mildred L. Batchelder Award* for "a book considered to be the most outstanding of those books originally published in a foreign country and subsequently translated and published in the United States" was given to Pantheon Books for *In the Land of Ur: The Discovery of Ancient Mesopotamia*, written in German by Hans Baumann and translated by Stella Humphries.

British Book Awards: Awards given in Great Britain were the *Carnegie Medal 1970* for "the most outstanding book of the year," won by Leon Garfield and Edward Blishen for *The God Beneath the Sea* (Longman Pantheon); and the *Kate Greenaway Medal 1970*, "for the most distinguished work in the illustration of a children's book," won by John Burningham for *Mr. Gumpy's Outing* (Cape).

Book World's Children's Spring Book Festival Awards: The award in the Picture Book Division was won by *All upon a Store* (Crowell), by Jean George and illustrated by Don Bolognese. There was no first prize given in the Middle Books Division. *Reggie and Nilma* (Farrar), by Louise Tanner, won the award in the Older Books Division.

National Book Committee Award: The National Book Award for children's literature was presented to Lloyd Alexander for *The Marvelous Misadventures of Sebastian* (Dutton).

Lynn de Grummond Delaune

LIVESTOCK. See Agriculture; International Live Stock Exposition.

LOS ANGELES suffered its worst earthquake in nearly 40 years on Feb. 9, 1971. The quake killed 62, injured 1,000, and caused over $350 million in property damage. Yet the disaster, which hit just after 6 A.M., would have been much worse had it occurred several hours later, when the freeways, schools, and other public places would have been filled with people. As it was, freeway bridges were destroyed, schools were shaken, and hospitals badly damaged. The worst tragedy occurred at the Veterans' Hospital in suburban Sylmar, where 46 persons lost their lives. Others were buried in the building's rubble for days, awaiting rescue. The quake measured 6.6 on the Richter scale, a severe jolt, but not the disastrous earthquake that scientists had been predicting would hit the area.

Political Developments. A California Supreme Court ruling voided certain provisions of the Los Angeles city charter. The provisions permitted the apportionment of city legislative districts on the basis of registered voters rather than on the number of residents. This allowed a deviation of as much as 10 per cent in the size of such districts.

Voters defeated proposed city-charter and county-administrative reforms. The proposed reorganization would have increased the authority of the mayor and city council and transferred administrative functions from the board of supervisors to a chief county executive officer.

Money caused typical problems in Los Angeles. The city's school board was forced to cut $20 million from its budget, firing 500 substitute and provisional teachers and 1,000 other employees in the process. The cutbacks also forced the board to shorten the high school day.

City Police tried an experimental program in 1971 aimed at curbing juvenile delinquency. In this program, called Operation Sweep, the police detained youngsters picked up as truants during the daytime until their parents came to claim them. During one week, police reported a 30 per cent reduction in daytime burglaries and auto thefts.

The police did not fare as well on other fronts. Five policemen were indicted by a federal grand jury on charges of violating civil rights. In one of the incidents in question, two Mexicans were fatally shot.

The 1970 Census showed that the Los Angeles metropolitan area had passed Chicago to become the nation's second largest, with a population of 7,036,887. The city itself remained in third place behind New York and Chicago, with a population of 2,816,061. Blacks account for about 18 per cent of the city's residents.

On July 10, Mayor Samuel W. Yorty dedicated the new Los Angeles Convention and Exhibition Center.   J. M. Banovetz

LOUISIANA. See NEW ORLEANS; STATE GOVT.

LUMBER. See FOREST AND FOREST PRODUCTS.

LUNS, JOSEPH M. A. H. (1911-   ), who had been foreign minister of the Netherlands since 1952, became secretary-general of the North Atlantic Treaty Organization (NATO) on Oct. 1, 1971. He succeeded Manlio Brosio of Italy.

Luns was born in Rotterdam on Aug. 28, 1911. After attending high schools in Amsterdam and Brussels, he studied law from 1932 to 1937 at the University of Leyden and the University of Amsterdam. In 1938, he took courses at both the London School of Economics and the University of Berlin. In the same year, he entered the foreign service and was assigned to the Netherlands ministry of foreign affairs. He served in Bern, Switzerland, in 1940 and 1941; in Lisbon, Portugal from 1941 to 1943; and in London from 1943 to 1949. From 1949 to 1952, he was a member of the Netherlands permanent delegation to the United Nations.

Luns' term as foreign minister was by far the longest of any Western foreign minister. During the 1950s, he helped to guide the successful economic union of the Netherlands, Belgium, and Luxembourg.

Luns is imposing in both his height (6 feet 5½ inches) and his impeccable dress, and has a dry, off-beat sense of humor. He once told an interviewer that he leaves all dinner parties punctually at 10:30 unless he wants to show how much he enjoyed himself. In that case, he stays until 10:35.   Michael Reed

LUXEMBOURG was the scene of a historic achievement for Europe on June 23, 1971, when the European Community (Common Market) negotiators successfully ended talks on Great Britain's entry into the community. The negotiators met in the Kirchberg European Center in Luxembourg. See EUROPE.

Inflation, despite moderate economic growth, became more extreme in 1971 than at any time since the post-Korean War boom. A leap in wages emphasized the difficulties that followed when foreign iron and steel customers bought less of Luxembourg's products. New industries, being established to diversify the economy, include aluminum and ferroalloys, automotive assemblies, electrical batteries, photographic supplies, and rubber products.

Acieries Reunies de Burbach-Eich-Dudelange, a major European steel producer with revenue greater than the Luxembourg government's, concluded a merger with the West German steel concern of Roechling. The Luxembourg company made record profits of $400 million in 1971.

Facts in Brief. Population: 344,000. Government: Grand Duke Jean; President and Prime Minister Pierre Werner. Monetary Unit: Luxembourg franc. Foreign Trade: exports, $11,610,000,000; imports, $11,362,000,000 (including Belgium). Principal Exports: iron and steel, machinery.   Kenneth Brown

MAGAZINE. See PUBLISHING.

MAINE. See STATE GOVERNMENT.

MALAGASY REPUBLIC was alive with political turmoil and rumors of plots in 1971. In February, President Philibert Tsiranana formed a new government by reshuffling the ministry portfolios among the same Cabinet members. The main result of the Cabinet change was the demotion of André Resampa from first to second vice-president. Resampa was also removed as head of the powerful ministry of the interior and placed in charge of the ministry of agriculture. Before the Cabinet change, Resampa was widely considered as the most likely man to succeed Tsiranana.

On June 1, Resampa and several other officials were arrested on charges of complicity with a foreign government. Tsiranana accused the United States of being involved in a plot with Malagasy officials to overthrow the government. Five U.S. Embassy employees were deported, and, at Tsiranana's request, the U.S. ambassador was recalled.

Presidential Politics. Even though Tsiranana was reportedly in poor health, he appeared to be preparing his campaign for re-election to a third seven-year term as president. Elections were scheduled for March, 1972. He traveled throughout the country making speeches, and exerted his control over the ruling Social Democratic Party (PSD). Before his fall from power, Resampa had virtually run the PSD.

Tsiranana's most likely opponent in the 1972 presidential race is Richard Andriamanjato, leader of the opposition Congress Party for the Independence of Madagascar.

Rebel Uprising. On April 1, rebels under Monja Jaona, leader of the leftist Monima Party, attempted to start a rebellion in the southern province of Tulear. They attacked a military base, and 30 persons were killed in the fighting. The government outlawed the Monima Party and executed two of its leaders. The government reported that 857 persons were held for questioning. On April 23, Monja Jaona was arrested.

The rebels were dissatisfied with the system of fixed livestock prices, and the revolt was triggered by unrest during a period of drought. Even though he is a leftist, Monja Jaona was defended by a Roman Catholic newspaper, which denounced the government's indifference to the plight of the peasants.

South African Ties. Malagasy favored establishing a dialogue with white-ruled South Africa. Malagasy's trade with South Africa has been increasing. In June, diplomatic relations between the two nations were established. In August, Malagasy and South Africa agreed to establish a permanent commission for expanding mutual cooperation.

Facts in Brief. Population: 7,112,000. Government: President Philibert Tsiranana. Monetary Unit: franc. Foreign Trade: exports, $145,000,000; imports, $170,000,000. Principal Exports: coffee, vanilla, rice. George Shepherd

MALAWI. President Hastings Kamuzu Banda visited the Republic of South Africa in August, 1971, the first black African head of state ever to do so. Banda has been the leading black advocate of establishing contacts with South Africa's white-minority government.

Officially, Banda was returning South African Prime Minister Balthazar Johannes Vorster's 1970 visit to Malawi. But he was more interested in securing the loans and trade arrangements that South Africa had promised. He returned to Malawi with an agreement for a $17-million loan to create a new capital at Lilongwe, northwest of the present capital, Zomba, and a promise for all the military and economic assistance that Malawi might need. Banda also discussed development loans for projects such as an international airport.

Banda's Reception. Banda became the first black to be given full ceremonial honors in South Africa, including dining with whites. Although his travel routes were supposedly a secret, black Africans managed to discover where he would be, and thousands turned out to greet him. Many of the country's black leaders hailed his reception as a sign of a new, dignified status for South African blacks. White South Africans used the visit to improve their image in the world.

Leaders of other black African nations generally condemned the Banda visit as a dangerous precedent, possibly leading to the emergence of a South African neocolonialism. In Malawi, however, Banda's policies appeared to be popular.

In July, Malawi established the first black African embassy in South Africa. South Africa also sent an ambassador to Malawi.

Malawi virtually withdrew from all Organization of African Unity (OAU) activities. Malawi's policies of collaboration with South Africa were strongly criticized at OAU meetings.

Political Developments. On July 6, Banda was made president for life. He had refused to accept the honor earlier, claiming that he was not sufficiently well known to his countrymen.

In the general elections held in March, only candidates of the ruling Malawi Congress Party were permitted to run. However, party delegates were allowed to select candidates before the elections. Thirteen incumbent members of Parliament were not nominated as candidates.

The Cabinet was reorganized in April. Banda himself took over the ministries of agriculture and natural resources. On February 15, the International Monetary Fund announced that Malawi had introduced a new monetary unit, the kwacha.

Facts in Brief. Population: 4,764,000. Government: President Hastings Kamuzu Banda. Monetary Unit: kwacha. Foreign Trade: exports, $59,000,000; imports, $99,000,000. Principal Exports: tobacco, tea, peanuts. George Shepherd

MALAYSIA made significant strides in 1971 toward a return to representative government. The restrictive measures adopted after the racial riots in May, 1969, were eased by Prime Minister Abdul Razak. The prime minister also lifted the government's ban on public rallies for election campaigns, although he maintained the ban on debates involving racially sensitive issues. The National Operations Council, which had run the country for 22 months, was dissolved on February 19, and Parliament, which had been suspended, was reconvened.

The United Malay National Organization, the alliance that governed the nation, underwent changes, with younger factions replacing the more conservative leadership. In response to demands for increased special concessions to Malaysians, the Malay Chinese Association (MCA) finally agreed to accept Bahasa Malay as the national language. But Prime Minister Razak had trouble finding representative Chinese to serve in his government. The MCA was rapidly losing its influence with younger Chinese, and though Dato Ong, leader of the Sarawak United People's Party, did join the Cabinet, a noticeable imbalance remained.

In June, the government launched its second Five-Year Development Plan. Although it was ambitious, Malaysian resources were adequate to meet the fiscal requirements of the targets set. The plan called for spending $4.8 billion between 1971 and 1976. More emphasis was placed on agriculture, with plans to open up 200,000 acres of new land to farming. Malaysians were to receive preferred treatment on both the use and the ownership of such land. The plan also called for the creation of 600,000 jobs during the same period, and again, special efforts were to be made to ensure that Malaysians would be favored.

Communist guerrilla activity increased in 1971, despite efforts to cooperate with the neighboring Thais in wiping out gangs using the border as hide-out areas. More important, Communist activity moved south, with special camps being found at Perak and Ipoh. Curfews were promptly enforced, martial law was invoked, and the tin mines at Perak were closed for a time.

Relations with Peking improved slightly during the year. Pernas, a state trading agency, was authorized to expand commercial relations with China. The United States, however, was still Malaysia's major trading partner.

Facts in Brief. Population: 11,522,000. Government: Paramount Ruler Abdul Halim Muazzam; Prime Minister Abdul Razak. Monetary Unit: Malaysian dollar. Foreign Trade: exports, $1,680,-000,000; imports, $1,389,000,000. Principal Exports: rubber, tin, timber. *John N. Stalker*

MALI. See AFRICA.

MALIK, ADAM (1917-   ), an Indonesian diplomat, became president of the 26th United Nations General Assembly in September, 1971. He succeeded Edvard Hambro of Norway.

Malik was born on July 22, 1917, in the village of Pematangsiantar in north Sumatra. Like most of Indonesia, the area was under Dutch colonial rule.

Malik attended a Dutch primary school and a Moslem religious school. He spent his youth in Medan, Sumatra, where he joined the Indonesian independence movement. In 1934, Malik was jailed by the Dutch for his nationalist activities.

In 1937, Malik founded Antara, a news agency. It was run by a small group of revolutionary nationalists including Sukarno, who later became president of Indonesia. The Dutch again jailed Malik, and he was not freed until 1942, when Japan took Java. In 1947, Sukarno charged Malik with plotting a coup and had him jailed again. Malik escaped, however, and convinced Sukarno of his loyalty and desire to serve Indonesia.

Malik began his career in government service as a legislator. He served as ambassador to Russia from 1959 to 1963, when he became minister of trade. In 1966, he became minister of foreign affairs.

Malik is married and has four sons and a daughter. He reads voraciously, and also likes photography and big-game hunting. *Michael Reed*

MANITOBA. See CANADA.

Sultan Abdul Halim Muazzam, newly elected Paramount Ruler of Malaysia, ceremonially kisses the state dagger at his coronation. His queen is beside him.

MANUFACTURING. President Richard M. Nixon told the American people on Aug. 15, 1971, that "the time has come for a new economic policy. Its targets are unemployment, inflation, and international speculation." This new policy was prompted, in part, by the persistent sluggishness of the economic recovery from the recession of 1969 and 1970. Industrial production picked up slightly in November, buoyed by gains in consumer goods and business equipment. However, through October, 1971, it had fallen by slightly more than 1 per cent from the pre-General Motors strike level in the third quarter of 1970 and 5 per cent from the prerecession production peak of September, 1969. Unemployment hovered around 6 per cent through the first 11 months of 1971, closing the year at slightly under that mark.

In reviewing the first 11 months of the recovery, *The Wall Street Journal* noted that industrial production rose only 3.6 per cent, the smallest gain for any similar period of recovery of the five post-World War II recessions. Confirmation of the sputtering recovery came from the Federal Reserve System (Fed), whose figures for October showed industrial production was up only 1.2 per cent from the September average of 106.1 per cent (1967=100).

The rise in consumer goods and business equipment was particularly disappointing, with the September-to-October advance only 0.1 per cent and 0.4 per cent, respectively. For the recovery to have more substance, these two categories must increase at a faster rate in 1972. The November industrial output figure of 107 per cent of the 1967 average seemed to indicate an upturn was in store.

The Department of Commerce figures on durable goods supported the view that "the recovery is flat." New orders for October, at $31.06 billion, were only slightly better than September's $31.03 billion. However, orders in the capital-goods and defense industries did increase. Capital-goods orders for the same period were up $400 million, to $6.8 billion, and up $1 billion from October, 1970.

Total shipments of durable goods in November, at $32.2 billion, were up 3.6 per cent from October's $31.2 billion. The October figure was, in turn, down $140 million from September. Shipments of durables rose 2.2 per cent to $31.85 billion and unfilled orders increased $400 million or 0.05 per cent to $74.9 billion.

New Plants and Equipment. Capital spending in the third quarter scored the first significant gain in more than two years. The National Industrial Conference Board (NICB) reported that the nation's leading 1,000 manufacturing firms increased their capital appropriations by 12 per cent in this period. This was a positive sign, because it came while output was still flat and capacity was being used at the low rate of 73 per cent. Equally important, this gain came during the 90 days of the President's wage-price freeze, when investment decisions

were being held up pending clarification of rules. The need to modernize facilities in order to increase productivity (output per man-hour) and to meet the new standards for pollution control were viewed by the NICB as the key to the appropriation rise.

The need for better productivity was underscored by third-quarter results that showed a drop in productivity, with a resultant sharp rise in unit labor costs. Productivity in manufacturing declined at an annual rate of 2.1 per cent, following increases of 6.7 per cent and 8.4 per cent in the second and first quarters. Unit labor costs rose at an annual rate of 6.7 per cent in the third quarter, compared with a decline of 1 per cent in the second quarter and a rise of 1.4 per cent in the first quarter.

Total investment in new plants and equipment was estimated by the McGraw-Hill Economics Department at $81.44 billion, compared to an actual investment of $79.7 billion in 1970.

Productivity Is Key. When viewed in relation to productivity in other industrial nations, the situation in the United States is poor. Between 1965 and 1970, the yearly gain in output per man-hour in the United States was 2.1 per cent, placing it last. The United States ranked behind such competitive countries as Great Britain, Italy, Germany, France, Sweden, the Netherlands, and Japan, in that order. The gains in these countries ranged from a low of 3.6 per cent for Great Britain, to a high of 14.2 per cent for Japan.

Many U.S. economists claim the small productivity growth is due to the relatively small portion of the gross national product (GNP) that is represented by capital outlays. The trade magazine *American Machinist* made a study of capital investment for the 1960s in the same countries covered by the productivity study. It shows U.S. capital investment to be 13 per cent of GNP. Again, the United States trails the other industrial nations, who invest from a low of 14 per cent by Great Britain and Italy, to a high of 17 per cent by Japan.

Taking into account the inflationary pressures of 1971, McGraw-Hill estimated that "U.S. industry will be putting less new equipment in place this year than last."

Concern was voiced by James M. Roche, chairman of General Motors, for the deteriorating competitive position of U.S. products—domestically as well as internationally. According to Roche, the increase in average hourly compensation in the United States over the last five years was greater than output per man-hour. This resulted in an increase of unit labor costs of 3.9 per cent per year—higher than that in any of the other leading 11 industrial nations, with the exception of Canada.

Labor. The key development of 1971 was organized labor's breach with President Nixon's Pay Board. The board was charged with maintaining guidelines for noninflationary pay increases during

A new fabric cutter that uses laser beams was hailed as the first major
advance in apparel manufacturing since the invention of the sewing machine.

Phase 2 of the wage-price controls. At their biennial convention, AFL-CIO officials spoke of gains of 15 per cent for 1971 and 6 per cent or more for 1972, despite the board's 5.5 per cent guideline.

Even with the strains of the wage-price freeze, relative harmony prevailed on the labor front. The Department of Labor reported that some 3,830 strikes began in the first nine months, an 18.6 per cent decline from the 1970 level, and the fewest since 1967. These strikes involved nearly 2.7 million workers, a 5.5 per cent increase over 1970.

Contract settlements in the first nine months covered 2.8 million workers in some key industries—railroad, auto, agricultural implement, can, aluminum, steel, copper, communications, and apparel. In the manufacturing industries, the average wage rise was 7.1 per cent, up from 6.7 per cent a year earlier and 6 per cent for all of 1970. See LABOR.

Machine Tool Orders were down. The 1970 levels were, in turn, off 47 per cent from the 1969 level. In the first 10 months of 1971, new orders totaled $692.1 million, some $112 million less than the $804.25 million booked in the same period in 1970. This represented a drop of 9 per cent in domestic business and 34 per cent in foreign orders. Industry shipments for the 10-month period were $825 million, down 33 per cent from the $1.23-billion for the same period in 1970.

In an effort to reverse the slump in orders, General Electric (GE), which supplies numerical controls to the machine tool industry, and 29 manufacturers initiated a "buy now–pay later" plan. The manufacturers agreed to produce a sizable inventory of machine tools in advance of orders. GE would then pay for the manufacturers' advertisements to help sell the tools. Both GE and the toolmakers were betting that such machine tools will be in the lead of a resurging economy.

Electrical Industry. The National Electrical Manufacturers Association (NEMA) estimated that shipments for the electrical industry would reach a record $47.5 billion for 1971, up 4.5 per cent. The largest single increase was in the power-equipment segment, which registered a 10 per cent increase, from $4.8 billion to $5.3 billion. Building equipment scored the second largest gain, 7.5 per cent, from $1.6 billion to $1.7 billion. Consumer products and industrial electronics and communications, the two largest dollar categories, each scored increases of 5 per cent, from $10 billion to $10.5 billion, and from $14.6 billion to $15.3 billion, respectively.

Despite the fact that some segments of the industry were under strong competitive pressure from abroad, Chris J. Witting, chairman of NEMA, attributed the industry's continued growth in part to its concentration on research and development. Witting, who is president of Crouse-Hinds Company of Syracuse, N.Y., reported that a National

Science Foundation survey revealed that the electrical industry's spending in this area was "a full 50 per cent higher than that of any other industry."

Rubber. The Rubber Manufacturers Association (RMA) indicated that the industry would ship 185-million passenger tires to market, a gain of 10 per cent over 1970. That figure surpassed the record year of 1969, when 177 million units were shipped. Record shipments were also indicated for truck and bus tires. Shipments to manufacturers were expected to reach 10 million, a gain of 17 per cent over 1970. The replacement market was expected to account for 18.3 million, up 20 per cent, for a total of 28 million, or a 12 per cent overall rise.

Consumption of rubber also reached a record level, 2.7 million long tons. This surpassed the 1969 record of 2.6 million, and was up 9 per cent over 1970. Synthetic rubber accounted for 78 per cent of the 1971 total.

In what could be a development of long-term significance to the tire industry, B.F. Goodrich announced a new process that it claims cuts in half the cost of producing radial tires. Called Gyrocore, the new process cushions a belt of wire between two double textile belts.　　　　　George J. Berkwitt

MARINE CORPS, U.S. See NATIONAL DEFENSE.
MARYLAND. See BALTIMORE; STATE GOVERNMENT.
MASSACHUSETTS. See BOSTON; STATE GOVT.
MAURITANIA. See AFRICA.

McCLOSKEY, PAUL NORTON, JR. (1927-   ), a congressman from California, announced on July 9, 1971, that he would seek the Republican nomination for President. McCloskey said he would enter the presidential primaries in New Hampshire and California in a direct challenge to President Richard M. Nixon. He said he had three objectives in his candidacy: To pressure Mr. Nixon to end the war in Vietnam more quickly, to revitalize the Republican Party through increased voter registration, and to serve as a "rallying point" for new leadership.

McCloskey first attracted national attention in 1967 when, as a "peace candidate," he defeated Shirley Temple Black in a special congressional election. Even though he maintained no illusions about winning the presidential nomination, he entered the race because he thought it "essential to the American form of government that dissenting views be presented clearly and squarely for the decision of those who are governed."

Born in San Bernardino, Calif., McCloskey served in the Marine Corps as an enlisted man from 1945 to 1947, then attended Occidental College and the California Institute of Technology. He served as a Marine Corps officer from 1950 to 1952 during the Korean War, and received the Navy Cross, the Silver Star, and the Purple Heart.

McCloskey married Caroline Wadsworth in 1945. They have four children.　　　　　Allan Davidson

McGOVERN, GEORGE STANLEY (1922-   ), on Jan. 18, 1971, became the first of the Democratic Party presidential hopefuls to declare his candidacy. In announcing his candidacy early, McGovern declared: "The kind of campaign I intend to run will rest on candor and reason; it will be rooted not in the manipulation of fears and divisions, but in a national dialogue based on mutual respect and common hope. That kind of campaign takes time."

A member of the Democratic Party's liberal wing, the South Dakota senator, in 1963, was the first to criticize Vietnam policy publicly, and has been a consistent critic of the war ever since. He has stated that "Vietnam is the most grievous manifestation of a world view that is based on what we are afraid of rather than on what we stand for," and that the result has been "the cruelest, most barbaric, and most stupid war in our national history."

A bomber pilot who flew 35 combat missions in World War II, McGovern served two terms in the U.S. House of Representatives and two more in the U.S. Senate, where he became a leading antiwar and antipoverty spokesman. In 1968, he made a belated and unsuccessful attempt to gain the Democratic presidential nomination.

A tall, soft-spoken scholar, McGovern has a Ph.D. degree in history from Northwestern University. In 1943, he married Eleanor Stegeberg. The McGoverns have five children.　　Allan Davidson

McMAHON, WILLIAM (1908-   ), a veteran of 22 years in the Australian Parliament, became prime minister March 10, 1971. He succeeded John G. Gorton, who was deposed as head of the Liberal Party after a party dispute. The Liberals are the larger of the two parties in Australia's governing coalition. McMahon, who lost two earlier tries for the leadership of his party, had been named Australia's external affairs minister in 1969.

McMahon was born in Sydney. He studied theology before switching courses to obtain a law degree from the University of Sydney. After World War II, he also earned a degree in economics from the university. He was first elected to Parliament in 1949.

In his long government career, McMahon served as minister for navy and air, for primary industry, for social services, and for labor and national service during the period from 1951 to 1966. He was federal treasurer from 1966 to 1969, and served on the board of governors of the International Monetary Fund and the World Bank. At the time he was chosen as party leader, McMahon was Australia's minister for foreign affairs.

McMahon is known as a physical fitness zealot and is an amateur golfer and squash player. In 1965, when he was 57, he married the former Sonia Hopkins, a svelte blonde socialite who is 24 years his junior. They have a son and a daughter.　Ed Nelson

MEDICARE

MEDICARE payments by recipients were increased in 1971 for both the voluntary medical insurance premium and the hospital insurance program. The new rate of $5.60 per month for the medical insurance premium became effective on July 1. This voluntary medical insurance program supplements the basic hospital insurance part of Medicare by helping to pay doctor bills and a wide variety of other medical expenses in and out of the hospital. About 19.5 million persons 65 and over are enrolled for this supplementary protection.

The increase in the hospital insurance program became effective on Jan. 1, 1972. Medicare patients are now required to pay the first $68 of their hospital bill instead of the $60 that they formerly paid. The amount of the payment is supposed to be equal to the cost of one day's hospitalization.

Payment of hospital bills is provided for under Part A of Medicare, the part for which all Americans 65 years of age or older are eligible. Medicare records indicate that about 20 per cent of those eligible will enter a hospital in any given year.

Another payment under the hospital insurance program was also increased on Jan. 1, 1972. The Medicare patient must pay $17 a day for each day he is hospitalized after the 61st day and ending with the 90th day. The payment formerly was $15 per day. The cost of treatment in an extended-care facility or nursing home was increased by $1 per day from the 21st through the 100th day.

Medicaid Regulations. The Department of Health, Education, and Welfare issued a series of regulations to prevent fraudulent abuse of the Medicaid program. The new regulations require:

■ That states file annual information returns showing the amounts they have paid to those providing service.

■ That state agencies report each case of suspected fraud.

■ That physicians be required to certify a patient's continuing need for in-patient care on or before the 12th day of a hospital stay and again no later than the 18th day.

■ That state Medicaid agencies provide annually for a medical review and treatment plan for each patient.

■ That inspections be made on short notice by medical review teams under state authority to determine the adequacy of services to meet each patient's needs.

New Recommendations. The 1971 Advisory Council on Social Security and Medicare completed its comprehensive review of the social security and Medicare programs and submitted its report on April 1. The council's recommendations included providing Medicare for social security disability beneficiaries and expanding the coverage to include payment for out-of-hospital drugs requiring a prescription.   Joseph P. Anderson

MEDICINE posted new gains in 1971 in the struggle to control hepatitis. Recent discoveries concerning serum hepatitis have changed long-held beliefs about the nature of this liver disorder. Although both serum and infectious hepatitis are thought to be caused by viruses, the infectious agents responsible have yet to be isolated. An antigen, however, was found in the blood of an Australian aborigine in 1963. Called the Australia antigen, it is now known to exist in the blood of all hepatitis carriers and patients with serum hepatitis. This has made possible the development of a test substance to screen blood for the hepatitis virus.

In February, the U.S. government for the first time licensed a substance called "Hepatitis-Associated Anti-body (anti-Australia antigen, human)." The substance may bring this kind of safety testing within the capabilities of most hospitals and blood banks. Blood transfusions are known to cause more than 30,000 cases of hepatitis a year, and from 1,500 to 3,000 are fatal. The American Association of Blood Banks announced that, beginning on October 1, all blood banks had to test donor blood and blood components for Hepatitis-Associated Antigen. If the antigen was found, the blood had to be rejected.

In March, New York University Medical Center researchers directed by Dr. Saul Krugman reported that they had succeeded in immunizing a small group of children against serum hepatitis. The studies were done on 60 children from 3 to 10 years old at Willowbrook State School on Staten Island during the period from 1965 to 1970. Dr. Krugman said his group had tested two types of immunizations on these children, both involving the Australia antigen. One type was active immunization using a heat-treated serum called MS2. "One inoculation gave enough protection to prevent some cases and to modify others," Dr. Krugman reported, but "two inoculations were more effective than one." The second type was passive immunization using a special gamma globulin containing about 100,000 times the amount of antibody found in the commercial supply of gamma globulin. Dr. Krugman's team said that the special gamma globulin had proved "extraordinarily effective in preventing serum hepatitis."

Sickle Cell Anemia. In May, two scientists at Rockefeller University, New York City, reported that they had successfully checked the sickling of red blood cells taken from patients with sickle cell anemia. Anthony Cerami, a cell biologist, and chemist James M. Manning added potassium cyanate to the blood in test-tube experiments and found that it prevented 80 per cent of the treated cells from becoming sickle-shaped, which impairs the transmission of blood to the tissues. Their research, they say, is controversial and still too preliminary to talk about in terms of possible treatment of the disease in the human body.

Acupuncture: The Chinese Needle Treatment

When James Reston of *The New York Times* and *The Year Book* Board of Editors developed appendicitis during a trip to Peking in July, 1971, the Chinese treated him with the best of their medical skills. They used Western-style surgery to remove his appendix, and the ancient Chinese art of acupuncture to relieve his postoperative pain. The acupuncture treatment—three long, slender needles skillfully inserted into his knees and right elbow and then twirled—was just a minor application of one of the most popular medical techniques in use in China today.

Acupuncture is an ancient treatment method, having been used in China for thousands of years. Only recently, however, has it been used as a painkiller and as an anesthetic for surgery. Visiting Canadian doctors watched open-heart surgery performed on a woman in May. To kill the pain, needles were inserted into her wrists and forearms. She showed no evidence of pain as the surgeon cut through her ribs. During the operation, the patient drank a glass of orange juice.

There is no known scientific basis for the practice of acupuncture. According to legend, acupuncture was developed 3,600 years ago by Emperor Shih Huang-Ti who noticed that arrow wounds received in battle sometimes relieved ailments in other parts of the body.

Over the centuries, Chinese doctors worked out an elaborate theory of the flow of "vital energy" along 12 invisible pathways of the body, called meridians. Imbalance in the flow caused disease. Needles inserted at points along the meridians would change the flow and restore balance and health.

The needles are not inserted at the point of pain, but at specific places, generally some distance from the place where the symptoms are felt. According to acupuncture practitioners, any disease that is caused by, or causes, a physiological malfunction of the body can be corrected by this technique. For example, hay fever, asthma, duodenal ulcer, appendicitis, colitis, and migraine are all physiological disturbances, and, as such,

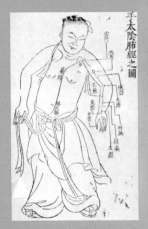

Ancient acupuncture chart drawn by a Chinese doctor

may be successfully treated by acupuncture. But emphysema, a cataract, or a broken bone, are anatomical alterations that no physiological process can affect, so they cannot be treated by acupuncture.

Most American physicians are skeptical of the claims made for acupuncture. Some think the needles may kill pain by interfering with a nerve's ability to send messages. A needle through a nerve could block sensations to a particular part of the body, thus numbing it. This is only a theory, however, and there is no evidence to support it.

Other physicians believe that the successes of acupuncture can be attributed to the placebo effect, a phenomenon well known to every American doctor. "There's really no difference between acupuncture and lots of other 'cures' that people believe in. They all work for certain things," says Dr. Edgar Berman, physician to former Vice-President Hubert H. Humphrey.

The Chinese counter this with evidence that they have produced the same anesthetic effects in acupuncture experiments with rabbits and cats. And as far as anyone can determine, animals cannot "believe" in their treatment.

Some physicians also suggest that Chinese surgeons using acupuncture as an anesthetic probably rely on the combined effects of acupuncture and drugs. But the Chinese have assured American observers that no drugs are used. If further investigation confirms this, and rules out the possibility that drugs given for other purposes may have an anesthetic effect, Western neurophysiologists are almost certain to begin a systematic study of this form of treatment.

Dr. Samuel Rosen of New York's Mount Sinai School of Medicine, who recently visited China, says, "I have no explanation for this phenomenon, but science has no explanation for many observations that still elude investigation. Neither have Chinese medical men, as they frankly concede. They are investigating acupuncture anesthesia diligently. That the effect is present cannot be denied."

Foster Stockwell

427

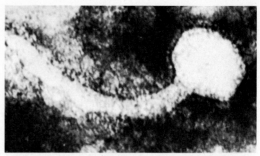

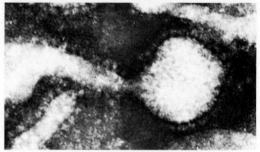

Dan H. Moore of the Institute for Medical Research found particles in human milk, *top,* that are like the viruses that cause breast cancer in mice, *bottom.*

Sickle cell anemia is an incurable, hereditary blood disorder that affects blacks almost exclusively. It results from an abnormality in the formation of the blood protein, hemoglobin, that causes the blood cells to change their shape if they are deprived of oxygen. This prevents an adequate supply of blood from reaching the tissues, and clots form in small blood vessels.

The Foundation for Research and Education in Sickle Cell Disease has started a program to alert black Americans to the dangers of the inherited blood disorder. Because there is no known cure for sickle cell anemia, the foundation will emphasize detection.

Cancer Research. After more than a decade of trying, researchers at M. D. Anderson Hospital and Tumor Institute in Houston reported in July that they had obtained tiny spherical particles of a C type virus from living cells of a cancer patient. Specialists say that the achievement opens many doors for explaining the role of viruses in human cancer and, hopefully, for doing something about it. The new virus has been named ESP-1 for Dr. Elizabeth S. Priori, who led the research efforts.

Of 113 known viruses capable of causing cancers in animals, some 30 are classified as C type. In various animal species, they cause such types of cancer as lymphomas, leukemias, and sarcomas. Yet, until this discovery, the expected C type viruses of man remained elusive. The virus was found in human cells grown in laboratory flasks, after being culled from fluid taken from a child who had Burkitt's lymphoma cancer. The virus has not been proved to cause cancer in man, although it is suspect.

On December 23, President Richard M. Nixon signed the National Cancer Act, authorizing $1.6-billion over three years for research programs.

In February, a team of scientists at the University of Washington Medical School and the U.S. Public Health Hospital in Seattle reported the strongest clue yet that some cases of human leukemia can be caused by a virus. In treating a 16-year-old girl for acute lymphoblastic leukemia, physicians, under the direction of Dr. Philip J. Fialkow, irradiated her body with massive doses of X rays in an effort to kill all blood-forming cells. They then injected into her veins millions of bone marrow cells donated by her healthy 10-year-old brother. The new therapy enabled the patient to live several extra weeks. She died later, however, from an infection that complicated a recurrence of her leukemia. From chromosomal studies, it was learned that when the leukemia recurred, it was in the bone marrow cells from her brother, not in her own. The doctors reported that they did not know what mechanism had caused the normal, nonleukemic bone marrow cells to become leukemic, but they suspected it might be a virus. — Theodore F. Treuting

MEMORIALS dedicated or announced in 1971 include the following:

Winston Churchill Memorial. A bronze statue of Sir Winston Churchill 12 feet high, to stand in Parliament Square in London, was commissioned in March. Designed by Welsh sculptor Ivor Roberts Jones, it will show the wartime leader bare-headed, wearing a military-style greatcoat, and grasping a walking stick. The statue will be completed in 1973.

Leif Ericson Memorial. An 11½-foot-tall bronze statue of Leif Ericson, the Viking explorer who many scholars believe visited America before Christopher Columbus, was dedicated on May 23 in Leif Ericson Park in Brooklyn, N.Y. The statue was designed by New York artist Arnold Bergier. It stands on a 5½-foot granite base.

Lyndon Baines Johnson Memorial. A library housing 31 million pages of documents, 500,000 photographs of former President Johnson, and thousands of bits of memorabilia of his career was dedicated on May 22 in Austin, Tex. Among those attending the dedication of the travertine marble building on the University of Texas campus was President Richard M. Nixon. Dominating the library's interior is the Great Hall, a tremendous room with 60-foot-high ceilings. On the south wall of the room, a panel of photographs depict the former President's political career. On the north wall, artists have carved a presidential seal 34 feet in diameter.

John F. Kennedy Memorial. The world première of a Mass by composer Leonard Bernstein marked the spectacular opening of the John F. Kennedy Center for the Performing Arts in Washington, D.C., on September 8. The building's Grand Foyer is 600 feet long and 60 feet high. The foyer is dominated by a 7-foot bust of the late President, the work of the sculptor Robert Berks. It stands on a travertine marble pedestal 8 feet tall. The doors to the opera house open directly opposite the bust. The opera house, which is the central auditorium in the center, seats more than 2,200 persons.

Abraham Lincoln Memorial. The home of Abraham Lincoln in Springfield, Ill., was designated a national historical site on August 18. The brown, two-story frame house is the only home Lincoln ever owned. Three of his four children were born there, and one died there. He purchased the home in 1844, and he and his family lived there until 1861. The federal government plans to spend up to $2 million to purchase land in the four-block area surrounding the Lincoln home, and more than $5 million to restore a number of houses, sheds, and sidewalks in the area.

Ottmar Mergenthaler Memorial. A bronze plaque honoring Ottmar Mergenthaler, inventor of the Linotype machine, was unveiled in Baltimore on June 25. The Linotype, patented in 1884, revolutionized the printing industry and journalism, because it cast type automatically. The Maryland chapter of Sigma Delta Chi, national journalistic society, unveiled the plaque to mark the site as "an historic site in journalism."

Mormon Memorial. A columned building of traditional Mormon design was dedicated on September 4 at Nauvoo, Ill. A monument to the Church of Latter-day Saints and its role in the settlement of the West, it will be used as a Visitors Center at Nauvoo, which was the home of the Mormons from 1838 to 1846. It stands on a 16-acre site overlooking the Mississippi River from which the followers of Joseph Smith moved west 125 years ago to the church's eventual home in Salt Lake City, Utah.   Foster Stockwell

The John F. Kennedy Center for the Performing Arts, which stands beside the Potomac River in Washington, D.C., was opened to the public on September 8.

MENTAL HEALTH. Results of the largest federal survey on the use of marijuana on American college campuses were released in February, 1971. They showed that 31 per cent of the students had used marijuana at least once, and 14 per cent of them "had used it every week or two." In this latter group, 79 per cent said that they found that the continued use of marijuana was "satisfying." The same percentage said that alcohol was satisfying, but only 50 per cent put the continued use of tobacco in that category.

The survey was conducted by the National Institute of Mental Health. The data were collected for the institute under the direction of Peter H. Rossi of the Department of Social Relations at Johns Hopkins University, in Baltimore. It was compiled from questionnaires given to 10,000 students.

In an article published in the *Journal of the American Medical Association* in April, Dr. Harold Kolansky and Dr. William T. Moore of the Philadelphia Association for Psychoanalysis warned that marijuana in moderate to heavy amounts may create serious psychological problems, even among users who have no predisposition to mental illness. Their report was based on a study of 38 persons between 13 and 24 years of age, all of whom smoked two or more marijuana cigarettes two or more times a week. The researchers said the tested patients showed "very poor social judgment, poor attention span, poor concentration, confusion, anxiety, depression, apathy, indifference, passivity, and often slowed and slurred speech."

Schizophrenia. In April, a team of New Jersey researchers reported that they had developed a new treatment for schizophrenia. The ailment, one of the most serious and baffling mental disorders, is characterized by hallucinations, delusions, generally disorganized thinking, and impairment of emotional response. Dr. Carl Pfeiffer of the New Jersey Neuropsychiatric Institute said the therapy is based on the concept that schizophrenia is primarily a biochemical disorder in the brain, and that trace elements play a key role in maintaining a sound mind. He said there is increasing evidence that the majority of schizophrenic cases are caused by a combination of a lack of zinc and too much copper in the body.

Mental Retardation. Equipment that may some day allow doctors to check a dozen blood indicators simultaneously for signs of mental retardation in babies was developed by Dr. John A. Ambrose of the U.S. Center for Disease Control in Atlanta, Ga. Dr. Ambrose has used the equipment to check for two indicators, but he said the testing capacity of the device could be greatly expanded within five years. The equipment chemically analyzes a tiny speck of blood to determine the level of phenylalanine and tyrosine, two amino acids whose imbalance can cause severe retardation. Theodore F. Treuting

MEXICO. Terrorism, and acts of violence including kidnapings, bank robberies, and student disturbances, were major preoccupations of the Mexican government in 1971. The terrorist activities were carried out for the most part by members of an urban guerrilla movement dissatisfied with the ruling Institutional Revolutionary Party (PRI) and its policies. The student unrest reflected an impatience among Mexico's young people for quick solutions to the country's deep-rooted social and economic problems. One incident alone, a clash involving about 8,500 students of the Polytechnic Institute in Mexico City on June 10, resulted in at least 9 students killed and 160 wounded.

On September 1, in his first State of the Union address since taking office, President Luis Echeverría Alvárez warned that extreme leftists, by defying the law, were jeopardizing the security of the nation. He reiterated his inaugural address promise that he would continue to steer the economy in such a way as to achieve a more equitable distribution of the national income.

Throughout most of 1971, the economy showed a downward trend. This was attributable in part to a 10 per cent reduction in government spending, a move the regime hoped would help it handle a huge national debt piled up by overspending, overborrowing, and wasteful expenditures. To further relieve the situation, President Echeverría took such unpopular measures as cutting down drastically on foreign borrowing, ending wasteful state subsidies, and halting graft and corruption in government circles. Underscoring the near stagnation of several sectors of the economy was the meager 1.1 per cent increase in the January-to-August output of basic industries. Overall, it was estimated that the real growth rate for 1971 would probably be from 5 to 6 per cent, as compared with 7.7 per cent in 1970.

Economic Moves. During the year, the government acted to eliminate industrial protectionism in order to spur competition. Among the new measures was one providing tax incentives for investors whose enterprises and projects contribute to the export of manufactured goods. It also proposed a new Industrial Promotion Law, applicable to all industries that were at least 51 per cent Mexican owned. The law would broaden considerably the base for fiscal incentives and tax exemptions. In addition, it would place a fundamental emphasis on industrial decentralization and regional development. Meanwhile, there were indications that during the next few years, the continuing problem of unemployment and marginal employment would grow worse. Early in 1971, it was estimated that no more than 50 per cent of the population was productive; employment opportunities, on the other hand, were growing at only 3.2 per cent a year. A further complication in the employment picture stemmed from a new Mexican antipollution law, considered one of

Octavio Senties, left, accepted appointment as mayor of Mexico City after Alfonso Martinez Dominquez, right, resigned under political pressure.

Latin America's toughest, that went into effect on March 24 in the Federal District. To comply with its requirements, many industries would be forced to slow production or close down temporarily while corrective facilities were installed.

Record Crops Reported. Overall, agricultural output in 1971 was considerably higher than had been forecast because of better than expected rainfall in most farm areas during the summer. There were record sugar, coffee, and wheat harvests, and improved corn, oil-producing seeds, tomato, and sorghum crops.

Plans for various projects announced during the year included a $400-million atomic energy plant at Laguna Verda. The Pemex oil agency announced it planned a $1.44-billion 1971 investment program. The government approved the projected Las Truchas iron ore and steel mill complex in Michoacan; the mill was to have a yearly production capacity of 1.5 million tons of ingot by 1975. Work was intensified at the Pena Colorado iron ore project in Colima, which would have an estimated annual output of 1.5 million metric tons of pellets when completed.

Facts in Brief. Population: 54,253,000. Government: President Luis Echeverría Alvárez. Monetary Unit: peso. Foreign Trade: exports, $1,398,-000,000; imports, $2,461,000,000. Principal Exports: cotton, sugar, coffee. Mary C. Webster

MICHENER, ROLAND (1900-   ), made the first state tour to Europe by a Canadian governor general when he visited Belgium, the Netherlands, and Luxembourg for 19 days in April. Arriving on HMCS *Preserver*, he received a particularly warm welcome in the Netherlands, where people recalled that Holland's Queen Juliana lived in Canada during World War II and that Canadian troops helped to liberate the Netherlands at the end of that war.

In October, the governor general and his wife Norah attended the 2,500th anniversary celebration of the Persian Empire, given by the Shah of Iran at Persepolis. This visit followed a short stay in June by the empress of Iran at Rideau Hall in Ottawa, the governor general's official residence. During the year, the governor general also entertained the prime minister of Malaysia and President Josip Broz Tito of Yugoslavia at Rideau Hall.

In May, the governor general welcomed Queen Elizabeth II to British Columbia at the start of her centennial-year tour of the Pacific province. Governor General Michener also toured the province extensively. As the queen's formal representative in Canada, his major function is to improve relations and enhance Canada's image abroad. Since he became governor general in 1967, Michener has traveled more than 120,000 miles while making official tours in Canada. D.M.L. Farr

MICHIGAN. See DETROIT; STATE GOVERNMENT.

MIDDLE EAST. There was no real progress toward an Arab-Israeli settlement in 1971, despite intensive efforts by the major powers and the United Nations (UN) and intermittent indications that the principals were ready to negotiate. While the attitude of some Arab states toward Israel was one of restraint, some Arab leaders, notably President Muammar al-Qadhaafi of Libya, continued to call for liberation of occupied Arab territory by force. And Egyptian President Anwar al-Sadat said there was no alternative to new fighting.

Egyptian and Israeli forces, nevertheless, continued the cease-fire along the Suez Canal by tacit agreement after it officially expired in March. Concern over a possible resumption of hostilities rose briefly in September when Israeli fighters shot down a Russian-built bomber for allegedly photographing Israeli positions. Egyptian gunners retaliated by destroying an Israeli transport plane. Nothing further came of the clash, however, and most observers attributed the incidents to a continuing war of nerves.

Diplomatic Efforts. The pressure for a settlement shifted to the diplomatic front. In February, UN special representative Gunnar Jarring sent identical memoranda to Egypt and Israel asking for their conditions for a settlement. In his reply, Egypt's Sadat was to prove far more adept than his predecessor, Gamal Abdel Nasser, at winning international support for his country's position. Consequently, he was more difficult for Israel to deal with. Sadat agreed in principle to the reopening of the Suez Canal, an end to belligerency, and negotiations for a peace treaty in return for Israeli withdrawal from occupied territories as specified in UN Resolution 242 of November, 1967, which also promised Israel a secure frontier. He also specified that a UN force be stationed at Sharm el-Sheikh, at the southern tip of the Sinai Peninsula, and demanded settlement of the Palestine refugee problem.

Israel held firmly to its refusal to withdraw until a formal peace treaty had been signed. The Israelis also refused to yield Sharm el-Sheikh, the Golan Heights taken from Syria, or Jerusalem, which they declared to be irrevocably their capital. The Jarring mission was suspended in March.

Sadat's success in overcoming a political crisis at home in May left him as Egypt's undisputed leader. This and a new, 15-year treaty with Russia greatly strengthened his hand. He began saying in speeches that 1971 would be Egypt's year of decision, although, as time passed, a wry Egyptian joke suggested he might fall back on the Gregorian and Islamic calendars in case of need to prove his point. See EGYPT.

With the Jarring mission in abeyance, the initiative for a settlement shifted to the major powers. United States Secretary of State William P. Rogers visited the area to push a U.S. plan for a temporary agreement. It called for the reopening of the Suez Canal in return for an Israeli troop withdrawal for an unspecified distance from the canal's east bank. Its eagerness for even a temporary agreement found the United States at odds with its principal Middle Eastern ally. Israel continued to insist on direct peace negotiations and to reject either big-power or UN guarantees. The United States Senate voted a $500-million arms appropriation for Israel in December as the Congress sought to reaffirm its unconditional support for that nation.

Some observers, however, felt that the general Arab attitude was reasonable and that this put the United States in a difficult position as it tried to maneuver the deeply suspicious Israelis toward a settlement. Many other observers, of course, believed that the Israelis were justly suspicious. See ISRAEL.

Arabs Federate. Libya, Syria, and Egypt formed the Federation of Arab Republics on April 17. It linked in a common front three Arab countries with a combined population of 58 million and large human and material resources. The main purpose was viewed as a pooling of strength for the contest with Israel, but a successful merger would have other important consequences for the Arab world. The draft federal Constitution was approved by national referendums in Egypt and Syria, but internal disagreements delayed approval in Libya. A Federal Council, supported by the armed forces, would have the right to intervene to restore order in any of the member countries. This could provide an Arab regime with built-in safeguards against the uprisings that have repeatedly undermined internal stability for 25 years. Mohammed Haykal, influential editor of the semiofficial Egyptian newspaper *Al Ahram*, called the federation "a gleam of hope amid an Arab world which seems as though it wants to commit suicide from despair and failure before the gap between its ambitions and its capabilities."

Political realities weakened the effectiveness of the federation. Sudan had been invited to join, but declined to do so until it could set its own house in order after an attempted military coup in July. Libyan President Qadhaafi's political adventurism and interference in the attempted Morocco and Sudan coups was another problem. Syria's President Hafiz al-Asad was unable to form a national front of Syrian and Ba'athist leaders that would promote such federation aims as a common economic market and provisions for the exchange of workers. A meeting of the three heads of state in October produced nothing more than the election of Sadat as president of the Federal Council and the choice of Cairo as the capital.

Unrest and Discontent. The gap between Arab ambitions and capabilities underscored considerable political unrest and social discontent, not only in the Arab world but also in Turkey. To a lesser

Radiophoto from Amman, Jordan, shows Palestinian guerrillas captured by the Jordanian Army in July and held under guard in a detention pen near Amman.

extent, it reached Israel and even remote Afghanistan. Coups were attempted—and failed—in Morocco and Sudan. The Moroccan attempt against the monarchy was made in July by leaders of the armed forces, who had been considered the most loyal supporters of King Hassan II (see MOROCCO). The attempt in Sudan resulted in the destruction of the Sudanese Communist Party, largest in the Arab world, and the only one with a positive program of land and social reform (see SUDAN). Yemen and Iraq struggled to form workable governments that could deal effectively with economic and social problems created by long civil wars. A political split developed in Tunisia. Some members of the Central Bureau of the ruling Socialist Destour Party there challenged President Habib Bourguiba's choice of Prime Minister Hedi Nouira as his eventual successor. They also demanded the completion of the liberal reforms Bourguiba had promised two years earlier. See TUNISIA.

The Palestinian guerrilla movement was greatly reduced in scope and effectiveness by the Jordanian Army's vigorous pursuit and by its own inability to mount operations within Israel. King Hussein's determination to destroy the guerrillas as a threat to his rule caused Algeria and Iraq to break relations with Jordan. Libya canceled the annual subsidy it pledged to Jordan after the 1967 war. But Jordanian troops continued to drive the guerrillas from their

bases, and by midsummer very few were left. Israel estimated that the guerrillas had suffered 6,000 casualties since 1967. The Israeli-occupied Gaza Strip, with 168,000 refugees crowded into a 25-mile area, remained the only haven and breeding ground for Arab guerrillas. On November 28, Jordan's Premier Wasfi al-Tal was assassinated in Cairo by members of a Palestinian guerrilla execution squad. See JORDAN.

In Turkey, the government of Prime Minister Suleyman Demirel could not stem the mounting tide of anarchy. The Turkish armed forces stepped in as they had done in 1960. A memorandum by the commanders of the four armed services on March 12 demanded that Demirel resign or face the prospect of a military coup. Martial law was imposed.

Demirel was replaced as prime minister by Nihat Erim, a senator and law professor, as a compromise candidate acceptable to the four major parties. Erim won passage of several constitutional amendments in support of his promise to the military to carry out reforms. See ERIM, NIHAT.

An unexpected element in the Turkish crisis was the appearance of violence and urban terrorism on a large scale. The Turkish Peoples' Liberation Army (TPLA) advocated violent change in the constitutional system. It carried out a series of bank robberies and acts of terrorism. The violence culminated in the kidnaping of four U.S. airmen in

433

"Back up first and we'll negotiate later."

March and the kidnap-murder of Israeli Consul-General Ephraim Elrom in May in Istanbul. Most of the TPLA members were university students, and many of them reportedly were trained in Syria by Ba'athists and Palestinian guerrillas and supplied with arms smuggled across the Turkish-Syrian border.

After martial law was imposed in April, army and police units began a systematic crackdown on terrorism. In October, a military court in Ankara handed down death sentences for Deniz Gecmis, urban TPLA leader, and 17 followers for the kidnapings. See TURKEY.

New Oil Agreements. The signing of the Teheran and Tripoli agreements between the major oil companies and the oil-producing countries of the region paved the way for a new burst of economic development. The agreements, which set higher posted prices for Middle Eastern oil exports, would yield an additional $1.2 billion per year. As a result, oil production showed dramatic increases—48 per cent for Abu Dhabi, 28 per cent for Saudi Arabia, 20 per cent for Iran, and 16.3 per cent for Iraq, the first significant gain in years in that country. A drop in Venezuelan production left Iran and Saudi Arabia the world's leading oil exporters. The added oil revenue more than offset huge new expenditures for arms, in some cases as much as 10 per cent of the gross national product. William Spencer

434

MILLS, WILBUR DAIGH (1909-   ), congressman from Arkansas, was closely watched in 1971 as a possible candidate for the Democratic presidential nomination. During the latter half of the year, he traveled to more than 30 states, making speeches and testing his popularity. In spite of his professed noncandidacy, "Wilbur watching" became a major activity of political analysts and the White House during the early part of the year.

As Chairman of the House Ways and Means Committee, Mills ranks as one of the most powerful political figures in the United States. His power in economic matters is virtually equal to that of President Richard M. Nixon. "If the White House were to rate the independent powers of the world with which it must deal according to their formidability," said political reporter Hugh Sidey in *Life* magazine, "Mills would probably rank just below Germany and above France." A loner, Mills collects his own data and is widely respected for the breadth of his knowledge of the economy and his political acumen.

Mills was born in Kensett, Ark., the son of a general store owner. The store is still operated by his younger brother and their 86-year-old mother. Mills graduated from Hendrix College in 1930 and Harvard Law School in 1933. He has been in the House since 1939 and Chairman of Ways and Means since 1958. Allan Davidson

MINERALOGY. See GEOLOGY.

MINES AND MINING. A spirit of pessimism pervaded the American Mining Congress's 1971 convention in Las Vegas, Nev., in November. Weak minerals prices, foreign expropriations, sluggish markets, rising pollution-abatement costs, and an unfriendly legislative atmosphere were major concerns. The most serious expropriation reported was that of the Kennecott Copper Corporation's El Teniente mine in Chile, in which the company lost a 49 per cent equity interest. Mine operators' problems were heightened by an oversupply of some metals. Aluminum, copper, silver, nickel, and molybdenum were declining in price from oversupply.

The Coal Industry. For several years, coal was regarded as an obsolete fuel, but it actually provides almost 67 per cent of the nation's fuel needs. The estimated year-end tonnage for 1971 was 600 million tons. A projection by *U.S. News and World Report* indicated production of 700 million tons annually by 1975 and 850 million by 1980. Even here, however, the picture was clouded by a prolonged strike in October by 80,000 soft coal miners. The strike shut down soft coal mining in 20 states.

Mine operators were also concerned by a move by Congress in September to regulate strip mining, or mining at the surface. Strip mining provides nearly 40 per cent of the national coal output. More than 2 million acres have been devastated by the $200-million-a-year strip mining industry.

Mine Safety. The Federal Coal Mine Health and Safety Act, passed in 1969 and put into effect in 1970, continued to be a subject of controversy. Some 120 fatalities among miners were reported through August. Edward D. Failor, a lawyer and businessman without mining experience, was appointed to the new post of enforcer of federal coal-mine safety standards for the U.S. Bureau of Mines. In an 80-page report issued by the General Accounting Office in June, the Bureau of Mines was accused of failing to enforce federal safety laws.

New Copper Reserves. Rich new copper deposits are being explored in remote areas of the world. The volcanic island of Bougainville, in the southwest Pacific Ocean between New Guinea and the British Solomons, is expected to yield 30 million tons of ore a year. In the wilds of Indonesia, near West Irian, an American company began opening a rich copper ore deposit.

One of the world's largest deposits of high-grade bauxite, the ore that yields aluminum, is being mined by an international consortium in Boké, Guinea. In addition to the bauxite, Guinea has significant deposits of diamonds, gold, and iron ore, making it potentially one of the richest countries in western Africa. — Mary E. Jessup

MINNESOTA. See STATE GOVERNMENT.

MISSISSIPPI. See STATE GOVERNMENT.

MISSOURI. See ST. LOUIS; STATE GOVERNMENT.

MONEY, including demand deposits as well as notes and coin held by the U.S. public, grew at the exceptionally rapid annual rate of 10.5 per cent during the first half of 1971. Although the rate slowed to about 6 per cent during the latter half of the year, even this lower rate was unusually expansionary by recent standards. From 1957 to 1969, the growth rate was only 3.3 per cent.

Monetary growth during the first three quarters of 1971 was as high as for any similar period since World War II. In contrast, the money supply was virtually stagnant in 1969–a factor that the monetarists, led by University of Chicago economist Milton Friedman, interpreted as a major cause of the 1970 recession in business activity. Monetary growth resumed in 1970 at a moderate rate of 5 per cent before the acceleration early in 1971.

The public held a total of $51.1 billion in currency at midyear, up 7 per cent from mid-1970. Currency comprised 23 per cent of the U.S. money stock. Significantly, this percentage has grown in recent years despite the widespread use of credit cards. Currency comprised only 14 per cent of the money stock in 1929. Some experts have speculated that much U.S. currency had been held by foreigners since the 1930s when the dollar developed into the main international reserve currency. The 1971 dollar crisis, following years of inflation in the United States and deficits in its balance of international payments, raised some question about continued foreign holdings of U.S. dollars.

The table below shows the distribution of currency in circulation by type (including currency held as bank reserves) and by denomination as of June, 1971. The Federal Reserve System (Fed) issues almost all paper notes while the U.S. Treasury Department issues all the coin:

Type of currency	Amount	Per cent
Federal reserve notes	$51,304,000,000	87.9
Treasury currency		
Standard silver dollars	482,000,000	0.8
Fractional coins	5,990,000,000	10.3
U.S. notes	321,000,000	0.5
Monies in process of retirement	296,000,000	0.5
Total	$58,393,000,000	100.0

Denomination	Amount	Per cent
Coin	$ 6,472,000,000	11.0
$1	2,277,000,000	3.9
$2	136,000,000	0.2
$5	3,099,000,000	5.3
$10	9,137,000,000	15.6
$20	19,144,000,000	32.9
$50	5,075,000,000	8.7
$100	12,596,000,000	21.6
$500, $1,000, $5,000, $10,000	459,000,000	0.8
Total	$58,393,000,000	100.0

Source: Federal Reserve Bulletin

The table shows that coin comprised 11 per cent of currency in circulation in June, 1971, well above the 7.6 per cent of a decade earlier when there was an acute coin shortage in the United States. The old 90-per-cent-silver dimes, quarters, halves, and dollars technically were still listed as "in circulation" in 1971, although nearly all of these coins had already been melted down for their silver value or were being hoarded in coin collections.

As the table shows, the $20 bill remained by far the most popular note in dollar value, followed by the $100 note. There were actually more $20s in circulation than $10s or $5s, and more $100s than $50s.

Mints and assay offices began distributing the new copper-nickel sandwich-type Eisenhower dollars in 1971. Public demand was unprecedented for a special minting of 40-per-cent silver Eisenhower dollars, the first silver dollar to be minted by the United States since 1935, for sale at $3, as well as for proof mintings of the silverless coins at $10. Also authorized was the production of 20 million proof coins–highly polished to a jewellike finish–at $10 each. Despite the flurry of demand for the old 90-per-cent-silver standard dollars and halves during the 1960s, these relatively heavy coins had generally not been as popular as smaller, lower-valued coins. Because of this, officials predicted that there would be an adequate supply of the copper-nickel Eisenhower dollars and Kennedy halves in the future.

Great Britain switched to decimal currency units instead of the pound, shillings, and pence in February. There was relatively little confusion as British shoppers adjusted to the system. — William G. Dewald

MONTANA. See STATE GOVERNMENT.

MOROCCO. A conspiracy by senior military officers to depose King Hassan II narrowly missed its mark on July 10, 1971. During a celebration of Hassan's 42nd birthday, cadets from the Ahermoumou Military School invaded the summer palace at Skhirat, south of Rabat, and opened fire. In the confusion, General Mohammed Medbouh, head of the royal household and presumed leader of the attempted coup, was killed by his own men. The Moroccan Army quickly broke up the rebellion. In all, about 97 persons were killed, including the Belgian ambassador, and 158 were wounded.

Hassan gave General Mohammed Oufkir, minister of the interior, emergency powers to deal with the rebels. A military court executed four generals and six other senior officers. Ironically, the coup attempt developed among those considered most loyal to the king. Resentment had focused on reports of wide corruption in government and Hassan's inability or unwillingness to do more than dismiss ministers implicated in it.

New Cabinet. On August 6, Hassan named a new Cabinet of 15 ministers replacing a 29-member unit dismissed on August 4. It was headed by Mohamed Karim Lamrani, former minister of finance. General Oufkir, new defense minister, was given the job of rebuilding the decimated general staff. His predecessor in the chief of staff function, General Bachir Bouhali, was killed in the attempted coup.

The new Cabinet included 10 ministers from the previous group. Four retained their old positions. Hassan said the Cabinet was to institute reforms in education, the economy, administration, and justice.

A treason trial for 191 persons accused of plotting to overthrow the monarchy ended in September. Many were members of the National Union of Popular Forces, one of the two opposition political parties. Five were sentenced to death and many received prison terms from a military court.

Morocco's family-planning program proceeded slowly. The five-year program aimed to provide birth-control devices for 600,000 women by 1973. However, Dr. Abdelkader Laraqui said in May it had reached only about 33,000 women. He said medical progress had cut the death rate to 17 per 1,000 persons per year, but that each year saw 50 births per 1,000 population, for a 3.3 per cent annual increase.

Facts in Brief. Population: 16,454,000. Government: King Hassan II; Prime Minister Mohamed Karim Lamrani. Monetary unit: dirham. Foreign Trade: exports, $488,000,000; imports, $686,000,-000. Principal Exports: phosphates, citrus fruits, tomatoes. William Spencer

Regular Army troops loyal to Moroccan King Hassan II rounded up rebels outside a Rabat radio station after their attempted coup failed.

MOTION PICTURES. For the American motion-picture industry, 1971 was a year filled with terrifying contradictions. Attendance continued to drop, sinking at times to as little as 6 million a week, and averaging about 15 million a week for the year. And yet, in several instances, the profits from a mere handful of pictures were sufficient to pull an entire studio into the black. Outstanding in this regard was Paramount's *Love Story*, with a towering domestic gross of well over $50 million. The miracle worker at Warner Brothers was *Summer of '42*, with a strong assist from *Klute*. And 20th Century-Fox was pleasantly surprised with *The French Connection*, Metro-Goldwyn-Mayer (M-G-M) with *Shaft* and *Get Carter*, and Cinerama was frankly astonished by the runaway success of its boy-loves-rat shocker, *Willard*.

Significantly, all of these pictures were modestly budgeted and, for the most part, had no expensive big-name stars. Clearly, the public was buying stories instead of personalities. But this simply posed the question—what kind of stories? Judging from the variety of pictures that moved into the hit class in 1971, there were no clear-cut answers to that question. *Love Story* was regarded as romantic and old-fashioned, yet it sold tickets. But so did *Carnal Knowledge*, as cold and cynical a portrait of the manipulative male animal as the motion-picture screen has ever presented. And *The Stewardesses*, a 3-D sexploitation picture, went well over the $10-million mark on a limited number of playdates. What was it to be, romance or reality?

One Thing Was Certain. The youth market, so resolutely courted during 1970 because it supposedly accounted for 74 per cent of the filmgoing public, was virtually boycotting youth-oriented movies. Dennis Hopper, of *Easy Rider* fame, got nowhere with *The Last Movie*, which he both directed and starred in. His easy-riding companion, Peter Fonda, fared no better performing similar chores in *The Hired Hand*. And completing the *Easy Rider* triumvirate, Jack Nicholson failed to score either as the director of *Drive, He Said* or as the star of *A Safe Place* (along with Orson Welles and Tuesday Weld)—despite the success of *Carnal Knowledge*, in which he starred. Such successors to the wildly popular *Woodstock* as *Medicine Ball Caravan* and *Celebration at Big Sur*, essentially rock LP records with a video accompaniment, were losers. Even more disappointing were the youth-oriented drug films—*Dusty and Sweets Magee*, *Panic in Needle Park*, *Cisco Pike*, *Born to Win*, and others. Youths were obviously turned off by precisely the kind of pictures all the experts anticipated would turn them on. Stanley Kubrick's *A Clockwork Orange*, appearing at the very end of the year, seemed a good deal closer to the mark, with its odd mixture of violence, sex, and social criticism.

Unexpectedly, nostalgia seemed to figure largely in the popularity of many of the 1971 films. It was

Many critics predicted an Academy Award for director Peter Bogdanovich's *The Last Picture Show,* which skillfully portrays small-town Texas life in 1951.

perhaps only incidental in *Carnal Knowledge*, which picked up its college heroes, Jack Nicholson and Art Garfunkel, in the late 1940s, the late 1950s, and the late 1960s. But it was central to the success of *Summer of '42*, and worked strongly in favor of *The Last Picture Show*, which looked back to the early 1950s. *Fiddler on the Roof*, the big musical of the year, also seems to have benefited from this rosy glow, as did the "little" musical, *The Boy Friend*.

On the other hand, the one positive new element in the "now" film scene was the emergence of a Negro audience receptive to pictures by Negro artists and depicting the black communities. Black militant Melvin Van Peebles' *Sweet Sweetback* was a runaway success. It was expected to gross over $20-million—most of it coming from black support. *Shaft*, *The Organization*, and *Black Jesus* also garnered enough support in Negro centers to encourage further ventures in this area, despite the relative failures of such efforts as *Brother John* (with Sidney Poitier) and *The Great White Hope* (with James Earl Jones). In the black community as well as the white, the primary consideration seems to be the theme of a picture, rather than the stars.

Film Censorship. Films with a strong sexual content diminished markedly in 1971. The tide had begun to recede in 1970, when neither *Myra Breckinridge* nor *Beyond the Valley of the Dolls* racked up important grosses. With significantly few excep-

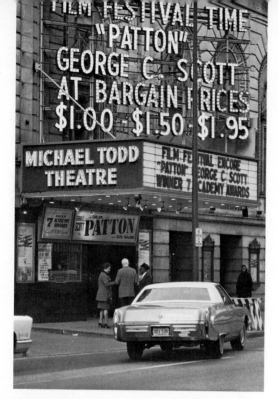

Bargain prices posted on a marquee in Chicago reflect a nationwide effort by the industry to lure moviegoers back to theaters in cities' central business districts.

tions, the major studios made sure in 1971 that relatively few of their pictures went into release with the hated X rating. Newspapers in some 40 cities exercised a kind of moral blackout, refusing either to advertise or review X-rated pictures. In some instances, the ban extended even to the R-rated films. In June, the National Council of Churches and the Catholic Office for Motion Pictures jointly declared that they would no longer support the Production Code and Rating Administration of the Motion Picture Association of America because of what they termed the gross laxness of its application.

As a result, the film companies became increasingly careful and often willingly submitted to suggested trims that might change an X to an R or an R to a GP (all ages admitted). In the battle for better ratings, Aaron Stern, a New York psychologist appointed to head the rating board in July, became a significant figure.

No small part of Stern's concern was with the marked upswing in violence in American films. Although no definite correlation between movie violence and crime in the streets has ever been established, the gratuitous killings, knifings, and beatings found in such films as *Get Carter*, *Villain*, *The Hunting Party*, *Light at the Edge of the World*, and *Straw Dogs* convinced many that the time had come to clamp down on the excesses of sadism even as, a

few years earlier, they had attempted to clamp down on excesses of sexuality in films. Stern seemed to be in complete agreement, precipitating a battle between film makers who felt that on-screen violence was necessary to depict the violence of our times and production companies that would rather have their pictures released with an R or GP.

The Industry. Consolidation seemed to be the new watchword. In June, Columbia Pictures announced its intention of closing down its studios in the heart of Hollywood, and moving out to Burbank to share Warner Brothers' facilities. Soon after, Paramount began exploratory talks with Universal, and then 20th Century-Fox, on the possibilities of sharing facilities. Late in December, Fox announced that it was closing its New York home office and shifting everything to California. With an eye on diminishing box-office returns, the industry was tightening its belt—even though the profit-and-loss statements tended to be on the bright side. Unfortunately, the sale of landholdings, the auctioning of costumes and props, and the leasing of films to television often made the profit statements seem better than they really were.

Since many studios admittedly lacked the production capital necessary to start a new film, enterprising independent producers began to tap money sources completely outside the industry. In this way, many producers could make their pictures for considerably less than if done under studio auspices, with approximately a 40 per cent studio overhead charged against them.

Quaker Oats was the first to realize the potentials of this situation, and backed Wolper Productions with $3 million for the production *Willie Wonka and the Chocolate Factory*. The oil-rich Jicarillo Apache Indian tribe came up with $2 million for *A Gunfight*, co-starring Kirk Douglas and Johnny Cash.

New Developments. By 1971, the word *cassette* had become a fearsome one in the film vocabulary. Both the Writers Guild and the Screen Actors Guild almost went on strike because they could not come to terms with the producers on their share of profits generated by this still-experimental field. But the results turned up in Newark, N.J., and a few smaller cities by a new firm called Computer Cinema gave some indication of the potential. Theater admissions were off by as much as 40 per cent on the nights that pictures were available via closed-circuit television to occupants of hotel rooms. Even so, most observers agree that the cassettes will not come into their own until 1975, at the earliest.

Meanwhile, videotronics continue to upset the settled ways of the studio film makers. Consolidated Film Industries, one of the largest film-processing laboratories, unveiled a new, electronic editing machine that can reduce by two-thirds the time it normally takes to cut a picture. Arthur Knight

See also AWARDS AND PRIZES.

MUSEUMS. It became possible in 1971 for museums in the United States to achieve accreditation. By midyear, 16 museums had matched the standards set by the American Association of Museums.

Objects Versus People. The museum problem most debated concerned the relative importance of two responsibilities—how a museum should divide its resources between the obligation to preserve, study, and interpret objects, and the need to serve the culturally deprived people in its community. As one solution, 18 museums in New York City helped the city's Department of Cultural Affairs in a new museums collaborative program. The program staff experimented with exhibitions and educational projects in makeshift quarters close to inner city people. The Philadelphia Museum of Art established a Department of Urban Outreach. It set out to involve the museum actively with such community organizations as neighborhood art centers.

Gifts and Grants. The National Endowment for the Arts allotted $1 million to museums throughout the country in the first half of 1971, and planned to appropriate about $4 million more in the fiscal year that began July 1. The National Endowment for the Humanities, in its largest museum grant so far, provided $1 million for the Museum of African Arts and the Frederick Douglass Institute in Washington, D.C.

The citizens of St. Louis County, Missouri, voted to raise taxes to help support three museums. The Joslyn Art Museum in Omaha, Nebr., received a private gift of $1 million, and the Field Museum of Natural History in Chicago received a donation of $500,000 from industry, both for building improvements. In Washington, D.C., the Corcoran Gallery of Art obtained a $200,000 foundation grant to improve the security of its collections. Smaller grants enabled the California Academy of Sciences to strengthen its junior academy program and the National Gallery of Art in Washington, D.C., to develop a photographic archive.

Grants from the National Science Foundation helped to support research by the Field Museum of Natural History, the Illinois State Museum, and the Los Angeles County Museum of History and Science. Congress appropriated $600,000 for research, publication, and training programs to raise the standards of museum work.

Exhibits and Buildings. The American Museum of Natural History in New York City installed a Hall of Peoples of the Pacific. The Denver Art Museum moved into its new $6-million building. In Minneapolis, the Walker Art Center also moved into a new $4.5-million building. The Cleveland Museum of Art completed a modern education wing. Ralph H. Lewis

The new Hall of the Peoples of the Pacific, built at a cost of $1 million, opened May 18 at the American Museum of Natural History in New York City.

MUSIC, CLASSICAL

The performing arts, most notably music, were given a dazzling new cultural center in which to display their attractions in 1971. On September 8, the massive $70-million John F. Kennedy Center for the Performing Arts was officially opened in Washington, D.C.

Earlier in the year, on May 27, a gala preview of the facilities brought a fashionable crowd and raised $240,000 for the center's educational fund. The official opening in September, which featured the première performance of Leonard Bernstein's mixed media *Mass*, was prefaced by performances designated as a dress rehearsal and preview, respectively. On September 9, the center's Concert Hall, a new home for the National Symphony, was inaugurated under the baton of Antal Dorati, who was beginning his second year as music director of the orchestra. On September 10, the Opera House followed the Bernstein work with a second première, Alberto Ginastera's *Beatrix Cenci*. Performed by the Opera Society of Washington, it proved to be another example of the composer's flair for the Renaissance horror story.

Queen Elizabeth II of England in June named Georg Solti Knight Commander of the Order of the British Empire. He cannot, however, be addressed as Sir Georg until he secures British citizenship. His years as music director of the Royal Opera House, Covent Garden, London, ended on July 4, and he devoted most of the autumn to working with the Chicago Symphony Orchestra.

In August, September, and October, Solti led the orchestra through the first European tour of its 80-year history. The schedule at home included a concert production of Arnold Schönberg's *Moses and Aron*, which received its first New York performance from the touring Chicagoans in November. Despite his heavy Chicago commitment, Solti retained his European affiliations with the London Philharmonic Orchestra, the Orchestre de Paris, the Opera in Paris, and Covent Garden, where he will return as a guest conductor.

The Boston Symphony Orchestra marked its 90th birthday in 1971 by touring Europe for the first time in 15 years. Conductors for the tour were William Steinberg, Michael Tilson Thomas, and Arthur Fiedler. As if to emphasize its importance in the musical life of the South, the Atlanta Symphony, with Robert Shaw conducting, made the most ambitious tour of its history. The orchestra visited 25 cities in 13 states.

The Financial Situation of orchestras was difficult, but manageable, during the year. On June 30, the deadline set by the Ford Foundation on its project to fortify endowments arrived. Of 60 participating orchestras, 55 raised $88 million during the period from 1966 to 1971 to meet their goals; 5 failed to make them. One of the latter was the Kansas City Philharmonic, which was so broke that it had to cancel part of its spring schedule.

One solution to the chronic financial problems faced by the orchestras was to build new audiences, especially among younger people. Pierre Boulez, who had made his presence known mightily in his first weeks as music director of the New York Philharmonic, was pioneering along these lines in two cities. In Cleveland, where he was winding up his engagement as principal guest conductor, he offered two informal evenings with himself and the Cleveland Orchestra. His New York plans were more formidable – an invasion of Greenwich Village for "Prospective Encounters" between young listeners and the performers during which music would be both played and discussed. The Boston Symphony called on its young associate conductor, Michael Tilson Thomas, to lead four special programs designed to attract young people.

Lorin Maazel, a 41-year-old American conductor, was named music director of the Cleveland Orchestra, effective with the 1972-1973 season. Born in France, Maazel has made most of his reputation in Europe. In the autumn, he directed a United States tour of the New Philharmonic Orchestra of London, with which he is affiliated.

An unqualified record in the history of the New York Philharmonic was set by Leonard Bernstein, who, 28 years and 1 month after his debut with the orchestra, conducted it in public for the 1,000th time.

Leopold Stokowski, nearing 90, was ill in London during the summer, but was back at work in the autumn. He received the Henry Elias Howland Memorial Prize from Yale University for his services to music. In October, 1972, he is to direct the Philadelphia Orchestra in a special concert marking the 60th anniversary of his initial appearance in Philadelphia. He led the Philadelphia Orchestra to international fame from 1912 to 1938.

Anniversaries of Note included the 450th of the death of Josquin des Pres, which brought a group of music scholars to New York in June to speak (if not sing) of his fame. Artur Rubinstein marked the 65th anniversary of his American debut by playing two big concertos (the Rachmaninoff No. 2 and Brahms Second) in a single program with Eugene Ormandy and the Philadelphia Orchestra.

Musicians and dancers perform in Leonard Bernstein's controversial *Mass*, which marked the opening of the John F. Kennedy Center for the Performing Arts.

Pittsburgh opened a new concert hall on September 10. Heinz Hall for the Performing Arts is a remodeled downtown movie palace.

The Council of Europe, meeting in Strasbourg, France, late in 1971, recommended that European orchestras adopt the standard pitch of the United States and Great Britain. Concert "A" (the "A" above middle "C") is nominally a tone of 440 cycles per second, but it has shifted both up and down in the course of musical history, and on the European continent in recent years it has tended to rise, creating a serious problem for singers and performers on stringed instruments.

The Metropolitan Opera opened its 87th season on September 20, the 22nd and last under the direction of Rudolf Bing. Verdi's *Don Carlo* was the opening-night opera with Martina Arroyo the prima donna of the evening.

In the house on opening night were Goeran Gentele, who will succeed Bing in the autumn of 1972, and Rafael Kubelik, who will become music director (see KUBELIK, RAFAEL). Five new productions were set for the 1971-1972 season, Carl Weber's *Der Freischütz*, Richard Wagner's *Tristan und Isolde*, Claude Debussy's *Pelléas et Mélisande*, Gaetano Donizetti's *The Daughter of the Regiment*, and Giuseppe Verdi's *Otello*. *Freischütz* had not been produced at the Metropolitan since 1929.

The Opera Company of Boston announced a season that will contain the first American-staged production of the whole of Louis Hector Berlioz's *Les Troyens*. Abridged and concert versions have been heard in the past.

In Chicago, the Lyric Opera opened with Gioacchino Rossini's *Semiramide*, and staged Wagner's *Das Rheingold* as the first chapter in its initial presentation of the composer's "Ring" cycle.

Carlisle Floyd's *Susannah*, a staple of the New York City Opera since 1956, wore out its original scenery and got a new production, an unprecedented event in contemporary American opera production. In addition to fall and spring seasons at home, the New York company was now appearing in Washington, D.C., and Los Angeles.

In its 49th year, the San Francisco Opera offered a sophisticated season of scores from all the major operatic nations of Europe. But the Juilliard American Opera Center staged the farthest-out opera of the year, *The Losers* by Harold Farberman. It dealt with the violent world of a motorcycle gang.

A new Ford Foundation program announced in October provided cash reserve grants for performing arts groups, especially those with recurring "cash-flow crises" and a weight of accumulative deficits. Fifteen opera companies were among the beneficiaries; none was more elated than the Dallas

Gian Carlo Menotti's *The Most Important Man*, premièred by the New York City Opera in March, deals with a black scientist who can control the world.

Opera, which marked its 15th season with the help of a $751,000 Ford Foundation grant that ended the threat of bankruptcy.

The Recording Industry had a transitional year in which costs made new ventures a gamble and major technological changes seem close at hand. Even so, the autumn brought a group of complete Wagner operas led by eminent conductors: *Parsifal* from Boulez, *Tannhaüser* from Solti, *Die Meistersinger* from Herbert Von Karajan, and *Lohengrin* from Kubelik, all of them high-budget projects. Kubelik, Solti, and Bernard Haitink all completed editions of the Gustav Mahler symphonies.

Although there was a great deal of discussion of four-channel recording for the classical record customer, there were two major drawbacks—a limitation of available four-channel material to hear, and a lack of uniform industry standards as to how a four-channel recording should be made. Until these matters are cleared up, consumer reaction is likely to be cautious. See RECORDINGS.

On the other hand, the application of Dolby noise-reduction techniques to the commercially recorded cassette and home recording yielded the kind of marked improvement that could make a substantial difference in the role of cassettes in the struggle that is going on among rival modes of tape recording.   Robert C. Marsh

See also AWARDS AND PRIZES.

MUSIC, POPULAR. A nationwide movement by young people to seek peace and salvation through Jesus Christ inspired the creation of songs espousing Christ in 1971. For the first time in popular music, a "Jesus rock movement" flourished. The religious movement drew material from such diverse sources as Ed Ames, Johnny Rivers, Al DeLory, George Harrison, Three Dog Night, Ocean, and Helen Reddy. What was significant about using Christ as the theme for pop songs was the willingness of pop radio stations to play them, especially since many of them feature hard rock'n'roll rhythms.

Young people bought millions of these recordings, including the $10 two-record album of the "rock opera" *Jesus Christ Superstar. Superstar* not only sold more than 3 million copies, but this work by two young Britishers, composer Andrew Lloyd Webber and lyricist Tim Rice, also sparked a Broadway production, a touring company, and a motion picture, which was slated for shooting early in 1972.

Rock's hard core, which dominated the pop scene during 1969 and 1970, was being softened in 1971. An abundance of artists created a style that pleased both the youth and adults. Carole King, James Taylor, and Neil Diamond wrote and sang their own songs, while the Carpenters, a brother-sister duo, became the nation's top domestic attraction.

The dramatic, ear-shattering, hard-rock school was ruled by an American group, the Grand Funk

Railroad, which was sold out wherever it played. Nevertheless, it could not gain the plaudits of critics.

A British group, Black Sabbath, led the foreign brigade of hard-rock groups that found American audiences still willing to pay to see English touring bands. And tour they did, in a full-scale invasion: Elton John (whose act consisted of singing and piano playing coupled with circus shenanigans), and the Who, Bee Gees, Humble Pie, Ten Years After, Cat Stevens, Traffic, and Emerson, Lake and Palmer. In addition, Engelbert Humperdinck and Tom Jones, two stalwart sexy singers, crisscrossed the United States amassing hundreds of thousands of dollars apiece to take back home.

Canadian Performers. While British acts have been commonplace in the United States since the Beatles' invasion in 1964, Canadian artists suddenly caught fire. The Guess Who, the Stampeders, the Poppy Family, Ocean, and Gordon Lightfoot were Canada's most popular export items. The Guess Who, from Winnipeg, became Canada's first pop act to earn seven gold records in the United States with a sound that drew on the best of rock music's dynamics.

This dynamics, less sophisticated in the 1950s and 1960s, was featured in a series of "revival" package groups that toured the country. Back into the spotlight came such performers of the 1950s as Bill Haley, Chuck Berry, Bo Diddley, the Coasters, Bobby Ridell, Jerry Lee Lewis, and the Shirelles.

The Beach Boys, an act identified with the "surfin'" music of 1963 and 1964, began playing before audiences after a two-year self-imposed exile. The Beach Boys had formerly been the leading American contemporary rock group. Their new look —long hair and beards—plus an involvement with message songs about the environment and man's struggle for dignity, endeared them anew to the crowd that had danced to their music in high school.

Old Favorites Return. Several other artists found their careers rekindling. The Mamas and Papas began work on an album as the initial step toward a cross-country tour. Sonny and Cher, the husband-wife deep-voiced duo; Paul Anka; and Perry Como were again in demand.

The theme from the film *Love Story*, with music by Francis Lai, drew a record number of interpretations. More than 30 artists recorded Carl Sigman's lyrics, and Andy Williams' single emerged as the top hit. Although *Love Story* began the year as the film that produced the most recordings, *Fiddler on the Roof*, released in November, promised to match this. Joan Baez, the priestess of peace and nonviolence, recorded a song with a man's lyric about destruction during the Civil War and earned her first gold single for "The Day They Drove Old Dixie Down."

Groups splintered as individual members sought solo careers. Paul Stokey and Mary Travers, for-

A Lot of Soul

Louis (Satchmo) Armstrong was a magician. He could make people respond to his music even in countries where few understood a word that he sang or spoke. He could play a tune in a completely original way, one others liked and found easy to imitate.

He was a pristine artist, an original. He played a major role in developing the jazz trumpet in New Orleans, but his influence went far beyond that. When he died on July 6, 1971, in New York City, he was internationally regarded as an American goodwill ambassador. People everywhere responded to this happy man who mopped his face with an ever-present white handkerchief, rolled his big eyes, and smiled his dazzling smile.

The year before he died, Satchmo was the subject of several concerts celebrating his 70th birthday—a significant birthday, because Satchmo had recovered from a two-year illness and was able to appear in Los Angeles at one of the concerts. He made few public appearances during the last year of his life, and when he did appear, it was as a vocalist.

Yet it was originally his adroitness with a cornet, then a trumpet, that earned Armstrong his place in musical history. He could reach F above high C with ease, a feat unheard of in the late 1920s. His stratospheric musical flights became a sought-after effect when he played with big bands.

Armstrong learned to play the cornet at the Waif's Home for Boys in New Orleans, and he first met trumpeter Joe (King) Oliver shortly after that. Armstrong joined Oliver's famous Creole Jazz Band in Chicago in 1922. In 1924, he moved to the renowned Fletcher Henderson band in New York City, and a year later he began recording as leader of his own small group.

Armstrong's playing was marked by his pure tone, the continuity of his phrasing, and his sophisticated improvisation. He was head and shoulders above the other professionals playing during his early years. The most striking technical aspect of his playing during the 1920s was his use of legato—long, smooth runs without breaks between the notes. Armstrong developed long melodic lines, usually

followed by short, rapidly descending phrases, and this sound became his hallmark, even years later when he turned such pop tunes as "When It's Sleepy Time Down South" and "Mack the Knife" into mass-audience gems.

Armstrong recorded his first solo on cornet on March 31, 1923, playing "Chimes Blues" with King Oliver. By 1970, when he recorded his last albums ("Louis Armstrong and Friends" and "Louis Country and Western Armstrong"), he had made about 1,500 records.

From his earliest days, Armstrong liked to sing, and his gravelly voice became a trademark along with his trumpet playing. It was this one-two punch that enabled him to become an international star in the 1930s.

Satchmo's sense of humor shone through his vocals so that audiences laughed with him. He considered himself an entertainer, not merely a jazz musician, a stance that propelled him into motion pictures. His first film was *Pennies from Heaven* in 1936.

After World War II, he began to take advantage of his international popularity. He performed with his sextet in Europe from 1948 to 1952 and made his first personal appearance in Japan in 1954. In 1960, he toured parts of eastern and western Africa, first for an American soft drink firm and then under the aegis of the U.S. Department of State. But he never toured the Republic of South Africa because of its apartheid.

Armstrong was respected, even loved, by fellow musicians, who called him "Pops." But he was not free of controversy. He chided the modern school of musicians who developed the "bebop" style in the 1950s, and he frustrated the jazz world by praising Guy Lombardo's "sweet-sounding" band.

Armstrong led an integrated combo (clarinet, trombone, piano, bass, and drums), and he would not play in cities—including New Orleans—that required him to segregate his band. When Armstrong died, Earl (Fatha) Hines, with whom he recorded in 1928, said: "The world lost a champion who had an awful lot of soul."

Eliot Tiegel

Satchmo

One of Motown's hottest properties, the Jackson Five, continued its sensational rise, and made its first television special in September.

merly of Peter, Paul and Mary, made the best-selling charts with singles. So did Graham Nash and Stephen Stills of Crosby, Stills, Nash, and Young. Paul McCartney of the Beatles teamed with his wife Linda. John Lennon began shooting musical darts at McCartney, and Ringo Starr recorded swing era and country music favorites. George Harrison joined the religious movement with the hit "My Sweet Lord."

The Jazz Scene. The 18th annual Newport Jazz Festival was canceled during the second day of its four-day program. Hairy youths stormed the park during the third concert over the July 4 weekend, forcing the cancellation. The 14th annual Monterey Jazz Festival in September avoided booking the kinds of rock-jazz bands that attract this kind of young people and saved itself with a program of Kansas City blues, mainstream jazz, and stellar high school musicians.

Top jazz stars of 1970 included Pharaoh Sanders, Bobby Hutcheson-Harold Land, Miles Davis, and England's Mark-Almond group. Carl Tjader rejoined Fantasy, his first label, and was promptly "rediscovered." Stan Kenton, George Shearing, and the Four Freshmen started a movement to have their own mail-order record companies after they found themselves labeled "uncommercial" by the big companies.   Eliot Tiegel

See also AWARDS AND PRIZES.

MUSKIE, EDMUND SIXTUS (1914-   ), was the leading contender in 1971 for the Democratic presidential nomination. A Democratic senator from Maine since 1959, Muskie was formerly a state representative, Democratic national committeeman, and governor of Maine. He gained national prominence as the 1968 Democratic vice-presidential candidate.

Muskie became an active candidate during the summer of 1971. Between Labor Day and the end of the year, he visited more than half the states. He announced his candidacy on Jan. 4, 1972.

The rugged-looking 6-foot 4-inch senator has a reputation for honesty and moderation, but he has been widely criticized for indecisiveness on major issues and for what a writer in *The New York Times* called a lack of "pizzazz, savvy, and chutzpa."

Muskie was born in Rumford, Me., one of six children of an immigrant tailor. The family name was shortened from Marciszewski when his father entered the United States. Muskie spoke only Polish until the age of 4.

Muskie received a B.A. degree from Bates College in 1936 and a law degree from Cornell University Law School in 1939. In 1954, he became Maine's first Roman Catholic governor and the first Polish-American elected governor in the United States. Muskie married Jane Gray of Waterville in 1948. They have five children.   Allan Davidson

445

NATIONAL DEFENSE. The United States proceeded with its scheduled cutbacks in military power in 1971. The U.S. armed forces dropped more than 200,000 men during the year from the 2,874,000 in service on January 1. The decline was scheduled to continue until the official goal of about 2.5 million men is reached in mid-1972. The U.S. arsenal of land-based intercontinental ballistic missiles (ICBM's) fell more than 35 per cent behind that of Russia. The United States, however, continued to hold a considerable lead in strategic bombers and in submarine-launched ballistic missiles. The Navy was scheduled to reduce its strength to 658 major warships by mid-1972, the smallest U.S. fleet since 1950. See ARMED FORCES OF THE WORLD.

This reduction in U.S. military strength resulted primarily from a long-range policy that Secretary of Defense Melvin R. Laird termed "a national security strategy of realistic deterrence" in his annual defense report on March 9. This was an outgrowth of President Richard M. Nixon's "strategy for peace." It followed the President's concept of "sufficiency" rather than "superiority" in nuclear deterrent power and overall military strength.

Laird said, "This new strategy is designed to prevent wars by furthering the President's goal of building a viable structure of peace based on adequate strength, true partnership, and meaningful negotiations." He added that this "takes account of the strategic, fiscal, manpower, and political realities while steering a prudent middle course between two policy extremes—world policeman or new isolationism." The new strategy emphasized the following aims:

■ Prevention of wars by negotiation from a position of strength.

■ Support of U.S. allies who will contribute to the "total force," thus relieving some of the burden on the United States.

■ Reduction of U.S. troop strength overseas by withdrawing from South Vietnam and other areas where local forces have grown stronger.

■ Limiting of military manpower to 2.5 million troops, all volunteers, by July 1, 1973, when the Administration hopes to end the draft.

■ Cutting of the defense budget to 7 per cent of the gross national product, the total value of all U.S. goods and services produced during the fiscal year.

The "Total-Force" Concept was the key to U.S. strategy. This concept combines the nuclear and conventional arms of the United States and its allies, with new emphasis on the National Guard and reserve forces. This approach assumed that the reduction in regular armed forces would be more than compensated for by the improvement in allied forces and reserves.

Conventional forces would be augmented first in an emergency by the National Guard and the reserves, not by draftees. This reversed the policy followed during the Vietnam War build-up, which drew almost entirely on draftees.

Under the total-force concept, the United States would provide the overall shield for deterring strategic nuclear war. "Theater," or regional, nuclear war would be deterred by U.S. nuclear forces augmented by the nuclear weapons of certain allies.

Laird recognized that nuclear capability alone is not enough to deter aggression. In addition, the U.S. and allied forces need "sufficient conventional capability."

Quick conventional response to an emergency in Europe would involve deploying divisions based in the United States, plus National Guard men and reserves. The North Atlantic Treaty Organization (NATO) would have about 20 divisions ready in central Europe, including 4⅓ U.S. divisions. The United States has 31 air squadrons in Europe, with about 600 jet fighters and bombers. These would be joined by several squadrons from U.S. bases.

Marines are available in the Mediterranean and Caribbean seas, on the Atlantic and Pacific coasts, and on Okinawa. The Army has troops in Hawaii, the continental United States, and Europe that are ready for deployment within a few hours or a few days. The Navy's Sixth Fleet in the Mediterranean and the Seventh Fleet in the Far East can also respond on short notice.

Localized wars would be primarily the responsibility of the nation that is directly threatened, according to Laird. Nevertheless, he said, the United States would provide military and economic assistance if U.S. interests or obligations were at stake.

Depending upon the interpretation of this policy, the United States could deploy air and sea support and could also engage in another Korea- or Vietnam-type war with ground combat troops.

Sufficient Nuclear Force. The formula for a reliable, realistic, strategic nuclear deterrent was explained by John S. Foster, Jr., director of defense research and engineering, in testimony before the Senate Foreign Relations Committee on June 16. He spelled out the four "sufficiency criteria" for nuclear deterrence:

■ Maintain an adequate second-strike capability to deter an all-out surprise attack on our strategic forces.

■ Provide no incentive for Russia to strike the United States first in a crisis.

■ Make certain that Russia cannot cause greater urban and industrial destruction in a nuclear war than the United States could inflict on Russia.

■ Defend against damage from small attacks or accidental launches.

Since 1967, U.S. strategic nuclear forces have remained about the same size, except for the gradual retirement of aging B-52 bombers. There are 1,000 Minuteman ICBM's, 54 Titan II ICBM's, 656

The Calley Case

It was the longest court-martial in U.S. Army history. It ended after more than four months of testimony, a parade of more than 100 witnesses, and some 700 exhibits placed in evidence–amassing 15,000 pages of trial record. On March 29, 1971, the six-officer jury–a colonel, four majors, and a captain–five of whom were Vietnam combat veterans, returned its verdict: First Lieutenant William Laws Calley, Jr., was guilty of the premeditated murder of at least 22 Vietnamese civilians in the village of My Lai 4 on March 16, 1968.

The verdict rocked the nation. It set off a nationwide storm of protest that reached state legislatures, the Congress, and the White House. A *Newsweek* magazine survey conducted by the Gallup Organization indicated that Americans disapproved the verdict by an overwhelming majority of 8 to 1. Seventy per cent of those polled felt that Calley was being made a scapegoat for others at higher levels of military and civilian authority.

State legislatures called for his release. Flags flew at half mast throughout the nation. Nearly 100,000 telegrams, running 100-to-1 against the verdict, flooded the White House. There were pro-Calley rallies, marches, and petitions. A strange song called "The Battle Hymn of Rusty Calley," about "a little boy who wanted to grow up to be a soldier," sold 200,000 copies within three weeks of the verdict. "War is hell," read a bumper sticker, "free Lieutenant Calley."

The White House responded quickly to the pro-Calley sentiment. On April 1, President Richard M. Nixon took the unprecedented step of intervening to block Calley's imprisonment. The President ordered Calley released from the stockade at Fort Benning, Ga. Calley was to be held under house arrest in his own apartment at Fort Benning until the review of his case had been completed –a review in which Mr. Nixon would personally take part.

The appeals machinery began. In August, Lieutenant General Albert O. Conner, commander of the Third Army, concluded on the basis of a review by a team of Army legal officers

Calley leaves stockade

that the guilty verdict had been "correct in law and fact," but that the life sentence imposed by the court-martial had been too harsh. The review panel had recommended that the sentence be cut to 45 years, but Conner reduced it to 20, with parole possible in about 7 years.

Conner's review was but the first step in an appeals process that will eventually take the case to the Army Judge Advocate General, the civilian U.S. Court of Military Appeals, the Secretary of the Army, and, finally, the President. The sentence can be reduced further, but never increased.

But whatever the eventual outcome, the Calley case will be on the public's mind for a long time. It invited a rare and profound soul-searching in the United States.

Not all Americans disagreed with the verdict. To many, it was clear that Calley, whatever his reasons, was a mass murderer. But "can we not still say there is a bit of Calley in most of us?" asked a New York psychiatrist. "Who shares the guilt?" asked *Time* and other magazines. People argued questions of military orders versus individual conscience, "war crimes" standards set by the Nuremberg Trials, and the ultimate responsibility for My Lai. But the issues remained unresolved.

There was the troublesome question of Calley himself. Clearly not cast in the hero's mold, he dropped out of college after a year of failing grades. Rejected by the Army, he drifted through a series of odd jobs. In July, 1966, he tried the Army again, and this time he was accepted. He was sent to Officer Candidate School at Fort Benning, where he graduated in the bottom third of his class. "He shouldn't have been there in the first place," said a Pentagon colonel. "But . . . holes in the screen got bigger and bigger, and Calley slipped through."

Many who felt compassion for Calley still had little stomach for the act. "There were mothers with babies in their arms," said a senior officer. "How can you shut your eyes to that?" Perhaps the national response was summed up best by one of the jurors. "I wanted to believe it didn't happen," he said.

Allan Davidson

447

Polaris and Poseidon missiles on 41 submarines, and some 550 long-range bombers. The bombers will be reduced to a total of about 520 by mid-1972.

The strategic force, however, was being improved. The B-52s were shifted to inland bases where they will be safer from surprise attacks by Russian submarine missiles. The needed warning time to prepare for an enemy missile attack was cut from 15 minutes to 2 or 3 minutes. This became possible through the use of space satellites and over-the-horizon radar, which blankets Russia and China.

The B-52 bombers will get help in penetrating hostile defenses from the short-range attack missile (SRAM). Now in early production, SRAM is designed to knock out enemy missile defense batteries along the way to the B-52's target. Development started on a longer-range cruise missile that will act as a decoy for the B-52. It projects a false radar image that is as large as the bomber. The Air Force continued development of the B-1 swing-wing bomber, which is described as more elusive than the B-52.

Of the 1,000 Minuteman ICBM's, 550 were being equipped with multiple independent re-entry vehicle (MIRV) warheads. Each of the more-advanced Minuteman III warheads will carry two or three nuclear bombs of about 250 kilotons each, the equivalent of about 250,000 tons of TNT. More than 100 ICBM's have been converted to the Minuteman III model, reportedly accurate to within a quarter of a mile.

Thirty-one Polaris-missile submarines will be converted to carry the Poseidon missile. The Poseidon can carry approximately 10 MIRV warheads a distance of 2,800 miles. Four Poseidon-missile submarines were expected to be ready by the end of 1971.

The Navy was researching the underwater long-range missile system (ULMS), a jumbo version of the Polaris-Poseidon. This system would fire a missile more than 5,000 miles. An extended-range Poseidon (EXPO) was also being studied.

Strategic Defense against enemy attack lagged behind U.S. offensive capabilities. The number of jet interceptors dropped from 565 to 484. The number of Hercules antiaircraft missile batteries fell from 76 to 48. There were eight Hawk batteries for defense against low-flying planes and five Bomarc ground-to-air antiaircraft missile squadrons. The United States had a total of 900 air-defense missiles.

Some provision was made to improve the air defenses. Research was being carried out on an over-the-horizon radar for the United States. Under development was an airborne warning and control system (AWACS) plane that would detect and track hostile planes flying at any altitude.

Early warning against enemy missiles, now provided by the ballistic missile early warning system

"Even in the new Army we'll stick with the old salute, lieutenant."

(BMEWS) and the "forward scatter" over-the-horizon radar, was augmented by seven coastal radars. The coastal radars would provide a short-notice alert against enemy submarine-missile launches. The satellite early warning system was initiated on May 5 with the successful launching of the missile detector.

The United States still had no active defense against enemy missiles, however. The Safeguard antiballistic missile (ABM) defense system was still in the early stages of construction at three sites—Grand Forks Air Force Base (AFB) in North Dakota, Malmstrom AFB in Montana, and Whiteman AFB in Missouri.

On February 19, many radio and television stations announced a national emergency and went off the air following a false alert sent by the National Emergency Warning Center. It took 40 minutes to correct the error, but most U.S. citizens were unaware that a warning had been issued.

Conventional Forces, according to Laird's program, would provide 13⅓ Army divisions (a loss of ⅓ division) and 3 Marine divisions in fiscal 1972. There would be 21 Air Force wings; 11 Navy attack wings (a loss of 1); and 3 Marine Corps wings. The Navy would have 16 aircraft carriers (a loss of 2); 55 nuclear attack submarines (an increase of 4); 227 escort ships (an increase of 1); and 75 amphibious assault ships (a loss of 6). There would also be

4 jumbo C-5A airlift squadrons (an increase of 2); 13 other airlift squadrons (a loss of 2); and 98 troopships, cargo ships, and tankers.

The land forces totaled 25⅔ divisions in 1971, including 13⅔ Army divisions, 3 Marine Corps divisions, 8 National Guard divisions, and 1 Marine Reserve division. There were also 21 Army Reserve brigades.

The Army had 3 brigades in Vietnam at the end of 1971. In Europe, for NATO defense, the Army had 4⅓ divisions. In Berlin, there was 1 brigade, with 2 brigades of the 1st Infantry Division available in the United States. There were 4 other Army divisions in the United States and 1 in South Korea.

The Air Force had about 2,200 tactical planes. The Navy had 11 carrier attack wings, with 1,300 sea-based planes. The Marines had about 500 fighters and attack planes operating from carriers.

The Navy's 16 aircraft carriers included 1 nuclear carrier, 8 Forrestal class, 3 Midway class, and 4 older flattops. Two nuclear carriers were being built. In addition, the Navy had about 90 attack submarines and 225 destroyers and amphibious ships, plus 155 logistics and support ships.

The Navy embarked on a $3.3-billion shipbuilding program for fiscal 1972. The new vessels included five high-speed atomic submarines, a nuclear frigate, seven new destroyers, and six support ships.

Technical problems and cost increases caused some trouble for the Navy's F-14 jet-fighter project. But the Navy moved ahead with plans for using an existing engine in the plane to save money. This, however, lowered the performance of the swingwing fighter, designed for use by the Navy's carrier task forces.

The Air Force budgeted $415 million to continue development of its F-15 jet fighter. The fighter would carry short- and medium-range missiles in addition to a cannon.

The Defense Budget submitted to Congress for fiscal 1972 was $77 billion. The Army was allotted $21 billion; the Navy, $21.3 billion; and the Air Force, $22.9 billion. Defense agencies received $1.6-billion; defense-wide services $4.6 billion; and civil defense, $77 million.

The Department of Defense had planned to add only $1.1 billion for incentives to attract an all-volunteer force. Congress, however, raised military pay by $2.4 billion. This military and civilian pay increase was delayed by Mr. Nixon's wage-price freeze.

Extending the Draft. In September, Congress voted to extend the draft after a three-month lapse in the draft law. President Nixon signed the bill on September 28, reinstating the draft for two more years. The new law also ended student deferments for those beginning college in the fall of 1971.

Extension of the old draft law, which expired on June 30, was delayed by Congress. There was a lengthy debate on the question of adding an amend-

U.S. Troops in Vietnam

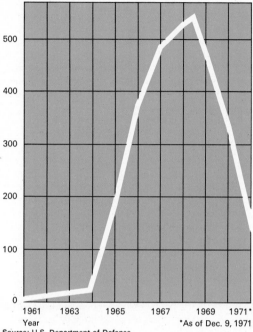

Thousands

Year *As of Dec. 9, 1971
Source: U.S. Department of Defense

ment to the bill calling for the withdrawal of U.S. troops from Vietnam.

Draft calls were suspended after June 30. The Department of Defense had projected draft calls of about 8,000 men a month during the second half of 1971 and into 1972. Voluntary enlistments were expected to increase during that period.

The first call-up under the new draft law was issued on September 30. The defense department ordered 10,000 men to be drafted during the last three months of the year. The Selective Service System said that men with lottery numbers above 125 were relatively safe from the draft in 1971. The total number of draftees for 1971 was estimated at 98,000 men, the lowest figure since 1962.

Drug and Racial Problems. The Department of Defense was troubled with the increasing problems of drug abuse and racism in the armed forces. It ordered medical examinations of troops before their departure from Vietnam. The department provided drug treatment and an amnesty program for drug users who requested treatment.

Racial strife broke out on military bases in Vietnam, Europe, and the United States. The defense department instituted educational and equal-opportunity programs to reduce the friction. Lloyd H. Norman

NATIONALIST CHINA. See FORMOSA (TAIWAN).
NAVY, U.S. See NATIONAL DEFENSE.
NEBRASKA. See STATE GOVERNMENT.

NEPAL. The expiration of a trade and transit treaty with India in 1971 provoked a sharp dispute between the two neighbors. Nepal, a landlocked nation, was totally dependent on India for outlets to the world markets. Thus, India virtually controlled Nepal's trade. The Nepalese, however, insisted on controlling their own overseas shipments, and they also wanted such transit facilities as warehouses in Indian ports. The dispute was finally resolved in September with the signing of a new treaty that incorporated many of Nepal's demands.

Because movement of essential goods was suspended during the quarrel, Nepal's industrial and agricultural development was seriously hampered, and the government was forced to institute a new austerity program. King Mahendra Bir Bikram Sha Deva continued to push his land-reform program, but the program came under sharp criticism in the Nepalese press.

Student protests against the educational system erupted in June. All were dissatisfied with the severe examination standards under which only 20 per cent of the university students were graduated.

Facts in Brief. Population: 11,441,000. Government: King Mahendra Bir Bikram Sha Deva; Prime Minister Kirti Nidhi Bista. Monetary Unit: rupee. Foreign Trade: exports, $29,000,000; imports, $39,000,000. Principal Exports: jute, rice, timber, oilseeds. John N. Stalker

NETHERLANDS. Demonstrators showed hostility toward Emperor Hirohito and Empress Nagato of Japan when they visited the Netherlands in October, 1971. A rock smashed the windshield of their car, and Japanese Embassy windows were broken. Householders flew Dutch flags at half-mast in memory of thousands of their countrymen who died in Japanese prison camps after the fall of Netherlands East Indies (now Indonesia) in 1942.

Voters in the April 28 national elections ended the majority rule of Petrus J. S. de Jong's four-party conservative coalition. After 63 days of negotiations, Barend W. Biesheuvel, 51, leader of the Protestant Anti-Revolutionary Party, formed a five-party coalition government on July 1. The new coalition, with a moderately conservative Cabinet, adds the new Democrat Socialist '70 Party, a small group of right-wing Socialists, to the four former partners, the Anti-Revolution and Catholic People's parties, the Christian Historical Union, and the Liberals. The coalition controls 82 seats in the 150-seat lower house, the Second Chamber.

Inflation Danger. The new Administration faced heavy inflationary pressure that slowed the rate of growth. The gross national product grew by only 4 per cent, compared with 6 per cent in 1970. The new Cabinet abolished its power to intervene in collective labor agreements and in fixing prices.

The previous government's price and wage con-

trols had led to social unrest and threatened worker-employer cooperation. Unemployment rose late in the year, particularly in the industrialized Randstad region in the west. The government floated the guilder on May 9, in effect devaluating the U.S. dollar, to counter a heavy dollar inflow.

New Bishop. Leaders of the Rotterdam Pastoral Council resigned in February in protest against the appointment by Pope Paul VI of a conservative, Monsignor Adrian Simonis, as their new bishop. At his consecration on March 21, Bishop Simonis pledged to "modernize the church without internal dissension." He supports celibacy for priests and opposes birth control.

Joseph Luns, foreign minister for 18 years and one of Europe's most prominent and colorful personalities, in October became secretary-general of the North Atlantic Treaty Organization.

Facts in Brief. Population: 13,342,000. Government: Queen Juliana; Prime Minister Barend W. Biesheuvel. Monetary Unit: guilder. Foreign Trade: exports, $11,765,000,000; imports, $13,391,000,000. Principal Exports: machinery, chemicals, textiles, meats, flower bulbs. Kenneth Brown

NEVADA. See STATE GOVERNMENT.

NEW BRUNSWICK. See CANADA.

NEW HAMPSHIRE. See STATE GOVERNMENT.

NEW JERSEY. See STATE GOVERNMENT.

NEW MEXICO. See STATE GOVERNMENT.

NEW ORLEANS. The nation's first Black Panther trial presided over by a black judge and tried before a predominantly black jury was held in New Orleans in 1971. Twelve Black Panthers, nine men and three women, were accused of the attempted murder in September, 1970, of five New Orleans policemen. In July, during the course of the trial, the male defendants led an uprising at the Orleans Parish Prison, where they were being held, to protest what they called the "corrupt judicial system." That system, however, acquitted all 12 defendants on August 6 after the jury of 10 black and 2 white men spent 31 minutes deliberating.

Two buildings housing Black Panther offices were fire-bombed on January 12. Reportedly the fires were set in retaliation for the arrest of blacks in the Desire Street housing project. Firemen summoned to battle the fires were repulsed by residents throwing rocks and bottles.

The Causes. Economic and racial causes for such unrest were plentiful in New Orleans. The city experienced a 14.5 per cent growth in its black population during the 1960s while the total population fell 5.4 per cent to a 1970 count of 593,471 persons. Although 45 per cent of the city's residents are black, a report on school integration released by the U.S. Department of Health, Education, and Welfare (HEW) in June showed that the number of blacks in predominantly white schools in New Orleans had actually fallen, from 8.8 per cent in 1968 to 7.8 per cent in 1970.

Another HEW report, released in July, indicated that 14.8 per cent of New Orleans' population received some form of welfare assistance. This gave New Orleans the third highest relief dependency rate among the nation's 26 largest urban areas.

Garrison Arrested. A well-known New Orleans figure, District Attorney Jim C. Garrison, experienced a perverse turn in his political fortune in 1971. Garrison, who achieved national renown for his investigations into the assassination of President John F. Kennedy, was arrested by federal agents in New Orleans on June 30. Nine others, including two New Orleans policemen, were arrested with Garrison. All 10 were charged with illegal gambling, bribery to obstruct law enforcement, interstate transportation of pinball machines to be used for gambling, and conspiracy to commit those acts.

Garrison denied that he was involved in the pinball operation and immediately retaliated by ordering the arrest of the two federal prosecutors on charges of extortion, intimidation, and defamation of character. However, he later dropped the charges.

Construction began in August on a $113-million domed stadium in downtown New Orleans, destined to be the world's largest.   J. M. Banovetz

NEW YORK. See NEW YORK CITY; STATE GOVERNMENT.

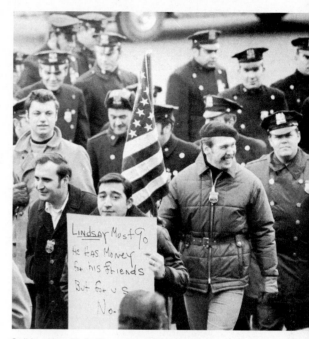

Striking New York City policemen protested outside the New York State Supreme Court Building in January after the court ordered them to return to work.

NEW YORK CITY. The shadow of bankruptcy continued to hover over New York City in 1971. Mayor John V. Lindsay's administration attempted to hold off stringent pay demands from city employees' unions and threatened reductions in state financial assistance. The results were declining municipal services and another round of crippling strikes.

City Workers Strike. Eighty per cent of the police force, about 21,000 men, joined in a weeklong strike in January. Crime was held in check, however, by the round-the-clock efforts of 5,000 nonstrikers and the department's officer corps. The strikers were fined two days' pay for each day of absence and were put on probation for a year. In March, policemen won a retroactive pay increase through court action.

In June, striking members of the Municipal Employees' Union opened and jammed 27 of the 29 drawbridges leading to Manhattan Island and blocked major arteries with maintenance equipment. A work stoppage at sewage-treatment plants caused an estimated 1 billion gallons of raw sewage to be dumped into the East and Harlem rivers. The union wanted a pension system for its employees.

Welfare Cuts. Fiscal problems forced Mayor Lindsay to reject a record $2.4-billion welfare budget, and in April, he fired 800 full-time city employees and 2,000 part-time and temporary workers. The state budget cuts touched off rioting in Browns-

ville, a neighborhood where 80 per cent of the residents are on welfare.

When Congress shelved the welfare-reform issue, the city estimated it would have to raise an additional $100 million to sustain welfare services. The city budget was already running about $300 million in the red, so welfare cuts were made.

A report produced by *Time* magazine in April noted that 11 firms with annual sales in excess of $15 billion were moving out of the city. General Telephone and Electronics Corporation reported that 50 per cent of its executives refused transfer to its New York office in 1970. A 1971 Bureau of Labor Statistics report showed that living costs in New York City were 16 per cent over Chicago or Los Angeles.

The Knapp Commission, appointed by Mayor Lindsay to investigate police corruption, uncovered widespread graft in the city's police department. The commission's undercover agents testified that virtually every plainclothesman and many uniformed policemen had accepted bribes. The investigation produced its first federal grand jury indictments against several police officers in November.

The 1970 Census showed that New York is still the nation's largest city. The city had 7,894,862 persons in 1970, up 1.5 per cent from 1960, while the metropolitan area registered 11,571,899 persons, up 8.2 per cent.   J. M. Banovetz

See also LINDSAY, JOHN V.

NEW ZEALAND. Its future trade status became a major concern of New Zealand in 1971. For years, the output from its highly efficient sheep and dairy industries had been given preferential status by Great Britain. But the impending entry of Britain into the European Community (Common Market) meant that new trading partners had to be found. Accordingly, New Zealand not only sought new markets in the Pacific Basin, but it also stimulated exports to Australia, Japan, and the United States.

The discovery and exploitation of a large variety of mineral ore deposits, including black ironsand on North Island, stimulated a whole new area of development. The discovery of vast fields of natural gas along the Taranaki coast also gave promise of a new industry. New Zealand's economic future was also assured by the Conservative government's determination to hold back inflation by retaining the wage and price freezes it had instituted in 1970.

Facts in Brief. Population: 2,912,000. Government: Governor General Sir Arthur E. Porritt; Prime Minister Keith J. Holyoake. Monetary Unit: New Zealand dollar. Foreign Trade: exports, $1,225,000,000; imports, $1,243,000,000. Principal Exports: wool, lamb and mutton.   John N. Stalker

NEWFOUNDLAND. See CANADA.

NEWSPAPER. See PUBLISHING.

NICARAGUA. See LATIN AMERICA.

NIGER. See AFRICA.

NIGERIA, by 1971, had made a remarkable recovery from the civil war with secessionist Biafra (now the country's Central Eastern State). Communications had largely been restored, and many Nigerians had returned from exile. Most Nigerians were reconciled to the unity drive of Major General Yakubu Gowon, the head of the Federal Military Government. Gowon visited the Central Eastern State in January, 1971, for the first time since the civil war ended in January, 1970.

The federal government continued its harsh policy toward persons convicted of armed robbery. By September 8, 70 armed robbers had been executed since the end of the civil war.

African Relations. Nigeria was among the most vigorous opponents of South Africa's racism. Gowon told British officials that Great Britain might lose its oil interests and its trade with Nigeria if it supplied arms to South Africa. Nigeria is now the second largest oil producer in Africa, and oil has become the greatest source of revenue for the Nigerian government. This fact has strengthened its position in Africa and in world politics.

Gowon played a major role at the Organization of African Unity in gaining recognition for the military regime that seized power in Uganda in January. Even though Tanzania opposed recognition for Uganda, this did not prevent Nigeria and Tanzania from re-establishing diplomatic ties in June. Nigeria

also resumed relations with Zambia in July. Relations with those countries had been broken during the Nigerian civil war. In April, Gowon visited Cameroon and discussed a maritime border settlement with President Ahmadou Ahidjo.

Other Foreign Affairs. In February, Nigeria recognized the People's Republic of China as the only legal government of all the Chinese people. The two nations agreed to establish diplomatic relations. Nigeria also voted in October to seat the Peking government in the United Nations.

Nigeria hosted a private conference in March on U.S.-African relations sponsored by the Afro-American Institute. Senator Edmund S. Muskie (D., Me.) was a key speaker. The event, however, was marred by the death of Whitney M. Young, Jr., director of the National Urban League, in Lagos on March 11.

Canadian Minister of External Affairs Mitchell Sharp visited Nigeria in March. Sharp announced that the Canadian International Development Agency was granting Nigeria a $20-million interest-free loan to purchase Canadian-made locomotives.

Facts in Brief. Population: 68,580,000. Government: Federal Military Government Head Yakubu Gowon. Monetary Unit: pound. Foreign Trade: exports, $1,242,000,000; imports, $1,053,000,000. Principal Exports: crude petroleum, cacao, peanut oil.   George Shepherd

NIMERI, JAFIR MUHAMMAD (1931-   ), became the first elected president of the Sudan on Oct. 12, 1971. In a referendum conducted between September 15 and October 1, he received 98.6 per cent of the vote. In addition to being president, Major General Nimeri is also the prime minister.

Nimeri was born in Omdurman, Sudan, in 1931. He was educated for an army career at the Sudan Military College, graduating in 1952 as a second lieutenant. Three years later, he was promoted to company commander and served in the northern command for two years. In 1957, he joined the armored corps and helped to build it up.

After participating in the revolution of October, 1964, which overthrew a military dictatorship, Nimeri went to Egypt and West Germany for advanced military training. He also received military training in the United States and graduated from the Command and General Staff School at Fort Leavenworth, Kans., in June, 1966.

Nimeri has ruled the country since May, 1969, when, as a colonel, he came to power through a military coup. From then until his election to the presidency in 1971, he served as chairman of the Revolutionary Council.

His rule was briefly interrupted in July, 1971, by an attempted leftist coup. The rebellion was put down within 72 hours, however, and Nimeri was returned to power. See SUDAN.   Darlene R. Stille

NIXON,RICHARD MILHOUS. As President Nixon shaped new foreign and domestic policies in 1971, the American people gained more insight into his philosophy and his personality. Abandoning his "low profile," the President launched a bold new economic policy and inaugurated a new era of East-West diplomacy (see PRESIDENT OF THE UNITED STATES). In a pre-presidential election year, the chief executive traveled extensively and granted journalists several long interviews to make his views known to the voters. Highlight of the Nixon family's year, however, was the marriage of the President's elder daughter Patricia to Edward Finch Cox on June 12. See Close-Up.

Unusual Interviews. The President granted four long and revealing interviews in one month. The first, with a British journalist, appeared in the London *Sunday Telegraph* in February and was published by *The Washington Post* on March 6. In the interview, the President explained that he was a "progressive" who was unable to embrace the welfare philosophy of New Deal programs. This, he said, was because he had been reared by deeply religious parents in the Puritan tradition of self-help.

His second interview, published on March 10, was with *The New York Times* columnist C. L. Sulzberger. In this discussion, the President declared that he "seriously doubted if we would ever have another war." He stated that he believed the war in Vietnam was drawing to a close.

The third interview, granted to nine women correspondents, was held in his Oval Office in the White House on March 11 and lasted 75 minutes. Drinking tea in front of a fireplace, Mr. Nixon spoke of his wife and family. He told the reporters that a President needs a wife of character to support him, and declared that his wife Pat was "in that tradition."

On March 15, Mr. Nixon was interviewed on the National Broadcasting Company's "Today" television show. In this fourth appearance, Mr. Nixon said that he had no plans for "image making," and did not care that he was regarded as "rather stuffy." Nonetheless, through these interviews, the American people were able to learn more about the personal views of their rather reticent President.

On April 6, four newspaper editors and two reporters interviewed the President in a live newscast. This interview took place during the final session of the annual convention of the American Society of Newspaper Editors in Washington, D.C.

Presidential Visits. In 1971, President Nixon became the first President to have visited all 50 states. (Franklin D. Roosevelt had visited all 48 states during his term in office.) On October 8, the President completed his 50th state visit when he attended the 35th annual Mountain State Festival in Elkins,

President Nixon danced with the bride, Mrs. Nixon with the groom, at White House reception following daughter Tricia's wedding in the Rose Garden.

White House Weddings

The wedding of President Richard M. Nixon's daughter, Patricia (Tricia), was a major social event in 1971. Tricia married Edward Finch Cox in the Rose Garden of the White House on June 12. Hundreds of reporters, photographers, and television cameramen descended upon Washington, D.C., to record every detail of the event.

The couple were married by Edward Gardiner Latch, chaplain of the U.S. House of Representatives. Tricia had four bridal attendants, including her sister Julie Nixon Eisenhower.

Tricia was the eighth daughter of a President to be married in the White House. Among the 400 guests at her wedding were two previous White House brides, Lynda Bird Johnson Robb and 87-year-old Alice Roosevelt Longworth.

Surrounded by Secret Service men and television crews, Lynda Bird, the daughter of President Lyndon B. Johnson, married Charles S. Robb on Dec. 9, 1967, in the East Room. Tricia's wedding probably brought back happy memories for Lynda Bird, but it must have been a foreign scene for Alice Longworth.

It was an entirely different era when President Theodore Roosevelt's daughter, Alice, married Nicholas Longworth, a congressman from Ohio, in the East Room on Feb. 17, 1906. The wedding, probably the most spectacular in the history of the White House, was witnessed by 1,000 guests. Afterward, a wedding breakfast was served for 700. Pope Pius X and heads of governments sent priceless gifts.

Those were pretelevision days, but the public was kept well informed by ambitious newspaper reporters. Many people traveled to Washington, D.C., just to stand outside the White House on the wedding day, and enterprising businessmen sold souvenirs of the wedding.

In contrast, the first White House wedding of a President's daughter did not create much of a stir. On March 9, 1820, Maria Hester Monroe, daughter of President James Monroe, married Samuel Lawrence Gouverneur, the President's personal secretary. There were only about 40 guests, and newspapers gave the wedding little coverage.

The second White House wedding united President John Tyler's daughter, Elizabeth, and William Nevison Waller. The ceremony was held in the East Room on Jan. 31, 1842. It was more impressive than the first wedding, with Cabinet members and other high government officials attending. Still, the wedding received little attention in the newspapers.

President Ulysses S. Grant's daughter, Ellen (Nellie), married Algernon Charles Frederick Sartoris, an Englishman, on May 21, 1874. This was the first White House wedding to arouse widespread public interest. Walt Whitman wrote a poem in honor of the occasion.

Two daughters of President Woodrow Wilson were married in the White House within six months in 1913 and 1914. On Nov. 25, 1913, Jessie Wilson married Francis Bowes Sayre in the East Room. Theirs was a large and elegant wedding, even though it did not match the Alice Roosevelt spectacular. The House of Representatives sent Jessie a diamond necklace, and the Senate gave her a 14-piece silver service. Gifts poured in from foreign rulers and dignitaries.

Her sister's wedding, however, was a quiet event. Eleanor Wilson, then 24, married Secretary of the Treasury William Gibbs McAdoo, 50, in the Blue Room on May 7, 1914. There were only 80 guests. The wedding was subdued in deference to the President's wife, who was seriously ill.

Daughters of Presidents, though, were not the only ones to marry in the White House. A President's son, John Quincy Adams II, was married there in 1828. Even a President, Grover Cleveland, was married in the White House, in 1886. And nieces of Presidents Wilson and Rutherford B. Hayes also were married there.

There have been many other weddings in the White House, but the exact number is not known. Vague accounts have been given of weddings early in White House history. By the most commonly accepted estimate, Patricia Nixon Cox's wedding was the 16th to be held at the Executive Mansion.

Darlene R. Stille

Mr. and Mrs. Edward F. Cox

Ensign David Eisenhower is handed his naval commission by his father-in-law, the President, on March 12, *left*. David's wife, Julie Nixon Eisenhower, *below left*, wears a cast after a toe was crushed by a cartload of books. While in California in August to deed 372 acres along the Mexican border to the state for use as a park, Mrs. Nixon steps over the border and greets a crowd of cheering Mexicans, *below*.

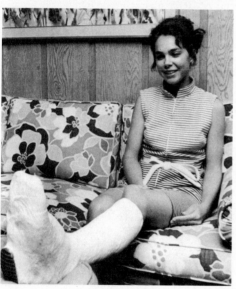

W.Va. He had visited the 49th state, Delaware, on October 5, when he met with Republican Party fund-raisers who were planning a "salute to the President" dinner for November.

On March 12, the President spoke at his son-in-law David Eisenhower's commencement at the Naval Officers Training School in Newport, R.I. In his speech, Mr. Nixon warned against the nation's "new isolationists."

On September 26, the President met Emperor Hirohito of Japan at Elmendorf Air Force Base in Alaska. This marked the first time in history that a U.S. President had met with a Japanese emperor.

The coming year promised to be an exciting year for presidential travel. On July 15, the President announced that he would visit China in 1972. He also planned to visit Russia.

The First Family. In August, Mrs. Nixon visited Virginia, Michigan, Minnesota, Oregon, and California to inspect public recreational facilities and to turn over 4,200 acres of government land for public use. Her trip focused national attention on the President's "legacy of parks" program.

Because of an injury to her foot in August, Julie Nixon Eisenhower was forced to cut short her career as a full-time elementary-school teacher in Florida. A toe on her left foot was crushed by a falling cartload of books. Her husband David, assigned to a guided-missile cruiser, began his three-year tour of active Navy duty in March. Carol L. Thompson

NOBEL PRIZES in literature, peace, economics, and science were presented at ceremonies in Stockholm, Sweden, on Dec. 10, 1971. They were awarded by the Norwegian Storting (legislative) Nobel Committee, Oslo.

Literature Prize was awarded to Pablo Neruda, 67, a Chilean poet and diplomat, and perhaps the finest Latin American poet living today. Neruda, who was born Neftalí del Carman Reyes Basoalto, first published poems at the age of 17, and several volumes of his verse had appeared by the time he was 20. He won wide acclaim for these works, and, in an old tradition of government recognition of artists, later served as Chilean consul to several countries. In 1970, he was named ambassador to France by Chilean President Salvador Allende Gossens. During the Spanish Civil War, between 1936 and 1938, he turned to Communism, and in 1945 he was elected a Communist Senator in Chile. He was forced into hiding and exile from 1948 to 1952. Neruda was awarded the Stalin Prize in 1950, and the Lenin Peace Prize in 1953. Except for a brief surrealistic period around 1930, his poetry has always been clear and lyrical, infused with love and politics. His best-known volumes of poetry include *Crepuscular* (1923), *Twenty Poems of Love and One Desperate Song* (1924), *Residence on Earth* (1931; 1935), and *The Furies and the Pains* (1939).

Peace Prize was awarded to West German Chancellor Willy Brandt, 58, for his success in building bridges between Communist and non-Communist nations. The Nobel committee honored Brandt for the "concrete initiatives leading to a relaxation of tension" that he had taken both as foreign minister in 1966 and as chancellor since 1969. It stressed the signing of the treaty to prevent the spread of nuclear weapons, the signing of friendship treaties by West Germany with Poland and Russia, and Brandt's "efforts to obtain for the people of West Berlin the fundamental human rights of personal security and full freedom of movement." As a youth, Brandt joined the Social Democratic Party and openly opposed the Nazis. In 1933, he fled to Norway.

Economic Science Prize was awarded to Simon Kuznets, 70, an American economist and statistician noted for his factual studies of business cycles, economic growth, and national income. He has long been the leader of the effort to provide systematic statistical measurement of economic behavior and its results. The organizing theme of his investigations is that the economic growth of a nation is necessarily tied to a thoroughgoing transformation of its economic structure. He was born in Kharkov, Russia, but has spent all his adult life in the United States. He has taught at the University of Pennsylvania, Johns Hopkins University, and Harvard.

Chemistry Prize was awarded to Gerhard Herzberg, 66, of Canada. The German-born physicist was honored for his "contributions to the knowledge of the electronic structure and geometry of molecules, especially free radicals." (Free radicals are fragments of molecules that combine easily with other molecules.) In his research, Herzberg determined the structure of two free radicals, methyl and methylene.

Physics Prize was awarded to Dennis Gabor, 71, a Hungarian-born British engineer. Gabor invented holography, a process for making three-dimensional photographs without using a lens. Holography uses coherent beams of light to record a whole image, rather than just the flat surface of ordinary photographs. The light is provided by laser beams.

Physiology and Medicine Prize was awarded to Earl W. Sutherland, Jr., 55, for his "discoveries concerning the mechanisms of the action of hormones." In 1956, he discovered a complex molecule called cyclic AMP that mediates the action of many hormones and regulates important activities in cells. Sutherland found that there is a tiny amount of cyclic AMP in almost every living cell–even in bacteria. He also discovered that hormones can change the amount of cyclic AMP in a cell, and thus affect the cell's action.   Foster Stockwell

NORTH ATLANTIC TREATY ORGANIZATION (NATO). See EUROPE.

NORTH CAROLINA. See STATE GOVERNMENT.

NORTH DAKOTA. See STATE GOVERNMENT.

NORTHERN IRELAND. See GREAT BRITAIN.

NORWAY. Prime Minister Per Borten resigned on March 2, 1971, after a political scandal. Borten's five-year-old, four-party coalition fell after Borten admitted he leaked a classified state paper–a report of a conversation between Norway's ambassador to Belgium and Jean-Francois Deniau, a member of the European Community (Common Market) Commission. It was published in an Oslo newspaper and shown to an anti-Common Market pressure group in Norway. The report said Norway's demands for lasting special arrangements for agriculture and fisheries made Common Market membership impossible.

A Labor Party government replaced Borten's, whose Center Party had refused an appeal by its partners–the Conservative, Liberal, and Christian People's parties–to continue the coalition. On March 10, the Labor Party leader, Trygve M. Bratteli, accepted an invitation from King Olav V to form a new government. Bratteli declared: "The new government will handle Norway's relations with the European Community on the basis of the decision of the Storting [legislature] in June, 1970." The Storting had instructed the government to negotiate Norway's entry as a full member. Bratteli's government has 74 of the 150 seats in the Storting; the old coalition had 76. His first task was to stop the drift of public opinion away from Common Market entry. He asked for $210,000 for an information campaign and sent trade unionists on fact-finding missions to the market's Brussels headquarters. On June 17, the Storting voted, 113 to 37, to continue Common Market negotiations for membership.

Fishing Rights are the central issue in the negotiations. Norwegian fisheries are bigger than those of the six charter members combined. According to Common Market policy, fishermen from any member country may fish in the territorial waters of all the others. Norway wants to preserve its 12-mile coastal waters limit. The negotiators indicated they recognize Norway's special problems with fisheries.

The Labor government faced a crisis in June over its plans to fight inflation. It had decided to raise both taxes and deductions for national pensions. Bratelli's reaching an agreement with the leaders of two of the four non-Socialist parties brought him the support he needed and avoided a political battle.

Women's Liberation action in municipal elections in Oslo on September 27 gave women the majority in the City Council. They won 45 of the 85 seats.

Facts in Brief. Population: 3,944,000. Government: King Olav V; Prime Minister Trygve Martin Bratteli. Monetary Unit: krone. Foreign Trade: exports, $2,455,000,000; imports, $3,697,000,000 Principal Exports: ships and boats, aluminum, paper and pulp, fish. Kenneth Brown

See also BRATTELI, TRYGVE M.

NOVA SCOTIA. See CANADA.

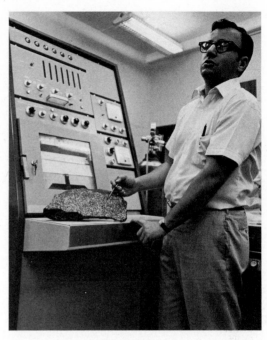

Thomas A. Vogel, Michigan State University geologist, points to a basaltic inclusion found in the first piece of granite ever recovered from the ocean floor.

OCEAN. The U.S. deep-sea drilling project continued coring operations in the Atlantic and Pacific oceans and in the Caribbean and Mediterranean seas in 1971. Scientists found that sediment cores taken from the North Pacific become progressively older as they are taken from the ocean bottom from east to west. That finding is consistent with the theory of sea-floor spreading. Younger sediments drawn from the boundary trenches between what appear to be massive plates of the earth's crust were found to be compact, hard, and highly deformed. This suggests they are being scraped off the ocean floor and crumpled against the continent as the ocean crust passes beneath the continental block.

Evidence of climatic change, revealed by microfossils in the sediments, showed that the Pacific Northwest was never warmer over the past 2 million years than it is today. Other findings of the drilling project helped to explain how the Isthmus of Panama was probably formed by a combination of sea floor rising and ridge drifting in an area that was once a deep-sea trench, the northwest extension of which still exists off the coast of Central America and Mexico. Sediments in the Mediterranean suggest that the entire area has alternately been above and under water.

International Exploration. In 1971, the United States took the first major steps in the International Decade of Ocean Exploration (IDOE) program.

This is part of the expanded program of oceanic exploration adopted by the Intergovernmental Oceanographic Commission of the United Nations Educational, Scientific, and Cultural Organization (UNESCO) in 1969. A program of oceanographic research and exploration, it focused on man's use of, and impact on, the oceans. IDOE launched a series of research projects in environmental quality, environmental forecasting, and seabed assessment. The environmental quality experiments seek to achieve a detailed understanding of the stirring and mixing processes at work in the Atlantic, Pacific, and Indian oceans, and how they affect dispersal or concentration of heavy metals, chlorinated hydrocarbons, and petrochemicals from oil spills in the deep sea.

An important element of the environmental forecasting program is the investigation of the part that medium-scale eddies play in the general circulation of the oceans. Just how large and widespread these eddies are is not known, but their total kinetic energy is so large that they must be accounted for in the dynamics of any ocean models.

Seabed Disarmament Treaty. In July, President Richard M. Nixon asked the U.S. Senate to ratify a treaty prohibiting the installation of nuclear weapons on the ocean floor. The treaty, the result of two years of intensive negotiations in Geneva, Switzerland, and in the United Nations, was signed on February 11, by U.S., Russian, and British officials in Washington, D.C., Moscow and London, and by representatives of 60 other nations in Washington. By August 1, it had been signed by 69 nations. In essence, the treaty bars placing nuclear weapons and other weapons of mass destruction on the ocean floor beyond a 12-mile coastal "seabed zone."

Sea Grant Colleges. In a landmark ceremony on September 17, Oregon State University, Texas A&M University, the University of Rhode Island, and the University of Washington were designated by Secretary of Commerce Maurice H. Stans as the first four sea grant colleges. The National Sea Grant College and Program Act of 1966 is aimed at promoting marine resource development in the same way that land grant colleges stimulated agricultural development.

The National Council on Marine Resources and Engineering Development issued its fourth and last annual report to the President entitled, "Marine Science Affairs," in April. Shortly thereafter, the council ceased existence.

On Aug. 16, the President signed a bill establishing a 25-member National Advisory Committee for Oceans and Atmosphere to serve principally as the advisory arm of the National Oceanic and Atmospheric Administration. Arthur G. Alexiou

OHIO. See CLEVELAND; STATE GOVERNMENT.

OKLAHOMA. See LATTING, PATIENCE SEWELL; STATE GOVERNMENT.

OLD AGE. The White House Conference on Aging was held in Washington, D.C., from Nov. 28 to Dec. 2, 1971. With more than 3,000 voting delegates and several hundred observers, the conference provided a comprehensive public discussion of the problems and status of elderly people in today's society.

Early in the year, there was much criticism of the way the conference was being organized. This criticism was given publicity by the Special Senate Committee on Aging, under the chairmanship of Senator Frank Church (D., Ida.), which held hearings in March and April on the conduct of the conference. Among the critics was Nelson Cruikshank, president of the National Council of Senior Citizens, who charged that the technical committees producing the materials for study by the conference participants were dominated by Republicans. There were also complaints that minority groups and the elderly poor were not adequately represented in the membership of committees or among the delegates.

At the time these charges were being made, the Nixon Administration was moving to include more representatives of these groups in the conference. It was also moving to increase the money appropriated by Congress for programs under the Administration on Aging from $29.5 million for 1971 and 1972 to $39.5 million. Also, to the satisfaction of most critics, Arthur S. Flemming, former Secretary of Health, Education, and Welfare under President Dwight D.

Eisenhower, was recruited to serve as full-time chairman of the conference.

Action Promised. During the conference, a set of recommendations from the 14 sections that constituted its working organization was published, and the White House designated 1972 as the time for action on the conference recommendations. To get action, including the passage of legislation, President Richard M. Nixon has created a Cabinet-level Committee on Aging within the Domestic Council, which advises him on domestic legislation and policy. The chairman of this committee is Health, Education and Welfare Secretary Elliot L. Richardson.

The White House Conference recommended against mandatory retirement at a fixed age, and proposed that people be allowed and encouraged to work, at least on a part-time basis, as long as they want to and can do the work with competence. Nevertheless, there is a trend toward earlier voluntary retirement, which was illustrated late in 1971 when a number of automobile workers retired at from 55 to 60 years of age with pensions of $500 a month after 30 years on the job. In general, the high productivity of American technology has provided the basis for greater flexibility of the work career after the age of 45. Some people may prefer to trade some of their earning power for more leisure during their 40s and 50s, and to continue working, at least part time, until they are 70.

Longer Life. The outlook for a longer active adult life for the average person was a matter of intense discussion during the year among authorities on aging. Most medical and biological experts kept their fingers crossed with respect to the widely publicized claims of Dr. Alex Comfort, director of research on aging at University College in London. In a magazine article, Dr. Comfort asked for a major government subsidy for research on ways to slow down the aging process in human beings. He wrote: "We know that human aging can almost certainly be slowed, and we know how to set about trying. Science has two ways of making people live longer: It can stop their dying before their time, or it can try to slow down the figurative clock that controls aging, so that old age and death take longer to arrive."

Dr. Comfort pointed out that if we had a cure for the two leading causes of death to elderly people—cancer and heart disease—this would increase the average length of life after age 65 by only 2 years, from the present 14.5 years to 16.5 years. He predicted, however, that "By the year 1990, we will know of an experimentally tested way of slowing down age changes in man that offers an increase of 20 per cent in the life span." He added that the extra 10 to 15 years will be years of middle-aged vigor and activity, not years of tired old age. Robert J. Havighurst

ONTARIO. See CANADA.

OPERA. See MUSIC, CLASSICAL.

OREGON. See STATE GOVERNMENT.

PACIFIC ISLANDS. The United States decision to pull back from its positions on mainland Asia had subsidiary effects on the Pacific Islands in 1971. The most important of these was the signing of an accord between President Richard M. Nixon and Japan's Prime Minister Eisaku Sato that called for the reversion of Okinawa and the other Ryukyu Islands to Japan in July, 1972. Part of the agreement called for the continued maintenance of U.S. military bases on Okinawa, although the number of troops would be substantially reduced. Militant Japanese leftists opposed to the treaty rioted in Tokyo in November, but the Sato government pushed the agreement through Parliament.

Change in Micronesia. The U.S. withdrawal from Asia also began to have a marked effect in the United Nations-mandated islands of Micronesia, which were under American control. Special military surveys were conducted in 1971 regarding the feasibility of reopening U.S. bases that had been established there during World War II. American defense planning, however, ran into considerable opposition from the Micronesians, who not only pressed for greater independence from the United States, but also were considerably alarmed over the proposed reactivation of the bases. In a series of meetings in Hawaii between Micronesian leaders and American officials, the Micronesians agreed to opt for a "free association" with the United States, which would handle foreign affairs and defense. Micronesians, however, would have complete control over internal affairs. The major point still to be decided was whether or not the Micronesians would be able to abrogate the agreement if it proved unsatisfactory.

Economic Development. The effort to encourage growth of a tourist industry in many of the islands was hindered by the general economic slowdown during the year. The Cook Islands became the center of attention due to new experiments in aquaculture and the artificial spawning of mullet. Special tests were to be conducted on the islands, which, if successful, would give many of the islands self-sufficiency in food and other products.

Fiji and Tonga, newly independent, enjoyed a relatively stable year as they began to work out the economic arrangements for their survival. Tonga finally created a banking system to handle its exchange problems.

French authorities continued to exercise strict control over the Society Islands, but Tahitians were showing increasing resistance to colonial rule. New Hebrides experienced something of a land boom, especially on Espiritu Santo, as speculators tried to market land in both Australia and the United States. By year-end this was sharply restricted as it became evident that the international control commission would invalidate many titles.   John N. Stalker

PAINTING. See Visual Arts.

PAKISTAN. A long-expected civil war erupted between the nation's two provinces in 1971. The year began with hope, after the first free election in more than 10 years. It ended with East Pakistan a devastated province, with millions of its population seeking refuge in camps in India, and with perhaps 150,000 persons killed in what had at first been a civil war but which later flared into an all-out war with India. See Asia; India.

The crisis dated back to the election of Dec. 7, 1970, in which Sheik Mujibur Rahman and his Awami (People's) League won 167 seats, or a majority of the 300 seats in the National Assembly. But the voters also gave Mujibur a mandate to improve the lot of the aggrieved province, which had long felt itself cruelly exploited by the power elite of West Pakistan, 1,000 miles away across the breadth of India.

General Agha Mohammed Yahya Khan, Pakistan's president and strongman, went to the East's capital, Dacca, in March to discuss with Mujibur Rahman the terms on which the new Assembly would draft a constitution and form a civilian government. Mujibur Rahman, or "Mujib," as he was known affectionately by his followers, was a nationalist spellbinder who had spent years in prison for the cause of East Pakistan. He presented the general with six conditions. These called for the creation of

The emblem of Bangla Desh, the newly proclaimed Bengali nation, is unfurled in Chudanga, East Pakistan, by members of the militant Awami League.

a federal state, with the powers of the national government limited to defense and foreign affairs. Mujibur called for separate currencies for the East and West, for giving control of all taxation to the states, for separate reserve banks, and for its own militia for East Pakistan.

Yahya Khan found the terms unacceptable. They were also rejected by former Foreign Minister Zulfikar Ali Bhutto, who, with 88 seats, emerged as the most powerful leader in West Pakistan. An ambitious leftist, Bhutto saw no future for himself or his program in an Assembly dominated by Mujibur.

The Break. While the talks in Dacca dragged on, the general kept moving his troops east. On March 25, they struck. Centers of East Pakistan (or Bengal) nationalism, such as the University of Dacca, were attacked; Indian squatter areas were set on fire; and Mujibur himself was arrested and flown to West Pakistan. With the troops sweeping the countryside and with the non-Bengali vigilantes burning, looting, and raping, the exodus of millions to India began. Among those who escaped were many Awami League leaders who, in a symbolic ceremony just inside East Pakistan, set up a Bangla Desh (Bengal State) government and proclaimed East Pakistan independent. At the same time, India began to train guerrillas of the Mukti Bahini (Liberation Army).

Events now began to move swiftly. In the fall, Yahya Khan proscribed 79 of the Awami League's 167 Assembly members and ordered by-elections for December. He also announced that a team of experts would draft a new constitution by December 20. It was a futile move. On December 3, the Indian Army launched an all-out attack across the borders of East Pakistan. India's policy, which favored autonomy for East Pakistan, had been shrewd and carefully planned. The Indians had trained guerrillas in the spring and summer and, during the monsoon rains in July, had begun infiltrating them into Pakistan. Thereafter, the Indian Army had begun to exert pressure on the borders of East Pakistan, drawing the Pakistani Army away from the hinterland and thus enabling the guerrillas to have a free hand.

On December 16, the Pakistani Army surrendered, and India proclaimed East Pakistan a free territory. As a result of powerful civilian and military pressure, Yahya Khan resigned the presidency; his successor, Zulfikar Ali Bhutto, was sworn in on December 20. Sheik Mujibur Rahman, who remained under arrest in West Pakistan, was named president in absentia of Bangla Desh by his adherents, who clamored for his release.

Facts in Brief. Population: 135,455,000. Government: President Zulfikar Ali Bhutto. Monetary Unit: rupee. Foreign Trade: exports, $723,000,000; imports, $1,151,000,000. Principal Exports: textiles, jute, cotton.   Mark Gayn

PANAMA. United States jurisdiction over the Panama Canal Zone remained a major preoccupation of this Central American country in 1971. On October 11, General Omar Torrijos Herrera, the National Guard commander who rules Panama, declared the time might soon come "for one generation to offer its lives" to recover sovereignty over the U.S.-controlled zone.

Torrijos was referring to negotiations with the United States over an extension of the Panama Canal Treaty. These negotiations, which had lapsed in 1967, were resumed on June 29 in Washington, D.C. Panama was willing to give the United States full rights to operate and defend, as well as improve or supplement, the canal. But in return, it wanted a treaty with a fixed time limit, plus an increased share of the fees and total sovereignty over the entire zone. The United States was prepared to grant substantial territorial and commercial concessions, but it was reluctant to surrender all sovereignty.

By late fall, the positions of both nations had hardened to such an extent that an impasse appeared unavoidable. On October 5, Panama placed its case before the United Nations.

Facts in Brief. Population: 1,562,000. Government: Provisional Government President Demetrio B. Lakes. Monetary Unit: balboa. Foreign Trade: exports, $114,000,000; imports, $353,000,000. Principal Exports: bananas, shrimp.   Mary C. Webster

PAN AMERICAN GAMES. The United States won most of the medals and most of the gold medals in the Pan American Games in Cali, Colombia, in 1971. Cuba surprisingly finished second in total medals and gold medals.

The quadrennial Western Hemisphere competition, held July 30 through August 13, attracted 4,150 athletes from 30 national teams. Of the 194 gold medals in 24 sports, the United States won 105, Cuba 30, Canada 19, Brazil 9, Mexico 7, Argentina 6, Colombia 5, and Jamaica 4. Of the 595 total medals, the United States won 218, Cuba 105. Cuba had taken only eight gold medals in the 1967 Pan American Games, in Winnipeg, Canada.

The Cubans won 5 of the 8 gold medals in men's gymnastics, 4 of 10 in boxing, and 3 of 8 in fencing. In team sports, they won in baseball, men's volleyball, and women's volleyball. In track and field, Pedro Perez, their 19-year-old triple jumper, set a world record of 57 feet 1 inch.

The U.S. team won 20 of the 24 gold medals in men's track and field, 5 of 13 (Canada also took 5) in women's track and field, 16 of 17 in men's swimming and diving, 8 of 16 (Canada also took 8) in women's swimming and diving, all 6 in women's gymnastics, 19 of 32 in weight lifting, 9 of 12 in shooting, 7 of 10 in free-style wrestling, 5 of 8 in fencing, and all 3 in synchronized swimming.

Brazil won men's and women's basketball, and

Robert McAdoo of the United States took this rebound away from Cuba's Pedro Garcia, but the Cubans upset the U.S. basketball team in the Pan American Games.

PARAGUAY. The three-year old confrontation between the Roman Catholic Church and the state continued to smolder during 1971. The church constituted the only major opposition to the government, which had remained in the firm control of President Alfredo Stroessner for 16 years.

On February 27, the quarrel broke out into the open with the arrest of a Uruguayan priest, Uberfil Monzón, whom the government charged was connected with the Tupamaros guerrillas operating in Uruguay (see URUGUAY). Subsequently, Uruguayan Bishop Andrés Rubio García was attacked by a mob at Asunción airport when he flew in to secure the priest's release. Church authorities blamed members of the government for the mob action, and excommunicated 30 persons, including Interior Minister Sabino Montanaro. The government repudiated the excommunications and declared them "unconstitutional interference with the power of authorities to enforce civil laws."

In May, Paraguay declared a 90-day state of siege in Asunción and the provinces of Itapúa and Alto Paraná. It maintained that "international subversive organizations" were at work in the country.

Facts in Brief. Population: 2,531,000. Government: President Alfredo Stroessner. Monetary Unit: guaraní. Foreign Trade: exports, $64,000,000; imports, $76,000,000. Principal Exports: meat, timber, oilseeds.   Mary C. Webster

all three yachting classes. Soccer, rowing, and field hockey were dominated by Argentina, cycling by Colombia, and equestrian events by Canada.

In Men's Basketball, the U.S. team, composed mostly of lesser-known collegians, failed to gain the finals. The United States, Brazil, and Cuba—the three strongest teams—were grouped in the same preliminary round robin because of questionable seeding. Each finished with two wins and a loss, and only two could advance to the finals.

Entering the final preliminary game between Brazil and Cuba, those two would gain the finals (and the United States would be eliminated)only if Brazil beat Cuba by 5 points. Though leading in that game by 11 points with less than 2 minutes to play, Brazil won the game by exactly 5 points.

John Crosby, a gymnast from New Haven, Conn., won eight medals (two gold, five silver, one bronze). Frank Heckl, a swimmer from Los Angeles, won six gold medals and one silver. Roxanne Pierce of Kensington, Md., won three gold and two bronze medals in women's gymnastics. Francis Higginson of Placerville, Calif., won three gold medals in pistol shooting. Frank Shorter of Boulder, Colo., a distance runner, and Don Quarrie of Jamaica, a sprinter, won two track titles each. Perhaps the major upset of the games was the victory of Jack Howard, a soldier from Springfield, Mo., in the cycling road race, a Latin American specialty.   Frank Litsky

PARENTS AND TEACHERS, NATIONAL CONGRESS OF (PTA), reaffirmed its commitment to youth in 1971 by changing its bylaws to assure a greater role for young people in PTA planning and policy formulation. Five governing commissions were established, each including a member between 16 and 21 years of age. The five young people elected in 1971 are: David John Asai of Kahului, Hawaii, commission on leadership development; Carole Ann Chapman of Evansville, Ind., commission on education; Paul Corning of Seattle, commission on individual development; Christopher Davidson of Tabor, N.J., commission on membership, organization extension, and program services; and Kenneth Robinson of Nashville, Tenn., commission on health and welfare.

Delegates to the 75th annual convention held in Oklahoma City, in May, elected the following officers: Mrs. John M. Mallory of Endicott, N.Y., president; Mrs. J. M. Herndon of Columbia, S.C., first vice-president; Gilmore B. Seavers, who is president of Shippensburg (Pa.) State College, second vice-president; and also four regional vice-presidents.

Resolutions adopted by the convention included one that work be expanded with the Corporation for Public Broadcasting and with public broadcasting stations to complement and strengthen the educational process.   Joseph P. Anderson

461

PEACE CORPS. On March 1, 1971, the Peace Corps celebrated its 10th anniversary. Then, on July 1, the Peace Corps was incorporated into Action, a new antipoverty agency composed of several volunteer organizations. The Peace Corps retained its name and basic identity (see POVERTY). In November, 93 Peace Corps officials faced dismissal when Action director Joseph H. Blatchford announced strict enforcement of a rule limiting Peace Corps service to five years.

Almost 50,000 Americans had served as Peace Corps volunteers during its first 10 years. There were 8,535 Peace Corps volunteers and trainees in 1971, compared with 9,225 in 1970 and about 12,000 in 1969. There were 26,543 applicants for the Peace Corps in 1971, down from the 27,500 in 1970. A stepped-up recruiting campaign included an appeal for skilled and experienced workers.

Volunteers were serving in 56 countries during 1971, compared to the all-time high of 60 the previous year. Panama ended its agreement with the Peace Corps in February. It was the first Latin American country to do so.

The average Peace Corps volunteer was a college graduate, but the newly sought-after skilled recruits do not necessarily need degrees. Most volunteers were between the ages of 21 and 27.   William McGaffin

PENNSYLVANIA. See PHILADELPHIA; STATE GOVT.

PERSIAN GULF EMIRATES. Agreement on an amended federal constitution brought the Union of Arab Emirates close to formal existence in July, 1971. Six of the Trucial States signed the agreement on July 18, despite old antipathies between many of the rulers. Ras al Khaymah objected to the constitution, which would give veto rights over legislation to some of the member states, but not all of them. The federation consists of the emirates of Abu Dhabi, Ajman, Dubai, Fujaira, Sharja, and Umm al Qaiwain.

Great Britain then began to negotiate an alliance with the union to replace a patchwork of treaties with the Trucial States. Some dated back to 1820. British forces were to withdraw from the Persian Gulf in January, 1972.

Bahrain and Qatar, the largest and richest of the gulf states, rejected membership in the union, which was formalized on December 2 as the Union of Arab Emirates. Bahrain declared its independence in August, was admitted to the Arab League, and then became the 130th member of the United Nations (UN) on September 21. Qatar also declared its independence and joined the Arab League. The Sultanate of Oman became the 131st UN member on September 30.

An $82-million coastal road linking four federation members opened in October.   William Spencer

Persian Gulf States

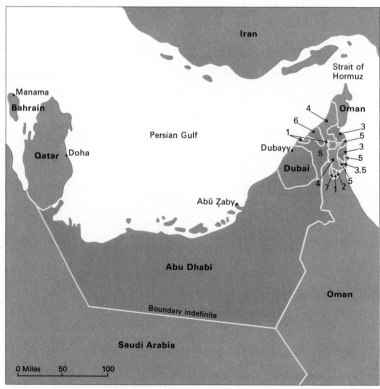

Federation of
Arab Emirates

Approximate areas of influence:
1. Ajman
2. Dubai
3. Fujairah
4. Ra's al Khaymah
5. Sharjah
6. Umm al Qaywayn
7. Ajman and Oman

PERSONALITIES OF 1971. For the third consecutive year, President Richard M. Nixon was the man most admired by Americans, according to the Gallup Poll. Others on the list of the 10 most admired men, in order: evangelist Billy Graham; Senator Edward M. Kennedy (D., Mass.); former President Lyndon B. Johnson, up from seventh in 1970; Senator Hubert H. Humphrey (D., Minn.), up from ninth in 1970; Vice-President Spiro T. Agnew; consumer advocate Ralph Nader; Pope Paul VI; Bob Hope; and Governor George Wallace of Alabama.

Dropped from the 1970 list were Senator Edmund S. Muskie (D., Me.), Governor Ronald Reagan, and former President Harry S. Truman.

Israeli Prime Minister Golda Meir was the most admired woman, replacing Mamie Eisenhower, who dropped to fifth. Mrs. Meir was followed in order by: Mrs. Nixon; Mrs. Joseph (Rose) Kennedy; Indian Prime Minister Indira Gandhi; Mrs. Eisenhower; Mrs. Aristotle (Jacqueline Kennedy) Onassis; Mrs. Lyndon (Lady Bird) Johnson; Mrs. John (Martha) Mitchell; Senator Margaret Chase Smith; and U.S. Representative Shirley Chisholm (D., N.Y.).

Dropped from the 1970 list were Mrs. Robert (Ethel) Kennedy, and Mrs. Martin Luther (Coretta) King.

President Nixon was also selected as "Man of the Year" by *Time* magazine.

Other Personalities in the news in 1971 included the following:

Bacall, Lauren, threatened to sue Pan American World Airways for using a photograph of her late husband, Humphrey Bogart, to advertise flights to Casablanca. The advertisements were captioned, "Play it again, Sam," the line Bogart made famous in the movie *Casablanca,* when he asked piano player Dooley Worth to play "As Time Goes By." "Is there no limit to what people will do to make a buck?" Miss Bacall asked. "Bogart didn't do this sort of advertising when he was alive, so why should they be able to make him do it when he is dead?"

Basksha, Ali Sabzei, of Khaveh, a village near Teheran, Iran, became the proud father of a daughter in 1971. Basksha, a farmer, claims to be 140 years old. The child was born to his third wife, Mah Soltan (Sultan of the Moon), 30. Basksha said that he hoped to have another child soon "as one child alone creates anxiety for the mother."

Beckett, Samuel B., the celebrated Irish author, poet, and playwright, who won the 1969 Nobel Prize for literature, was offered a rare opportunity to improve his writing skills. In March, he received a solicitation for correspondence study with the Famous Writers' School.

Bennet, Linda, of Heywood, England, was sent home when school authorities forbade her to wear hot pants to class. Linda's incensed father withdrew her from the school and hired a private tutor. Linda was 5 years old.

Bologna, Pat, 63, economic forecaster and the editor and publisher of *Yearly Market, Economic and Political Letter,* correctly predicted the summer Dow Jones industrial stock averages and other 1971 economic events. Among the 200 subscribers to his Xeroxed annual reports are bank presidents and managing partners of brokerage houses. But Bologna (pronounced ba LOH nya) does not work for a large brokerage house or a bank. He is the proprietor of a two-man,

FBI chief J. Edgar Hoover made his first public social appearance in three years in May at a dinner for Mrs. Martha Mitchell, wife of the U.S. attorney general.

five-chair shoeshine stand in the heart of Wall Street. According to *The Wall Street Journal,* the finger-stained economist is one of the most respected and authoritative experts on the Street. He is also reputed to give one of the best shoeshines in New York City. "I have an agreement with the brokerage industry," Bologna says. "If they promise not to shine shoes, I promise not to sell securities. Last year, they almost broke their promise."

Brand, Stewart, the youthful founder and editor of one of the most successful U.S. publishing ventures in recent years, *The Whole Earth Catalog,* published *The Last Whole Earth Catalog* in August. Its 447 crammed-full pages, priced at $5, sold nearly 500,000 copies. Brand explained he was ending the publication in order to open the way for a multitude of similar ventures. "Ideas we've had," he said, "and evaluations we've made are free for recycling." The catalogs provide information ranging from grinding your own grains to building geodesic domes.

Bulpitt, Stan, of Scarsdale, Conn., owns and operates probably the largest blender in the world—a 150-gallon-capacity machine that looks something like a concrete mixer. Bulpitt uses his blender to make compost. By grinding up kitchen scraps, discarded flowers, leaves, tree cuttings, newspapers, and other refuse, Bulpitt recycles these waste materials and provides an excellent soil conditioner. Bulpitt's machine, which has saved the town of Scarsdale about $43,000 annually, has earned him the title of "compost king."

Campos, Eddie, drove his $6,500 Continental Mark III onto the front lawn of the Ford Motor Company assembly plant in Pico Rivera, Calif., poured gasoline on it, and set it on fire. "I saved up for five years to buy that car new," Campos said, "and it turned out to be a lemon. I had it towed in for repairs 10,000 times and everybody just laughed at me—the dealers I took it to, the Ford people. I couldn't get any satisfaction." A deputy sheriff at the scene described Campos as "perfectly sober, perfectly rational, and completely disgusted."

Castro, Fidel, appeared at a sugar-cane cutting ceremony in Camagüey, Cuba, and promised he would cut his remarks short. "We are facing a very hot day," he said, observing that many persons had collapsed from the heat. "I promise you that I won't be very long." An hour and a half later, he began his closing remarks.

Dutka, Jacques, a Columbia University mathematician, performed what may be the most prodigious mathematical computation of all time in October. He calculated the square root of 2—that number which, when multiplied by itself, equals 2—to more than 1-million decimal places. His computations cover 200 tightly spaced computer printout pages. Dutka claims a practical use for his digits. The square root of 2, it seems, is an "irrational number," one that runs on in random fashion without any predictable pattern. Dutka's list is thus a "naturally occurring" series of random numbers, free of the subtle biases that might exist in other lists. Random numbers are useful for a wide variety of academic, military, and industrial applications. Next, Dutka says, he will tackle pi (3.14159....).

Elliott, Mama Cass, formerly of the Mamas and the Papas singing group, who married Donald von Wiedenman in June, remarked: "He's the first man I've met who has enough bread to support me." Wiedenman, whose nickname is "The Baron," works in a Los Angeles bakery.

Estes, Billie Sol, the Texas financial wonder who was sentenced to 15 years in prison in 1963, was paroled in July. Estes had been jailed for a scheme to extract money from farmers for nonexistent fertilizer tanks. "He was a real gentleman," said warden W. E. Zachem, speaking of Estes' six and one-half years at La Tuna federal prison in El Paso, Tex. Granted parole on the condition that he refrain from engaging in "promotional activities," Estes said, "Business and money are no longer my gods."

Fefferman, Charles L., a 22-year-old mathematician, in September became the youngest full professor in University of Chicago history. A mathematical genius who graduated from Princeton University with a Ph.D. at 19, Fefferman was appointed to the highest faculty rank with lifetime tenure. Fefferman's specialty is the Fourier analysis. "In my opinion, he is the best man to have appeared in the area of his specialty in the last 10 or 20 years," said Alberto Calderon, chairman of the department. The son of a Washington, D.C., economist, Fefferman entered Princeton at 14.

Feldman, Saul, told a September gathering of the American Sociological Association of a seldom-mentioned but widespread prejudice in the United States— heightism. Feldman, a Cleveland sociologist, said that the American male under 5 feet 8 inches tall is a victim of discrimination that is widely reflected in our society and even in our language. The question never is, "What is your height?" he explained, but, "How tall are you?" In addition, customers can be "short-changed," and persons who lack vision are "short-sighted." It is also reflected in our institutions, Feldman told the delegates. Motion pictures prefer tall leading men. A University of Pittsburgh study showed that recent business graduates over 6 feet 2 inches tall received higher starting salaries. And all presidential elections since 1900 have been won by the taller of the contenders. Feldman is 5 feet 4 inches tall.

Garr, John J., bought Podunk Center, Iowa, the most famous "hick town" in the United States, for

Baseball's Hall of Fame opened slowly for Satchel Paige. He was named to a special niche for old Negro league stars in February, won full membership in July.

$10,000 in January. The 1-acre town includes a gas station, a grocery store with a cafe, and a four-unit motel. Garr, the operator of a tavern and mail-order business in Hollywood, Calif., refused to disclose his plans for the town.

Gillespie, Dizzy, 53, announced in August that he would run for the presidency of the United States. If he wins, said the "bop" trumpet player, he will appoint Muhammad Ali as secretary of state because, "he has charisma, and a sincerity about his actions and his demeanor that will go very well in foreign affairs."

Graham, Bill, owner of the Fillmore East in New York City, a converted movie house that became the rock center of the United States, closed it and its sister, the Fillmore West in San Francisco, in June. Rock groups had become too greedy, he said. They were shunning his establishments to entertain in bigger sports arenas where they could make more money.

Gregory, Dick, stopped eating on April 24 to protest the war in Vietnam. Sticking to a strict liquid diet of about a gallon of water or fruit juice a day, and running 5 to 10 miles daily, the 38-year-old black comedian dropped from his normal 158 pounds to 117 in late June and expected to level off at about 70. "Everytime I see food now I think of the war," Gregory said. "That plate actually turns into Vietnam. I think of them cats on both sides who are hungry."

Hartford, Huntington, multimillionaire heir to the Great Atlantic and Pacific Tea Company (A & P stores) fortune, auctioned off most of his extensive art collection at New York City's Parke-Bernet Galleries in February. "I needed the cash," he explained.

Hoffman, Abbie, made the front pages again in 1971 when it was widely reported that he had his long hair cut. Hoffman, a defendant in the Chicago 7 conspiracy trial, told 1,500 Drew University students in Madison,

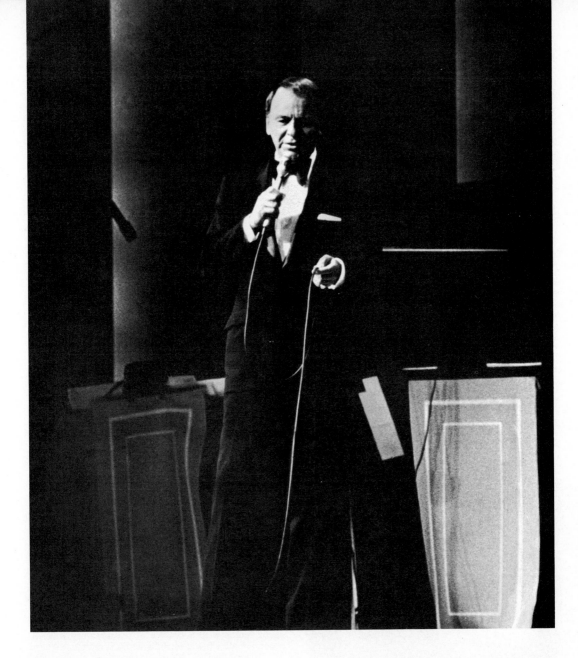

Frank Sinatra, 56, who announced his retirement in 1971, made it official with his last public appearance at the Los Angeles Music Center Pavilion on June 14.

N.J., that the current hip culture had become fraudulent. "Every time I turn on the television," he said, "I see movie stars with long hair. . . . The youth cult has been taken over by Warner Brothers and Columbia Records." *Life* magazine later reported it was all a hoax. Hoffman's abundant head of hair was still intact.

Meredith, James H., 38, who in 1962 became the first black to enroll in the University of Mississippi, announced in June that he was moving his family back to Mississippi from New York City. The South, he said, "on a person-to-person, day-to-day basis, is a more livable place for blacks. . . ."

Paukstys, Victoria, 16, a senior at Austin High School in Chicago, received the Outstanding Teen-Ager of the Year award for her discovery of a new blood-identifying process. She used a lima bean extract that requires no refrigeration and is cheaper than serums now used. Her process may turn out to be a significant contribution to blood banks throughout the United States. Victoria began work on her project when she was in the eighth grade.

Perelman, S. J., a well-known humorist, completed a trip around the world in 80 days when he returned to London's Reform Club, his starting point, on May 24. Perelman set off with his secretary on March 5 to emulate the famous journey of Phileas Fogg in the Jules Verne classic novel *Around the World in 80 Days*. The first letter Perelman opened upon his return was a notice from the Reform Club membership committee that he was behind in his dues.

Plimpton, George, author and sportsman, admitted to a strange new obsession in 1971. He is totally convulsed by the Cookie Monster on television's "Sesame Street." "He's marvelous," said Plimpton. "You always know exactly what he's going to do—consume something." Plimpton was not the only adult fascinated by one of the show's characters. *The Wall Street Journal* reported that Captain Daniel Nichols, an Army helicopter pilot decorated for guiding his ship through crippling Viet Cong fire, explained: "I owe it all to clean living and my Rubber Duckie, sir."

Satin, a 1-year-old cat, disappeared from a motel in Illinois while the Tiala family was moving from Towanda, Pa., to Forest Lake, Minn. Giving her up for lost, the Tialas continued on to their new home. Eleven months later, Mrs. Tiala received a call from an old Towanda neighbor. Satin had returned there—an 880-mile journey across four states.

Sutton, Willie, claimed to be the best example of the adage that crime does not pay. The famous bank robber, who was freed from prison in 1970, told a meeting of ex-convicts in New York City in 1971 that he had taken more than $200,000 and had nothing to show for it. "The money I stole never did me any good," he said. He urged the ex-convicts to consider "on-the-level" ways of earning a living.

Tolvish, Steve, was always at home to callers. For a time, he had the only residence in Philadelphia that was taller than it was wide or long—and had a folding door. A former mailer for a printing firm, but unemployed at the time, Tolvish, 54, lived in a telephone booth. He stored his belongings in a suitcase on top of the booth, and, as might be expected under the circumstances, he slept standing up. He also was occasionally interrupted. "When people wanted to use the phone,"

Long-time screen star Gloria Swanson, who began her career in the early 1920s, joined the all-new cast of long-running Broadway hit *Butterflies Are Free* in 1971.

he said, "they knocked on the door. I woke up and got out." Later, a benefactor found more normal accommodations for Tolvish after a newspaper described his plight.

Toy Token Tom, an 8-inch worm from Surrey, England, won the Brighton Worm Prix in March by scooting across the 2-foot course in a record-setting 1 minute 7 seconds. At two-hundredths of a mile per hour, Toy Token Tom was clearly the fastest worm alive. He topped the previous record, held by the late Wippie Willie, by more than a minute. Tom's owner, a toy company executive, attributed Tom's speed to a "secret diet."

Trudeau, Pierre Elliott, Canadian prime minister, shook hands with Secretary of the Treasury John B. Connally soon after being introduced by President Richard M. Nixon at the White House in December and quipped, "I'll count my fingers."

Vitek, Robert, 19, was sentenced by a municipal judge in Cleveland to spend three hours with four hogs and eight piglets for calling a policeman a pig. The pigpen sentence was in lieu of 30 days in jail. Surprisingly, Vitek was happy with the ruling. "I don't think the court could have made a better decision," he said. "I'm no hippie radical."

Yasgur, Max, put his farm up for sale in 1971. Located in the rolling Catskills, 90 miles upstate from New York City, Yasgur's 660-acre dairy farm became a part of the national folklore as the site of the Woodstock Music and Art Fair in August, 1969. Yasgur's farm, where an estimated 300,000 to 500,000 rock fans spent a three-day weekend that became immortalized as the Woodstock Nation, was put up for sale in November at $1,000 an acre. The farm contains two ponds that were referred to by *The National Observer* as "the twin skinny-dipping capitals of the world."   Allan Davidson

Happiest personality of the year was the ubiquitous "Smiley," whose radiance beamed from T-shirts, hats, purses, and other places too numerous to mention.

PERU. The revolutionary government headed by President Juan Velasco Alvarado pleaded with business for closer cooperation in 1971. The ruling generals apparently realized that the government's ambitious development programs, announced on July 28, could succeed only if the private sector, too, stepped up its investments.

In the background were an estimated 2 million persons who were either unemployed or underemployed. They represented 29.5 per cent of the work force, the highest figure in Peruvian history. The important mining companies were losing money, and production was down, seemingly because of endless labor conflicts. This, in turn, meant lower export earnings and reduced tax revenue for the republic. The regime wanted the support of private industry, and showed an inclination to crack down on outrageous labor demands for wages and benefits. It even appeared ready to risk a showdown with the Communist-dominated General Confederation of Peruvian Workers, which represented most of the miners and was pushing for immediate state seizure of all mining operations. Its demands, however, ran counter to the government's "gradualist" minerals policy, which called for service-contract arrangements on new production and a slow take-over of all mineral marketing by the state-owned mining company, Mineroperu.

In mid-October, Mineroperu officially became responsible for the marketing of all Peru's copper production, and while it completely controlled and handled all other minerals and metals exports, the actual take-overs still remained on a gradual basis. To underscore its desire to promote both public and private firms, the government set up the Financiera de Desarrollo corporation in March to channel local and foreign capital into private as well as public development schemes.

Up to midyear, the gross national product was rising at an annual rate of 3.5 per cent. The strongest areas were construction (up 18 per cent), government (10 per cent), and manufacturing (5 per cent). Fishing, however, declined by 30 per cent, while the added value of the mining sector receded 12 per cent. Because of labor disputes, generally weaker international commodity prices, and a lower level of fish meal shipments, exports between January and June dropped 24 per cent. Copper sales alone were off $67 million as compared to the same period in 1970. Imports, meanwhile, expanded 21 per cent, creating a serious balance of payments problem.

On November 3, Peru became the third Latin American nation to recognize China.

Facts in Brief. Population: 14,536,000. Government: President Juan Velasco Alvarado; Prime Minister Ernesto Montagne Sanchez. Monetary Unit: sol. Foreign Trade: exports, $1,044,000,000; imports, $603,000,000. Principal Exports: fish meal, copper, sugar.   Mary C. Webster

PET. Many breeders and sellers were accused in 1971 of misrepresenting inferior dogs as purebreds to eager buyers. The demand for dogs has increased greatly, and an estimated $300 million was spent on the purchase of dogs in 1971, with 8,000 pet shops and 75,000 breeders striving to meet the demand. Many buyers were defrauded, according to consumer advocates, because they erroneously equated pedigrees and registration papers with quality. Dogs may be registered with the American Kennel Club (AKC) even if they come from inferior breeding stock.

In some cases, registration papers were switched, according to Richard Beaucamp, editor of *Kennel Review*, who wrote: "Some unscrupulous breeders claim a bitch has 10 puppies in a litter when she only has 6. . . . They get four extra papers that they can sell or use for other dogs." Beaucamp advocated a government-backed dual registration system for dogs such as is used in Canada. A Canadian breeder can provide two kinds of certificates depending on the quality of the dog. Registered dogs in Canada must also have a nose print or tattoo on record to prevent puppy switching and theft.

The U.S. Department of Agriculture (USDA), in December, took the first steps under a new law to regulate dog sales. Breeders and dealers who sell dogs to pet shops and other breeders must now have federal licenses. The identity of a dog will be checked in this way by the USDA and minimum standards will be set for care and shipping. Pet shops or breeders that sell directly to the public are exempt from the law, however, which in effect weakens the reforming aspect of the law.

Dog Shows. A liver-and-white springer spaniel, Ch. Chinoe's Adamant James, owned by Milton Prickett of Lexington, Ky., took best-in-show honors at both the Westminster Kennel Club show in New York City in February and the International Kennel Club show in Chicago in April. The New York show had 3,031 dogs entered, and 3,649 were entered in Chicago. For the first time in the Westminster's 95-year history, a black standard schnauzer made it to the final judging by winning the working group. The dog, Ch. Pavo de la Steingasse, is owned by Mrs. Margaret S. Smith of Dallas. Black standard schnauzers are rare and usually do not have much quality. Veteran show observers could not recall one having won in any major U.S. dog show before, let alone the prestigious Westminster.

Cruft's, the world's largest show, drew 8,431 dogs in London in February. Best-in-show was taken by Ranacon Swashbuckler, a German shepherd, owned by Zada Ahmed Husain of London.

Breed Standings. Based on AKC registration figures, poodles were the most popular breed of dog in the United States for the 11th straight year. They were followed by German shepherds, dachshunds, beagles, miniature schnauzers, Saint Bernards,

Ch. Chinoe's Adamant James, springer spaniel, greets owner Milton Prickett, Lexington, Ky., after winning top honors at the Westminster Kennel Club show.

Irish setters, and collies. The Saint Bernards and Irish setters were newcomers to the top eight. Pekingese and chihuahuas dropped to 9th and 11th place. Labrador retrievers were 10th.

Trixie, a mixed-breed dog, was awarded the Ken-L Ration gold medal as Dog Hero of the year. In April, Trixie ran for help when her 2-year-old master Ricky Sherry of Lynn, Mass., tumbled into a pond. Then, she showed rescuers where Ricky was by swimming around him.

Cats. In its 1971 All-American awards, *Cats* magazine selected as *Cat of the Year* Lowlands Zeus of Lin-Lea, a cream Persian male owned by Ralph and Judy Beery of Duarte, Calif. Second best *Cat of the Year* was Glen Otty's Toshee, a black manx male owned by Ruth and Ellen Carlson of West Chicago, Ill. Chosen third best *Cat of the Year* was Madali Hi-Tone of Lee Crest, a seal point Siamese male, owned by Mrs. Fred L. Grew of Gibraltar, Mich. *Opposite Sex Shorthair of the Year* was Nile's Meresa V of Vel-Vet, a ruddy Abyssinian female owned by Georgia Morgan of Baton Rouge, La. *Opposite Sex Longhair of the Year* was Minnewaska's Kaia, a blue Persian female owned by Mr. and Mrs. Roy Vegoe of Glenwood, Minn. *Kitten of the Year* was Babalong Candy Cane of Kitwillows, owned by John Stevens of Richmond, B.C., Canada. *Alter of the Year* was Couer de Lion's Gwyn Ap Pawys' Rhys, owned by Kathryn C. Morgan. 　　　　　Theodore M. O'Leary

PETROLEUM AND GAS. Consumption of petroleum products grew by more than 4 per cent in 1971, or about 15 million barrels a day, and most estimates agreed that consumption would continue to increase by at least that rate through the 1970s.

The growing increase in the demand for oil led government officials, oilmen, and others to talk in 1971 of an "energy gap." Oil accounts for fully 43 per cent of the nation's energy needs—and natural gas from the oil fields supplies another 32 per cent. Conservationists worried that pressures for unlimited growth would not only create additional pollution problems, but also could eventually result in crippling shortages.

Industry spokesmen argued for higher prices and higher profits to finance expanded explorations for oil and natural gas. At midyear, the Federal Power Commission approved sharply higher prices for natural gas produced in the southern Louisiana area, the nation's major source of natural gas, and in the Rocky Mountain area. The commission said the increases were a "major step to deal with the critical shortage of natural gas in the United States." Consumer groups protested, claiming the new rates would mean increases of 5 to 6 cents per thousand cubic feet of gas.

Alaska Pipeline. It had been thought that the opening of the great North Slope discovery field on the Arctic Coast of Alaska would end U.S. worries about future sources of oil, but the social issues caught up with industry plans. Miles of four-foot-wide pipe lay rusting in Alaska while environmentalists battled in Congress and in the courts in 1971 to prevent the oil companies from building a 786-mile pipeline across Alaska to bring the North Slope oil to a shipping point at the southern Alaska port of Valdez.

In a suit filed on October 5, Eskimos, banding together as the Arctic Slope Native Association, filed a claim to the entire 76,000-acre North Slope area, included in 413,000 acres that had been leased by Alaska to private oil companies for nearly $1 billion. On December 14, a bill to settle natives' land claims passed Congress. It was signed by the President on December 18. The bill gave 40 million acres and $926.5 million to Alaska's 60,000 Eskimos, Indians, and Aleuts. The bill excluded from native acquisition, however, the 12-mile corridor set aside for the Alaskan oil pipeline. At year-end, the construction of the pipeline was being held up by various court and Administration actions. A settlement of the dispute with the natives and with conservation groups did not appear to be in the immediate offing.

Other Sources of natural gas and oil deposits were being sought with increased vigor during the year. The Atomic Energy Commission set off another in its series of underground nuclear explosions in Nevada in June to determine if nuclear power can unlock new sources of natural gas. Also in June, a consortium of 33 oil companies began probing the Atlantic shelf region, seeking sedimentary rock formations that may indicate hidden deposits.

Foreign Sources. Africa and the Middle East account for 80 per cent of the known oil in the ground. Together with Indonesia and Venezuela, these areas supply 85 per cent of the oil exported from producing countries to consuming nations. Canada is the source of most of the rest of the world's exported oil. The United States receives the bulk of the oil that it imports from Canada and Venezuela.

Present scarcities of oil and future new sources played a key role in 1971 in an international power play that momentarily threatened both Europe and the United States with critical losses of supplies. The Middle East and North African nations could see that the great oil and gas discoveries being made in the North Sea might someday make Europe semi-independent of their oil. And Venezuela feared the same distant possibility of oil-income loss in the North Slope discoveries.

After a series of threats to cut off oil supplies, and repeated warnings and confrontations, the 10-nation Organization of Petroleum Exporting Countries wrung major concessions from the international oil companies. Venezuela immediately increased prices to U.S. buyers by 25 per cent – and the yearly 12 per cent increase in gasoline prices was certain to continue in Europe.   Edwin W. Darby

PHILADELPHIA elected a new mayor in 1971, and many observers predicted a new mayoral style for the city. Democrat Frank L. Rizzo was elected in November to succeed Mayor James H. J. Tate, who was ineligible to run for a third consecutive term. Rizzo, former Philadelphia police commissioner, has a reputation as "an exceedingly tough cop." As police commissioner, his philosophy of meeting "force with superior force" was credited with maintaining one of the lowest crime rates among the nation's 10 largest cities.

The voters, on November 2, also approved a $91-million bond issue to finance more than 100 improvement projects in the city. Included among the projects were water-supply and sewer-systems improvements and continuing improvements to Philadelphia International Airport.

The bond-issue referendum came in the midst of continuing concern over the costs of government. The city's schools have been in particular jeopardy. The city, at one point, considered reducing the length of the school year. While their costs have been increasing by from 15 to 20 per cent a year, the property tax base from which half the schools' revenue must come has been growing by only 1 per cent a year.

Transportation problems caused frustration in 1971. Plans for an expressway through the city were canceled, and an experiment with park-and-ride facilities failed. When the Delaware Bridge Authority provided park-and-ride facilities for commuters, auto traffic on the bridge was cut by less than 4 per cent. Even that minor improvement was seen as only temporary.

The Philadelphia Plan, a model scheme to increase the employment of blacks in the building trades, was beset by legal problems. The plan required that a certain percentage of jobs on all federally supported building projects be reserved for black workers. However, this was alleged to violate the ban on employment quotas contained in the 1964 Civil Rights Act. A lower court ruling dismissed the allegation, but that decision was appealed. Meanwhile, almost no progress was made toward increasing the number of black workers in the building trades.

The Philadelphia Bicentennial Corporation selected a site in August for the city's part of the nation's 1976 bicentennial celebration. It chose an area covering parts of Camden, N.J.; Philadelphia; and Pettys Island in the Delaware River.

The 1970 census-showed few population changes in the city. The nation's fourth largest city declined in population by 53,903 persons to a new total of 1,948,609. However, the metropolitan area population was up 10.9 per cent to 4,817,914 persons. There was a relatively small increase in Philadelphia's nonwhite population, which accounted for 34.4 per cent of the total in 1970.   J. M. Banovetz

PHILIPPINES. A hotly disputed off-year election in 1971 developed into one of the bloodiest in the 25-year history of the Republic of the Philippines. Between the start of the campaigning on July 9 and the closing of the polls on November 8, there were 206 known dead and 217 wounded.

Despite growing fears that the violence would escalate disastrously on election day, about 80 per cent of the electorate turned out to vote. In what was considered a severe setback for President Ferdinand E. Marcos and his ruling Nacionalista Party, the voters gave the Liberal Party 6 of the 8 senatorial seats at stake, for a total of 8 in the 24-seat Senate. Most of the 15,085 other municipal and provincial offices at stake, however, went to the Nacionalista Party, whose candidates were mostly unopposed.

Marcos Criticized. During the campaign, the Marcos Administration was accused of graft, corruption, and failure to control the runaway cost of living. President Marcos was accused, too, of planning to circumvent a constitutional limit of two terms by putting his wife Imelda up for the presidency in 1973. In addition, critics accused Marcos early in the campaign of using the threat of Communist subversion to suspend indefinitely the right of habeas corpus and of authorizing the police to search houses without warrants.

The suspension had been announced by Marcos on August 23, two days after 10 persons were killed and 74 wounded in a terrorist grenade attack on a Liberal Party rally in Manila. The government had identified the terrorists as Mao-Marxist members of the New People's Army, an antigovernment group operating out of central Luzon as an offshoot of the Marxist-oriented Hukbalahap guerrillas.

A Senate Committee, in a report issued on September 6 after a 12-month study, denied that there was a "clear and present danger of a Communist-inspired insurrection or rebellion." The immediate problem in central Luzon, the report said, was poverty, lawlessness, and corruption in government. On September 21, President Marcos modified his original order by restoring the guarantee against indeterminate detention in 39 of the republic's 65 provinces. The right of habeas corpus, however, remained suspended in Manila, parts of Luzon, and all of Mindanao Island.

A number of anti-American incidents occurred during 1971. On January 22, the headquarters of two U.S.-owned oil companies, Esso and Caltex, were damaged by bombs presumably thrown by members of the Philippines' People's Revolutionary Front. Later, on February 12, a bomb exploded on the grounds of the U.S. Embassy in Manila.

Facts in Brief. Population: 41,220,000. Government: President Ferdinand E. Marcos. Monetary Unit: peso. Foreign Trade: exports, $1,067,000,000; imports, $1,210,000,000. Principal Exports: wood, coconut products, sugar.   Paul C. Tullier

PHOTOGRAPHY. The year 1971 was one of dramatic upheaval in the industry, profession, and hobby of photography. The German camera industry, hard pressed by labor shortages, rising costs, and competition from Japan, retrenched. Voigtlander, one of the German manufacturers and the oldest active name in photography, went off the market. Zeiss-Ikon stopped producing cameras for amateurs, and put all its emphasis on professional equipment. Rollei moved much of its production to Singapore, where it would also produce lenses for Schneider and Zeiss, and lens shutters for Compur and Prontor. Japan, too, facing increasing labor costs, was building plants in less-developed areas of Asia, such as Hong Kong, Formosa, South Korea, and Singapore.

Everywhere, the photographic industry was facing public pressure to change its basic chemistry because of concern over pollution and the dwindling supply of silver. The already-feasible print-stabilization process, which requires no wash water, was extended by Kodak to industrial X-ray use. Perhaps the most promising note came from Edith Weyde, who had developed the silver-halide diffusion-transfer process for Agfa-Gevaert in 1941. She announced a new imaging system at Chicago's Photo-Expo '71 that uses minimal quantities of costly silver. Her photographic material would be processed by heat, without fixation or washing.

New Cameras. Heightened competition brought significant improvements in camera hardware. Leitz began producing an M5 Leica, the first rangefinder camera to have through-the-lens metering. Bell & Howell introduced a new Canon F1 35mm camera in an apparent move to break the Nikon's lead in the advanced-35mm market. By year's-end, Nippon Kogaku had announced the first new Nikon camera in 12 years, the F2.

Electronics and automation were applied to most new products. Many of these developments were already standard in home-movie cameras and in the great variety of moderate-priced cameras with non-removable lenses. Now they were applied to the more complex, higher-priced interchangeable-lens 35mm single-lens reflex cameras. The new Canon and Nikon models featured solid state electronic shutter-timing mechanisms that were more precise and more dependable, and had a broader range of speeds than the traditional mechanical escapement. Most medium-priced cameras and a few deluxe models had automatic electric-eye exposure control.

Nikon and Canon marketed electronic-flash cameras in which setting the camera focus automatically adjusted the lens aperture, and Polaroid devised a flash system in which the camera focus controlled louvers in front of the light. Most automatic flash units, however, used an ultra-speed photocell circuit to control the amount of current into the flashtube by measuring the light reflected from the subject.

Market Decline. For the professional photographer, however, all these improvements were offset by deterioration of his markets. A continued slump in advertising reduced the number of possible high-fee advertising-illustration jobs, and magazines, faced with reduced advertising revenues, moved away from picture-story articles. One of the two remaining large outlets for the photo-essay, *Look*, ceased publication. *Travel & Camera* also ceased publication, leaving only two major camera magazines, *Popular Photography* and *Modern Photography*. In efforts to fill the void, *Camera 35* doubled its schedule to become a monthly.

The dwindling outlets for photojournalism spurred amateur and professional alike to seek new outlets. The American Society of Magazine Photographers, facing drastic changes in the profession, took a new name, Society of Photographers in Communication, and opened its ranks to students. Galleries opened to display and sell prints.

Movie Cameras. On the movie front, Kodak introduced a new XL camera and Ektachrome 160 film, an 8mm combination for home movies by available light. At the other end of the motion-picture scale, the Imax cine-system achieved a $2\frac{1}{4}$ x $3\frac{1}{4}$ film size by running 70mm film through a camera and projector horizontally. Shown on a four-story concave screen in Toronto's Cinesphere, the system was hailed for its ability to project spectacular realism.

Rus Arnold

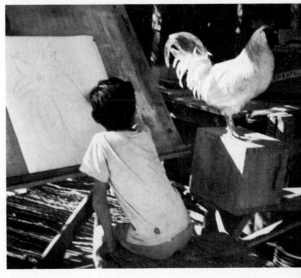

Among the award-winning photographs of 1971 were "Martha," *above*, taken by 16-year-old Emily Wheeler of Fairfax, Va.; an action shot of two teen-age surfers by Clarence Maki of Honolulu, Hawaii; and a picture of a boy trying to draw a rooster that insisted on continually "turning the wrong way," taken by Juan Manuel Diaz Almada of Mexicali, Mexico.

PHYSICS research produced few conclusive results of fundamental importance in 1971. Some work, however, offered exciting prospects for the future, and steady progress occurred in many areas.

Elementary Particles. A new look into the interactions between protons was provided by the successful operation of the intersecting storage rings (ISR) at the European Center for Nuclear Research (CERN) in Geneva, Switzerland. This instrument causes two beams of high-energy protons to collide almost head-on. In order to equal the energy thus made available for interactions, a conventional proton beam hitting a stationary target would have to be over a trillion electron volts in energy – some 20 times higher than present accelerators can provide.

In April, Carlo Rubbia of Harvard University presented results at the American Physical Society meeting in Washington, D.C., that he and an international team of scientists had obtained in the first studies of such interactions using the ISR. The range of the force between protons at the energies possible with this instrument departed sharply from the regular increase that had been observed with such interactions at lower energies. Clarification of why this is true will depend on further measurements with the ISR and with large accelerators now being built. The new accelerators will provide high interaction rates with dense stationary targets.

Nuclear Physics. In February, Amnon Marinov, an Israeli physicist, and a team of British collaborators announced evidence for the production of a super-heavy element having 112 protons in its nucleus. It is believed to be chemically similar to mercury. Such an element is of special interest because of theoretical predictions that nuclei containing this number of protons should decay slowly by emitting charged particles or by undergoing fission, unlike most other heavy nuclei, which decay rapidly.

Evidence for the new element was obtained by examining the fission fragments and the energy spectrum of alpha particles emitted by two tungsten blocks that had been irradiated by 24-billion-electron-volt protons in the CERN proton synchrotron. The scientists theorized that the high-energy protons that bombarded the blocks could have caused recoiling tungsten nuclei, or fragments thereof, to combine with other nuclei into objects that rapidly decay to element 112.

The announcement met with considerable skepticism from many physicists, largely because contaminants could have produced the observed effects. Nevertheless, nuclear laboratories throughout the world made plans to look for the new element in materials that have been heavily bombarded at a high-energy accelerator. A considerable amount of detailed study of nuclear interactions is being carried on using heavy-ion accelerators, and this technique is likely to produce the most extensive systematic study of superheavy nuclei.

Solids. Fundamental understanding of the physical properties of solid matter depends on knowing how energy is distributed among the atoms of which it is composed. In crystalline solids, the regular array of atoms that is repeated many times to make up the crystal lattice is a special object of study. Theoretical physicists who study solids frequently treat the crystal lattice mathematically in a simplified fashion – because such simplifications adequately describe the experimental data, and because of limitations in mathematical technique.

In April, Rodney J. Baxter of the Australian National University in Canberra published the results of a solution to the so-called "eight vertex model" of a crystal lattice. Here the lattice is visualized as a square array of atoms, each forming the vertex for the eight possible even number of couplings to the four nearest neighbor atoms. Cubic lattices such as those of ice crystals fit this model.

Baxter found that near the critical temperature where magnetic properties of the lattice change, thermal properties depend in a special way on how the energy at the vertex varies with the coupling configuration. Until now, scientists always believed that such a dependence could be ignored. Baxter's work will no doubt motivate experimentalists to take a more careful look at how real three-dimensional solids behave.   Thomas O. White

PLASTICS. See CHEMICAL INDUSTRY.

POETRY. The world of poetry experienced no major events in 1971. It seemed, after the change-filled 1960s, as if American poets needed a respite, a period of stocktaking and reassessment. The effects of the 1960s were obvious everywhere, especially in the extreme proliferation of a poetic style based on the free rhythms and natural phrasings of William Carlos Williams and his imitators. Indeed, the style, which had seemed innovative 10 years earlier, was now so common, its diction and verse were so predictable, that complaints of monotony were voiced, and observers predicted a new change, perhaps toward a revived traditionalism.

Yet, for the present, the common style prevailed. Even so stalwart an elder conservative as Stanley Kunitz published a book, *The Testing Tree*, in which he abandoned traditional rhyme and meter for the popular free forms. It seemed less a personal capitulation than another sign of the implacable Americanization of poetry. This was confirmed in virtually all the thousands of "little magazines."

In part, these versifying multitudes of new poets were products of the expanded poetry-writing classes in colleges and universities. But, more basically, they represented the liberalization and decommercialization of American culture that started in the 1960s and was gathering steam in the 1970s. The combined effect has been to turn more and more young people to poetry and other arts.

The Golden Cache of Ogden Nash

I don't mind eels
Except as meals.
*And the way they feels.**

These somewhat less than immortal lines are typical of the "slightly goofy and cheerfully sour" work of America's best-known practitioner of zany verse, Ogden Nash, who died on May 19, 1971, at the age of 68. For more than 40 years, the tall, courtly poet poked fun at human foibles with his witty, unconventional, often preposterous rhyming schemes and his wry sense of satire. In the process, he admittedly "maltreated and mishandled every known rule of grammar, prosody, and spelling."

He wrote mainly about "the minor idiocies of humanity," which meant that he was never at a loss for material. Like a fellow Baltimorean, H. L. Mencken, Nash found much that was funny among the pretensions and poses of man. But, unlike Mencken, his humor was always gentle and whimsical, never malicious.

His last poem, submitted to *The New Yorker* magazine shortly before he died, was about Henry Henley, who dreamed of becoming a great navigator but who
. . . as a courting swain on the
lake in Central Park
attempted simultaneously
to row and woo,
Thereby achieving temporary fame
as the only adult unaccompanied
by a child to ground his
boat in the Children's Zoo.†
Henry's plight ("You Steer and I'll Toot") was the 353rd poem Nash had submitted to the magazine. The first, written while he was an advertising copywriter, appeared on Jan. 11, 1930:
I sit in an office at 244 Madi-
son Avenue,
And say to myself you have a
responsible job, havenue?
He wrote all his verse in longhand on yellow lined paper. "Sometimes," he said, "a poem is suggested by some human foible, and sometimes by the play on words. I'm very fond of the English language. I tease it, and you tease only things you love."

Anyone who could explain that Captain John Smith did not belong to B'nai B'rith; or that two pints still make one cavort; or that, to a baby, a bit of talcum is always walcum, must have loved the language very much.

In his poem—"A Brief Guide to Rhyming *or* How Be the Little Busy Doth?"—he offered a defense:
English is a language than which
none is sublimer,
But it presents certain
*difficulties for the rhymer.**
Nash was born in Rye, N.Y., in 1902 into a family that traced its forebears back to pre-Revolutionary days. Nashville, Tenn., was named for an ancestor. He attended St. George's School in Newport, R.I., and then became a "quarter-bred Harvard alumnus," dropping out after his freshman year to earn a living. After brief and unhappy trials as a teacher, a bond salesman, and an advertising copywriter, and a fling at serious "poetry" about "beauty, truth, and eternity," he began to write his nonsensical verse.

In a career that spanned four decades, Nash authored some two dozen books of poems, including *I'm a Stranger Here Myself, You Can't Get There from Here,* and numerous children's books, among them *The Untold Adventures of Santa Claus.* In 1943, he collaborated with S. J. Perelman and Kurt Weill on a hit Broadway musical, *One Touch of Venus.* Later, he wrote verses for composer Camille Saint-Saëns' *Carnival of Animals,* and Sergei Prokofiev's symphonic fairy tale *Peter and the Wolf.*

In 1931, Nash married Frances Rider Leonard, about whom he wrote:
There are people I ought to wish I was;
But under the circumstances,
I prefer to continue my life as me—
*For nobody else has Frances.**
In a poem that appeared in *The New York Times* shortly after his death, fellow poet Judith Viorst offered this tribute:

And how shall we explain to
a generation communing
in communes with macro-
biotic foods and pipes full
of hashish
That the world has become a
far far better world for having
become a little Ogden
Nashish?††   Allan Davidson

Ogden Nash

Black Poets. Perhaps the most difficult new development to appraise is the explosive emergence since 1967 of radical black poetry. The catalyst in the early 1960s had been LeRoi Jones. As poet, dramatist, and critic, he had insisted that black writers align themselves with radical activists under the banners of Malcolm X, the Muslims, and the Black Panthers. As early as 1965, Jones proclaimed: "Only a united black consciousness can save black people from annihilation at the white man's hands."

After the killings of Martin Luther King, Malcolm X, George Jackson, and others, the point seemed forceful. Following Jones, such poets as Don L. Lee (*We Walk the Way of the New World*), Sonia Sanchez (*We a BaddDDD People*), David Henderson (*De Mayor of Harlem*), Lucille Clifton (*Good Times*), Nikki Giovanni (*Black Feeling, Black Talk, Black Judgment*), Etheridge Knight (*Poems from Prison*), Audre Lorde (*Cables to Rage*), and Mari Evans (*I Am a Black Woman*) took up the work of defining and cultivating black consciousness.

An important factor in their work was the Broadside Press in Detroit, established and operated by Dudley Randall, an elder black poet whose own writing had been decidely tame compared with the work of the younger poets he befriended. So central to radical black consciousness did his Broadside Press become that another elder poet, Pultizer Prize-winner Gwendolyn Brooks, renounced her New York publisher and declared she would give all her work to Broadside. At the same time, younger poets who had been published first by Broadside were reaching out through new magazines and publishing houses, and the number of poets in the radical black movement increased to the hundreds, even thousands. The movement was helped by two important anthologies—*The New Black Poetry* (1969), edited by Clarence Major, and *We Speak as Liberators* (1970), edited by Orde Coombs. Its unifying and inspiring effect among black radicals was undeniable, but its ultimate poetic meaning, especially in terms of its stridency and extremes of verbal experimentation, was harder to judge.

Other Books. Meanwhile, other important books of the year were *The Will to Change*, by Adrienne Rich, and *The Book of Nightmares*, by Galway Kinnell. The writing of these two established poets, in its integration of personal and political, metaphysical and radical themes, represented the flowering of the movement of the 1960s. Indeed, some critics believed that this new naturalness in combining social and cultural values had been unknown in Western literature since the time of Dante or Villon. It brought to a culmination in total human relevance the process begun some 50 years earlier by Ezra Pound when he forced, often awkwardly, the yoking of cultural history and modern economics in his *Cantos*.   Hayden Carruth

See also AWARDS AND PRIZES.

POLAND abandoned ambitious but unrealistic planning in 1971 and embarked on a moderate reform course under its new Communist Party leader, Edward Gierek. The new government acted quickly to end the strikes that caused the fall of Gierek's predecessor, Wladyslaw Gomulka, in December, 1970. Family allowances and pensions were substantially increased in January. On February 15, the food price increases that started the strikes and rioting were canceled. A large Russian loan made these concessions possible.

Prices of meat and milk products were raised on March 19 to stimulate agricultural production. In April, the government promised to abolish by the end of 1971 the unpopular compulsory deliveries to the state by farmers of meat, potatoes, and grain. In the interest of what Gierek called "harmonious development," most industrial plan targets were drastically cut back. A new version of the 1971 five-year plan recognized consumer demands. It provides for a shift of investment toward consumer goods output, a substantial growth in real incomes, the construction of more housing, and more funds for previously neglected services.

The Purge of many old and unpopular trade union and party leaders from Gomulka's administration improved factory morale. The demotion of the hard-line General Mieczyslaw Moczar in June was followed by a purge of his supporters and other hard-liners.

But, despite the talk of restoring the role and authority of the Sejm (legislature) and giving nonparty members a bigger role in running the country, Gierek trod warily in the political field.

Gierek's governing style, involving frequent face-to-face meetings with the people, appeared to be popular. So did the cautious reconciliation with the Roman Catholic Church. The most tangible gain in this change was the legal rights of possession to church-owned land in the former German territories. The transfer was made on September 1. The successes led Premier Piotr Jaroszewicz to claim on September 20 that the party had "won general and active support for its policy." Gierek appeared to enjoy full Russian support, and responded with repeated assurances of Polish loyalty to the Warsaw Pact and to COMECON, the East European trade union. Poland also moved toward closer cooperation with Czechoslovakia and East Germany. But it continued to keep its economic lines to the west open, hoping to attract capital investment.

Facts in Brief. Population: 33,541,000. Government: Communist Party First Secretary Edward Gierek; State Council Chairman Józef Cyrankiewicz; Premier Piotr Jaroszewicz. Monetary Unit: zloty. Foreign Trade: exports, $3,547,000,000; imports, $3,607,000,000. Principal Exports: coal, meat, ships and boats.   Chris Cviic

POLLUTION. See ENVIRONMENT.

POPULATION, WORLD. The human race multiplied at an unprecedented pace in 1971. By the end of the year, the United Nations (UN) estimated the world's population at approximately 3.74 billion. More than 73 million people had been added during the year, the greatest annual increase ever recorded.

Since 1951, the world population has increased by 1.25 billion persons. There were 2.5 billion persons in 1951 increasing at the rate of 25 million a year. But, as of 1971, an estimated 1 billion persons are being added every 15 years. At this rate, UN experts predict a world population of 5 billion by 1985 and more than 6 billion by the year 2000.

Critical Areas. More than 80 per cent of the births recorded in 1971 were in the developing countries in Africa, Asia, and Latin America. The latest statistics available from the United Nations revealed that Latin America has the highest rate of population growth, about 3 per cent a year. However, Asia leads all other areas of the world in sheer numbers, adding about 48 million persons a year.

India's 1971 census showed it now has a population of 547 million. This represents an increase of almost 108 million persons, or 24.6 per cent, since 1961. At the present 2.4 per cent annual rate of increase, India will have a population of 1 billion by the year 2000, almost double the present count.

The populations of the developing countries double every 20 to 30 years. However, in the more advanced nations, the populations double only every 70 to 175 years. The United States had a sharp decline in the rate of population growth in 1971. According to a National Fertility Study released by Princeton University in November, the total fertility rate (the number of children per woman of childbearing age) dropped to 2.2 during July and August, almost the "zero population growth" level. However, to achieve "zero population growth," the total fertility rate would have to continue at 2.11 for about 70 years. The National Center for Health Statistics reported that the general fertility rate (the number of children per 1,000 women of child-bearing age) fell about 12 per cent between February and July to 77.5, reflecting a decline in the U.S. birth rate. See VITAL STATISTICS.

Birth-Control Programs. By 1971, 23 nations had official family-planning programs. Unofficial support was given to birth-control programs by 15 other nations. The U.S. Congress appropriated $100-million in 1971 for worldwide research and population-control programs. The U.S. Department of Health, Education, and Welfare estimated that from $224 to $272 million in federal and private funds were used for population research and family-planning programs that were conducted in the United States in 1971.

The UN Fund for Population Activities grew from $4 million in 1969 to $35 million in 1971. The United States pledged $12.5 million. Robert C. Cook

PORTUGAL. The National Assembly enacted into law in August, 1971, a package of liberalizing reforms proposed by Prime Minister Marcello Caetano. They included a new press law, reforms guaranteeing freedom of worship for religious minorities, and constitutional changes giving overseas possessions more autonomy.

Editors had reservations about the press law, however. It abolished censorship, but provided up to two years in prison for publishing stories against the "common good" or "national interest." Journalists' Union secretary Antonio dos Santos, one of the law's strongest critics, was arrested in August and held without charge or access to legal advice. A month earlier, Daniel Cabrita, secretary of the bank clerks' union, who protested the makeup of a union delegation, was also arrested and held without formal charges. On July 26, armed police broke up a march by bank clerks protesting Cabrita's arrest.

In June, the Portuguese hosted a meeting of the North Atlantic Treaty Organization's Ministerial Council. United States Vice-President Spiro T. Agnew visited Portugal on July 26.

Facts in Brief. Population: 9,820,000. Government: President Américo Deus Rodrigues Thomaz; Prime Minister Marcello Caetano. Monetary Unit: escudo. Foreign Trade: exports, $946,000,000; imports, $1,556,000,000. Principal Exports: textiles, wine, fish. Kenneth Brown

POSTAL SERVICE. In a sweeping postal reform, the corporate-style U.S. Postal Service replaced the 182-year-old Post Office Department on July 1, 1971. The government-owned, but independent, authority was created by the Postal Reorganization Act of 1970. The Postal Service has the power to appoint postmasters and fix postal rates and pay.

A Board of Governors, appointed by President Richard M. Nixon, chose Winton M. Blount to be its chairman and the Postal Service's first postmaster general. Blount was also the last of 62 postmasters general to serve under the old Post Office Department. In late October, he resigned, expecting to run for the U.S. Senate from Alabama in 1972. Merrill A. Hayden was appointed acting postmaster general.

Collective bargaining with the postal unions became the new method of setting pay. The first union contract was signed on July 20.

Better Service Promised. Various plans designed to increase efficiency and provide faster service were set into operation. Blount made a commitment guaranteeing overnight delivery of 95 per cent of all air-mail letters addressed to cities within a 600-mile radius. He promised to deliver, by the following day, 95 per cent of local first-class mail deposited before 5 P.M.

Blount also initiated a bulk-mail system consisting of 33 specially designed, automated plants to handle parcel post. The plants were scheduled for completion in 1975. A preferential-mail network, which will process letters automatically, was expected to be in full operation by 1976.

In May, a postal rate increase raised the cost of a first-class stamp from 6 cents to 8 cents and an air-mail stamp from 10 cents to 11 cents. The rate on first-class post cards went from 5 cents to 6 cents; on air-mail post cards, from 8 cents to 9 cents.

The U.S. Postal Service handled 87 billion pieces of mail in the fiscal year that ended June 30, compared with 84.8 billion the previous fiscal year. It employed about 729,000 persons and operated almost 32,000 local post offices.

Other Major Developments:

• The position of Postal Consumer Advocate was established to help customers with problems.

• Indictments were brought against 54 commercial pornography dealers in fiscal 1971, and 23 of them were convicted.

• After a new antipornography law went into effect on February 1, complaints about the receipt of sexually oriented mail dropped 41 per cent. A householder now can stop all sexually oriented advertising from coming through the mails to his home by filling out a form at his local post office.

• Airport security was tightened to protect valuable registered air-mail shipments. A Postal Service security force was also created to protect postal buildings and employees and to reduce thefts.   William McGaffin

POVERTY. A report issued in 1971 showed that the number of poor people increased in 1970 for the first time since the Bureau of the Census began keeping such records in 1959. The bureau said that the number of Americans below the poverty level increased from 24.3 million in 1969 to 25.5 in 1970. The poverty level is based on the Social Security Administration's classification, which covers nonfarm households where total income is less than $1,954 for an individual, $2,525 for a couple, and $3,968 for a family of four.

The report showed that more than 30 per cent of those in poverty are Negroes. About 9 per cent are persons of Spanish-speaking background, and about 60 per cent are other whites.

The study also showed that the poverty population is growing faster in the suburbs than in the cities. Metropolitan areas accounted for about 90 per cent of the 1.2 million increase of persons living in poverty in 1970. The central cities' poverty population grew by 400,000 to a total of 8.2 million. The one-year increase in the suburbs, meanwhile, exceeded 650,000 – reaching a total of 5.2 million. Thus, about 30 per cent of the nation's poor now live in the central cities, and about 21 per cent live in the metropolitan areas surrounding them.

A New Agency. In a move to consolidate government voluntary-action programs, President Richard M. Nixon proposed a new agency, on March 24, that

would administer the following programs: Volunteers in Service to America (VISTA), auxiliary and special volunteer programs in the Office of Economic Opportunity (OEO), the Foster Grandparents Program, the Retired Senior Volunteer Program (RSVP), the Service Corps of Retired Executives (SCORE), and the Active Corps of Executives (ACE). The President said the new agency would be called Action.

Mr. Nixon explained that his major purpose was to enlarge the role of voluntary action on community problems. The new agency would assign volunteers to work under the technical supervision of other federal, state, and local agencies and private sponsors. The services of local part-time volunteers would be sought, and they would be assisted, when necessary, by full-time volunteers.

The U.S. Senate and the House of Representatives approved the plan for the new agency, and it was established on July 1. President Nixon named Joseph H. Blatchford as director of Action. At the time of his appointment, Blatchford was serving as director of the Peace Corps. The President also announced that as of July 1 the functions of the Peace Corps, VISTA, and several other volunteer service agencies had been merged under the agency. The final component of the reorganization plan calls for legislative action to transfer the Teachers Corps, now under the Office of Education, to the new agency.

Role for VISTA. Under the reorganization plan, VISTA will continue to play the major role in providing full-time volunteers in domestic antipoverty programming. Since January, 1965, more than 2,000 persons have served on a full-time basis as VISTA volunteers in 1,000 communities. The VISTA volunteers have come from every age group and every walk of life. About 8 per cent have been over 50 years of age, 22 per cent have had a high school education, and 22 per cent have had professional skills. They have worked with local residents in obtaining services, in defining objectives, and in mobilizing neighborhoods to focus on specific problems. The experience of the VISTA program will form the heart of the domestic program in Action.

OEO Program Development. A complete review was undertaken of all OEO programs in 1971, with the view of weeding out unsuccessful projects and those that have achieved their objectives. As a result, a substantial number of projects were terminated or re-funded for the last time. Funds freed by the termination of projects and additional new funds were concentrated in a variety of new experimental and demonstration programs.

In community development, the major new approaches were in programs for the Spanish-speaking poor and in housing. A series of steps were taken to provide opportunities for higher education to promising Spanish-speaking youth, to train indigenous

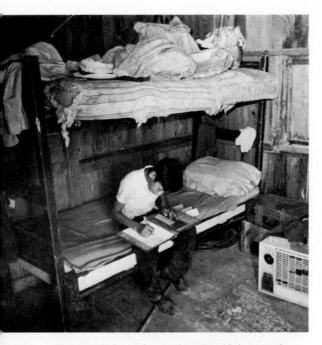

The son of migrant farmworkers does his homework in a bedroom he shares with his brother and parents in a two-room, $17-a-week shack near Miami, Fla.

informational services, including health, nutrition, homemaking, and child care.

■ That the print media acknowledge their obligation to the entire public by regularly publishing listings of the informational services offered by government, nonprofit, and other public interest organizations in fields such as nutrition and health.

■ That industry and trade associations conduct programs to educate the public, especially the poor.

■ That strong support be given to any nondiscriminatory means by which the poor and disadvantaged can secure more convenient low-cost access to information services and extension education.

United Nations Volunteers. After months of planning and debate, the United Nations General Assembly voted to establish an international corps of men and women to work in developing countries. The new agency will be called United Nations Volunteers (UNV). A provisional UNV office was opened in New York in January, 1971.

For the first year, most volunteers will be assigned to existing United Nations projects in developing countries. The volunteers will be recruited by their individual countries, with each country covering the costs of recruiting, selecting, and transporting them to their assignments and back home again. The United Nations and the host government will pay the allowance for volunteers during their tours of duty.   Joseph P. Anderson

POWELL, LEWIS FRANKLIN, JR. (1907-   ), was confirmed as an associate justice of the Supreme Court of the United States by an 89-to-1 vote in the Senate on December 6. Powell filled one of the vacancies created by the retirement of justices Hugo L. Black and John M. Harlan in September.

Powell was born on Sept. 19, 1907, in Suffolk, Va. He earned his bachelor's and law degrees at Washington and Lee University in 1931, and a master's degree at Harvard University in 1932. In 1932, he joined the Richmond law firm of Hunton, Williams, Gay, and Gibson, one of the oldest in Virginia. In 1964, he served as president of the American Bar Association.

Powell brings to the Supreme Court the Southern voice that President Richard M. Nixon had sought. That voice, however, is more of the "new South" than the old. In 1959, for example, while serving on the Richmond school board, Powell calmly helped to integrate the city's schools. While the integration issue raged in other Virginia towns, Richmond schools integrated without a single school closing. But Powell has remained unswerving in the middle of the road. On one hand, he said that "wealth, social position, and race . . . affect the standards of justice available." On the other, he feels that demonstrators go beyond constitutional rights of free speech and petition "by occupying buildings and tying up traffic in the streets."   Michael Reed

leaders and resource mobilizers, and to create a variety of technical-assistance institutions that are necessary to provide central direction and leadership to local programs.

The OEO created a national housing development center that provides a central computerized revolving fund to ensure maximum use of all funds provided by state, regional, and local housing development corporations. The national center also provides a core-training and technical-assistance resource to strengthen existing corporations and promote the establishment of new ones.

Advertising Impact on the Poor. The Federal Trade Commission (FTC) received a statement by OEO Communications Director William Sharp outlining the special needs of the poor and disadvantaged for assistance from the advertising media and advertisers. Sharp said studies have shown that the poor and disadvantaged get most of their information, news, entertainment, product information, and education from the advertising-supported mass media. Studies have also revealed that, due to conditions beyond individual control, the poor are the least trained or prepared to deal with the impact of modern advertising and advertising media on their lives.

Sharp submitted the following recommendations:

■ That radio and television stations be required to reserve 3 to 5 per cent of their total programming for

PRESIDENT OF THE UNITED STATES

Richard Milhous Nixon shifted course dramatically in 1971 to meet the challenge of inflation at home and the demands of shifting power blocs overseas. An economic conservative who dislikes government intervention, he adopted wage and price controls to check the disastrous combination of rising prices and growing unemployment. A strong anti-Communist, he accepted an invitation to visit mainland China, supported the admission of China to the United Nations (UN), and began preparations for visits to Peking in February and Moscow in May, 1972.

The New Economic Policy. During the first half of 1971, the President repeatedly urged industry and labor to follow voluntary guidelines for curbing inflation. On April 13, the President's Council of Economic Advisers issued its third "inflation alert," warning of rising prices. On June 29, he named Secretary of the Treasury John B. Connally as his chief economic adviser.

Meeting with representatives of the major steel companies and the steelworkers on July 6, he urged them to negotiate a "constructive contract settlement." Despite his plea, the United Steelworkers of America on August 1 negotiated a three-year contract providing an average annual wage increase of more than 30 per cent. The major steel companies then announced that prices on almost all types of steel would rise an average 8 per cent. In a surprise move on August 15, President Nixon announced that he was taking drastic steps to curb inflation.

Acting under emergency powers extended by Congress, the President placed a 90-day nationwide freeze on all wages and prices, supervised by a Cost of Living Council. He ordered federal spending reduced by $4.7 billion. In addition, the President asked Congress to repeal the 7 per cent automobile excise tax and to establish a one-year, 10 per cent investment tax credit to stimulate the economy. He placed a four-month 10 per cent surcharge on most imports, and ended the American dollar's ties to gold.

In a Labor Day speech, the President urged Americans to dedicate themselves to "a new prosperity without war and without inflation." He

The President got a friendly welcome in Idaho Falls, Ida., soon after announcing the wage-price freeze. Most Americans approved of his new economic program.

stressed the need for increased productivity to stabilize the economy. On September 9, he told a joint session of Congress that he would not extend the freeze, which was known as Phase 1, but would take whatever steps were necessary to control inflation.

During Phase 1, the President set up the machinery for Phase 2, which began when the freeze ended on November 13. He established a 7-member Price Commission and a 15-member Pay Board under the Cost of Living Council. C. Jackson Grayson, Jr., was named chairman of the Price Commission; George H. Boldt became chairman of the Pay Board; Donald Rumsfeld was director of the Cost of Living Council. Phase 2 provided for average pay raises of no more than 5.5 per cent a year and average price increases of up to 2.5 per cent. See ECONOMY, THE; LABOR.

In a series of announcements in December, the President continued his economic surprises by agreeing to a formal devaluation of the dollar. See INTERNATIONAL TRADE AND FINANCE.

The New China Policy. On July 15, the President told a startled national television audience that he planned to visit China before May, 1972. For 21 years, the United States had refused to recognize the People's Republic of China and had opposed seating that government in the UN.

Arrangements for the trip to China were made by the President's adviser on national security affairs,

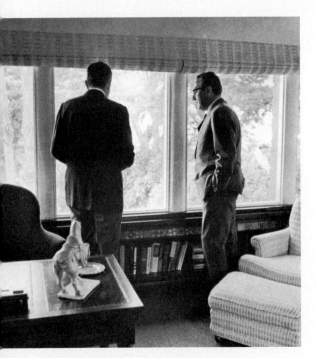

Henry A. Kissinger's first trip to China in July was one of the year's best-kept secrets. He reported on the trip to the President at the western White House.

Henry A. Kissinger. He made a secret trip to Peking in July on the President's behalf and another in October to make further arrangements for the presidential visit. On October 12, the White House announced that President Nixon also planned to visit Russia in 1972. The President scheduled meetings with the leaders of Canada, France, Great Britain, Japan, and West Germany, to take place earlier.

There had been signs earlier in the year that the Administration was softening its stand on China. The United States Table Tennis Association team was invited to visit China in April. During the period of "Ping-pong diplomacy" that followed, a special presidential commission headed by Henry Cabot Lodge recommended that the United States support China's admission to the UN. Then on June 10, the President announced the end of a 20-year trade embargo against the Chinese.

On September 16, the President declared that the United States would vote to seat the Peking regime in the UN, but would oppose the expulsion of Nationalist China. However, on October 25, the UN General Assembly voted to seat the People's Republic and to expel the Nationalist Chinese.

War in Indochina. Despite continued pressure from Senate doves, President Nixon refused to set a "date certain" for the final withdrawal of U.S. troops from Indochina. His program of gradual withdrawal continued throughout the year. He announced, on April 7, that his objective was the withdrawal of 100,000 more American soldiers from South Vietnam by December 1.

The withdrawal program moved even faster than promised. On September 1, the U.S. command in Saigon announced that there would be only 177,000 American troops in Vietnam by December 1. On March 4, the President had declared that allied operations in Laos had successfully blocked the flow of supplies from North Vietnam.

Relations with Congress. In his State of the Union message to Congress on January 22, Mr. Nixon proposed the reorganization of the executive branch of government to make it more responsive to the nation's needs. He suggested that the Departments of State, Treasury, Defense, and Justice remain unchanged. All other departments would be merged into four new departments: Human Resources, Community Development, Natural Resources, and Economic Development. He also made a plea for welfare reform and for revenue sharing with the states. The slow-moving first session of the 92nd Congress did not act on any of these suggestions.

Congressional irritation with the Administration was partly responsible for the Senate's refusal to pass the foreign aid bill on October 29. Relations between the Administration and the Senate Foreign Relations Committee were particularly sensitive because of the committee's disagreement on the conduct of the war in Indochina.

President Nixon gives a briefing on his new economic policy that shocked the nation when it was announced in August as Phase 1 of a plan to halt inflation.

On August 31, the President invoked executive privilege in refusing to divulge the five-year plan for foreign military aid drawn up by the Department of Defense. Dissatisfaction with the military aspects of the foreign aid program and the UN's action on the China vote were prime factors leading to the Senate's defeat of the foreign aid bill.

On November 18, both houses of Congress agreed to extend the foreign aid program, which had expired at midnight, November 15, until December 8. Then, in December, the program was extended until February, 1972. See CONGRESS OF THE UNITED STATES.

Budget. On January 29, President Nixon sent Congress a $229.2-billion budget for fiscal 1972. He termed the budget "expansionary but not inflationary." Despite Administration efforts to keep the deficit figure down, Connally reported in September that the 1972 deficit would be about $28 billion, instead of the $11.6 billion originally estimated.

The Supreme Court. On October 21, President Nixon nominated an assistant attorney general, William H. Rehnquist, and Virginia lawyer Lewis F. Powell, Jr., to fill two vacant seats on the Supreme Court of the United States. Both candidates were regarded as conservatives who would favor a narrow interpretation of the Constitution. The Senate confirmed Powell on December 6, Rehnquist on December 10.

President Nixon has named 4 of the 9 justices now serving on the Supreme Court, and has repeatedly stated his determination to appoint conservatives with a strong interest in preserving "law and order."

Before Powell and Rehnquist were named, a list of six other potential candidates (including two women) was widely publicized. The American Bar Association advised that none of the six was suitable. See COURTS AND LAWS; POWELL, LEWIS F., JR.; REHNQUIST, WILLIAM H.

Civil Rights. Housing and busing were volatile issues for the President in 1971. On February 17, he declared that it is not the government's responsibility to provide low-cost housing in the suburbs for low-income families. It is, he said, the government's responsibility to prevent racial discrimination in housing. In a major policy statement on June 11, President Nixon declared that he would enforce existing rules barring discrimination in housing, but he would not force local communities to accept low-income housing.

On August 3, the President reaffirmed his opposition to busing to achieve racial balance in the schools. He directed Health, Education, and Welfare Secretary Elliot L. Richardson and Attorney General John N. Mitchell to hold the busing of schoolchildren to the minimum required by law.

Presidential Politics. It was becoming clear that the big issue of the 1972 election would be the condition of the economy. Withdrawal of troops from Indochina had defused the Vietnam War as a prime political issue.

After the President announced his new economic policy, a Gallup Poll reported him leading all Democratic presidential contenders. His plans to visit both China and Russia in 1972 also appeared to strengthen his political position.

At a fund-raising Republican Party dinner on November 9, President Nixon proposed an "agenda for America," indicating that the 1972 Republican campaign would be based on a platform of "peace and prosperity." He spoke in New York City and Chicago on the same evening, and the speeches were broadcast on closed-circuit television to Republican gatherings in 18 other cities. See REPUBLICAN PARTY.

Other Presidential Actions: On April 1, the President intervened in the trial of Army Lieutenant William L. Calley, who had been convicted of premeditated murder during a 1968 search-and-destroy mission at My Lai, a hamlet in South Vietnam. After his conviction, the President ordered Calley returned to his base pending a review. Presidential adviser John Ehrlichman said that the President would personally review the case before the final sentence was imposed. See NATIONAL DEFENSE (Close-Up).

In June, the President named Robert F. Froehlke

as secretary of the Army. On September 20, President Nixon nominated Mrs. Romana A. Banuelos as treasurer of the United States. The Senate confirmed her appointment in December. Mr. Nixon appointed Earl L. Butz as secretary of agriculture in November. He was confirmed by the Senate on December 2. See AGRICULTURE; BUTZ, EARL L.

The President pressed for an agreement to limit the export of Japanese textiles to the United States. It was finally negotiated on October 15. See JAPAN.

Mr. Nixon gave the go-ahead signal for an underground nuclear test explosion at Amchitka in the Aleutian Islands on October 27. On November 5, he created a new National Security Council Intelligence Committee chaired by Kissinger.

President Nixon got a cool reception when he addressed a meeting of top labor leaders on November 19 in Miami Beach, Fla. He was attempting to win support for his Phase 2 program by confronting his labor critics head-on. Labor leaders felt that the new economic policies tended to favor business over labor.   Carol L. Thompson.

See also Section One, FOCUS ON THE ECONOMY; FOCUS ON THE NATION; FOCUS ON THE WORLD.
PRINCE EDWARD ISLAND. See CANADA.
PRISON. See CRIME.
PRIZES. See AWARDS AND PRIZES; NOBEL PRIZES; PULITZER PRIZES.

President and Mrs. Nixon entertained Prime Minister Emilio Colombo of Italy, at left, at a state dinner in the White House in February.

PROTESTANT. Growth of institutional religion continued to taper off in 1971, and in some areas there was evidence of actual decline. Church building reached a 13-year low, and the Gallup Poll reported that Protestant church attendance showed little change. Only 38 per cent of those who claimed to be Protestants said that they went to church on any particular Sunday. The National Council of Churches cut its staff and activities because of a shortage of funds.

Typical of denominational adjustments was the action of the Episcopal Church. At the beginning of the year, it reduced the number of its staff executives from 205 to 103. Along with most denominations, however, the Episcopal Church still anticipated substantial budget deficits. Yet, cost-cutting and fund-raising drives enabled many denominations to hold their own.

A decline in posts available for ministers led to the first surplus of clerics in many years. Although the surplus was modest, there were signs of a trend toward "tent-making" ministries, in which men and women support themselves through secular employment in order to be able to carry on part-time religious ministry.

A youth-based "Jesus Revolution" attracted attention in 1971. It challenged traditional religious views through its emphasis on emotional, ecstatic, and communal religion. Thoughtful Protestants expressed some reservations about the durability of the revival. The majority, however, adopted wait-and-see and mildly positive attitudes, seeming to welcome the Jesus Movement as being at least partly authentic, in continuity with some dimensions of historic Christianity. In the face of the general drift from the churches on the part of youth, there seemed to be a tolerance of dramatic and emotional religion and even an expectation that it could enliven the tired, routine denominations. See RELIGION.

Ecumenism Slows. There were no major new mergers, and ecumenical institutions suffered as a result of financial problems, some apathy, and some continuing reaction to their more controversial theological statements or social policies. There were some surprises, however. For example, 19 theologians from churches as diverse as the Friends, the Southern Baptist Convention, moderate Protestant groups, and Roman Catholicism, issued a statement of agreement on the meaning of the Eucharist (or Holy Communion, or the Lord's Supper). Roman Catholic theologian Harry J. McSorley called this "one of the most dramatic achievements of the ecumenical-theological dialogue that has taken place on many levels, nationally or internationally."

Polarization appeared to recede. But the national meetings of some denominations evidenced the deep splits that afflict several large church bodies. Southern Baptists, for example, who gathered in St. Louis in June for their annual meeting, once again faced the troubling issues of Biblical authority. The voting "Messengers" advised the Baptist Sunday School Board to obtain a new writer of a commentary on the Book of Genesis for a series of publications on the Bible. The original publication had been censured at the 1970 convention.

The Presbyterian Church in the United States, in its assembly in July at Massanetta Springs, Va., lived up to its billing as a divided church body. The moderates prevailed slightly in vote after vote on public policy, doctrine, and administration of the church. But several congregations and individuals later tried to split from the main body.

The Lutheran Church-Missouri Synod, a once staid and familial denomination now often described as America's most polarized church, also saw close votes in its biennial convention in Milwaukee in July. Conservatives dominate the administration, but moderates fought them to a standstill and prevailed in many decisive votes. They denied the synod's president, J. A. O. Preus, his wishes to have synodical statements of doctrine possess "binding force" on a virtual par with that of the Bible and historic Lutheran confessions or creeds. Despite the leadership's wariness, they resolved to continue on a cautious ecumenical path.

Social and Personal Issues. Various peace, social action, and militant causes received noticeably less attention in 1971. Debates shifted somewhat from these matters to issues that affected people in more private spheres. Churchmen lined up on both sides of the abortion debate. The majority of moderate Protestants evidently favored some sort of abortion-law reform, though many drew back from supporting "abortion on demand." To counter what they saw to be an unreflective support of change, several prestigious theologians, among them J. Robert Nelson of Boston University School of Theology, Albert C. Outler of Southern Methodist University, and Paul Ramsey of Princeton University, sponsored a statement criticizing most of the newer Protestant expressions supporting abortion.

The freedom of expression in public media had led to what many labeled a "pornography explosion." On the local level, at least, many Protestant groups tried to find ways to counter the new portrayals of sexuality on stage and screen, and to discourage or restrict the flow of pornographic books and magazines. The legal status of pornography was so poorly defined, however, that it was difficult to mount a coherent national campaign, and traditional Protestant support of free expression led to uncertainty and ambiguity in the programs.

One of the most widely publicized "new freedoms" in religious circles had to do with the more open ministry to homosexual communities. Former Pentecostalist minister Troy Perry and other leaders successfully organized parishes that were devoted chiefly to helping homosexuals. Their ministries were

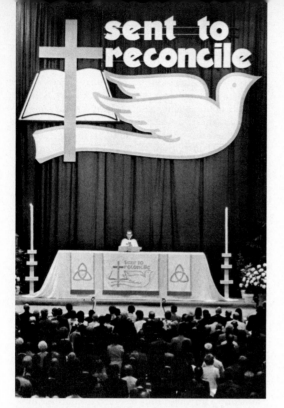

sent to reconcile

The Lutheran Church-Missouri Synod, holding its convention in Milwaukee in July, struggled for agreement between liberal and conservative views.

determine its own doctrine and to order its own worship," the members wrote. They recommended that Parliament should no longer have final authority over either the Anglican Church's worship or its doctrine.

Two Protestant bodies were involved in conflict over apartheid policies in South Africa. Anglican Dean Gonville A. ffrench-Beytagh of St. Mary's Cathedral in Johannesburg was arrested by South African security police, and a number of prointegration American Methodists and Congregationalists were ordered to leave South Africa. In November, ffrench-Beytagh was convicted on three counts of terrorism and was sentenced to five years in prison. He had been charged with urging others to prepare for a violent revolution.

President Jean B. Bokeleale, head of the Church of Christ in the Congo, visited the United States and told executives of mission agencies that Protestantism has no hope in the Congo if it is regarded as "white Western Christianity." Bokeleale, ordained in the Christian Church (Disciples of Christ), said that Africans find denominational competition impossible to justify.

That indigenous, post-colonial Christianity can prosper in the non-Western world seemed clear from the experience of Indonesia. There, during the past five years, as many as 2.5 million Indonesians have converted to Christianity.   Martin E. Marty

applauded by those who saw them as a further extension of Christian acceptance and were deplored by those who saw in several Biblical passages explicit denunciation of homosexual expression.

Efforts to alter women's conception of their role in the churches and to improve their situation were effective. The United Church of Christ, in its convention, declared itself boldly committed to seeking more women ministers. Two of the three largest Lutheran bodies were ordaining women, an action only recently authorized by both. Mrs. Lois H. Stair was elected moderator of The United Presbyterian Church in the United States of America, the first woman to head that denomination. Mrs. Marcus Rohlfs was elected president of the American Baptist Convention. Mrs. Kiyoko Takeda Cho of Tokyo became one of the six presidents of the World Council of Churches.

In Other Lands. In Northern Ireland, tension, hatred, and open violence between Roman Catholics and Protestants increased, particularly in and around Belfast. While some evangelical leaders, notably the militant Ian Paisley, injected religious motives into the disputes, most observers recognized that the roots of the controversy were basically economic.

In Great Britain, a commission envisaged far-reaching changes in the languishing Anglican Church. "The Church must have greater freedom to

PSYCHOLOGY. Larry Stein and C. David Wise of the Wyeth Laboratories in Philadelphia studied the chemical nature of the mental disease schizophrenia in 1971. They focused their research on the loss of interest in the rewards and incentives of everyday life that characterize the disease.

According to Stein and Wise, the mental disorder is caused by abnormal metabolism of dopamine, one of the principal substances found in every brain. Dopamine is an intermediate chemical produced in the synthesis of another chemical, neurotransmitter norepinephrine, which is essential to the thinking process. Dopamine can be metabolized by 6-hydroxydopamine (6-HD), which is also present in every brain, but normally only in low concentrations.

Experiments with Rats. Stein and Wise raised the concentration of 6-HD in the brains of rats by injecting the chemical directly into the bloodstream. After the injections, the rats developed abnormalities of behavior that paralleled traits in human schizophrenics. First noted was a rat's loss of interest in stimuli that are usually powerful incentives. In one experiment, rats trained to drink milk from a tube during a regular daily 45-minute session acted as if they were no longer interested in the milk.

Following repeated administration of 6-HD, rats developed a catatoniclike syndrome, and could be placed in bizarre postures that they maintained for several minutes. Further experiments showed that chlorpromazine, a tranquilizer helpful to human schizophrenics, reduced or prevented the harmful effects of 6-HD on the behavior of rats.

Malnutrition and the Mind. Undernourishment in the first few years of life may permanently impair thinking processes, according to Lois Brockman and Henry Ricciuti of the Cornell University Medical Center in New York City. They studied 20 children, ranging in age from 1 to 3½ years, who were severely malnourished. The children were given 10 different sorting tests soon after admission to the hospital, and tested again in the same way after several months of dietary treatment. The investigators found that the more severe the malnutrition, the greater the impairment of ability to perform sorting tasks.

On all tests, the malnourished children performed more poorly than other children of the same age. Moreover, there was no measurable improvement in performance of malnourished children following nutritional therapy. The poorer performance did not seem to be due to apathy or lack of interest in the tasks, but rather to deficits in their thinking processes. The investigators acknowledged that their results do not demonstrate permanent impairment of ability, because their study lasted only a few months. Nevertheless, they pointed out that other scientists conducting similar studies have obtained evidence that impairments caused by undernutrition in the first years of life may be permanent.   Robert W. Goy

PUBLISHING. The printed word proved in 1971 to be the "hot" medium that communications expert Marshall McLuhan has said it is. It actively involved both readers and writers in ways that the "cool" electronic media do not seem able to do. Newspapers, magazines, and books all made big news in communications and became more involved in local, national, and international events.

The most obvious case in point, of course, was the "Pentagon Papers" published in June by *The New York Times* and other daily newspapers (see Close-Up). But there were many other important instances of involvement and commitment by newspapers and the other print media.

In October, Eugene C. Pulliam, publisher of the Phoenix, Ariz., *Republic* and the Indianapolis, Ind., *Star and News*, pre-empted the front page of these and six other papers he publishes for an editorial entitled "Will the Federal Bureaucracy Destroy Individual Freedom in America?" According to the *Republic,* it was "the first time any American newspaper has devoted its entire front page to an editorial." The same editorial appeared in two Washington, D.C., newspapers, the *Post* and the *Star*, as a paid advertisement.

In Philadelphia, the *Inquirer* brought legal action against both the state and the city directors of welfare, claiming that under Pennsylvania's "right-to-know" law the newspaper is entitled to inspect and copy the records of welfare recipients. The Pennsylvania Supreme Court agreed: "The people of Pennsylvania are entitled to nothing less than this. . . . Free people and a free land cannot exist if governmental affairs are run *in camera* [in private]."

In many cases, federal, state, and local governments made real efforts to bridge what seemed to be an ever-widening gap. The Nixon Administration, for instance, employs more public relations professionals and imagemakers than any other presidential staff in history. Many publishers and journalists, on the other hand, argued that the government interferes with the freedom of the press. They cited such practices as: the use of false press credentials by government investigators, serving journalists with grand-jury and congressional-committee subpoenas to force them to reveal confidential sources of information, antitrust suits against merged newspapers and multimedia businesses, threatening to raise postal rates for newspapers and magazines by as much as 142 per cent over the next five years, and certain applications of the wage-price freeze.

Despite these and other difficulties, the print media either made gains or just about held their own during the year. In April, the American Newspaper Publishers Association reported that some 334 morning and 1,429 evening newspapers were published in the United States, making a grand total of 1,763.

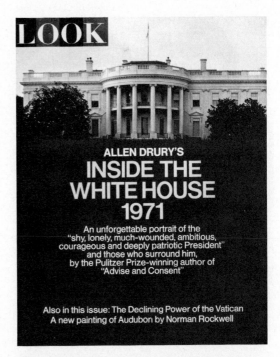

The last issue of *Look* magazine hit the newsstands in October, 1971. The publication was suspended because increased costs would wipe out profits.

The Pentagon Papers

On Sunday, June 13, 1971, a two-line, three-column headline appeared on the front page of *The New York Times*. It was far from sensational: "Vietnam Archive: Pentagon Study Traces 3 Decades of Growing U.S. Involvement." But the article that followed precipitated a momentous and historic confrontation between the press and the government that temporarily silenced one of the nation's most respected newspapers and, in effect, put the First Amendment to the U.S. Constitution on trial.

At the heart of the matter was a secret, 7,000-page, 47-volume "History of U.S. Decision-Making Process on Vietnam Policy" that became known as the "Pentagon Papers." It had been compiled by order of U.S. Secretary of Defense Robert S. McNamara shortly before he left his Pentagon post in 1968. In it were many documents, memoranda, proposals, and orders that traced the growing involvement of the United States in the Vietnam War.

The highly classified material had been obtained from an "anonymous" source in March by Neil Sheehan, Washington correspondent of the *Times*. The *Times* subsequently refused to name the "anonymous" source. However, Daniel Ellsberg, a 40-year-old research associate of the Massachusetts Institute of Technology, admitted he had leaked the information. Ellsberg had worked on the study in 1969 while employed by the Rand Corporation, a private firm doing research work for the government. (He was indicted on June 28 on charges of violating the Espionage Act and theft of government property.)

The *Times* officials who reviewed the material faced several key decisions. Should the *Times* publish what was obviously a historic and relevant document with an immediate bearing on an on-going crisis in the United States? And if so, how much, and in what format?

They decided to publish it in serial form. In deep secrecy, a staff was assembled to analyze and condense the mass of material into a five-part series. Eventually, about 75 *Times* employees—all sworn to secrecy—were brought into the effort.

Publication of the first installment caught the public as well as the government off guard. But when the second installment appeared, the government acted: U.S. Attorney General John N. Mitchell telegraphed the newspaper, asking that it cease publication of the report and return all of the material to the government. Mitchell cited a provision in the espionage law that provided for a 10-year sentence for anyone convicted of willingly revealing secret defense information that could endanger the country's safety.

The *Times* refused to comply. Its refusal was based on the premise that the principle of prior restraint was being invoked and that the government's move constituted an act of censorship forbidden by the First Amendment. The papers, it insisted, were historical records and in no way damaging to national security.

Thus, two principles essential to a free and viable society collided head-on: the *Times'* insistence on its rights under the First Amendment's guarantee of freedom of the press, and the government's insistence on the need to prevent disclosure of information that could endanger lives or the national security and jeopardize delicate negotiations being carried out with foreign powers.

With the issue joined, the government took its case to Manhattan's federal court, where a temporary restraining order against publication was granted. Five days later, a second hearing began in the same court; it, too, upheld the restraining order. Ultimately, 14 days after initial publication, the case reached the Supreme Court of the United States. The case had become a cause célèbre; other newspapers had begun to publish portions of the papers.

On Wednesday, June 30, shortly after 2 P.M., Chief Justice Warren E. Burger delivered the court's four-sentence ruling. By a vote of 6 to 3, the orders restraining *The New York Times* and *The Washington Post*—which had also tried to publish the material—from publishing the "Pentagon Papers" were dissolved. The great tradition of the First Amendment had once again been reaffirmed. Paul C. Tullier

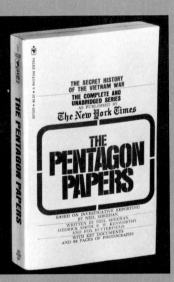

A historic controversy

This was down 10 from the previous year, but involved a total circulation of 62,107,527, a small gain of about 50,000 readers.

Ad linage, by and large, was down in both newspapers and magazines – as much as 10 per cent on some metropolitan dailies – and enough to make publishers call for increased productivity from their employees and greater efficiency from new technological developments.

Trend to Offset. Eight per cent of the U.S. dailies abandoned traditional letterpress printing for offset during the year. That means more than 40 per cent of all U.S. dailies are now printed by the offset process. This, however, represents only 13 per cent of the total circulation, because the smaller circulation newspapers (35,000 and under) find the shift to offset most profitable. This same trend to offset and to photocomposition also applies to the printing of magazines and books.

Biggest news in the magazine field was the closing of *Look* with its October 19 issue after 34 years of publication. The magazine reportedly had a before-taxes loss of $5 million in 1970 and was expecting a similar loss in 1971. Publisher-founder Gardner Cowles blamed the slack economy in general; network television, which cut deeply into ad revenue; and rising costs – particularly postal rates.

Another publication, *Business Management*, which circulated mostly among 200,000 corporate executives, suspended publication with its October issue. Its publisher, Crowell Collier and MacMillan, said that insufficient advertising volume and the resultant low margin of profits had forced the demise.

Top Editors Resign. Norton Simon, Inc., a billion-dollar conglomerate that expanded into publishing in 1967, sold its 640,000-circulation magazine, *The Saturday Review*, as well as its other major holding in the field, the trade book division of *McCall's*. Norman Cousins, one-time owner of *The Saturday Review* and its editor for 31 years, found himself unable to work with the magazine's new owner, Communication / Research / Machines, Incorporated, and resigned.

In another shakeup, Willie Morris, editor since 1967 of the prestigious but financially troubled 300,000-circulation *Harper's Magazine*, resigned on March 4 and took six members of the editorial staff with him.

Crowded Book Shelves. Well over 36,000 new titles and new editions of books were published in 1971 compared to some 29,000 in 1969. As A. J. McCaffrey, vice-president of the Association of American Publishers pointed out, "This poses a major problem for book dealers whose shelves are already jammed."

Major titles of the year included Lyndon B. Johnson's *The Vantage Point: Perspectives of the Presidency, 1963-1969,* and Joseph P. Lash's biography of Eleanor Roosevelt, *Eleanor and Franklin.* Malcolm Merritt

PUERTO RICO. The United States and Puerto Rico eased a long-standing dispute on Jan. 11, 1971, when the United States signed a formal agreement ceding most of the U.S. Navy-controlled island of Culebra to Puerto Rico. The Navy had been using the 10-square-mile island off Puerto Rico for target practice since the end of World War II. But some tensions remained, because of a clause granting the United States "several years" to evacuate the island.

A serious student riot broke out on the University of Puerto Rico campus in San Juan on March 11 when members of several radical student groups clashed over the question of Puerto Rican independence from the United States. Two policemen and one student were killed before order was restored.

The whole issue of U.S.-Puerto Rican relations remained an overriding one in 1971 as it had in years past. On August 19, Puerto Rico's two major political parties, the New Progressives and the Popular Democrats, agreed to sponsor a referendum on whether the government should request the U.S. Congress to grant Puerto Ricans the right to vote in U.S. presidential elections.

Facts in Brief. Population: 2,733,000. Government: Governor Luis A. Ferré. Monetary Unit: U.S. dollar. Foreign Trade: exports, $1,606,000,000; imports, $2,262,000,000. Principal Exports: food products, textiles, clothing. Paul C. Tullier

Pro-independence Puerto Rican demonstrators waving Yankee-Go-Home signs clog a downtown street during a U.S. governors' conference in San Juan in September.

PULITZER PRIZES

PULITZER PRIZES in journalism, letters, and music were announced in New York City on May 3, 1971. The following awards were made:

Journalism

Public Service. A gold medal to the *Winston-Salem* (N.C.) *Journal and Sentinel*, for its reporting of environmental problems. The aggressive campaigns of the news and editorial staffs aroused the community and prevented strip-mining on thousands of acres of land in an area popular with tourists.

General Local Reporting. $1,000 to the staff of the *Akron* (Ohio) *Beacon Journal* for its coverage of the tragedy at Kent State University, where four students were killed by Ohio National Guard men on May 4, 1970. The staff was commended for giving a balanced presentation in spite of wild rumors 'surrounding the incident.

Special Local Reporting. $1,000 to William H. Jones, 35, of the *Chicago Tribune* for a six-part exposé dealing with the bribery of policemen to refer sick people to private ambulance companies. Jones took first-aid training and then worked as an ambulance driver. His investigation resulted in 16 indictments, 10 of them against policemen. Jones has been with the *Tribune* for six years. He has a master's degree in journalism from Northwestern University.

National Reporting. $500 each to Lucinda Franks, 31, and Thomas Powers, 30, of United Press International (UPI) for "The Story of Diana: The Making of a Terrorist." This 12,000-word study described the life and death of Diana Oughton, a radical student who died when a house described as a "bomb factory" in New York City's Greenwich Village exploded. Miss Franks was born in Chicago and educated at Vassar. She joined UPI in 1968. Powers is a New Yorker who majored in English literature at Yale University. He joined UPI in 1967.

International Reporting. $1,000 to Jimmie L. Hoagland, 31, of the *Washington Post* for articles on apartheid in South Africa. He was born in Rock Hill, S.C., and graduated from the University of South Carolina. He has been the *Post* correspondent in Africa since 1969. The previous year, he was a Ford Foundation Fellow in international reporting at Columbia University.

Editorial Writing. $1,000 to Horance G. Davis, Jr., 46, professor of journalism at the University of Florida for 15 years, for more than 30 editorials for *The Gainesville* (Fla.) *Sun* in favor of peaceful desegregation of Gainesville schools. Born in Manchester, Ga., he began his career in journalism as a correspondent for Jacksonville's *Florida Times-Union*. He is national vice-president for campus affairs for Sigma Delta Chi, the professional journalistic society.

Editorial Cartooning. $1,000 to Paul Conrad, 46, of the *Los Angeles Times*, for all his 1970 editorial cartooning for the *Times*. Conrad also won a Pulitzer Prize in 1964 for his work on *The Denver Post*. Born in Cedar Rapids, he graduated from the University of Iowa in 1950, where he began drawing cartoons for *The Daily Iowan*. He has been with the *Times* since 1964.

Spot News Photography. $1,000 to John P. Filo, 21, photography student at Kent State University, for his picture of a screaming girl kneeling over a student slain on May 4, 1970, at Kent State. A native of Natrona Heights, Pa., Filo graduated in 1971 and works for *The Valley Daily News* and *Daily Dispatch* of Tarentum and New Kensington, Pa.

Feature Photography. $1,000 to Jack Dykinga, 28, of the *Chicago Sun-Times* for photographs of children at the Lincoln and Dixon State Schools for the Retarded in Illinois that revealed overcrowding and other serious conditions. A native Chicagoan, he attended Lisle and Elmhurst Colleges in Illinois. He began his career with Metro News, a free-lance group of photographers. The Chicago-Press Photographers Association awarded *The Sun-Times* 6 of 32 awards for his work in 1969.

Commentary. $1,000 to William A. Caldwell, 64, associate editor of the Hackensack, N.J., *Record*, for "Simeon Stylites," a daily column on local events in Bergen County, N.J., that he has been writing for more than 40 years. His articles urged members of the community to become more active in local affairs. Caldwell was born in Butler, Pa., and has been with the Hackensack paper since 1926. He received an honorary LL.D. degree from Rutgers University in 1970.

Criticism. $1,000 to Harold C. Schonberg, 55, senior music critic of *The New York Times* since 1960. Born in New York City, he began piano lessons at the age of 3 and became a critic when he was 21. Schonberg received an A.B. degree *cum laude* from Brooklyn College in 1937 and an A.M. degree in music and English from New York University in 1938. He joined the *Times* in 1950.

Letters

Drama. $1,000 to Paul Zindel, 35, for the off-Broadway play *The Effect of Gamma Rays on Man-in-the-Moon Marigolds*, which he wrote in 1962. It began its long run at the New Theater on April 7, 1970. The play centers on a teen-age girl and takes its title from a school essay she wrote on experiments with atomic energy. Zindel earned B.S. and M.S. degrees in science from Wagner College in New York City and taught high school chemistry and physics in Staten Island, where he was born.

History. $1,000 to James MacGregor Burns, 53, professor of government, Williams College, for *Roosevelt: The Soldier of Freedom*, the second of two volumes on the life of Franklin D. Roosevelt. This volume also won a 1971 National Book Award. Born in Melrose, Mass., Burns received a B.A. degree from Williams College in 1939, where he has taught since 1947. During World War II, he was an Army combat historian in the Pacific.

Biography. $1,000 to Lawrance R. Thompson, 65, Holmes Professor of Belles-Lettres, Princeton, N.J., for *Robert Frost: The Years of Triumph, 1915-1938*. Born in Franklin, N.H., he received his Ph.D. degree from Columbia University in 1939.

Poetry. $1,000 to William S. Merwin, 43, poet, critic, and translator, for *The Carrier of Ladders*, his seventh book of poetry. He also translates poetry from Spanish, French, Portuguese, and Latin. Born in New York City, he received an A.B. degree from Princeton University in 1947.

General Nonfiction. $1,000 to John Toland, 58, for *The Rising Sun*, the story of Japan during World War II. He is a 1936 graduate of Williams College. He began to write when he was 40 years old and has held a variety of jobs that included teaching actors and running a gift shop.

Music. $1,000 to Mario Davidovsky, 37, associate professor of music at City College of New York and lecturer in music at Columbia University, for *Synchronisms No. 6*, for piano and electronic sound. Born in Buenos Aires, Davidovsky came to the United States in 1958. His numerous honors include election to the American Institute of Arts and Letters. He composes chamber music and orchestral works as well as electronic music. Lillian Zahrt

QUEBEC. See CANADA.

RACING. See AUTOMOBILE RACING; BOATS AND BOATING; HORSE RACING; TRACK AND FIELD.

RADIO. Business improved in 1971, but radio was subjected to as much pressure from the government and angry citizens groups as was television. The biggest headache for music stations–particularly those playing rock music–was the policy statement issued on March 6 by the Federal Communications Commission (FCC). The FCC ordered broadcasters to screen out any records with lyrics that might "promote or glorify the use of illegal drugs." Songs cited as drug-oriented included "I like Marijuana," "Acid Queen," and "Cocaine Blues."

The warning drew immediate and sharp reaction. The FCC policy was strongly protested as "censorship" by rock music stations, disk jockeys, record companies, and even news commentator Walter Cronkite of the Columbia Broadcasting System (CBS). In a rather ambiguous effort to clarify its statement, the FCC later said it did not actually ban any records, but merely warned stations of their responsibility to act "in the public's best interest."

Prudent broadcasters, however, were convinced that they might lose their licenses if they played any offending disks. On March 10, Max Leon, owner of WDAS (AM-FM) in Philadelphia, fired his son, Steve, as FM program director when the younger Leon insisted on playing Arlo Guthrie's "Coming into Los Angeles." That song's lyrics are about smuggling a "couple of 'keys' [kilos]" into Los Angeles.

In October, Clay T. Whitehead, director of the White House Office of Telecommunications Policy (OTP), startled radio executives by proposing a plan to liberalize all broadcast regulation and virtually deregulate radio. He recommended that OTP and the FCC first set up one or two radio "deregulatory" test markets.

FM Radio continued its slow but steady climb. In March, the National Association of FM Broadcasters launched a drive to persuade Detroit automakers to reduce prices on FM car radios and improve construction of the radios.

FM broadcasters tried to build their strength on music and let AM radio handle news and information. The American Broadcasting Company (ABC) adopted a progressive-rock format for all its FM stations in 1971. In May, CBS began to convert programming on all its owned and operated FM stations to music only (mainly rock) and to all news on its AM outlets.

Station Sales. More stations were bought and sold at higher prices than ever before. Observers attributed the brisk traffic to growing uncertainty over the effect of federal regulations, challenges on license-renewals, and the FCC ruling prohibiting ownership of more than one full-time station in any market.

Time-Life sold its four AM and four FM stations in April for more than $11 million. The McLendon Corporation sold KLIF (AM), Dallas, to Fairchild Industries in May for $10.5 million and KABL (AM-FM), Oakland-San Francisco, to Starr Broadcasting in July for $10.8 million.

In June, the National Broadcasting Company put its six AM and FM stations up for sale. In October, Kaiser Broadcasting announced that it would sell its radio interests (asking price over $8 million), to concentrate on television. However, no deals had been made by either of the companies by the end of the year.

National Public Radio, which is funded by the Corporation for Public Broadcasting, went on the air on May 3. About 90 of the 457 noncommercial radio stations in the United States are participating in the network, which operates for only an hour and a half each day, Monday through Friday. It features a news and public affairs show, "All Things Considered," that is broadcast in the early evening. The network plans to establish a morning news service in the future, and then weekend programs of music, drama, and cultural entertainment. It will also provide a funnel through which foreign radio broadcasts, such as those of the British Broadcasting Corporation, can reach an audience in the United States. Previously, the Corporation for Public Broadcasting had put its resources into noncommercial television exclusively. June Bundy Csida

See also AWARDS AND PRIZES; TELEVISION.

RAILROAD. See TRANSPORTATION.

RECORDINGS

RECORDINGS. The music and recording industries marketed a new plaything in 1971 – four-channel, or surround, sound. This new concept in listening offers four channels instead of the two used in stereophonic sound. Promoters labeled it as quadraphony, quadrasonic, quadfonic, or quadriphonic sound.

In the fall of 1971, four-channel music was being sold on both tapes and records, with 13 major Japanese electronics companies geared up to supply the sound equipment. Columbia Records was the first major firm to get the new music on records and tapes. Radio Corporation of America (RCA) released its quadrasonic music on eight-track cartridges. Ampex went with tapes and LP's. Among the first small record companies to develop quad albums were Ovation and Project 3 Records.

Two methods of recording quad sound were being developed, and they were competing to become the standard. Matrix (or simulated) four-channel reproduction involves recording four channels on tape and reducing them to two for a record. A decoder device converts them to four channels when played. Discrete, or individual, four-channel reproduction involves recording four separate channels of sound on tape and transferring them to an album.

Sales Go Up. Despite tight money conditions in the United States, 1970 record and tape sales figures, released in 1971, totaled $1.66 billion. That was a 4.7 per cent rise over 1969 sales of $1.59 billion. In 1970, record sales accounted for $1.18 billion, with prerecorded tape sales totaling $478 million, up from the previous year's $416 million. Record companies reported that eight-track and cassette sales accounted for from 30 to 35 per cent of their income.

Bootlegging. Record manufacturers and music publishers began legal action against "bootleggers" to stop the illegal duplication of records and tapes. Record companies also notified retail shops that if they were caught selling unauthorized albums or tapes, they would not be sold products that were legitimately produced. Recording companies also worked to get Congress to extend coverage of the existing copyright bill by 1973 to cover the actual recordings themselves.

A new, thin plastic record made its appearance in 1971. It is so thin that shoppers often thought the record had been left out of the package. RCA and Music Corporation of America began pressing records for themselves and clients, using an 80- to 90-gram weight instead of the standard 140 grams.

Best-selling albums by classical artists included *Love Story* by the Philadelphia Orchestra, *Themes from Death in Venice* by the Bavarian Radio Symphony, and *Peter Rabbit and the Tales of Beatrix Potter*, all motion picture scores, plus Joshua Rifkin playing Scott Joplin piano rags.   Eliot Tiegel

Before the rock opera *Jesus Christ Superstar* opened on Broadway, Oct. 12, 1971, the record album on which the show is based sold more than 3 million copies.

RED CROSS. Delegates to the 46th National Convention held in Washington, D.C., May 17 to 19, 1971, heard E. Roland Harriman, chairman of the board of governors, outline the role of the agency in the 1970s. He said that it will emphasize:

■ Involving and serving the entire community, particularly the youth.

■ Continuing efforts to obtain humane treatment of war prisoners.

■ Evaluating Red Cross fund-raising techniques.

■ Extending Red Cross blood-program activities to help nonmember community blood banks recruit volunteer donors.

■ Modernizing disaster policy in view of new liberalized disaster insurance programs. The Red Cross will now concentrate on the immediate needs of victims, because federal and private insurance programs now provide more long-term aid.

The following actions were taken:

■ Several young volunteers were elected as youth members of the 50-member board of governors. They included Nicholas T. Lemesh, 24, of Pittsburgh; Pamela Matthews, 20, of Boston; and Elaine Musselman, 27, of Louisville.

■ A new statement providing for increased coordination of relief efforts on behalf of disaster victims between the American Red Cross and the U.S. government's Office of Emergency Preparedness was adopted.　　　　Joseph P. Anderson

REHNQUIST, WILLIAM HUBBS (1924-　　), became the fourth justice of the Supreme Court of the United States to be appointed by President Richard M. Nixon. He was confirmed by the Senate in a 68 to 26 vote on Dec. 10, 1971. Rehnquist filled one of the vacancies created by the retirement of justices Hugo L. Black and John M. Harlan.

Rehnquist was born on Oct. 1, 1924, in Milwaukee, and attended grade school and high school there. He earned his undergraduate and law degrees at Stanford University and a master's degree at Harvard University. In 1952, he went to Washington, D.C., to serve as law clerk for the late Supreme Court Justice Robert H. Jackson. In 1953, he went to Phoenix to practice law, and he became active in Arizona politics as a conservative Republican. He was a strong supporter of Barry M. Goldwater in the 1964 presidential campaign. In 1969, he returned to Washington as assistant attorney general.

Rehnquist's nomination was opposed by some who believed that he did not fully support all constitutional guarantees of liberty. Some black leaders claimed he was a racist, and some civil rights proponents objected to his views on the surveillance of individuals.

Rehnquist has been described as a hard worker and, by President Nixon, a "lawyer's lawyer." He married Natalie Cornell of San Diego in 1953. They have three children.　　　　Michael Reed

RELIGION. Emotionalism—a so-called "inner revolution"—dominated religion in the United States in 1971. In other parts of the world, interreligious conflict aggravated the problems of many nations.

Interest in African, primitive, Eastern, and occult religions continued in the United States. But the focus changed to a Protestant-based emphasis that had effects far beyond Protestantism. In its tendency toward innocence, simplism, communalism, and a desire for immediacy and experience, it typified the general nature of much of the nation's recent spiritual search.

The Jesus Revolution was chiefly a movement of the young. It began on the Pacific Coast and spread eastward through a campus network. Its members turned to Jesus for inspiration. The movement was interpreted by many observers as a reaction against the radical social activist commitments of youth in recent years.

The revolution produced "Jesus people" who cherished ecstatic versions of faith, many of them rooted in older American revivalist experience. Leaders of conservative evangelical denominations supported many versions, sometimes cautiously and sometimes enthusiastically. There were at least superficial likenesses between the theology of the Jesus movement and these denominations, though the young people almost unanimously criticized formalism in all denominations.

The more exotic element called itself the "Jesus Freaks." They were the heirs of the hippie movement, but they showed signs that they were not interested in the drug culture. Their spokesmen advocated communal life and showed how to achieve spiritual "highs" without drugs. They published a number of underground newspapers.

Sons and daughters of more affluent churchgoers formed the "straight people" versions of the movement. Their doctrinal position was roughly comparable to that of evangelist Billy Graham, who was a hero to some of them. Others discarded the polished and programmed features of Graham's campaigns and sought freer forms of expression.

They carried on ministries among communes and on campuses—wherever youth gathered. A number of celebrities, including singer Pat Boone, gave leadership. They conducted public baptisms on beaches or in swimming pools. They used slogans, buttons, balloons, bumper stickers, cheers, and songs to elaborate their simple affirmations.

Television and magazines gave considerable space to the Jesus Revolution. The public also heard the sounds of the movement through recordings of *Jesus Christ Superstar*, such revived Gospel songs as "Amazing Grace," and new country-and-soul hymns on Gospel themes. Off-Broadway, there was John-Michael Tebelak's *Godspell*, which was derived from themes in Matthew's Gospel, but presented in modern settings. Thus, through the mass media, the

Niebuhr: Relevant Theologian

Reinhold Niebuhr

"Religious faith is basically a trust that life, however difficult and strange, has ultimate meaning." Thus wrote theologian Reinhold Niebuhr, who died at the age of 78 on June 1, 1971. He was regarded as a giant in the field of theology by Protestant and Roman Catholic scholars alike, and he influenced many political and social leaders of his time. His Protestant neo-orthodoxy restated some traditional Christian beliefs in a way that neglected neither Biblical history nor modern scientific and social thought.

In his theology, Niebuhr stressed original sin, which he defined as pride, the "universality of self-regard in everybody's motives, whether they are idealists or realists or whether they are benevolent or not." Niebuhr rejected utopianism, the belief "that increasing reason, increasing education, increasing technical conquests of nature make for moral progress, that historical development means moral progress."

Though his arguments forged a new direction for Protestantism in America, it was in the arena of practical politics that he became best known to the public. He wrote more than 20 books, and his teaching and writings influenced many public figures, particularly those who were leaders in the Democratic Party during the 1950s and 1960s. George F. Kennan, the diplomat and adviser to Presidents on Russian affairs, called Niebuhr "the father of us all" in recognition of his role in encouraging intellectuals to help shape national policies. He also influenced such statesmen and political analysts as Paul H. Nitze, Dean Acheson, McGeorge Bundy, Louis J. Halle, Hans J. Morgenthau, and Arthur M. Schlesinger, Jr.

"The tragedy of man," Niebuhr said, "is that he can conceive self-perfection but he cannot achieve it." He asserted that mankind should not passively accept evil, but should strive for moral solutions to all problems. Niebuhr suggested that in the struggle for good, institutional change is likely to be more effective than a change of heart.

He decried clergymen who offered salvation on what he considered simplistic terms. The evangelist Billy Graham and Norman Vincent Peale were among those he contradicted. Their "wholly individualistic conceptions of sin," he said, were "almost completely irrelevant" to the collective problems of the nuclear age. He objected especially to the idea that religious conversion could cure race prejudice, economic injustice, or political chicanery. The remedy for these evils, Niebuhr said, lay in social changes spurred by Christian realism. In this sense, man could be an agent of history by coming to terms with it and working to alter his environment.

Niebuhr's own life illustrated his beliefs. He was born June 21, 1892, in Wright City, Mo., the son of the pastor of a German Lutheran congregation. At the age of 10, he decided to be a minister because, as he told his father, "You're the most interesting man in town." He was ordained in 1915 and became the pastor of an Evangelical church in Detroit. During the next 13 years, he became an active advocate of the rights of labor in industrial Detroit. He criticized such industrialists as Henry Ford, and became an active Socialist and a leader of the "social gospel" movement among Protestants.

In 1928, he became an assistant professor at Union Theological Seminary in New York City. He served as its dean from 1950 to 1960. He was gradually disillusioned by Marxism, Fascism, pacifism, and the social gospel movement, and in the process, he developed the fundamentals of his influential theology.

At the outset of World War II, he favored American intervention, declaring that, "The halting of totalitarian aggression is a prerequisite to world peace and order." After the United States became involved in the war in Vietnam, he became one of the leading critics of American policy in the Far East.

Niebuhr's principal writings, the titles of which point to his philosophy, included *Does Civilization Need Religion?* (1927); *Moral Man and Immoral Society* (1932); *Beyond Tragedy* (1937); the two-volume *Nature and Destiny of Man* (1941 and 1943); and *Faith and Politics* (1968).   Foster Stockwell

stage, and word of mouth, the Jesus movement reached into many areas of national life. It typified the general religious mood that seemed to have pervaded the country.

Jewish leaders expressed concern over the fact that many young Jews were joining these Christian forces. But, while Judaism had no exact parallels, the new interest of the young in the Cabala and other Jewish mystical traditions, and in Hasidism—a kind of Jewish revivalism based upon joy—matched the revolution's spirit. So did Catholic Pentecostalism, also a minority phenomenon, which attracted some notice. These, the continuing vogue for Eastern experience, and interest in "bodily awareness" emphases, sensitivity centers, and similar offerings, showed Americans to be decidedly experience-hungry during their inner revolution.

Less Tension. The inward turning meant that many Americans looked away from the role religion traditionally has played in the public sphere, and the tension over religious issues that had divided the nation eased slightly. Church-state affairs, matters affecting the overlap of civil and religious realms, remained controversial, however. Most notable of these issues was governmental support of private and parochial education, generally forbidden, at least on elementary school and secondary school levels, by the Supreme Court of the United States.

The continuing debate did not follow classic Protestant-versus-Roman Catholic-versus-Jew lines. Many non-Catholics were sympathetic to Catholics who were trying to ensure the survival of their schools, and many Catholics voiced their distaste or lack of interest in the continued survival of the parochial system.

Religious Conflict was more evident in other parts of the world, where religious beliefs aggravated what were basically economic, social, and territorial disputes. Both sides in the Arab-Israeli near-warfare frequently referred to the conflict as a kind of "holy war."

The newest sphere of international tension was in East Pakistan. The conflict between Hindu and Moslem caused some of the savagery and suffering. In India, Hindus frequently criticized Prime Minister Indira Gandhi for cooperating with Moslems. The ultimate religious outcome of India's victory over Pakistan in a two-week war that ended in surrender on December 16 was not yet apparent as the year ended. In Vietnam, Buddhists criticized President Nguyen Van Thieu for his devotion to Roman Catholic causes and institutions.

China came into new prominence in Western eyes late in the year. Students of "secular religions," as Maoism might be called, should get the opportunity now to observe their clash with the inherited faiths. China displayed several of these before it was so effectively sealed off completely to non-Chinese eyes in the early 1950s.   Martin E. Marty

U.S. Church Membership Reported for Bodies with 150,000 or More Members*

African Methodist Episcopal Church	1,166,301
African Methodist Episcopal Zion Church	940,000
American Baptist Association	790,000
American Baptist Convention	1,472,478
American Lutheran Church	2,543,293
Armenian Church of North America, Diocese of the (including Diocese of California)	300,000
Assemblies of God	1,064,631
Baptist Missionary Association of America	187,246
Christian Church (Disciples of Christ)	1,424,479
Christian Churches and Churches of Christ	1,020,751
Christian Methodist Episcopal Church	466,718
Christian Reformed Church	285,628
Church of God (Anderson, Ind.)	150,198
Church of God (Cleveland, Tenn.)	272,276
Church of God in Christ	425,000
Church of Jesus Christ of Latter-day Saints	2,073,146
Church of the Brethren	182,614
Church of the Nazarene	383,284
Churches of Christ	2,400,000
Conservative Baptist Association of America	300,000
Episcopal Church	3,285,826
Exarchate of the Russian Orthodox Church in North and South America	152,973
Free Will Baptists	186,136
Greek Orthodox Archdiocese of North and South America	1,950,000
International Church of God in Christ (Evanston, Ill.)	500,000
Jehovah's Witnesses	388,920
Jewish Congregations	5,870,000
Lutheran Church in America	3,106,844
Lutheran Church Missouri Synod	2,788,536
National Baptist Convention of America	2,668,799
National Baptist Convention, U.S.A., Inc.	5,500,000
National Primitive Baptist Convention	1,523,000
Orthodox Church in America	1,000,000
Polish National Catholic Church of America	282,411
Presbyterian Church in the U.S.	958,195
Progressive National Baptist Convention, Inc.	521,692
Reformed Church in America	367,606
Regular Baptist Churches, General Association of	210,000
Reorganized Church of Jesus Christ of Latter-day Saints	152,670
Roman Catholic Church	48,214,729
Salvation Army, The	326,924
Seventh-day Adventists	420,419
Southern Baptist Convention	11,628,032
Spiritualists, International General Assembly of	164,072
Unitarian Universalist Association	265,408
United Church of Christ	1,960,608
United Methodist Church	10,671,774
United Pentecostal Church, Inc.	250,000
United Presbyterian Church in the U.S.A.	3,087,213
Wisconsin Evangelical Lutheran Synod	381,321

*Majority of figures are for the years 1970 and 1971. Source: National Council of Churches, *Yearbook of American Churches for 1972.*

493

REPUBLICAN PARTY

REPUBLICAN PARTY. Republicans won a special congressional election in Pennsylvania and the mayoral elections in Cleveland and Indianapolis in 1971. H. John Heinz III was hailed as a new Republican star when he won Pennsylvania's special congressional election on November 2. He retained his party's seat in the House of Representatives, beating Democrat John E. Connelly, a millionaire cruiseship owner, by a 2 to 1 margin to fill the vacancy created by the death in April of Republican Representative Robert J. Corbett. Heinz, 33, is an executive in the Heinz food-canning company. He was regarded as a potential candidate for governor of Pennsylvania after his victory in the only congressional election in November, 1971.

Mayoral Gains. In Cleveland, the Republicans elected a mayor for the first time in 30 years. County Auditor Ralph J. Perk defeated Democrat James M. Carney and Arnold R. Pinkney, a black Democrat running as an independent, on November 2. Perk's surprise success, achieved with the help of white ethnic voters, was a setback for retiring black Democratic Mayor Carl B. Stokes. Stokes had tried to demonstrate black political power by electing Pinkney as his successor.

In Indianapolis, the Republicans won another large city contest on November 2 when Mayor Richard G. Lugar, a strong supporter of President Richard M. Nixon, won re-election easily. He defeated Democrat John Neff.

Election Losses. Republicans were disappointed, however, in the Kentucky governorship race. Republican Governor Louis B. Nunn, who ended 20 years of Democratic rule with his election in 1967, was ineligible to succeed himself. Republican hopes of keeping the office were frustrated by Lieutenant Governor Wendell Ford, a Democrat, who ran up a margin of 60,000 votes over Republican Thomas D. Emberton. The Kentucky loss reduced to 20 the number of state capitols under Republican control.

In Virginia, Democrat Henry E. Howell, Jr., defeated Republican George R. Shafran and Democrat George J. Kostel in a special election for lieutenant governor in November. Howell ran as an independent. His victory gave him a strong base from which to launch a drive for governor in 1973.

Republicans failed to dislodge Democrats from their power bases in most major cities. In Chicago, Richard E. Friedman, an independent running with Republican backing, was crushed on April 6 by the landslide vote that returned Democrat Richard J. Daley to an unprecedented fifth term as mayor. On November 2, liberal Republican Thacher Longstreth lost the Philadelphia mayoralty race to Democrat Frank L. Rizzo. In San Francisco, Republican Harold S. Dobbs was one of 10 opponents who failed to block the re-election of Democratic Mayor Joseph L. Alioto.

Lindsay's Switch. Republicans lost control of New York City on August 11, when Mayor John V. Lindsay switched to the Democratic Party. This created serious problems for Republicans, because Lindsay's action made him New York state's most important Democrat and a potential candidate for governor in 1974. There was also the possibility that he might be a contender for the Democratic presidential nomination in 1972. Lindsay had long been in trouble with the Republican Party and had feuded with Governor Nelson A. Rockefeller. He won re-election in 1969 as a liberal independent and apparently felt he had a brighter future as a Democrat. See LINDSAY, JOHN VLIET.

President Nixon took no part in the 1971 campaigns and had no comment after the elections. No clear-cut patterns emerged from them despite the traditional claims and counterclaims of party spokesmen. "I believe the results foreshadow a Democratic trend that will carry through to November, 1972," said Senator Hubert H. Humphrey (D., Minn.). But Senator Robert J. Dole (R., Kans.), Republican national chairman, said, "Overall, I believe that it is clear that Republicans are continuing to build strength toward the 1972 presidential elections."

In the Senate, Republican ranks were split between liberals and conservatives. Senator Hugh D. Scott, Jr., of Pennsylvania, a moderate-to-liberal,

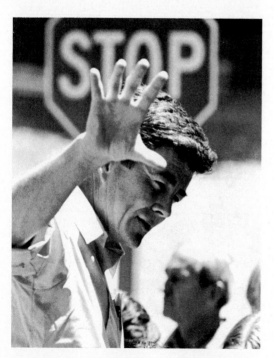

Congressman Paul N. McCloskey, Jr., (R., Calif.), one of the Republican challengers for the 1972 presidential nomination, gives an antiwar speech in Woodside, Calif.

won re-election as Senate Republican leader on January 21, defeating Senator Howard H. Baker, Jr., of Tennessee by four votes. Baker is a member of the conservative bloc.

Looking Ahead to 1972, Republicans were encouraged by President Nixon's continued lead over all potential Democratic challengers in the national opinion polls. For the Democrats, the problem of unseating an incumbent President was further complicated by the Republicans' money advantages. In a single night, November 10, President Nixon helped his party raise $5 million for the 1972 campaign. He addressed $500-a-plate "Salute to the President" dinners in New York City and Chicago. His speeches were heard at dinners in 18 other cities via closed-circuit television.

On July 23, the Republican National Committee chose San Diego, Calif., as the site for the 1972 Republican National Convention. President Nixon favored San Diego, calling it his "lucky city." However, San Diego's residents, fearing 1968-Chicago-style demonstrations, were less than enthusiastic about the prospect. In September, a citizens' group unsuccessfully sought an injunction against the use of city tax revenues for the convention.

The Republican Committee on Delegates and Organizations recommended on July 22 that half the members of state delegations to the 1972 Republican National Convention be women. The committee also called for equitable representation of minorities and youth.

Congressman Paul N. McCloskey, Jr., a liberal California Republican, on July 9 challenged President Nixon for the Republican presidential nomination. He planned to enter the 1972 primaries in California and New Hampshire. While McCloskey has virtually no chance of winning the nomination, he felt that his announced candidacy would bring pressure on the President to end the war in Indochina. He said he would enter a slate of antiwar delegates in the California primary. Although McCloskey spoke at "Dump Nixon" rallies, he still contended that the struggle for change should take place within the major political parties. See McCLOSKEY, PAUL N., JR.

A challenge from a conservative Republican came on December 29, when Congressman John M. Ashbrook of Ohio announced his candidacy. He claimed Mr. Nixon was drifting toward the left.

Outspoken Vice-President Spiro T. Agnew aroused much debate in 1971 as to whether he was a political asset or a liability. Rumors persisted that the President was thinking of dropping Agnew from the 1972 Republican ticket. Agnew, however, did not appear concerned, saying that if Mr. Nixon selected a different running mate, he would support the choice. See AGNEW, SPIRO T.   William McGaffin

See also AMERICAN PARTY; DEMOCRATIC PARTY; ELECTIONS.

RETAILING. Retailers were keeping their hopes high throughout 1971, but the big wave of buying never quite gathered real force until the Christmas selling season – the period when about 40 per cent of all retail sales are made. Retailers faced the last quarter with some optimism, but still feeling the tremors of the new (and still unclear) economic policy. Nevertheless, retail sales picked up after the 90-day wage-price freeze, especially for durable goods. Sales of soft goods experienced more modest gains. In November, retail sales jumped an estimated $600 million, up 13.5 per cent over November, 1970, and, during the Christmas selling season, sales jumped an estimated 8 to 9 per cent in volume and 11 to 12 per cent in dollars over 1970.

Disposable consumer income (income after taxes) continued to rise in 1971. The increase was unusually large in the first and second quarters, but slowed down somewhat thereafter to close the year with the rate of increase averaging about 7 per cent. Consumers had more money to put away or spend but, during the first half of the year, as in 1970, they were saving an abnormally high percentage of their incomes, nearly 8 per cent as compared with an average of 6.3 per cent from 1962 to 1970. The consumer savings rate dropped below 8 per cent during the third quarter for the first time since the second quarter of 1970.

Consumer Survey. Clearly the public was remaining cautious in the early stages of the freeze. As late as the end of September, more than a month after President Richard M. Nixon announced the government's broad new attack on inflation and economic problems, the University of Michigan's respected Survey Research Center reported that "a basic improvement in consumer sentiment has yet to materialize."

Consumer Debt. Signs of some movement could be seen, however. For example, the September figure on consumer debt showed that the public piled up $999 million in new debt, a record for any month, topping the previous record of $974 million set in the boom month of October, 1968. Such a commitment to installment debt seemed to indicate a new willingness to spend and a new confidence. However, analysis showed that the greater part of the increase was accounted for by purchases of new automobiles. Automobile sales were boosted by the public's apparent reasoning that the freeze, along with its elimination of the 7 per cent excise tax, offered a bargain buying opportunity. New-car sales in 1971 were expected to set a record at more than 10 million units.

Sears, Roebuck and Company, the nation's largest retailer, was showing sales gains of close to 9 per cent at the close of the year. Even after adjusting for inflation, that rate of growth would indicate a good, if not spectacular, year for retailing.   Edwin W. Darby

RHODE ISLAND. See STATE GOVERNMENT.

RHODESIA found the pressures of British and United States economic sanctions suddenly eased in late 1971. In November, Great Britain negotiated a settlement with the government of Prime Minister Ian D. Smith, and the U.S. Congress lifted the ban on importing Rhodesian chrome.

Sir Alex Douglas-Home, the British foreign secretary, visited Rhodesia in November. The visit was demanded by British Conservatives who had grown tired of what they called ineffectual United Nations (UN) sanctions. When they met, Smith and Douglas-Home were able to agree on a settlement. The British House of Commons voted to accept the agreement on December 1. However, the approval of the Rhodesian people was still needed.

Complicated Plan. The terms announced in November were far from the original "no independence before majority African rule" policy of former British Prime Minister Harold Wilson's Labour Government in 1968. Great Britain will grant independence as soon as Rhodesia arranges for wider black African political representation. This is to be done by a complicated formula in which those who qualify for a so-called "upper roll," based on their education and wealth, will be allowed to vote. To be placed on the upper roll, blacks must have a $2,700 yearly income or have property worth $5,400; or be secondary school graduates and have a yearly income of $1,800 or property worth $3,600.

When the number of black voters equals 6 per cent of the registered whites, two new parliamentary seats for blacks will be created. This process will be repeated for each bloc of black voters equal to 6 per cent of the white voters, until parity is reached in Parliament. Then, 10 more parliamentary seats will be created to be filled by either blacks or whites. At this point, black Africans could achieve majority rule. Also, a new constitution will be drawn up, containing some safeguards for the rights of blacks.

World Reaction. This formula obviously left little chance for black majority rule in this century. The British government, however, maintained it was the only way to prevent Rhodesia from becoming completely racially segregated and aligned with South Africa.

Black African nations generally reacted negatively. The Organization of African Unity denounced the settlement as a "sellout," and the UN continued the economic sanctions against Rhodesia. The United States was expected to support the settlement reluctantly.

Facts in Brief. Population: 5,594,000. Government: President Clifford Dupont; Prime Minister Ian D. Smith. Monetary Unit: Rhodesian dollar. Foreign Trade: exports, $318,000,000; imports, $279,000,000. Principal Exports: tobacco, asbestos, copper.   George Shepherd

ROADS AND HIGHWAYS. See BUILDING AND CONSTRUCTION; TRANSPORTATION.

ROMAN CATHOLIC CHURCH. The synod of Bishops, an advisory body created by Vatican II to share in the government of the church, in 1971 rejected the principle of optional celibacy for Latin Rite priests. The synod convened in Rome from September 30 to November 6. Although 107 bishops voted against the ordination of married men to the priesthood, 87 supported a statement endorsing their ordination in special cases. Pope Paul VI has the power to permit ordination of married men, and the closeness of the vote may incline him to exercise this power in cases of special pastoral need. In a statement on justice and peace, the synod endorsed the principle of conscientious objection to wars.

An unprecedented synod event was an address by the British economist Barbara Ward. She maintained that the church should conduct its own affairs "in a strict spirit of justice and poverty."

The synod did not explicitly discuss the candidacy of priests in politics but warned that ordinarily "no priest should become a leader or active militant of any political faction." (As in 1970, several priests ran for political office in the United States.)

John Cardinal Heenan of London urged the bishops to sell church treasures and donate the proceeds to the poor. This echoed a proposal made earlier in the year by Cardinal Maurer of Sucre, Bolivia, and supported by many of the Latin American clergy.

During the days of the synod, Father Maximilian Kolbe, a Polish Franciscan, was beatified by Pope Paul, a step toward canonization as a saint. The Franciscan martyr had volunteered to take the place of the father of a family who had been marked for execution in the Nazi death camp at Auschwitz during World War II.

Peace, War, and Politics. Addressing a working-class audience on Jan. 1, 1971, Pope Paul urged the peoples of the world to demand that their leaders avoid war. Then, on January 12, a federal grand jury in Harrisburg, Pa., named or formally indicted 13 persons, 10 of them priests or nuns, on the charge of conspiracy to kidnap Henry A. Kissinger, special assistant to President Richard M. Nixon, and to blow up the heating systems of federal buildings in Washington, D.C. The priests included Fathers Daniel and Philip Berrigan, Catholic antiwar militants.

At the annual January meeting of the Inter-American Cooperation Program in Washington, D.C., many Latin American theologians called for a theology of "liberation" from the evils of the capitalistic system. Progressive Roman Catholics were in the vanguard of the social reform movement in Latin America, often in conflict with national political regimes. Archbishop Helder Camara of Brazil has been a key figure in this peaceful revolution. Numerous instances of political repression and torture of priests were reported during 1971, especially in Brazil.

Ukrainian Request. Pope Paul refused to recognize a patriarchate for the Ukraine, thereby rejecting Joseph Cardinal Slipyj who had been proposed by the Ukrainian Catholics for the patriarchate. At the synod, Cardinal Slipyj said that Ukrainian Catholics were victims of church diplomacy as well as Communist persecution. Sixteen Ukrainian bishops held their own "synod" in Rome during the official synod, but there was no talk of a schism.

In July, Pope Paul asked that Jerusalem be protected "by a special statute guaranteed by international treaty." This evoked protests from certain leaders in the Catholic-Jewish dialogue who spoke against the internationalization of Jerusalem or the holy places.

Joseph Cardinal Mindszenty arrived in Rome after 15 years of voluntary exile in the United States Embassy in Budapest. This climaxed a long period of negotiations between the Vatican and Hungary.

All of Ulster's bishops issued a statement condemning the "war of violence" conducted by the provisional wing of the Irish Republican Army in Northern Ireland. In August, Pope Paul broke a two-year silence on the Ulster troubles, blaming "exceptional security measures" for the worsening of the troubles. These measures allowed the imprisonment of Catholic suspects without trial.

The Vatican Press announced that the Archbishop of Hanoi had consecrated Father Paul Nang as Bishop of Vinh.

Relief for Poor Refugees. The American Bishops' Catholic Relief Services sent approximately $8-million worth of supplies to refugees in Pakistan from March to September.

In March, the United States Bishops' Antipoverty Campaign announced it had raised $8.4 million. This is the largest total ever reached in a single national collection.

Celibacy and Abortion. In a survey, the National Federation of Priests' Councils, in the United States, voted overwhelmingly in favor of optional celibacy for priests. In the survey, conducted by the National Opinion Research Center, only 27 per cent of the priests queried rejected all artificial contraception, but there was little indication of any change in their condemnation of abortion and premarital sex.

In June, Lawrence Cardinal Shehan of Baltimore ordained six married men as deacons, and John Cardinal Dearden of Detroit ordained 13 to the same order. Pope Paul simplified certain rules for marriage cases in church courts. Previously, cases of alleged nullity of marriage often had dragged on for years in these courts.

Women in the Church. In May, Pope Paul addressed a letter to Maurice Cardinal Roy, the Canadian president of the Pontifical Commission on Justice and Peace, in which discrimination against women was discussed. The pope wrote that legisla-

Pope Paul greets Joseph Cardinal Mindszenty of Hungary, who flew to Vatican City in September, thus ending 15 years' exile in U.S. Embassy in Budapest.

tion should be "directed to protecting her vocation and at the same time recognizing her equal rights to participate in cultural, economic, social, and political life."

Civil Laws. American prelates in 1971 tended to restrict their efforts mainly to informing their own coreligionists about upcoming legislation. The New York state bishops, for instance, informed Catholics about reforms in abortion laws and designated the week of April 25 as "Right to Life Week." In view of the financial plight of the parochial schools, however, the American bishops made public appeals to taxpayers and legislators for support of religious schools. They asked for aid for those features of Roman Catholic education that serve "a secular purpose."

In June, the Supreme Court of the United States struck down a Pennsylvania law that permitted "the purchase of secular services" and a Rhode Island nonpublic teachers' salary supplement act. This prompted the bishops to plead for legislation that would provide for some form of aid to parents of parochial-school children. At the Knights of Columbus annual dinner in New York City in August, President Nixon announced that he could be counted on to help stop the trend away from aid to religious schools.

Publications. Hans Kung, a Swiss Catholic theologian, published in April the highly controversial *Infallible? An Inquiry.* The book's theme was that the church is not infallible, but merely indefectible, and that it has made grave errors but, nevertheless, communicates the gospel without fail.

During the year, various textbooks that were published on sex education were severely criticized by ultraconservative Catholics. Likewise, publishers issued new catechisms utilizing new psychological approaches for adults and for students.

In June, the Vatican issued a catechetical directory that caused some Catholic educators to raise a storm of protest. The protest subsided when it was explained that it was not intended as a catechism but as "a service for local commissions of episcopal conferences responsible for the supervision of catechisms."

The Worldwide Membership of the Roman Catholic church remained fairly stable in 1971. Gains in missionary countries compensated for losses in countries such as the Netherlands, where there was a drop in church attendance. In the United States, according to the *Official Catholic Directory* for 1971, the total Catholic population increased by 342,640 over 1970's total of 48,214,749. However, the number of priests declined by 1,031, sisters by 7,286, and seminarians by about 3,000. The number of converts dipped from 92,670 in 1970 to 84,534 in 1971, and there were 290,695 fewer students enrolled in Catholic schools.   John B. Sheerin

ROMANIA continued to cultivate good relations with all countries, especially Communist regimes, in 1971. Its close friendship with China, however, caused severe Russian displeasure and brought attacks in the Hungarian press and that of other Warsaw Pact nations. The Warsaw Pact countries worried Romania by holding military exercises along Romania's frontiers.

President Nicolae Ceausescu's 25-day trip to Asia in June, particularly his heavily publicized visit to China, earned him a cold reception when he went to Moscow on June 26. He had already heard bitter recriminations in Mongolia. A meeting of Warsaw Pact leaders in the Crimea in August discussed "the unity of the Socialist bloc." Romania, although absent, was probably high on the agenda.

Emergency Meeting. A joint session of the Romanian Communist Party Central Committee, the Cabinet, and the State Council was held in August. The meeting endorsed Ceausescu's foreign policy, including that toward China. Li Teh-cheng, head of the Chinese People's Army political department, led a military delegation to Romania in late August. He publicly urged the Romanians to continue their independent stand with China's support. Warsaw Pact pressure stopped abruptly after August 23, Romania's national holiday. Military maneuvers in Bulgaria in September followed those in Hungary in July and August, but without Russian

or Romanian participation. All share borders with Romania. As soon as the crisis was over, Romania began to play it down, denying any resemblance to the situation that preceded the 1968 invasion of Czechoslovakia.

On July 9, Ceausescu launched a campaign to combat "cosmopolitan attitudes and artistic fashions borrowed from the capitalist world." It led to the removal of some Western television programs and films. Many Western observers saw the campaign primarily as Ceausescu's attempt to deny Russia any excuse for direct military intervention.

Economic Problems. Romania continued in economic difficulty in 1971. Aftereffects of the disastrous floods in 1970 were still felt. A drive was launched to increase agricultural production for export to reduce Romania's growing balance-of-payments deficit with Western countries. West Germany became Romania's main Western trading partner.

Facts in Brief. Population: 20,616,000. Government: Communist Party General Secretary and State Council President Nicolae Ceausescu; Prime Minister Ion Gheorghe Maurer. Monetary Unit: leu. Foreign Trade: exports, $1,851,000,000; imports, $1,960,000,000. Principal Exports: food, lumber, fuel.   Chris Cviic

ROTARY INTERNATIONAL. See SERVICE CLUBS.

ROWING. See SPORTS.

RUBBER. See MANUFACTURING.

RUSSIA. A cautiously conservative domestic policy stood in sharp contrast to Russia's vigorous foreign policy in 1971. The greatest activity occurred in Europe, the Middle East, Asia, and North America. During the year, Russia aligned itself more closely with India (and against China and Pakistan), and increased its visibility in the Middle East. It also sought new ties in the Western Hemisphere, particularly with Canada and some Latin American countries.

The lively Russian foreign policy activity during the year reflected the growth of Soviet global commitments. Many of the policy steps were in response to moves by rival powers.

In Europe, Russia's main objective early in 1971 was to consolidate its hold over its East European bloc after Poland's workers rioted and forced a leadership change in December, 1970. In February, 1971, Edward Gierek, Poland's new party leader, obtained a Russian loan. In Czechoslovakia, Moscow continued to back Communist Party leader Gustav Husak's conservative regime rather than the deeply unpopular and discredited hard-line Stalinists who, nevertheless, remained a potential alternative should Husak fail. Hungary's moderate reformers also enjoyed continuing Russian support. But East Germany's veteran party leader, Walter Ulbricht, was eased out in May at Moscow's insistence because of his unyielding opposition to the present Soviet policy of reaching friendlier relations with West Germany.

All East European trade-bloc members, including Romania, accepted the Russian-sponsored long-term program for economic integration at the end of July. The decision was a success for Russia's policy of keeping a tight economic grip on Eastern Europe. But Romania's open flirtation with China, symbolized by President Nicolae Ceausescu's highly publicized trip to China in June, provoked a sharp anti-Romanian campaign in the press of Hungary and other Warsaw Pact countries.

China's growing links with Romania and Yugoslavia led to an unsuccessful campaign of threats (including border military maneuvers) against Romania and Yugoslavia in July and August. But in September, the Kremlin suddenly switched to a more conciliatory line toward Romania, and on September 22, Communist Party leader Leonid I. Brezhnev visited Yugoslavia. During the visit, he gave qualified reaffirmation to Yugoslavia's right to an "independent road to Socialism."

In the West, Russian diplomacy continued to press for a European security conference sanctioning the status quo in Europe and leading to full recognition of East Germany by the West. Russia recognized the seriousness of the prior conditions the West insisted on before joining such a conference or

ratifying West Germany's 1970 treaties with the Soviet Union and Poland. The West wanted an agreement giving West Berlin access to East Berlin, and providing secure transportation, economic, and social links between the two. West Berlin's right to be represented internationally by West Germany also was important. A four-power agreement resulted on August 23. See GERMANY, WEST.

West German Chancellor Willy Brandt's sudden visit to the Crimea in September marked a gain for Brezhnev because Brandt supported the Soviet Union's call for a European security conference soon. But Brezhnev's much-publicized visit to France in October was only a partial success. He signed two agreements there on October 27. One provided for stronger technical, scientific, and economic cooperation between France and Russia. The other called for the French automobile firm, Renault, to aid in building a truck factory in Russia.

Russian relations with Britain reached their lowest point in many years when Britain expelled 105 Soviet diplomats and other officials as spies on September 24. But the mild Soviet retaliation supported the belief that Russia was eager to maintain its present diplomatic offensive in Europe. See ESPIONAGE.

In the Middle East, Russia was involved in several complex situations. On January 15, at the official opening of Egypt's Aswan High Dam, built

View along Kalinin Prospekt in Moscow includes a placard for the 24th congress of Russia's Communist Party. The congress had been delayed for a full year.

with Russian help, Nikolai V. Podgorny, chairman of the Supreme Soviet Presidium, announced that Russia would provide about $180 million toward furnishing electricity to 4,000 Egyptian villages. The project will take five years to complete, and cost about $275 million. But relations with Egypt became strained after the May purge of Vice-President Aly Sabri and pro-Russian officials.

On May 27 the two governments concluded a 15-year treaty of friendship and cooperation. It provided for consultation in case either country is attacked or threatened. But the two countries were wary of each other's moves for the rest of the year.

Egypt's close cooperation with the anti-Communist Sudan complicated the situation further. An unsuccessful Communist coup there in July led to violent and bloody reprisals against the local Communist Party. Libya's active help in the Sudanese countercoup strained relations with Moscow.

In Asia. Russia reacted with suspicion and propaganda attacks to the July 15 announcement that President Richard M. Nixon would visit Peking in 1972. On August 9, Russia and India signed a treaty of peace, friendship, and cooperation. The treaty seemed as much a gesture against China as it was a move to protect India against Pakistan.

After a pause of several months, the Russo-Chinese controversy revived in April and increased

Leonid Rigerman and his mother leave the U.S. Embassy in Moscow with passports following a long struggle to win Russian recognition of their U.S. citizenship.

in July and August. In April, China's *Red Flag* referred to the "intensification" of Russia's change into a "fascist dictatorship." After President Nixon's announcement that he would visit China, Russia charged indirectly that China and the United States were secretly allied against Russia.

The Sino-Soviet dispute quieted after the announcement that Nixon would also visit Moscow. It revived again in November, however, with an article in the Russian magazine *International Affairs* criticizing China's foreign policy. In December, Russia backed India in the bloody, two-week India-Pakistan war, while China and the United States sided with Pakistan.

U.S. Relations. In February, President Nixon called U.S. relations with Russia "mixed." But Russia and the United States continued their strategic arms limitation talks. The fifth round of these negotiations ended September 24 in Helsinki with tentative agreements on ways to limit the risk of an accidental nuclear war and to improve communications between the two superpowers by switching to a satellite rather than using the teleprinter "hot line" between Moscow and Washington, D.C. The sixth round began on November 15 in Vienna with fairly optimistic hopes for major progress soon. The United States in November agreed to sell grain worth $136 million to Russia, $118 million worth from the Continental Grain Company of New York and Cargill, Incorporated, of Minneapolis. The deal was larger than all American exports to Russia in 1970.

Relations with Canada. Russia continued to exploit sharp and growing differences between Canada and the United States in 1971 to establish a position on the American continent. Canadian Prime Minister Pierre Elliott Trudeau visited Russia in May, and Premier Aleksei N. Kosygin paid a return visit to Canada in October. During his visit, Kosygin seemed to be offering Canada an economic and political alternative to its close relationship with the United States. Canada and Russia had already formed working groups to study business cooperation in the fields of architecture, construction and building materials, forest industries, nonferrous metals, electric power, and oil and gas industries. See CANADA.

In Latin America, Russia granted a $27-million loan to Bolivia in August. It also signed an aid agreement to Chile on May 28.

In Domestic Politics, the main event of 1971 was the Communist Party's 24th congress. It was held, after a year's delay, in Moscow's Palace of Congresses from March 30 to April 9. No changes occurred at the top of the party. The congress confirmed Brezhnev's supremacy in the Politburo, which was enlarged from 11 to 15 members.

The key congress theme, the demand for greater discipline, reflected the leaders' growing concern over the extent and persistence of political dissent. The congress endorsed the local party organizations' call for greater control over all aspects of public life. This set back the government apparatus, which had enjoyed some autonomy since Nikita S. Khrushchev's fall in 1964. (Khrushchev's "subjective" leadership was criticized, but his name was not mentioned. His death on September 11 received only brief notices in the Soviet press.)

The congress decided on a minor purge by requiring the exchange of party cards. Liberals' fears that Stalin and Stalinism would be revived did not materialize, but the persecution of prominent and active dissenters continued. So did harassment of Western news correspondents known to be in touch with them.

The role played by Russian psychiatric institutions in the torture of political dissidents was described in detail in illegal publications reaching the West. Western psychiatrists' protests against the misuse of psychiatry provoked the government newspaper *Izvestia* into an official denial in October.

Trials of Jews accused of trying to hijack an airliner in late 1970 and, more generally, of anti-Russian, Zionist propaganda were held in May and June. On May 20, Professor Andrey Sakharov, who heads the unofficial Human Rights Committee, protested the persecution and harassment of Russia's Jewish community. He appealed to the authorities to grant visas to those Jews who wish to emigrate to Israel. Russia increased the rate of Jewish emigration and, by the end of December, an estimated 10,000 Russian Jews – 10 times the 1970 total – had been allowed to leave. The policy led to restiveness among some of the country's other non-Russian groups.

The Economy. Russia's 1971-1975 plan was approved by the congress and published on April 11. It foresees an increase of 35 to 40 per cent in Russia's national income, 80 to 85 per cent of it to be achieved by higher labor productivity. Industrial output is to increase by from 42 to 46 per cent by 1975, with 87 to 90 per cent of that increase from higher productivity. The new awareness of the consumer and his needs seemed a direct consequence of the Polish workers' riots in December, 1970. Premier Kosygin said satisfaction of consumer needs had become the major objective of government economic policy. Brezhnev went further, calling defense of workers' legitimate rights a basic trade-union task. An October 28 resolution by the party's Central Committee specified wallpaper, curtains, hats, furs, and women's underwear among goods whose output is to go up 90 per cent by 1975. A bulletin reporting the state of the consumer goods market is to be published in Moscow. But Kosygin told the congress that heavy industry "is, and remains, the foundation of the country's economic might." Light industries' output is to grow no faster than it did from 1966 to 1970. This certainly casts a shadow over Russia's ability to satisfy, even remotely, the potentially huge consumer demand that exists in Russia.

In Agriculture, the outlook is brighter, especially in light of large investments earmarked for it. The new five-year plan calls for increases of 16 per cent in the average grain output, 23 per cent in meat production, and 15 per cent in dairy products while the population increases an estimated 6.3 per cent.

Officially, Russia's modest economic reform of 1965 was not abandoned. The party congress emphasized, however, the increased party role in the direct management of the economy. The 1965 reform had sought to reduce that role by allowing managers to make more decisions. The congress also stressed the continued importance of central planning.

The party congress opened a campaign for stricter labor discipline as a way to reduce the huge labor turnover – 4 million people a year. The campaign also aims for more rational use of raw materials and reserves. The first nine months of 1971 saw economic growth of 8 per cent, compared to 8.3 per cent a year earlier.

Facts in Brief. Population: 248,760,000. Government: Communist Party General Secretary Leonid I. Brezhnev; Premier Aleksei N. Kosygin; Supreme Soviet Presidium Chairman Nikolai V. Podgorny. Monetary Unit: ruble. Foreign Trade: exports, $12,000,000,000; imports, $11,739,000,000. Principal Exports: machinery, fuels.　　Chris Cviic

RWANDA. See AFRICA.

SAFETY. The Occupational Safety and Health Act, which affects more than 57 million employees in over 4 million places of employment, became effective on April 28, 1971. Safety officials hailed it as the most significant law ever enacted to protect the employee in the workplace. The legislation applies to all industries affected by commerce, except mining and railroads, which are governed by other federal laws. The National Safety Council called the new law "perhaps the single most important event in the history of the safety movement."

The new law is administered by the Department of Labor and enforced by the Occupational Safety and Health Review Commission, a quasi-judicial body appointed by President Richard M. Nixon. Another agency recently established within the Department of Health, Education, and Welfare – the National Institute of Occupational Safety and Health – has responsibility for research, training, and related activities. The secretary of labor is authorized to announce the standards, or rules, for avoiding hazards. The act calls for safety and health inspections of workplaces to determine compliance with the law.

Automobile Safety. Although the new law was a significant development, it did not ease the mounting concern of safety officials over the continuing injuries at home, on the highway, and at play. More than 16 million motor-vehicle accidents involving

Doll's flameproof pajamas resist a match in Secretary of Commerce Maurice Stans's demonstration. Such sleepwear for children will be required starting in 1973.

seat have buckled their safety belts. Cars manufactured after August, 1975, must have passive devices –perhaps airbags– to protect the occupants automatically.

Recreational Safety. With more free time, Americans have been expanding their recreational activities and at the same time meeting new hazards. Efforts to make traveling safer in this area have focused on snowmobile problems. A rising number of states have passed legislation limiting the use of snowmobiles, which were blamed for 102 deaths and an untold number of injuries in 1970.

The Federal Boating Act, designed to protect the estimated 40 million persons who go boating every year, was signed into law in 1971. During the previous five years, about 7,000 persons were killed in boating accidents. Drownings, increasing each year, totaled 7,300 in 1970.

One of the most important, and most neglected, aspects of safety–protection of the individual in his home as a consumer–received long-overdue attention in 1971. New safety standards were developed, and existing ones upgraded, for such products as lawn mowers, glazing materials used in buildings, flammable fabrics, and safety closures for packaging hazardous products. Standards were being developed for such products as children's toys and infant furniture. Howard Pyle

SAILING. See BOATS AND BOATING.

27.7 million drivers occurred during 1971. In 1970, they caused about $4.7 billion in property damage. Because of this, efforts have increased to improve highways, tighten automobile safety standards, and maintain programs of recalling vehicles that may have defective parts.

The federal government is heavily involved with the problem of reducing automobile accident fatalities and injuries. The Department of Transportation, for example, is pressing for improved protection for occupants.

Cars manufactured after Aug. 15, 1973, if they

ST. LOUIS tried a new approach to citizen participation in 1971. The East-West Gateway Coordinating Council, representing local government units throughout the metropolitan area, established a Regional Citizen Forum with financial help from the Danforth Foundation and the Department of Housing and Urban Development (HUD).

The 27-member forum was designed to represent a broad cross section of the St. Louis area's leaders and citizens. It seeks ways to involve citizens in efforts to resolve environmental pollution, housing, law enforcement, transportation, governmental reform, and other problems.

The council developed a new dimension in representation by adding six "regional citizens" to the board specifically to represent five sectors: blacks, business and labor, and the educational and religious communities.

Population Decline. The St. Louis metropolitan area had a 1970 population of 2,363,768. Although this represented a 12.3 per cent increase during the 1960s, the city of St. Louis suffered the most severe population decline of any major U.S. city. Population fell 17 per cent to 622,236 persons, of whom 254,191 (40.9 per cent) were black. The city's black population had been 28.6 per cent of the total in 1960. The white population of the city fell by 31 per cent, indicating that blacks would be in the majority before the next census.

Accidental Deaths and Death Rates

| | 1970 | | 1971† | |
	Number	Rate††	Number	Rate††
Motor Vehicle	54,800	26.9	55,000	26.7
Work	14,200	7.0	14,390	6.9
Home	26,500	13.0	26,500	12.8
Public	22,000	10.8	22,000	10.7
Total*	114,000	56.0	114,000	55.3

†For 12-month period up to Nov. 1, 1971.
††Deaths per 100,000 population.
*The total does not equal the sum of the four classes because *Motor Vehicle* includes some deaths also included in *Work* and *Home*.
Source: National Safety Council estimates

do not incorporate passive restraint systems, must have an ignition interlock system. These will prevent the cars from starting until those sitting in the front

The city added 270 men to its police force during the year and achieved a 2.6 per cent reduction in its crime rate. This was accomplished despite an increasing national crime rate and a 17 per cent increase in crime in the city's suburbs. In the continuing battle against crime, the city launched a major street and alley lighting program.

The Department of Health, Education, and Welfare reported that 14.7 per cent of the city's residents were on welfare as of February, 1971. St. Louis ranked fifth among major cities in the percentage of population receiving public aid. This was a marked increase over the 12.5 per cent in February, 1970.

Housing. St. Louis devoted a great deal of attention to urban renewal during the year. Derelict buildings were torn down and Operation Breakthrough, an experiment in mass-produced housing sponsored by HUD, was launched.

The U.S. Department of Justice filed suit against the suburb of Blackjack in June, charging that the suburb was illegally attempting to block construction of lower-income housing. After learning of the planned housing project, the residents of Blackjack had incorporated their community and had passed a zoning law prohibiting multifamily housing.

St. Louis fared well under the new Amtrak system of passenger rail service. Two routes were set up that give St. Louis direct connections with both Chicago and Washington, D.C.   J. M. Banovetz

SALVATION ARMY designated 1971 as the "Children's Year." Theme of this international crusade was "Every Child Matters." The program grew out of strong concern that the Army was not in touch with the children of today.

In a personal letter sent to every Salvation Army officer in the world, General Erik Wickberg invited them to join him in trying to make the entire Salvation Army "child conscious"; to critically examine current children's activities and produce a strategy for the 1970s; to generate interest and enthusiasm among children; to contact children that are unfamiliar with the Army; and to lead children to commit themselves to Christ and His service. Related programs that have been an integral part of Army activities since its founding were to be given new emphasis. These include personal contact, individual guidance, group projects, Sunday school, cradle roll, and junior soldiers. Colonel William Larson was appointed to serve as director of the International Children's Year Crusade.

The Fourth Soldiers National Seminar on Evangelism was held at the Christian Conference Center of the Navigators near Colorado Springs, Colo., in July. The 110 delegates who attended were selected from Salvation Army Corps in all parts of the United States. The age range of the delegates was 18 to 55, but 41 were 30 years old or less, indicating a growing emphasis on youth.   Joseph P. Anderson

SAN FRANCISCO. Incumbent Mayor Joseph L. Alioto won re-election to his second term on Nov. 2, 1971. Alioto, a Democrat, won despite a federal grand jury indictment charging him with nine counts of bribery, conspiracy, and mail fraud.

The continuing conflict over the "Manhattanization" of San Francisco, the systematic obliteration of the city's skyline by high-rise office buildings, erupted anew in February after U.S. Steel announced plans to build a hotel-office tower complex on pilings over the bay. Conservationists objected strongly to the plan. Their Save Our Bay campaign was successful in stopping both U.S. Steel's plans and landfill operations that were already underway.

An unprecedented proposal to halt the construction of more high-rise buildings in the city was presented to voters on the November 2 ballot. The measure would have limited the height of future buildings to six stories. The proposal was defeated by a margin of 65,607 votes. Since 1960, 21 new skyscrapers have been built in San Francisco, and another 23 are scheduled for the next five years.

Police and Teachers. San Francisco's Committee on Crime produced a massive condemnation of the city's police force, reporting that it was archaic, inefficient, incompetent, and more concerned with politics than professionalism. Mayor Alioto and Police Chief Alfred Nelder disagreed.

San Francisco's schools were closed for 19 days when teachers went on strike on March 24. The teachers won a 5 per cent pay increase and a reduction in the size of classes.

The city's plan to achieve racial balance through busing met with public opposition, particularly from the Chinese-American community. Parents in Chinatown felt that busing their children to schools in other areas would defeat efforts to preserve their cultural heritage. The Supreme Court of the United States ruled in August against their efforts to halt the busing plan, stating that integration laws apply to all races. See CIVIL RIGHTS.

Oil Spills. The worst oil spill in the history of San Francisco Bay occurred on January 18. Two Standard Oil tankers collided in fog, spilling approximately 1 million gallons of oil into the bay. The slick spread along the California coast, killing birds, fish, and other wildlife. A second spill occurred on September 17. A Standard Oil tanker spilled about 20,000 gallons of oil into the bay while it was unloading at a dock.

Population Data. The 1970 census showed that San Francisco ranked as the nation's 13th largest city with a population of 715,674, of whom 13.4 per cent were black. The count represented a 3.3 per cent decline from the city's 1960 total of 740,316. Although only 13th in size as a city, San Francisco, with Oakland, formed the sixth largest metropolitan area, with 3,109,519 persons.   J. M. Banovetz

SASKATCHEWAN. See CANADA.

SAUDI ARABIA. The Teheran agreement signed on Feb. 14, 1971, between the oil-producing Persian Gulf states and the major international oil companies ensured Saudi Arabia vastly increased oil revenue. Saudi Arabia's share was expected to be 81 per cent higher than in 1970, when royalties exceeded $1 billion. The Trans-Arabian Pipeline, which carries Saudi oil to Mediterranean ports, reopened in 1971. It had been closed for nine months because of political differences with Syria that kept repair crews from repairing a break.

King Faisal visited U.S. President Richard M. Nixon in Washington on May 27. He also visited several Arab and Asian countries. Signing of the first Saudi-Iranian trade agreement followed his trip to Iran.

Deposits of gold, silver, copper, and zinc worth an estimated $82.5 billion were discovered in central Arabia, further diversifying Saudi Arabia's resource base. The new Jizan Dam, with a storage capacity of more than 2.5 billion cubic feet of water, went into operation in March.

Facts in Brief. Population: 7,551,000. Government: King and Prime Minister Faisal. Monetary Unit: riyal. Foreign Trade: exports, $2,001,000,000; imports, $750,000,000. Principal Exports: petroleum and petroleum products.   William Spencer

SCHOOL. See COURTS AND LAWS; EDUCATION; Section One, FOCUS ON EDUCATION.

SCIENCE AND RESEARCH. Increasing demands for practical payoffs from basic research plagued scientists in 1971. Along with government officials, they re-examined the role of science in society.

The demand for practical results was at the heart of efforts by the American Cancer Society and New York philanthropist Mary Lasker to initiate a massive campaign to cure cancer. As spelled out in a bill introduced by Senator Edward M. Kennedy (D., Mass.) and later backed by President Richard M. Nixon, the campaign would establish a federal agency responsible solely for cancer research. The new agency would be modeled after the National Aeronautics and Space Administration (NASA), and would not be related to the government's main body for biomedical research, the National Institutes of Health (NIH). It was believed that the creation of a new agency might prompt Congress to pour ever-increasing funds into cancer research, and allow for a more "businesslike" and "goal-directed" management of the research.

In defending the campaign, its supporters and their congressional allies spoke of "breakthroughs" possibly leading to a cancer cure in the near future, if only enough money was spent. Most scientists, however, lined up in opposition to the campaign, fearing that the fragmentation of cancer research from the other health sciences in the NIH would retard, rather than promote, progress in curing the disease. They also believed that a "businesslike" approach would lead to mediocre, rather than creative, experimentation. Moreover, they argued that the basic knowledge necessary to undertake a massive assault against cancer was lacking.

Nevertheless, the bill sailed through the Senate by a vote of 79 to 1 on July 7. In the House of Representatives, however, the opposition from the scientific community coalesced behind Representative Paul G. Rogers (D., Fla.), chairman of the Health Subcommittee, who managed to hold the bill in committee in hopes of effecting some sort of compromise that would satisfy the scientists. On November 16, the House passed, 350 to 5, a bill that would increase government spending on cancer research, but keep the effort closely tied to NIH.

In his budget for fiscal 1972, President Nixon allowed modest increases in funds for research, thereby ending a two-year freeze in the level of government support for science. But here, too, the emphasis was on practical payoffs. Much of the increase went to weapons development, environmental problems, highway safety, air-traffic control, and reduction of crime. This trend also influenced the budget of the National Science Foundation (NSF), bastion of federal support for basic research.

Employment Problems. An apparent excess of basic research scientists accounted, at least in part,

U.S. Science and Technology Budget

Millions of dollars

Source: National Science Foundation

for this shift to the support of pragmatic work. An NSF survey of over 300,000 scientists found 2.6 per cent of them out of work. Chemists and physicists accounted for more than half the unemployed. While the plight of scientists was mild compared to the 6 per cent overall national unemployment, the Nixon Administration, nonetheless, saw it as a serious waste of highly trained manpower. It responded on April 2 with a $42-million program for aid to jobless scientists.

Another NSF study predicted a surplus of between 18,000 and 66,000 science graduates with Ph.D. degrees by 1980. The government responded to this with cutbacks in its support to graduate education.

High-Energy Research. Hardest hit by the shift of funds away from basic research was high-energy physics. This study of subatomic particles consumes comparatively large sums of money and offers in return only basic knowledge with no immediate practical applications. Physicists eagerly awaited the opening of a new $250-million particle accelerator in Batavia, Ill., but an older facility, the Princeton-Penn accelerator in New Jersey, was closed. Congressional overseers of scientific funding began to discuss which of the country's six remaining accelerators would have to be shut down next.

The Princeton-Penn accelerator may have a future in cancer research as one of several laboratories converted to new usage. Among the other laboratories slated for conversion to cancer research was the Army's former center for chemical and biological warfare research at Fort Detrick, Md. Another biological warfare center in Pine Bluff, Ark., was transferred to the Food and Drug Administration.

Pollution-Free Fuel. The search for new sources of nonpolluting energy was an area of intensive research in 1971. To develop such a fuel source, President Nixon asked Congress, on June 4, to spend $2-billion in the next decade for the development of a fast-breeder reactor. Fueled by plutonium, a fast-breeder reactor converts the most plentiful isotope of uranium, U^{238}, into more plutonium while producing steam that can be used to generate electricity. Immediately after President Nixon's announcement, however, a group of scientists brought suit to halt this development program, claiming that it would create a serious radiation hazard.

Scientists took an increasingly active role in political issues involving science in 1971. A group called the Federation of American Scientists, with a distinguished membership that included several former Department of Defense officials, actively lobbied in Congress. They opposed Defense Department claims of a threat from rapidly expanding Russian military research, NASA's planned reusable space shuttle, and the Atomic Energy Commission's test of a 5-megaton atomic warhead on Amchitka, in the Aleutian Islands.   Robert J. Bazell

SCOTT, GEORGE C. (1927-   ), was awarded the 1970 Oscar as best actor for his performance as General George S. Patton in the motion picture *Patton*. Despite his nomination, Scott refused to attend the Academy Awards ceremony on April 14, 1971. Also in 1971, he received a television Emmy award for "outstanding single performance" in the "Hallmark Hall of Fame" production of Arthur Miller's drama *The Price*.

Scott was born in Wise, Va., on Oct. 18, 1927. His mother died when he was 8 and he was reared mostly by his sister Helen. He joined the Marines when he was 17, served four years, and then enrolled at the University of Missouri School of Journalism. While a student there, he played the lead role in *The Winslow Boy* and realized that acting was for him.

After playing more than 150 roles in stock, Scott got his big break playing the title role in *Richard III* for the New York Shakespeare Festival in 1957. He also won acclaim in motion pictures, being nominated for Academy Awards for his role as the prosecutor in *Anatomy of a Murder* (1959) and as the gambler in *The Hustler* (1961). Scott's film credits also include the roles of General Buck Turgidson in *Dr. Strangelove* (1964), the doctor in *Petulia* (1968), and a gangster in *The Last Run* (1971).

Scott is married to actress Colleen Dewhurst. They have two sons.   Lillian Zahrt

SCULPTURE. See VISUAL ARTS.

SENEGAL. Political intrigue stalked Senegal's ruling circle in 1971. Jean Collin, the French-born minister of finance and economic affairs, was removed from his post in April and made minister of interior because of an anonymous letter accusing him of corruption. The letter blamed him for the country's economic troubles and contended that he favored French interests over those of the Senegalese.

A group of government supporters vigorously defended Collin by pointing out that the repeated poor peanut harvests, declining world prices for peanuts, and a reduction in direct French subsidies were responsible for Senegal's economic stagnation. However, the Collin affair became a rallying point for the political opposition.

There were student disorders at the University of Dakar in February. The students staged a strike and distributed literature denouncing the government of President Leopold Sedar Senghor. They were protesting poor housing conditions and the increased cost of their meals. The government closed the university on February 26, and it was reopened on March 18 with tighter administrative controls.

Facts in Brief. Population: 4,035,000. Government: President Leopold Sedar Senghor; Prime Minister Abdou Diouf. Monetary Unit: CFA franc. Foreign Trade: exports, $152,000,000; imports, $193,000,000. Principal Exports: peanuts and peanut oil, phosphates.   George Shepherd

SERVICE CLUBS

SERVICE CLUBS expanded their cooperative community-service projects in 1971. They also increased their emphasis on international exchange and cooperation, strengthened their means of communication with young people, and initiated activities designed to recruit new members.

Kiwanis International held its 56th annual convention in San Francisco, June 27 to 30. The highlight of the convention was the unveiling of the 1971-1972 Kiwanis International Major Emphasis Program, "Unite for Progress in Operation Drug Alert and Project Environment."

The program was aimed at maximizing achievement through service projects selected, planned, and implemented by Kiwanians, youth, and young adults working together in any area; extending the "Operation Drug Alert" program; and strengthening efforts to protect natural resources and improve the quality of our environment through both individual and community action.

Delegates also voted to approve two amendments to the Kiwanis constitution and bylaws. The first raised the per capita dues each club pays to Kiwanis International from $4.50 to $5.50 per year. The increase became effective Oct. 1, 1971. The second amendment restructured the committee format of Kiwanis, and also became effective as of October 1. Wes H. Bartlett, of Algona, Iowa, was elected president of Kiwanis International.

Lions International established its 25,000th club in 1971. The new club is in Fred, Tex.

Among the Leo clubs granted a charter in 1971 was one that represented a historical first for Lions International. The new Leo club's members are all students of the Model Secondary School for the Deaf in Washington, D.C.

To maintain Lions International's steady growth in membership, the board of directors adopted a far-ranging membership-retention program. Key to the program is a series of efforts to help members strengthen their clubs by means of a major service activity; a major fund-raising project; good public relations both within and without the club; good meetings; good association spirit; and good induction, indoctrination, and involvement procedures.

The Lions new international headquarters office building was completed in 1971. The new address is Lions International Office Building, York and Cermak Roads, Oak Brook, Ill. 60521.

The 54th annual convention of the International Association of Lions Clubs was held in Las Vegas, Nev., June 22 to 25, 1971. Robert J. Uplinger of Syracuse, N.Y., was elected president of Lions International.

Rotary International urged its clubs and members to bridge the generation gap through such activities as grants for study abroad, youth exchange, career conferences, youth centers, scout sponsorship, and job training.

There was a record increase in Rotary Clubs in 1971. On July 26, there were 14,900 clubs and an estimated 704,500 Rotarians living in 149 countries and geographical regions. Rotaract, Rotary International's three-year-old service organization for young adults, chartered its 1,000th club.

The Rotary Foundation trustees established a new program to provide 25 awards for one year's study in another country to teachers of the mentally, physically, and educationally handicapped. These awards will be made in 1973 and 1974. The trustees will also grant 25 new technical-training awards for candidates in developing countries.

Urs Burkard, 18, of Zurich, Switzerland, was the $500 grand prizewinner in the Rotary second world-wide poster art contest for secondary school students. He designed and painted the poster judged to best exemplify the contest theme, "World Peace Through World Understanding." The Zurich Rotary Club entered his poster in the contest.

More than 17,000 Rotarians from 73 countries attended the 62nd annual international convention held in Sydney, Australia, May 16 to 20. Ernst G. Breitholtz of Kalmar, Sweden, was elected president of Rotary International.   Joseph P. Anderson

SHIPS AND SHIPPING. See TRANSPORTATION.

SHOOTING. See SPORTS.

SIERRA LEONE. See AFRICA.

SKATING. See HOCKEY; ICE SKATING.

SKIING. The world's most successful skiers in 1971 were Gustavo Thoeni, a 20-year-old Italian customs guard, and Annamarie Proell, a 17-year-old Austrian. Among the best Americans were three members of the Cochran family of Richmond, Vt.—20-year-old Marilyn, 19-year-old Barbara, and 18-year-old Bob.

Thoeni and Miss Proell won the World Cup overall titles, decided in 24 competitions (9 special slalom, 8 giant slalom, and 7 downhill) in the United States, Canada, and Europe. France won the Nations Cup competition for overall team honors, and Austria was second.

Thoeni scored 155 of a possible 225 points. Next were Henri Duvillard of France with 135 points and Patrick Russel of France with 125. Tyler Palmer of Kearsarge, N.H., making his first European tour, finished 10th, the only American man in the top 20.

Cochran Girls Excel. The women's leaders were Miss Proell with 210 points, Michele Jacot of France with 177, and Isabelle Mir of France with 133. Only two American women ranked among the top 16, Barbara Cochran in 8th place and sister Marilyn in 11th. But in the 1971-1972 International Ski Federation seedings, Barbara was ranked first in giant slalom and Marilyn first in special slalom.

Both Cochran girls won World Cup races. Barbara took the special slalom and giant slalom in South Lake Tahoe, Calif., and Marilyn the special slalom in Beaupré, Canada. In the French championships in La Plagne in March, Marilyn won the special slalom, giant slalom, and combined titles.

U.S. Championships. In the U.S. Alpine Championships staged from March 12 to 14 in Aspen, Colo., Bob Cochran won the downhill, giant slalom, and combined. The special slalom went to Otto Tschudi of Norway. A week earlier, in the National Collegiate Athletic Association championships in Lead, S. Dak., Tschudi won three titles in leading Denver University to the team championship.

The women's national champions were Barbara Cochran in special slalom; Cheryl Bechdolt of Tahoe City, Calif., in downhill; Laurie Kreiner of Timmons, Canada, in giant slalom; and Judy Crawford of Toronto, Canada, in combined.

Professional skiers competed in nine U.S. meets on dual slalom or giant slalom courses. Vladimir (Spider) Sabich of Kyburz, Calif., was the leading money winner with $21,188.

Money was the main issue as the International Olympic Committee attempted to disqualify 10 outstanding amateur skiers from the 1972 Olympic Games. The 10 were accused of violating Olympic rules by taking $50 a day for teaching skiing in California. After six nations, including France and Austria, threatened to boycott the 1972 games, the International Olympic Committee backed down and allowed the skiers to enter the Olympics. Frank Litsky

SOCCER. Pelé, the world's most celebrated player, bid an emotional farewell to international competition in 1971. He played his final game for the Brazilian national team on July 18, before a record crowd of 130,000 in Rio de Janeiro, Brazil, as well as an international television audience. At halftime, he jogged around the field, stripped off his shirt, and waved it to the crowd as tears streamed down his cheeks. He planned to continue playing for the Santos club, but will make few appearances overseas. At 30, Pelé (Edson Arantes do Nascimento) is a millionaire, and his businesses demand his time.

Arsenal of London and Celtic of Glasgow had highly successful years. Arsenal won the English League first division title and the English Association Cup, only the second team to achieve this feat in the 1900s. Celtic swept the Scottish first division, Scottish League Cup, and Scottish Association Cup.

Ajax of Amsterdam won the European Cup, Chelsea of England the European Cup-Winners Cup, and Leeds United of England the European Fairs Cup. Hota of New York gained the U.S. National Challenge Cup with a 6-4 overtime victory over the Los Angeles Yugoslavs.

Professional soccer struggled with small crowds in the United States. The North American Soccer League expanded to eight teams, losing Kansas City but adding New York City, Toronto, and Montreal. Dallas won the league title. Frank Litsky

Pelé, retiring from international competition, trots around Rio de Janeiro stadium to a standing ovation at his last game with the Brazilian Nationals.

SOCIAL SECURITY benefit increases of 10 per cent were authorized in legislation passed by Congress and signed into law by President Richard M. Nixon on March 17, 1971. The benefit increase, retroactive to Jan. 1, 1971, raised total monthly benefits by about $270 million to $2.9 billion.

Under the new payment schedule, minimum benefits for individuals rise from $64 to $70.40, and from $96 to $105.60 for couples. Average payments rise from $114 to $126 for a retired worker, and from $199 to $219 for a retired couple. A widowed mother with children will receive an average social security benefit of about $324, up from $295. For a disabled worker with a wife and one or more children, the new average monthly payment will be increased from $269 to $296.

Under the new law, social security taxes on employers and employees are levied on the first $9,000 of earnings instead of $7,800. This means the maximum social security tax will rise from $405.60 to $468.

Advisory Council Report. The Advisory Council on Social Security issued a report containing 22 general recommendations in a section on cash benefits. It included the following:
- Provide a guarantee that social security benefits will increase automatically with increases in prices.
- Reflect in future consideration of cash benefit levels the adequacy of benefit amounts for regularly

employed, low-paid workers, and the relationship of general benefit levels to living levels of current workers.

■ Increase the maximum amount of annual earnings taxable and creditable toward benefits to $12,000 in 1974, and thereafter automatically adjust it to rising earning levels.

■ Shorten by three the number of years over which a man's earnings are averaged in figuring benefits amounts, and the period used to determine the amount of covered employment needed for him to qualify for benefits. These criteria thus would be the same as for women. Also, reduced benefits should be provided for dependent widowers at the age of 60, as they are now for dependent widows.

■ Raise to $2,000 the annual amount that can be earned without having any benefits withheld, and deduct $1 from social security benefits for each $2 earned above that amount.

■ Increase widows' and dependent widowers' benefits so that one who comes on the rolls at 65 or older would receive all of the benefits he or she would have been eligible for at age 65.

■ Eliminate the requirement that a divorcée must show that she lost support or a potential source of support when her former husband retired, became disabled, or died, in order to qualify for benefits based on his earnings.   Joseph P. Anderson

SOCIAL WELFARE. The U.S. House of Representatives approved an omnibus bill covering welfare, social security, and Medicare on June 22, 1971. The measure was hailed as the most important piece of social legislation adopted by Congress since New Deal days. However, in late summer, with the bill awaiting action in the Senate, President Richard M. Nixon urged a one-year delay on welfare reform as part of his new economic program. Should the program eventually be approved by the Senate and signed into law, it will affect the lives of 35 million people and will cost $12 billion annually. The following were included in the bill:

■ A federally guaranteed income for poor families– $2,400 a year for a couple with two children, and up to $3,600 for larger families–on condition that at least one parent register and accept suitable employment.

■ Permission for states to finance higher minimum-income levels, as the great majority do, but protection against the soaring caseload cost by guaranteeing federal funds for all expenses above each state's 1971 welfare budget.

■ Federal welfare benefits under the Family Assistance Plan to the "working poor"–families with marginal income. As a family's earnings increase, the benefits decline, vanishing when the total reaches $4,320 a year for a family of four.

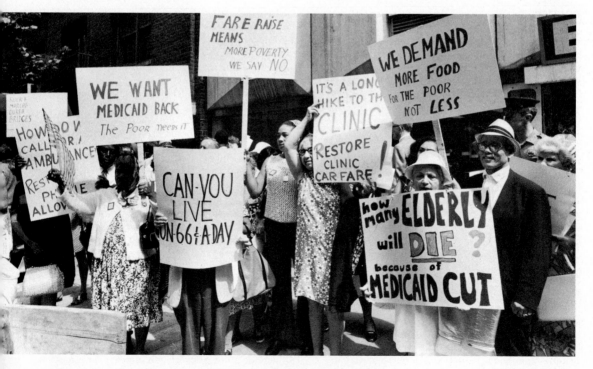

Elderly citizens protested aid cutbacks outside the office of Governor Nelson A. Rockefeller of New York. Many states reduced welfare benefits in 1971.

- Federal payment of all other major "adult" welfare expenses, such as payments to the aged, blind, and disabled, over a three-year period. Minimum monthly payments would be $150 for an individual and $200 for a couple.
- A 5 per cent increase in all social security benefits effective June 1, 1972. There would be an acceleration in the payroll tax beginning in 1975, and an increase in the wage base against which the social security tax is levied from $7,800 to $9,000.
- An automatic escalation in social security benefits as the Consumer Price Index rises.
- A $300-million income-tax reduction for older people by increasing the retirement income credit.
- An extensive new federal child-care program that would make it easier for welfare mothers to take jobs.
- Eligibility for hospital and medical insurance under Medicare for 1.5 million people receiving disability benefits under the social security and railroad retirement programs.

Supreme Court Ruling. On January 12, the Supreme Court of the United States ruled that state and local officials have the right to cut off public assistance to families that refuse to let caseworkers into their homes for inspection visits without search warrants. The majority of the justices held that the visits made in the case at issue were to protect children as well as to detect fraud. Joseph P. Anderson

SOMALIA. See AFRICA.

SOUTH AFRICA, REPUBLIC OF, sought to change its racist image but was, nevertheless, embroiled in constant racial conflict during 1971. Clergymen who opposed the white-minority government's policy of separating the races were often harassed and sometimes imprisoned. Security police arrested 20 persons on February 18 under the Terrorism Act. All were said to be members of African unity movements. Offices of churches and student groups were raided by police on February 25. Police said they were looking for evidence that the organizations handled money for a political prisoners' defense fund. On March 7, police in Port Elizabeth opened fire on thousands of Coloreds (persons of mixed racial stock) who were protesting higher bus fares. Ten protestors were wounded.

On the other side of the racial violence, the South West African People's Organization apparently planted a land mine that killed two policemen on May 22. The incident occurred in Namibia (South West Africa), and the guerrillas evidently escaped across the Zambian border. South Africa declared it would pursue terrorists across the Zambian border.

A Major Treason Trial in Johannesburg ended in October with the conviction of Anglican Dean Gonville ffrench-Beytagh. The Anglican clergyman was sentenced to five years in prison on charges of plotting to violently overthrow the government, conveying funds to the African underground, and distributing subversive literature. The dean denied the charges.

In June, Cosomo Desmond, a Roman Catholic priest, was placed under house arrest. He had written a book, *The Discarded People*, attacking the government's removal policy, which set up Bantustans, or separate homelands for blacks.

Foreign Relations. South Africa tried to establish a dialogue with black African states, and Ghana, the Ivory Coast, and Uganda responded favorably to the proposal. However, most black African countries rejected South Africa's overtures.

Although South Africa claimed to be virtually self-sufficient, it continued to seek arms abroad. Great Britain broke the United Nations boycott on arms to supply naval helicopters, France sold some Mirage fighter planes, and the United States allowed some light aircraft to be sold to South Africa.

Facts in Brief. Population: 21,065,000. Government: President Jacobus Fouche; Prime Minister Balthazar Johannes Vorster. Monetary Unit: rand. Foreign Trade: exports, $2,175,000,000; imports, $3,922,000,000. Principal Exports: gold, diamonds, wool. George Shepherd

SOUTH AMERICA. See LATIN AMERICA and articles on various countries.

SOUTH CAROLINA. See STATE GOVERNMENT.

SOUTH DAKOTA. See STATE GOVERNMENT.

SOUTH WEST AFRICA. See AFRICA.

SOUTHERN YEMEN, which had changed its official name to the People's Democratic Republic of Yemen, sought further to blunt charges that the country was Communist-controlled and was being used to further Russian and Chinese interests. National Liberation Front (NLF) leaders urged exiled leaders of the preindependence struggle to return and join in a coalition government, but failed. Government forces and rebels calling themselves the National Deliverance Army clashed periodically during the year.

In May, a 101-member Provisional Supreme People's Council took office as the nation's legislative body. On August 1, Presidential Council Chairman Salim Ali Rubayya resigned. But on August 8, he was reappointed and the three-man Presidential Council was reshuffled. Prime Minister Muhammad Ali Haitham was replaced by Ali Nasir Hassani, who continued as minister of defense.

Southern Yemen received aid from various countries as it struggled to develop its meager resources. Countries from which it received support included China, Libya, North Korea, and Romania.

Facts in Brief. Population: 1,302,000. Government: Presidential Council Chairman Salim Ali Rubayya; Prime Minister Ali Nasir Hassani. Monetary Unit: dinar. Foreign Trade: exports, $146,000,000; imports, $201,000,000. Principal Exports: petroleum products, cotton. William Spencer

SPACE EXPLORATION

United States astronauts David R. Scott and James B. Irwin drove an automobile on the moon in 1971. The *Apollo 15* astronauts covered a total of 17.4 miles in their little electric car, exploring the area around Hadley Rille on July 30 and 31 and August 1.

Both the United States and Russia also made unmanned flights to Mars. A U.S. spacecraft was the first to travel from the earth into orbit around another planet. The *Mariner 9* craft journeyed 250-million miles in 5½ months to reach its Mars orbit on November 13. Two Russian spacecraft reached Mars within the next three weeks. One dropped a Soviet pennant onto the surface of the planet. Part of the second made a soft landing. But because of hurricane-force winds and dust storms, it transmitted signals to earth for only 20 seconds after its landing on December 2.

Tragedy also marked the year. Three Soviet cosmonauts died when their spacecraft malfunctioned during its return to the earth on June 30, after an earth-orbiting flight that lasted a record 24 days.

The Russian disaster and the near calamity on the U.S. *Apollo 13* mission 14 months earlier gave significance to the continuing technical discussions on the possibility of developing compatible docking facilities on both U.S. and Soviet manned spacecraft.

After U.S. engineers corrected the design errors found through the investigation of the *Apollo 13* accident, the U.S. made two more successful lunar landings. Astronauts Alan B. Shepard, Jr., Stuart A. Roosa, and Edgar D. Mitchell flew on *Apollo 14* in February. Shepard and Mitchell landed on February 5 on the Fra Mauro highlands south of the equator on the west side of the visible face of the moon. Scott, Alfred M. Worden, and Irwin took *Apollo 15* to the moon in July. Scott and Irwin landed in the mountainous Hadley-Apennine region.

Apollo 15 was the first in a final group of three flights to use the battery-powered electric auto and other equipment designed to increase the time and extent of lunar exploration. Scott and Irwin were able to stay on the moon more than 66 hours, about double the previous record of 33½ hours spent by the *Apollo 14* crew. Each was outside the lunar module more than 18 hours, again double the time on *Apollo 14*. The 17.4 miles driven by car compared with the previously longest traverse of only about 2.5 miles covered on foot by Shepard and Mitchell, who hauled their scientific gear in a two-wheeled cart. About 168 pounds of lunar material were returned to earth on *Apollo 15*.

Apollo 15 astronaut David Scott climbs into Rover, the battery-powered car that he and astronaut James Irwin drove over 17 miles on the moon's surface.

New Discoveries. One of the most surprising discoveries by the lunar motorists was that Hadley Rille is terraced and consists of many horizontal layers of lunar soil. A core sample that the astronauts took by drilling 8 feet deep nearby, produced 58 distinct layers indicating stages in the history of the moon.

Another surprise was the growing evidence that the moon is still a volcanically active planetary body. Analysis of data sent by seismometers at three loca-

tions, following the *Apollo 15* mission, pinpointed a source of moonquakes approximately 500 miles below the surface of the southwestern part of the visible face, west of the crater Tycho. Gary Latham of the Lamont-Doherty Geological Observatory at Columbia University, principal investigator of the seismic experiments, speculated that the source of these moonquakes may be a pocket of molten lava a few dozen miles in diameter.

Another clue that the moon is not "dead" was contained in an exciting but controversial report that indicated the possibility of finding water on the moon, perhaps in pockets far below the surface. John W. Freeman of Rice University said two instruments detected gas of the same molecular weight as water

vapor for about 14 hours on March 7. The instruments, called suprathermal ion detectors, were put in place by Charles Conrad, Jr., and Alan L. Bean on the *Apollo 12* flight to the Ocean of Storms in November, 1969, and by Shepard and Mitchell on the *Apollo 14* flight. The vapor evidently escaped into space.

At about the same time, Latham said, the seismic instruments indicated many small moonquakes. With only two scientific stations operating on the moon at the time, the scientists could not establish the source of the gas discharge or of the seismic activity.

Measuring the Moon's Distance. Astronomical observatories around the world began making precise determinations of the 250,000-mile distance between the earth and the moon. They did it by shining laser beams on reflectors placed on the moon by astronauts, and measuring the time the beams take to return to earth. With a full set of three reflectors – those placed by Neil A. Armstrong and Edwin E. Aldrin, Jr., in July, 1969, in the Sea of Tranquility, and those at Fra Mauro and Hadley-Apennine – astronomers could measure accurately to within a few inches. They will now be able to record minute wobbles in the earth's rotation by regularly checking the earth-moon distance.

The returned lunar rocks and soil were distributed among more than 200 teams of scientists in the United States and 15 other countries for study. Some of the Apollo material was exchanged for a bit of the soil returned from the Sea of Fertility in 1970 by the unmanned Soviet *Luna 16* spacecraft.

The unmanned Soviet Lunokhod roving vehicle, meanwhile, in October, completed 6.5 miles of travel on the moon during 10½ months of operation on the Sea of Rains. The 1,660-pound, eight-wheeled vehicle ceased functioning after transmitting to earth more than 20,000 pictures and a vast amount of information on the chemical and physical properties of the surface of the moon.

The Mars Probes. *Mariner 9* carried two television cameras and other instruments toward Mars. They were designed to transmit pictures and information on surface temperatures and composition, atmospheric conditions, the field of gravity, and the two Martian moons. The transmissions were expected to last for three months or more after its November arrival. But the first observations were hampered by a planetwide dust storm, whipped up by winds apparently in excess of 180 miles per hour.

An Atlas-Centaur rocket launched *Mariner 9* from Cape Kennedy, Fla., on May 30. It was the second of two spacecraft that were intended to be placed in complementary Mars orbits. The first plunged into the Atlantic Ocean on May 8, after its Centaur stage went out of control.

Mariner 9 is now in an orbit that revolves around Mars every 12 hours and crosses its equator at an angle of 64 degrees. At its closest point, Mariner comes within 870 miles of the planet. It swings out to a distance of 10,650 miles.

An agreement between the National Aeronautics and Space Administration (NASA) and the Soviet Academy of Sciences called for rapid exchanges of the findings by *Mariner 9* and the Soviet *Mars 2* and *Mars 3*, which were launched May 19 and 28 and arrived in Mars orbit November 27 and December 2.

Mariner 9 returned to earth a picture of the Martian moon Phobos showing it to be an irregular-shaped rock about 15 miles long. It also sent a pic-

James Irwin pauses to salute the flag he and David Scott placed on the moon. Visible behind the lunar module Falcon is the 13,000-foot Hadley Delta.

ture of a crater over 60 miles in diameter that one scientist said was an extinct volcano.

The Cosmonaut's Deaths were caused by a seal failure in the Russian *Soyuz 11* spacecraft. The failure led to a sudden decompression that killed Lieutenant Colonel Georgi T. Dobrovolsky, 43, Vladislav N. Volkov, 35, and Viktor I. Patsayev, 38. A special government investigating commission said there were many possible reasons for the seal failure.

Theirs was the second three-man spacecraft to dock with the *Salyut 1* space station, which was in orbit from April 19 to October 11. The first spacecraft, *Soyuz 10*, carried cosmonauts Vladimir A. Shatalov, Alexei S. Yeliseyev, and Nikolai N. Rukavishnikov on a two-day flight.

Soyuz 11 went into orbit June 6 and docked with *Salyut 1* the next day. The three cosmonauts boarded the space station, and, during their 24 days in space, made medical observations of one another and carried out scientific experiments. In one experiment, they observed crops, forests, and water formations in the region east of the Caspian Sea. The fatal accident occurred after they had returned to *Soyuz 11*, separated, and started back to earth. The tragedy tended to divert attention from the fact that the Soviet spacemen had achieved a major milestone in flying the first long-duration space station.

China, for the second year in a row, launched an instrumented earth-orbiting spacecraft on March 3. It weighed 486 pounds, considerably more than the 386-pound satellite that they launched on April 24, 1970. No details regarding the launching were given by Peking, and they did not give the new satellite a name. In Washington, it was designated *China 2.* Experts believe that a new launching rocket, or at least a new upper stage of the rocket, was used by the Chinese to place the spacecraft in orbit.

International Cooperation. United States and Russian space engineers agreed, at a June meeting in Houston, to study the feasibility of joint space rendezvous and docking experiments. The studies were based on the premise that the first such project could be the docking of an Apollo spacecraft with a manned orbital station of the Salyut type, perhaps in 1974. A subsequent effort might be the docking of a manned spacecraft of the Soyuz type and an orbital scientific station of the type of the U.S. Skylab, scheduled to be launched in 1973.

The first of a series of major steps to advance space weather forecasting during the 1970s was taken on August 16 with the launch of a French satellite, *Éole,* by a U.S. Scout rocket from Wallops Island, Virginia. *Éole's* task was to measure the speed and direction of winds and the temperatures and pressures of the air at altitudes of about 9 miles in the Southern Hemisphere. The information was collected by balloons launched from three sites in Argentina and radioed to the satellite, which relayed them to the earth. See WEATHER.

Russia's *Soyuz 11*, shown just before its launching on June 6, set a 24-day space-flight record. But its three crewmen were dead when it landed June 30.

Plans for the next few years call for global cooperation in the use of satellites, aircraft, ships, and ocean buoys to collect information that will be fed into master computers to program the total weather of the earth. The goal is to achieve accurate worldwide, two-week forecasts by the late 1970s.

The Communications Satellite Corporation (Comsat) introduced the first of its *Intelsat 4* satellites in January and the second in December. Each satellite can carry about 5,000 telephone messages or 12 television transmissions simultaneously – three to seven times the capacity of previous satellites.

Other 1971 Satellites included:

- *Explorer 43*, carrying 12 instruments to measure radiation and magnetic fields. It was placed in a highly elliptical orbit on March 13, and reached an altitude of 129,000 miles above the earth.
- Two satellites to study the sun and the mechanisms of solar flares. These were the Orbiting Solar Observatory, *OSO 7*, and the Naval Research Laboratory's *Solrad 10*.
- Two satellites launched for the United States by Italian engineers with U.S. Scout vehicles from the San Marco platform in the Indian Ocean off the coast of Kenya, Africa. These were the *San Marco 3*, carrying three experiments to study the thin upper atmosphere, and *Explorer 45* with six instruments to observe the dynamic relationships in the earth's radiation belts.

Soviet scientists announced in January that their *Venera 7* spacecraft, which had landed on Venus in December, 1970, sent signals for 23 minutes after landing. The signals indicated a surface temperature of about 890° F. and an atmospheric pressure 90 times that of the earth. This tended to confirm previous indications that no human being could survive on the planet because of the high temperatures and great atmospheric pressure.

Space Shuttle. Planning moved forward, in 1971, for the reusable space shuttle. This has emerged as the principal U.S. flight hardware-development program for the 1970s. Contracted studies were completed on a fully reusable two-stage vehicle that would require a minimum of repair work after each flight. The studies were extended, however, to consider ways to cut operational costs and development costs.

NASA decided in October to design the orbiter stage of the shuttle so that its hydrogen and oxygen tanks would be discarded on each flight, thus substantially reducing the size of the vehicle that must be brought back to earth intact. This change resulted in a major development-cost reduction, but increased the expected operating cost somewhat above the previous target of $100 a pound for the round trip from the earth to orbit.

On Jan. 5, 1972, President Richard M. Nixon authorized NASA to proceed with a $5.5-billion program to develop the space shuttle. The first manned orbital flight was set for 1978. The plan for developing the booster stage was to be established in early 1972.

The shuttle is planned to replace all U.S. launch vehicles except the smallest, the Scout, and the largest, the Saturn 5, which is used for the Apollo lunar missions. The *Mark 2* shuttle will be able to launch a payload of almost 65,000 pounds into a due-east orbit.

Representatives of the European Space Conference and NASA began detailed technical discussions of potential arrangements for international cooperation in developing the shuttle and other major items of space hardware. But European spokesmen indicated that funds for their share of the costs could be made available only if plans were dropped for the development of a *Europa 3* launch vehicle. The new vehicle would be about as large as the U.S. Atlas-Centaur.

Congress appropriated $3.298 billion for NASA in the fiscal year that began July 1, a slight increase over the $3.269 billion of the previous year. The slight increase reversed a steady decline that had been underway since 1966.

President Nixon, in March, appointed James C. Fletcher, president of the University of Utah, to serve as NASA administrator. The post had been vacant since Thomas O. Paine resigned in September, 1970.　　　　　　　　　　　　　Jay Holmes

SPAIN. General Francisco Franco promised 100,000 cheering Spaniards on Oct. 1, 1971, to continue to rule Spain "as long as God gives me life and preserves my faculties of judgment." He spoke at a political rally in Madrid marking the 35th anniversary of his appointment as chief of state. His pledge ended rumors that he would soon hand the reins over to Prince Juan Carlos, whom he has designated as future king. Franco reduced the sentences of almost everyone in Spanish jails, including political prisoners. He also pardoned several former ministers implicated in the Matesa credit scandal, which involved mishandling of government export loans.

Labor problems appeared the same month, however. About 11,000 miners in Asturias were on strike and 24,000 Barcelona auto workers locked out. Both groups ignored official channels for their complaints.

Church and State. Spanish Roman Catholic bishops voted in February to end the official partnership between state and church. They also rejected the draft of a new concordat (agreement) between Madrid and the Vatican. Their action was taken as a sign of the decline of conservative influence among the Spanish hierarchy. The unacceptable document was returned to the Holy See, leaving the 1953 concordat in effect pending a new agreement. Events following the death of Archbishop Casimiro Morcillo of Madrid in June underlined the church-state rift. Under the concordat, Franco may nominate new bishops. Before he could do so in this key diocese, the Vatican named a progressive, Cardinal Enrique y Tarancon, the Archbishop of Toledo and Primate of Spain, to fill the post temporarily.

Terrorism Law. A committee of the Cortes (legislature) drafted a law on October 6 providing from 30 years' imprisonment to death for terrorism. Such offenses would be tried by military courts. The bill supplemented another, passed earlier in the year, increasing fines on nonpolitical dissenters and authorizing government officials to impose fines of up to $30,000 and three months in jail without trial. Communists were arrested in police sweeps in Seville, Salamanca, Murcia, and Madrid. Many were jailed for operating Communist Party cells. These measures reflected a growing pressure from powerful right wing elements in the army to hold back a rising demand for greater political freedom.

Wine Crop Disaster. Mildew, resulting from the rainy summer, ruined nearly 90 per cent of the grape harvest. Only the southernmost areas, where sherry and Malaga wines are produced, escaped. The Toledo area alone had losses totaling $15-million.

Facts in Brief. Population: 33,947,000. Government: President Francisco Franco; Vice-President Luis Carrero Blanco. Monetary Unit: peseta. Foreign Trade: exports, $2,344,000,000; imports, $4,717,000,000. Principal Exports: fruits and vegetables, machinery, chemicals.　　　　Kenneth Brown

SPORTS. The legal relationship between professional athletes and their teams came under severe scrutiny in 1971. The ultimate decision rested with Congress and the Supreme Court of the United States, and what they decided might well revolutionize the structure of professional team sports.

The player contracts in the four major team sports – baseball, football, basketball, and hockey – contain a reserve, or option, clause that binds a player to his team, sometimes for an additional year and sometimes in perpetuity. The most publicized challenge to these clauses came in the lawsuit of Curt Flood, a $110,000-a-year outfielder for the Washington Senators, against organized baseball. He challenged a 1922 Supreme Court ruling that gave antitrust exemption to professional baseball.

Professional basketball found itself under fire, too. The rival leagues – the National Basketball Association (NBA) and the American Basketball Association (ABA) – agreed to merge, afraid that if they did not, their dollar war for outstanding college players would bankrupt many teams. The NBA Players Association, however, obtained a court order forbidding a merger without congressional approval.

A federal court voided one long-standing rule – the NBA's rule forbidding the use of college players until their class had graduated. In other words, undergraduates could not play professional basketball. The court called the rule illegal, and the NBA reluctantly accepted undergraduate "hardship" cases. The ABA already had such a hardship rule.

Television Bonanza. For the first time, a World Series baseball game was played at night, an accommodation to television, and the game attracted a TV audience estimated at 61 million persons. It appeared likely that all future World Series weekday games would be played at night. During the year, major league baseball signed a four-year, $70-million contract with the National Broadcasting Company (NBC) covering the World Series, All-Star games, and the Game of the Week. Major league teams collected $40.4 million during the year from national television and local television and radio. Professional football's television and radio income for the year was $66 million.

The marriage of sports and television, as successful as it was, was threatened by the prospect of cable television and its greater financial rewards for club owners and players. The incredible $20-million gross from the Joe Frazier-Muhammad Ali heavyweight title fight came mostly from this form of closed-circuit television in theaters and arenas. See BOXING.

Among the Winners in 1971 sports competition were:

Curling. Donald Duguid led his Winnipeg rink to its second consecutive world and Canadian champion-

Climbing to 14,500 feet and floating past the Jungfrau, an American entry, The Circus Knie, heads for Italy in the 10th High Alpine Dolder Ballooning Week.

Shamateurism

An outdated code hobbles amateur athletes in the United States. Its impractical, unrealistic restrictions force American amateurs to cheat and resort to sham in order to compete. Because of it, amateurism in the United States should really be called "shamateurism."

The amateur code, promulgated during the Victorian era, was originally intended to protect the gentleman athlete from associating with professionals. Because professionals earned their livelihood from sport, they devoted more time to training and were more proficient than amateurs. Without competition between the two, the gentleman athlete did not need to expose himself to defeat at the hands of a social unequal.

Today's amateur, however, is rated on the basis of performance, not social class, and he must devote several hours daily to his sport. It is common for a swimmer to practice from four to seven hours each day, for a trackman to run 150 miles a week, and for a diver to practice three times a day. He is in no danger of being victimized by someone better trained.

Unfortunately, despite the change in status for the amateur athlete, the rules that govern him have not changed. They fail to take into account that amateurs are no longer merely gentlemen finding something to do in their leisure. Amateurs have become extremely serious athletes intent on bettering existing records or improving performances, and are prepared to devote time to the practice sessions necessary to achieve those ends. It has long been apparent that the code proclaimed in about 1896 does not apply today. But amateurism has its own imperatives, based on this archaic definition, and the old rules still stand.

The outcome of this failure to modernize is nothing less than a system that encourages cheating, condones dishonesty, and sustains hypocrisy. Virtually no one lives up to either the letter or the spirit of what is loosely known as the "amateur code." There is, for example, a very stringent rule against amateur athletes taking advantage of their athletic fame for economic gain. It is ignored, of course, because it is virtually impossible not to reap some benefit once one has achieved fame as an athlete.

What the code has taught them, then, is certainly not anything about honor or gentlemanly conduct. They have learned that laws can be flouted, that there is a way to beat the system, which is out of touch with reality.

Interpreting and enforcing our amateur code is a closely related problem. What is not acceptable in this country is flagrantly practiced throughout the world with impunity, and what is not acceptable in one sport is permitted in another. In certain European countries, a well-known track athlete can own a sporting goods store under his own name. In the United States, an athlete would be barred for such an act. In the closed societies of Eastern Europe, amateur athletes are fully subsidized for participating in sports; U.S. athletes would be banned from international competition if this happened.

To U.S. athletes, this lack of uniformity in enforcing the code is clearly an unacceptable double standard. While they do not object to the conduct of their European counterparts, they demand the same treatment for themselves.

We need a realistic and rational set of values that does not penalize the amateur, *per se*. It must be a set of rules that allows the amateur to compete and to plan his life as a normal citizen, rather than as one who is denied certain occupations and restricted in a manner that his fellow citizens would not tolerate.

We need a definition of amateur that is broad enough to allow the athlete freedom of movement and decision. It might allow amateur athletes to endorse products, or engage in professions in which part of their usefulness would arise from their athletic prowess. It should allow the athlete to accept reasonable compensation for time lost because of practice or competition. Such provisions would legitimize practices that are already in effect, but are illegal under the letter of the amateur code. Such a redefinition would allow the amateur to compete honestly, live honestly, and serve sports honestly.   John B. Kelly, Jr.

John B. Kelly, Jr.

ships. The Canadians won nine straight matches in the world competition in March at Megeve, France.

Fencing. Russia won 4 of the 8 world championships in July in Vienna, Austria, its winners including Vasily Stankovich in foil and Grigory Kriss in épée. In the U.S. championships in June in Berkeley, Calif., Alex Orban of the Bronx, N.Y., won in saber, and Harriet King of San Francisco won in women's foil, each for the fourth time.

Handball. Paul Haber of Chicago won the U.S. Handball Association four-wall title for the fifth time in six years, but lost to Pat Kirby of Brooklyn in the Amateur Athletic Union (A.A.U.) four-wall final. Steve Sandler of New York won his sixth A.A.U. one-wall title.

Rowing. The Harvard Lightweights won the Thames Challenge Cup for lightweight eights and their spares captured the Wyfold Challenge Cup for coxless fours in the Henley Royal Regatta in England. Jim Dietz of the Bronx, a Diamond Challenge Sculls finalist at Henley, won the single sculls in the U.S. championships and the Lucerne Regatta in Switzerland.

Shooting. Army Major Lones Wigger of Carter, Mont., flew back from the Pan American Games in Cali, Colombia, slept four hours, and then won the U.S. smallbore rifle title at Camp Perry, Ohio, in August. Staff Sergeant John A. Smith of Stroh, Ill., won titles in all-round and center-fire pistol shooting.

Weight Lifting. Russia took 6 of the 9 titles in the world championships in September in Lima, Peru. The only U.S. medalist was Ken Patera of Minneapolis, second among the superheavyweights. Vasily Alekseyev of the Soviet Union won the superheavyweight title, and broke all four world records for his class.

Wrestling. Dan Gable of Waterloo, Iowa, won the lightweight title in the world free-style championships in Sofia, Bulgaria, one of three medals won by Americans. Russia captured 5 of the 10 titles. Bulgaria won the Greco-Roman competition, beating Russia, which had not lost this event since 1953. Gable pinned all five opponents in the U.S. amateur championships.

Other Champions. *Archery*, world champions: men, John Williams, Cranesville, Pa.; women, Emma Gapchenko, Russia. U.S. champions: men, John Williams, Cranesville, Pa.; women, Doreen Wilber, Jefferson City, Iowa. U.S. professional indoor champions: men, Jim Riley, Bellbrook, Ohio; women, Ann Butz, Suffern, N.Y. *Badminton*, U.S. champions: men, Muljadi, Indonesia; women, Noriko Takagi, Japan. *Biathlon*, world champion: Dieter Speer, East Germany. *Billiards*, U.S. open pocket title: Steve Mizerak, Carteret, N.J. *Bobsledding*, world champions: four-man, Switzerland (Rene Stadler, driver); two-man, Italy (Giafranco Gaspari, driver). A.A.U. champions: four-man, U.S. Air Force (Jim Hickey, driver); two-man, U.S. Navy (Paul Lamey, driver). *Canoeing*, world champions: men's canoe, Reinhold Kauder, West Germany; men's kayak, Siegbert Horn, East Germany; women's kayak, Angelika Bahmann, East Germany. U.S. champions: men's canoe (1,000 meters), Andy Weigand, Arlington, Va.; men's kayak (1,000 meters), Tony Ralphs, Newport Beach, Calif.; women's kayak (500 meters), Mrs. Marcia Smoke, Niles, Mich. *Casting*, U.S. all-around champion: Zack Willson, Powell, Ohio. *Cycling*, Tour de France winner: Eddy Merckx, Belgium. World road racing champions: professional, Eddy Merckx; amateur, Regis Ovion, France; women's amateur, Anna Konkina, Russia. *Gymnastics*, A.A.U. all-around champions: men, Yoshiaki Takei, Georgia Southern College; women, Linda Metheny, Tuscola, Ill. National Collegiate Athletic Association (NCAA) all-around champion: Yoshi Hayasaki, University of Washington, *Horseshoe pitching*, U.S. champion: Curtis Day, Frankfort, Ind. *Lacrosse*, U.S. champions: NCAA,

Cornell; club, Long Island Athletic Club. *Luge* (tobogganing), world champions: men, Karl Brunner, Italy; women, Elisabeth Demleitner, West Germany. *Modern pentathlon*, world champion: Boris Onishenko, Russia. *Motorcycling*, grand national champion: Dick Mann, Richmond, Calif. *Polo*, U.S. champions: open, Oak Brook, Ill.; 20 goal, Green Hill Farms, Tulsa. *Rodeo*, all-around champion: Phil Lyne, George West, Tex. *Roller skating*, North American champions: men, Michael Jacques, Norwood, Mass.; women, April Allen, Houston. *Snowmobiling*, world championship derby winner: Mike Trapp, Woodruff, Wis. *Softball*, U.S. champions: men, Welty Way, Cedar Rapids, Iowa; women, Raybestos Brakettes, Stratford, Conn. *Squash racquets*, U.S. champions: men, Colin Adair, Montreal; women, Mrs. Terry Thesieres, Bala-Cynwyd, Pa. *Squash tennis*, U.S. open champion: Pedro Bacallao, New York. *Surfing*, U.S. champions: men, David Nuuhiwa, Huntington Beach, Calif.; women, Mrs. Joyce Hoffman Langor, Del Mar, Calif. *Table tennis*, world champions: men's team, China; women's team, Japan; men, Stellan Bengtsson, Sweden; women, Lin Hui-ching, China. U.S. champions: men, Dal Joon Lee, Parma, Ohio; women, Mrs. Connie Sweeris, Grand Rapids, Mich. *Team handball*, U.S. champion: Adelphi University. *Volleyball*, U.S. champions: men, Santa Monica (Calif.) Y.M.C.A.; women, Los Angeles Renegades Red; intercollegiate, University of California, Los Angeles. *Water skiing*, world champions: men, George Athans, Kelowna, British Columbia; women, Christy Weir, McQueeney, Tex. U.S. champions: men, Mike Suyderhoud, Petaluma, Calif.; women, Mrs. Liz Allan Shetter, Richmond, Va. Frank Litsky

See also articles on individual sports; Section One, Focus on Sports; Section Two, New Game Plan for Sports in the '70s.

STAMP COLLECTING

STAMP COLLECTING. President Richard M. Nixon's order on June 10, 1971, allowing trade in nonstrategic materials with China, made it possible for U.S. collectors to obtain Chinese stamps that had been banned in the United States for 20 years. Initially, publishers of some leading U.S. stamp catalogs said they already had enough stamps to list and keep up with. Within a month, however, stamp magazines were advertising the stamps. But stamps of North Korea, North Vietnam, Cuba, and Rhodesia remained on the forbidden list.

Because of a lengthy postal strike, the British government authorized private mail services for which local operators issued their own stamps. These stamps, known as "Cinderellas" among collectors, provided a bonanza for some collectors. Some contended, however, that too many of the stamps were issued to make them of much value. Among those whose likenesses appeared on the British Cinderellas were Winston Churchill and John F. Kennedy.

Stamp Issues. One of the most unusual stamp issues of the year came in June from Nicaragua. It consisted of 10 stamps, each showing a mathematical equation "that changed the face of the earth." One of the stamps displayed Albert Einstein's $E = mc^2$, the equation that played such an important part in the development of atomic energy.

A pane of 100 8-cent U.S. flag stamps, erroneously issued without perforations, was discovered in May

Artist Thomas Hart Benton stands beside an enlargement of the nation's first
8-cent stamp, issued on May 8. The design was taken from a mural by Benton.

in Boise, Ida. It brought $15,500 at an auction in New York City in August. Prior to the auction, the stamps were cut into pairs and blocks. Pairs brought from $270 to $275. Blocks of four brought from $600 to $625, and the block with the plate number sold for $3,000.

Great Britain completed the decimalization of its stamps, begun in June, 1970. Nondecimal stamps will be invalid for postage after Aug. 15, 1973.

In August, the *American Philatelist*, journal of the American Philatelic Society, reported that the U.S. Eisenhower 6-cent definitive stamp had been counterfeited. While the genuine stamp had been produced from engravings, the spurious stamp was lithographed on paper a shade whiter than that of the genuine stamp. The society also placed on its caution list gold-embossed stamps from some of the French-community nations of Africa. The society's watchdog committee said these were excessively priced. The U.S. Treasury also warned that importation of such stamps was illegal.

Stamp dealers were enthusiastic about the publication of *Fundamentals of Philately* by L. N. Williams and M. Williams. It was published by the American Philatelic Society, State College, Pa. David Lidman of *The New York Times* called the book "conceivably the definitive book on what stamp collecting is all about . . . the Williams masterwork is not likely to be outdated." Theodore M. O'Leary

STATE GOVERNMENT. The concerns of the state governments mirrored those of the nation in 1971 – financial uncertainty, increasing drug abuse, pollution control, and the problems of youth. For the state legislatures, there was an additional concern, the responsibility to reapportion their legislatures and congressional districts.

The financial squeeze on state budgets became particularly acute. With the dip in the economy, revenue from state income and sales taxes at times did not meet the increased financial demands created by growing welfare rolls and the rising costs of state services. Some states cut back on welfare benefits, while others funded welfare programs by using up accumulated budget surpluses. The financial dilemma made new tax legislation the dominant theme for most of the 50 state legislatures that met in either regular or special sessions in 1971.

Money and Taxes. More than half the states raised taxes in 1971. Individual income taxes were increased in 13 states and newly adopted in 3 others – Ohio, Pennsylvania, and Rhode Island. Connecticut, after adopting an income tax, repealed it at a special session because of strong public opposition.

New corporate income taxes were adopted in Ohio and Florida, and existing ones were increased in more than a dozen other states.

Sales-tax rates were raised in five states: Connecticut, from 5 to 6.5 per cent; Minnesota and

New York, from 3 to 4 per cent; Tennessee, from 3 to 3.5 per cent; and Texas, from 3.25 to 4 per cent. Voters in Montana rejected a sales-tax proposal.

Taxes on gasoline and tobacco were favorite sources for revenue. At least 8 states raised gasoline taxes, and cigarette taxes were raised in 17.

A California Supreme Court decision, handed down in August, could drastically change the tax structure of nearly every state. The California court found that the state's system of financing schools primarily from local property taxes caused great inequities among districts in the quality of education offered. Wealthy neighborhoods can afford better educational facilities than poorer areas. In December, a federal court in Texas made a similar ruling. If these decisions are sustained, it could mean that most states would have to increase their support of public education. See COURTS AND LAWS; EDUCATION.

Several states turned to state lotteries as a means of increasing revenue. Legislatures in Connecticut, Pennsylvania, and Massachusetts approved lotteries in 1971. They were already in operation in New Hampshire, New Jersey, and New York.

Total state tax receipts for fiscal 1971 reached $51.5 billion, a rise of 7.3 per cent above the fiscal 1970 total of $48 billion. The rate of increase was about half that of the previous year, due primarily to the nationwide economic slump. However, state appropriations were again at record levels.

Reapportionment. The politically important task of reapportionment, which could affect the political control of state legislatures and Congress for the next 10 years, absorbed a substantial amount of state lawmakers' time in 1971. By the end of the year, 29 states had reapportioned their legislatures, and 19 had restructured their congressional districts. But the redistricting process was not without its problems. Court challenges were raised on legislative redistricting in at least 16 states. Other suits questioned the constitutionality of congressional remapping.

Environmental Protection continued to be a major concern of the states. Indiana became the first state to ban detergents containing more than 3 per cent phosphates. The ban becomes effective in 1973. Minnesota approved a $1-surcharge on all automobile sales to finance the recycling of junked cars. Missouri adopted its first strip-mining regulation. Oregon banned nonreturnable beverage containers and required 5-cent deposits on beer and soft-drink bottles. Rhode Island gave its governor the power to stop all commerce, travel, and other activities contributing to pollution if the state director of health determines that an "air-pollution episode" exists. Several states passed legislation allowing citizens to file class-action suits against polluters.

Youth-Related Actions. With nearly half the nation's population under 25 years of age, questions relating to the rights and activities of youth have become increasingly important. A major change came in June, 1971, when the 38th state legislature ratified the 26th Amendment to the U.S. Constitution. This granted 18- to 21-year-olds the right to vote in all elections.

Other privileges of adulthood were also given to this age group by several state legislatures. Eight states passed legislation setting the age of majority at 18. They were California, Illinois, Michigan, New Mexico, North Carolina, Tennessee, Vermont, and Washington. In all eight states they may enter into contracts, own property, and make wills. The National Governors' Conference gave unanimous approval to a resolution urging all states to consider lowering the age of majority to 18. The states were also concerned with the increase in youthful crime.

The states generally were combating drug abuse with better educational programs on drugs. There was also a trend toward reducing the punishment for first-offense possession and use of marijuana, while increasing the penalties for drug pushers.

In other areas of crime control, the states concentrated on providing more community-based youth service bureaus. Massachusetts started a Parole Volunteers Program to aid youthful offenders. Kansas appropriated about $1 million for rehabilitation facilities for juvenile offenders. Arkansas set up a youth rehabilitation treatment facility.

Violent Crime. The states took action on broad fronts to reduce violence. Armed guards were hired in some instances to patrol campuses, courts, and legislatures. The California Supreme Court and the court of appeals required a search of persons entering the courts' chambers. The Ohio Supreme Court, like California, placed security officers in the court. Rhode Island began training a security force to prevent courtroom disruptions.

Individual state legislatures also took security precautions. In New York, plainclothesmen were placed in Senate galleries. Security police, searches of visitors, or both, were employed in the Louisiana, Michigan, Ohio, and Wisconsin legislatures. The National Legislative Conference appointed a Committee on Legislative Security and Training to study the problem and make recommendations.

Campus violence, meanwhile, subsided considerably in 1971. The previous year, more than 30 state legislatures had adopted measures to curb student disorders.

Prison Reform. The deaths of 43 inmates and hostages resulting from the prisoner uprising at New York State's Attica Correctional Facility in September shocked the nation. Largely overlooked in the wake of the tragedy were the efforts underway in many states to improve correctional policies.

Florida, Illinois, Indiana, Massachusetts, Mississippi, New Hampshire, and Washington were among the states whose legislatures revised state cor-

Selected Statistics on State Governments

State	Population*	Governor	Legislature*** Senate (D.)	(R.)	House (D.)	(R.)	State tax rev.††	Tax rev. per capita	Enrollment in schools Elem.‡	High‡
Alabama	3,444	George C. Wallace (D.)	35	0	104	2	$710	$204.18	426	379
Alaska	302	William A. Egan (D.)	10	10	31	9	102	326.05	52	28
Arizona	1,772	Jack Williams (R.)	12	18	26	34	523	282.92	305	135
Arkansas	1,923	Dale Bumpers (D.)	34	1	98	2	380	195.38	252	211
California	19,953	Ronald Reagan (R.)	20	19‡‡	43	37	5,675	280.64	2,864	1,769
Colorado	2,207	John A. Love (R.)	14	21	27	38	514	225.03	307	243
Connecticut	3,032	Thomas A. Meskill (R.)	18	17‡‡	99	78	796	258.22	454	208
Delaware	548	Russell W. Peterson (R.)	6	13	16	23	222	398.17	74	59
Florida	6,789	Reubin Askew (D.)	33	15	81	38	1,587	225.42	782	646
Georgia	4,590	Jimmy Carter (D.)	50	6	172	22‡‡	991	212.47	705	394
Hawaii	771	John A. Burns (D.)	16	8‡‡	34	17	373	472.39	102	78
Idaho	713	Cecil Andrus (D.)	16	19	29	41	187	255.98	93	89
Illinois	11,115	Richard B. Ogilvie (R.)	29	29	87	90	3,142	230.66	1,500	857
Indiana	5,195	Edgar D. Whitcomb (R.)	21	28‡‡	46	53‡‡	1,054	199.90	749	482
Iowa	2,825	Robert Ray (R.)	13	37	37	63	637	223.30	374	286
Kansas	2,249	Robert Docking (D.)	8	32	41	84	463	205.11	357	155
Kentucky	3,219	Wendell H. Ford (D.)	27	11	73	27	760	231.67	456	261
Louisiana	3,643	John J. McKeithen (D.)	38	1	104	1	989	268.60	509	333
Maine	995	Kenneth M. Curtis (D.)	14	18	65	84‡‡‡	229	228.14	177	68
Maryland	3,922	Marvin Mandel (D.)	33	10	120	22	1,146	286.56	524	393
Massachusetts	5,689	Francis W. Sargent (R.)	27	13	177	62‡‡	1,494	259.52	650	518
Michigan	8,875	William G. Milliken (R.)	19	19	58	52	2,544	282.74	1,228	953
Minnesota	3,805	Wendell R. Anderson (D.)	67**		135**		1,099	283.19	489	432
Mississippi	2,218	William L. Waller (D.)	50	2	119	2†	517	232.39	312	222
Missouri	4,677	Warren E. Hearnes (D.)	25	9	112	51	827	174.07	684	355
Montana	694	Forrest H. Anderson (D.)	30	25	49	55	136	191.86	107	69
Nebraska	1,485	J. James Exon (D.)	(Unicameral)**		49		294	194.74	187	142
Nevada	490	D. N. O'Callaghan (D.)	13	7	18	22	173	340.27	74	53
New Hampshire	739	Walter R. Peterson (R.)	9	15	148	249‡‡	118	155.47	95	64
New Jersey	7,168	William T. Cahill (R.)	16	24	40	39†	1,501	205.62	978	504
New Mexico	1,016	Bruce King (D.)	28	14	48	22	294	285.69	153	128
New York	18,241	Nelson A. Rockefeller (R.)	22	30‡‡	71	79	6,248	339.74	1,922	1,555
North Carolina	5,082	Robert W. Scott (D.)	43	7	97	23	1,297	252.04	836	356
North Dakota	619	William L. Guy (D.)	12	36‡‡	40	58	142	227.59	91	56
Ohio	10,652	John J. Gilligan (D.)	13	20	45	54	1,773	164.46	1,698	727
Oklahoma	2,559	David Hall (D.)	39	9	78	21	541	207.25	350	277
Oregon	2,091	Tom McCall (R.)	16	14	26	34	444	205.85	281	199
Pennsylvania	11,795	Milton J. Shapp (D.)	27	23	112	90‡‡	3,094	260.42	1,260	1,098
Rhode Island	951	Frank Licht (D.)	41	9	75	24†	272	283.42	111	77
South Carolina	2,592	John C. West (D.)	44	2	113	11	600	228.58	393	244
South Dakota	666	Richard S. Kneip (D.)	11	24	30	45	122	181.69	88	78
Tennessee	3,924	Winfield Dunn (R.)	19	13†	56	43	740	185.44	571	329
Texas	11,198	Preston Smith (D.)	29	2	140	10	2,188	190.95	1 578	1,262
Utah	1,059	Calvin L. Rampton (D.)	12	16	38	31	269	244.67	165	139
Vermont	446	Deane C. Davis (R.)	8	22	52	95†††	141	307.99	64	39
Virginia	4,648	Linwood Holton (R.)	33	7	73	24†††	1,041	220.74	683	396
Washington	3,409	Daniel J. Evans (R.)	29	20	48	51	1,126	326.57	443	375
West Virginia	1,744	Arch A. Moore, Jr. (R.)	23	11	68	32	436	248.99	222	178
Wisconsin	4,419	Patrick J. Lucey (D.)	13	20	65	34‡‡	1,423	317.98	586	408
Wyoming	332	Stanley K. Hathaway (R.)	11	19	20	40†	93	274.24	47	40

*Numbers in thousands   †Also one independent   ‡Numbers in thousands, for 1971

**Nonpartisan   ††Amount in millions, for 1971   ‡‡One vacancy

***As of Dec. 31, 1971   †††Also three independents   ‡‡‡Two vacancies

rections systems in 1971. Many of the changes were aimed at easing the transition when inmates leave prison and return to society. They included prisoner furloughs, work-release programs, and community prerelease centers. Illinois, one of the leaders, removed its arbitrary licensing and registration restrictions that barred felons from many jobs. Other Illinois reforms allow prisoners to pursue outside education, volunteer for conservation projects, speak to groups on crime, and visit their homes on furlough.

Transportation. The states gave increased attention to automobile safety, car insurance, and mass-transportation problems. With the success of no-fault insurance in Massachusetts, similar laws were passed in at least six states.

In the automobile-safety field, New York required rear window defrosters on most new cars beginning with 1974 models. Bumpers on future models were required to withstand 5-mile-per-hour barrier crashes under laws adopted in several states.

Illinois approved a $900-million transportation bond issue, the largest in the state's history. The bonding will provide $600 million for freeways, $200 million for mass transit, and $100 million for airports. The measure was passed by the legislature under provisions of Illinois's new Constitution, which allows long-range financing without state-wide referendum. By contrast, in New York, the voters rejected a $2.5-billion bond issue for highways and rapid transit.

Massachusetts took a pioneering step among the states when it won a $3.5-million federal grant to plan a balanced transportation system for Boston. The purpose of Boston's planning program is to increase local decision making and allow evaluation of transportation facilities before they are built.

Health, Education, Welfare. The states approved record education budgets and continued a trend toward providing aid to nonpublic schools and universities through scholarships. New approaches to state aid were taken after the Supreme Court of the United States ruled on June 28 that certain types of state financial aid to parochial schools are illegal. See Section One, FOCUS ON EDUCATION.

Illinois provided $6.7 million for private higher education and $20.5 million for textbooks and auxiliary services in grants to parents of pupils in private schools. A $5-million appropriation will fund innovative programs in both private and public schools, and $4.5 million will go to poor families with children in private schools.

Minnesota provided income tax credits of up to $140 for each child in private secondary schools and up to $100 for each child in private elementary schools. Students entering private colleges were made eligible for a $500 subsidy. Other states acting in 1971 to aid private schools included New York,

Mr. and Mrs. Edward Henry, first to win $1 million in New Jersey state lottery, wept when Governor William Cahill presented Henry with millionaire's certificate.

Nebraska, North Carolina, Oregon, and Vermont.

In the area of health, there was a trend toward legislation permitting juveniles to get medical assistance, without parental consent, for drug abuse, communicable diseases, or pregnancies. At least 14 states allowed juveniles to seek one or all of these services.

As welfare rolls grew, relief requirements were made more stringent in many states and benefits were reduced in others. New York, for instance, required welfare recipients to pick up their checks at state employment offices and to produce an identification photograph. California reduced payments to recipients with outside income.

Federal-State Relations. President Richard M. Nixon received strong support for his revenue-sharing program from both governors and state legislative groups. For much of the year, a deadlock existed between the congressional proponents of revenue sharing and Representative Wilbur Mills (D., Ark.), chairman of the House Ways and Means Committee. Mills maintained that the federal government had its own revenue problems without allocating regularly scheduled amounts to the states. However, by year-end, Mills had modified his position. He introduced his own federal aid bill, which would provide aid to states and local governments, raising hopes that some form of revenue sharing would pass Congress in 1972.   Robert H. Weber

521

STEEL INDUSTRY. Production for the first nine months of 1971 totaled 97.5 million tons, a decline of 5.8 per cent from the total for the same period in 1970. At year-end, however, the industry began staging a comeback. Both November and December figures showed a rise in production. Although the United States experienced a 6.9 per cent decline in raw steel output in 1970 from its 1969 record level, it remained the world leader with 20.1 per cent of world production. However, its lead narrowed, with Russia – producing nearly 128 million tons – less than 4 million behind. Japan, in third place, continued its rapid year-to-year gains in raw steel output, surpassing 100 million tons for the first time.

The U.S. Industry consisted of more than 200 companies with plants in 37 states. The industry's biggest merger in recent years took place with acquisition of the Granite City (Ill.) Steel Company by the National Steel Corporation. The merged company, with annual sales of about $1.4 billion, will be the nation's third largest steel producer, behind U.S. Steel and Bethlehem Steel.

United States steelworkers gained a 30 per cent increase in wages, as well as other benefits, in a new three-year contract agreed to with major domestic steel producers on August 1 on the eve of a threatened strike. In the wake of the steel pact, tens of thousands of steelworkers were laid off, as steel users drew from inventories stockpiled against the strike. Because the contract went into effect on August 1, its initial pay and benefit increases were exempt from the wage-price freeze proclaimed by President Richard M. Nixon on August 15.

In December, the Price Commission ruled that U.S. Steel could raise prices of its entire steel mill line by an average of no more than 3.6 per cent from December, 1971, to August, 1972. Republic Steel was granted a 3.4 per cent increase for the same period. On August 5, however, U.S. Steel had put through increases of 8 per cent on structural steel and bar products, which account for 55 per cent of their product mix, narrowly escaping the mid-August freeze.

Steel Imports continued to take an important share of the steel market even though steel producers of the European Community (Common Market) and Japan were subject to self-imposed limitations on exports to the United States. Their failure to honor their commitments of maintaining 1968 proportions of exports affected domestic manufacturers of stainless alloy and tool steels. Those serving the Pacific Coast were hit particularly hard. Total imports of all types of steel in the first half of 1971 set a record at slightly more than 9 million tons.

Automobiles again were the major market for steel. The 50 per cent rise in residential building during the year and new mass-transit systems under design or construction in several U.S. cities also provided important markets. — Mary E. Jessup

STOCKS AND BONDS. The slow recovery from the recession prompted President Richard M. Nixon to forsake his original economic game plan in 1971. On August 15 he announced an incomes policy that would control prices and wages. The initial reaction to his new economic policy advanced the Dow Jones average of 30 industrial stocks a record 32.93 points to 888 on August 15, and set a daily record of 31,730,000 shares traded on the New York Stock Exchange (NYSE). But uncertainties about the new policies and continued sluggishness in the economy resulted in a gradual loss of all of the initial increases in October and November. From early September to late November, the market dropped more than 100 points. The succession of yearly lows climaxed on November 23, when the Dow Jones dropped 5.18 points to below the 800 barrier. At 797.97, it was at its lowest point since Dec. 1, 1970. However, it rallied in late November with a 17.96-point gain on November 26, and a 46-point gain over the remainder of the month.

The market peaked again in mid-December with the announcement by President Nixon on December 15 of a U.S. agreement to devalue the dollar in an attempt to solve the world currency crisis. In the week following the President's statement, issued jointly with President Georges Pompidou of France, the Dow Jones jumped to 885. By the end of the year, the market had regained 92 points since Thanksgiving, closing at 890.2. Although its imminent penetration had been predicted, the 1,000 mark on the Dow Jones eluded the market again. Standard and Poor's index of 500 stocks ended the year at 102, up 10 points from a year earlier.

Continued decline in interest rates early in 1971 attracted record borrowing by cash-starved corporations and governments. By March, interest rates started rising again. The net federal debt rose to $326 billion in August, up $17 billion from the end of 1970. It had increased $6 billion in the like period a year earlier. Over $6 billion in new issues of corporate bonds and stocks were sold in March. Despite a deteriorated credit rating and higher borrowing costs, New York City issued $258 million in bonds in April, a record amount for a city.

Mutual Funds. For the first time in the history of mutual funds, there were net redemptions of shares for several months beginning in May. The industry was further shaken by an out-of-court settlement of a suit to prohibit sale of a mutual fund management company for more than its nominal book value. New Securities and Exchange Commission (SEC) chairman William J. Casey feared that if the precedent were allowed to stand, it would keep new firms from the mutual fund business.

In March, the SEC released a long-awaited study of mutual funds. It reported no evidence of any destabilizing price effects from large transactions, but recommended that institutional investors disclose

Stock Prices: 1,000 Mark Missed Again

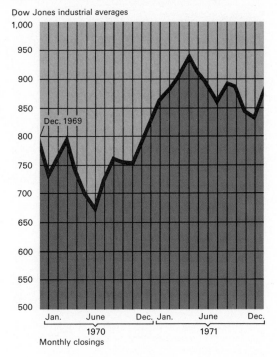

Dow Jones industrial averages

Monthly closings

chairman Casey favored computerizing stock ownership because of the rash of stock-certificate thefts. He said that only one of the recent broker failures was directly attributable to theft, but that it had been a factor in others.

Merrill Lynch – the largest U.S. broker – received $20 million in industry support to merge with bankrupt Goodbody & Company. Requirements were tightened generally by disallowing the use of securities rather than cash for capitalization. Several brokers raised capital by issuing their own stock for the first time. Brokers overall had a good profit year after several bad years, although the figures for 1970 showed half of the firms had losses.

The Federal Securities Investor Protection Corporation (SIPC) was established in January to insure individual deposits of securities with brokers up to $50,000, including up to $20,000 in cash. SIPC resources are based on assessments of brokers and backed by a $1-billion standby credit from the Department of the Treasury. A $55-million NYSE trust fund to reimburse customers of 10 bankrupt member firms was fully committed at the beginning of 1971 and had to be supplemented by $20 million to cover customers of three more bankrupt firms before the SIPC took over. President Nixon named Byron D. Woodside, formerly with the Defense Production Administration in Washington, D.C., as the first SIPC chairman in January. William G. Dewald

more information about transactions, and be prevented from participating in corporate take-overs. The SEC proposed that previously unregulated hedge funds (private funds) as well as offshore funds (outside the United States) be subjected to controls.

A New Fee Schedule was adopted by the NYSE at the urging of the SEC. The main provision was that brokers would negotiate commissions on trades in excess of $500,000. In addition, a schedule of rates was adopted that offered a descending scale of commissions – the larger the transaction, the lower the commission rate. The new schedule was expected to reduce the commissions slightly from the previous levels including the $15 surcharge per transaction, which was dropped.

Ralph S. Saul, 48, resigned on March 16 as president of the American Stock Exchange (AMEX) to become vice-chairman of the First Boston Corporation, an investment banking house. He was replaced in May by Paul Kolton, 47, executive vice-president of AMEX for nine years. Ralph W. Haack, NYSE president, announced in October he would not seek a second term in 1972.

Tightening Controls. The National Association of Securities Dealers began to publish trading volume in addition to price data for the 2,800 unlisted stocks in its automated quotations system. The Federal Reserve System computerized its bookkeeping transfers of treasury securities to limit thefts. SEC

SUDAN endured a brief revolution in 1971. Despite an attempted leftist coup in July, the government of Major General Jafir Muhammad Nimeri, which had been ruling for two years, clung to power. The difficulty began in January, when the Sudan joined with Egypt, Libya, and Syria to form a federation of Arab states. This association was opposed by the Sudanese Communists and left-wing army officers.

On July 19, leftist army officers led by Major Hashem al-Ata attempted to overthrow the government. They managed to hold power for about three days. Ata indicated that he would include Communists in the new government.

Iraq, which was opposed to the Arab federation, immediately recognized the Ata government and dispatched a delegation to Khartoum. However, the plane in which they were traveling mysteriously crashed in Saudi Arabia.

Nimeri's Countercoup. On July 22, Libya forced a British airliner carrying two rebel Sudanese officers to land at Bengasi. Libyan authorities took the two officers into custody. That same day, loyal troops and officers staged a countercoup in the Sudan, returning Nimeri to power.

Nimeri dealt harshly with the rebels. Major Ata and three other officers were executed on July 23 by a firing squad. Within the next three days, seven more officers were executed, including the two who were captured in Libya, in spite of a British plea for

523

clemency. On July 28, Abdul Khalek Mahgoub, the leader of the Sudanese Communist Party, was hanged. He had denied any knowledge of the antigovernment plot, and Russia had appealed for his life.

Nimeri then broke diplomatic relations with Iraq and expelled two Bulgarian and Russian diplomats. He recalled his ambassadors from Bulgaria, Great Britain, Italy, Kenya, Russia, and Yugoslavia.

In August, Nimeri purged his government of four ministers who had been linked to the Communist Party and dismantled the Communist-controlled Sudanese Trade Union Federation. He brought four prominent southerners into the Cabinet in an effort to end the 10-year-old conflict with Africans in the Sudan's three southern provinces.

On October 12, Nimeri was sworn in as the first elected president of the Sudan. He had won an overwhelming vote of confidence in a September referendum. See NIMERI, JAFIR MUHAMMAD.

Facts in Brief. Population: 16,498,000. Government: President and Prime Minister Jafir Muhammad Nimeri. Monetary Unit: Sudanese pound. Foreign Trade: exports, $298,000,000; imports, $288,000,000. Principal Exports: cotton, gum arabic, peanuts.   George Shepherd

SUPREME COURT OF THE UNITED STATES. See COURTS AND LAWS.

SWAZILAND. See AFRICA.

SWEDEN was brought almost to a standstill in 1971 by what Social Democrats called "a luxury strike." On February 4, 600 supervisors on the state railroads walked out. In 14 days, 10,000 middle- and upper-level government employees were involved, closing courts, welfare services, construction work, and commuting facilities. Industry had to lay off thousands. The government retaliated by locking out 30,000 employees, including 25,000 teachers. The two unions involved demanded pay raises up to 22 per cent.

A lockout of 3,000 union members among the armed forces' 5,300 officers was threatened. It was called off when Prime Minister Olof Palme introduced a bill to force 47,000 government employees back to work. Pay negotiations broke down on June 21 when employers rejected a Swedish Confederation of Trade Unions demand for a 30 per cent raise over three years. They agreed on 27.9 per cent.

The price freeze on goods and services, imposed in 1970, was extended for six months in March. A new constitution proposed in August would take more power from King Gustaf VI Adolf and allow 18-year-olds to vote.

Facts in Brief. Population: 8,171,000. Government: King Gustaf VI Adolf; Prime Minister Olof Palme. Monetary Unit: krona. Foreign Trade: exports, $6,761,000,000; imports, $7,006,000,000. Principal Exports: machinery, paper and pulp, iron and steel.   Kenneth Brown

One lonely student sits in a classroom in Stockholm, Sweden, after government lockout idled about 25,000 teachers on February 19, during a wave of strikes.

SWIMMING. Shane Gould, a 14-year-old Australian girl new to international competition, and Mark Spitz, a 21-year-old American who is an old hand at record-breaking, were the best swimmers in 1971.

Miss Gould, 5 feet 8 inches and 130 pounds, set world free-style records for 200 meters (2 minutes 5.8 seconds), 400 meters (4 minutes 21.2 seconds), 800 meters (8 minutes 58.1 seconds), and 1,500 meters (17 minutes 0.6 seconds), and tied the record for 100 meters (58.9 seconds). Her victory in May over Debbie Meyer of Sacramento, Calif., prompted Miss Meyer to abandon thoughts of retiring.

Spitz set world records for the 200-meter free-style (1 minute 53.5 seconds), 100-meter butterfly (55 seconds), and 200-meter butterfly (2 minutes 3.9 seconds, which stood only until Hans Fassnacht of West Germany did 2 minutes 3.3 seconds four days later). Spitz won four titles in the Amateur Athletic Union (A.A.U.) national outdoor championships in August in Houston; two in the National Collegiate Athletic Association (NCAA) championships in March in Ames, Iowa (Indiana won its fourth straight team title); two in the important Santa Clara, Calif., invitational meet in July; two in the United States-East German meet in September in Leipzig, and two in the United States-Russian-British meet, also in September, in Minsk.

International Meets. The two September meets in Europe proved stunning triumphs for the U.S.

team. They won 24 of the 28 events against East Germany, and 27 of 29 (with 5 world records) against Russia and Great Britain. In the Pan American Games, held from July 30 to August 14 in Cali, Colombia, the United States won 14 of the 15 events for men and 8 of the 14 for women.

The Year's Records. The world-record toll was heavy–9 of the 16 records for men and 7 of the 15 for women were broken in 1971 (with another women's record tied). The male record-breakers were Spitz (twice), Fassnacht, Tom McBreen of San Mateo, Calif. (4 minutes 2.1 seconds for the 400-meter free-style), Roland Matthes of East Germany (56.7 seconds for the 100-meter backstroke, and 2 minutes 5.6 seconds for the 200-meter backstroke), Graham Windeatt of Australia (8 minutes 28.6 seconds for the 800-meter free-style), and two American relay teams.

Women's records were bettered by Miss Gould (three times), 13-year-old Cathy Calhoun of Alhambra, Calif. (17 minutes 19.2 seconds for the 1,500-meter free-style), Ellie Daniel of Drexel Hill, Pa. (2 minutes 18.4 seconds for the 200-meter butterfly), and two U.S. relay teams.

Other leading U.S. swimmers included Frank Heckl, Mike Burton, Susie Atwood, Ann Simmons, and Linda Johnson, all from California. The best American divers were Cynthia Potter and Micki King among the women and Dick Rydze and Mike Finneran among the men. *Frank Litsky*

SWITZERLAND. Feminists who fought for 50 years against male prejudice and indifference finally won the right for women to vote on Feb. 7, 1971. In an all-male referendum, women were enfranchised by 621,403 votes to 323,596.

Women then voted for the first time in a June 6 national referendum that approved antipollution and tax-reform measures. One of the new measures gives the parliament power to legislate heavy penalties for pollution of air, water, and the environment, and to wage war on noise. Concern over pollution has risen because of the postwar growth of population, industry, and aircraft noise.

The four-party ruling coalition retained control of the Swiss legislature. In December, legislators picked Nello Celio as president for 1972.

Switzerland raised the value of the franc by 7 per cent in May. The change, coupled with the U.S. imposition of a four-month surcharge on imports in August, dismayed industrialists.

Labor shortages continued. In September, only 51 people of working age were registered as unemployed. The shortage closed 11 mountain frontier posts with Italy. Helicopter patrols took over.

Facts in Brief. Population: 6,476,000. Government: President Rudolf Gnaegi. Monetary Unit: franc. Foreign Trade: exports, $5,135,000,000; imports, $6,551,000,000. Principal Exports: machinery, chemicals, clocks and watches. *Kenneth Brown*

SYRIA. Acting President Hafiz al-Asad was elected Syria's 14th president in March, 1971, receiving 99.2 per cent of the 1.9 million votes cast. He was the only candidate and the first Syrian head of state from the powerful Alawite religious sect. An amendment to the 1969 provisional Constitution provided for a referendum to elect a "president of the republic" for a seven-year term.

With the election, the ruling Ba'ath Party moved to fulfill its pledge to restore representative government. It set up a Peoples' Council of 173 members, 87 of them Ba'athists, to serve as the supreme legislative body. Other Syrian parties were represented with the next largest bloc, 11, belonging to the Socialist Union. The council was Syria's first legislature since the National Assembly was dissolved in 1966 after a military coup.

New Cabinet. In April, Asad appointed a new Cabinet of 28 members, with Major-General Abd al-Rahman Khalafawi, interior minister in the previous Cabinet, as his new prime minister. Asad traveled to other Arab countries, explaining Syrian foreign policy and seeking to reduce Syria's self-imposed isolation. The government restored diplomatic relations with Morocco, and it agreed to exchange workers with Lebanon. Border restrictions between the two neighbors were lifted.

Relations with Jordan worsened, however. They had improved after Asad's 1970 coup. But King Hussein refused a Syrian offer to mediate with Palestinian guerrillas, and Syria closed the border in July, 1971. After reported border clashes between the two nations in August, Syria broke diplomatic relations with Jordan on August 12.

Joins Federation. Syria took an important step toward Arab unity when it joined with Libya and Egypt in signing the charter of the Federation of Arab Republics. Syrians later voted their approval of a new federation Constitution.

The new alignment offered a possible solution to the Ba'ath Party's search for popular support. Syrians were growing suspicious of military or civilian coups. Efforts to form a Progressive National Front similar to Egypt's Arab Socialist Union were unsuccessful despite a general amnesty and minority party representation in the Cabinet and Peoples' Council.

In trade, Russia agreed to buy $4 million worth of Syrian tobacco. A Chinese-built cotton-spinning mill was opened in Hama in March and China agreed to build a second one. The 1971 budget, balanced at $718 million, showed a smaller deficit in the balance of payments. Italy replaced Russia as Syria's major export market.

Facts in Brief. Population: 6,373,000. Government: President Hafiz al-Asad; Prime Minister Abd al-Rahman Khalafawi. Monetary Unit: pound. Foreign Trade: exports, $203,000,000; imports, $360,000,000. Principal Export: cotton. *William Spencer*

TAIWAN. See FORMOSA.

TANZANIA came close to war with neighboring Uganda in 1971. President Julius K. Nyerere refused to recognize Uganda's new military government headed by General Idi Amin Dada, which he called reactionary. Nyerere opposed the acceptance of Amin's government at such international institutions as the Organization of African Unity (OAU). Adding to the tension, former Ugandan President Apollo Milton Obote settled in Tanzania after his overthrow in January. Amin promised a reward to anyone who returned Obote to Uganda. By August, border fighting broke out between troops of the two nations.

Border Situation. In July, Amin had closed Uganda's border with Tanzania. He accused Tanzania of interfering in Uganda's internal affairs and of planning an invasion. Tanzania denied this and accused Amin of using the border dispute to rally support for his coup and reunite warring factions of the Ugandan Army.

The secretary-general of the Commonwealth of Nations sought to mediate the dispute. In September, Amin accepted the proposal but Tanzania rejected it, charging that this was a ploy to win recognition for the Amin government.

Political Unrest existed on both the island of Zanzibar and the mainland. Tanzania's first treason trial ended on February 9, when four persons were sentenced to life in prison for plotting to assassinate President Nyerere.

In May, 19 men were tried and convicted of conspiring to overthrow the island government on Zanzibar. All of them were sentenced to death. Charges of prisoner torture were reportedly made against the island's government.

Liberation Movements. Tanzania continued its important role on the liberation committee of the OAU and remained a major channel of support for the Mozambique Liberation Front. The Swedish government funneled increased support to African liberation movements through Tanzania. In January, the Russian ambassador to Tanzania presented President Nyerere with the Lenin Centenary Jubilee Medal for his efforts at aiding liberation movements.

Tanzania continued its close relations with China. With Chinese aid and manpower, remarkable progress was made on the new Tanzam Railroad, which will connect the capital and port city of Dar es Salaam with Lusaka, Zambia.

When the United Nations voted on China's entry in October, Tanzania was one of the sponsors of the successful resolution calling for the seating of the Peking government. See UNITED NATIONS (UN).

Facts in Brief. Population: 13,952,000. Government: President Julius K. Nyerere. Monetary Unit: shilling. Foreign Trade: exports, $239,000,000; imports, $271,000,000. Principal Exports: coffee, cotton, sisal, diamonds. George Shepherd

TAXATION. The first session of the 92nd Congress passed a new tax bill on Dec. 9, 1971, that was designed to stimulate the economy and ease the federal tax burden on individuals with low incomes. The tax reductions had been suggested by President Richard M. Nixon on August 15, to reinforce his new economic policy. Mr. Nixon signed the bill into law on December 11.

Included in the new law was a 7 per cent tax credit for investment in new equipment. This was intended to encourage industry to invest in new machinery. The 7 per cent automobile excise tax, formerly paid by car manufacturers, was retroactively eliminated.

Exemptions Increased. The new tax law increased the personal exemption for 25 million personal-income-tax payers from $650 to $675 for 1971 and to $750 for 1972. It also increased the tax-free allowance for persons with a low income. Savings to most individuals would be small, but it was estimated that about 2.8 million individuals with low incomes would no longer have to pay federal income taxes. Nevertheless, the tax burden for many individuals would remain heavy, because social security tax rates, affecting 63 million people, were scheduled to rise on Jan. 1, 1972.

The total tax cut provided for in the new law was estimated at $26 billion by 1973. At the same time, the federal deficit was growing. In July, the deficit for fiscal 1971 was estimated at $23.2 billion.

After much debate and the threat of a presidential veto, Congress attached a rider to the tax bill that would provide financing for presidential campaigns with a $1 tax checkoff for the candidate of the taxpayer's choice. The President had threatened to veto the tax bill if the provisions of the rider were effective in 1972. However, a compromise was worked out, and the campaign funds will not be available until 1976.

The Tax Burden. On March 18, the U.S. Bureau of the Census released a study, based on 1968 statistics, showing who bears the heaviest tax burden in the United States. Most U.S. families – those with incomes ranging from $4,000 to $49,000 a year – pay out about 30 per cent of their income in direct or indirect taxes. Poor families earning less than $2,000 pay 50 per cent of their income in taxes. However, they actually receive a negative tax benefit of 57 per cent. Although they pay out 50 per cent of their incomes in taxes, they receive 106.5 per cent of their income in various government benefits, such as welfare and social security payments. Families with incomes of $50,000 or more pay 45 per cent of their income in taxes, but they receive less than 1 per cent in government benefits.

State and Local Taxes. State tax collections in fiscal 1971 reached $51.5 billion. This was $3.5 billion, or 7.3 per cent, more than in fiscal 1970. In 1971, 18 states collected 10 per cent or more in increased revenue than in 1970. The greatest percentage rises were in New Hampshire (25 per cent) and Idaho (20.2 per cent).

Once again, New York and California led in the amount of tax revenue collected. In all, seven major states collected nearly half of all state tax revenue: New York, California, Illinois, Pennsylvania, Michigan, Texas, and Ohio.

State per-capita tax collections varied. Twenty-three states collected $250 or more in taxes per capita; 11 states collected $220 to $249; 7 collected $200 to $219; 6, $180 to $199; and 3 states collected less than $180 per capita.

In fiscal 1971, 43 states collected personal income taxes and 45 states collected general sales and gross-receipts taxes.

According to figures released by the Bureau of the Census, the six greatest sources of tax revenue for the state governments in fiscal 1971 were as follows: general sales and gross receipts, $15.5 billion; individual income, $10.1 billion; motor fuels, $6.6 billion; corporate income, $3.4 billion; tobacco products, $2.5 billion; alcoholic beverages, $1.5 billion.

In fiscal 1971, local tax collections amounted to some $43.3 billion, about 15.8 per cent less than the total state tax revenue collected.   Carol L. Thompson

TELEPHONE AND TELEGRAPH. See COMMUNICATIONS.

TELEVISION experienced a traumatic year in 1971, the 25th anniversary of commercial telecasting. A record number of shows (35) were dropped during the year, including the oldest of them all, "The Ed Sullivan Show," which had run 23 years. Ironically, several of these shows still had strong audience ratings. They were dropped because studies by advertising agencies, sponsors, and networks indicated that their viewers were either too young, or too old, or not affluent enough to be the perfect consumer.

Among the missing were "Lassie," Lawrence Welk, Jim Nabors, Andy Griffith, Red Skelton, Danny Thomas, "Hogan's Heroes," "Family Affair," "Beverly Hillbillies," and "Green Acres."

In their place, the networks provided an unprecedented number of movie "superstars." Jimmy Stewart, Henry Fonda, Anthony Quinn, Glenn Ford, Shirley MacLaine, Rock Hudson, and Tony Curtis all debuted as television series "regulars" in 1971. By year's end, however, cancellations were in on Fonda, MacLaine, and Quinn. Among the older shows, "Marcus Welby, M.D.," and the "Flip Wilson Show" continued as the nation's top-rated series. The most popular new show was "All in the Family," an irreverent, "relevant" comedy satirizing bigotry.

Law and Order was the most prevalent theme in the fall, with more than 20 series pursuing the cause of justice. Every conceivable type of law man was represented, ranging from a blind insurance detective ("Longstreet") to a moonlighting cop-turned-priest ("Sarge").

Again, the foremost dramatic series were British Broadcasting Corporation imports: "The Six Wives of Henry VIII"; and two brilliant "Masterpiece Theater" presentations, "The First Churchills" and Thomas Hardy's "Jude the Obscure" on the Public Broadcasting Service (PBS) network.

Outstanding specials included: "Hogan's Goat" (PBS); "The Great American Dream Machine" (PBS); Arthur Miller's "The Price"; "The Neon Ceiling"; and "The Electric Company." The latter, a PBS reading program for 7- to 10-year-olds, was a worthy post-graduate course to the heralded "Sesame Street," which was carried on more stations (300) during 1971 than any other show on American television.

A Troubled Year. Broadcasters were in a constant state of agitation during 1971. Network profits fell because of the ailing economy and the loss of cigarette advertising. Vital prime-time revenue also dropped because the Federal Communications Commission (FCC) ordered the networks to return a nightly half-hour of prime time to affiliated stations. The FCC had hoped the move would lead to creative local programming, but most affiliated stations filled the time with reruns of network shows.

Broadcasters were under more pressure than ever

"All in the Family," the CBS spoof on bigotry, won an Emmy as best comedy series on TV; and Jean Stapleton, standing, was named best comedy actress.

before from minority and other citizen groups who demanded a voice in programming and employment practices. The American Broadcasting Company (ABC) bowed to the Italian-American Civil Rights League, and agreed not to use the terms Mafia and Cosa Nostra on "The FBI" series.

Broadcasters were also pressured by the government. The Administration of President Richard M. Nixon was incensed by "The Selling of the Pentagon," the Emmy-winning documentary about Pentagon public relations. This Columbia Broadcasting System (CBS) documentary was first aired on February 23. Vice-President Spiro T. Agnew called it "distorted" and "disreputable." CBS president Frank Stanton risked citation for contempt of Congress when he refused to give the House Investigations Sub-committee *out-takes* (film edited out of the final program).

In January the FCC, prodded by Action for Children's Television (ACT) and other citizen groups, launched an inquiry into commercial television's lucrative but woefully substandard children's programming. ACT proposed that broadcasters be required to set aside 14 hours weekly, without commercials, for quality children's fare.

By July, the commission had heard from more than 60,000 concerned parents, and in October, it formed a special task force on children's program-

ming. A prime responsibility of the task force, said FCC Chairman Dean Burch, would be to evaluate the surgeon general's long-awaited study of the effect of television violence on children. The study was scheduled for release by the end of 1971.

In October, Clay T. Whitehead, director of the White House Office of Telecommunications Policy called for eliminating the Fairness Doctrine and for longer license periods for television stations. The Fairness Doctrine refers to the broadcasters' duty to present all sides of controversial issues. Whitehead recommended replacing it with a law giving an individual the right to buy time. He also proposed that the government remove itself from program regulation.

Although Whitehead said he was not prepared at the time to speak officially for the White House, some broadcasters were cautiously optimistic that his startling speech heralded a reversal of attitude by the Administration toward television and radio. See RADIO.

Cable television (CATV) had more than 5 million subscribers in over 2,500 communities in 1971, but further growth of CATV was stymied by the FCC's failure to lift its freeze on cable service in big cities. Relief was promised before the end of 1971 by the FCC.   June Bundy Csida

See also AWARDS AND PRIZES.

TENNESSEE. See STATE GOVERNMENT.

Keith Mitchell aged from 18 to 56 as Henry in superb BBC series "The Six Wives of Henry VIII." Rosalie Crotchley played Henry's last wife, Catherine Parr.

©British Broadcasting Corp.

TENNIS enjoyed a spectacular year on the court in 1971. Off the court, it suffered through another year of the power struggle between the professional players and the national federations.

There were many winners, among them John Newcombe, Rod Laver, and Ken Rosewall of Australia, and Arthur Ashe of Gum Spring, Va.—all contract professionals—and Stan Smith of Pasadena, Calif., and Jan Kodes of Czechoslovakia, independent professionals. The winners among the women included Billie Jean King of Long Beach, Calif., Margaret Smith Court of Australia, and two bright newcomers—19-year-old Evonne Goolagong of Australia and 16-year-old Chris Evert of Fort Lauderdale, Fla.

Men's Competition. The 25-year-old Newcombe won the Wimbledon in England, beating Smith in a five-set final. Kodes won the French title on a clay court and gained the finals of the U.S. championship on grass and the Italian championship on clay. Ashe was an Australian finalist and United States and Italian semifinalist.

Smith beat Kodes in four sets for the U.S. title on September 15, at Forest Hills, N.Y. Smith was a Wimbledon finalist, an Italian and a French quarterfinalist, and the winner of the International Lawn Tennis Federation (ILTF) Grand Prix circuit. He also led the United States to a 3-2 victory over Romania in the Davis Cup challenge round.

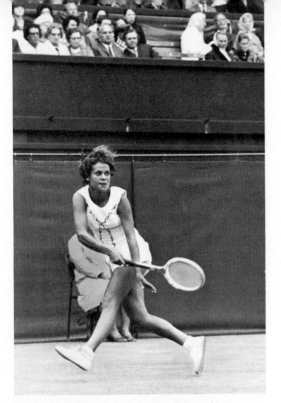

Evonne Goolagong, Australia's aborigine tennis prodigy, vaulted to stardom by beating Margaret Smith Court, also Australian, for the Wimbledon women's title.

Laver became the first tennis player to reach $1-million in career earnings. He won $289,841 during the year.

Rosewall won the Australian and South African championships and reached the Wimbledon semi-finals. He won $50,000, the largest purse in tennis history, by beating Laver in the final of the World Championship of Tennis in Dallas in November.

Women's Competition. Mrs. King, United States and German champion and Wimbledon semifinalist, became the first woman in any sport to win $100,000 in one year. Much of her earnings came on the new Virginia Slims professional circuit for women. Mrs. Court won her 10th Australian title in 12 years, lost the Wimbledon final to Miss Goolagong, and then stopped playing to await the birth of her first baby.

Miss Goolagong, the daughter of an Australian aboriginal sheepshearer, won the Wimbledon and French titles (see GOOLAGONG, EVONNE). She passed up the U.S. Open.

The uneasy truce between World Championship Tennis, the group representing the contract pros, and the ILTF, representing the national federations, seemingly ended when the ILTF banned the contract pros from its tournaments, including Wimbledon and Forest Hills, in 1972.　Frank Litsky

TEXAS. See DALLAS; HOUSTON; STATE GOVERNMENT.

THAILAND. United States troop withdrawals from Southeast Asia – and Thailand in particular – had a drastic effect on the Thai economy as well as the nation's politics in 1971. The military was also affected. Early in the year, the government announced it was withdrawing its 12,000-man force from South Vietnam. The troops were needed at home to combat a growing insurgency that, by the end of the year, had assumed serious proportions.

The continued withdrawal of American troops as well as the moth-balling of some of the U.S. air bases in Thailand meant a further decline in the once-booming economy. To bolster it, the government instituted new austerity programs and cut imports sharply. Exports also began to drop; rice, once a major export, became a glut on the market. There was a surplus of about a million tons in Bangkok alone.

The Thais, no longer able to depend so freely on U.S. support, began negotiating new trade agreements with the People's Republic of China. To stimulate an atmosphere of cordiality, the government even eased its restrictions on Chinese Communist propaganda. It was this search for a new, less Western-oriented alignment that finally brought a stunning political change in the country.

On November 17, Prime Minister Thanom Kittikachorn abolished the three-year-old Constitution, dissolved Parliament, and proclaimed martial law. Thailand was to be ruled by a National Executive Council composed of nine men, seven of them military officers. The Council was headed by Kittikachorn, who had previously been an army field marshal. It marked an end to representative government in Thailand for the foreseeable future.

The new military regime promised a new constitution and elections, but no definite dates were set. In effect, the Thais were resorting to an old pattern in which the military executed a coup whenever the country's political leaders tried to establish new policies that were at odds with military thinking. There had been more than a dozen such coups in 40 years.

The necessity of working out new relations with China and the growth of rebel movements in Thailand had probably precipitated the move. The new government took a more cautious policy by eliminating from high positions those known to be overly friendly to the Chinese. They were also successful in persuading the United States to slow down its rate of withdrawal from Thailand. A new priority was given to the suppression of various rebel movements within the country.

Facts in Brief. Population: 38,070,000. Government: King Phumiphon Aduldet; National Executive Council Chairman Thanom Kittikachorn. Monetary Unit: baht. Foreign Trade: exports, $697,000,000; imports, $1,253,000,000. Principal Exports: rice, rubber, corn, tin, teak, jute. John N. Stalker

THEATER

The New York stage was a medium with a message in 1971. Audiences were supposed not only to enjoy themselves, but also to examine their values, attitudes, and aims. This was revealed by the triple meaning of *Follies*, the title of the year's best musical. *Follies* were the opulent musical extravaganzas of the 1930s, and also the foibles of the leading characters, two former showgirls who were once bitter rivals for the same man. Played by Dorothy Collins and Alexis Smith, the two meet backstage 30 years later. As they relive old conflicts, they start new intrigues. The spectacular "Loveland" number reveals the girls' individual follies and those of their husbands. While celebrating the past, the musical demonstrates that it is folly to try to change the past.

Two musical revivals that offered their nostalgia straight were *No, No, Nanette* (1925) and *On the Town* (1944). *Nanette* has a farcical plot about a rich Bible publisher, three flappers, and his wife, played by 60-year-old Ruby Keeler, tap-dancing as energetically as ever. *On the Town* tells the tale of three sailors on shore leave in a 1940s New York City that today seems more like never-never land than the area outside the theater.

The frustrations of New York City life in the 1970s were turned to comic effect by Neil Simon in *The Prisoner of Second Avenue*. Peter Falk and Lee Grant played a typical middle-aged couple who suffer the petty annoyances and major catastrophes that surround the urban apartment dweller.

Off-Broadway, serious comedies by young writers made audiences think as well as laugh. John Guare's *The House of Blue Leaves*, judged the season's best by drama critics, is a cartoon that deals knockout blows to some American dreams. Hero Artie aspires to Hollywood stardom from his lowly job in a zoo. He has absolutely no talent, and a fatal gift for choosing the wrong women. His girl friend is even worse than his demented wife.

Robert Montgomery, a 23-year-old Yale drama student, "responded" in play form to characters and incidents from Dostoevsky's novel *The Idiot*, and called his play *Subject to Fits*. The phrase is used by the epileptic hero, Prince Myshkin, to describe himself, whereas the others are all "subject to life." Like the novel, the play asks, "Can absolute good exist in the world today?"

Religious Themes. The same question is evoked by two musicals based on the life of Christ, *Godspell*, off Broadway, and the Broadway rock opera *Jesus Christ Superstar*. *Godspell* is an energetic presentation of parables and scenes from the Gospel according to St. Matthew. Jesus, His friends, and His disciples are depicted as lovable circus clowns.

Jesus Christ Superstar, by Andrew Lloyd Webber, 23, and Tim Rice, 26, is more ambitious. Before the musical opened, the record album had been acclaimed by many, including numerous church groups. To recount the last days of Jesus, the authors use contemporary idiom and music to indicate that average people then (as now), because of their limitations, could react only in ordinary ways when faced with the extraordinary. The crowds see Christ in their own terms, not as a mystery, but as a

Follies, the big Broadway hit musical, featured lavishly gowned, Ziegfeld-type showgirls and tunes reminiscent of musical shows in the 1920s and 1930s.

"superstar." For the Broadway stage, however, Tom O'Horgan turned the simple story into a spectacular display of vulgarity, showing Jesus in sequins, a painted and effeminate Herod, circus floats, and a crucifixion in three-D with fireworks.

Satire was David Rabe's weapon against the clichés of happy home life that are pictured on television and in films. A veteran returns from Vietnam in *Sticks and Bones*, Rabe's version of *The Best Years of Our Lives*, a sentimental film of the 1940s about returning veterans and their understanding home folks. The hero is blind, but he refuses to accept his disability, and is outraged instead. The play implies that his family, not he, needs rehabilitation.

The Public Theater of the New York Shakespeare Festival presented *Sticks*, Rabe's *The Basic Training of Pavlo Hummel*, and Richard Wesley's *The Black Terror*, all outstanding new works. The last-named was set in "the very near future given the nature of American society" and dealt with black revolution. An expert assassin, trained in Vietnam, first carries out the orders of the revolution's leaders and then begins to question the need for violence. "Themes of black struggle" also were presented in a series of plays offered by the Negro Ensemble Company, an impressive acting company in its fifth season.

Contemporary Themes. Two plays depicted recent incidents and actual people who were outspoken critics of the American scene. *Lenny* by Julian Barry uses large segments of the late comedian

New York Theater Openings in 1971

Plays

Abelard and Héloïse, by Ronald Millar; with Keith Michell and Diana Rigg. Directed by Robin Phillips, produced by Elliot Martin. Opened March 10.

All Over, by Edward Albee; with Jessica Tandy and Colleen Dewhurst. Directed by John Gielgud, produced by Theater 1971. Opened March 27.

And Miss Reardon Drinks a Little, by Paul Zindel; with Julie Harris, Estelle Parsons, and Nancy Marchand. Directed by Melvin Bernhardt, produced by James B. McKenzie. Opened February 25.

Antigone, by Sophocles; with Philip Bosco and Martha Henry. Directed by John Hirsch, produced by Repertory Theater of Lincoln Center. Opened May 13.

The Dance of Death, by August Strindberg; with Rip Torn and Viveca Lindfors. Directed by Alfred Ryder, produced by Leo Kerz. Opened April 28.

A Doll's House, by Henrik Ibsen; with Claire Bloom and Donald Madden. Directed by Patrick Garland, produced by Hillard Elkins. Opened January 13.

An Enemy of the People, by Henrik Ibsen, translated by Arthur Miller, with Stephen Elliott and Philip Bosco. Directed by Jules Irving, produced by Repertory Theater of Lincoln Center. Opened March 11.

Father's Day, by Oliver Hailey; with Brenda Vaccaro and Biff McGuire. Directed by Donald Moffat, produced by Joseph Kipness. Opened March 16.

Four on a Garden, by Abe Burrows; with Sid Caesar and Carol Channing. Directed by Abe Burrows, produced by David Merrick. Opened January 30.

Hedda Gabler, by Henrik Ibsen; with Claire Bloom and Donald Madden. Directed by Patrick Garland, produced by Hillard Elkins. Opened February 17.

How the Other Half Loves, by Alan Ayckbourn; with Phil Silvers and Sandy Dennis. Directed by Gene Saks, produced by Michael Myerberg. Opened March 29.

The Incomparable Max, by Jerome Lawrence and Robert E. Lee, based on Max Beerbohm's works; with Clive Revill and Richard Kiley. Directed by Gerald Freedman, produced by Michael Abbott. Opened October 19.

Lenny, by Julian Barry; with Cliff Gorman. Directed by Tom O'Horgan, produced by Jules Fisher. Opened May 26.

Mary Stuart, by Friedrich Schiller, translated by Stephen Spender; with Salome Jens and Nancy Marchand. Directed by Jules Irving, produced by Repertory Theater of Lincoln Center. Opened November 11.

Metamorphoses, based on Ovid, adapted by Arnold Weinstein; with Paul Sand and Penny White. Directed by Paul Sills, produced by Zev Bufman. Opened April 22.

A Midsummer Night's Dream, by William Shakespeare; with Alan Howard and Sara Kestelman. Directed by Peter Brook, produced by the David Merrick Arts Foundation. Opened January 20.

Murderous Angels, by Conor Cruise O'Brien; with Jean-Pierre Aumont and Lou Gossett. Directed by Gordon Davidson, produced by Phoenix Theatre. Opened December 20.

No Place to Be Somebody, revival, by Charles Gordone; with Terry Alexander and Henry Baker. Directed by Charles Gordone, produced by Ashton Springer. Opened September 22.

Old Times, by Harold Pinter; with Mary Ure, Rosemary Harris, and Robert Shaw. Directed by Peter Hall, produced by Roger L. Stevens. Opened November 16.

The Philanthropist, by Christopher Hampton; with Alec McCowen. Directed by Robert Kidd, produced by David Merrick. Opened March 15.

The Playboy of the Western World, by John Millington Synge. Directed by John Hirsch, produced by the Repertory Theater of Lincoln Center. Opened January 7.

The Prisoner of Second Avenue, by Neil Simon; with Lee Grant and Peter Falk. Directed by Mike Nichols, produced by Saint Subber. Opened November 11.

Solitaire, Double Solitaire, by Robert Anderson; with Richard Venture and Joyce Ebert. Directed by Arvin Brown, produced by Gilbert Cates. Opened September 30.

The School for Wives, by Molière, translated by Richard Wilbur; with Brian Bedford. Directed by Stephen Porter, produced by Phoenix Theatre. Opened February 16.

Scratch, by Archibald MacLeish, based on Stephen Vincent Benét's story "The Devil and Daniel Webster," with Patrick Magee and Will Geer. Directed by Peter Hunt, produced by Stuart Ostrow. Opened May 6.

Twigs, by George Furth; with Sada Thompson. Directed by Michael Bennett, produced by Frederick Brisson. Opened November 14.

Unlikely Heroes, by Philip Roth, adapted by Larry Arrick; with Michael Tolan and Lou Jacobi. Directed by Larry Arrick, produced by Robert Livingston. Opened October 26.

Musicals

Ain't Supposed to Die a Natural Death, book, lyrics, and music by Melvin Van Peebles. Directed by Gilbert Moses, produced by Eugene V. Wolsk. Opened October 20.

Ari, based on Leon Uris' *Exodus*, book and lyrics by Leon Uris, music by Walt Smith. Directed by Lucia Victor, produced by Ken Gaston. Opened January 15.

Earl of Ruston, book and lyrics by C. C. Courtney and Ragan Courtney, music by Peter Link. Directed by C. C. Courtney, produced by David Black. Opened May 5.

Follies, book by James Goldman, music and lyrics by Stephen Sondheim. Directed by Harold Prince and Michael Bennett, produced by Harold Prince. Opened April 4.

Frank Merriwell, music and lyrics by Skip Redwine and Larry Frank, book by Skip Redwine, Larry Frank, and Heywood Gould. Directed by N. Kenyon, produced by S. Farber. Opened April 24.

The Grass Harp, based on the novel by Truman Capote, book and lyrics by Kenward Elmslie, music by C. Richardson; Directed by Ellis Rabb, produced by Theater 1972. Opened November 2.

Inner City, book and lyrics by Eve Merriam, music by Helen Miller; with Joy Garrett and Carl Hall. Directed by Tom O'Horgan, produced by Joseph Kipness. Opened December 12.

Johnny Johnson, revival, book and lyrics by Paul Green, music by Kurt Weill. Directed by Jose Quintero, produced by Timothy Gray. Opened April 11.

Jesus Christ Superstar, conceived by Tom O'Horgan, music by Andrew Lloyd Webber, lyrics by Tim Rice. Directed by Tom O'Horgan, produced by Robert Stigwood. Opened October 12.

No, No, Nanette, revival, book by Otto Harbach and Frank Mandel, music by Vincent Youmans, lyrics by Irving Caesar and Otto Harbach. Directed by Burt Shevelove, produced by Pyxidium Ltd. Opened January 19.

On the Town, revival, book and lyrics by Betty Comden and Adolph Green, music by L. Bernstein. Directed by Ron Field, produced by Jerry Schlossberg. Opened October 31.

70, Girls, 70, book by Fred Ebb and Norman L. Martin, music by John Kander, lyrics by Fred Ebb. Directed by Paul Aaron, produced by Arthur Whitelaw. Opened April 15.

Soon, book by Martin Duberman, music by Joseph M. Kookoolis and Scott Fagan, lyrics by Scott Fagan. Directed by Gerald Freedman, produced by Bruce Stark. Opened January 12.

To Live Another Summer, to Pass Another Winter, musical from Israel by Hayim Hefer, music by Dov Seltzer. Directed by J. Karmon, presented by L. Soloway. Opened October 21.

Two Gentlemen of Verona, based on Shakespeare's comedy, book by John Guare and Mel Shapiro, lyrics by John Guare, music by Galt MacDermot. Opened December 1.

Wild and Wonderful, music and lyrics by Bob Goodman, book by Phil Phillips. Directed by Burry Fredrik, produced by Rick Hobard. Opened December 7.

You're a Good Man, Charlie Brown, revival, based on "Peanuts" by Charles M. Schulz; book by John Gordon, music and lyrics by Clark Gesner. Opened June 1.

Lenny Bruce's monologues denouncing hypocrisy in morals, language, social behavior, and religion. Cliff Gorman's interpretation of Lenny brought balance to the play by stressing the leading character's inner complexities.

The Trial of the Catonsville Nine, by Father Daniel Berrigan, is a documentary based on the actual testimony given in the trial at which he, his brother Philip, and seven others were found guilty of destroying draft files in Catonsville, Md. The play effectively uses self-questioning as a counterpoint to the actual questions at the trial, and ultimately focuses on a major question, "What is one's Christian duty in the face of what he considers to be public evil?"

New plays by Edward Albee and Paul Zindel did not live up to expectations. Albee's *All Over* is a vague, abstract, and stilted play. Five people—family and friends—closest to a dying man await word that it is "all over." Seemingly reminiscing about the departing loved one, thay are actually talking about themselves. Paul Zindel's *And Miss Reardon Drinks a Little* is a mood piece about three sisters, schoolteachers. Although perceptively depicted and expertly acted, they are not very interesting people.

Royal Shakespeare Company of England produced two distinguished imports. Peter Brook staged an imaginative and entertaining production of *A*

Rosemary Harris and Robert Shaw trade memories in *Old Times*, Harold Pinter's first full-length play in six years. It premièred in November on Broadway.

Midsummer Night's Dream. The company returned in the fall with Harold Pinter's *Old Times*. A casual visit to a husband and wife from her old friend turns into the unknown and the feared. Pinter's use of implication suggests something more—the unspoken word, the relationship undone, the world estranged. By the end, the established relationships are changed. The intruder, or the past, is more firmly rooted in the household than is the wife, or the present.

In Other Cities, major revivals included Eugene O'Neill's *Long Day's Journey into Night* at Catholic University in Washington, D.C. Helen Hayes's interpretation of the tormented mother, Mary Tyrone, was hailed as definitive. Leo Brady directed.

Tennessee Williams chose to try out his new play, *Out Cry*, in Chicago, where he first achieved national recognition for *The Glass Menagerie*. *Out Cry* also treats a brother and sister, but this time they are the entire cast. Eileen Herlie and Donald Madden played actors deserted by a touring company that considers them mad. Left in a theater, they perform a two-character play written by the brother, acting out their desperation and loneliness. Williams described the play as "a dramatic metaphor . . . about how the vulnerable can be strong."   Alice Griffin

See also AWARDS AND PRIZES.

TOGO. See AFRICA.

TORNADOES. See DISASTERS; WEATHER.

TOYS. See GAMES, MODELS, AND TOYS.

TRACK AND FIELD. Pat Matzdorf, meticulously coached since high school, and Delano Meriwether, who never had a coach, were track and field's most spectacular performers in 1971. Matzdorf is a 21-year-old University of Wisconsin junior from Sheboygan, Wis., and Meriwether, a 28-year-old hematologist involved in leukemia research in Baltimore. Matzdorf raised the world high-jump record to 7 feet 6¼ inches on July 3, during the meet between the United States and Russia in Berkeley, Calif. Meriwether won the national title in the Amateur Athletic Union (A.A.U.) outdoor 100-yard dash in Eugene, Ore., on June 25, only a year after he had taken up running.

Earlier in the year, Matzdorf won many honors, but Reynaldo Brown defeated him in June in both the National Collegiate Athletic Association (NCAA) and A.A.U. outdoor title meets. Matzdorf's performance against the Russians was therefore all the more astonishing. He bettered his personal record of 7 feet 3 inches, Dick Fosbury's American record of 7 feet 4¼ inches, and Russian Valery Brumel's world record of 7 feet 5¾ inches.

Meriwether never ran until the summer of 1970, when he tried it for fun and liked it. Indoor promoters, sensing a box-office attraction, invited him to their 1971 winter meets, and he won his share of races. Wearing a white hospital shirt, yellow trunks, and striped suspenders, he looked like a poor relative, but he very quickly became a crowd favorite.

The little technique Meriwether did have was acquired by reading an instruction book. He missed many workouts because he was so busy with his medical work, and he was injured often because he did not know how to loosen his muscles. Despite those obstacles, he defeated a horde of world-class sprinters and won the A.A.U. 100-yard dash in a wind-aided 9 seconds flat.

Ryun and Liquori. Jim Ryun had to pass up the June A.A.U. title meet. Ryun, history's fastest miler, retired in 1969 at the age of 22, a victim of staleness. He returned to the sport in the winter of 1971, equaled the world indoor record for the mile, and hooked up with Marty Liquori, an old foe, in a widely heralded outdoor race on May 16 in Philadelphia. Liquori, a Villanova University senior, beat Ryun in a tingling race by two feet in 3 minutes 54.6 seconds.

Ryun was hardly discouraged. "You win and you lose," he said. "I have nothing to redeem myself for." But the problems ahead were too much. Ryun moved from Kansas to Eugene, Ore., only to find that the high pollen count in Eugene aggravated his hay fever. Because of the hay fever, he could not run in the A.A.U. championships in Eugene, and later he cut short a summer tour of Europe because the hay fever left him so weak.

Meanwhile, Liquori won the NCAA and A.A.U.

miles, ran well in Europe, and, until he injured a heel, established himself as a favorite for the 1,500-meter title in the 1972 Olympic Games in Munich, West Germany. Another early favorite was Kipchoge Keino of Kenya, the 1968 Olympic champion.

Other Stars. Despite improvement by athletes from many nations, notably East Germany, the United States remained the strongest nation in track. Its men soundly defeated the Russians in July. Then they won 20 of the 24 gold medals in the quadrennial Pan American Games in Cali, Colombia, in August, even though many of the best American athletes were absent, touring Europe on their own (see PAN AMERICAN GAMES). Meanwhile, the East Germans were the major winners in the European championships in Helsinki, Finland, in August, though the individual stars were Valery Borzov, a Russian sprinter, and Juha Vaatainen, a Finnish distance runner, each winning two titles.

Rod Milburn, a sophomore at Southern University, and John Smith, a junior at the University of California, Los Angeles, broke world records in the A.A.U. championships and became 1972 Olympic favorites. Milburn's time of 13 seconds for the 120-yard high hurdles wiped out the oldest (1959) record in the book—13.2 by Martin Lauer of West Germany and others. Smith's time of 44.5 seconds for the 440-yard dash demolished Lee Evans' record.

New World Track and Field Records Established in 1971

Subject to recognition by the International Amateur Athletic Federation (IAAF)

Event	Holder	Country	Where made	Date	Record
Men					
200 meters	Don Quarrie	Jamaica	Cali, Colombia	August 3	0:19.8*
440 yards	John Smith	U.S.A.	Eugene, Ore.	June 26	0:44.5
2 miles	Emiel Puttemans	Belgium	Edinburgh, Scotland	August 21	8:17.8
120-yard high hurdles	Rod Milburn	U.S.A.	Eugene, Ore.	June 25	0:13.0
High jump	Pat Matzdorf	U.S.A.	Berkeley, Calif.	July 3	7 ft. 6¼ in.
Triple jump	Pedro Perez	Cuba	Cali, Colombia	August 5	57 ft. 1 in.
Women					
100 meters	Renate Stecher	E. Germany	Berlin	July 31	0:11.0*
800 meters	Hildegard Falck	W. Germany	Stuttgart	July 11	1:58.3
1,500 meters	Karin Burneleit	E. Germany	Helsinki	August 15	4:09.6
1 mile	Ellen Tittel	W. Germany	Sittard, Netherlands	August 20	4:35.4
100-meter hurdles	Karin Balzer	E. Germany	Berlin	July 31	0:12.6
440-yard relay	Hughes, Wedgeworth, Render, Davis	U.S.A.	Bakersfield, Calif.	July 9	0:44.6
1,600-meter relay	Kuhne, Lohse, Seidler, Zehrt	E. Germany	Helsinki	August 15	3:29.3
1-mile relay	Stroy, Laing, Norman, Toussaint	U.S.A.	Durham, N.C.	July 17	3:38.7
3,200-meter relay	Tittel, Schenk, Merten, Falck	W. Germany	Lubeck, W. Germany	July 25	8:16.8
High jump	Ilona Gusenbauer	Austria	Vienna	September 4	6 ft. 3½ in.
Shot-put	Nadezhda Chizhova	U.S.S.R.	Moscow	August 29	67 ft. 0¼ in.*
Discus throw	Faina Melnik	U.S.S.R.	Munich	September 4	212 ft. 10½ in.

*Equals record.

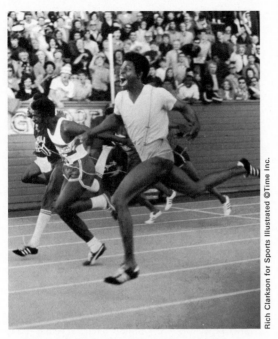

Delano Meriwether, right, narrowly beat Jim Green and Don Quarrie to the tape to win the 100-yard dash in a windy 9 seconds at the National A.A.U. meet in June.

Rich Clarkson for Sports Illustrated © Time Inc.

TRANSPORTATION industries in the United States found their financial situation modestly improved in 1971. A modest year-end strengthening in the general economy eased the depressed situation, but the industries' basic problems of rising costs, labor difficulties, and unresponsive government regulation persisted.

During 1971, legislation passed in recent years began to be implemented. As a result, transportation industries found themselves increasingly concerned with such social considerations as ecology, environment, and safety.

The year also saw the first serious attempts in many years to deal with the problems of economic regulation. There were three major legislative proposals. The first, the Surface Transportation Act of 1971, was backed by regulated surface carriers. Its major provisions include more financial assistance, greater relief from property taxes, approval of more requests for route abandonment by surface carriers, and increased federal regulation of waterway operators and those highway carriers that handle agricultural commodities.

The other two proposals were made by the Department of Transportation (DOT). The DOT proposals were similar to those of the carriers, but they emphasized *deregulation* (less government control), particularly for highway transportation, placing greater reliance on natural market forces.

The total U.S. transportation bill for 1971 was about $205 billion, a 4.1 per cent increase over 1970, according to preliminary estimates of the Transportation Association of America (TAA). This was the first time the nation's dollar expenditures on transportation exceeded $200 billion. The figure included all types of private and public transportation, with $95 billion spent on freight and $110-billion for passenger transportation. The TAA's preliminary estimates of total U.S. mainland traffic volume were:

Freight	1970	1971
(billions of intercity ton-miles)		
Rail	773.0	750.0
Truck	412.0	428.0
Pipeline	431.0	443.0
Rivers and canals	190.0	190.0
Lakes	116.0	111.0
Air	3.4	3.2
Total	1,925.4	1,925.2
Passenger		
(billions of intercity passenger-miles)		
Auto	1,026	1,067.0
Private air	10	10.0
Public commercial air	104	106.0
Bus	25	25.0
Rail	11	10.0
Water	4	4.0
Total	1,180	1,222.0

Serious efforts to develop plans and programs to achieve a more balanced transportation system also characterized the transportation year. On March 31, President Richard M. Nixon called for "a truly

Milburn won in five major meets—NCAA, A.A.U., U.S.-U.S.S.R., U.S.-Africa, and the Pan American Games. Steve Prefontaine, a precocious sophomore distance runner from the University of Oregon, made the same sweep. Smith skipped the Russian meet but won in the other four.

Though the world record of 224 feet 5 inches for the discus throw was bettered three times, each record performance was tainted. Jay Silvester of Smithfield, Utah, the 34-year-old record holder, had a throw of 230 feet 11 inches disallowed because the meet was unsanctioned and another of 229 feet 9½ inches put under a cloud because of sanctioning problems. Ricky Bruch of Sweden threw 230 feet ½ inch only to find that his discus was a quarter-ounce light.

Women's Events. Women's track received unusual attention in 1970 because of the many world records set by Chi Cheng, a Formosan who is now a college student in Pomona, Calif. Thigh injuries cut short her 1971 season and threatened her career.

After losing to the Russian team, U.S. women won 5 of the 13 gold medals in the Pan American Games.

Cross Country. Prefontaine and Frank Shorter, who won the major cross-country races in 1970, repeated in 1971. Prefontaine beat Garry Bjorklund of the University of Minnesota by 40 yards in leading Oregon to the NCAA championship. Shorter beat Steve Stageberg by 150 yards in leading the Florida Track Club to A.A.U. honors. *Frank Litsky*

balanced transportation system." The President urged "the people of this nation to join with the Department of Transportation and also with state and local officials in re-evaluating our goals and reaffirming our commitment to a balanced transportation system for these United States."

DOT Actions in 1971 were mostly a series of stopgap measures. The department began to implement legislation it had spearheaded in 1970 involving airports, mass transit, maritime transport, and railroads.

In September, DOT released its long-awaited statement on national transportation policy. The document dealt with the problems of imbalance in the promotion and regulation of transportation and favored some deregulation, expansion of user charges, greater pollution controls, revenue sharing with the states, and increased planning. To many, the statement was disappointing. It seemed to be more a description of the nation's transportation problems than a prescription for dealing with them.

The DOT was deeply involved in supporting three major proposals of the Nixon Administration: the proposed federal revenue-sharing program through a transportation trust fund, Cabinet reorganization, and an "Emergency Public Interest Protection Act" to deal with labor problems.

Airlines

The U.S. airline industry pulled out of its economic tailspin in 1971 after suffering the greatest losses in history in 1970. Major factors in the improvement were a 6 per cent fare increase effective in May, increased traffic (largely business travel) that started in September, and extensive cost reductions, achieved through layoffs, reductions in flights, and deferred capital expenditures.

The Air Transport Association estimated that the 11 trunk carriers would have a bookkeeping pretax profit of $25 million in 1971 as compared with an $87 million loss in 1970. The $25 million profit, however, reflected $33 million in federal government refunds of previously posted delivery position options for the supersonic transport (SST) that was canceled in 1971. See AVIATION.

Railroads

It became increasingly clear during the year that railroad service would deteriorate further if nothing was done to restore the industry's financial viability. Earnings would decline even more, and additional railroads would be forced into bankruptcy.

Large segments of the railroad industry contined to be in such serious financial trouble that there was a very real danger that the nation's rail system might collapse. After years of low earnings, the railroads were lacking the money necessary to make improvements.

The first nine months of 1971 saw some earnings recovery for the railroads over the depressed levels of 1970. Rate increases, some concessions by labor on

work rules, and the transfer of passenger service deficits to the new nationwide rail passenger system, Amtrak, brought the improvement. However, after midyear, the industry was hurt by both internal and external labor disputes.

Consequently, the U.S. railroad industry's rate of return remained perilously low during 1971–2.5 per cent compared with 1.7 per cent for 1970. This level was still far below the 6 per cent return the Interstate Commerce Commission indicated the railroads would have to attain if they were to provide needed service improvements. The industry's rate of return has not exceeded 3 per cent since the 1966 rate of 3.90 per cent.

The Reading Company, corporate parent of the Reading Railroad, filed a bankruptcy petition on November 23, contending that it could not pay $11-million in debts and taxes. The Reading's petition for reorganization was the fifth such move made in the last five years by eastern railroads, and it underscored their serious financial problems.

To make up for past deficiencies and to expand for the future, railroads must undertake one of the largest capital improvement programs of any industry in history–$36 billion over 11 years. That estimate was made by a rail industry study group, America's Sound Transportation Review Organization (ASTRO). The $36 billion compared with a current net capital investment for the entire industry of $28 billion. Of the $36 billion, ASTRO proposed that the federal government provide $10 billion in the form of loans, tax incentives, and loan guarantees.

Passenger Trains. Despite strong objections to reductions in service and the loss of jobs, the National Railroad Passenger Corporation formally started operation on May 1, with all but three passenger-carrying railroads (Southern, Denver & Rio Grande; Western; and Rock Island). The country's first nationwide rail passenger system was initially called Railpax, then renamed Amtrak (*Am* for American, *tr* for travel, and *ak* for track).

Late in the year, Amtrak requested an additional $170 million in federal financial aid for fiscal 1973. Some rail executives expressed the view that they would like to see Amtrak succeed, but thought that no company or government agency could operate long-haul intercity passenger service profitably without heavy subsidies. They believe that the government must be prepared to subsidize all passenger operations heavily if it feels such service is socially necessary and in the public interest.

Trucking

Trucking companies made a very strong earnings comeback in 1971. An improved economy, higher freight rates, and greater labor stability caused the rally. Industry earnings for the first half of 1971 soared to $200 million from only $58 million during the strike-depressed first half of 1970. Earnings for all of 1970 were $208 million.

Amtrak-Intercity Passenger Routes

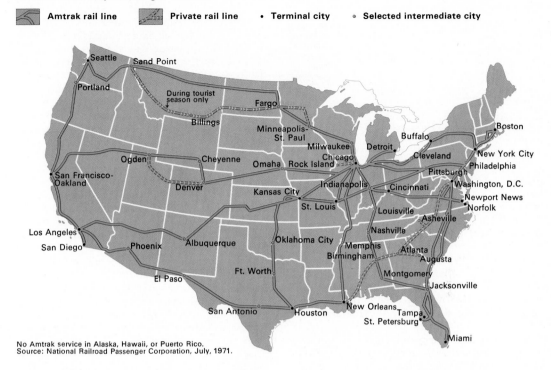

Amtrak rail line   Private rail line   • Terminal city   ○ Selected intermediate city

No Amtrak service in Alaska, Hawaii, or Puerto Rico.
Source: National Railroad Passenger Corporation, July, 1971.

Trucking earnings were helped by intercity freight tonnage increasing about 4 per cent over 1970. Rate increases of 4 per cent in both January and July helped to offset higher labor costs. Improved productivity also helped, particularly among long-haul carriers. Many of the latter switched from two-man sleepers to one-man relay systems.

Highways

The DOT reported in mid-1971 that more than 31,900 miles (more than 75 per cent) of the planned 42,500-mile Interstate Highway System was open to traffic. Construction was underway on another 4,020 miles, and engineering or right-of-way work was in process on 4,900 miles. Only 1,637 miles (4 per cent) of the system had yet to advance beyond the preliminary planning stages.

Major bottlenecks in the program continued to be links in urban areas, which were controversial because of disputes over routes, displacement of housing, and other factors.

Ocean Shipping

During 1971, financial problems continued to mount for U.S. shipping companies. A serious erosion of the nation's trade competitiveness, a badly deteriorating balance of payments position, rate cutting caused by substantial overcapacity on major trade routes, and costly longshoremen strikes at East, West, and Gulf coast ports were the causes of the difficulty.

Twice within seven weeks, President Nixon invoked Taft-Hartley Act procedures in longshoremen strikes. On October 6, the President used the act to force an end to the 16-week West Coast dockworkers strike. On November 26, he used the act again to halt an eight-week strike at Gulf and Atlantic ports.

The Maritime Program to revitalize the U.S. Merchant Marine, which became law in October, 1970, progressed slowly during 1971. The new program included plans for building 30 new ships a year over a 10-year period. However, faced with problems of overcapacity and labor unrest, shipping operators were hesitant to place orders for more tonnage with U.S. yards.

As a result, more than $60 million of the fiscal 1971 construction subsidy budget was carried over into fiscal 1972. When added to the $230 million already appropriated, the 1972 program totaled $290 million. There was growing concern that if the money was not used soon by U.S. operators, it would be difficult to obtain an equivalent appropriation for fiscal 1973.

World Shipping. According to Lloyd's Register of Shipping, 1,939 merchant ships were under construction on Sept. 30, 1971, a decrease from 2,028 for the same period in 1970. Shipbuilding orders, including those under construction, increased to 4,126 from 1970's 4,077.

Gross tonnage of vessels on the total world order

book increased to a record 84.1 million compared with 69.7 million gross tons on Sept. 30, 1970:

Leading Countries	Total Tonnage Under Construction and on Order*
Japan	32,926,937
Sweden	6,496,850
France	5,488,794
Great Britain & Northern Ireland	5,315,976
Spain	5,251,621
West Germany	5,164,246
Denmark	3,972,968
Norway	3,793,233
Italy	2,925,699
Netherlands	2,450,882
Yugoslavia	2,085,541
United States	1,993,852
Poland	1,411,300

*As of Sept. 30, 1971
Source: Lloyd's Register of Shipping

Urban Mass Transit

Financial problems continued to plague city mass transportation in 1971. The American Transit Association estimated that transit companies lost more than $360 million in 1971 as operating costs continued to soar while passenger volume and revenues lagged. This loss compared with $288 million in 1970 and $220 million in 1969.

In a few cities where new and innovative services were provided, such as Washington, D.C., and Philadelphia, better public transportation apparently attracted some motorists away from their automobiles. But, nationwide, there was no pause in the decline of the public's patronage of transit systems. Traffic dropped to a new low of 7.2 billion passengers, compared with 7.3 billion passengers in 1970 and 23 billion in 1945.

Transit officials stressed that existing legislation dealt only with long-term solutions to transit problems—acquisition, construction, and improvement of facilities and equipment—and did not provide funds to alleviate operating deficits while long-term remedies were being worked out. Public officials applied increasing pressure for interim emergency operating subsidies to keep essential transit systems operating until they could be placed on a firm financial footing. Legislation for such aid was introduced by a number of key senators and congressmen.

DOT officials, however, were reluctant to provide such funds. They held that operating subsidies might result in transit organizations becoming too willing to accept high wage demands, or too reluctant to initiate unpopular fare increases, because they could keep turning to the federal government to cover mounting operating losses.

Nevertheless, Secretary of Transportation John A. Volpe reported to Congress on Nov. 22, 1971, that the subject was receiving further study by the Administration. He indicated that he was leaving the door open to consider the growing need for operating subsidies.
Kenneth E. Schaefle

TRAVEL. International tourism increased by 9 per cent in 1971. It accounted for about 182 million visits across international borders and for expenditures of about $25 billion, including fares.

Despite an uncertain United States economy, the 1971 volume of travel was greater than ever, though the traveler became more price-conscious. The travel industry established record-breaking traffic and revenue figures at home and abroad, and remained the third largest U.S. industry. The United States was host to 13.8 million foreign visitors, a 5 per cent gain over 1970. Their expenditures registered an 11 per cent gain to a new high of $3 billion.

American Travel Abroad not only increased at a greater rate than did foreign travel to the United States, but also at a greater rate than the world travel market as a whole. An estimated 22.9 million Americans traveled abroad, spending $5.6 billion. This sent the travel deficit to a new high of $2.6-billion. Canada attracted 14.7 million Americans, a gain of 3 per cent over 1970; 1.9 million Americans traveled to Mexico, a gain of 6 per cent; and 6.3-million went overseas, a gain of 8 per cent.

For the third consecutive year, Great Britain remained the number-one overseas destination for Americans. About 1.75 million Americans visited there last year and spent about $336 million. Conversely, the United States attracted 310,000 Britishers, and Japanese visitors ran a close second, sending 280,000 to the United States.

Canada provided the United States with 10.1-million visitors who remained more than 48 hours. About 1.2 million visitors came from Mexico, and 2.5 million from overseas.

Domestic Travel Grew 7 per cent, despite the stagnant economy. American tourists spent approximately $60 billion on transportation, lodging, food, and commercial travel attractions.

During the last quarter of 1971, the international readjustment of currency values, which followed the Nixon Administration's wage-price freeze, inhibited some Americans from traveling to Europe, Japan, and other lands where the dollar bought less. On the other hand, it stimulated their travel within the United States and in Mexico, Canada, and those Caribbean and Western Hemisphere countries whose currencies remained at a stable relationship to the dollar. Travel to the United States from Europe and Japan, however, was stimulated because their currencies went further here.

Congress authorized the U.S. Travel Service to allocate matching funds to regions, states, and cities of the United States to encourage them to develop and improve facilities for international visitors. The National Tourism Resources Review Commission, which was authorized by Congress in October, 1970, began a study of transportation, communications, tourism resources, tourism needs, and foreign tourism. Initial reports on foreign tourism and tourism in

Visitors to Disney World's Magic Kingdom walk down Main Street, U.S.A., past Victorian-style restaurants and shops to Cinderella Castle, background.

©Walt Disney Productions

TREVINO, LEE (1939-), posted one of the greatest winning streaks in golf history in 1971. During the period from April 22 to July 30, the happy-go-lucky Texan won four tournaments (including the U.S., Canadian, and British Opens) and $210,000 in prize money. Although an emergency appendectomy sidelined him for a time, Trevino won a total of $231,202 during the year. He was named Professional Golfer of the Year by the Professional Golfers Association (PGA).

Trevino had to borrow money to enter the U.S. Open in 1967. But he won that tournament for the first time in 1968, and he quickly became one of the leading money winners on the pro golf tour. In addition, his relaxed, wisecracking manner has made him one of the most popular golfers. He refuses to give in to tension. "When you're hot, you're hot," he quipped during the tense final round of the British Open. "When you're not, you're not."

Trevino was born in Dallas, and quit school after the seventh grade to work at a Dallas golf course. He joined the Marine Corps at 17, and played on a service golf team. When he was discharged at 21, he got a job as a professional at a Dallas pitch-and-putt course. He lives with his wife Claudia and their two children in El Paso, Tex.   Joseph P. Spohn

TRINIDAD AND TOBAGO. See WEST INDIES.

TRUCIAL STATES. See PERSIAN GULF EMIRATES.

TRUCK AND TRUCKING. See TRANSPORTATION.

American life were scheduled to be made early in 1972.

Air Travel. Troubled by mounting losses and increased competition from charter airlines bargains, the scheduled air carriers sought to outdo each other in offering a variety of low transatlantic fares. By December, however, they reached a basic agreement. For one year, beginning April 1, 1972, round-trip economy fare, New York-London, will be $404 in winter, $556 in summer, and $454 in the in-between seasons. Round-trip 22-to-45-day excursion fares will range from a low of $224 to $314 between New York and European cities.

The scheduled airlines carried 170 million passengers a total of 133 billion passenger-miles. They lost somewhat less than in 1970, when losses amounted to more than $200 million.

The operation of illegal charters reached such proportions during the summer that the Civil Aeronautics Board sought injunctions against their operators. Furthermore, when some operators failed to reimburse the carriers in full, thousands of travelers, mostly young people, were stranded in Europe.

Transatlantic steamship traffic decreased by 8.5 per cent. The U.S. recession cut down on this relatively expensive means of travel to Europe. Also, more vessels were being shifted from this service to the cruise market.   Lynn Beaumont

TRUDEAU, PIERRE ELLIOTT. The Canadian prime minister's year was filled with personal milestones in 1971. The 51-year-old bachelor became a family man on March 4 when he married Margaret Sinclair, 22, the beautiful daughter of a former Cabinet minister, in British Columbia. They met in Tahiti in 1969. Their first child, a son, Jason, was born in Ottawa on December 25. Trudeau's insistence on keeping his public and private lives apart, plus his flair for the dramatic, meant that his marriage surprised the country, as well as most of his aides.

In his public role, Trudeau devoted much attention in 1971 to Canada's economic problems. High unemployment, combined with trade difficulties with the United States related to the temporary U.S. import surcharge, created major worries for the Trudeau administration. In world affairs, Trudeau opened a Canadian window to the north, across the Arctic toward Russia, in a move to diversify Canada's contacts.

Trudeau spent more than 50 days outside Canada in 1971. In January, he toured the Indian Ocean countries before attending a Commonwealth Conference in Singapore. In April, he spent eight days in the Caribbean with his bride. In May, he visited Russia. A trip to Yugoslavia and Great Britain in August was cut short by the trade crisis with the United States. In December, he met with President Richard M. Nixon.   David M. L. Farr

TRUMAN, HARRY S.

TRUMAN, HARRY S. (1884-   ), the 33rd President of the United States, celebrated his 87th birthday and his 52nd wedding anniversary in 1971.

Senator Hubert H. Humphrey (D., Minn.) paid a surprise birthday visit at the Truman home in Independence, Mo., on May 8. Senator Humphrey called Mr. Truman "one of the greatest men of all time." That same day, Winton M. Blount, who was then postmaster general, also visited the former President. Blount later attended ceremonies at the nearby Truman Library, where a new 8-cent stamp commemorating Missouri's 150 years of statehood was dedicated. Two days earlier, Mr. Truman had rejected an attempt to waive the combat requirement and present him with the Medal of Honor.

Also on May 8, a new portrait of Mr. Truman was unveiled. Missouri artist Thomas Hart Benton had painted the former President earlier in the year.

In January, Mr. Truman was briefly hospitalized for an intestinal aliment. Vice-President Spiro T. Agnew visited him while he was in the hospital. Mr. and Mrs. Truman celebrated their 52nd wedding anniversary on June 28 at Research Hospital in Kansas City, Mo., where Mrs. Truman was undergoing a routine physical examination.

On May 15, Mr. Truman announced that he supported President Richard M. Nixon's opposition to a reduction in the number of U.S. troops stationed in Europe.   Carol L. Thompson

TUNISIA. President Habib Bourguiba resumed his duties in June, 1971, after 5½ months treatment and convalescence in the United States and Switzerland for hepatitis and nervous depression. The ruling Destour Party closed ranks behind him in support of his measures for political liberalization.

At the party's long-delayed national congress in October, Bourguiba refused an offer to be president for life. He nominated Prime Minister Hedi Nouira to succeed him in 1974, at the end of his third presidential term.

Tunisia restored diplomatic relations with Syria after a two-year break. It made a trade agreement that would double the exchange of goods with Egypt to $7 million. The National Assembly approved payment of $15 million to Italy for property nationalized in 1964. West Germany and Tunisia signed an agreement increasing from 9,300 to 12,000 the number of Tunisian emigrant workers sent to Germany during the year.

The French National Petroleum Company made a major oil strike near Sfax. The discovery promised to double Tunisia's oil production to 9 million tons annually.

Facts in Brief. Population: 5,154,000. Government: President Habib Bourguiba; Prime Minister Hedi Nouira. Monetary Unit: dinar. Foreign Trade: exports, $181,000,000; imports, $305,000,000. Principal Exports: petroleum, phosphates. William Spencer

TURKEY. A threatened military coup forced the resignation of Prime Minister Suleyman Demirel on March 12, 1971. Senior military officers demanded that the government halt anarchy and begin needed reforms or else face a take-over. Their ultimatum followed months of disorders that culminated in the kidnaping of four U.S. airmen in March and the kidnap-murder of Israeli Consul General Ephraim Elrom in Istanbul in May.

On March 19, Turkey's four major political parties compromised on a coalition Cabinet headed by Republican People's Party deputy Nihat Erim (see ERIM, NIHAT). The Erim Cabinet labored to bring order and progress back to Turkey. Martial law was imposed in several provinces in April, and the army rounded up hundreds of suspects for questioning and trial by special military courts. Changes in the penal code imposed harsh penalties for political violence, kidnapings, and related crimes. Other changes restricted individual rights somewhat. Many believed that the abuse of such rights had brought on the crisis. Many who had advocated violent social change were given long prison terms after October trials.

Facts in Brief. Population: 37,056,000. Government: President Cevdet Sunay; Prime Minister Nihat Erim. Monetary Unit: lira. Foreign Trade: exports, $604,000,000; imports, $920,000,000. Principal Exports: cotton, hazel nuts. William Spencer

UGANDA. Army officers led by Major General Idi Amin Dada overthrew the government of President Apollo Milton Obote on Jan. 25, 1971, while he was attending a Commonwealth of Nations conference in Singapore. Obote went into exile in Tanzania, and Amin was named president of Uganda on February 20. See AMIN, IDI.

The body of Sir Edward Mutesa III (King Freddie), former president and king of the Baganda tribe who died in exile in England in 1969, was brought back for burial on March 31. Since the Baganda is the largest tribe in Uganda, this was seen as a move to consolidate support for Amin's government.

Relations between Uganda and Tanzania broke down after Amin seized power. Tanzania refused to recognize the Amin regime as the legal government of Uganda. In August, fighting broke out between Tanzanian and Ugandan troops along the border. In September, Uganda accused Tanzania of bombing Ugandan villages. There was renewed fighting in October. See AFRICA; TANZANIA.

Facts in Brief. Population: 8,981,000. Government: President Idi Amin Dada. Monetary Unit: shilling. Foreign Trade: exports, $249,000,000; imports, $121,000,000. Principal Exports: coffee, cotton, copper. George Shepherd

UNION OF SOVIET SOCIALIST REPUBLICS (U.S.S.R.). See RUSSIA.

UNITED ARAB REPUBLIC (U.A.R.). See EGYPT.

540

UNITED NATIONS (UN). The long-awaited arrival of the People's Republic of China and the selection of a new secretary-general highlighted the 26th session of the UN General Assembly in 1971, and lifted hopes for a dramatic new era of international political reality. But neither new presence was able to deal immediately with the political and humanitarian tangles in the wake of the bloody India-Pakistan war, the Middle East peace impasse, the continuing frustrations of racism in Africa, or the virtual bankruptcy of the world organization.

By a vote of 76 to 35 on October 25, the General Assembly welcomed the Peking delegation to the UN forum after 22 years of political isolation. Despite an intensive diplomatic effort by the United States, the UN also ousted Nationalist China (Formosa), whose foreign minister Chow Shu-kai accused the world body of "betrayal" of UN Charter principles before he led his delegation from the hall. Widespread jubilation among delegates after the historic vote, including a display of hand-clapping exuberance by the Tanzanian ambassador, drew an unusual White House protest against "undisguised glee" at the American diplomatic defeat.

The Chinese, after perfunctory criticism of U.S. military involvement in Asia, surprised most diplomats by virtually ignoring the United States and launching blistering attacks against Russia.

China emphasized it was not a "superpower" involved in the "aggression, control, subversion, interference, and bullying" that Russia and the United States carried out against smaller nations. It accused Russia of abandoning real Socialism for "social-imperialism," or socialism in words, imperialism in deeds. Red-faced Russians sputtered that China's claims were as "absurd as fried ice" and aimed at putting on "an excellent show" for those who wish to witness the "disintegration" of relations between China and Russia.

War in Pakistan. The two-week war between India and Pakistan in December afforded even broader opportunities for bitter clashes between the Russians, who supported India's invasion and occupation of East Pakistan, and China, which lined up with the United States in support of West Pakistan.

Three Soviet vetoes blocked attempts by the 15-member Security Council to pass a mandatory order for both sides to cease firing and withdraw their forces. The Council finally passed the matter to the Assembly, which voted 104 to 11 on December 7 for the cease-fire and withdrawal call. India, however, rejected the recommendation until it unilaterally declared a cease-fire after Dacca fell on December 16 and the infant nation of Bangla Desh rose from the ruins of East Pakistan.

Pakistani Foreign Minister Zulfikar Ali Bhutto, brushing tears from his eyes, denounced the UN as a "fraud and a farce" as he led his delegation in a dramatic walkout from Council chambers. He charged his country was being "dismembered" as the UN looked on. "You do not need a secretary-general, you need a chief executioner," he lashed out. A week later, he was named president of his country after Agha Mohammed Yahya Khan's resignation. See PAKISTAN.

After war's end, the Council finally passed a resolution calling for strict observance of the cease-fire and the dispatch of a special UN representative to coordinate relief efforts for the 10 million Bengalis who had fled across India's borders. The vote was 13 to 0, with Russia and Poland abstaining.

Middle East Impasse. UN diplomats expressed keen disappointment at what some called the "sorry spectacle" of the Council's inaction during the India-Pakistan conflict, a frustration also reflected in the paralysis of Middle East peace efforts during 1971. Three separate negotiations – special UN mediator Gunnar Jarring's talks, a U.S. move to get an interim agreement to open the Suez Canal, and Big Four talks in New York City – were at least temporarily abandoned by the year's end.

The Jarring talks had been resumed on January 5, after a four-month suspension. But Israel adamantly refused to commit itself to withdrawal from occupied territory before the talks resumed, despite Egypt's assurances it would sign a peace treaty stipulating permanent and secure Israeli borders. This again threw the talks into diplomatic limbo.

On December 13, the General Assembly voted 79 to 7, with 36 abstentions, that "acquisition of territory by force is inadmissible . . . and must be restored." It also called on Israel to agree to Jarring's request, and it reaffirmed the validity of Security Council resolution 242. That resolution, passed in November, 1967, said that peace would be based on the withdrawal of Israeli forces from occupied territory, the ending of Arab belligerency, and the acknowledging of sovereignty of every nation and its right to peace and security.

China rejected a proposed enlargement of the Big Four to the Big Five, charging that "dirty political deals" were being hatched in those negotiations, with no regard for Palestinian political aspirations. The Assembly also "strongly urged" Israel to stop annexing territory, destroying houses, moving people, and deporting and torturing political prisoners. A three-man commission charged those practices existed, but Israel denied the charges. The Security Council again called on Israel to rescind its annexation of Jerusalem and restore that city's "international status."

New Secretary-General. Secretary-General U Thant, the 62-year-old Burmese who had held the job since Dag Hammarskjöld's death in 1961, declared in January he had "no intention whatsoever" of accepting another term. Austrian ambassador to the UN Kurt Waldheim, 53, former foreign minister of his country, was named Thant's successor on

The flagpole awaits a new Chinese flag, following UN vote on October 25 to seat Communist China. A few days later, their delegation arrived in New York.

December 21 after three secret voting sessions. His five-year term of office in the $62,500-a-year post began on Jan. 1, 1972.

During his tenure, Thant was sometimes criticized for maintaining a diplomatic silence on world issues. But in February he called U.S. incursions in Laos "one more deplorable episode" in the Indochina war, and labeled as "senseless violence" the civil strife in Northern Ireland.

The Growing Deficit. Thant, in his last address to the Assembly, lamented the virtual bankruptcy of the United Nations. Despite a current deficit of between $50 and $70 million, the UN had approved an all-time high budget of $213 million. United States delegate Representative Edward J. Derwinski (R., Ill.) told the Assembly the United States intended to cut back its contribution by from 31 to 25 per cent. The shaky international economy threatened further shrinkage of many UN economic and social activities.

Former General Assembly President Edvard Hambro of Norway reported his committee on UN finances found no solution to increasing UN deficits, such as the $10-million Cyprus peacekeeping debt, the $21-million deficit from the Middle East, and another $11 million from Congo (Kinshasa), now known as the Zaïre Republic. The 3,117-man UN Peace Force on Cyprus was extended, however, for six months to June 15, 1972.

Delegates reeled in disbelief when the U.S. Senate voted on October 29–four days after the ouster of Nationalist China and the admission of Peking to the UN–to kill the entire U.S. foreign aid program. That vote was later rescinded, but UN programs already suffering deficits, such as the UN Relief and Works Agency (UNRWA), which services 1.4 million Palestinian refugees in the Middle East, were expected to be adversely affected.

Aid slowdowns were expected to interrupt the progress of the Second Development Decade, going into its third year. Paul Hoffman, first administrator of the Marshall Plan, announced his retirement as of January, 1972, as head of the UN Development Program. This agency fostered $265 million worth of pre-investment projects in nearly 100 developing countries in 1970. The Assembly prepared a list of 25 "least developed" countries, ranging from Afghanistan to Yemen, to facilitate identification of their development needs.

New Treaties. Two conventions–one prohibiting the development, production, and stockpiling of biological weapons and toxins, the other setting procedures for determining international liability for damages caused by objects launched into outer space–were approved by the Assembly and opened for signature.

A Soviet proposal for a World Disarmament Conference, vigorously opposed by the Peking delegation, was deferred by the Assembly until 1972. Another Soviet proposal for a treaty to ban the establishment of national sovereignty on the moon remained under consideration. The Assembly declared the Indian Ocean a "zone of peace for all time," and asked for further study on procedures to ban all warships, arms, naval maneuvers and intelligence, and weapons tests from that area.

Africa and Decolonization. The resignation of Representative Charles C. Diggs (D., Mich.), a black, as a special U.S. delegation member climaxed another year's frustration over the UN's inability to deal with racist policies of the white-minority governments in the Republic of South Africa and Portuguese-controlled Angola and Mozambique.

Diggs said he found American hypocrisy in talking for, but voting against, anti-apartheid measures "stifling." The Assembly had called on the United States to rescind congressional action that would allow the purchase of Rhodesian chromium, thus flouting a 1966 mandatory ban instituted by the Security Council.

A British compromise with Ian Smith's white-minority government in Rhodesia, which had declared its independence in November, 1965, was announced on November 25. Two days later, the compromise was rejected by the UN General Assembly as unacceptable because independence would come before majority rule. The British plan would allow legal independence immediately, with unimpeachable provisions ensuring majority rule later. See RHODESIA.

The United States and Great Britain withdrew in January from a special committee on decolonization. They objected to "unrealistic" demands and Assembly votes.

With only Micronesia, a U.S. trust territory, and New Guinea, an Australian mandate, waiting for independence, the UN turned its attention to a number of island territories for investigation. They included the U.S. and British Virgin Islands, Guam, the Seychelles, and the Bahamas.

World Court. Namibia, the African name given to the territory of South West Africa, was the subject of World Court action. It is still administered by South Africa despite UN revocation in 1966 of a post-World War I mandate. The 15-member tribunal at The Hague ruled 13 to 2 on June 21 that South Africa is "under obligation to withdraw its administration from Namibia immediately and thus put an end to its occupation of the territory." Great Britain and France voted against the ruling. Earlier in 1971, the court refused requests by South Africa to hold a plebiscite in South West Africa and to choose a judge ad hoc to participate in future rulings.

The Security Council followed up the World Court ruling by asking that all countries recognize the illegality of South Africa's presence in Namibia. It asked all countries to withdraw or refuse to establish consuls there and to make no treaties with South Africa concerning the territory.

Late in the year, India asked the World Court to determine jurisdiction of a Pakistani complaint to the International Civil Aviation Organization, after India barred Pakistani flights over its territory.

Other Actions. Five new Security Council members were elected for the 1972-1973 term. Guinea, India, Panama, the Sudan, and Yugoslavia replaced Burundi, Nicaragua, Poland, Sierra Leone, and Syria. The UN also admitted Bahrain, Bhutan, Oman, Qatar, and the Union of Arab Emirates to membership in 1971, expanding to 132 nations.

The UN also delved into the social problems of crime and drugs. It ordered a study of crime and its social effects and approved a convention on LSD, mescaline, and other psychotropic substances.

Two Near East countries, Yemen and Iran, received the first teams of the UN volunteers, an international peace corps. The General Assembly approved the creation of a permanent Coordinator for Disaster Relief. A convention was also approved for the protection of journalists on dangerous missions in armed conflict. It provides for the issuance of a universally recognized safe-conduct card.

George Bush, former Republican congressman from Texas, became U.S. ambassador to the UN on March 2. He replaced Charles Yost, who had held the post two years. See BUSH, GEORGE.   Betty Flynn

U.S. CONSTITUTION. The 26th Amendment to the Constitution, granting 18-year-olds the right to vote, was officially certified on July 5, 1971, in a ceremony held at the White House. The 26th Amendment guarantees that "The right of citizens of the United States, who are 18 years of age or older, to vote shall not be denied or abridged by the United States or any state on account of age."

The amendment's journey to ratification began on March 10, when it received unanimous Senate approval. It then passed the House of Representatives on March 23 by a vote of 400 to 19 and was sent to the states for ratification.

Record Ratification. State legislatures quickly ratified the proposed amendment, with Minnesota approving it moments after the House passage. To be adopted, an amendment to the Constitution must be ratified by a minimum of 38 states, three-fourths of the 50 states. On June 30, Ohio became the 38th state to ratify the amendment, completing the process in a record two months and seven days.

The 26th Amendment was designed to eliminate confusion caused by the 1970 Supreme Court ruling that 18-year-olds could vote in federal elections. Before the amendment was added to the Constitution, only three states allowed 18-year-olds to vote in state and local elections – Alaska, Georgia, and Kentucky. The voting-age minimum in Massachusetts, Minnesota, and Montana for state and local elections was

19, and in Hawaii, Maine, and Nebraska, it was 20. The remaining states had a voting age of 21 and over.

The discrepancy in age requirements between federal and state and local elections could have caused much confusion and increased election costs. Separate federal and state voter-registration lists would have been needed in states where the age requirement was higher than 18.

Ratification of the 26th Amendment made an added estimated 11.5 million young people eligible to vote in all elections held in the United States.

School Prayers. Another constitutional amendment proposed during the year would have permitted voluntary prayers in public schools. However, it was defeated in the House on November 8. The vote was 240 for passage and 162 against, less than the two-thirds majority needed to pass a proposed constitutional amendment.

This proposed amendment was also prompted by a Supreme Court decision. In 1963, the court ruled that prayers in public schools violated the 1st and 14th amendments, with regard to separation of church and state and the rights of the individual.

Sponsors of the proposed amendment said that the public wanted prayers in public schools. However, 38 major religious denominations opposed it. Congressional opponents also believed that to pass such an amendment would be dangerously toying with the Constitution. Darlene R. Stille

U.S. GOVERNMENT. The three branches of the federal government—the executive, legislative, and judicial—were in uneasy balance in 1971. President Richard M. Nixon and Congress struggled for control of foreign and military policy. Congress, controlled by the Democrats, refused to pass much of the President's domestic program. Mr. Nixon, however, retained firm control of the nation's foreign policy. And, through his power of appointment, he added two more conservatives to the Supreme Court of the United States.

The Executive Branch. In his State of the Union message to Congress on January 22, President Nixon proposed a drastic reorganization of the executive branch of the government. The departments of State, Treasury, Defense, and Justice were to be left unchanged. Four new departments—Human Resources, Community Development, Natural Resources, and Economic Development—would take over the functions of all remaining departments. In November, the President announced that he had abandoned his plan to merge the Department of Agriculture into the four new departments. Congress, however, did not act on the President's suggestion in 1971. See PRESIDENT OF THE UNITED STATES.

On February 8, John B. Connally, former Democratic governor of Texas, was confirmed by the Senate as secretary of the treasury, succeeding David M. Kennedy. When Postmaster General Winton M.

Blount took over as director of the new U.S. Postal Service on July 1, he lost his Cabinet rank. On December 2, Earl L. Butz was confirmed by the Senate as secretary of agriculture, succeeding Clifford M. Hardin. See BUTZ, EARL L.; CABINET.

In May, plans for the reorganization of the postal system were announced. Fifteen postal regions were to be consolidated into five. The postal rate for first-class mail rose from 6 cents to 8 cents an ounce; special delivery stamps, from 45 cents to 60 cents. See POSTAL SERVICE.

As the President began to put his new economic policy into effect in August, a whole new administrative structure was established to oversee the program. The President's Cost of Living Council, established on August 15, was to guide the nation through Phase 2 of the wage and price controls aimed at halting inflation. On October 22, the President established a Pay Board and a Price Commission to administer the program. In December, Mr. Nixon agreed to devalue the U.S. dollar by 7.89 per cent. See ECONOMY, THE.

The Legislative Branch. The first session of the 92nd Congress clashed with the President in both the foreign and domestic fields. Senate doves persistently asked the Administration to set a date for the withdrawal of all U.S. troops from Vietnam. An amendment attached to a military procurement bill specifically stated that it was the sense of the Congress that all troops be withdrawn from Indochina, subject only to the release of all U.S. prisoners of war. The President flatly refused to follow Senate advice, however.

The Administration also withstood Senate pressure to reduce the number of U.S. troops in Europe. Senate disagreement with the President was reflected in the Senate's vote to kill the foreign aid bill on October 29. But in December, Congress extended foreign aid funding to February, 1972.

In the domestic field, Congress refused to act on Administration requests for revenue sharing. Major legislation passed by the first session of the 92nd Congress included an extension of the Selective Service System, increased social security benefits, tax reform, and an extension of the President's power to control wages and prices. See CONGRESS; NATIONAL DEFENSE; SOCIAL SECURITY; TAXATION.

The Judicial Branch. It has been President Nixon's good fortune to appoint four justices to the Supreme Court of the United States: Chief Justice Warren E. Burger, in 1969; Justice Harry Blackmun, in 1970; and Justices Lewis F. Powell, Jr., and William H. Rehnquist in 1971. These four justices of conservative outlook now outnumber the liberal faction on the high court. Mr. Nixon's newest appointees, Justices Powell and Rehnquist, were confirmed by the Senate in December. See COURTS AND LAWS; POWELL, LEWIS F., JR.; REHNQUIST, WILLIAM H.

In June, the high court acted to limit the power of

Diplomatic Corps*

Official ambassadors representing the United States of America in other countries and their counterparts to the United States.

Country	From U.S.A.	To U.S.A.
Afghanistan	Robert G. Neumann	Abdullah Malikyar
Argentina	John Davis Lodge	Carlos Manuel Muniz
Australia	Walter L. Rice	Sir James Plimsoll
Austria	John P. Humes	Karl Gruber
Barbados	Eileen R. Donovan	Valerie Theodore McComie
Belgium	Vacant	Walter Loridan
Bolivia	Ernest V. Siracusa	Edmundo Valencia Ibanez
Brazil	William M. Rountree	Joao Augusto de Araujo Castro
Bulgaria	Horace G. Torbert, Jr.	Luben Guerassimov
Burma	Edwin W. Martin	U San Maung
Burundi	Thomas Patrick Melady	Nsanze Terence
Cambodia	Emory C. Swank	Sonn Voeunsai
Cameroon	Lewis Hoffacker	Francois Xavier Tchoungui
Canada	Adolph W. Schmidt	Marcel Cadieux
Central African Republic	Melvin L. Manfull	Christophe Maidou
Ceylon	Robert Strausz-Hupé	Neville T. D. Kanakaratne
Chad	Terence A. Todman	Lazare Massibe
Chile	Nathaniel Davis	Orlando Letelier
Colombia	Leonard J. Saccio	Douglas Botero-Boshell
Congo (Kinshasa)	Sheldon B. Vance	Pierre Ileka
Costa Rica	Walter C. Ploeser	Rafael Alberto Zuniga
Cyprus	David H. Popper	Zenon Rossides
Czechoslovakia	Vacant	Ivan Rohal-Ilkiv
Dahomey	Vacant	Wilfred De Souza
Denmark	Fred J. Russell	Eyvind Bartels
Dominican Republic	Francis E. Meloy, Jr.	S. Salvador Ortiz
Ecuador	Findley Burns, Jr.	Carlos Mantilla-Ortega
El Salvador	Henry E. Catto, Jr.	Julio A. Rivera
Ethiopia	E. Ross Adair	Vacant
Finland	Val Peterson	Olavi Munkki
Formosa	Walter P. McConaughy	James C. H. Shen
France	Arthur K. Watson	Charles Lucet
Gabon	John A. McKesson III	Gaston-Robert Bouckat-Bou-Nziengui
Gambia	G. Edward Clark	Vacant
Germany, West	Kenneth Rush	Rolf Pauls
Ghana	Fred L. Hadsel	Ebenezer Moses Debrah
Great Britain	Walter H. Annenberg	The Earl of Cromer
Greece	Henry J. Tasca	Basil George Vitsaxis
Guatemala	William G. Bowdler	Julio Asensio-Wunderlich
Guinea	Albert W. Sherer, Jr.	Elhadj Mory Keita
Guyana	Spencer M. King	Rahman B. Gajraj
Haiti	Clinton E. Knox	René Chalmers
Honduras	Hewson A. Ryan	Roberto Galvez Barnes
Hungary	Alfred Puhan	Karoly Szabo
Iceland	Luther I. Replogle	Gudmundur I. Gudmundsson
India	Kenneth B. Keating	Lakshmi Kant Jha
Indonesia	Francis J. Galbraith	Sjarif Thajeb
Iran	Vacant	Amir-Aslan Afshar
Ireland	John D. J. Moore	William Warnock
Israel	Walworth Barbour	Yitzhak Rabin
Italy	Graham A. Martin	Egidio Ortona
Ivory Coast	John F. Root	Timothée N'Guetta Ahoua
Jamaica	Vincent de Roulet	Sir Egerton R. Richardson
Japan	Armin H. Meyer	Nobuhiko Ushiba
Jordan	L. Dean Brown	Abdul Hamid Sharaf
Kenya	Robinson McIlvaine	Leonard Oliver Kibinge
Korea, South	Philip C. Habib	Dong Jo Kim
Kuwait	William A. Stoltzfus, Jr.	Salem S. Al-Sabah
Laos	G. McMurtrie Godley	Prince Khammao
Lebanon	William B. Buffum	Najati Kabbani
Lesotho	Charles J. Nelson	Mothusi T. Mashologu
Liberia	Samuel Z. Westerfield, Jr.	S. Edward Peal
Libya	Joseph Palmer II	Abdulla al-Suwesi
Luxembourg	Kingdon Gould, Jr.	Jean Wagner
Malawi	William C. Burdett	Nyemba Wales Mbekeani
Malaysia	Jack W. Lydman	Tan Sri Ong Yoke Lin
Mali	Robert O. Blake	Seydou Traoré
Malta	John C. Pritzlaff, Jr.	Joseph Attard Kingswell
Mexico	Robert H. McBride	José Juan de Olloqui
Morocco	Stuart W. Rockwell	Badreggine Senoussi
Nepal	Carol C. Laise	Kul Shekhar Sharma
Netherlands	J. William Middendorf II	Baron Rijnhard B. Van Lynden
New Zealand	Kenneth Franzheim II	Frank Corner
Nicaragua	Turner B. Shelton	Guillermo Sevilla-Sacasa
Niger	Roswell D. McClelland	Georges M. Condat
Nigeria	John E. Reinhardt	Joe Iyalla
Norway	Philip K. Crowe	Arne Gunneng
Pakistan	Joseph S. Farland	Nawabzada Agha Mohammad Raza
Panama	Robert M. Sayre	Jose Antonio de la Ossa
Paraguay	J. Raymond Ylitalo	Roque J. Avila
Peru	Taylor G. Belcher	Fernando Berckemeyer
Philippines	Henry A. Byroade	Eduardo Z. Romualdez
Poland	Walter J. Stoessel, Jr.	Witold Trampczynski
Portugal	Ridgway B. Knight	Joao M. Hall-Themido
Romania	Leonard C. Meeker	Corneliu Bogdan
Russia	Jacob D. Beam	Anatoliy F. Dobrynin
Rwanda	Robert F. Corrigan	Fidèle Nkundabagenzi
Saudi Arabia	Nicholas G. Thacher	Ibrahim Al-Sowayel
Senegal	G. Edward Clark	Andre Jean Coulbary
Sierra Leone	Vacant	Jacob A. C. Davies
Singapore	Charles T. Cross	Ernest Steven Monteiro
Somalia	Vacant	Abdullahi Ahmed Addou
South Africa	John G. Hurd	Johan S. F. Botha
Spain	Vacant	Jaime Arguelles
Swaziland	Charles J. Nelson	S. T. Msindazwe Sukati
Sweden	Jerome H. Holland	Hubert de Besche
Switzerland	Shelby Davis	Felix Schnyder
Tanzania	Claude G. Ross	Gosbert Marcell Rutabanzibwa
Thailand	Leonard Unger	Sunthorn Hongladarom
Togo	Dwight Dickinson	Epiphane Ayi Mawussi
Trinidad and Tobago	Vacant	Sir Ellis Emmanuel Innocent Clarke
Tunisia	John A. Calhoun	Slaheddine El Goulli
Turkey	William J. Handley	Melih Esenbel
Uganda	Clarence C. Ferguson, Jr.	Mustapha Ramathan
Upper Volta	Donald B. Easum	Paul Rouamba
Uruguay	Charles W. Adair, Jr.	Hector Luisi
Venezuela	Robert McClintock	Julio Sosa-Rodriguez
Vietnam, South	Ellsworth Bunker	Bui Diem
Yugoslavia	Malcolm Toon	Toma Granfil
Zambia	Oliver L. Troxel, Jr.	Unia Gostel Mwila

*As of Dec. 31, 1971. Sources: U.S. Dept. of State and Congressional Record

Estimated U.S. Budget for Fiscal 1972*

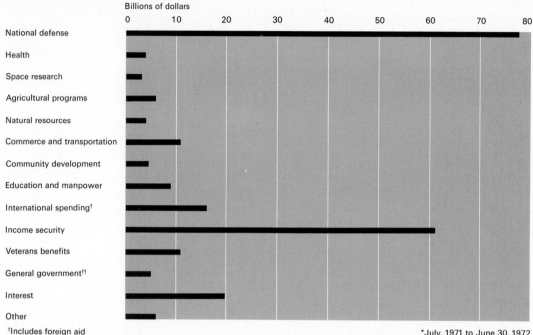

Billions of dollars

| | 0 | 10 | 20 | 30 | 40 | 50 | 60 | 70 | 80 |

National defense

Health

Space research

Agricultural programs

Natural resources

Commerce and transportation

Community development

Education and manpower

International spending†

Income security

Veterans benefits

General government††

Interest

Other

†Includes foreign aid
††Includes law enforcement

*July, 1971 to June 30, 1972
Source: U.S. Office of Management and Budget

the executive branch by refusing to allow the Department of Justice to suppress publication of the so-called "Pentagon Papers." The controversial, classified documents dealt with the history of U.S. involvement in Indochina. See PUBLISHING.

In major decisions in 1971, the Supreme Court ruled that draft-exempt status may not be granted to conscientious objectors who object only to a particular war, and that state programs reimbursing parochial schools for teaching nonreligious subjects are unconstitutional. It refused to hear a challenge to the legality of the war in Vietnam and refused to delay a November underground nuclear bomb test on Amchitka Island in the Aleutians.

On August 31, Chief Justice Burger declared that lower court judges must not interpret the Supreme Court rulings on school desegregation to mean that racial balance is required in every school in the nation. See EDUCATION.

Other Actions. The new National Rail Passenger Corporation (Amtrak) began to operate commuter service in May. Amtrak offered roughly half the service formerly available to commuters. See TRANSPORTATION.

The 26th Amendment to the Constitution became effective on July 5. The amendment set 18 as the minimum voting age for all federal, state, and local elections. See U.S. CONSTITUTION.   Carol L. Thompson

UPPER VOLTA. See AFRICA.

URUGUAY. The stability of President Jorge Pacheco Areco's government was threatened repeatedly in 1971 by bands of urban-centered left-wing Tupamaros guerrillas. On September 11, the president assumed personal responsibility for the elimination of the revolutionaries, and, for the first time in Uruguay's history, the armed forces were ordered to take full control of the antiguerrilla operations. In a defiant show of strength, the Tupamaros responded by freeing 106 of their comrades from a prison in Montevideo and then releasing British Ambassador Geoffrey H. S. Jackson. The Tupamaros had held the ambassador as a hostage for eight months despite strenuous government efforts to locate and release him. In the public outcry that followed, the police as well as the prison security forces were accused of collusion in permitting the escape.

In the November 28 presidential elections, Pacheco was succeeded by Juan Maria Bordaberry. He was to take office in February, 1972. See BORDABERRY, JUAN MARIA.

Facts in Brief. Population: 2,956,000. Government: President Jorge Pacheco Areco. Monetary Unit: peso. Foreign Trade: exports, $233,000,000; imports, $233,000,000. Principal Exports: meat, wool, hides and skins.   Mary C. Webster

UTAH. See STATE GOVERNMENT.

UTILITIES. See COMMUNICATIONS; ENERGY; PETROLEUM AND GAS.

VENEZUELA. Economic nationalism, as proclaimed by President Rafael Caldera during a speech celebrating Venezuelan independence on July 5, surged forward in 1971. A new banking law sharply limited the activities of foreign banks, while a new investment law under consideration would strongly curtail foreign investments in manufacturing.

The natural gas industry, with estimated reserves of 30 trillion cubic feet, was nationalized on July 30, and Congress deleted from the final version of the law the government's proposal to pay "just compensation" for the gas. The government also extended its control over all Venezuelan oil operations and imposed new financial burdens on oil firms prior to reversion of their concessions to the state. About 75 per cent of the 40-year-old concessions would so revert in 1983 and 1984. The foreign companies involved had thought that only such assets as oil reserves, wells, pipelines, and other essential facilities would revert to the state without compensation. They discovered that the government could also lay claim to ownership of tankers, refineries, and other installations.

Facts in Brief. Population: 11,158,000. Government: President Rafael Caldera. Monetary Unit: bolívar. Foreign Trade: exports, $2,638,000,000; imports, $1,869,000,000. Principal Exports: petroleum, petroleum products, iron ore.   Mary C. Webster

VERMONT. See STATE GOVERNMENT.

U.S. soldiers line up at heroin-detection center before leaving South Vietnam. The new program has proven effective in discovering hard-drug users.

VETERANS returned to civilian life in 1971 at the rate of 85,000 a month, and an increasing number took advantage of the educational benefits that were voted by Congress in 1970. During the fiscal year ended June 30, 1971, some 1.6 million veterans were in schools, colleges, and job-training programs. This group included 917,000 veterans who were studying at the college level, a 36 per cent increase over 1970. Sizable increases were also reported in vocational rehabilitation training for disabled veterans and educational assistance for dependents of deceased or permanently and totally disabled veterans.

The 8 out of 10 returning veterans who wanted immediate employment, however, discovered that there were fewer jobs than in 1970. This was especially true for the untrained and inexperienced. In the 20-to-24 age group, the jobless rate reached nearly 15 per cent, and for young black veterans, it was 21 per cent. Expressing concern about the growing number of returning veterans who could not find employment, President Richard M. Nixon announced a Jobs for Veterans Program in October. It was designed to focus national attention on the employment potential of the Vietnam veteran. He directed Secretary of Labor James D. Hodgson to assume leadership of a more intensive effort to find job-training and employment opportunities for veterans. He called upon business, organized labor, veterans' organizations, and state and local govern-

ments for their support and cooperation. An advisory committee of 100 members representing these groups was named by the President to assist with the program. James F. Oates, retired chairman of the Equitable Life Assurance Society of the United States, was appointed chairman of Jobs for Veterans.

Heroin Addiction was reported in large numbers of returning Vietnam veterans in 1971. From the beginning, figures varied greatly. Dr. Jerome H. Jaffe, President Nixon's special consultant on narcotics and dangerous drugs, claimed that 4.5 per cent of those returning from Vietnam were addicted. Other U.S. officials claimed that the actual figure was from 10 to 15 per cent. On September 4, the Pentagon claimed that its tests showed that only 3.6 per cent of the servicemen were addicts. Several programs were suggested to help these men break the habit and keep others from becoming addicted.

GI Loan Benefits. Changes in the 1970 Veterans Housing Act, greater flexibility in administrative policies and procedures, and new legislation approved in 1971 made the housing outlook considerably brighter for veterans. Major changes included the following:

▪ Expiration dates for all Veterans Administration (VA) housing benefits were abolished. Nearly 9 million World War II and Korean War veterans had eligibility for VA benefits restored by this change.

▪ Veterans now can use their VA benefits to refinance existing property loans, provided the new loan is for a dwelling owned and occupied by the veteran.

- Direct loans are guaranteed for the purchase of mobile homes, condominiums, and home sites.
- The cost of loans was reduced by eliminating a 0.5 per cent funding fee previously paid by post-Korean veterans, and the maximum rate of interest was reduced from 8.5 to 7.5 per cent.

Conventions. The American Legion held its 53rd annual national convention in Houston from August 27 to September 2. John H. Geiger of Des Plaines, Ill., was elected national commander.

The American Legion high school oratorical contest was won by 16-year-old William H. White of San Antonio, Tex. White won an $8,000 college scholarship.

John C. Glunt, 17, of Kirkwood, Mo., was elected president of the 1971 American Legion Boys Nation at its 26th annual session, held July 23 to 30, in Washington, D.C.

The American Veterans Committee held its 28th convention from June 11 to 13, at Vacation Valley, Pa. Raymond Bramucci of Hazlet, N.J., was elected national chairman.

Veterans of Foreign Wars held its 72nd annual national convention in Dallas, Tex., from August 13 to August 20. Joseph L. Vicites, Uniontown, Pa., was elected commander in chief.   Joseph P. Anderson

South Vietnam's President Nguyen Van Thieu casts his ballot during National Assembly elections in August, 1971. He later ran unopposed for the presidency.

VIETNAM. In a controversial, uncontested election held on Oct. 3, 1971, Nguyen Van Thieu was re-elected to a second four-year term as president of the Republic of (South) Vietnam. In the largest voter turnout in recent South Vietnamese history, Thieu received 91.5 per cent of the 6,311,853 votes cast. Before the election, he said that he would step down if he received less than 50 per cent of the votes. Anything less, he said, would be interpreted as a vote of no-confidence in himself and his vice-presidential running mate, Tran Van Huong.

Thieu's victory was achieved despite considerable antigovernment agitation in the months preceding the election. The agitation ranged in scope from appeals to the voters to boycott the election to scattered antigovernment street demonstrations in Saigon and other parts of the country. One of the more serious antigovernment demonstrations occurred in Hue on October 2 when 3,000 students attacked the police with fire bombs. The demonstrators were dispersed with tear gas and the University of Hue was closed for the remainder of the day to prevent the students from regrouping.

Initially, Thieu was opposed by Vice-President Nguyen Cao Ky, who officially entered the race on July 5, and General Duong Van Minh, who formally announced his candidacy on July 26. Both men withdrew later, however. They charged that President Thieu had rigged the election in his favor by forcing

through the National Assembly a law that, in effect, drastically restricted the number of candidates eligible for election.

Under the law, a presidential candidate's nomination paper required the signature of either 40 deputies and senators or 100 members of the elected provincial councils. Inasmuch as Thieu controlled majorities in both the assembly and the provincial councils, his two opponents felt that their chances of securing the needed endorsements were poor if not nonexistent. Many foreign diplomats as well as official U.S. election observers were equally skeptical of the "democratic" aspects of a contest that, in effect, was restricted to only one candidate.

Despite considerable post-election bitterness, complete with charges of fraud leveled by the anti-Thieu factions, Thieu was inaugurated without incident on October 31. Coincidentally with the inauguration ceremonies, the government freed the first of nearly 3,000 Viet Cong prisoners due to be released under an amnesty announced in Saigon earlier in the year. The prisoner-of-war issue remained one of the major stumbling blocks in the efforts of President Richard M. Nixon to negotiate a peaceful settlement of the war in Vietnam. See ASIA.

Economic Reforms. The South Vietnamese government instituted a number of economic reforms in March. Included were measures designed to encourage private and corporate investors to use the

Vietnamese banking system rather than Chinese moneylenders. Most preferred to deal with the Chinese, whose records were not subject to government scrutiny and therefore were not subject to analysis for tax purposes. The reforms permitted deposits to be made anonymously in Vietnamese banks, and government economists predicted that not only private savings would rise but also that much more money would be available for investment purposes.

According to a report on food production in the Far East issued by the United Nations Food and Agriculture Organization on August 22, farm production in South Vietnam increased by 8 per cent in 1970 and would probably rise even higher in 1971. The increase, according to the report, "reflected more settled conditions in the rice-producing areas that are being rapidly planted to high-yielding varieties."

North Vietnam held elections on April 11 for a new National Assembly for the first time since 1964. There were 529 candidates for the 420 seats. Among those re-elected as deputies were President Ton Duc Thang; Premier Pham Van Dong; Le Duan, first secretary of the ruling Workers (Communist) Party; and Truong Chinh, chairman of the National Assembly. All were re-elected to their leadership posts when the National Assembly held its first session on June 7.

On October 10, it was announced that a joint Russian-North Vietnamese committee had been created to formulate long-range economic, trade, cultural, scientific, and technological relations between the two countries. The announcement was made at the conclusion of a six-day visit to Hanoi by Russian Presidium Chairman Nikolai V. Podgorny and a committee of experts. Earlier, on March 18, the Norwegian government announced that it would establish diplomatic relations with North Vietnam. Norway became the first member of the North Atlantic Treaty Organization to establish diplomatic ties with North Vietnam.

Other pacts signed by the North Vietnamese government in 1971 included one by which Sweden agreed to allocate $14.5 million in foreign aid. Another agreement provided that Cuba will exchange products with North Vietnam.

Facts in Brief. (North) Population: 23,387,000. Government: President Ton Duc Thang; Premier Pham Van Dong. Monetary Unit: dong. Foreign Trade: exports, $51,000,000; imports, $134,000,000. Principal Exports: agricultural products, minerals. (South) Population: 19,297,000. Government: President Nguyen Van Thieu; Vice-President Tran Van Huong; Prime Minister Tran Thien Khiem. Monetary Unit: piastre. Foreign Trade: exports, $7,000,000; imports, $325,000,000. Principal Exports: rubber, tea, feathers.   Paul C. Tullier

VIETNAM WAR. See ASIA.

VIRGINIA. See STATE GOVERNMENT.

VISUAL ARTS. Anniversary honors in 1971 went to Albrecht Dürer, the great German artist of the Renaissance period. The 500th anniversary of his birth was marked by exhibitions in many museums. Large collections of this printmaker's graphic works exist in the major museums in the United States, and outstanding exhibitions were held in Boston, Chicago, New York City, and Washington, D.C. (see CELEBRATIONS). The 90th birthday of Pablo Picasso was also observed with various exhibitions.

At a time when museum activity continues brisk, despite rapidly increasing economic restrictions, two exhibitions held in New York City may point to the future when the "show from within" – an exhibition gathered entirely from the resources of the museum itself – will become more frequent. "Ways of Looking" at the Museum of Modern Art was a compact history of modern art, while the Metropolitan Museum showed "Florentine Painting," a rearrangement of its Italian galleries.

Nonetheless, several large and impressive exhibitions testified to the vitality of the loan exhibition. In the area of older art, chief among these was the large "Caravaggio and His Followers" at the Cleveland Museum of Art, Caravaggio initiated a dramatic realism about 1600 that was still of great importance in the 1800s. The Minneapolis Institute of Arts sponsored the traveling exhibition "Dutch 18th Century Painting," an introduction of this little-known art – always eclipsed by the grandeur of the great men of the previous century.

The Salvador Dali Museum, first American museum dedicated solely to the works of a living artist, was opened near Cleveland by the owners of the world's largest collection of that artist's work. The museum, displaying 300 works, was opened by Mr. and Mrs. A. Reynolds Morse. An interfaith chapel opened at the Texas Medical Center in Houston. It is decorated only by 14 large paintings by the late Mark Rothko. The chapel is the first American place of worship devoted exclusively to the work of a major contemporary American artist.

Museums and galleries throughout the United States continued to confront new forms of the visual arts, representing either an interest in new materials and technologies, or new attitudes toward making art objects. The Los Angeles County Museum of Art, presenting "Art and Technology," acted as intermediary in introducing artists to industrial firms with whom they worked on individual projects. Although it drew criticism and posed problems, the exhibit without question will be important in the presently evolving idea of art's possibilities.

The Boston Museum of Fine Arts concluded its centennial year with "Earth, Air, Fire, Water," a compilation of happenings, environments, process, and concept art. The newly opened Walker Art Center offered a similar exhibition in Minneapolis, "New Works for New Spaces." The Everson Mu-

Canadian sculptor Armand Vaillancourt designed this new fountain for San Francisco's Embarcadero Plaza. Made of concrete, it was dedicated in April.

seum in Syracuse, N.Y., showed "Air," in which all the works involved the use of that element in a significant way.

"Four Americans in Paris," the Stein family collection, was one of the year's unusual exhibitions. It was sponsored by the Museum of Modern Art, New York City. During the years before World War I, writer Gertrude Stein and her brothers met and befriended many artists who later became famous, such as Henri Matisse and Picasso. Many works of art owned by the family were reunited for the exhibition.

Exotic Exhibitions of the year were simultaneously presented by The Art Institute of Chicago. "Ukiyo-e Prints and Paintings, The Primitive Period (1680-1745)" showed the rare "floating world" woodcuts and paintings of Japan in the early 1700s, where the subject matter was taken from the world of everyday life. The display focused on works made before the introduction of color printing. Shown at the same time was "The Art of the Sepik River," severe and beautiful works from primitive New Guinea.

Two prestigious exhibitions during the year pointed to the continuing fascination with the "multiple," the reproduction in limited edition of three-dimensional works of art. The Philadelphia Museum of Art presented "Multiples," a large exhibition with an interesting catalog, itself a mul-

tiple. The Museum of Modern Art offered a retrospective view of the production of the Gemini G.E.L. studios in Los Angeles, a pioneer in multiples.

Exhibitions of 19th century art included the Los Angeles County Museum of Fine Arts' organization of the work of the French Romantic painter Théodore Géricault; and a carefully chosen group of paintings by Paul Cézanne was assembled by The Art Institute of Chicago in conjunction with the Phillips Gallery in Washington, D.C., to honor the latter's 50th anniversary.

Large exhibitions of decorative arts were those at the Minneapolis Institute of Arts, where "Art Deco" displayed thousands of items from every realm of the functional arts in the now fanatically admired 1920s style; and at the Metropolitan Museum of Art, where the première exhibition of the newly opened Costume Institute showed elegant clothing from the museum's extensive collections.

Major American Artists accorded large exhibitions in 1971 included Andy Warhol, with an exhibition at the Whitney Museum of American Art in New York City and Barnett Newman at the Museum of Modern Art. The Whitney also showed a selection of the more than 2,000 items given to the museum by the estate of the American painter Edward Hopper, who died in 1967.

The Artist's Uneasiness with his former ivory tower role showed clearly in 1971 in New York City.

Women's Liberation moved into the artistic arena, establishing a central clearing house, *The Women's Art Registry*, that listed biographies along with slides of work. In addition, the Guggenheim Museum was forced to cancel a show of "conceptual" works by Hans Haacke, because it felt the content was too specifically critical of real estate practices that created slum dwellings in New York City.

Seth Siegelaub, a young experimental art dealer, distributed his Artist's Reserved Rights and Transfer and Sale Agreement nationally. In effect, the document is a contract that becomes binding upon the original purchaser and each subsequent purchaser of a work of art once it is entered into voluntarily. At each resale, the artist is to be given 15 per cent of the increase in the value of the work, and other rights as well. For instance, the artist is to be given all reproduction rights, told whom his works are sold to, and consulted on exhibition rights.

Sculpture Exhibition. The outstanding traditional sculpture exhibition of the year was the Walker Art Center's showing of the bronzes of Joan Miró in Minneapolis. Important public monumental works produced included a 32-foot-high, multiton, abstract sculpture with rearrangeable parts, made by Jacob Agam, for the Juilliard School in New York City. Also striking was the Embarcadero Plaza Fountain, a five-sided pool with massive squared concrete tubes set up in San Francisco by the Canadian sculptor Armand Vaillancourt.

Christo, a European artist known in the United States for his projects involving wrapping up buildings and other large objects, experienced one of his few failures when a large curtain meant to hang across a valley near Rifle, Colo., collapsed and tore apart. The bright orange vinyl curtain was 1,200 feet long.

Record Prices. As for almost a decade, art works brought huge prices at auctions. This was perhaps even more significant in 1971, when economic recession threatened. An etching by Rembrandt was sold for $83,000, the world record for a print. The famous bronze sculpture by Degas, *The Little 14-Year-Old Dancer*, was sold for $380,000. And in a very complex transaction, billionaire J. Paul Getty paid the second-highest price ever paid at auction for a painting when he bought Titian's *Death of Actaeon* for more than $4 million. The Getty transaction was held up because the British government refused to permit the export of the Titian painting for one year, so an attempt could be made to raise money to buy the painting for a British museum, and thus keep it in England. The highest single art auction total ever reached in the United States was set in 1971 when 74 works from the collections of Norton Simon were sold for $6.5 million.   Joshua Kind

See also AWARDS AND PRIZES.

VITAL STATISTICS. There were fewer births and deaths in the United States in 1971 than in 1970. The number of marriages also declined slightly.

From January to September, 1971, there were 2,673,000 live births recorded, about 3 per cent fewer than in the same period of 1970. During the first nine months of 1971, 1,654,000 marriages were performed, 0.5 per cent fewer than in 1970.

There were an estimated 567,000 divorces between January and September, 1971, 16,000 more

The Little 14-Year-Old Dancer, a 37½-inch-high statue by Degas, sold for $380,000 at an auction in New York City in 1971, a record price for sculpture.

U. S. Vital Statistics	1970*	1971*
Live births	3,668,000	3,632,000
Birth rate†	18.0	17.7
Infant deaths (under age 1)	73,400	70,600
Deaths	1,920,000	1,920,000
Death rate†	9.4	9.3
Marriages	2,166,000	2,186,000
Divorces	721,000	754,000

*12 months through September.
†Per 1,000 population.
Source: U.S. Public Health Service

than in 1970. The divorce rate increased by 6 per cent in 1971, compared with a 12 per cent rise in 1970.

In the first nine months of 1971, 1,438,000 deaths were recorded, 0.1 per cent fewer than during the same 1971 period. Provisional figures showed that heart disease was still the leading cause of death, with a rate of 360.3 per 100,000 persons. Cancer ranked second, with a rate of 162.0.   Darlene R. Stille

WALLACE, GEORGE CORLEY (1919-   ), governor of Alabama and 1968 American Independent Party presidential candidate, indicated in August, 1971, that he would be a serious presidential candidate in 1972. "The only thing that would keep me out," Wallace said, "is a meaningful change in direction in the Nixon Administration or the Democratic Party." He added that he had "no realistic hopes that such miracles will come to pass." He particularly criticized the busing of students to achieve racial balance in public schools. In the 1968 presidential election, Wallace received 9,897,141 votes, or 13.5 per cent of the votes cast, and carried five states.

Wallace was born on Aug. 25, 1919, in Clio, Ala. He received a law degree from the University of Alabama in 1942, and served in the Army Air Force from 1942 to 1945. He became an assistant attorney general of Alabama in 1946 and was elected to the state legislature in 1947. He served as judge for the Third Judicial Circuit in Alabama from 1953 to 1958. In 1962, he was elected governor. Because Alabama law does not allow a governor to succeed himself, Wallace's first wife, Lurleen, ran and won in 1966. Wallace served as her administrative assistant until her death in 1968. He was elected to his present term in 1970. On Jan. 4, 1971, Wallace married Cornelia Ellis Snively, 31.   Allan Davidson

WASHINGTON. See STATE GOVERNMENT.

WASHINGTON, D.C. The District of Columbia gained representation in Congress in 1971 for the first time in almost a century. Walter E. Fauntroy, a Democrat, was chosen in a special election on March 23 to serve in the U.S. House of Representatives. Congressman Fauntroy, who immediately joined the Black Caucus in the House, filled an unusual position. The District's congressman does not have a vote on the floor of the House. But he does have a seat on the House District Committee (where he is able to vote), receives a full congressional salary, and enjoys all of the other privileges and prerogatives of a congressman. See FAUNTROY, WALTER E.

Antiwar Dissenters again focused on Washington in 1971. In March, a bomb exploded in a washroom in the U.S. Capitol. The bomb, allegedly planted by an antiwar group, damaged several surrounding offices and the Senate barbershop, and imperiled the already fragile west front of the Capitol. The blast marked the fourth time in the building's history that it had been the scene of violence.

Some 1,000 Vietnam War veterans staged a five-day antiwar demonstration in April, camping on the Mall near the Capitol. In a dramatic scene in front of the Capitol, many of the veterans threw away their medals and battle ribbons.

The largest mass arrest in the nation's history took place in Washington in May. Thousands of antiwar militants mounted a campaign of civil disruption in an effort to close down the nation's government. Police arrested 13,400 persons during the disruptions, 7,200 of them in a single day. The massive arrests overflowed the city's jails and forced the use of a Washington Redskins football practice field as a temporary detention facility for large numbers of those arrested.

Prisoner Labor. The National Capital Housing Authority indicated that prisoners may be used to renovate all of the city's 10,000 public housing units. The authority was enthusiastic about a successful experiment using about 300 inmates from the Lorton Reformatory to repair vacant and vandalized public housing apartments. Even though the inmates were paid prevailing wages for their work, the Housing Authority realized considerable savings. Inmate labor eliminates the need to provide profits for private contracting firms.

Census Profile. The Washington, D.C., metropolitan area grew more rapidly than any other major metropolitan center on the East Coast during the 1960s. The area had a population of 2,861,123 in 1970. It rose from 10th to 7th among metropolitan areas in the United States. In the city itself, the population declined 1 per cent to 756,510 persons. Of that total, 71.1 per cent were black, giving Washington the largest percentage of black residents of any major U.S. city.   J. M. Banovetz

WEATHER. Winter brought generally warm and dry weather to the South and West of the United States in 1971. By early spring, a severe drought had set in in the Southwest and in southern Florida, and it continued until late summer. The drought eventually encompassed some northern states, such as Montana. With the coming of fall, however, rains fell in most drought areas.

The South Atlantic Ocean was the spawning ground for an unusually large number of tropical storms in 1971. The hurricanes Doria, Edith, Fern, and Ginger invaded the land, and Ginger achieved a record life of 24 days. Tornado damage in the United States was also costly. By May, an estimated 141 persons had been killed by tornadoes, nearly twice the total for 1970. About 90 of these deaths occurred in Louisiana, Mississippi, and Tennessee on February 21. See DISASTERS.

Weather Satellites. The first Improved Tiros Operational Satellite, *ITOS-A*, was launched from the National Aeronautics and Space Administration (NASA) test range at Lompoc, Calif., on Dec. 11, 1970, and it operated well throughout 1971. In addition to cameras for daylight cloud pictures, it has infrared cameras that can take pictures of clouds at night. A severe blow struck the operational satellite program, however, when *ITOS-B* failed to achieve orbit on Oct. 23, 1971.

In late summer, the French put a weather satellite,

Water levels dropped as much as an inch a day in Everglades National Park during Florida's drought, and dried-up canal beds such as this were common.

tion will be studied through a special GARP Atlantic Tropical Experiment. This experiment is designed primarily to determine the effects of the tropical cloud clusters in transporting heat, water vapor, and momentum on the global circulation. This observational experiment is scheduled to begin in the South Atlantic in 1974.

Making the greatest use of meteorological data is one of the major concerns of GARP. A group of meteorologists met at Princeton University in April to consider how to get the best results from satellite weather data. They considered several numerical atmospheric models for utilizing the information.

Climate Change Network. NOAA announced a program in 1971, designed to study the poorly understood effects of human activities on weather and climate. The program will complement existing efforts to monitor physical, chemical, and biological aspects of man's environment. It will also establish a network of observation stations to measure long-term atmospheric changes.

In cooperation with the Department of Housing and Urban Development, NOAA is developing a storm-evacuation mapping program for flood-prone areas along the Atlantic and Gulf coasts. The maps, the first of which was developed for Slidell, La., and was released in July, delineate areas of flooding at various heights of storm tide as well as evacuation routes. William G. Collins

Éole, into orbit. It will monitor the movements of a fleet of 500 constant-level balloons sent into the atmosphere of the Southern Hemisphere. This balloon-satellite system will provide data on the wind patterns of the upper atmosphere.

Weather Modification. Cloud seeding efforts were intensified, partly as a consequence of the Florida drought. The seeding by the National Oceanic and Atmospheric Administration's (NOAA) Experimental Meteorology Laboratory in Florida was expanded to try to provide more rain and thus alleviate the drought. Early analysis of the results showed that on almost every day of seeding there was some precipitation that could be credited to the seeding efforts. The Bureau of Reclamation and the U.S. Air Force started a similar project in Texas because of the severe drought there.

Atmospheric Research. Plans for the Global Atmospheric Research Program (GARP) were detailed in 1971. This is a program of the World Meteorological Organization and the International Council of Science Unions. It is scheduled to begin about 1976. It will use satellites, constant-level balloons, and various measuring instruments to test a series of theoretical models and relevant aspects of the atmosphere's behavior, in an effort to describe more precisely the physical processes of weather and their interactions.

The tropical aspects of the global weather circula-

WEBER, JOSEPH (1919-   ), a noted American physicist, by 1971 had amassed considerable evidence indicating that he has detected gravitational waves. Albert Einstein predicted the existence of these waves in 1916 in his general theory of relativity. Using detectors that are large metal cylinders suspended in vacuums, Weber appears to have discovered an incredibly strong source of gravitational waves very close to the center of our Galaxy, the Milky Way.

Weber was born in Paterson, N. J., on May 17, 1919. He graduated from the U.S. Naval Academy in 1940, and also attended the Naval Postgraduate School in Monterey, Calif. In 1948, he resigned from the Navy and began graduate work in physics at the Catholic University of America. This led to a Ph.D. degree in 1951. He taught electrical engineering at the University of Maryland throughout his graduate work and until 1959, when he became a professor of physics there. He is the author of *General Relativity and Gravitational Waves* (1961).

Weber did most of his gravitational-wave work alone over a period of more than a decade. Even his outside interests – classical music, mountaineering, and photography – are those characterized by independent effort. He married in 1942, and now has four sons. His wife Anita, died unexpectedly of a stroke in 1971. Michael Reed

WEIGHT LIFTING. See SPORTS.

WEST INDIES. Regional cooperation remained a primary concern of a number of Caribbean countries during 1971. In April, representatives of the Bahamas, Barbados, and Trinidad and Tobago attended the first annual board meeting of the Caribbean Development Bank in St. John, Antigua. To increase tourism and industrial expansion in the area, the group unanimously endorsed plans designed to increase economic, social, and cultural exchanges among its members.

In July, representatives of the British Commonwealth of Nations countries in the Caribbean met in Grenada, the Windward Islands, and formally adopted procedures designed to form a new political union of the former British territories in the area. Such a union, known as the Federation of the West Indies, had been founded in 1958 and dissolved in 1962.

The Bahamas, Barbados, and Trinidad and Tobago, all sugar producers, sent representatives to a meeting in London in June to discuss the sugar terms offered to Great Britain pending its entry into the European Community (Common Market). All three endorsed the terms. As an indication of regional cooperation on an international level, Brazil announced in August that it would sign a pact permitting Trinidad and Tobago to fish within Brazil's 200-mile territorial limits, the first such pact Brazil had signed.

In Other Developments, Barbados held a general election on Sept. 9, 1971. The Barbados Democratic Labor Party, headed by Prime Minister Errol W. Barrow, increased its majority from 15 to 18 seats in the 24-seat House of Assembly. On May 24, the Peoples' National Movement Party (PNM) in Trinidad and Tobago won all 36 seats in a parliamentary election. Eric Eustace Williams, as leader of the PNM, retained his post as prime minister.

Facts in Brief. Bahamas. Population: 162,000. Government: Governor Sir Francis Cumming-Bruce; Prime Minister Lynden O. Pindling. Monetary Unit: dollar. Foreign Trade: exports, $54,000,-000; imports, $202,000,000. Principal Exports: cement, pulpwood, rum, salt.

Barbados. Population: 263,000. Government: Governor General Sir Arleigh Winston Scott; Prime Minister Errol W. Barrow. Monetary Unit: East Caribbean dollar. Foreign Trade: exports, $43,000,-000; imports, $114,000,000. Principal Exports: sugar, molasses, rum.

Trinidad and Tobago. Population: 1,104,000. Government: Governor General Sir Solomon Hochoy; Prime Minister Eric Eustace Williams. Monetary Unit: dollar. Foreign Trade: exports, $482,000,000; imports, $541,000,000. Principal Exports: petroleum and petroleum products, sugar, ammonium sulfate. Paul C. Tullier

WEST VIRGINIA. See State Government.

WILDLIFE. See Conservation.

WILSON, FLIP (1933-), a black comedian, starred in one of television's most popular variety shows in 1971. Wilson's success stems from a brand of ethnic humor that is devoid of racial rancor. "What you see is what you get," one of his most famous lines, best describes Wilson's comic routines. He relies heavily for humor on bodily movements and Deep South dialect rather than on snappy punch lines. Wilson's comic character portrayals, such as Geraldine and the Reverend Leroy of the Church of What's Happening Now, highlighted "The Flip Wilson Show" on the National Broadcasting Company (NBC) network. It was the first successful weekly variety show hosted by a black.

Clerow (Flip) Wilson is one of 18 children born to a poverty-stricken family in Jersey City, N.J. His parents separated when he was 8 years old, and he grew up in foster homes. At the age of 16 he joined the Air Force, where he received the nickname Flip, for flipped-out.

During the 1950s and early 1960s, he earned a meager living playing in small night clubs. Then, in 1965, Wilson made his television debut on Johnny Carson's "Tonight Show."

Wilson has been married twice, and he has four children. Darlene R. Stille

WISCONSIN. See State Government.

WRESTLING. See Sports.

WYOMING. See State Government.

YEMEN struggled through a year of political and financial crisis in 1971, the aftermath of eight years of civil war. Yemen's first Consultative Council, elected in March and April, chose a three-member executive body to advise the president (Republican Council chairman) and his Cabinet. The council represented urban, tribal, and other social groups. But actual executive power remained in the hands of President Abdul Rahman Iryani, Major General Hassan al-Amri, the armed forces commander, and senior tribal leader Shaikh Muhammad Uthman.

Prime Minister Muhsin al-Ayni resigned in February. In May, Iryani named Ahmad Noman as prime minister. The immediate problem for Noman and his Cabinet was a $20-million budget deficit. The government did not have enough funds on hand to pay army and civil service salaries or subsidies to the Yemeni tribes. Foreign debts, most of them to Russia and China, totaled $186 million.

Noman's efforts received little support, and he resigned on July 20. General Amri formed a new Cabinet on August 23, but he resigned after nine days and former Prime Minister al-Ayni returned to office.

Facts in Brief. Population: 5,000,000. Government: Republican Council Chairman Abdul Rahman Iryani; Prime Minister Muhsin al-Ayni. Monetary Unit: ryal. Foreign Trade: exports, $1,000,000; imports, $11,000,000. Principal Exports: coffee, qat, hides and skins, cotton. William Spencer

YOUNG MEN'S CHRISTIAN ASSOCIATION

(YMCA) membership reached an all-time high of more than 7 million early in 1971. The new international division of the U.S. YMCA began an expanded program. The division, which for the first time brings all the international activities of the National Council into one group, will be responsible for:

▪ World service, which includes development and strengthening of YMCA's overseas. In this area, the council works with YMCA's in 36 countries.

▪ International student service, which helps students from other countries studying in the United States and arranges and supervises student exchanges.

▪ The Center for International Management Studies, which arranges the international exchange of business executives.

▪ International programs for local associations, which includes planning international travel, conferences, and volunteer service opportunities for youth and young adults, and educational travel for all members and professional staff.

Rix G. Rogers, general secretary of the Montreal YMCA since 1968, was named general secretary for the National Council of Canadian YMCA's. Robert W. Harlan was appointed executive director of the National Council of Young Men's Christian Associations of the United States. He has been executive director of the Pacific Region.   Joseph P. Anderson

YOUNG WOMEN'S CHRISTIAN ASSOCIATION

(YWCA) began in 1971 to work toward the goal, set by the 1970 national convention, of "the elimination of racism wherever it exists and by any means necessary." Armed with suggestions from the staff and others, the YWCA National Board outlined a nationwide program to attack one of the major problems of our time, racism.

The first major step, taken early in 1971, was termed an Action Audit for Change. It was carried out in two phases. First, the YWCA itself was thoroughly scrutinized for evidence of racism. Next came a broader study of the effects of racism in the community the YWCA serves and the community's institutions.

Then in March, a series of workshops were held in 15 communities across the nation. The workshops were designed to show YWCA executives how to put local antiracism activities into effect.

From April to September, 16 community institutes were conducted by the YWCA National Board. Those attending the institutes learned how racism appears in such areas as housing, health, drug abuse, education, environment, employment, poverty, child development, communications, and the administration of justice.

Many members felt that participants in all these antiracism activities should be brought together for a conference.   Joseph P. Anderson

YOUTH ORGANIZATIONS made history in 1971 by planning the White House Conference on Youth. About 1,500 delegates, 1,000 of them between 14 and 24 years of age, attended the conference in Estes Park, Colo., in April. This marked the first time that the conference was planned by and for youth. It was also the first time the regular conference on children and youth was split into two conferences. A separate conference on the problems of children had been held in Washington, D.C., in December, 1970 (see CHILD WELFARE).

The youth delegates called for an immediate end to the Vietnam War and withdrawal of all U.S. forces and logistical support by the end of 1971. Their report on the Estes Park meeting was submitted to President Richard M. Nixon.

Boy Scouts of America (BSA) adopted the following program revisions:

▪ Project SOAR (Save Our American Resources) will continue throughout 1972.

▪ Two national jamborees will be conducted in the United States in 1973, one in the East and one in the West.

▪ A boy may become a Boy Scout if he has completed the 5th grade or is 11 years of age.

▪ Operation Reach, an effort to help solve the drug-abuse problem in America, was to begin in 1972.

The U.S. Department of Labor Manpower Ad-

Girls second, third, and fourth from left wear new senior Girl Scout uniform with optional pants. Adult leader at far left has a new uniform, too.

ministration awarded a $700,000 Public Service Careers contract to the BSA to train 200 disadvantaged persons as Scout officials. These officials will work with Scout troops in economically depressed areas.

The 61st annual meeting of the Boy Scouts was held from May 26 to 28 in Atlanta, Ga. Norton Clapp of Tacoma, Wash., was elected president.

Boys' Clubs of America established a new Urban Affairs Service to help determine how Boys' Clubs can help solve urban problems.

The 65th annual convention was held in Atlanta, Ga., from May 16 to 20. Pelton Stewart, 18, of San Francisco was named Boy of the Year.

Camp Fire Girls held its third Horizon Club Conference, "Aware '71," in three different parts of the United States. Over a thousand boys and girls attended the conference. The first meeting was held at North Texas State University in Denton from June 22 to 26. A West Coast conference was held at the University of California, Davis, from June 24 to 28. The final meeting was at Georgetown University in Washington, D.C., from July 5 to 9.

The issues identified as the ones in which Camp Fire Girls are most interested include democratic citizenship, drug abuse, racial prejudice, the right to dissent, women's liberation, and changing moral values. On November 2, a decision to admit boys to the Camp Fire Girls Horizon Club was announced.

Four-H Clubs adopted the 1971 theme, "4-H Bridges the Gap." Four-H members were active in fighting air and water pollution; improving the nutrition of all people; fighting drug addiction and smoking; aiding the mentally retarded and physically handicapped; building more pleasant, safe surroundings; and learning about and understanding people of other cultures.

The national 4-H Club conference was held in the new 4-H Club center in Chevy Chase, Md., from April 18 to 23, with 235 delegates from the 50 states, the District of Columbia, and Puerto Rico attending. A highlight of the conference was a reception at the White House for the delegates. Mrs. Richard M. Nixon was cited as a Partner-in-4-H.

Future Farmers of America (FFA) expanded award opportunities in 1971 by offering more awards for off-farm occupations. Areas in which new awards were presented included agricultural processing, agricultural product sales and service, outdoor recreation, and soil, water, and air management.

The FFA continued to assist other countries in initiating their own Future Farmers organizations and arranging student exchange activities. Through the FFA's Work Experience Abroad program, 23 FFA members were placed on farms in Europe and South America for three months, and 50 students from Europe and South America were placed on farms in the United States. A new membership category opened in 1971, the FFA Alumni Association.

It is for former active, collegiate, or honorary members, and both present and former professional vocational agricultural educators.

Girl Scouts of the United States of America discussed the needs and interests of girls and women in minority groups in several regional and national conferences. Girl Scout Councils throughout the nation received grants from the Julie (Mrs. David) Eisenhower Fund. Mrs. Eisenhower donated $81,-000 to Girl Scouts to enable them to extend and maintain Girl Scouting in low-income areas. The money represented her share of profits from a crewel kit she designed that was marketed through *Family Circle* magazine.

The Reader's Digest Foundation helped 23 Senior Girl Scout service projects in 1971. Among them were a community drug-education center, day camps for children of migrant workers, inner-city programs for children, and services for children in rural poverty areas.

Through Eco-Action, the nationwide ecological program, Girl Scouts across the nation have adopted a "watershed." Within this area, they have cooperated with government and community agencies to try to eliminate sources of water pollution and to improve the total environment. Two pilot projects set up with the National Fish and Wildlife Service of the U.S. Department of the Interior enable girls to explore career possibilities and learn about the purpose, operation, and problems of a refuge or hatchery.

New senior and adult girl uniforms with optional pants suits were introduced in 1971. This was the first uniform change for the 14- to 17-year-old senior girls in 12 years.

Girls Clubs of America (GCA) adopted the following goals for its second 25 years of service:

▪ A 25 per cent increase in Girls Club centers. There are 172 centers affiliated with GCA in the United States and Canada.

▪ A 25 per cent increase in GCA membership. There are now more than 100,000 members.

▪ The establishment of two new regional offices in the northeastern and southwestern United States.

▪ A jubilee expansion and development fund of $1.25 million.

Junior Achievement (JA) approved the continuation of two programs of economic education. The first is designed to provide meaningful summer employment. It is called JA Job Apprenticeship Program. The second is called Practical Business Economics, and is designed to help members understand how private enterprise works. The annual Junior Achievers Conference was held at the University of Indiana, Bloomington, from August 15 to 20. Jinny Sands, 17, of Peoria, Ill., was named Miss Junior Achievement of 1971. Anthony Abowd, an 18-year-old from Detroit, was selected as President of the Year. — Joseph P. Anderson

YUGOSLAVIA introduced far-reaching constitutional changes in 1971, but its foreign policy remained independent, aligned with neither the East nor the West. President Josip Broz Tito's program of constitutional reforms ran into strong opposition from Communist Party conservatives in March and April, but the 79-year-old Tito overcame the opposition at a dramatic meeting of top party leaders in April.

On June 30, the Federal Assembly adopted 23 constitutional amendments transferring most central government powers to Yugoslavia's six republics and two autonomous regions. The federal government remains responsible for defense, foreign affairs, and broad economic policy.

New Government. On July 29, the Federal Assembly elected the new 22-man collective presidency, which includes members from all of the republics. Tito will preside over it until 1976. Also on July 29, the Assembly elected Yugoslavia's new prime minister; Djemal Bijedic became the first Moslem to hold that post. His government inherited a grave economic situation from its predecessor, which had devalued the dinar in January and then tried to curb Yugoslavia's rampant inflation and shrink its huge trade deficit in July.

That deficit amounted to $854 million at the end of June, 62 per cent higher than a year earlier. But inflation was running at the rate of 17 per cent at the end of the year, causing unrest and strikes among low-paid workers.

The government continued to tolerate free discussion in factories, at the universities, and within the Communist Party. But disagreements within the party compelled the leadership to postpone until 1972 the party conference scheduled for October.

Foreign Affairs. Tito went to Italy in March, and visited Pope Paul VI. In October, he visited the United States, Canada, and Great Britain. President Richard M. Nixon endorsed Tito's independent policy, and promised to help double U.S. imports from Yugoslavia, which have been running about $100 million annually.

Yugoslavia's relations with Russia continued to be difficult through the spring and summer of 1971. The Belgrade newspaper *Politika* complained in June that Russia was openly supporting anti-Tito emigrants from Yugoslavia.

However, Russian party chief Leonid I. Brezhnev visited Yugoslavia in September. During his visit, he recognized, with some qualifications, Yugoslavia's independent "road to socialism."

Facts in Brief. Population: 21,030,000. Government: President Josip Broz Tito; Prime Minister Djemal Bijedic. Monetary Unit: dinar. Foreign Trade: exports, $1,679,000,000; imports, $2,872,-000,000. Principal Exports: machinery, meat, chemicals. *Chris Cviic*

ZAIRE. See Congo (Kinshasa).

ZAMBIA. Relations with several other nations were strained in 1971. President Kenneth David Kaunda refused to recognize the military regime that seized power in Uganda in January. In March, he accused Portugal of blocking shipments of goods to Zambia in retaliation for the January kidnaping of five Portuguese workers by revolutionaries in Mozambique. Portugal claimed that Zambia was responsible for the kidnaping, but Kaunda denied the charge. Portugal denied blocking shipments to Zambia. Zambia re-established diplomatic relations, broken in 1967, with Nigeria in July.

The University of Zambia was shut down on July 15, after students took over the campus to protect 10 students who wrote a letter protesting Kaunda's policy toward South Africa. It was reported in April that Kaunda had been in contact with the South African government since 1968.

The United Progressive Party (UPP) was formed in August to provide Socialist opposition to the ruling United National Independence Party. In September, about 75 UPP members were arrested and charged with encouraging guerrilla activity.

Facts in Brief. Population: 4,612,000. Government: President Kenneth David Kaunda; Vice-President Mainza Chona. Monetary Unit: kwacha. Foreign Trade: exports, $1,073,000,000; imports, $437,000,000. Principal Exports: copper, zinc, lead, foodstuffs. *Darlene R. Stille*

ZOOLOGY. Investigators pressed the study of aggression in various species of animals in 1971. Many hoped that the research might lead to better understanding and controlling human aggression. Arthur Cherkin and Richard O. Meinecke of the University of California, Los Angeles, found that adult male rabbit pairs, which are aggressive toward each other and cannot be caged together, become docile if they are allowed to recover together from anesthesia. The experimental rabbits were selected for their aggressive nature, anesthetized together in a cage, and allowed to remain together for seven days after recovery from the anesthetic (sodium pentobarbital). The same rabbits, re-isolated after the seven-day period and then paired again, resumed their aggressive behavior. Other rabbits, not allowed to recover from anesthesia together, showed attack behavior consistently throughout the testing period.

It is possible that the groggy rabbits did not resume their aggressive behavior because they only gradually became aware that another rabbit was present. Their senses were dulled during the slow emergence from anesthesia. The scientists suggested that aggressive human mental patients might respond to anesthetic treatments similarly.

Homing Pigeon's Secret. The effect of the earth's magnetic field on the homing behavior of pigeons has been considered for many years, but results have been inconclusive. In 1971, William T.

Keeton of Cornell University designed a new experiment to solve the problem, and obtained convincing results. He attached magnets to pigeons to interfere with the effect of the earth's magnetic field on them. Experienced birds showed some disorientation under totally overcast skies, but not under clear skies. First-flight birds showed disorientation under both types of sky. Birds wearing nonmagnetic bars showed no disorientation. This indicates that either the sun or the earth's magnetic field is apparently sufficient to orient experienced pigeons, while first-flight birds need both cues.

Tail Eaters. Skinks, a type of ground lizard, automatically break off their tails when they flee from an enemy. The severed tails continue to thrash about after they are dropped, probably to distract a predator while the skink escapes. Many skinks that drop their tails also store fat there, so discarding the tail results in a loss of fat reserves. Donald R. Clark, Jr., of Texas A&M University found that many skinks with large fat reserves in the tail return to the place where they dropped the tail and eat it, thus recovering the fat reserves.

Cornell University's Laboratory of Ornithology has reported the discovery of the only known pouched bird. Male American finfoots, which are related to rails and coots, have pleats of skin beneath each wing that form cavities into which the young fit comfortably.   Barbara N. Benson

ZOOS AND AQUARIUMS. The unsettled economic climate in the United States seemed to be reflected in the change in fortunes that U.S. zoos suffered in 1971. Elaborate plans for a new Minnesota state zoo near St. Paul came to naught when the state legislature failed to authorize construction funds. Inflationary forces caused cuts in services or increased fees at several zoos, including the Philadelphia Zoo, America's oldest. On the other hand, a new zoo was begun near Columbia, S.C., and voters in the St. Louis metropolitan area approved increased tax support for that city's famous museums and zoo.

Conservation Themes. During Earth Week, from April 18 to 24, New York City's Bronx Zoo featured a "graveyard" of extinct species. Brookfield Zoo near Chicago presented each autumn visitor with a booklet enabling zoo visitors to take a self-guided tour of vanishing species.

Collaborative breeding projects for endangered species became ever-more common. Through the cooperation of the Bronx Zoo, the Brookfield Zoo, and the National Zoo in Washington, D.C., the Houston Zoo had four of the five known captive specimens of the St. Vincent Island parrot. Similarly, a transfer of golden lion marmosets from Phoenix, Ariz., to San Antonio, Tex., established another potential breeding colony for this species. The lone mountain gorilla at the Tel Aviv Zoo in Israel was sent as a mate to the bachelor male in Oklahoma City, Okla.,

and a male Indian rhinoceros at Basel, Switzerland, was mated with a female from West Berlin, Germany.

New Exhibits. The huge World of Birds building at the Bronx Zoo was completed in 1971. In Chicago, Lincoln Park Zoo unveiled new moated outdoor enclosures for large cats and for small mammals, and Shedd Aquarium opened a $1-million coral-reef tank. Stocks of large animals, including 20 white rhinoceroses, were gathered together by the San Diego Zoological Society for its San Pasqual Wild Animal Park. New children's zoos opened at Sedgwick County Zoo near Wichita, Kans., and at the Milwaukee County Zoo. At Canada's Vancouver Aquarium, killer whales frolicked in a spacious new pool.

Notable Births. Aardvark births became commonplace in Miami, Fla., where three females produced young in 1971. One was also born in Tacoma, Wash. The National Zoo in Washington, D.C., recorded the first birth of a bongo, a rare large forest antelope, and the hatching of a kagu, a rare New Caledonian bird. Golden eagles hatched and reared two young at the Topeka, Kans., zoo.

In 1971, the principal professional organization, the American Association of Zoological Parks and Aquariums, left the National Recreation and Parks Association. The move was made so that the association could act more effectively on problems that are peculiar to zoos.   George B. Rabb

ZUMWALT, ELMO RUSSELL, JR. (1920-   ), chief of naval operations, instituted controversial reforms in naval personnel policies that resulted in higher enlistment and re-enlistment rates in 1971. Zumwalt had become the youngest chief of naval operations in the history of the U.S. Navy on July 1, 1970. He was chosen for the post over 33 senior admirals. A vice-admiral when he was appointed in April, 1970, he became a full admiral that May.

Zumwalt immediately set about humanizing and modernizing the Navy by treating personnel with "20th-century common sense." He eliminated outdated regulations and make-work projects and relaxed dress codes for enlisted men.

Zumwalt was born on Nov. 29, 1920, in Tulare, Calif. Both of his parents were physicians, and he had also intended to become a physician. Instead, he attended the U.S. Naval Academy. He began his naval career as an ensign on destroyers during World War II and was awarded a Bronze Star. After the war, he held a variety of posts from Naval Reserve Officer Training Corps instructor to commanding officer on destroyers.

In 1961, Zumwalt entered the National War College for 10 months of study. He was assigned to the office of an assistant secretary of defense in 1962. From 1968 to 1970, he was commander of the U.S. Naval Forces in Vietnam. Zumwalt married Mouza Coutelais-du-Roche in 1945.   Darlene R. Stille

World Book Supplement

In its function of keeping all WORLD BOOK owners up-to-date,
THE WORLD BOOK YEAR BOOK herewith offers significant
new articles from the 1972 edition of THE WORLD BOOK
ENCYCLOPEDIA. These articles should be indexed in
THE WORLD BOOK ENCYCLOPEDIA by means of
THE YEAR BOOK cross-reference tabs.

560 **Motion Picture**
An enlarged and revised article that tells the history of
films and includes an account of the steps in making a film.

590 **Environmental Pollution**
A new article about a major concern of the entire world.

George C. Scott in *Patton*

Charlie Chaplin in *Easy Street*

Ginger Rogers
and Fred Astaire in *Swing Time*

Snow White and the Seven Dwarfs

Boris Karloff in *Frankenstein*

MOTION PICTURE

MOTION PICTURE is one of the most popular forms of art and entertainment throughout the world. Every week, millions of people go to the movies. Many millions more watch movies on television. In addition, TV networks use motion-picture techniques to film many of the programs that appear on television each week.

Motion pictures are a major source of information as well as of entertainment. Movies can take us back into history. They can re-create the lives of great men and women. Motion pictures can introduce us to new ideas and help us explore serious social issues. Students learn from educational films in school. Industries use movies to train employees and to advertise their products. Governments use films to inform and influence their own citizens and people in other countries.

The motion picture is a major art form, as are, for example, painting and writing. An artist expresses himself by using paint, and a writer by using words. The film maker expresses his ideas through a motion-picture camera. By using the camera in different ways, the film maker can express different points of view. Even the most realistic-looking movie shows only the film maker's version of reality. He can point the camera up at a man and make him appear a hero on the screen. He can point the camera down and make the same man seem insignificant.

We can enjoy many forms of art and entertainment by ourselves. For example, we can enjoy reading a poem or looking at a painting by ourselves. But we usually enjoy a motion picture most when we watch it with others. An exciting scene increases in suspense when we feel the tension sweeping through the audience. We usually enjoy a movie less if we see it in a nearly empty theater or on television.

In some ways, movies resemble stage plays. Both use performers, settings, and dialogue. However, the playwright usually must confine his performers to a single setting until a scene or act ends. He must use dialogue as the main tool to tell his story. In a play, the char-

Arthur Knight, the contributor of this article, is Professor of Cinema at the University of Southern California and the author of The Liveliest Art, *a history of motion pictures.*

Clark Gable and Vivien Leigh
in *Gone with the Wind*

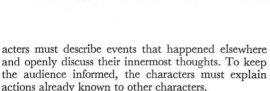

John Barrymore
and Greta Garbo in *Grand Hotel*

King Kong

acters must describe events that happened elsewhere and openly discuss their innermost thoughts. To keep the audience informed, the characters must explain actions already known to other characters.

Unlike the playwright, the film maker can *show* rather than *tell* his story. In movies, action is more important than words. The film maker can change the setting as often as he wishes. For example, he may film parts of his picture in a desert, on a mountain, and in a large city. He can also film scenes from different angles. Later, through a technique called *editing*, he can select the angle that most effectively expresses a dramatic point. Through editing, the film maker can also show events happening at the same time in different places.

The motion picture is an art form that has become a gigantic industry. A movie may cost up to several million dollars to make and require the skills of many hundreds of workers. Highly technical devices, including cameras, sound-recording equipment, and projectors, are needed to film and show movies. In fact, motion pictures could not exist without many of the scientific and technical discoveries made during the 1900's. For this reason, motion pictures have been called the art form of the 20th century.

Motion pictures have become perhaps the most democratic of the arts. Most art forms can appeal to a small, specialized audience and still survive. But most movies cost so much money to make that they must attract large audiences to show a profit. As a result, most film makers attempt to please as many people as possible, regardless of their economic, educational, or social background. Few motion pictures can succeed without broad public support.

The movies have a brief history, compared with such art forms as music and painting. The beginning of the movies dates back only to the late 1800's. By the early 1900's, film makers had already developed distinctive artistic theories and techniques. However, movies received little scholarly attention until the 1960's. Today, the motion picture is recognized as a major art form. Hundreds of books have been printed about films. Many universities and colleges offer degrees in motion pictures, and many more offer courses.

John Wayne in *Red River*

2001: A Space Odyssey

Laurence Olivier, *right*, in a scene from *Hamlet* (1948), directed by Olivier; Universal Studios

A Filmed Version of *Hamlet* has given many people their first opportunity to see this great tragedy by William Shakespeare. Movies of books and plays help students understand literature.

Most people consider motion pictures important mainly as a form of entertainment. But movies are also widely used in education. In addition, TV stations, government agencies, and industrial firms use films to provide information or to influence people's attitudes. The making of home movies has also become a popular hobby.

Entertainment. Most people go to the movies to relax or to escape from their cares for a few hours. They may want to lose themselves in a romantic story, laugh at a popular comedian, or see a part of the world they could never afford to visit in real life. Nearly all the most popular films in motion-picture history have emphasized pure entertainment. They include the historical romance *Gone with the Wind* (1939) and the musicals *Mary Poppins* (1964) and *The Sound of Music* (1965).

Most television stations broadcast many hours of motion pictures a day. Nearly all movies on TV were originally shown in theaters and then sold to television. However, some movies are made especially for TV.

A film maker may try to educate as well as entertain his audience. For example, *I Am a Fugitive from a Chain Gang* (1932) shows the brutality of chain gangs. Political corruption is the theme of *Mr. Smith Goes to Washington* (1939) and *All the King's Men* (1950). *Paths of Glory*

(1957) and *Catch-22* (1970) attack war as senseless. *Pinky* (1949) and *In the Heat of the Night* (1967) deal with racial prejudice.

People disagree over whether motion pictures reflect or help create our society. For example, some people believe that violence in films encourages viewers to behave violently in real life. But others say violence is part of life and movies only mirror that fact.

Education. Motion pictures made especially for educational purposes have become important teaching aids in the classroom. Teachers use such films in teaching geography, history, mathematics, and the physical and social sciences. Movies in the physical sciences use slow motion, cartoons, and other special techniques to demonstrate processes that otherwise could not be seen or studied thoroughly. For example, a film can slow down the formation of crystals so a science class can study this process.

Teachers also use motion pictures made originally to be shown in theaters. Such movies as *Abe Lincoln in Illinois* (1939) and *The Howards of Virginia* (1940) help in teaching American history. An English film about juvenile delinquency, *The Loneliness of the Long-Distance Runner* (1962), has become a standard teaching aid in the social sciences. Many great novels and plays have been filmed. Such movies help students understand and appreciate literature.

Some elementary schools, junior high schools, and high schools in the United States have courses in making motion pictures. In making movies, students learn to express themselves, as they do in painting, writing, or any other art.

Hospitals and medical schools film operations so students can watch doctors at work. Athletic teams take movies of their games and later examine the films to learn what mistakes the players made. Boxers, golfers, and other athletes also study movies to learn how to improve their skills.

Most educational films in the United States are made by schools and commercial firms. City, county, and state educational agencies, as well as colleges and universities, make these films available through film libraries. Some state university film libraries have as many as 7,000 films. In Canada, the National Film Board, a federal government agency, produces educational films. Many films produced by the board have won international awards.

Information. Television stations use motion pictures to inform as well as to entertain their viewers. TV networks and stations may cancel entertainment programs

Scene from *The Living Desert* (1953); © Walt Disney Productions

A Documentary Film presents factual information in a dramatic way. This scene, from a documentary about desert animals, shows a kangaroo rat trying to escape from a rattlesnake.

to present films of special interest at the moment. On the death of a great world leader, for example, they may show films that trace his career. TV networks and stations also make and broadcast many *documentary films*—nonfiction movies that present factual information in a dramatic way. These documentaries deal with a variety of subjects, such as pollution, the popularity of football, and the history of presidential elections.

For many years, movie theaters showed newsreels in addition to feature films. But movie newsreels ended with the rapid development of TV in the 1950's. The newsreels could not be changed often enough to compete with the up-to-the-minute news coverage on TV.

Several U.S. government agencies have long created motion pictures dealing with problems and achievements in their fields. During the 1930's, under President Franklin D. Roosevelt, the federal government sponsored a number of documentaries on national problems. For example, *The Plow That Broke the Plains* (1936) described the great drought in the Dust Bowl of the Southwest. *The River* (1937) stressed the need to control flooding and to bring electricity to the Tennessee Valley. Both films were factual yet poetic statements about major problems of the day.

During World War II (1939-1945), the government used motion pictures to help soldiers understand why the United States was at war. All the warring nations used motion pictures for propaganda purposes. While the Germans and Japanese occupied countries in Europe and Asia, they showed propaganda films praising their way of life and attacking the United States and its allies. After these countries were liberated, the Americans showed films sympathetically describing life in the United States. Today, the U.S. Information Agency (USIA) and the U.S. Information Service (USIS) produce motion pictures describing the American way of life for viewers in other countries.

Many states produce films to attract tourists or new industry. Such films show a state's beauty or recreational facilities or its industrial resources.

Today, nearly every major industrial firm has its own motion-picture unit or a film company that regularly makes movies for it. Many firms make films as part of their public relations programs. These films may tell the history of the company or explain how its products make life easier and more pleasant. Companies distribute such films free to schools and various adult groups. Businesses also use movies to train salesmen and to teach personnel how to use equipment.

A familiar industrial film is the television commercial. To produce a one-minute commercial, a company may spend tens of thousands of dollars, more than the cost of some full-length feature films.

Movies as a Hobby. Millions of people enjoy taking their own motion pictures at family gatherings and on vacation trips. Home movies began to develop as a hobby in the 1920's, following the invention of low-cost film that could be used in small cameras. The popularity of home movies has increased steadily over the years with the continual improvement in cameras and projectors and the development of low-cost color and sound film.

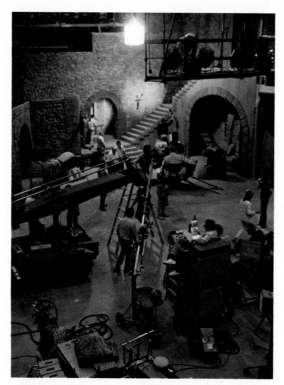

A Sound Stage bustles with activity before filming begins. Technicians ready the lights, camera, and sound-recording equipment in preparation for the director's call for "Action!"

From about 1915 to the late 1940's, large movie studios in and near Hollywood, Calif., made nearly all American motion pictures. Procedures in moviemaking varied little from one studio to another. Each studio had its own story department, which read literary works published in all parts of the world. If the department found a story that it believed would make a good motion picture, it recommended the story to a group of producers. If one of the producers liked the story, he took it to the studio's vice-president in charge of production. Finally, if the vice-president approved the story, it was turned over to one or more writers employed by the studio.

The studio writers were responsible for creating an acceptable movie script from the story. After the script gained studio approval, another department prepared a budget breakdown. This breakdown estimated how much the story would cost to film. If the studio decided the cost was reasonable, it assigned a director to the project. The producer, director, and heads of appropriate departments then selected the cast, cameraman, composer, and other key personnel. As far as possible, everyone working on the film was selected from people on the studio payroll. The studio used outsiders only

Unless otherwise credited, the photographs in this section were taken for WORLD BOOK *at Universal Studios by John Hamilton, Globe Photos.*

when everyone else was busy, a specialist was needed, or a role required a certain performer.

The studio production system began to decline during the late 1940's with the rise of independent producers. By the late 1940's, television had captured a large share of the moviegoing audience. Studios reduced the number of pictures they made and released many of their producers, directors, stars, writers, and other personnel. Many of these producers—as well as some leading directors, stars, and writers—then became independent producers and established their own film companies. The independent producer would find his own story and hire key personnel to work on the picture. The producer would then take his project to the various studios until he found one willing to provide money for the picture. Instead of being a salaried employee of a studio, the independent producer became a partner who would receive a major share of the film's profits if there were any.

Major studios still produce some movies, but the trend has increasingly been toward independent production. This section of the article describes chiefly how a movie is made by an independent producer. But the key personnel and many of the steps involved in moviemaking also apply to motion pictures produced by major studios.

The People Who Make a Motion Picture

Making a motion picture requires the skills of people in hundreds of different occupations. Many of these people—for example, carpenters, electricians, and painters—perform about the same work they would do anywhere else. But others perform jobs that are special to motion pictures. The most important of these people include: (1) the producer, (2) the director, (3) the writer, (4) the cameraman, (5) the actors and actresses, (6) the costume and set designers, (7) the editor, and (8) the composer.

The Producer is the only person involved in the production of a motion picture from its beginning until its release to the theaters. The producer finds the story to be filmed and helps prepare the budget. He hires the director and writer and works with them in developing the script. The producer helps select the actors and actresses and approves the design of the costumes and sets. During the making of the movie, he supervises the work of the director, editor, and composer. Finally, he helps create publicity campaigns to stir public interest in the motion picture when it is released.

The Director is probably the single most important person involved in the actual making of a motion picture. With the producer and other personnel, the director determines the final script, selects the cast, and arranges the work schedules. He also participates in approving the costumes and sets. Most important, the director supervises the filming of the motion picture. He guides the performances of the actors and actresses and decides how each scene should be interpreted and photographed. The director usually has many people to assist him, but the basic responsibility for the quality of the picture rests with him. Some directors also serve as producers.

Designing Sets and Costumes is one of the first steps in making a movie. The designers, *left,* examine a selection of sketches for a film's sets and *props* (furnishings). In a studio costume workshop, *right,* seamstresses finish costumes designed for several different films.

The Writer prepares the motion-picture script, also called the *scenario* or *screenplay.* The script may be an original story developed by the writer or an adaptation of a novel or a stage play. Many writers work only in the movies. If the film is to be based on a current novel or play, however, the producer may hire its author to adapt the work for the screen.

The Cameraman operates the cameras during the filming of a picture. He is also called a *cinematographer.* A good cameraman must be able to use the various kinds of motion-picture cameras and lenses. He must also know how to use light and color effectively. In addition, the cameraman must have a knowledge of composition so that the arrangement of the people and objects in each shot will produce the desired effect.

An inventive cameraman is invaluable to a director. The cameraman can suggest the best camera angles to express various ideas. For example, if a scene calls for men dragging a heavy load up a hill, the cameraman can emphasize the feeling of strain by shooting the scene from below and at an angle. The cameraman can also create special effects and visual tricks. By rocking the camera, for example, he can create the impression of an earthquake.

The Actors and Actresses in motion pictures range from *extras,* who appear on the screen as part of a crowd, to internationally famous stars. Some movie performers have built careers around a particular kind of role, such as that of a brutal gangster, a witty butler, or a bad-tempered old woman.

A Makeup Artist applies cosmetics to an actress before a day's shooting begins. The makeup will help make her coloring look natural under the bright lights needed for filming.

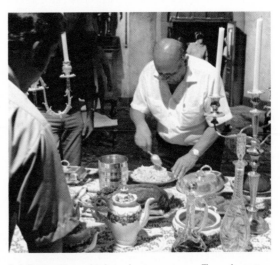

Set Decorators obtain and arrange props. These decorators are arranging props for a banquet scene. Most studios have prop departments that make and store an enormous variety of objects.

Preparing to Shoot a Scene on a sound stage, *left*, the director explains the action to actor Anthony Quinn. The cameraman lines up the angle from which he will film the scene. The script supervisor records the director's instructions on a copy of the script, *above*. The script contains the dialogue, a description of the action, and the camera angles for each scene.

Many actors and actresses work both in movies and on the stage. However, movie acting differs greatly from stage acting. On the stage, an actor completes his entire role during the course of a performance lasting from two to three hours. For a motion picture lasting the same length of time, the actor's scenes may take weeks to film. The movie actor may also have to play his scenes out of the natural order of the story. The same scene may be shot repeatedly until the director is satisfied. Thus, the movie actor must keep control of his part to make the development of his character understandable.

Cracking the Clapper Board is the final step before the director calls for the action to begin. The board shows the number of the shot to be photographed. The clapper boy brings the bar down sharply, announces the number of the shot, and filming starts.

The Designers. A costume designer creates the clothing worn by the performers in a movie. A set designer plans the scenery. If the motion picture takes place during a particular period of history, the designers must do research to learn what people wore and how buildings and furnishings looked at that time. The costume designer then prepares sketches of the clothing to be worn in the film, and the set designer makes blueprints and sometimes models of the sets. After these designs are approved by the producer and director, the costumes and sets are made. Both the costumes and the sets are designed so the performers can move about freely. The sets are also designed so the cameras can easily photograph all the action.

The Editor, or *cutter*, works with the director in selecting the most effective shots taken of the various scenes of a motion picture. The editor must then assemble these shots—which number in the hundreds—into an understandable story.

The Composer writes the background music for a motion picture. He tries to suit his music to the mood and action of the various scenes. Many composers conduct their own music when it is recorded for the film. Music from the film may also be recorded for release on phonograph records and tapes. Recordings of the entire score or of individual songs from a film can provide an important source of income for the movie and help advertise it.

Steps in Making a Motion Picture

Finding a Property is the first step in making a motion picture. A *property* is the story on which a motion picture can be based. Some properties are original stories. That is, they have never appeared in any other

Shooting a Scene. The cameraman is filming the action from a movable perch above the set. A technician called a *boom man* guides a microphone to pick up the dialogue as the actors move about. The dialogue is recorded on magnetic tape and later transferred onto the sound track.

form. However, most properties come from such sources as novels, plays, and musical comedies. Producers may pay an author hundreds of thousands of dollars for the right to make a movie out of his best-selling book or popular play.

Many properties come from literary classics. For example, several of William Shakespeare's plays and many of Charles Dickens' novels have been adapted for motion pictures. *Dr. Jekyll and Mr. Hyde*, Robert Louis Stevenson's famous horror story, has been filmed many times in many countries.

The success of a particular picture often leads producers to make similar movies. For example, if a picture about motorcycle gangs attracts large audiences, other producers may rush to make additional motorcycle movies.

Financing the Motion Picture. Most major motion pictures cost millions of dollars to make. But most independent producers do not have that much money to make a major movie, and so they ask the studios for financing.

In a typical case, an independent producer finds a property he wants to film. He then hires a director, writer, performers, and other key personnel. The producer then presents the project to a studio. If the studio likes the project, it will agree to finance it. Many factors determine whether a studio will back a film. The property may be desirable, such as a best-selling novel. The

Special Effects are used to produce illusions. This scene calls for soldiers to blast a double door open with machine-gun fire. To achieve this effect, small explosives are taped to the sides of the doors not being filmed, *left*. At the proper moment, the charges are set off to give the illusion that bullets are shattering the wood, *center*. The photo, *right*, shows the damaged door as it will appear in the movie.

Filming on Location, *left,* can provide a movie with realistic settings that might be difficult, as well as more costly, to create at a studio. But on-location filming also has disadvantages. For example, personnel and equipment must be transported to the location. In isolated areas, trees may have to be cleared and roads built.

The Back Lot, *below,* consists of permanent outdoor sets erected on the grounds of a studio. The sets are full-sized reproductions of houses, other buildings, and streets. Most of the structures consist only of realistic fronts supported by wooden braces. Studios often use the same sets over and over in different films.

John Hamilton, Globe Photos

Universal Studios

director may have a record of making profitable pictures, or the performers may be especially popular with the public.

Most studios offer an independent producer a *step deal.* A step deal gives the studio the right to withdraw financing at any point up to the time filming is ready to begin. For example, the studio may pull out of a project if it does not like the script.

Preparing the Script. After the money has been promised to make a picture, the script is written. Writing the script can take many months. The writer may prepare many versions before one finally meets with general approval. The scriptwriter usually works closely with the producer and director. Some directors write their own scripts.

Writing for motion pictures is a highly specialized craft. The scriptwriter not only provides dialogue for the characters, but he may also indicate various camera shots to help tell the story, explain an idea, or establish a mood. A writer may create long scenes that have no dialogue, such as scenes of a battle or a chase. But his script still must describe in detail the action that makes up such scenes.

Budgeting. After the script has been approved, it is turned over to the studio production department for budgeting. The production department estimates the cost of the sets and of the use of studio facilities. It also estimates how much the filming to be done outside the studio will cost. Such filming is called *location shooting.* The production department also estimates the salaries needed to pay the many people involved in the production of the movie. If the studio finds the total estimated cost of the picture acceptable, it completes arrangements with the independent producer to finance the project.

Casting a Motion Picture. The critical or financial success of a motion picture often depends largely on the actors and actresses. Casting thus requires much

care. If an actor appears in a role unsuited to him, the movie may be ruined, no matter how good the script and the directing.

When casting a movie, the producer and director must decide whether to use stars. Some pictures are built around a star. A producer may even wait until a certain star is available before beginning his project. Some producers feel that star names increase a picture's chances of making money. A star's popularity at the box office may also help a producer get studio financing for his picture.

In some cases, a producer may prefer not to use stars in his picture. The picture may not have a role big enough for a star, or the producer may believe that the presence of a star would distract the audience from the story. A producer may also feel that an unfamiliar actor will help make a role more believable. If a picture is being made on a small budget, a producer may decide that a star would be too expensive.

Filming a Motion Picture begins after the script has been approved, the casting completed, the sets and costumes designed, and the locations selected. Filming usually takes several months. To save time and money, a director does not necessarily shoot the scenes of a picture in the order they will appear on the screen. For example, he may begin shooting scenes from the middle or the end of the film. He may shoot all the scenes involving the stars at one time and all the scenes at a particular location another time. The director thus must have a clear idea of the emotional and narrative flow of his picture.

In many movies, all or most of the shooting takes place in studio buildings called *sound stages*. These large, windowless buildings resemble airplane hangars. These are called sound stages because both pictures and dialogue are recorded in them. A network of electric cables crosses the floor of a sound stage. These cables supply power for the lights and other equipment. The floor is also cluttered with partitions, machinery, and wires. The cameras are mounted on large, self-powered vehicles called *dollies*. Microphones and dozens of powerful lights hang down just out of range of the cameras.

Many movies are filmed partly or entirely on location. In shooting a picture on location, the cast and other personnel may travel to several parts of the world. Craftsmen can build studio sets that resemble African jungles or the streets of Rome. But many producers feel that filming on the actual location makes a movie more realistic. In addition, filming on location is sometimes less costly than creating the setting at a studio.

But shooting on location also has disadvantages. The cast, camera crew, technicians, and equipment must be transported to the location. Generators must be brought to provide power for lights and other electrical equip-ment. The personnel must be housed and fed. In some areas, trees and bushes must be cleared and roads built so trucks can carry personnel and equipment. Each day, the film that has been shot must be flown or driven to a laboratory to be developed. The next day, the developed film must be returned so the results can be viewed and the scenes reshot if necessary.

Editing a Motion Picture. The film shot each day during the filming of a movie is called that day's *rushes*. After a day's shooting, the editor and director review the preceding day's developed rushes and select the most effective shots. The editor assembles each day's selected shots into what is called a *rough cut*.

After all shooting is completed, the editor works on improving the rough cut. It often takes as long to edit a movie as it does to film it.

In editing a motion picture, the editor has to keep many things in mind. He must blend the individual shots into a logical progression that tells the story clearly. The editor must also be able to sense when a shot has made its point and the audience can move to the next point. Editing also involves a sensitivity to rhythm and tempo. For example, abrupt changes in shots create visual excitement that would be suitable for a gunfight but might destroy a romantic scene.

Composing the Music. Most composers prefer to be hired for a film as early as possible to absorb its mood and style. In addition, they can then suggest sequences where music could effectively replace dialogue or where music and action could be effectively combined. But in most cases, the composer is hired after nearly all the principal photography has been completed. As a result, he can only add musical accents to scenes already filmed.

Before the editing is completed, the composer sketches various themes, which he submits to the producer and

The Film Editor, *left,* operates a machine called the Movieola. Two reels of film, like those at his left, run through the machine. The dark film has the pictures, and the light film carries the dialogue. The editor examines the film on the Movieola screen, *above,* and selects the shots he wants. He then organizes these shots so they tell the film's story.

Recording Sound Effects for a western film requires the creation of many different sounds. For example, the seated man is rubbing a leather purse to produce the sound of a saddle while bouncing on a wagon seat to make the noise of a buckboard.

director for approval. With them, he also selects places in the film where music could be particularly effective, as in romantic scenes or during action passages. In addition, he can write music to bridge awkward or abrupt shifts from one sequence of scenes to the next.

Generally, a composer can write a motion picture score in three to six weeks. But if music runs throughout the film, it may take him considerably longer. The composer writes the final score against a detailed, shot-by-shot—almost second-by-second—breakdown of the film. On the written score, the composer notes where dialogue begins and ends, where significant action occurs, and where screams or other important sounds

must be heard. A composer may write a magnificent score, but it will be a failure if the music drowns the dialogue or does not accent the film's visual high points.

When the score is ready to be recorded for the film, the studio's music department contacts the musicians' union, which supplies the necessary musicians. The music is then recorded. As the conductor leads the orchestra, he watches the film so that the music matches the action.

Dubbing. When we watch a motion picture, we hear the dialogue, music, and other sounds in the movie as they come through loudspeakers. All these sounds have been recorded along one side of the motion-picture film called the *sound track*. But this sound track is really a composite of dozens of separate sound tracks. For each different kind of sound in a movie, a separate track, or recording, is made. There are individual tracks for dialogue, for music, and for all special sounds, such as boat whistles, crowd noises, or forest fires. All these separate sound tracks are blended together through a complicated process called *dubbing* to make the composite sound track we hear in a movie.

Dubbing requires that the various sounds be balanced delicately against one another. For example, a scene may show two men whispering on a boat in a fog. The sounds would include their voices, the put-put of the boat's motor, the lapping of the water against the boat, and the moan of a distant foghorn. These sounds must be mixed so that none overpowers the others.

Dubbing takes place in a small projection room after editing is nearly completed. The producer, director, and at least three technicians called *mixers* participate in the dubbing sessions. The technicians sit behind a *sound console* and face the viewing screen. The console is a long desk with controls to *fade in* (switch on) and *fade out* (switch off) each sound and to regulate its volume. Each technician is responsible for certain sounds. He has a specially prepared script that tells at precisely

Recording the Music for a movie takes place in a special studio, *left*. The conductor leads the orchestra as he follows the film's action on the screen. In a control room, *above*, a technician supervises the recording of the music on magnetic tape. The composer, at his right, offers suggestions.

At a Dubbing Session, technicians called *mixers* blend the individual sound tracks for the dialogue, music, and sound effects onto a master tape. The mixers watch the screen action as they operate controls on their *sound console* to switch on and balance the various sounds.

what moment, as the film runs through the projector, each of his sounds must be faded in and out. All the sounds for each shot are thus blended onto a *master tape*. The tape is played back immediately after each shot. If the sounds are not perfectly balanced, the tape is erased and the dubbing repeated until the director, producer, and technicians are satisfied. This procedure continues until the master tape for the entire film is completed. The master tape is then used to produce the composite sound track.

The Sneak Preview. Before releasing their films to the theaters, many producers show them unannounced at *sneak previews*. At a preview, the new movie is shown in addition to the advertised feature. Preview audiences are asked to fill out cards that reveal their reactions to the film. These reactions influence the final editing of the movie. Preview audiences may complain that some scenes are boring or that they do not understand certain scenes. To overcome such criticisms, the film may be re-edited in many places. To tighten up the action, minor cuts may be made or entire scenes dropped. Previously discarded scenes may be restored to clarify points in the story that the audience may find confusing. After the movie has been tested in previews, the final editing is completed.

Publicity and Advertising can play an important part in making a movie a financial success. Publicity for a new picture begins with the announcement that a property has been acquired and continues through nearly every phase of production. At first, the studio publicity department handles the publicity campaign. It sends many stories to newspapers and radio and television stations on casting and other items that might be of interest.

As a film nears completion, the studio exploitation department takes over the publicity campaign. The exploitation department tries to stimulate the maximum amount of public interest in a picture just before its release. The department may recommend that an album of the film's music be issued. It may also arrange for the picture's stars, director, or producer to appear on TV interview shows. If the film is based on a book, the book may be reissued in paperback, with advertising for the film on the cover. Sometimes, a studio will employ an author outside the movie industry to write a novel based on an original screenplay. The novel is then published at the same time that the motion picture is released.

Meanwhile, the producer works closely with the studio advertising department on developing newspaper and, perhaps, television ads for the film. These ads try to capture the public's imagination and make people want to see the picture.

Releasing a Motion Picture. After the final editing has been completed and the advertising campaign approved, a motion picture is ready for release to the theaters. Most films open on a *first-run* basis in downtown theaters in major U.S. cities. Generally after a picture no longer attracts enough customers at a first-run theater, it is shown at *second-run* neighborhood theaters. The picture is also exhibited in smaller towns and, usually, in many other countries. The film may finally appear on television.

Unless a motion picture is remarkably popular, it will be exhibited on a large scale in the United States for only a few months. During this brief time, public response largely determines whether the picture makes a profit.

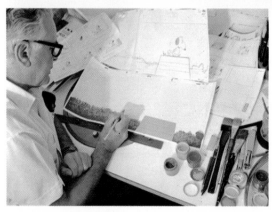

The Storyboard on the wall, *left,* is a series of drawings that portrays the action and gives the dialogue for an animated movie. The music for the film, *above,* is carefully timed so it matches each sequence of action on the storyboard.

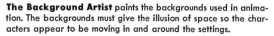

The Background Artist paints the backgrounds used in animation. The backgrounds must give the illusion of space so the characters appear to be moving in and around the settings.

The Animator draws the characters. He must create a series of drawings for each movement made by a character. He must also match each character's actions to the dialogue and sound effects.

Animation is the technique of making motion-picture cartoons from a series of drawings. A feature-length animated movie may require a million separate drawings and take three years to complete.

The first step in making an animated movie is finding a story. Many animated films are made for children and are based on fairy tales and children's books. After a story has been selected, an artist-writer prepares a *storyboard,* which serves as the film's script. The storyboard resembles a giant comic strip. It consists of rough sketches that portray the action of the story, with the dialogue printed with each sketch.

After the director and other key personnel approve the storyboard, the music and dialogue are recorded.

The photographs in this section were taken for WORLD BOOK *at Bill Melendez Productions in Los Angeles by John Hamilton, Globe Photos.*

The composer carefully follows the storyboard to make sure his music matches each sequence of the action.

Layout artists then work with the director to determine what settings will be drawn, how each character will act and look, and how the story can best be broken into scenes. After these decisions have been made, the layout artists prepare drawings to guide two other groups of artists—*background artists* and *animators.*

The background artists draw all the backgrounds for the film. Backgrounds include everything that will appear on the screen except the characters. The animators make separate drawings of the characters. They work from a *timing chart,* which indicates the number of *frames* (separate pictures) needed to express each word of the recorded dialogue. The animators must create the exact number of drawings required by the dialogue. In one episode, for example, a character may answer the phone by saying "Hello." The timing chart shows

The Animator's Drawings are traced in black ink onto sheets of transparent celluloid called *cels, above.* Other artists then paint on the reverse side of the cels all the colors needed for each character's clothes, hair, and skin, *right.*

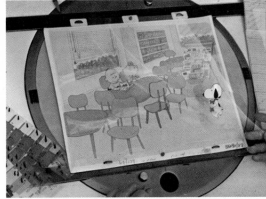

The Completed Cels are assembled over the proper backgrounds. The cels shown above are from a movie about the characters in the comic strip "Peanuts." At the left, a technician places a cel of Charlie Brown over a background showing the inside of a library. At the right, she adds a cel of Snoopy.

that the word "Hello" requires eight frames. The animator thus must make eight drawings in which the character's mouth moves in sequence to form the word. He must also include all the character's body movements.

After the animators complete their drawings, another group of artists traces them onto sheets of transparent celluloid called *cels.* The cels are then sent to the painting department, where the proper colors are applied to the reverse side of the cels.

Technicians collect the completed cels and sort them into scenes. The cels and backgrounds are then sent to the camera department, where the cels are photographed frame by frame over the proper background. An *exposure sheet* tells the camera operator what cels and background he needs for each frame. After the photography is completed, the sound track is added. Prints of the film are then made, and the picture is released.

Cels and Backgrounds Are Photographed one frame at a time with a special camera. The *exposure sheet* at the cameraman's left tells him what background and cels he needs for each frame.

A 35-MILLIMETER MOTION-PICTURE CAMERA

A soundproof cover called a *blimp* prevents noise made by the camera from reaching the microphone. The blimp houses two reels. The *supply reel* holds the unexposed film. As the film moves through the camera, it is exposed by light entering through the lens. The exposed film winds onto the *take-up reel*. Controls on the camera are used to focus the lens and change the camera's position.

Mitchell Camera Corp.

Blimp

Lens

Eyepiece for seeing through lens

MITCHELL

Knobs for focusing

Wheels to control horizontal and vertical camera movement

The Shutter controls the length of time that light strikes the film. When the shutter is open, light travels through the lens and an opening called the *aperture* onto the unexposed film. A register pin holds the film motionless until one frame has been exposed. The pin then withdraws, and the shutter closes. A claw is next inserted into the sprocket holes. It pulls the film to the next frame. This cycle is repeated 24 times a second.

When we watch a motion picture, we are actually seeing many thousands of separate still pictures. In each picture, the position of the subject is slightly different. Each picture is flashed on the screen for a fraction of a second, but we do not see the separate pictures. Instead, we see smooth, continuous movement because of a condition of the eye called *persistence of vision*. For example, when the eye sees an object under a bright light, the visual image of that object will persist for one-tenth of a second after the light has been turned off. In this way, each picture on the motion-picture screen is presented to the eye before the preceding image has faded out. See EYE (Persistence of Vision).

The Camera used to take motion pictures operates much like a still camera. In both cameras, light from objects enters through a lens and exposes the film. But a motion-picture camera takes pictures at a much faster rate.

The movie camera performs a number of precise operations to produce the series of pictures, or frames, that appear on the exposed film. As the camera photographs a subject, it repeatedly stops and starts the film and opens and closes the shutter. The shutter regulates

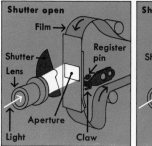
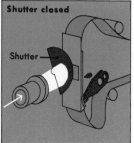

Shutter open

Film

Register pin

Shutter Lens

Aperture

Light

Claw

Shutter closed

Shutter

PHOTOGRAPHING A SOUND TRACK ON FILM

The sound track is photographed on film by a beam of light, shown in white. The beam shines from a recording lamp through a lens, which shapes it into a wedge, shown in brown. The wedge shines on a mirror vibrating from electrical impulses produced by the master tape recording of the sound track. As the mirror vibrates, it moves the wedge up and down across a slit in another lens. This action exposes a pattern of light on the film. The pattern is converted into sound when the film is run through a projector.

A 35-MILLIMETER COMPOSITE PRINT

The composite print carries both the sound track and the pictures. A narrow black band separates each frame. When the movie is projected on the screen at the proper speed, the bands are not seen and the action appears continuous. The composite print shown here has two identical sound tracks side by side. The use of two tracks improves the quality of sound reproduction.

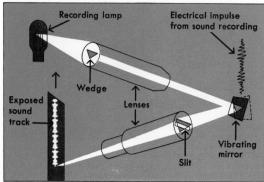

Recording lamp

Electrical impulse from sound recording

Wedge

Exposed sound track

Lenses

Vibrating mirror

Slit

WORLD BOOK diagrams by Mas Nakagawa

Frame

Sound track

Sprocket hole

Universal Studios

A 35-MILLIMETER PROJECTOR

The projector shines a beam of light from the lamphouse through the film as it moves through the projection unit. The soundhead helps convert the sound track into amplified sound.

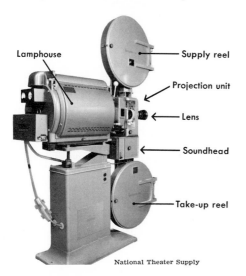

Lamphouse

Supply reel

Projection unit

Lens

Soundhead

Take-up reel

National Theater Supply

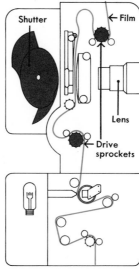

Shutter

Film

Lens

Drive sprockets

The Movement of Film through the projector is controlled by drive sprockets. Teeth in the sprockets fit into the film's sprocket holes and pull the film through the projector. As the film moves past the shutter, it is stopped and started repeatedly. This is called *intermittent movement*. After passing through the projection unit, the film runs through the soundhead without interruption. This is called *continuous movement*. The loops of film near the sprockets help maintain an even flow of film from intermittent movement to continuous movement.

HOW LIGHT TRAVELS THROUGH A PROJECTOR

A powerful bulb shines an intense light onto a metal reflector in the lamphouse. This light is concentrated into a beam. A revolving shutter controls the passage of the beam through the projection unit. When a frame of film is in position between the aperture and the lens, the shutter opens. The beam shines through the film and projects the picture onto the screen. The shutter then closes and cuts off the beam while the film advances to the next frame.

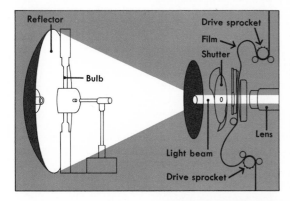

Reflector

Drive sprocket

Film

Shutter

Bulb

Lens

Light beam

Drive sprocket

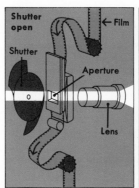

Shutter open

Film

Shutter

Aperture

Lens

Shutter closed

Shutter

SOUND REPRODUCTION IN A THEATER

Light from an exciter lamp is concentrated into a beam in a photocell. The beam shines through the sound track and strikes a solar cell. The solar cell converts the beam into electrical impulses. These impulses are strengthened by an amplifier. Finally, the strengthened impulses are changed into sound waves in a speaker behind the screen.

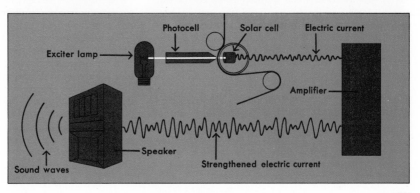

Photocell

Solar cell

Electric current

Exciter lamp

Amplifier

Speaker

Sound waves

Strengthened electric current

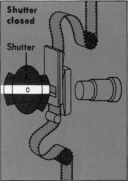

the length of time that the light strikes the film. When the shutter is open, the film is motionless and light passes through the lens and exposes a frame. The shutter then closes, and a device called a *claw* is inserted into small, evenly spaced *sprocket holes* along each edge of the film. Using the holes, the claw pulls the film forward to the next frame. The shutter opens, and light passing through the lens exposes the motionless frame. This cycle is repeated 24 times a second.

Film for motion pictures is a flexible strip of celluloid coated with chemicals that are sensitive to light. Both black-and-white and color film can be used in a standard motion-picture camera. Motion-picture film is made in several standard widths, which are expressed in millimeters. Film widths for movies shown in theaters are either 35 millimeters (about $1\frac{3}{8}$ inches) or 70 millimeters (about $2\frac{3}{4}$ inches). Most film for use in schools is 16 millimeters (about $\frac{5}{8}$ of an inch). Most cameras used to take home movies use 8-millimeter film, which is a little more than $\frac{1}{4}$ of an inch wide.

Sound in a motion picture is recorded on a narrow band along one side of the film called the *sound track*. During the production of a movie, the dialogue, music, and sound effects are first recorded on separate magnetic tapes. These tapes are carefully blended onto a composite master tape through a process called *dubbing*. To learn about the process, see the section of this article *How a Motion Picture Is Made (Dubbing)*. This master tape is then recorded on the exposed film, making a complete sound and picture print. As the film passes through the projector, the sound track is converted into the sounds we hear in the theater.

The Projector flashes the exposed frames of film onto the screen. Inside the projector, drive sprockets pull the film past a powerful beam of light.

The projector, like the camera, stops and starts the film 24 times each second. Each time the projector stops the film, a revolving shutter opens and a frame is flashed on the screen. While the film moves to the next frame, the shutter revolves and shuts out the light from the beam. The viewer's persistence of vision fills in the periods of darkness, making the action appear continuous. In reality, the screen is dark for a longer period of time than it is lit. If the images were projected continuously rather than as separate frames, the viewer would see the motion picture as a blur on the screen.

The Screen used in movie theaters has a highly reflective surface that gives a clear picture with bright colors. The screen may be covered with tiny beads of glass or painted with titanium dioxide or a mixture of white lead and white zinc. The speakers are placed behind the screen so that the sound seems to come from the picture itself. There are 20 to 40 holes in each square inch of the screen to allow the sound to project through.

MOTION PICTURE / The Motion-Picture Industry

Movies are a billion-dollar industry in the United States. Americans pay more than $1\frac{1}{4}$ billion yearly to see movies. The payroll for people working in the industry amounts to over $1 billion a year. Motion-picture theater buildings in the United States are valued at more than $2\frac{1}{2}$ billion.

The motion-picture industry is divided into three branches—production, distribution, and exhibition. This section deals with distribution and exhibition. It also discusses attempts by government and private organizations to censor movies and the industry's attempts at self-regulation. The section ends with a discussion of motion-picture festivals and awards. For information on motion-picture production, see the section *How a Motion Picture Is Made*.

Distribution and Exhibition. From about 1915 to the late 1940's, the Hollywood studios controlled the three major branches of the American motion-picture industry. The studios not only made the movies, but they also distributed them to the theaters, most of which they owned. In the late 1940's, the Supreme Court of the United States ruled that studio control over production, distribution, and exhibition was an unfair monopoly. The court ordered the studios to give up any one of the three functions. The studios chose to give up their role as exhibitors, and by 1952 they had sold all their theaters.

During the late 1940's, the studios also began to cut their production of new films, partly because of competition from television. The studios discovered that, in most cases, they could earn more money distributing movies made by independent producers than by making and distributing their own pictures. Today, studios receive a large part of their income from distribution activities. In addition to the studios, there are also many distributing companies that specialize in renting films to theaters.

The distributor charges the film's producer a fee of 30 to 50 per cent of all the money the film takes in. A new producer may have to pay a larger fee to attract a distributor than does an established producer with a record of profitable films. The distributor also charges for making the copies of the film sent to the theaters. In addition, he charges for advertising and publicizing the film. The costs of copying the film, advertising, and publicity come out of the first money the film takes in. The producer receives money only after these costs and the distribution fees have been deducted. The distributor can thus make a profit on a picture, while the film's producer may earn nothing.

Theater owners place bids with distributors for the films they want to exhibit. The decrease in the number of films produced has forced exhibitors to bid higher and higher against one another for the right to rent desirable films. To recover the ever-increasing cost of rentals, exhibitors have raised ticket prices. The higher prices have helped make the public very selective in its moviegoing. As a result of the high prices and competition from TV, movie attendance has dropped sharply. In the United States, about 90 million persons attended the movies weekly during the late 1940's. By the late 1960's, the figure had dropped to less than 30 million persons a week. During the same period, the number of theaters declined from about 17,000 to about 10,000, including drive-ins.

Censorship and Self-Regulation. During the first half of the 1900's, several state and local governments had censorship boards that reviewed all movies before they could be shown in their areas. Some civic and religious groups also had censorship boards that advised members whether they believed a movie to be offensive. The censors were concerned largely with what they considered an objectionable emphasis on sex. The government boards could ban a picture from being shown in their city or state. Attacks by private censorship groups could affect a film's chance of succeeding at the box office.

Censorship remained an important factor in the American movie industry until the 1950's. Beginning in 1952, the Supreme Court made a series of decisions that eliminated the legal reasons that permitted local and

The Academy Awards are given annually for outstanding achievements in film making. Here, actress Greer Garson presents Humphrey Bogart with the 1951 award for best actor.

United Press Int.

ACADEMY AWARD WINNERS

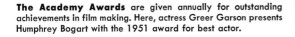

BEST PICTURE

1927-28	Wings	1942	Mrs. Miniver	1957	The Bridge on the River Kwai
1928-29	The Broadway Melody	1943	Casablanca	1958	Gigi
1929-30	All Quiet on the Western Front	1944	Going My Way	1959	Ben-Hur
		1945	The Lost Weekend	1960	The Apartment
1930-31	Cimarron	1946	The Best Years of Our Lives	1961	West Side Story
1931-32	Grand Hotel	1947	Gentleman's Agreement	1962	Lawrence of Arabia
1932-33	Cavalcade	1948	Hamlet	1963	Tom Jones
1934	It Happened One Night	1949	All the King's Men	1964	My Fair Lady
1935	Mutiny on the Bounty	1950	All About Eve	1965	The Sound of Music
1936	The Great Ziegfeld	1951	An American in Paris	1966	A Man for All Seasons
1937	The Life of Émile Zola	1952	The Greatest Show on Earth	1967	In the Heat of the Night
1938	You Can't Take It with You	1953	From Here to Eternity	1968	Oliver!
1939	Gone with the Wind	1954	On the Waterfront	1969	Midnight Cowboy
1940	Rebecca	1955	Marty	1970	Patton
1941	How Green Was My Valley	1956	Around the World in 80 Days		

BEST DIRECTOR

1927-28	Frank Borzage (Seventh Heaven), Lewis Milestone (Two Arabian Knights)	1950	Joseph L. Mankiewicz (All About Eve)
1928-29	Frank Lloyd (The Divine Lady)	1951	George Stevens (A Place in the Sun)
1929-30	Lewis Milestone (All Quiet on the Western Front)	1952	John Ford (The Quiet Man)
1930-31	Norman Taurog (Skippy)	1953	Fred Zinnemann (From Here to Eternity)
1931-32	Frank Borzage (Bad Girl)	1954	Elia Kazan (On the Waterfront)
1932-33	Frank Lloyd (Cavalcade)	1955	Delbert Mann (Marty)
1934	Frank Capra (It Happened One Night)	1956	George Stevens (Giant)
1935	John Ford (The Informer)	1957	David Lean (The Bridge on the River Kwai)
1936	Frank Capra (Mr. Deeds Goes to Town)	1958	Vincente Minnelli (Gigi)
1937	Leo McCarey (The Awful Truth)	1959	William Wyler (Ben-Hur)
1938	Frank Capra (You Can't Take It with You)	1960	Billy Wilder (The Apartment)
1939	Victor Fleming (Gone with the Wind)	1961	Robert Wise and Jerome Robbins (West Side Story)
1940	John Ford (The Grapes of Wrath)		
1941	John Ford (How Green Was My Valley)	1962	David Lean (Lawrence of Arabia)
1942	William Wyler (Mrs. Miniver)	1963	Tony Richardson (Tom Jones)
1943	Michael Curtiz (Casablanca)	1964	George Cukor (My Fair Lady)
1944	Leo McCarey (Going My Way)	1965	Robert Wise (The Sound of Music)
1945	Billy Wilder (The Lost Weekend)	1966	Fred Zinnemann (A Man for All Seasons)
1946	William Wyler (The Best Years of Our Lives)	1967	Mike Nichols (The Graduate)
1947	Elia Kazan (Gentleman's Agreement)	1968	Sir Carol Reed (Oliver!)
1948	John Huston (The Treasure of Sierra Madre)	1969	John Schlesinger (Midnight Cowboy)
1949	Joseph L. Mankiewicz (A Letter to Three Wives)	1970	Franklin J. Schaffner (Patton)

state boards to function. In 1965, the last strong state censorship board—that of New York State—went out of existence. Some private censorship groups still exist, but they have less influence than such groups had earlier in the 1900's.

The movie industry's efforts to regulate itself date back to 1922, when the studios established the Motion Picture Producers and Distributors of America. This organization reviewed scripts before filming began, attempting to catch and delete material it felt might be considered offensive.

In 1945, the organization became the Motion Picture Association of America. In 1968, the association adopted a classification system. Instead of reviewing scripts before production, the association rates the completed film as to its suitability for various age groups. The association classifies films into four categories: *G*—general, all ages admitted; *GP*—general, all ages admitted, but parental guidance suggested; *R*—restricted, persons under the age of 17 must be accompanied by a parent or guardian; *X*—no one under the age of 17 admitted (the age may vary in different parts of the United States).

Festivals and Awards. The first film festival opened in Venice, Italy, in 1932. Today, hundreds of festivals are held every year in Europe, North America, and South America. The best-known festivals include those in Cannes, France; London; Moscow; New York City; and San Sebastián, Spain. Many festivals show new feature pictures and give prizes for the best pictures and

--- BEST ACTOR ---

1927-28	Emil Jannings (*The Way of All Flesh, The Last Command*)	1948	Laurence Olivier (*Hamlet*)
1928-29	Warner Baxter (*In Old Arizona*)	1949	Broderick Crawford (*All the King's Men*)
1929-30	George Arliss (*Disraeli*)	1950	José Ferrer (*Cyrano de Bergerac*)
1930-31	Lionel Barrymore (*A Free Soul*)	1951	Humphrey Bogart (*The African Queen*)
1931-32	Fredric March (*Dr. Jekyll and Mr. Hyde*), Wallace Beery (*The Champ*)	1952	Gary Cooper (*High Noon*)
		1953	William Holden (*Stalag 17*)
1932-33	Charles Laughton (*The Private Life of Henry VIII*)	1954	Marlon Brando (*On the Waterfront*)
		1955	Ernest Borgnine (*Marty*)
1934	Clark Gable (*It Happened One Night*)	1956	Yul Brynner (*The King and I*)
1935	Victor McLaglen (*The Informer*)	1957	Alec Guinness (*The Bridge on the River Kwai*)
1936	Paul Muni (*The Story of Louis Pasteur*)	1958	David Niven (*Separate Tables*)
1937	Spencer Tracy (*Captains Courageous*)	1959	Charlton Heston (*Ben-Hur*)
1938	Spencer Tracy (*Boys Town*)	1960	Burt Lancaster (*Elmer Gantry*)
1939	Robert Donat (*Goodbye, Mr. Chips*)	1961	Maximilian Schell (*Judgment at Nuremberg*)
1940	James Stewart (*The Philadelphia Story*)	1962	Gregory Peck (*To Kill a Mockingbird*)
1941	Gary Cooper (*Sergeant York*)	1963	Sidney Poitier (*Lilies of the Field*)
1942	James Cagney (*Yankee Doodle Dandy*)	1964	Rex Harrison (*My Fair Lady*)
1943	Paul Lukas (*Watch on the Rhine*)	1965	Lee Marvin (*Cat Ballou*)
1944	Bing Crosby (*Going My Way*)	1966	Paul Scofield (*A Man for All Seasons*)
1945	Ray Milland (*The Lost Weekend*)	1967	Rod Steiger (*In the Heat of the Night*)
1946	Fredric March (*The Best Years of Our Lives*)	1968	Cliff Robertson (*Charly*)
1947	Ronald Colman (*A Double Life*)	1969	John Wayne (*True Grit*)
		1970	George C. Scott (*Patton*)

--- BEST ACTRESS ---

1927-28	Janet Gaynor (*Seventh Heaven, Street Angel, Sunrise*)	1951	Vivien Leigh (*A Streetcar Named Desire*)
		1952	Shirley Booth (*Come Back Little Sheba*)
1928-29	Mary Pickford (*Coquette*)	1953	Audrey Hepburn (*Roman Holiday*)
1929-30	Norma Shearer (*The Divorcee*)	1954	Grace Kelly (*The Country Girl*)
1930-31	Marie Dressler (*Min and Bill*)	1955	Anna Magnani (*The Rose Tattoo*)
1931-32	Helen Hayes (*The Sin of Madelon Claudet*)	1956	Ingrid Bergman (*Anastasia*)
1932-33	Katharine Hepburn (*Morning Glory*)	1957	Joanne Woodward (*The Three Faces of Eve*)
1934	Claudette Colbert (*It Happened One Night*)	1958	Susan Hayward (*I Want to Live!*)
1935	Bette Davis (*Dangerous*)	1959	Simone Signoret (*Room at the Top*)
1936	Luise Rainer (*The Great Ziegfeld*)	1960	Elizabeth Taylor (*Butterfield 8*)
1937	Luise Rainer (*The Good Earth*)	1961	Sophia Loren (*Two Women*)
1938	Bette Davis (*Jezebel*)	1962	Anne Bancroft (*The Miracle Worker*)
1939	Vivien Leigh (*Gone with the Wind*)	1963	Patricia Neal (*Hud*)
1940	Ginger Rogers (*Kitty Foyle*)	1964	Julie Andrews (*Mary Poppins*)
1941	Joan Fontaine (*Suspicion*)	1965	Julie Christie (*Darling*)
1942	Greer Garson (*Mrs. Miniver*)	1966	Elizabeth Taylor (*Who's Afraid of Virginia Woolf?*)
1943	Jennifer Jones (*The Song of Bernadette*)	1967	Katharine Hepburn (*Guess Who's Coming to Dinner*)
1944	Ingrid Bergman (*Gaslight*)		
1945	Joan Crawford (*Mildred Pierce*)		
1946	Olivia de Havilland (*To Each His Own*)	1968	Katharine Hepburn (*The Lion in Winter*), Barbra Streisand (*Funny Girl*)
1947	Loretta Young (*The Farmer's Daughter*)		
1948	Jane Wyman (*Johnny Belinda*)	1969	Maggie Smith (*The Prime of Miss Jean Brodie*)
1949	Olivia de Havilland (*The Heiress*)	1970	Glenda Jackson (*Women in Love*)
1950	Judy Holliday (*Born Yesterday*)		

the best performances. Some festivals specialize in a particular kind of film, such as cartoons.

Many cities hold film festivals primarily to attract tourists. But the festivals also serve as a kind of international fair for distributors looking for profitable new films. In addition, the festivals give critics and film students an opportunity to learn what is happening in motion pictures around the world. The London and New York City festivals are especially popular with critics and students. Both festivals are held in autumn. They show the best motion pictures that appeared at other festivals earlier in the year.

A number of organizations make film awards. The best-known awards are made each spring by the Academy of Motion Picture Arts and Sciences. These awards, called the *Academy Awards* or *Oscars*, are presented for outstanding achievements in film making during the preceding year.

Glamorous Stars help make the Academy Awards an exciting event. Burt Lancaster and Elizabeth Taylor won the 1960 Oscars, as the statuettes are called, for best actor and best actress.

Academy of Motion Picture Arts and Sciences

——— BEST SUPPORTING ACTOR ———	——— BEST SUPPORTING ACTRESS ———
1927-28 No Award	**1927-28** No Award
1928-29 No Award	**1928-29** No Award
1929-30 No Award	**1929-30** No Award
1930-31 No Award	**1930-31** No Award
1931-32 No Award	**1931-32** No Award
1932-33 No Award	**1932-33** No Award
1934 No Award	**1934** No Award
1935 No Award	**1935** No Award
1936 Walter Brennan (*Come and Get It*)	**1936** Gale Sondergaard (*Anthony Adverse*)
1937 Joseph Schildkraut (*The Life of Émile Zola*)	**1937** Alice Brady (*In Old Chicago*)
1938 Walter Brennan (*Kentucky*)	**1938** Fay Bainter (*Jezebel*)
1939 Thomas Mitchell (*Stagecoach*)	**1939** Hattie McDaniel (*Gone with the Wind*)
1940 Walter Brennan (*The Westerner*)	**1940** Jane Darwell (*The Grapes of Wrath*)
1941 Donald Crisp (*How Green Was My Valley*)	**1941** Mary Astor (*The Great Lie*)
1942 Van Heflin (*Johnny Eager*)	**1942** Teresa Wright (*Mrs. Miniver*)
1943 Charles Coburn (*The More the Merrier*)	**1943** Katina Paxinou (*For Whom the Bell Tolls*)
1944 Barry Fitzgerald (*Going My Way*)	**1944** Ethel Barrymore (*None But the Lonely Heart*)
1945 James Dunn (*A Tree Grows in Brooklyn*)	**1945** Anne Revere (*National Velvet*)
1946 Harold Russell (*The Best Years of Our Lives*)	**1946** Anne Baxter (*The Razor's Edge*)
1947 Edmund Gwenn (*Miracle on 34th Street*)	**1947** Celeste Holm (*Gentleman's Agreement*)
1948 Walter Huston (*The Treasure of Sierra Madre*)	**1948** Claire Trevor (*Key Largo*)
1949 Dean Jagger (*Twelve O'Clock High*)	**1949** Mercedes McCambridge (*All the King's Men*)
1950 George Sanders (*All About Eve*)	**1950** Josephine Hull (*Harvey*)
1951 Karl Malden (*A Streetcar Named Desire*)	**1951** Kim Hunter (*A Streetcar Named Desire*)
1952 Anthony Quinn (*Viva Zapata!*)	**1952** Gloria Grahame (*The Bad and the Beautiful*)
1953 Frank Sinatra (*From Here to Eternity*)	**1953** Donna Reed (*From Here to Eternity*)
1954 Edmond O'Brien (*The Barefoot Contessa*)	**1954** Eva Marie Saint (*On the Waterfront*)
1955 Jack Lemmon (*Mister Roberts*)	**1955** Jo Van Fleet (*East of Eden*)
1956 Anthony Quinn (*Lust for Life*)	**1956** Dorothy Malone (*Written on the Wind*)
1957 Red Buttons (*Sayonara*)	**1957** Miyoshi Umeki (*Sayonara*)
1958 Burl Ives (*The Big Country*)	**1958** Wendy Hiller (*Separate Tables*)
1959 Hugh Griffith (*Ben-Hur*)	**1959** Shelley Winters (*The Diary of Anne Frank*)
1960 Peter Ustinov (*Spartacus*)	**1960** Shirley Jones (*Elmer Gantry*)
1961 George Chakiris (*West Side Story*)	**1961** Rita Moreno (*West Side Story*)
1962 Ed Begley (*Sweet Bird of Youth*)	**1962** Patty Duke (*The Miracle Worker*)
1963 Melvyn Douglas (*Hud*)	**1963** Margaret Rutherford (*The V.I.P.'s*)
1964 Peter Ustinov (*Topkapi*)	**1964** Lila Kedrova (*Zorba the Greek*)
1965 Martin Balsam (*A Thousand Clowns*)	**1965** Shelley Winters (*A Patch of Blue*)
1966 Walter Matthau (*The Fortune Cookie*)	**1966** Sandy Dennis (*Who's Afraid of Virginia Woolf?*)
1967 George Kennedy (*Cool Hand Luke*)	**1967** Estelle Parsons (*Bonnie and Clyde*)
1968 Jack Albertson (*The Subject Was Roses*)	**1968** Ruth Gordon (*Rosemary's Baby*)
1969 Gig Young (*They Shoot Horses, Don't They?*)	**1969** Goldie Hawn (*Cactus Flower*)
1970 John Mills (*Ryan's Daughter*)	**1970** Helen Hayes (*Airport*)

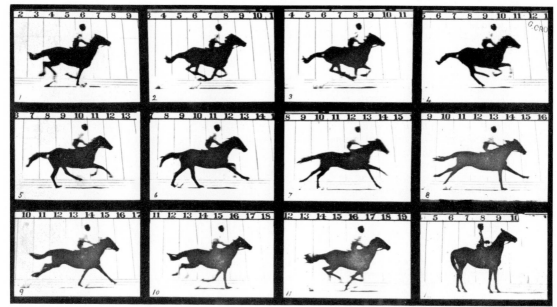

The First Successful Photographs of Motion were pictures of a horse. Eadweard Muybridge, a San Francisco photographer, took the pictures in the 1870's using 24 still cameras.

The idea of portraying things in motion has interested man since earliest times. In paintings in Altamira Cave in Spain, prehistoric artists tried to show animals running by painting them with many legs. Ancient Egyptian and Greek bas-reliefs portray figures in the act of moving.

About 65 B.C., the Roman poet Lucretius discovered the principle of the persistence of vision. About 200 years later, the Egyptian astronomer Ptolemy experimentally proved the principle.

During the 1800's, many men experimented with devices that would make pictures appear to move. In 1832, Joseph Antoine Ferdinand Plateau, a Belgian scientist, developed the *phenakistoscope*, the first device that gave pictures the illusion of movement. Plateau placed two disks a few inches apart along a rod. He painted pictures of an object or a person along the edge of one disk. Each picture slightly advanced the subject's position. Slots were cut in the other disk. When both disks were rotated at the same speed, the pictures seemed to move as they came into view in the slots.

The first successful photography of motion took place in 1877 and 1878, when Eadweard Muybridge, a San Francisco photographer, made instantaneous photos of a running horse. Muybridge set up 24 cameras in a row, with strings stretched across a race track to the shutter of each camera. When the horse ran by, it broke each string in succession, tripping the shutters.

The Invention of Motion Pictures. During the late 1800's, inventors in France, Great Britain, and the United States tried to find ways to make and project motion pictures. These experimenters included Thomas Armat, Thomas A. Edison, Charles F. Jenkins, and Woodville Latham of the United States; William Friese-Greene and Robert W. Paul of Great Britain; and the brothers Louis and Auguste Lumière and Étienne Jules Marey of France. After many failures, success came to several pioneers at about the same time. No one knows who first produced and projected movies.

In 1887, Edison began work on a device to make pictures appear to move. He succeeded in 1889, after Hannibal W. Goodwin, an American clergyman, had developed a transparent celluloid film base that was tough but flexible. This base could hold a coating, or *film*, of chemicals sensitive to light. A series of pictures could be photographed on the film and moved rapidly through a camera. Previously, most photographs were taken on glass plates that had to be changed after each exposure. George Eastman, a pioneer in making photographic equipment, manufactured the film.

Using the Eastman film, Edison or his assistant William Kennedy Laurie Dickson invented the *kinetoscope*. Historians are not sure which man invented the device. The kinetoscope was a cabinet in which 50 feet of film revolved on spools. A person looked through a peephole in the cabinet to watch the pictures move.

In 1894, Edison opened the Kinetoscope Parlor in New York City. The parlor had two rows of coin-operated kinetoscopes. The kinetoscope also appeared in London and Paris in 1894. In spite of the kinetoscope's success, Edison believed that moving pictures were only of passing interest. However, other inventors in the United States and Europe disagreed. Using the principles of the kinetoscope, they developed improved cameras and projection equipment.

Motion pictures were projected on a screen publicly for the first time on Dec. 28, 1895. In a Paris café, the Lumière brothers showed some simple scenes, including that of a train arriving at a station. Within a few months, movies were being shown in all the major cities of Europe.

Edison finally recognized that motion pictures had commercial possibilities and adapted a projector invented by Armat. Using this device, which he called the *projecting kinetoscope*, Edison presented the first public exhibition of motion pictures projected on a screen in the United States. The exhibition took place at Koster and Bial's Music Hall in New York City on April 23, 1896. The program included a few scenes from a prize fight, a performance by a dancer, and scenes of waves rolling onto a beach.

Early Motion Pictures. Pioneer film makers recognized that movies gave them an opportunity to record people and objects in vivid motion. They photographed crowds, horses, parades, waterfalls, and almost anything

else that moved. By 1900, motion pictures had become a popular attraction in amusement arcades, music halls, traveling fairs, wax museums, and vaudeville theaters in many countries.

Film makers throughout the world adopted 35 millimeters as the standard size for movie film. Thus, a movie made in one country could be used in projectors in all other countries. Language differences presented no problem either. Until the late 1920's, movies were silent. That is, no sound came from the motion picture. The film makers inserted *titles*—printed dialogue and descriptions of action—into the film at appropriate places between scenes. To convert a film into another language, the original titles were simply cut out and translated titles were inserted.

At first, movies flourished simply because they were a novelty. The sense of reality particularly impressed audiences. When the screen showed ocean waves breaking on the shore, women raised their skirts to keep them dry. But audiences soon recognized that the motion picture's sense of realism was merely an illusion. They became bored, attendance declined, and the motion picture faced extinction.

The Movies Tell Stories. One development saved movies from extinction—they began to tell stories. As early as 1899, a French magician named Georges Méliès arranged short filmed scenes into a storytelling sequence. Méliès filmed hundreds of charming fairy tales and science fiction stories. He wrote and directed his films, acted in them, and designed the settings. Méliès thus became the film industry's first artist.

Edwin S. Porter, an American director, made the first motion pictures using modern film techniques to tell a story. Porter's most important film was *The Great Train Robbery* (1903), an 11-minute movie describing

The First Important Movie was *The Great Train Robbery, above,* directed by Edwin S. Porter in 1903. The movie described a train robbery and the pursuit and capture of the bandits. Porter was the first director to use modern motion-picture techniques to tell a story.

Bettmann Archive

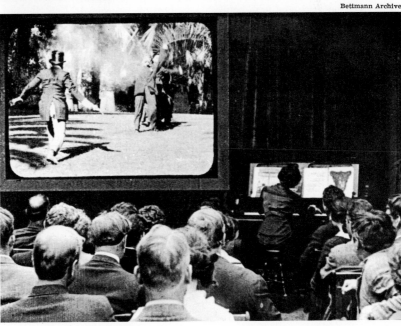

The First Movie Theaters were called *nickelodeons, right.* Most were stores converted into theaters by adding chairs. The nickelodeons charged 5 cents. They showed silent movies, while a pianist played music that suited the action on the screen.

The Birth of a Nation, directed by D. W. Griffith, was the first motion-picture epic. The film dealt with the American Civil War and the period that followed. The movie was particularly famous for its spectacular battle scenes. A cameraman can be seen at the lower left.

a train robbery and the pursuit and capture of the robbers.

Porter was perhaps the first director to recognize that a motion picture need not be filmed in the strict sequence of the action. The story of *The Great Train Robbery* switches back and forth between a number of settings, and so Porter realized it was impractical to shoot the story in sequence. Instead, he filmed all the scenes for each setting at one time and later edited the individual shots into an understandable story. Porter also created suspense by alternating scenes of the robbers escaping with scenes of a posse being formed to catch them. Porter's pioneer work in filming and editing set the standard for directors throughout the world for several years.

The Nickelodeon. *The Great Train Robbery* was a tremendous hit at music halls, vaudeville houses, and wherever else it was shown. The film's success led to the establishment of *nickelodeons*—the first motion-picture theaters. Most nickelodeons were stores converted into primitive theaters by the addition of chairs. The nickelodeons charged 5 cents and showed a variety of films accompanied by piano music. Audiences consisted mainly of laborers, many of them immigrants who could not read and write.

By 1907, there were about 5,000 nickelodeons throughout the United States. The sudden growth of the nickelodeon increased the demand for motion pictures. Many studios were formed to produce movies to satisfy this demand.

The Birth of Hollywood. During the first years of the 1900's, most movies were made in New York City and in Fort Lee, N.J. But film makers soon realized that the Los Angeles area had a climate and a variety of natural scenery especially well suited to making movies. In 1907, the first movie was made in Los Angeles. In 1911, the Nestor Company built the first studio in a district of Los Angeles called Hollywood. Within a few years, more studios were built and Hollywood became the motion-picture capital of the world.

D. W. Griffith. Many film historians credit D. W. Griffith, an American director, with single-handedly creating the art of motion pictures. Between 1908 and 1913, Griffith directed hundreds of short films. In these films, Griffith developed basic film-making techniques still used today.

Before Griffith's time, directors always kept the camera in a fixed position when filming in the studio. The camera was placed about a dozen feet from the performing area and at a right angle to it. In that way, the camera could photograph all the action and there was never any need to rearrange the lighting. But Griffith cared more about making his films dramatic than about the cost of rearranging the lights. He moved the camera closer and closer to the actors until, finally, the entire screen might be filled with a close-up of a face, a hand, or a pistol. Griffith did not invent the close-up, but he was the first film maker to demonstrate how it could be used dramatically and expressively.

Griffith also introduced the use of additional camera angles. Until his time, all the action in a scene had been taken in a single shot from a single camera position. Griffith moved his camera around the playing area to maintain the center of attention as it shifted from one part of the scene to another. By photographing a single scene from several viewpoints, Griffith could mingle long shots with close-ups. This technique provided visual variety and permitted him to emphasize whatever was important in the scene.

The breaking up of scenes into several shots also led Griffith to improve editing techniques. Griffith discovered he could create tensions within a scene through the rhythm of his editing. For example, many short scenes in succession would create a feeling of great excitement. Griffith also learned that, through editing, he could flash backward in time or show what a character was dreaming or thinking.

In two masterpieces, *The Birth of a Nation* (1915) and *Intolerance* (1916), Griffith proved that the motion picture was a major art form. *The Birth of a Nation* was the screen's first epic. It attempted to re-create episodes in the American Civil War and the Reconstruction period that followed in the South. The action is seen through the eyes of two families—one Northern and one Southern. *Intolerance* was an even more ambitious film that wove together stories from four periods in history.

The Rise of Stars. The first motion-picture performers were not identified by name on the screen. In fact, some performers preferred to remain unknown because movie acting was considered degrading compared with acting on the stage. But starting in 1910, a few of the more popular personalities were identified by name. In 1910, the famous stage star Sarah Bernhardt appeared in a film version of one of her best-known plays, *The Lady of the Camellias*. Movie acting then quickly became respectable.

The American public soon singled out certain performers as special favorites. These performers were the first movie stars. The earliest stars included the cowboy actor Bronco Billy Anderson and the comedian John Bunny. Later stars of the silent films included Theda Bara, Charlie Chaplin, Douglas Fairbanks, William S. Hart, Buster Keaton, Mary Pickford, and Rudolph Valentino.

Mack Sennett and Silent Comedy. Mack Sennett, a Canadian, entered motion pictures in 1909 as a writer and actor at the Biograph Studio in New York City. By 1912, he had opened the Keystone Studio in Glendale, a Los Angeles suburb. In a short time, Sennett began producing a flood of wildly creative comedies. Nearly every major comic performer in American silent films worked at Keystone. They included Fatty Arbuckle, Charlie Chaplin, Charlie Chase, Marie Dressler, Harry Langdon, Harold Lloyd, Mabel Normand, and Gloria Swanson. Many of Sennett's films featured a group of oddly dressed policemen called the Keystone Cops.

In his comedies, Sennett made brilliant use of trick photography and an editing technique that placed special emphasis on precise timing. He would edit a scene so that a speeding train would just miss hitting an automobile by a split second. Sennett sometimes reversed the film so that the characters seemed to be moving backward. He also speeded up or slowed down the film to achieve comic effects. Sennett even combined animated cartoon characters with live actors. Keystone comedies raced along at such a swift pace that the audience had little opportunity to notice that the action defied the laws of logic and gravity.

Movies Become Big Business. By 1912, motion pictures had begun to move out of nickelodeons and into real theaters, many of which had been used for stage plays. Movies became longer and more expensive to make. Film makers tried to attract a new audience—the middle class, which had avoided movies as unworthy of their attention. Movie companies began to film popular novels and plays, and they hired the biggest names in the theater to star in them.

During World War I (1914-1918), motion-picture production almost stopped in Europe because of shortages of materials and power. But the European people demanded movies as never before to escape for a few hours from the burdens of war. They especially liked the cheerful, glamorous movies made in the United States. American studios moved into the rich European market, using the profits to make pictures that were bigger, better, and even more glamorous.

The ever-increasing demand for movies led the American motion-picture industry to adopt more efficient methods of production. Thomas H. Ince, owner of Thomas H. Ince Pictures, is credited with introducing mass-production methods to film making. At first, Ince directed all the pictures produced by his studio. But by 1915, studio production had grown to the point where it became physically impossible for Ince to direct every film personally. To guide his movies through production, Ince appointed a group of super-

From left to right, Louise Fazenda, Charlie Murray, and Ford Sterling in a scene from a 1917 Keystone comedy; Keystone Studio

Silent Comedies directed by Mack Sennett emphasized improbable and violent situations. Nearly all the important silent comedy stars worked for Sennett at his Keystone Studio.

visors called *producers*. Each producer was responsible directly to Ince, and each had control over a certain number of pictures.

Ince planned the production of each film systematically. He allowed a certain number of days for shooting on location and a certain number of days for shooting on the studio stages. Ince would have up to 10 or more pictures in various states of production at one time and so could rotate his movies through the studio facilities. In this way, he made full use of all his facilities all the time. Ince's "factory system" dominated Hollywood film making until the 1950's.

By the mid-1920's, most of the major Hollywood studios had been established. They included Columbia, Metro-Goldwyn-Mayer, Paramount, RKO, United Artists, Universal, and Warner Brothers. The heads of the major studios approved of Ince's system. The studio heads were businessmen, not artists. They cared chiefly about making profitable films, building chains of theaters to show their films, and further penetrating the worldwide market. The Ince system served them well in making money. But the system also restricted the creativity of the directors, who had to meet strict shooting schedules and thus could not experiment with new ideas. For this reason, much of the development of motion pictures as an art form during the 1920's took place in Europe.

New Techniques in Photography. Many of the most impressive motion pictures of the 1920's came from Germany. The German film makers became especially noted for their brilliant photographic techniques.

Almost all German movies of the 1920's were filmed entirely in huge, magnificently equipped studios in what is now East Berlin. All the sets—even if the script called for a modern street or a fortress on a rocky cliff—were built on gigantic stages. These elaborate studio facilities gave a director complete control over his picture. He could select his camera angles, place his lights, and arrange his actors without worrying about bad weather or other matters that often disrupt filming on location.

German directors preferred dark, moody backgrounds with the dramatic elements in a scene, such as an actor's face or hands, sharply lighted. The directors carefully arranged the performers and objects in each shot to achieve striking visual effects.

German directors introduced the *subjective* use of the camera—perhaps their greatest contribution to the art of motion pictures. Until about 1919, directors used the camera as a disinterested observer that looked at a scene or a character from the outside. However, the German directors wanted to express the inner emotional states of their characters and discovered they could do so by the imaginative use of the camera. As early as 1919, director Robert Wiene used unusual camera angles in *The Cabinet of Dr. Caligari* to suggest the world as seen by a madman. But the movie that revolutionized motion pictures through the creative use of the camera was *The Last Laugh* (1924), directed by F. W. Murnau.

The camera work in *The Last Laugh* is so expressive that the story is told entirely without titles. The film opens with a shot of the busy lobby of the Hotel Atlantic as seen from a descending elevator. The elevator gate opens, and the camera *dollies* (moves) across the lobby to the revolving doors of the entrance.

Emil Jannings in a scene from *The Last Laugh* (1924); Bettmann Archive

The Creative Use of the Camera by German film makers in the 1920's revolutionized the art of motion pictures. In *The Last Laugh*, director F. W. Murnau used expressive photography to capture a doorman's feeling of humiliation when he is transferred to the job of washroom attendant.

Outside the doors is an elderly doorman, played by the great German actor Emil Jannings.

The doorman, proudly strutting in his glamorous uniform, greets the arriving and departing guests. The camera takes a closer shot and looks up at the doorman's majestic figure. A few moments later, a taxi arrives with a large trunk on its roof. The doorman looks for a porter, finds none, and struggles to take down the trunk himself. This shot is taken from above, diminishing the figure of the doorman while emphasizing the weight of the trunk. The doorman, exhausted by his struggle, leaves his post to rest. The hotel manager sees him resting and transfers him to the humiliating position of washroom attendant.

Most of the remainder of the film shows how the man reacts in horror and shame to his loss of status at the hotel. During one famous scene, at a wedding party, he becomes drunk and collapses in a chair. The room is shown spinning around, reflecting the confusion and dizziness in the man's mind.

New Techniques in Editing. While German directors were developing more expressive use of the camera, Russian film makers were pioneering in new editing techniques. In their experimental editing, the Russians arranged different shots into different sequences and cut shots to different lengths. Their experiments led to a new kind of editing called *montage.*

About 1922, the Russian film maker Lev Kuleshov demonstrated the effectiveness of montage. He inserted a close-up shot of the expressionless face of an actor at various points in a film. He placed the close-up among shots of a bowl of soup, a dead woman, and a child with a teddy bear. Kuleshov then showed the film to an audience. The viewers believed the actor showed hunger at seeing the bowl of soup, grief at seeing the dead woman, and delight at seeing the child with the teddy bear. The demonstration proved that a director could suggest an emotion or an idea by arranging shots in a certain order.

The greatest Russian film director, teacher, and theorist was Sergei Eisenstein. His first film, *Strike* (1924), was so effective that the Russian government invited him to make a picture celebrating the 20th anniversary of an unsuccessful revolution in Russia in 1905. Eisenstein made *Potemkin* (1925), a motion picture based on a mutiny among the crew of the Russian battleship *Potemkin.* The film focused worldwide attention on Russian movies for the first time.

Potemkin shows Eisenstein's effective use of montage. In one shot, for example, soldiers fire their rifles. In the next shot, a woman clutches her stomach in agony. The viewer believes he has seen the troops shooting the woman, though this act is not shown.

Eisenstein also used editing to create powerful visual effects. In *Potemkin*, he built a sequence starting with the figure of a lone woman mourning at the coffin of a murdered sailor. A sequence of shots gradually added more people until, at the end, it seems as if the entire city has come to mourn.

The Movies Talk. A few motion pictures used sound before 1900. But these films depended on a mechanical hookup with a phonograph, and it was difficult to ad-

just the sound to the action on the screen. In the mid-1920's, Bell Telephone Laboratories developed a system that successfully coordinated sound on records with the projector. In 1926, Warner Brothers used the system, called Vitaphone, in *Don Juan*, a silent film with music and sound effects on record. In 1927, Warner produced *The Jazz Singer* starring Al Jolson. The picture was basically a silent film with a few songs by Jolson. But in one sequence, the actor spoke a few lines. *The Jazz Singer* revolutionized motion pictures and ended the era of silent films.

Meanwhile, a sound system called Movietone had been developed. In this system, sound was photographed directly on the film. The sound-on-film system was far superior to the sound-on-record method and was soon used for all talking pictures.

By 1929, the public demanded only sound movies. Theater owners rushed to install sound equipment, which was in short supply. Owners who could not get the equipment closed their theaters until it was available. Public enthusiasm for sound pictures became so great that U.S. movie attendance increased from 60 million persons in 1927 to 110 million in 1929.

The first years of sound were actually a setback in the artistic development of motion pictures. Silent films were at the peak of their achievement in the late 1920's. When sound first became popular, several great European silent films were being shown in U.S. theaters. But the public ignored them, preferring talkies. In contrast to the brilliance of many silent films, the first talkies were clumsy, stiff, and self-conscious.

Many silent film stars had voices unsuited to sound films. For example, some had thick foreign accents, and others had voices that were too high-pitched. The careers of such stars ended almost immediately with

Edward G. Robinson, *right*, in a scene from *Little Caesar* (1930), directed by Mervyn Le Roy; Bettmann Archive

Gangster Movies were among the most popular of the early sound films. *Little Caesar*, which portrayed the rise and fall of a mobster, became the most imitated gangster picture.

Hollywood Musicals of the 1930's became noted for their elaborate staging. Dance director Busby Berkeley staged this spectacular World War I musical number in *Gold Diggers of 1933*.

talkies. But some other silent film stars, such as Greta Garbo and the comedy team of Stan Laurel and Oliver Hardy, successfully adjusted to sound.

Movies in the 1930's. During the early 1930's, Hollywood's most notable successes were musicals, gangster films, and newspaper movies. The musicals included *42nd Street* (1933) and *Gold Diggers of 1933* (1933). Among the most popular gangster movies were *Little Caesar* (1930), *The Public Enemy* (1931), and *Scarface* (1932). *The Front Page* (1931) was one of the best of the fast-paced and wisecracking newspaper movies.

During the early 1930's, Hollywood also produced several popular horror movies. *Dracula* (1931) was about a vampire. *Frankenstein* (1931) dealt with a man-made monster. *The Mummy* (1932) described how a mummy came back to life after lying for thousands of years in a tomb. The success of these movies led to many later films based on the same characters.

Sound-recording methods improved greatly during the 1930's. In addition, creative directors throughout the world used sound in imaginative ways. For exam-

ple, the French director René Clair deliberately used the wrong sounds for certain scenes in *Le Million* (1931). In a scene of a fight for a jacket backstage at the Paris Opera, the action is accompanied by the cheers, shouts, and whistles of a crowd at a soccer match.

After about 1933, musical scores became increasingly important. The 1935 American film *The Informer* had an almost operatic score composed by Max Steiner. After the unexpected success of this picture, a full musical accompaniment became a status symbol in movies.

By the mid-1930's, sound movies had developed a new group of outstanding stars. The leading actors included Wallace Beery, James Cagney, Gary Cooper, W. C. Fields, Clark Gable, Cary Grant, Charles Laughton, Fredric March, the Marx brothers, and Spencer Tracy. The most popular actresses included Joan Crawford, Bette Davis, Marlene Dietrich, Greta Garbo, Jean Harlow, Katharine Hepburn, and Mae West.

Most of the important directors of the 1930's had begun their careers in silent films. In England, Alfred Hitchcock became internationally famous for directing such thrillers as *The 39 Steps* (1935) and *The Lady Vanishes* (1938). Jean Renoir became one of France's leading directors with two dramas of social criticism—*Grand Illusion* (1937) and *The Rules of the Game* (1939). John Ford of the United States directed many outstanding adventure and western films, including *The Lost Patrol* (1934) and *Stagecoach* (1939). Ernst Lubitsch began his directing career in Germany but settled in the United States in 1922. He won fame for such sophisticated and witty comedies as *Trouble in Paradise* (1932) and *Ninotchka* (1939).

The 1930's closed triumphantly with *Gone with the Wind* (1939), directed by Victor Fleming and starring Clark Gable and Vivien Leigh. The 220-minute Civil War drama was one of the longest films up to that time. It has been rereleased many times and has become one of the biggest money-makers in film history.

Orson Welles. Late in 1939, RKO studios invited Orson Welles, a 24-year-old American director and actor, to come to Hollywood to make a motion picture of his own choosing. Welles had won a reputation as a "boy wonder" for his work both in radio and on the stage. His experience gave him special understanding of the possibilities of sound and dialogue in movies. Welles directed two landmark motion pictures—*Citizen Kane* (1941) and *The Magnificent Ambersons* (1942). The second film is only partly Welles's work because RKO took the movie out of his hands before completion. Just as *The Birth of a Nation* and *Intolerance* stood as signposts to the future of silent films, so did Welles's two pictures show the way for later sound motion pictures.

Welles produced, directed, and starred in *Citizen Kane*. The film is the story of Charles Foster Kane, a powerful American newspaper publisher who closely resembles William Randolph Hearst, then one of the most powerful men in the United States. In the film, Welles used many experimental photographic techniques, such as startling camera angles and dramatic lighting that cast deep shadows over much of the screen. The camera continually stressed the most important character, gesture, or incident in a scene. To achieve the effects Welles wanted, Gregg Toland, the cameraman, developed new camera lenses and new styles of lighting.

Welles revolutionized the use of the sound track in *Citizen Kane*. Earlier film scores served simply as an operatic or symphonic accompaniment to the movie. For *Citizen Kane*, composer Bernard Herrmann wrote a score to reflect the shifting moods of the story and to tie scenes together. From his radio experience, Welles introduced an off-screen narrator to describe portions of the action. He inserted a variety of off-screen voices to establish swiftly what an entire community was thinking about a topic. Welles cut away from one voice beginning a sentence to another completing it. He used the camera and sound track to compress time. For example, Welles condensed the long decline of Kane's marriage into three minutes of screen time by quickly showing a series of quarrels between Kane and his wife at the breakfast table.

In *The Magnificent Ambersons*, Welles used dialogue realistically. He allowed his characters to interrupt one another or talk at the same time instead of permitting them to complete a sentence. In earlier sound movies, a character would complete a sentence or speech before the next character would begin talking.

Postwar American Movies. During World War II (1939-1945), the American motion-picture industry operated largely as it had before the war. However, great changes took place in the industry after the war ended. By the late 1940's, television had attracted a large portion of the moviegoing public. The studios reduced the number of pictures they made and released many of the directors, performers, producers, and writers they had under contract. Many of these people formed their own independent companies.

Many of the independent producers used their freedom from studio control to introduce serious themes into films. Stanley Kramer produced *Home of the Brave* (1949), a film about racial discrimination. Otto Preminger produced and directed *The Man with the Golden Arm* (1956), a drama about drug abuse. Such subjects might have frightened many studio heads, who believed movies should only entertain.

To lure the public from television, the movie studios developed such wide-screen processes as CinemaScope and Todd-AO and allowed their pictures to get bigger, more expensive, and more spectacular than ever. The studios produced such epics as *Ben-Hur* (1959), *Mutiny on the Bounty* (1962), and *Cleopatra* (1963). But motion pictures like these must take in enormous sums of money before they can even begin to show a profit. Most of the motion-picture spectacles were financial disasters. Some studios then turned to producing films that could not be seen on television. Such pictures

Orson Wells and Ruth Warrick in a scene from *Citizen Kane* (1941);
Culver Pictures

Orson Welles produced, directed, and starred in *Citizen Kane*. Welles experimented with many photographic effects in the film. He used this striking angle, for example, to stress the coldness between the main character, Charles Foster Kane, and his wife.

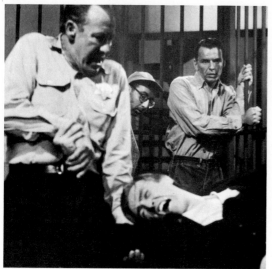

Scene from *The Man with the Golden Arm* (1956), directed by Otto Preminger; the John Springer Collection, Bettmann Archive

Scene from *The Bicycle Thief* (1949), directed by Vittorio De Sica; Culver Pictures

Postwar American Motion Pictures broke new ground in treating controversial subjects. *The Man with the Golden Arm,* starring Frank Sinatra, *right rear,* examined drug addiction.

Italian Films gained international attention after World War II with such realistic movies as *The Bicycle Thief.* The film concerned a man and his son searching for a stolen bicycle.

stressed abnormal sexual behavior, nudity, and obscene language. The emphasis on sex and nudity in movies continued into the 1970's.

Postwar European Movies. European motion-picture production nearly ceased during World War II. However, Europeans resumed making films as soon as the war ended. Many of these films introduced new styles and gifted directors to audiences in many countries.

Italy became the first country to capture worldwide attention for its films after the war. A group of talented Italian directors made a series of intensely realistic movies showing the miseries of war and the problems of returning to peacetime living. Their film style became known as *neorealism.* The neorealists worked against natural backgrounds whenever possible, both in the cities and in the countryside. They used nonprofessional actors whenever possible.

The first neorealist film was *Open City* (1945), directed by Roberto Rossellini. In an almost documentary style, it shows the struggles of the Italian people under the German occupation. Director Vittorio De Sica used the streets of Milan to film *The Bicycle Thief* (1949), a grim story of a man and his son trying to find a bicycle the man needs for his job. Neorealism served as a training school for later Italian directors who became internationally famous. The most notable of these directors were Michelangelo Antonioni and Federico Fellini.

Both Antonioni and Fellini developed personal styles. Antonioni directed moody studies of characters apparently adrift without a sense of purpose in modern society. His best-known films include *L'Avventura* (1960) and *Blow-Up* (1966). Fellini gained international acclaim in the 1950's for several realistic pictures, especially *La Strada* (1954) and *La Dolce Vita* (1959). He later turned to symbolic fantasies, as in *8½* (1963).

France. The most important development in postwar French movies was the appearance of a group of talented young directors who began what was called the *new wave* in film making. Most of these directors were originally film critics.

Most of the new wave films dealt with modern French life and centered on young people. In addition, nearly all the films cost comparatively little money. But the new wave movies had little else in common. Instead, each picture was marked by the individual style of its director. The major new wave directors and their first important films included Claude Chabrol (*The Cousins,* 1959); Jean Luc Godard (*Breathless,* 1959); Louis Malle (*The Lovers,* 1958); François Truffaut (*The 400 Blows,* 1959); and Roger Vadim (*And God Created Woman,* 1956).

Godard and Truffaut gained the greatest international recognition during the 1960's. Godard aroused much debate because of his experiments in editing and photography and because of the Marxist philosophy in some of his pictures. His best-known films of the 1960's include *Weekend* (1967) and *La Chinoise* (1968). Truffaut became noted for his gentle, realistic motion pictures about a young man named Antoine Doinel, a character based on Truffaut himself. Doinel appears in *The 400 Blows* and *Stolen Kisses* (1968).

England. Between 1945 and 1960, the English film industry was known largely for a series of light comedies and for the work of directors David Lean and Sir Carol Reed. Lean directed one of the greatest English postwar films, the romantic drama *Brief Encounter* (1945). Reed became known for several moody dramas, notably *Odd Man Out* (1946) and *The Third Man* (1949).

Beginning in 1959, English motion pictures were revolutionized by a series of films that realistically examined English working-class life. The film that started the trend was *Room at the Top* (1959), directed by Jack Clayton. Important movies that followed included *Saturday Night and Sunday Morning* (1960), directed by Karel Reisz; *A Kind of Loving* (1962), directed by John Schlesinger; and *The Loneliness of the Long-Distance Runner* (1962), directed by Tony Richardson.

Postwar Asian Movies. Since the late 1940's, Asian countries have produced more motion pictures yearly than have European countries and the United States combined. Formosa, Hong Kong, India, Japan, and South Korea rank among the world's leading producers.

Few Asian films were shown in Western countries before the late 1940's. Since then, Asian motion pictures—particularly those made in India and Japan—have become popular in the West. The film industry of India achieved international attention through the work of director Satyajit Ray. He became particularly noted for a series of three motion pictures describing the growth of a boy to manhood in modern India. The series, known as the *Apu Trilogy*, consists of *Pather Panchali* (1954), *The Unvanquished* (1956), and *The World of Apu* (1959). Western film critics and audiences especially admire Japanese movies dealing with the legends and history of Japan. The director Akira Kurosawa earned international praise for his films *Rashomon* (1950) and *Seven Samurai* (1954).

Motion Pictures Today. The American motion-picture industry struggled desperately for economic survival during the late 1960's and early 1970's. About 80 per cent of all films produced lost money. Nearly every studio was in serious financial trouble, and unemployment in some movie craft unions in Hollywood reached 90 per cent.

A few motion pictures, however, made large profits during the late 1960's and early 1970's. They included *The Graduate* (1968), *Easy Rider* (1969), *Airport* (1970), *Love Story* (1970), *M*A*S*H* (1970), and *Carnal Knowledge* (1971). Several films aimed primarily at black audiences, such as *Shaft* (1971), were also box-office successes in cities with large Negro populations.

During the 1960's, historians, scholars, and educators began to take great interest in the history of motion pictures and in motion pictures as an art form. Before the 1960's, movies had received little serious scholarly attention. For many years, most information on motion pictures appeared in newspaper gossip columns and *fan magazines* and dealt largely with sensational or scandalous stories about the stars.

Since the early 1960's, hundreds of hard-cover and paperback books have been published on motion pictures. These books trace the history of films, analyze the work of important directors and stars, and provide instructions on how to make movies. Publishers have issued collections of significant articles written years ago about films as well as reprints of historically important material, such as filmscripts. A selected list of important books on motion pictures appears on the next page.

Interest in film study grew enormously in American colleges and universities during the 1960's and early 1970's. In 1960, only about half a dozen universities offered degrees in motion pictures. Today, about 50 institutions of higher learning offer degrees, and more than 200 offer at least one course in films.

During the 1960's and early 1970's, colleges and universities trained many young people in the art of directing films. These directors reject the traditional studio system of making movies. They prefer to shoot on location, using relatively inexpensive portable equipment available in 16 millimeters. They do not consider theaters important and exhibit their films at colleges and before film societies. Some critics believe the artistic survival of motion pictures lies with these directors.

In 1967, the U.S. government established the American Film Institute under the National Endowment for the Arts. The institute is supported jointly by the government, the movie industry, and private organizations. It develops programs in movie appreciation, teacher training, scholarship and research, film production, and film preservation. In 1969, the institute opened the Center for Advanced Film Studies in Beverly Hills, Calif. The center tries to help independent and student film makers build a career in motion pictures.

The American Film Institute is sponsoring one of the most ambitious film scholarship projects ever attempted. The institute is preparing a 19-volume reference work that will list all significant production information on every motion picture that has ever been produced in the United States. Such information will include the names of the performers, the producer, and the director of every movie.   ARTHUR KNIGHT

From left to right, Elliott Gould, Donald Sutherland, and Tom Skerritt in a scene from *M*A*S*H* (1970), directed by Robert Altman; © 1969 Aspen Productions and Twentieth Century-Fox Film Corp.

A Satirical Approach to Military Life made *M*A*S*H* one of the most discussed American movies of the early 1970's. The film dealt with three young Army surgeons during the Korean War.

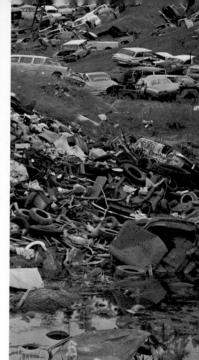

Environmental Pollution damages man's surroundings. Gases and smoke in the air, chemicals and other substances in water, and solid wastes on land are all common forms of pollution.

ENVIRONMENTAL POLLUTION

ENVIRONMENTAL POLLUTION is a term that refers to all the ways by which man pollutes his surroundings. Man dirties the air with gases and smoke, poisons the water with chemicals and other substances, and damages the soil with too many fertilizers and pesticides. Man also pollutes his surroundings in various other ways. For example, people ruin natural beauty by scattering junk and litter on the land and in the water. They operate machines and motor vehicles that fill the air with disturbing noise. Nearly everyone causes pollution in some way.

Environmental pollution is one of the most serious problems facing mankind today. Air, water, and soil—all harmed by pollution—are necessary to the survival of all living things. Badly polluted air can cause illness, and even death. Polluted water kills fish and other marine life. Pollution of soil reduces the amount of land available for growing food. Environmental pollution also brings ugliness to man's naturally beautiful world.

Everyone wants to reduce pollution. But the pollution problem is as complicated as it is serious. It is complicated because much pollution is caused by things that benefit people. For example, exhaust from automobiles causes a large percentage of all air pollution. But the automobile provides transportation for millions of peo-

ple. Factories discharge much of the material that pollutes air and water, but factories provide jobs for people. Too much fertilizer or pesticide can ruin soil, but fertilizers and pesticides are important aids to the growing of crops.

Thus, to end or greatly reduce pollution immediately, people would have to stop using many things that benefit them. Most people do not want to do that, of course. But pollution can be gradually reduced in several ways. Scientists and engineers can work to find ways to lessen the amount of pollution that such things as automobiles and factories cause. Governments can pass and enforce laws that require businesses and individuals to stop, or cut down on, certain polluting activities. And—perhaps most importantly—individuals and groups of people can work to persuade their representatives in government, and also persuade businesses, to take action toward reducing pollution.

Man has always polluted his surroundings. But throughout much of history, pollution was not a major problem. Most people lived in uncrowded rural areas, and the *pollutants* (waste products) they produced were widely scattered. People had no pollution-causing machines or motor vehicles. The development of crowded industrial cities in the 1700's and 1800's made pollution a major problem. People and factories in these cities put huge amounts of pollutants into small areas. During the 1900's, urban areas continued to develop and automobiles and other new inventions made pollution steadily worse. By the mid-1900's, pollution had affected the water in every major lake and river and the air over every major city in the United States and other industrial countries. Since the late 1960's, millions of people have become alarmed by the dangers of pollution. Large numbers of people are now working to reduce pollution.

Alan McGowan, the contributor of this article, is the Scientific Administrator of the Center for the Biology of Natural Systems at Washington University. Jack W. Hudson, the critical reviewer, is Professor of Zoology and Chairman of the Section of Ecology and Systematics at Cornell University.

There are several kinds of environmental pollution. They include air pollution, water pollution, soil pollution, and pollution caused by solid wastes, noise, and radiation.

All parts of the environment are closely related to one another. (The study of the relationships among living things, and between living things and other parts of the environment, is called *ecology* [see ECOLOGY]). Because of the close relationships, a kind of pollution that chiefly harms one part of the environment may also affect others. For example, air pollution harms the air. But rain washes pollutants out of the air and deposits them on the land and in bodies of water. Wind, on the other hand, blows pollutants off the land and puts them into the air.

Air Pollution turns clear, odorless air into hazy, smelly air that harms health, kills plants, and damages property. Man causes air pollution by pouring hundreds of millions of tons of gases and *particulates* into the atmosphere each year. Particulates are tiny particles of solid or liquid matter. One of the most common forms of air pollution is smog.

Most air pollution results from *combustion* (burning) processes. The burning of gasoline to power motor vehicles and the burning of coal to heat buildings and help manufacture products are examples of such processes. Each time a fuel is burned in a combustion process, some type of pollutant is released into the air. The pollutants range from small amounts of colorless poison gas to clouds of thick black smoke.

Weather conditions can help reduce the amount of pollutants in the air. Wind scatters pollutants, and rain and snow wash them into the ground. But in many areas, pollutants are put into the air faster than weather conditions can dispose of them. In crowded cities, for example, thousands of automobiles, factories, and fur-

AIR POLLUTION Most of the gases and particles that man puts into the air come from *combustion* (burning) processes. The furnaces in factories, homes, and office buildings; the engines in automobiles, airplanes, and other motor vehicles; and the burning of garbage and trash are the chief sources of pollution from combustion. The pollutants from these sources have a wide variety of effects, as shown below.

WORLD BOOK diagram by George Suyeoka

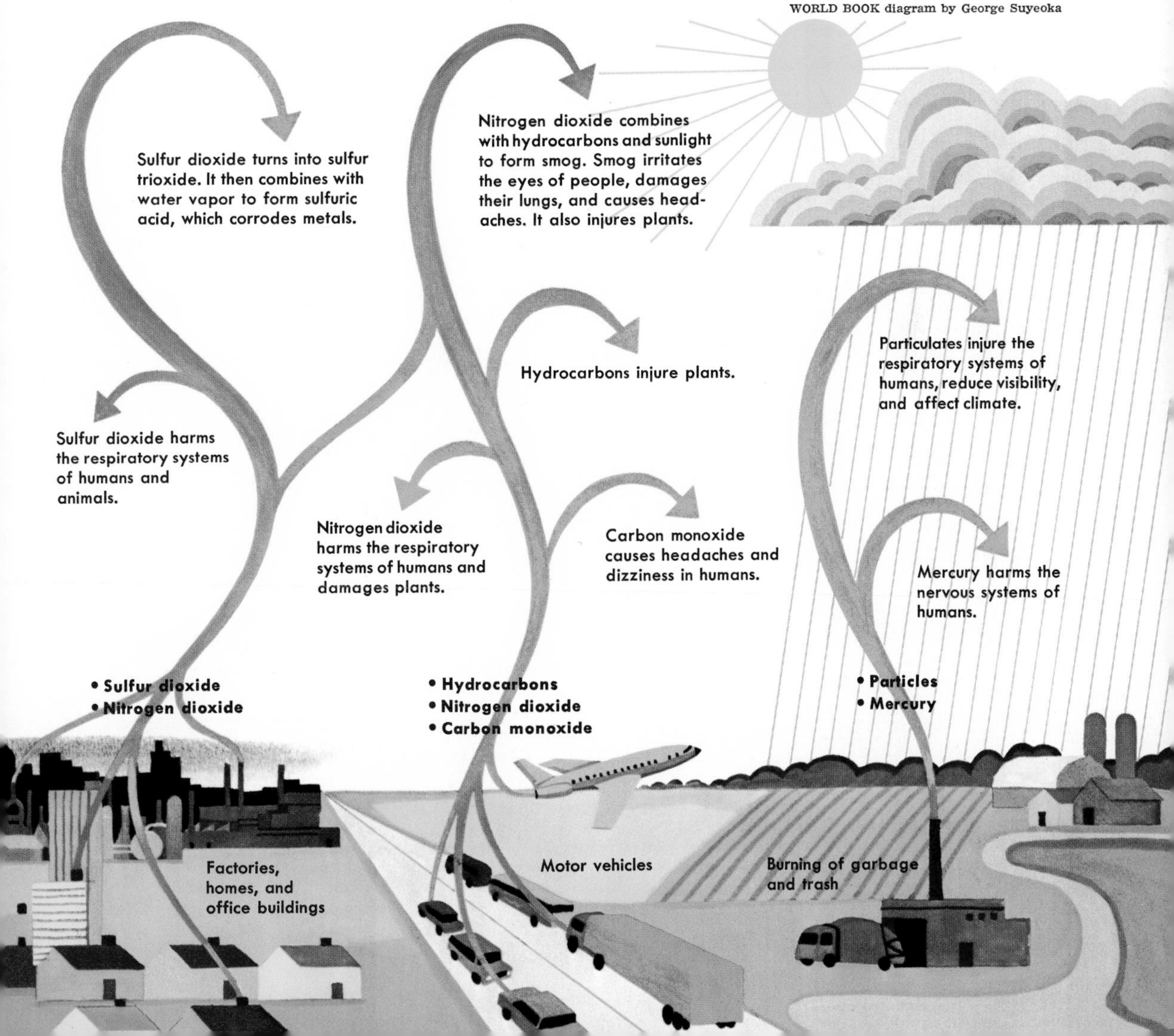

Sulfur dioxide turns into sulfur trioxide. It then combines with water vapor to form sulfuric acid, which corrodes metals.

Nitrogen dioxide combines with hydrocarbons and sunlight to form smog. Smog irritates the eyes of people, damages their lungs, and causes headaches. It also injures plants.

Hydrocarbons injure plants.

Particulates injure the respiratory systems of humans, reduce visibility, and affect climate.

Sulfur dioxide harms the respiratory systems of humans and animals.

Nitrogen dioxide harms the respiratory systems of humans and damages plants.

Carbon monoxide causes headaches and dizziness in humans.

Mercury harms the nervous systems of humans.

• **Sulfur dioxide**
• **Nitrogen dioxide**

• **Hydrocarbons**
• **Nitrogen dioxide**
• **Carbon monoxide**

• **Particles**
• **Mercury**

Factories, homes, and office buildings

Motor vehicles

Burning of garbage and trash

naces may add tons of pollutants to a small area of the atmosphere each day.

At times, weather conditions cause pollutants to build up over an area instead of clearing them away. One such condition—called *thermal inversion*—occurs when a layer of warm air settles over a layer of cooler air that lies near the ground. The warm air holds down the cool air and prevents pollutants from rising and scattering. A serious pollution problem results when a thermal inversion occurs over a city that is pouring tons of pollutants into the air.

The most serious result of air pollution is its harmful effect on human health. Both gases and particulates burn people's eyes and irritate their lungs. Particulates can settle in the lungs and worsen such respiratory diseases as asthma and bronchitis. Some experts believe that particulates may even help cause such diseases as cancer, emphysema, and pneumonia. In cities throughout the world, long periods of heavy air pollution have caused illness and death rates to increase dramatically.

Air pollution also harms plants. Poisonous gases in the air can restrict the growth of, and eventually kill, nearly all kinds of plants. Forests in Tennessee, citrus groves near Los Angeles, and vegetable gardens in New Jersey have all been seriously damaged by air pollution.

Most materials get dirty and wear out more quickly in polluted air than they do in clean air. Polluted air even harms such hard and strong materials as concrete and steel. In some cities, statues and other art objects that stood outdoors for hundreds of years have been moved indoors because today's air pollution threatened to destroy them.

Air pollutants may also affect the weather. Both gases and particulates can cause changes in the average temperatures of an area. Particulates scatter the sun's rays and reduce the amount of sunlight that reaches the ground. Such interference with sunlight may cause average temperatures in an area to drop. Some gases, including carbon dioxide, allow sunlight to reach the ground, but prevent the sunlight's heat from rising out of the atmosphere and flowing back into space. This development, called a *greenhouse effect*, may cause average temperatures to rise.

For more details on air pollution, see the WORLD BOOK articles on AIR POLLUTION and SMOG.

Water Pollution reduces the amount of pure, fresh water that is available for such necessities as drinking and cleaning, and for such activities as swimming and fishing. The pollutants that affect water come mainly from industries, farms, and sewerage systems.

WATER POLLUTION

Most of the pollutants that man puts into water come from treated and untreated sewage, from agricultural drainage, and from industrial wastes. The pollutants reduce valuable supplies of pure, fresh water by upsetting the natural cycles that work to keep water clean. By upsetting the cycles, the pollutants harm the animals and plants that live in the water.

WORLD BOOK diagram by George Suyeoka

Untreated sewage   Treated sewage

Untreated Sewage contains large amounts of wastes from animal and plant matter. The wastes decay in water, and some of the water's oxygen is used up in the decaying process. If too much oxygen is used, animals and plants in the water cannot survive.

Treated Sewage contains nitrates and phosphates. These substances cause large amounts of *algae* (tiny, one-celled plants) to grow. The algae multiply quickly, and also die quickly. After they die, they decay and use up oxygen.

Industries dump millions of gallons of waste products into bodies of water each year. These wastes include chemicals, wastes from animal and plant matter, and hundreds of other substances. Wastes from farms include animal wastes, fertilizers, and pesticides. Most of these materials drain off farm fields and into nearby bodies of water. Sewerage systems carry wastes from homes, offices, and industries into water. Nearly all cities have waste treatment plants that remove some of the most harmful wastes from sewage. But even most of the treated sewage contains material that harms water.

Natural cycles work to absorb small amounts of wastes in bodies of water. During a cycle, wastes are turned into useful, or at least harmless, substances. Bacteria called *aerobic bacteria* use oxygen to decay natural wastes such as dead fish and break them down into chemicals, including nitrates, phosphates, and carbon dioxide. These chemicals, called *nutrients*, are used as food by *algae* (tiny, one-celled plants) and other green plants in the water. The algae serve as food for microscopic animals called *zooplankton*. Small fish, such as minnows, eat the zooplankton, and the small fish, in turn, are eaten by larger fish. The large fish eventually die and bacteria break them down, beginning the cycle again.

The same natural cycles work on wastes poured into water by man. Bacteria break down chemicals and other wastes and turn them into nutrients, or else into substances that will not harm fish or sea plants. But if too much waste matter is poured into the water, the whole cycle will begin to break down, and the water becomes dirtier and dirtier. The bacteria that work to decay the wastes use up too much oxygen during the decaying process. As more and more oxygen is used up, less and less oxygen is available for the animals and plants in the water. Animals and plants then die, adding even more wastes to the water. Finally, the water's entire oxygen supply is used up and, without oxygen, *anaerobic bacteria*, rather than aerobic bacteria, decay wastes. The anaerobic decaying process causes wastes to give off smelly gases.

Nutrients in water cause a similar process—called *nutrient enrichment*, or *eutrophication*—to take place. Nutrients that man adds to water, such as nitrates from agricultural fertilizers and phosphates from detergents in sewage, greatly increase the growth of algae in water. As larger amounts of algae grow, larger amounts also die. The dead algae become wastes, and, as they decay, they use up the water's oxygen supply.

The addition of heated water to a body of water also upsets cycles. Heated water can kill animals and plants that are accustomed to living at lower temperatures. It also reduces the amount of oxygen that water can hold. The addition of heated water is called *thermal pollution*. Most heated water comes from industries and power plants that use water for cooling.

For more details on water pollution, see WATER (How Man Poisons Water).

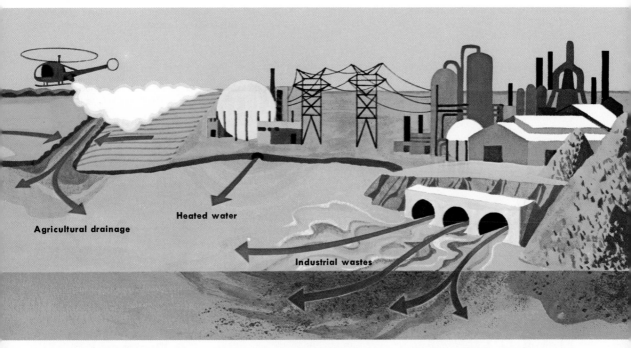

Agricultural Drainage includes animal wastes, which decay; fertilizers, which increase the growth of algae; and pesticides, which kill animals and plants.

Heated Water kills animals and plants that are accustomed to living in cooler water. Most heated water comes from industries that use water for cooling.

Industrial Wastes include chemicals, wastes from animal and plant matter, and hundreds of other substances. They ruin water by upsetting natural cycles.

ENVIRONMENTAL POLLUTION

Soil Pollution damages the thin layer of fertile soil that covers much of the earth's land and is essential for growing food. Natural processes took thousands of years to form the soil that supports crops. But, through careless treatment, man can destroy soil in just a few years.

In nature, cycles similar to those that keep water clean work to keep soil fertile. Wastes, including dead plants and waste from animals, form a substance in the soil called *humus*. Bacteria decay the humus and break it down into nitrates, phosphates, and other nutrients. The nutrients feed growing plants, and when the plants die the cycle begins again.

Man uses fertilizers and pesticides to grow more and better crops. Fertilizers add extra nutrients to the soil and increase the amount of a crop that can be grown on an area of land. But the use of large amounts of fertilizer may decrease the ability of bacteria to decay humus and produce nutrients naturally.

Pesticides destroy weeds and insects that harm crops. But pesticides may also harm bacteria and other helpful organisms in the soil.

Much damage to soil results from *erosion*. Erosion is the wearing away of soil. It can result from the removal of trees, grass, and other plants that hold soil in place. Wind can then blow the bare soil away and rain can wash it away. Careless farming methods are a major cause of erosion. The clearing of land for construction projects, such as roads and real estate developments, also causes erosion.

For more information on soil and how it is damaged, see the articles on SOIL and EROSION.

Solid Wastes are probably the most visible forms of pollution. Man throws away billions of tons of solid material each year. Much of this waste ends up littering roadsides, floating in lakes and streams, and collecting in ugly dumps. The almost countless examples of solid wastes include junked automobiles, tires, refrigerators, and stoves; cans and other packaging materials; and scraps of metal and paper. Such solid pollutants are most common in the heavily populated areas in and near cities. Piles of animal wastes, and of slag and other wastes from mining processes, pollute much land away from cities.

Solid wastes present a serious problem because most of the methods used to dispose of them result in some type of damage to the environment. When the wastes are put into open dumps, they ruin the attractiveness of the surrounding areas. Dumps also provide homes for disease-carrying animals, such as cockroaches and rats. Some solid wastes can be destroyed by burning them. But burning produces smoke that causes air pollution. When wastes are dumped in water, they contribute to various forms of water pollution.

In 1970, nearly 4 billion tons of solid wastes were produced in the United States. This amounted to an average of about 5 pounds of solid wastes for each person in the country each day. Most solid wastes are disposed of in open dumps. But in many areas, especially near large cities, the land available for dumping is running out. In the meantime, the production of solid wastes is increasing rapidly. In addition, more and more wastes that are difficult to dispose of are being produced. Tin and steel cans that rust and can be absorbed by the soil are being replaced by aluminum cans that stay in their original state for many years. Paper and cardboard packaging that decays and burns easily is being replaced by plastics that will not decay and that give off harmful gases when burned.

HOW MERCURY REACHES MAN

Mercury comes from many sources and reaches people in several ways. It travels directly through air and water, and it collects in the tissues and organs of animals and plants that man eats. Mercury is a dangerous pollutant because, in large doses, it can harm the human nervous system.

WORLD BOOK diagram by Mas Nakagawa

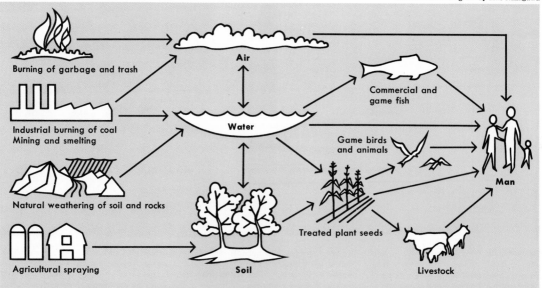

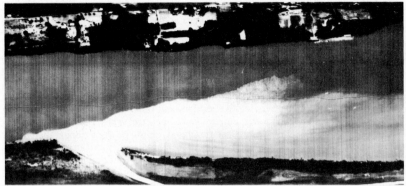

Thermal Pollution occurs when heated water is added to a body of water. In this photo, taken with special film called *infrared* film, heated water appears much lighter than the rest of the water in the river. The heated water is coming from a nuclear power plant, and is being carried downstream by the river's current.

U.S. Geological Survey

Other Kinds of Pollution. Some things that pollute the environment cannot be classified as air, water, or soil pollutants, or as solid wastes. They travel through and affect various parts of the environment. These pollutants include noise, radiation, pesticides, and such metals as mercury and lead.

Noise is especially troublesome in urban areas. People in and near cities are exposed to loud noise much of the time. The noise comes from such things as airplanes, automobiles, buses, motorcycles, trains, trucks, construction projects, and industries. The noise causes discomfort in people. In extreme cases, loud noise can damage hearing or even cause deafness. See SOUND (Noise).

Radiation is an invisible pollutant that can be highly dangerous. Some radiation reaches the earth from the sun and outer space. Larger amounts come from radioactive materials, such as fallout from nuclear weapons and waste materials from nuclear power plants and from various electronic devices. Scientists have not determined exactly what effects small amounts of radiation have on humans. But exposure to large amounts of radiation is believed to result in cancer and in harmful changes in reproductive cells. International agreements have banned most testing of nuclear weapons in the atmosphere and have helped eliminate the largest sources of radiation. But the number of electronic devices that produce small amounts of radiation is steadily increasing. These devices include lasers, X-ray machines, color television sets, and microwave ovens. Scientists are trying to determine if frequent exposure to the small amounts of radiation that come from such sources can harm people. See FALLOUT; RADIATION.

Pesticides affect more than the natural cycles in soil and water. Much pesticide material never reaches the insects or other pests it is intended to kill. Instead, tiny particles of the pesticide travel through the air and water, sometimes for hundreds of miles. Humans and animals that come in direct contact with the pesticide take it into their bodies, and the material collects in tissues and organs. Humans and animals also take in pesticides indirectly when they eat organisms that contain the material. For example, a large fish can take in heavy amounts of pesticide by eating smaller fish that have the material in their bodies. A human may then eat the large fish and acquire the highly concentrated pesticide material the fish contains. When materials are passed from one organism to another in this way, they travel through what is called a *food chain*.

As with radiation, scientists do not yet understand the exact effects of small amounts of pesticides. However, they know that some pesticides, including DDT, have been responsible for the deaths of many birds, fish, and other animals.

Millions of tons of mercury, lead, and other *heavy metals* are put into the water and air each year in the form of liquids and gases. Most of these materials come from combustion processes in industries or motor vehicle engines. Heavy metals, like pesticides, are long lasting and can spread over large areas. They too collect in tissues and organs and can pass through food chains. Most heavy metals are highly poisonous, and, in large amounts, can affect the human nervous system.

Noise Pollution is a problem in urban areas. Loud noises annoy people and, under some circumstances, can cause damage to hearing. Noises are measured in units called *decibels*. The chart below shows the approximate decibel level from some sources of noise and effects various decibel levels can have.

WORLD BOOK graph

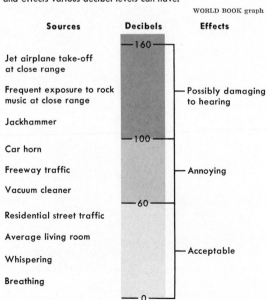

Sources	Decibels	Effects
	— 160 —	
Jet airplane take-off at close range		
Frequent exposure to rock music at close range		— Possibly damaging to hearing
Jackhammer		
	— 100 —	
Car horn		
Freeway traffic		— Annoying
Vacuum cleaner		
	— 60 —	
Residential street traffic		
Average living room		
Whispering		— Acceptable
Breathing		
	— 0 —	

Man has continuously developed new inventions and processes that have improved his way of life. Such developments are called *technological advances*. Technological advances help man, but many of them also bring about harm to the environment. In addition to technological causes, there are economic and social causes of pollution.

Technological Causes. Many environmental pollution problems are a result of the rapid advances in technology that have been made since about the end of World War II (1945). Technological advances in agriculture, industry, and transportation have greatly improved man's way of life. But most of the advances were made without consideration of the effects they would have on the environment.

The automobile engine is an example of a very useful technological development that harms the environment. Through the years, automobiles have been made more and more powerful. Most cars being built today have about three times as much horsepower as most cars built in the 1940's. Because of this, the new cars produce much more polluting exhaust than the older ones did. In order to make engines more powerful, automobile manufacturers had to increase *compression ratios*. That is, they increased the pressure and—as a result—the temperature at which combustion takes place in the engines' cylinders. The higher temperatures during combustion cause chemical reactions that put large amounts of nitrogen oxide gases into the engines' exhausts. In addition, high compression engines require special gasolines that burn evenly to prevent

"knocking" noises. A compound of lead called *tetraethyl lead* has been added to gasolines to prevent "knocking." But this poisonous lead also goes into the engines' exhaust. The increased production of nitrogen oxides and lead, along with an increased use of automobiles for transportation, has helped create the dangerous air pollution that often hangs over cities.

The sewage treatment plant is an example of a technological development that was designed to protect the environment, but which can cause pollution nevertheless. Most treatment plants prevent dangerous *organic wastes* (wastes from animal and plant matter) from upsetting the natural cycles in water. The plants use bacteria and oxygen to break down the wastes and turn them into inorganic nutrients. But when the nutrients are put into the water, they upset natural cycles by increasing the growth of algae. Scientists and engineers are working to develop sewage treatment plants that will also remove inorganic nutrients from sewage.

Some products of advanced technology contribute to environmental pollution in more than one way. For example, plastics are a troublesome solid waste because they will not break down and cannot be absorbed by the soil. Plastics also indirectly cause pollution when they are produced. Large amounts of electricity are needed to produce plastics. As a result, plastic production helps create a demand for more electric power plants. Electric power plants that burn fuel, such as coal, are a major source of air pollution.

Economic Causes. Many pollution problems have developed because methods of preventing pollution are

ENERGY AND POLLUTION

The use of energy is related to pollution. Most methods of producing energy result in some kind of pollution. The graph, *right*, shows how demand for energy, such as that from an electric power plant, *below*, has increased.

Robert H. Glaze, Artstreet

ENERGY CONSUMED PER PERSON IN THE U.S.

Kilowatt-hours of energy from coal, hydroelectric power, natural gas, nuclear power, and petroleum consumed per person each year*

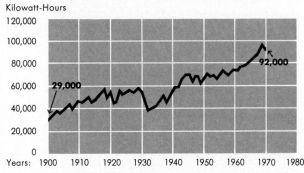

Kilowatt-Hours

120,000
100,000
80,000
60,000 — 29,000
40,000
20,000
0

Years: 1900 1910 1920 1930 1940 1950 1960 1970 1980

92,000

SOURCES OF ENERGY CONSUMED IN THE U.S.

Total kilowatt-hours of energy consumed in 1970 — 20,100,000,000,000*

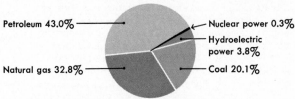

Petroleum 43.0%

Nuclear power 0.3%

Hydroelectric power 3.8%

Natural gas 32.8%

Coal 20.1%

*One kilowatt-hour equals work done by one kilowatt in one hour; one kilowatt equals 1.34 horsepower.
Source: U.S. Bureau of Mines

expensive. Many waste products could somehow be reused. But such practices have seldom been followed, partly because of the high costs involved.

The use of *feed lots* (large pens) in raising livestock is an example of how economical farming methods can result in pollution. When livestock graze on large areas of land, their waste products become part of the natural cycles that fertilize the soil. But much farmland has become too valuable to be used for the grazing of livestock. Farmers can make more money by using land for growing crops and by keeping livestock in feed lots. Pollution results because animals in feed lots deposit large amounts of wastes on small areas. The soil in the feed lots cannot absorb all the waste, and much of it runs off the feed lots and pollutes nearby bodies of water. In addition, the farmers must use chemical fertilizers on the farmland to replace the natural fertilizers that are provided by livestock. Much of this fertilizer also runs off the land and pollutes water.

In industry, sulfur is an example of a pollutant that is allowed to exist for economic reasons. Sulfur is released in the form of sulfur dioxide when coal is burned. Industries in the United States that use coal for fuel put about 6 million tons of sulfur dioxide into the atmosphere each year. This is approximately the same amount of sulfur that chemical industries use to produce sulfuric acid, a widely used industrial chemical. Most of the sulfur in industrial smoke could be captured and reused by the sulfuric acid producers. But a practical and inexpensive method for capturing sulfur is not yet available. Until such a method is developed, mining new

supplies of sulfur for the sulfuric acid industry will be much easier and cheaper.

Social Causes. Man's desire for convenience is another cause of pollution. Many man-made materials that pollute the environment were developed to save people time, work, or money. With effort, some of the pollution from these materials could be eliminated. But, just as prevention of pollution is often considered too expensive, it is often considered too inconvenient.

The use of throwaway packaging materials is an example of how demands for convenience cause pollution. Such forms of packaging as aluminum and steel cans and glass bottles could be saved and reused. Cans can be melted down and reused. Bottles can be refilled, or ground up and used as a raw material again. But many people prefer to throw away containers rather than save and return them for reuse. Thus, metal and glass, which are difficult to dispose of, pile up in dumps and litter streets and countrysides.

The use of automobiles instead of public transportation is another example of pollution that results from a desire for convenience. In nearly every city in the United States, automobiles are more widely used than buses or trains. People find it more convenient to drive a car directly to their destinations than to wait for a bus or train that might take them out of their way or take a little more time. This widespread use of the automobile makes it the country's chief source of air pollution. If more people rode buses and trains instead of automobiles, the number of motor vehicles on the road would decrease and air pollution would be greatly reduced.

SOLID WASTES

The production of solid wastes is increasing so rapidly, *right*, that disposing of them has become a major problem. Solid wastes include garbage and trash, *below*, as well as wastes from agriculture, manufacturing, and mining.

Owen Franken

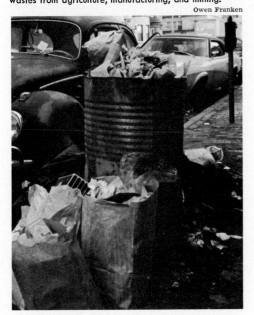

SOLID WASTES GENERATED IN THE U.S.

Tons of agricultural, manufacturing, mineral, and municipal wastes generated each year

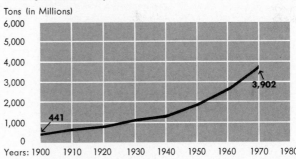

Sources: 1960 and 1970 estimates are from the U.S. Environmental Protection Agency; estimates for other years are based on the gross national product, the total value of goods and services produced.

SOURCES OF SOLID WASTES GENERATED IN THE U.S.

Total solid wastes generated in 1970—3,902,000,000 tons

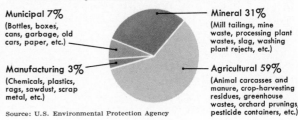

Municipal 7%
(Bottles, boxes, cans, garbage, old cars, paper, etc.)

Mineral 31%
(Mill tailings, mine waste, processing plant wastes, slag, washing plant rejects, etc.)

Manufacturing 3%
(Chemicals, plastics, rags, sawdust, scrap metal, etc.)

Agricultural 59%
(Animal carcasses and manure, crop-harvesting residues, greenhouse wastes, orchard prunings, pesticide containers, etc.)

Source: U.S. Environmental Protection Agency

Some lakes and rivers may already be so badly polluted that they may not be able to regain their health even if all pollution is stopped. Some soil has been too badly eroded to support crops any more. But in most areas, effective programs to prevent pollution could greatly improve environmental conditions.

Several different approaches can be used to control pollution. Waste products can be saved and used again. New technological developments can help prevent pollution from older ones. Restrictions can be placed on the use of materials that pollute. These approaches may result in much less convenience and much higher costs, however.

Recycling. The reprocessing of waste products for reuse is called *recycling*. Many kinds of wastes can be recycled. Some, including cans and newspapers, can be used over and over again for the same purposes. Cans can be melted down and used to make new cans. Old newspapers can be turned into pulp and then made into clean newsprint. Other materials, such as glass bottles and automobile tires, can be reused for other purposes. Ground-up glass can serve as an ingredient in roadbuilding materials. Old tires can be melted into solid material that is useful in making filters for sewage treatment plants.

New Technological Developments do much to control pollution caused by older technology. For example, several types of devices have been developed to prevent particulates from leaving industrial smokestacks. These devices include filters that trap particulates that would otherwise be released into the air with gases. Other devices use processes by which static electricity keeps particulates from escaping into the air. Still other devices wash out particulates with chemical sprays.

Devices have also been invented to reduce the pollution that comes from automobile engines. These devices work to make the engines burn less fuel, to allow them to burn fuel containing little or no lead, and to make combustion processes more complete.

An important development in agriculture is the use of biological controls instead of pesticides. Biological controls involve the use of various types of insects and bacteria to control pests. Other new developments have improved the effectiveness of water treatment facilities and provided various new ways to dispose of solid wastes.

Restrictions on the use of materials that pollute can be extremely effective in controlling pollution. But the restrictions may also cause inconvenience and require changes in ways of life.

The use of some harmful materials has been stopped or reduced without major problems resulting. For example, the United States government has banned the use of the dangerous pesticide DDT for all except essential purposes. Farmers have found other less harmful pesticides to replace DDT. Oil companies have begun producing gasoline that does not have lead added to it, because lead is responsible for much of the pollution in

WASTE RECYCLING

Recycling processes help reduce solid wastes by turning waste materials into new, useful materials. Paper is one of the most common products that is recycled. Others include aluminum and glass.

WORLD BOOK diagram

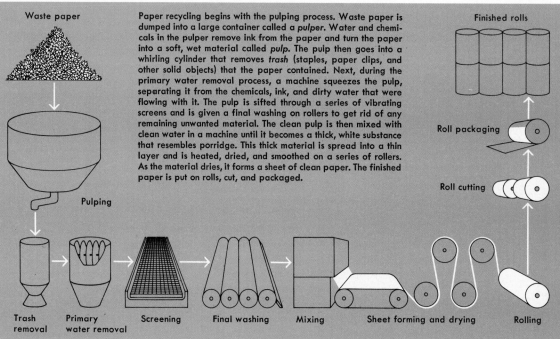

Waste paper

Paper recycling begins with the pulping process. Waste paper is dumped into a large container called a *pulper*. Water and chemicals in the pulper remove ink from the paper and turn the paper into a soft, wet material called *pulp*. The pulp then goes into a whirling cylinder that removes *trash* (staples, paper clips, and other solid objects) that the paper contained. Next, during the primary water removal process, a machine squeezes the pulp, separating it from the chemicals, ink, and dirty water that were flowing with it. The pulp is sifted through a series of vibrating screens and is given a final washing on rollers to get rid of any remaining unwanted material. The clean pulp is then mixed with clean water in a machine until it becomes a thick, white substance that resembles porridge. This thick material is spread into a thin layer and is heated, dried, and smoothed on a series of rollers. As the material dries, it forms a sheet of clean paper. The finished paper is put on rolls, cut, and packaged.

Finished rolls

Roll packaging

Roll cutting

Pulping

Trash removal | Primary water removal | Screening | Final washing | Mixing | Sheet forming and drying | Rolling

AIR POLLUTION CONTROL DEVICES

Industries use several devices to prevent particulates from entering the atmosphere. Fabric filters trap particulates as air flows through the filters. Electrostatic precipitators have electrodes that attract particulates by giving them an electric charge. Mechanical collectors force air to swirl around in a chamber, and particulates drop out of the air as they strike the walls of the chamber. Scrubbers wash particulates out of the air as the air passes through chemical sprays.

WORLD BOOK diagram by Mas Nakagawa

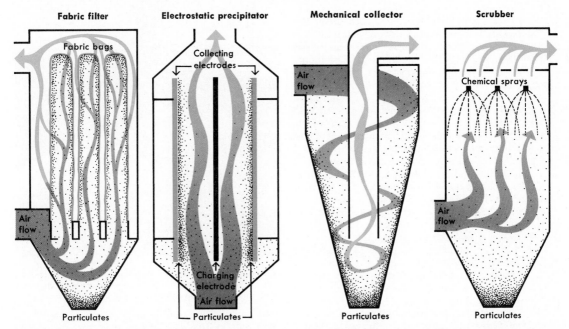

| Fabric filter | Electrostatic precipitator | Mechanical collector | Scrubber |

automobile exhausts. Automobile manufacturers have modified engines so that leaded gasoline is not essential for the engines to run properly.

Other restrictions could cause major problems. For example, some cities are considering banning private automobiles in crowded downtown areas. This would mean that more mass transportation systems would have to be developed, and that people would have to give up the convenience of using private cars downtown.

Government Action. Federal, state, and local governments have taken many steps to control pollution. They have passed laws limiting the amount of pollution that such things as automobiles, industries, and sewage treatment plants can put into the environment. They conduct and support research that leads to better understandings of environmental problems. They also provide money for antipollution programs.

The United States government passed its first important pollution control law in 1899. That law made it a crime to dump any liquid wastes except those from sewers into navigable waters. The law could have been extremely effective in lessening water pollution, but it was almost never enforced. Until the 1960's, few other significant federal pollution laws were passed. But during and since the 1960's, much legislation has been passed to deal with all types of pollution. In 1970, several federal pollution programs were combined under an independent federal agency called the Environmental Protection Agency. This agency is directly

responsible to the President. It has the power to set and enforce pollution standards, conduct research, and assist state and local governments in pollution control.

Most local and state governments have developed some kind of pollution control program. The programs vary widely, depending on the types of and seriousness of pollution problems in the area. The most common state and local pollution laws prohibit such activities as burning of trash in the open air and dumping of untreated sewage in water. In some areas, interstate agencies are being set up to control pollution that originates in one state and affects another.

The governments of most other industrial countries have also taken action against pollution. Canada, Japan, and many European countries have environmental problems similar to those of the United States and have passed laws to deal with them. In some areas, international agreements on pollution control are being developed.

Private Organizations. Groups of citizens throughout the United States have formed organizations to fight pollution. Most of these organizations are concerned with local problems. But many also work on regional, national, and international problems.

Private groups are responsible for much of the action governments and industries have taken to control pollution. They call public attention to pollution problems and put pressure on government and industry officials to act on the problems.

Man has caused some environmental pollution for as long as he has existed. Since prehistoric times, he has put wastes in water and caused smoke by burning fuel. But early people did not live crowded together, and they had no pollution-causing machines. Thus, pollution was light and spread out over large areas.

Pollution problems first arose during ancient times, when large numbers of people began living together in cities. As cities grew, pollution grew with them. But environmental problems seldom became extremely serious or widespread until the late 1700's and early 1800's, during a period called the Industrial Revolution. The Industrial Revolution began in England and spread to other European countries and to the United States. It was characterized by the development of factories and by cities that became overcrowded with factory workers. Coal was used to power most of the factories and to heat most of the homes in the cities. As a result, the air over such industrial cities as London became filled with huge amounts of smoke and soot. In addition, poor sanitation facilities allowed raw sewage to get into water supplies in some cities. The polluted water caused typhoid fever and other illnesses.

In the United States, air pollution problems in industrial cities became particularly serious in the 1900's. By the 1930's, smoke and soot from steel mills, power plants, railroads, and heating plants filled the air over many Eastern and Midwestern cities. In some cities, such as Pittsburgh and St. Louis, pollution frequently became so thick that motorists had to use headlights to see during daylight hours.

Since the 1950's, air pollution from coal burning has been greatly reduced in most parts of the world. Nearly all railroads and many industries and home heating plants now use cleaner fuels, such as oil and natural gas. In addition, many industries that still use coal have taken steps to control the pollution from their furnaces. Epidemics from disease-carrying germs in city

International Harvester Company

A Mobile Pollution Laboratory in New York City can take accurate measurements of air pollution anywhere in the city. Most large cities have set up agencies to deal with pollution.

water supplies are also no longer a major problem in most parts of the world. Cities now treat their water and keep it as free from germs as possible.

But in spite of these improvements, environmental pollution has become more serious and widespread since World War II than ever before. Technological advances, including more powerful automobiles and new chemicals, have helped cause this increase in pollution. In addition, the population of urban areas and the wealth of many people grew. More people meant more wastes of every kind. Greater wealth meant more people could own such things as automobiles. Factories turned out more products than ever before.

Gradually, public concern over environmental pollution grew. It became especially widespread in the late 1960's. Large numbers of people began objecting to the air pollution, water pollution, and solid wastes that they saw around them. More dramatic environmental tragedies—shown on television and reported in magazines and newspapers—also pointed up the seriousness of the pollution problem. These included oil spills that ruined beaches and killed wildlife, thick blankets of air pollution that lasted for days over cities, and waterways that had become nearly dead from pollution.

A highlight of the antipollution movement took place on April 22, 1970. On that day, called *Earth Day*, more than 20 million persons throughout the United States participated in antipollution demonstrations and other activities. Since then, the antipollution movement has continued to grow.   ALAN McGOWAN

Critically reviewed by JACK W. HUDSON

Sam Falk, Monkmeyer

An Oil-Soaked Beach resulted from a leak in an offshore oil well near Santa Barbara, Calif., in 1969. Oil spills have caused serious pollution problems in many parts of the world.

Section Five

Dictionary Supplement

This section lists important words to be included in the 1972 edition of THE WORLD BOOK DICTIONARY. This dictionary, first published by Field Enterprises Educational Corporation in 1963, keeps abreast of our living language with a program of continuous editorial revision. The following supplement has been prepared under the direction of the editors of THE WORLD BOOK ENCYCLOPEDIA and Clarence L. Barnhart, editor in chief of THE WORLD BOOK DICTIONARY. It is presented as a service to owners of the dictionary and as an informative feature to subscribers of THE WORLD BOOK YEAR BOOK.

A

Age of Aquarius, (in astrology) an age of unprecedented freedom and fellowship now newly dawning upon earth.
[< Latin *Aquārius* < *aqua* water]
anomalous water, polywater.
A·quar·i·an (ə kwãr′ē ən), *adj.* of or having to do with the Age of Aquarius. —*n.* a person belonging to this age, especially when of a younger generation.
Art De·co (ärt dā′kō), a style of ornate, geometrical, and colorful decoration that originated in France in the 1920's. [< French *Art Déco* (ratif) Decorative Art]

B

body clock, the rhythm or cycle of the body's normal activities.
Brans-Dick·e theory (brans′-dik′ē), a theory that predicts a lesser degree of curvature for electromagnetic waves passing through a strong gravitational field than that predicted by Einstein's general theory of relativity. [< Carl *Brans* and Robert *Dicke*, American physicists]
bread (bred), *n.* **4.** *U.S. Slang.* money: *... you're one of those who will never like cop out on the true scene and split for the Establishment bread* (New Yorker).
bust[2] (bust), *v.i.* **7.** *U.S. Slang.* to arrest: *I have never been busted for pot ...* (Time).
byte (bīt), *n.* a unit of eight bits in a computer memory. [< *b*(inar)*y* (digi)*t e*(ight)]

C

cal·ci·to·nin (kal′sə tō′nən), *n.* a hormone that regulates the level of calcium in body fluids, secreted by the thyroid gland.
carbon fiber, a strong, light synthetic fiber used in plastics, made by carbonizing acrylic fiber.
cas·sette (ka set′), *n.* **2.** a cartridge of videotape to play on a home television set: *The video cartridge, or cassette, will transform television by the mid-1970's* (Saturday Review). **3.** a case of baked clay, usually round with a flat bottom, in which china and other delicate ware are enclosed while baking; sagger. [< French *cassette* small case < *casse* case[2]]
central dogma, a theory in molecular biology which maintains that only DNA can act as a template or blueprint for the formation of RNA. This theory was considered fundamental until challenged by Teminism.
chip[1] (chip), *n., v.,* **chipped, chipping.** —*n.* **10.** a tiny piece of silicon imprinted or engraved with one or more microcircuits. [< verb]
con·sum·er·ism (kən sü′mə riz-əm), *n.* **2.** a movement to protect the consumer from unsafe or defective products.
co-opt (kō opt′), *v.t.* **2.** to take over; secure for oneself; adopt: *Williams believes that white power corrupted and then co-opted [Martin Luther] King by making him believe that he*

had power (Time). [< Latin *cooptāre* < *com-* together with + *optāre* choose, elect]
coun·ter·cul·ture (koun′tər kul′-chər), *n.* a group, especially of young people, opposed to traditional standards, customs, etc., of their society: *When their own children desert to the "counterculture" and in effect become strangers, Middle Americans say in bewilderment, "Either we neglected them or we spoiled them"* (Time).

D

da·ta·bank (dā′tə bank′), *n.* **1.** a large collection of records stored on a computer system from which specialized data may be extracted. **2.** such a computer system with its data. **3.** the place where such a computer system is located.
da·ta·base (dā′tə bās′), *n.* databank.
decision table, a table listing all the conditions of a problem and the possible actions to be taken, used to help make decisions, plans, etc.
demand pull, *Economics.* a rise in price caused by increased demand that exceeds supply.
di·ox·in (dī ok′sən), *n.* a very powerful poison used in certain weed-killing compounds that has been found to cause deformities in fetuses.
do·jo (dō′jō), *n., pl.* **-jos.** a place where judo, karate, etc., is taught. [< Japanese *dōjo*]
do·pa·mine (dō′pə mēn), *n.* a hormone of the adrenal glands that controls nerve function: *These hormones, particularly dopamine, play an intimate role in the tremors experienced by patients with Parkinson's disease* (Science News). [< *dop*(a) + *amine*]
do·pant (dō′pənt), *n.* an impure substance added in very small amounts to a semiconductor to vary its conductive properties. [< *dope* + *-ant*]
DOT (no periods), Department of Transportation.

E

element 104, an artificial, radioactive chemical element, the first of the transactinide series, produced in the form of various isotopes chiefly by bombarding californium with carbon ions; rutherfordium; kurchatovium.
element 105, hahnium.
encounter group, a group of people, especially people with different backgrounds, who get together to increase their self-awareness, sensitivity to others, and common interests or mutual objectives; T-group.
en·vi·ron·men·tal·ist (en vī′rən-men′tə list), *n.* **2.** a person who studies the environment and such problems as its pollution.

F

floor-through (flôr′thrü′, flōr′-), *n.* an apartment that takes up an entire floor: *in a floor-through*

ground floor apartment (New Yorker).
fu·tur·ol·o·gy (fyü′chə rol′ə jē), *n.* the study and forecasting of the future, especially of developments in the sciences and their effects upon society.

G

gate[1] (gāt), *n., v.,* **gat·ed, gat·ing.** —*n.* **14.** an electronic circuit with two or more input terminals and one output terminal, used to connect printed circuits, microcircuit chips, etc.
gene pool, the aggregation of genes that make up the genotype of a species.
genetic engineering, the manipulation of genes or of genetic processes to create new traits or organisms: *The development of techniques for isolating pure genes brings us one step closer to practical genetic engineering* (World Book Year Book).
greenhouse effect, the excessive accumulation of heat and water vapor in the earth's atmosphere caused by increased presence of pollutants which retain more solar radiation.
green revolution, the recent introduction of new, high-yielding strains of wheat, rice, etc., into Asia, resulting in revolutionary changes in the economy of many poor countries.
groove (grüv), *n., v.,* **grooved, groov·ing.** —*n.* **6.** *Slang.* something groovy or first-rate: *The show was a groove.*
grunt (grunt), *n.* **4.** *Slang.* an enlisted soldier in the United States Army or Marine Corps infantry, especially in combat in Vietnam. [< verb]
guaranteed income, a proposed annual minimum income below which the government will provide compensation.
guerrilla theater, theater performance especially on the street to dramatize opposition to war, discrimination, etc.

H

hahn·i·um (hä′nē əm), *n.* an artificial, radioactive chemical element produced by bombarding californium with nitrogen nuclei; element 105. *Symbol;* Ha; *at. wt.:* (C[12]) 260; *at. no.:* 105; *half-life:* 1.6 seconds. [< New Latin *Hahnium* < Otto *Hahn*, 1879–1968, a German radiochemist]
hard·hat (härd′hat′) *n.* **2.** *U.S.* a construction worker. **3.** a militant opponent of leftist views. **4.** a bowler or derby.
hash[2] (hash) *n. Slang.* hashish.
has·sle (has′əl), *n., v.,* **-sled, -sling.** —*v.t.* to annoy persistently; harass: *He [Jesus Christ] wore long hair and a beard, and when they hassled him, he taught more love* (Time).
head (hed), *n., pl.* **heads** or (*for def. 7*) **head,** *adj., v.* —*n.* **31.** *Slang.* a drug user or addict; an acidhead, pothead, etc.
head-hunt·er (hed′hun′tər), *n.*

2. *Informal.* a person who recruits executives for business.

his·to·com·pat·i·bil·i·ty (his'tō-kəm pat'ə bil'ə tē), *n.* a condition in which grafted or transplanted tissue is accepted by surrounding tissue.

hot pants, very short, close-fitting pants worn by women and girls.

hype (hīp), *v.,* **hyped, hyp·ing,** *n. Slang.* something that stimulates sales or interest; a publicity stunt, campaign, etc. [alteration of *hypo*²]

I

IC (no periods), **1.** immediate constituent. **2.** integrated circuit.

im·mu·no·flu·o·res·cence (i-myü'nō flü'ə res'əns), *n.* the use of a fluorescent dye to identify antibodies and antigens.

integrated circuit, an electronic circuit of many parts assembled at the same time and often combined with other such circuits in an electronic device, such as a television set or computer.

in·ter·me·di·a² (in'tər mē'dē ə), *n.* mixed media. [< *inter-* + *media*]

J

Jo·seph·son junction (jō'zəf-sən), an electronic unit of two separated superconductors that generate microwave radiation when alternating current is applied to them. [< Brian *Josephson,* a British scientist]

L

Las·sa fever (las'ə, lä'sə), a very contagious, fatal virus disease characterized by high fever, cardiac infection, and a rash with subcutaneous hemorrhage. It was discovered in Lassa, Nigeria.

L-do·pa (el'dō'pə), *n.* a form of the amino acid dopa, used as a drug to relieve the symptoms of Parkinson's disease; levodopa.

LEAA, Law Enforcement Assistance Administration.

le·vo·do·pa (lē'vō dō'pə), *n.* L-dopa.

love beads, a long string or chain of beads worn around the neck as a love symbol or for ornament.

low profile, manner, behavior, style, performance, etc., that is inconspicuous, moderate, or unexceptional: *. . . the unpretentious Mme. Ricci all the while maintained a low profile that made her the antithesis of her headline-making contemporary, Coco Chanel* (Time).

luminal art, a form of art that uses electric lights to create moving or flashing patterns, images, etc.

lu·mi·nist (lü'mə nist), *n.* **1.** a luminarist. **2.** a person who produces luminal art.

Lys·tro·sau·rus (lis'trə sôr'əs), *n.* a small herbivorous reptile of the Triassic period whose remains were discovered in South Africa, Asia, and Antarctica. [< New Latin *Lystro* + Greek *saûros* lizard]

M

mac·ro·bi·ot·ics (mak'rō bī ot'-iks), *n.* a dietary system derived from Zen Buddhism, based on the opposite qualities of yin and yang in various foods, and consisting chiefly of organically grown fruits, vegetables, and fish, usually accompanied by brown rice.

Ma·fi·a or **Maf·fi·a** (mä'fē ä), *n.* **2.** any secret society or exclusive set, circle, or clique: *the Diplomatic Mafia. The composers' Mafia, with its dedication to atonality . . .* (New Yorker). [see *mafia*]

mas·con (mas'kon), *n.* matter beneath the surface of the moon, marked by an increase in gravity: *Most scientists believe that the moon has mascons . . . which alter the orbital paths of spacecraft* (Science News). [< *mas*(s) *con*(centration)]

meth·yl·phen·i·date (meth'əl-fen'ə dāt), *n.* Ritalin: *The mild stimulant Ritalin* (*methylphenidate*), *widely used here for hyperactivity in children and for depression in persons past 40. . .* (Science News).

met·ri·cate (met'rə kāt), *v.t.,* **-cat·ed, -cat·ing.** to change to the metric system: *Nine-tenths of the world is already metricated, or going metric* (New Scientist).

met·ri·ca·tion (met'rə kā'shən), *n.* the act or process of changing to the metric system.

mil·i·tar·y-in·dus·tri·al com·plex (mil'ə ter'ē in dus'trē əl), the military branch of a government and all of the businesses supplying its needs: *We hear many dark mutterings about the vested interest of the military-industrial complex in war . . .* (Harper's).

minimal art, a form of painting and sculpture in which the simplest or most basic shapes, colors, etc., are used: *. . . sculptors have produced forms in aluminum, plastics, and other industrial materials which remain severely geometrical, deliberately anonymous, and almost totally impersonal. Such work has been called minimal art* (Sir Herbert Read).

mo·gul (mō'gul, mō gul'), *n.* **3.** a bump or snow mound on a ski run. [< *Mogul*]

mon·e·tar·ism (mon'ə ter iz'əm, mun'-), *n. Economics.* the theory that the money supply of a country determines the shape of its economy.

mon·o·pole (mon'ə pōl'), *n. Physics.* a hypothetical particle having a single magnetic pole, either north or south.

mul·ti·me·di·a (mul'ti mē'dē ə), *n.* mixed media.

N

narc (närk), *n. U.S. Slang.* a Federal narcotics agent.

Nax·a·lite (nak'sə līt), *n.* one of a group of Communist extremists in northern India. [< *Naxal*(bari), West Bengal village + -*ite*¹]

negative income tax, guaranteed income: *a negative income tax . . . [pays] taxes to the poor in exactly the same way that those who are better off now pay taxes to the Internal Revenue Service* (New York Times).

Nix·on Doctrine (nik'sən), a declaration made by President Richard M. Nixon in Guam in 1969, that the United States would avoid further military involvement like that in Vietnam and that Asian countries would have to deal themselves with aggression.

no-fault insurance (nō'fôlt'), automobile insurance that covers a policyholder against accidents regardless of who is at fault.

noise pollution, a concentration of excessively loud sound or noise by traffic, jet planes, etc.

no-knock (nō'nok'), *adj.* involving or authorizing forcible entry into a suspect's quarters without having to give warning or identification.

O

Ost·po·li·tik (ôst'pō'li tēk'), *n.* a policy of West Germany which seeks to establish normal diplomatic and trade relations with the Communist countries of eastern Europe. [< German *Ostpolitik* Eastern policy]

OTB (no periods), off-track betting.

P

pe·riph·er·al (pə rif'ər əl), —*n.* any of the input or output equipment of a computer, such as the keyboard, magnetic tape, or printout unit. —**pe·riph'er·al·ly,** *adv.*

pig¹ (pig), *n., v.,* **pigged, pig·ging. 6.** *Slang.* a derogatory term for a police officer.

plate (plāt), *n., v.,* **plat·ed, plat·ing.** —*n.* **27.** (in plate tectonics) one of the series of vast, platelike parts making up the crust of the earth: *Basically the idea is that both oceans and continents consist of rigid crustal plates—six major and several minor ones* (New Scientist).

plate tectonics, a theory that the earth's crust is divided into a series of vast, platelike parts that move or drift as distinct land masses.

po·lar·ize (pō'lə rīz), *v.,* **-ized, -iz·ing.** to divide into opposing sides or extremes; split into opposite camps or factions: *People are tired of being polarized on emotional issues . . .* (Time).

pol·y I:C (pol'ē ī'sē'), a chemical substance resembling double-stranded RNA core viruses, used to stimulate the body to produce interferon. [< *polyi*(nosinic:poly)-*c*(ytidylic acid)]

pol·y·wa·ter (pol'ē wôt'ər, -wot'-), *n.* a polymeric form of water that has about four times the molecular weight and fifteen times the viscosity of ordinary water; anomalous water: *Polywater . . . appears when water vapor condenses in minute capillary tubes . . . It is denser than ordinary water, and it does not freeze* (Science News).

PRONUNCIATION KEY: h**a**t, **ā**ge, c**ã**re, f**ä**r; l**e**t, **ē**qual, t**ė**rm; **i**t, **ī**ce; h**o**t, **ō**pen, **ô**rder; **oi**l, **ou**t; c**u**p, p**u̇**t, r**ü**le, **ū**se; **ch**ild; lo**ng**; **th**in; **ᴛн**en; **zh**, measure; **ə** represents **a** in about, **e** in taken, **i** in pencil, **o** in lemon, **u** in circus.

603

pot·head (pot′hed′), *n.* a person using or addicted to marijuana.

priority mail, *U.S.* a class of mail consisting of first-class matter weighing over 12 ounces and air mail weighing over 8 ounces.

pros·ta·glan·din (pros′tə glan′dən), *n.* any of 6 basic hormonelike substances that enter the blood stream from various parts of the body, including blood platelets, and to some extent control fever and inflammation and influence action of the heart, blood vessels, bronchial tubes, etc. [< *prosta*(te) *gland* (from the earlier belief that the substances originated there) + *-in*]

psy·chot·o·gen·ic (sī kot′ō jen′ik), *adj.* inducing or causing a psychotic state: *a psychotogenic agent or drug.*

R

rap[4] (rap), *v.,* **rapped, rap·ping,** *n. U.S. Slang.* —*v.i.* to talk informally; converse: *Young Cubans rap in this American-made political documentary, and are seen at work, school, and play* (New Yorker). —*n.* informal talk; conversation. [< *rap*(port)]

rif·am·pi·cin (rif′əm pī′sən), *n.* a semisynthetic antibiotic drug which inhibits the development of bacteria and the replication of viruses. [origin uncertain]

right on, *U.S. Slang.* perfectly right; entirely correct or true.

rip·off (rip′ôf′, -of′), *n. U.S. Slang.* **1.** a theft or robbery. **2.** an exploitation.

ruth·er·for·di·um (ruᴛʜ′ər fôr′dē əm), *n.* the American name for element 104. [< Lord Ernest *Rutherford,* 1871–1937 a British physicist]

S

sensitivity training, the development of feelings and attitudes that make people aware of feelings and attitudes of others considered as groups, such as women, blacks, etc.

sex·ism (sek′siz əm), *n.* discrimination against women in employment, politics, etc.

sex·ist (sek′sist), *n.* a person who favors or practices sexism. —*adj.* based on or characterized by sexism: *a sexist society, sexist laws.*

Sey·fert galaxy (sē′fərt), any of a class of spiral galaxies with very bright, compact centers. [< Carl K. *Seyfert,* an American astronomer]

Silent Majority, *U.S.* that part of the American population, thought to be a majority, which opposes militant dissidents and radicals but does not voice its opposition.

ski·doo (ski dü′, skē′dü), *n.* **1.** a kind of small snowmobile, usually seating two. **2. Ski-Doo.** a trademark for this vehicle.

split (split), *v.,* **split, split·ting,** *n., adj.* **5.** *U.S. Slang.* to leave a place; go away: *My old lady and I split after we got busted* (New York Sunday News).

star·quake (stär′kwāk′), *n.* a rup-

ture in the crust of a star, detected by sudden acceleration in its radiation emission: *Starquakes may change a pulsar's pulse* (New Scientist).

straight (strāt), *adj.* **4.** *Informal.* conventional; orthodox. **6.** *Slang.* a person who acts in a conventional manner or holds orthodox views: *The Silent Majority . . . that includes blue and white collars, small businessmen, professionals, and assorted "straights"* (Time).

street theater, 1. theater performance on the street. **2.** guerrilla theater.

T

tach·y·on (tak′ē on), *n. Physics.* a hypothetical particle that travels faster than light: *At the velocity of light a tachyon would possess infinite energy and momentum; as the particle lost energy, it would speed up, until at zero energy its velocity would be infinite!* (New Scientist). [< Greek *tachý*(s) swift + *on,* as in *ion*]

tee·ny-bop·per (tē′nē bop′ər), *n. Slang.* a teen-ager, especially a girl, who shuns adult conventions and adopts hippie ways: *Teenyboppers . . . flee to 4th Avenue in revolt against their parents* (Maclean's).

Tem·in·ism (tem′ə niz′əm), *n.* a theory in molecular biology which maintains, in contravention to the central dogma, that RNA can act as a blueprint or template for the formation of DNA. [< Howard M. *Temin,* an American biochemist who proposed this theory]

T-group (tē′grüp′), *n.* encounter group. [< (Sensitivity) *T*(raining) *group*]

thermal pollution, the discharge of heated effluents into water or air causing pollution destructive to surrounding plant and animal life.

thy·ris·tor (thī ris′tər), *n.* a transistor having the characteristics of a thyratron. [< *thyr*(atron) + (trans)*istor*]

thy·ro·cal·ci·to·nin (thī′rō kal′sə tō′nən), *n.* calcitonin.

tie-dye (tī′dī′), *v.,* **-dyed, -dye·ing,** *n.* —*v.t.* to dye (cloth) by tying parts of the material in tight knots so that the cloth inside the knot will not absorb the dye: *Simple bias-cut skirts are made of panne velvet tie-dyed by hand to rare shades* (New Yorker). —*n.* fabric tie-dyed.

trade-off (trād′ôf′, -of′), *n.* an even or fair exchange: *There would have to be at least implicit trade-offs giving higher prices to industry and higher real wages and salaries to employees* (London Times).

trans·ac·ti·nides (trans ak′tə nīdz), *n.pl.* the series of chemical elements whose atomic numbers extend beyond the actinides, from element 104 through element 112.

trans·ac·ti·nide series (trans-ak′tə nīd), the transactinides.

trash[1] (trash), *n.* **5.** *Slang.* act of vandalism.
—*v.t.* **2.** to treat or discard as worthless. **3.** *Slang.* to vandalize.
—*v.i. Slang.* to engage in van-

dalism: *. . . campus revolutionaries intent on destroying all freedom except their own are now turning to what they call 'trashing'—the setting of fires, hurling of rocks, smashing of windows* (New Yorker).

tri·bol·o·gy (trī bol′ə jē), *n.* the study of friction, wear, and lubrication. [< Greek *tríbos* a rubbing (< *tríbein* to rub) + English *-logy*]

U

un·bun·dle (un bun′dəl), *v.t., v.i.,* **-dled, -dling.** to separate an offer involving a number of elements grouped as a unit, such as rent and maintenance service: *International Business Machines' decision to "unbundle" its prices in Europe . . . heralds the end of an era* (London Times).

u·ni·sex (yü′nə seks′), *n.* a denial of distinction between the sexes: *. . . the triumph of unisex . . . which undermines what is sound in the cause of women's protest* (Harper's). —*adj.* of or having to do with such a denial.

unit pricing, a method of pricing foods or other merchandise by showing both the total price and the cost per pound, ounce, or other agreed-upon unit of measure.

urban guerrilla, a person who engages in terrorist activities in the cities.

V

video cartridge or **cassette,** a cartridge of film or videotape for use on a television set converted to show film or tape.

W

wa·fer (wā′fər), *n.* **6.** a tiny disk of silicon or ceramic material imprinted or engraved with one or more microcircuits.

Wan·kel engine (wang′kəl; *German* vän′kəl), an internal-combustion engine in which the difference in shape of a triangular rotor revolving within a cylinder makes firing chambers that replace conventional pistons and cylinders. [< Felix *Wankel,* a German engineer, who designed it]

Weath·er·man (weᴛʜ′ər mən), *n., pl.* **-men.** *U.S.* a member of the Revolutionary Youth Movement, an organization engaged in violent revolutionary activities.

Women's Liberation or **Women's Lib** (lib), a movement of active feminists demanding equal rights with men in all areas of life: *The abstract, damnation-dealing fury of some Women's Lib cells indeed resemble that of Weathermen gatherings* (Atlantic).

worry beads, a small string of colored beads to finger as a pastime or relaxation.

Z

zilch (zilch), *n. U.S. Slang.* nothing at all; zero: *The Senator's lady . . . says she knows that her real political power is approximately zilch* (Harper's). [origin uncertain]

Section Six

Index

How to Use the Index

This index covers the contents of the 1970, 1971, and 1972 editions of THE WORLD BOOK YEAR BOOK.

Each index entry is followed by the edition year (in *italics*) and the page numbers, as:

BURMA, *72*–255, *71*–236, *70*–252

This means that information about Burma begins on the pages indicated for each of the editions.

An index entry that is the title of an article appearing in THE YEAR BOOK is printed in capital letters, as: **AUTOMOBILE.** An entry that is not an article title, but a subject discussed in an article of some other title, is printed: **Tires.**

The various "See" and "See also" cross references in the index list are to other entries within the index. Clue words or phrases are used when two or more references to the same subject appear in the same edition of THE YEAR BOOK. These make it easy to locate the material on the page, since they refer to an article title or article subsection in which the reference appears, as:

Bangla Desh: Asia, *72*–220; Pakistan, *72*–459

The indication *"il."* means that the reference is to an illustration only. An index entry in capital letters followed by *"WBE"* refers to a new or revised WORLD BOOK ENCYCLOPEDIA article that is printed in the supplement section, as:

MOTION PICTURE, *WBE, 72*–560

A

AARON, HENRY LOUIS, 71–184
Abdul Halim Muazzam, 72–422
Abernathy, Ralph David, 70–278
Abortion: health and disease, 72–377; Protestant, 72–483; Roman Catholic, 72–497, 71–456
ABRAMS, CREIGHTON WILLIAMS, 69–198
Abyssinia. See ETHIOPIA
Accelerator: particle, il., 71–434
Accidents. See DISASTERS; SAFETY
Acheson, Dean G., 72–309, 71–449
Action: Peace Corps, 72–462; poverty, 72–476
Acupuncture, 72–427
Adams, Nick, 69–298
Adams, Roger, 72–309
ADEN. See SOUTHERN YEMEN, PEOPLE'S REPUBLIC OF
Adoption, 71–253
ADVERTISING, 72–198, 71–184, 70–198
Bacall, Lauren, 72–463; drugs, 72–322; photography, 72–471; poverty, 72–477; publishing, 72–487, 71–446; radio, 71–450, 70–482; regulation, 71–139; television, 71–486
Advocacy, 70–213
Aerospace industry, 71–317. See also AVIATION
AFGHANISTAN, 72–199, 71–185, 70–199
AFRICA, 72–200, 71–186, 70–200; geology, 71–338; health and disease, 72–377; petroleum and gas, 72–469; Portugal, 71–437; Roman Catholic, 71–456, 70–489; United Nations, 72–543, 71–501. See also by name of country
Aga Khan IV, 70–452
Agajianian, Gregory Cardinal, 72–309
Agency for International Development, 71–375
Aggression: zoology, 72–557
Aging, 70–242
AGNEW, SPIRO THEODORE, 72–204, 71–190, 70–205, Nixon, Richard M., il., 70–442; President of the U.S., il., 70–472; Republican Party, 72–495, il., 71–453; space exploration, 70–506. See also Vice-President of the United States
Agnon, Shmuel Yosef, 71–283
AGRICULTURE, 72–205, 71–190, 70–205
Afghanistan, 72–199; archaeology, 71–198; Asia, 70–219; Australia, 71–209, 70–223; Brazil, 71–232; China, 72–282, 71–254; congress, 71–272; economy, 72–326, 70–323; Europe, 70–337; farm equipment, 70–412; food, 72–354, 71–329, 70–344; gardening, 72–363, 70–354; Great Britain, il., 71–345; labor, 71–372; livestock show, 72–390, 71–359; Malaysia, 72–422; Mexico, 72–431, 71–397; Nobel Prizes, 71–420; Russia, 72–501, 71–461; soil conservation, 70–294; Special Report, 72–59; United Arab Republic, 71–499; Vietnam, 72–549; youth organizations, 72–556, 70–550
Agriculture, U. S. Department of: agriculture, 72–206, 71–193, 70–208; Butz, Earl L., 72–255; chemical industry, 71–250; congress, 72–295; Hardin, Clifford M., 70–364; pets, 72–467; U.S. government, 70–538
Ahidjo, Ahmadou, 72–257
Air defense system, 71–414
Air Force, 72–217, 71–201, 70–217
Air Force, U.S.: Laos, 71–373; Libya, 71–379; national defense, 72–446, 71–412, 70–437
Air pollution: automobile, 72–228, 71–212; aviation, 71–214; botany, 71–230; city, 72–285; electronics, 72–335, 70–332; environment, 72–339, 71–319; health and disease, 71–348; Japan, 71–363; Los Angeles, 71–388; manufacturing, 71–390; New York City, 71–416; petroleum, 71–431; pollution, 70–464; Venice, 71–151; weather, 71–512
Aircraft carrier, 71–414
Airlines. See AVIATION
Airplane Model, 71–337
Airport: Australia, 71–209, 70–224; aviation, 72–231, 70–227; Congress, 71–272; travel, 71–497, 70–531
Akers, Milburn P., 71–283
Akufo-Addo, Edward, 71–340
Alabama: celebrations, 70–262; Wallace, George C., 71–196
Alaska: Canada, 70–257; conservation, 72–298, 70–294; environment, 72–339; forests, 70–348; geology, 70–355; Indian, American, 72–387, 71–357, 70–376; personalities, 70–456; petroleum, 72–468, 70–457; state government, 70–513
Al-Azhari, Ismail, 70–302
ALBANIA, 72–209, 71–194
Albee, Edward: theater, 72–533

ALBERT, CARL BERT, 72–209; Congress, il., 72–295; Democratic party, 72–315
Alberta: Canada, 72–263, 71–243, 70–259; census, 72–266
Alcoholism: safety, 71–462
Alcindor, Lew, 72–241
ALDRIN, EDWIN EUGENE, JR., 70–209; astronauts, 72–224, 70–220; space exploration, 70–47, 70–504; Special Report, 70–64
Alexander, Ben, 70–302
Alexander, Sir Harold R. L. G., 70–302
Alexis, Patriarch, 71–299
Alfven, Hannes O., 71–420
Algae, 70–246
ALGERIA, 72–210, 71–194, 70–209
Africa, 71–190
Ali, Muhammad. See Clay, Cassius
Alien. See IMMIGRATION AND EMIGRATION
Alioto, Joseph L., elections, 72–334; San Francisco, 72–503, 70–496
Allen, George V., 71–283
Allen, James E., Jr.: deaths, 72–309; education, 71–307, 70–41, 70–326
ALLENDE GOSSENS, SALVADOR, 71–195 Chile, 72–280, 71–253; Latin America, il., 71–377
Allergy, 72–244
Alliance for Progress, 72–408
Alliluyeva, Svetlana, il., 71–425
Aluminum, 72–211
Alvarez, Luis Walter, 70–213
Amalrik, Andrei, 71–462
Amateur: sports, 72–516; tennis, 70–520
Amateur Athletic Union: sports, Focus, 71–54; track and field, 72–533, 70–525
Ambassador. See DIPLOMAT
Amchitka, 72–298
Ameba: biology, 71–228
American Civil Liberties Union, 71–263
American Dental Association, 72–317
American Indian. See INDIAN, AMERICAN
American Institute of Architects, 71–199
American Legion, 72–548, 71–505, 70–539
AMERICAN LIBRARY ASSOCIATION, 72–210, 71–196, 70–210
awards, 72–234, 71–216; library, 71–378; literature for children, 72–419, 71–387
American Medical Association, 72–377
AMERICAN PARTY, 72–211, 71–196, 70–210; Wallace, George C., 72–552, 71–196
American Revolution Bicentennial. See American Bicentennial, U. S.
American Veterans Committee, 72–548, 71–505, 70–539
AMIN, IDI, 72–211; Africa, 72–202; Tanzania, 72–526; Uganda, 72–549
Amino acids: astronomy, 72–224; biochemistry, 72–243
Ammonia, 70–267
Amtrak: transportation, 72–536; U.S. government, 72–546
Andean Common Market, 71–374
Anders, William A., 70–220
Anders, General Wladyslaw, 71–283
Anderson, Judith Edna B., 72–309
Andretti, Mario, 70–226
Andrews, George W., 72–309
Anemia, 72–426, 71–198
Anesthesia, 72–427
Anglican, 72–484
Angola: Africa, 72–202, 71–186, 70–202
ANGUILLA, 70–211; Great Britain, 70–362; West Indies, 70–548
Animal. See AGRICULTURE; CONSERVATION; Livestock; INTERNATIONAL LIVESTOCK EXPOSITION; PET; Wildlife; ZOOLOGY; ZOOS AND AQUARIUMS
Anne, Princess, 72–373, il., 70–451
Anniversaries. See CELEBRATIONS
Annulment, 71–457
Ansermet, Ernest A., 70–302
Antarctica: geology, 71–337
Anthony, John J., 71–283
ANTHROPOLOGY, 72–211, 71–196, 70–211. See also ARCHAEOLOGY
Antiballistic missile system: armed forces, 70–217; Canada, 70–257; Congress, 70–287; national defense, 72–448, 71–414, 70–437
Antibiotics, 70–318
Antibodies, 70–242
Antiques, 72–378
Antitrust laws: chemical industry, 70–267; drugs, 70–319
Apartheid, 72–212, 70–503
Apollo, Project: astronauts, 72–223; Focus, 70–47; space exploration, 72–510, 71–471, 70–504; Special Report, 70–64
Aquariums. See ZOOS AND AQUARIUMS
Arabia. See MIDDLE EAST; SAUDI ARABIA; YEMEN

ARAB EMIRATES, FEDERATION OF, 70–212; Persian Gulf Emirates, 72–462
Arab League, 72–462
Arab Republics, Federation of: Egypt, 72–333; Libya, 72–412; Middle East, 72–432; Syria, 72–525
Arabs: Chad, 72–276; Israel, 70–382; Jordan, 72–397, 71–365; Libya, 71–379; Middle East, 72–432, 71–400, 70–419; Persian Gulf Emirates, 71–425; religion, 70–484; United Nations, 71–501
Aramburu, Pedro Eugenio, 71–200
Arana Osorio, Carlos, 71–376
ARCHAEOLOGY, 72–212, 71–198, 70–212; waste disposal, 71–80. See also ANTHROPOLOGY
Archery, 72–517, 71–476, 70–511
ARCHITECTURE, 72–213, 71–199, 70–213 awards and prizes, 72–233, 71–215, 70–231; building and construction, 71–234; city, 72–192; fairs and expositions, 71–325; memorials, 72–429; Venice, 71–149. See also BUILDING AND CONSTRUCTION
Arctic: Canada, 70–257; celebrations, 70–263; conservation, 70–294; energy, 72–337; ocean, 70–444; petroleum, 70–457
Arenales Catalán, Emilio, 70–302
ARGENTINA, 72–215, 71–200, 70–216 bridges, 70–251; Latin America, 72–408, 71–374; Levingston, Roberto, 71–378
Arkansas: Mills, Wilbur, 72–434; state government, 72–519
ARMED FORCES OF THE WORLD, 72–216, 71–201, 70–217; Asia, 72–223; Europe, 72–346; world affairs, 72–20. See also NATIONAL DEFENSE and the names of the various countries and areas of the world
Armstrong, Frank A., 70–302
Armstrong, Louis: deaths, 72–309; music, popular, 72–444, 71–410
ARMSTRONG, NEIL ALDEN, 70–218; astronauts, 72–224, 71–206, 70–220; museums, 71–406; space exploration, 70–47, 70–204; Special Report, 70–64
Army, 72–217, 71–201, 70–217
Army, U.S.: national defense, 72–446, 71–412, 70–438; U.S. government, 71–504
Arts: Algeria, 70–209; Australia, 70–174; awards and prizes, 72–233, 71–215, 70–231; Canadian literature, 72–272; Focus, 72–47, 71–47, 70–53; literature, 72–415; literature for children, 72–417, 70–406; museums, 72–439. See also ARCHITECTURE; DANCING; LITERATURE; MOTION PICTURES; MUSIC; PAINTING; POETRY; SCULPTURE; THEATER; VISUAL ARTS
Asad, Hafiz al-, 72–525
Asbestos, 71–210
Ash, Roy L., 71–140
Ashbrook, John M., 72–495
ASIA, 72–218, 71–202, 70–218; agriculture, 72–59; food, 72–354; religion, 71–455; Roman Catholic, 71–455; Russia, 72–500. See also by name of country
Asquith of Yarnbury, Baroness, 70–302
Assad, Hafez al-, 71–483
Assassination: crime, 72–97; Jordan, 72–397; Kenya, 70–387; Roman Catholic, 71–455; Uganda, 71–499
ASTRONAUTS, 72–223, 71–206, 70–219. See also SPACE EXPLORATION; also names of individual astronauts
ASTRONOMY, 72–224, 71–207, 70–220 science, Focus, 72–35; space exploration, 72–510, 70–504
Astrophysics: astronomy, 72–224; science, 72–235; Weber, Joseph, 72–553
Aswan High Dam: Middle East, 71–401; United Arab Republic, 71–499
Athenagoras I, 72–323
Atlanta, 70–331
Atlantic City, 71–246
Atmosphere: air pollution, 70–464; weather, 72–553
Atomic Energy: armed forces, 72–217; awards, 72–234; 71–217, 70–233; conservation, 72–298; energy, 72–337, 71–316, 70–334; environment, 72–341; France, 72–362; India, 71–355; Mexico, 72–431; national defense, 72–446, 71–414; petroleum, 72–469; physics, 72–472, 71–434; science, 72–505; United Nations, 71–503
Atomic weight, 71–250
ATP, 71–226
Attica, N.Y.: civil rights, 72–287; crime, 72–304; state government, 72–519
Auctions and sales: Hartford, Huntington, 72–464; hobbies, 72–378, 71–348; motion pictures, 71–405; painting and sculpture, 70–449; stamp collecting, 72–518; visual arts, 72–549, 71–508

AUSTRALIA, 72–226, 71–209, 70–222
mining, 70–423; McMahon, William, 72–425; New Guinea, 71–415, 70–439; New Zealand, 70–440; Roman Catholic, 71–455; *Special Report,* 70–160; *Trans-Vision®,* 70–177
Australopithecus, 72–212, 70–211
AUSTRIA, 72–227, 71–210, 70–224
Czechoslovakia, 72–305; Kreisky, Bruno, 71–367; skiing, 70–500
Autographs, 72–378
Automation: energy, 71–317; labor, 70–393; photography, 72–470
AUTOMOBILE, 72–228, 71–210, 70–224
advertising, 72–198; Canada, 72–258; China, 71–256; disasters, 72–318, 71–295; economy, 71–300; electronics, 71–313; fairs, 72–349; insurance, 72–388, 71–358; labor, 71–368; manufacturing, 71–390; pollution, 70–465; retailing, 72–495; rubber, 72–425; Russia, *il.,* 72–502, 71–462, 70–495; space exploration, 72–510; state government, 72–521; steel industry, 72–522; transportation, *il.,* 71–494, 70–529; travel, 70–531; trucking, 72–536, 71–495; Woodcock, Leonard, 71–513
AUTOMOBILE RACING, 72–230, 71–212, 70–226
Auvray, Jean-Gabriel, 72–342
Avalanche, 71–338
AVIATION, 72–231, 71–213, 70–227; Australia, 72–227; awards, 72–235, 71–217; Cameroon, 72–257; Canadian literature, 71–246; celebrations, 70–264; Congress, 72–297; Cuba, 72–305; disasters, 72–318, 71–293, 70–314; espionage, 72–342; fairs, 72–349, 70–341; France, 70–353; games, models, and toys, 72–363; Germany, 72–367; labor, 71–373; Middle East, 71–400, 70–420; national defense, 72–446, 71–414, 70–437; noise, 70–132; regulation, 71–133; transportation, 72–536, 71–493, 70–528; travel, 72–538, 71–496, 70–530; United Nations, 70–537
Awami League: Asia, 72–222; Pakistan, 72–459
AWARDS AND PRIZES, 72–233, 71–215, 70–231; Dallas, 72–306; Nobel prizes, 72–456, 71–420; Pulitzer prizes, 72–488, 71–448. See also by name of organization and activity
Axelrod, Julius, 71–420
Ayub Khan, Mohammed, 70–449

B

BACALL, LAUREN, 71–218; personalities, 72–463; theater, 71–489
Bacci, Antonio Cardinal, 72–309
Backhaus, Wilhelm, 70–302
Badminton, 72–517, 71–476, 70–511
Baer, Arthur (Bugs), 70–302
Baggs, William C., 70–302
Bahamas, 72–554, 71–512, 70–548
Bahrain, 72–462, 71–425
Balaban, Barney, 72–309
Balaguer, Joaquín, 71–377
Balance of payments: economy, 70–325; Europe, 70–340; Great Britain, 70–359, 70–380; travel, 70–531
Ballard, Edna, 72–309
Ballet: Australia, 71–210; dancing, 72–306, 71–282, 70–300
Ballooning, *il.,* 72–515
BALTIMORE, 72–236, 71–219; memorials, 72–429
Banda, Hastings Kamuzu: Africa, 72–200; Malawi, 72–421, 71–389
BANDARANAIKE, SIRIMAVO, 71–219
Ceylon, 72–276, 71–248
Bangla Desh: Asia, 72–220; Pakistan, 72–459
BANKS AND BANKING, 72–236, 71–219, 70–233
Africa, 71–188; economy, 72–326, 70–320; Europe, 72–344; *Focus,* 71–32; housing, 72–381, 70–371; India, 70–374; international trade, 72–390, 71–359, 70–379; Ireland, 71–361; Latin America, 71–375; money, 72–435, 71–402; post office, 71–437; poverty, 71–438; stocks and bonds, 71–481; veterans, 72–547
Banuelos, Romana A.: immigration, 72–385; president of the U.S., 72–482
BANZER SUAREZ, HUGO, 72–238; Bolivia, 72–247
Baptist, 72–483, 71–445, 70–476
Barbados, 72–554, 71–512, 70–548
Barber, Anthony, 72–372, 71–322
Barbirolli, Sir John: deaths, 71–283; music, 71–406
Barley, 72–206
Barrientos Ortuño, René: Bolivia, 70–245; deaths, 70–302

Barton, Derek H. R., 70–443
BASEBALL, 72–238, 71–221, 70–236
Aaron, Henry L., 71–184; Blue, Vida, 72–238; Kuhn, Bowie K., 70–389; Mays, Willie, 71–392; personalities, *il.,* 72–464; sports, 72–55, 72–129, 72–515, 71–55, 70–59, 70–508
BASKETBALL, 72–240, 71–224, 70–238
Pan American games, 72–461; sports, 72–515; sports, 72–56
Basksha, Ali Sabzei, 72–463
Basques, 71–474
Basutoland. See LESOTHO
Baudouin I, *il.,* 71–266
Baunsgaard, Hilmar, 72–316
Bauxite: Australia, 71–210; mines and mining, 72–435
Beall, J. Glenn, Jr., 72–309, 71–453
Bean, Alan L., 71–472, 70–505
Beatles, the: music, 72–445, 71–409; Starr, Ringo, 71–429
Beberman, Max, 72–309
Bechuanaland. See Botswana
Becket, Welton D., 70–302
Beckett, Samuel, 72–463, 70–443
Beckwith, Jonathan, 70–35
Beethoven, Ludwig van: celebrations, 71–246; music, 71–406
Begley, Ed, 71–283
Belding, Don, 70–302
Belgian Congo. See CONGO (KINSHASA)
BELGIUM, 72–242, 71–226, 70–240
civil rights, 69–273; Congo (Kinshasa), *il.,* 71–266; Europe, *il.,* 69–336; tunnels, 70–251
Beliveau, Jean, 72–379
BELLOW, SAUL, 72–463
Belyayev, Pavel I., 71–283
Ben Bella, Ahmed, 72–210
Ben Salah, Ahmed, 70–532
Benediktsson, Bjarni, 71–283
Bengal. See Bangla Desh
Bennet, Linda, 72–463
Benson, Edgar J., 72–258
Benton, Thomas Hart: stamp collecting, *il.,* 72–518; Truman, Harry S., 72–540
Beran, Josef Cardinal, 70–302
Berlin: Europe, *il.,* 72–348, 71–324, 70–339; Germany, 72–365, 71–338, 70–356
Berne, Eric L., 71–283
Bernstein, Leonard, 72–440, 70–430
Berrigan, Daniel and Philip: civil rights, 72–288; crime, 72–304; Roman Catholic, 72–496; theater, 72–533
Bertrand, Jean-Jacques, 70–260
Beverages, 72–355, 71–329
Bhutto, Zulkifar Ali: Asia, 72–222; Pakistan, 72–460
Biafra: *il.,* 70–203; Nigeria, 72–452, 71–417, 70–440
Biathlon, 72–517, 71–476
Bicentennial, U.S.: fairs, 72–349, 71–326, 70–342; Philadelphia, 72–469
Bijedic, Djemal, 72–557
Billiards, 72–517, 71–476, 70–511
BIOCHEMISTRY, 72–243, 71–226, 70–241
dentistry, 71–291; photosynthesis, 71–251; psychology, 72–484
Biography: Canadian literature, 72–271, 71–246, 70–261; Johnson, Lyndon B., 72–397; literature, 72–413, 71–381, 70–401; literature for children, 72–417, 70–406; Pulitzer prizes, 72–489, 71–449, 70–481. See also DEATHS OF NOTABLE PERSONS; PERSONALITIES; also names of individuals
Biological warfare: Europe, 72–346; United Nations, 72–542
BIOLOGY, 72–245, 71–228, 70–242
astronomy, 72–224; awards and prizes, 72–235, 71–217, 70–233; biochemistry, 72–243, 71–226, 70–241; botany, 72–248, 71–230, 70–246; Nobel prizes, 70–444; old age, 70–445; psychology, 70–477; science, 70–35; space exploration, 70–507; zoology, 72–557, 71–515, 70–551
Birds: conservation, 70–294; psychology, 71–446; zoology, 72–557, 71–515, 70–552
Birmingham: environment, 72–339
Birnbaum, Martin, 71–283
Birth control: China, 72–283; drugs, 71–298; health, 72–377; India, 71–355; Ireland, 72–392; medicine, 70–414; Morocco, 72–436; population, 72–475, 71–436, 70–465; Roman Catholic, 72–497, 70–489
Births: population, 72–475; vital statistics, 72–551; zoos, 72–558
Bista, Kirti Nidhi, 71–415
Black, Hugo L.: courts, 72–302; deaths, 72–309
Black, Shirley Temple, 70–452
Black Panthers: Chicago, 72–279; civil rights, 72–286, 71–261; New Orleans, 72–450, 71–415

BLACKMUN, HARRY ANDREW, 71–229; courts, 71–277
Blacks. See Negro
Blaiberg, Philip: deaths, 70–302; medicine, 70–413
Blakeney, Allan, 72–264
Blanchfield, Florence A., 72–309
Blanda, George, 71–331
BLATCHFORD, JOSEPH HOFFER, 70–243; Peace Corps, 70–451; poverty, 72–476
Blindness: handicapped, 72–376, 71–347, 70–364; social security 70–501
Blood: medicine, 72–428; Paukstys, Victoria, 72–465
BLOUNT, WINTON MALCOLM, 70–244
Cabinet, 72–255; postal service, 72–475
BLUE, VIDA, 72–246; baseball, 72–238; sports, 72–130
Blumenthal, Richard, 70–93
BOATS AND BOATING, 72–246, 71–229, 70–244
personalities, *il.,* 71–428; rowing, 71–475, 70–510; sports, 72–517
Bobsledding, 72–517, 71–476, 70–511
Boe, Roger, 70–453
Boehm, Edward M., 70–302
Boeing 747, 72–232, 71–496
Bogan, Louise: deaths, 71–283; poetry, 71–436
Boles, John, 70–302
BOLIVIA, 72–247, 71–230, 70–245
Banzer Suarez, Hugo, 72–238; Latin America, 71–374
Bologna, Pat, 72–463
Bonds. See STOCKS AND BONDS
Bonilla, Jesse, 71–426
Book publishing: Brand, Stewart, 72–463; Canadian Library Association, 72–271; fairs, 72–349; Johnson, Lyndon B., 72–397; poetry, 72–474, 71–435; publishing, 72–487, 71–447; Roman Catholic, 72–498; stamp collecting, 72–518. See also LITERATURE
BORDABERRY, JUAN MARIA, 72–247
Borlaug, Norman: agriculture, 71–194; Nobel prizes, 71–420; *Special Report,* 72–61
Borman, Frank: astronauts, 71–206, 70–219; space exploration, 70–507
Born, Max, 71–283
Borten, Per, 72–456
BOSTON, 72–248, 71–230, 70–245
architecture, *il.,* 70–215; celebrations, 71–246; Democratic Party, 72–315; elections, 72–334; museums, 71–406; music, 72–440, 71–406; state government, 72–521; visual arts, 72–549, 71–507
BOTANY, 72–248, 71–230, 70–246; agriculture, 71–190; gardening, 72–363, 71–337, 70–354; geology, 72–364; Green Revolution, 72–59. See also AGRICULTURE; GARDENING
Botstein, Leon, 71–426
Botswana: Africa, 70–204; Rhodesia, 71–455
Bottling, 71–92
Bouché, Louis, 70–302
Boulez, Pierre, 72–440
Boulogne, Charles (Father Damien), 70–302
Boumediene, Houari, 72–210, 71–194, 70–209
BOURASSA, J. ROBERT, 71–231; Canada, 72–238; *il.,* 71–242; Quebec, 72–264, 71–244
Bourguiba, Habib, 72–540, 71–498, 70–532
Bourke-White, Margaret, 72–309
BOWLING, 72–248, 71–231, 70–246
BOXING, 72–249, 71–231, 70–246
Frazier, Joe, 71–336
Boy Scouts of America, 72–555, 71–514, 70–550
Boyd Orr, Lord, 72–309
Boys' Clubs of America, 72–556, 71–514, 70–550
Bracken, John, 70–302
Brackett, Charles, 70–302
Bragg, Sir William Lawrence, 72–309
Brain: psychology, 71–446, 70–477
Brakes, 71–313
Brand, Stewart, 72–463
BRANDT, WILLY, 70–247; Europe, *il.,* 71–323; Germany, East, 71–338; Germany, West, 72–366, 71–340, 70–355; Nobel prizes, 72–456; personalities, 71–425; Russia, 72–499
BRATELLI, TRYGVE M., 72–250; Norway, 71–456
BRAZIL, 72–250, 71–232, 70–248
building and construction, 70–251; Latin America, 72–408, 71–374; Médici, Emílio, 70–413; Protestant, 72–484, 71–446; soccer, 72–507, 71–467; West Indies, 72–554
Breadbasket, Operation, 70–276
Breedlove, Craig, 72–120
Breger, Dave, 71–283
Brezhnev, Leonid Ilyich: Bulgaria, 72–254; communism, 70–283; Czechoslovakia, *il.,*

72–305; Germany, 72–367; Hungary, 72–383; Russia, 72–499, 71–458, 70–493; Yugoslavia, 72–557
Bridge and Tunnel: building and construction, 72–253, 71–235, 70–250; disasters, 71–297; Prince Edward Island, 70–260
BRIDGE, CONTRACT, 72–252, 71–234, 70–249
Briggs, Walter O., Jr., 71–283
Briscoe, Robert, 70–302
British Columbia: Canada, 72–263, 71–243, 70–259; census, 72–266; tunnels, 70–251
British Commonwealth. See **GREAT BRITAIN;** also articles on the various countries of the Commonwealth
British Guiana. See **GUYANA**
British West Indies. See **Caribbean Islands; Jamaica; Trinidad and Tobago; West Indies**
Broadcasting: advertising, 72–199; Agnew, Spiro T., 72–204; awards, 72–233. See also **RADIO; TELEVISION**
Brock, William E., III, 71–453
BROOKS, ANGIE ELIZABETH, 70–249; United Nations, *il.,* 70–535
Brown, John Mason, 70–303
Brown, Oscar, Jr., *il.,* 71–450
Brownlee, John D. M., 70–303
Bruce, Ailsa Mellon, 70–303
Bruce, Louis R., Jr., 70–376
Buckley, James: elections, 71–310; Republican Party, 71–453
Buddhism: religion, 71–451, 70–483; Vietnam, 70–545
Budget, national: armed forces, 71–201; Congress, 72–291, 71–267; economy, 72–326; Mayo, Robert P., 70–412; national defense, 72–449, 71–412, 70–437; President of the U.S., 72–481, 71–441, 70–473; science and research, 71–464; taxation, 71–484, 70–519
Buganda, 70–532
BUILDING AND CONSTRUCTION, 72–252, 71–234, 70–249
architecture, 72–214, 71–199; Australia, 71–209; banks and banking, 72–237, 70–234; Boston, 70–245; chemical industry, 70–265; Chicago, 71–252, 70–269; Dallas, 72–306, 70–300; dam, 70–251; energy, 71–315, 70–332; forest products, 70–348; highways, 72–537, 71–495; housing, 72–381, 71–352, 70–371; Houston, 71–353; labor, 72–404, 71–371; library, 72–411, 71–378; Los Angeles, 70–409; Philadelphia, 72–469; San Francisco, 72–503; steel, 71–480; theater, 71–490; transportation, 70–529; Washington, D.C., 70–546. See also **ARCHITECTURE**
BULGARIA, 72–254, 71–236, 70–252; Algeria, 71–195; Eastern Orthodox, 72–323
Bullock, Dan, 70–303
Bulpitt, Stan, 72–463
Bunche, Ralph J., 72–309
Burch, Dean, 70–519
BURGER, WARREN EARL, 70–252; arts, 70–56; courts and laws, 71–278, 70–294; U.S. government, 72–544, 70–538
Burke, Billie, 71–283
BURMA, 72–255, 71–236, 70–252
Burnett, Leo, 72–309
Burnham, L.F.S., 72–375, 71–346
BURNS, ARTHUR FRANK, 71–236; banks and banking, 72–236, 71–219, 70–235; economy, *il.,* 72–328, *il.,* 70–324; *Special Report,* 70–85
Burns, David, 72–309
Bus: disasters, 72–318, 71–295, 70–316; transportation, 70–529
BUSH, GEORGE H.W., 72–255: President of the U.S., 71–443; United Nations, 72–543, 71–503
Business. See **ECONOMY, THE**
Busing, school: civil rights, 72–286; education, 72–331; President of the U.S., 72–481, 71–442; San Francisco, 72–503
BUTZ, EARL L., 72–255; agriculture, 72–205; U.S. government, 72–544
Byington, Spring, 72–309
Byrd, Harry F., Jr., 71–453
Byrd, Richard E., 71–394

C

CABINET, 72–255, 71–237, 70–253
Butz, Earl L., 72–255; Canada, 72–260, 71–239; Connally, John B., Jr., 71–272; Hodgson, James D., 71–351; Morton, Rogers C.B., 71–403; President of the U.S., 72–480, 71–443; Richardson, Elliot L., 71–455; *Special Report,* 70–82. See also names of Cabinet members
Cable, submarine, 71–265, 70–280

Cable television: communications, 72–290; television, 72–528, 71–486
Caetano, Marcelo Alves, 71–437, 70–466
Cahill, William T., 70–486
Cairo (U.A.R.), 70–262
Caldecott medal, 72–419, 70–408
CALDERA, RAFAEL, 70–253; Venezuela, 72–547, 71–505, 70–539
Calderón Guardia, Rafael A., 71–283
Caldwell, Dean, 71–426
Calendar: 1972, 72–625; 1971, 71–629; 1970, 70–627. See also **CELEBRATIONS; CHRONOLOGY 1971** (pages 8 to 14)
California: architecture, *il.,* 71–199; bridge, 70–251; Chavez, Cesar, 71–249; conservation, 71–273, 70–293; courts and laws, 72–303; crime, 71–278; dams, 70–251; Democratic party, 70–310; disasters, 72–319; education, 72–330; geology, 72–365; Los Angeles, 72–420, 71–388, 70–408; Nixon, Richard M., 70–443; pollution, 70–463; San Francisco, 72–503, 71–464, 70–496; state government, 72–519; taxation, 72–527
California, University of, 70–328
CALLEY, WILLIAM LAWS, Jr., 72–256; national defense, 72–447; President of the U.S., 72–482; Stevenson, Adlai, 72–153
CAMBODIA, 72–256, 71–237, 70–253
Asia, 72–222, 71–222; China, 71–255; Nol, Lon, 71–420; President of the U.S., 71–440; Thailand, 72–487; Vietnam, 71–506; world affairs, 71–19
Camera, 72–470, 71–432, 70–460
CAMEROON, 72–257; Africa, 71–187, 70–204
Camp Fire Girls, 72–556, 71–514, 70–550
Campos, Eddie, 72–463
CANADA, 72–258, 71–238, 70–254
banks, 72–237, 71–221; bridge, 71–235; celebrations, 71–246; China, 71–255; coin collecting, 72–289; dancing, 71–282; economy, 72–324; environment, 71–320; fairs and expositions, 71–326; fishing industry, 71–328; Formosa, 71–333; international trade, 71–360; Jews, 71–365; labor, 70–393; libraries, 71–245; Michener, Roland, 72–431, 71–397, 70–417; mining, 71–401; music, popular, 72–443; Nigeria, 72–452; Russia, 72–500; Trudeau, Pierre E., 72–539, 71–497, 70–531
CANADIAN LIBRARY ASSOCIATION, 72–271, 71–245, 70–261
CANADIAN LITERATURE, 72–271, 71–245, 70–261
Canal, 72–299
Cancer: biochemistry, 71–226; dentistry, 70–312; medicine, 72–428, 71–393, 70–414; science, 72–504
Canoeing, 72–517, 71–476, 70–511
Canterbury, 71–248
Capital punishment: courts and laws, 72–302; crime, 70–304
Capote, Truman, 71–426
Carbon monoxide, 71–208
Cárdenas, Lázaro, 71–283
Cardinals, Sacred College of: Roman Catholic, 70–490
Caribbean Islands, 72–410, 71–377, 70–397. See also **WEST INDIES**
Carlucci, Frank, 71–438
Carnap, Rudolf, 71–283
Carswell, G. Harrold, 71–504
Cartoon: arts, *Focus,* 71–48; awards, 72–233, 71–216; Pulitzer prizes, 72–488, 71–448, 70–481; *Special Report,* 70–147
Cary, William L., 71–140
Casey, William Joseph, stocks and bonds, 72–523
Cash, Johnny, 71–410
Casper, Billy, 71–341
Cassette: electronics, 71–314; motion pictures, 72–438, 71–405; recordings, 71–450
Casson, Sir Lewis, 70–303
Casting, 72–517, 71–476
Castle, Irene, 70–303
Castro, Fidel: Cuba, 72–305; personalities, 72–464
Cat: personalities, 72–465; pets, 72–468, 71–430, 70–457
Cates, General Clifton B., 71–283
Cather, Willa, 70–415
Cavanagh, Jerome P., 70–312
Cayton, Horace R., 71–283
Ceausescu, Nicolae: communism, 70–283; Romania, 72–498, 71–457, 70–491
CELEBRATIONS, 72–272, 71–246, 70–262
Australia, 71–209, 70–160; Boston, 70–245; British Columbia, 72–263; Bulgaria, 70–252; calendar 1972, 72–625; calendar 1971, 71–629; calendar 1970, 70–627; Canadian literature, 71–245; civil liberties, 71–263; coin collecting, 72–289; conservation, 71–

273; Dickens, Charles, 71–246; Europe, 70–337; fairs, 72–349, 71–326, 70–342; France, *il.,* 72–349; Greece, *il.,* 72–374; handicapped, 72–377; Iran, 72–392; Manitoba, 71–243; music, 72–440; painting and sculpture, 70–447; Truman, Harry S., 71–498; United Nations, 71–500; visual arts, 72–549; weather, 71–511
Celibacy, 72–497
Cell, 71–228
Censorship: arts, 70–54; Great Britain, 72–373; motion pictures, 72–437; Portugal, 72–475; radio, 72–489
CENSUS, 72–274, 71–517, 70–264
Canada, 72–265; city, 72–284; housing, 72–382; poverty, 72–476; Russia, 71–461; St. Louis, 71–463; state government, 71–476; taxation, 72–526; Washington, D.C., 72–552
Central African Republic, 71–190, 70–203
Central America. See **LATIN AMERICA**
Central American Common Market, 71–374
Central Intelligence Agency: espionage, 70–336
Cerf, Bennett, 72–309
Cernan, Eugene, 70–504
CEYLON, 72–276, 71–248, 70–265; Asia, 72–222; Bandaranaike, Sirimavo, 71–219
CHABAN-DELMAS, JACQUES MICHEL PIERRE, 70–265
CHAD, 72–276; Africa, 70–202; Libya, 72–412
Chambers, Lenoir, 71–283
Chanel, Coco: deaths, 72–309; fashion, 72–350
Chapin, Dwight L., 72–96
Charles, Prince, 71–423, *il.,* 70–362
CHAVEZ, CESAR ESTRADA, 71–249; labor, *il.,* 71–371
CHEMICAL INDUSTRY, 72–277, 71–249, 70–265
drugs, 71–298, 70–318; environment, 72–341, 71–321; St. Louis, 70–495
Chemical warfare, 70–291
CHEMISTRY, 72–278, 71–250, 70–267
astronomy, 70–222; awards and prizes, 72–234, 71–217, 70–233; biochemistry, 72–243, 71–226, 70–241; botany, 70–246; chemical industry 71–249, 70–265; gardening, 72–363; Nobel prizes, 72–456, 71–420, 70–443
CHESS, 72–278, 71–251, 70–268
Fischer, Bobby, 72–353; sports, 72–54
Chiang Ching, *il.,* 71–256
Chiang Ching-kuo, 72–361, 71–333
Chiang Kai-shek, 72–360, 70–349
CHICAGO, 72–279, 71–252, 70–269
architecture, 72–213, 71–199, 70–215; building and construction, 71–234; celebrations, 72–272; city, 72–185; civil rights, 70–278; courts and laws, 72–302; crime, 71–278; Democratic party, 72–315; education, 72–330; elections, 72–335; museums, *il.,* 70–428; music, classical, 72–442, 71–406, 70–429; music, popular, 71–409; Republican party, 72–494; transit, 70–530; visual arts, 72–550, 71–507; zoos, 72–558, 70–116
"Chicago 7": civil rights, 71–263; courts, 71–277
CHI CHENG, 71–252; track and field, 72–535, 71–492
CHILD WELFARE, 72–279, 71–253, 70–269
dentistry, 70–312; education, 70–326; health and disease, 70–366; mental health, 72–430, 70–416; rubella, 70–99; Salvation Army, 72–503; social security, 70–502; television, 72–528
Childress, Libby, 71–427
Childs, Marquis W., 71–448
CHILE, 72–280, 71–253, 70–270; Allende Gossens, Salvador, 71–195; Cuba, 72–305; Latin America, *il.,* 72–406, 71–374; mining, 72–434, 70–423; Nobel prizes, 72–456
CHINA, 72–280, 71–254, 70–270
acupuncture, 72–427; Africa, 72–202; agriculture, 72–66; Albania, 72–209, 71–194, 70–209; armed forces, 72–217, 71–201, 70–217; Asia, 72–221, 70–218; Burma, 71–236, 70–252; Canada, 72–261, 71–241, 70–257; Ceylon, 72–276; Communism, 70–282; espionage, 72–342; fashion, 72–349; food, 72–354; Formosa, 72–360, 71–333, 70–349; hobbies, 71–349; international relations, 70–20; Malaysia, 72–422, 71–389; Mongolia, 70–424; Nigeria, 72–452; population, 71–436; President of the U.S., 72–480; religion, 72–493, 71–451; Romania, 72–498; Russia, 72–499, 71–459, 70–492; space exploration, 72–513, 71–474; sports, 72–53; stamp collecting, 72–526; Tanzania, 72–526; Thailand, 72–529; United Arab Republic, 70–553; United Nations, 71–500, 70–537; U.S. affairs, 72–24; Vietnam, 70–544; world affairs, 72–18

CHISHOLM, SHIRLEY ANITA, 72–283
Democratic party, 72–316
Chittenden, Keith, 70–453
Cholera: Chad, 72–276; health and disease, 72–377, 71–347; India, 72–386
Chou En-lai: China, 72–280, 71–255, 70–272; Communism, 70–282
Christ Uniting, Church of, 71–445
Christian Church. See **EASTERN ORTHODOX; PROTESTANT; RELIGION; ROMAN CATHOLIC; SALVATION ARMY**
Christo, 72–551
Church membership: religion, 72–493, 71–452; Roman Catholic, 72–498, 71–457
Churchill, Winston, 72–429, 70–415
Ciannelli, Eduardo, 70–303
CITY, 72–284, 71–257, 70–274; architecture, 72–214, 70–215; census, 72–274, 71–520; civil rights, 71–261, 70–278; crime, 72–97, 70–296; Democratic party, 72–315, 70–311; Detroit, 72–317; economy, 71–300, 70–323; education, 72–41; elections, 72–333, 70–330; housing, 70–371; Moynihan, Daniel, 70–427; Republican party, 70–486; *Special Report,* 72–179; sports, 72–134; taxation, 72–483; transit, 72–538, 71–495, 70–530; *Trans-Vision,* 72–161; waste disposal, 71–80; *WBE,* 71–562; zoos and aquariums, 71–516
City planning, 71–215
Civil Aeronautics Board: aviation, 72–231, 71–213, 70–227; regulatory agencies, 71–132; travel, 72–539
Civil disorders. See **CIVIL RIGHTS; CITY; Protests**
CIVIL RIGHTS, 72–286, 71–259, 70–277
Chicago, 70–269; consumer affairs, 72–300; courts and laws, 72–301, 71–276, 70–295; democracy, 70–309; Democratic party, 72–316; education, 72–331, 71–307, 70–329; Fauntroy, Walter E., 72–352; Great Britain, 72–372; housing, 70–371; Jews, 72–396; Jordan, Vernon E., Jr., 72–398; labor, 71–373, 70–390; library, 71–378; literature, 71–383, 70–402; Los Angeles, 71–388; Philadelphia, 72–469; President of the United States, 72–481, 71–442; Protestant, 71–445; publishing, 72–485, 71–447; radio, 71–449; United Nations, 70–537. See also **Protests**
Civil service, 72–185, 70–501
Civil war: Iraq, 71–361; Jordan, 71–365; Nigeria, 71–417; Yemen, 71–513
Civil War, U.S., 71–394
Clark, Joseph James, 72–309
Clark, Walter Van Tilburg, 72–311
Clay, Cassius: boxing, 72–249, 71–231, 70–246; *Focus,* 72–54
Clement, Frank Goad, 70–303
Clemente, Roberto, 72–239
Cleva, Fausto, 72–505
CLEVELAND, 72–288, 71–264; city, 71–258; Democratic party, 70–311; elections, 70–331; music, 72–440, 71–406; Republican party, 72–494; Salvation Army 70–495; visual arts, 72–549
Clothing, 70–411. See also **FASHION**
Clubs. See **Organizations**
Coal: economy, 72–329; energy, 72–336, 71–314; mines and mining, 72–434, 71–401, 70–423; safety, 71–463
Coe, Albert B., 71–283
Coffee: Ethiopia, 72–343; agriculture, *il.,* 71–192
Cohen, Isadore M., 71–427
Coin, 70–423
COIN COLLECTING, 72–289
hobbies, 72–349, 70–368; money, 72–435
Cold War. See **COMMUNISM; NATIONAL DEFENSE**
Cole, Kenneth R., Jr., 70–85
Collecting: *Special Report,* 71–111
Collin, Jean, 72–505
COLLINS, MICHAEL, 70–279; astronauts, 70–220; space exploration, 70–504; *Special Report,* 70–64
Collyer, Clayton (Bud), 70–303
COLOMBIA, 72–289, 71–264, 70–280
Latin America, 72–409, 71–374, 70–397; Pastrana Borrero, Misael, 71–424
COLOMBO, EMILIO, 71–264; Italy, 72–394; President of the U.S., *il.* 72–482
Colombo, Joseph A., Sr., 72–304
Colonialism: Africa, 71–186; Pacific Islands, 71–423; United Nations, 70–537
Colorado: education, *il.,* 72–332; energy, *il.,* 70–333; tunnels, 72–254
Columbia River, 72–253
Comet, 71–207
Comfort, Dr. Alex, 72–458
Comic strip. See **Cartoon**
Commerce. See **ECONOMY, THE; INTERNATIONAL TRADE AND FINANCE**

Commerce, U.S. Department of: fairs, 72–348; ocean, 71–421; Stans, Maurice H., 70–511; weather, 71–510
Common Market: Austria, 72–227; Denmark, 72–316; economy, 72–324, 71–305, 70–323; Europe, 72–344, 71–322, 70–337; *Focus,* 72–29; France, 72–361, 70–352; Great Britain, 72–370, 71–344; Greece, 71–346; international trade, 72–391; Latin America, 72–408, 71–374, 70–395; Norway, 72–456, 71–421; world affairs, 72–20, 70–19
Commonwealth of Nations. See **GREAT BRITAIN;** also articles on various countries of the Commonwealth
COMMUNICATIONS, 72–290, 71–264, 70–280; Canada, 70–256; electronics, 71–313, 70–332; regulations, 71–129. See also **LITERATURE; MOTION PICTURES; POSTAL SERVICE; PUBLISHING; RADIO; RECORDINGS; SPACE EXPLORATION; Telephone and Telegraph; TELEVISION; TRANSPORTATION**
COMMUNISM, 70–282
Africa, 72–202; Allende Gossens, Salvador, 71–195; armed forces, 71–201; Asia, 72–222, 71–202; Cambodia, 72–256; Ceylon, 72–276, 71–248; Chile, 71–253; Congo (Brazzaville), 71–266; economy, 71–305; Finland, 72–352; Honecker, Erich, 72–380; India, 71–355; Indonesia, 72–387, 71–357; international education, 71–99; Jews, 71–365; Laos, 72–405, 71–373; Malaysia, 72–422, 71–389; national defense, 71–411; Philippines, 72–470; Southern Yemen, 72–509; Sudan, 72–523; Thailand, 71–487; Vietnam, 71–506; world affairs, 70–18. See also articles on individual Communist countries
Compton-Burnett, Dame Ivy, 70–303
COMPUTERS, 70–285; agriculture, 71–193; botany, 71–231; Canada, 72–265; communications, 72–290, 71–265; electronics, 70–331; games, 71–336; invention, 70–380; manufacturing, 71–392, 70–411; sports, 72–123; stocks and bonds, 70–515; travel, 70–531
Concrete, 71–234
Confederate States, 71–395
CONGO (BRAZZAVILLE), 71–266; 70–202
CONGO (KINSHASA), 72–290, 71–266; Africa, 70–200; Protestant, 72–484
CONGRESS OF THE UNITED STATES, 72–291, 71–267, 70–286
advertising, 72–198, 71–185, 70–198; agriculture, 72–205, 71–193; Albert, Carl, 72–209; automobile, 72–229, 71–212; aviation, 72–232, 71–214; banks and banking, 72–237, 70–235; basketball, 72–241; Black Caucus, *il.,* 72–287; cabinet, 70–253; census, 71–523; child welfare, 72–279; Chisholm, Shirley, 72–283; city, 72–284; civil rights, 72–287; conservation, 72–298, 71–273; consumer affairs, 72–300, 71–274; courts and laws, 70–294; crime, 72–303, 71–278, 70–296; democracy, 70–309; Democratic party, 72–315, 71–289, 70–310; Dole, Robert J., 72–322; drugs, 72–322, 70–319; economy, 72–327, 71–305; education, 71–308, 70–324; elections, 72–334, 71–310, 70–330; environment, 71–320; Fauntroy, Walter E., 72–352; fishing, 72–354, 71–328; forest, 72–360, 71–333; foundations, 70–349; games, 70–353; health, 72–377; housing, 71–352; Humphrey, Hubert, 72–383; immigration and emigration, 71–354, 70–374; Indian, American, 71–356, 70–376; insurance, 71–357; international trade, 71–359; invention, 70–380; Jackson, Henry M., 72–395; Latin America, 72–406; McCloskey, Paul N., Jr., 72–425; McCormack, John W., 71–392; McGovern, George S., 72–425; Medicare, 70–412; Mills, Wilbur, 72–434; mines, 72–434; money, 71–402; Muskie, Edmund S., 72–445; national defense, 72–446; ocean, 71–421; 70–445; old age, 72–458, 70–446; petroleum, 71–431; population, 72–475, 71–436; post office, 71–437, 70–467; poverty, 71–438, 70–468; President of the U.S., 72–478, 71–441, 70–473; regulatory agencies, 71–129; Republican party, 72–494, 71–453, 70–486; retailing, 70–487; safety, 71–463; science, 72–504; Scott, Hugh D., 72–497; social security, 72–507, 71–468, 70–501; social welfare, 72–508, 71–469; space exploration, 72–514; *Special Report,* 72–137; state government, 72–521; taxation, 72–526, 70–518; television, 70–520; transportation, 72–535, 71–494; travel, 72–538, 70–531; United Nations, 72–542; U.S. affairs, 72–26; U.S. government, 72–544, 71–504;

veterans, 71–505; voting, 71–312; Washington, D.C., 72–552, 71–510; women's rights, 72–287
CONNALLY, JOHN BOWDEN, JR., 71–272; cabinet, 72–256; Canada, 72–258; economy, *il.,* 72–328; President of the U.S., 72–478, 71–443; U.S. government, 72–544
Connecticut: architecture, 71–199; Republican party, 71–453; state government, 72–518
Conniff, Frank, 72–311
Connolly, Maureen, 70–303
Conrad, Charles, Jr., 71–472, 70–505
Conscientious objectors, 72–302
CONSERVATION, 72–298, 71–273, 70–292
agriculture, 71–193; chemical industry, 70–266; energy, 71–316, 70–334; environment, 72–339, 71–319; Europe, 71–325; forestry, 72–360, 71–333; hunting and fishing, 72–384, 71–354; petroleum, 72–469, 71–431; pollution, 70–463; Venice, 71–148; zoology, 70–552; zoos and aquariums, 72–558, 71–516, 70–126, 70–552. See also **ENVIRONMENT; POLLUTION**
Conservative party (Britain), 72–370, 71–342, 70–359
Conservative party (New York), 71–453
Constantine, Lord Learie N., 72–311
Constitution: Canada, 72–261, 71–240; Chicago, 72–279; Morocco, 71–402; Rhodesia, 71–454; Somalia, 71–469; state government, 71–479; Tunisia, 71–498; Yugoslavia, 72–557
Constitution, U.S.: civil rights, 71–262; Congress, 72–297; state government, 72–519
Construction. See **BUILDING AND CONSTRUCTION**
CONSUMER AFFAIRS, 72–300, 71–274
advertising, 72–198, 71–185; banks, 70–235; drugs, 71–298; economy, 71–303, 70–321; fishing industry, 70–344; food, 72–354, 71–329, 70–344; insurance, 72–388; Knauer, Virginia H., 70–388; Nader, Ralph, 71–410; petroleum, 72–468; price index, *il.,* 71–303; regulation, 72–139; retailing, 72–495, 71–454, 70–487; safety, 71–463; state government, 70–514
Continental drift: geology, 72–365, 71–337, 70–354; ocean, 71–421
Contract, 72–551
Cook Islands, 72–459
Cooper, Leroy Gordon, 71–206
Copland, Aaron, 71–406
Copper: Australia, 71–210; Chile, 72–280; mining, 72–434, 71–401, 70–423; Peru, 72–467, 71–430
Copyright: celebrations, 71–246
Corbett, Robert J., 72–311
Corn, 72–206, 71–190
Cornfeld, Bernard, 71–481
Coruna, Juan V., 72–304
Cost of living, 72–325
Cost of Living Council: labor, 72–402; President of the U.S., 72–480
Costa E Silva, Arthur Da, 70–248
Costa Rica, 72–409, 71–375, 70–396
Cotton, 72–206, 71–191, 70–206
Council of Europe: Europe, 70–339; Greece, 70–363
Counterfeiting, 70–424
Court-martial, 70–295
COURTS AND LAWS, 72–301, 71–276, 70–294; baseball, 71–221; Calley, William L., 72–447; Chicago, 71–252; civil rights, 72–286, 71–263, 70–278; computer, 70–285; conservation, 71–273; consumer affairs, 71–275; crime, 70–297; drugs, 72–322; education, 72–330; environment, 72–341; invention, 70–380; Jews, 71–365; labor, 71–373; Los Angeles, 72–420; New Orleans, 72–450, 70–439; Pentagon Papers, 72–486; publishing, 72–485, 71–447; religion, 70–485; Roman Catholic, 72–497, 71–456; Russia, 71–461; social welfare, 71–469; sports, 72–515; state government, 72–519, 71–476; taxation, 71–483; United Nations, 71–503, 70–537; U.S. government, 72–504. See also **CONGRESS OF THE UNITED STATES; STATE GOVERNMENT**
Cox, Edward F., 72–454
Cranko, John, 72–308
Crewe, Albert V., 71–251
CRIME, 72–303, 71–278, 70–296
Africa, 72–204; archaeology, 72–213; aviation, 72–231, 70–229; Brazil, 70–248; city, 72–284, 70–275; coin collecting, 70–368; Congress, 71–268; courts and laws, 72–301; Cuba, 70–297; Dallas, 71–280; drugs, 72–322; espionage, 71–321; food, 72–355; labor, 71–373; Los Angeles, 72–420; money, 70–424; museums, 71–405; national affairs, 70–24; New Orleans, 72–450, 71–415;

Nigeria, 72–452; recordings, 72–490; San Francisco, 72–503, 70–496; *Special Report*, 72–93; state government, 72–519; travel, 70–531; United Nations, 70–537; 71–510; Washington, D.C., 70–546. See also **Assassination; Kidnaping; Terrorism; Violence**
Criticism, 71–298
Crosby, Caresse, 71–283
Cross, James R., 71–238
Cross country, 71–492
Crow, John O., 72–387
Cruz, Carlos (Teo), 71–283
CRUZ, RAMÓN ERNESTO, 72–304
CUBA, 72–305, 71–279, 70–297; Castro, Fidel, 72–463; Chile, 71–253; espionage, 72–343; Pan American games, 72–460
Cultural centers, 72–429
Cunningham, Walter, 72–224
Curling, 72–515, 71–475, 70–510
Cushing, Richard Cardinal: Boston, 71–230; deaths, 71–285
Cyanocarbon, 72–278
Cybernetics. See **COMPUTERS.**
Cyclamates: advertising, 70–198; drugs, 71–298, 70–318; foods, 71–329; U.S. government, 70–538
Cycling, 72–517, 71–476, 70–511
Cyprus, 70–537
Cyrankiewicz, Jozef, 71–436
CZECHOSLOVAKIA, 72–305, 71–279, 70–298
Austria, 70–224; Communism, 70–285; democracy, 70–309; Husák, Gustav, 70–373; international affairs, 70–18; Roman Catholic Church, 71–456; Russia, 72–498, 70–492

D

DAHOMEY, 72–306, 71–280; Africa, 70–202
Dairying, *il.,* 71–192
Dalai Lama, 70–484
Daley, Richard J.: Chicago, 72–279, 70–269; Democratic party, 72–315; elections, 72–335
Dali, Salvador, 72–549
DALLAS, 72–306, 71–280, 70–300; memorials, 71–394
Dam: Australia, 71–209; building and construction, 72–253, 71–235, 70–251; forest, *il.,* 72–360; Mexico, 70–416; Pakistan, 71–423; Tanzania, 70–517; United Arab Republic, 71–499
Dameshek, William, 70–303
DANCING, 72–306, 71–281, 70–300
awards, 71–215
Daniels, Bebe, 72–311
Darcy, Thomas F., 71–448
Data processing. See **COMPUTERS**
David, Edward E., Jr., 71–465
David-Neel, Alexandra, 70–303
Davis, Benjamin O., Sr., 71–285
Davis, Hallie Flanagan, 70–303
DAVIS, WILLIAM GRENVILLE, 72–308; Ontario, 72–264
Dawson, William L., 71–285
Day-care center, 72–280
Day, Helen H., 71–285
Dayan, Moshe, *il.,* 71–362
DDT: chemical industry, 72–266; conservation, 70–294; environment, 71–321; science, 71–36; U.S. government, 70–538
Deafness, 72–376
Deaths: safety, 72–502; vital statistics, 72–551
DEATHS OF NOTABLE PERSONS, 72–309, 71–283, 70–302
architecture, 71–200; Eastern Orthodox Churches, 71–299; fashion, 72–350; Great Britain, 71–342; interior design, 70–378; jazz, 70–434; music, 72–444, 71–406; poetry, 72–473, 71–436; Protestant, 70–477; religion, 72–492
Decathlon, 70–525
Decay, dental, 72–317
DeChamplain, Raymond C., 72–342
Deer, 72–384
Defense. See **ARMED FORCES OF THE WORLD; NATIONAL DEFENSE**
Defense, U.S. Department of: Laird, Melvin R., 70–394; national defense, 72–446, 71–411; U.S. government, 70–538
De Gaulle, Charles: deaths, 71–285; Europe, 70–337; France, 71–334, 70–350; world affairs, 71–19
DeGroot, Dudley S., 71–285
DeKruif, Paul, 72–311
Delbruck, Max, 70–444
Demirel, Suleyman, 72–433, 72–540, 71–498
DEMOCRACY, 70–309
Afghanistan, 71–185; Africa, 71–188; Algeria, 72–210; Argentina, 72–215; Brazil, 71–233, 70–248; civil rights, 72–286, 71–263; Ecuador, 71–305; education, 70–327;

Ghana, 70–357; Greece, 72–374, 71–346, 70–363; Indonesia, 70–377; Iraq, 70–381; Latin America, 71–374; Lesotho, 71–378; Malaysia, 72–422; Morocco, 71–402; New Guinea, 71–415; Pacific Islands, 71–423; Portugal, 72–475, 71–437, 70–466; Rhodesia, 72–496; Russia, 70–493; science, 70–496; South Africa, 72–509; Spain, 70–508; Thailand, 72–529; Uganda, 71–499; Vietnam, 72–548
DEMOCRATIC PARTY, 72–315, 71–289, 70–310
Chicago, 70–269; Congress, 72–291, 71–267; elections, 72–333, 71–310; Humphrey, Hubert H., 72–383; Jackson, Henry M., 72–395; Kennedy, Edward M., 72–398; Lindsay, John V., 72–412; McGovern, George S., 72–425; Mills, Wilbur D., 72–434; Muskie, Edmund S., 72–445; Republican party, 71–453; state government, 71–476, 70–511
Demography. See **POPULATION, WORLD; CENSUS, U. S.**
Demonstrations. See **CIVIL RIGHTS; Protests; Violence**
Dempsey, Sir Miles, 70–303
DENMARK, 72–316, 71–290, 70–312; Europe, 72–346, 71–322; tunnels, 70–251
Dent, Harry S., 70–85
DENTISTRY, 72–317, 71–291, 70–312
Derleth, August, 72–311
Desalinization, 70–203
Desegregation: adoption, 71–253; Boston, 72–248; civil rights, 72–286; courts, 70–295; education, 72–331, 71–309, 70–329; Houston, 72–382, 71–388; Los Angeles, 71–388; Parents and Teachers Association, 71–424; President of the U.S., 72–481, 71–442; San Francisco, 72–503; taxation, 71–483; U.S. government, 71–504. See also **CIVIL RIGHTS**
Deshalit, Amos, 70–303
Detergents: chemical industry, 72–277; environment, 72–341
DETROIT, 72–317, 71–291, 70–312; elections, 70–331
Devaluation. See **MONEY**
De Vaux, Roland, 72–311
Devlin, Bernadette, 70–361
Dewey, Thomas E., 72–311
Diabetes: drugs, 71–298; medicine, 71–393
Diamond: Africa, 70–204; astronomy, 70–222
Díaz Ordaz, Gustavo: Mexico, 70–416
Dickens, Charles: celebrations, 71–246; literature, 71–382
Dictionary: *World Book Encyclopedia Dictionary* supplement, 72–602, 71–607, 70–597
DIPLOMAT, 71–292, 70–313; Argentina, 71–200; China, 71–255; U.S. government, 72–545
Dirksen, Everett M.: death, 70–303; gardening, 71–337; Republican Party, 70–487
Disarmament: armed forces, 72–216; Europe, 72–346; ocean, 72–457; President of the U.S., 70–472; Russia, 72–500; United Nations, 72–542, 71–503, 70–534; world affairs, 71–18, 70–20. See also **Peace**
DISASTERS, 72–318, 71–293, 70–314; agriculture, 71–190; astronauts, 72–224; Brazil, 71–233; Bulgaria, 72–254; forests, 72–360; geology, 71–338; health, 71–377; Kenya, 72–398; ocean, 70–444; Pakistan, 71–423; Peru, 71–429; Quebec, 72–264; Red Cross, 72–491, 70–483; space exploration, 72–510; weather, 70–547. See also **Violence**
Discus throwing, 72–534
Disease. See **HEALTH AND DISEASE; MEDICINE**
DISN, 72–278
Disney World: fairs, 72–349; travel, *il.,* 72–539
District of Columbia. See **WASHINGTON, D.C.**
Divorce: Italy, 72–394, 71–363; vital statistics, 72–551, 71–509, 70–546
Dixon, Margaret, 71–285
DNA: biochemistry, 71–226; biology, 72–245
Dobrovolsky, Georgi T., 72–311
Dodd, Thomas J., 72–311
Dodge, Anna Thompson, 71–285
Dogs, 72–467, 71–430, 70–457
DOLE, ROBERT J., 72–322
Domestic animals, 72–212
Dominican Republic, 72–410, 71–377, 70–397
Donahey, William, 71–285
Dos Passos, John R., 71–285
Douglas-Home, Sir Alec: Great Britain, 72–372, 71–342; Rhodesia, 72–496
Douglass, Truman B., 70–305
Dowding, Lord Hugh C. T., 71–285
Doyle, Adrian Conan, 71–285
Draft. See **Selective Service**
Drama. See **THEATER**
Draper, Dorothy, 70–378

Drought, 72–552
DRUGS, 72–322, 71–298, 70–318; child welfare, 72–280; crime, 72–103, 70–297; medicine, 71–393, 70–415; mental health, 72–430, 70–416; music, popular, 71–409; national defense, 72–449; poverty, 71–439; radio, 71–449; rubella, 70–99; state government, 72–519, 71–477; United Nations, 72–543; veterans, 72–547; weight lifting, 71–475
Dryden, Ken, 72–379
Duan, Le, 71–507
Dubček, Alexander, 71–279, 70–298
Dubilier, William, 70–305
DuBridge, Lee A., 71–464
Duke, Vernon, 70–305
Dulles, Allen W., 70–305
Duncan, Donald F., 72–311
Dupré, Marcel, 72–311
Durand, Ruth Sawyer, 71–285
Dürer, Albrecht: celebrations, 72–272; visual arts, 72–549
Dutch elm disease, 72–248, 71–337
Dutka, Jacques, 72–464
Duvalier, François, 72–311, 71–377, 70–397
DUVALIER, JEAN-CLAUDE, 72–323; Haiti, 72–375
Dyer, Rolla E., 72–311

E

Eagle, 72–299
Earth Day: conservation, 71–273; environment, 71–319
Earthquakes: astronomy, 71–208; disasters, 72–318, 71–295, 70–317; geology, 72–365, 71–338, 70–355; Los Angeles, 72–420; Peru, 71–429; space exploration, 72–511, 70–505
East Germany. See **GERMANY**
East Pakistan. See **Bangla Desh**
EASTERN ORTHODOX CHURCHES, 72–323, 71–299, 70–320
Eastman, Max, 70–305
Eaton, William J., 71–448
ECHEVERRÍA ÁLVAREZ, LUIS, 71–299; Mexico, 72–430, 71–396
Eckert, William D., 72–311
Eclipse, 71–207
Ecology. See **ENVIRONMENT**
Econometrics, 70–443
Economics: inflation, 72–77; Nobel prizes, 72–456, 71–420
ECONOMY, THE, 72–324, 71–300, 70–320
advertising, 72–198, 71–184; Africa, 71–188; agriculture, 72–205, 71–190, 70–207; Algeria, 71–194; anthropology, 72–211; Argentina, 72–215; Asia, 71–206; Australia, 72–226; Austria, 71–210, aviation, 72–231, 71–213; banks, 72–236; boats, 71–230; Brazil, 72–250, 71–232; building and construction, 72–252, 71–234; Canada, 72–258; census, 70–264; chemical industry, 72–277; China, 71–255; city, 72–284; civil rights, 72–286; Congress, 72–291; Czechoslovakia, 72–305; education, 72–41, 72–330; elections, 72–334; engineering, 72–339; Ethiopia, 72–343; Europe, 72–344; *Focus,* 72–29, 71–29, 70–29; food, 72–68; France, 72–361; Germany, West, 72–366, 71–340; Great Britain, 72–371, 71–344; Greece, 72–374; housing, 72–381, 71–352; inflation, 72–77; insurance, 71–357, international education, 71–99; Japan, 72–395, 71–66, 71–364; labor, 72–401; library, 72–411; Luxembourg, 71–389; manufacturing, 72–423; Mexico, 72–430, 71–396; money, 72–435, 71–402; Norway, 71–421; Paraguay, 71–424; Peru, 71–429; President of the U.S., 72–478, 70–474; regulatory agencies, 71–126; retailing, 72–495, 71–454; Russia, 72–501, 71–460; sports, 72–118; state government, 72–518; steel, 72–522, 71–479; stocks and bonds, 72–522, 71–480; Thailand, 72–529; transportation, 71–493; travel, 71–496; U.S. affairs, 72–23; U.S. government, 71–504; *Focus,* 72–20; Vietnam, 72–548. See also **BANKS AND BANKING; MANUFACTURING; INTERNATIONAL TRADE; LABOR**
Ecotage, 72–298
ECUADOR, 72–329, 71–305, 70–398
fishing industry, 72–353
Ecumenical movement: Eastern Orthodox, 72–323; Jews and Judaism, 70–386; Protestant, 72–483, 71–445, 70–476
Edmonton, 72–265
EDUCATION, 72–330, 71–307, 70–326
Afghanistan, 71–185; American Library Association, 70–210; Baltimore, 72–236; Boston, 72–248; Canadian Library Associa-

tion, 72–271, 71–245, 70–261; child guidance, 70–261; China, 72–283, 71–256; civil rights, 72–286, 70–277; congress, 72–295, 71–268; courts, 72–311, 70–295; democracy, 70–309; engineering, 72–339, 71–317, 70–335; Ethiopia, 71–322; Focus, 72–41, 71–41, 70–41; foundations, 71–334; handicapped, 72–376, 71–347, 70–364; health, 71–348; Houston, 72–382, 71–353; Indian, American, 71–357; international understanding, 71–95; library, 72–411, 70–399; Los Angeles, 71–388; Morocco, 71–402; museums, 72–439, 71–405, 70–427; New York City, 70–439; Parents and Teachers, National Congress of, 72–461, 71–424, 70–451; Philadelphia, 72–469; poverty, 71–438, 70–469; President of the U.S., 71–442; Protestant, 71–445; Roman Catholic, 72–497, 71–456; Salvation Army, 71–463; San Francisco, 72–503; service clubs, 70–499; "Sesame Street," 71–485; state government, 72–519, 71–479, 70–512; taxation, 71–483; Tunisia, 71–505; United Nations, 70–536; U.S. constitution, 72–544; U.S. government, 71–504; Venezuela, 71–505; veterans, 72–547; zoos and aquariums, 72–558. See also **Foundations; Protests; Universities and Colleges**

Edwards, Cliff, 72–311
Edwards, James, 71–285
Edwards, Philip A., 72–311
Egal, Mohammed Ibrahim, 70–503
EGYPT, 72–333. See also **UNITED ARAB REPUBLIC**, 71–499, 70–533
Africa, 71–188; archaeology, 71–198, 70–212; celebrations, 70–262; Iran, 71–360; Israel, 72–393; Kuwait, 71–367; library, 71–412; Middle East, 72–432, 71–398, 70–419; Russia, 72–500; United Nations, 71–541
EHRLICH, PAUL R., 71–309
Ehrlichman, John: President of the U.S., 70–473; Special Report, 70–84
Eisenhower, David, 72–455, 71–419
Eisenhower, Dwight D.: coin collecting, 72–289; deaths, 70–304; hobbies, 71–349
Eisenhower, Edgar N., 72–311
Eisenhower, Julie Nixon: Girl Scouts, 72–556; Nixon, Richard M., 72–455, 71–419, 70–442
Eisenhower, Mamie: Nixon, Richard M., il., 71–418; personalities, 71–425
Elbrick C. Burke, 70–248
ELECTIONS, 72–333, 71–310, 70–330; advertising, 71–185; Africa, 71–187; Agnew, Spiro T., 71–190; Algeria, 72–210; American Party, 72–211; Austria, 72–227, 71–210; Baltimore, 72–236; Belgium, 72–242; Boston, 72–248; Brazil, 71–232; Canada, 72–260, 71–243; Ceylon, 71–248; Chicago, 72–279; Chile, 71–253; city, 72–285, 71–258; civil rights, 72–286; Congo (Kinshasa), 71–266; Congress, 71–267; Cruz, Ramón E., 72–304; Dallas, 72–306; democracy, 70–309; Democratic party, 72–315, 71–289, 70–310; Denmark, 72–316; Dominican Republic, 71–129; Finland, 71–328; France, 72–362; Germany, West, 71–340; Great Britain, 71–342; House, 71–270; Houston, 72–383; India, 72–385; Indonesia, 72–387; inflation, 72–91; Iran, 72–392; Japan, 71–363; Kennedy, Edward M., 72–398; Korea, South, 72–400; Kuwait, 72–400; Lebanon, 71–377; Mexico, 71–396; Netherlands, 72–450; New Orleans, 71–415; Nixon, Richard M., 71–418; Pakistan, 71–423; Philadelphia, 72–469; Philippines, 72–470; President of the U.S., 72–482, 71–443; Republican party, 72–494, 71–453, 70–486; Rhodesia, 71–454; Senate, 71–269; South Africa, 71–470; state government, 72–519, 71–476; Stevenson, Adlai E., 72–158; Sweden, 71–481; Tanzania, 71–483; television, 71–484; U.S. affairs, 72–26, 71–25; Vietnam, 72–548, 71–506; Wallace, George C., 72–552; West Indies, 72–554
Electric power: Australia, 72–253, 71–209; Canada, il., 71–244; dam, 71–235; energy, 72–336, 71–314; India, 71–355; Quebec, 72–264; regulation, 71–133; waste disposal, 71–86. See also **ENERGY**
Electrical Equipment: computer, 70–285; energy, 70–332; labor, 71–371; manufacturing, 72–424, 71–392, 70–411
Electromagnetism, 71–435
Electronic surveillance, 72–302
ELECTRONICS, 72–335, 71–313, 70–331; handicapped, 71–347; invention, 70–381; manufacturing, 71–391, 70–411; motion pictures, 72–438; photography, 72–470; recordings, 70–482; visual arts, 71–509

Elements, 71–250
Eliot, George Fielding, 72–311
Elizabeth II: Australia, 71–209; Austria, 70–224; Canada, 72–263; Great Britain, 72–373, 70–362; Manitoba, 71–243; Michener, Roland, 72–431; music, 72–440; personalities, il., 71–426
Ellington, Duke, 70–434
Elliott, Mama Cass, 72–464
Elm, 71–337
El Salvador, 72–409, 70–395
Ellsberg, Daniel, 72–486
Emigration. See **IMMIGRATION AND EMIGRATION**
Employment, 72–301. See also **LABOR; Unemployment**
ENERGY, 72–336, 71–314, 70–332; automobile, 71–212; environment, 72–341; mines, 72–434; petroleum, 72–468, 71–431; science, 72–505; transportation, 70–529
Engine: automobile, 72–229; automobile racing, 72–230; aviation, 72–231; boats, 72–246; energy, 72–336
ENGINEERING, 72–339, 71–317, 70–335 awards, 72–235, 71–217; building, 72–253; electronics, 70–331; Engle, Joe H., 72–223; Switzerland, 70–517
English language. See Dictionary
Entertainment. See **MOTION PICTURES; MUSIC, CLASSICAL; MUSIC, POPULAR; RADIO; RECORDINGS; TELEVISION; THEATER**
ENVIRONMENT, 72–339, 71–319; agriculture, 72–208, 71–193; architecture, 72–213; Canada, 72–260; chemical industry, 72–277; city, 72–179, 72–285; Congress, 72–272; conservation, 72–298; dams, 72–253; economy, 71–304; Ehrlich, Paul R., 71–309; energy, 72–337, 71–316; Europe, 71–325; Focus, 71–34; games, 71–336; gardening, 72–363; international education, 71–96; medicine, 71–394; museums, 71–405; ocean, 72–457; petroleum, 72–469, 71–431; President of the U.S., 71–443; science, 71–465; Special Report, 71–79; San Francisco, 72–503; state government, 72–519, 71–477; Train, Russell E., 71–492; U.S. government, 71–504; weather, 72–553. See also **CONSERVATION; POLLUTION**
ENVIRONMENTAL POLLUTION: WBE, 72–590
Environmental Protection Agency: chemical industry, 72–277; environment, 71–319, 72–339
Enzyme, 70–241
Epidemics, 72–377
Epidemiology, 71–226
Episcopalian, 72–483, 70–476
EQUATORIAL GUINEA, 70–335; Africa, 70–202; United Nations, 70–536
Erickson, Jon, il., 70–452
Ericson, Leif, 72–429
Erikson, Erik H., 71–449
ERIM, NIHAT, 72–342; Middle East, 72–433; Turkey, 72–540
Eritrea, 72–343, 71–187, 70–202
Erlichman, John D., 71–443
Eshkol, Levi, 70–305
Eskimo, 71–377
ESPIONAGE, 72–342, 71–321, 70–336; Russia, 72–499
ESPOSITO, PHIL ANTHONY, 72–343; hockey, 72–378
Estes, Billie Sol, 72–464
Ethics: Congress, 70–291; courts, 70–295; Special Report, 72–117
ETHIOPIA, 72–343, 71–322, 70–336; Africa, 71–186; Somalia, 71–469
Etna, Mt., il., 72–364
EUROPE, 72–344, 71–322, 70–337; banks, 72–237; conservation, 72–273; Focus, 72–19, 71–20; food, 72–354; national defense, 72–449. See also by name of country
European Economic Community. See **Common Market**
European Free Trade Association, 71–322, 71–340
Evangelism, 70–476
Evans, Herbert M., 72–311
Everglades, 72–273
Evolution, 71–197
Excise taxes: state government, 70–512
Exhibitions. See **FAIRS AND EXPOSITIONS; VISUAL ARTS**
Exploration: anthropology, il., 71–197; archaeology, 71–198; Australia, 70–223. See also **SPACE EXPLORATION**
Explosions: disasters, 72–320, 71–295, 70–317
Exports. See **INTERNATIONAL TRADE AND FINANCE**
Eye, 70–332

F

Fairchild, John Burr, 71–427
Fairchild, Sherman M., 72–311
FAIRS AND EXPOSITIONS, 72–348, 71–325, 70–340
agriculture, il., 72–208; architecture, 71–199; interior design, 71–358; livestock show, 72–390, 71–359, 70–379; pet, 72–469, 71–430, 70–457; photography, 70–460; visual arts, 72–549
Faisal, Abdel Aziz Al Saud al Faisal, 72–504, 71–464, 70–496
Famine: Afghanistan, 72–199; food, 71–329; Kenya, 72–398
Fanning, Lawrence S., 72–311
Farm Equipment, 70–412
Farnsworth, Philo T., 72–311
FASHION, 72–349, 71–327, 70–342; Great Britain, 71–346; personalities, 71–427; retailing, 71–454. See also **INTERIOR DESIGN; Textile**
FAULKNER, ARTHUR BRIAN DEANE, 72–352; Great Britain, 72–372
FAUNTROY, WALTER EDWARD, 72–352; Washington, D.C., 72–552
Federal Aviation Administration, 71–214
Federal Bureau of Investigation, 72–303, 71–321
Federal Communications Commission: communications, 72–290, 71–265; publishing, 71–447; radio, 72–489, 71–449, 70–482; Special Report, 71–129; television, 71–486, 70–519
Federal Housing Administration, 72–381
Federal Power Commission: energy, 71–316; petroleum, 71–431; Special Report, 71–133
Federal Reserve Board: banks, 72–236, 71–219, 70–233; Burns, Arthur F., 71–236; economy, 71–32
Federal Trade Commission: advertising, 72–198, 71–185; automobile, 72–228; consumer affairs, 72–300, 71–275; safety, 72–502; Special Report, 71–137
Fefferman, Charles L., 72–464
Feld, Eliot, 72–307
Feldman, Saul, 72–464
Fencing, 72–517, 71–475, 70–510
Fernandel, 72–311
Fernando Póo. See Equatorial Guinea
Ferré, Luis A., 71–444, 70–480
Fertilizer: chemical industry, 72–277, 71–249; Special Report, 72–65
Festivals: celebrations, 72–272; dancing, 70–302; jazz, 72–445, 71–410; popular music, 71–409, 70–433; theater, 71–490
ffrench-Beytagh, Gonville, 72–509
Fiction. See **LITERATURE**
Field, Marshall V, il., 70–478
Figueres Ferrer, José, 71–375
Fiji: Pacific Islands, 72–459, 71–423, 70–446; United Nations, 71–503
Filibuster, 72–156
Film, 71–434, 70–460
FINCH, ROBERT HUTCHISON, 70–343; Cabinet, 71–237; pollution, 70–463; President of the U.S., 71–443
FINLAND, 72–352, 71–328, 70–344; labor, 70–393
Fio Rito, Ted ,72–311
Fires: disasters, 72–320, 71–295, 70–317; forestry, 72–360, 71–333, 70–348; Los Angeles, il., 71–388
FISCHER, BOBBY, 72–353; chess, 72–278; sports, 72–54
Fischer, Louis, 71–285
FISHING INDUSTRY, 72–353, 71–328, 70–344; environment, 71–320; Europe, 72–345, 71–323; food, 72–355, 70–344; hunting and fishing, 72–384, 71–353, 70–373; Norway, 72–457; Peru, 70–456; pollution, 70–464; science, 71–36; West Indies, 72–554
Fitzpatrick, Daniel R., 72–305
Fitzpatrick, Thomas, 71–444
FITZSIMMONS, FRANK EDWARD, 72–354; labor, il., 72–402
Flanders, Ralph E., 71–285
Fleischmann, Raoul H., 70–305
Fleisher, Leon, 71–407
Fleming, Lady Amalia: civil rights, 72–288; Greece, 72–374
Fleming, Peter, 72–311
Flood, Curt: baseball, 72–240, 71–221; sports, 72–515, 71–55
Floods: Brazil, 72–320, il., 72–251; disasters, 71–296, 70–317; Philippines, 71–432; Romania, 71–457; weather, 72–553
Florida: conservation, 72–299, 71–273, 70–293; fairs, 72–349; state government, 72–518; weather, il., 72–553

Florigens, 72–248
Flowers, 72–363, 71–337, 70–354
Fluoridation, 70–312
Fly, Claude, 71–505
FOOD, 72–354, 71–329, 70–344
Afghanistan, 72–199; agriculture, 72–206, 71–190, 70–205; Brazil, 71–233; consumer affairs, 72–301; expenditures for, *il.,* 71–192; fishing, 72–353, 71–328, 70–344; health, 70–365; India, 72–386; poverty, 71–438; *Special Report,* 72–59· Vietnam, 72–549. See also **AGRICULTURE**
Food and Agriculture Organization, 72–354, 71–329
Food and Drug Administration: chemical industry, 72–277; drugs, 72–322, 71–298, 70–318; food, 72–354; games, models, and toys, 72–363, 71–337
FOOTBALL, 72–356, 71–330, 70–345; labor, 71–372; *Focus,* 72–55, *Special Report,* 72–118; 70–509. See also **SOCCER**
Ford, Corey, 70–305
Ford, Edward H., 71–285
Ford Foundation: dancing, 70–300; library, 70–399; music, 72–440; population, 71–436
Foreign aid: Asia, 72–219; Congress, 72–295; Ethiopia, 72–343; Indonesia, 72–387; President of the U.S., 72–480; Southern Yemen, 72–509
Foreign exchange: Africa, 71–189; banks, 70–235; economy, 70–324; international trade, 71–359. See also **MONEY**
FOREST AND FOREST PRODUCTS, 72–360, 71–333, 70–348
Canada, *il.,* 70–257
Forman, James, 70–475; *il.,* 70–483
FORMOSA, 72–360, 71–333, 70–349; Asia, 72–218; Chi Cheng, 71–252; dams, 72–253
Forster, Edward M., 71–285
Fortas, Abe: courts and laws, 70–294; U.S. government, 70–538
Fosdick, Harry Emerson, 70–305
Fossils: anthropology, 70–300; botany, 71–231; geology, 72–364, 71–337
FOUNDATIONS, 71–334, 70–349
awards, 72–233, 71–216, 70–232; library, 72–411; museums, 72–439, 71–406. See also **Ford Foundation**
Four-H Clubs, 72–556, 71–514, 70–550
FRANCE, 72–361, 71–334, 70–350; Algeria, 72–210; armed forces, 70–217; aviation, 72–232; banks, 70–235; Chaban-Delmas, Jacques, 70–265; Chad, 72–276; espionage, 72–342; Europe, 72–344, 71–322, 70–337; Great Britain, 72–370; international trade, 70–379; Jews, 72–396, 71–365; labor, 71–373; Pacific Islands, 71–423; Pompidou, Georges, 70–465; space exploration, 71–474; travel, 70–531; world affairs, 70–19
Francis, Thomas, Jr., 70–305
Franco, Francisco: Spain, 72–514, *il.,* 71–440
FRANJIEH, SULEIMAN, 71–336
Fraser, Malcolm, 72–226
FRAZIER, JOSEPH (JOE), 71–336; boxing, 72–249, 71–231, 70–246
Freedom of speech, 71–447
Freedoms Foundation, 72–234, 70–232
French Canadians, 70–254
French Polynesia, 72–459
Freud, Sigmund, 70–415
Frisch, Ragnar, 70–443
Froehlke, Robert, F., 72–482
Frog jumping, 71–429
Fruit: agriculture, 70–205
Fuel. See ENERGY
Fulton, James G., 72–311
Furniture: hobbies, 72–378; interior design, 72–389, 71–358, 70–378
Future Farmers of America, 72–556, 71–514, 70–550

G

Gabor, Dennis, 72–456
Galaxy, 72–224, 71–207
Gallegos, Rómulo, 70–305
Gallop, Sam, 72–311
Galvão, Henrique C.M., 71–285
GAMBIA, 72–362, 71–336, 70–203
Gambling: horse racing, 72–380; state government, 72–519, 70–509
GAMES, MODELS, AND TOYS, 72–363, 71–336, 70–353. See also **BRIDGE, CONTRACT; CHESS; SPORTS**
Gamma globulin, 72–426
Gandhi, Indira Nehru, 72–385, 71–355, 70–374
Gandhi, Mohandas K.: celebrations, 70–262; religion, 70–485
GARDENING, 72–363, 71–337, 70–354
Gardner, Erle Stanley, 71–285

Gardner, John William, 70–23, 70–25
Garland, Judy, 70–306
Garlic, 71–428
Garment industry, 71–371
Garr, John J., 72–464
Garrison, Jim C., 72–451
Gary (Ind.), 71–258
Gas. See PETROLEUM AND GAS
Gas turbine: automobile, 72–229; energy, 72–336
Gasoline, 71–431
Gell-Mann, Murray, 70–444
General Motors: automobile, 71–210; economy, 71–301; energy, 71–314; manufacturing, 71–390; Nader, Ralph, 71–410
Genetics: biochemistry, 71–226; biology, 72–245, 71–228; medicine, 71–394; science, 70–35
Gentele, Goeran, 72–442, 71–408
GEOLOGY, 72–364, 71–337, 70–354
awards, 72–235, 71–217; energy, 72–337; moon, 72–505; ocean, 72–457, 71–421, 70–444; space exploration, 72–510
Georgia: memorials, 71–395; visual arts, 71–508
German measles, 70–99
GERMANY, 70–355
armed forces, 70–217; banks, 70–235; Brandt, Willy, 70–247; democracy, 70–309; espionage, 70–336; Europe, 71–324, 70–337; Heinemann, Gustav W., 70–366; international trade, 70–379; Poland, 70–463; pollution, *il.,* 70–465
GERMANY, DEMOCRATIC REPUBLIC OF (EAST), 72–365, 71–338
Czechoslovakia, 72–305; Honecker, Erich, 72–380; Russia, 72–498
GERMANY, FEDERAL REPUBLIC OF (WEST), 72–366, 71–340; chemical industry, 71–250; disasters, *il.,* 72–318; economy, 72–324; espionage, 71–321; fairs, 72–349; labor, 71–373; Nobel prizes, 72–456; photography, 72–470; Poland, 71–436; Russia, 72–499, 71–458; world affairs, 72–19, 71–20
Gerstmann, Josef, 70–305
Geyelin, Philip L., 71–448
Ghali, Paul, 71–285
GHANA, 72–367, 71–340, 70–357
South Africa, 72–509
Ghiorso, Albert, 71–251
Gibraltar: Great Britain, 70–362; Spain, 71–474
Gibson, Kenneth, 71–261
GIEREK, EDWARD, 71–341; Poland, 72–474, 71–436
Gilbert, Billy, 72–311
Gilbert, L. Wolfe, 71–285
Gilbert Islands, 71–423
Gillespie, Dizzy, 72–464
Gimbel, Adam, 70–306
Giminez, Divaldo, 70–453
GIRI, VARAHAGIRI VENKATA, 70–357; India, 70–374
Girl Scouts, 72–556, 71–514, 70–550
Girls Clubs of America, 72–556, 71–514, 70–551
Gisby, Paul, 70–453
Glacier, 71–338
Glass, 71–92
Glueck, Nelson, 72–311
Goetze, Albrecht E.R., 72–311
Goldberg, Larry, 71–427
Goldberg, Rube, 71–285
Goldrich, David, 71–427
GOLF, 72–367, 71–341, 70–358
sports, 72–56; Trevino, Lee, 72–539
Gomez, Thomas, 72–311
Gomulka, Wladyslaw, 71–436
Gonorrhea, 72–377, 71–348
Goodell, Charles E., 71–453
GOODPASTER, ANDREW JACKSON, 70–359
Europe, 72–347, 70–339
GOOLAGONG, EVONNE, 72–369
tennis, 72–528
Gorcey, Leo, 70–306
Gordon, Dorothy L., 71–285
Gordon, Richard, 70–505
Gordon, Roy G., 72–278
Gordone, Charles, 71–449
Gore, Albert, 71–453
Gori, Alberto, 71–285
Gorton, John Grey, 72–226, 71–209, 70–222
Goslin, Leon A., 72–311
Gould, Shane, 72–524
Government. See CITY; STATE GOVERNMENT; U.S. GOVERNMENT
Governors of the States: Democratic party, 72–315, 71–289, 70–311; elections, 72–334, 71–310, 70–330; Republican party, 72–494, 71–453; Rockefeller, Nelson, 70–486; state government, 72–520, 71–478
Gowon, Yakubu, 72–452, 71–417

Grace, Gerald, 71–427
Graham, Bill, 72–464
Graham, Billy: celebrations, *il.,* 71–247; religion, 72–491, 71–452, 70–476
Graham, Robin Lee, *il.,* 71–428
Granatelli, Andy, 70–226
Grand jury, 72–302
Grant, Earl, 71–285
Grapes, 71–372
Grau San Martín, Ramón, 70–306
GRAVELY, SAMUEL LEE, JR., 72–369
Gravitational Radiation, 72–553, 70–463
GREAT BRITAIN, 72–370, 71–342, 70–359
Africa, 72–202; Anguilla, 70–211; Arab Emirates, 70–212; archaeology, *il.,* 72–213; armed forces, 70–217; Asia, 72–220; Australia, 70–163; banks, 72–237; Ceylon, 71–248; communications, 72–290; economy, 72–32, 72–324, 71–305; espionage, 72–342, 71–321; Europe, 72–344, 71–322; France, 72–361; Guyana, 70–363; Heath, Edward R.G., 71–348; international trade, 72–391, 70–379; Iran, 72–392, 71–360; Jews, 72–396; labor, 70–393; Laos, 71–373; Lesotho, 71–378; money, 72–435, 71–402; New Zealand, 72–452, 71–416, 70–440; Pacific islands, 71–423; Persian Gulf Emirates, 72–462, 71–435; Protestant, 72–484, 70–476; Rhodesia, 72–496, 71–454, 70–487; Russia, 72–499; stamp collecting, 72–517; travel, 71–497; tunnel, 71–236; United Nations, 72–543, 70–535; visual arts, 72–551; West Indies, 72–554; world affairs, 72–20
Great Lakes, 71–316
GREECE, 72–374, 71–346, 70–363
Albania, 71–194; archaeology, *il.,* 71–198; Bulgaria, 72–254; civil rights, 72–288, 71–263
Greek Orthodox Church, 72–323, 71–299
Green, Mitzi, 70–306
Greenfield, Burton J., 71–427
Gregory, Dick, 72–464
Grogan, Mrs. John, 71–428
Gropius, Walter: architecture, 70–214; deaths, 70–306
Gross national product: comparative chart, *il.,* 71–303; economy, 72–325, 71–300, 70–320; Europe, 71–324; Latin America, 72–408; manufacturing, 72–423
Groves, Lt. Gen. Leslie R., 71–285
Grunitzky, Nicolas: deaths, 70–306
Guaranteed income, 72–508
Guatemala, 72–409, 71–374, 70–396
Gubser, Joseph, 71–428
Guided missiles: armed forces, 72–216, 71–201, 70–217; Canada, 72–262; France, 72–362; national defense, 72–446, 71–414, 70–437
Guinea: Africa, 71–188; mines, 72–435; United Nations, 71–503. See also **EQUATORIAL GUINEA; Portuguese Guinea**
Gum, Colin S., 72–225
Gun control, 72–304
Gunther, John J., 71–285
Guthrie, Arlo, 70–453
Guthrie, Sir Tyrone, 72–311
GUYANA, 72–375, 71–346, 70–363; Venezuela, 71–505
Gymnastics, 72–517, 71–476, 70–511

H

Hagen, Walter, 70–306
Hahnium, 71–251
Haile Selassie I: Ethiopia, 72–343, 71–322, 70–336
Haise, Fred W., Jr.: astronauts, 71–206; space exploration, 71–471
HAITI, 72–375; Duvalier, Jean-Claude, 72–323; Latin America, 71–377, 70–397
Haldeman, Harold R.: President of the U.S., 70–473; *Special Report,* 70–85
HAMBRO, EDVARD I., 71–347; United Nations, 71–500
Handball, 72–517, 71–475, 70–510
HANDICAPPED, 72–376, 71–347, 70–364
Hanrahan, Edward V.: Chicago, 72–279; courts, 72–302
HARDIN, CLIFFORD MORRIS, 70–364; agriculture, 72–205, 70–208; cabinet, 72–255
Harlan, John M.: courts, 72–302; deaths, 72–311
Harlow, Bryce N., 71–443, 70–84
Harness Racing, 72–380, 71–352, 70–370
Harridge, Will, 72–311
Harris, Fred R., 72–316
Harris, Patricia Roberts, 72–316
Hart, Sir Basil Liddell, 71–285
Hart, Thomas C., 72–311
Hartford, Huntington, 72–464

Hartley, Fred A., Jr., 70–306
Harvard University, 70–327
Hassan II, 72–436, 71–402, 70–425
Hassell, Odd, 70–443
Hatcher, Richard G., 71–258
Hathaway, Dame Sybil of Sark, 70–453
Haviland, John Kenneth, 70–453
Hawaii: crime, 72–93; labor, 71–373
Hawkins, Coleman, 70–306
Hayes, George (Gabby), 70–306
HAYNSWORTH, CLEMENT FURMAN, JR., 70–365; Congress, 71–267; courts, 70–294; U.S. government, 70–538
Hayward, Leland, 72–311
Haywood, Spencer, 72–240
Head Start, Project: education, 70–43; poverty, 71–439, 70–469
HEALTH AND DISEASE, 72–377, 71–347, 70–365; agriculture, il, 72–205; air pollution, 71–320; archaeology, 71–198; China, 71–256; dentistry, 72–317, 71–291, 70–312; drugs, 70–318; environment, 72–341; food, 72–355, 71–329; Hogness, John R., 72–380; hospitals, 70–371; Kenya, 72–398; Latin America, 72–409; Medicare, 72–426, 71–393, 70–412; medicine, 72–426, 71–393, 70–413; mental health, 72–430, 71–396, 70–416; noise, 70–137; old age, 71–422; poverty, 71–439, 70–469; safety, 72–501; state government, 72–521, 71–479, 70–514. See also MEDICINE
Health, Education, and Welfare, U.S. Department of: drugs, 70–318; Finch, Robert H., 70–343; health, 72–377; Medicare, 72–426; Richardson, Elliot L., 71–455; science, 70–496; U.S. government, 71–504, 70–538
Heard, Alexander: education, 71–307; President of the U.S., 71–442
Heart: electronics, 71–313; medicine, 71–393, 70–413
HEATH, EDWARD R. G., 71–348
  Europe, 72–344; Germany, 72–367; Great Britain, 72–370, 71–342; world affairs, 72–20
Heating: energy, 71–315; petroleum, 71–431
Heckel, Erich, 71–285
Heflin, Van, 72–312
HEINEMANN, GUSTAV WALTER, 70–366
  Germany, 70–356
Heisman Trophy, 72–359
Hellyer, Paul, 70–254
Hemingway, Ernest, 71–380
Hendrix, Jimi, 71–285
Henie, Sonja, 70–306
Henning, Anne, 72–384
Hepatitis, 72–426
Herbert, Sir Alan P., 72–312
Herman, St., 71–299
Hernandez, Juan G., 71–285
Hersh, Seymour M., 71–448
Hershey, Alfred D., 70–444
Herzberg, Gerhard, 72–456
Heyerdahl, Thor, il., 71–197, 70–212; il., 70–453
HICKEL, WALTER JOSEPH, 70–366; cabinet, 71–237, 70–253; conservation, 70–292; environment, 71–320
Hickenlooper, Bourke B., 72–312
Hicks, Louise Day, 72–334
High-fidelity, 71–313
High jump, 72–533
Highway. See ROADS AND HIGHWAYS
Hijacking: aviation, 71–214; Great Britain, 71–345; Japan, 71–364; Middle East, 71–400; travel, 71–497; U.S. government, 71–504
Hinduism: Asia, 72–220; religion, 72–493, 70–485
Hirohito: Japan, 72–395; Netherlands, 72–450; Nixon, Richard M., 72–455
Hirsch, Max, 70–306
History: awards and prizes, 70–231; Canadian literature, 72–271, 71–246, 70–262; literature, 72–414, 71–383, 70–402; Pulitzer prizes, 72–488, 71–449, 70–481
Ho Chi Minh: deaths, 70–306; Vietnam, 70–545
HOBBIES, 72–378, 71–348, 70–367; coin collecting, 72–289; collecting, 71–111; stamp collecting, 72–517. See also GAMES, MODELS, AND TOYS; PET; SPORTS
HOCKEY, 72–378, 71–349, 70–368; Esposito, Phil, 72–343; Orr, Bobby, 71–422
Hodges, Johnny, 71–285
Hodgins, Eric, 72–312
HODGSON, JAMES DAY, 71–351; President of the U.S., 71–443
Hoffa, James R., 72–354
Hoffman, Abbie, 72–464
Hoffman, Julius J., 71–277
Hoffman, Paul, 72–542
Hofstadter, Richard, 71–285

HOGNESS, JOHN RUSTEN, 72–380
Holland. See NETHERLANDS
Holland, Spessard L., 72–312
Holman, Libby, 72–312
Holography, 72–456, 71–313
Holton, A. Linwood, Jr., 70–486
Holum, Dianne, 72–384
Holyoake, Keith J., 71–416, 70–440
Homing pigeon, 72–557
Homo habilis, 70–211
Homosexuality, 72–483
Honduras: Cruz, Ramón, 72–304; Latin America, 72–410, 71–374, 70–395
HONECKER, ERICH, 72–380; Germany, 72–365
Hoover, J. Edgar, il., 72–463
Hope, Bob, il., 71–419
Hormones: biochemistry, 72–243; botany, 71–230; Nobel prizes, 72–456
Hornung, Paul, 72–123
HORSE RACING, 72–380, 71–351, 70–369; harness racing, 71–352, 70–370
Horseshoe pitching, 72–517, 71–476, 70–511
Horticulture, 72–248. See also GARDENING
Horton, Edward Everett, 71–285
Horton, William C., 70–306
HOSPITAL, 70–371; Medicare, 72–426, 70–412; medicine, 70–413
Hotel, 71–497, 70–531
Houphouet-Boigny, Felix, 72–200
HOUSING, 72–381, 71–352, 70–371; anthropology, 72–211; Baltimore, 72–236; banks, 72–237; building and construction, 72–252, il., 71–235; Canada, 70–256; census, 72–274, 71–523; Chicago, 72–279, 71–252; city, 72–284, 71–257, 70–276; Cleveland, 71–264; courts, 72–302; Detroit, 71–291; forest, 72–360; New York City, 71–416, 70–439; President of the U.S., 72–481; St. Louis, 72–503, 71–463; veterans, 72–547
Housing and Urban Development, U.S. Department of: building and construction, 72–252; crime, 72–304; Romney, George W., 70–491
Houssay, Bernardo Alberto, 72–312
HOUSTON, 72–382, 71–353, 70–372; banks, 72–237; classical music, 71–406; visual arts, 72–549; waste disposal, 71–87
Howard, Richard, 71–449
Howe, Gordie, 72–379
Hoxha, Enver, 71–194
Humphrey, George M., 71–285
Humphrey, Hubert Horatio, 72–383
  Democratic party, 71–290
HUNGARY, 72–383, 71–353, 70–373; celebrations, 71–248; Jews, 71–365
Hunger: food, 70–344; health, 70–365; Nigeria, 70–440
HUNTING AND FISHING, 72–384, 71–353, 70–373
  sports, 72–517
Huntley, Chet., il., 71–427
Hurricane: disasters, 72–320, 71–295, 70–314; insurance, 70–377; weather, 70–547
Husain, Zakir, 70–306
HUSÁK, GUSTAV, 70–373; Czechoslovakia, 72–305, 71–279, 70–298; Russia, 72–498, 70–492
Hussein I: Jordan, 72–397, 71–365, 70–386; Middle East, 71–400
Hutchinson, Margarete, 71–428
Huxtable, Ada Louise: architecture, 71–200; Pulitzer prizes, 71–449
Hydrogen, 71–208
Hydroplanes, 72–246

I

Iacocca, Lee A., 71–212
Ice Hockey. See HOCKEY
ICE SKATING, 72–384, 71–354, 70–374
Iceland: Europe, 72–348; geology, 72–365
Idaho: dam, 71–235; forest, il., 72–360; taxation, 72–527
Idris I, 70–399
Ifni, 70–425
Illinois: Chicago, 72–279, 71–252, 70–269; memorials, 72–429; music, 70–431; pollution, 70–464; state government, 72–519, 71–479, 70–512; waste disposal, il., 71–82
IMMIGRATION AND EMIGRATION, 72–385, 71–354, 70–374; Great Britain, 71–344; Israel, 72–394; Jews, 72–396; Switzerland, 71–482
Immunization: health, 72–377; medicine, 72–426
Imports. See INTERNATIONAL TRADE AND FINANCE
Income Tax: economy, 70–325; state government, 72–518, 70–512; taxation, 72–526, 70–518

INDIA, 72–385, 71–355, 70–374; agriculture, 72–59; Asia, 72–218, 71–206; disasters, il., 72–321; food, 70–344; Giri, Varahagiri Venkata, 70–357; health, 72–377; mining, 70–423; Nepal, 72–450, 71–415, 70–438; Pakistan, 72–460, 71–423; population, 72–475; Protestant, 71–446; religion, 72–493, 70–485; Russia, 72–500; United Nations, 72–541
INDIAN, AMERICAN, 72–387, 71–356, 70–376 anthropology, 72–212, 71–197; Canadian Library Association, 70–261; Canadian literature, 72–272; census, 72–274; museums, 70–428; petroleum, 72–469
Indiana, 72–519, 70–514
Indianapolis, 72–494
Indochina: Asia, 72–221. See also CAMBODIA; LAOS; VIETNAM
INDONESIA, 72–387, 71–357, 70–376
  Malik, Adam, 72–422; New Guinea, 71–415, 70–439; Protestant, 72–484
INDUSTRY. See MANUFACTURING. See also ECONOMY, THE; INTERNATIONAL TRADE; LABOR; also entries on specific industries, countries, and states
Inflation: building, 72–252; consumer affairs, 72–300; economy, 72–327, 71–300; Focus, 72–29, 71–29; France, 72–361; Germany, 72–367; labor, 72–401; Luxembourg, 72–420; Netherlands, 72–450; old age, 71–422; President of the U.S., 72–478; retailing, 71–454; Special Report, 72–77
Ingram, Rex, 70–306
Insect: chemical industry, 70–266; WBE, 70–554
Insulin: biochemistry, 71–227; chemistry, 70–268
INSURANCE, 72–388, 71–357, 70–377; consumer affairs, 72–301; crime, 72–304; health, 72–377; hospital, 70–371; medicare, 72–426, 71–393; state government, 72–521; stocks and bonds, 72–523. See also SOCIAL SECURITY
Intelligence, 71–196
Intelligence services, 72–482. See also ESPIONAGE
Interest rates, 71–219, 70–233
Interior, U.S. Department of the: Cabinet, 71–237; conservation, 70–292; environment, 72–341; fishing industry, 72–354; Hickel, Walter J., 70–366; Indian, American, 72–387; Morton, Robert C.B. 71–403; U.S. government, 71–504
INTERIOR DESIGN, 72–389, 71–358, 70–378; awards, 71–215
Internal Revenue Service: library, 71–378; taxation, 71–483
International cooperation: communications, 72–290; environment, 71–319; Europe, 71–325; ocean, 72–457; space exploration, 72–512
International Court of Justice, 72–200, 71–503, 70–537
International education, 71–95
International Labor Organization, 70–443
INTERNATIONAL LIVE STOCK EXPOSITION, 72–390, 71–359, 70–379
International Monetary Fund: banks and banking, 72–237, 71–221, 70–235; economy, 70–31, 70–324; international trade, 71–360, 70–379
INTERNATIONAL TRADE AND FINANCE, 72–390, 71–359, 70–379
  Africa, 72–202, 71–188; agriculture, 72–206, 71–193; Argentina, 72–215; Asia, 72–219; Austria, 72–227; automobile, 72–228, 71–210; banks, 72–237; Canada, 72–258, 71–242; chemical industry, 72–277; drugs, 72–322; economy, 72–324, 71–305; Europe, 72–344, 71–322; fairs and expositions, 72–348, 71–325; Finland, 72–352; fishing industry, 72–353; food, 72–68; inflation, 72–86; Japan, 72–395, 71–72, 71–364; Latin America, 71–374; Mexico, 72–408, 71–397; Nepal, 70–442; New Zealand, 71–416; petroleum, 71–431; South Africa, 71–470; steel, 72–522, 71–479; travel, 72–538, 71–496; United Nations, 71–503; U.S. affairs, 71–25
Interstate Commerce Commission, 71–135
INVENTION, 70–380
  automobile, 71–212; electronics, 71–313, 70–331; handicapped, 72–377, 71–347; Ireland, 70–382; manufacturing, 72–425, 71–391, 70–411; photography, 72–470, 70–460; recordings, 72–490. See also BANKS AND BANKING; ECONOMY, THE; STOCKS AND BONDS
Investments. See BANKS AND BANKING; ECONOMY, THE; STOCKS AND BONDS
Iowa, 71–477
IRAN, 72–392, 71–360, 70–381
  celebrations, 72–272

IRAQ, 72–392, 71–361, 70–381
    Kuwait, 71–367; Middle East, 71–400; Sudan, 72–523
IRELAND, 72–392, 71–361, 70–382; Europe, 72–345, 71–322. See also **Northern Ireland**
Iron: Australia, 70–223; mines, 71–401, 70–423. See also **STEEL INDUSTRY**
Irrigation, 72–66
Irtron, 71–207
Irwin, James B.: astronauts, 72–223; space exploration, 72–510
Iryani, Abdul Rahman, 72–554
Ishak, Yusof bin, 71–285
Islam, 70–484
Isotope, 72–278
ISRAEL, 72–393, 71–362, 70–382; Jordan, 72–397, 70–386; Lebanon, 72–410, 70–398; Libya, 71–379; Meir, Golda, 70–415; Middle East, 72–432, 71–398, 70–419; Saudi Arabia, 71–464; United Arab Republic, 71–499, 70–533; United Nations, 72–541, 71–501, 70–534. See also **JEWS**
ITALY, 72–394, 71–363, 70–383; Austria, 72–227; Colombo, Emilio, 71–264; Jews, 72–396; Formosa, 71–333; Trans-Vision, 71–161; Venice, 71–143
Ivory Coast: Africa, 70–202; Cameroon, 72–257; South Africa, 72–509

J

Jacklin, Tony, 71–341
JACKSON, GLENDA, 72–394
JACKSON, HENRY MARTIN, 72–395
    Democratic party, 72–316
Jackson, Jesse: city, 70–276; civil rights, 72–287, 70–278; il., 70–469
Jacobs, Hirsch, 71–285
Jaffe, Jerome H., 72–322
JAPAN, 72–395, 71–363, 70–384
    agriculture, 71–194; architecture, 71–199; Asia, 72–219, 71–206; Australia, 70–165; automobile, 72–228; building and construction, 71–234; China, 72–281; economy, 72–324, 71–305, 70–324; electronics, 72–335; espionage, 72–343; fairs, 71–325, 70–340; food, 72–68; international trade, 72–391; Korea, North, 72–399; Netherlands, 72–450; New Guinea, 70–439; New Zealand, 71–416, 70–440; Okinawa, 71–423; Pacific islands, 72–459; photography, 72–470; Protestant, 71–446; religion, 71–451; space exploration, 71–474; steel, 71–479; Special Report, 71–59; tunnels, 72–254; world affairs, 72–20
Jarring, Gunnar V.: Middle East, 72–432, 71–399; United Nations, 72–541, 71–501
Jaspers, Karl, 70–306
Jawara, Sir Dawda Kairaba, 71–336
Jazz: Armstrong, Louis, 72–444; arts, 71–49; music, popular, 72–445, 71–410
Jenkins, Roy, 72–370
Jersey City, 72–334
Jerusalem: Israel, 72–393, 70–382; religion, 70–485; Roman Catholic, 72–497
"Jesus Revolution": Protestant, 72–483 religion, 72–491
Jewelry, 71–327
JEWS, 72–396, 71–364, 70–385; church membership, 71–452; civil rights, 72–288; religion, 72–493, 71–451, 70–485; Russia, 72–501, 71–462. See also **ISRAEL**
Job Corps, 71–439, 70–468
Jobs for Veterans, 72–547
Johnson, Alex, 72–240
Johnson, Alvin, 72–312
JOHNSON, LYNDON BAINES, 72–397, 71–365, 70–386
    architecture, 72–215; inflation, 72–83; library, 72–411; literature, 72–413; memorials, 72–429, 71–394
Jonathan, Leabua, 72–411, 71–378
Jones, Bobby, 72–312
Jones, Brian, 70–306
Jones, LeRoi, 72–474
Joplin, Janis, 71–285
JORDAN, 72–397, 71–365, 70–386
    Iraq, 71–361; Israel, 72–393; Middle East, 72–433, 71–400, 70–420; Syria, 72–525; world affairs, 71–19
JORDAN, VERNON EULION, JR., 72–398 civil rights, 72–286
Journalism. See **Newspapers and Magazines; PUBLISHING**
Juan Carlos, Prince, 72–514, 70–508
Judiciary. See **COURTS AND LAWS**
Judo, 71–476, 70–511
Juliana: Indonesia, 72–388
Junior Achievement, 72–556, 71–514, 70–551
Jury, 71–276

Justice, Department of: drugs, 72–322; Mitchell, John N., 70–423; President of the U.S., 71–442; U.S. government, 71–504

K

Kadar, Janos, 71–353
Kahane, Meir, 72–396
Kahn, Louis, 72–213
Kansas: Dole, Robert J., 72–322; state government, 72–519
Kaplan, Morris, 72–312
Karageorgevich, Peter P., 71–285
Karate, 71–476
Karjalainen, Ahti, 72–352, 71–328
Karloff, Boris, 70–306
Karns, Roscoe, 71–286
Karras, Alex, 72–121
Karrer, Paul, 72–312
Kasavubu, Joseph, 70–307
Kashmir, 72–222
Katchen, Julius, 70–307
Katz, Bernard, 71–420
Kaunda, Kenneth David: Africa, 72–200; Great Britain, 71–345; Zambia, 72–557, 71–515, 70–551
Kaye, Danny, il., 71–488
KENNEDY, DAVID MATTHEW, 70–387; Cabinet, 71–237; economy, il., 70–321; President of the U.S., 71–443
KENNEDY, EDWARD MOORE, 72–398; Democratic party, 72–315, 71–290, 70–311
Kennedy, John F.: memorial, 72–429, 71–394, 70–415
Kennedy, Joseph P., 70–306
Kent, Rockwell, 72–312
Kent State University: civil rights, 71–261; President of the U.S., 71–442
Kentucky: Democratic party, 72–315; elections, 72–334; Republican party, 72–494
KENYA, 72–398, 71–366, 70–387; Africa, 70–200; democracy, 70–309
Kenyatta, Jomo: Kenya, 72–398, 71–366, 70–387
Keogh, James, 70–85
Kerensky, Alexander F., 71–286
Kerouac, Jack, 70–306
Kerr, Clark, 70–454
Keyserling, Leon H., 71–353
Keyes, Frances Parkinson, 71–286
Khaury, Herbert B., 70–454
Khorana, Har Gobind: biochemistry, il., 71–227; biology, 71–228
Khrushchev, Nikita S.: deaths, 72–312; Russia, 72–501
Kidd, Billy, 71–466
Kidnaping: Argentina, 71–200; Brazil, 71–233; Canada, 71–238; Latin America, 71–374; Spain, 71–474; Uruguay, 71–505
Kierans, Eric W., 72–260
Kiesinger, Kurt Georg, 70–355
Kim Chung Nam, 70–454
Kim Il-sung, 71–367
King, Billie Jean, 72–528
King, Dennis, 72–312
King, Frank, 70–307
King, Martin Luther, Jr., 70–415
Kinney, Dallas, 71–448
KINSELLA, JOHN, 72–399
KISSINGER, HENRY A., 70–387; China, 72–280; President of the U.S., 72–480, 70–473; Special Report, 70–86; world affairs, 72–18
Kittikachorn, Thanom, 72–529
Kiwanis International, 72–506, 71–465, 70–499
Klein, Herbert G., 70–85
KNAUER, VIRGINIA H., 70–388 consumer affairs, 72–300
Knight, Dame Laura, 71–286
Knudsen, Semon E., 70–226
Kolbe, Maximilian, 72–496
KOREA, 70–388; United Nations, 70–537
KOREA, NORTH, 72–399, 71–367
KOREA, SOUTH, 72–400, 71–367; Asia, 72–218; national defense, 71–411
Kosygin, Aleksei Nikolaevich: Canada, 72–262; China, 70–274; Communism, 70–282; Europe, il., 71–323; Germany, West, 71–340; Romania, 71–457; Russia, 72–500, 71–458
Krag, Jens Otto, 71–420
KREISKY, BRUNO, 71–367; Austria, 72–227, 71–210
Kroyt, Boris, 70–307
KUBELIK, RAFAEL, 72–400
KUHN, BOWIE KENT, 70–389; baseball, 70–238
Kurds: Iraq, 72–392, 71–361, 70–381; Middle East, 71–400; Syria, 70–517
Kusmanovich, Svetom, 70–454
KUWAIT, 72–400, 71–367, 70–389
Kuznets, Simon, 72–456
Ky, Nguyen Cao, 72–548, 70–545

L

LABOR, 72–401, 71–368, 70–389
    advertising, 71–185; agriculture, 71–190, 70–205; Argentina, 71–200, 70–216; Australia, 72–227; automobile, 71–210; baseball, 72–238; Belgium, 72–243, 71–226; building and construction, 72–252, 71–234; Canada, 72–260, 71–242; Chavez, Cesar, 71–249; celebrations, 70–262; Chicago, 70–269; city, 72–182; civil rights, 70–277; Colombia, 70–280; communications, 72–290; Congress, 71–272; courts, 70–296; Detroit, 71–291; economy, 72–325, 71–300, 70–320; education, 71–308; engineering, 72–339, 71–317; Europe, 70–340; Fitzsimmons, Frank E., 72–354; France, 72–361, 71–334; Great Britain, 72–372, 71–344, 70–361; handicapped, 70–364; immigration, 72–385, 70–374; Italy, 72–394, 71–363, 70–383; Los Angeles, 71–388; manufacturing, 72–423, 71–390, 70–410; Mexico, 71–396; music, 71–407, 70–428; New York City, 71–416; old age, 72–458, 70–445; Philadelphia, 71–432, 70–459; post office, 71–437; poverty, 70–469; President of the U.S., 72–478, 71–443; San Francisco, 71–464; shipping, 72–537; South Africa, 71–470; Spain, 71–474; sports, 71–474, 70–508; steel industry, 72–522, 71–479; theater, 71–488; transportation, 71–493, 70–529; U.S. government, 71–504; veterans, 72–547; Woodcock, Leonard, 71–513
Labor, U.S. Department of: Hodgson, James D., 71–351; labor, 72–404; safety, 72–501; Shultz, George, 70–499
Labour Party (Britain), 72–370, 71–342, 70–359
Lacrosse, 72–517, 71–476, 70–511
LAIRD, MELVIN ROBERT, 70–394; espionage, 70–336; national defense, 72–446, 71–411, 70–435
Lamorisse, Albert, 71–286
Land conservation, 71–274
Land reform, 71–432
Landrieu, Moon, 71–415
Landslides, 72–321
Language: archaeology, 70–213; Belgium, 72–242; Canada, 70–256; Canadian literature, 72–272; psychology, 71–446
Lanusse, Alejandro Augustín, 72–215
LAOS, 72–405, 71–373, 70–394; Asia, 72–218, 71–202; Vietnam, 71–506
Laporte, Pierre: Canada, 71–238; deaths, 71–286
Lascaux caves, 70–246
Laser: Australia, 72–227; dentistry, 72–317; electronics, 71–313; manufacturing, il., 72–424; space exploration, 72–512
Lassa fever, 71–394
LATIN AMERICA, 72–406, 71–374, 70–394; Canada, 71–241; President of the U.S., 70–472; Roman Catholic, 72–496. See also by name of country
Latin American Free Trade Association, 71–374
LATTING, PATIENCE SEWELL, 72–410 elections, il., 72–334
Laubach, Frank C., 71–286
Laver, Rod, 72–528, 70–520
Lawless, Theodore K., 72–312
Laws. See **COURTS AND LAWS**
Leacock, Stephen, 71–246
Lead poisoning, 70–366
League of Nations, 71–347, 70–262
Leakey, Mary, 70–211
Learning, 71–41
LEBANON, 72–410, 71–377, 70–398; Franjieh, Suleiman, 71–336; Middle East, 71–400, 70–422
Lee, Gypsy Rose, 71–286
Lee, Manfred B., 72–312
Legislation. See **CONGRESS OF THE UNITED STATES; PRESIDENT OF THE UNITED STATES; STATE GOVERNMENT**
Lehman, Robert, 70–307
Leloir, Luis F., 71–420
Lemass, Sean F., 72–312
Lenin, V. I.: celebrations, 71–247; international education, 71–99
Leone, Giovanni, 72–394
Leopold, Nathan F., 72–312
LESOTHO, 72–411, 71–378; Africa, 71–187
Lessinger, Leon M., 71–42
Leukemia, 72–428
LEVINGSTON, ROBERTO MARCELO, 71–378 Argentina, 72–215, 71–200
Lewis, Joe E., 72–312
Lewis, John L., 70–307; labor, 70–392
Lewis, Oscar, 71–286

Ley, Herbert, 70–319
Ley, Willy, 70–307
Liberia: Africa, 70–203; Brooks, Angie, 70–249
LIBRARY, 72–411, 71–378, 70–399; American Library Association, 72–210, 71–196, 70–210; awards, 71–216; Canadian Library Association, 72–271, 71–245, 70–261; Johnson, Lyndon B., 72–397; memorials, 72–429
Library of Congress: celebrations, 71–246; library, 72–411, 71–378
LIBYA, 72–412, 71–379, 70–399; Africa, 71–188; bridges, 72–253; Chad, 72–276; Egypt, 72–333; Middle East, 72–432, 71–400; Qadhaafi, Muammar Muhammad al-, 71–449; Sudan, 72–523
Lichens, 71–230
Lieberman, Elias, 70–307
Liechtenstein: civil rights, 72–288; Europe, 72–348
Life, 72–35
Light, 72–225
Limongello, Mike, 72–248
Lincoln, Abraham, 72–429
LINDSAY, JOHN VLIET, 72–412; *Apollo 11, il.,* 70–80; Democratic party, 72–315, 70–311; New York City, 72–451; Republican party, 72–494, 70–486; United Nations, *il.,* 71–500
Lin Piao, 72–281, 71–254, 70–272
Lions International, 72–506, 71–466, 70–499
Liquori, Marty, 72–534
Liston, Charles (Sonny), 72–312
Literacy, 70–41
LITERATURE, 72–412, 71–380, 70–400
awards and prizes, 72–233, 71–216, 70–231; Bellow, Saul, 72–243; Canadian, 72–271, 71–245, 70–261; celebrations, 72–272; Nobel prizes, 72–456, 71–420, 70–443; poetry, 72–472, 71–435; publishing, 71–447, 70–480; Pulitzer prizes, 72–489, 71–449, 70–481; Russia, 70–494. See also **THEATER**
LITERATURE FOR CHILDREN, 72–416, 71–384, 70–404
Liturgy, 70–489
Liu Shao-chi, 70–272
Livestock: agriculture, 72–205, 71–190, 70–205; meat, 71–329; show, 72–390, 71–359, 70–379
Living, cost of, 71–300
Livingstone, David, 72–273
Lleras Restrepo, Carlos, 70–280
Lloyd, Harold, 72–312
Lockheed Corporation: aviation, 72–231; banks, 72–238
LODGE, HENRY CABOT, JR., 70–408; United Nations, 71–500
Loesser, Frank, 70–307
Logan, Ella, 70–307
Lollobrigida, Gina, 71–428
Lomax, Lewis E., 71–286
Lombardi, Vincent T., 71–286
Lombardo, Carmen, 72–312
London: classical music, 71–408; Great Britain, 70–363; memorials, 72–429; zoo, 70–117
Longevity, 72–458
López Mateos, Adolfo, 70–307
LOS ANGELES, 72–420, 71–388, 70–408; city, *il.,* 70–276; disasters, 72–319; elections, 70–331; geology, 72–365; visual arts, 72–549, 71–507
Louisiana: bridges, 70–251; New Orleans, 72–450, 71–415, 70–439; state government, 72–519; taxation, 72–527
Lovell, James A.: astronauts, 72–224, 71–206; space exploration, 71–471
Low, Frank J., 71–207
Lowe, Edmund, 72–312
Luge, 72–517
Lumber industry. See **FORESTRY AND FOREST PRODUCTS**
LUNS, JOSEPH M.A.H., 72–420
Netherlands, 72–450
Luria, Salvador E., 70–444
Lutheran, 72–483, 71–445, 70–476
LUXEMBOURG, 72–420, 71–389, 70–409
Lynch, John, 72–392, 70–382
Lynd, Robert S., 71–286

M

Maazel, Lorin, 72–440
Macdonald, Donald S., 71–240
MacEachen, Allan J., 71–240
Machine. See **ENGINE AND ENERGY; MANUFACTURING**
Machine tools, 72–424, 71–391, 70–411
Macias Nguema, Francisco, 70–335
Mackey, Guy J., 72–312
MacLane, Barton, 70–307
Macleod, Iain N.: death, 71–286; Great Britain, 71–342

Maclure, William, 72–365
Macneil, Robert Lister, 71–286
Madagascar. See **MALAGASY REPUBLIC**
Maffei 1, 72–224
Maga, Hubert, 72–306
Magazines: advertising, 72–198, 70–198; literature, 70–404; photography, 72–471, 71–432, 70–462; poetry, 71–435; publishing, 72–487, 71–446, 70–480
Magnetic fields, 72–557
Magnetism: space exploration, 70–505
Maharaja of Jaipur, Sawai Man Singh, 71–286
Mahendra, 72–450, 71–415, 70–438
Maine: Muskie, Edmund S., 72–445; state government, 70–512
MALAGASY REPUBLIC, 72–421; Africa 70–204
MALAWI, 72–421, 71–389; Africa, 70–202
MALAYSIA, FEDERATION OF, 72–422, 71–389, 70–409; Asia, 71–206; Australia, 72–226; New Zealand, 70–440; Thailand, 71–487
Mali, 71–188, 70–202
MALIK, ADAM, 72–422
Malta, 72–347
Man: anthropology, 71–196, 70–211; biology, 70–242
Mandal, Bishnu, 71–428
Manitoba: Canada, 72–263, 71–243, 70–259; Canadian literature, 71–245; celebrations, 71–247; census, 72–266
Mann, Erika, 70–307
Manry, Robert N., 72–312
Mansfield, Mike, *il.,* 72–145
Manson, Charles M., 72–304
Mantle, Mickey: baseball, 70–237; personalities, *il.,* 70–455
MANUFACTURING, 72–423, 71–390, 70–410
Asia, 70–219; automobile, 72–228, 71–210; aviation, 72–231, 71–214; boats, 72–246; chemical industry, 72–277, 71–249; drugs, 72–322; economy, 72–325, 71–302; electronics, 72–335; energy, 71–314, 70–333; engineering, 71–317; environment, 72–339; fishing, 71–328; labor, 71–371; production index, *il.,* 71–303; steel industry, 72–522, 71–479. See also **INVENTION; TECHNOLOGY**
Manush, Henry A., 72–313
Mao Tse-tung, 72–281, 71–254, 70–270
Marbles, 71–429
March, Hal, 71–286
Marciano, Rocky, 70–307
Marcos, Ferdinand Edralin, 72–470, 71–432, 70–460
Marijuana: courts, 70–295; crime, 70–297; drugs, *il.,* 71–298, 70–319; mental health, 72–430; state government, 72–519, 71–477, 70–514
Marine Corps, U.S., 72–446, 71–412
Marland, Sidney, 72–376, 71–307
Marriage: immigration and emigration, 71–354; Roman Catholic, 71–455; vital statistics, 72–551, 71–509
Mars (planet): astronomy, *il.,* 70–221; botany, 70–246; space exploration, 72–510, 70–48, 70–506
Martin, Harold E., 71–448
Martinelli, Giovanni, 70–307
Maryland: Baltimore, 72–236; 71–219; conservation, 72–298
Masella, Benedetto Cardinal, 71–286
Maslow, Abraham H., 71–286
Mass culture, 70–53
Massachusetts: Boston, 72–248, 71–230; consumer affairs, 71–275; insurance, 71–358; Kennedy, Edward M., 72–398; state government, 72–519, *il.,* 71–476
Mathematics: archaeology, 72–212; Dutka, Jacques, 72–464
Matter: astronomy, 71–207; biochemistry, 71–226; chemistry, 71–250; physics, 72–472, 71–434
Matzdorf, Pat, 72–533
Mauriac, François, 71–286
Mauritania, 71–194
Mauritius, 71–190
Maxwell, Gavin, 70–307
"Mayflower," 71–248
MAYO, ROBERT P.: President of the U.S., 72–443, 70–412
Mayors, 72–315
MAYS, WILLIE HOWARD, 71–392
Mboya, Tom: Africa, *il.,* 70–200; deaths, 70–307; democracy, 70–309; Kenya, 70–387
McCarey, Leo, 70–307
McCartney, Paul, 70–454
McCLOSKEY, PAUL NORTON, JR., 72–425
Republican party, 72–495
McCORMACK, JOHN WILLIAM, 71–392; Congress, 71–268; crime, 71–278

McCracken, Paul W., *il.,* 72–328
McCulloch, Warren S., 70–307
McDivitt, James A.: astronauts, 70–220; space exploration, 70–504
McGill, Ralph, 70–307
McGOVERN, GEORGE STANLEY, 72–425
Democratic party, 72–316
McHugh, James F., 70–307
McKay, David O., 71–286
McLain, Dennis, 72–240, 71–221
McLaren, Bruce: automobile racing, 71–212
McMahon, Horace, 72–313
McMAHON, WILLIAM, 72–425; Australia, 72–226
Meany, George, 72–402, *il.,* 71–372
Measles, 72–377, 71–348, 70–99
Meat: agriculture, 72–206, 70–206; Chicago, *il.,* 71–252; food, 72–355, 71–329, 70–344; labor, 71–371; New Zealand, 71–416; production, *il.,* 71–192. See also **Livestock**
Medicaid, 72–426, 70–412
MEDICARE, 72–426, 71–393, 70–412; Canada, 71–243; old age, 71–422; social welfare, 72–509
MÉDICI, EMÍLIO GARRASTAZÚ, 70–413; Brazil, 72–250, 70–248
MEDICINE, 72–426, 71–393, 70–413
awards and prizes, 71–216, 70–233; biochemistry, 72–244; child welfare, 72–280; dentistry, 71–291, 70–312; drugs, 72–322, 71–298, 70–318; education, 71–308; electronics, 71–313; foundations, 71–334; Nobel prizes, 72–456, 71–420, 70–444; old age, 72–458, 70–445; Roman Catholic, 71–457; rubella, 70–99; state government, 70–514. See also **DRUGS; HEALTH AND DISEASE; MENTAL HEALTH**
Medicine, Institute of, 72–380
MEIR, GOLDA, 70–415; Israel, 72–393, 71–362, 70–382
Mekong River, 71–235
MEMORIALS, 72–429, 71–394, 70–415
architecture, 72–215; coins, 72–289; music, 72–440; visual arts, 72–508; Washington, D.C., 71–510
Memory, 70–243
Mendoza y Amor, Benjamin, 71–455
MENTAL HEALTH, 72–430, 71–396, 70–416; child welfare, 70–270; psychology, 72–484; Pulitzer prizes, 71–449; Russia, 72–501
Mental retardation: handicapped, 71–347; mental health, 72–430, 71–347
Merchant marine. See **Ship**
Mercury: chemical industry, 71–250; environment, 71–320; fishing, 71–328
Meredith, James H., 72–465
Mergenthaler, Ottmar, 72–429
Meriwether, Delano, 72–533
Meteorology. See **WEATHER**
Methodist, 71–445, 70–477
Mexican-American, 71–388
MEXICO, 72–430, 71–396, 70–416
agriculture, 72–61; anthropology, 70–212; crime, 70–297; dam, 70–251; drugs, 70–319; Echeverría Alvárez, Luis, 71–299; immigration, 70–374; labor, 71–373; Latin America 72–409; President of the U.S., 71–444; soccer, 71–467
Meyer, Agnes E., 71–286
Meyer, Debbie, 71–482, 70–516
Meyer, Dr. Harry M., 70–104
Miami, 72–315
Michel, F. Curtis, 70–220
MICHENER, ROLAND, 72–431, 71–397, 70–417
Michigan: conservation, 71–273; Detroit, 72–317, 71–291, 70–312; hunting and fishing, 72–384; Roman Catholic, 71–456; state government, 72–519
Micronesia, 72–459
Microscope: biology, *il.,* 72–245; chemistry, 72–278; electronics, 72–335
MIDDLE EAST, 72–432, 71–398, 70–419; international relations, 71–17, 70–17; petroleum, 72–469; President of the U.S., 72–441; Roman Catholic, 71–456; Russia, 72–499; United Nations, 72–541, 71–501. See also under names of countries
Mies van der Rohe, Ludwig: architecture, 70–216; deaths, 70–307; interior design, 70–378
Milk, 71–196
Milky Way, 72–224
MILLS, WILBUR DAIGH, 72–434; state government, 72–521
Mindszenty, Joseph Cardinal, 72–497
MINES AND MINING, 72–434, 71–401, 70–423; Africa, 70–204; Australia, 72–227, 71–210, 70–223; disasters, 72–320, 71–296, 70–318; Latin America, 72–409;

Lewis, John L., 70–392; Mexico, 72–431; New Zealand, 72–452; Peru, 72–467, 71–430, 70–456; safety, 71–463; Saudi Arabia, 72–504; tunnels, 70–251; U.S. government, 71–504. See also **PETROLEUM AND GAS**
Minh, Duong Van, 72–548
Minneapolis: building, il., 72–253; visual arts, 72–549
Minnesota: city, 71–258; conservation, 72–298; courts, 72–303; hunting, 72–384; state government, 72–518
Mint, 71–402
Mirza, Iskander, 70–307
Mishima, Yukio, 71–286
Missile. See Guided Missile
Mississippi: disasters, 70–314; Meredith, James H., 72–465; state government, 72–519
Missouri: celebrations, 72–272; St. Louis, 72–502, 71–463, 70–495; state government, 72–519
Mitchell, Arthur, 72–306
Mitchell, Edgar D.: astronauts, 72–223; space exploration, 72–510
MITCHELL, JOHN NEWTON, 70–423; elections, 71–312; Pentagon papers, 72–486; publishing, 71–447; U.S. government, 71–504; voting, 71–312
Mitchell, Martha, il., 72–463
Mitrione, Dan A., 71–505
Mobile home, 72–381, 70–372
Mobutu, Joseph, 72–290, 71–266
MODEL BUILDING. See GAMES, MODELS, AND TOYS
Model Cities Program, 71–257
Mohammed Zahir Shah, 72–199, 71–185, 70–199
Moholy-Nagy, Sibyl: architecture, 72–215; deaths, 72–313
Molecule: astronomy, 72–224, 70–222; chemistry, 72–278; Nobel prizes, 72–456
Mondadori, Arnoldo, 72–313
Mondlane, Eduardo Chivambo, 70–307
MONEY, 72–435, 71–402, 70–423
Africa, 72–203; Argentina, 72–216; Asia, 72–219; Austria, 72–227; banks and banking, 72–236, 71–219, 70–233; Belgium, 72–243; building and construction, 70–249; coin collecting, 72–289, 71–349, 70–368; Costa Rica, 72–409; Denmark, 70–312; economy, 72–324, 71–300; Ecuador, 71–305; Europe, 72–344, 71–324, 70–340; France, 72–361, 70–352; Gambia, 72–362; Germany, 72–367, 71–340, 70–356; inflation, 72–77; international trade, 72–390, 71–359, 70–379; Ireland, 71–361; Japan, 72–396; Nigeria, 71–417; Philadelphia, 72–459; Philippines, 71–432; retailing, 71–454; stocks and bonds, 72–522; supply, il., 71–303; travel, 72–538; U.S. affairs, 72–25; Vietnam, 71–506
MONGOLIAN PEOPLE'S REPUBLIC, 70–424. See also **OUTER MONGOLIA**
Mononucleosis, 70–414
Montana, 72–519
Montreal: Canada, 72–265, 71–238, 70–260; fairs and expositions, 72–349, 71–326, 70–340; Quebec, 71–244; waste disposal, il., 71–85
Moody, Orville, 70–358
Moon: astronauts, 72–223, 71–206; astronomy, 71–208, 70–220; science, 70–35; space exploration, 72–510, 71–471, 70–47, 70–504; *Special Report,* 70–64
Moore, Douglas S., 72–307
Mormon: memorials, 72–429; Protestant, 71–446; Smith, Joseph F., 71–467
MOROCCO, 72–436, 71–402, 70–425
Africa, 71–188; Libya, 72–412; Middle East, 72–433
Morrison, James D., 72–313
Morse, Arthur D., 72–313
MORTON, ROGERS CLARK BALLARD, 71–403; conservation, 72–298; Indian, American, 72–387
Moslem: Asia, 72–220; Chad, 72–276; religion, 72–493; 70–484
MOTION PICTURES, 72–437, 71–403, 70–425; arts, 72–47; awards, 72–235, 71–218; Jackson, Glenda, 72–394; photography, 72–471; popular music, 71–409; Scott, George C., 72–505; *WBE,* 72–560
Motlotlehi Moshoeshoe II, 72–411
Motorboat racing, 72–246, 71–230, 70–244
Motorcycling, 72–517, 71–476, 70–511
Mountain climbing: Japan, 71–364; Nepal, 71–415; personalities, 71–426
Mowbray, Alan, 70–308
MOYNIHAN, DANIEL PATRICK, 70–427; city, 70–274; *Special Report,* 70–85; President of the U.S., 71–443

Mozambique: Africa, 72–202, 71–186, 70–202; dams, 70–251
Mujibur Rahman: Asia, 72–222; India, 72–385; Pakistan, 72–459
Multiple sclerosis, 72–244
Mulzac, Hugh N., 72–313
Murphy, Audie, 72–313
Murphy, Johnny, 71–286
Murphy, Robert, 72–313
Murray, Mary, 70–454
MUSEUMS, 72–439, 71–405, 70–427
archaeology, 72–213; architecture, 71–199; Boston, 70–245; celebrations, 71–246; collecting, 71–125; painting, 70–447; sculpture, 70–497; visual arts, 72–549, 71–507
MUSIC, CLASSICAL, 72–440, 71–406, 70–428
Australia, 71–210; awards, 72–233, 71–215, 70–231; dancing, 72–307; Kubelik, Rafael, 72–400; literature for children, 72–417, 71–386, 70–406; memorials, 72–429; Pulitzer prizes, 72–489, 71–449; recordings, 72–490, 71–450, 70–482; Stravinsky, Igor, 72–310
MUSIC, POPULAR AND JAZZ, 72–443, 71–409, 70–433; arts, 71–49; Graham, Bill, 72–464; health, 71–451; radio, 72–489; recordings, 72–490, 70–482; religion, 72–491; theater, 72–530
Musicals, 72–530, 71–488, 70–522
Muskie, Edmund Sixtus, 72–445; civil rights, 72–288; Democratic party, 72–316, 71–290
Mutesa II, Sir Edward, 70–308
Mutual funds, 72–522
My Lai, 72–256

N

NADER, RALPH, 71–410; consumer affairs, 72–300, 71–275; democracy, 70–309; drugs, 71–298; economy, 70–325; environment, 72–339; fishing industry, 70–344; safety, 70–495
Nagel, Conrad, 71–286
Namath, Joe, 72–120, 70–347
Namibia: Africa, 72–200, 71–188; United Nations, 72–543, 71–501
Narcotics: courts and laws, 70–295; drug addiction, 70–319; mental health, 70–416; Mexico, 70–416; state government, 70–514. See also **DRUGS**
Nash, Ogden: deaths, 72–313; poetry, 72–473
Nasser, Gamal Abdel: deaths, 71–286; Jordan, 71–366; Middle East, 71–400; United Arab Republic, 71–499, 70–533
NATO. See North Atlantic Treaty Organization
National Aeronautics and Space Administration. 72–223, 71–206. See also **SPACE EXPLORATION**
National Council of Churches, 71–445
NATIONAL DEFENSE, 72–446, 71–411, 70–435
armed forces, 71–201, 70–217; Asia, 72–218, 71–203; Canada, 72–258; Congress, 72–297, 71–267, 70–287; espionage, 70–336; Goodpaster, Andrew J., 70–359; Korea, South, 72–400, 71–367; Laos, 71–373; President of the U.S., 72–480; science, 70–496; Spain, 71–474; Thailand, 71–487, 70–521; veterans, 72–547; Vietnam, 70–541
National forests, 71–333
National Guard, 72–446, 71–477
National Institutes of Health, 72–504
National Labor Relations Board, 71–373
National monuments, 72–429
NATIONAL PARKS, 71–588
conservation, 72–298, 71–272, 70–293; forests, 72–360; memorials, 70–415
National Science Foundation, 70–497
National Security Council, 70–473
National Urban League, 72–398
Nationalization: Chile, 72–280; Guyana, 72–375; Latin America, il., 72–406; Sudan, 71–481; Tanzania, 71–483; Venezuela, 72–547
Natural gas. See PETROLEUM AND GAS
Nauvoo, 72–429
Navy: armed forces, 72–216, 71–201, 70–217; Asia, 72–223; national defense, 70–437; Puerto Rico, 71–448
Navy, U.S.: Gravely, Samuel L., Jr., 72–369; national defense, 72–446, 71–412; Puerto Rico, 72–487, 71–448; Zumwalt, Elmo R., Jr., 72–558
Ne Win, 72–255, 70–252
Nebraska, 72–521
Nebula, 72–225
Néel, Louis E., 71–420
Negro: awards, 72–234, 71–216; Baltimore, 72–236; banks, il., 70–234; census, 72–267; city, 72–284; 71–258, 70–276; civil rights, 72–286, 71–259, 70–277; dancing, 72–306;

Democratic party, 72–315; education, 72–330, 71–41; elections, 72–334, 71–311, 70–331; Gravely, Samuel L. Jr., 72–369; Houston, 72–382; Jews, 72–396, 70–385; labor, 71–373; Los Angeles, 71–388, 70–408; motion pictures, 72–437; music, classical, 71–408; New Orleans, 72–450; Philadelphia, 72–469; poetry, 72–474; Protestant, 71–445, 70–475; publishing, il., 71–447; radio, 71–449; Roman Catholic, 70–491; sports, 71–55; Sudan, 71–481
Nelson, Eric H., 71–287
NEPAL, 72–451, 71–415, 70–438
Neruda, Pablo, 72–456
Nervous system, 72–245
Netcher, Rose Dolly, 71–287
NETHERLANDS, 72–450, 71–415, 70–438
building and construction, il., 70–250; dam, il., 72–254; electronics, 72–335; Indonesia, 72–388; Luns, Joseph, 72–420; Roman Catholic, il., 71–456
Neutra, Richard J.: architecture, 71–200; deaths, 71–287
Nevins, Allan, 72–313
New Brunswick: Canada, 72–263, 71–243, 70–259; census, 72–267
NEW GUINEA, 71–415, 70–439
New Hampshire: architecture, il., 72–214; state government, 72–519; taxation, 72–527
New Jersey: elections, 70–330; Republican party, 70–486; state government, 72–519
New Mexico, 72–519
NEW ORLEANS, 72–450, 71–415, 70–439
New York (state): city, 70–276; crime, 72–304; elections, 70–331; geology, 72–364; health, 72–377; mental health, 71–396; popular music, 70–432; religion, 70–485; Republican party, 71–453, 70–486; Roman Catholic, 71–457; social welfare, il., 72–508; state government, 72–519, 70–512; taxation, 72–527
NEW YORK CITY, 72–451, 71–416, 70–439
architecture, il., 72–251; building and construction, 72–252, 71–234; celebrations, 71–247; city, il., 72–285; *Special Report,* 72–181; civil rights, 72–263; communications, 72–290; dancing, 71–281; Democratic party, 70–311; Earth Day, il., 71–295; education, 72–331, 71–307, 70–327; energy, 72–336, il., 70–334; fairs, 72–348; horse racing, 72–380; housing, 71–352; Lindsay, John V., 72–412; medicine, il., 70–413; memorials, 72–429; museums, 72–439, 71–406; music, 72–440, 71–406, 70–428; publishing, il., 70–480; Republican party, 72–494; theater, 72–530; tunnels, 70–251; United Nations, 71–503; visual arts, 72–549, 71–507; waste disposal, 71–87; zoos, 72–558, 71–516, 70–120, 70–552
NEW ZEALAND, 72–452, 71–416, 70–440
Europe, 72–344
Newark, 71–258
Newfoundland: Canada, 72–263, 71–243, 70–259; census, 72–267
Newman, Alfred, 71–287
Newman, Barnett, 71–287
Newscasting, 71–486
Newspapers: advertising, 70–198; awards and prizes, 72–233, 71–215, 70–232; Baltimore, 71–219; courts, 72–302; Greece, 72–374; photography, 71–432, 70–462; publishing, 71–485, 71–466, 70–478; Pulitzer prizes, 72–488, 71–448, 70–481; Tanzania, 71–483
N'Gouabi, Marien, 71–266
Niagara Falls, il., 70–292
Nicaragua: Latin America, 72–410, 71–377, 70–395; stamp collecting, 72–517
Nicklaus, Jack, 72–367, 71–341
Niebuhr, Reinhold: deaths, 72–313; religion, 72–492
NIGERIA, 72–452, 71–417, 70–440; Africa, 71–188, 70–200; Great Britain, 70–362; United Nations, 70–534
Nikolayev, Andrian G., 71–473
NIMERI, JAFAR MUHAMMAD, 72–452
Africa, 72–204; Sudan, 72–523, 71–481
Niven, Paul K., Jr., 71–287
Nixon, Patricia, 72–454, 71–419, 70–443
NIXON, RICHARD MILHOUS, 72–453, 71–418, 70–441
Apollo 11, 70–78; Canada, il., 70–254; civil rights, 72–286; Europe, 70–338; football, 70–348; hobbies, 72–378; national affairs, il., 70–24; personalities, 71–425, 70–451; photography, il., 70–461; President of the U.S., 72–478, 71–444; Protestant, 71–446, 70–476; religion, 71–452; Republican party, 72–494; Roman Catholic, 70–491; Truman, Harry S., 70–532. See also **PRESIDENT OF THE UNITED STATES**

Nixon, Tricia, 72–454
Nkrumah, Kwame, 72–367
Noailles, Viscountess Marie-Laure de, 71–287
NOBEL PRIZES, 72–456, 71–420, 70–443
No-fault insurance, 72–388
Noise pollution: aviation, 71–214; environment, 71–321; Special Report, 70–131
NOL, LON, 71–420; Asia, 71–204; Cambodia, 72–256, 71–237
Norin, 72–61
Norodom, Sihanouk, 70–253
North Atlantic Treaty Organization: armed forces, 72–217, 71–201, 70–217; Canada, 70–256; espionage, 71–321, 70–336; Europe, 72–346, 71–324, 70–337; Luns, Joseph, 72–420; national defense, 72–446, 71–412
North Carolina, 72–519
North Vietnam. See VIETNAM
Northern Ireland: civil rights, 70–279; Faulkner, Brian, 72–352; Great Britain, 72–372, 71–345, 70–361; Ireland, 72–392, 71–361; Protestant, 70–476; religion, 71–451; Roman Catholic, 72–497
Northern Rhodesia. See ZAMBIA
Northwest Passage: ocean, 70–444; petroleum, 70–458
NORWAY, 72–456, 71–421, 70–444; Bratteli, Trygve M., 72–250; celebrations, 72–273, 71–246; Europe, 72–345, 71–322; Hambro, Edvard I., 71–347; Vietnam, 72–549
Nova Scotia: Canada, 72–263, 71–243, 70–259; census, 72–267
Nu, U, 72–255
Nuclear physics, 71–217. See also Atomic Energy; PHYSICS
Nuclear nonproliferation treaty, 70–287
Nursing, 71–463
Nutrition: anthropology, 71–196; archaeology, 71–198; food, 72–355; psychology, 72–485, 70–478; zoology, 71–515
Nyasaland. See MALAWI; RHODESIA
Nye, Gerald P., 72–313
Nyerere, Julius, 72–526, 71–483, 70–517

O

OAS. See Organization of American States
Oats, 72–206, 71–192, 70–206
Oberammergau, 71–451
Obituaries. See DEATHS OF NOTABLE PERSONS
Obote, Apollo Milton: Africa, 72–202; Amin, Idi, 72–211; Tanzania, 72–526, 71–499, 70–532; Uganda, 72–540
O'Brien, Lawrence F., 72–316, il., 71–289
OCEAN, 72–457, 71–421, 70–444
    biology, il., 70–243; electronics, 71–313; petroleum, 71–431; waste disposal, 71–83; zoology, 70–551
O'Daniel, W. Lee, 70–308
Office of Economic Opportunity, 72–476
Off-track betting, 72–380
O'Hara, Barratt, 70–308
Ohio: Cleveland, 72–288, 71–264; music, 71–406; state government, 72–518
Oil. See PETROLEUM
Okinawa: Asia, 72–218; Japan, 70–384; Pacific Islands, 72–459, 71–423, 70–446
Oklahoma, 72–209
Oklahoma City, 72–410
OLD AGE, 72–458, 71–422, 70–445
Olson, Charles: deaths, 71–287; poetry, 71–436
OLYMPIC GAMES: Japan, 72–396; skiing, 72–506, 71–467; South Africa, 71–470. See also SPORTS
Oman, 71–425
Ongania, Juan Carlos, 71–200, 70–216
Ontario: Canada, 72–264, 71–243, 70–259; census, 72–267; Davis, William, 72–308
Opera: celebrations, 70–264; Kubelik, Rafael, 72–400; labor, il., 70–390; music, 72–440, 71–408, 70–428; music, popular, 71–409; Sydney, 70–170; theater, 72–530
Opportunity funding, 71–438
Orange Bowl, 72–359
Orchestra. See Symphony
Oregon: forest, 72–360; state government, 72–519
Organization of African Unity, 72–201, 71–186
Organization of American States, 71–374, 70–394
Organizations: advertising, 72–199; agriculture, 71–193; architecture, 71–199, 70–213; awards and prizes, 72–233, 70–231; conservation, 70–292; consumer affairs, 71–275; education, 70–329; engineering, 70–335; gardening, 72–363, 71–337; handicapped, 72–376; museums, 72–439; service clubs, 72–506, 71–465; veterans, 72–547, 71–505,

70–539; zoos and aquariums, 72–558. See also YOUTH ORGANIZATIONS; also names of specific organizations
Ormandy, Eugene, 71–406
ORR, ROBERT GORDON (BOBBY), 71–422; hockey, 71–349
Orthodox Church in America, 72–323
Osaka: architecture, 71–199; fairs, 71–325
Ottawa, il., 70–258
Ovando Candia, Alfredo, 71–230, 70–245
Owen, Sir A. David K., 71–287
Owen, William James, 71–321

P

Pacheco Areco, Jorge, 72–546, 71–505, 70–538
PACIFIC ISLANDS, 72–459, 71–423, 70–446
    mines, 72–435; New Zealand, 71–416. See also NEW GUINEA
Packaging, 71–329, 70–345
Paige, Satchel, il., 72–464
Paine, Thomas O., 71–474
PAINTING, 70–447
    awards, 72–233, 71–215; Canadian literature, 71–245; literature, 71–383; visual arts, 72–549, 71–507
Paisley, Ian, 70–361
PAKISTAN, 72–459, 71–423, 70–449
    agriculture, 72–62, 71–194; Asia, 72–218; disasters, 72–294; India, 72–398; religion, 72–493; Roman Catholic, 72–497; United Nations, 72–541; Yahya Khan, Agha Mohammed, 72–548
Paleontology. See Fossils
Palestine. See ISRAEL; JORDAN; MIDDLE EAST
Palestinians: Jordan, 72–397, 71–365; Kuwait, 71–367; Lebanon, 71–377; Middle East, 72–433, 71–400
Palmer, Arnold, 72–369, 70–359
Palmer, Dewey H., 72–313
PANAMA, 72–460, 71–424, 70–450
    Latin America, 72–409
PAN AMERICAN GAMES, 72–460
Papadopoulous, George, 72–374
Papanicolaou, Christos, 71–491
Papen, Franz von, 70–308
Papua. See NEW GUINEA
PARAGUAY, 72–461, 71–424; Latin America, 70–398
Parathyroid hormone, 72–243
PARENTS AND TEACHERS, NATIONAL CONGRESS OF, 72–461, 71–424, 70–451
Paris: building and construction, 70–250; fairs, 72–349, 70–341; France, 72–361; library, 71–378; music, 71–408; zoo, 70–117
Park, Chung Hee, 72–400, 70–388
Parkinson's disease, 70–415
Parkman, Dr. Paul D., 70–102
Parks, 70–293. See also NATIONAL PARKS; ZOOS AND AQUARIUMS
Parliament (Canada), 72–261, 70–255
Parole, 72–109
Particle, 71–434, 70–462
Particle accelerator, 72–505
PASTRANA BORRERO, MISAEL, 71–424; Colombia, 72–289, 71–264
Patent. See INVENTIONS
Pathet Lao, 72–405
Patsayev, Viktor I., 72–313
Paukstys, Victoria, 72–465
PAUL VI: religion, 70–483; Roman Catholic Church, 72–496, 71–455, 70–489; Uganda, 70–532
Paumgartner, Bernhard, 72–313
Pay Board: economy, 72–329; inflation, 72–88; labor, 72–402; President of the U.S., 72–480
Peace: Africa, 71–186; Asia, 71–206; Middle East, 71–398; national defense, 71–411, 70–437; Nigeria, 71–417; national defense, 70–437; Nobel prizes, 72–456, 71–420, 70–443; ocean, 72–457; President of the U.S., 71–440, 70–471; Roman Catholic, 72–496; United Nations, 71–501, 70–534; Vietnam, 70–541
"Peanuts," 70–147
PEACE CORPS, 72–462, 71–425, 70–451
    Africa, 70–202; Blatchford, Joseph, 70–243; Libya, 70–400; poverty, 72–476; service clubs, 70–499; United Nations, 72–543
Pearson, Drew, 70–308
Pegler, Westbrook, 70–308
Pelé (Edson Arantes do Nascimento), 72–507, 71–467
Penn Central Railroad: economy, 71–302; transportation, 71–494
Penney, James Cash, 72–313

Pennsylvania: labor, 71–373; Philadelphia, 72–469, 71–432, 70–459; state government, 72–518
Pentagon Papers: civil rights, 72–288; courts, 72–302; Johnson, Lyndon B., 72–397; publishing, 72–485
Pentathlon: sports, 72–517, 71–476, 70–511; track and field, 70–525
Pentecostals, 72–483
Percy, Charles H., il., 72–144
Perelman, S.J., 72–465
Periodontal disease, 70–312
Perk, Ralph J., 72–288
Perlea, Jonel, 71–406
Perls, Frederick S., 71–287
Peron, Juan, 71–200
PERSIAN GULF EMIRATES, 72–462, 71–425; Middle East, 71–401; Saudi Arabia, 72–504
PERSONALITIES, 72–463, 71–425, 70–451. See also Biography
PERU, 72–467, 71–429, 70–456; archaeology, 72–212; disasters, 71–294; geology, 71–338; Latin America, il., 70–398
Pesticides: chemical industry, 72–277, 70–266; environment, 72–341, 71–321; gardening, 72–363; medicine, 70–414
PET, 72–467, 71–430, 70–457
Peter II (Yugoslavia), 71–285
Petkevich, John M., 72–385
PETROLEUM AND GAS, 72–468, 71–431, 70–457
    Africa, 71–190; Algeria, 72–210; Australia, 71–210; Canada, 71–241, 70–257; Colombia, 70–397; conservation, 70–292; economy, 71–302; energy, 72–336, 71–314; environment, 72–341, 71–320; Iran, 70–381; Iraq, 72–392; Israel, 71–362; Kuwait, 71–367; Libya, 72–412, 71–379; Mexico, 71–397; Middle East, 72–434, 71–401, 70–422; Netherlands, 70–438; New Zealand, 72–452; Nigeria, 72–452; Nova Scotia, 72–263; ocean, 71–421; Peru, 70–456; pollution, 70–463; regulation, 71–133; San Francisco, 72–503; Saudi Arabia, 72–504, 71–464; transportation, il., 70–527; Tunisia, 72–540; United Arab Republic, 71–499; Venezuela, 72–547, 71–505; Venice, 71–148
Petrosian, Tigran, 72–278
Petty, Richard, 72–230
PHILADELPHIA, 72–469, 71–432, 70–459
    architecture, 72–214; building and construction, 70–250; civil rights, 71–260; elections, 70–330; fairs and expositions, 71–326; money, 71–402; music, 71–406; "Philadelphia plan," 70–390; Republican party, 72–494; transit, 70–530; visual arts, 72–550; zoos, 72–558
Philanthropy: museums, 72–439; Red Cross, 72–491; service clubs, 72–506
PHILIPPINES, 72–470, 71–432, 70–460
    agriculture, 72–60; anthropology, 72–211; Asia, 72–218, 71–206; Roman Catholic, 71–455
Phonograph. See RECORDINGS
PHOTOGRAPHY, 72–470, 71–432, 70–460
    awards, 72–233, 71–216, 71–218, 70–232; Pulitzer prizes, 72–488, 71–448, 70–481
Photometer, 72–278
Photosynthesis, 71–251
PHYSICS, 72–472, 71–434, 70–462
    astronomy, 70–222; awards and prizes, 72–234, 71–217, 70–233; electronics, 72–335, 71–313; Nobel prizes, 72–456, 71–420, 70–443; science, 72–505
Physiology: biochemistry, 72–243; biology, 72–245; Nobel prizes, 71–420; psychology, 71–446
Piccard, Jacques, 70–444
Pigeon: zoology, 72–557
Pike, James A., 70–308
Pimen, Metropolitan, 72–323
Pipinelis, Panayotis, 71–287
Pire, Dominique Georges, 70–308
Pittsburgh, 72–442, 71–407, 70–330
Plastics: boats, 70–244; chemical industry, 72–277, 71–249, 70–265; interior design, 72–389, 71–358; recordings, 72–490
Plants, 71–230
Plate tectonics, 72–365
Plaza Lasso, Galo, 72–408
Plimpton, George, 72–466
Plunkett, Jim, 71–332
Pluto, 72–225
Plymouth, 71–248
Podgorny, Nikolai V., 72–549
Podunk, 72–464
POETRY, 72–472, 71–435
    awards and prizes, 72–234, 71–216, 70–231; Canadian, 72–271, 71–246, 70–262; literature, 70–403; literature for children, 72–417; 71–386, 71–406; Nobel prizes, 72–456; Pulitzer prizes, 72–489, 71–449, 70–481

POLAND, 72–474, 71–436, 70–463
espionage, 72–342; Gierek, Edward, 71–341; Jews, 72–396; Russia, 72–498

Pole vault, 71–491, 70–525

Police: aviation, 71–214; civil rights, 71–261; courts and laws, 70–295; crime, 72–105, 72–303, 71–278, 70–297; Los Angeles, 72–420; New York City, 72–451; St. Louis, 72–503; San Francisco, 72–503; state government, 70–514; Washington, D.C., 71–510

Political parties: Congress, 71–267; U.S. affairs, 71–25. See also **AMERICAN PARTY; COMMUNISM; DEMOCRATIC PARTY; RE-PUBLICAN PARTY** as well as names of other parties

POLLUTION, 70–463; automobile, 72–228; aviation, 71–214; Baltimore, 71–219; Canada, 72–261, 71–240; chemical industry, 72–277, 71–250, 70–266; Congress, 71–272; economy, 71–304; energy, 72–336; environment, 72–339, 71–319; fishing, 72–353; food, 72–355; health and disease, 71–348; Houston, 72–383; international education, 71–96; Japan, 71–71, 71–363; manufacturing, 71–390; Mexico, 72–430; museums, 70–427; New York City, 70–439; personalities, 71–427; photography, 72–470; President of the U.S., 71–443; science, 72–505, 71–34; *Special Report,* 71–79; state government, 72–519, 71–477, 70–514; Switzerland, 72–525; taxation, 71–484; United Nations, 70–536; United States, *Focus,* 71–23; *WBE,* 72–590. See also **CONSERVATION; ENVIRONMENT**

Polo, 71–476, 70–511

Polynesia. See **PACIFIC ISLANDS**

POMPIDOU, GEORGES JEAN RAYMOND, 70–465; Europe, 72–344, 70–337; France, 72–361, 71–334, 70–350; President of the U.S., *il.,* 71–444

Pope. See **PAUL VI**

Popular music. See **MUSIC, POPULAR**

POPULATION, WORLD, 72–475, 71–436, 70–465
Africa, 72–203; awards, 72–234; Canada, 72–265, 72–274; China, 72–282; city, 72–182, 72–284; Cleveland, 72–288; Dallas, 71–280; Detroit, 72–317; Ehrlich, Paul R., 71–309; energy, 71–316; Great Britain, 71–344; immigration and emigration, 72–385, 71–354; Jews, 72–396; Russia, 71–461; vital statistics, 72–551. See also **CENSUS**

Pornography: arts, 70–54; Denmark, 70–312; literature, 71–380; motion pictures, 71–403, 70–426; postal service, 72–476, 71–437; Protestant, 72–483; publishing, 71–446

Ports and harbors, 71–243

PORTUGAL, 72–475, 71–437, 70–466
Africa, 72–202, 71–186; Rhodesia, 71–454; United Nations, 72–501, 70–537; Zambia, 72–557

Portuguese Guinea, 71–186

POSTAL SERVICE, 72–475. See also **POST OFFICE,** 71–437, 70–467
Blount, Winton M., 70–244; cabinet, 72–255; communications, 70–281; Congress, 71–268; hobbies, 71–349; labor, 71–372; President of the U.S., 70–474; stamp collecting, 72–517, 70–367; U.S. government, 72–544

Potatoes, 71–192, 70–206

POVERTY, 72–476, 71–438, 70–468
agriculture, 72–209; Boy Scouts, 71–514; civil rights, 70–291; food, 70–344; health, 70–365; Roman Catholic, 70–491; social welfare, 71–469

Powdermaker, Hortense, 71–287

Powell, Cecil Frank, 70–308

Powell, Enoch, 70–360

POWELL, LEWIS FRANKLIN, JR., 72–477; courts, 72–302; President of the U.S., 72–481

Prayers, school, 72–544

Presbyterians: Protestant, 72–483, 71–445; women's rights, 72–484

PRESIDENT OF THE UNITED STATES, 72–478, 71–440, 70–471
Agnew, Spiro T., 72–204; agriculture, 70–208; Asia, 72–221, 71–204; automobile, 72–229; awards, 70–232; banks, 72–237; building and construction, 71–234, 70–249; Cabinet, 72–255, 71–237, 70–253; Calley, William, Jr., 72–256; child welfare, 70–269; China, 72–280; city, 70–285, 70–274; civil rights, 71–259, 70–277; Congress, 72–291, 71–267, 70–286; conservation, 72–298, 71–273, 70–292; consumer affairs, 72–300; courts, 72–302; crime, 72–303; Democratic party, 72–315; drugs, 72–322; economy, 72–29, 72–323, 71–30, 71–300, 70–325; education, 72–331, 71–307; elections, 71–

310; environment, 72–339, 71–319; Europe, 71–324; fairs and expositions, 71–326; forests, 72–360, 71–333; health, 72–377; housing, 71–352; immigration and emigration, 71–354; Indian, American, 72–387, 71–356; inflation, 72–77; insurance, 72–388; international trade, 72–390, 71–359; Italy, 71–363; Japan, 70–384; labor, 72–401; Latin America, 70–394; library, 71–378; memorials, 72–429, 71–394; Mexico, 71–397; music, 71–406; national affairs, 70–23; national defense, 72–446, 71–411, 70–435; ocean, 72–457; old age, 72–458, 71–422; Pacific Islands, 72–459; petroleum, 71–431; Philippines, 70–460; population, 70–465; post office, 70–467; poverty, 72–476, 71–438, 70–468; publishing, 71–446; Republican party, 71–453, 70–486; Romania, 70–491; Russia, 72–500; safety, 70–495; science and research, 72–504, 71–464; social security, 70–501; social welfare, 72–508, 71–469, 70–502; space exploration, 70–48, 70–506; sports, 72–53; state government, 72–521, 71–479; stocks and bonds, 72–522; taxation, 72–526, 71–483, 70–518; transportation, 72–535, 70–530; U.S. affairs, 72–23, 71–23; U.S. government, 72–544, 70–537; veterans, 72–547, 70–539; Vietnam, 71–504, 70–543; voting, 71–312; Washington, 72–546; world affairs, 72–18, 71–19; Yugoslavia, 71–515. See also the names of the various Presidents

Price Commission: inflation, 72–88; labor, 72–403; President of the U.S., 72–480

Prices: agriculture, 72–205; automobile, 72–229; consumer affairs, 72–300; economy, 72–324; steel, 72–522

Primaries. See **ELECTIONS**

Prince Edward Island: Canada, 72–264, 71–244, 70–260; census, 72–268

Printing: memorials, 72–429; publishing, 72–487

Prison: civil rights, 72–287; courts and laws, 71–278, 72–108; crime, 72–304; state government, 72–519, 71–477; Washington, D.C., 72–552

Prisoners of war, 71–451

Privacy, 72–288

Proell, Annamarie, 72–506

Promethium, 72–224

Protein: biochemistry, 72–244, 71–226, 70–241; biology, 70–242; food, 72–355

PROTESTANT, 72–483, 71–444, 70–475
church membership, 71–452; Great Britain, 70–361; religion, 72–491, 70–485

Protests: Africa, 70–200; Algeria, 72–210; architecture, 71–199; Argentina, 70–216; Asia, *il.,* 72–222, 70–218; Canada, 70–261; civil rights, 71–261; Congo, 72–290; conservation, 71–273; Czechoslovakia, 70–298; democracy, 70–309; education, *il.,* 72–332, 71–30, 70–326; Ethiopia, 72–343, 70–336; France, 71–334; golf, *il.,* 70–358; Gregory, Dick, 72–464; Houston, 70–372; Indian, American, 72–387, 71–356; Indonesia, 71–357; Ireland, 72–393; Italy, 70–383; Korea, *il.,* 70–388; Lebanon, 72–410; literature, 71–383, 70–403; Malaysia, 70–409; medicine, *il.,* 70–414; music, popular, 70–385; national affairs, 71–25, 70–26; Nepal, 72–450, 70–438; Netherlands, 71–415, 70–438; New York City, 71–416; Okinawa, 71–423; Philippines, 71–432; President of the U.S., 71–441; Puerto Rico, 72–487; radio, 71–449; Russia, 71–462, 70–493; science, 70–496; Senegal, 72–505; Spain, 71–474; sports, 71–53; television, 71–484; Turkey, 71–498, 70–532; Vietnam, 70–543; Washington, D.C., 72–552; Zambia, 72–557. See also **Violence; Terrorism**

Proton, 72–472, 71–434

Proust, Marcel, 72–273

Prouty, Winston L., 72–313

Psychiatry. See **MENTAL HEALTH**

PSYCHOLOGY, 72–484, 71–446, 70–477
child welfare, 72–280; collecting, 71–124; mental health, 72–430; zoology, 72–557, 71–515

PTA. See **PARENTS AND TEACHERS, NATIONAL CONGRESS OF**

Public health: dentistry, 72–317; food, 72–355; health and disease, 72–377, 71–348; mental health, 71–396

Public opinion: advertising, 72–198; Calley, William, Jr., 72–447; Democratic party, 72–316

Public utilities, 72–336

Public welfare. See **SOCIAL WELFARE**

PUBLISHING, 72–485, 71–446, 70–478
advertising, 72–198, 70–198; American Library Association, 72–210; arts, 70–55;

awards and prizes, 72–233, 70–232; Great Britain, 72–373; Russia, 71–461. See also **Book publishing; LITERATURE; Magazines; Newspapers**

PUERTO RICO, 72–487, 71–448, 70–480

PULITZER PRIZES, 72–488, 71–448, 70–481
architecture, 71–200

Puller, Lewis B., 72–313

Pulsar, 72–225, *il.,* 71–313, 70–220

Pyne, Joe, 71–287

Q

Qabus bin Said, 71–425

QADHAAFI, MUAMMAR MUHAMMAD AL-, 71–449; Libya, 72–412, 71–379

Quark, 70–462

Quasi-star (quasar), 70–221

Qatar, 72–462

Quebec: Bourassa, J. Robert, 71–231; building and construction, 71–235; Canada, 72–258, 72–264, 71–238, 71–244, 70–260; census, 72–268

Quinine, 71–298

R

Racing. See **AUTOMOBILE RACING; BOATS AND BOATING; HORSE RACING; SKATING; SKIING; SPORTS; TRACK AND FIELD**

Racism: Africa, 72–200; crime, 72–97; Great Britain, 70–360; labor, 70–390; Malaysia, 70–409; national defense, 72–449; South Africa, 72–509; sports, 71–55, 70–508; United Nations, 72–543, 70–537; YWCA, 72–555. See also **CIVIL RIGHTS; Negro**

Rademacher, Hans, 70–308

Radiation, 71–207

RADIO, 72–489, 71–449, 70–482
advertising, 71–184, 70–198; awards, 72–233, 71–216, 70–232; Great Britain, 72–373, 70–362; regulation, 71–129

Radioactivity, 71–434

Railpax, 71–494

Railroad: Australia, 71–209; banks, 71–220; celebrations, 70–264; Chicago, 70–269; Cleveland, 72–288; China, *il.,* 70–273; Congress, 71–272; disasters, 72–320, 71–297, 70–318; economy, 71–302; labor, 72–404, 71–371; manufacturing, 71–392; President of the U.S., 71–443; railpax, 71–494; regulation, 71–136; safety, 70–495; transportation, 72–536, 71–493, 70–528; travel, 71–497; tunnel, 71–236; Washington, D.C., 71–510; Zambia, 70–551

Rainmaking, 71–510

Raman, Sir Chandrasekhara Venkata, 71–287

Ramani, Radhakrishna, 71–287

Rapacki, Adam, 71–287

Razak, Abdul, 72–422, 71–389

Reading, Lady Stella, 72–313

Reagan, Ronald Wilson, 71–453

Reapportionment, 72–519, 71–523

Recidivism, 72–107

RECORDINGS, 72–490, 71–450, 70–482
awards, 72–233, 71–215; electronics, 72–335, 71–314; motion pictures, 72–438; music, 71–406, 70–431; music, classical, 72–443; popular music, 71–409

RED CROSS, 72–491, 71–451, 70–483
Korea, North, 72–399

Reed, William R. 72–313

Refugees: United Nations, 70–534

Regulatory agencies: aviation, 71–213; consumer affairs, 71–274; *Special Report,* 71–126

Rehabilitation. See **HANDICAPPED**

REHNQUIST, WILLIAM HUBBS, 72–491; courts, 72–302; President of the U.S., 72–481

Reith, Lord John C.W., 72–313

Relativity, 71–474

Relief. See **SOCIAL WELFARE**

RELIGION, 72–491, 71–451, 70–483; Asia, 72–220; civil rights, 70–278; courts and laws, 72–302, 71–277; Eastern Orthodox, 72–323, 71–299, 70–320; education, 71–109; Great Britain, 72–372, 70–361; international education, 71–109; Jews and Judaism, 72–396, 71–364, 70–385; literature, 70–402; music, popular, 72–443; Nixon, Richard M., 70–442; Protestant, 72–483, 71–444, 70–475; Roman Catholic, 72–496, 71–455, 70–489; Salvation Army, 72–503, 71–463, 70–495; theater, 72–530; U.S. constitution, 72–544; world affairs, 70–17; YMCA, 72–555; YWCA, 72–555

Remarque, Erich Maria, 71–287

Rembrandt van Rijn: celebrations, 70–263; painting, 70–447

Representatives, House of. See **CONGRESS**
Reproduction, 70–242
REPUBLICAN PARTY, 72–494, 71–453, 70–486; Agnew, Spiro T., 71–190; Congress, 72–291, 71–267; Democratic party, 72–315; Dole, Robert J., 72–322; elections, 71–310, 70–330; McCloskey, Paul, 72–425; President of the U.S., 72–482, 71–443; state government, 71–476, 70–511
Research. See **INVENTION; SCIENCE AND RESEARCH**
RETAILING, 72–495, 71–454, 70–487
advertising, 72–198; automobile, 72–228; food, 72–355, 70–344; interior design, 72–389; photography, 70–460; recordings, 72–490
Reuther, Walter: deaths, 71–287; labor, 71–370
Revolution: Africa, 72–202; Argentina, 72–215; Asia, 72–222; Bolivia, 72–247; Cameroon, 72–257; Ceylon, 72–276; Chad, 72–276; Ecuador, 72–329; Egypt, 72–333; Ethiopia, 72–343; Kenya, 72–398; Latin America, 72–406; Malagasy Republic, 72–421; Morocco, 72–436; Sudan, 72–523; *Special Report,* 71–105; Uganda, 72–540; Uruguay, 72–546. See also **Civil War; Terrorism; Violence**
Reza Pahlavi, Mohammed, 72–392
Rhizobitoxine, 70–246
Rhode Island: building, 70–250; state government, 72–518; taxation, 72–527
RHODESIA, 72–496, 71–454, 70–487
Africa, 72–202; civil rights, 70–279; Great Britain, 72–372; United Nations, 72–543, 70–537
Rice: agriculture, 72–206, 71–194, 70–206; Asia, 70–219; Indonesia, 70–376; *Special Report,* 72–60; Vietnam, 71–506
RICHARDSON, ELLIOT LEE, 71–455; President of the U.S., 71–443
Rickets, 71–198
Rifle shooting, 72–517, 71–475, 70–510
Rindt, Jochen, 71–287
Rio Grande, 71–397
Rio Muñi. See **EQUATORIAL GUINEA**
Rippon, Geoffrey, 72–370
Ritter, Thelma, 70–308
Rivers. See **Waterways**
Rivers, L. Mendel, 71–267
Rizzo, Frank L.: elections, 72–334; Philadelphia, 72–469
RNA: biochemistry, 71–226; biology, 71–228, 70–243
Roads and highways: bridge and tunnel, 70–250; Dallas, 70–300; Latin America, 72–409; New Orleans, 70–439; safety, 72–501, 71–462; transportation, 72–537; 71–495, 70–529; tunnel, 70–251
Robarts, John P., 71–243
Robbins, Jerome, 72–307
Robertson, A. Willis, 72–313
Robertson, Oscar, 72–241
Robertson, Walter S., Sr., 71–287
Robichaud, Louis J., 71–243
Robinson, Brooks, *il.,* 71–221
Rochester (N.Y.), 70–216
Rockefeller, Nelson Aldrich: Argentina, 70–216; Democratic party, 71–289; Latin America, 70–394; painting, 70–449; Republican party, 71–453, 70–486
Rockets, 72–512. See also **Guided Missile; SPACE EXPLORATION**
Rodale, J. I., 72–313
Rodeo, 72–517, 71–476
ROGERS, WILLIAM PIERCE, 70–488
Africa, 71–186; Greece, 72–374; Middle East, 72–432, 71–399
Rojankovsky, Feodor, 72–313
Rolfe, Robert A., 70–308
Roller skating, 72–517, 71–476, 70–511
Rolls-Royce: automobile, *il.,* 72–229; Great Britain, 72–372
ROMAN CATHOLIC CHURCH, 72–496, 71–455, 70–489
church membership, 71–452; education, 72–331, 72–43; Great Britain, 72–372, 70–361; Hungary, 70–373; Italy, 72–394, 71–363; Jews, 72–396, 70–386; Netherlands, 72–450, 71–415; Paraguay, 72–461, 71–424; Poland, 72–474; religion, 72–493, 71–451, 70–483; Spain, 72–514
ROMANIA, 72–498, 71–457, 70–491; Hungary, 72–383; President of the U.S., *il.,* 70–475; Russia, 72–499
Romanoff, Dmitri Michael, 72–313
Romantic Movement, 72–47
ROMNEY, GEORGE WILCKEN, 70–491; city, *il.,* 71–258; housing, 70–372
Roosa, Stuart A.: astronauts, 72–223; space exploration, 72–510

Roosevelt, Franklin D.: memorials, 71–395; Washington, D.C., 71–510
Rosewall, Ken, 72–528, 71–487
Rossiter, Clinton L., 71–287
Rotary International, 72–506, 71–466, 70–499
Rothko, Mark, 71–287
Rous, F. Peyton, 71–287
Rowing, 72–517, 71–475, 70–510
Ruanda-Urundi. See **Burundi; Rwanda**
Rubber: labor, 71–371; manufacturing, 72–425, 70–411
Rubella, 72–377, 70–99
Rubeola, 72–377
Ruckelshaus, William D., 71–319
Rugs and carpets, 72–389
Rumor, Mariano, 71–363, 70–383
Rumsfeld, Donald, 72–480, 71–438, 70–468
Running: track and field, 72–533, 71–491, 70–525
Russell, Bertrand A. W., 71–284
Russell, Louis B., *il.,* 71–429
Russell, Richard B., 72–314
RUSSIA, 72–498, 71–458, 70–492
Africa, 72–202, 70–202; agriculture, 72–206; armed forces, 71–201, 70–217; Asia, 72–223, 70–218; astronauts, 72–224; aviation, 72–232, 70–230, *il.,* 70–228; Bulgaria, 72–254, 71–236, 70–252; Canada, 72–261; China, 72–281, 71–256, 70–274; civil rights, 72–288; communications, 70–281; Communism, 70–282; Czechoslovakia, 72–305, 71–280, 70–298; dams, 72–253; dancing, 72–308; Eastern Orthodox Churches, 71–299; energy, 72–336, *il.,* 71–315; espionage, 72–342, 71–321; Europe, 72–347, 71–324, 70–339; fairs, 72–349; Finland, 72–352, 70–344; fishing, 72–353; France, 71–335; Germany, 72–367, 71–340, 70–356; Hungary, 72–383; India, 72–386; Israel, 72–394; Jews, 72–396, 71–365; Laos, 71–373; Middle East, 71–398, 70–419; Mongolia, 70–424; Nobel prizes, 71–420; Roman Catholic, 71–456; Romania, 72–498, 71–457, 70–491; skiing, 71–467; space exploration, 72–510, 71–471, 70–504; United Arab Republic, 71–499; United Nations, 72–541, 70–534; Vietnam, 72–549, 70–544; world affairs, 72–18, 71–17, 70–18; Yugoslavia, 72–557, 70–551
Russian Orthodox Church, 72–323, 70–320
Ryan, William M., 72–314
Ryder, David, 70–455
Ryerson, Edward L., 72–314
Ryun, Jim, 72–534, 70–525

S

Sachs, Nelly, 71–287
SADAT, ANWAR, 71–462; Egypt, 72–333; Middle East, 72–432; United Arab Republic, 71–499
SAFETY, 72–501, 71–462, 70–495
automobile, 72–228, 71–212, 70–225; aviation, 72–231; building, 72–252; drugs, 70–318; electronics, 71–313; energy, 71–317; games, models, and toys, 70–353; gardening, 72–363; mining, 72–435, 71–407, 70–423; old age, 70–446; space exploration, 71–471; state government, 72–521; toys, 72–363. See also **DISASTERS**
Sagendorph, Robb, 71–287
Sahara, 71–338
Sailing, 72–246, 71–229, 70–244
Saint: Eastern Orthodox Churches, 71–299; Roman Catholic, 71–455
Saint Kitts-Nevis, 70–211
ST. LOUIS, 72–502, 71–463, 70–495
architecture, 72–214
Salazar, António de Oliveira, 71–287, 70–466
SALT: armed forces, 72–216; Europe, 72–346; Russia, 72–500, 71–460; world affairs, 72–19, 71–18
SALVATION ARMY, 72–503, 71–463, 70–495
Samuelson, Paul A., 71–420
San Diego: celebrations, 70–264; Republican party, 72–495; zoo, 70–121
SAN FRANCISCO, 72–503, 71–464, 70–496; elections, 72–334; music, 72–442, 71–408, 70–429; transit, 70–530
Sandburg, Carl: memorials, 70–415
Saragat, Giuseppe, 72–394
Sarnoff, David, 72–314
Saskatchewan: Canada, 72–264, 71–245, 70–261; census, 72–269; mining, 71–401
Satellite, artificial. See **SPACE EXPLORATION**
Sato, Eisaku: Japan, 72–395, 71–363, 70–384; Pacific islands, 72–459
Saturday Evening Post, 70–479
Saturn (planet), 71–207

Saud ibn Abdul Aziz: deaths, 70–308; Saudi Arabia, 70–496
SAUDI ARABIA, 72–504, 71–464, 70–496
Savings and loan associations, 71–220, 70–234
Savio, Mario, 71–428
Sawant, Vasudeva, 70–455
Sawchuck, Terry, 71–287
Scandinavia. See **DENMARK; FINLAND; NORWAY; SWEDEN**
Schacht, Hjalmar H.G., 71–288
Schalk, Ray (Cracker), 71–288
Schenk, Ard, 72–384
Schizophrenia: mental health, 72–430; psychology, 72–484
Schmitt, Harrison H., 72–223
Schnakenberg, Henry 71–288
School. See **EDUCATION**
School-lunch program, 72–295
Schopf, Johann David, 72–365
Schulz, Charles M., 70–147
Schweickart, Russell L., 70–504
SCIENCE AND RESEARCH, 72–504, 71–464, 70–496
agriculture, 71–193; astronauts, 72–223; awards, 72–234, 71–217; *Focus,* 72–35, 71–34; gardening, 72–363; literature, 72–415; literature for children, 72–418, 71–385; museums, 72–439; national defense, 72–446; ocean, 72–457; space exploration, 72–510, 71–473; weather, 72–553. See also the various sciences
Scopes, John T., 71–288
Scotland, 71–248
Scott, David R.: astronauts, 72–223; space exploration, 72–510, 70–504
SCOTT, GEORGE C., 72–505
SCOTT, HUGH D., JR., 70–497; Republican party, 72–494, *il.,* 70–486
Scott, Sir Walter, 72–273
Scranton, William W.: civil rights, 71–261; education, 71–307; President of the U.S., 71–442
SCULPTURE, 70–497. See also **PAINTING AND SCULPTURE**
awards, 72–233; memorials, 72–429, 71–394; visual arts, 72–550, 71–508; Ziolkowski, Korczak, 71–429
Sealab, 70–444
Seattle, 71–221
Seaver, Tom, *il.,* 70–236
Securities and Exchange Commission: Casey, William, 72–522; regulatory agencies, 71–136; stocks and bonds, 72–522, 70–515
Seferis, George, 72–314
Seldes, Gilbert, 71–47
Selective Service: birth dates for, 71–413; Congress, 72–297; courts and laws, 71–276; national defense, 72–449, *il.,* 70–436; Tarr, Curtis W., 71–483
Seminole Indians, 71–357
Senanayake, Dudley, 70–265
Senate, U.S., *Special Report,* 72–137. See also **CONGRESS**
SENEGAL, 72–505; Africa, 70–202; Gambia, 72–362, 71–336, 70–202
Senties, Octavio, *il.,* 72–431
Servan-Schreiber, Jean-Jacques, 71–334
SERVICE CLUBS, 72–506, 71–465, 70–499
"Sesame Street," 71–485
Sevastianov, Vitaly I., 71–473
Shahn, Ben, 70–308
Sharp, Mitchell, 70–257
Shaughnessy, Clark D., 71–288
Sheep, 71–209
Sheil, Bernard James, 70–308
Shepard, Alan B., Jr.: astronauts, 72–223, 71–206, 70–219; space exploration, 72–510
Sheridan, Clare C., 71–288
Ship: Canada, *il.,* 72–264, 70–258; disasters, 72–320, 71–296, 70–318; ocean, 70–444; petroleum, 70–458; pollution, 70–464; Somalia, 71–469; Suez Canal, 70–421; transportation, 72–537, 71–495; travel, 71–497. See also **Waterways**
Shipbuilding: Great Britain, 72–372; national defense, 71–414; transportation, 72–537
Shivkov, Todor, 72–254
Shooting, 71–475, 70–510
Short story, 71–380
Shot put, 72–534
SHULTZ, GEORGE PRATT, 70–499; Cabinet, 71–237; economy, *il.,* 72–328; labor, *il.,* 71–372, 70–390; President of the U.S., 71–443
Sicily, *il.,* 72–364
Sickle cell anemia, 72–426
SIERRA LEONE, 70–500; Africa, 72–204
Siffert, Jo, 72–314
Sihanouk, Norodom: Asia, 71–204; Cambodia, 71–237, 70–253; China, 71–255

Silberman, Charles E., 71–45
Silver, 72–435, 70–424
Simpson, O. J., il., 70–346
Sinatra, Frank, il., 72–465
Sinclair, Archibald H. M., 71–288
Singapore, 72–218, 70–264
Sirik Matak, 72–256
Sitwell, Sir Osbert, 70–308
Skating. See HOCKEY; ICE SKATING
Skeet shooting, 70–510
SKIING, 72–506, 71–466, 70–500
Skink, 72–558
Skouras, Spyros P., 72–314
Skulnik, Menasha, 71–288
Skyworks, 71–509
Slavinsky, Michel, il., 71–460
Sleep, 70–551
Slim, Mongi, 70–308
Smallwood, Joseph R., 72–263, 71–243, 70–259
Smith, Helen Sobel, 70–308
Smith, Ian, 72–496, 71–454, 70–487
SMITH, JOSEPH FIELDING, 71–467
Smith, Len, 71–428
Smith, Stan, 72–528
Smoking: advertising, 72–199, 71–185, 70–198; dentistry, 70–312; health, il., 70–366
Smuggling, 71–405
Snake River, 72–254
Snowmobiling: games, 72–363; sports, 72–517, 71–476
Sobolev, Leonid S., 72–314
Socarras Ramírez, Armando, 70–455
SOCCER, 72–507, 71–467, 70–500
Social Credit Party, 72–263
Social sciences. See ANTHROPOLOGY; ARCHAEOLOGY
SOCIAL SECURITY, 72–507, 71–468, 70–501
child welfare, 70–269; Congress, 72–297, 71–272; economy, 71–33; Medicare, 72–426, 71–393
SOCIAL WELFARE, 72–508, 71–469, 70–502
agriculture, 71–193; Boston, 72–248; Canada, 70–256; Chicago, 72–279; child welfare, 72–279, 71–253; Congress, 72–297, 71–267, 70–291; courts and laws, 71–276, 70–295; dentistry, 70–312; food, 72–355, 71–329; Great Britain, 71–345; handicapped, 70–364; health, 70–365; hospital, 70–371; Medicare, 71–393, 70–412; New York City, 72–451; old age, 71–422, 70–445; poverty, 72–476, 71–438, 70–468; Red Cross, 71–451; St. Louis, 72–503; social security, 71–468; state government, 72–521, 71–479, 70–511; veterans, 71–505. See also CHILD WELFARE
Socialism: Austria, 72–227, 71–210; Burma, 70–252; Ceylon, 72–255, 71–248; Chile, 72–280; Peru, 70–456
Softball, 72–517, 71–476
Soika, Giordani, 71–145
Soil conservation, 71–193, 70–294
Solti, Georg, 72–440
Solzhenitsyn, Alexander I.: Nobel prizes, 71–420; Russia, 71–462
SOMALIA, 71–469, 70–503; Africa, 71–187, 70–202; Kenya, 70–387
Song My, 70–543
Sonic boom, 70–132
Sorghum, 72–206
South, The, 71–289
SOUTH AFRICA, REPUBLIC OF, 72–509, 71–470, 70–503
Africa, 72–200, 71–186, 70–200; anthropology, 72–212; Great Britain, 71–344; Kenya, 72–398; Malagasy Republic, 72–421; Malawi, 72–421, 71–389; Nigeria, 72–452; Protestant, 72–484; Rhodesia, 71–454; United Nations, 72–543, 71–501, 70–537; Zambia, 72–557
South America. See LATIN AMERICA
South Carolina: celebrations, 71–248; library, 71–378
SOUTHERN YEMEN, PEOPLE'S REPUBLIC OF, 72–509, 71–470, 70–503
Souvanna Phouma, 72–405, 71–373, 70–394
Souza, Paul Emile de, 71–280
Soviet Union. See RUSSIA
Soybeans, 72–206, 71–191, 70–206
SPACE EXPLORATION, 72–510, 71–471, 70–504
astronauts, 72–223, 71–206, 70–219; astronomy, 72–224, 70–220; awards, 71–217; botany, 70–246; communications, 71–264, 70–280; electronics, 72–335; Europe, 71–325, 70–340; fairs, 70–349; Focus, 70–47; games, 72–363; photography, 70–460; science, 70–35, 70–496; Special Report, 70–64; stamp collecting, 70–367; television, 70–519; United Nations, 72–542, 70–551; weather, 70–552, 71–510, 70–547

SPAIN, 72–514, 71–474, 70–508
Africa, 70–202; Equatorial Guinea, 70–335; Great Britain, 70–362; health, 72–377; Jews, 71–365; Morocco, 70–425; President of the U.S., il., 71–440; Protestant, 71–446; St. Louis, 71–463
Spanish-Americans: census, 72–274; Houston, 72–382; poverty, 72–476
Special Drawing Rights: banks, 71–221, 70–235; economy, 70–31, 70–324; international trade, 71–360, 70–379
Spectroscopy, 70–268
Speech, 71–446
Spitz, Mark, 72–524
Spock, Dr. Benjamin, 70–279
SPORTS, 72–515, 71–474, 70–508; celebrations, 70–262; Focus, 72–53, 71–53, 70–59; Pan American Games, 72–460; South Africa, 71–470; Special Report, 72–118. See entries under the different sports; OLYMPIC GAMES
Squash racquets, 72–517, 71–476, 70–511
Squash tennis, 72–517
Stafford, Jean, 71–449
Stafford, Thomas P.: astronauts, 72–224; space exploration, 70–504
STAMP COLLECTING, 72–517; celebrations, 72–272; gardening, 70–354; hobbies, 71–348, 70–367; poetry, 71–436
Stanley, Henry, 72–273
Stanley, Wendell M., 72–314
STANS, MAURICE HUBERT, 70–511; safety, il., 72–502
Starkie, Enid M., 71–288
Starr, Ringo, 71–429
Starr, Steve, 71–448
State Department, U.S.: diplomat, 72–545, 71–292, 70–313; Rogers, William P., 70–488; U.S. government, 70–538
STATE GOVERNMENT, 72–518, 71–476, 70–511
census, U.S., 71–522; Chicago, 72–279; consumer affairs, 72–301, 71–275; courts and laws, 71–276; Democratic party, 72–315, 71–289, 70–311; economy, 70–323; education, 72–41; elections, 71–310; Medicare, 72–426, 70–412; poverty, 70–468; social welfare, 72–508, 70–502; taxation, 72–526, 71–483, 70–519; U.S. constitution, 72–543; voting, 71–312
STEEL INDUSTRY, 72–522, 71–479, 70–514
Brazil, 72–251; China, 72–282; interior design, 71–358; Japan, il., 71–58; Mexico, 72–431; President of the U.S., 72–478
Steele, Wilbur Daniel, 71–288
Steiner, Max R., 72–314
Stereophonic sound: electronics, 72–335; recordings, 72–490
Stern, Otto, 70–308
Stevens, Siaka P., 72–204
Stevenson, Adlai E., III, 72–137, 71–310
Stewart, J. George, 71–288
Stewart, Jackie, 72–230
STOCKS AND BONDS, 72–522, 71–480, 70–515
banks, 72–238, 71–220; Bologna, Pat, 72–463; city, 70–276; Detroit, 71–291; economy, 72–326, 71–29, 71–302, 70–29, 70–321; insurance, 70–377; Japan, il., 71–62; regulation, 71–136
Stokes, Carl B.: city, 71–258; Cleveland, 72–288, 71–264
Stokowski, Leopold, 72–440
Storms, 72–320
Stravinsky, Igor, 72–310, 72–314
Strikes: city, il., 72–285; communications, 72–290; France, 72–361; Italy, 72–394; labor, 72–404; New York City, 72–451; Sweden, 72–524
Stroessner, Alfredo, 72–461, 71–424
Students for a Democratic Society, 70–327
Submarine: armed forces, 72–216, 70–217; national defense, 72–448; ocean, 70–444
Suburbs: census, 72–274; city, 72–284, 71–259; Detroit, 72–317
Subway: Mexico, il., 70–417; New York City, 71–416; transit, 71–481; tunnel, 71–236
SUDAN, 72–523, 70–516
Africa, 72–204, 71–188; Libya, 72–412; Middle East, 72–433, 71–400; Nimeri, Jafir Muhammad, 72–452; Russia, 72–500
Suez Canal, 71–401, 70–421
Sugar, 71–279
Suharto, 72–387, 71–357, 70–376
Suicide, 70–416
Sukarno, 71–288
Sullivan, Brian, 70–308
Sullivan, Pat, 72–359
Sullivan Trophy, 72–399
Sultanoff, Morton, 71–288
Sun, 71–207
Sunay, Cevdet, 72–342

Supersonic aircraft: aviation, 72–232, 71–215; Congress, 72–297; Stevenson, Adlai E., III, 72–153
Supreme Court of the United States: arts, 70–56; baseball, 72–240; Blackmun, Harry Andrew, 71–229; Burger, Warren E., 70–252; civil rights, 72–286, 70–277; Congress, 72–297, 71–267, 70–286; courts and laws, 72–301, 71–276, 70–294; education, 72–331, 72–44, 70–329; elections, 71–312; Haynsworth, Clement F., Jr., 70–365; Pentagon Papers, 72–486; Powell, Lewis F., 72–477; President of the U.S. 72–481; Rehnquist, William H., 72–491; religion, 70–485; social welfare, 72–509; sports, 72–54; state government, 70–511; taxation, 71–483; U.S. government, 72–544, 71–504, 70–538
Surfing, 72–517, 71–476, 70–511
Surinam, 72–375, 71–346, 70–363
Sutherland, Earl W., Jr., 72–456
Sutton, Willie, 72–466
Suzuki, Mosaburo, 71–288
Svedberg, Theodore, 72–314
Svedberg, Theodore, 72–314
Swann Islets, 72–410
Swanson, Gloria, il., 72–466
Swarthout, Gladys, 70–308
Swaziland, 70–203
SWEDEN, 72–524, 71–481, 70–516
celebrations, 72–272; labor, 71–373
Swigert, John L.: astronauts, 71–206; space exploration, 71–471
SWIMMING, 72–524, 71–481, 70–516
Kinsella, John, 72–399; personalities, il., 70–452
SWITZERLAND, 72–525, 71–482, 70–517
banks and banking, 71–220; civil rights, 72–288; espionage, 72–342; tunnels, 72–254
Sydney, 70–162
Symphony orchestra: Kubelik, Rafael, 72–400; music, classical, 72–440, 71–406
Synthetics, 70–345
SYRIA, 72–525, 71–483, 70–517
Egypt, 72–333; Middle East, 72–432
Syvertsen, George, 71–288
Szell, George: deaths, 71–288; music, 71–406

T

Table tennis: China, 72–280; President of the U.S., 72–480; sports, 72–517, 72–53, 71–476, 70–511
Taft, Robert A.: elections, 71–310; Republican party, 71–453
Taft, William Howard, 71–395
Tahiti, 71–423
Taiwan. See FORMOSA
Tal, Wasfi al-, 72–397
Tamm, Igor Y., 72–314
Tansie, Russell H., 70–455
Tantalum, 72–227
TANZANIA, 72–526, 71–483, 70–517; Africa, 72–202, 70–202; anthropology, 70–211; Nigeria, 72–452; Uganda, 72–540
Tape recordings: electronics, 72–314; music, 71–408; recordings, 72–490, 71–450
Tariffs. See INTERNATIONAL TRADE
TARR, CURTIS W., 71–483
Tate, James H. J., 71–288
TAXATION, 72–526, 71–483, 70–518
agriculture, 70–208; automobile, 72–229; banks, 70–235; Canada, 72–262, 71–240; city, 70–274; Cleveland, 72–288; congress, 72–297, 70–291; courts and laws, 72–303, 71–277; economy, 70–325; education, 72–41, 72–330; Finland, 72–353; foundations, 70–349; Great Britain, 72–371; Norway, 71–421; Ontario, 70–259; petroleum, 71–431, 70–459; President of the United States, 70–474; social security, 72–507; sports, 72–131; state government, 72–518, 71–477, 70–512; Sweden, 71–481
Taylor, Richard D., 71–288
Taylor, Robert, 70–308
Teacher: education, 72–330, 71–308, 70–329; labor, 71–372; Los Angeles, 71–388; Philadelphia, 71–432
Team handball, 72–517
Technology: automobile, 72–228; awards, 72–234, 71–217; building and construction, 72–252, 71–234; chemistry, 72–278; electronics, 72–335; handicapped, 72–377; international education, 71–98; mining, 72–431; motion pictures, 71–405; ocean, 71–441; photography, 70–470, 71–432; recordings, 71–450; space exploration, 72–514; visual arts, 71–509; waste disposal, 71–84. See also ENGINEERING; INVENTION; MANUFACTURING; SCIENCE AND RESEARCH

Teen-agers: elections, 71–312; state government, 71–479. See also **Youth; YOUTH ORGANIZATIONS**

Telephone and telegraph: Australia, 71–209; communications, 72–290, 71–265, 70–281; labor, 72–404; manufacturing, 71–391

Telescope: astronomy, 72–224, 71–208, 70–222; electronics, 72–335

TELEVISION, 72–527, 71–484, 70–519
advertising, 71–184, 70–198; Agnew, Spiro T., 71–205; arts, 72–47; Australia, 71–209; awards, 72–233, 71–215, 70–232; Cabinet, 70–253; communications, 70–281; education, 72–332, 71–309; electronics, 70–331; manufacturing, 70–412; mental health, 71–396; regulation, 71–129; soccer, 71–467; sports, 72–515, 71–474; visual arts, 71–509; Wilson, Flip, 72–554

Tennessee, 72–519, 70–263

TENNIS, 72–528, 71–486, 70–520; Goolagong, Evonne, 72–369; sports, 72–56, 70–508

Territo, Carmelo Lo Guasto, 70–456

Terrorism: Argentina, 71–200; aviation, 71–213; Brazil, 71–233; Canada, 71–238; civil rights, 71–263; Latin America, 71–374; Uruguay, 71–505. See also **Protests**

Texarkana, 71–41

Texas: agriculture, 72–209; Bush, George H.W., 72–255; Dallas, 72–306, 71–280, 70–300; dams, 70–251; Houston, 72–382, 71–353; 70–372; hunting and fishing, 72–384; Johnson, Lyndon B., 72–397, 71–365; library, 72–411; memorials, 72–429, 71–394; state government, 72–519

Textile: fashion, 71–327, 70–342; interior design, 70–378; manufacturing, 71–391, 70–411

THAILAND, 72–529, 71–487, 70–521; Asia, 72–218; food, 72–68; national defense, 71–412

THANG, TON DUC, 70–521

Thant, U: *Apollo 11, il.,* 70–80; United Nations, 72–541, 71–500, 70–534

Thatcher, W. Ross: deaths, 72–314; Saskatchewan, 72–264

THEATER, 72–530, 71–488, 70–522
arts, 72–48, 71–48; Australia, 71–210; awards and prizes, 72–235, 71–215, 71–218, 70–231; Bacall, Lauren, 71–218; China, 72–283; civil rights, 70–278; dancing, 72–306, 71–281, 70–300; motion pictures, 72–437; Pulitzer prizes, 72–488, 71–449, 70–481; recordings, *il.,* 72–490; *WBE,* 70–578. See also **MOTION PICTURES**

Theology: Niebuhr, Reinhold, 72–492; Protestant, 71–445

Thermoluminescent dating, 72–213

Thieu, Nguyen Van, 72–548, 71–506, 70–545

Thoeni, Gustavo, 72–506

Thomas, Michael Tilson, 71–406

Thompson, William, 72–314

Threlfall, David, 70–455

Tibet, 70–484

Tiger, Dick, 72–314

Timber. See **FORESTRY AND FOREST PRODUCTS**

Tims, John Francis, 70–309

Tinbergen, Jan, 70–443

Tiny Tim, 70–454

Tiselius, Arne, 72–314

Titian, 72–551

Tito: Canada, 72–262; Yugoslavia, 72–557, 71–515

Tobacco: agriculture, 71–191, 70–206; Australia, 70–223; radio, 70–482; television, 70–519

Tobago. See **Trinidad-Tobago**

Todorov, Stanko, 72–254

TOGO, 70–525; service clubs, 70–499

Tokyo, 71–320

Tolbutamide, 71–393

Tolvish, Steve, 72–466

Tombalbaye, François, 72–276

Tonga, 72–459, 71–423, 70–446

Tornadoes: disasters, 72–320, 71–297, 70–318; Pakistan, 71–423

Toronto: building and construction, 72–252, 70–250; Davis, William G., 72–308; Ontario, 72–264

Torres, Juan Jose, 72–247

Torrijos, Omar, 72–460, 70–450

Tourism. See **FAIRS AND EXPOSITIONS; TRAVEL**

Toys. See **GAMES, MODELS, AND TOYS**

TRACK AND FIELD, 72–533, 71–491, 70–525
Chi Cheng, 71–252; Pan American Games, 72–460; sports, 71–54

Trade. See **ECONOMY, THE; INTERNATIONAL TRADE**

Trade fairs. See **FAIRS AND EXPOSITIONS**

TRAIN, RUSSELL ERROL, 71–492; conservation, 70–292

Trampoline, 71–476

Trans-Vision®, 72–161, 71–161, 70–177

Transit: city, 71–259; Congress, 71–272; Mexico, *il.,* 70–417; New York City, 71–416; old age, 71–422; steel industry, 71–480; transportation, 72–538, 71–495, 70–530; Washington, D.C., 70–546

TRANSPORTATION, 72–535, 71–493, 70–527
city, 72–195; Congress, 71–272; Philadelphia, 72–469; regulation, 71–133; state government, 72–521. See also **AUTOMOBILE; AVIATION; DISASTERS; Railroad; Ship; TRAVEL; Trucking; Waterways**

Transportation, U.S. Department of: aviation, 72–231; insurance, 72–388; transportation, 72–535, 71–493, 70–528; U.S. government, 71–504; Volpe, John A., 70–546

TRAVEL, 72–538, 71–496, 70–530
aviation, 72–231; Europe, 70–340; fairs, 72–348; Pacific islands, 72–459; transportation, 72–535

Treasury Department, 71–272, 70–387

Treaties, 71–424

Trees, 72–248

TREVINO, LEE, 72–539
golf, 72–367

Trinidad-Tobago, 72–554, 71–512, 70–548

Triolet, Elsa, 71–288

Trucking: Chicago, 71–252; disasters, 72–318, 71–295; labor, 71–371; regulation, 71–135; transportation, 72–536, 71–495

TRUDEAU, PIERRE ELLIOTT, 72–539, 71–497, 70–531; Canada, 72–258, 71–238, 70–254; Russia, 72–500

TRUMAN, HARRY S., 72–540, 71–498, 70–532

Tshombe, Moise, 70–309

Tsiranana, Philibert, 72–421

Tubman, William V.S., 72–314

Tufts, Sonny, 71–288

TUNISIA, 72–540, 71–498, 70–532
Africa, 71–188; Algeria, 71–194; Middle East, 72–433

Tunnel: building and construction, 72–254, 71–236, 70–251; France, 71–335

Tunney, John V., 71–310

TURKEY, 72–540, 71–498, 70–532
bridge, 71–235; disasters, *il.,* 71–296; Eastern Orthodox, 72–323; Erim, Nihat, 72–342; Middle East, 72–433

Turnbull, Andrew W., 71–288

Turner, Roscoe, 71–288

Tussaud, Madame, 71–248

Typhoon, 72–320, 71–294, 70–317

Tyrol, 72–227

U

UGANDA, 72–540, 71–499, 70–532
Africa, 72–202; Amin, Idi, 72–211; Kenya, 72–398; Nigeria, 72–452; South Africa, 72–509; Tanzania, 72–526; Zambia, 72–557

Ukraine, 72–497

Ulbricht, Walter: Germany, 72–365, 71–338; Russia, 72–498

Ullman, James Ramsey, 72–314

Ulster. See **Northern Ireland**

Unemployment: Africa, 72–204; Canada, 72–262; economy, 72–325, 71–300; engineering, 72–339; labor, 72–401, 71–368; manufacturing, 71–390; Peru, 72–467; science, 72–504; veterans, 72–547

UNESCO: awards, 72–234, 71–217; United Nations, 70–536; Venice, 71–154

Ungaretti, Giuseppe, 71–288

Union of Soviet Socialist Republics. See **RUSSIA**

Unitarian Universalist, 71–445

UNITED ARAB REPUBLIC, 71–499, 70–533. See also **EGYPT**

United Church of Christ, 70–476

UNITED NATIONS, 72–541, 71–500, 70–534, 69–515
Africa, 72–200, 71–188; Asia, 72–221; Brooks, Angie, 70–249; Bush, George H.W., 72–255; China, 72–280; conservation, 72–299; food, 72–354; 71–329, 70–344; Formosa, 72–360; Germany, East, 71–338; Hambro, Edvard, 71–347; Israel, 72–393; library, 72–411; Malik, Adam, 72–422; Middle East, 72–432, 71–399, 70–419; ocean, 72–457; Persian Gulf Emirates, 72–462; population, 71–436, 70–466; Portugal, 71–437; poverty, 72–477; Rhodesia, 70–488; world affairs, 72–18, 70–18; Yost, Charles W., 70–549

U.S. CONSTITUTION, 72–543

UNITED STATES GOVERNMENT, 72–544, 71–504, 70–537
agriculture, 70–208; aviation, 71–213; banks, 72–236, 70–235; Cabinet, 72–255, 71–237, 70–253; census, 71–518, 70–264; chemical industry, 72–277, 70–266; civil rights, 72–288; communications, 70–280; Congress, 72–291, 71–267, 70–286; conservation, 72–298, 71–273; consumer affairs, 72–300, 71–274; constitution, 72–543; courts and laws, 71–276, 70–294; democracy, 70–309; diplomat, 71–292, 70–313; drugs, 72–322; economy, 72–324, 71–300; education, 72–331, 71–307; elections, 71–310; environment, 72–339, 71–319; *Focus,* 71–23; housing, 71–352; immigration, 72–385, 71–354; Indian, American, 72–387, 71–356; inflation, 72–77; labor, 72–402, 70–423; national defense, 72–446, 71–411, 70–435; ocean, 71–421; old age, 72–458; Peace Corps, 71–425, 70–451; Pentagon Papers, 72–486; postal service, 72–475, 71–437, 70–467; poverty, 72–476, 71–438, 70–468; President of the United States, 72–478, 71–440, 70–471; publishing, 71–447; Puerto Rico, 71–448; regulatory agencies, 71–126; safety, 71–463; science, 72–504, 71–464, 70–496; Social Security, 71–468, 70–501; space exploration, 70–48, 70–506; *Special Report,* 70–82; state government, 72–521, 71–479, 70–511; taxation, 71–483, 70–518; television, 72–527; transportation, 71–493, 70–528; veterans, 71–505, 70–539; weather, 71–510. See also biographies of individual government officials and entries on various government agencies

UNITED STATES OF AMERICA. See various states and cities and various specific subjects

Universities and colleges: celebrations, 70–262; civil rights, 71–261; dancing, 71–282; democracy, 70–309; education, 72–41, 72–330; 71–307, 70–326; engineering, 72–339, 71–317, 70–335; France, 71–334; insurance, 71–357; Japan, 70–385; library, 70–399; mental health, 72–430; national affairs, 71–25; ocean, 72–458; President of the U.S., 71–441; sports, 71–53, 71–474; state government, 71–477, 70–512; theater, amateur, 70–524. See also **SPORTS**

Unser, Al, 72–230, 71–212

Uranium, 71–210

Urban renewal. See **CITY; City Planning**

Urban transportation. See **Roads and Highways; Transit**

Uris, Norman B., 71–429

URUGUAY, 72–546, 71–505, 70–538
Bordaberry, Juan Maria, 72–247; Latin America, 71–374

Utah, 70–264

Ute Indians, 72–212

V

Vaccine: medicine, 70–414; rubella, 70–99

Van-Hay, Geoffrey, 71–429

Vancouver, 72–265

Vanderbilt, Harold S., 71–288

Vanderschuit, John, 71–429

Vatican Council II, 71–455

Veeck, Bill, 72–130

Velasco Alvarado, Juan: Latin America, 72–408; Peru, 72–467

Velasco Ibarra, José María, 72–329, 71–305

Velázquez, Diego, 71–508

Venereal disease, 72–377, 71–347

VENEZUELA, 72–547, 71–505, 70–539
Caldera, Rafael, 70–253; Guyana, 71–346; Latin America, 72–409

Venice: *Special Report,* 71–143

Venus: astronomy, 72–225; space exploration, 72–514

Vermont: chemical industry, 72–277; state government, 72–521, 70–512

VETERANS, 72–547, 71–505, 70–539

Veterans of Foreign Wars, 72–548, 71–505, 70–539

Vice-President of the United States: Afghanistan, 71–185; Agnew, Spiro T., 72–204, 71–190; education, 71–307; elections, 71–310; radio, 71–449; space explorations, 70–48; television, 71–486. See also names of vice-presidents

Vienna: celebrations, 70–264; music, 70–429

VIETNAM, 72–548, 71–506, 70–541; armed forces, 72–217; arts, 72–48; Asia, 72–218, 71–202, 70–218; Australia, 72–226; Cambodia, 72–256; China, 72–281; civil rights, 71–261; Congress, 71–267; democracy, 70–309; espionage, 70–336; inflation, 72–83; Laos, 72–405, 71–373, 70–394; literature,

72–414, 71–383; Lodge, Henry Cabot, Jr., 70–408; national affairs, 71–24; national defense, 72–446, 71–411; Pentagon Papers, 72–486; Philippines, 70–435; President of the U.S., 72–480, 71–440, 70–471; Red Cross, 71–451; Roman Catholic, 71–456; Sweden, 70–516; Thailand, 72–529; Thanq, Ton Duc, 70–521; United Nations, 71–503, 70–534; U.S. affairs, 72–24; world affairs, 70–17.

Violence: astronomy, 71–208; Canada, 72–258; city, 72–284, 71–257, 70–275; civil rights, 71–261, 70–287; Colombia, 72–289; Congress, il., 72–291; courts, 70–296; crime, 72–97, 72–304, 71–278; education, 71–307; elections, 71–310; France, 71–334; Great Britain, 71–372; India, 71–355; insurance, 71–357; Latin America, 71–374; Los Angeles, 71–388; Malaysia, 71–389; Mexico, 72–430; Middle East, 71–400; motion pictures, 72–438; national affairs, 70–23; New Orleans, 72–450, 71–415; New York City, 71–416; New Zealand, 71–416; Northern Ireland, 71–345; Philippines, 72–470; popular music, 71–409; prisons, 72–287; South Africa, 72–509; Spain, 72–514; state government, 72–519, 70–512; television, 71–477; Turkey, 72–433, 72–540; U.S. affairs, 72–25; Uruguay, 72–546; Washington, D.C., 72–552; West Indies, 71–512; world affairs, 70–17. See also **CIVIL RIGHTS; Protests; Terrorism**

Virgin Islands, 71–421

Virginia: elections, 72–335, 70–330; memorials, 71–394; Republican party, 72–494, 70–486; state government, 71–479

Virus: biology, 71–394; medicine, 72–426, 70–414; rubella, 70–102

VISTA, 72–476, 71–439

VISUAL ARTS, 72–549, 71–507
awards and prizes, 71–215; literature for children, 71–386; museums, 71–405; Venice, 71–151

VITAL STATISTICS, 72–551, 71–509, 70–546
population, 72–475, 70–465. See also **CENSUS**

Vocational education, 71–463

Volcano: geology, il., 72–364; space exploration, 72–510, 71–473

Voletich, Mario, 70–456

Volkov, Vladimir N., 72–314

Volleyball, 72–517, 71–476, 70–511

VOLPE, JOHN ANTHONY, 70–546; New Orleans, 70–439; transportation, 71–494, 70–528; U.S. government, 71–504

Volunteer Corps, 71–503

Von Euler, Ulf S., 71–420

Vorster, Balthazar Johannes, 71–470

Voting: civil rights, 70–277; elections, 72–333, 71–268, 71–312; Europe, 72–348; Great Britain, 70–363; state government, 71–479; Switzerland, 71–482; U.S. Constitution, 72–543. See also **ELECTIONS**

W

Wages, 72–401, 71–31. See also **LABOR**
Waldheim, Kurt, 72–541
Wallace, David A., 71–288
WALLACE, GEORGE CORLEY, 72–552
American Party, 72–211, 71–196, 70–210
Wallenda, Karl, 71–429
Walsh, James E., 71–457
Walters, Jack, 72–384
War: Asia, 72–218, 71–17, 71–202; Cambodia, 72–256; India, 72–385; Korea, South, 72–400; Laos, 72–405, 71–373; Latin America, 70–395; national defense, 72–446; Nigeria, 71–417, 71–440; Pakistan, 72–459; religion, 72–493, 71–451, 70–483; Vietnam, 70–521; Yemen, 72–549. See also **ARMED FORCES OF THE WORLD; NATIONAL DEFENSE**
Warburg, Otto H., 71–288
Warhol, Andy, 70–456
Warren, Constance, 72–314
Warsaw Pact: armed forces, 72–217; Europe, 72–346
Washington, Walter E., 71–258

Washington (state): dam, 71–235; Jackson, Henry M., 72–395; state government, 72–519, 71–235
WASHINGTON, D.C., 72–552, 71–510, 70–546
architecture, 72–215; building, 72–252; city, 71–258; civil rights, 70–278; Congress, 71–268; courts and laws, 71–278; Fauntroy, Walter E., 72–352; memorials, 72–429, 71–395; music, 72–440
Waste disposal: agriculture, 71–193; Chicago, 72–279; environment, 72–341, 71–320; manufacturing, 71–391; *Special Report,* 71–79
Water: Afghanistan, 72–199; China, 72–66; conservation, 72–299, 71–273; dam, 70–251; disasters, 70–317; pollution, 70–463; tunnels, 70–251; weather, 72–552
Water pollution: Canada, 71–240; energy, 71–316; environment, 72–341, 71–319; fishing, 71–328; Girl Scouts, 72–556; health and disease, 71–348; pollution, 70–463
Water polo, 71–476, 70–511
Water Skiing, 72–517, 71–476, 70–511
Waterways: dams, 70–251; environment, 72–341; Panama, 71–424; Suez Canal, 70–421
Weapons. See **ARMED FORCES; Guided Missiles; NATIONAL DEFENSE**
WEATHER, 72–552, 71–510, 70–547
Australia, 71–209; disasters, 72–320, 71–294, 70–314; Germany, East, 71–339; space exploration, 72–510, 71–507
WEBER, JOSEPH, 72–553
Webster, Sir David, 72–314
Weddings: Canada, il., 72–258; Nixon, Richard M., 72–454
Weigel, Helene, 72–314
Weight lifting, 72–517, 71–475, 70–510
Weinberger, Caspar W., 71–139
Welfare. See **CHILD WELFARE; SOCIAL WELFARE**
Welty, Eudora, 71–380
West Germany. See **GERMANY, WEST**
WEST INDIES, 72–554, 71–512, 70–548; Anguilla, 70–211; Caribbean Islands, 70–397; Latin America, 71–374, 70–394; weather, 70–547
West Irian. See **NEW GUINEA**
Westmoreland, William Childs: il., 71–427
Whaling, 72–354
Wheat: agriculture, 72–206, 71–194, 70–206; Australia, 71–209; food, 71–329; *Special Report,* 72–60
Wheeler, Earle G., il., 71–411
White, Josh, 70–309
White, Kevin H.: Boston, 72–248; elections, 72–334
Whitehead, Clay T., 72–528
Whooping crane, 70–294
Widener, Gertrude D., 71–288
Wildlife: conservation, 72–299, 71–273, 70–293; energy, 70–334; hunting and fishing, 72–384, 71–353, 70–373; science, 71–36; zoology, 72–557, 70–551; zoos and aquariums, 71–516, 70–114, 70–552
Williams, T. Harry, 71–449
Williams, Ted, 70–238
Williams, Tennessee, 72–533
WILSON, FLIP, 72–554, il., 71–486
Wilson, (James) Harold, 72–370, 71–342, 70–359
Wine, 72–514
Winter sports, 72–517. See also **HOCKEY; ICE SKATING; SKIING**
Wiretapping, 72–288
Wisconsin: astronomy, 71–208; civil rights, 71–263; conservation, 72–298; crime, 71–278; hunting and fishing, 72–384; state government, 72–519
Women: advertising, il., 72–199; child welfare, 72–280; civil rights, 72–287, 71–262; Congress, 72–296; courts and laws, 72–302; education, 72–332; elections, 71–313; Europe, 72–348; Germany, West, 71–340; horse racing, 70–370; Ireland, 72–393; Latting, Patience, 72–410; Norway, 72–457; personalities, il., 71–427; Protestant, 72–484; Roman Catholic, 72–407; Switzerland, 72–525, 71–482, 70–517; visual arts, 72–551, 70–517; West Indies, 71–512
Wood, Leonard S., 70–309

Wood, Robert E., 70–309
WOODCOCK, LEONARD, 71–513; labor, il., 71–369
Woods, Harry MacGregor, 71–288
Wool, 71–209, 70–224
Worden, Alfred M.: astronauts, 72–223; space exploration, 72–510
Wordsworth, William, 71–248
World Book Encyclopedia: ALA award, 71–196, 70–210; dictionary supplement, 71–607, 70–597; photography, 70–462
World Council of Churches: Africa, 72–201; Protestant, 71–444; religion, 70–483; Roman Catholic, 70–489
World Court, 72–543
World Health Organization, 72–377, 71–347
World Series, 72–239, 71–221, 70–236
World's Fair. See **FAIRS AND EXPOSITIONS**
Wrestling, 72–517, 71–475, 70–511
Wright, Mary Clabaugh, 71–288
Wright, Quincy, 71–288
Wuorinen, Charles, 71–449
Wyeth, Andrew, 71–507
Wylie, Philip G., 72–314
Wyndham, John, 70–309

X

X-ray star, 72–224

Y

Yablonski, Joseph A., 71–288
Yachting. See **BOATS AND BOATING**
YAHYA KHAN, AGHA MOHAMMED, 70–548; Asia, 72–222; Pakistan, 72–459, 71–423, 70–404
Yakir, Pyotr, 70–493
Yarbrough, Lee Roy, 70–226
Yasgur, Max, 72–466
YEMEN, 72–554, 71–513, 70–549
Saudi Arabia, 71–464. See also **SOUTHERN YEMEN, PEOPLE'S REPUBLIC OF**
York, 72–273
York, Rudy, 71–288
Yorty, Samuel W.: Democratic party, 72–316; Los Angeles, 72–420, 70–408
YOST, CHARLES WOODRUFF, 70–549; advertising, 72–437; United Nations, 71–503
Young, Whitney M., Jr.: civil rights, 72–286; deaths, 72–314
YOUNG MEN'S CHRISTIAN ASSOCIATION, 72–555, 71–513, 70–549
YOUNG WOMEN'S CHRISTIAN ASSOCIATION, 72–555, 71–513, 70–549
Youth: Africa, 72–204; child welfare, 72–279; city, 72–285; elections, 72–333; motion pictures, 72–437; PTA, 72–437; Protestant, 72–483; Red Cross, 72–491; religion, 72–491; state government, 72–519; U.S. affairs, 72–26; U.S. Constitution, 72–543
YOUTH ORGANIZATIONS, 72–555, 71–514, 70–550
service clubs, 70–499; Young Men's Christian Association, 72–555, 71–513, 70–549; Young Women's Christian Association, 72–555, 71–513, 70–549
YUGOSLAVIA, 72–557, 71–515, 70–551
Bulgaria, 71–236; Hungary, 72–383; Roman Catholic, 71–456; Romania, 70–491

Z

Zaïre. See **CONGO (KINSHASA)**
ZAMBIA, 72–557, 71–515, 70–551
Africa, 72–202, 71–188; mining, 71–401; Rhodesia, 71–455; South Africa, 72–509
Zoitakis, George, 72–374
ZOOLOGY, 72–557, 71–515, 70–551
archaeology, 72–212; conservation, 72–299
ZOOS AND AQUARIUMS, 72–558, 71–516, 70–552; personalities, 71–429; *Special Report,* 70–114
Zulus, 71–470
ZUMWALT, ELMO RUSSELL, JR., 72–558, il., 72–143

Acknowledgments

The publishers of the 1972 WORLD BOOK YEAR BOOK gratefully acknowledge the courtesy of the following artists, photographers, publishers, institutions, agencies, and corporations for the illustrations in this volume. Credits should be read from left to right, top to bottom, on their respective pages. All entries marked with an asterisk (*) denote illustrations created exclusively for THE WORLD BOOK YEAR BOOK. All maps were created by the WORLD BOOK Cartographic Staff. All charts and diagrams were prepared by artists of The WORLD BOOK YEAR BOOK staff unless otherwise noted.

Chronology

8 Pictorial Parade; NASA; Wide World; Pictorial Parade
9 Wide World; Wide World; Wide World; Wide World; United Press Int.
10 Pictorial Parade; Pictorial Parade; United Press Int.; Wide World; United Press Int.
11 United Press Int.; NASA; United Press Int.; Wide World
12 *The Detroit News*; APIS; Wide World; United Press Int.
13 United Press Int.; Wide World; Pictorial Parade; Wide World

Focus Reports

16 Wide World; United Press Int.; United Press Int.; Pictorial Parade; United Press Int.; Gumé Nuñez*
17 David Hurn*
18-19 Wide World
20 Pictorial Parade
22 United Press Int.; Wide World; Wide World; Wide World; Wide World; Wide World; Gumé Nuñez*
23 Robert Isear*
24-26 Wide World
28 Wide World; Joe Kordick, *Chicago Sun-Times*; United Press Int.; United Press Int.; Wide World; Wide World; Gumé Nuñez*
29 Robert Isear*
32 United Press Int.
34 William S. Young, *San Francisco Chronicle*; NASA; Dr. Marion I. Barnhart, Wayne State University School of Medicine; Pictorial Parade; Henry Groskinsky, *Life* © Time Inc.; Gumé Nuñez*
35 Gene Trindl*
37 Hale Observatories
38 Joel Cole*
40 Sybil Shackman, Monkmeyer; Children's Television Workshop; United Press Int.; Fred Stein, *Chicago Daily News*; Gumé Nuñez*
41 Dan Budnik*
43 Harris and Ewing
44 *Catholic School Journal*
46 CBS Television; Ted Streshinsky; Zodiac; Kenneth Primack*; United Press Int.; Gumé Nuñez*
47 Dan Budnik*
48 United Press Int.
49 ABC Pictures Corporation
50 Jack Hamilton, Globe

52 Wide World; *London Daily Express;* Vernon J. Biever; Wide World; Wide World; Wide World; Gumé Nuñez*
53 J. R. Eyerman*
54 Wide World
55 United Press Int.

Special Reports

58-59 Dave Burnett, Camera 5; Ted Spiegel, Rapho Guillumette
60 *Toronto Star*
61 F. Botte, FAO
62-64 Richard Swanson, Black Star
67 Mark Gayn, *Toronto Star*
69 Guy Gillette, Photo Researchers
71 Ashvin Gatha, Rapho Guillumette
73 Richard Swanson, Black Star
74 Paolo Koch, Rapho Guillumette
76-89 George Roth*
92 Ted Streshinsky*
93 Van Bucher, Photo Researchers
95 Ted Streshinsky*
96-98 Martin J. Dain, Magnum
100 Joe Covello, Black Star
102 Rohn Engh, Photo Researchers
105 Ted Streshinsky*
106 Marcia Keegan, Photo Researchers
111-115 A. Salbosa, Pix*
116 Ted Streshinsky*
119-133 John Huehnergarth*
136-152 Yoichi Okamoto*; Joel Cole*
154-155 Yoichi Okamoto
157 Thomas J. Wagner
158 Yoichi Okamoto
160 Parker Heath*; Archie Lieberman

Trans-Vision® and Special Report

161 Portland, Oregon Development Commission; Joel Cole*; Katrina Thomas, Photo Researchers
162 Farrell Grehan, DPI; Marc Garanger, Rapho Guillumette; Irene Stack
163 Farrell Grehan, DPI; Marc St. Gil, Black Star; Tom Stack
166-174 Parker Heath*
176 Arvil A. Daniels, Photo Researchers; M. E. Warren
177 William A. Graham; The Rouse Company; M. E. Warren; William A. Graham
179-180 Richard Gordon
181 George E. Jones III, Photo Researchers

183	Joseph Sterling
184	George Hall
185	Joseph Sterling; Kenneth Primack*
186	George Hall; F. B. Grunzweig, Photo Researchers; George Hall
187	Archie Lieberman
188-189	Joseph Sterling; Katrina Thomas, Photo Researchers; Joseph Sterling
191	George Hall
192-193	Joseph Sterling
194	George Hall
195	Joseph Sterling; Ann E. Hubbard, Photo Researchers

Year on File

198	*Newsweek*
199	Henry Gill, *Chicago Daily News*
200-205	Wide World
208	U.S. Dept. of Agriculture
211-213	Wide World
214	George Cserna, American Institute of Architects
215	Ezra Stoller, American Institute of Architects
216-221	United Press Int.
222	Ken Regan, Camera 5
223	NASA
225	Pictorial Parade
226-230	Wide World
232	United Press Int.
236-238	Wide World
241	Robert B. Tai
244	William S. Young, *San Francisco Chronicle*
245-249	Wide World
251	Pictorial Parade
253	Federal Reserve Bank of Minneapolis
254	Photoreporters
256	Pictorial Parade
257	François Sully, *Newsweek*
259	Vancouver Province
261	©Toronto Star Syndicate
264	Wide World
273	APIS
279	U.S. Dept. of Agriculture
281	Wide World
282	United Press Int.
285	*The New York Times*
287	Wally McNamee, *Newsweek*
289	U.S. Treasury
291-296	Wide World
299	New York Zoological Society
301	*The New York Times*
303	Wide World
305	Czechoslovak News Agency
307	Hannes Killian, Stuttgart
309	United Press Int.
310	Wide World
312	Wide World; Wide World; Alfred Eisenstaedt, *Life* © Time Inc.
313-315	Wide World
318	Pictorial Parade
319	J. R. Eyerman, Black Star
321	Wide World
323	Sovfoto
325	Wide World
328	The White House
331	*The Detroit News*
332	*Pueblo Star-Journal*
333	United Press Int.
334	Wide World
336	*The New York Times*
340	Henry Groskinsky, *Life* © Time Inc.
342	Wide World
344-345	Photoreporters
348	Wide World
350	Pictorial Parade
351	Stephen Ladner; Pictorial Parade
353	Wide World
354	*The New York Times*
355	Kenneth Primack*
357	Henry Gill, *Chicago Daily News*
359	Les King, Auburn University
360	Wide World
362	Pictorial Parade
364	Wide World
366	Eastfoto
368	Wide World
370-371	Pictorial Parade
373	Camera Press from Pix
374-375	Wide World
376	Derek Bayes
379	Wide World
382	Mobile Americana Corporation
384	Wide World
386	Photoreporters
388-407	Wide World
411	Lyndon Baines Johnson Library
415	Martha Holmes
416	From Tomi Ungerer's *The Beast of Monsieur Racine*. Publisher: Farrar, Straus and Giroux
417	From John Burningham's *Mr. Gumpy's Outing*. Publisher: Holt, Rinehart and Winston
418	From William Steig's *Amos & Boris*. Publisher: Farrar, Straus and Giroux
422	Wide World
424	Hughes Aircraft Company
427	Bibliothèque Nationale, Paris
428	Institute for Medical Research, Camden, N.J.; Nural H. Sarkar, Institute for Medical Research, Camden, N.J.
429	John F. Kennedy Center for the Performing Arts
431-436	Wide World
437	Columbia Pictures Industries, Inc.
439	Lawrence Fried
441	Fletcher Drake
442	Fred Fehl
444	*Newsweek*
445	Leroy Patton, *Ebony*
447	Wide World
451	*New York Daily News*
453-454	Wide World
455	The White House; United Press Int.; United Press Int.
457	Michigan State University
459-463	United Press Int.
464	Bernard Gotfryd, *Newsweek*
465	Wide World
466	Henry Grossman; Wide World
467-468	Wide World
471	Scholastic/Kodak Photography Awards: Emily Wheeler; 1971 Kodak International Newspaper Snapshot Awards: Clarence Maki; 1971 Kodak International Newspaper Snapshot Awards: Juan Manuel Diaz Almada
473-477	Wide World
478-479	Walter Bennett, *Time*
480-481	The White House
482	Wide World
484	United Press Int.
485	Cowles Communications, Inc.
486	Staff photo
487	Wide World
490	Solter & Sabinson, Inc.
492-497	Wide World
499	Sovfoto
500	Wide World
502-507	United Press Int.
508	*The New York Times*
510-512	NASA
513	Sovfoto
515	William A. Graham
516	John B. Kelly, Inc.
518	United Press Int.
521	Wide World
524	Photoreporters
527	CBS Television
528	© BBC
529	*London Daily Express*
530-531	Van Williams
533	Sy Friedman, Zodiac
535	Rich Clarkson, *Sports Illustrated* © Time Inc.
539	© Walt Disney Productions
542	Wide World; Tony Rollo, *Newsweek*
547-548	Wide World
550	Ted Streshinsky
551	Park-Bernet Galleries, Inc.
553	Wide World
555	Girl Scouts of the United States of America

624

January

1   **New Year's Day.**

6   **Epiphany,** 12th day after Christmas, celebrates visit of the Three Wise Men.

16   **Jaycee Week** through January 22, marks founding of Jaycees.
World Religion Day, emphasizes need for world religious unity.

18   **92nd Congress** reconvenes for second session.

19   **Robert E. Lee's Birthday,** celebrated as a legal holiday in most Southern States.

21   **Monte Carlo Automobile Rally,** through January 29, in Monaco.

30   **Holiday of the Three Hierarchs.** Eastern Orthodox holy day, commemorating Saints Basil, Gregory, and John Chrysostom.

February

1   **National Freedom Day.**
American Heart Month through February 29.
Boy Scouts of America Anniversary Celebration through February 29.

2   **Ground-Hog Day.** Legend says six weeks of winter weather will follow if ground hog emerges to see its shadow.

3   **Winter Olympic Games,** Sapporo, Japan, through February 12.

12   **Abraham Lincoln's Birthday,** celebrated in 26 states.

14   **Saint Valentine's Day,** festival of romance and affection.

15   **Mardi Gras,** last celebration before Lent, observed in New Orleans and many Roman Catholic countries.

16   **Ash Wednesday,** first day of Lent, the 40-day period, not including Sundays, that precedes Easter.

20   **Brotherhood Week** through February 26.

21   **George Washington's Birthday,** according to law, is now legally celebrated by federal employees and the District of Columbia on the third Monday in February, not on the actual anniversary, the 22nd. Forty-two states also follow this practice.

28   **Easter Seal Campaign** through April 4.

29   **Purim,** observed on the 14th day of the Hebrew month of Adar, commemorates the delivery of Jews through the death of the ancient Persian despot Haman.
Leap Year Day.

March

1   **Red Cross Month** through March 31.

3   **World Day of Prayer.**

7   **Volunteers of America Week** through March 13.

12   **Girl Scout Week** through March 18, marking 60th birthday of U.S. Girl Scouts.

17   **St. Patrick's Day** honoring the patron saint of Ireland.

19   **Camp Fire Girls Birthday Week** through March 25, marks 62nd birthday of the organization.

26   **Holy Week** through April 1, commemorates suffering and Resurrection of Jesus Christ.

26   **Palm Sunday,** marks Jesus' final entry into Jerusalem along streets festively covered with palm branches.

30   **Passover** or Pesah, first day, starting the 15th day of the Hebrew month of Nisan. The eight-day festival celebrates the deliverance of the ancient Jews from bondage in Egypt.
Maundy Thursday. Celebrates Christ's injunction to love each other.

31   **Good Friday,** marks the death of Jesus on the cross. It is observed as a public holiday in 17 states.

April

1   **April Fools' Day.**
Cancer Control Month through April 30.

2   **Easter Sunday,** commemorating the Resurrection of Jesus Christ.

9   **National Boys' Club Week** through April 15.
Pan American Week through April 15.

16   **National Library Week** through April 22.

23   **National YWCA Week** through April 29.

28   **National Arbor Day.**

30   **Daylight Saving Time Begins** at 2 A.M. in most of the United States.
Walpurgis Night, according to legend the night of the witches' Sabbath gathering in Germany's Harz Mountains.

May

1   **May Day,** observed as a festival of spring in many countries.
Law Day, U.S.A.
Mental Health Week through May 6.

7   **National Music Week** through May 13.

8   **Salvation Army Week** through May 14.

11   **Ascension Day,** 40 days after Easter Sunday, commemorating the ascent of Jesus into heaven.

14   **Mother's Day.**

19   **Shabuot,** Jewish Feast of Weeks, marks the revealing of the Ten Commandments to Moses on Mount Sinai.

21   **Whitsunday** or Pentecost, the seventh Sunday after Easter, commemorating the descent of the Holy Spirit upon Jesus' 12 apostles.

22   **National Maritime Day.**

27   **Indianapolis 500-Mile Race** in Indianapolis, Ind.

29   **Memorial Day,** according to law, is the last Monday in May.

June

3   **Queen's Official Birthday,** marked by trooping of the colors in London.

5   **Stratford Festival,** drama and music, Ontario, Canada, through October 21.

6   **D-Day,** commemorates the day the Allies landed to assault the German-held continent of Europe in 1944.

11   **National Flag Week** through June 17.

14   **Flag Day,** commemorates adoption of the Stars and Stripes in 1777 as the official U.S. flag.

18   **Father's Day.**

21   **First Day of Summer** (2:06 A.M., E.S.T.).

27   **Freedom Week** through July 4.

A Preview Of 1972

January
S	M	T	W	T	F	S
						1
2	3	4	5	6	7	8
9	10	11	12	13	14	15
16	17	18	19	20	21	22
23	24	25	26	27	28	29
30	31					

February
S	M	T	W	T	F	S
		1	2	3	4	5
6	7	8	9	10	11	12
13	14	15	16	17	18	19
20	21	22	23	24	25	26
27	28	29				

March
S	M	T	W	T	F	S
			1	2	3	4
5	6	7	8	9	10	11
12	13	14	15	16	17	18
19	20	21	22	23	24	25
26	27	28	29	30	31	

April
S	M	T	W	T	F	S
						1
2	3	4	5	6	7	8
9	10	11	12	13	14	15
16	17	18	19	20	21	22
23	24	25	26	27	28	29
30						

May
S	M	T	W	T	F	S
	1	2	3	4	5	6
7	8	9	10	11	12	13
14	15	16	17	18	19	20
21	22	23	24	25	26	27
28	29	30	31			

June
S	M	T	W	T	F	S
				1	2	3
4	5	6	7	8	9	10
11	12	13	14	15	16	17
18	19	20	21	22	23	24
25	26	27	28	29	30	

A Preview Of 1972

July

S	M	T	W	T	F	S
						1
2	3	4	5	6	7	8
9	10	11	12	13	14	15
16	17	18	19	20	21	22
23	24	25	26	27	28	29
30	31					

August

S	M	T	W	T	F	S
		1	2	3	4	5
6	7	8	9	10	11	12
13	14	15	16	17	18	19
20	21	22	23	24	25	26
27	28	29	30	31		

September

S	M	T	W	T	F	S
					1	2
3	4	5	6	7	8	9
10	11	12	13	14	15	16
17	18	19	20	21	22	23
24	25	26	27	28	29	30

October

S	M	T	W	T	F	S
1	2	3	4	5	6	7
8	9	10	11	12	13	14
15	16	17	18	19	20	21
22	23	24	25	26	27	28
29	30	31				

November

S	M	T	W	T	F	S
			1	2	3	4
5	6	7	8	9	10	11
12	13	14	15	16	17	18
19	20	21	22	23	24	25
26	27	28	29	30		

December

S	M	T	W	T	F	S
					1	2
3	4	5	6	7	8	9
10	11	12	13	14	15	16
17	18	19	20	21	22	23
24	25	26	27	28	29	30
31						

July

1 **Dominion Day** (Canada) celebrates the confederation of the provinces in 1867. **Battle of Gettysburg** commemorative ceremonies in Gettysburg, Pa., through July 3.

4 **Independence Day,** marks Continental Congress's adoption of Declaration of Independence in 1776.

14 **Bastille Day** (France), commemorates popular uprising against Louis XVI in 1789 and seizure of the Bastille, the infamous French prison.

15 **Saint Swithin's Day.** According to legend, if it rains on this day, it will rain for 40 days.

16 **Captive Nations Week** through July 22.

20 **Moon Day,** the anniversary of man's first landing on the moon in 1969. **Tishah B'ab,** Jewish fast day, on ninth day of Hebrew month of Ab, marking Babylonians' destruction of the First Temple in Jerusalem in 587 B.C.; Roman destruction of the Second Temple in A.D. 70; and Roman suppression of Jewish revolt in 135.

25 **Salzburg International Music and Drama Festival,** Salzburg, Austria, through August 30.

August

14 **V-J Day** (original), marks Allied victory over Japan in 1945.

15 **Feast of the Assumption,** Roman Catholic and Eastern Orthodox holy day celebrates the ascent of the Virgin Mary into heaven.

19 **National Aviation Day.**

20 **Edinburgh International Festival,** music, drama, and film, through September 9.

26 **Summer Olympic Games,** Munich, West Germany, through September 10.

September

4 **Labor Day** in the United States and Canada.

9 **Rosh Hashanah,** or Jewish New Year, the year 5733 beginning at sunset. It falls on the first day of the Hebrew month of Tishri and lasts for two days.

10 **National Hispanic Heritage Week** through September 16.

17 **Citizenship Day.** **Constitution Week,** through September 23, commemorating signing of U.S. Constitution in Philadelphia, on Sept. 17, 1787.

18 **Yom Kippur,** or Day of Atonement, most solemn day in the Jewish calendar, marking the end of the period of penitence.

22 **First Day of Autumn** (5:33 P.M., E.S.T.). **Harvest Moon,** the full moon nearest the autumnal equinox of the sun, shines with special brilliance for several days and helps farmers in the Northern Hemisphere to get more field work done after sunset.

23 **Sukkot,** or Feast of Tabernacles, begins the nine-day Jewish observance, which originally celebrated the end of harvest season.

October

1 **National Employ the Physically Handicapped Week** through October 7. **National 4-H Week** through October 7.

2 **Child Health Day**

8 **Fire Prevention Week** through October 14. **National Y-Teen Week** through October 14.

9 **Thanksgiving Day,** Canada. **Columbus Day** commemorates Columbus' discovery of America in 1492. Previously celebrated on October 12. **Ramadan** begins, the ninth month of the Moslem calendar observed by fasting. **Leif Ericson Day,** celebrating early Norse explorer of North America.

21 **National Day of Prayer.**

22 **American Education Week** through October 28.

23 **Veterans Day,** formerly Armistice Day, is now observed on the fourth Monday in October.

29 **Daylight Saving Time Ends** and standard time resumes at 2 A.M.

31 **Halloween,** or All Hallows' Eve. **Reformation Day,** celebrated by Protestants, marks the day in 1517 when Martin Luther nailed his Ninety-Five Theses of protest to the door of a church in Wittenberg, Germany. **United Nations Children's Fund (UNICEF) Day.**

November

1 **All Saints' Day,** observed by the Roman Catholic Church since the 8th century.

5 **Guy Fawkes Day** (Great Britain) marks the failure of a plot to blow up King James I and Parliament in 1605 with ceremonial burning of Guy Fawkes in effigy.

7 **Anniversary of 1917 Bolshevik Revolution,** Russia's national holiday, through November 8. **Election Day.**

10 **Christmas Seal Campaign** through December 31.

13 **National Children's Book Week** through November 19.

23 **Thanksgiving Day.**

December

1 **Hanukkah,** or Feast of Lights, Jewish holiday beginning on the 25th day of the Hebrew month of Kislev and lasts eight days, celebrates the Jewish defeat of the Syrian tyrant Antiochus IV in 165 B.C. and the rededication of The Temple in Jerusalem.

2 **Pan American Health Day.**

3 **Advent,** first Sunday in the month-long Christian season preceding Christmas.

6 **Saint Nicholas Day,** observed in parts of Europe by the giving of gifts.

10 **Human Rights Week** through December 16.

11 **Nobel Peace Prize Presentation,** in Stockholm, Sweden.

15 **Bill of Rights Day,** marks the ratification of that document in 1791.

21 **First Day of Winter** (1:13 P.M., E.S.T.).

25 **Christmas.**

31 **New Year's Eve.**